Lecture Notes in Computer Science   11240

Commenced Publication in 1973
Founding and Former Series Editors:
Gerhard Goos, Juris Hartmanis, and Jan van Leeuwen

More information about this series at http://www.springer.com/series/7410

Amos Beimel · Stefan Dziembowski (Eds.)

Theory of Cryptography

16th International Conference, TCC 2018
Panaji, India, November 11–14, 2018
Proceedings, Part II

 Springer

Editors
Amos Beimel
Ben Gurion University
Beer Sheva, Israel

Stefan Dziembowski
University of Warsaw
Warsaw, Poland

ISSN 0302-9743 ISSN 1611-3349 (electronic)
Lecture Notes in Computer Science
ISBN 978-3-030-03809-0 ISBN 978-3-030-03810-6 (eBook)
https://doi.org/10.1007/978-3-030-03810-6

Library of Congress Control Number: 2018960441

LNCS Sublibrary: SL4 – Security and Cryptology

This Springer imprint is published by the registered company Springer Nature Switzerland AG
The registered company address is: Gewerbestrasse 11, 6330 Cham, Switzerland

Preface

The 16th Theory of Cryptography Conference (TCC 2018) was held during November 11–14, 2018, at the Cidade de Goa hotel, in Panaji, Goa, India. It was sponsored by the International Association for Cryptologic Research (IACR). The general chairs of the conference were Shweta Agrawal and Manoj Prabhakaran. We would like to thank them for their hard work in organizing the conference.

The conference received 168 submissions, of which the Program Committee (PC) selected 50 for presentation (with two pairs of papers sharing a single presentation slot per pair). Each submission was reviewed by at least three PC members, often more. The 30 PC members (including PC chairs), all top researchers in our field, were helped by 211 external reviewers, who were consulted when appropriate. These proceedings consist of the revised version of the 50 accepted papers. The revisions were not reviewed, and the authors bear full responsibility for the content of their papers.

As in previous years, we used Shai Halevi's excellent Web-review software, and are extremely grateful to him for writing it, and for providing fast and reliable technical support whenever we had any questions. Based on the experience from previous years, we again made use of the interaction feature supported by the review software, where PC members may anonymously interact with authors. This was used to ask specific technical questions, such as suspected bugs. We felt this approach helped us prevent potential misunderstandings and improved the quality of the review process.

This was the fifth year that TCC presented the Test of Time Award to an outstanding paper that was published at TCC at least eight years ago, making a significant contribution to the theory of cryptography, preferably with influence also in other areas of cryptography, theory, and beyond. This year the Test of Time Award Committee selected the following paper, published at TCC 2005: "Evaluating 2-DNF Formulas on Ciphertexts" by Dan Boneh, Eu-Jin Goh, and Kobbi Nissim. This paper was selected for introducing compact two-operation homomorphic encryption and developing new bilinear map techniques that led to major improvements in the design of cryptographic schemes. The authors were also invited to deliver a talk at TCC 2018. A Best Student Paper Award was given to Tianren Liu for his paper "On Basing Search SIVP on NP-Hardness."

The conference also featured two other invited talks, by Moni Naor and by Daniel Wichs.

We are greatly indebted to many people who were involved in making TCC 2018 a success. First of all, a big thanks to the most important contributors: all the authors who submitted papers to the conference. Next, we would like to thank the PC members for their hard work, dedication, and diligence in reviewing the papers, verifying the correctness, and in-depth discussion. We are also thankful to the external reviewers for their volunteered hard work and investment in reviewing papers and answering questions, often under time pressure. For running the conference itself, we are very grateful to the general chairs, Shweta Agrawal and Manoj Prabhakaran. We appreciate the sponsorship from the IACR, Microsoft Research, IBM, and Google. We also wish to thank IIT Madras and IIT Bombay for their support. Finally, we are thankful to the TCC Steering Committee as well as the entire thriving and vibrant TCC community.

November 2018

Amos Beimel
Stefan Dziembowski
TCC 2018 Program Chairs

TCC 2018

The 16th Theory of Cryptography Conference

Goa, India

November 11–14, 2018

Sponsored by the *International Association for Cryptologic Research*

General Chairs

Shweta Agrawal   Indian Institute of Technology, Madras, India
Manoj Prabhakaran   Indian Institute of Technology, Bombay, India

Program Committee

Masayuki Abe   NTT and Kyoto University, Japan
Divesh Aggarwal   National University of Singapore, Singapore
Shweta Agrawal   Indian Institute of Technology, Madras, India
Gilad Asharov   Cornell Tech, USA
Amos Beimel (Co-chair) Ben-Gurion University, Israel
Andrej Bogdanov   The Chinese University of Hong Kong, SAR China
Zvika Brakerski   Weizmann Institute of Science, Israel
Nishanth Chandran   Microsoft Research, India
Stefan Dziembowski   University of Warsaw, Poland
  (Co-chair)
Sebastian Faust   TU Darmstadt, Germany
Marc Fischlin   TU Darmstadt, Germany
Iftach Haitner   Tel Aviv University, Israel
Martin Hirt   ETH Zurich, Switzerland
Pavel Hubáček   Charles University in Prague, Czech Republic
Aggelos Kiayias   University of Edinburgh, UK
Eyal Kushilevitz   Technion, Israel
Anna Lysyanskaya   Brown University, USA
Tal Malkin   Columbia University, USA
Eran Omri   Ariel University, Israel
Chris Peikert   University of Michigan – Ann Arbor, USA
Krzysztof Pietrzak   IST Austria, Austria
Antigoni Polychroniadou Cornell University, USA
Alon Rosen   IDC Herzliya, Israel
Mike Rosulek   Oregon State University, USA
Vinod Vaikuntanathan   MIT, USA
Ivan Visconti   University of Salerno, Italy
Hoeteck Wee   CNRS and ENS, France

Mor Weiss   Northeastern University, USA
Stefan Wolf   University of Lugano, Switzerland
Vassilis Zikas   University of Edinburgh, UK

TCC Steering Committee

Ivan Damgård   Aarhus University, Denmark
Shai Halevi (Chair)   IBM Research, USA
Huijia (Rachel) Lin   UCSB, USA
Tal Malkin   Columbia University, USA
Ueli Maurer   ETH, Switzerland
Moni Naor   Weizmann Institute of Science, Israel
Manoj Prabhakaran   Indian Institute of Technology, Bombay, India

Additional Reviewers

Aydin Abadi
Shashank Agrawal
Adi Akavia
Navid Alamati
Ghada Almashaqbeh
Bar Alon
Joel Alwen
Prabhanjan Ananth
Megumi Ando
Benny Applebaum
Frederik Armknecht
Christian Badertscher
Saikrishna
    Badrinarayanan
Karim Baghery
Marshall Ball
Fabio Banfi
Laasya Bangalore
Carsten Baum
Aner Ben-Efraim
Fabrice Benhamouda
Nir Bitansky
Jonathan Bootle
Cecilia Boschini
Florian Bourse
Elette Boyle
Anne Broadbent
Brent Carmer

David Cash
Anrin Chakraborti
Yilei Chen
Ilaria Chillotti
Wutichai Chongchitmate
Michele Ciampi
Ran Cohen
Xavier Coiteux-Roy
Sandro Coretti
Geoffroy Couteau
Dana Dachman-Soled
Pratish Datta
Bernardo David
Jean Paul Degabriele
Akshay Degwekar
Apoorvaa Deshpande
Nico Döttling
Lisa Eckey
Naomi Ephraim
Omar Fawzi
Serge Fehr
Matthias Fitzi
Nils Fleischhacker
Georg Fuchsbauer
Eiichiro Fujisaki
Steven Galbreith
Chaya Ganesh
Adria Gascon

Romain Gay
Peter Gazi
Ran Gelles
Badih Ghazi
Satrajit Ghosh
Irene Giacomelli
Junqing Gong
Dov Gordon
Paul Grubbs
Cyprien de Saint Guilhem
Siyao Guo
Divya Gupta
Arne Hansen
Patrick Harasser
Prahladh Harsha
Julia Hesse
Minki Hhan
Ryo Hiromasa
Justin Holmgren
Kristina Hostakova
Yuval Ishai
Muhammad Ishaq
Zahra Jafargholi
Tibor Jager
Aayush Jain
Abhishek Jain
Daniel Jost
Bruce Kapron

Tomasz Kazana
Dakshita Khurana
Jiseung Kim
Sam Kim
Fuyuki Kitagawa
Susumu Kiyoshima
Karen Klein
Ilan Komargodski
Orestis Konstantinidis
Venkata Koppula
Lucas Kowalczyk
Daniel Kraschewski
Mukul Kulkarni
Ashutosh Kumar
Rajendra Kumar
Benjamin Kuykendall
Rio LaVinge
Changmin Lee
Moon Sung Lee
Nikos Leonardos
Xiao Liang
Jyun-Jie Liao
Chengyu Lin
Huijia (Rachel) Lin
Feng-Hao Liu
Qipeng Liu
Tianren Liu
Yi-Kai Liu
Chen-Da Liu Zhang
Alex Lombardi
Julian Loss
Steve Lu
Yun Lu
Vadim Lyubashevsky
Urmila Mahadev
Mohammad Mahmoody
Subhamoy Maitra
Nikolaos Makriyannis
Takahiro Matsuda
Christian Matt
Jeremias Mechler
Peihan Miao

Daniele Micciancio
Michele Minelli
Konstantinos Mitropoulos
Tarik Moataz
Fabrice Mouhartem
Tamer Mour
Pratyay Mukherjee
Priyanka Mukhopadhyay
Marta Mularczyk
Jörn Müller-Quade
Kartik Nayak
Tobias Nilges
Chinmay Nirkhe
Ryo Nishimaki
Sai Lakshmi Bhavana
    Obbattu
Maciej Obremski
Miyako Ohkubo
Georgios Panagiotakos
Omer Paneth
Anat Paskin-Cherniavsky
Valerio Pastro
Serdar Pehlivanoglu
Renen Perlman
Giuseppe Persiano
Thomas Peters
Christopher Portmann
Srinivasan Raghuraman
Govind Ramnarayan
Samuel Ranellucci
Michael Raskin
Michael Riabzev
João Ribeiro
Silas Richelson
Felix Rohrbach
Lior Rotem
Paul Rösler
Manuel Sabin
Katerina Samari
Alessandra Scafuro
Giannicola Scarpa
Peter Scholl

Adam Sealfon
Sruthi Sekar
Yannick Seurin
Sina Shiehian
Tom Shrimpton
Luisa Siniscalchi
Veronika Slivova
Pratik Soni
Nick Spooner
Akshayaram Srinivasan
Martjin Stam
John Steinberger
Noah
    Stephens-Davidowitz
Qiang Tang
Stefano Tessaro
Ni Trieu
Rotem Tsabary
Yiannis Tselekounis
Margarita Vald
Prashant Vasudevan
Muthuramakrishnan
Venkitasubramaniam
Daniele Venturi
Satyanarayana Vusirikala
Hendrik Waldner
Petros Wallden
Michael Walter
Xiao Wang
Christopher Williamson
David Wu
Keita Xagawa
Yu Yu
Shota Yamada
Takashi Yamakawa
Kevin Yeo
Eylon Yogev
Thomas Zacharias
Mark Zhandry
Jiamin Zhu
Dionysis Zindros
Giorgos Zirdelis

Contents – Part II

MPC Protocols

Topology-Hiding Computation Beyond Semi-Honest Adversaries 3
  Rio LaVigne, Chen-Da Liu-Zhang, Ueli Maurer, Tal Moran,
  Marta Mularczyk, and Daniel Tschudi

Secure Computation Using Leaky Correlations (Asymptotically
Optimal Constructions) 36
  Alexander R. Block, Divya Gupta, Hemanta K. Maji, and Hai H. Nguyen

Fine-Grained Secure Computation 66
  Matteo Campanelli and Rosario Gennaro

On the Structure of Unconditional UC Hybrid Protocols 98
  Mike Rosulek and Morgan Shirley

Order-Revealing Encryption and Symmetric Encryption

Impossibility of Order-Revealing Encryption in Idealized Models 129
  Mark Zhandry and Cong Zhang

A Ciphertext-Size Lower Bound for Order-Preserving Encryption
with Limited Leakage 159
  David Cash and Cong Zhang

Ciphertext Expansion in Limited-Leakage Order-Preserving Encryption:
A Tight Computational Lower Bound 177
  Gil Segev and Ido Shahaf

Towards Tight Security of Cascaded LRW2 192
  Bart Mennink

Information-Theoretic Cryptography II and Quantum Cryptography

Continuous NMC Secure Against Permutations and Overwrites,
with Applications to CCA Secure Commitments 225
  Ivan Damgård, Tomasz Kazana, Maciej Obremski, Varun Raj,
  and Luisa Siniscalchi

Best Possible Information-Theoretic MPC 255
  Shai Halevi, Yuval Ishai, Eyal Kushilevitz, and Tal Rabin

Secure Certification of Mixed Quantum States with Application
to Two-Party Randomness Generation   282
    Frédéric Dupuis, Serge Fehr, Philippe Lamontagne, and Louis Salvail

Classical Proofs for the Quantum Collapsing Property
of Classical Hash Functions   315
    Serge Fehr

LWE-Based Cryptography

Traitor-Tracing from LWE Made Simple and Attribute-Based   341
    Yilei Chen, Vinod Vaikuntanathan, Brent Waters, Hoeteck Wee,
    and Daniel Wichs

Two-Message Statistically Sender-Private OT from LWE   370
    Zvika Brakerski and Nico Döttling

Adaptively Secure Distributed PRFs from LWE   391
    Benoît Libert, Damien Stehlé, and Radu Titiu

iO and Authentication

A Simple Construction of iO for Turing Machines   425
    Sanjam Garg and Akshayaram Srinivasan

Succinct Garbling Schemes from Functional Encryption Through
a Local Simulation Paradigm   455
    Prabhanjan Ananth and Alex Lombardi

FE and iO for Turing Machines from Minimal Assumptions   473
    Shweta Agrawal and Monosij Maitra

The MMap Strikes Back: Obfuscation and New Multilinear Maps Immune
to CLT13 Zeroizing Attacks   513
    Fermi Ma and Mark Zhandry

Return of GGH15: Provable Security Against Zeroizing Attacks   544
    James Bartusek, Jiaxin Guan, Fermi Ma, and Mark Zhandry

The Security of Lazy Users in Out-of-Band Authentication   575
    Moni Naor, Lior Rotem, and Gil Segev

ORAM and PRF

Is There an Oblivious RAM Lower Bound for Online Reads?   603
    Mor Weiss and Daniel Wichs

Perfectly Secure Oblivious Parallel RAM......................... 636
   T.-H. Hubert Chan, Kartik Nayak, and Elaine Shi

Watermarking PRFs Under Standard Assumptions: Public Marking
and Security with Extraction Queries............................ 669
   Willy Quach, Daniel Wichs, and Giorgos Zirdelis

Exploring Crypto Dark Matter: New Simple PRF Candidates
and Their Applications....................................... 699
   Dan Boneh, Yuval Ishai, Alain Passelègue, Amit Sahai, and David J. Wu

Author Index 731

Contents – Part I

Memory-Hard Functions and Complexity Theory

Provable Time-Memory Trade-Offs: Symmetric Cryptography
Against Memory-Bounded Adversaries 3
    Stefano Tessaro and Aishwarya Thiruvengadam

Static-Memory-Hard Functions, and Modeling the Cost of Space vs. Time. . . 33
    Thaddeus Dryja, Quanquan C. Liu, and Sunoo Park

No-signaling Linear PCPs 67
    Susumu Kiyoshima

On Basing Search SIVP on NP-Hardness 98
    Tianren Liu

Two-Round MPC Protocols

Two-Round MPC: Information-Theoretic and Black-Box 123
    Sanjam Garg, Yuval Ishai, and Akshayaram Srinivasan

Perfect Secure Computation in Two Rounds. 152
    Benny Applebaum, Zvika Brakerski, and Rotem Tsabary

Two-Round Adaptively Secure Multiparty Computation
from Standard Assumptions 175
    Fabrice Benhamouda, Huijia Lin, Antigoni Polychroniadou,
    and Muthuramakrishnan Venkitasubramaniam

Zero Knowledge

One-Message Zero Knowledge and Non-malleable Commitments 209
    Nir Bitansky and Huijia Lin

Smooth NIZK Arguments 235
    Charanjit S. Jutla and Arnab Roy

Round-Optimal Fully Black-Box Zero-Knowledge Arguments
from One-Way Permutations 263
    Carmit Hazay and Muthuramakrishnan Venkitasubramaniam

Round Optimal Black-Box "Commit-and-Prove" 286
    Dakshita Khurana, Rafail Ostrovsky, and Akshayaram Srinivasan

Information-Theoretic Cryptography

On the Power of Amortization in Secret Sharing: *d*-Uniform Secret Sharing
and CDS with Constant Information Rate. 317
   Benny Applebaum and Barak Arkis

Information-Theoretic Secret-Key Agreement: The Asymptotically Tight
Relation Between the Secret-Key Rate and the Channel Quality Ratio 345
   Daniel Jost, Ueli Maurer, and João L. Ribeiro

Information-Theoretic Broadcast with Dishonest Majority
for Long Messages 370
   Wutichai Chongchitmate and Rafail Ostrovsky

Oblivious Transfer in Incomplete Networks 389
   Varun Narayanan and Vinod M. Prabahakaran

Trapdoor Permutations and Signatures

Injective Trapdoor Functions via Derandomization: How Strong
is Rudich's Black-Box Barrier?. 421
   Lior Rotem and Gil Segev

Enhancements are Blackbox Non-trivial: Impossibility of Enhanced
Trapdoor Permutations from Standard Trapdoor Permutations 448
   Mohammad Hajiabadi

Certifying Trapdoor Permutations, Revisited. 476
   Ran Canetti and Amit Lichtenberg

On the Security Loss of Unique Signatures 507
   Andrew Morgan and Rafael Pass

Coin-Tossing and Fairness

On the Complexity of Fair Coin Flipping. 539
   Iftach Haitner, Nikolaos Makriyannis, and Eran Omri

Game Theoretic Notions of Fairness in Multi-party Coin Toss 563
   Kai-Min Chung, Yue Guo, Wei-Kai Lin, Rafael Pass,
   and Elaine Shi

Achieving Fair Treatment in Algorithmic Classification 597
   Andrew Morgan and Rafael Pass

Functional and Identity-Based Encryption

Upgrading to Functional Encryption   629
  Saikrishna Badrinarayanan, Dakshita Khurana, Amit Sahai,
  and Brent Waters

Impossibility of Simulation Secure Functional Encryption Even with
Random Oracles   659
  Shashank Agrawal, Venkata Koppula, and Brent Waters

Registration-Based Encryption: Removing Private-Key Generator
from IBE   689
  Sanjam Garg, Mohammad Hajiabadi, Mohammad Mahmoody,
  and Ahmadreza Rahimi

Author Index   719

MPC Protocols

Topology-Hiding Computation Beyond Semi-Honest Adversaries

Rio LaVigne[1]($\boxtimes$), Chen-Da Liu-Zhang[2], Ueli Maurer[2], Tal Moran[3], Marta Mularczyk[2], and Daniel Tschudi[4]

[1] MIT, Cambridge, USA
rio@mit.edu
[2] ETH Zurich, Zürich, Switzerland
{lichen,maurer,mumarta}@inf.ethz.ch
[3] IDC Herzliya, Herzliya, Israel
talm@idc.ac.il
[4] Aarhus University, Aarhus, Denmark
tschudi@cs.au.dk

Abstract. Topology-hiding communication protocols allow a set of parties, connected by an incomplete network with unknown communication graph, where each party only knows its neighbors, to construct a complete communication network such that the network topology remains hidden even from a powerful adversary who can corrupt parties. This communication network can then be used to perform arbitrary tasks, for example secure multi-party computation, in a topology-hiding manner. Previously proposed protocols could only tolerate passive corruption. This paper proposes protocols that can also tolerate fail-corruption (i.e., the adversary can crash any party at any point in time) and so-called semi-malicious corruption (i.e., the adversary can control a corrupted party's randomness), without leaking more than an arbitrarily small fraction of a bit of information about the topology. A small-leakage protocol was recently proposed by Ball et al. [Eurocrypt'18], but only under the unrealistic set-up assumption that each party has a trusted hardware module containing secret correlated pre-set keys, and with the further two restrictions that only passively corrupted parties can be crashed by the adversary, and semi-malicious corruption is not tolerated. Since leaking a small amount of information is unavoidable, as is the need to abort

R. Lavigne—This material is based upon work supported by the National Science Foundation Graduate Research Fellowship under Grant No. 1122374. Any opinion, findings, and conclusions or recommendations expressed in this material are those of the authors(s) and do not necessarily reflect the views of the National Science Foundation. Research also supported in part by NSF Grants CNS-1350619 and CNS-1414119, and by the Defense Advanced Research Projects Agency (DARPA) and the U.S. Army Research Office under contracts W911NF-15-C-0226 and W911NF-15-C-0236.

T. Moran—Supported in part by ISF grant no. 1790/13 and by the Bar-Ilan Cybercenter.

M. Mularczyk—Research was supported by the Zurich Information Security and Privacy Center (ZISC).

D. Tschudi—Work partly done while author was at ETH Zurich. Author was supported by advanced ERC grant MPCPRO.

© International Association for Cryptologic Research 2018
A. Beimel and S. Dziembowski (Eds.): TCC 2018, LNCS 11240, pp. 3–35, 2018.
https://doi.org/10.1007/978-3-030-03810-6_1

the protocol in case of failures, our protocols seem to achieve the best possible goal in a model with fail-corruption.

Further contributions of the paper are applications of the protocol to obtain secure MPC protocols, which requires a way to bound the aggregated leakage when multiple small-leakage protocols are executed in parallel or sequentially. Moreover, while previous protocols are based on the DDH assumption, a new so-called PKCR public-key encryption scheme based on the LWE assumption is proposed, allowing to base topology-hiding computation on LWE. Furthermore, a protocol using fully-homomorphic encryption achieving very low round complexity is proposed.

1   Introduction

1.1   Topology-Hiding Computation

Secure communication over an insecure network is one of the fundamental goals of cryptography. The security goal can be to hide different aspects of the communication, ranging from the content (secrecy), the participants' identity (anonymity), the existence of communication (steganography), to hiding the topology of the underlying network in case it is not complete.

Incomplete networks arise in many contexts, such as the Internet of Things (IoT) or ad-hoc vehicular networks. Hiding the topology can, for example, be important because the position of a node within the network depends on the node's location. This could in information about the node's identity or other confidential parameters. The goal is that parties, and even colluding sets of parties, can not learn anything about the network, except their immediate neighbors.

Incomplete networks have been studied in the context of communication security, referred to as secure message transmission (see, e.g. [DDWY90]), where the goal is to enable communication between any pair of entities, despite an incomplete communication graph. Also, anonymous communication has been studied extensively (see, e.g. [Cha81, RC88, SGR97]). Here, the goal is to hide the identity of the sender and receiver in a message transmission. A classical technique to achieve anonymity is the so-called mix-net technique, introduced by Chaum [Cha81]. Here, *mix* servers are used as proxies which shuffle messages sent between peers to disable an eavesdropper from following a message's path. The onion routing technique [SGR97, RC88] is perhaps the most known instantiation of the mix-technique. Another anonymity technique known as *Dining Cryptographers networks*, in short DC-nets, was introduced in [Cha88] (see also [Bd90, GJ04]). However, none of these approaches can be used to hide the network topology. In fact, message transmission protocols assume (for their execution) that the network graph is public knowledge.

The problem of *topology-hiding communication* was introduced by Moran et al. [MOR15]. The authors propose a broadcast protocol in the cryptographic setting, which does not reveal any additional information about the network topology to an adversary who can access the internal state of any number of passively corrupted parties (that is, they consider the semi-honest setting). This allows to achieve topology-hiding MPC using standard techniques to transform broadcast channels into secure point-to-point channels. At a very high level, [MOR15] uses a series of nested multi-party computations, in which each node is emulated by a secure computation of its neighbor. This emulation then extends to the entire graph recursively. In [HMTZ16], the authors improve this result and provide a construction that makes only black-box use of encryption and where the security is based on the DDH assumption. However, both results are feasible only for graphs with logarithmic diameter. Topology hiding communication for certain classes of graphs with large diameter was described in [AM17]. This result was finally extended to allow for arbitrary (connected) graphs in [ALM17a].

A natural next step is to extend these results to settings with more powerful adversaries. Unfortunately, even a protocol in the setting with fail-corruptions (in addition to passive corruptions) turns out to be difficult to achieve. In fact, as shown already in [MOR15], some leakage in the fail-stop setting is inherent. It is therefore no surprise that all previous protocols (secure against passive corruptions) leak information about the network topology if the adversary can crash parties. The core problem is that crashes can interrupt the communication flow of the protocol at any point and at any time. If not properly dealt with by the protocol, those outages cause shock waves of miscommunication, which allows the adversary to probe the network topology.

A first step in this direction was recently achieved in [BBMM18] where a protocol for topology-hiding communication secure against a fail-stop adversary is given. However, the resilience against crashes comes at a hefty price; the protocol requires that parties have access to secure hardware modules which are initialized with correlated, pre-shared keys. Their protocol provides security with abort and the leakage is arbitrarily small.

In the information-theoretic setting, the main result is negative [HJ07]: any MPC protocol in the information-theoretic setting inherently leaks information about the network graph. They also show that if the routing table is leaked, one can construct an MPC protocol which leaks no additional information.

1.2 Comparison to Previous Work

In [ALM17a] the authors present a broadcast protocol for the semi-honest setting based on random walks. This broadcast protocol is then compiled into a full topology-hiding computation protocol. However, the random walk protocol fails spectacularly in the presence of fail-stop adversaries, leaking a lot of information about the structure of the graph. Every time a node aborts, any number of walks get cut, meaning that they no longer carry any information. When this happens, adversarial nodes get to see which walks fail along which edges, and can get a good idea of where the aborting nodes are in the graph.

We also note that, while we use ideas from [BBMM18], which achieves the desired result in a trusted-hardware model, we cannot simply use their protocol and substitute the secure hardware box for a standard primitive. In particular, they use the fact that each node can maintain an encrypted "image" of the entire graph by combining information from all neighbors, and use that information to decide whether to give output or abort. This appears to require both some form of obfuscation and a trusted setup, whereas our protocol uses neither.

1.3 Contributions

In this paper we propose the first topology-hiding MPC protocol secure against passive and fail-stop adversaries (with arbitrarily small leakage) that is based on standard assumptions. Our protocol does not require setup, and its security can be based on either the DDH, QR or LWE assumptions. A comparison of our results to previous works in topology-hiding communication is found in Table 1.

Theorem 1 (informal). *If DDH, QR or LWE is hard, then for any MPC functionality $\mathcal{F}$, there exists a topology-hiding protocol realizing $\mathcal{F}$ for any network graph G leaking at most an arbitrarily small fraction p of a bit, which is secure against an adversary that does any number of static passive corruptions and adaptive crashes. The round and communication complexity is polynomial in the security parameter κ and $1/p$.*

Table 1. Adversarial model and security assumptions of existing topology-hiding broadcast protocols. The table also shows the class of graphs for which the protocols have polynomial communication complexity in the security parameter and the number of parties.

Adversary	Graph	Hardness Asm.	Model	Reference
Semi-honest	log diam.	Trapdoor Perm.	Standard	[MOR15]
	log diam.	DDH	Standard	[HMTZ16]
	cycles, trees, log circum.	DDH	Standard	[AM17]
	arbitrary	DDH or QR	Standard	[ALM17a]
Fail-stop	arbitrary	OWF	Trusted Hardware	[BBMM18]
Semi-malicious & fail-stop	arbitrary	DDH or QR or LWE	Standard	[This work]

Our topology-hiding MPC protocol is obtained by compiling a MPC protocol from a topology-hiding broadcast protocol leaking at most a fraction p of a bit. We note that although it is well known that without leakage any functionality can be implemented on top of secure communication, this statement cannot be directly lifted to the setting with leakage. In essence, if a communication protocol is used multiple times, it leaks multiple bits. However, we show that our broadcast protocol, leaking at most a fraction p of a bit, can be executed sequentially and in parallel, such that the result leaks also at most the same fraction p. As a consequence, any protocol can be compiled into one that hides topology and known results on implementing any multiparty computation can be lifted to the topology hiding setting. However, this incurs a multiplicative overhead in the round complexity.

We then present a topology hiding protocol to evaluate any poly-time function using FHE whose round complexity will amount to that of a single broadcast execution. To do that, we first define an enhanced encryption scheme, which we call *Deeply Fully-Homomorphic Public-Key Encryption* (DFH-PKE), with similar properties as the PKCR scheme presented in [AM17, ALM17a] and provide an instantiation of DFH-PKE under FHE. Next, we show how to obtain a protocol using DFH-PKE to evaluate any poly-time function in a topology hiding manner.

We also explore another natural extension of semi-honest corruption, the so-called *semi-malicious* setting. As for passive corruption, the adversary selects a set of parties and gets access to their internal state. But in addition, the adversary can also set their randomness during the protocol execution. This models the setting where a party uses an untrusted source of randomness which could be under the control of the adversary. This scenario is of interest as tampered randomness sources have caused many security breaches in the past [HDWH12, CNE+14]. In this paper, we propose a general compiler that enhances the security of protocols that tolerate passive corruption with crashes to semi-malicious corruption with crashes.

2 Preliminaries

2.1 Notation

For a public-key pk and a message m, we denote the encryption of m under pk by $[m]_{pk}$. Furthermore, for k messages $m_1, \ldots, m_k$, we denote by $[m_1, \ldots, m_k]_{pk}$ a vector, containing the k encryptions of messages m_i under the same key pk.

For an algorithm $A(\cdot)$, we write $A(\cdot \, ; U^*)$ whenever the randomness used in $A(\cdot)$ should be made explicit and comes from a uniform distribution. By $\approx_c$ we denote that two distribution ensembles are computationally indistinguishable.

2.2 Model of Topology-Hiding Communication

Adversary. Most of our results concern an adversary, who can *statically passively corrupt* an arbitrary set of parties $\mathcal{Z}^p$, with $|\mathcal{Z}^p| < n$. Passively corrupted parties follow the protocol instructions (this includes the generation of randomness), but the adversary can access their internal state during the protocol.

A *semi-malicious* corruption (see, e.g., [AJL+12]) is a stronger variant of a passive corruption. Again, we assume that the adversary selects any set of semi-malicious parties $\mathcal{Z}^s$ with $|\mathcal{Z}^s| < n$ before the protocol execution. These parties follow the protocol instructions, but the adversary can access their internal state and can additionally choose their randomness.

A *fail-stop* adversary can adaptively crash parties. After being crashed, a party stops sending messages. Note that crashed parties are not necessarily corrupted. In particular, the adversary has no access to the internal state of a crashed party unless it is in the set of corrupted parties. This type of fail-stop adversary is stronger and more general than the one used in [BBMM18], where only passively corrupted parties can be crashed. In particular, in our model the adversary does not necessarily learn the neighbors of crashed parties, whereas in [BBMM18] they are revealed to it by definition.

Communication Model. We state our results in the UC framework. We consider a synchronous communication network. Following the approach in [MOR15], to model the restricted communication network we define the $\mathcal{F}_{\text{NET}}$-hybrid model. The $\mathcal{F}_{\text{NET}}$ functionality takes as input a description of the graph network from a special "graph party" P_{graph} and then returns to each party P_i a description of its neighborhood. After that, the functionality acts as an "ideal channel" that allows parties to communicate with their neighbors according to the graph network.

Similarly to [BBMM18], we change the $\mathcal{F}_{\text{NET}}$ functionality from [MOR15] to deal with a fail-stop adversary.

Functionality $\mathcal{F}_{\text{NET}}$

The functionality keeps the following variables: the set of crashed parties $\mathcal{C}$ and the graph G. Initially, $\mathcal{C} = \varnothing$ and $G = (\varnothing, \varnothing)$.

Initialization Step:

1: The party P_{graph} sends graph G' to $\mathcal{F}_{\text{NET}}$. $\mathcal{F}_{\text{NET}}$ sets $G = G'$.
2: $\mathcal{F}_{\text{NET}}$ sends to each party P_i its neighborhood $\mathbf{N}_G(P_i)$.

Communication Step:

1: If the adversary crashes party P_i, then $\mathcal{F}_{\text{NET}}$ sets $\mathcal{C} = \mathcal{C} \cup \{P_i\}$.
2: If a party P_i sends the command (SEND, j, m), where $P_j \in \mathbf{N}_G(P_i)$ and m is the message to P_j, to $\mathcal{F}_{\text{NET}}$ and $P_i \notin \mathcal{C}$, then $\mathcal{F}_{\text{NET}}$ outputs (i, m) to party P_j.

Observe that since $\mathcal{F}_{\text{NET}}$ gives local information about the network graph to all corrupted parties, any ideal-world adversary should also have access to this information. For this reason, similar to [MOR15], we use in the ideal-world the functionality $\mathcal{F}_{\text{INFO}}$, which contains only the Initialization Step of $\mathcal{F}_{\text{NET}}$.

To model leakage we extend $\mathcal{F}_{\text{INFO}}$ by a leakage phase, where the adversary can query a (possibly probabilistic) leakage function $\mathcal{L}$ once. The inputs to $\mathcal{L}$ include the network graph, the set of crashed parties and arbitrary input from the adversary.

We say that a protocol leaks one bit of information if the leakage function $\mathcal{L}$ outputs one bit. We also consider the notion of leaking a fraction p of a bit. This is modeled by having $\mathcal{L}$ output the bit only with probability p (otherwise, $\mathcal{L}$ outputs a special symbol $\perp$). Here our model differs from the one in [BBMM18], where in case of the fractional leakage, $\mathcal{L}$ always gives the output, but the simulator is restricted to query its oracle with probability p over its randomness. As noted there, the formulation we use is stronger. We denote by $\mathcal{F}_{\text{INFO}}^{\mathcal{L}}$ the information functionality with leakage function $\mathcal{L}$.

Functionality $\mathcal{F}_{\text{INFO}}^{\mathcal{L}}$

The functionality keeps the following variables: the set of crashed parties $\mathcal{C}$ and the graph G. Initially, $\mathcal{C} = \varnothing$ and $G = (\varnothing, \varnothing)$.

Initialization Step:

1: The party P_{graph} sends graph $G' = (V, E)$ to $\mathcal{F}_{\text{INFO}}^{\mathcal{L}}$. $\mathcal{F}_{\text{INFO}}^{\mathcal{L}}$ sets $G = G'$.
2: $\mathcal{F}_{\text{INFO}}^{\mathcal{L}}$ sends to each party P_i its neighborhood $\mathbf{N}_G(P_i)$.

Leakage Step:

1: If the adversary crashes party P_i, then $\mathcal{F}_{\text{INFO}}^{\mathcal{L}}$ sets $\mathcal{C} = \mathcal{C} \cup \{P_i\}$.
2: If the adversary sends the command (LEAK, q) to $\mathcal{F}_{\text{INFO}}^{\mathcal{L}}$ for the first time, then $\mathcal{F}_{\text{INFO}}^{\mathcal{L}}$ outputs $\mathcal{L}(q, \mathcal{C}, G)$ to the adversary.

Security Model. Our protocols provide security with abort. In particular, the adversary can choose some parties, who do not receive the output (while the others still do). That is, no guaranteed output delivery and no fairness is provided. Moreover, the adversary sees the output before the honest parties and can later decide which of them should receive it.

Technically, we model such ability in the UC framework as follows: First, the ideal world adversary receives from the ideal functionality the outputs of the corrupted parties. Then, it inputs to the functionality an *abort vector* containing a list of parties who do not receive the output.

Definition 1. *We say that a protocol Π topology-hidingly realizes a functionality $\mathcal{F}$ with $\mathcal{L}$-leakage, in the presence of an adversary who can statically passive corrupt and adaptively crash any number of parties, if it UC-realizes $(\mathcal{F}_{\text{INFO}}^{\mathcal{L}} \parallel \mathcal{F})$ in the $\mathcal{F}_{\text{NET}}$-hybrid model.*

2.3 Background

Graphs and Random Walks. In an undirected graph $G = (V, E)$ we denote by $\mathbf{N}_G(P_i)$ the neighborhood of $P_i \in V$. The k-neighborhood of a party $P_i \in V$ is the set of all parties in V within distance k to P_i.

In our work we use the following lemma from [ALM17a]. It states that in an undirected connected graph G, the probability that a random walk of length $8|V|^3\tau$ covers G is at least $1 - \frac{1}{2^\tau}$.

Lemma 1 ([ALM17a]). *Let $G = (V, E)$ be an undirected connected graph. Further let $\mathcal{W}(u, \tau)$ be a random variable whose value is the set of nodes covered by a random walk starting from u and taking $8|V|^3\tau$ steps. We have*

$$\Pr_{\mathcal{W}}[\mathcal{W}(u, \tau) = V] \geq 1 - \frac{1}{2^\tau}.$$

PKCR Encryption. As in [ALM17a], our protocols require a public key encryption scheme with additional properties, called *Privately Key Commutative and Rerandomizable encryption*. We assume that the message space is bits. Then, a PKCR encryption scheme should be: privately key commutative and homomorphic with respect to the OR operation[1]. We formally define these properties below.

Let $\mathcal{PK}$, $\mathcal{SK}$ and $\mathcal{C}$ denote the public key, secret key and ciphertext spaces. As any public key encryption scheme, a PKCR scheme contains the algorithms KeyGen : $\{0,1\}^* \to \mathcal{PK} \times \mathcal{SK}$, Encrypt : $\{0,1\} \times \mathcal{PK} \to \mathcal{C}$ and Decrypt : $\mathcal{C} \times \mathcal{SK} \to \{0,1\}$ for key generation, encryption and decryption respectively (where KeyGen takes as input the security parameter).

Privately Key-Commutative. We require $\mathcal{PK}$ to form a commutative group under the operation $\circledast$. So, given any $\mathrm{pk}_1, \mathrm{pk}_2 \in \mathcal{PK}$, we can efficiently compute $\mathrm{pk}_3 = \mathrm{pk}_1 \circledast \mathrm{pk}_2 \in \mathcal{PK}$ and for every pk, there exists an inverse denoted pk^{-1}.

This group must interact well with ciphertexts; there exists a pair of efficiently computable algorithms AddLayer : $\mathcal{C} \times \mathcal{SK} \to \mathcal{C}$ and DelLayer : $\mathcal{C} \times \mathcal{SK} \to \mathcal{C}$ such that

- For every public key pair $\mathrm{pk}_1, \mathrm{pk}_2 \in \mathcal{PK}$ with corresponding secret keys sk_1 and sk_2, message $m \in \mathcal{M}$, and ciphertext $c = [m]_{\mathrm{pk}_1}$,

$$\mathsf{AddLayer}(c, \mathrm{sk}_2) = [m]_{\mathrm{pk}_1 \circledast \mathrm{pk}_2}.$$

- For every public key pair $\mathrm{pk}_1, \mathrm{pk}_2 \in \mathcal{PK}$ with corresponding secret keys sk_1 and sk_2, message $m \in \mathcal{M}$, and ciphertext $c = [m]_{\mathrm{pk}_1}$,

$$\mathsf{DelLayer}(c, \mathrm{sk}_2) = [m]_{\mathrm{pk}_1 \circledast \mathrm{pk}_2^{-1}}.$$

Notice that we need the secret key to perform these operations, hence the property is called *privately* key-commutative.

OR-Homomorphic. We also require the encryption scheme to be OR-homomorphic, but in such a way that parties cannot tell how many 1's or 0's were OR'd (or who OR'd them). We need an efficiently-evaluatable homomorphic-OR algorithm, HomOR : $\mathcal{C} \times \mathcal{C} \to \mathcal{C}$, to satisfy the following: for every two messages $m, m' \in \{0,1\}$ and every two ciphertexts $c, c' \in \mathcal{C}$ such that $\mathsf{Decrypt}(c, \mathrm{sk}) = m$ and $\mathsf{Decrypt}(c, \mathrm{sk}) = m'$,

$$\{(m, m', c, c', \mathrm{pk}, \mathsf{Encrypt}(m \vee m', \mathrm{pk}; U^*))\}$$
$$\approx_c$$
$$\{(m, m', c, c', \mathrm{pk}, \mathsf{HomOR}(c, c', \mathrm{pk}; U^*))\}$$

Note that this is a stronger definition for homomorphism than usual; usually we only require correctness, not computational indistinguishability.

In [HMTZ16], [AM17] and [ALM17a], the authors discuss how to get this kind of homomorphic OR under the DDH assumption, and later [ALM17b] show how

---

[1] PKCR encryption was introduced in [AM17, ALM17a], where it had three additional properties: key commutativity, homomorphism and rerandomization, hence, it was called Privately Key Commutative and *Rerandomizable* encryption. However, rerandomization is actually implied by the strengthened notion of homomorphism. Therefore, we decided to not include the property, but keep the name.

to get it with the QR assumption. For more details on other kinds of homomorphic cryptosystems that can be compiled into OR-homomorphic cryptosystems, see [ALM17b].

Random Walk Approach [ALM17a]. Our protocol builds upon the protocol from [ALM17a]. We give a high level overview. To achieve broadcast, the protocol computes the OR. Every party has an input bit: the sender inputs the broadcast bit and all other parties use 0 as input bit. Computing the OR of all those bits is thus equivalent to broadcasting the sender's message.

First, let us explain a simplified version of the protocol that is unfortunately not sound, but gets the basic principal across. Each node encrypts its bit under a public key and forwards it to a random neighbor. The neighbor OR's its own bit, adds a fresh public key layer, and it forwards the ciphertext to a randomly chosen neighbor. Eventually, after about $O(\kappa n^3)$ steps, the random walk of every message visits every node in the graph, and therefore, every message will contain the OR of all bits in the network. Now we start the backwards phase, reversing the walk and peeling off layers of encryption.

This scheme is not sound because seeing where the random walks are coming from reveals information about the graph! So, we need to disguise that information. We will do so using correlated random walks, and will have a walk running down each direction of each edge at each step (so 2× number of edges number of walks total). The walks are correlated, but still random. This way, at each step, each node just sees encrypted messages all under new and different keys from each of its neighbors. So, intuitively, there is no way for a node to tell anything about where a walk came from.

3   Topology-Hiding Broadcast

In this section we present a protocol, which securely realizes the broadcast functionality $\mathcal{F}_{\text{BC}}$ (with abort) in the $\mathcal{F}_{\text{NET}}$-hybrid world and leaks at most an arbitrarily small (but not negligible) fraction of a bit. If no crashes occur, the protocol does not leak any information. The protocol is secure against an adversary that (a) controls an arbitrary static set of passively corrupted parties and (b) adaptively crashes any number of parties. Security can be based either on the DDH, the QR or the LWE assumption. To build intuition we first present the simple protocol variant which leaks at most one bit.

Functionality $\mathcal{F}_{\text{BC}}$

When a party P_i sends a bit $b \in \{0, 1\}$ to the functionality $\mathcal{F}_{\text{BC}}$, then $\mathcal{F}_{\text{BC}}$ sends b to each party $P_j \in \mathcal{P}$.

3.1   Protocol Leaking One Bit

We first introduce the broadcast protocol variant BC-OB which leaks at most one-bit. The protocol is divided into n consecutive phases, where, in each phase, the parties execute a modification of the random-walk protocol from [ALM17a]. More specifically, we introduce the following modifications:

Single Output Party: There will be n phases. In each phase only one party, P_o, gets the output. Moreover, it learns the output from exactly one of the random walks it starts.

To implement this, in the respective phase all parties except P_o start their random walks with encryptions of 1 instead of their input bits. This ensures that the outputs they get from the random walks will always be 1. We call these walks *dummy* since the contain no information. Party P_o, on the other hand, starts exactly one random walk with its actual input bit (the other walks it starts with encryptions of 1). This ensures (in case no party crashes) that P_o actually learns the broadcast bit.

Happiness Indicator: Every party P_i holds an *unhappy-bit* u_i. Initially, every P_i is happy, i.e., $u_i = 0$. If a neighbor of P_i crashes, then in the next phase P_i becomes unhappy and sets $u_i = 1$. The idea is that an unhappy party makes all phases following the crash become dummy.

This is implemented by having the parties send along the random walk, instead of a single bit, an encrypted tuple $[b, u]_{\mathrm{pk}}$. The bit u is the OR of the unhappy-bits of the parties in the walk, while b is the OR of their input bits and their unhappy-bits. In other words, a party P_i on the walk homomorphically ORs $b_i \vee u_i$ to b and u_i to u.

Intuitively, if all parties on the walk were happy at the time of adding their bits, b will actually contain the OR of their input bits and u will be set to 0. On the other hand, if any party was unhappy, b will always be set to 1, and $u = 1$ will indicate an abort.

Intuitively, the adversary learns a bit of information only if it manages to break the one random walk which P_o started with its input bit (all other walks contain the tuple $[1, 1]$). Moreover, if it crashes a party, then all phases following the one with the crash abort, hence, they do not leak any information.

More formally, parties execute, in each phase, protocol RandomWalkPhase. This protocol takes as global inputs the length T of the random walk and the P_o which should get output. Additionally, each party P_i has input (d_i, b_i, u_i) where d_i is its number of neighbors, u_i is its unhappy-bit, and b_i is its input bit.

Protocol RandomWalkPhase(T, P_o, $(d_i, b_i, u_i)_{P_i \in \mathcal{P}}$)

Initialization Stage:

1: Each party P_i generates $\mathrm{T} \cdot d_i$ keypairs $(\mathrm{pk}_{i \to j}^{(r)}, \mathrm{sk}_{i \to j}^{(r)}) \leftarrow \mathsf{KeyGen}(1^\kappa)$ where $r \in \{1, \ldots, \mathrm{T}\}$ and $j \in \{1, \ldots, d_i\}$.

2: Each party P_i generates $\mathtt{T} - 1$ random permutations on d_i elements $\left\{\pi_i^{(2)}, \ldots, \pi_i^{(\mathtt{T})}\right\}$

3: For each party P_i, if any of P_i's neighbors crashed in any phase before the current one, then P_i becomes unhappy, i.e., sets $u_i = 1$.

Aggregate Stage: Each party P_i does the following:

1: **if** P_i is the recipient P_o **then**

2:     Party P_i sends to the first neighbor the ciphertext $[b_i \vee u_i, u_i]_{\mathsf{pk}_{i \to 1}^{(1)}}$ and the public key $\mathsf{pk}_{i \to 1}^{(1)}$, and to any other neighbor P_j it sends ciphertext $[1,1]_{\mathsf{pk}_{i \to j}^{(1)}}$ and the public key $\mathsf{pk}_{i \to j}^{(1)}$.

3: **else**

4:     Party P_i sends to each neighbor P_j ciphertext $[1,1]_{\mathsf{pk}_{i \to j}^{(1)}}$ and the key $\mathsf{pk}_{i \to j}^{(1)}$.

5: **end if**

6: // Add layer while ORing own input bit

7: **for** any round r from 2 to $\mathtt{T}$ **do**

8:     For each neighbor P_j of P_i, do the following (let $k = \pi_i^{(r)}(j)$):

9:     **if** P_i did not receive a message from P_j **then**

10:         Party P_i sends ciphertext $[1,1]_{\mathsf{pk}_{i \to k}^{(r)}}$ and key $\mathsf{pk}_{i \to k}^{(r)}$ to neighbor P_k.

11:     **else** // AddLayer and HomOR are applied component-wise

12:         Let $c_{j \to i}^{(r-1)}$ and $\overline{\mathsf{pk}}_{j \to i}^{(r-1)}$ be the ciphertext and the public key P_i received from P_j. Party P_i computes $\overline{\mathsf{pk}}_{i \to k}^{(r)} = \overline{\mathsf{pk}}_{j \to i}^{(r-1)} \circledast \mathsf{pk}_{i \to k}^{(r)}$ and $\hat{c}_{i \to k}^{(r)} \leftarrow \mathsf{AddLayer}\left(c_{j \to i}^{(r-1)}, \mathsf{sk}_{i \to k}^{(r)}\right)$.

13:         P_i computes $[b_i \vee u_i, u_i]_{\overline{\mathsf{pk}}_{i \to k}^{(r)}}$ and $c_{i \to k}^{(r)} = \mathsf{HomOR}\left([b_i \vee u_i, u_i]_{\overline{\mathsf{pk}}_{i \to k}^{(r)}}, \hat{c}_{i \to k}^{(r)}, \overline{\mathsf{pk}}_{i \to k}^{(r)}\right)$.

14:         Party P_i sends ciphertext $c_{i \to k}^{(r)}$ and public key $\overline{\mathsf{pk}}_{i \to k}^{(r)}$ to neighbor P_k.

15:     **end if**

16: **end for**

Decrypt Stage: Each party P_i does the following:

1: For each neighbor P_j of P_i, if P_i did not receive a message from P_j at round $\mathtt{T}$ of the Aggregate Stage, then it sends ciphertext $e_{i \to j}^{(\mathtt{T})} = [1,1]_{\overline{\mathsf{pk}}_{j \to i}^{(\mathtt{T})}}$ to P_j.

Otherwise, P_i sends to P_j $e_{i \to j}^{(\mathtt{T})} = \mathsf{HomOR}\left([b_i \vee u_i, u_i]_{\overline{\mathsf{pk}}_{j \to i}^{(\mathtt{T})}}, c_{j \to i}^{(\mathtt{T})}, \overline{\mathsf{pk}}_{j \to i}^{(\mathtt{T})}\right)$.

2: **for** any round r from $\mathtt{T}$ to 2 **do**

3:     For each neighbor P_k of P_i:

4:     **if** P_i did not receive a message from P_k **then**

5:         Party P_i sends $e_{i \to j}^{(r-1)} = [1,1]_{\overline{\mathsf{pk}}_{j \to i}^{(r-1)}}$ to neighbor P_j, where $k = \pi_i^{(r)}(j)$.

6:     **else**

7:         Denote by $e_{k \to i}^{(r)}$ the ciphertext P_i received from P_k, where $k = \pi_i^{(r)}(j)$. Party P_i sends $e_{i \to j}^{(r-1)} = \mathsf{DelLayer}\left(e_{k \to i}^{(r)}, \mathsf{sk}_{i \to k}^{(r)}\right)$ to neighbor P_j.

8:     **end if**

9: **end for**

> 10: If P_i is the recipient P_o, then it computes $(b, u) = \mathsf{Decrypt}(\mathsf{e}^{(1)}_{1 \to i}, \mathsf{sk}^{(1)}_{i \to 1})$ and
> **outputs** (b, u, u_i). Otherwise, it **outputs** $(1, 0, u_i)$.

The actual protocol BC-OB consists of n consecutive runs of the random walk phase protocol RandomWalkPhase.

Protocol BC-OB$(\mathsf{T}, (d_i, b_i)_{P_i \in \mathcal{P}})$

Each party P_i keeps bits b_i^{out}, u_i^{out} and u_i, and sets $u_i = 0$.
for o from 1 to n **do**
    Parties jointly execute
    $((b_i^{tmp}, v_i^{tmp}, u_i^{tmp})_{P_i \in \mathcal{P}}) = \mathsf{RandomWalkPhase}(\mathsf{T}, P_o, (d_i, b_i, u_i)_{P_i \in \mathcal{P}})$.
    Each party P_i sets $u_i = u_i^{tmp}$.
    Party P_o sets $b_o^{out} = b_o^{tmp}$, $u_o^{out} = v_o^{tmp}$.
end for
For each party P_i, **if** $u_i^{out} = 0$ **then** party P_i outputs b_i^{out}.

The protocol BC-OB leaks information about the topology of the graph during the execution of RandomWalkPhase, in which the first crash occurs. (Every execution before the first crash proceeds almost exactly as the protocol in [ALM17a] and in every execution afterwards all values are blinded by the unhappy-bit u.) We model the leaked information by a query to the leakage function $\mathcal{L}_{OB}$. The function outputs only one bit and, since the functionality $\mathcal{F}^{\mathcal{L}}_{\mathrm{INFO}}$ allows for only one query to the leakage function, the protocol leaks overall one bit of information.

The inputs passed to $\mathcal{L}_{OB}$ are: the graph G and the set $\mathcal{C}$ of crashed parties, passed to the function by $\mathcal{F}^{\mathcal{L}}_{\mathrm{INFO}}$, and a triple (F, P_s, T'), passed by the simulator. The idea is that the simulator needs to know whether the walk carrying the output succeeded or not, and this depends on the graph G. More precisely, the set F contains a list of pairs (P_f, r), where r is the number of rounds in the execution of RandomWalkPhase, at which P_f crashed. $\mathcal{L}_{OB}$ tells the simulator whether any of the crashes in F disconnected a freshly generated random walk of length T', starting at given party P_s.

Function $\mathcal{L}_{OB}((F, P_s, \mathsf{T}'), \mathcal{C}, G)$

if for any $(P_f, r) \in F$, $P_f \notin \mathcal{C}$ **then** Return 0.
else
    Generate in G a random walk of length T' starting at P_s.
    Return 1 if for any $(P_f, r) \in F$ removing party P_f after r rounds disconnects
    the walk and 0 otherwise.
end if

We prove the following theorem in Sect. A.1.

Theorem 2. *Let κ be the security parameter. For $\mathsf{T} = 8n^3(\log(n) + \kappa)$ the protocol BC-OB$(\mathsf{T}, (d_i, b_i)_{P_i \in \mathcal{P}}))$ topology-hidingly realizes $\mathcal{F}^{\mathcal{L}_{OB}}_{\mathrm{INFO}} \| \mathcal{F}_{\mathrm{BC}}$ (with abort)* *in the $\mathcal{F}_{\text{NET}}$ hybrid-world, where the leakage function $\mathcal{L}_{OB}$ is the one defined as above. If no crashes occur, then there is no abort and there is no leakage.*

3.2   Protocol Leaking a Fraction of a Bit

We now show how to go from BC-OB to the actual broadcast protocol BC-FB$_p$ which leaks only a fraction p of a bit. The leakage parameter p can be arbitrarily small. However, the complexity of the protocol is proportional to $1/p$. As a consequence, $1/p$ must be polynomial and p cannot be negligible.

The idea is to leverage the fact that the adversary can gain information in only one execution of RandomWalkPhase. Imagine that RandomWalkPhase succeeds only with a small probability p, and otherwise the output bit b is 1. Moreover, assume that during RandomWalkPhase the adversary does not learn whether it will fail until it can decrypt the output.

We can now, for each phase, repeat RandomWalkPhase ρ times, so that with overwhelming probability one of the repetitions does not fail. A party P_o can then compute its output as the AND of outputs from all repetitions (or abort if any repetition aborted). On the other hand, the adversary can choose only one execution of RandomWalkPhase, in which it learns one bit of information (all subsequent repetitions will abort). Moreover, it must choose it before it knows whether the execution succeeds. Hence, the adversary learns one bit of information only with probability p.

What is left is to modify RandomWalkPhase, so that it succeeds only with probability p, and so that the adversary does not know whether it will succeed. We only change the Aggregate Stage. Instead of an encrypted tuple $[b, u]$, the parties send along the walk $\lfloor 1/p \rfloor + 1$ encrypted bits $[b^1, \ldots, b^{\lfloor 1/p \rfloor}, u]$, where u again is the OR of the unhappy-bits, and every b^k is a copy the bit b in RandomWalkPhase, with some caveats. For each phase o, and for every party $P_i \neq P_o$, all b^k are copies of b in the walk and they all contain 1. For P_o, only one of the bits, b^k, contains the OR, while the rest is initially set to 1.

During the Aggregate Stage, the parties process every ciphertext corresponding to a bit b^k the same way they processed the encryption of b in the RandomWalkPhase. Then, before sending the ciphertexts to the next party on the walk, the encryptions of the bits b^k are randomly shuffled. (This way, as long as the walk traverses an honest party, the adversary does not know which of the ciphertexts contain dummy values.) At the end of the Aggregate Stage (after T rounds), the last party chooses uniformly at random one of the $\lfloor 1/p \rfloor$ ciphertexts and uses it, together with the encryption of the unhappy-bit, to execute the Decrypt Stage as in RandomWalkPhase.

The information leaked by BC-FB$_p$ is modeled by the following function $\mathcal{L}_{FB_p}$.

Function $\mathcal{L}_{FB_p}((F, P_s, \mathbf{T}'), \mathcal{C}, G)$

Let $p' = 1/\lfloor 1/p \rfloor$. With probability p', return $\mathcal{L}_{OB}((F, P_s, \mathbf{T}'), \mathcal{C}, G)$ and with probability $1 - p'$ return $\perp$.

A formal description of the modified protocol ProbabilisticRandomWalkPhase$_p$ and a proof of the following theorem can be found in Sect. A.2.

Theorem 3. *Let κ be the security parameter. For $\tau = \log(n) + \kappa$, $T = 8n^3\tau$, and $\rho = \tau/(p' - 2^{-\tau})$, where $p' = 1/\lfloor 1/p \rfloor$, protocol BC-FB$_p(T, \rho, (d_i, b_i)_{P_i \in \mathcal{P}})$ topology-hidingly realizes $\mathcal{F}_{\text{INFO}}^{\mathcal{L}_{FB_p}} \| \mathcal{F}_{\text{BC}}$ (with abort) in the $\mathcal{F}_{\text{NET}}$ hybrid-world, where the leakage function $\mathcal{L}_{FB_p}$ is the one defined as above. If no crashes occur, then there is no abort and there is no leakage.*

4 From Broadcast to Topology-Hiding Computation

We showed how to get topology-hiding broadcasts. To get additional functionality (e.g. for compiling MPC protocols), we have to be able to compose these broadcasts. When there is no leakage, this is straightforward: we can run as many broadcasts in parallel or in sequence as we want and they will not affect each other. However, if we consider a broadcast secure in the fail-stop model that leaks at most 1 bit, composing t of these broadcasts could lead to leaking t bits.

The first step towards implementing any functionality in a topology-hiding way is to modify our broadcast protocol to a topology-hiding all-to-all multibit broadcast, without aggregating leakage. Then, we show how to sequentially compose such broadcasts, again without adding leakage. Finally, one can use standard techniques to compile MPC protocols from broadcast. In the following, we give a high level overview of each step. A detailed description of the transformations can be found in the full version [LLM+18].

All-to-all Multibit Broadcast. The first observation is that a modification of BC-FB$_p$ allows one party to broadcast multiple bits. Instead of sending a single bit b during the random-walk protocol, each party sends a vector $\vec{b}$ of bits encrypted separately under the same key. That is, in each round of the Aggregate Phase, each party sends a vector $[\vec{b_1}, \ldots, \vec{b_\ell}, u]$.

We can extend this protocol to all-to-all multibit broadcast, where each party P_i broadcasts a message $(b_1, \ldots, b_k)$, as follows. Each of the vectors $\vec{b_i}$ in $[\vec{b_1}, \ldots, \vec{b_\ell}, u]$ contains nk bits, and P_i uses the bits from $n(i-1)$ to ni to communicate its message. That is, in the Aggregate Stage, *every* P_i homomorphically OR's $\vec{b_i} = (0, \ldots, 0, b_1, \ldots, b_k, 0, \ldots, 0)$ with the received encrypted vectors.

Sequential Execution. All-to-all broadcasts can be composed sequentially by preserving the state of unhappy bits between sequential executions. That is, once some party sees a crash, it will cause all subsequent executions to abort.

Topology-Hiding Computation. With the above statements, we conclude that any MPC protocol can be compiled into one that leaks only a fraction p of a bit in total. This is achieved using a public key infrastructure, where in the first round the parties use the topology hiding all-to-all broadcast to send each public key to every other party, and then each round of the MPC protocol is simulated with an all-to-all multibit topology-hiding broadcast. As a corollary, any functionality $\mathcal{F}$ can be implemented by a topology-hiding protocol leaking any fraction p of a bit.

5 Efficient Topology-Hiding Computation with FHE

One thing to note is that compiling MPC from broadcast is rather expensive, especially in the fail-stop model; we need a broadcast for every round. However, we will show that an FHE scheme with additive overhead can be used to evaluate any polynomial-time function f in a topology-hiding manner. Additive overhead applies to ciphertext versus plaintext sizes and to error with respect to all homomorphic operations if necessary. We will employ an altered random walk protocol, and the total number of rounds in this protocol will amount to that of a single broadcast. We remark that FHE with additive overhead can be obtained from subexponential iO and subexponentially secure OWFs (probabilistic iO), as shown in [CLTV15].

5.1 Deeply-Fully-Homomorphic Public-Key Encryption

In the altered random walk protocol, the PKCR scheme is replaced by a deeply-fully-homomorphic PKE scheme (DFH-PKE). Similarly to PKCR, a DFH-PKE scheme is a public-key encryption scheme enhanced by algorithms for adding and deleting layers. However, we do not require that public keys form a group, and we allow the ciphertexts and public keys on different levels (that is, for which a layer has been added a different number of times) to be distinguishable. Moreover, DFH-PKE offers full homomorphism.

This is captured by three additional algorithms: $\mathsf{AddLayer}_r$, $\mathsf{DelLayer}_r$, and HomOp_r, operating on ciphertexts with r layers of encryption (we will call such ciphertexts level-r ciphertexts). A level-r ciphertext is encrypted under a level-r public key (each level can have different key space).

Adding a layer requires a new secret key sk. The algorithm $\mathsf{AddLayer}_r$ takes as input a vector of level-r ciphertexts $[\![\vec{m}]\!]_{\mathsf{pk}}$ encrypted under a level-r public key, the corresponding level-r public key $\mathbf{pk}$, and a new secret key sk. It outputs a vector of level-$(r+1)$ ciphertexts and the level-$(r+1)$ public key, under which it is encrypted. Deleting a layer is the opposite of adding a layer.

With HomOp_r, one can compute any function on a vector of encrypted messages. It takes a vector of level-r ciphertexts encrypted under a level-r public key, the corresponding level-r public key $\mathbf{pk}$ and a function from a permitted set $\mathcal{F}$ of functions. It outputs a level-r ciphertext that contains the output of the function applied to the encrypted messages.

Intuitively, a DFH-PKE scheme is secure if one can simulate any level-r ciphertext without knowing the history of adding and deleting layers. This is captured by the existence of an algorithm Leveled-Encrypt$_r$, which takes as input a plain message and a level-r public key, and outputs a level-r ciphertext. We require that for any level-r encryption of a message $\tilde{m}$, the output of AddLayer$_r$ on that ciphertext is indistinguishable from the output of Leveled-Encrypt$_{r+1}$ on $\tilde{m}$ and a (possibly different) level-$(r+1)$ public key. An analogous property is required for DelLayer$_r$. We will also require that the output of HomOp$_r$ is indistinguishable from a level-r encryption of the output of the functions applied to the messages. We refer to the full version [LLM+18] for a formal definition of a DFH-PKE scheme and an instantiation from FHE.

Remark. If we relax DFH-PKE and only require homomorphic evaluation of OR, then this relaxation is implied by any OR-homomorphic PKCR scheme (in PKCR, additionally, all levels of key and ciphertext spaces are the same, and the public key space forms a group). Such OR-homomorphic DFH-PKE would be sufficient to prove the security of the protocols BC-OB and BC-FB$_p$. However, for simplicity and clarity, we decided to describe our protocols BC-OB and BC-FB$_p$ from a OR-homomorphic PKCR scheme.

5.2 Topology-Hiding Computation from DFH-PKE

To evaluate any function f, we modify the topology-hiding broadcast protocol (with PKCR replaced by DFH-PKE) in the following way. During the Aggregate Stage, instead of one bit for the OR of all inputs, the parties send a vector of encrypted inputs. At each round, each party homomorphically adds its input together with its id to the vector. The last party on the walk homomorphically evaluates f on the encrypted inputs, and (homomorphically) selects the output of the party who receives it in the current phase. The Decrypt Stage is started with this encrypted result.

Note that we still need a way to make a random walk dummy (this was achieved in BC-OB and BC-FB$_p$ by starting it with a 1). Here, we will have an additional input bit for the party who starts a walk. In case this bit is set, when homomorphically evaluating f, we (homomorphically) replace the output of f by a special symbol. We refer to the full version [LLM+18] for a detailed description of the protocol and a proof of the following theorem.

Theorem 4. *For security parameter κ, $\tau = \log(n) + \kappa$, $T = 8n^3\tau$, and $\rho = \tau/(p' - 2^{-\tau})$, where $p' = 1/\lfloor 1/p \rfloor$, the protocol DFH-THC$(T, \rho, (d_i, \mathsf{input}_i)_{P_i \in \mathcal{P}}))$ topology-hidingly evaluates any poly-time function f, $\mathcal{F}_{\mathrm{INFO}}^{\mathcal{L}_{FB_P}} \| f$ in the $\mathcal{F}_{\mathrm{NET}}$ hybrid-world.*

6   Security Against Semi-malicious Adversaries

In this section, we show how to generically compile our protocols to provide in addition security against a semi-malicious adversary. The transformed protocol proceeds in two phases: Randomness Generation and Deterministic Execution. In the first phase, we generate the random tapes for all parties and in the second phase we execute the given protocol with parties using the pre-generated random tapes. The tapes are generated in such a way that the tape of each party P_i is the sum of random values generated from each party. Hence, as long as one party is honest, the generated tape is random.

Randomness Generation. The goal of the first phase is to generate for each party P_i a uniform random value r_i, which can then be used as randomness tape of P_i in the phase of Deterministic Execution.[2]

Protocol GenerateRandomness

1: Each party P_i generates $n+1$ uniform random values $s_i^{(0)}, s_i^{(1)}, \ldots, s_i^{(n)}$ and sets $r_i^{(0)} := s_i^{(0)}$.
2: **for** any round r from 1 to n **do**
3:      Each party P_i sends $r_i^{(r-1)}$ to all its neighbors.
4:      Each party P_i computes $r_i^{(r)}$ as the sum of all values received from its (non-crashed) neighbors in the current round and the value $s_i^{(k)}$.
5: **end for**
6: Each party P_i outputs $r_i := r_i^{(n)}$.

Lemma 2. *Let G' be the network graph without the parties which crashed during the execution of GenerateRandomness. Any party P_i whose connected component in G' contains at least one honest party will output a uniform value r_i. The output of any honest party is not known to the adversary. The protocol GenerateRandomness does not leak any information about the network-graph (even if crashes occur).*

Proof. First observe that all randomness is chosen at the beginning of the first round. The rest of the protocol is completely deterministic. This implies that the adversary has to choose the randomness of corrupted parties independently of the randomness chosen by honest parties.

If party P_i at the end of the protocol execution is in a connected component with honest party P_j, the output r_i is a sum which contains at least one of the values $s_j^{(r)}$ from P_j. That summand is independent of the rest of the summands and uniform random. Thus, r_i is uniform random as well.

Any honest party will (in the last round) compute its output as a sum which contains a locally generated truly random value, which is not known to the adversary. Thus, the output is also not known to the adversary.

Finally, observe that the message pattern seen by a party is determined by its neighborhood. Moreover, the messages received by corrupted parties from honest parties are uniform random values. This implies, that the view of the adversary in this protocol can be easily simulated given the neighborhood of

---

[2] To improve overall communication complexity of the protocol the values generated in the first phase could be used as local seeds for a PRG which is then used to generate the actual random tapes.

corrupted parties. Thus, the protocol does not leak any information about the network topology.   □

Transformation to Semi-malicious Security. In the second phase of Deterministic Execution, the parties execute the protocol secure against passive and fail-stop corruptions, but instead of generating fresh randomness during the protocol execution, they use the random tape generated in the first phase.

Protocol EnhanceProtocol(Π)

1: The parties execute GenerateRandomness to generate random tapes.
2: If a party witnessed a crash in GenerateRandomness, it pretends that it witnessed this crash in the first round of the protocol Π.
3: The parties execute Π, using the generated randomness tapes, instead of generating randomness on the fly.

Theorem 5. *Let $\mathcal{F}$ be an MPC functionality and let Π be a protocol that topology-hidingly realizes $\mathcal{F}$ in the presence of static passive corruptions and adaptive crashes. Then, the protocol EnhanceProtocol(Π) topology-hidingly realizes $\mathcal{F}$ in the presence of static semi-malicious corruption and adaptive crashes. The leakage stays the same.*

Proof. (sketch) The randomness generation protocol GenerateRandomness used in the first phase is secure against a semi-malicious fail-stopping adversary. Lemma 2 implies that the random tape of any semi-malicious party that can interact with honest parties is truly uniform random. Moreover, the adversary has no information on the random tapes of honest parties. This implies that the capability of the adversary in the execution of the actual protocol in the second phase (which for fixed random tapes is deterministic) is the same as for an semi-honest fail-stopping adversary. This implies that the leakage of EnhanceProtocol(Π) is the same as for Π as the randomness generation protocol does not leak information (even if crashes occur).   □

As a corollary of Theorems 3 and 5, we obtain that any MPC functionality can be realized in a topology-hiding manner secure against an adversary that does any number of static semi-malicious corruptions and adaptive crashes, leaking at most an arbitrary small fraction of information about the topology.

7   LWE Based OR-Homomorphic PKCR Encryption

In this section, we show how to get PKCR encryption from the LWE. The basis of our PKCR scheme is the public-key crypto-system proposed in [Reg09].
LWE PKE scheme [Reg09] Let κ be the security parameter of the cryptosystem. The cryptosystem is parameterized by two integers m, q and a probability distribution χ on $\mathbb{Z}_q$. To guarantee security and correctness of the encryption scheme, one can choose $q \geq 2$ to be some prime number between κ^2 and $2\kappa^2$, and

let $m = (1 + \epsilon)(\kappa + 1) \log q$ for some arbitrary constant $\epsilon > 0$. The distribution χ is a discrete gaussian distribution with standard deviation $\alpha(\kappa) := \frac{1}{\sqrt{\kappa} \log^2 \kappa}$.

Key Generation: *Setup:* For $i = 1, \ldots, m$, choose m vectors $\mathbf{a}_1, \ldots, \mathbf{a}_m \in \mathbb{Z}_q^{\kappa}$ independently from the uniform distribution. Let us denote $A \in \mathbb{Z}_q^{m \times \kappa}$ the matrix that contains the vectors $\mathbf{a}_i$ as rows.
Secret Key: Choose $\mathbf{s} \in \mathbb{Z}_q^{\kappa}$ uniformly at random. The secret key is $\mathbf{sk} = \mathbf{s}$.
Public Key: Choose the error coefficients $e_1, \ldots, e_m \in \mathbb{Z}_q$ independently according to χ. The public key is given by the vectors $b_i = \langle \mathbf{a}_i, \mathbf{sk} \rangle + e_i$. In matrix notation, $\mathbf{pk} = A \cdot \mathbf{sk} + \mathbf{e}$.
Encryption: To encrypt a bit b, we choose uniformly at random $\mathbf{x} \in \{0,1\}^m$. The ciphertext is $c = (\mathbf{x}^\mathsf{T} A, \mathbf{x}^\mathsf{T} \mathbf{pk} + b\frac{q}{2})$.
Decryption: Given a ciphertext $c = (c_1, c_2)$, the decryption of c is 0 if $c_2 - c_1 \cdot \mathbf{sk}$ is closer to 0 than to $\lfloor \frac{q}{2} \rfloor$ modulo q. Otherwise, the decryption is 1.

Extension to PKCR. We now extend the above PKE scheme to satisfy the requirements of a PKCR scheme. For this, we show how to rerandomize ciphertexts, how add and remove layers of encryption, and finally how to homomorphically compute XOR. We remark that it is enough to provide XOR-Homomorphic PKCR encryption scheme to achieve an OR-Homomorphic PKCR encryption scheme, as was shown in [ALM17a].

Rerandomization: We note that a ciphertext can be rerandomized, which is done by homomorphically adding an encryption of 0. The algorithm Rand takes as input a cipertext and the corresponding public key, as well as a (random) vector $\mathbf{x} \in \{0,1\}^m$.

Algorithm $\mathsf{Rand}(c = (c_1, c_2), \mathbf{pk}, \mathbf{x})$

return $(c_1 + \mathbf{x}^\mathsf{T} A, c_2 + \mathbf{x}^\mathsf{T} \mathbf{pk})$.

Adding and Deleting Layers of Encryption: Given an encryption of a bit b under the public key $\mathbf{pk} = A \cdot \mathbf{sk} + \mathbf{e}$, and a secret key $\mathbf{sk}'$ with corresponding public key $\mathbf{pk}' = A \cdot \mathbf{sk}' + \mathbf{e}'$, one can add a layer of encryption, i.e. obtain a ciphertext under the public key $\mathbf{pk} \cdot \mathbf{pk}' := A \cdot (\mathbf{sk} + \mathbf{sk}') + \mathbf{e} + \mathbf{e}'$. Also, one can delete a layer of encryption.

Algorithm $\mathsf{AddLayer}(c = (c_1, c_2), \mathbf{sk})$

return $(c_1, c_1 \cdot \mathbf{sk} + c_2)$

Algorithm $\mathsf{DelLayer}(c = (c_1, c_2), \mathbf{sk})$

return $(c_1, c_2 - c_1 \cdot \mathbf{sk})$

Error Analysis. Every time we add a layer, the error increases. Hence, we need to ensure that the error does not increase too much. After l steps, the error in the public key is $\mathrm{pk}_{0\dots l} = \sum_{i=0}^{l} \mathbf{e}_i$, where $\mathbf{e}_i$ is the error added in each step.

The error in the ciphertext is $c_{0\dots l} = \sum_{i=0}^{l} \mathbf{x}_i \sum_{j=0}^{i} \mathbf{e}_j$, where the $\mathbf{x}_i$ is the chosen randomness in each step. Since $\mathbf{x}_i \in \{0,1\}^m$, the error in the ciphertext can be bounded by $m \cdot \max_i\{|\mathbf{e}_i|_\infty\} \cdot l^2$, which is quadratic in the number of steps.

Homomorphic XOR: A PKCR encryption scheme requires a slightly stronger version of homomorphism. In particular, homomorphic operation includes the rerandomization of the ciphertexts. Hence, the algorithm hXor also calls Rand. The inputs to hXor are two ciphertexts encrypted under the same public key and the corresponding public key.

Algorithm $\mathrm{hXor}(c = (c_1, c_2), c' = (c_1', c_2'), \mathrm{pk})$

Set $c'' = (c_1 + c_1', c_2 + c_2')$.
Choose $\mathbf{x} \in \{0,1\}^m$ uniformly at random.
return $\mathrm{Rand}(c'', \mathrm{pk}, \mathbf{x})$

Appendix

A   Topology-Hiding Broadcast

This section contains supplementary material for Sect. 3.

A.1   Protocol Leaking One Bit

In this section we prove Theorem 2 from Sect. 3.1.

Theorem 2. *Let κ be the security parameter. For $\mathrm{T} = 8n^3(\log(n)+\kappa)$ the protocol $BC\text{-}OB(\mathrm{T}, (d_i, b_i)_{P_i \in \mathcal{P}})$ topology-hidingly realizes $\mathcal{F}_{\mathrm{INFO}}^{\mathcal{L}_{OB}} \| \mathcal{F}_{\mathrm{BC}}$ (with abort) in the $\mathcal{F}_{\mathrm{NET}}$ hybrid-world, where the leakage function $\mathcal{L}_{OB}$ is the one defined as above. If no crashes occur, then there is no abort and there is no leakage.*

Proof. **Completeness.** We first show that the protocol is complete. To this end, we need to ensure that the probability that all parties get the correct output is overwhelming in κ. That is, the probability that all non-dummy random walks (of length $\mathrm{T} = 8n^3(\log(n) + \kappa)$) reach all nodes is overwhelming.

By Lemma 1, a walk of length $8n^3\tau$ does not reach all nodes with probability at most $\frac{1}{2^\tau}$. Then, using the union bound, we obtain that the probability that there is a party whose walk does not reach all nodes is at most $\frac{n}{2^\tau}$. Hence, all n walks (one for each party) reach all nodes with probability at least $1 - \frac{n}{2^\tau}$. If we want this value to be overwhelming, e.g. $1 - \frac{1}{2^\kappa}$, we can set $\tau := \kappa + \log(n)$.

Soundness. We now need to show that no environment can distinguish between the real world and the simulated world, when given access to the adversarially-corrupted parties. We first describe on a high level the simulator $\mathcal{S}_{OB}$ and argue that it simulates the real execution.

In essence, the task of $\mathcal{S}_{OB}$ is to simulate the messages sent by honest parties to passively corrupted parties. Consider a corrupted party P_c and its honest neighbor P_h. The messages sent from P_h to P_c during the Aggregate Stage are ciphertexts, to which P_h added a layer, and corresponding public keys. Since P_h is honest, the adversary does not know the secret keys corresponding to the sent public keys. Hence, $\mathcal{S}_{OB}$ can simply replace them with encryptions of a pair $(1,1)$ under a freshly generated public key. The group structure of keys in PKCR guarantees that a fresh key has the same distribution as the composed key (after executing AddLayer). Semantic security implies that the encrypted message can be replaced by $(1,1)$.

Consider now the Decrypt Stage at round r. Let $\mathbf{pk}^{(r)}_{c \to h}$ be the public key sent by P_c to P_h in the Aggregate Stage (note that this is not the key discussed above; there we argued about keys sent in the opposite direction). $\mathcal{S}_{OB}$ will send to P_c a fresh encryption under $\mathbf{pk}^{(r)}_{c \to h}$. We now specify what it encrypts.

Note that the only interesting case is when the party P_o receiving output is corrupted and when we are in the round r in which the (only one) random walk carrying the output enters an area of corrupted parties, containing P_o (that is, when the walk with output contains from P_h all the way to P_o only corrupted parties). In this one message in round r the adversary learns the output of P_o. All other messages are simply encryptions of $(1,1)$.

For this one meaningful message, we consider three cases. If any party crashed in a phase preceding the current one, $\mathcal{S}_{OB}$ sends an encryption of $(1,1)$ (as in the real world the walk is made dummy by an unhappy party). If no crashes occurred up to this point (round r in given phase), $\mathcal{S}_{OB}$ encrypts the output received from $\mathcal{F}_{BC}$. If a crash happened in the given phase, $\mathcal{S}_{OB}$ queries the leakage oracle $\mathcal{L}_{OB}$, which essentially executes the protocol and tells whether the output or $(1,1)$ should be sent.

Simulator. Below, we present the pseudocode of the simulator. The essential part of it is the algorithm PhaseSimulation, which is also illustrated in Fig. 1.

Simulator $\mathcal{S}_{OB}$

1. $\mathcal{S}_{OB}$ corrupts passively $\mathcal{Z}^p$.
2. $\mathcal{S}_{OB}$ sends inputs for all parties in $\mathcal{Z}^p$ to $\mathcal{F}_{BC}$ and receives the output bit b^{out}.
3. For each $P_i \in \mathcal{Z}^p$, $\mathcal{S}_{OB}$ receives $\mathbf{N}_G(P_i)$ from $\mathcal{F}^{\mathcal{L}}_{INFO}$.
4. Throughout the simulation, if $\mathcal{A}$ crashes a party P_f, so does $\mathcal{S}_{OB}$.
5. Now $\mathcal{S}_{OB}$ has to simulate the view of all parties in $\mathcal{Z}^p$.
   In every phase in which P_o should get the output, first of all the Initialization Stage is executed among the parties in $\mathcal{Z}^p$ and the T key pairs are generated for every $P_i \in \mathcal{Z}^p$. Moreover, for every $P_i \in \mathcal{Z}^p$ the permutations $\pi_i^{(r)}$ are generated, defining those parts of all random walks, which pass through parties in $\mathcal{Z}^p$.

The messages sent by parties in $\mathcal{Z}^p$ are generated by executing the protocol RandomWalkPhase. The messages sent by correct parties $P_i \notin \mathcal{Z}^p$ are generated by executing PhaseSimulation(P_o, P_i), described below.

6. $\mathcal{S}_{OB}$ sends to $\mathcal{F}_{BC}$ the abort vector (in particular, the vector contains all parties P_o who should receive their outputs in phases following the first crash and, depending on the output of $\mathcal{L}_{OB}$, the party who should receive its output in the phase with first crash).

Algorithm PhaseSimulation(P_o, P_i)

If $P_o \in \mathcal{Z}^p$, let w denote the random walk generated in the Initialization Stage (at the beginning of the simulation of this phase), which starts at P_o and carries the output bit. Let ℓ denote the number of parties in $\mathcal{Z}^p$ on w before the first correct party. If $P_o \notin \mathcal{Z}^p$, w and ℓ are not defined.

For every $P_j \in \mathcal{Z}^p \cap \mathbf{N}_G(P_i)$, let $\mathrm{pk}_{j \to i}^{(r)}$ denote the public key generated in the Initialization Stage by P_j for P_i and for round r.

Initialization Stage

1: For every neighbor $P_j \in \mathcal{Z}^p$ of the correct P_i, $\mathcal{S}_{OB}$ generates T key pairs $(\mathrm{pk}_{i \to j}^{(1)}, \mathrm{sk}_{i \to j}^{(1)}), \ldots, (\mathrm{pk}_{i \to j}^{(T)}, \mathrm{sk}_{i \to j}^{(T)})$.

Aggregate Stage

1: In round r, for every neighbor $P_j \in \mathbf{N}_G(P_i) \cap \mathcal{Z}^p$, $\mathcal{S}_{OB}$ sends $([1, 1]_{\mathrm{pk}_{i \to j}^{(r)}}, \mathrm{pk}_{i \to j}^{(r)})$ to P_j.

Decrypt Stage

1: **if** $\mathcal{A}$ crashed any party in any phase before the current one or $P_o \notin \mathcal{Z}^p$ **then**
2:     In every round r and for every neighbor $P_j \in \mathbf{N}_G(P_i) \cap \mathcal{Z}^p$, $\mathcal{S}_{OB}$ sends $[1, 1]_{\mathrm{pk}_{j \to i}^{(r)}}$ to P_j.
3: **else**
4:     In every round r and for every neighbor $P_j \in \mathbf{N}_G(P_i) \cap \mathcal{Z}^p$, $\mathcal{S}_{OB}$ sends $[1, 1]_{\mathrm{pk}_{j \to i}^{(r)}}$ to P_j unless the following three conditions hold: (a) P_i is the first party not in $\mathcal{Z}^p$ on w, (b) P_j is the last party in $\mathcal{Z}^p$ on w, and (c) $r = 2T - \ell$.
5:     If the three conditions hold (in particular $r = 2T - \ell$), $\mathcal{S}_{OB}$ does the following. If $\mathcal{A}$ did not crash any party in a previous round, $\mathcal{S}_{OB}$ sends $[b^{out}, 0]_{\mathrm{pk}_{j \to i}^{(r)}}$ to party P_j.
6:     Otherwise, let F denote the set of pairs $(P_f, s - \ell + 1)$ such that $\mathcal{A}$ crashed P_f in round s. $\mathcal{S}_{OB}$ queries $\mathcal{F}_{\mathrm{INFO}}^{\mathcal{L}_{OB}}$ for the leakage on input $(F, P_i, T - \ell)$. If the returned value is 1, it sends $[1, 1]_{\mathrm{pk}_{j \to i}^{(r)}}$ to P_j. Otherwise it sends $[b^{out}, 0]_{\mathrm{pk}_{j \to i}^{(r)}}$ to party P_j.
7: **end if**

We prove that no environment can tell whether it is interacting with $\mathcal{F}_{\text{NET}}$ and the adversary in the real world or with $\mathcal{F}_{\text{INFO}}^{\mathcal{L}}$ and the simulator in the ideal world.

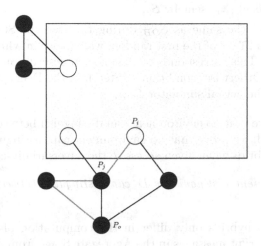

Fig. 1. An example of the algorithm executed by the simulator $\mathcal{S}_{OB}$. The filled circles are the corrupted parties. The red line represents the random walk generated by $\mathcal{S}_{OB}$ in Step 5, in this case of length $\ell = 3$. $\mathcal{S}_{OB}$ simulates the Decrypt Stage by sending fresh encryptions of $(1, 1)$ at every round from every honest party to each of its corrupted neighbors, except in round $2\mathsf{T} - 3$ from P_i to P_j. If no crash occurred up to that point, $\mathcal{S}_{OB}$ sends encryption of $(b^{out}, 0)$. Otherwise, it queries the leakage oracle about the walk of length $\mathsf{T} - 3$, starting at P_i.

Hybrids and Security Proof.

Hybrid 1. $\mathcal{S}_1$ simulates the real world exactly. This means, $\mathcal{S}$ has information on the entire topology of the graph, each party's input, and can simulate identically the real world.

Hybrid 2. $\mathcal{S}_2$ replaces the real keys with the simulated public keys, but still knows everything about the graph as in the first hybrid.

More formally, in each random walk phase and for each party $P_i \in \mathcal{P} \setminus \mathcal{Z}^p$ where $\mathbf{N}_G(P_i) \cap \mathcal{Z}^p \neq \varnothing$, $\mathcal{S}_2$ generates T key pairs $(\text{pk}_{i \to j}^{(1)}, \text{sk}_{i \to j}^{(1)})$, ..., $(\text{pk}_{i \to j}^{(\mathsf{T})}, \text{sk}_{i \to j}^{(\mathsf{T})})$ for every neighbor $P_j \in \mathbf{N}_G(P_i) \cap \mathcal{Z}^p$. In each round r of the corresponding Aggregate Stage and for every neighbor $P_j \in \mathbf{N}_G(P_i) \cap \mathcal{Z}^p$, $\mathcal{S}_2$ does the following. P_i receives ciphertext $[b, u]_{\text{pk}_{* \to i}^{(r)}}$ and the public key $\text{pk}_{* \to i}^{(r)}$ destined for P_j. Instead of adding a layer and homomorphically OR'ing the bit b_i, $\mathcal{S}_2$ computes $(b', u') = (b \lor b_i \lor u_i, u \lor u_i)$, and sends $[b', u']_{\text{pk}_{i \to j}^{(r)}}$ to P_j. In other words, it sends the same message as $\mathcal{S}_1$ but encrypted with a fresh public key. In the corresponding Decrypt Stage, P_i will get back a ciphertext from P_j encrypted under this exact fresh public key.

Hybrid 3. $\mathcal{S}_3$ now simulates the ideal functionality during the Aggregate Stage. It does so by sending encryptions of $(1,1)$ instead of the actual messages and unhappy bits. More formally, in each round r of the Aggregate Stage and for all parties $P_i \in \mathcal{P} \setminus \mathcal{Z}^p$ and $P_j \in \mathbf{N}_G(P_i) \cap \mathcal{Z}^p$, $\mathcal{S}_3$ sends $[1,1]_{\mathrm{pk}_{i \to j}^{(r)}}$ instead of the ciphertext $[b,u]_{\mathrm{pk}_{i \to j}^{(r)}}$ sent by $\mathcal{S}_2$.

Hybrid 4. $\mathcal{S}_4$ does the same as $\mathcal{S}_{OB}$ during the Decrypt Stage for all steps except for round $2\mathrm{T} - \ell$ of the first random walk phase in which the adversary crashes a party. This corresponds to the original description of the simulator except for the 'Otherwise' condition of Step 6 in the Decrypt Stage.

Hybrid 5. $\mathcal{S}_5$ is the actual simulator $\mathcal{S}_{OB}$.

In order to prove that no environment can distinguish between the real world and the ideal world, we prove that no environment can distinguish between any two consecutive hybrids when given access to the adversarially-corrupted nodes.

Claim 1. *No efficient distinguisher D can distinguish between Hybrid 1 and Hybrid 2.*

Proof: The two hybrids only differ in the computation of the public keys that are used to encrypt messages in the Aggregate Stage from any honest party $P_i \in \mathcal{P} \setminus \mathcal{Z}^p$ to any dishonest neighbor $P_j \in \mathbf{N}_G(P_i) \cap \mathcal{Z}^p$.

In Hybrid 1, party P_i sends to P_j an encryption under a fresh public key in the first round. In the following rounds, the encryption is sent either under a product key $\overline{\mathrm{pk}}_{i \to j}^{(r)} = \overline{\mathrm{pk}}_{k \to i}^{(r-1)} \circledast \mathrm{pk}_{i \to j}^{(r)}$ or under a fresh public key (if P_i is unhappy). Note that $\overline{\mathrm{pk}}_{k \to i}^{(r-1)}$ is the key P_i received from a neighbor P_k in the previous round.

In Hybrid 2, party P_i sends to P_j an encryption under a fresh public key $\mathrm{pk}_{i \to j}^{(r)}$ in every round.

The distribution of the product key used in Hybrid 1 is the same as the distribution of a freshly generated public-key. This is due to the (fresh) $\mathrm{pk}_{i \to j}^{(r)}$ key which randomizes the product key. Therefore, no distinguisher can distinguish between Hybrid 1 and Hybrid 2. ■

Claim 2. *No efficient distinguisher D can distinguish between Hybrid 2 and Hybrid 3.*

Proof: The two hybrids differ only in the content of the encrypted messages that are sent in the Aggregate Stage from any honest party $P_i \in \mathcal{P} \setminus \mathcal{Z}^p$ to any dishonest neighbor $P_j \in \mathbf{N}_G(P_i) \cap \mathcal{Z}^p$.

In Hybrid 2, party P_i sends to P_j in the first round an encryption of $(b_i \vee u_i, u_i)$. In the following rounds, P_i sends to P_j either an encryption of $(b \vee b_i \vee u_i, u \vee u_i)$, if message (b,u) is received from neighbor $\pi_i^{-1}(j)$, or an encryption of $(1,1)$ if no message is received.

In Hybrid 3, all encryptions that are sent from party P_i to party P_j are replaced by encryptions of $(1,1)$.

Since the simulator chooses a key independent of any key chosen by parties in $\mathcal{Z}^p$ in each round, the key is unknown to the adversary. Hence, the semantic security of the encryption scheme guarantees that the distinguisher cannot distinguish between both encryptions.   ∎

Claim 3. *No efficient distinguisher D can distinguish between Hybrid 3 and Hybrid 4.*

Proof: The only difference between the two hybrids is in the Decrypt Stage. We differentiate two cases:

- A phase where the adversary did not crash any party in this or any previous phase. In this case, the simulator S_3 sends an encryption of (b_W, u_W), where $b_W = \bigvee_{P_j \in W} b_j$ is the OR of all input bits in the walk and $u_W = 0$, since no crash occurred. S_4 sends an encryption of $(b^{out}, 0)$, where $b^{out} = \bigvee_{P_i \in \mathcal{P}} b_i$. Since the graph is connected, $b^{out} = b_W$ with overwhelming probability, as proven in Corollary 1. Also, the encryption in Hybrid 4 is done with a fresh public key which is indistinguishable with the encryption done in Hybrid 3 by OR'ing many times in the graph, as shown in Claim 2.1 in [ALM17a].
- A phase where the adversary crashed a party in a previous phase or any round different than $2T - \ell$ of the first phase where the adversary crashes a party. In Hybrid 4 the parties send an encryption of $(1, 1)$. This is also the case in Hybrid 3, because even if a crashed party disconnected the graph, each connected component contains a neighbor of a crashed party. Moreover, in Hybrid 4, the messages are encrypted with a fresh public key, and in Hybrid 3, the encryptions are obtained by the homomorphic OR operation. Both encryptions are indistinguishable, as shown in Claim 2.1 in [ALM17a].   ∎

Claim 4. *No efficient distinguisher D can distinguish between Hybrid 4 and Hybrid 5.*

Proof: The only difference between the two hybrids is in the Decrypt Stage, at round $2T - \ell$ of the first phase where the adversary crashes.

Let F be the set of pairs (P_f, r) such that $\mathcal{A}$ crashed P_f at round r of the phase. In Hybrid 4, a walk W of length T is generated from party P_o. Let W_1 be the region of W from P_o to the first not passively corrupted party and let W_2 be the rest of the walk. Then, the adversary's view at this step is the encryption of $(1, 1)$ if one of the crashed parties breaks W_2, and otherwise an encryption of $(b_W, 0)$. In both cases, the message is encrypted under a public key for which the adversary knows the secret key.

In Hybrid 5, a walk W_1' is generated from P_o of length $\ell \leq T$ ending at the first not passively corrupted party P_i. Then, the simulator queries the leakage function on input $(F, P_i, T - \ell)$, which generates a walk W_2' of length $T - \ell$ from P_i, and checks whether W_2' is broken by any party in F. If W_2' is broken, P_i sends an encryption of $(1, 1)$, and otherwise an encryption of $(b_W, 0)$. Since the walk W' defined as W_1' followed by W_2' follows the same distribution as W, $b_W = b^{out}$ with overwhelming probability, and the encryption with a fresh public key which is indistinguishable with the encryption done by OR'ing many times in the graph, then it is impossible to distinguish between Hybrid 4 and Hybrid 5. ∎

This concludes the proof of soundness. □

A.2 Protocol Leaking a Fraction of a Bit

In this section, we give a formal description of the random-walk phase protocol $\mathsf{ProbabilisticRandomWalkPhase}_p$ for the broadcast protocol $\mathsf{BC\text{-}FB}_p$ from Sect. 3.2. Note that this protocol should be repeated ρ times in the actual protocol. The boxes indicate the parts where it differs from the random-walk phase protocol $\mathsf{RandomWalkPhase}$ for the broadcast protocol leaking one bit (cf. Sect. 3.1).

Protocol $\mathsf{ProbabilisticRandomWalkPhase}_p(\mathbf{T}, P_o, (d_i, b_i, u_i)_{P_i \in \mathcal{P}})$

Initialization Stage:

1: Each party P_i generates $\mathbf{T} \cdot d_i$ keypairs $(\mathrm{pk}_{i \to j}^{(r)}, \mathrm{sk}_{i \to j}^{(r)}) \leftarrow \mathsf{KeyGen}(1^\kappa)$ where $r \in \{1, \ldots, \mathbf{T}\}$ and $j \in \{1, \ldots, d_i\}$.

2: Each party P_i generates $\mathbf{T} - 1$ random permutations on d_i elements $\left\{\pi_i^{(2)}, \ldots, \pi_i^{(\mathbf{T})}\right\}$

3: For each party P_i, if any of P_i's neighbors crashed in any phase before the current one, then P_i becomes unhappy, i.e., sets $u_i = 1$.

Aggregate Stage: Each party P_i does the following:

1: **if** P_i is the recipient P_o **then**

2:     Party P_i sends to the first neighbor the public key $\mathrm{pk}_{i \to 1}^{(1)}$ and the ciphertext $\boxed{[b_i \vee u_i, 1, \ldots, 1, u_i]_{\mathrm{pk}_{i \to 1}^{(1)}}}$ ($\lfloor 1/p \rfloor - 1$ ciphertexts contain 1), and to any other neighbor P_j it sends $\boxed{[1, \ldots, 1, 1]_{\mathrm{pk}_{i \to j}^{(1)}}}$ and the public key $\mathrm{pk}_{i \to j}^{(1)}$.

3: **else**

4:     Party P_i sends to each neighbor P_j ciphertext $\boxed{[1, \ldots, 1, 1]_{\mathrm{pk}_{i \to j}^{(1)}}}$ and the public key $\mathrm{pk}_{i \to j}^{(1)}$.

5: **end if**

6: // Add layer while ORing own input bit

7: **for** any round r from 2 to $\mathbf{T}$ **do**

8:     For each neighbor P_j of P_i, do the following (let $k = \pi_i^{(r)}(j)$):

9:     **if** P_i did not receive a message from P_j **then**

10:        Party P_i sends $\boxed{[1, \ldots, 1, 1]_{\mathrm{pk}_{i \to k}^{(r)}}}$ and $\mathrm{pk}_{i \to k}^{(r)}$ to neighbor P_k.

11:    **else**

12:        Let $c_{j \to i}^{(r-1)}$ and $\overline{\mathrm{pk}}_{j \to i}^{(r-1)}$ be the ciphertext and the public key P_i received from P_j. Party P_i computes $\overline{\mathrm{pk}}_{i \to k}^{(r)} = \overline{\mathrm{pk}}_{j \to i}^{(r-1)} \circledast \mathrm{pk}_{i \to k}^{(r)}$ and $\hat{c}_{i \to k}^{(r)} \leftarrow \mathsf{AddLayer}\left(c_{j \to i}^{(r-1)}, \mathrm{pk}_{i \to k}^{(r)}\right)$.

13:      Party P_i computes $\boxed{[b_i \vee u_i, \ldots, b_i \vee u_i, u_i]_{\overline{\mathrm{pk}}_{i \to k}^{(r)}}}$ and

$$\boxed{\mathsf{c}_{i \to k}^{(r)} = \mathsf{HomOR}\left([b_i \vee u_i, \ldots, b_i \vee u_i, u_i]_{\overline{\mathrm{pk}}_{i \to k}^{(r)}}, \hat{\mathsf{c}}_{i \to k}^{(r)}\right)}.$$

14:      Party P_i sends ciphertext $\mathsf{c}_{i \to k}^{(r)}$ and public key $\overline{\mathrm{pk}}_{i \to k}^{(r)}$ to neighbor P_k.

15:    **end if**

16: **end for**

Decrypt Stage: Each party P_i does the following:

1: For each neighbor P_j of P_i:

2: **if** P_i did not receive a message from P_j at round T of the Aggregate Stage **then**

3:      Party P_i sends ciphertext $\mathsf{e}_{i \to j}^{(\mathrm{T})} = [1,1]_{\overline{\mathrm{pk}}_{j \to i}^{(\mathrm{T})}}$ to P_j.

4: **else**

5:      $\boxed{\begin{array}{l}\text{Party } P_i \text{ chooses uniformly at random one of the first } \lfloor 1/p \rfloor \text{ ciphertexts} \\[4pt] \text{in } \mathsf{c}_{j \to i}^{(\mathrm{T})}. \text{ Let } \bar{\mathsf{c}}_{j \to i}^{(\mathrm{T})} \text{ denote the tuple containing the chosen ciphertext and} \\[4pt] \text{the last element of } \mathsf{c}_{j \to i}^{(\mathrm{T})} \text{ (the encryption of the unhappy bit). Party } P_i \\[4pt] \text{computes and sends } \mathsf{e}_{i \to j}^{(\mathrm{T})} = \mathsf{HomOR}\left([b_i \vee u_i, u_i]_{\overline{\mathrm{pk}}_{j \to i}^{(\mathrm{T})}}, \bar{\mathsf{c}}_{j \to i}^{(\mathrm{T})}\right) \text{ to } P_j.\end{array}}$

6: **end if**

7: **for** any round r from T to 2 **do**

8:      For each neighbor P_k of P_i:

9:      **if** P_i did not receive a message from P_k **then**

10:         Party P_i sends $\mathsf{e}_{i \to j}^{(r-1)} = [1,1]_{\overline{\mathrm{pk}}_{j \to i}^{(r-1)}}$ to neighbor P_j, where $k = \pi_i^{(r)}(j)$.

11:      **else**

12:         Denote by $\mathsf{e}_{k \to i}^{(r)}$ the ciphertext P_i received from P_k, where $k = \pi_i^{(r)}(j)$.
        Party P_i sends $\mathsf{e}_{i \to j}^{(r-1)} = \mathsf{DelLayer}\left(\mathsf{e}_{k \to i}^{(r)}, \mathsf{sk}_{i \to k}^{(r)}\right)$ to neighbor P_j.

13:      **end if**

14: **end for**

15: If P_i is the recipient P_o, then it computes $(b, u) = \mathsf{Decrypt}(\mathsf{e}_{1 \to i}^{(1)}, \mathsf{sk}_{i \to 1}^{(1)})$ and **outputs** (b, u, u_i). Otherwise, it **outputs** $(1, 0, u_i)$.

Security Proof of the Protocol Leaking a Fraction of a Bit.
  In this section we prove Theorem 3 from Sect. 3.2.

Theorem 3. *Let κ be the security parameter. For $\tau = \log(n) + \kappa$, $T = 8n^3\tau$ and $\rho = \tau/(p' - 2^{-\tau})$, where $p' = 1/\lfloor 1/p \rfloor$, the protocol $\mathsf{BC\text{-}FB}_p\left(T, \rho, (d_i, b_i)_{P_i \in \mathcal{P}}\right)$ topology-hidingly realizes $\mathcal{F}_{\mathrm{INFO}}^{\mathcal{L}_{FB_p}} || \mathcal{F}_{\mathrm{BC}}$ (with abort) in the $\mathcal{F}_{\mathrm{NET}}$ hybrid-world, where the leakage function $\mathcal{L}_{FB_p}$ is the one defined as above. If no crashes occur, then there is no abort and there is no leakage.*

Proof. **Completeness.** We first show that the protocol is complete. That is, that if the adversary does not crash any party, then every party gets the correct output (the OR of all input bits) with overwhelming probability. More specifically, we show that if no crashes occur, then after ρ repetitions of a phase, the party P_o outputs the correct value with probability at least $1 - 2^{-(\kappa + \log(n))}$. The overall completeness follows from the union bound: the probability that all n parties output the correct value is at least $1 - 2^{-\kappa}$.

Notice that if the output of any of the ρ repetitions intended for P_o is correct, then the overall output of P_o is correct. A given repetition can only give an incorrect output when either the random walk does not reach all parties, which happens with probability at most $2^{-\tau}$, or when the repetition fails, which happens with probability $1 - p'$. Hence, the probability that a repetition gives the incorrect result is at most $1 - p' + 2^{-\tau}$. The probability that all repetitions are incorrect is then at most $(1 - p' + 2^{-\tau})^\rho \leq 2^{-(\kappa + \log(n))}$ (the inequality holds for $0 \leq p' - 2^{-\tau} \leq 1$).

Soundness. We show that no environment can distinguish between the real world and the simulated world, when given access to the adversarially-corrupted nodes. The simulator $\mathcal{S}_{FB}$ for BC-FB$_p$ is a modification of $\mathcal{S}_{OB}$. Here we only sketch the changes and argue why $\mathcal{S}_{FB}$ simulates the real world.

In each of the ρ repetitions of a phase, $\mathcal{S}_{FB}$ executes a protocol very similar to the one for $\mathcal{S}_{OB}$. In the Aggregate Stage, $\mathcal{S}_{FB}$ proceeds almost identically to $\mathcal{S}_{OB}$ (except that it sends encryptions of vectors $(1, \ldots, 1)$ instead of only two values). In the Decrypt Stage the only difference between $\mathcal{S}_{FB}$ and $\mathcal{S}_{OB}$ is in computing the output for the party P_o (as already discussed in the proof of Theorem 2, $\mathcal{S}_{FB}$ does this only when P_o is corrupted and the walk carrying the output enters an area of corrupted parties). In the case when there were no crashes before or during given repetition of a phase, $\mathcal{S}_{OB}$ would simply send the encrypted output. On the other hand, $\mathcal{S}_{FB}$ samples a value from the Bernoulli distribution with parameter p and sends the encrypted output only with probability p, while with probability $1 - p$ it sends the encryption of $(1, 0)$. Otherwise, the simulation is the same as for $\mathcal{S}_{OB}$.

It can be easily seen that $\mathcal{S}_{FB}$ simulates the real world in the Aggregate Stage and in the Decrypt Stage in every message other than the one encrypting the output. But even this message comes from the same distribution as the corresponding message sent in the real world. This is because in the real world, if the walk was not broken by a crash, this message contains the output with probability p. The simulator encrypts the output also with probability p in the two possible cases: when there was no crash ($\mathcal{S}_{FB}$ samples from the Bernoulli distribution) and when there was a crash but the walk was not broken ($\mathcal{L}_{FB}$ is defined in this way).

Simulator. The simulator $\mathcal{S}_{FB}$ proceeds almost identically to the simulator $\mathcal{S}_{OB}$ given in the proof of Theorem 2 (cf. Sect. A.1). We only change the algorithm PhaseSimulation to ProbabilisticPhaseSimulation and execute it ρ times instead of only once.

Algorithm ProbabilisticPhaseSimulation(P_o, P_i)

If $P_o \in \mathcal{Z}^p$, let w denote the random walk generated in the Initialization Stage (at the beginning of the simulation of this phase), which starts at P_o and carries the output bit. Let ℓ denote the number of parties in $\mathcal{Z}^p$ on w before the first correct party. If $P_o \notin \mathcal{Z}^p$, w and ℓ are not defined.

For every $P_j \in \mathcal{Z}^p \cap \mathbf{N}_G(P_i)$, let $\mathrm{pk}_{j \to i}^{(r)}$ denote the public key generated in the Initialization Stage by P_j for P_i and for round r.

Initialization Stage

1: For every neighbor $P_j \in \mathcal{Z}^p$ of the correct P_i, $\mathcal{S}_{FB}$ generates $\mathbf{T}$ key pairs $(\mathrm{pk}_{i \to j}^{(1)}, \mathrm{sk}_{i \to j}^{(1)}), \dots, (\mathrm{pk}_{i \to j}^{(\mathbf{T})}, \mathrm{sk}_{i \to j}^{(\mathbf{T})})$.

Aggregate Stage

1: In round r, for every neighbor $P_j \in \mathbf{N}_G(P_i) \cap \mathcal{Z}^p$, $\mathcal{S}_{FB}$ sends the tuple $([1, \dots, 1]_{\mathrm{pk}_{i \to j}^{(r)}}, \mathrm{pk}_{i \to j}^{(r)})$ (with $\lfloor 1/p \rfloor + 1$ ones) to P_j.

Decrypt Stage

1: **if** $P_o \notin \mathcal{Z}^p$ or $\mathcal{A}$ crashed any party in any phase before the current one

2: or in any repetition of the current phase **then**

3:    In every round r and for every neighbor $P_j \in \mathbf{N}_G(P_i) \cap \mathcal{Z}^p$, $\mathcal{S}_{FB}$ sends $[1, 1]_{\mathrm{pk}_{j \to i}^{(r)}}$ to P_j.

4: **else**

5:    In every round r and for every neighbor $P_j \in \mathbf{N}_G(P_i) \cap \mathcal{Z}^p$, $\mathcal{S}_{FB}$ sends $[1, 1]_{\mathrm{pk}_{j \to i}^{(r)}}$ to P_j unless the following three conditions hold: (a) P_i is the first party not in $\mathcal{Z}^p$ on w, (b) P_j is the last party in $\mathcal{Z}^p$ on w, and (c) $r = 2\mathbf{T} - \ell$.

6:    If the three conditions hold (in particular $r = 2\mathbf{T} - \ell$), $\mathcal{S}_{FB}$ does the following. If $\mathcal{A}$ did not crash any party in a previous round,

7:    $\mathcal{S}_{FB}$ samples a value x from the Bernoulli distribution with parameter p'. If $x = 1$ (with probability p'), $\mathcal{S}_{FB}$ sends to P_j the ciphertext $[b_{out}, 0]_{\mathrm{pk}_{j \to i}^{(r)}}$ and otherwise it sends $[1, 0]_{\mathrm{pk}_{j \to i}^{(r)}}$.

8:    Otherwise, let F denote the set of pairs $(P_f, s - \ell + 1)$ such that $\mathcal{A}$ crashed P_f in round s. $\mathcal{S}_{FB}$ queries $\mathcal{F}_{\mathrm{INFO}}^{\mathcal{L}_{FB_p}}$ for the leakage on input $(F, P_i, \mathbf{T} - \ell)$. If the returned value is 1, it sends $[1, 1]_{\mathrm{pk}_{j \to i}^{(r)}}$ to P_j. Otherwise it sends $[b^{out}, 0]_{\mathrm{pk}_{j \to i}^{(r)}}$ to party P_j.

9: **end if**

Hybrids and Security Proof. We consider similar steps as the hybrids from Sect. A.1.

Hybrid 1. $\mathcal{S}_1$ simulates the real world exactly. This means, $\mathcal{S}_1$ has information on the entire topology of the graph, each party's input, and can simulate identically the real world.

Hybrid 2. $\mathcal{S}_2$ replaces the real keys with the simulated public keys, but still knows everything about the graph as in the first hybrid.

More formally, in each subphase of each random walk phase and for each party $P_i \in \mathcal{P} \setminus \mathcal{Z}^p$ where $\mathbf{N}_G(P_i) \cap \mathcal{Z}^p \neq \varnothing$, $\mathcal{S}_2$ generates T key pairs

$(\text{pk}_{i\rightarrow j}^{(1)}, \text{sk}_{i\rightarrow j}^{(1)}), \ldots, (\text{pk}_{i\rightarrow j}^{(\text{T})}, \text{sk}_{i\rightarrow j}^{(\text{T})})$ for every neighbor $P_j \in \mathbf{N}_G(P_i) \cap \mathcal{Z}^p$. Let $\alpha := \lfloor \frac{1}{p} \rfloor$. In each round r of the corresponding Aggregate Stage and for every neighbor $P_j \in \mathbf{N}_G(P_i) \cap \mathcal{Z}^p$, $\mathcal{S}_2$ does the following: P_i receives ciphertext $[b_1, \ldots, b_\alpha, u]_{\text{pk}_{*\rightarrow i}^{(r)}}$ and the public key $\text{pk}_{*\rightarrow i}^{(r)}$ destined for P_j. Instead of adding a layer and homomorphically OR'ing the bit b_i, $\mathcal{S}_2$ computes $(b_1', \ldots, b_\alpha', u') = (b_1 \vee b_i \vee u_i, \cdots, b_\alpha \vee b_i \vee u_i, u \vee u_i)$, and sends $[b_{\sigma(1)}', \cdots, b_{\sigma(\alpha)}', u']_{\text{pk}_{i\rightarrow j}^{(r)}}$ to P_j, where σ is a random permutation on α elements. In other words, it sends the same message as $\mathcal{S}_1$ but encrypted with a fresh public key. In the corresponding Decrypt Stage, P_i will get back a ciphertext from P_j encrypted under this exact fresh public key.

Hybrid 3. $\mathcal{S}_3$ now simulates the ideal functionality during the Aggregate Stage. It does so by sending encryptions of $(1, \ldots, 1)$ instead of the actual messages and unhappy bits. More formally, let $\alpha := \lfloor \frac{1}{p} \rfloor$. In each round r of a subphase of a random walk phase and for all parties $P_i \in \mathcal{P} \setminus \mathcal{Z}^p$ and $P_j \in \mathbf{N}_G(P_i) \cap \mathcal{Z}^p$, $\mathcal{S}_3$ sends $[1, 1, \ldots, 1]_{\text{pk}_{i\rightarrow j}^{(r)}}$ instead of the ciphertext $[b_1, \ldots, b_\alpha, u]_{\text{pk}_{i\rightarrow j}^{(r)}}$ sent by $\mathcal{S}_2$.

Hybrid 4. $\mathcal{S}_4$ does the same as $\mathcal{S}_{FB}$ during the Decrypt Stage for all phases and subphases except for the first subphase of a random walk phase in which the adversary crashes a party.

Hybrid 5. $\mathcal{S}_5$ is the actual simulator $\mathcal{S}_{FB}$.

The proofs that no efficient distinguisher D can distinguish between Hybrid 1, Hybrid 2 and Hybrid 3 are similar to the Claims 1 and 2. Hence, we prove indistinguishability between Hybrid 3, Hybrid 4 and Hybrid 5.

Claim 5. *No efficient distinguisher D can distinguish between Hybrid 3 and Hybrid 4.*

Proof: The only difference between the two hybrids is in the Decrypt Stage. We differentiate three cases:

- A subphase l of a phase k where the adversary did not crash any party in this phase, any previous subphase, or any previous phase. In this case, $\mathcal{S}_3$ sends with probability p an encryption of (b_W, u_W), where $b_W = \bigvee_{u \in W} b_u$ is the OR of all input bits in the walk and $u_W = 0$ (since no crash occurs), and with probability $1 - p$ an encryption of $(1, 0)$. On the other hand, $\mathcal{S}_4$ samples r from a Bernoulli distribution with parameter p, and if $r = 1$, it sends an encryption of $(b_{out}, 0)$, where $b_{out} = \bigvee_{i \in [n]} b_i$, and if $r = 0$ it sends an encryption of $(1, 0)$. Since the graph is connected, $b_{out} = b_W$ with overwhelming probability, as proven in Corollary 1. Also, the encryption in Hybrid 4 is done with a fresh public key which is indistinguishable with the encryption done in Hybrid 3 by OR'ing many times in the graph, as shown in Claim 2.1. in [ALM17a].
- A subphase l of a phase k where the adversary crashed a party in a previous subphase or a previous phase.
  In Hybrid 3 the parties send encryptions of $(1, 1)$. This is also the case in Hybrid 4, because even if a crashed party disconnected the graph, each connected component contains a neighbor of a crashed party. Moreover, in Hybrid

4, the messages are encrypted with a fresh public key, and in Hybrid 3, the encryptions are obtained by the homomorphic OR operation. Both encryptions are indistinguishable, as shown in Claim 2.1. in [ALM17a].

■

Claim 6. *No efficient distinguisher D can distinguish between Hybrid 4 and Hybrid 5.*

Proof: The only difference between the two hybrids is in the Decrypt Stage of the first subphase of a phase where the adversary crashes.

Let F be the set of pairs (P_f, r) such that $\mathcal{A}$ crashed P_f at round r of the phase. In Hybrid 4, a walk W of length T is generated from party P_o. Let W_1 be the region of W from P_o to the first not passively corrupted party and let W_2 be the rest of the walk. Then, the adversary's view at this step is the encryption of $(1,1)$ if one of the crashed parties breaks W_2 or if the walk became dummy (which happens with probability $1 - p$, since the ciphertexts are permuted randomly and only one ciphertext out of $\frac{1}{p}$ contains b_W). Otherwise, the adversary's view is an encryption of $(b_W, 0)$. In both cases, the message is encrypted under a public key for which the adversary knows the secret key.

In Hybrid 5, a walk W_1' is generated from P_o of length $\ell \leq \mathsf{T}$ ending at the first not passively corrupted party P_i. Then, the simulator queries the leakage function on input $(F, P_i, \mathsf{T} - \ell)$. Then, with probability p it generates a walk W_2' of length $\mathsf{T} - \ell$ from P_i, and checks whether W_2' is broken by any party in F. If W_2' is broken, P_i sends an encryption of $(1,1)$, and otherwise an encryption of $(b_W, 0)$. Since the walk W' defined as W_1' followed by W_2' follows the same distribution as W, $b_W = b^{out}$ with overwhelming probability, and the encryption with a fresh public key which is indistinguishable with the encryption done by OR'ing many times in the graph, then it is impossible to distinguish between Hybrid 4 and Hybrid 5.   ■

This concludes the proof of soundness.   □

References

[AJL+12] Asharov, G., Jain, A., López-Alt, A., Tromer, E., Vaikuntanathan, V., Wichs, D.: Multiparty computation with low communication, computation and interaction via threshold FHE. In: Pointcheval, D., Johansson, T. (eds.) EUROCRYPT 2012. LNCS, vol. 7237, pp. 483–501. Springer, Heidelberg (2012). https://doi.org/10.1007/978-3-642-29011-4_29

[ALM17a] Akavia, A., LaVigne, R., Moran, T.: Topology-hiding computation on all graphs. In: Katz, J., Shacham, H. (eds.) CRYPTO 2017. LNCS, vol. 10401, pp. 447–467. Springer, Cham (2017). https://doi.org/10.1007/978-3-319-63688-7_15

[ALM17b] Akavia, A., LaVigne, R., Moran, T.: Topology-hiding computation on all graphs. Cryptology ePrint Archive, Report 2017/296 (2017). http://eprint.iacr.org/2017/296

[AM17] Akavia, A., Moran, T.: Topology-hiding computation beyond logarithmic diameter. In: Coron, J.-S., Nielsen, J.B. (eds.) EUROCRYPT 2017. LNCS, vol. 10212, pp. 609–637. Springer, Cham (2017). https://doi.org/10.1007/978-3-319-56617-7_21

[BBMM18] Ball, M., Boyle, E., Malkin, T., Moran, T.: Exploring the boundaries of topology-hiding computation. In: Nielsen, J.B., Rijmen, V. (eds.) EURO-CRYPT 2018. LNCS, vol. 10822, pp. 294–325. Springer, Cham (2018). https://doi.org/10.1007/978-3-319-78372-7_10

[Bd90] Bos, J., den Boer, B.: Detection of disrupters in the DC protocol. In: Quisquater, J.-J., Vandewalle, J. (eds.) EUROCRYPT 1989. LNCS, vol. 434, pp. 320–327. Springer, Heidelberg (1990). https://doi.org/10.1007/3-540-46885-4_33

[Cha81] Chaum, D.L.: Untraceable electronic mail, return addresses, and digital pseudonyms. Commun. ACM 24(2), 84–90 (1981)

[Cha88] Chaum, D.: The dining cryptographers problem: unconditional sender and recipient untraceability. J. Cryptol. 1(1), 65–75 (1988)

[CLTV15] Canetti, R., Lin, H., Tessaro, S., Vaikuntanathan, V.: Obfuscation of probabilistic circuits and applications. In: Dodis, Y., Nielsen, J.B. (eds.) TCC 2015. LNCS, vol. 9015, pp. 468–497. Springer, Heidelberg (2015). https://doi.org/10.1007/978-3-662-46497-7_19

[CNE+14] Checkoway, S., et al.: On the practical exploitability of dual EC in TLS implementations. In: USENIX Security Symposium, pp. 319–335 (2014)

[DDWY90] Dolev, D., Dwork, C., Waarts, O., Yung, M.: Perfectly secure message transmission. In: 31st FOCS, pp. 36–45. IEEE Computer Society Press, October 1990

[GJ04] Golle, P., Juels, A.: Dining cryptographers revisited. In: Cachin, C., Camenisch, J.L. (eds.) EUROCRYPT 2004. LNCS, vol. 3027, pp. 456–473. Springer, Heidelberg (2004). https://doi.org/10.1007/978-3-540-24676-3_27

[HDWH12] Heninger, N., Durumeric, Z., Wustrow, E., Halderman, J.A.: Mining your PS and QS: detection of widespread weak keys in network devices. In: USENIX Security Symposium, vol. 8, p. 1 (2012)

[HJ07] Hinkelmann, M., Jakoby, A.: Communications in unknown networks: preserving the secret of topology. Theoret. Comput. Sci. 384(2–3), 184–200 (2007)

[HMTZ16] Hirt, M., Maurer, U., Tschudi, D., Zikas, V.: Network-hiding communication and applications to multi-party protocols. In: Robshaw, M., Katz, J. (eds.) CRYPTO 2016. LNCS, vol. 9815, pp. 335–365. Springer, Heidelberg (2016). https://doi.org/10.1007/978-3-662-53008-5_12

[LLM+18] Lavigne, R., Liu-Zhang, C.-D., Maurer, U., Moran, T., Mularczyk, M., Tschudi, D.: Topology-hiding computation beyond semi-honest adversaries. Cryptology ePrint Archive, Report 2018/255 (2018). https://eprint.iacr.org/2018/255

[MOR15] Moran, T., Orlov, I., Richelson, S.: Topology-hiding computation. In: Dodis, Y., Nielsen, J.B. (eds.) TCC 2015. LNCS, vol. 9014, pp. 159–181. Springer, Heidelberg (2015). https://doi.org/10.1007/978-3-662-46494-6_8

[RC88] Reiter, M.K., Crowds, R.A.: Anonymity for web transaction. ACM Trans. Inf. Syst. Secur. **1**(1), 66–92 (1988)

[Reg09] Regev, O.: On lattices, learning with errors, random linear codes, and cryptography. J. ACM (JACM) **56**(6), 34 (2009)

[SGR97] Syverson, P.F., Goldschlag, D.M., Reed, M.G.: Anonymous connections and onion routing. In: 1997 Proceedings of IEEE Symposium on Security and Privacy, pp. 44–54. IEEE (1997)

Secure Computation Using Leaky Correlations (Asymptotically Optimal Constructions)

Alexander R. Block[1]([✉]), Divya Gupta[2], Hemanta K. Maji[1],
and Hai H. Nguyen[1]

[1] Department of Computer Science, Purdue University, West Lafayette, IN, USA
{block9,hmaji,nguye245}@purdue.edu
[2] Microsoft Research, Bangalore, India
divya.gupta@microsoft.com

Abstract. Most secure computation protocols can be effortlessly adapted to offload a significant fraction of their computationally and cryptographically expensive components to an offline phase so that the parties can run a fast online phase and perform their intended computation securely. During this offline phase, parties generate private shares of a sample generated from a particular joint distribution, referred to as the *correlation*. These shares, however, are susceptible to leakage attacks by adversarial parties, which can compromise the security of the secure computation protocol. The objective, therefore, is to preserve the security of the honest party despite the leakage performed by the adversary on her share.

Prior solutions, starting with n-bit leaky shares, either used 4 messages or enabled the secure computation of only sub-linear size circuits. Our work presents the first 2-message secure computation protocol for 2-party functionalities that have $\Theta(n)$ circuit-size despite $\Theta(n)$-bits of leakage, a qualitatively optimal result. We compose a suitable 2-message secure computation protocol in parallel with our new 2-message *correlation extractor*. Correlation extractors, introduced by Ishai, Kushilevitz, Ostrovsky, and Sahai (FOCS–2009) as a natural generalization of privacy amplification and randomness extraction, recover "fresh" correlations from the leaky ones, which are subsequently used by other cryptographic protocols. We construct the first 2-message correlation extractor that produces $\Theta(n)$-bit fresh correlations even after $\Theta(n)$-bit leakage.

Our principal technical contribution, which is of potential independent interest, is the construction of a family of multiplication-friendly linear secret sharing schemes that is simultaneously a family of small-bias distributions. We construct this family by randomly "twisting then permuting" appropriate Algebraic Geometry codes over constant-size fields.

A. R. Block, H. K. Maji, and H. H. Nguyen—The research effort is supported in part by an NSF CRII Award CNS-1566499, an NSF SMALL Award CNS-1618822, and an REU CNS-1724673.

A. Beimel and S. Dziembowski (Eds.): TCC 2018, LNCS 11240, pp. 36–65, 2018.
https://doi.org/10.1007/978-3-030-03810-6_2

1   Introduction

Secure multi-party computation (MPC) allows mutually distrusting parties to compute securely over their private data. Secure computation of most functionalities requires expensive public-key primitives such as oblivious transfer, even in the semi-honest setting.[1] We can effortlessly adjust most of these existing secure computation protocols so that they offload a significant fraction of their complex operations to an offline preprocessing phase. Subsequently, during an online phase, parties can implement extremely fast secure computation protocols. In fact, several specialized protocols optimize MPC for this online-offline paradigm [4,6,7,15,18,28,29,31,37].

For instance, in the two-party setting, we envision this offline phase as a secure implementation of a *trusted dealer* who generates private albeit correlated shares (r_A, r_B) for Alice and Bob, respectively, sampled from an appropriate joint distribution (R_A, R_B), referred to as a *correlation*. This versatile framework allows the implementation of this trusted dealer using computational hardness assumptions, secure hardware, trusted hardware, or physical processes. Furthermore, this offline phase is independent of the final functionality to be computed, as well as the parties' private inputs.

A particularly useful correlation is the *random oblivious transfer correlation*, represented by ROT. One sample of this correlation generates three random bits x_0, x_1, b and provides private shares $r_A = (x_0, x_1)$ to Alice, and $r_B = (b, x_b)$ to Bob. Note that Alice does not know the choice bit b, and Bob does not know the other bit x_{1-b}. Let $\mathcal{F}$ be the class of functionalities that admit 2-message secure computation protocols in the ROT-hybrid [10,26]. Note that $\mathcal{F}$ includes the powerful class of functions that have a decomposable randomized encoding [3,5,25]. Alice and Bob can compute the required ROTs in the offline phase. Then, they can compute *any* functionality from this class using 2-messages, a protocol exhibiting optimal message complexity[2] and (essentially) optimal efficiency in the usage of cryptographic resources.

However, the private share of the honest party is susceptible to leakage attacks by an adversary, both during the generation of the shares and the duration of storing the shares. We emphasize that the leakage need not necessarily reveal individual bits of the honest party's share. The leakage can be on the entire share and encode crucial global information that can potentially jeopardize the security of the secure computation protocol. This concern naturally leads to the following fundamental question.

"Can we preserve the security and efficiency of the secure computation during the online phase despite the adversarial leakage on the honest party's shares?"

Using the class $\mathcal{F}$ of functionalities (defined above) as a yardstick, let us determine the primary hurdle towards a positive resolution of this question. In

---

[1] A semi-honest adversary follows the prescribed protocol but is curious to find additional information.

[2] Message complexity refers to the number of messages exchanged between Alice and Bob.

the sequel, $\mathcal{F}_{m/2} \subset \mathcal{F}$ is the set of all two-party functionalities that have a 2-message protocol in $\mathsf{ROT}^{m/2}$-hybrid, i.e., parties start with $m/2$ independent samples[3] from the ROT correlation. In the leaky correlation setting where an adversary has already leaked global information from the private share of the honest party, our objective is to design an (asymptotically) optimal secure computation protocol for the functionalities in $\mathcal{F}_{m/2}$. That is, starting with leaky correlations (of size n), we want to compute any $F \in \mathcal{F}_{m/2}$ such that $m = \Theta(n)$ via a 2-message protocol despite $t = \Theta(n)$ bits of leakage. We note that this task is equivalent to the task of constructing a secure computation protocol for the particular functionality $\mathsf{ROT}^{m/2}$ that also belongs to $\mathcal{F}_{m/2}$. This observation follows from the parallel composition of the secure protocol implementing the functionality $\mathsf{ROT}^{m/2}$ from leaky correlations with the 2-message protocol for F in the $\mathsf{ROT}^{m/2}$-hybrid. To summarize, our overall objective of designing optimal secure computation protocols from leaky ROT correlations reduces to the following equivalent goal.

"Construct a 2-message protocol to compute $\mathsf{ROT}^{m/2}$ securely, where $m = \Theta(n)$, from the leaky $\mathsf{ROT}^{n/2}$ correlation in spite of $t = \Theta(n)$ bits of leakage."

Note that in the $\mathsf{ROT}^{n/2}$-hybrid, both parties have private share of size n bits. The above problem is identical to *correlation extractors* introduced in the seminal work of Ishai, Kushilevitz, Ostrovsky, and Sahai [26].

Correlation Extractors. Ishai et al. [26] introduced the notion of correlation extractors as an interactive protocol that takes a leaky correlation as input and outputs a new correlation that is secure. Prior correlation extractors either used four messages [26] or had a sub-linear production [9,22], i.e., $m = o(n)$. We construct the first 2-message correlation extractor that has a linear production and leakage resilience, that is, $m = \Theta(n)$ and $t = \Theta(n)$. Note that even computationally secure protocols can use the output of the correlation extractor in the online phase. Section 1.1 formally defines correlation extractors, and we present our main contributions in Sect. 1.2.

1.1 Correlation Extractors and Security Model

We consider the standard model of Ishai et al. [26], which is also used by the subsequent works, for 2-party semi-honest secure computation in the preprocessing model. In the preprocessing step, a trusted dealer draws a sample of shares (r_A, r_B) from the joint distribution of correlated private randomness (R_A, R_B). The dealer provides the secret share r_A to Alice and r_B to Bob. Moreover, the adversarial party can perform an arbitrary t-bits of leakage on the secret share of the honest party at the end of the preprocessing step. We represent this leaky correlation hybrid[4] as $(R_A, R_B)^{[t]}$.

---

[3] Each sample of ROT gives two bits to each party; (x_0, x_1) to the first party and (b, x_b) to the second party. Therefore each party receives m-bit shares.

[4] That is, the functionality samples secret shares (r_A, r_B) according to the correlation (R_A, R_B). The adversarial party sends a t-bit leakage function $\mathcal{L}$ to the functionality

Definition 1 (Correlation Extractor). *Let (R_A, R_B) be a correlated private randomness such that the secret share of each party is n-bits. An (n, m, t, ε)- correlation extractor for (R_A, R_B) is a two-party interactive protocol in the $(R_A, R_B)^{[t]}$-hybrid that securely implements the $\mathsf{ROT}^{m/2}$ functionality against information-theoretic semi-honest adversaries with ε simulation error.*

Note that the size of the secret shares output by the correlation extractor is m-bits. We emphasize that no leakage occurs during the correlation extractor execution. The t-bit leakage cumulatively accounts for all the leakage before the beginning of the online phase. We note that, throughout this work, we shall always normalize the total length of the input shares of each party to n-bits.

1.2 Our Contribution

Recall that $\mathcal{F}_{m/2} \subset \mathcal{F}$ is the set of all two-party functionalities that have a 2-message protocol in the $\mathsf{ROT}^{m/2}$-hybrid. We prove the following results.

Theorem 1 (Asymptotically Optimal Secure Computation from Leaky Correlations). *There exists a correlation (R_A, R_B) that produces n-bit secret shares such that for all $F \in \mathcal{F}_{m/2}$ there exists a 2-message secure computation protocol for F in the leaky $(R_A, R_B)^{[t]}$-hybrid, where $m = \Theta(n)$ and $t = \Theta(n)$, with exponentially low simulation error.*

The crucial ingredient of Theorem 1 is our new 2-message (n, m, t, ε)-correlation extractor for $\mathsf{ROT}^{n/2}$. We compose the 2-message secure computation protocol for functionalities in $\mathcal{F}_{m/2}$ in the $\mathsf{ROT}^{m/2}$-hybrid with our correlation extractor. Our work presents the first 2-message correlation extractor that has a linear production and a linear leakage resilience (along with exponentially low insecurity).

Theorem 2 (Asymptotically Optimal Correlation Extractor for ROT). *There exists a 2-message (n, m, t, ε)-correlation extractor for $\mathsf{ROT}^{n/2}$ such that $m = \Theta(n)$, $t = \Theta(n)$, and $\varepsilon = \exp(-\Theta(n))$.*

The technical heart of the correlation extractor of Theorem 2 is another correlation extractor (see Theorem 3) for a generalization of the ROT correlation. For any finite field $\mathbb{F}$, the *random oblivious linear-function evaluation* correlation over $\mathbb{F}$ [36, 42], represented by $\mathsf{ROLE}(\mathbb{F})$, samples random $a, b, x \in \mathbb{F}$ and defines $r_A = (a, b)$ and $r_B = (x, z)$, where $z = ax + b$. Note that, for $\mathbb{F} = \mathsf{GF}[2]$, we have $(x_0 + x_1)b + x_0 = x_b$; therefore, the $\mathsf{ROLE}(\mathsf{GF}[2])$ correlation is identical to the ROT correlation. One share of the $\mathsf{ROLE}(\mathbb{F})$ correlation has secret share size $2 \lg |\mathbb{F}|$. In particular, the correlation $\mathsf{ROLE}(\mathbb{F})^{n/2\lg|\mathbb{F}|}$ provides each party with $n/2 \lg |\mathbb{F}|$ independent samples from the $\mathsf{ROLE}(\mathbb{F})$ correlation and the secret share size of each party is n-bits for suitable constant sized field $\mathbb{F}$.

---

and receives the leakage $\mathcal{L}(r_A, r_B)$ from the functionality. The functionality sends r_A to Alice and r_B to Bob. Note that the adversary does not need to know its secret share to construct the leakage function because the leakage function gets the secret shares of both parties as input.

Theorem 3 (Asymptotically Optimal Correlation Extractor for ROLE($\mathbb{F}$)). *There exists a 2-message (n, m, t, ε)-correlation extractor for* ROLE$(\mathbb{F})^{n/2\lg|\mathbb{F}|}$ *such that $m = \Theta(n)$, $t = \Theta(n)$, and $\varepsilon = \exp(-\Theta(n))$.*

In Fig. 4, we present our correlation extractor that outputs fresh samples from the same ROLE($\mathbb{F}$) correlation. Finally, our construction obtains multiple ROT samples from *each* output ROLE($\mathbb{F}$) sample using the OT embedding technique of [9]. Figure 1 positions our contribution vis-à-vis the previous state-of-the-art. In particular, Fig. 1 highlights the fact that our result simultaneously achieves the best qualitative parameters. Our results are also quantitatively better than the previous works and we discuss the concrete performance numbers we obtain for Theorem 3 and Theorem 2 below. For more detailed numerical comparison with prior works [9, 22, 26], refer to Sect. 5.

	Correlation Description	Message Complexity	Number of OTs Produced $(m/2)$	Number of Leakage bits (t)	Simulation Error (ε)
IKOS [26]	ROT$^{n/2}$	4	$\Theta(n)$	$\Theta(n)$	$2^{-\Theta(n)}$
GIMS [22]	ROT$^{n/2}$	2	$n/\operatorname{poly}\lg n$	$(1/4 - g)n$	$2^{-gn/m}$
	IP$\left(\mathbb{K}^{n/\lg|\mathbb{K}|}\right)$	2	1	$(1/2 - g)n$	2^{-gn}
BMN [9]	IP$\left(\mathbb{K}^{n/\lg|\mathbb{K}|}\right)$	2	$n^{1-o(1)}$	$(1/2 - g)n$	2^{-gn}
Our Result	ROT$^{n/2}$	2	$\Theta(n)$	$\Theta(n)$	$2^{-\Theta(n)}$
	ROLE$(\mathbb{F})^{n/2\lg|\mathbb{F}|}$	2	$\Theta(n)$	$\Theta(n)$	$2^{-\Theta(n)}$

Fig. 1. A qualitative summary of our correlation extractor constructions and a comparison to prior relevant works. Here $\mathbb{K}$ is a finite field and $\mathbb{F}$ is a finite field of constant size. The IP$(\mathbb{K}^s)$ is a correlation that samples random $r_A = (u_1, \ldots, u_s) \in \mathbb{K}^s$ and $r_B = (v_1, \ldots, v_s) \in \mathbb{K}^s$ such that $u_1 v_1 + \cdots + u_s v_s = 0$. All correlations are normalized so that each party gets an n-bit secret share. The parameter g is the gap to maximal leakage resilience such that. $g > 0$.

Performance of Correlation Extractors for ROLE($\mathbb{F}$) (Theorem 3). Our correlation extractor for ROLE($\mathbb{F}$) relies on the existence of suitable Algebraic Geometry (AG) codes[5] over finite field $\mathbb{F}$, such that $|\mathbb{F}|$ is an even power of a prime and $|\mathbb{F}| \geqslant 49$. We shall use $\mathbb{F}$ that is a finite field with characteristic 2.

As the size of the field $\mathbb{F}$ increases, the "quality" of the Algebraic Geometry codes get better. However, the efficiency of the BMN OT embedding protocol [9] used to obtain the output ROT in our construction decreases with increasing $|\mathbb{F}|$. For example, with $\mathbb{F} = \mathrm{GF}\left[2^{14}\right]$ we achieve the highest production rate $m/n = 16.32\%$ if the fractional leakage rate is $t/n = 1\%$. For leakage rate $t/n = 10\%$, we achieve production rate $m/n = 10\%$. Figure 7 (Sect. 5) and Fig. 9 (Sect. 6) summarize these tradeoffs for various choices of the finite field $\mathbb{F}$.

---

[5] Once the parameters of the AG code are fixed, it is a one-time cost to construct its generator matrix.

Performance of Correlation Extractors for ROT (Theorem 2). We know extremely efficient algorithms that use multiplications over $\mathbb{GF}[2]$ to emulate multiplications over any $\mathbb{GF}[2^s]$ [12,14]. For example, we can use 15 multiplications over $\mathbb{GF}[2]$ to emulate one multiplication over $\mathbb{GF}[2^6]$. Therefore, we can use 15 samples of $\mathsf{ROLE}(\mathbb{GF}[2])$ to perform one $\mathsf{ROLE}(\mathbb{GF}[2^6])$ with perfect semi-honest security. Note that, by applying this protocol, the share sizes reduce by a factor of $6/15$. In general, using this technique, we can convert the leaky $\mathsf{ROLE}(\mathbb{GF}[2])$ (equivalently, ROT) correlation, into a leaky $\mathsf{ROLE}(\mathbb{F})$ correlation, where $\mathbb{F}$ is a finite field of characteristic 2, by incurring a slight multiplicative loss in the share size. Now, we can apply the correlation extractor for $\mathsf{ROLE}(\mathbb{F})$ discussed above. By optimizing the choice of the field $\mathbb{F}$ (in our case $\mathbb{F} = \mathbb{GF}[2^{10}]$), we can construct a 2-message correlation extractor for ROT with fractional leakage rate $t/n = 1\%$ and achieve production rate of $m/n = 4.20\%$ (see Fig. 8, Sect. 5). This is several orders of magnitude better than the production and resilience of the IKOS correlation extractor and uses less number of messages.[6]

High Leakage Resilience Setting. Ishai et al. [27] showed that $t < n/4$ is necessary to extract even one new sample of ROT from the leaky $\mathsf{ROLE}(\mathbb{F})^{n/2\lg \mathbb{F}}$ correlation. Our construction, when instantiated with a suitably large constant-size field $\mathbb{F}$, demonstrates that if $t \leqslant (1/4 - g)n$ then we can extract $\Theta(n)$ new samples of the ROT correlation. The prior construction of [22] only achieves a sub-linear production by using sub-sampling techniques.

Theorem 4 (Near Optimal Resilience with Linear Production). *For every $g \in (0, 1/4]$, there exists a finite field $\mathbb{F}$ with characteristic 2 and a 2-message (n, m, t, ε)-correlation extractor for $(R_A, R_B) = \mathsf{ROLE}(\mathbb{F})^{n/2\lg |\mathbb{F}|}$, where $t = (1/4 - g)n$, $m = \Theta(n)$, and $\varepsilon = \exp(-\Theta(n))$.*

The production $m = \Theta(n)$ depends on the constant g, the gap to optimal fractional resilience. We prove Theorem 4 in the full version of our work [8]. Section 5 shows that we can achieve linear production even for $t = 0.22n$ bits of leakage using $\mathbb{F} = \mathbb{GF}[2^{10}]$.

Correlation Extractors for Arbitrary Correlations. Similar to the construction of IKOS, we can also construct a correlation extractor from *any* correlation and output samples of *any* correlation; albeit it is not round optimal anymore. However, our construction achieves overall better production and leakage resilience than IKOS because our correlation extractor for ROT has higher production and resilience. Figure 2 outlines a comparison of these two correlation extractor construction for the general case.

---

[6] Even optimistic estimates of the parameters m/n and t/n for the IKOS construction are in the order of 10^{-6}.

Kilian
[30]   Randomized   One-sided   Randomized   One-sided   Randomized
$(R_A, R_B)^{[t]}$ ──────→ ROT$^{[t]}$ ──Encoding──→ ROLE$^{[t]}$ ──Corr. Ext.──→ ROT$^{[t]}$ ──Encoding──→ ROLE$^{[t]}$ ──Corr. Ext.──→ ROT ──Encoding──→ (R'_A, R'_B)

IKOS Correlation Extractor

Kilian
[30]   Bilinear   ROLE Corr.   OT Embed.   Randomized
$(R_A, R_B)^{[t]}$ ──────→ ROT$^{[t]}$ ──Mult.──→ ROLE$^{[t]}$ ──Ext.(Fig. 4)──→ ROLE ──[9]──→ ROT ──Encoding──→ (R'_A, R'_B)

Our 2-message Correlation Extractor

Fig. 2. General correlation extractors that extract arbitrary correlations from arbitrary correlations. Above is the expanded IKOS [26] correlation extractor and below is ours. Our main contribution is shown in highlighted part. For brevity, it is implicit that there are *multiple samples* of the correlations. The ROLE correlations are over suitable constant size fields. The superscript "(t)" represents that the correlation is secure against adversarial leakage of only one a priori fixed party.

1.3   Other Prior Relevant Works

Figure 1 already provides the summary of the current state-of-the-art in correlation extractors. In this section, we summarize works related to combiners: extractors where the adversary is restricted to leaking individual bits of the honest party's secret share. The study of OT combiners was initiated by Harnik et al. [24]. Since then, there has been work on several variants and extensions of OT combiners [23,28,33,34,39]. Recently, Ishai et al. [27] constructed OT combiners with nearly optimal leakage resilience. Among these works, the most relevant to our paper are the ones by Meier, Przydatek, and Wullschleger [34] and Przydatek, and Wullschleger [39]. They use Reed-Solomon codes to construct two-message error-tolerant[7] combiners that produce fresh ROLEs over large fields[8] from ROLEs over the same field. Using multiplication friendly secret sharing schemes based on Algebraic Geometry Codes introduced by Chen and Cramer [13], a similar construction works with ROLEs over fields with appropriate constant size. We emphasize that this construction is *insecure* if an adversary can perform even 1-bit global leakage on the whole secret of the other party. In our construction, we crucially rely on a family of linear codes instead of a particular choice of the linear code to circumvent this bottleneck. Section 1.4 provides the principal technical ideas underlying our correlation extractor construction.

In the malicious setting, the feasibility result on malicious-secure combiners for ROT is reported in [28]. Recently, Cascudo et al. construct a malicious-secure combiner with high resilience, but $m = 1$ [11]. The case of malicious-secure correlation extractors remains entirely unexplored.

---

[7] A sample (r_A, r_B) is an *erroneous sample* if it is not in the support of the distribution (R_A, R_B), i.e., it is an incorrect sample. An error-tolerant combiner is a combiner that is secure even if a few of the input samples are erroneous.

[8] The size of the fields increases with n, the size of the secret shares produced by the preprocessing step.

1.4   Technical Overview

At the heart of our correlation extractor constructions is a 2-message ROLE($\mathbb{F}$)-to-ROLE($\mathbb{F}$) extractor, where we start with leaky $(R_A, R_B)^{[t]} = \left(\text{ROLE}(\mathbb{F})^{n/2 \lg |\mathbb{F}|} \right)^{[t]}$ and produce fresh secure sample of ROLE$(\mathbb{F})^{m/2 \lg |\mathbb{F}|}$. The field $\mathbb{F}$ is a constant-size field with characteristic 2, say $\mathbb{F} = \mathbb{GF} \left[2^6 \right]$, and each party gets n-bit shares. Below, we discuss some of the technical ideas underlying this construction.

This correlation extractor relies on the existence of a family of linear codes over $\mathbb{F}$ with suitable properties that we define below. For this discussion, let us assume that $s \in \mathbb{N}$ is the block-length of the codes. Let $\mathcal{J}$ be an index set, and we denote the family of linear codes with block-length s as follows: $\mathcal{C} = \{C_j : j \in \mathcal{J}\}$. This family of code $\mathcal{C}$ needs to have the following properties.

1. **Multiplication Friendly Good Codes.** Each code $C_j \subseteq \mathbb{F}^s$ in the family $\mathcal{C}$ is a *good code*, i.e., its rate and distance is $\Theta(s)$. Further, the Schur-product[9] of the codes, i.e., $C_j * C_j$, is a linear code with distance $\Theta(s)$. Such codes can be used to perform the multiplication of two secrets by multiplying their respective secret shares in secure computation protocols, hence the name.

2. **Small Bias Family.** Intuitively, a small bias family defines a pseudorandom distribution for linear tests. Let $S = (S_1, \ldots, S_s) \in \mathbb{F}^s$ and its corresponding linear test be defined as $L_S(x_1, \ldots, x_s) := S_1 x_1 + \cdots + S_s x_s$. Consider the distribution D of $L_S(c)$ for a random $j \in \mathcal{J}$ and a randomly sampled codeword $c \in C_j$. If $\mathcal{C}$ is a family of ρ-biased distributions, then the distribution D has statistical distance at most ρ from the output of $L_S(u)$ for random element $u \in \mathbb{F}^s$. For brevity, we say that the family $\mathcal{C}$ "ρ-fools the linear test L_S." The concept of small bias distributions was introduced in [1,35] and has found diverse applications, for example, [2,17,20,35].

   An interesting property of any linear code $C \subseteq \mathbb{F}^s$ is the following. A random codeword $c \in C$ can 0-fool every linear test L_S such that S is *not* a codeword in the dual of C. However, if S is a codeword in the dual of the code C, then the linear test L_S is clearly not fooled.

   So, a randomly chosen codeword from one fixed linear code cannot fool *all* linear tests. However, when we consider an appropriate family of linear codes, then a randomly chosen codeword from a randomly chosen code in this family can fool *every* linear test.

We construct such a family of codes over small finite fields $\mathbb{F}$ that can be of potential independent interest. Our starting point is an explicit Algebraic Geometry code $C \subseteq \mathbb{F}^s$ that is multiplication friendly [19,21]. Given one such code C, we randomly "twist then permute" the code to define the family $\mathcal{C}$. We emphasize that the production of our correlation extractor relies on the bias

---

[9] Consider a linear code $C \subseteq \mathbb{F}^s$. Let $c = (c_1, \ldots, c_s)$ and $c' = (c'_1, \ldots, c'_s)$ be two codewords in the code C. We define $c * c' = (c_1 c'_1, \ldots, c_s c'_s) \in \mathbb{F}^s$. The Schur-product $C * C$ is defined to be the linear span of all $c * c'$ such that $c, c' \in C$.

being small. So, it is crucial to construct a family with extremely small bias. Next, we describe our "twist then permute" operation.

Twist then Permute.[10] Suppose $C \subseteq \mathbb{F}^s$ is a linear code. Pick any $\lambda = (\lambda_1, \ldots, \lambda_s) \in (\mathbb{F}^*)^s$, i.e., for all $i \in [s]$, $\lambda_i \neq 0$. A λ-*twist* of the code C is defined as the following linear code

$$C_\lambda := \{(\lambda_1 c_1, \ldots, \lambda_s c_s) : (c_1, \ldots, c_s) \in C\}.$$

Let $\pi : \{1, \ldots, s\} \to \{1, \ldots, s\}$ be a permutation. The π-*permutation* of the λ-twist of C is defined as the following linear code

$$C_{\pi,\lambda} := \{(\lambda_{\pi(1)} c_{\pi(1)}, \ldots, \lambda_{\pi(s)} c_{\pi(s)}) : (c_1, \ldots, c_s) \in C\}.$$

Define $\mathcal{J}$ as the set of all (π, λ) such that $\lambda \in (\mathbb{F}^*)^s$ and π is a permutation of the set $\{1, \ldots, s\}$. Note that if C is multiplication friendly good code, then the code $C_{\pi,\lambda}$ continues to be multiplication friendly good code. A key observation towards demonstrating that $\mathcal{C}$ is a family of small bias distributions is that the following two distributions are identical (see Claim 2).

1. Fix $S \in \mathbb{F}^s$. The output distribution of the linear test L_S on a random codeword $c \in C_j$, for a random index $j \in \mathcal{J}$.
2. Let $T \in \mathbb{F}^s$ be a random element of the same weight[11] as S. The output distribution of the linear test L_T on a random codeword $c \in C$.

Based on this observation, we can calculate the bias of the family of our codes. Note that there are a total of $\binom{s}{w}(q-1)^w$ elements in $\mathbb{F}^s$ that have weight w. Let A_w denote the number of codewords in the dual of C that have weight w. Our family of codes $\mathcal{C}$ fools the linear test L_S with $\rho = A_w \cdot \binom{s}{w}^{-1} (q-1)^{-w}$, where w is the weight of $S \in \mathbb{F}^s$.

We obtain precise asymptotic bounds on the weight enumerator A_w of the dual of the code C to estimate the bias ρ, for $w \in \{0, 1, \ldots, s\}$. This precise bound translates into higher production m, higher resilience t, and exponentially low simulation error ε of our correlation extractor. We remark that for our construction if C has a small dual-distance, then the bias cannot be small.

Remark. The performance of the code C supersedes the elementary Gilbert-Varshamov bound. These Algebraic Geometry codes are one of the few codes in mathematics and computer science where explicit constructions have significantly better quality than elementary randomized constructions. So, elementary randomization techniques are unlikely to produce any (qualitatively) better

---

[10] In the literature there are multiple definitions for the *equivalence* of two linear codes. In particular, one such notion (cf., [38]), states that two codes are equivalent to each other if one can be twisted-and-permuted into the other code. For clarity, we have chosen to explicitly define the "twist then permute" operation.

[11] The weight of $S \in \mathbb{F}^s$ is defined as the number of non-zero elements in S.

parameters for this approach, given that the estimations of the weight enumerator in this work are asymptotically optimal. Therefore, finding *better randomized techniques* to construct the family of multiplication friendly good codes that is also a family of small-bias distributions is the research direction that has the potential to reduce the bias. This reduction in the bias can further improve the production and leakage resilience of our correlation extractors.

2 Preliminaries

We denote random variables by capital letters, for example X, and the values taken by small letters, for example $X = x$. For a positive integer n, we write $[n]$ and $[-n]$ to denote the sets $\{1, \ldots, n\}$ and $\{-n, \ldots, -1\}$, respectively. Let $\mathcal{S}_n$ be the set of all permutations $\pi : [n] \to [n]$. We consider the field $\mathbb{F} = \mathrm{GF}[q]$, where $q = p^a$, for a positive integer a and prime p. For any $c = (c_1, \ldots, c_\eta) \in \mathbb{F}^\eta$, define the function $\mathrm{wt}(c)$ as the cardinality of the set $\{i : c_i \neq 0\}$. For any two $x, y \in \mathbb{F}^\eta$, we let $x * y$ represent the point-wise product of x and y. That is, $x * y = (x_1 y_1, x_2 y_2, \ldots, x_\eta y_\eta) \in \mathbb{F}^\eta$. For a set Y, U_Y denotes the uniform distribution over the set Y, and $y \xleftarrow{\$} Y$ denotes sampling y according to U_Y. For any vector $x \in \mathbb{F}^\eta$ and a permutation $\pi \in \mathcal{S}_\eta$, we define $\pi(x) := (x_{\pi(1)}, \ldots, x_{\pi(\eta)})$.

2.1 Correlation Extractors

We denote the functionality of 2-choose-1 bit Oblivious Transfer as OT and Oblivious Linear-function Evaluation over a field $\mathbb{F}$ as OLE($\mathbb{F}$). Also, we denote the Random Oblivious Transfer Correlation as ROT and Random Oblivious Linear-function Evaluation Correlation over the field $\mathbb{F}$ as ROLE($\mathbb{F}$). When $\mathbb{F} = \mathrm{GF}[2]$, we denote ROLE($\mathbb{F}$) by ROLE.

Let η be such that $2\eta \lg |\mathbb{F}| = n$. In this work, we consider the setting when Alice and Bob start with η samples of the ROLE($\mathbb{F}$) correlation and the adversary performs t-bits of leakage. We give a secure protocol for extracting multiple secure OTs in this hybrid. Below we define such an correlation extractor formally using initial ROLE($\mathbb{F}$) correlations.

Leakage Model. We define our leakage model for ROLE($\mathbb{F}$) correlations as follows:

1. **η-ROLE correlation generation phase.** Alice gets $r_A = \{(a_i, b_i)\}_{i \in [\eta]} \in \mathbb{F}^{2\eta}$ and Bob gets $r_B = \{(x_i, z_i)\}_{i \in [\eta]} \in \mathbb{F}^{2\eta}$ such that for all $i \in [\eta]$, a_i, b_i, x_i is uniformly random and $z_i = a_i x_i + b_i$. Note that the size of secret share of each party is n bits.
2. **Corruption and leakage phase.** A semi-honest adversary corrupts either the sender and sends a leakage function $L : \mathbb{F}^\eta \to \{0,1\}^t$ and gets back $L(x_{[\eta]})$. Or, it corrupts the receiver and sends a leakage function $L : \mathbb{F}^\eta \to \{0,1\}^t$ and gets back $L(a_{[\eta]})$. Note that w.l.o.g. any leakage on the sender (resp., receiver) can be seen as a leakage on $a_{[\eta]}$ (resp., $x_{[\eta]}$). We again emphasize that this leakage need not be on individual bits of the shares, but on the entire share, and thus can encode crucial global information.

We denote by (R_A, R_B) the above correlated randomness and by $(R_A, R_B)^{[t]}$ its t-leaky version. Recall the definition for (n, m, t, ε)-correlation extractor (see Definition 1, Sect. 1.1). Below, we give the correctness and security requirements.

The *correctness* condition says that the receiver's output is correct in all $m/2$ instances of ROT. The *privacy* requirement says the following: Let $(s_0^{(i)}, s_1^{(i)})$ and $(c^{(i)}, z^{(i)})$ be the output shares of Alice and Bob, respectively, in the ith ROT instance. Then a corrupt sender (resp., receiver) cannot distinguish between $\{c^{(i)}\}_{i \in [m/2]}$ (resp., $\left\{ s_{1-c^{(i)}}^{(i)} \right\}_{i \in [m/2]}$) and $r \xleftarrow{\$} \{0, 1\}^{m/2}$ with advantage more than ε. The *leakage rate* is defined as t/n and the *production rate* is defined as m/n.

2.2 Fourier Analysis over Fields

We give some basic Fourier definitions and properties over finite fields, following the conventions of [40]. To begin discussion of Fourier analysis, let η be any positive integer and let $\mathbb{F}$ be any finite field. We define the *inner product* of two complex-valued functions.

Definition 2 (Inner Product). *Let $f, g \colon \mathbb{F}^\eta \to \mathbb{C}$. We define the* inner prod-*uct of f and g as*

$$\langle f, g \rangle := \mathop{\mathbb{E}}_{x \xleftarrow{\$} \mathbb{F}^\eta} \left[f(x) \cdot \overline{g(x)} \right] = \frac{1}{|\mathbb{F}|^\eta} \sum_{x \in \mathbb{F}^\eta} f(x) \cdot \overline{g(x)},$$

where $\overline{g(x)}$ is the complex conjugate of $g(x)$.

Next, we define general *character functions* for both $\mathbb{F}$ and $\mathbb{F}^\eta$.

Definition 3 (General Character Functions). *Let $\psi \colon \mathbb{F} \to \mathbb{C}^*$ be a group homomorphism from the additive group $\mathbb{F}$ to the multiplicative group $\mathbb{C}^*$. Then we say that ψ is a character function of $\mathbb{F}$.*

Let $\chi \colon \mathbb{F}^\eta \times \mathbb{F}^\eta \to \mathbb{C}^*$ be a bilinear, non-degenerate, and symmetric map defined as $\chi(x, y) = \psi(x \cdot y) = \psi(\sum_i x_i y_i)$. Then, for any $S \in \mathbb{F}^\eta$, the function $\chi(S, \cdot) := \chi_S(\cdot)$ is a character function of $\mathbb{F}^\eta$.

Given χ, we have the *Fourier Transformation*.

Definition 4 (Fourier Transformation). *For any $S \in \mathbb{F}^\eta$, let $f \colon \mathbb{F}^\eta \to \mathbb{C}$ and χ_S be a character function. We define the map $\widehat{f} \colon \mathbb{F}^\eta \to \mathbb{C}$ as $\widehat{f}(S) := \langle f, \chi_S \rangle$. We say that $\widehat{f}(S)$ is a Fourier Coefficient of f at S and the linear map $f \mapsto \widehat{f}$ is the Fourier Transformation of f.*

Note that this transformation is an invertible linear map. The Fourier inversion formula is given by the following lemma.

Lemma 1 (Fourier Inversion). *For any function $f \colon \mathbb{F}^\eta \to \mathbb{C}$, we can write $f(x) = \sum_{S \in \mathbb{F}^\eta} \widehat{f}(S) \chi_S(x)$.*

2.3 Distributions and Min-Entropy

For a probability distribution X over a sample space U, entropy of $x \in X$ is defined as $H_X(x) = -\lg \Pr[X = x]$. The min-entropy of X, represented by $\mathbf{H}_\infty(X)$, is defined to be $\min_{x \in \mathsf{Supp}(X)} H_X(x)$. The binary entropy function, denoted by $\mathbf{h_2}(x) = -x \lg x - (1-x) \lg(1-x)$ for every $x \in (0,1)$.

Given a joint distribution (X, Y) over sample space $U \times V$, the marginal distribution Y is a distribution over sample space V such that, for any $y \in V$, the probability assigned to y is $\sum_{x \in U} \Pr[X = x, Y = y]$. The conditional distribution $(X|y)$ represents the distribution over sample space U such that the probability of $x \in U$ is $\Pr[X = x|Y = y]$. The average min-entropy [16], represented by $\widetilde{\mathbf{H}}_\infty(X|Y)$, is defined to be $-\lg \mathbb{E}_{y \sim Y}[2^{-\mathbf{H}_\infty(X|y)}]$.

Imported Lemma 1 ([16]). *If $\mathbf{H}_\infty(X) \geq k$ and L is an arbitrary ℓ-bit leakage on X, then $\widetilde{\mathbf{H}}_\infty(X|L) \geqslant k - \ell$.*

Lemma 2 (Fourier Coefficients of a Min-Entropy Distribution). *Let $X \colon \mathbb{F}^\eta \to \mathbb{R}$ be a min-entropy source such that $\mathbf{H}_\infty(X) \geqslant k$. Then $\sum_S |\widehat{X}(S)|^2 \leqslant |\mathbb{F}|^{-\eta} \cdot 2^{-k}$.*

2.4 Family of Small-Bias Distributions

Definition 5 (Bias of a Distribution). *Let X be a distribution over $\mathbb{F}^\eta$. Then the bias of X with respect to $S \in \mathbb{F}^\eta$ is defined as $\mathsf{Bias}_S(X) := |\mathbb{F}|^\eta \cdot |\widehat{X}(S)|$.*

Dodis and Smith [17] defined small-bias distribution families for distributions over $\{0,1\}^\eta$. We generalize it naturally for distributions over $\mathbb{F}^\eta$.

Definition 6 (Small-bias distribution family). *A family of distributions $\mathcal{F} = \{F_1, F_2, \cdots, F_k\}$ over sample space $\mathbb{F}^\eta$ is called a ρ^2-biased family if for every non-zero vector $S \in \mathbb{F}^\eta$ following holds:*

$$\mathop{\mathbb{E}}_{i \xleftarrow{\$} [k]} \mathsf{Bias}_S(F_i)^2 \leqslant \rho^2.$$

Following extraction lemma was proven in previous works over $\{0,1\}^\eta$.

Imported Lemma 2 ([2,17,20,35]). *Let $\mathcal{F} = \{F_1, \ldots, F_\mu\}$ be ρ^2-biased family of distributions over the sample space $\{0,1\}^\eta$. Let (M, L) be a joint distribution such that the marginal distribution M is over $\{0,1\}^\eta$ and $\widetilde{\mathbf{H}}_\infty(M|L) \geq m$. Then, the following holds: Let J be a uniform distribution over $[\mu]$. Then,*

$$\mathsf{SD}\left((F_J \oplus M, L, J), (U_{\{0,1\}^\eta}, L, J)\right) \leq \frac{\rho}{2}\left(\frac{2^\eta}{2^m}\right)^{1/2}.$$

A natural generalization of above lemma for distributions over $\mathbb{F}^\eta$ gives the following.

Theorem 5 (Min-entropy extraction via masking with small-bias distributions). *Let $\mathcal{F} = \{F_1, \ldots, F_\mu\}$ be a ρ^2-biased family of distributions over the sample space $\mathbb{F}^\eta$ for field $\mathbb{F}$ of size q. Let (M, L) be a joint distribution such that the marginal distribution M is over $\mathbb{F}^\eta$ and $\widetilde{\mathbf{H}}_\infty(M|L) \geqslant m$. Then, the following holds: Let J be a uniform distribution over $[\mu]$. Then,*

$$\mathrm{SD}\left((F_J \oplus M, L, J), (U_{\mathbb{F}^\eta}, L, J)\right) \leqslant \frac{\rho}{2}\left(\frac{|\mathbb{F}|^\eta}{2^m}\right)^{1/2}.$$

We provide the proof of this result in the full version of our work [8].

2.5   Distribution over Linear Codes

Let $C = [\eta, \kappa, d, d^\perp, d^{(2)}]_{\mathbb{F}}$ be a linear code over $\mathbb{F}$ with generator matrix $G \in \mathbb{F}^{\kappa \times \eta}$. We also use C to denote the uniform distribution over codewords generated by G. For any $\pi \in \mathcal{S}_\eta$, define $G_\pi = \pi(G)$ as the generator matrix obtained by permuting the columns of G under π.

The **dual code** of C, represented by $C^\perp$, is the set of all codewords that are orthogonal to every codeword in C. That is, for any $c^\perp \in C^\perp$, it holds that $\langle c, c^\perp \rangle = 0$ for all $c \in C$. Let $H \in \mathbb{F}^{(\eta-\kappa) \times \eta}$ be a generator matrix of $C^\perp$. The distance of $C^\perp$ is $d^\perp$.

The **Schur product code** of C, represented by $C^{(2)}$, is the span of all codewords obtained as a Schur product of codewords in C. That is, $C^{(2)} = C * C := \langle c * c' : c, c' \in C \rangle \subseteq \mathbb{F}^\eta$, where $c * c'$ denotes the coordinate-wise product of c and c'. The distance of $C^{(2)}$ is $d^{(2)}$.

3   Family of Small-Bias Distributions with Erasure Recovery

In this section, we give our construction of the family of small-bias distributions $\{C_j\}_{j \in \mathcal{J}}$ such that each C_j is a linear code and $C_j * C_j$ supports erasure recovery. Recall that $C_j * C_j$ is the linear span of all $c * c'$ such that $c, c' \in C_j$. We formally define the requirements for our family of distributions in Property 1.

Property 1. A family of linear code distributions $\mathcal{C} = \{C_j : j \in \mathcal{J}\}$ over $\mathbb{F}^{\eta^*}$ satisfy this property with parameters δ and γ if the following conditions hold.

1. **$2^{-\delta}$-bias family of distributions.** For any $0^{\eta^*} \neq S \in \mathbb{F}^{\eta^*}$, $\mathbb{E}\left[\mathrm{Bias}_S(C_j)^2\right] \leqslant 2^{-\delta}$, where the expectation is taken over $j \xleftarrow{\$} \mathcal{J}$.
2. **γ-erasure recovery in Schur Product.** For all $j \in \mathcal{J}$, the Schur product code of C_j, that is $C_j * C_j = C_j^{(2)}$, supports the erasure recovery of the first γ coordinates. Moreover, the first γ coordinates of C_j and $C_j^{(2)}$ are linearly independent of each other.

3.1 Our Construction

Figure 3 presents our construction of a family of linear codes which satisfies Property 1 and Theorem 6 gives the parameters for our construction.

Family of small-bias distributions with erasure recovery in the product distribution:

Fix a linear code $C = [\eta^*, \kappa, d, d^\perp, d^{(2)}]_{\mathbb{F}}$ with generator matrix $G \in \mathbb{F}^{\kappa \times \eta^*}$, where $|\mathbb{F}| = q$ and $\kappa \geqslant d^{(2)}$, where $d^{(2)}$ is the distance of $C * C$. Let γ be a fixed natural number (to be determined later during parameter setting) such that $C * C$ supports γ-erasure recovery. We construct the family of small-bias distributions $\{C_{\pi,\lambda} : \pi \in \mathcal{S}_{\eta^*}, \lambda \in (\mathbb{F}^*)^{\eta^*}\}$ over $\mathbb{F}^{\eta^*}$ as follows.

1. Let $\lambda \in (\mathbb{F}^*)^{\eta^*}$. Define $G_\lambda = [\lambda_1 G_1, \dots, \lambda_{\eta^*} G_{\eta^*}] \in \mathbb{F}^{\kappa \times \eta^*}$, where G_i is the ith column of G and $\lambda_i G_i$ is the multiplication of G_i by λ_i.
2. Let $\pi \in \mathcal{S}_{\eta^*}$. Define $G_{\pi,\lambda} = \pi(G_\lambda) \in \mathbb{F}^{\kappa \times \eta^*}$, where $\pi(G_\lambda)$ is the permutation of the columns of G_λ according to permutation π. Then $C_{\pi,\lambda}$ is the uniform distribution over the linear code generated by $G_{\pi,\lambda}$.

(Enc, Dec) for $C_{\pi,\lambda}$: Let $(\mathsf{Enc}_C, \mathsf{Dec}_C)$ be the encoder and decoder for the code C.

- $\mathsf{Enc}(m)$: Compute $c = (c_1, \dots, c_{\eta^*}) = \mathsf{Enc}_C(m)$. Compute $c * \lambda = (\lambda_1 c_1, \dots, \lambda_{\eta^*} c_{\eta^*})$. Output $\pi(c * \lambda)$.
- $\mathsf{Dec}(x)$: Compute $c' = (c'_1, \dots, c'_{\eta^*}) = \pi^{-1}(x)$. Compute $c' * \lambda' = (\lambda_1^{-1} c'_1, \dots, \lambda_{\eta^*}^{-1} c'_{\eta^*})$. Output $\mathsf{Dec}_C(c' * \lambda')$.

(Enc, Dec) for $(C_{\pi,\lambda} * C_{\pi,\lambda})$: Let $(\mathsf{Enc}_{C^{(2)}}, \mathsf{Dec}_{C^{(2)}})$ be the Encoder and Decoder for the linear code $C^{(2)} = C * C$.

- $\mathsf{Enc}(m)$: Compute $c = (c_1, \dots, c_{\eta^*}) = \mathsf{Enc}_{C^{(2)}}(m)$. Compute $c * \lambda * \lambda = (\lambda_1^2 c_1, \dots, \lambda_{\eta^*}^2 c_{\eta^*})$. Output $\pi(c * \lambda * \lambda)$.
- $\mathsf{Dec}(x)$: Compute $c' = (c'_1, \dots, c'_{\eta^*}) = \pi^{-1}(x)$. Compute $c' * \lambda' * \lambda' = (\lambda_1^{-2} c'_1, \dots, \lambda_{\eta^*}^{-2} c'_{\eta^*})$. Output $\mathsf{Dec}_{C^{(2)}}(c' * \lambda' * \lambda')$.

Fig. 3. Our construction of a family of small bias linear code distributions.

At a high level, the linear code C is a suitable algebraic geometric code over constant size field $\mathbb{F}$ of block length $\eta^* = \gamma + \eta$. The parameters of the code C are chosen such that C is a $2^{-\delta}$-biased family of distributions under our "twist-then-permute" operation, and $C * C$ supports erasure recovery of any γ coordinates. The precise calculation of the parameters of the code C can be found in the full version of our work [8]. Our family of linear codes satisfies the following theorem.

Theorem 6. *The family of linear code distributions $\{C_{\pi,\lambda} : \pi \in \mathcal{S}_{\eta^*}, \lambda \in (\mathbb{F}^*)^{\eta^*}\}$ over $\mathbb{F}^{\eta^*}$ given in Fig. 3 satisfies Property 1 for any $\gamma < d^{(2)}$, where $d^{(2)}$ is the distance of the Schur product code of C, and $\delta = [d^\perp + \eta^*/(\sqrt{q}-1) - 1] \cdot [\lg(q-1) - \mathbf{h_2}(1/(q+1))] - (\eta^*/(\sqrt{q}-1)) \lg q$, where $\mathbf{h_2}$ denotes the binary entropy function.*

Proof. We first prove erasure recovery followed by the small-bias property.

γ-erasure Recovery in Schur Product code. First we note that permuting or re-ordering the columns of a generator matrix does not change its distance, distance of the Schur product, or its capability of erasure recovery (as long as we know the mapping of new columns vis-à-vis old columns). Let $\mathcal{I}_\gamma = \{i_1, \ldots, i_\gamma\}$ be the indices of the erased coordinates of codeword in $C^{(2)}_{\pi,\lambda}$. Hence to show erasure recovery of the coordinates $\mathcal{I}_\gamma$ of a codeword of $C^{(2)}_{\pi,\lambda}$, it suffices to show erasure recovery of the γ erased coordinates $\mathcal{J}_\gamma = \{j_1, \ldots, j_\gamma\}$ of a codeword of $C^{(2)}_\lambda$, where C_λ is the uniform codespace generated by G_λ, and $\pi(j_k) = i_k$, $\forall k \in [\gamma]$.

Note that since $\gamma < d^{(2)}$, the code $C^{(2)}$ supports erasure recovery of *any* γ coordinates. Thus it suffices to show that this implies that $C^{(2)}_\lambda$ also supports the erasure recovery of *any* γ coordinates. Note that since $\lambda \in (\mathbb{F}^*)^{\eta^*}$, multiplication of the columns of G according to λ does not change its distance or distance of the Schur product. Then we do the following to perform erasure recovery of γ coordinates in $C^{(2)}_\lambda$. Let $c^{(2)} \in C^{(2)}_\lambda$ be a codeword with erased coordinates $\mathcal{J}_\gamma = \{j_1, \ldots, j_\gamma\}$, and let $\mathcal{J}_\eta = \{j'_1, \ldots, j'_\eta\}$ be the coordinates of $c^{(2)}$ that have not been erased. For every $j \in \mathcal{J}_\eta$, compute $c_j = (\lambda_j^{-1})^2 c^{(2)}_j$. Then the vector $(c_j)_{j \in \mathcal{J}_\eta}$ is a codeword of $C^{(2)}$ with coordinates c_i erased for $i \in \mathcal{J}_\gamma$. Since $C^{(2)}$ has γ erasure recovery, we can recover the c_i for $i \in \mathcal{J}_\gamma$. Once recovered, for every $i \in \mathcal{J}_\gamma$, compute $c^{(2)}_i = \lambda_i^2 c_i$. This produces the γ erased coordinates of $c^{(2)}$ in $C^{(2)}_\lambda$. Finally, one can map the $c^{(2)}_i$ for $i \in \mathcal{J}_\gamma$ to the coordinates $\mathcal{I}_\gamma$ using π, recovering the erasures in $C^{(2)}_{\pi,\lambda}$.

$2^{-\delta}$-bias Family of Distributions. Let $C, C_\lambda, C_{\pi,\lambda}$ be the uniform distribution over the linear codes generated by $G, G_\lambda, G_{\pi,\lambda}$, respectively. Recall that $d^\perp$ is the dual distance for C. Note that $C_\lambda, C_{\pi,\lambda}$ have dual-distance $d^\perp$ as well. Let $\eta^* = \eta + \gamma$. Since $\mathsf{Bias}_S(C_{\pi,\lambda}) = |\mathbb{F}|^{\eta^*} |\widehat{C_{\pi,\lambda}}(S)|$ for every $S \in \mathbb{F}^{\eta^*}$, it suffices to show that

$$\mathop{\mathbb{E}}_{\pi,\lambda} \left[\widehat{C_{\pi,\lambda}}(S)^2 \right] \leqslant \frac{1}{|\mathbb{F}|^{2\eta^*} \cdot 2^\delta}.$$

To begin, first recall the definition of $C_{\pi,\lambda}$:

$$C_{\pi,\lambda} := \{\pi(\lambda_1 c_1, \ldots, \lambda_{\eta^*} c_{\eta^*}) \mid (c_1, \ldots, c_{\eta^*}) \in C\}.$$

Next, given any $S \in \mathbb{F}^{\eta^*}$, define $\mathcal{S}(S) := \{\pi(\lambda_1 S_1, \ldots, \lambda_{\eta^*} S_{\eta^*}) \in \mathbb{F}^{\eta^*} \mid \forall \pi \in \mathcal{S}_{\eta^*} \wedge \lambda \in (\mathbb{F}^*)^{\eta^*}\}$. Note that $\mathcal{S}(S)$ is equivalently characterized as

$$\mathcal{S}(S) = \{T = (T_1, \ldots, T_{\eta^*}) \in \mathbb{F}^{\eta^*} \mid \mathsf{wt}(T) = \mathsf{wt}(S)\}.$$

It is easy to see that $|\mathcal{S}(S)| = \binom{\eta^*}{w_0}(q-1)^{\eta^*-w_0}$, where $w_0 = \eta^* - \mathsf{wt}(S)$; i.e., w_0 is the number of zeros in S. We prove the following claim.

Claim 1. *For any $S \in \mathbb{F}^{\eta^*}$, we have $\widehat{C_{\pi,\lambda}}(S) = \widehat{C}(\pi^{-1}(S) * \lambda)$.*

Proof. Notice that by definition for any $x \in C_{\pi,\lambda}$, we have $C_{\pi,\lambda}(x) = C(c)$ since $x = \pi(\lambda_1 c_1, \ldots, \lambda_{\eta^*} c_{\eta^*})$ for $c \in C$. This is equivalently stated as $C_{\pi,\lambda}(\pi(c * \lambda)) = C(c)$. For $x = \pi(\lambda_1 y_1, \ldots, \lambda_{\eta^*} y_{\eta^*}) \in \mathbb{F}^{\eta^*}$ and any $S \in \mathbb{F}^{\eta^*}$, we have

$$S \cdot x = \sum_{i=1}^{\eta^*} S_i x_i = \sum_{i=1}^{\eta^*} S_i(\lambda_{\pi(i)} y_{\pi(i)}) = \sum_{i=1}^{\eta^*} (S_{\pi^{-1}(i)})\lambda_i y_i = (\pi^{-1}(S) * \lambda) \cdot y.$$

where $S \cdot x$ is the vector dot product. By definition of $\chi_S(x)$, this implies $\chi_S(x) = \chi_y(\pi^{-1}(S) * \lambda)$. Using these two facts and working directly from the definition of Fourier Transform, we have

$$\widehat{C_{\pi,\lambda}}(S) = \frac{1}{|\mathbb{F}|^{\eta^*}} \sum_{x \in \mathbb{F}^{\eta^*}} C_{\pi,\lambda}(x)\overline{\chi_S(x)}$$

$$= \frac{1}{|\mathbb{F}|^{\eta^*}} \sum_{c \in \mathbb{F}^{\eta^*}} C_{\pi,\lambda}(\pi(\lambda_1 c_1, \ldots, \lambda_{\eta^*} c_{\eta^*}))\overline{\chi_S(\pi(\lambda_1 c_1, \ldots, \lambda_{\eta^*} c_{\eta^*}))}$$

$$= \frac{1}{|\mathbb{F}|^{\eta^*}} \sum_{c \in \mathbb{F}^{\eta^*}} C(c)\overline{\chi_c(\pi^{-1}(S) * \lambda)} = \widehat{C}(\pi^{-1}(S) * \lambda).$$

This proves Claim 1. $\qquad\square$

It is easy to see that $\mathsf{wt}(\pi^{-1}(S) * \lambda) = \mathsf{wt}(S)$, so $(\pi^{-1}(S) * \lambda) = T \in \mathcal{S}(S)$. From this fact and Claim 1, we prove the following claim.

Claim 2. *For any $S \in \mathbb{F}^n$, $\underset{\pi,\lambda}{\mathbb{E}}\left[\widehat{C_{\pi,\lambda}}(S)^2\right] = \underset{T \xleftarrow{\$} \mathcal{S}(S)}{\mathbb{E}}\left[\widehat{C}(T)^2\right]$.*

Proof. Suppose we have codeword $x \in C_{\pi,\lambda}$ such that $\pi(\lambda_1 c_1, \ldots, \lambda_\eta^* c_\eta^*) = x$, for some codeword $c \in C$. Let $\{i_1, \ldots, i_{w_0}\}$ be the set of indices of 0 in c; that is, $c_j = 0$ for all $j \in \{i_1, \ldots, i_{w_0}\}$. Then for any permutation π, the set $\{\pi(i_0), \ldots, \pi(i_{w_0})\}$ is the set of zero indices in x. Note also that for any index $j \notin \{\pi(i_0), \ldots, \pi(i_{w_0})\}$, we have $x_j \neq 0$. If this was not the case, then we have $x_j = c_{\pi^{-1}(j)}\lambda_{\pi^{-1}(j)} = 0$. Since $j \notin \{\pi(i_0), \ldots, \pi(i_{w_0})\}$, this implies $\pi^{-1}(j) \notin \{i_0, \ldots, i_{w_0}\}$, which further implies that $c_{\pi^{-1}(j)} \neq 0$. This is a contradiction since $\lambda \in (\mathbb{F}^*)^{\eta^*}$. Thus any permutation π must map the zeros of S to the zeros of c, and there are $w_0!(\eta^* - w_0)!$ such permutations. Notice now that for any $c_k = 0$, λ_k can take any value in $\mathbb{F}^*$, so we have $(q-1)^{w_0}$ such choices. Furthermore, if $c_k \neq 0$ and $\lambda_k c_k = x_{\pi^{-1}(k)} \neq 0$, then there is exactly one value $\lambda_k \in \mathbb{F}^*$ which satisfies this equation. Putting it all together, we have

$$
\begin{aligned}
\mathop{\mathbb{E}}_{\pi,\lambda}\left[\widehat{C_{\pi,\lambda}}(S)^2\right] &= \frac{1}{\eta^*!(q-1)^{\eta^*}}\sum_{\pi,\lambda}\widehat{C_{\pi,\lambda}}(S)^2 = \frac{1}{\eta^*!(q-1)^{\eta^*}}\sum_{\pi,\lambda}\widehat{C}\left(\pi^{-1}(S)*\lambda\right)^2 \\
&= \frac{(w_0!(\eta^*-w_0)!(q-1)^{w_0})}{\eta^*!(q-1)^{\eta^*}}\sum_{T\in\mathcal{S}(S)}\widehat{C}(T)^2 \\
&= \frac{w_0!(\eta^*-w_0)!}{\eta^*!(q-1)^{\eta^*-w_0}}\sum_{T\in\mathcal{S}(S)}\widehat{C}(T)^2 \\
&= \left(\binom{\eta^*}{w_0}(q-1)^{\eta^*-w_0}\right)^{-1}\sum_{T\in\mathcal{S}(S)}\widehat{C}(T)^2 = \mathop{\mathbb{E}}_{T\xleftarrow{\$}\mathcal{S}(S)}\left[\widehat{C}(T)^2\right].
\end{aligned}
$$

where the first line of equality follows from Claim 1. This proves Claim 2.   □

With Claim 2, we now are interested in finding δ such that for $0^{\eta^*}\neq S\in\mathbb{F}^{\eta^*}$

$$
\mathop{\mathbb{E}}_{T\xleftarrow{\$}\mathcal{S}(S)}\left[\widehat{C}(T)^2\right] \leq \frac{1}{|\mathbb{F}|^{2\eta^*}2^\delta}.
$$

We note that since C is a linear code, C has non-zero Fourier coefficients only at codewords in $C^\perp$.

Claim 3. *For all $S\in\mathbb{F}^{\eta^*}$, $\widehat{C}(S) = \begin{cases} \dfrac{1}{|\mathbb{F}|^{\eta^*}} & S\in C^\perp \\ 0 & otherwise. \end{cases}$*

Let $A_w = |C^\perp\cap\mathcal{S}(S)|$, where $w = \eta^*-w_0 = \mathsf{wt}(S)$. Intuitively, A_w is the number of codewords in $C^\perp$ with weight w. Then from Claim 3, we have

$$
\mathop{\mathbb{E}}_{T\xleftarrow{\$}\mathcal{S}(S)}\left[\widehat{C}(T)^2\right] = \frac{|C^\perp\cap\mathcal{S}(S)|}{|\mathbb{F}|^{2\eta^*}\binom{\eta^*}{\eta^*-\mathsf{wt}(S)}(q-1)^{\mathsf{wt}(S)}} = \frac{A_w}{|\mathbb{F}|^{2\eta^*}\binom{\eta^*}{w}(q-1)^w}.
$$

Now, our goal is to upper bound A_w. Towards this goal, the weight enumerator for the code $C^\perp$ is defined as the following polynomial:

$$
W_{C^\perp}(x) = \sum_{c\in C^\perp} x^{\eta^*-\mathsf{wt}(c)}.
$$

This polynomial can equivalently be written in the following manner:

$$
W_{C^\perp}(x) = \sum_{w\in\{0,\dots,\eta^*\}} A_w x^{\eta^*-w}.
$$

Define $a = \eta^*-d^\perp$.

Imported Theorem 1 (Exercise 1.1.15 from [41]). *We have the relation*

$$
W_{C^\perp}(x) = x^{\eta^*} + \sum_{i=0}^{a} B_i(x-1)^i, where
$$

$$B_i = \sum_{j=\eta^*-a}^{\eta^*-i} \binom{\eta^*-j}{i} A_j \geq 0 \qquad A_i = \sum_{j=\eta^*-i}^{a} (-1)^{\eta^*+i+j} \binom{j}{\eta^*-i} B_j.$$

For weight $w \in \{d^\perp, \ldots, \eta^*\}$, we use the following expression to estimate A_w.

$$A_w = \binom{\eta^*-w}{\eta^*-w} B_{\eta^*-w} - \binom{\eta^*-w+1}{\eta^*-w} B_{\eta^*-w+1} + \cdots \pm \binom{\eta^*-d^\perp}{\eta^*-w} B_{\eta^*-d^\perp}$$

Since we are interested in the asymptotic behavior (and not the exact value) of A_w, we note that $\lg A_w \sim \lg \Gamma(w)$, where

$$\Gamma(w) = \max \left\{ \binom{\eta^*-w}{\eta^*-w} B_{\eta^*-w}, \binom{\eta^*-w+1}{\eta^*-w} B_{\eta^*-w+1}, \ldots, \binom{\eta^*-d^\perp}{\eta^*-w} B_{\eta^*-d^\perp} \right\}.$$

Thus, it suffices to compute $\Gamma(w)$ for every w, and then the bias. We present this precise asymptotic calculation in the full version of our work [8]. This calculation yields

$$\delta = \left(d^\perp + \frac{\eta^*}{\sqrt{q}-1} - 1 \right) \left(\lg(q-1) - \mathbf{h_2}\left(\frac{1}{q+1} \right) \right) - \frac{\eta^*}{\sqrt{q}-1} \lg q,$$

which completes the proof. □

4   Construction of Correlation Extractor

Our main sub-protocol for Theorem 3 takes $\mathsf{ROLE}(\mathbb{F})$ as the initial correlation and produces secure $\mathsf{ROLE}(\mathbb{F})$. Towards this, we define a $\mathsf{ROLE}(\mathbb{F})$-to-$\mathsf{ROLE}(\mathbb{F})$ extractor formally below.

Definition 7 ($(\eta, \gamma, t, \varepsilon)$-$\mathsf{ROLE}(\mathbb{F})$-to-$\mathsf{ROLE}(\mathbb{F})$ extractor). *Let $(R_A, R_B) = (\mathsf{ROLE}(\mathbb{F}))^\eta$ be correlated randomness. An $(\eta, \gamma, t, \varepsilon)$-$\mathsf{ROLE}(\mathbb{F})$-to-$\mathsf{ROLE}(\mathbb{F})$ extractor is a two-party interactive protocol in the $(R_A, R_B)^{[t]}$-hybrid that securely implements the $(\mathsf{ROLE}(\mathbb{F}))^\gamma$ functionality against information-theoretic semi-honest adversaries with ε simulation error.*

Let $(u_i, v_i) \in \mathbb{F}^2$ and $(r_i, z_i) \in \mathbb{F}^2$ be the shares of Alice and Bob, respectively, in the ith output ROLE instance. The *correctness* condition says that the receiver's output is correct in all γ instances of ROLE, i.e., $z_i = u_i r_i + v_i$ for all $i \in [\gamma]$. The *privacy* requirement says the following: A corrupt sender (resp., receiver) cannot distinguish between $\{r_i\}_{i\in[\gamma]}$ (resp., $\{u_i\}_{i\in[\gamma]}$) and $U_{\mathbb{F}^\gamma}$ with advantage more than ε.

In Sect. 4.1, we give our construction for Theorem 3. Later, in Sect. 4.3, we build on this to give our construction for Theorem 2.

4.1 Protocol for ROLE($\mathbb{F}$) correlation extractor

As already mentioned in Sect. 1.4, to prove Theorem 3, our main building block will be $(\eta, \gamma, t, \varepsilon)$-ROLE($\mathbb{F}$)-to-ROLE($\mathbb{F}$) extractor (see Definition 7). That is, the parties start with η samples of the ROLE($\mathbb{F}$) correlation such that size of each party's share is $n = 2\eta \log |\mathbb{F}|$ bits. The adversarial party gets t bits of leakage. The protocol produces (ROLE($\mathbb{F}$))$^\gamma$ with simulation error ε. We give the formal description of the protocol, inspired by the Massey secret sharing scheme [32], in Fig. 4. Note that our protocol is round-optimal and uses a family of distributions $\mathcal{C} = \{C_j\}_{j \in \mathcal{J}}$ that satisfies Property 1 with parameters δ and γ.

$(\eta, \gamma, t, \varepsilon)$-ROLE($\mathbb{F}$)-to-ROLE($\mathbb{F}$) Extractor:

Let $\mathcal{C} = \{C_j : j \in \mathcal{J}\}$ be a family of distributions over $\mathbb{F}^{\eta+\gamma}$ satisfying Property 1 for appropriate values of δ and γ.

Hybrid (Random Correlations): Client A gets random $(a_{[\eta]}, b_{[\eta]}) \in \mathbb{F}^{2\eta}$ and Client B gets random $(x_{[\eta]}, z_{[\eta]}) \in \mathbb{F}^{2\eta}$ such that for all $i \in \{1, 2, \ldots, \eta\}$, $a_i x_i + b_i = z_i$.

1. *Code Generation.* Client B samples $j \xleftarrow{\$} \mathcal{J}$.
2. *ROLE Extraction Protocol.*
   (a) Client B picks random $r = (r_{-\gamma}, \ldots, r_{-1}, r_1, \ldots, r_\eta) \sim C_j$ and computes $m_{[\eta]} = r_{[\eta]} + x_{[\eta]}$. Client B sends $(m_{[\eta]}, j)$ to client A.
   (b) Client A picks the same distribution C_j as client B. Client A picks random $u = (u_{-\gamma}, \ldots, u_{-1}, u_1, \ldots, u_\eta) \sim C_j$ and random $v = (v_{-\gamma}, \ldots, v_{-1}, v_1, \ldots, v_\eta) \sim C_j^{(2)}$. Client A computes $\alpha_{[\eta]} = u_{[\eta]} - a_{[\eta]}$, and $\beta_{[\eta]} = a_{[\eta]} * m_{[\eta]} + b_{[\eta]} + v_{[\eta]}$ and sends $(\alpha_{[\eta]}, \beta_{[\eta]})$ to Client B.
   (c) Client B computes $t_{[\eta]} = (\alpha_{[\eta]} * r_{[\eta]}) + \beta_{[\eta]} - z_{[\eta]}$. Cleint B performs erasure recovery on $t_{[\eta]}$ for $C_j^{(2)}$ to obtain $t_{[-\gamma]}$.
   (d) Client A outputs $\{u_i, v_i\}_{i \in \{-\gamma, \ldots, -1\}}$ and Client B outputs $\{r_i, t_i\}_{i \in \{-\gamma, \ldots, -1\}}$

Fig. 4. ROLE($\mathbb{F}$)-to-ROLE($\mathbb{F}$) extractor protocol.

Next, we use the ROT embedding technique from [9] to embed σ ROTs in each fresh ROLE($\mathbb{F}$) obtained from above protocol. For example, we can embed two ROTs into one ROLE($\mathrm{GF}\left[2^6\right]$). Using this we get production $m = 2\sigma\gamma$, i.e., we get $m/2 = \sigma\gamma$ secure ROTs. We note that the protocol from [9] is round-optimal, achieves perfect security and composes in parallel with our protocol in Fig. 4. Hence, we maintain round-optimality (see Sect. 4.2).

Correctness of Fig. 4. The following lemma characterizes the correctness of the scheme presented in Fig. 4.

Lemma 3 (Correctness). *If the family of distributions $\mathcal{C} = \{C_j\}_{j \in \mathcal{J}}$ satisfies Property 1, i.e., erasure recovery of first γ coordinates in Schur product, then for all $i \in \{-\gamma, \ldots, -1\}$, it holds that $t_i = u_i r_i + v_i$.*

Proof. First, we prove the following claim.

Claim 4. *For all $i \in [\eta]$, it holds that $t_i = u_i r_i + v_i$.*

This claim follows from the following derivation.

$$
\begin{aligned}
t_i &= \alpha_i r_i + \beta_i - z_i = (u_i - a_i)r_i + (a_i m_i + b_i + v_i) - z_i \\
&= u_i r_i - a_i r_i + a_i(r_i + x_i) + b_i + v_i \\
&= u_i r_i + a_i x_i + b_i + v_i - z_i \\
&= u_i r_i + v_i
\end{aligned}
$$

From the above claim, we have that $t_{[\eta]} = u_{[\eta]} * r_{[\eta]} + v_{[\eta]}$. From the protocol, we have that $u, r \in C_j$ and $v \in C_j^{(2)}$. Consider $\tilde{t} = u * r + v \in C_j^{(2)}$. Note that $t_i = \tilde{t}_i$ for all $i \in [\eta]$. Hence, when client B performs erasure recovery on $t_{[\eta]}$ for a codeword in $C_j^{(2)}$, it would get $\tilde{t}_{[-\gamma]}$. This follows from erasure recovery guarantee for first γ coordinates by Property 1. $\qquad\square$

Security of Fig. 4. To argue the security, we prove that the protocol is a secure implementation of $(\mathsf{ROLE}(\mathbb{F}))^\gamma$ functionality against an information-theoretic semi-honest adversary that corrupts either the sender or the receiver and leaks at most t-bits from the secret share of the honest party at the beginning of the protocol. At a high level, we prove the security of our protocol by reducing it exactly to our unpredictability lemma.

Lemma 4 (Unpredictability Lemma). *Let $\mathcal{C} = \{C_j \colon j \in \mathcal{J}\}$ be a $2^{-\delta}$-biased family of linear code distributions over $\mathbb{F}^{\eta^*}$, where $\eta^* = \gamma + \eta$. Consider the following game between an honest challenger $\mathcal{H}$ and an adversary $\mathcal{A}$:*

1. *$\mathcal{H}$ samples $m_{[\eta]} \sim U_{\mathbb{F}^\eta}$.*
2. *$\mathcal{A}$ sends a leakage function $\mathcal{L} \colon \mathbb{F}^\eta \to \{0,1\}^t$.*
3. *$\mathcal{H}$ sends $\mathcal{L}(m_{[\eta]})$ to $\mathcal{A}$.*
4. *$\mathcal{H}$ samples $j \xleftarrow{\$} \mathcal{J}$. $\mathcal{H}$ samples a uniform random $(r_{-\gamma}, \ldots, r_{-1}, r_1, \ldots, r_\eta) \in C_j$. $\mathcal{H}$ computes $y_{[\eta]} = r_{[\eta]} + m_{[\eta]}$ and sends $(y_{[\eta]}, j)$ to $\mathcal{A}$.*
   $\mathcal{H}$ picks $b \xleftarrow{\$} \{0,1\}$. If $b = 0$, then $\mathcal{H}$ sends $\mathsf{chal} = r_{[-\gamma]}$ to $\mathcal{A}$; otherwise (if $b = 1$) $\mathcal{H}$ sends $\mathsf{chal} = u_{[\gamma]} \sim U_{\mathbb{F}^\gamma}$.
5. *$\mathcal{A}$ sends $\tilde{b} \in \{0,1\}$.*

The adversary $\mathcal{A}$ wins the game if $b = \tilde{b}$. For any $\mathcal{A}$, the advantage of the adversary is $\varepsilon \leq \frac{1}{2}\sqrt{\frac{|\mathbb{F}|^\gamma 2^t}{2^\delta}}$.

Proof. Let $M_{[\eta]}$ be the distribution corresponding to $m_{[\eta]}$. Consider $M'_{[\eta+\gamma]} = (0^\gamma, M_{[\eta]})$. By Imported Lemma 1, $\tilde{\mathbf{H}}_\infty(M' | \mathcal{L}(M')) \geq \eta \log |\mathbb{F}| - t$. Recall that $\mathcal{C} = \{C_j : j \in \mathcal{J}\}$ is a $2^{-\delta}$-bias family of distributions over $\mathbb{F}^{\eta+\gamma}$. Then, by Theorem 5, we have the following as desired:

$$
\mathrm{SD}\left((C_\mathcal{J} \oplus M', \mathcal{L}(M'), \mathcal{J}), (U_{\mathbb{F}^{\eta+\gamma}}, \mathcal{L}(M'), \mathcal{J})\right) \leq \frac{1}{2}\left(\frac{2^t \cdot |\mathbb{F}|^{\eta+\gamma}}{2^\delta \cdot |\mathbb{F}|^\eta}\right)^{\frac{1}{2}} = \frac{1}{2}\sqrt{\frac{|\mathbb{F}|^\gamma 2^t}{2^\delta}}.
$$

$\qquad\square$

We note that this lemma crucially relies on a family of small-bias distributions. Next, we prove the following security lemma.

Lemma 5. *The simulation error of our protocol is $\varepsilon \leq \sqrt{\frac{|\mathbb{F}|^{\gamma} 2^t}{2^{\delta}}}$, where t is the number of bits of leakage, and γ and δ are the parameters in Property 1 for the family of distributions $\mathcal{C}$.*

Proof. We first prove Bob privacy followed by Alice privacy.

Bob Privacy. In order to prove privacy of client B against a semi-honest client A, it suffices to show that the adversary cannot distinguish between Bob's secret values $(r_{-\gamma}, \ldots, r_{-1})$ and $U_{\mathbb{F}^{\gamma}}$. We show that the statistical distance of $(r_{-\gamma}, \ldots, r_{-1})$ and $U_{\mathbb{F}^{\gamma}}$ given the view of the adversary is at most ε, where ε is defined above.

We observe that client B's privacy reduces directly to our unpredictability lemma (Lemma 4) for the following variables. Let $X_{[\eta]}$ be the random variable denoting B's input in the initial correlations. Then, $X_{[\eta]}$ is uniform over $\mathbb{F}^{\eta}$. Note that the adversary gets $L = \mathcal{L}(X_{[\eta]})$ that is at most t-bits of leakage. Next, the honest client B picks $j \xleftarrow{\$} \mathcal{J}$ and a random $r = (r_{-\gamma}, \ldots, r_{-1}, r_1, \ldots, r_{\eta}) \in C_j$. Client B sends $m_{[\eta]} = r_{[\eta]} + x_{[\eta]}$. This is exactly the game between the honest challenger and an semi-honest adversary in the unpredictability lemma (see Lemma 4). Hence, the adversary cannot distinguish between $r_{[-\gamma]}$ and $U_{\mathbb{F}^{\gamma}}$ with probability more than ε.

Alice Privacy. In order to prove privacy of client A against a semi-honest client B, it suffices to show that the adversary cannot distinguish between Alice's secret values $(u_{-\gamma}, \ldots, u_{-1})$ and $U_{\mathbb{F}^{\gamma}}$. We show that the statistical distance of $(u_{-\gamma}, \ldots, u_{-1})$ and $U_{\mathbb{F}^{\gamma}}$ given the view of the adversary is at most ε, where ε is defined above by reducing to our unpredictability lemma (see Lemma 4).

Let $A_{[\eta]}$ denote the random variable corresponding to the client A's input $a_{[\eta]}$ in the initial correlations. Then, without loss of generality, the adversary receives t-bits of leakage $\mathcal{L}(A_{[\eta]})$. We show a formal reduction to Lemma 4 in Fig. 5. Given an adversary $\mathcal{A}$ who can distinguish between $(u_{-\gamma}, \ldots, u_{-1})$ and $U_{\mathbb{F}^{\gamma}}$, we construct an adversary $\mathcal{A}'$ against an honest challenger $\mathcal{H}$ of Lemma 4 with identical advantage. It is easy to see that this reduction is perfect. The only differences in the simulator from the actual protocol are as follows. In the simulation, the index j of the distribution is picked by the honest challenger $\mathcal{H}$ instead of client B. This is identical because client B is a semi-honest adversary.

Also, the simulator $\mathcal{A}'$ generates $\beta_{[\eta]}$ slightly differently. We claim that the distribution of $\beta_{[\eta]}$ in the simulation is identical to that of real protocol. This holds by correctness of the protocol: $t_{[\eta]} = u_{[\eta]} * r_{[\eta]} + v_{[\eta]} = (\alpha_{[\eta]} * r_{[\eta]}) + \beta_{[\eta]} - z_{[\eta]}$. Hence, $\beta_{[\eta]} = (u_{[\eta]} * r_{[\eta]} + v_{[\eta]}) - (\alpha_{[\eta]} * r_{[\eta]}) + z_{[\eta]} = w_{[\eta]} - (\alpha_{[\eta]} * r_{[\eta]}) + z_{[\eta]}$, where $w_{[-\gamma, \eta]}$ is chosen as a random codeword in $C_j^{(2)}$. This holds because in the real protocol $v_{[-\gamma, \eta]}$ is chosen as a random codeword in $C_j^{(2)}$ and $u_{[-\gamma, \eta]} * r_{[-\gamma, \eta]} \in C_j^{(2)}$. Here, we denote by $[-\gamma, \eta]$ the set $\{-\gamma, \ldots, -1, 1, \ldots, \eta\}$. $\qquad \square$

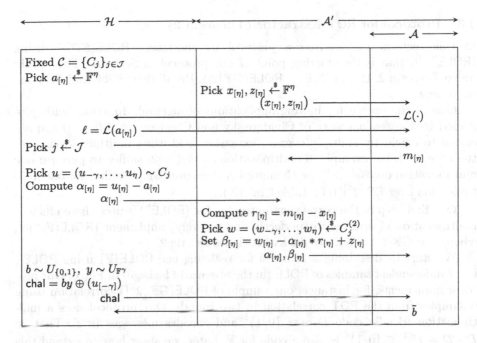

Fig. 5. Simulator for Alice Privacy.

4.2 OT Embedding

The second conceptual block is the ROT embedding protocol from [9], referred to as the BMN embedding protocol, that embeds a constant number of ROT samples into one sample of $\mathsf{ROLE}(\mathbb{F})$, where $\mathbb{F}$ is a finite field of characteristic 2. The BMN embedding protocol is a two-message perfectly semi-honest secure protocol. For example, asymptotically, [9] embeds $(s)^{1-o(1)}$ samples of ROT into one sample of the $\mathsf{ROLE}(\mathbb{GF}[2^s])$ correlation. However, for reasonable values of s, say for $s \leq 2^{50}$, a recursive embedding embeds $s^{\log 10/\log 32}$ samples of ROT into one sample of the $\mathsf{ROLE}(\mathbb{GF}[2^s])$ correlation, and this embedding is more efficient than the asymptotically good one. Below, we show that this protocol composes in parallel with our protocol in Fig. 4 to give our overall round optimal protocol for (n, m, t, ε)-correlation extractor for $\mathsf{ROLE}(\mathbb{F})$ correlation satisfying Theorem 3.

We note that the BMN embedding protocol satisfies the following additional properties. (1) The first message is sent by client B, and (2) this message depends only on the first share of client B in $\mathsf{ROLE}(\mathbb{F})$ (this refers to r_i in Fig. 4) and does not depend on the second share (this refers to t_i in Fig. 4). With these properties, the BMN embedding protocol can be run in parallel with the protocol in Fig. 4. Also, since the BMN protocol satisfies perfect correctness and perfect security, to prove overall security, it suffices to prove the correctness and security of our protocol in Fig. 4. This holds because we are in the semi-honest information theoretic setting.

4.3 Protocol for ROT Extractor (Theorem 2)

In this section, we describe a protocol to construct $(\mathsf{ROLE}(\mathbb{F})^\eta)^{[t]}$ using $(\mathsf{ROLE}^n)^{[t]}$, that is the starting point of our protocol in Sect. 4.1. This would prove Theorem 2. Here, $\mathsf{ROLE} := \mathsf{ROLE}(\mathbb{GF}[2])$. Recall that ROLE and ROT are equivalent.

One of the several fascinating applications of algebraic function fields pioneered by the seminal work of Chudnovsky and Chudnovsky [14], is the application to efficiently multiply over an extension field using multiplications over the base field. For example, 6 multiplications over $\mathbb{GF}[2]$ suffice to perform one multiplication over $\mathbb{GF}[2^3]$, or 15 multiplications over $\mathbb{GF}[2]$ suffice for one multiplication over $\mathbb{GF}[2^6]$ (cf., Table 1 in [12]).

Our first step of the correlation extractor for $(\mathsf{ROLE}^n)^{[t]}$ uses these efficient multiplication algorithms to (perfectly and securely) implement $(\mathsf{ROLE}(\mathbb{F})^\eta)^{[t]}$, where $\mathbb{F} = \mathbb{GF}(2^\alpha)$ is a finite field with characteristic 2.

We start by describing a protocol for realizing one $\mathsf{ROLE}(\mathbb{F})$ using ROLE^ℓ, i.e., ℓ independent samples of ROLE (in the absence of leakage) in Fig. 6. Our protocol implements, for instance, one sample of $\mathsf{ROLE}(\mathbb{GF}[2^3])$ correlation using 6 samples from the ROT correlation in two rounds. Our protocol uses a multiplication friendly code $\mathcal{D}$ over $\{0,1\}^\ell$ and encodes messages in $\mathbb{F}$. That is, $\mathcal{D} * \mathcal{D} = \mathcal{D}^{(2)} \subset \{0,1\}^\ell$ is also a code for $\mathbb{F}$. Later, we show how to extend this to the leakage setting.

Protocol for ROLE($\mathbb{F}$) in ROLE$^\ell$ hybrid:

Let $\mathcal{D} \subset \{0,1\}^\ell$ be a multiplication friendly code that encodes messages in $\mathbb{F} = \mathbb{GF}(2^\alpha)$. Let $(\mathsf{Enc}_{\mathcal{D}}, \mathsf{Dec}_{\mathcal{D}})$ (resp., $\mathsf{Enc}_{\mathcal{D}^{(2)}}, \mathsf{Dec}_{\mathcal{D}^{(2)}}$) be encoding and decoding procedures for $\mathcal{D}$ (resp., $\mathcal{D}^{(2)}$).

Hybrid ROLE$^\ell$: Client A and client B have access to a single call to ROLE$^\ell$ functionality. Client A will play as the sender and client B will play as the receiver.
Inputs: Client A has inputs $a_0, b_0 \in \mathbb{F}$ and client B has inputs $x_0 \in \mathbb{F}$.

1. Client A picks a random codeword $a_{[\ell]} \sim \mathsf{Enc}_{\mathcal{D}}(a_0)$ and $b_{[\ell]} \sim \mathsf{Enc}_{\mathcal{D}^{(2)}}(b_0)$ Client A sends $a_{[\ell]}, b_{[\ell]}$ as sender inputs to ROLE$^\ell$ functionality.
2. Client B picks a random codeword $x_{[\ell]} \sim \mathsf{Enc}_{\mathcal{D}}(x_0)$ and sends $x_{[\ell]}$ as receiver input to ROLE$^\ell$. Client B gets $z_{[\ell]} \in \{0,1\}^\ell$ as output. Client B runs $\mathsf{Dec}_{\mathcal{D}^{(2)}}(z_{[\ell]})$ to obtain $z_0 \in \mathbb{F}$.
3. Client A outputs a_0, b_0 and Client B outputs x_0, z_0.

Fig. 6. Perfectly secure protocol for ROLE($\mathbb{F}$) in ROLE$^\ell$ hybrid.

Security Guarantee. It is easy to see that the protocol in Fig. 6 is a perfectly secure realization of ROLE($\mathbb{F}$) in the ROLE$^\ell$-hybrid against a semi-honest adversary using the fact that $\mathcal{D}$ is a multiplication friendly code for $\mathbb{F}$. Moreover, [26] proved the following useful lemma to argue t-leaky realization of ROLE($\mathbb{F}$) if the perfect oracle call to ROLE$^\ell$ is replaced by a t-leaky oracle.

Imported Lemma 3 ([26]). *Let π be a perfectly secure (resp., statistically ε secure) realization of f in the g-hybrid model, where π makes a single call to g. Then, π is also a perfectly secure (resp., statistically ε secure) realization of $f^{[t]}$ in the $g^{[t]}$-hybrid model.*

Using the above lemma, we get that the protocol in Fig. 6 is a perfect realization of $(\mathsf{ROLE}(\mathbb{F}))^{[t]}$ in $(\mathsf{ROLE}^{\ell})^{[t]}$-hybrid. Finally, by running the protocol of Fig. 6 in parallel for η samples of $\mathsf{ROLE}(\mathbb{F})$ and using Imported Lemma 3, we get a perfectly secure protocol for $(\mathsf{ROLE}(\mathbb{F})^{\eta})^{[t]}$ in $(\mathsf{ROLE}^{\eta\ell})^{[t]}$-hybrid.

Round Optimality. To realize the round-optimality in Theorem 2, we can run the protocols in Figs. 6 and 4 in parallel. We note that the first messages of protocols in Figs. 6 and 4 can be sent together. This is because the first message of client B in protocol of Fig. 4 is independent of the second message in Fig. 6. The security holds because we are in the semi-honest information theoretic setting. Hence, overall round complexity is still 2.

5   Parameter Comparison

5.1   Correlation Extractor from $\mathsf{ROLE}(\mathbb{F})$ (Theorem 3)

In this section, we compare our correlation extractor for $\mathsf{ROLE}(\mathbb{F})$ correlation, where $\mathbb{F}$ is a constant size field, with the BMN correlation extractor [9].

BMN Correlation Extractor [9]. The BMN correlation extractor emphasizes high resilience while achieving multiple ROTs as output. Roughly, they show the following. If parties start with the $\mathsf{IP}\big(\mathsf{GF}\big[2^{\Delta n}\big]^{1/\Delta}\big)$ correlation, then they (roughly) achieve $\frac{1}{2} - \Delta$ fractional resilience with production that depends on (Δn). Here, Δ has to be the inverse of an even natural number $\geqslant 4$.

In particular, the $\mathsf{IP}\big(\mathsf{GF}\big[2^{n/4}\big]^{4}\big)$ correlation[12] achieves the highest production using the BMN correlation extractor. The resilience of this correlation is $(\frac{1}{4} - g)$, where $g \in (0, 1/4]$ is a positive constant. Then the BMN correlation extractor produces at most $(n/4)^{\log 10/\log 38} \approx (n/4)^{0.633}$ fresh samples from the ROT correlation as output when $n \leq 2^{50}$. This implies that the production is $m \approx 2 \cdot (n/4)^{0.633}$, because each ROT sample produces private shares that are two-bits long. For $n = 10^3$, the production is $m \leqslant 66$, for $n = 10^6$ the production is $m \leqslant 5,223$, and for $n = 10^9$ the production is $m \leqslant 413,913$. We emphasize that the BMN extractor *cannot* increase its production any further by sacrificing its leakage resilience and going below $1/4$.

Our Correlation Extractor for $\mathsf{ROLE}(\mathbb{F})$. We shall use $\mathbb{F}$ such that $q = |\mathbb{F}|$ is an even power of 2. For the suitable Algebraic Geometry codes [19] to exist, we need $q \geqslant 49$. Since, the last step of our construction uses the OT embedding

---

[12] Recall that the inner-product correlation $\mathsf{IP}\big(\mathbb{K}^{s}\big)$ over finite field $\mathbb{K}$ samples random $r_A = (u_1, \ldots, u_s) \in \mathbb{K}^s$ and $r_B = (v_1, \ldots, v_s) \in \mathbb{K}^s$ such that $u_1 v_1 + \cdots + u_s v_s = 0$.

Field $\mathbb{F}$	# of OTs Embedded Per ROLE$(\mathbb{F})$ [9]	Production $(\alpha = m/n)$
$\mathbb{GF}\left[2^6\right]$	2	4.83%
$\mathbb{GF}\left[2^8\right]$	3	11.39%
$\mathbb{GF}\left[2^{10}\right]$	4	15.59%
$\mathbb{GF}\left[2^{14}\right]$	5	16.32%
$\mathbb{GF}\left[2^{20}\right]$	6	14.31%

Fig. 7. The production rate of our correlation extractor for ROLE$(\mathbb{F})$, where $\beta = t/n = 1\%$ rate of leakage using different finite fields.

Field $\mathbb{F} = \mathbb{GF}\left[2^s\right]$	Bilinear Comp. Mult. $\mu_2(s)$ [12]	$n' = \frac{s}{\mu_2(s)}n$	$\beta' = \frac{\mu_2(s)}{s}\beta$	OT Embed. [9]	α'	$\alpha = \frac{s}{\mu_2(s)}\alpha'$
$\mathbb{GF}\left[2^6\right]$	15	$\frac{6}{15}n$	2.50%	2	4.05%	1.62%
$\mathbb{GF}\left[2^8\right]$	24	$\frac{8}{24}n$	3.00%	3	10.07%	3.35%
$\mathbb{GF}\left[2^{10}\right]$	33	$\frac{10}{33}n$	3.30%	4	13.86%	4.20%
$\mathbb{GF}\left[2^{14}\right]$	51	$\frac{14}{51}n$	3.64%	5	14.46%	3.97%
$\mathbb{GF}\left[2^{20}\right]$	81	$\frac{20}{81}n$	4.05%	6	12.48%	3.08%

Fig. 8. The production rate of our correlation extractor for ROT. We are given n-bit shares of the $\mathrm{ROT}^{n/2}$ correlation, and fix $\beta = t/n = 1\%$ fractional leakage. Each row corresponds to using our ROLE$(\mathbb{F})$-to-ROT correlation extractor as an intermediate step. The final column represents the production rate $\alpha = m/n$ of our ROT-to-ROT correlation extractor corresponding to the choice of the finite field $\mathbb{F}$.

technique introduced by BMN [9], we need to consider only the smallest fields that allow a particular number of OT embeddings. Based on this observation, for fractional resilience $\beta = (t/n) = 1\%$, Fig. 7 presents the achievable production rate $\alpha = (m/n)$. Note that the Algebraic Geometry codes become better with increasing q, but the BMN OT embedding becomes worse. So, the optimum $\alpha = 16.32\%$ is achieved for $\mathbb{F} = \mathbb{GF}\left[2^{14}\right]$. For $n = 10^3$, for example, the production is $m = 163$, for $n = 10^6$ the production is $m = 163,200$, and for $n = 10^9$ the production is $m = 163,200,000$. In Fig. 9 (Sect. 6), we demonstrate the trade-off between leakage rate (Y-axis) with production rate (X-axis). We note that even in the high leakage setting, for instance, for $\beta = 20\%$, we have $\alpha \approx 3\%$. Hence, the production is $m \approx 30$, for $n = 10^6$ the production is $m \approx 30,000$, and for $n = 10^9$ the production is $m \approx 30,000,000$. Our production is overwhelmingly higher than the BMN production rate.

5.2   Correlation Extractor for ROT (Theorem 2)

In this section we compare our construction with the GIMS [22] correlation extractor from ROT. The IKOS [26] correlation extractor is a feasibility result with minuscule fractional resilience and production rate.

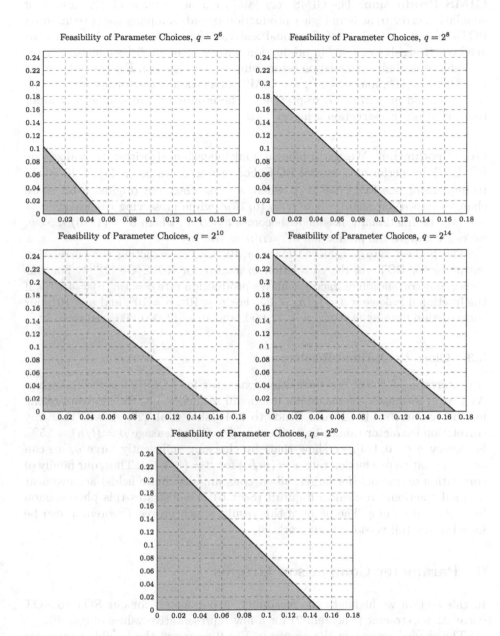

Fig. 9. A comparison of the feasibility regions for our correlation extractors for ROLE($\mathbb{F}$) for various finite fields $\mathbb{F}$ of characteristic 2. For each plot, the X-axis represents the relative production rate $\alpha = m/n$ and the Y-axis represents the fractional leakage resilience $\beta = t/n$.

GIMS Production. The GIMS correlation extractor for ROT [22] trades-off simulation error to achieve higher production by sub-sampling the precomputed ROTs. For $\beta = (t/n) = 1\%$ fractional leakage, the GIMS correlation extractor achieves (roughly) $m = n/4p$ production with $\varepsilon = m \cdot 2^{-p/4}$ simulation error. To achieve negligible simulation error, suppose $p = \log^2(n)$. For this setting, at $n = 10^3$, $n = 10^6$, and $n = 10^9$, the GIMS correlation extractor obtains $m = 3$, $m = 625$, and $m = 277,777$, respectively. These numbers are significantly lower than what our construction achieves.

Our Production. We use a bilinear multiplication algorithm to realize one ROLE$(\mathbb{F})$ by performing several ROT. For example, we use $\mu_2(s) = 15$ ROTs to implement one ROLE$(\mathbb{GF}[2^s])$, where $s = 6$. Thus, our original n-bit share changes into n'-bit share, where $n' = (6/15)n$ while preserving the leakage $t = \beta n$. So, the fractional leakage now becomes $t = \beta' n'$, where $\beta' = (15/6)\beta$. Now, we can compute the production $m' = \alpha' n' = \alpha n$.

The highest rate is achieved for $s = 10$, i.e., constructing the correlation extractor for ROT via the correlation extractor for ROLE$(\mathbb{GF}[2^{10}])$. For this choice, our correlation extractor achieves production rate $\alpha = (m/n) = 4.20\%$, if the fractional leakage is $\beta = (t/n) = 1\%$. For $n = 10^3$, $n = 10^6$, and $n = 10^9$, our construction obtains $m = 42$, $m = 42,000$, and $m = 42,000,000$, respectively.

5.3   Close to Optimal Resilience

An interesting facet of our correlation extractor for ROLE$(\mathbb{F})$ is the following. As $q = |\mathbb{F}|$ increases, the maximum fractional resilience, i.e., the intercept of the feasibility curve on the Y-axis, tends to $1/4$. Ishai et al. [27] showed that any correlation extractor cannot be resilient to fractional leakage $\beta = (t/n) = 25\%$. For every $g \in (0, 1/4]$, we show that, by choosing sufficiently large q, we can achieve positive production rate $\alpha = (m/n)$ for $\beta = (1/4 - g)$. Thus, our family of correlation extractors (for larger, albeit constant-size, finite fields) achieve near optimal fractional resilience. Figure 9 (Sect. 6) demonstrates this phenomenon for a few values of q. The proof of this result, which proves Theorem 4, can be found in the full version of our work [8].

6   Parameter Comparison Graphs

In this section we highlight the feasibility of parameters for our ROT to ROT correlation extractor (Theorem 2) for a few representative values of $q = |\mathbb{F}|$.

The shaded regions in the graphs in Fig. 9 represent the feasible parameter choices. In particular, the X-axis represents the production rate m/n and the Y-axis represents the leakage rate t/n given our parameter choices. The full version of the paper [8] details the calculation of the feasible parameters.

Note that, as the size of the field $\mathbb{F}$ increases, the quality of the algebraic geometric code used in our construction increases. This observation translates into higher possible production values and leakage resilience, which is illustrated by increasing $q = 2^6$ to $q = 2^{14}$. However, as the size of the field $\mathbb{F}$ increases, the efficiency of the BMN embedding [9] reduces, potentially reducing the overall production rate (for example, increasing $q = 2^{14}$ to $q = 2^{20}$).

Finally, as noted earlier, the feasibility graphs demonstrate that our family of correlation extractors achieve near optimal fractional resilience. That is, as the size of the field $\mathbb{F}$ increases, the fractional leakage resilience approaches $1/4$, which is optimal [27].

References

1. Alon, N., Goldreich, O., Håstad, J., Peralta, R.: Simple constructions of almost k-wise independent random variables. In: 31st FOCS, pp. 544–553. IEEE Computer Society Press, October 1990
2. Alon, N., Roichman, Y.: Random cayley graphs and expanders. Random Struct. Algorithms 5(2), 271–284 (1994)
3. Applebaum, B.: Garbled circuits as randomized encodings of functions: a primer. Cryptology ePrint Archive, Report 2017/385 (2017). http://eprint.iacr.org/2017/385
4. Applebaum, B., Damgård, I., Ishai, Y., Nielsen, M., Zichron, L.: Secure arithmetic computation with constant computational overhead. In: Katz, J., Shacham, H. (eds.) CRYPTO 2017. LNCS, vol. 10401, pp. 223–254. Springer, Cham (2017). https://doi.org/10.1007/978-3-319-63688-7_8
5. Applebaum, B., Ishai, Y., Kushilevitz, E.: Cryptography in NC⁰. In: 45th FOCS, pp. 166–175. IEEE Computer Society Press, October 2004
6. Beaver, D.: Efficient multiparty protocols using circuit randomization. In: Felgenbaum, J. (ed.) CRYPTO 1991. LNCS, vol. 576, pp. 420–432. Springer, Heidelberg (1992). https://doi.org/10.1007/3-540-46766-1_34
7. Ben-David, A., Nisan, N., Pinkas, B.: FairplayMP: a system for secure multi-party computation. In: Ning, P., Syverson, P.F., Jha, S. (eds.) ACM CCS 2008, pp. 257–266. ACM Press, October 2008
8. Block, A.R., Gupta, D., Maji, H.K., Nguyen, H.H.: Secure computation using leaky correlations (asymptotically optimal constructions). Cryptology ePrint Archive, Report 2018/372 (2018). https://eprint.iacr.org/2018/372
9. Block, A.R., Maji, H.K., Nguyen, H.H.: Secure computation based on leaky correlations: high resilience setting. In: Katz, J., Shacham, H. (eds.) CRYPTO 2017. LNCS, vol. 10402, pp. 3–32. Springer, Cham (2017). https://doi.org/10.1007/978-3-319-63715-0_1
10. Canetti, R.: Security and composition of multiparty cryptographic protocols. J. Cryptology 13(1), 143–202 (2000)
11. Cascudo, I., Damgård, I., Farràs, O., Ranellucci, S.: Resource-efficient OT combiners with active security. In: Kalai, Y., Reyzin, L. (eds.) TCC 2017. LNCS, vol. 10678, pp. 461–486. Springer, Cham (2017). https://doi.org/10.1007/978-3-319-70503-3_15
12. Cenk, M., Özbudak, F.: On multiplication in finite fields. J. Complex. 26(2), 172–186 (2010)
13. Chen, H., Cramer, R.: Algebraic geometric secret sharing schemes and secure multi-party computations over small fields. In: Dwork, C. (ed.) CRYPTO 2006. LNCS, vol. 4117, pp. 521–536. Springer, Heidelberg (2006). https://doi.org/10.1007/11818175_31

14. Chudnovsky, D.V., Chudnovsky, G.V.: Algebraic complexities and algebraic curves over finite fields. Proc. Natl. Acad. Sci. **84**(7), 1739–1743 (1987)
15. Damgård, I., Pastro, V., Smart, N., Zakarias, S.: Multiparty computation from somewhat homomorphic encryption. In: Safavi-Naini, R., Canetti, R. (eds.) CRYPTO 2012. LNCS, vol. 7417, pp. 643–662. Springer, Heidelberg (2012). https://doi.org/10.1007/978-3-642-32009-5_38
16. Dodis, Y., Ostrovsky, R., Reyzin, L., Smith, A.: Fuzzy extractors: How to generate strong keys from biometrics and other noisy data. SIAM J. Comput. **38**(1), 97–139 (2008). http://dx.doi.org/10.1137/060651380
17. Dodis, Y., Smith, A.: Correcting errors without leaking partial information. In: Gabow, H.N., Fagin, R. (eds.) 37th ACM STOC, pp. 654–663. ACM Press, May 2005
18. Döttling, N., Ghosh, S., Nielsen, J.B., Nilges, T., Trifiletti, R.: TinyOLE: Efficient actively secure two-party computation from oblivious linear function evaluation. In: Thuraisingham, B.M., Evans, D., Malkin, T., Xu, D. (eds.) ACM CCS 17, pp. 2263–2276. ACM Press, October/November 2017
19. Garcia, A., Stichtenoth, H.: On the asymptotic behaviour of some towers of function fields over finite fields. J. Number Theory **61**(2), 248–273 (1996)
20. Goldreich, O., Wigderson, A.: Tiny families of functions with random properties: a quality-size trade-off for hashing. Random Struct. Algorithms **11**(4), 315–343 (1997). https://doi.org/10.1002/(SICI)1098-2418(199712)11:4(315::AID-RSA3)3.0.CO;2-1
21. Goppa, V.D.: Codes on algebraic curves. In: Soviet Math. Dokl., pp. 170–172 (1981)
22. Gupta, D., Ishai, Y., Maji, H.K., Sahai, A.: Secure computation from leaky correlated randomness. In: Gennaro, R., Robshaw, M. (eds.) CRYPTO 2015. LNCS, vol. 9216, pp. 701–720. Springer, Heidelberg (2015). https://doi.org/10.1007/978-3-662-48000-7_34
23. Harnik, D., Ishai, Y., Kushilevitz, E., Nielsen, J.B.: OT-combiners via secure computation. In: Canetti, R. (ed.) TCC 2008. LNCS, vol. 4948, pp. 393–411. Springer, Heidelberg (2008). https://doi.org/10.1007/978-3-540-78524-8_22
24. Harnik, D., Kilian, J., Naor, M., Reingold, O., Rosen, A.: On robust combiners for oblivious transfer and other primitives. In: Cramer, R. (ed.) EUROCRYPT 2005. LNCS, vol. 3494, pp. 96–113. Springer, Heidelberg (2005). https://doi.org/10.1007/11426639_6
25. Ishai, Y., Kushilevitz, E.: Perfect constant-round secure computation via perfect randomizing polynomials. In: Widmayer, P., Ruiz, F.T., Bueno, R.M., Hennessy, M., Eidenbenz, S., Conejo, R. (eds.) ICALP 2002. LNCS, vol. 2380, pp. 244–256. Springer, Heidelberg (2002). https://doi.org/10.1007/3-540-45465-9_22
26. Ishai, Y., Kushilevitz, E., Ostrovsky, R., Sahai, A.: Extracting correlations. In: 50th FOCS, pp. 261–270. IEEE Computer Society Press, October 2009
27. Ishai, Y., Maji, H.K., Sahai, A., Wullschleger, J.: Single-use OT combiners with near-optimal resilience. In: 2014 IEEE International Symposium on Information Theory, Honolulu, HI, USA, 29 June–4 July 2014, pp. 1544–1548 (2014)
28. Ishai, Y., Prabhakaran, M., Sahai, A.: Founding cryptography on oblivious transfer – efficiently. In: Wagner, D. (ed.) CRYPTO 2008. LNCS, vol. 5157, pp. 572–591. Springer, Heidelberg (2008). https://doi.org/10.1007/978-3-540-85174-5_32
29. Keller, M., Orsini, E., Scholl, P.: MASCOT: Faster malicious arithmetic secure computation with oblivious transfer. In: Weippl, E.R., Katzenbeisser, S., Kruegel, C., Myers, A.C., Halevi, S. (eds.) ACM CCS 2016, pp. 830–842. ACM Press, October 2016

30. Kilian, J.: A general completeness theorem for two-party games. In: 23rd ACM STOC, pp. 553–560. ACM Press, May 1991

31. Malkhi, D., Nisan, N., Pinkas, B., Sella, Y.: Fairplay - secure two-party computation system. In: Proceedings of the 13th USENIX Security Symposium, 9–13 August 2004, San Diego, pp. 287–302 (2004)

32. Massey, J.L.: Some applications of coding theory in cryptography. In: Codes and Ciphers: Cryptography and Coding IV, pp. 33–47 (1995)

33. Meier, R., Przydatek, B.: On robust combiners for private information retrieval and other primitives. In: Dwork, C. (ed.) CRYPTO 2006. LNCS, vol. 4117, pp. 555–569. Springer, Heidelberg (2006). https://doi.org/10.1007/11818175_33

34. Meier, R., Przydatek, B., Wullschleger, J.: Robuster combiners for oblivious transfer. In: Vadhan, S.P. (ed.) TCC 2007. LNCS, vol. 4392, pp. 404–418. Springer, Heidelberg (2007). https://doi.org/10.1007/978-3-540-70936-7_22

35. Naor, J., Naor, M.: Small-bias probability spaces: Efficient constructions and applications. In: 22nd ACM STOC, pp. 213–223. ACM Press, May 1990

36. Naor, M., Pinkas, B.: Computationally secure oblivious transfer. J. Cryptology 18(1), 1–35 (2005)

37. Nielsen, J.B., Nordholt, P.S., Orlandi, C., Burra, S.S.: A new approach to practical active-secure two-party computation. In: Safavi-Naini, R., Canetti, R. (eds.) CRYPTO 2012. LNCS, vol. 7417, pp. 681–700. Springer, Heidelberg (2012). https://doi.org/10.1007/978-3-642-32009-5_40

38. Pless, V.: Introduction to the Theory of Error-Correcting Codes, vol. 48. Wiley (2011)

39. Przydatek, B., Wullschleger, J.: Error-tolerant combiners for oblivious primitives. In: Aceto, L., Damgård, I., Goldberg, L.A., Halldórsson, M.M., Ingólfsdóttir, A., Walukiewicz, I. (eds.) ICALP 2008. LNCS, vol. 5126, pp. 461–472. Springer, Heidelberg (2008). https://doi.org/10.1007/978-3-540-70583-3_38

40. Rao, A.: An exposition of bourgain's 2-source extractor. ECCCTR: Electronic Colloquium on Computational Complexity Technical reports (2007)

41. Vladut, S., Nogin, D., Tsfasman, M.: Algebraic Geometric Codes: Basic Notions. American Mathematical Society, Boston (2007)

42. Wolf, S., Wullschleger, J.: Oblivious transfer is symmetric. In: Vaudenay, S. (ed.) EUROCRYPT 2006. LNCS, vol. 4004, pp. 222–232. Springer, Heidelberg (2006). https://doi.org/10.1007/11761679_14

Fine-Grained Secure Computation

Matteo Campanelli[✉] and Rosario Gennaro

The City College of New York, New York, USA
matteo.campanelli@gmail.com, rosario@ccny.cuny.edu

Abstract. This paper initiates a study of *Fine Grained Secure Computation*: i.e. the construction of *secure computation primitives* against "moderately complex" adversaries. We present definitions and constructions for *compact* Fully Homomorphic Encryption and Verifiable Computation secure against (*non-uniform*) NC^1 adversaries. Our results do not require the existence of one-way functions and hold under a widely believed separation assumption, namely $NC^1 \subsetneq \oplus L/poly$. We also present two application scenarios for our model: *(i)* hardware chips that prove their own correctness, and *(ii)* protocols against rational adversaries potentially relevant to the *Verifier's Dilemma* in smart-contracts transactions such as Ethereum.

1 Introduction

Historically, Cryptography has been used to protect information (either in transit or stored) from unauthorized access. One of the most important developments in Cryptography in the last thirty years, has been the ability to protect not only information but also the *computations* that are performed on data that needs to be secure. Starting with the work on secure multiparty computation [Yao82], and continuing with ZK proofs [GMR89], and more recently Fully Homomorphic Encryption [Gen09], verifiable outsourcing computation [GKR08, GGP10], SNARKs [GGPR13, BCI+13] and obfuscation [GGH+16] we now have cryptographic tools that protect the secrecy and integrity not only of data, but also of the programs which run on that data.

Another crucial development in Modern Cryptography has been the adoption of a more "fine-grained" notion of computational hardness and security. The traditional cryptographic approach modeled computational tasks as "easy" (for the honest parties to perform) and "hard" (infeasible for the adversary). Yet we have also seen a notion of *moderately hard* problems being used to attain certain security properties. The best example of this approach might be the use of moderately hard inversion problems used in blockchain protocols such as Bitcoin. Although present in many works since the inception of Modern Cryptography, this approach was first formalized in a work of Dwork and Naor [DN92].

In the second part of this work we consider the following model (which can be traced back to the seminal paper by Merkle [Mer78] on public key cryptography).

A. Beimel and S. Dziembowski (Eds.): TCC 2018, LNCS 11240, pp. 66–97, 2018.
https://doi.org/10.1007/978-3-030-03810-6_3

Honest parties will run a protocol which will cost[1] them C while an adversary who wants to compromise the security of the protocol will incur a $C' = \omega(C)$ cost. Note that while C' is asymptotically larger than C, it might still be a feasible cost to incur – the only guarantee is that it is substantially larger than the work of the honest parties. For example in Merkle's original proposal for public-key cryptography the honest parties can exchange a key in time T but the adversary can only learn the key in time T^2. Other examples include primitives introduced by Cachin and Maurer [CM97] and Hastad [Has87] where the cost is the space and parallel time complexity of the parties, respectively.

Recently there has been renewed interest in this model. Degwekar et al. [DVV16] show how to construct certain cryptographic primitives in NC^1 [resp. AC^0] which are secure against all adversaries in NC^1 [resp. AC^0]. In conceptually related work Ball et al. [BRSV17] present computational problems which are "moderately hard" on average, if they are moderately hard in the worst case, a useful property for such problems to be used as cryptographic primitives.

The goal of this paper is to initiate a study of *Fine Grained Secure Computation*. By doing so we connect these two major developments in Modern Cryptography. The question we ask is if it is possible to construct *secure computation primitives* that are secure against "moderately complex" adversaries. We answer this question in the affirmative, by presenting definitions and constructions for the task of Fully Homomorphic Encryption and Verifiable Computation in the fine-grained model. In our constructions, our goal is to optimize at the same time (for the extent to which it is possible) in terms of depth, size, round and communication complexity. Our constructions rely on a widely believed complexity separation[2]. We also present two application scenarios for our model: (i) hardware chips that prove their own correctness and (ii) protocols against rational adversaries including potential solutions to the *Verifier's Dilemma* in smart-contracts transactions such as Ethereum.

1.1 Our Results

Our starting point is the work in [DVV16] and specifically their public-key encryption scheme secure against NC^1 circuits. Recall that $AC^0[2]$ is the class of Boolean circuits with constant depth, unbounded fan-in, augmented with parity gates. If the number of AND (and OR) gates of non constant fan-in is constant we say that the circuit belongs to the class $AC^0_Q[2] \subset AC^0[2]$.

Our results can be summarized as follows:

- We first show that the techniques in [DVV16] can be used to build a somewhat homomorphic encryption (SHE) scheme. We note that because honest parties are limited to NC^1 computations, the best we can hope is to have a scheme that is homomorphic for computations in NC^1. However our scheme can only support computations that can be expressed in $AC^0_Q[2]$.

---

[1] We intentionally refer to it as "cost" to keep the notion generic. For concreteness one can think of C as the running time required to run the protocol.

[2] A separation implied by $L \neq NC^1$. See Sect. 1.1 for more details.

– We then use our SHE scheme, in conjunction with protocols described in [GGP10, CKV10, AIK10], to construct verifiable computation protocols for functions in $\mathsf{AC}^0_Q[2]$, secure and input/output private against any adversary in NC^1.

Our somewhat homomorphic encryption also allows us to obtain the following protocols secure against NC^1 adversaries: *(i)* constant-round 2PC, secure in the presence of semi-honest static adversaries for functions in $\mathsf{AC}^0_Q[2]$; *(ii)* *Private Function Evaluation* in a two party setting for circuits of constant *multiplicative* depth without relying on universal circuits. These results stem from well-known folklore transformations and we do not prove them formally.

The class $\mathsf{AC}^0_Q[2]$ includes many natural and interesting problems such as: fixed precision arithmetic, evaluation of formulas in 3CNF (or kCNF for any constant k), a representative subset of SQL queries, and S-Boxes [BP11] for symmetric key encryption.

Our results (like [DVV16]) hold under the assumption that $\mathsf{NC}^1 \subsetneq \oplus\mathsf{L}/\mathsf{poly}$, a widely believed worst-case assumption on separation of complexity classes. Notice that this assumption does not imply the existence of one-way functions (or even $\mathsf{P} \neq \mathsf{NP}$). Thus, our work shows that it is possible to obtain "advanced" cryptographic schemes, such as somewhat homomorphic encryption and verifiable computation, even if we do not live in Minicrypt[34].

COMPARISON WITH OTHER APPROACHES. One important question is: on what features are our schemes better than "generic" cryptographic schemes that after all are secure against *any* polynomial time adversary.

One such feature is the type of assumption one must make to prove security. As we said above, our schemes rely on a very mild worst-case complexity assumption, while cryptographic SHE and VC schemes rely on very specific assumptions, which are much stronger the above.

For the case of Verifiable Computation, we also have information-theoretic protocols which are secure against *any* (possibly computationally unbounded) adversary. For example the "Muggles" protocol in [GKR08] which can compute any (log-space uniform) NC function, and is also reasonably efficient in practice [CMT12]. Or, the more recent work [GR18], which obtains efficient VC for functions in a subset of $\mathsf{NC} \cap \mathsf{SC}$. Compared to these results, one aspect in which our protocol fares better is that our Prover/Verifier can be implemented with a constant-depth circuit (in particular in $\mathsf{AC}^0[2]$, see Sect. 4) which is not possible for the Prover/Verifier in [GKR08, GR18], which needs[5] to be in TC^0. Moreover our protocol is non-interactive (while [GKR08, GR18] requires $\Omega(1)$ rounds of interaction) and because our protocols work in the "pre-processing model"

---

[3] This is a reference to Impagliazzo's "five possible worlds" [Imp95].

[4] Naturally the security guarantees of these schemes are more limited compared to their standard definitions.

[5] The techniques in [GKR08, GR18] are based on properties of finite fields. Arithmetic in such fields can be carried out by circuits of constant depth with threshold gates (TC^0), but not in $\mathsf{AC}^0[2]$.

we do not require any uniformity or regularity condition on the circuit being outsourced (which are required by [GKR08, CMT12]). Finally, out verification scheme achieves input and output privacy.

Another approach to obtain information-theoretic security for Verifiable Computation is to use the framework of randomized encodings (RE) [IK00a, AIK04] (e.g. [GGH+07] which uses related techniques). In this work we build scheme with additional requirements: *compact* homomorphic encryption[6] and *overall efficient* verification for verifiable computation[7]. We do not see how to achieve these additional requirements via current RE-based approaches. We further discuss these and other limitations of directly using RE in Appendix D.

1.2   Overview of Our Techniques

HOMOMORPHIC ENCRYPTION. In [DVV16] the authors already point out that their scheme is linearly homomorphic. We make use of the *re-linearization* technique from [BV14] to construct a leveled homomorphic encryption.

Our scheme (as the one in [DVV16]) is secure against adversaries in the class of *(non-uniform)* NC^1. This implies that we can only evaluate functions in NC^1 otherwise the evaluator would be able to break the semantic security of the scheme. However we have to ensure that the *whole* homomorphic evaluation stays in NC^1. The problem is that homomorphically evaluating a function f might increase the depth of the computation.

In terms of circuit depth, the main overhead will be (as usual) the computation of multiplication gates. As we show in Sect. 3 a single homomorphic multiplication can be performed by a depth two $AC^0[2]$ circuit, but this requires depth $O(\log(n))$ with a circuit of fan-in two. Therefore, a circuit for f with $\omega(1)$ multiplicative depth would require an evaluation of $\omega(\log(n))$ depth, which would be out of NC^1. Therefore our first scheme can only evaluate functions with constant multiplicative depth, as in that case the evaluation stays in $AC^0[2]$.

We then present a second scheme that extends the class of computable functions to $AC^0_Q[2]$ by allowing for a negligible error in the correctness of the scheme. We use techniques from a work by Razborov [Raz87] on approximating $AC^0[2]$ circuits with low-degree polynomials – the correctness of the approximation (appropriately amplified) will be the correctness of our scheme.

REUSABLE VERIFIABLE COMPUTATION. The core of our approach is the construction in [CKV10], to derive Verifiable Computation from Homomorphic Encryption. The details of this approach follow. Recall that we are working in a model with an expensive preprocessing phase (executed by the Client only once and before providing any inputs to the Server) and an inexpensive online phase. The online phase is in turn composed by two algorithms, an algorithm

---

[6] Where the ciphertexts do not grow in size with each homomorphic operation.

[7] Where not only the circuit depth is constant but also the size of the circuit is quasilinear – the size of the verification circuit should be $O(\text{poly}(\lambda)(n + m))$ where n and m are the size of the input and output respectively.

to encode the input for the Server and one to check its response. In the preprocessing phase in [CKV10], the Client selects a random input r, encrypts it as $c_r = E(r)$ and homomorphically compute $c_{f(r)}$ an encryption of $f(r)$. During the online phase, the Client, on input x, computes $c_x = E(x)$ and submits the ciphertexts c_x, c_r in random order to the Server, who homomorphically computes $c_{f(r)} = E(f(r))$ and $c_{f(x)} = E(f(x))$ and returns them to the Client. The Client, given the message c_0, c_1 from the Server, checks that $c_b = c_{f(r)}$ (for the appropriate bit b) and if so accepts $y = D(c_{f(x)})$ as $y = f(x)$. The semantic security of E guarantees that this protocol has soundness error $1/2$. This error can be reduce by "scaling" this approach replacing the two ciphertexts c_x and c_r with $2t$ ciphertexts (t distinct encryptions of x and t encryptions of random values $r_1, \ldots, r_t$) sent to the prover after being shuffled through a random permutation. The scheme as described is however one-time secure, since a malicious server can figure out which one is the test ciphertext $c_{f(r)}$ if it is used again. To make this scheme "many-times secure", [CKV10] uses the paradigm introduced in [GGP10] of running the one-time scheme "under the hood" of a different homomorphic encryption key each time.

When applying these techniques in our fine-grained context the main technical challenge is to guarantee that they would also work within NC^1. In particular, we needed to ensure that: *(i)* the constructions can be computed in low-depth; *(ii)* the reductions in the security proofs can be carried out in low-depth. We rely on results from [MV91] to make sure a random permutation can be sampled by an appropriately low-depth scheme[8] Moreover, we cannot simply make black-box use of the one-time construction in [CKV10]. In fact, their construction works only for homomorphic encryption schemes with deterministic evaluation, whereas the more expressive of our constructions (Sect. 3.3) is randomized[9].

1.3 Application Scenarios

The applications described in this section refer to the problem of Verifying Computation, where a Client outsources an algorithm f and an input x to a Server, who returns a value y and a proof that $y = f(x)$. The security property is that it should be infeasible to convince the verifier to accept $y' \neq f(x)$, and the crucial efficiency property is that verifying the proof should cost less than computing f (since avoiding that cost was the reason the Client hired the Server to compute f).

HARDWARE CHIPS THAT PROVE THEIR OWN CORRECTNESS Verifiable Computation (VC) can be used to verify the execution of hardware chips designed by untrusted manufacturers. One could envision chips that provide (efficient) *proofs of their correctness* for every input-output computation they perform. These proofs must be *efficiently verified* in less time and energy than it takes to re-execute the computation itself.

---

[8] More precisely, that a permutation statistically indistinguishable from a random one can be sampled in AC^0.

[9] See also Remark C.1.

When working in hardware, however, one may not need the full power of cryptographic protection against *any* malicious attacks since one could bound the computational power of the malicious chip. The bound could be obtained by making (reasonable and evidence-based) assumptions on how much computational power can fit in a given chip area. For example one could safely assume that a malicious chip can perform at most a constant factor more work than the original function because of the basic physics of the size and power constraints. In other words, if C is the cost of the honest Server in a VC protocol, then in this model the adversary is limited to $O(C)$-cost computations, and therefore a protocol that guarantees that successful cheating strategies require $\omega(C)$ cost, will suffice. This is exactly the model in our paper. Our results will apply to the case in which we define the cost as the depth (i.e. the parallel time complexity) of the computation implemented in the chip.

RATIONAL PROOFS. The problem above is related to the notion of composable Rational Proofs defined in [CG15]. In a Rational Proof (introduced by Azar and Micali [AM12, AM13]), given a function f and an input x, the Server returns the value $y = f(x)$, and (possibly) some auxiliary information, to the Client. The Client in turn pays the Server for its work with a reward based on the transcript exchanged with the server and some randomness chosen by the client. The crucial property is that this reward is maximized in expectation when the server returns the correct value y. Clearly a *rational* prover who is only interested in maximizing his reward, will always answer correctly.

The authors of [CG15] show however that the definition of Rational Proofs in [AM12, AM13] does not satisfy a basic compositional property needed for the case in which many computations are outsourced to many servers who compete with each other for rewards (e.g. the case of volunteer computations [ACK+02]). A "rational proof" for the single-proof setting may no longer be rational when a large number of "computation problems" are outsourced. If one can produce T "random guesses" to problems in the time it takes to solve 1 problem correctly, it may be preferable to guess! That's because even if each individual reward for an incorrect answer is lower than the reward for a correct answer, the total reward of T incorrect answers might be higher (and this is indeed the case for some of the protocols presented in [AM12, AM13]).

The question (only partially answered in [CG15, CG17] for a limited class of computations) is to design protocols where the reward is strictly connected, not just to the correctness of the result, but to the amount of work done by the prover. Consider for example a protocol where the prover collects the reward only if he produces a proof of correctness of the result. Assume that the cost to produce a valid proof for an incorrect result, is higher than just computing the correct result and the correct proof. Then obviously a rational prover will always answer correctly, because the above strategy of fast incorrect answers will not work anymore. While the application is different, the goal is the same as in the previous verifiable hardware scenario.

THE VERIFIER'S DILEMMA. In blockchain systems such as Ethereum, transactions can be expressed by arbitrary programs. To add a transaction to a block miners have to verify its validity, which could be too costly if the program is too complex. This creates the so-called *Verifier's Dilemma* [LTKS15]: given a costly valid transaction Tr a miner who spends time verifying it is at a disadvantage over a miner who does not verify it and accept it "uncritically" since the latter will produce a valid block faster and claim the reward. On the other hand if the transaction is invalid, accepting it without verifying it first will lead to the rejection of the entire block by the blockchain and a waste of work by the uncritical miner. The solution is to require efficiently verifiable proofs of validity for transactions, an approach already pursued by various startups in the Ethereum ecosystem (e.g. TrueBit[10]). We note that it suffices for these proofs to satisfy the condition above: i.e. we do not need the full power of information-theoretic or cryptographic security but it is enough to guarantee that to produce a proof of correctness for a false transaction is more costly than producing a valid transaction and its correct proof, which is exactly the model we are proposing.

1.4 Future Directions

Our work opens up many interesting future directions.

First of all, it would be nice to extend our results to the case where cost is the actual running time, rather than "parallel running time"/"circuit depth" as in our model. The techniques in [BRSV17] (which presents problems conjectured to have $\Omega(n^2)$ complexity on the average), if not even the original work of Merkle [Mer78], might be useful in building a verifiable computation scheme where if computing the function takes time T, then producing a false proof of correctness would have to take $\Omega(T^2)$.

For the specifics of our constructions it would be nice to "close the gap" between what we can achieve and the complexity assumption: our schemes can only compute $\mathsf{AC}^0_\mathsf{Q}[2]$ against adversaries in NC^1, and ideally we would like to be able to compute all of NC^1 (or at the very least all of $\mathsf{AC}^0[2]$).

Finally, to apply these schemes in practice it is important to have tight concrete security reductions and a proof-of-concept implementations.

2   Preliminaries

For a distribution D, we denote by $x \leftarrow D$ the fact that x is being sampled according to D. We remind the reader that an ensemble $\mathcal{X} = \{X_\lambda\}_{\lambda \in \mathbb{N}}$ is a family of probability distributions over a family of domains $\mathcal{D} = \{D_\lambda\}_{\lambda \in \mathbb{N}}$. We say two ensembles $\mathcal{D} = \{D_\lambda\}_{\lambda \in \mathbb{N}}$ and $\mathcal{D}' = \{D'_\lambda\}_{\lambda \in \mathbb{N}}$ are statistically indistinguishable if $\frac{1}{2} \sum_x |D(x) - D'(x)| < \mathsf{neg}(\lambda)$. Finally, we note that all arithmetic computations (such as sums, inner product, matrix products, etc.) in this work will be over $GF(2)$ unless specified otherwise.

---

[10] TrueBit: https://truebit.io/.

Definition 2.1 (Function Family). *A function family is a family of (possibly randomized) functions* $F = \{f_\lambda\}_{\lambda \in \mathbb{N}}$, *where for each* λ, f_λ *has domain* D_λ^f *and co-domain* R_λ^f. *A class* $\mathcal{C}$ *is a collection of function families.*

In most of our constructions $D_\lambda^f = \{0,1\}^{d_\lambda^f}$ and $R_\lambda^f = \{0,1\}^{r_\lambda^f}$ for sequences $\{d_\lambda^f\}_\lambda, \{d_\lambda^f\}_\lambda$.

In the rest of the paper we will focus on the class of $\mathcal{C} = \mathsf{NC}^1$ of functions for which there is a polynomial $p(\cdot)$ and a constant c such that for each λ, the function f_λ can be computed by a Boolean (randomized) fan-in 2, circuit of size $p(\lambda)$ and depth $c \log(\lambda)$. In the formal statements of our results we will also use the following classes: AC^0, the class of functions of polynomial size and constant depth with $\mathsf{AND}, \mathsf{OR}$ and NOT gates with unbounded fan-in; $\mathsf{AC}^0[2]$, the class of functions of polynomial size and constant depth with $\mathsf{AND}, \mathsf{OR}, \mathsf{NOT}$ and PARITY gates with unbounded fan-in.

Given a function f, we can think of its *multiplicative depth* as the degree of the lowest-degree polynomial in $\mathrm{GF}(2)$ that evaluates to f. We denote by $\mathsf{AC}^0_{\mathrm{CM}}[2]$ the class of circuits in $\mathsf{AC}^0[2]$ with *constant multiplicative depth*. We say that a circuit has *quasi-constant multiplicative depth* if it has a constant number of gates with non-constant fan-in (an example is a circuit composed by a single AND of fan-in n). We denote the class of such circuits by $\mathsf{AC}^0_{\mathrm{Q}}[2]$. See Appendix A for a formal treatment.

LIMITED ADVERSARIES. We define adversaries also as families of randomized algorithms $\{A_\lambda\}_\lambda$, one for each security parameter (note that this is a non-uniform notion of security). We denote the class of adversaries we consider as $\mathcal{A}$, and in the rest of the paper we will also restrict $\mathcal{A}$ to NC^1.

INFINITELY-OFTEN SECURITY. We now move to define security against all adversaries $\{A_\lambda\}_\lambda$ that belong to a class $\mathcal{A}$. Our results achieve an "infinitely often" notion of security, which states that for all adversaries outside of our permitted class $\mathcal{A}$ our security property holds infinitely often (i.e. for an infinite sequence of security parameters rather than for every sufficiently large security parameter). This limitation seems inherent to the techniques in this paper and in [DVV16]. We informally denote with $\mathcal{X} \sim_A \mathcal{Y}$ the fact that two ensembles $\mathcal{X}$ and $\mathcal{Y}$ are indistinguishable by NC^1 adversaries for an infinite sequence of parameters Λ. See also Appendix A.

3   Fine-Grained SHE

We start by recalling the public key encryption from [DVV16] which is secure against adversaries in NC^1.

The scheme is described in Fig. 1. Its security relies on the following result, implicit in [IK00a][11]. We will also use this lemma when proving the security of our construction in Sect. 3.

---

[11] Stated as Lemma 4.3 in [DVV16].

Lemma 3.1 ([IK00a]). *If* $\mathsf{NC}^1 \subsetneq \oplus\mathsf{L/poly}$ *then there exist distribution* $\mathcal{D}_\lambda^{kg}$ *over* $\{0,1\}^{\lambda\times\lambda}$, *distribution* $\mathcal{D}_\lambda^f$ *over matrices in* $\{0,1\}^{\lambda\times\lambda}$ *of full rank, and infinite set* $\Lambda \subseteq \mathbb{N}$ *such that*

$$\mathbf{M}^{kg} \sim_\Lambda \mathbf{M}^f$$

where $\mathbf{M}^f \leftarrow \mathcal{D}_\lambda^f$ *and* $\mathbf{M}^{kg} \leftarrow \mathcal{D}_\lambda^{kg}$.

The following result is central to the correctness of the scheme PKE in Fig. 1 and is implicit in [DVV16].

Lemma 3.2 ([DVV16]). *There exists sampling algorithm* KSample *such that* $(\mathbf{M}, \mathbf{k}) \leftarrow$ KSample(1^λ), $\mathbf{M}$ *is a matrix distributed according to* $\mathcal{D}_\lambda^{kg}$ *(as in Lemma 3.1),* $\mathbf{k}$ *is a vector in the kernel of* $\mathbf{M}$ *and has the form* $\mathbf{k} = (r_1, r_2, \ldots, r_{\lambda-1}, 1) \in \{0,1\}^\lambda$ *where* r_i-s *are uniformly distributed bits.*

- PKE.Keygen$_{\mathsf{sk}}(1^\lambda)$:
    1. Sample $(\mathbf{M}, \mathbf{k}) \leftarrow$ KSample(1^λ);
    2. Output $(\mathsf{pk} = \mathbf{M}, \mathsf{sk} = \mathbf{k})$.
- PKE.Enc$_{\mathsf{pk}=\mathbf{M}}(\mu)$:
    1. Sample $\mathbf{r} \leftarrow_{\!s} \{0,1\}^\lambda$;
    2. Let $\mathbf{t}^\mathsf{T} = (0 \ldots 0\ 1) \in \{0,1\}^\lambda$;
    3. Output $\mathbf{c}^\mathsf{T} = \mathbf{r}^\mathsf{T}\mathbf{M} + \mu\mathbf{t}^\mathsf{T}$.
- PKE.Dec$_{\mathsf{sk}=\mathbf{k}}(\mathbf{c})$:
    1. Output $\langle \mathbf{k}, \mathbf{c} \rangle$

Fig. 1. PKE construction [DVV16]

Theorem 3.1 ([DVV16]). *Assume* $\mathsf{NC}^1 \subsetneq \oplus\mathsf{L/poly}$. *Then, the scheme* PKE $=$ (PKE.Keygen, PKE.Enc, PKE.Dec) *defined in Fig. 1 is a Public Key Encryption scheme secure against* NC^1 *adversaries. All algorithms in the scheme are computable in* $\mathsf{AC}^0[2]$.

3.1 Leveled Homomorphic Encryption for $\mathsf{AC}^0_{\mathrm{CM}}[2]$ Functions Secure Against NC^1

We denote by $\boldsymbol{x}[i]$ the i-th bit of a vector of bits $\boldsymbol{x}$. Below, the scheme PKE $=$ (PKE.Keygen, PKE.Enc, PKE.Dec) is the one defined in Fig. 1. Our SHE scheme is defined by the following four algorithms:

- HE.Keygen$_{\mathsf{sk}}(1^\lambda, L)$: For key generation, sample $L + 1$ key pairs $(\mathbf{M}_0, \mathbf{k}_0), \ldots, (\mathbf{M}_L, \mathbf{k}_L) \leftarrow$ PKE.Keygen(1^λ), and compute, for all $\ell \in \{0, \ldots, L-1\}$, $i, j \in [\lambda]$, the value

$$\boldsymbol{a}_{\ell,i,j} \leftarrow \mathsf{PKE.Enc}_{\mathbf{M}_{\ell+1}}(\mathbf{k}_\ell[i] \cdot \mathbf{k}_\ell[j]) \in \{0,1\}^\lambda$$

We define $\mathbf{A} := \{a_{\ell,i,j}\}_{\ell,i,j}$ to be the set of all these values. t then outputs the secret key $\mathsf{sk} = \mathbf{k}_L$, and the public key $\mathsf{pk} = (\mathbf{M}_0, \mathbf{A})$. In the following we call $\mathsf{evk} = \mathbf{A}$ the evaluation key.

We point out a property that will be useful later: by the definition above, for all $\ell \in \{0, \ldots, L-1\}$ we have

$$\langle \mathbf{k}_{\ell+1}, a_{\ell+1,i,j} \rangle = \mathbf{k}_\ell[i] \cdot \mathbf{k}_\ell[j]. \tag{1}$$

- $\mathsf{HE.Enc_{pk}}(\mu))$: Recall that $\mathsf{pk} = \mathbf{M}_0$. To encrypt a message μ we compute $v \leftarrow \mathsf{PKE.Enc_{M_0}}(\mu)$. The output ciphertext contains v in addition to a "level tag", an index in $\{0, \ldots, L\}$ denoting the "multiplicative depth" of the generated ciphertext. The encryption algorithm outputs $c := (v, 0)$.
- $\mathsf{HE.Dec_{k_L}}(c)$: To decrypt a ciphertext[12] $c = (v, L)$ compute $\mathsf{PKE.Dec_{k_L}}(v)$, i.e.

$$\langle \mathbf{k}_L, v \rangle$$

- $\mathsf{HE.Eval_{evk}}(f, c_1, \ldots, c_n)$: where $f : \{0,1\}^n \to \{0,1\}$: We require that f is represented as an arithmetic circuit in $\mathrm{GF}(2)$ with addition gates of unbounded fan-in and multiplication gates of fan-in 2. We also require the circuit to be *layered*, i.e. the set of gates can be partitioned in subsets (layers) such that wires are always between adjacent layers. Each layer should be composed homogeneously either of addition or multiplication gates. Finally, we require that the number of multiplications layers (i.e. the multiplicative depth) of f is L.
  We homomorphically evaluate f gate by gate. We will show how to perform multiplication (resp. addition) of two (resp. many) ciphertexts. Carrying out this procedure recursively we can homomorphically compute any circuit f of multiplicative depth L.

Ciphertext Structure During Evaluation. During the homomorphic evaluation a ciphertext will be of the form $c = (v, \ell)$ where ℓ is the "level tag" mentioned above. At any point of the evaluation we will have that ℓ is between 0 (for fresh ciphertexts at the input layer) and L (at the output layer). We define homomorphic evaluation only among ciphertexts at the same level. Since our circuit is layered we will not have to worry about homomorphic evaluation occurring among ciphertexts at different levels. Consistently with the fact a level tag represents the multiplicative depth of a ciphertext, addition gates will keep the level of ciphertexts unchanged, whereas multiplication gates will increase it by one. Finally, we will keep the invariant that the output of each gate evaluation $c = (v, \ell)$ is such that

$$\langle \mathbf{k}_\ell, v \rangle = \mu \tag{2}$$

where μ is the correct plaintext output of the gate. We prove our construction satisfies this invariant in Appendix B.

---

[12] We are only requiring to decrypt ciphertexts that are output by $\mathsf{HE.Eval}(\cdots)$.

Homomorphic Evaluation of Gates:

- *Addition gates.* Homomorphic evaluation of an addition gates on inputs $c_1, \ldots, c_n$ where $c_i = (\boldsymbol{v}_i, \ell)$ is performed by outputting

$$c_{\text{add}} = (\boldsymbol{v}_{\text{add}}, \ell) := \left(\sum_i \boldsymbol{v}_i, \ell \right)$$

- *Multiplication gates.* We show how to multiply ciphertexts c, c' where $c = (\boldsymbol{v}, \ell)$ and $c' = (\boldsymbol{v}', \ell)$ to obtain an output ciphertext $c_{\text{mult}} = (\boldsymbol{v}_{\text{mult}}, \ell + 1)$. The homomorphic multiplication algorithm will set

$$\boldsymbol{v}_{\text{mult}} := \sum_{i,j \in [\lambda]} h_{i,j} \cdot \boldsymbol{a}_{\ell+1,i,j}$$

where $h_{i,j} = \boldsymbol{v}[i] \cdot \boldsymbol{v}'[j]$ for $i, j \in [\lambda]$.
The final output ciphertext will be

$$c_{\text{mult}} := (\boldsymbol{v}_{\text{mult}}, \ell + 1).$$

The following theorem states the security of our scheme under our complexity assumption.

Theorem 3.2 (Security). *The scheme* HE *is CPA secure against* NC^1 *adversaries (Definition A.5) under the assumption* $\mathsf{NC}^1 \subsetneq \oplus \mathsf{L}/\text{poly}$.

3.2   Efficiency and Homomorphic Properties of Our Scheme

Our scheme is secure against adversaries in the class NC^1. This implies that we can run HE.Eval only on functions f that are in NC^1, otherwise the evaluator would be able to break the semantic security of the scheme. However we have to ensure that the *whole* homomorphic evaluation stays in NC^1. The problem is that homomorphically evaluating f has an overhead with respect to the "plain" evaluation of f. Therefore, we need to determine for which functions f, we can guarantee that HE.Eval$(F, \ldots)$ will stay in NC^1. The class of such functions turns out to be the class of functions implementable in constant multiplicative depth, i.e. $\mathsf{AC}^0_{\text{CM}}[2]$[13].

These observations, plus the fact that the invariant in Eq. 2 is preserved throughout homomorphic evaluation, imply the following result.

Theorem 3.3. *The scheme* HE *is leveled* $\mathsf{AC}^0_{CM}[2]$-*homomorphic. Key generation, encryption, decryption and evaluation are all computable in* $\mathsf{AC}^0_{CM}[2]$.

---

[13] In terms of circuit depth, the main overhead when evaluating f homomorphically is given by the multiplication gates (addition, on the other hand, is "for free" — see definition of HE.Eval above). A single homomorphic multiplication can be performed by a depth two $\mathsf{AC}^0[2]$ circuit, but this requires depth $\Omega(\log(n))$ with a circuit of fan-in two. Therefore, a circuit for f with $\omega(1)$ multiplicative depth would require an evaluation of $\omega(\log(n))$ depth, which would be out of NC^1. On the other hand, observe that for any function f in $\mathsf{AC}^0[2]$ with constant multiplicative depth, the evaluation stays in $\mathsf{AC}^0[2]$. This because there is a constant number (depth) of homomorphic multiplications each requiring an $\mathsf{AC}^0[2]$ computation.

3.3   Beyond Constant Multiplicative Depth

In the previous section we saw how our scheme is homomorphic for a class of constant-depth, unbounded fan-in arithmetic circuits in GF(2) with *constant multiplicative depth*. We now show how to overcome this limitation by first extending techniques from [Raz87] to approximate $AC^0[2]$ circuits with low-degree polynomials and then designing a construction that internally uses our scheme HE from Sect. 3.1.

Approximating $AC_Q^0[2]$ in $AC_{CM}^0[2]$. Our approach to homomorphically evaluate a function $f \in AC_Q^0[2]$ is as follows. Instead of evaluating f we evaluate f^*, an approximate version of f that is computable in $AC_{CM}^0[2]$. The function f^* is randomized and we will denote by n' the number of random bits f^* takes in input (in addition to the n bits of the input x). If $\hat{x} = \mathsf{Enc}(x)$ and $\hat{r} = \mathsf{Enc}(r)$ where r is uniformly random in $\{0,1\}^{n'}$, then decrypting $\mathsf{HE.Eval}(f^*, \hat{x}, \hat{r})$[14] yields $f(x)$ with constant error probability. One way to reduce error could be to let evaluation compute f^* s times with s random inputs. However, this requires particular care to avoid using majority gates in the decryption algorithm. With this goal in mind we extend the output of the approximating function f^*. When performing evaluation we will then perform s evaluations of f', the "extension" of f^* This additional information will be returned (encrypted) from the evaluation algorithm and will allow correct decryption with overwhelming probability and in low-depth (and without majority gates).

In the next constructions we will make use of the functions GenApproxFun, GenDecodeAux and DecodeApprox, here only informally defined[15]. The function GenApproxFun(f) returns the (extended) approximating function f'; the function GenDecodeAux(f) returns a constant-size string $\mathbf{aux}_f$ used to decode (multiple) output of $f'(x)$; the function DecodeApprox($\mathbf{aux}_f, y_1^{\mathrm{out}}, \ldots, y_s^{\mathrm{out}}$) returns $f(x)$ w.h.p. if each y_s^{out} is an output of $f'(x; r)$ for random r.

Homomorphic Evaluations of $AC_Q^0[2]$ Circuits. Below is our construction for a homomorphic scheme that can evaluate all circuits in $AC_Q^0[2]$ in $AC^0[2]$. This time, in order to evaluate circuit C, we perform several homomorphic evaluations of the randomized circuit C' (as in Lemma B.2). To obtain the plaintext output of C we can decrypt all the ciphertext outputs and use DecodeApprox. Notice that this scheme is still compact. As we use a randomized approach to evaluate f, the scheme HE' will be implicitly parametrized by a soundness parameter s. Intuitively, the probability of a function f being evaluated incorrectly will be upper bounded by 2^{-s}.

For our new scheme we will use the following auxiliary functions:

---

[14] In the evaluation algorithm we ignore the distinction between deterministic and random input.

[15] The reader can find additional details in Appendix B.

Definition 3.1 (Auxiliary Functions for HE'). *Let* $f : \{0,1\}^n \to \{0,1\}$ *be represented as an arithmetic circuit as in* HE *and* pk *a public key for the scheme* HE *that includes the evaluation key. Let* s *be a soundness parameter. We denote by* f' *be as above; let* $n' = O(n)$ *be the number of additional bits* f' *will take as random input.*

- SampleAuxRandomness$_s$(pk, f') :
    1. *Sample* $s \cdot n'$ *random bits* $r_1^{(1)}, \ldots, r_{n'}^{(1)}, \ldots, r_1^{(s)}, \ldots, r_{n'}^{(s)}$;
    2. *Compute* $\hat{r}_{aux} := \{\hat{r}_j^{(i)} \mid \hat{r}_j^{(i)} \leftarrow \mathsf{HE.Enc}_{pk}(r_j^{(i)}), i \in [s], j \in [n']\}$;
    3. *Output* $\hat{r}_{aux}$.
- EvalApprox$_s$(pk, f', $c_1, \ldots, c_n$, $\hat{r}_{aux}$) :
    1. *Let* $\hat{r}_{aux} = \{\hat{r}_j^{(i)} \mid i \in [s], j \in [n']\}$.
    2. *For* $i \in [s]$, *compute* $c_i^{out} \leftarrow \mathsf{HE.Eval}_{evk}(f', c_1, \ldots c_n, \hat{r}_1^{(i)}, \ldots, \hat{r}_{n'}^{(i)})$;
    3. *Output* $c = (c_1^{out}, \ldots, c_s^{out})$.[16]

The new scheme HE' with soundness parameter s follows. Notice that the evaluation function outputs an auxiliary string $\mathbf{aux}_f$ together with the proper ciphertext c. This is necessary to have a correct decoding in decryption phase.

- Key generation and encryption are the same as in HE.
- HE'.Eval$_{pk}(f, c_1, \ldots, c_n)$:
    1. Compute $f' \leftarrow \mathsf{GenApproxFun}(f)$;
    2. Compute $\hat{r}_{aux} \leftarrow \mathsf{SampleAuxRandomness}_s(pk, f')$;
    3. $\mathbf{aux}_f \leftarrow \mathsf{GenDecodeAux}(f)$;
    4. $c \leftarrow \mathsf{EvalApprox}_s(pk, f', c_1, \ldots, c_n, \hat{r}_{aux})$;
    5. Output $(c, \mathbf{aux}_f)$.
- HE'.Dec$_{sk}(c = (c_1^{out}, \ldots, c_s^{out}), \mathbf{aux}_f)$:
    1. Let $y_i^{out} \leftarrow \mathsf{HE.Dec}_{sk}(c_i^{out})$ for $i \in [s]$;
    2. Output $\mathsf{DecodeApprox}_f(\mathbf{aux}_f, y_1^{out}, \ldots, y_s^{out})$.

The following theorem summarizes the properties of this construction.

Theorem 3.4. *The scheme* HE' *above with soundness parameter* $s = \Omega(\lambda)$ *is leveled* $\mathsf{AC}_Q^0[2]$*-homomorphic. Key generation, encryption and evaluation can be computed in* $\mathsf{AC}_{CM}^0[2]$. *Decryption is computable in* $\mathsf{AC}_Q^0[2]$.

4 Fine-Grained Verifiable Computation

In this section we describe our private verifiable computation scheme. Our constructions are based on the techniques in [CKV10] to obtain (reusable) verifiable computation from fully homomorphic encryption; see Sect. 1.2 for a high-level description.

---

[16] Recall that the output of the expanded approximating function f' is a bit string and thus each c_i^{out} encrypts a bit string.

4.1 A One-time Verification Scheme

In Figure 2 we describe an adaptation of the one-time secure delegation scheme from [CKV10]. We make non-black box use of our homomorphic encryption scheme HE′ (Sect. 3.3) with soundness parameter $s = \lambda$. Notice that. during the preprocessing phase, we fix the "auxiliary randomness" for EvalApprox (and thus for HE′.Eval) once and for all. We will use that same randomness for all the input instances. This choice does not affect the security of the construction. We remind the reader that we will simplify notation by considering the evaluation key of our somewhat homomorphic encryption scheme as part of its public key.

If x is a vector of bits $x_1, \ldots, x_n$, below we will denote with HE′.Enc(x) the concatenation of the bit by bit ciphertexts HE′.Enc$(x_1), \ldots,$ HE′.Enc(x_n). We denote by HE′.Enc$(\bar{0})$ the concatenation of n encryptions of 0, HE′.Enc(0).

Let $f : \{0,1\}^n \rightarrow \{0,1\}^m$ be a function and GenApproxFun, SampleAuxRandomness and EvalApprox as described in Section 3.3 and Definition 3.1.

- VC.KeyGen$(1^\lambda, f) \rightarrow (\mathsf{pk_W}, \mathsf{sk_D})$: We assume function f represented as
  1. Generate a pair of keys $(\mathsf{pk}, \mathsf{sk}) \leftarrow$ HE′.Keygen(1^λ).
  2. Generate the approximating function $f' \leftarrow$ GenApproxFun(f) and auxiliary string $\mathbf{aux}_f \leftarrow$ GenDecodeAux(f);
  3. Generate the ciphertext of the auxiliary random input for homomorphic evaluation $\hat{r}_{\mathsf{aux}} \leftarrow$ SampleAuxRandomness$_\lambda(\mathsf{pk}, f')$
  4. Compute t independent encryptions $\hat{r}_i =$ HE′.Enc$_{\mathsf{pk}}(\bar{0})$ and the homomorphic evaluations $\hat{w}_i = \hat{f}(\hat{r}_i) =$ EvalApprox$_s(\mathsf{pk}, f', \hat{r}_i, \hat{r}_{\mathsf{aux}})$ for $i \in [t]$;
  5. $\mathsf{pk_W} \leftarrow (\mathsf{pk}, f', \hat{r}_{\mathsf{aux}})$, $\mathsf{sk_D} \leftarrow (\{(\hat{r}_i, \hat{w}_i)_{i \in [t]}\}, \mathbf{aux}_f)$.
- VC.ProbGen$_{\mathsf{sk_D}}(x) \rightarrow (q_x, s_x)$:
  1. Compute t independent encryptions $\hat{r}_{i+t} =$ HE′.Enc$_{\mathsf{pk}}(x)$ for $i \in [t]$.
  2. Sample a random permutation $\pi \leftarrow_\$ S_{2t}$.
  3. $q_x \leftarrow (\hat{z}_{\pi(1)}, \ldots, \hat{z}_{\pi(2t)}) = (\hat{r}_1, \ldots, \hat{r}_{2t})$; $s_x \leftarrow \pi$
- VC.Compute$_{\mathsf{pk_W}}(q_x) \rightarrow a_x$:
  1. Compute $\hat{y}_i = \hat{f}(\hat{z}_i) =$ EvalApprox$_s(\mathsf{pk}, f', \hat{z}_i, \hat{r}_{\mathsf{aux}})$ for $i \in [2t]$.
  2. $a_x = (\hat{y}_1, \ldots, \hat{y}_{2t})$.
- VC.Verify$_{\mathsf{sk_D}}(s_x, a_x)$:
  1. Check if $\hat{w}_i = \hat{y}_i$ for all $i \in [t]$.
  2. Check if HE′.Dec$_{\mathsf{sk}}(\hat{y}_{\pi(t+1)}, \mathbf{aux}_f) = \cdots =$ HE′.Dec$_{\mathsf{sk}}(\hat{y}_{\pi(2t)}, \mathbf{aux}_f)$.
  3. If either of the two tests above fails, return $\bot$; otherwise return HE′.Dec$_{\mathsf{sk}}(\hat{y}_{\pi(t+1)}, \mathbf{aux}_f)$.

Fig. 2. One-Time Delegation Scheme $\mathcal{VC}$

The scheme $\mathcal{VC}$ in Figure 2 has overwhelming completeness and is one-time secure when t is chosen $\omega(\log(\lambda))$. We prove these results in Appendix C.

Remark 4.1 (Efficiency of $\mathcal{VC}$). In the following we consider the verifiable computation of a function $f : \{0,1\}^n \rightarrow \{0,1\}^m$ computable by an $\mathsf{AC}^0_\mathsf{Q}[2]$ circuit of size S.

- VC.KeyGen is computable by an $AC^0[2]$ circuit of size $O(\text{poly}(\lambda)S)$;
- VC.ProbGen is computable by an $AC^0[2]$ circuit of size $O(\text{poly}(\lambda)(m+n))$;
- VC.Compute is computable by an $AC^0[2]$ circuit of size $O(\text{poly}(\lambda)S)$;
- VC.Verify is computable by a $AC^0[2]$ circuit of size $O(\text{poly}(\lambda)(m+n))$.

The (constant) depth of VC.ProbGen and VC.Verify is independent of the depth of f[17].

4.2   A Reusable Verification Scheme

We obtain our reusable verification scheme $\overline{\mathcal{VC}}$ applying the transformation in [CKV10] from one-time sound verification schemes through fully homomorphic encryption. The core idea behind this transformation is to encapsulate all the operations of a one-time verifiable computation scheme (such as $\mathcal{VC}$ in Fig. 2) through homomorphic encryption. We instantiate this transformation with the simplest of our two somewhat homomorphic encryption schemes, HE (described in Sect. 3.1). The full construction of $\overline{\mathcal{VC}}$ is in Appendix C (Fig. 3).

Remark 4.2 (Efficiency of $\overline{\mathcal{VC}}$). The efficiency of $\overline{\mathcal{VC}}$ is analogous to that of $\mathcal{VC}$ with the exception of a circuit size overhead of a factor $O(\lambda)$ on the problem generation and verification algorithms and of $O(\lambda^2)$ for the computation algorithm. The (constant) depth of $\overline{\mathcal{VC}}$.ProbGen and $\overline{\mathcal{VC}}$.Verify is independent of the depth of f.

Theorem 4.1 (Completeness of $\overline{\mathcal{VC}}$). *The verifiable computation scheme $\overline{\mathcal{VC}}$ has overwhelming completeness (Definition A.10) for the class $AC_Q^0[2]$.*

Theorem 4.2 (Many-Times Soundness of $\overline{\mathcal{VC}}$). *Under the assumption that $NC^1 \subsetneq \oplus L/\text{poly}$ the scheme $\overline{\mathcal{VC}}$ is many-times secure against NC^1 adversaries whenever t is chosen to be $\omega(\log(\lambda))$ in the underlying scheme $\mathcal{VC}$.*

A   Additional Preliminaries

A.1   Infinitely-Often Computational Indistinguishability

Definition A.1 (Infinitely-Often Computational Indistinguishability). *Let $\mathcal{X} = \{X_\lambda\}_{\lambda \in \mathbb{N}}$ Let $\mathcal{Y} = \{Y_\lambda\}_{\lambda \in \mathbb{N}}$ be ensembles over the same domain family, $\mathcal{A}$ a class of adversaries, and Λ an infinite subset of $\mathbb{N}$. We say that $\mathcal{X}$ and $\mathcal{Y}$*

---

[17] Further details on the complexity of $\mathcal{VC}$ follow. All the algorithms are in $AC_{CM}^0[2]$, except for the online stage. In fact, VC.Verify and VC.ProbGen are in $AC^0[2]$. Moreover, they are not in $AC_Q^0[2]$ as they perform in parallel a non-constant (polylogarithmic) number of decryptions and permutations respectively, and these involve non-constant fan-in gates. Notice that even though the online stage is not in $AC_Q^0[2]$ we still have a gain at verification time (although not in an asymptotic sense). This because of the specific structure of these circuits. Consider for example what happens when implementing VC.Verify or VC.ProbGen with a fan-in two circuit. Their depth will be $c(\log(n) + \log(\lambda))$ for a constant c. Contrast this with a circuit f in $AC_Q^0[2]$ of constant depth D that we may want to verify. With fan-in two, the depth of f will become $c'D\log(n)$ (for a constant c'), which may be significantly larger.

are infinitely often computational indistinguishable with respect to set Λ and the class $\mathcal{A}$, denoted by $\mathcal{X} \sim_{\Lambda, \mathcal{A}} \mathcal{Y}$ if there exists a negligible function ν such that for any $\lambda \in \Lambda$ and for any adversary $A = \{A_\lambda\}_\lambda \in \mathcal{A}$

$$|\Pr[A_\lambda(X_\lambda) = 1] - \Pr[A_\lambda(Y_\lambda) = 1]| < \nu(\lambda)$$

When $\mathcal{A} = \mathsf{NC}^1$ we will keep it implicit and use the notation $\mathcal{X} \sim_\Lambda \mathcal{Y}$ and say that $\mathcal{X}$ and $\mathcal{Y}$ are Λ-computationally indistinguishable.

In our proofs we will use the following facts on infinitely-often computationally indistinguishable ensembles. We skip their proof as, except for a few technicalities, it is analogous to the corresponding properties for standard computational indistinguishability[18].

Lemma A.1 (Facts on Λ-Computational Indistinguishability).

- **Transitivity:** *Let $m = \mathsf{poly}(\lambda)$ and $\mathcal{X}^{(j)}$ with $j \in \{0, \ldots, m\}$ be ensembles. If for all $j \in [m]$ $\mathcal{X}^{(j-1)} \sim_\Lambda \mathcal{X}^{(j)}$, then $\mathcal{X}^{(0)} \sim_\Lambda \mathcal{X}^{(m)}$.*
- **Weaker than statistical indistinguishability:** *Let $\mathcal{X}, \mathcal{Y}$ be statistically indistinguishable ensembles. Then $\mathcal{X} \sim_\Lambda \mathcal{Y}$ for any infinite $\Lambda \subseteq \mathbb{N}$.*
- **Closure under NC^1:** *Let $\mathcal{X}, \mathcal{Y}$ be ensembles and $\{f_\lambda\}_{\lambda \in \mathbb{N}} \in \mathsf{NC}^1$. If $\mathcal{X} \sim_\Lambda \mathcal{Y}$ for some Λ then $f_\lambda(\mathcal{X}) \sim_\Lambda f_\lambda(\mathcal{Y})$.*

A.2   Circuit Classes

For a gate g we denote by $\mathsf{type}_C(g)$ the type of the gate g in the circuit C and by $\mathsf{parents}_C(g)$ the list of gates of C whose output is an input to C (such list may potentially contain duplicates).

We define the multiplicative depth of a circuit as follows:

Definition A.2 (Multiplicative Depth). *Let C be a circuit, we define the multiplicative depth of C as $\mathsf{md}(g_{out})$ where g_{out} is its output gate and the function md, from the set of gates to the set of natural numbers is recursively defined as follows:*

$$\mathsf{md}(g) := \begin{cases} 1 & \textit{if } \mathsf{type}_C(g) = \mathsf{input} \\ \max\{\mathsf{md}(g') : g' \in \mathsf{parents}_C(g)\} & \textit{if } \mathsf{type}_C(g) = \mathsf{XOR} \\ \displaystyle\sum_{g' \in \mathsf{parents}_C(g)} \mathsf{md}(g') & \textit{if } \mathsf{type}_C(g) \in \{\mathsf{AND}, \mathsf{OR}\} \end{cases}$$

where the sum in the last case is over the integers.

The following two circuit classes will appear in several of our results.

Definition A.3 (Circuits with Constant Multiplicative Depth). *We denote by $\mathsf{AC}^0_{CM}[2]$ the class of circuits in $\mathsf{AC}^0[2]$ with constant multiplicative depth.*

---

[18] We refer the reader to [Gol01].

Definition A.4 (Circuits with Quasi-Constant Multiplicative Depth).
For a circuit C we denote by $S_{\omega(1)}(C)$ the set of AND *and* OR *gates in C
with non-constant fan-in. We say that C has quasi-constant multiplicative depth
if $|S_{\omega(1)}(C)| = O(1)$. We shall denote by* $\mathsf{AC}^0_Q[2]$ *the class of circuits in* $\mathsf{AC}^0[2]$
with quasi-constant multiplicative depth.

A.3   Public-Key Encryption

A public-key encryption scheme
$\mathsf{PKE} = (\mathsf{PKE.Keygen}, \mathsf{PKE.Enc}, \mathsf{PKE.Dec})$ is a triple of algorithms which operate
as follow:

- **Key Generation.** The algorithm $(\mathsf{pk}, \mathsf{sk}) \leftarrow \mathsf{PKE.Keygen}(1^\lambda)$ takes a unary
  representation of the security parameter and outputs a public key encryption
  key pk and a secret decryption key sk.
- **Encryption.** The algorithm $c \leftarrow \mathsf{PKE.Enc}_{\mathsf{pk}}(\mu)$ takes the public key pk and
  a single bit message $\mu \in \{0, 1\}$ and outputs a ciphertext c. The notation
  $\mathsf{PKE.Enc}_{\mathsf{pk}}(\mu; r)$ will be used to represent the encryption of a bit μ using
  randomness r.
- **Decryption.** The algorithm $\mu^* \leftarrow \mathsf{PKE.Dec}_{\mathsf{sk}}(c)$ takes the secret key sk and
  a ciphertext c and outputs a message $\mu^* \in \{0, 1\}$.

Obviously we require that $\mu = \mathsf{PKE.Dec}_{\mathsf{sk}}(\mathsf{PKE.Enc}_{\mathsf{pk}}(\mu))$

Definition A.5 (CPA Security for PKE).   *A scheme* PKE *is IND-CPA
secure if for an infinite $\Lambda \subseteq \mathbb{N}$ we have*

$$(\mathsf{pk}, \mathsf{PKE.Enc}_{\mathsf{pk}}(0)) \sim_\Lambda (\mathsf{pk}, \mathsf{PKE.Enc}_{\mathsf{pk}}(1))$$

where $(\mathsf{pk}, \mathsf{sk}) \leftarrow \mathsf{PKE.Keygen}(1^\lambda)$.

Remark A.1 (Security for Multiple Messages). Notice that by a standard hybrid
argument and Lemma A.1 we can prove that any scheme secure according to
Definition A.5 is also secure for multiple messages (i.e. the two sequences of
encryptions bit by bit of two bit strings are computationally indistinguishable).
We will use this fact in the constructions in Sect. 4, but we do not provide the
formal definition for this type of security. We refer the reader to 5.4.2 in [Gol09].

Somewhat Homomorphic Encryption. A public-key encryption scheme is
said to be homomorphic if there is an additional algorithm Eval which takes a
input the public key pk, the representation of a function $f : \{0, 1\}^l \to \{0, 1\}$ and
a set of l ciphertexts $c_1, \ldots, c_l$, and outputs a ciphertext c_f[19].

We proceed to define the homomorphism property. The next notion of $\mathcal{C}$-
homomorphism is sometimes also referred to as "somewhat homomorphism".

---

[19] Notice that the syntax of Eval can also be extended to return a sequence of encryptions for the case of multi-output functions. We will use this fact in Sect. 3.3. See
also Remark A.1.

Definition A.6 ($\mathcal{C}$-homomorphism). *Let $\mathcal{C}$ be a class of functions (together with their respective representations). An encryption scheme* PKE *is $\mathcal{C}$-homomorphic (or, homomorphic for the class $\mathcal{C}$) if for every function f_λ where $f_\lambda \in \mathcal{F}\{f_\lambda\}_{\lambda \in \mathbb{N}} \in \mathcal{C}$ and respective inputs $\mu_1, \ldots, \mu_n \in \{0, 1\}$ (where $n = n(\lambda)$), it holds that if $(\mathsf{pk}, \mathsf{sk}) \leftarrow$ PKE.Keygen(1^λ) and $c_i \leftarrow$ PKE.Enc$_\mathsf{pk}(\mu_i)$ then*

$$\Pr[\mathsf{PKE.Dec}_\mathsf{sk}(\mathsf{Eval}_\mathsf{pk}(F, c_1, \ldots, c_n)) \neq F(\mu_1, \ldots, \mu_n)] = \mathsf{neg}(\lambda),$$

As usual we require the scheme to be non-trivial by requiring that the output of Eval is compact:

Definition A.7 (Compactness). *A homomorphic encryption scheme* PKE *is compact if there exists a polynomial s in λ such that the output length of* Eval *is at most $s(\lambda)$ bits long (regardless of the function f being computed or the number of inputs).*

Definition A.8. *Let $\mathcal{C} = \{\mathcal{C}_\lambda\}_{\lambda \in \mathbb{N}}$ of arithmetic circuits in $GF(2)$. A scheme* PKE *is leveled $\mathcal{C}$-homomorphic if it takes 1^L as additional input in key generation, and can only evaluate depth-L arithmetic circuits from $\mathcal{C}$. The bound $s(\lambda)$ on the ciphertext must remain independent of L.*

A.4   Verifiable Computation

In a *Verifiable Computation* scheme a Client uses an untrusted server to compute a function f over an input x. The goal is to prevent the Client from accepting an incorrect value $y' \neq f(x)$. We require that the Client's cost of running this protocol be smaller than the cost of computing the function on his own. The following definition is from [GGP10] which allows the client to run a possibly expensive pre-processing step.

Definition A.9 (Verifiable Computation Scheme). *We define a verifiable computation scheme as a quadruple of algorithms $\mathcal{VC} = ($VC.KeyGen, VC.ProbGen, VC.Compute, VC.Verify$)$ where:*

1. VC.KeyGen$(f, 1^\lambda) \rightarrow (\mathsf{pk}_W, \mathsf{sk}_D)$: *Based on the security parameter λ, the randomized key generation algorithm generates a public key that encodes the target function f, which is used by the Server to compute f. It also computes a matching secret key, which is kept private by the Client.*
2. VC.ProbGen$_{\mathsf{sk}_D}(x) \rightarrow (q_x, s_x)$: *The problem generation algorithm uses the secret key sk_D to encode the function input x as a public query q_x which is given to the Server to compute with, and a secret value s_x which is kept private by the Client.*
3. VC.Compute$_{\mathsf{pk}_W}(q_x) \rightarrow a_x$: *Using the Client's public key and the encoded input, the Server computes an encoded version of the function's output $y = F(x)$.*
4. VC.Verify$_{\mathsf{sk}_D}(s_x, a_x) \rightarrow y \cup \{\bot\}$: *Using the secret key sk_D and the secret "decoding" s_x, the verification algorithm converts the worker's encoded output into the output of the function, e.g., $y = f(x)$ or outputs $\bot$ indicating that a_x does not represent the valid output of f on x.*

The scheme should be complete, i.e. an honest Server should (almost) always return the correct value.

Definition A.10 (Completeness). *A delegation scheme* $\mathcal{VC}$, *with* $\mathcal{VC} =$ (VC.KeyGen, VC.ProbGen, VC.Compute, VC.Verify), *has overwhelming completeness for a class of functions* $\mathcal{C}$ *if there is a function* $\nu(n) = \mathsf{neg}(\lambda)$ *such that for infinitely many values of* λ, *if* $f_\lambda \in \mathcal{F} \in \mathcal{C}$, *then for all inputs* x *the following holds with probability at least* $1 - \nu(n)$: $(\mathsf{pk_W}, \mathsf{sk_D}) \leftarrow$ VC.KeyGen(f_λ, λ), $(q_x, s_x) \leftarrow$ VC.ProbGen$_{\mathsf{sk_D}}(x)$ *and* $a_x \leftarrow$ VC.Compute$_{\mathsf{pk_W}}(q_x)$ *then* $y = f_\lambda(x) \leftarrow$ VC.Verify$_{\mathsf{sk_D}}(s_x, a_x)$.

To define soundness we consider an adversary who plays the role of a malicious Server who tries to convince the Client of an incorrect output $y \neq f(x)$. The adversary is allowed to run the protocol on inputs of her choice, i.e. see the *queries* q_{x_i} for adversarially chosen x_i's before picking an input x and attempt to cheat on that input. Because we are interested in the parallel complexity of the adversary we distinguish between two parameters l and m. The adversary is allowed to do l rounds of adaptive queries, and in each round she queries m inputs. Jumping ahead, because our adversaries are restricted to NC^1 circuits, we will have to bound l with a constant, but we will be able to keep m polynomially large.

Experiment $\mathbf{Exp}_A^{\mathsf{Verif}}[\mathcal{VC}, f, \lambda, l, m]$

$\quad (\mathsf{pk_W}, \mathsf{sk_D}) \leftarrow$ VC.KeyGen(f, λ);

$\quad \mathcal{I} \leftarrow \emptyset$;

$\quad$ For $i = 1, \ldots, i = l$;

$\quad\quad \{x_{(i-1)m}, \ldots x_{im-1}\} \leftarrow A_\lambda(\mathsf{pk_W}, \mathcal{I})$;

$\quad\quad \{(q_j, s_j) : (q_j, s_j) \leftarrow$ VC.ProbGen$_{\mathsf{sk_D}}(x_j), j \in \{(i-1)m, \ldots, im\}\}$

$\quad\quad \mathcal{I} \leftarrow \mathcal{I} \cup \{x_{(i-1)m}, \ldots x_{im-1}\} \cup \{q_{(i-1)m}, \ldots q_{im-1}\}$;

$\quad \hat{a} \leftarrow A_\lambda(\mathsf{pk_W}, \mathcal{I})$;

$\quad \hat{y} \leftarrow$ VC.Verify$_{\mathsf{sk_D}}(s_{lm}, \hat{a})$

$\quad$ If $\hat{y} \neq \perp$ and $\hat{y} \neq f(x_{lm})$, output 1, else 0.

Remark A.2 In the experiment above the adversary "tries to cheat" on the last input presented in the last round of queries (i.e. x_{lm}). This is without loss of generality. In fact, assume the adversary aimed at cheating on an input presented before round l, then with one additional round it could present that same input once more as the last of the batch in that round.

Definition A.11 (Soundness). *We say that a verifiable computation scheme is* (l, m)-*sound against a class* $\mathcal{A}$ *of adversaries if there exists a negligible function* $\mathsf{neg}(\lambda)$, *such that for all* $A = \{A_\lambda\}_\lambda \in \mathcal{A}$, *and for infinitely many* λ *we have that*

$$\Pr[\mathbf{Exp}_A^{\mathsf{Verif}}[\mathcal{VC}, f, \lambda, l, m] = 1] \leq \mathsf{neg}(\lambda)$$

Assume the function f we are trying to compute belongs to a class $\mathcal{C}$ which is smaller than $\mathcal{A}$. Then our definition guarantees that the "cost" of cheating is higher than the cost of honestly computing f and engaging in the Verifiable

Computation protocol $\mathcal{VC}$. Jumping ahead, our scheme will allow us to compute the class $\mathcal{C} = \mathsf{AC}^0[2]$ against the class of adversaries $\mathcal{A} = \mathsf{NC}^1$.

EFFICIENCY The last thing to consider is the efficiency of a VC protocol. Here we focus on the time complexity of computing the function f. Let n be the number of input bits, and m be the number of output bits, and S be the size of the circuit computing f.

- A verifiable computation scheme $\mathcal{VC}$ is **client-efficient** if circuit sizes of VC.ProbGen and VC.Verify are $o(S)$. We say that it is **linear-client** if those sizes are $O(\mathsf{poly}(\lambda)(n + m))$.
- A verifiable computation scheme $\mathcal{VC}$ is **server-efficient** if the circuit size of VC.Compute is $O(\mathsf{poly}(\lambda)S)$.

We note that the key generation protocol VC.KeyGen can be expensive, and indeed in our protocol (as in [GGP10, CKV10, AIK10]) its cost is the same as computing f – this is OK as VC.KeyGen is only invoked once per function, and the cost can be amortized over several computations of f.

B   Proofs for Homomorphic Encryption Constructions

B.1   Constant Multiplicative Depth

Lemma B.1. *The construction of* HE *(Sect. 3.1) satisfies Eq. 1 (ibid).*

Proof. For homomorphic addition:

$$\langle \mathbf{k}_\ell, \mathbf{v}_{\mathrm{add}} \rangle = \langle \mathbf{k}_\ell, \sum_i \mathbf{v}_i \rangle = \sum_i \langle \mathbf{k}_\ell, \mathbf{v}_i \rangle = \sum_i \mu_i$$

where μ_i is the plaintext corresponding to $\mathbf{v}_i$.
For homomorphic multiplication:

$$\langle \mathbf{k}_{\ell+1}, \mathbf{v}_{\mathrm{mult}} \rangle = \langle \mathbf{k}_{\ell+1}, \sum_{i,j \in [\lambda]} h_{i,j} \cdot \mathbf{a}_{\ell+1,i,j} \rangle$$

$$= \sum_{i,j \in [\lambda]} \left(h_{i,j} \cdot \langle \mathbf{k}_{\ell+1}, \mathbf{a}_{\ell+1,i,j} \rangle \right)$$

$$= \sum_{i,j \in [\lambda]} \left(h_{i,j} \cdot \mathbf{k}_\ell[i] \cdot \mathbf{k}_\ell[j] \right)$$

$$= \sum_{i,j \in [\lambda]} \left(\mathbf{v}[i] \cdot \mathbf{v}'[j] \cdot \mathbf{k}_\ell[i] \cdot \mathbf{k}_\ell[j] \right)$$

$$= \left(\sum_{i \in [\lambda]} \mathbf{v}[i] \cdot \mathbf{k}_\ell[i] \right) \cdot \left(\sum_{j \in [\lambda]} \mathbf{v}'[j] \cdot \mathbf{k}_\ell[j] \right)$$

$$= \langle \mathbf{k}_\ell, \mathbf{v} \rangle \cdot \langle \mathbf{k}_\ell, \mathbf{v}' \rangle$$

$$= \mu \cdot \mu'$$

where in the third and fourth equality we used respectively Eq. 1 and the definition of $h_{i,j}$, and μ, μ' are the plaintexts corresponding to $\mathbf{v}$ $\mathbf{v}'$ respectively.

$\square$

Theorem B.1 (Security). *The scheme* HE *is CPA secure against* NC^1 *adversaries (Definition A.5) under the assumption* $\mathsf{NC}^1 \subsetneq \oplus \mathsf{L/poly}$.

Proof. We are going to prove that there exists infinite $\varLambda \subseteq \mathbb{N}$ such that $(\mathsf{pk}, \mathsf{evk}, \mathsf{HE.Enc_{pk}}(0)) \sim_\varLambda (\mathsf{pk}, \mathsf{evk}, \mathsf{HE.Enc_{pk}}(1))$.

When using the notations $\mathbf{M}^\mathsf{f}$ and $\mathbf{M}^\mathsf{kg}$ we will always denote matrices distributed respectively according to $\mathcal{D}_\lambda^\mathsf{f}$ and $\mathcal{D}^\mathsf{kg}$, where $\mathcal{D}_\lambda^\mathsf{f}$ and $\mathcal{D}^\mathsf{kg}$ are the distributions defined in Lemma 3.1.

We will define the (randomized) encoding procedure $\mathsf{E} : \{0,1\}^{\lambda \times \lambda} \to \{0,1\}^\lambda$ defined as

$$\mathsf{E}(\mathbf{M}, b) = \mathbf{r}^\mathsf{T}\mathbf{M} + (0 \ldots 0\ b)^\mathsf{T},$$

where r is uniformly distributed in $\{0,1\}^\lambda$. The functions we will pass to E will be distributed either according to $\mathbf{M}^\mathsf{kg}$ or $\mathbf{M}^\mathsf{f}$. Notice that: *(i)* $\mathsf{E}(\mathbf{M}^\mathsf{kg}, b)$ is distributed identically to $\mathsf{HE.Enc_{pk}}(b)$; *(ii)* $\mathsf{E}(\mathbf{M}^\mathsf{f}, b)$ corresponds to the uniform distribution over $\{0,1\}^\lambda$ because (by Lemma 3.1) $\mathbf{M}^\mathsf{f}$ has full rank and hence $\mathbf{r}^\mathsf{T}\mathbf{M}^\mathsf{f}$ must be uniformly random.

We will denote with $\mathbf{M}_1^\mathsf{kg}, \ldots, \mathbf{M}_L^\mathsf{kg}$ the matrices $\mathbf{M}_1, \ldots, \mathbf{M}_L$ used to construct the evaluation key in HE.Keygen (see definition). Recall these matrices are distributed according to $\mathcal{D}^\mathsf{kg}$ as in Lemma 3.1.

We will also define the following vectors:

$$\alpha_\ell^\mathsf{kg} := \{\mathsf{E}(\mathbf{M}_{\ell+1}^\mathsf{kg}, \mathbf{k}_\ell[i]\cdot\mathbf{k}_\ell[j]) \mid i, j \in [\lambda]\} \quad \alpha_\ell^\mathsf{f} := \{\mathsf{E}(\mathbf{M}_{\ell+1}^\mathsf{f}, \mathbf{k}_\ell[i]\cdot\mathbf{k}_\ell[j]) \mid i, j \in [\lambda]\},$$

where $\mathbf{k}_\ell$ is defined as in HE.Keygen and the matrices in input to E will be clear from the context. Notice that all the elements of α_ℓ^kg are encryptions, whereas all the elements of α_ℓ^f are uniformly distributed.

We will use a standard hybrid argument. Each of our hybrids is parametrized by a bit b. This bit informally marks whether the hybrid contains an element indistinguishable from an encryption of b.

- $\mathcal{E}^b := (\mathbf{M}_0^\mathsf{kg}, \mathsf{E}(\mathbf{M}_0^\mathsf{kg}, b), \alpha_1^\mathsf{kg}, \ldots, \alpha_L^\mathsf{kg})$ where $\mathbf{M}_0^\mathsf{kg}$ corresponds to the public key of our scheme. Notice that $\alpha_\ell^\mathsf{kg} \equiv \{\boldsymbol{a}_{\ell,i,j} \mid i, j \in [\lambda]\}$ where $\boldsymbol{a}_{\ell,i,j}$ is as defined in HE.Keygen. This hybrid corresponds to the distribution $(\mathsf{pk}, \mathsf{evk}, \mathsf{HE.Enc_{pk}}(b))$.
- $\mathcal{H}_0^b := (\mathbf{M}_0^\mathsf{f}, \mathsf{E}(\mathbf{M}^\mathsf{f}, b), \alpha_1^\mathsf{kg}, \ldots, \alpha_L^\mathsf{kg})$. The only difference from $\mathcal{E}$ is in the first two components where we replaced the actual public key and ciphertext with a full rank matrix distributed according to $\mathcal{D}_\lambda^\mathsf{f}$ and a random vector of bits.
- For $\ell \in [L]$ we define

$$\mathcal{H}_\ell^b := (\mathbf{M}_0^\mathsf{f}, \mathsf{E}(\mathbf{M}^\mathsf{f}, b), \alpha_1^\mathsf{f}, \ldots, \alpha_\ell^\mathsf{f}, \alpha_{\ell+1}^\mathsf{kg}, \ldots, \alpha_L^\mathsf{kg}).$$

We will proceed proving that

$$\mathcal{E}^0 \sim_\Lambda \mathcal{H}_0^0 \sim_\Lambda \mathcal{H}_1^0 \sim_\Lambda \ldots \sim_\Lambda \mathcal{H}_L^0 \sim_\Lambda \mathcal{H}_L^1 \sim_\Lambda \ldots \sim_\Lambda \mathcal{H}_1^1 \sim_\Lambda \mathcal{H}_0^1 \sim_\Lambda \mathcal{E}^1$$

through a series of smaller claims. In the remainder of the proof Λ refers to the set in Lemma 3.1.

- $\mathcal{E}^0 \sim_\Lambda \mathcal{H}_0^0$: if this were not the case we would be able to distinguish $\mathbf{M}_0^{\mathrm{kg}}$ from $\mathbf{M}_0^{\mathrm{f}}$ for some of the values in the set Λ thus contradicting Lemma 3.1.
- $\mathcal{H}_{\ell-1}^0 \sim_\Lambda \mathcal{H}_\ell^0$ for $\ell \in [L]$: assume by contradiction this statement is false for some $\ell \in [L]$. That is

$$(\mathbf{M}_0^{\mathrm{f}}, \mathsf{E}(\mathbf{M}_0^{\mathrm{f}}, b), \alpha_1^{\mathrm{f}}, \ldots, \alpha_{\ell-1}^{\mathrm{f}}, \alpha_\ell^{\mathrm{kg}}, \ldots, \alpha_L^{\mathrm{kg}})$$
$$\not\sim_\Lambda$$
$$(\mathbf{M}_0^{\mathrm{f}}, \mathsf{E}(\mathbf{M}_0^{\mathrm{f}}, b), \alpha_1^{\mathrm{f}}, \ldots, \alpha_\ell^{\mathrm{f}}, \alpha_{\ell+1}^{\mathrm{kg}}, \ldots, \alpha_L^{\mathrm{kg}})$$

  Recall that, by definition, the elements of $\alpha_\ell^{\mathrm{kg}}$ are all encryptions whereas the elements of α_ℓ^{f} are all randomly distributed values. This contradicts the semantic security of the scheme PKE (by a standard hybrid argument on the number of ciphertexts).
- $\mathcal{H}_L^0 \sim_\Lambda \mathcal{H}_L^1$: the distributions associated to these two hybrids are identical. In fact, notice the only difference between these two hybrids is in the second component: $\mathsf{E}(\mathbf{M}^{\mathrm{f}}, 0)$ in $\mathcal{H}_L^0$ and $\mathsf{E}(\mathbf{M}^{\mathrm{f}}, 1)$ in $\mathcal{H}_L^1$. As observed above $\mathsf{E}(\mathbf{M}^{\mathrm{f}}, b)$ is uniformly distributed, which proves the claim.

All the claims above can be proven analogously for $\mathcal{E}^1, \mathcal{H}_0^1$ and $\mathcal{H}_\ell^1$-s.

$\square$

B.2   Quasi-constant Multiplicative Depth

Lemma B.2 ([Raz87]). *Let C be an $\mathsf{AC}_\mathsf{Q}^0[2]$ circuit of depth d. Then there exists a randomized circuit $C' \in \mathsf{AC}_{CM}^0[2]$ such that, for all x,*

$$\Pr[C'(x) \neq C(x)] \leq \epsilon,$$

where $\epsilon = O(1)$. The circuit C' uses $O(n)$ random bits and its representation can be computed in NC^0 from a representation of C.

Proof. Consider a circuit $C \in \mathsf{AC}_\mathsf{Q}^0[2]$ and let $K = O(1)$ be the total number of AND and OR gates with non-constant fan-in. We can replace every OR gate of fan-in $m = \omega(1)$ with a randomized "gadget" that takes in input m additional random bits and computes the function

$$\hat{g}_{\mathsf{OR}}(x_1, \ldots, x_m; r_1, \ldots, r_m) := \sum_{i \in [m]} x_i r_i.$$

This function can be implemented in constant multiplicative depth with one XOR gate and m AND gates of fan-in two. Let $\mathbf{x} = (x_1, \ldots, x_m)$ and $\mathbf{r} = (r_1, \ldots, r_m)$. The probabilistic gadget $\hat{g}_{\mathsf{OR}}$ has one-sided error. if $x_i = 0$ (i.e. if $\mathsf{OR}(\mathbf{x}) = 0$) then $\Pr[\hat{g}_{\mathsf{OR}}(\mathbf{x}; \mathbf{r}) = 0] = 1$; otherwise $\Pr[\hat{g}_{\mathsf{OR}}(\mathbf{x}; \mathbf{r}) = 1] = \frac{1}{2}$.

In a similar fashion, we can replace every unbounded fan-in AND gate with a randomized gadget in computing

$$\hat{g}_{\mathsf{AND}}(x_1, \ldots, x_m; r_1, \ldots, r_m) := 1 - \sum_{i \in [m]} (1 - x_i) r_i \, .$$

This gadget can also be implemented in constant-multiplicative depth and has one-sided error $1/2$. Finally, by applying the union bound we can observe that $\Pr[C'(x) \neq C(x)] \leq \epsilon$ for a constant ϵ, because we have only a constant number of gates to be replaced with gadgets for $\hat{g}_{\mathsf{OR}}$ or $\hat{g}_{\mathsf{AND}}$.

We only provide the intuition for why the transformations above can be carried out in NC^0. Assume the encoding of a circuit as a list of gates in the form $(g, t_g, in_1, \ldots, in_m)$ where g and t are respectively the index of the output wire of the gate and its type (possibly of the form "input" or "random input") and the in_i-s are the indices of the input wire of g. The transformation from C to C' needs to simply copy all the items in the list except for the gates of unbounded fan-in. We will assume the encoding conventions of C always puts these gates at the end of the list[20]. For each of such gates the transformation circuit needs to: add appropriate $r_1, \ldots, r_m$ to the list, add m AND gates and one XOR, possibly (if we are transforming an AND gate) add negation gates. All this can be carried out based on wire connections and the type of the gate (a constant-size string) and thus in NC^0.

□

In the construction above, we built C' by replacing every gate $g \in \mathsf{S}_{\omega(1)}(C)$ (as in Definition A.4) with a (randomized) gadget G_g. The output of each of these gadgets will be useful in order to keep the low complexity of the decryption algorithm in our next homomorphic encryption scheme. We shall use an "expanded" version of C', the multi-output circuit C'_{exp}.

Definition B.1 (Expanded Approximating Function). *Let C be a circuit in $\mathsf{AC}^0_Q[2]$ and let C' be a circuit as in the proof of Lemma B.2. We denote by $G_g(\mathbf{x}; \mathbf{r})$ the output of the gadget G_g when C' is evaluated on inputs $(\mathbf{x}; \mathbf{r})$. On input $(\mathbf{x}; \mathbf{r})$, the multi-output circuit C'_{exp} output $C'(\mathbf{x}; \mathbf{r})$ together with the outputs of the $O(1)$ gadgets G_g for each $g \in \mathsf{S}_{\omega(1)}(C)$. Finally, we denote with $\mathsf{GenApproxFun}$ the algorithm computing a representation of C'_{exp} from a representation of C.*

---

[20] This allows our NC^0 circuit to "know" which gates to copy and which ones to transform based on their position only.

Lemma B.3. *There exists a deterministic algorithm* DecodeApprox *computable in* $\mathsf{AC}^0[2]$ *with the following properties. For every circuit C in* $\mathsf{AC}^0_Q[2]$ *computing the function f, there exists* $\mathbf{aux}_f \in \{0,1\}^{O(1)}$ *such that for all* $\mathbf{x} \in \{0,1\}^n$

$$\Pr[\mathsf{DecodeApprox}(\mathbf{aux}_f, C'_{exp}(\mathbf{x}; \mathbf{r}^{(1)}), \ldots, C'_{exp}(\mathbf{x}; \mathbf{r}^{(s)})) = C(\mathbf{x})] \geq 1 - \mathsf{neg}(s),$$

where C' is an approximating circuit as in Lemma B.2, the probability is taken over the uniformly distributed bit vectors $\mathbf{r}^{(i)}$-s for $i \in [s]$, C'_{exp} is as in Definition B.1. Finally, there exists a function GenDecodeAux *that computes* $\mathbf{aux}_f$ *from a representation of C in* NC^0.

Proof. Before we provide a construction for DecodeApprox, let us observe how we can amplify the error of C'. Consider for example a gadget $\hat{g}_{\mathsf{OR}}$ constructed as in the proof of Lemma B.2, approximating an OR gate in C. If we repeat the execution of the gadget s times, every time using fresh random bit vectors $\mathbf{r}'^{(1)}, \ldots, \mathbf{r}'^{(s)}$, then we can correctly compute $\mathsf{OR}(\mathbf{x}')$ with overwhelming probability. Define $h_{\mathsf{OR}}(\mathbf{x}'; \mathbf{r}'^{(1)}, \ldots, \mathbf{r}'^{(s)}) := \mathsf{OR}(\hat{g}_{\mathsf{OR}}(\mathbf{x}; \mathbf{r}'^{(1)}), \ldots, \hat{g}_{\mathsf{OR}}(\mathbf{x}'; \mathbf{r}'^{(s)}))$. Clearly $\Pr[h_{\mathsf{OR}}(\mathbf{x}'; \mathbf{r}'^{(1)}, \ldots, \mathbf{r}'^{(s)}) = \mathsf{OR}(\mathbf{x}')] \geq 1 - 2^{-s}$. In a similar fashion we can define $h_{\mathsf{AND}}(\mathbf{x}'; \mathbf{r}'^{(1)}, \ldots, \mathbf{r}'^{(s)}) := \mathsf{AND}(\hat{g}_{\mathsf{AND}}(\mathbf{x}; \mathbf{r}'^{(1)}), \ldots, \hat{g}_{\mathsf{AND}}(\mathbf{x}'; \mathbf{r}'^{(s)}))$. It holds that $\Pr[h_{\mathsf{AND}}(\mathbf{x}'; \mathbf{r}'^{(1)}, \ldots, \mathbf{r}'^{(s)}) = \mathsf{AND}(\mathbf{x}')] \geq 1 - 2^{-s}$.

If C' were composed by a single gadget $\hat{g}_{\mathsf{OR}}$ (resp. $\hat{g}_{\mathsf{AND}}$) we could just let DecodeApprox be the same as h_{OR} (resp. h_{AND}) and we would be done. To deal with multiple gadgets, however, we need a more general approach. Consider some ordering on the gates in $S_{\omega(1)}$, i.e. let $S_{\omega(1)} = \{g_1, \ldots, g_K\}$. For sake of presentation, assume there are only gadgets approximating OR gates and let us temporarily ignore $\mathbf{aux}_f$. We can write each of the $C'_{exp}(\mathbf{x}; \mathbf{r}^{(j)})$ input to DecodeApprox as $(z^{(j)}, y_1^{(j)}, \ldots, y_K^{(j)})$ where $z^{(j)}$ is the output of $C'(\mathbf{x}, \mathbf{r}^{(j)})$ and $y_i^{(j)}$ is the output of the gadget corresponding to g_i when provided random bits from $\mathbf{r}^{(j)}$. Define y_i^* as $y_i^* := \mathsf{OR}(y_i^{(1)}, \ldots, y_i^{(s)})$. We then let the output of DecodeApprox be $z^{\hat{j}}$ where $\hat{j}$ is such that for all $i \in [K]$ it is the case that $y_i^{(\hat{j})} = y_i^*$. We let DecodeApprox output an arbitrary value if such $\hat{j}$ does not exist. However we can prove (Lemma B.4) that $\hat{j}$ exists with overwhelming probability. Denote by $V_{C,\mathbf{x}}(g_i)$ the value of the output wire of g_i when evaluating C on input $\mathbf{x}$. Clearly, by construction of C'_{exp}, $\Pr[z^{(\hat{j})} = C(\mathbf{x})] \geq \Pr[\forall i \; y_i^{(\hat{j})} = V_{C,\mathbf{x}}(g_i)]$ and by the proof of Lemma B.4 we can show that the right hand side probability is overwhelming.

To generalize this same approach to the scenario including both OR and AND gadgets we let the string $\mathbf{aux}_f$ include information on the type of gates in $S_{\omega(1)}$. This way DecodeApprox can use $\hat{g}_{\mathsf{OR}}$ or $\hat{g}_{\mathsf{AND}}$ accordingly. Clearly the representation of $\mathbf{aux}_f$ can be computed by a representation of C in NC^0.

$\square$

Lemma B.4. $\Pr[\exists \hat{j} \; \forall i \; y_i^{(\hat{j})} = y_i^*] \geq 1 - \mathsf{neg}(s).$

Proof. Let $\mathsf{S}_{\omega(1)} = \{g_1, \ldots, g_K\}$ and $V_{C,\mathbf{x}}(g_i)$ for $i \in [K]$ defined as in the proof of Lemma B.3. We have that

$$\Pr[\exists \hat{j} \ \forall i \ y_i^{(\hat{j})} = y_i^*] \geq \Pr[(\exists \hat{j} \ \forall i \ y_i^{(\hat{j})} = y_i^*) \wedge \ \forall i \ y_i^* = V_{C,\mathbf{x}}(g_i)]$$

$$= \Pr[\exists \hat{j} \ \forall i \ y_i^{(\hat{j})} = V_{C,\mathbf{x}}(g_i)] \Pr[\forall i \ y_i^* = V_{C,\mathbf{x}}(g_i)]$$

We now bound each of the two probabilities in the last product. Denote by $\mathcal{E}_{i,j}$ the event "$y_i^{(j)} = V_{C,\mathbf{x}}(g_i)$" and by $\overline{\mathcal{E}}_{i,j}$ its negation. Observe that

Remark B.1 (Efficiency of HE$'$ *in Sect. 3.3).* Given in input a function f not necessarily of constant multiplicative depth, GenApproxFun returns a function f' of constant multiplicative depth that approximates it. As stated in Lemma B.2, GenApproxFun is computable in NC^0 and so is GenDecodeAux. The function SampleAuxRandomness in AC$^0_{\mathrm{CM}}[2]$ and EvalApprox makes parallel invocations to HE.Eval which is computable in AC$^0_{\mathrm{CM}}[2]$ when provided in input a function in AC$^0_{\mathrm{CM}}[2]$ (Theorem 3.3). This fact will be useful when showing the completeness of the verifiable computation constructions in Sect. 4.

C   Proofs for Verifiable Computation Constructions

The following two auxiliary lemmas guarantee that the constructions in Figs. 2 and 3 are computable in AC$^0[2]$. We refer the reader to [Hag91, MV91] for the proof Lemma C.1.

Lemma C.1. [Hag91, MV91] *There are uniform* AC^0 *circuits* $C : \{0,1\}^{\mathsf{poly}(l)} \to [l]^l$ *of size* $\mathsf{poly}(l)$ *and depth* $O(1)$ *whose output distribution have statistical distance* $\leq 2^{-l}$ *from the uniform distribution over permutations of* $[l]$.

Lemma C.2. *There are uniform* AC$^0[2]$ *circuits* $C : [l]^l \times \{0,1\}^l \to \{0,1\}^l$ *of size* $O(l^2)$ *where* $C(\pi, (x_1, \ldots, x_l)) = (\pi(1), \ldots, \pi(l))$ *and* π *is a permutation.*

Proof. Let $\mathbf{x} = (x_1, \ldots, x_l)$ the bits to permute and let π be a permutation If π is represented as a permutation matrix with rows $\mathbf{r}_1, \ldots, \mathbf{r}_l$, we can permute $\mathbf{x}$ by simply performing l parallel inner products $\langle \mathbf{x}, \mathbf{r}_i \rangle$-s, which is in AC$^0[2]$. We now describe how to generate the permutation matrix from a binary representations $x_1, \ldots, x_{\lg(l)}$ of the integers in $[l]$. Let $f_i : \{0,1\}^{\lg(l)} \to \{0,1\}^l$ be the function that computes the i-th row of the permutation matrix. We can define f_i as follows:

$$f_i(x_1, \ldots, x_{\lg(l)}) := \mathsf{eq}([i-1]_2, (x_1, \ldots, x_{\lg(l)})),$$

where $[i-1]_2$ is the binary representation of $i-1$ and eq returns 1 if its two inputs (each of lenght $\lg(l)$) are equal. The function f_i is clearly in AC$^0[2]$.

$\square$

C.1   One-time scheme

Remark C.1 (On deterministic homomorphic evaluation). As pointed out in [CKV10], one requirement for the approach in Fig. 2 to work is for the homomorphic evaluation to be deterministic. We point out that once $\hat{r}_{aux}$ are fixed once and for all the homomorphic evaluation in VC.Compute is deterministic.

Lemma C.3 (Completeness of $\mathcal{VC}$). *The verifiable computation scheme $\mathcal{VC}$ in Fig. 2 has overwhelming completeness (Definition A.10) for the class $\mathsf{AC}^0_Q[2]$.*

Proof. The proof is straightforward and stems directly from the homomorphic properties of HE' (Theorem 3.4). In fact, by construction and by definition of HE' (Sect. 3.3), the distribution of the $\hat{w}_i$-s is identical to $\mathsf{HE'.Eval}_{pk}(f, \hat{r}_i)$. Analogously, the distribution of $\hat{y}_i$-s is identical to $\mathsf{HE'.Eval}_{pk}(f, \hat{z}_i)$.

□

Lemma C.4 (One-time Soundness). *Under the assumption that $\mathsf{NC}^1 \subsetneq \oplus\mathsf{L/poly}$ the scheme in Fig. 2 is $(1,1)$-sound (one time secure) against NC^1 adversaries whenever t is chosen to be $\omega(\log(\lambda))$.*

Proof. We follow the same proof structure as in the proof of Lemma 12 in [CKV10]. We will keep part of the analysis informal, emphasizing why this proof still works for low-depth circuits. We refer the reader to [CKV10] for further details.

The following observation will be crucial in the rest of the proof. Notice that, by construction and by definition of HE' (Sect. 3.3), the distribution of the $\hat{w}_i$-s is identical to $\mathsf{HE'.Eval}_{pk}(f, \hat{r}_i)$. Analogously, the distribution of $\hat{y}_i$-s is identical to $\mathsf{HE'.Eval}_{pk}(f, \hat{z}_i)$.

Consider an NC^1 adversary $\mathcal{A}^*$ that cheats with non-negligible probability in the one-time security experiment $\mathbf{Exp}_A^{\mathsf{Verif}}[\mathcal{VC}, f, \lambda, 1, 1]$ (Definition A.11). Let $(\hat{r}_1, \ldots, \hat{r}_t)$ be the independent copies of $\mathsf{HE'.Enc}_{pk_W}(\bar{0})$ and $(\hat{r}_{t+1}, \ldots, \hat{r}_{2t})$ the t independent copies of $\mathsf{HE'.Enc}_{pk_W}(x)$ as above. Whenever the verification algorithm accepts, the adversary must have responded correctly on $\hat{r}_1, \ldots, \hat{r}_t$ and incorrectly (and consistently) on $\hat{r}_{t+1}, \ldots, \hat{r}_{2t}$. Our goal is to bound the probability that the adversary succeeds in doing that.

First, notice that the view of the adversary is $(pk_W, \hat{r}_1, \ldots, \hat{r}_{2t})$, and identical to $(pk_W, \mathsf{HE'.Enc}_{pk_W}(\bar{0})^t, \mathsf{HE'.Enc}_{pk_W}(x)^t)$. By semantic security of the homomorphic encryption scheme, there exists an infinitely large set of parameters Λ such that $(pk_W, \mathsf{HE'.Enc}_{pk_W}(\bar{0})^t, \mathsf{HE'.Enc}_{pk_W}(x)^t) \sim_\Lambda (pk_W, \mathsf{HE'.Enc}_{pk_W}(\bar{0})^{2t})$. Consider a modified game where the adversary receives $(pk_W, \mathsf{HE'.Enc}_{pk_W}(\bar{0})^{2t})$. Denote by p the probability that the adversary succeeds in this game. By computational indistinguishability we have

$$\Pr[\mathcal{A}^* \text{ is correct on } (\hat{r}_1, \ldots, \hat{r}_t) \text{ and incorrect on } (\hat{r}_{t+1}, \ldots, \hat{r}_{2t})] \leq p + \mathsf{neg}(\lambda)$$

for all $\lambda \in \Lambda$. This inequality holds because we can test in NC^1 whether $\mathcal{A}^*$ cheats only on $(\hat{r}_{t+1}, \ldots, \hat{r}_{2t})$. Therefore, if the adversary's behavior differed significantly between the two games, one would be able to break the semantic security of the homomorphic scheme. Here we made use of the third fact in Lemma A.1.

We now proceed to upper bound p. Observe that

$$p = \Pr[\mathcal{A}^* \text{ is correct on } (\hat{z}_{\pi(1)}, \ldots, \hat{z}_{\pi(t)}) \text{ and incorrect on } (\hat{z}_{\pi(t+1)}, \ldots, \hat{z}_{\pi(2t)})]$$

where the $\hat{z}_{\pi(i)}$-s are defined as in Fig. 2. Because of Lemma C.1 that the distribution of π is statistically indistinguishable from that of a uniformly random permutation. Also, observe that the answers $\hat{y}_i$ of the adversary are independent of π. We can then conclude that $p \leq \frac{1}{\binom{2t}{t}} + \mathsf{neg}(t)$, which concludes the security analysis.

$\square$

C.2   Reusable scheme

Let $\mathcal{VC}$ be the verifiable computation scheme defined in Figure 2. The reusable verifiable computation scheme $\overline{\mathcal{VC}}$ = $(\overline{\mathsf{VC}}.\mathsf{KeyGen}, \overline{\mathsf{VC}}.\mathsf{ProbGen}, \overline{\mathsf{VC}}.\mathsf{Compute}, \overline{\mathsf{VC}}.\mathsf{Verify})$ is defined as follows.

- $\overline{\mathsf{VC}}.\mathsf{KeyGen}(1^\lambda, f) \to (\mathsf{pk_W}, \mathsf{sk_D})$: The key generation stage is the same as in $\mathcal{VC}$.
- $\overline{\mathsf{VC}}.\mathsf{ProbGen}_{\mathsf{sk_D}}(x) \to (\overline{q_x}, \overline{s_x})$:
    1. $(q_x, s_x) \leftarrow \mathsf{VC}.\mathsf{ProbGen}_{\mathsf{sk_D}}(x)$;
    2. Compute a fresh pair of keys $(\mathsf{pk}_x, \mathsf{sk}_x) \leftarrow \mathsf{HE}.\mathsf{Keygen}(1^\lambda)$;
    3. Compute $\hat{q}_x \leftarrow \mathsf{HE}.\mathsf{Enc}_{\mathsf{pk}_x}(q_x)$;
    4. $\overline{q_x} \leftarrow (\mathsf{pk}_x, \hat{q}_x)$; $\overline{s_x} \leftarrow (s_x, \mathsf{sk}_x)$
- $\overline{\mathsf{VC}}.\mathsf{Compute}_{\mathsf{pk_W}}(\overline{q_x}) \to \overline{a_x}$:
    1. $\hat{a}_x \leftarrow \mathsf{HE}.\mathsf{Eval}_{\mathsf{pk}_x}(\mathsf{VC}.\mathsf{Compute}(\cdot, f), \hat{q}_x)$.
    2. $\overline{a_x} \leftarrow \hat{a}_x$.
- $\overline{\mathsf{VC}}.\mathsf{Verify}_{\mathsf{sk_D}}(\overline{s_x}, \overline{a_x})$:
    1. $a_x \leftarrow \mathsf{HE}.\mathsf{Dec}_{\mathsf{sk}_x}(\hat{a}_x)$.
    2. return $\mathsf{VC}.\mathsf{Verify}_{\mathsf{sk_D}}(s_x, a_x)$.

Fig. 3. Transformation from one-time $\mathcal{VC}$ scheme to a *reusable* $\mathcal{VC}$ scheme

The following is a proof of the completeness of $\overline{\mathcal{VC}}$.

Proof (Of Theorem 4.1). The completeness of the reusable scheme follows directly from the completeness of the one-time scheme $\mathcal{VC}$ and the homomorphic properties of HE. Notice that we can use HE.Eval to homomorphically compute VC.Compute as the latter carries out a computation in $\mathsf{AC}^0_{\mathsf{CM}}[2]$ (although it is *approximating* a computation in $\mathsf{AC}^0_{\mathsf{Q}}[2]$).

$\square$

The following is a restatement of Theorem 4.2.

Theorem C.1 (Many-Times Soundness). *Under the assumption that* $\mathsf{NC}^1 \subsetneq \oplus\mathsf{L}/\mathsf{poly}$ *the scheme* $\overline{\mathcal{VC}}$ *in Fig. 3 is* $(O(1), \mathsf{poly}(\lambda))$*-sound (many-times secure) against* NC^1 *adversaries whenever* t *is chosen to be* $\omega(\log(\lambda))$ *in the underlying scheme* $\mathcal{VC}$.

Proof. By Lemma C.4 there exists an infinite set $\Lambda \subseteq \mathbb{N}$ of security parameters for which $\mathcal{VC}$ "is secure". By the proof of Lemma C.4, this set is also the set of parameters where the somewhat homomorphic encryption scheme HE "is secure". We will show that for all values in this same set Λ, the probability of success of any NC^1 adversary in $\mathbf{Exp}_A^{\mathsf{Verif}}[\overline{\mathcal{VC}}, f, \lambda, O(1), \mathsf{poly}(\lambda)]$ is negligible.

Assume by contradiction there exists an NC^1 adversary $\mathcal{A}^*$ that achieves non-negligible advantage in $\mathbf{Exp}_A^{\mathsf{Verif}}[\overline{\mathcal{VC}}, f, \lambda, O(1), \mathsf{poly}(\lambda)]$ for some $\lambda \in \Lambda$.

Claim: If $\overline{\mathcal{VC}}$ **is not secure for some** $\lambda^* \in \Lambda$ **then we can break the one-time security of** $\mathcal{VC}$. Let $l = O(1)$ be the number of rounds in the many-time soundness experiment for $\overline{\mathcal{VC}}$. Consider the following NC^1 adversary $\mathcal{A}_1$ for the experiment $\mathbf{Exp}_A^{\mathsf{Verif}}[\mathcal{VC}, f, \lambda, 1, 1]$:

- $\mathcal{A}_1$ obtains a pair a public key pk_W and sends it to $\mathcal{A}^*$;
- For all rounds $i \in \{1, \ldots, l-1\}$, $\mathcal{A}_1$ replies to $\mathcal{A}^*$ queries by generating a fresh pair of keys $(\mathsf{pk}, \mathsf{sk})$ and sending back encryptions of $\mathsf{HE.Enc}_\mathsf{pk}(\bar{0})$;
- At round l, $\mathcal{A}_1$ responds to all input queries but the last one as above. This, by experiment definition, is the input where $\mathcal{A}^*$ will try to cheat; we denote this input by x^*. Now $\mathcal{A}_1$ sends x^* as the only input query in the one-time security experiment and will receive back q^*. It will then obtain a fresh pair of keys $(\mathsf{pk}^*, \mathsf{sk}^*)$ and send $\mathsf{HE.Enc}_{\mathsf{pk}^*}(q^*)$ to $\mathcal{A}^*$.
- $\mathcal{A}^*$ will respond with $\hat{a}^*$ and $\mathcal{A}_1$ will send $\mathsf{HE.Dec}_{\mathsf{sk}^*}(\hat{a})$ to the challenger for one-time security experiment.

The advantage of $\mathcal{A}_1$ depends on how likely is $\mathcal{A}^*$ can successfully cheat in that interaction. Let p be the advantage of $\mathcal{A}_1$ in the one-time security experiment. Clearly, if p is close to the advantage of $\mathcal{A}^*$ in the many-times security experiment $\mathcal{A}_1$ breaks the security of the one-time scheme.

Claim: the advantage of $\mathcal{A}_1$ **is negligibly close to that of** $\mathcal{A}^*$ **in the many-time security game for security parameter** λ^*. We can prove this by relying on the semantic security of the homomorphic encryption and on a hybrid argument.

Let $L = lm$, the total number of input queries in the many-times security experiment. We now define the hybrids $H^{(j)}$ with $j \in \{0, \ldots, L\}$. We define $H^{(0)}$ to be the exactly the many-time security experiment. For $j \in [L]$ we define $H^{(j)}$ to be an experiment where we respond to input queries with $\mathsf{HE.Enc}_{\mathsf{pk}_f}(\bar{0})$ where pk_f is a fresh public key up to input query j and behaves the many-time security experiment from input query $j+1$ on. Notice that $H^{(L)}$ corresponds to the interaction with $\mathcal{A}_1$ above.

Denote by $A^{(j)}$ the output distribution of $\mathcal{A}^*$ when interacting with $H^{(j)}$. Intuitively, if the advantage of the $\mathcal{A}_1$ in the one-time experiment is significantly different from the advantage of $\mathcal{A}^*$ in the many-times security games, then $A^{(0)}$

and $A^{(L)}$ are not Λ-computationally indistinguishable. Therefore (by Lemma A.1), there exists $j \in [L]$ such that $A^{(j-1)} \not\sim_\Lambda A^{(j)}$.

Claim: If there exists $j \in [L]$ such that $A^{(j-1)} \not\sim_\Lambda A^{(j)}$ then we can break the semantic security of HE. Consider the following NC^1 adversary $\mathcal{A}_{CPA}$ which receives in input a "challenge" public key pk^*. $\mathcal{A}_{CPA}$ will interact with $\mathcal{A}^*$ simulating $H^{(j)}$ until receiving input query x_j. At this point it will compute q_j from $VC.ProbGen(x_j)$ and send to the CPA challenger (see Remark A.1) q_j and $\bar{0}$, receiving back an encryption c^* of either message under the public key pk^*. $\mathcal{A}_{CPA}$ will now send (pk^*, c^*) to $\mathcal{A}^*$ and continue simulating $H^{(j)}$ till the end of the experiment. The adversary $\mathcal{A}_{CPA}$ will check whether $\mathcal{A}^*$ cheated successfully at the end of the experiment and output (in the multiple-message CPA experiment) 1 if that is the case and 0 otherwise. This would allow $\mathcal{A}_{CPA}$ to have a noticeable advantage in the experiment thus breaking the semantic security of HE.

$\square$

D   On Approaches Based on Randomized Encodings

A randomized encoding of a function f is a randomized function $\hat{f}$ such that for any input x, the distribution of $\hat{f}(x)$ reveals $f(x)$, but nothing more about x. We observe that approaches based on low-depth information-theoretic affine randomized encodings (as constructed in [IK00a, IK02, AIK04] or as applied in [SYY99, AIK10, GGH+07]) may be used to obtain results similar to ours. Known ways to construct these tools, however, all seem to have significant limitations, which pushed us to look for different solutions.

EXAMPLE CONSTRUCTIONS. An example construction for homomorphic encryption: the encryptor could send to the evaluator a linearly homomorphic encryption of the inputs and the evaluator could reply with an affine (requiring only linear operations) randomized encoding of f computed on the ciphertexts. Possible constructions for verifiable computation could be based on [AIK10] or using a constant-round variant of [GKR08] for NC^1 circuits together with the approach in [GGH+07].

LIMITATIONS OF CONSTRUCTIONS FROM RE. Such approaches can yield homomorphic encryption for NC^1 circuits and verifiable computation in low-depth. Noticeably, such schemes would be (partly) implementable in NC^0 and the soundness of the (one-time) verifiable computation could hold unconditionally.

In our work, however, we are interested in *compact* homomorphic encryption schemes (where the ciphertexts do not grow in size with each homomorphic operation) and in verifiable computation schemes where the total (online) work of the verifier is approximately linear in the I/O size[21]. When using currently known constructions the techniques mentioned above seem to fail in both respects. One reason for this is that having the verifier (resp. evaluator) compute (resp. send)

---

[21] I.e. the size of the verification circuit should be $O(\text{poly}(\lambda)(n + m))$ where n and m are the size of the input and output respectively.

an *information-theoretic*[22] randomized encoding would require verification time (resp. communication complexity) to be at best $\Omega(n^2)$ (resp. $\Omega(2^d)$, where d is the depth of the fan-in two evaluation circuit). These lower bounds refer to the complexity of known constructions for information-theoretic randomized encodings [AIK04], which stem from two main approaches: the branching-program based one in [IK00a] and the "Yao-like" in [IK02] (Sect. 3). The former constructs randomized encodings computable in time $\Omega(\ell^2)$ and of the same size, where ℓ is the size of the (polynomial-size) branching program describing f (the related approach in [GGH+07] has output size and computation time of ℓ^3). The latter describes randomized encodings of size 2^d and computable in s^2 for circuits of size s and (logarithmic) depth d. The complexity of these encodings can be improved under the existence of PRGs with linear stretch (e.g. [AIK10] uses this fact to build verifiable computation with low online communication). Unfortunately it is not known how to build such primitives under the assumption $NC^1 \subsetneq \oplus L/poly$ [DVV16].

It would be worth investigating exactly the extent to which we can exploit such techniques in a context where low communication complexity and low sequential verification complexity are not constraints. We leave this as an open problem. We finally point out that some of these depth-reduction techniques can be applied to our results (naturally, with overheads similar to the ones pointed out above).

References

[ACK+02] Anderson, D.P., Cobb, J., Korpela, E., Lebofsky, M., Werthimer, D.: SETI@home: an experiment in public-resource computing. Commun. ACM **45**(11), 56–61 (2002)

[AIK04] Applebaum, B., Ishai, Y., Kushilevitz, E.: Cryptography in NC^0. In: Proceedings of the 45th Annual IEEE Symposium on Foundations of Computer Science, pp. 166–175 (2004)

[AIK10] Applebaum, B., Ishai, Y., Kushilevitz, E.: From secrecy to soundness: efficient verification via secure computation. In: Abramsky, S., Gavoille, C., Kirchner, C., Meyer auf der Heide, F., Spirakis, P.G. (eds.) ICALP 2010. LNCS, vol. 6198, pp. 152–163. Springer, Heidelberg (2010). https://doi. org/10.1007/978-3-642-14165-2_14

[AM12] Azar, P.D., Micali, S.: Rational proofs. In: Proceedings of the Forty-Fourth Annual ACM Symposium on Theory of Computing, pp. 1017–1028. ACM (2012)

[AM13] Azar, P.D., Micali, S.: Super-efficient rational proofs. In: Proceedings of the Fourteenth ACM Conference on Electronic Commerce, pp. 29–30. ACM (2013)

[BCI+13] Bitansky, N., Chiesa, A., Ishai, Y., Paneth, O., Ostrovsky, R.: Succinct non-interactive arguments via linear interactive proofs. In: Sahai, A. (ed.) TCC 2013. LNCS, vol. 7785, pp. 315–333. Springer, Heidelberg (2013). https:// doi.org/10.1007/978-3-642-36594-2_18

---

[22] These observations would not hold for the computational setting, which is out of the scope of this paper.

[BP11]   Boyar, J., Peralta, R.C.: A depth-16 circuit for the AES S-box. IACR Cryptology ePrint Archive (2011)

[BRSV17] Ball, M., Rosen, A., Sabin, M., Vasudevan, P.N.: Average-case fine-grained hardness. In: Electronic Colloquium on Computational Complexity (ECCC), vol. 24, p. 39 (2017)

[BV14]   Brakerski, Z., Vaikuntanathan, V.: Efficient fully homomorphic encryption from (standard) lwe. SIAM J. Comput. 43(2), 831–871 (2014)

[CG15]   Campanelli, M., Gennaro, R.: Sequentially composable rational proofs. In: Khouzani, M.H.R., Panaousis, E., Theodorakopoulos, G. (eds.) GameSec 2015. LNCS, vol. 9406, pp. 270–288. Springer, Cham (2015). https://doi.org/10.1007/978-3-319-25594-1_15

[CG17]   Campanelli, M., Gennaro, R.: Efficient rational proofs for space bounded computations. In: Rass, S., An, B., Kiekintveld, C., Fang, F., Schauer, S. (eds.) International Conference on Decision and Game Theory for Security, vol. 10575, pp. 53–73. Springer, Cham (2017). https://doi.org/10.1007/978-3-319-68711-7_4

[CKV10]   Chung, K.-M., Kalai, Y., Vadhan, S.: Improved delegation of computation using fully homomorphic encryption. In: Rabin, T. (ed.) CRYPTO 2010. LNCS, vol. 6223, pp. 483–501. Springer, Heidelberg (2010). https://doi.org/10.1007/978-3-642-14623-7_26

[CM97]   Cachin, C., Maurer, U.: Unconditional security against memory-bounded adversaries. In: Kaliski, B.S. (ed.) CRYPTO 1997. LNCS, vol. 1294, pp. 292–306. Springer, Heidelberg (1997). https://doi.org/10.1007/BFb0052243

[CMT12]   Cormode, G., Mitzenmacher, M., Thaler, J.: Practical verified computation with streaming interactive proofs. In: Proceedings of the 3rd Innovations in Theoretical Computer Science Conference, pp. 90–112. ACM (2012)

[DN92]   Dwork, C., Naor, M.: Pricing via processing or combatting junk mail. In: Brickell, E.F. (ed.) CRYPTO 1992. LNCS, vol. 740, pp. 139–147. Springer, Heidelberg (1993). https://doi.org/10.1007/3-540-48071-4_10

[DVV16]   Degwekar, A., Vaikuntanathan, V., Vasudevan, P.N.: Fine-grained cryptography. In: Robshaw, M., Katz, J. (eds.) CRYPTO 2016. LNCS, vol. 9816, pp. 533–562. Springer, Heidelberg (2016). https://doi.org/10.1007/978-3-662-53015-3_19

[Gen09]   Gentry, C.: A fully homomorphic encryption scheme. Stanford University (2009)

[GGH+07] Goldwasser, S., Gutfreund, D., Healy, A., Kaufman, T., Rothblum, G.N.: Verifying and decoding in constant depth. In: Proceedings of the Thirty-Ninth Annual ACM Symposium on Theory of Computing, pp. 440–449. ACM (2007)

[GGH+16] Garg, S., Gentry, C., Halevi, S., Raykova, M., Sahai, A., Waters, B.: Candidate indistinguishability obfuscation and functional encryption for all circuits. SIAM J. Comput. 45(3), 882–929 (2016)

[GGP10]   Gennaro, R., Gentry, C., Parno, B.: Non-interactive verifiable computing: outsourcing computation to untrusted workers. In: Rabin, T. (ed.) CRYPTO 2010. LNCS, vol. 6223, pp. 465–482. Springer, Heidelberg (2010). https://doi.org/10.1007/978-3-642-14623-7_25

[GGPR13] Gennaro, R., Gentry, C., Parno, B., Raykova, M.: Quadratic span programs and succinct NIZKs without PCPs. In: Johansson, T., Nguyen, P.Q. (eds.) EUROCRYPT 2013. LNCS, vol. 7881, pp. 626–645. Springer, Heidelberg (2013). https://doi.org/10.1007/978-3-642-38348-9_37

[GKR08] Goldwasser, S., Kalai, Y.T., Rothblum, G.N.: Delegating computation: interactive proofs for muggles. In: Proceedings of the Fortieth Annual ACM Symposium on Theory of Computing, pp. 113–122. ACM (2008)

[GMR89] Goldwasser, S., Micali, S., Rackoff, C.: The knowledge complexity of interactive proof systems. SIAM J. Comput. **18**(1), 186–208 (1989)

[Gol01] Goldreich, O.: Foundations of Cryptography: Basic Tools, vol. 1. Cambridge University Press, New York (2001)

[Gol09] Goldreich, O.: Foundations of Cryptography: Basic Applications, vol. 2. Cambridge University Press, New York (2009)

[GR18] Goldreich, O., Rothblum, G.N.: Simple doubly-efficient interactive proof systems for locally-characterizable sets. In: LIPIcs-Leibniz International Proceedings in Informatics, vol. 94. Schloss Dagstuhl-Leibniz-Zentrum fuer Informatik (2018)

[Hag91] Hagerup, T.: Fast parallel generation of random permutations. In: Albert, J.L., Monien, B., Artalejo, M.R. (eds.) ICALP 1991. LNCS, vol. 510, pp. 405–416. Springer, Heidelberg (1991). https://doi.org/10.1007/3-540-54233-7_151

[Has87] Hastad, J.: One-way permutations in NC0. Inf. Process. Lett. **26**(3), 153–155 (1987)

[IK00a] Ishai, Y., Kushilevitz, E.: Randomizing polynomials: a new representation with applications to round-efficient secure computation. In: Proceedings of the 41st Annual Symposium on Foundations of Computer Science, pp. 294–304. IEEE (2000)

[IK02] Ishai, Y., Kushilevitz, E.: Perfect constant-round secure computation via perfect randomizing polynomials. In: Widmayer, P., Eidenbenz, S., Triguero, F., Morales, R., Conejo, R., Hennessy, M. (eds.) ICALP 2002. LNCS, vol. 2380, pp. 244–256. Springer, Heidelberg (2002). https://doi.org/10.1007/3-540-45465-9_22

[Imp95] Impagliazzo, R.: A personal view of average-case complexity. In: Proceedings of Tenth Annual IEEE Structure in Complexity Theory Conference, pp. 134–147. IEEE (1995)

[LTKS15] Luu, L., Teutsch, J., Kulkarni, R., Saxena, P.: Demystifying incentives in the consensus computer. In: Proceedings of the 22nd ACM SIGSAC Conference on Computer and Communications Security, pp. 706–719. ACM (2015)

[Mer78] Merkle, R.C.: Secure communications over insecure channels. Commun. ACM **21**(4), 294–299 (1978)

[MV91] Matias, Y., Vishkin, U.: Converting high probability into nearly-constant time - with applications to parallel hashing. In: Proceedings of the Twenty-third Annual ACM Symposium on Theory of Computing, STOC 1991, pp. 307–316. ACM, New York (1991)

[Raz87] Razborov, A.A.: Lower bounds on the size of bounded depth circuits over a complete basis with logical addition. Math. Notes Acad. Sci. USSR **41**(4), 333–338 (1987)

[SYY99] Sander, T., Young, A., Yung, M.: Non-interactive cryptocomputing for NC1. In: Proceedings of the 40th Annual Symposium on Foundations of Computer Science, p. 554. IEEE Computer Society (1999)

[Yao82] Yao, A.C.: Protocols for secure computations. In: 23rd Annual Symposium on Foundations of Computer Science, SFCS 2008, pp. 160–164. IEEE (1982)

On the Structure of Unconditional UC Hybrid Protocols

Mike Rosulek[1][(✉)] and Morgan Shirley[2]

[1] Oregon State University, Corvallis, USA
rosulekm@eecs.oregonstate.edu
[2] University of Toronto, Toronto, Canada
shirley@cs.toronto.edu

Abstract. We study the problem of secure two-party computation in the presence of a trusted setup. If there is an unconditionally UC-secure protocol for f that makes use of calls to an ideal g, then we say that f *reduces to* g (and write $f \sqsubseteq g$). Some g are *complete* in the sense that *all* functions reduce to g. However, almost nothing is known about the power of an incomplete g in this setting. We shed light on this gap by showing a characterization of $f \sqsubseteq g$ for incomplete g.

Very roughly speaking, we show that f reduces to g if and only if it does so by the simplest possible protocol: one that makes a single call to ideal g and uses no further communication. Furthermore, such simple protocols can be characterized by a natural combinatorial condition on f and g.

Looking more closely, our characterization applies only to a very wide class of f, and only for protocols that are deterministic or logarithmic-round. However, we give concrete examples showing that both of these limitations are inherent to the characterization itself. Functions not covered by our characterization exhibit qualitatively different properties. Likewise, randomized, superlogarithmic-round protocols are qualitatively more powerful than deterministic or logarithmic-round ones.

1 Introduction

In 2-party secure function evaluation (SFE), Alice holds a private input $x \in X$, Bob holds a private input $y \in Y$, and the parties interact to learn $f(x, y)$ for some agreed-upon function $f : X \times Y \to Z$. Each party should learn no more than can be inferred from $f(x, y)$ alone, even when that party behaves adversarially.

Different functions f have different inherent complexities, and one way to compare the "cryptographic complexity" of functions is to use a *reduction*. The most natural reduction from f to g is a secure protocol for f where the parties are allowed to use an ideally-secure black-box for g (ideal here means that this black-box takes inputs from both parties, and reveals only the output of g). Depending on the security required of the protocol for f, we obtain reductions of various strengths that can resolve finer distinctions in cryptographic complexity.

M. Rosulek—Partially supported by NSF awards #114964 & #1617197.

A. Beimel and S. Dziembowski (Eds.): TCC 2018, LNCS 11240, pp. 98–126, 2018.
https://doi.org/10.1007/978-3-030-03810-6_4

Cryptographic Complexity and Related Work. In this work we exclusively focus on reductions between two-party, deterministic SFE functions with constant-size truth tables (meaning the function that is computed does not depend on the security parameter). We consider a reduction defined in terms of UC security [4] against computationally unbounded adversaries. We write $f \sqsubseteq g$ to denote that there is a UC-secure protocol securely realizing f against unbounded adversaries, that makes calls to an ideal g functionality (*i.e.*, a protocol in the "g-hybrid model").

After defining a notion of reducibility, the most natural step is to identify which objects are *complete* for the reduction. A function g is **complete** (under $\sqsubseteq$) if $f \sqsubseteq g$ for all f. Otherwise we say that g is **incomplete**.

Kilian [8] was the first to consider completeness of SFE functionalities, proving that the oblivious transfer function is complete. Although the result predates the UC model, a variant of the construction from [9] is likely to achieve UC security — *i.e.*, oblivious transfer is complete under the $\sqsubseteq$ reduction that we consider in this work. Later work characterized exactly which functions are complete (w.r.t. malicious, unconditional security): for symmetric SFE (where both parties receive the same output) [10], for asymmetric SFE (where only one party receives output) [11], for SFE where parties may receive different outputs [13], and even for randomized SFE functions [12,20].

When one or both of f, g are complete, the question of $f \sqsubseteq g$ is simple to answer. If g is complete, then $f \sqsubseteq g$. If f is complete but g is not, then $f \not\sqsubseteq g$. The goal of this line of work is to therefore **understand when $f \sqsubseteq g$, for f and g which are incomplete.**

Prabhakaran and Rosulek [21] gave an example of four functions that satisfy $f_1 \sqsubset f_2 \sqsubset f_3 \sqsubset f_4$ (where $f \sqsubset g$ means that $f \sqsubseteq g$ but $g \not\sqsubseteq f$). Maji, Prabhakaran and Rosulek [17] extended this result to show an *infinite* strict hierarchy $f_1 \sqsubset f_2 \sqsubset \cdots \sqsubset f_i \sqsubset \cdots$, and also showed an example of a pair of functions that are incomparable ($f \not\sqsubseteq g$ and $g \not\sqsubseteq f$). The same authors in [18] later proved several additional results of the form $f \not\sqsubseteq g$.

These results hint at a rich landscape of complexity with respect to the $\sqsubseteq$ reduction, but fall well short of revealing the entire picture. First, they are not complete characterizations, but give only necessary conditions for $f \sqsubseteq g$. Second, the techniques in these works apply only to f and g that have *semi-honest-secure* protocols. This leaves a large class of functions that are neither complete nor admit any semi-honest protocol (simple characterizations of both properties are known [1,10,14]). A canonical example of such a function is the so-called "spiral" function shown in Fig. 1c. Currently almost nothing is known about reductions involving such intermediate functions.

Other Related Work. We consider a reduction based on UC security against unbounded adversaries. Weaker reductions have been studied, but they do not turn out to illuminate many distinctions in complexity. For example, one may define a reduction based on *polynomial-time* UC security. It turns out that every SFE is either complete or trivial (it reduces to every other function) under this reduction [19].

In this paper we prove qualitative differences in the power of randomized and deterministic protocols, even when realizing deterministic functions using other deterministic functions (*i.e.*, we show specific, deterministic f and g where $f \sqsubseteq g$ via a randomized protocol but not by any deterministic protocol). In the two-party setting, Dodis and Micali [5] show such a separation among *complete* f and g, for a special class of protocols (in which one party does not speak). Beimel and Malkin [2] show specific f and (complete) g for which randomized protocols make exponentially fewer calls to g than deterministic protocols.

2   Overview of Our Results

Scope of Results: Incomplete, Non-Unilateral Functions. As mentioned in the introduction, the question of $f \sqsubseteq g$ is straight-forward when one of $\{f, g\}$ are complete. We therefore focus on characterizing $f \sqsubseteq g$ when both are incomplete.

We say that f is **unilateral** if there exists an input y^* for one of the parties (by symmetry, Bob) such that $f(\cdot, y^*)$ is a constant function. That is, by choosing input y^* Bob can *unilaterally* fix the output of f. We characterize $f \sqsubseteq g$, when f is non-unilateral. In Sect. 7.1 we show an example of unilateral f, g that do *not* obey the characterization, demonstrating that this restriction is tight.

Statement of Main Result. We show a complete and combinatorial characterization of $f \sqsubseteq g$, for a natural class of protocols. For this characterization, identify each function f with its 2-dimensional truth table (rows corresponding to Alice-inputs and columns to Bob-inputs). We say that f **embeds in** g if f appears as a submatrix of g, subject to some other restrictions (essentially, the other parts of g can't "interfere" with the f-submatrix—the formal definition is in Sect. 4). We then prove our main theorem:

Theorem 1. *The following are equivalent, when f and g are incomplete and f is non-unilateral.*

1. $f \sqsubseteq g$ *via a worst-case* $O(\log \kappa)$-*round protocol (where κ is the security parameter).*
2. $f \sqsubseteq g$ *via a deterministic protocol.*
3. $f \sqsubseteq g$ *via a deterministic protocol consisting of a single call to g and no additional communication.*
4. f *embeds in g.*

Technical Approach. The most involved part of our main theorem is proving $(1) \Rightarrow (3)$ and $(2) \Rightarrow (3)$. Intuitively this involves "compressing" an arbitrary protocol for $f \sqsubseteq g$ into a single call to g.

Our first step is to show that every secure protocol for $f \sqsubseteq g$ can be transformed into one with the following **instantaneous** property:

- With overwhelming probability, the protocol terminates immediately following some call to g.

- Strictly before this terminal call to g, the protocol transcript leaks negligible information about either party's inputs.

Our main technical tool is that of *frontier analysis*, which was introduced in [17] and extended in [16]. A *frontier* in the protocol is simply the collection of partial transcripts where some statistical condition is true for the first time. Roughly speaking, we define two frontiers for each party: one expressing "the first time the simulator is likely to extract" and another for "the first time honest parties can reliably predict the final output." We then argue that these frontiers must all be reached simultaneously, with overwhelming probability. As such, these events can happen only as the result of a call to g. Furthermore, the protocol can be safely truncated after reaching the frontiers (since both parties can already predict the final output). The result of truncation is a protocol with the "instantaneous" property described above. We complete the argument by showing how such an instantaneous protocol can be compressed from $O(\log \kappa)$ rounds to one round.

Tightness of the Characterization. Our main theorem does not characterize $f \sqsubseteq g$ when f is unilateral. This restriction is inherent, as we demonstrate with an example in Sect. 7.1. In Sect. 7.2 we also demonstrate an example f and g with the following properties:

1. f does not embed in g. Hence, by the classification theorem, $f \not\sqsubseteq g$ via any deterministic protocol or (randomized) logarithmic-round protocol.
2. $f \sqsubseteq g$ via a randomized protocol whose *expected* round complexity is constant, but whose *worst-case* round complexity is $r(\kappa)$ for any $r(\kappa) = \omega(\log \kappa)$.

This example demonstrates that our main characterization's limitation to $O(\log \kappa)$-round protocols is inherent.

Interestingly, the $\omega(\log \kappa)$-round protocol for $f \sqsubseteq g$ has the *instantaneous* property described above. Hence, the protocol leaks no information about the parties' inputs, until $f(x, y)$ is completely revealed in a single call to g. Yet there is no way to securely compress the protocol to just the "meaningful" call to g. Somehow, it is important that the "output-fixing" round is unpredictable.

Mysteriously, a similar structure appears in the protocols of Gordon *et al.* [6] that achieve fairness. These protocols leak nothing about the inputs until, in some secret round, the output is completely revealed. Analogously, Lindell and Rabin [15] show that the "output-fixing" round in a fair protocol cannot be predictable. We are not sure what fairness has to do with *unfair* multi-party computation with an incomplete hybrid functionality, and leave open this exploration for future work.

Ours is also one of the few examples of a $\omega(1)$ round-complexity lower bound for information-theoretic multi-party computation. Indeed, when g is complete, $f \sqsubseteq g$ is possible in constant rounds, for any f: first, obtain oblivious transfer from g in constant rounds [10,13], and from oblivious transfer obtain f in constant rounds [7].[1]

---

[1] Note that the round complexity of these protocols may depend on f and g (e.g., the circuit depth of f), but is constant with respect to the security parameter since we consider only functions with constant-size truth table.

3   Preliminaries

3.1   Secure Function Evaluation, UC Security

We assume the reader has familiarity with the UC framework (a brief overview is given in Appendix A). In this work we study deterministic 2-party secure function evaluation (SFE), in the universal composability (UC) framework [4] against computationally unbounded adversaries that corrupt parties *statically* (*i.e.*, once and for all before the protocol begins). We consider security-with-abort, meaning that malicious parties are allowed to learn their output first, and delay the honest parties from receiving output (perhaps indefinitely).

We use the following notation:

$f \sqsubseteq g$: there is a secure protocol (UC, unconditional) for f that uses calls to an ideal g (i.e., a secure protocol in the g-hybrid model).

$f \sqsubseteq_1 g$: $f \sqsubseteq g$ via a protocol that makes only a single call to g and uses no additional communication.

3.2   Combinatorial Properties of Complete/Incomplete f

We review some basics of 2-party SFE. Let f be a 2-party SFE with domain $X \times Y$. A fundamental property of SFE has to do with decomposing the function into "rectangles." Define $\text{rect}_f(x,y) = \{x' \mid f(x,y) = f(x',y)\} \times \{y' \mid f(x,y) = f(x,y')\}$. We refer to $\text{rect}_f(x,y)$ as a **rectangle** of f.

The characterization of [in]completeness for 2-party SFE is due to Kilian:

Theorem 2 ([10]). *f is **incomplete** if and only if: for all x, x', y, y',*

$$f(x,y) = f(x',y) = f(x,y') \implies f(x',y') = f(x,y).$$

A useful consequence of Theorem 2 is the following:

Observation 3. *Let f be incomplete. Then for all x,y, the value $\text{rect}_f(x,y)$ is uniquely determined by $f(x,y)$ and just one of $\{x,y\}$. Likewise, $f(x,y)$ is uniquely determined by $\text{rect}_f(x,y)$ and just one of $\{x,y\}$.*

Observation 3 implies that without loss of generality we can think of the parties as computing the function $(x,y) \mapsto \text{rect}_f(x,y)$ instead of the function $f(x,y)$.

Figure 1 shows three example functions, with the partition into rectangles given for the incomplete functions. Note that the second function has 4 rectangles: two rectangles with output 1, and two with output 2.

In this work we restrict our attention to **symmetric functions**, which give the same output $f(x,y)$ to both parties. One could easily consider asymmetric functions $f = (f_A, f_B)$ which give output $f_A(x,y)$ to Alice and $f_B(x,y)$ to Bob. However, a result of Kraschewski and Müller-Quade [13] shows that all incomplete functions (even asymmetric ones) are isomorphic to some symmetric

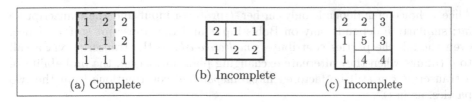

Fig. 1. Example SFE functions.

one.[2] Hence, our restriction to symmetric functions is without loss of generality, and our theorem statements can be interpreted to apply to asymmetric functions as well.

3.3   Properties of g-Hybrid Protocols for Incomplete g

Fix a 2-party protocol π, and let t be a partial transcript (*i.e.*, a prefix of a complete protocol transcript). We use $\Pr_\pi[t|xy]$ to denote the probability of obtaining a protocol transcript with prefix t, when both parties run the protocol honestly with respective inputs x and y.

Write t as a sequence of messages $t = (m_1,\ldots,m_k)$. Suppose Alice sends the odd-numbered messages. Then the choice of the odd-numbered (resp. even-numbered) messages depends only on the previous messages and x (resp. y), but not on y (resp. x). We can therefore write:

$$
\begin{aligned}
\Pr_\pi[t|xy] &= \prod_{i=1}^{k} \Pr_\pi[m_i|xy, m_1 \cdots m_{i-1}] \\
&= \left(\prod_{i \text{ odd}} \Pr_\pi[m_i|x, m_1 \cdots m_{i-1}] \right) \left(\prod_{i \text{ even}} \Pr_\pi[m_i|y, m_1 \cdots m_{i-1}] \right) \\
&\overset{\text{def}}{=} \Pr_\pi[t|x] \Pr_\pi[t|y] \qquad\qquad (\star)
\end{aligned}
$$

Here we are defining $\Pr_\pi[t|x]$ and $\Pr_\pi[t|y]$ to be equal to the parenthesized quantities. Essentially, $\Pr_\pi[t|x]$ is the probability that Alice behaves consistently with t when her input is x.

In the g-Hybrid Model. A similar property also holds when the parties can call an ideal functionality g (*i.e.*, protocols in the g-hybrid model), but only when g is *incomplete*, as we describe below.

When parties invoke g, its output is added to the joint transcript. From Observation 3 this is equivalent to adding $\mathsf{rect}_g(\tilde{x}, \tilde{y})$ to the transcript, where $\tilde{x}$ and $\tilde{y}$ were the inputs that the parties gave to this instance of g. Let $\tilde{X} \times \tilde{Y}$ be a particular rectangle in g. Then when g is incomplete we have:

$$
\Pr[\mathsf{rect}_g(\tilde{x}, \tilde{y}) = \tilde{X} \times \tilde{Y}] = \Pr[\tilde{x} \in \tilde{X}] \Pr[\tilde{y} \in \tilde{Y}]
$$

---

[2] If $f = (f_A, f_B)$ is incomplete then there is a symmetric function g such that (1) $g(x,y)$ can be computed from $x, f_A(x,y)$; (2) $g(x,y)$ can be computed from $y, f_B(x,y)$; (3) $f_A(x,y)$ can be computed from $x, g(x,y)$; (4) $f_B(x,y)$ can be computed from $y, g(x,y)$.

Alice's choice of $\tilde{x}$ depends only on her f-protocol input and the transcript so far; similarly $\tilde{y}$ depends only on Bob's input and the transcript so far. Hence, even though the parties contribute *simultaneously* to the transcript via a call to g (unlike when they alternate exchanging plain messages), the probability of a transcript can still be factored into *independent* contributions from the two parties, as in $(\star)$.

Stateless Parties/Adversaries. The "standard" way of defining a protocol is for each party to initially choose a random tape. Their subsequent behavior is a deterministic function of the random tape, their input, and the transcript so far.

However, $(\star)$ shows that Alice's view (including her private randomness) is independent of Bob's view (including his randomness), given the transcript. Therefore, *any g-hybrid protocol π can be purged of stateful randomness in the following way.* At each step, a stateless party can (1) sample a random tape conditioned on it being consistent with their private input and transcript so far; (2) use that (ephemeral) random tape to choose the next move in the protocol; (3) discard the ephemeral random tape. Note that this transformation may require exponential time, but we consider all parties to have unbounded computation. This transformation *also applies to adversaries*, so without loss of generality we consider only stateless adversaries.

4   Reducibility Characterization

We define the combinatorial condition at the heart of our main theorem. Intuitively, f embeds to g if one can identify a submatrix of g that "looks like" f. Of course, the outputs of f might be renamed relative to g. Such a submatrix property suffices for a semi-honest protocol for f using g, where parties simply use the subset of inputs of g that comprise the f-submatrix. However, such a protocol need not be secure in the presence of *malicious* adversaries, because other inputs of g may "interfere" with the f-submatrix. There are two main things that can go wrong, epitomized in the following examples:

$$f_1 = \begin{bmatrix} 1 & 3 \\ 1 & 4 \\ 2 & 4 \end{bmatrix} \not\sqsubseteq \begin{bmatrix} 1 & 3 & 5 \\ 1 & 4 & 6 \\ 2 & 4 & 7 \end{bmatrix} = g_1; \qquad f_2 = \begin{bmatrix} 1 & 3 \\ 2 & 4 \end{bmatrix} \not\sqsubseteq \begin{bmatrix} 1 & 3 \rightarrow 3 \\ 2 \leftarrow 2 & 4 \end{bmatrix} = g_2$$

Note that f_1 appears as the white submatrix of g_1. However, when a corrupt column-player cheats and uses the shaded column of g_1, he completely learns the row-players input, even though no column of f_1 legally allows this.

Similarly, f_2 appears as a submatrix of g_2. Consider a corrupt column-player who uses the shaded column of g_2. There is no *single* input for f_2 that "explains" the effect of this behavior for all possible inputs of the row-player. Concretely, there is no input of f_2 that guarantees an output in $\{2,3\}$.

The requirements for embedding are formalized in the following definition:

Definition 4. *For two functions α and β we say that α* **leaks no more than** *β if $\beta(y) = \beta(y') \Rightarrow \alpha(y) = \alpha(y')$ for all inputs y, y'. We say that α* **refines** *β if $\beta(y) \in \{\alpha(y), \bot\}$ for all inputs y.*

Let $f : X \times Y \to Z$ and $g : \widehat{X} \times \widehat{Y} \to \widehat{Z}$. Without loss of generality, assume $f(x, y) = \text{rect}_f(x, y)$ and $g(x, y) = \text{rect}_g(x, y)$. We say that f **embeds in** *g if:*

1. *(f appears as a submatrix in g) There exist two injective mappings, $A : X \to \widehat{X}$ and $B : Y \to \widehat{Y}$, and a third mapping, $C : \widehat{Z} \to Z \cup \{\bot\}$, such that $\forall x \in X, y \in Y : f(x, y) = C(g(A(x), B(y)))$.*
2. *(security guarantees) There exist mappings $\widehat{A} : \widehat{X} \to X$ and $\widehat{B} : \widehat{Y} \to Y$ such that the following hold:*
   (a) (g doesn't reveal too much information)
      – for all $\widehat{x} \in \widehat{X}$, $g(\widehat{x}, B(\cdot))$ leaks no more than $f(\widehat{A}(\widehat{x}), \cdot)$
      – for all $\widehat{y} \in \widehat{Y}$, $g(A(\cdot), \widehat{y})$ leaks no more than $f(\cdot, \widehat{B}(\widehat{y}))$
   (b) (there are no ambiguous g-inputs)
      – for all $\widehat{x} \in \widehat{X}$, $f(\widehat{A}(\widehat{x}), \cdot)$ refines $C(g(\widehat{x}, B(\cdot)))$.
      – for all $\widehat{y} \in \widehat{Y}$, $f(\cdot, \widehat{B}(\widehat{y}))$ refines $C(g(A(\cdot), \widehat{y}))$.

To understand this definition, it helps to see how the mappings $A, B, C, \widehat{A}, \widehat{B}$ relate to a secure protocol demonstrating $f \sqsubseteq_1 g$:

Lemma 5. *If f embeds in g, then $f \sqsubseteq_1 g$ via a deterministic protocol. This proves $(4) \Rightarrow [(1) \wedge (2) \wedge (3)]$ of Theorem 1 (stated in Sect. 2).*

Proof. Let f embed in g, with associated mappings as in Definition 4. The protocol for f is as follows:

– Alice sends input $A(x)$ to g where x is her f-input.
– Bob sends input $B(y)$ to g where y is his f-input.
– The parties both output $C(z)$ where z is the output they receive from g (they output $\bot$ if g gives output $\bot$).

Correctness follows from the first condition of Definition 4. Due to the symmetry in the definitions/protocol, we show security only against a malicious Alice.

Suppose Alice sends input $\widehat{x}$ to g. In the real protocol, Alice's view will consist of $g(\widehat{x}, B(y))$ and Bob's output will be $C(g(\widehat{x}, B(y)))$. In the ideal world, the simulator will do the following:

– The simulator sends $x^* = \widehat{A}(\widehat{x})$ to the ideal f, and obtains output $f(x^*, y) = C(g(A(x^*), B(y)))$.
– The simulator does not know Bob's input y but can choose any y' such that $f(x^*, y') = f(x^*, y)$. The simulator can give $g(\widehat{x}, B(y'))$ to Alice as her simulated view. From part 2a of Definition 4, we have that this is identical to the real view $g(\widehat{x}, B(y))$.
– The simulator checks whether $C(g(\widehat{x}, B(y))) = \bot$, and if so sends (DELIVER, 0) to f. In this case, Bob's real and ideal outputs will both be $\bot$. Otherwise, it sends (DELIVER, 1) to f and Bob will receive output $f(x^*, y)$.

Bob's ideal output is $f(x^*, y) = C(g(A(x^*), B(y)))$. From condition 2b of Definition 4, this matches the real output $C(g(\widehat{x}, B(y)))$.

Lemma 6. *For non-unilateral f, if $f \sqsubseteq_1 g$ via a deterministic protocol with simulation error[3] less than 1, then f embeds in g. This proves (3) $\Rightarrow$ (4) of Theorem 1 (stated in Sect. 2).*

Proof (Sketch). The full proof is in Appendix B. The fact that $f \sqsubseteq_1 g$ by some deterministic protocol immediately reveals part 1 of the embedding: there must be some set of mappings that Alice and Bob use to map f-inputs to g-inputs and g-outputs to f-outputs.

The main technical portion of this proof is that, if simulator mappings $\widehat{A}$ and $\widehat{B}$ do not follow the rules in parts 2a and 2b of Definition 4, then the simulation error is 1, which contradicts our assertion that the simulation error is less than 1. The intuition for these attacks is clear from the examples above.

5   Instantaneous Protocols

In this section we show how to transform any secure protocol in the g-hybrid model into one that has an "instantaneous" property (described further in Sect. 5.4). The results in this section apply to arbitrary protocols. Later in Sect. 6 we give further transformations that are restricted to deterministic or logarithmic-round protocols.

5.1   Frontier Basics

Recall that $\Pr_\pi[t|xy]$ refers to the probability that the protocol results in transcript with prefix t, when run honestly on inputs x and y. We write $\Pr_\pi[\mathcal{E}|txy]$ to denote the probability that event $\mathcal{E}$ happens, given that the parties run honestly with inputs x and y, and conditioned on t being a prefix of the transcript.

Let F be any set of partial protocol transcripts, with the property that if $t \in F$, and t is a prefix of t', then $t' \in F$. In other words, F describes an event in the protocol that happens and does not "unhappen." In this case we call F a **frontier**, using the terminology of [17].

It is sometimes helpful to associate the frontier F with its set of prefix-minimal elements, as these represents transcript where *some condition happened for the first time*. Let $\mathrm{first}(F)$ denote the prefix-minimal elements of F.

If F is a frontier, we use notation $\Pr_\pi[F|xy]$ to denote the probability that F is encountered when running the protocol honestly on inputs x and y. More formally:

$$\Pr_\pi[F|xy] \overset{\text{def}}{=} \sum_{t \in \mathrm{first}(F)} \Pr_\pi[t|xy]$$

---

[3] The simulation error of a protocol π is the maximum (supremum) over all environments of $|p_{\mathsf{real}} - p_{\mathsf{ideal}}|$, where p_{real} is the probability that the environment outputs 1 in the real interaction and p_{ideal} is the probability that it outputs 1 in the ideal interaction.

Finally, if F and G are two frontiers, then "$F < G$" denotes the event "either F happens strictly before G, or F happens and G never happens." More formally,

$$\Pr_\pi[F < G|xy] \overset{\text{def}}{=} \sum_{t \in \text{first}(F \backslash G)} \Pr_\pi[t|xy]$$

5.2 Our Frontiers

Our analysis relies on two types of frontiers that we introduce:

$F^x_{\text{A-ext}}$: captures the first time that the *simulator has extracted* with reasonable probability, in an ideal-world interaction involving a corrupt Alice running *honestly* on input x.

$F^x_{\text{A-out}}$: captures the first time that Alice's output becomes relatively fixed, in the following sense. If the parties continue with honest behavior from such a point in the protocol, and Alice has input x, then Alice has only one likely output, no matter what Bob's input is.

We define such a frontier for every input x. We also define analogous frontiers with respect to Bob.

We have already defined $\Pr_\pi[\cdot|xy]$ notation with respect to an honest execution of the protocol on inputs x, y. Since $F^x_{\text{A-ext}}$ refers to probabilities in an *ideal-model* interaction, we introduce notation to differentiate between the probabilities in real and ideal interactions. We write $\Pr_{\text{A-sim}}[\cdot|xy]$ to refer to probabilities induced by an ideal-model interaction among malicious Alice running the protocol honestly on input x, the simulator for corrupt Alice, and ideal honest Bob with input y. $\Pr_{\text{B-sim}}$ is defined analogously.

Definition 7. *At some point in an ideal interaction between corrupt Alice and the simulator, the simulator will at some point "extract" by sending an input to the ideal f. Define:*

$$\sigma_A(t, x) \overset{\text{def}}{=} \Pr_{\text{A-sim}}[\textit{simulator has previously extracted}|txy]$$

That is, $\sigma_A(t, x)$ is the probability that the simulator has extracted, given that the transcript so far is t. We define σ_B analogously.

In somewhat more detail, consider formally defining a simulator in terms of a its next-message function. Given as input its view so far (messages exchanged with the adversary and functionality and internal state), it outputs either (PROT, m) to indicate sending a simulated protocol message m to the adversary, or (EXT, x) to indicate sending an input x to the ideal functionality. Until the simulator talks to the ideal functionality, the only interaction is between the adversary and the simulator. As such, the simulator may be stateless for this period of time without loss of generality (by the same reasoning as in Sect. 3.3). The simulator's view certainly indicates whether extraction has happened (i.e., whether the view contains a EXT message). Since the moment of extraction (EXT message) is the first place that the simulator's view and the adversary-simulator transcript diverge, σ_A can be defined as a function of the transcript only.

Let $\sigma_A^*(t, x)$ denote the probability that the simulator has decided to extract "at this instant," i.e., in response to the most recent protocol message sent by the adversary. Formally, let $t = (t_1, \ldots, t_n)$ be the partial transcript, where Alice is corrupt and speaks first:

$$\sigma_A^*(t, x) \overset{\text{def}}{=} \Pr{}_\pi[t|x] \left(\prod_{\substack{i \text{ even} \\ i < n}} \Pr[\mathcal{S}(t_1 \cdots t_i) = (\text{PROT}, t_{i+1})] \right) \Pr[\mathcal{S}(t) = (\text{EXT}, \cdot)]$$

where $\mathcal{S}$ is the simulator's next-message function. Then

$$\sigma_A(t, x) = \sum_{i < n} \sigma_A^*\Big((t_1, \ldots, t_i), x\Big)$$

Note that before the simulator extracts, its view is perfectly independent of y in the ideal interaction. Its decision to extract, and hence the probability $\sigma_A(t, x)$, depends only on x and not on y.

With that in mind, note that we have defined σ_A to refer to the probability that extraction has happened *strictly in the past* (note $i < n$ in the summation above). Another way to interpret σ_A is "the probability that the transcript might be affected by the honest party's input y." Hence, as the transcript evolves, the value of σ_A cannot change as a result of a message sent by Alice. It can only change as a result of a message generated by the simulator, hence an output of g or a simulated Bob-message.

Finally, note that our terminology considers when the simulator *actually* extracts, and not when the simulator has *in principle* enough information to extract. Again, the important issue is whether the simulator has already contacted the ideal functionality, and therefore the transcript may be influenced by the honest party's input.

Definition 8. *Given a secure protocol π with simulation error ε, define the following for all inputs x, y:*

$$F_{A\text{-ext}}^x = \{t \mid \sigma_A(t, x) > 4\sqrt{\varepsilon}\}$$
$$F_{B\text{-ext}}^y = \{t \mid \sigma_B(t, y) > 4\sqrt{\varepsilon}\}$$

$$F_{A\text{-out}}^x = \left\{t \mid \forall y, y' : f(x, y) \neq f(x, y') \Rightarrow \min \left\{ \begin{array}{l} \Pr_\pi[out\ f(x, y)|txy], \\ \Pr_\pi[out\ f(x, y')|txy'] \end{array} \right\} < 1 - \sqrt{\varepsilon} \right\}$$

$$F_{B\text{-out}}^y = \left\{t \mid \forall x, x' : f(x, y) \neq f(x', y) \Rightarrow \min \left\{ \begin{array}{l} \Pr_\pi[out\ f(x, y)|txy], \\ \Pr_\pi[out\ f(x', y)|tx'y] \end{array} \right\} < 1 - \sqrt{\varepsilon} \right\}$$

Here $\Pr_\pi[out\ z|txy]$ refers to the probability that honest parties output z when starting the protocol at partial transcript t and running honestly with inputs x and y.

To understand $F_{A\text{-out}}^x$, observe that for $t \in F_{A\text{-out}}^x$ there is at most one output that can be induced with probability at least $1 - \sqrt{\varepsilon}$. It may be the case that no valid output can be induced with this probability, in which case only $\bot$ output is likely from starting point t.

Note that if ε is a negligible function of the security parameter, then $\sqrt{\varepsilon}$ is a larger function but also still negligible.

5.3   Properties of the Frontiers

We now show that, roughly speaking, all the frontiers that we have defined must occur simultaneously, with overwhelming probability. Proofs for the lemmas in this section are given in Appendix C. Note that all lemmas hold with the roles of Alice and Bob reversed.

Lemma 9. *For all x, y:* $\Pr_\pi[F^x_{A\text{-}ext} < F^y_{B\text{-}out} \mid xy] < 2\sqrt{\varepsilon}$.

Proof (sketch). A partial transcript $t \in F^x_{A\text{-}ext} \setminus F^y_{B\text{-}out}$ represents a situation where there is reasonable probability that the simulator would have extracted from Alice in the ideal-interaction ($t \in F^x_{A\text{-}ext}$), but in the real-interaction Alice can still induce two different outputs for Bob, each with good probability ($t \notin F^y_{B\text{-}out}$). Intuitively, the simulator has extracted prematurely. This event should be rare.

Next we show that $F^x_{A\text{-}out}$ is a point at which the honest parties can predict their eventual output.

Definition 10. *Fix x and let $t \in F^x_{A\text{-}out}$. Then there is at most one value z such that $\exists y : \Pr_\pi[out \; z \mid xyt] > 1 - \sqrt{\varepsilon}$. Let $\mathsf{guess}_A(t, x)$ denote this value z, and note that the value could be $\perp$. We extend the notation $\mathsf{guess}_A(t, x) = \perp$ in the case that $t \notin F^x_{A\text{-}out}$.*

Lemma 11. *For $z \neq \perp$ define $G^z = \{t \mid \mathsf{guess}_A(t, x) = z\}$. Then for all x, y:* $\Pr_\pi[G^{f(x,y)} \mid xy] > 1 - \varepsilon/2$. *Intuitively, upon reaching $F^x_{A\text{-}out}$, Alice can predict her eventual output with error at most $\varepsilon/2$.*

Lemma 12. *For all x, y (x not unilateral for f),* $\Pr_\pi[F^x_{A\text{-}out} < F^x_{A\text{-}ext} \mid xy] < 16\varepsilon$.

Proof (Sketch). A partial transcript $t \in F^x_{A\text{-}out} \setminus F^x_{A\text{-}ext}$ represents a situation where Alice can predict what the output will be ($t \in F^x_{A\text{-}out}$), but the simulator probably has not extracted yet ($t \notin F^x_{A\text{-}ext}$). This event should be rare, since in the ideal interaction Alice can gain no information about the f-output before the simulator extracts (assuming x is not a unilateral input, so that the output indeed depends on Bob's input).

Lemma 13. *For all x, y (y not unilateral),* $\Pr_\pi[F^y_{B\text{-}out} < F^x_{A\text{-}out} \mid xy] < 18\sqrt{\varepsilon}$.

Proof (Sketch). This follows from the fact that if $F^y_{B\text{-}out} < F^x_{A\text{-}out}$ then either $F^y_{B\text{-}out} < F^y_{B\text{-}ext}$ or $F^y_{B\text{-}ext} < F^x_{A\text{-}out}$, both of which are negligibly likely from Lemmas 9 and 12.

Lemma 14. *For all x, y', y (x, y' not unilateral),* $\Pr_\pi[F^{y'}_{B\text{-}out} < F^y_{B\text{-}out} \mid xy] < 42\sqrt{\varepsilon}$.

Proof (Sketch). If $F^{y'}_{B\text{-}out} < F^y_{B\text{-}out}$ then either $F^{y'}_{B\text{-}out} < F^x_{A\text{-}ext}$ or $F^x_{A\text{-}ext} < F^y_{B\text{-}out}$.

We can argue that the first case $F^{y'}_{B\text{-}out} < F^x_{A\text{-}ext}$ would be negligibly likely, if the parties run honestly on inputs x, y'. Unfortunately here we are using input y

for Bob. But consider the ideal interaction with corrupt Alice. We are interested in an event in which the simulator is not likely to have extracted from Alice ($t \notin F^x_{\text{A-ext}}$). Conditioned on the simulator not extracting, the protocol transcript is independent of Bob's input. Hence whatever is unlikely with input y' for Bob is also unlikely with input y for Bob.

The second case $F^x_{\text{A-ext}} < F^y_{\text{B-out}}$ is negligibly likely by Lemma 9.

5.4   Securely Truncating a Protocol

Lemma 15. *Let π be a secure protocol for f in the g-hybrid model. Define π' to be the following:*

- *On input x for Alice and y for Bob, both parties run π honestly on their given inputs.*
- *When the protocol transcript t reaches $F^{\tilde{x}}_{\text{A-out}}$ for any $\tilde{x}$, or reaches $F^{\tilde{y}}_{\text{B-out}}$ for any $\tilde{y}$, the parties terminate the protocol.*
- *Alice outputs $\mathsf{guess}_A(t,x)$ and Bob outputs $\mathsf{guess}_B(t,y)$.*

Then the truncated protocol π' is also a secure protocol for f.

Proof. Let ε denote the simulation error of π. First, we argue that π' is correct. Alice's output is $\mathsf{guess}_A(t,x)$, which differs from the correct answer $f(x,y)$ only in the following events:

- $t \notin F^x_{\text{A-out}}$ because the protocol reached $F^{x'}_{\text{A-out}}$ and terminated strictly before reaching $F^x_{\text{A-out}}$ for $x' \neq x$. By Lemma 14, this can happen only with probability $O(\sqrt{\varepsilon})$.
- $t \notin F^x_{\text{A-out}}$ because the protocol reached $F^y_{\text{B-out}}$ and terminated strictly before reaching $F^x_{\text{A-out}}$. By Lemma 13, this can happen only with probability $O(\sqrt{\varepsilon})$.
- $t \in F^x_{\text{A-out}}$ but $\mathsf{guess}_A(t,x) \neq f(x,y)$. By Lemma 11, this can only happen with probability $O(\varepsilon)$.

As for security, the only difference between π and π' is that π' truncates early based on some condition. But this condition is public and *independent of either party's private inputs*. Hence the simulation for π' works as follows. It simply runs the simulator for π but terminates the protocol when the transcript reaches the public termination condition.

Overall π' is a secure protocol with negligible simulation error $O(\sqrt{\varepsilon})$.

Observe that the new protocol π' has the "instantaneous" property discussed in Sect. 2. Importantly for our purposes in the next section, with overwhelming probability $1 - O(\sqrt{\varepsilon})$ the protocol terminates on a transcript that is both in $F^x_{\text{A-out}}$ and $F^y_{\text{B-out}}$. Such a transcript must end with a message produced by the simulator in both ideal interactions (i.e., when either party is corrupt). Hence the last protocol message must be an output of g, with overwhelming probability.

6   Collapsing Protocols to a Single Call to g

We complete our main theorem with the following lemmas.

Lemma 16. *If, for incomplete and non-unilateral f and g, $f \sqsubseteq g$ via a protocol with strict upper bound on number of rounds $r = O(\log \kappa)$, then f embeds in g. This proves (1) $\Rightarrow$ (4) of Theorem 1 (stated in Sect. 2).*

Proof (Sketch). The full proof is in Appendix D. Without loss of generality (from Lemma 15) the last step in π (in particular, the action in final round r) is a call to g with overwhelming probability.

We consider two cases. Consider a call to g that happens in the last round, following some partial transcript t. Imagine a new protocol where the parties simply "fast-forward" directly to this g-call by behaving as if the transcript so far was t. The result is a protocol consisting of a single call to g. If any call to g yields a *secure* protocol for f in this way, then we are done (we in fact have a *1-round* protocol for f).

In the other case, there may be no call to g during the final round of π that yields a secure protocol for f in this way. Intuitively, every time the protocol runs for the full r rounds there would have been a successful attack on the final call to g! Hence it must be negligibly unlikely that π would ever run for r rounds. We show that, in this case, truncating π after $r - 1$ rounds results in a secure protocol for f.

We can repeatedly apply this argument at most $r - 1$ times until we are guaranteed to obtain a 1-round protocol demonstrating $f \sqsubseteq_1 g$. The parameters are such that after truncating $r - 1$ rounds, the resulting protocol has simulation error $c^{r-1}\sqrt{\varepsilon}$ for some constant c. Such a protocol is secure as long as $r = O(\log \kappa)$, since $c^{O(\log \kappa)}\sqrt{\varepsilon} = \mathrm{poly}(\kappa)\sqrt{\varepsilon}$, which is negligible.

Corollary 17. *If $f \sqsubseteq g$ via a deterministic protocol (of any number of rounds) then f embeds in g. This proves (2) $\Rightarrow$ (4) of Theorem 1 (stated in Sect. 2).*

Proof. Deterministic protocols have zero simulation error (without loss of generality). Therefore, the same reasoning as in the previous proof applies but without any error accumulating with each round.

7   Tightness of the Characterization, Limitations

In this section we discuss why our main characterization does not extend (without modification) to consider unilateral functions or superlogarithmic-round, randomized protocols.

In Appendix E we discuss the possibility of extending our protocol model to allow parallel calls to g.

7.1   Unilateral Functions

Failure of Our Characterization on Unilateral Functions. In Fig. 2 we give f and g which are unilateral. Bob is the column-player and thus has 2 unilateral inputs labeled B and C.

First, we argue that $f \not\sqsubseteq_1 g$. Suppose for sake of contradiction that such a protocol exists. Consider the simulator for a corrupt Bob who runs the protocol semi-honestly, on f-input that is chosen uniformly at random. The only message that the simulator sees is Bob's input to g, after which the simulator must extract an output to send to f. The simulator gets only one bit of information about Bob's input (as there are only 2 possible g-inputs), while there are 3 possibilities for the extracted f-input. It follows that with constant probability the simulator must extract the wrong input, and this error will be evident in the output of f.

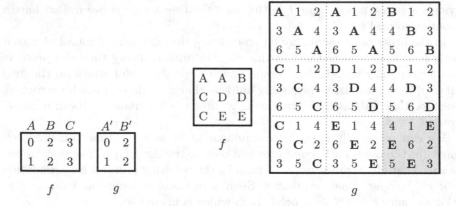

Fig. 2. Unilateral functions violating the main theorem.

Fig. 3. Functions violating the main theorem via a superlogarithmic-round protocol. Note that the bottom-right 3×3 submatrix is unlike the others.

However, there is a simple protocol for f using g: Alice sends her f input directly to g. If Bob has f-input A, he should choose g-input A'. In this case, the parties will see that the g-output is in $\{0, 1\}$ and they terminate with this as their f-output. Otherwise, if Bob has f-input B or C, he should choose g-input B'. In this case, the parties will see that the g output is 2, and then Alice will wait for Bob to send a plain message containing either "2" or "3." Alice takes this message to be her output.

It is simple to see that this protocol is secure against a malicious Alice. For a malicious Bob, the simulator does the following. If Bob chooses g-input A', then the simulator extracts Bob's ideal f-input as A and simulates the g-output to equal the ideal f-output. If Bob chooses g-input B', then the simulator gives 2 as the simulated g-output, then waits for a message from Bob (either "2" or "3") and uses this as the extracted ideal f-input. The reason the simulation is secure is that in the second case (Bob chooses g-input B'), the fact that this is a unilateral input means that the simulator doesn't need to know Alice's input to perfectly simulate the g-output. Hence the simulator can delay extraction until the second protocol message, where intuitively Bob resolves which unilateral input he has.

Hence, we have $f \sqsubseteq g$ via a protocol consisting of a single call to g, plus (in some cases) one extra message. It is a deterministic, constant-round protocol, and yet $f \not\sqsubseteq_1 g$. This example shows that our classification does not extend to unilateral functions.

7.2   Deterministic/Logarithmic-Round Protocols

Consider the functions f and g in Fig. 3. We first claim that f does not embed in g. Any embedding would map 3 f-columns into 3 distinct g-columns.[4] For any 3 columns of g, there exists a row for which these columns have distinct entries – this is simple (albeit time-consuming) to verify. However, there is no row in f that has three distinct values. Hence the embedding would contradict rule 2a of the embedding definition. Concretely, any candidate protocol for $f \sqsubseteq_1 g$ would allow a corrupt row-player to learn the column-player's input in its entirety, which is not allowed by f.

However, there is a protocol for f that uses g. We group the rows and columns of g into groups of three, as distinguished by the dotted lines in the figure. Associate the first row of f with the first row group of g, etc. Similarly, associate the first column of f with the first column group of g, etc. The protocol for f is as follows:

- Alice chooses a g-input from the row group associated with her f-input, uniformly at random.
- Bob chooses a g-input from the column group associated with his f-input, uniformly at random.
- They call g with their selected g-inputs.
- If the output of the g-call was in $\{A, B, C, D, E\}$, terminate the protocol with that output. Otherwise, repeat (with fresh random choices for the g-inputs).

The correctness of this protocol is clear. By only sending g-inputs in the group associated with their f-inputs, each party restricts any terminating output of g to be one that was possible given their f-input.

To see that the protocol is secure, consider the following simulation. Suppose corrupt Alice chooses some g-input (row). With probability 1/3, the simulator decides that the protocol will terminate at this round. It converts the g-input to an f-input (according to its row group), sends that f-input to the ideal f, then simulates the g-output as the ideal f-input. With probability 2/3, the simulator decides that the protocol will continue. Note that in any row, there are 2 non-terminal g-outputs (for example, in the second row only 3 and 4 are possible),

---

[4] Perhaps columns are mapped to rows if the roles of Alice and Bob are swapped during the embedding. The analysis is the same for this scenario.

which are equally likely no matter which column group Bob has selected. The simulator simply chooses one of these two with equal probability as the simulated g-output. Then the same process repeats.

The parties' inputs will "match" by giving a terminal output with probability $1/3$, meaning that the expected number of rounds is 3. The probability that the protocol continues for at least r rounds is $(2/3)^r$. We can get a protocol with a strict upper bound on round complexity by having the parties simply abort after some limit r number of rounds. If we set this limit as $r(\kappa) = \omega(\log \kappa)$, then the correctness of the protocol suffers by an amount $(2/3)^{\omega(\log \kappa)} = \kappa^{-\omega(1)}$, which is negligible. However, the simulation is still perfect, and the protocol is secure.

In summary, $f \sqsubseteq g$ via a randomized, (worst-case) superlogarithmic-round protocol, but f does not embed in g and so $f \not\sqsubseteq g$ via any deterministic protocol or any strict logarithmic-round protocol.

Acknowledgments. We thank the anonymous reviewers for their helpful comments.

A   UC Security Recap

A 2-party SFE task is a deterministic function $f : X \times Y \to Z$. We identify f with the following ideal functionality: The functionality waits for input $x \in X$ from Alice and input $y \in Y$ from Bob. If no party is corrupt, the functionality gives output $f(x, y)$ to both parties. If any party is corrupt, the functionality gives $f(x, y)$ to the adversary and waits for a command (DELIVER, b) from the adversary, where $b \in \{0, 1\}$. If $b = 0$, the functionality gives output $\bot$ to the honest party; if $b = 1$, the functionality gives $f(x, y)$ to the honest party. Hence, we consider **security with abort** — the functionality does not guarantee fairness or output delivery.

We assume basic familiarity with the UC framework, but briefly review the main concepts (specialized here for 2-party SFE). An execution in the framework begins with an *environment* $\mathcal{Z}$ (an arbitrary interactive TM) that chooses inputs for both of the *parties*. The parties interact with each other, and an ideal functionality for some function g, according to the protocol. The parties eventually give an output to the environment, who outputs a single bit. Throughout the entire interaction, there is an *adversary* $\mathcal{A}$ (an arbitrary interactive TM) who interacts arbitrarily with the environment. The adversary may also choose to *corrupt* one of the parties, which causes the party to come under complete control of the adversary. In that case, the party may deviate from the protocol. In this work we consider only **static** corruption, where the adversary must choose to corrupt a party before the protocol begins.

Given the description above, $\text{EXEC}[\pi, g, \mathcal{A}, \mathcal{Z}, 1^\kappa]$ denotes the probability that the environment outputs 1, when κ is the security parameter of the protocol.

A particular protocol of interest is the dummy protocol π_{dummy}. In this protocol, each party receives an input from the environment and sends it directly to the ideal functionality. When the ideal functionality delivers an output, the party gives it directly to the environment as output.

Definition 18. *We say f reduces to g, and write $f \sqsubseteq g$, if there exists a protocol π such that for all $\mathcal{A}$ there exists a $\mathcal{S}$ such that for all environments $\mathcal{Z}$, we have:*

$$\left| \text{EXEC}[\pi, g, \mathcal{A}, \mathcal{Z}, 1^{\kappa}] - \text{EXEC}[\pi_{dummy}, f, \mathcal{S}, \mathcal{Z}, 1^{\kappa}] \right| \text{ is negligible in } \kappa$$

We write $f \sqsubseteq_1 g$ if furthermore π has the following property: the parties make only one call to g and exchange no other messages.

In the execution of π_{dummy} we can think of $\mathcal{S}$ as simulating protocol π with $\mathcal{A}$. The security arises from the fact that the simulator communicates with the honest party via a single call to ideal f. This means that everything prior to the call $\mathcal{S}$ makes to ideal f must be independent of the honest party's input, and everything after that call must not affect the honest party's output. We call this event the *extraction*, as $\mathcal{S}$ must "extract" enough information about the input of $\mathcal{A}$ in order to correctly call f.

B   Proofs for the Reducibility Characterization

Lemma (Restatement of Lemma 6). *For non-unilateral f, if $f \sqsubseteq_1 g$ via a deterministic protocol with simulation error less than 1, then f embeds in g.*

Proof. During the deterministic protocol, Alice and Bob both map their f-inputs to g-inputs and then immediately terminate the protocol, meaning that they were each able to map the g-output to the same f-output. The input maps are A and B in the embedding. The output map is C in the embedding.

By symmetry, we only consider security against a malicious Alice.

Clearly, A is injective. If it is not, then choose some pair (x, x') where $A(x) = A(x')$. Choose y so that $f(x, y) \neq f(x', y)$ – since f is not unilateral, such an input exists. Consider two environments – they ask the parties to honestly run the protocol with inputs x, y and x', y respectively, and return 1 if the output is correct. In the real world, in both cases the parties will return the same output, so one of them is incorrect. Therefore, one of the environments has simulation error 1.

Because this protocol is UC-secure, there must be some method by which the simulator takes the parties' g-inputs and translate them to f-inputs upon extraction. Call these mappings for Alice and Bob $\widehat{A}$ and $\widehat{B}$, respectively. It suffices to show that these mappings satisfy 2a and 2b of Definition 4. We show that if the mappings violate Definition 4, then the simulation error of the protocol is 1.

(2a) Assume that $\widehat{A}$ violates part 2a. That is, there exists an $\widehat{x}$ where it is not the case that $g(\widehat{x}, B(\cdot))$ leaks no more than $f(\widehat{A}(\widehat{x}), \cdot)$. In particular, there is some pair (y, y') where $f(\widehat{A}(\widehat{x}), y) = f(\widehat{A}(\widehat{x}), y')$ but $g(\widehat{x}, B(y)) \neq g(\widehat{x}, B(y'))$.

Consider two environments:

- Adversary Alice uses input $\widehat{x}$, honest Bob uses input y, return 1 if Alice's view is $g(\widehat{x}, B(y))$.

- Adversary Alice uses input $\widehat{x}$, honest Bob uses input y', return 1 if Alice's view is $g(\widehat{x}, B(y'))$.

In the real world, both environments output 1 with probability 1. In the ideal world, the simulator's view in both environments is $f(\widehat{A}(\widehat{x}), y) = f(\widehat{A}(\widehat{x}), y')$. Since the simulator is deterministic, it must give the same simulated g-output for both environments. However, $g(\widehat{x}, B(y)) \neq g(\widehat{x}, B(y'))$, so in at least one of the environments the probability of outputting 1 is 0. Therefore, the simulation error is 1.

(2b) Assume that $\widehat{A}$ violates part 2b. Then there exists some $\widehat{x}$ and y where $C(g(\widehat{x}, B(y))) \notin \{f(\widehat{A}(\widehat{x}), y), \bot\}$. Consider the environment in which corrupt Alice uses g-input $\widehat{x}$ and honest Bob uses input y, and the environment outputs 1 if Bob's output is $C(g(\widehat{x}, B(y)))$. The environment outputs 1 with probability 1 in the real world. But in the ideal world, Bob's output is either $f(\widehat{A}(\widehat{x}), y)$ or $\bot$. This environment demonstrates a simulation error of 1.

C   Proofs for Frontier Properties

Lemma (Restatement of Lemma 9). *For all* x, y: $\Pr_\pi[F^x_{A\text{-ext}} < F^y_{B\text{-out}} \mid xy] < 2\sqrt{\varepsilon}$.

Proof. Let $\mathsf{bad} = \mathsf{first}(F^x_{A\text{-ext}} \setminus F^y_{B\text{-out}})$, whose probability we wish to bound. A partial transcript $t \in \mathsf{bad}$ represents a situation where there is reasonable probability that a simulator would have extracted an effective input for Alice ($t \in F^x_{A\text{-ext}}$), but in the protocol Alice can still induce two different outputs for Bob, each with good probability ($t \notin F^y_{B\text{-out}}$). Intuitively, the simulator has extracted prematurely. This event should be rare.

Consider the following strategy for corrupt Alice and environment:

- Run the protocol with input y for honest Bob, and Alice initially behaving semi-honestly with input x.
- If the protocol transcript avoids bad, then the adversary gives up and the environment outputs 0.
- Otherwise, when the partial transcript reaches $t \in \mathsf{bad}$ for the first time, then the properties of bad guarantee that there are two values x_0, x_1 such that $f(x_0, y) \neq f(x_1, y)$ and $\Pr_\pi[\text{out } f(x_c, y) \mid t x_c y] \geq 1 - \sqrt{\varepsilon}$ for both $c \in \{0, 1\}$.
- The adversary sends x_0, x_1 to the environment, who chooses a random $c \leftarrow \{0, 1\}$.
- The adversary switches strategies to run the protocol honestly with input x_c. The environment outputs 1 if Bob's eventual output is $f(x_c, y)$. Otherwise the environment outputs 0.

Let succ denote the event that the environment outputs 1.

In the real interaction, the environment outputs 1 only when the transcript hits bad and the adversary is successful in forcing Bob's output, which happens with probability at least $1 - \sqrt{\varepsilon}$ by the properties of bad. So:

$$\Pr_\pi[\text{succ}] \geq \Pr_\pi[\text{bad}|xy](1 - \sqrt{\varepsilon})$$

In the ideal interaction (between the adversary and simulator), Bob's output is now determined differently, as the output of the ideal f. There are two ways the environment outputs 0: (1) when the simulated transcript avoids bad; (2) when the transcript reaches bad but the simulator has already extracted. In the latter case, the environment's choice of c is independent of the simulator's extraction, so with further probability at least $1/2$ the honest Bob will not output $f(x_c, y)$. So:

$$\Pr_{\text{A-sim}}[\text{succ}] \leq (1 - (4\sqrt{\varepsilon})/2)\Pr_{\text{A-sim}}[\text{bad}|xy]$$

From the security of the protocol:

$$|\Pr_\pi[\text{succ}] - \Pr_{\text{A-sim}}[\text{succ}]| < \varepsilon$$
$$|\Pr_\pi[\text{bad}|xy] - \Pr_{\text{A-sim}}[\text{bad}|xy]| < \varepsilon$$

Hence:

$$
\begin{aligned}
\varepsilon &> \Pr_\pi[\text{succ}] - \Pr_{\text{A-sim}}[\text{succ}] \\
&\geq \Pr_\pi[\text{bad}|xy](1 - \sqrt{\varepsilon}) - (1 - 2\sqrt{\varepsilon})\Pr_{\text{A-sim}}[\text{bad}|xy] \\
&\geq \Pr_\pi[\text{bad}|xy](1 - \sqrt{\varepsilon}) - (1 - 2\sqrt{\varepsilon})(\Pr_\pi[\text{bad}|xy] + \varepsilon) \\
&= \Pr_\pi[\text{bad}|xy]\sqrt{\varepsilon} - \varepsilon(1 - 2\sqrt{\varepsilon}) \\
&> \Pr_\pi[\text{bad}|xy]\sqrt{\varepsilon} - \varepsilon
\end{aligned}
$$

Solving for $\Pr_\pi[\text{bad}|xy]$:

$$\Pr_\pi[\text{bad}|xy] < \frac{2\varepsilon}{\sqrt{\varepsilon}} = 2\sqrt{\varepsilon}$$

Lemma (Restatement of Lemma 11). *For $z \neq \perp$ define $G^z = \{t \mid \text{guess}_A(t, x) = z\}$. Then for all x, y: $\Pr_\pi[G^{f(x,y)}|xy] > 1 - \varepsilon/2$. Intuitively, upon reaching $F^x_{\text{A-out}}$, Alice can predict her eventual output with error at most $\varepsilon/2$.*

Proof. Define bad $= F^x_{\text{A-out}} \setminus G^{f(x,y)}$. Intuitively, these are the places in the protocol where $\text{guess}_A(t, x) \neq f(x, y)$.

From the correctness of the protocol, we have:

$$
\begin{aligned}
\varepsilon &> \Pr_\pi[\text{output not } f(x,y)|xy] \\
&\geq \sum_{t \in \text{first(bad)}} \Pr_\pi[t|xy]\Pr_\pi[\text{out guess}_A(t,x)|txy] \\
&\geq \sum_{t \in \text{first(bad)}} \Pr_\pi[t|xy](1 - \sqrt{\varepsilon}) = (1 - \Pr_\pi[G^{f(x,y)}|xy])(1 - \sqrt{\varepsilon})
\end{aligned}
$$

Solving for the probability expression:

$$\Pr_\pi[G^{f(x,y)}|xy] \geq 1 - \frac{\varepsilon}{1 - \sqrt{\varepsilon}} > 1 - \varepsilon/2$$

Lemma (Restatement of Lemma 12). *For all x, y, if x is not a unilateral input for f, then $\Pr_\pi[F^x_{\text{A-out}} < F^x_{\text{A-ext}} \mid xy] < 16\varepsilon$.*

Proof. Let $\text{bad} = \text{first}(F^x_{\text{A-out}} \setminus F^x_{\text{A-ext}})$, whose probability we wish to bound. A partial transcript $t \in \text{bad}$ represents a situation where Alice can predict what the output will be ($t \in F^x_{\text{A-out}}$), but the simulator probably has not extracted yet ($t \notin F^x_{\text{A-ext}}$). This event should be rare, since in the ideal world Alice can gain no information about the f-output before the simulator extracts.

Let x, y be given as in the premise of the lemma. Since x is not a unilateral input, let y' be such that $f(x, y) \neq f(x, y')$. Consider the following interaction with a corrupt Alice and environment:

- Alice initially runs the protocol honestly with input x. The environment randomly chooses input $y^* \leftarrow \{y, y'\}$ for Bob. If the transcript avoids bad then the adversary gives up and the environment outputs 0.
- Otherwise, if the partial transcript reaches $t \in \text{bad}$, there is a unique $z = \text{guess}_A(t, x)$ such that $\Pr_\pi[\text{out } z \mid tx] > 1 - \sqrt{\varepsilon}$. The adversary reports z to the environment.
- The environment outputs 1 if $z = f(x, y^*)$.

Let succ denote the probability that the environment outputs 1.

In the real interaction, the environment outputs 0 only if the transcript avoids bad or if $\text{guess}_A(t, x)$ is incorrect. By the union bound and Lemma 11,

$$\Pr_\pi[\neg\text{succ}] \leq \Pr_\pi[\neg\text{bad} \mid xy^*] + \Pr_\pi[\neg G^{f(x,y^*)} \mid xy^*] \leq 1 - \Pr_\pi[\text{bad} \mid xy^*] + \varepsilon/2$$

In the ideal interaction, the environment outputs 0 in the following (mutually exclusive) scenarios: (1) the simulated transcript avoids bad; (2) the transcript reaches bad and the simulator has not yet extracted. In the latter case, the adversary's view is independent of the environment's choice of y^*, and so the environment outputs 0 with probability at least $1/2$. Hence:

$$\Pr_{\text{A-sim}}[\neg\text{succ}] \geq \Pr_{\text{A-sim}}[\neg\text{bad} \mid xy^*] + \Pr_{\text{A-sim}}[\text{bad} \wedge \text{no extract} \mid xy^*]/2$$
$$\geq 1 - \Pr_{\text{A-sim}}[\text{bad} \mid xy^*] + \Pr_{\text{A-sim}}[\text{bad} \mid xy^*](1 - 4\sqrt{\varepsilon})/2$$
$$= 1 - \Pr_{\text{A-sim}}[\text{bad} \mid xy^*](\tfrac{1}{2} + 2\sqrt{\varepsilon})$$

Combining:

$$\varepsilon > \Pr_\pi[\text{succ}] - \Pr_{\text{A-sim}}[\text{succ}]$$
$$\geq \Pr_\pi[\text{bad} \mid xy^*] - \varepsilon/2 - \Pr_{\text{A-sim}}[\text{bad} \mid xy^*](\tfrac{1}{2} + 2\sqrt{\varepsilon})$$
$$\geq \Pr_\pi[\text{bad} \mid xy^*] - \varepsilon/2 - (\Pr_\pi[\text{bad} \mid xy^*] + \varepsilon)(\tfrac{1}{2} + 2\sqrt{\varepsilon})$$
$$= \Pr_\pi[\text{bad} \mid xy^*](\tfrac{1}{2} - 2\sqrt{\varepsilon}) - \varepsilon(1 - 2\sqrt{\varepsilon})$$

Solving for the probability expression:

$$\Pr_\pi[\text{bad} \mid xy^*] \leq \frac{\varepsilon(2 - 2\sqrt{\varepsilon})}{(\tfrac{1}{2} - 2\sqrt{\varepsilon})} < \frac{2\varepsilon}{1/4} = 8\varepsilon$$

Since $\Pr_\pi[\text{bad} \mid xy^*]$ is the average of $\Pr_\pi[\text{bad} \mid xy]$ and $\Pr_\pi[\text{bad} \mid xy']$, it follows that $\Pr_\pi[\text{bad} \mid xy] < 16\varepsilon$.

Lemma (Restatement of Lemma 13). *For all x, y, if y is not a unilateral input, then $\Pr_\pi[F^y_{\text{B-out}} < F^x_{\text{A-out}} | xy] < 18\sqrt{\varepsilon}$.*

Proof. By a union bound,

$$\Pr_\pi[F^y_{\text{B-out}} < F^x_{\text{A-out}} | xy] \leq \Pr_\pi[F^y_{\text{B-out}} < F^y_{\text{B-ext}} | xy] + \Pr_\pi[F^y_{\text{B-ext}} < F^x_{\text{A-out}} | xy]$$
$$\leq 16\varepsilon + 2\sqrt{\varepsilon} < 18\sqrt{\varepsilon}$$

Before proving Lemma 14, we introduce two helper lemmas:

Lemma 19. *For all x, y, if neither x nor y are a unilateral input, then $\Pr_\pi[F^y_{\text{B-out}} < F^x_{\text{A-ext}} | xy] < 34\sqrt{\varepsilon}$.*

Proof. By a union bound,

$$\Pr_\pi[F^y_{\text{B-out}} < F^x_{\text{A-ext}} | xy] \leq \Pr_\pi[F^y_{\text{B-out}} < F^y_{\text{B-ext}} | xy]$$
$$+ \Pr_\pi[F^y_{\text{B-ext}} < F^x_{\text{A-out}} | xy]$$
$$+ \Pr_\pi[F^x_{\text{A-out}} < F^x_{\text{A-ext}} | xy]$$
$$\leq 16\varepsilon + 2\sqrt{\varepsilon} + 16\varepsilon < 34\sqrt{\varepsilon}$$

Lemma 20. *Let F be any frontier in the protocol. For all x, y, y',*

$$\left| \Pr_\pi[F < F^x_{\text{A-ext}} | xy] - \Pr_\pi[F < F^x_{\text{A-ext}} | xy'] \right| < 6\sqrt{\varepsilon}$$

Proof. Let $G - F \setminus F^x_{\text{A-ext}}$. The main idea is that in the ideal interaction with corrupt Alice, it is unlikely that the simulator has extracted before the protocol has reached G. Conditioned on the simulator not yet extracting, the transcript is completely independent of Bob's input.

Consider running the ideal interaction and halting it when the transcript reaches either F or $F^x_{\text{A-ext}}$. Halting at this point is sufficient to determine whether the event $F < F^x_{\text{A-ext}}$ happened. We obtain two interactions depending on whether Bob is given input y or y'. In the terminology of Bellare-Rogaway [3], these are two *identical-until-bad games*, where the "bad" event is that the simulator extracts but $F^x_{\text{A-ext}}$ is not immediately reached. By the definition of $F^x_{\text{A-ext}}$, the bad event happens with probability at most $4\sqrt{\varepsilon}$. By the lemma in [3], this probability of the bad event bounds the distinguishing bias between the two games.

Then applying the security of the protocol we have:

$$\left| \Pr_\pi[F < F^x_{\text{A-ext}} | xy] - \Pr_\pi[F < F^x_{\text{A-ext}} | xy'] \right|$$
$$\leq \left| \Pr_{\text{A-sim}}[F < F^x_{\text{A-ext}} | xy] - \Pr_{\text{A-sim}}[F < F^x_{\text{A-ext}} | xy'] \right| + 2\varepsilon$$
$$< 4\sqrt{\varepsilon} + 2\varepsilon < 6\sqrt{\varepsilon}$$

Lemma (Restatement of Lemma 14). *For all x, y', y, with x, y' not unilateral, $\Pr_\pi[F^{y'}_{\text{B-out}} < F^y_{\text{B-out}} | xy] < 42\sqrt{\varepsilon}$.*

Proof. Let $\mathsf{bad} = \mathrm{first}(F^{y'}_{\mathsf{B}\text{-out}} \setminus F^{y}_{\mathsf{B}\text{-out}})$, whose probability we wish to bound. We partition bad into two parts: $\mathsf{bad}_1 = \mathsf{bad} \cap F^{x}_{\mathsf{A}\text{-ext}}$ and $\mathsf{bad}_2 = \mathsf{bad} \setminus F^{x}_{\mathsf{A}\text{-ext}}$.

Since $\mathsf{bad}_1 \subseteq F^{x}_{\mathsf{A}\text{-ext}} \setminus F^{y}_{\mathsf{B}\text{-out}}$ (i.e., the event $F^{x}_{\mathsf{A}\text{-ext}} < F^{y}_{\mathsf{B}\text{-out}}$ is true for these transcripts), Lemma 9 implies that

$$\Pr_\pi[\mathsf{bad}_1 | xy] < 2\sqrt{\varepsilon}.$$

Since bad_2 happens strictly before the $F^{x}_{\mathsf{A}\text{-ext}}$ event, Lemma 20 implies that

$$\left| \Pr_\pi[\mathsf{bad}_2 | xy] - \Pr_\pi[\mathsf{bad}_2 | xy'] \right| < 6\sqrt{\varepsilon}.$$

Since $\mathsf{bad}_2 \subseteq F^{y'}_{\mathsf{B}\text{-out}} \setminus F^{x}_{\mathsf{A}\text{-ext}}$, Lemma 19 implies that

$$\Pr_\pi[\mathsf{bad}_2 | xy'] < 34\sqrt{\varepsilon}.$$

Putting everything together, we have:

$$\begin{aligned}
\Pr_\pi[\mathsf{bad} | xy] &\leq \Pr_\pi[\mathsf{bad}_1 | xy] + \Pr_\pi[\mathsf{bad}_2 | xy] \\
&< 2\sqrt{\varepsilon} + \Pr_\pi[\mathsf{bad}_2 | xy'] + 6\sqrt{\varepsilon} \\
&< 2\sqrt{\varepsilon} + 34\sqrt{\varepsilon} + 6\sqrt{\varepsilon} \\
&= 42\sqrt{\varepsilon}
\end{aligned}$$

D   Proofs for Collapsing Protocols

In order to collapse a protocol to a single round, we use two important properties of instantaneous protocols. First, by Lemma 15 we can consider only protocols that end with a call to g. Second, by Lemma 20 before the final call to g the parties' inputs do not have a noticeable effect on the distribution of transcripts.

Lemma 21. *For all f and g there is a constant $c_{f,g}$ such that if $f \sqsubseteq_1 g$ via a protocol π with simulation error ε, then $f \sqsubseteq_1 g$ via a deterministic protocol π' with simulation error at most $c_{f,g}\varepsilon$.*

Proof. Since π consists of only one call to g, the only choices Alice, Bob, and the simulator can make in the protocol are:

- The mapping of Alice's f-input to her g-input
- The mapping of Bob's f-input to his g-input
- The mappings of either party's g-input to a suitable f-input in the simulator
- The mapping of the g-output to an f-output

The only ways that randomness can manifest in the protocol are in the choice of these mappings.

Let $c_{f,g}$ be the number of possible combinations of such mappings based on these random coins. This is certainly a constant, although it is perhaps very large.

Select the mapping combination that was most likely to be chosen in π. Consider the deterministic protocol π' constructed by locking in these choices at the start of the protocol. The probability that Alice, Bob, and the simulator in π match the behavior of π' is at least $1/c_{f,g}$. Then, if the simulation error of π' is δ, the simulation error of π must be at least $\delta/c_{f,g}$. Therefore, if π has simulation error ε, then π' must have simulation error at most $c_{f,g}\varepsilon$.

Given a protocol π with a strict upper limit of r rounds, $\mathsf{trunc}(\pi, i)$ is the protocol constructed by truncating π after $r - i$ rounds, outputting $\perp$ if π was not finished. Note that $\mathsf{trunc}(\pi, 0) = \pi$.

Let $\mathcal{R}$ be the transcripts of $\mathsf{trunc}(\pi, i)$ which are $r - i - 1$ rounds (that is, there is one action to go in the protocol) but have not terminated yet.

Lemma 22. *If π has simulation error ε, then for all x, y, y' and all i:*

$$\left| \Pr_{\mathsf{trunc}(\pi,i)} [\mathcal{R}|xy] - \Pr_{\mathsf{trunc}(\pi,i)} [\mathcal{R}|xy'] \right| < 6\sqrt{\varepsilon}$$

Proof. By Lemma 20 (in Appendix C) we know that this is true in $\mathsf{trunc}(\pi, 0) = \pi$, as these $\mathcal{R}$ transcripts are strictly before $F_{A\text{-ext}}^x$. Truncating doesn't change simulator extraction probabilities, as the simulator for $\mathsf{trunc}(\pi, i)$ just runs the simulator for π up until the truncated transcript. Therefore, the lemma still holds with respect to $\mathsf{trunc}(\pi, i)$.

Lemma 23. *If a protocol π is not ε-secure against malicious Alice, then there is an environment* ENV *for π with the following properties:*

1. ENV *chooses inputs for Bob uniformly at random*
2. $\Pr_\pi[\text{ENV outputs } 1] > \frac{1}{2} + \frac{\varepsilon}{4|Y|}$.
3. $\Pr_{A\text{-}sim}[\text{ENV outputs } 1] < \frac{1}{2} - \frac{\varepsilon}{4|Y|}$

Of course, a symmetrical lemma holds for protocol π that is insecure against malicious Bob.

Proof. Take an environment ENV_0 for which π has simulation error ε. Construct ENV as follows.

- Choose Bob's input y^* uniformly at random.
- Let $p(y)$ be the probability that ENV_0 chooses y. Let $p_{\max}$ be the maximum $p(y)$.
- Flip a coin with probability $1 - (p(y^*)/p_{\max})$. If it comes up heads, abort and return 0.
- Otherwise, run ENV_0.

Note that $\text{ENV} \equiv \text{ENV}_0$ conditioned on ENV not aborting. We abort with probability at most $(|Y|-1)/|Y|$ (as we never abort for the y where $p(y) = p_{\max}$). $(|Y|-1)/|Y|$ is a constant. The simulation error of ENV is therefore at least $\varepsilon/|Y|$.

At this point, possibly invert the output of ENV such that $\text{Pr}_\pi[\text{ENV outputs } 1]$ is greater than $\text{Pr}_{\text{A-sim}}[\text{ENV outputs } 1]$. This will not affect the simulation error.

The probability of ENV returning 1 in the real or simulated environments differs by $\varepsilon/|Y|$, and is centered around some constant p. That is, the probabilities are at least $p+\delta$ and at most $p-\delta$ respectively, where $\delta = \varepsilon/(2|Y|)$. Perform the following operations to ensure that the probability is centered around $1/2$ as required by the lemma.

1. If $p > 1/2$, run normally with probability $\frac{1}{2p}$. Otherwise, return 0.
2. if $p < 1/2$, run normally with probability $\frac{1}{2(1-p)}$. Otherwise, return 1.

This will "normalize" the average of the probabilities in the real and ideal world to $1/2$. This might shrink δ slightly – up to a factor of 2. The minimum value of δ is $\frac{\varepsilon}{4|Y|}$, as required by the lemma.

Define $\varepsilon_0 = \sqrt{\varepsilon}$ and $\varepsilon_i = (52nc)\varepsilon_{i-1} = (52nc)^i\varepsilon_0$ where $c = c_{f,g}$ is the constant defined in Lemma 21 and n is the maximum of $|X|$ and $|Y|$.

Lemma 24. *If* $\text{trunc}(\pi, i)$ *has simulation error at most* ε_i *then either* f *embeds in* g *or* $\text{trunc}(\pi, i+1)$ *has simulation error at most* ε_{i+1}.

Proof. Consider any partial transcript t where the next action in $\text{trunc}(\pi, i)$ is for the parties to make a call to g. Let protocol π_t be defined as follows: the parties "fast-forward" to t by imagining the transcript up to that round. They then complete the call to g and exit immediately afterwards.

If there is any π_t with simulation error less than $1/c$ (call such a t *good*), f embeds in g: by Lemma 21, there exists a single-round deterministic protocol for f in a g-hybrid world with simulation error less than 1. Then, by Lemma 6, f embeds in g.

Assume that there is no good t in round $r - i - 1$ of $\text{trunc}(\pi, i)$ (that is, in $\mathcal{R}$). We wish to bound the probability $\text{Pr}_{\text{trunc}(\pi, i)}[\mathcal{R}|xy]$ for all x, y in this case. Note that some $t \in \mathcal{R}$ may have simulation error when run against one malicious party but not the other. Let $\mathcal{R}_A$ be those t which have unacceptable simulation error against Alice, and let $\mathcal{R}_B$ be similarly defined for Bob. Then:

$$\Pr_{\text{trunc}(\pi,i)}[\mathcal{R}|xy] \leq \Pr_{\text{trunc}(\pi,i)}[\mathcal{R}_A|xy] + \Pr_{\text{trunc}(\pi,i)}[\mathcal{R}_B|xy]$$

Consider, then, the probability $\text{Pr}_{\text{trunc}(\pi,i)}[\mathcal{R}_A|xy]$. A symmetric argument will work for $\mathcal{R}_B$, and therefore we can use these to get a bound on the overall probability $\text{Pr}_{\text{trunc}(\pi,i)}[\mathcal{R}|xy]$.

For each t in $\mathcal{R}$, consider π_t. The simulation error is at least $1/c$, so by Lemma 23 we can construct an environment ENV_t satisfying:

1. ENV_t chooses inputs for Bob uniformly at random
2. $\text{Pr}_{\pi_t}[\text{ENV}_t \text{ outputs } 1] > \frac{1}{2} + \frac{1}{4|Y|c}$
3. $\text{Pr}_{\text{A-sim-for-}\pi_t}[\text{ENV}_t \text{ outputs } 1] < \frac{1}{2} - \frac{1}{4|Y|c}$

Fix a particular x and y. Consider the following attack:

- Alice runs on x, and the environment chooses input y^* for Bob uniformly at random.
- If the parties reach $t \in \mathcal{R}$, let ENV_t sample an input for Bob. If it samples y^*, run ENV_t, possibly allowing Alice to change her input maliciously. Otherwise, output 0.

The probability that during this attack we output 1 is the probability that we reached $\mathcal{R}$ times the probability that ENV_t chooses input y^* times the probability that ENV_t succeeds at its attack given y^*. These probabilities are independent.

$$\sum_{t \in \mathcal{R}_A} \sum_{y^*} \Pr_{\mathrm{trunc}(\pi,i)}[t|xy^*] \frac{1}{|Y|} \Pr_{\pi_t}[\mathsf{ENV}_t \text{ returns } 1|y^*]$$

If we eliminate the summations, we get the following expression:

$$\left(\Pr_{\mathrm{trunc}(\pi,i)}[\mathcal{R}_A|xy^*] \right) \left(\frac{1}{2} + \frac{1}{4|Y|c} \right)$$

By Lemma 22 we can replace y^* with the input for Bob we desire to bound probability against, y, with a small change in probability of reaching a transcript.

The probability the environment outputs 1 in the real world is therefore at least:

$$\left(\Pr_{\mathrm{trunc}(\pi,i)}[\mathcal{R}_A|xy] - 6\sqrt{\varepsilon} \right) \left(\frac{1}{2} + \frac{1}{4|Y|c} \right)$$

By a similar series of arguments, the probability the environment outputs 1 in the ideal world is at most:

$$\left(\Pr_{\text{A-sim-for-trunc}(\pi,i)}[\mathcal{R}_A|xy] + 6\sqrt{\varepsilon} \right) \left(\frac{1}{2} - \frac{1}{4|Y|c} \right)$$

Because the simulation error of $\mathrm{trunc}(\pi,i)$ is ε_i, the above expression is at most the following value:

$$\left(\Pr_{\mathrm{trunc}(\pi,i)}[\mathcal{R}_A|xy] + 6\sqrt{\varepsilon} + \varepsilon_i \right) \left(\frac{1}{2} - \frac{1}{4|Y|c} \right)$$

We know that, because $\mathrm{trunc}(\pi,i)$ has a simulation error of ε_i, the difference between the output probabilities in the real and ideal worlds is at most ε_i, which means that, in particular:

$$\varepsilon_i \geq \Pr_{\mathrm{trunc}(\pi,i)}[\mathcal{R}_A|xy] \frac{1}{2|Y|c} - 12\sqrt{\varepsilon} - \varepsilon_i \left(\frac{1}{2} - \frac{1}{4|Y|c} \right)$$

$$\Rightarrow \Pr_{\mathrm{trunc}(\pi,i)}[\mathcal{R}_A|xy] \leq \left(|Y|c + \frac{1}{2} \right) \varepsilon_i + 24|Y|c\sqrt{\varepsilon}$$

$$\Rightarrow \Pr_{\mathrm{trunc}(\pi,i)}[\mathcal{R}_A|xy] \leq (26|Y|c) \varepsilon_i$$

Recall that this is only against malicious Alice. We get the following bound without restricting which party is adversarial:

$$\Pr_{\mathsf{trunc}(\pi,i)}[\mathcal{R}|xy] \leq (52|Y|c)\,\varepsilon_i = \varepsilon_{i+1}$$

Truncating directly before $\mathcal{R}$, then, will only increase the simulation error to ε_{i+1}.

Lemma (Restatement of Lemma 16). *If, for incomplete and non-unilateral f and g, $f \sqsubseteq g$ using a protocol with security parameter κ and strict upper bound on number of rounds $r = O(\log \kappa)$, then f embeds in g.*

Proof. $\mathsf{trunc}(\pi, 0)$ has simulation error ε which is surely less than ε_0.

Either f embeds in g or we can apply the argument in Lemma 24 up to $r - 1$ times. If $r = O(\log \kappa)$, then we are left with a 1-round protocol $\mathsf{trunc}(\pi, r - 1)$ with simulation error $\varepsilon_r = (52nc)^{O(\log \kappa)}\sqrt{\varepsilon} = \mathsf{poly}(\kappa)\kappa^{-\omega(1)} = \kappa^{-\omega(1)}$ which is negligible. Then $f \sqsubseteq_1 g$, which by Lemma 6 means that f actually does embed in g.

E   Round Complexity and Parallel Calls to g

Our model encompasses protocols that make only a single call to g in each round. Requiring sequential calls to g is without loss of generality *with respect to security*, since in the UC model it cannot be *guaranteed* that calls happen in parallel. The adversary can without loss of generality schedule all the calls sequentially (learning the output of one before choosing an input to the next), resulting in a protocol in our model.

However, when considering round complexity, it is more realistic to allow protocols that make *parallel calls* to g. Although the adversary can schedule these parallel calls in sequence, we still consider the round complexity as that required by the *honest* parties. Most of our technical results apply to such protocols. More formally, consider protocols where at each step the parties may call n parallel instances of g, where n is agreed-upon by both parties. All of our results in Sect. 5.3 and most of the results in Sect. 6 apply to such protocols. In particular, we can collapse any $f \sqsubseteq g$ protocol of $O(\log \kappa)$ rounds to a single-round protocol that may make *many* parallel calls to g but uses no additional communication.

To extend our results, it suffices to show that such a protocol (many parallel calls to g, no additional communication) implies that f embeds in g. We have been currently unable to extend this step. The way we currently extract an embedding from a *single-call* protocol (Lemma 6) works by derandomizing the protocol, crucially using the fact that the number of possible actions in the protocol is *constant*. This property is not true when a protocol makes, say, $O(\kappa)$ parallel calls to g.[5]

---

[5] Our results hold as stated for protocols that call at most $O(\log \kappa)$ instances of g in parallel at a time, where the number of possible actions is polynomial in κ.

In Sect. 7.2 we gave a $\omega(\log \kappa)$-round protocol for specific f using specific g. We point out that this particular protocol *cannot* be made constant-round by making all the g-calls in parallel. The simple attack is to split the g-calls into two groups and use different effective inputs in both (e.g., Alice uses inputs from the first row-group in half of the calls, and second row-group in the other half). With very good probability, this attack leaks as much as evaluating f on two inputs. In particular, Alice can learn Bob's input in its entirety from this attack.

We conjecture that there is no $O(\log \kappa)$-round protocol for this f using this g, even when the protocol allows unlimited parallel calls to g in each round.

References

1. Beaver, D.: Perfect privacy for two-party protocols. In: Feigenbaum, J., Merritt, M. (eds.) Proceedings of DIMACS Workshop on Distributed Computing and Cryptography, vol. 2, pp. 65–77. American Mathematical Society (1989)
2. Beimel, A., Malkin, T.: A quantitative approach to reductions in secure computation. In: Naor, M. (ed.) TCC 2004. LNCS, vol. 2951, pp. 238–257. Springer, Heidelberg (2004). https://doi.org/10.1007/978-3-540-24638-1_14
3. Bellare, M., Rogaway, P.: The security of triple encryption and a framework for code-based game-playing proofs. In: Vaudenay, S. (ed.) EUROCRYPT 2006. LNCS, vol. 4004, pp. 409–426. Springer, Heidelberg (2006). https://doi.org/10.1007/11761679_25
4. Canetti, R.: Universally composable security: a new paradigm for cryptographic protocols. In: 42nd FOCS, pp. 136–145. IEEE Computer Society Press, October 2001
5. Dodis, Y., Micali, S.: Lower bounds for oblivious transfer reductions. In: Stern, J. (ed.) EUROCRYPT 1999. LNCS, vol. 1592, pp. 42–55. Springer, Heidelberg (1999). https://doi.org/10.1007/3-540-48910-X_4
6. Gordon, S.D., Hazay, C., Katz, J., Lindell, Y.: Complete fairness in secure two-party computation. In: Ladner, R.E., Dwork, C. (eds.) 40th ACM STOC, pp. 413–422. ACM Press, May 2008
7. Ishai, Y., Prabhakaran, M., Sahai, A.: Founding cryptography on oblivious transfer – efficiently. In: Wagner, D. (ed.) CRYPTO 2008. LNCS, vol. 5157, pp. 572–591. Springer, Heidelberg (2008). https://doi.org/10.1007/978-3-540-85174-5_32
8. Kilian, J.: Founding cryptography on oblivious transfer. In: 20th ACM STOC, pp. 20–31. ACM Press, May 1988
9. Kilian, J.: Uses of randomness in algorithms and protocols. Ph.D. thesis, Department of Electrical Engineering and Computer Science, Massachusetts Institute of Technology (1989)
10. Kilian, J.: A general completeness theorem for two-party games. In: 23rd ACM STOC, pp. 553–560. ACM Press, May 1991
11. Kilian, J.: More general completeness theorems for secure two-party computation. In: 32nd ACM STOC, pp. 316–324. ACM Press, May 2000
12. Kraschewski, D., Maji, H.K., Prabhakaran, M., Sahai, A.: A full characterization of completeness for two-party randomized function evaluation. In: Nguyen, P.Q., Oswald, E. (eds.) EUROCRYPT 2014. LNCS, vol. 8441, pp. 659–676. Springer, Heidelberg (2014). https://doi.org/10.1007/978-3-642-55220-5_36

13. Kraschewski, D., Müller-Quade, J.: Completeness theorems with constructive proofs for finite deterministic 2-party functions. In: Ishai, Y. (ed.) TCC 2011. LNCS, vol. 6597, pp. 364–381. Springer, Heidelberg (2011). https://doi.org/10.1007/978-3-642-19571-6_22

14. Kushilevitz, E.: Privacy and communication complexity. In: 30th FOCS, pp. 416–421. IEEE Computer Society Press, October/November 1989

15. Lindell, Y., Rabin, T.: Secure two-party computation with fairness - a necessary design principle. In: Kalai, Y., Reyzin, L. (eds.) TCC 2017. LNCS, vol. 10677, pp. 565–580. Springer, Cham (2017). https://doi.org/10.1007/978-3-319-70500-2_19

16. Maji, H.K., Ouppaphan, P., Prabhakaran, M., Rosulek, M.: Exploring the limits of common coins using frontier analysis of protocols. In: Ishai, Y. (ed.) TCC 2011. LNCS, vol. 6597, pp. 486–503. Springer, Heidelberg (2011). https://doi.org/10.1007/978-3-642-19571-6_29

17. Maji, H.K., Prabhakaran, M., Rosulek, M.: Complexity of multi-party computation problems: the case of 2-party symmetric secure function evaluation. In: Reingold, O. (ed.) TCC 2009. LNCS, vol. 5444, pp. 256–273. Springer, Heidelberg (2009). https://doi.org/10.1007/978-3-642-00457-5_16

18. Maji, H.K., Prabhakaran, M., Rosulek, M.: Cryptographic complexity classes and computational intractability assumptions. In: Yao, A.C.-C. (ed.) ICS 2010, pp. 266–289. Tsinghua University Press, Beijing (2010)

19. Maji, H.K., Prabhakaran, M., Rosulek, M.: A zero-one law for cryptographic complexity with respect to computational UC security. In: Rabin, T. (ed.) CRYPTO 2010. LNCS, vol. 6223, pp. 595–612. Springer, Heidelberg (2010). https://doi.org/10.1007/978-3-642-14623-7_32

20. Maji, H.K., Prabhakaran, M., Rosulek, M.: A unified characterization of completeness and triviality for secure function evaluation. In: Galbraith, S., Nandi, M. (eds.) INDOCRYPT 2012. LNCS, vol. 7668, pp. 40–59. Springer, Heidelberg (2012). https://doi.org/10.1007/978-3-642-34931-7_4

21. Prabhakaran, M., Rosulek, M.: Cryptographic complexity of multi-party computation problems: classifications and separations. In: Wagner, D. (ed.) CRYPTO 2008. LNCS, vol. 5157, pp. 262–279. Springer, Heidelberg (2008). https://doi.org/10.1007/978-3-540-85174-5_15

Order-Revealing Encryption and
Symmetric Encryption

Impossibility of Order-Revealing
Encryption in Idealized Models

Mark Zhandry[1]($\boxtimes$) and Cong Zhang[2]

[1] Department of Computer Science, Princeton University, Princeton, USA
mzhandry@princeton.edu
[2] Department of Computer Science, Rutgers University, New Brunswick, USA
cz200@cs.rutgers.edu

Abstract. An Order-Revealing Encryption (ORE) scheme gives a public procedure by which two ciphertexts can be compared to reveal the order of their underlying plaintexts. The ideal security notion for ORE is that *only* the order is revealed—anything else, such as the distance between plaintexts, is hidden. The only known constructions of ORE achieving such ideal security are based on cryptographic multilinear maps and are currently too impractical for real-world applications.

In this work, we give evidence that building ORE from weaker tools may be hard. Indeed, we show black-box separations between ORE and most symmetric-key primitives, as well as public key encryption and anything else implied by generic groups in a black-box way. Thus, any construction of ORE must either (1) achieve weaker notions of security, (2) be based on more complicated cryptographic tools, or (3) require non-black-box techniques. This suggests that any ORE achieving ideal security will likely be somewhat inefficient.

Central to our proof is a proof of impossibility for something we call *information theoretic ORE*, which has connections to tournament graphs and a theorem by Erdös. This impossibility proof will be useful for proving other black box separations for ORE.

Keywords: Black-box separations · Order-revealing encryption
Random oracle model · Generic group model

1 Introduction

Order preserving encryption (OPE) [1,3,4] and order revealing encryption (ORE) [5] have been proposed as useful tools to facilitate fast operations on encrypted databases, such as lookup and range queries.

Order Preserving Encryption (OPE). In OPE, plaintexts and ciphertexts are both integers, and encryption is monotonic: if $m_0 < m_1$, then $\mathsf{Enc}(k, m_0) < \mathsf{Enc}(k, m_1)$. Such a scheme allows, e.g., for binary search and range queries to be easily performed over encrypted data by replacing the plaintext comparisons with ciphertext comparisons. Boldyreva et al. [3] give an efficient construction using pseudorandom functions.

© International Association for Cryptologic Research 2018
A. Beimel and S. Dziembowski (Eds.): TCC 2018, LNCS 11240, pp. 129–158, 2018.
https://doi.org/10.1007/978-3-030-03810-6_5

While clearly, such a scheme will reveal the order of the underlying plain-texts, one may hope that nothing else is revealed; for example, the distance between plaintexts should not be learnable from the ciphertexts without the secret key. However, Boldyreva et al. also show that some additional leakage is necessary in OPE: any such scheme with polynomially-large ciphertexts will reveal some information beyond just the order of the plaintexts; in essence, their proof shows that the approximate distance of two plaintexts will be revealed. For their scheme, they instead prove a different notion of security, namely that encryption is indistinguishable from a random monotone function. Characteriz-ing the kind of information revealed by such a scheme is non-trivial, and has only been analyzed in certain cases such as uniformly random plaintexts [4]. Despite being limited to non-ideal security notions, OPE has been deployed in real products[1] and been studied in applied research [21,25,27].

Order Revealing Encryption (ORE). In order to circumvent Boldyreva et al.'s [3] impossibility result, Boneh et al. [5] define a relaxation called order *revealing* encryption. Here, ciphertexts are no longer necessarily integers. Instead, integer comparison for ciphertexts is replaced by a more general comparison procedure Comp. The correctness requirement is, roughly, that

$$\text{Comp}(\ \text{Enc}(k, m_0),\ \text{Enc}(k, m_1)\ ) = \begin{cases} \text{``} < \text{''} & \text{if } m_0 < m_1 \\ \text{``} = \text{''} & \text{if } m_0 = m_1 \\ \text{``} > \text{''} & \text{if } m_0 < m_1 \end{cases}$$

Boneh et al. give a construction using multilinear maps [7,13,16], and argue that their scheme reveals no information beyond the ordering of the plaintexts. We will call such an ORE scheme *ideal*. Alternate constructions achieving ideal leakage have since been proposed using multi-input functional encryption [5] or even single input functional encryption [9]. Unfortunately, as all known instan-tiations of functional encryption rely on multilinear maps anyway, all known constructions of ORE require multilinear maps as well.

Attacks on ORE. By considering more general comparison procedures for cipher-texts, ideal ORE provably leaks less information than OPE. Nevertheless, a series of works starting with Naveed et al. [14,18,23] have shown that when the adver-sary has a good estimate of the distribution of the data, even ideal ORE provides little protection. The problem is that the definition of ideal ORE, while precise, does not immediately provide any "semantically meaningful" guarantees for the privacy of the underlying data.

Despite these attacks, we still believe ORE is an interesting object to study for several reasons:

– ORE can still provide meaningful notions of security in some settings. For one example, suppose that each data point is sampled i.i.d. from some underlying

---

[1] e.g. https://www.skyhighnetworks.com, https://www.ciphercloud.com/, https://www.bluecoat.com/ and Cipherbase [2].

secret distribution D with large min-entropy (so all samples are distinct), and suppose the adversary has no side information about the data. Then ideal ORE provably hides the distribution D, since all the adversary will see is a random ordering. Note that in contrast, since OPE reveals approximate differences, it will also reveal the approximate scale of D.

- ORE represents one of the simplest functionalities for functional encryption that we do not know how to construct from traditional tools. As such, ORE represents a potential stepping stone toward more advanced functionalities.
- Finally, the comparison structure of ORE is shared with several other concepts in cryptography. For example, most collusion-resistant traitor tracing systems are built on top of *private linear broadcast* encryption [6], which is a form of encryption where there are N secret keys $sk_1, \ldots, sk_N$, and messages are encrypted to numbers j. Any sk_i for $i \geq j$ can decrypt, but any sk_i for $i < j$ cannot. For another example, positional witness encryption [17] also has a similar comparison structure, and is currently the best way to prove security of witness encryption under "instance-independent" assumptions.

However, all known ideal ORE schemes are built on heavy tools, such as multilinear maps, and current multilinear map candidates are quite inefficient, meaning the resulting constructions of order-revealing encryption are far from practical use. Therefore, a natural question is:

Is it possible to build ideal ORE from efficient tools so that it can be practical?

1.1 Our Work

We make a first attempt toward answering the above question by showing that natural constructions of ORE from several simple tools are impossible. Specifically, we give black box impossibility results for building ORE from symmetric key cryptography or public key encryption.

Theorem 1 (Informal). *There is no fully black box construction of an ORE scheme for a super-polynomial plaintext space from random oracles, or any object that can be constructed from random oracles in a black box way, including one-way functions, collision resistant hashing, PRGs, PRFs, and block ciphers.*

Theorem 2 (Informal). *There is no fully black box construction of an ORE scheme for a super-polynomial plaintext space from generic groups, or any object that can be constructed from cryptographic groups in a black box way, including public key encryption and non-interactive key agreement.*[2]

---

[2] There is some overlap in the implications of Theorems 1 and 2, as generic groups can also be used to build much of symmetric key cryptography. However, we still separate our black-box separations into these two theorems for a couple reasons. First, Theorem 1 is simpler, and serves to highlight the ideas that will be needed for Theorem 2. Second, the random oracle model is a very natural way to model

Thus, any black-box construction of order-revealing encryption will require tools with more involved structure, such as bilinear maps, multilinear maps, or lattice assumptions. Such tools tend to be less efficient than those needed to build symmetric cryptography or public key encryption. While we do not rule out non-black-box constructions, such constructions tend to be very inefficient. We, therefore, take our separations as evidence that some inefficiency is required to achieve order revealing encryption with ideal leakage.

In addition to proving Theorems 1 and 2, we also give a framework for proving black box separations for ORE from other cryptographic tools, which may be useful for extending our results.

1.2   Our Techniques

To prove our separation results, we start with an idealized model $\mathcal{M}$ capturing the primitive that we want to separate ORE from: in this work, we take $\mathcal{M}$ to be a random oracle or the generic group model [26].

We now imagine a very relaxed notion of order-revealing encryption using the model (relaxing the notion of ORE we consider only makes our separations stronger):

- There is no explicit decryption procedure.[3]
- The scheme is only partially correct, in that Comp may result in an incorrect answer, but is noticeably biased towards the correct answer.[4]
- The scheme (Gen, Enc, Comp) may make queries to the model $\mathcal{M}$.
- The algorithms are allowed to run arbitrary computations; the only restrictions are that (1) the number of queries to $\mathcal{M}$ is polynomially bounded, and (2) that the length of ciphertexts is polynomially bounded. Running times and key sizes can be unbounded.
- For simplicity in the following discussion, we will also assume the algorithms are deterministic, although our analysis readily applies to randomized schemes as well.
- The adversary can only make polynomially-many queries to $\mathcal{M}$ and can only see a polynomial number of ciphertexts, but we do not consider its computational power.

We next give a general recipe for proving that such a relaxed order-revealing encryption scheme does not exist. To prove impossibility, we proceed in three steps:

---

hash functions, and may capture many security properties desired of hash functions in addition to one-wayness and collision resistance (such as universal computational extractors). Our random oracle proof shows that *any* property that follows from a random oracle is insufficient for constructing ORE in a black-box way. In addition, to the best of our knowledge the random oracle and generic group models are incomparable, so providing both proofs gives the most complete separations.

[3] Though note that this is actually without loss of generality, since decryption can be derived from encryption and comparison by using a binary search.

[4] This is also essentially without loss of generality, as correctness can be boosted by running multiple instances of the scheme in parallel.

1. Compile any scheme satisfying the above requirements into one where Comp does not make any queries to $\mathcal{M}$.
2. Compile the resulting scheme into one where the entire scheme completely ignores $\mathcal{M}$. We call such ORE scheme information-theoretic ORE. This step may lose some level of correctness, so even starting from a perfectly correct scheme, the information-theoretic scheme will no longer be perfectly correct.
3. Finally, show that (even partially correct) information-theoretic ORE does not exist.

We now expand on the three steps above in reverse order:

Impossibility of Information-Theoretic ORE. In information-theoretic ORE, the public/secret key are allowed to be arbitrarily (e.g. exponentially) large, the running times of Gen, Enc, Comp are allowed to be arbitrary, while security must hold for arbitrary adversaries. There is no mention of a model $\mathcal{M}$; the only constraints are that ciphertexts must be polynomially bounded, and that the adversary sees only a polynomial number of ciphertexts.

First, since the scheme is deterministic, we can assume that $\mathsf{Comp}(u, v)$ only outputs "=" if u and v are actually the same. Indeed, if $\mathsf{Comp}(u, v) = $ "=" for $u \neq v$, it means that u, v could not simultaneously be valid encryptions of two messages under the same secret key (since then Comp would report "=" when the plaintexts are in fact not equal). Therefore, for $u \neq v$, if $\mathsf{Comp}(u, v) = $ "=", we can simply change the answer arbitrarily without affecting correctness. Hence, we will choose arbitrarily $\mathsf{Comp}(u, v) = $ "<" or $\mathsf{Comp}(u, v) = $ ">". By a similar argument, we can also assume that $\mathsf{Comp}(u, v) = $ "<" if and only if $\mathsf{Comp}(v, u) = $ ">".

Now, for such a scheme, we can construct an (exponentially large) graph $\mathcal{G}$ associated with the public key where nodes are all possible ciphertexts. There is a directed edge from node u to node v if $\mathsf{Comp}(u, v) = $ "<". Notice that any two distinct nodes have exactly one edge between them. $\mathcal{G}$ is therefore what is known as a tournament graph.

Let s be the number of nodes in $\mathcal{G}$, equivalently the number of ciphertexts. Let $[1, t]$ be plaintext space, which is assumed to be superpolynomial[5]. We show that $\log s$—the bit length of ciphertexts—must be superpolynomial, a contradiction.

This graph must have a significant amount of structure. In our setting, every key k corresponds to a set S of t nodes in $\mathcal{G}$, the encryptions of each of the plaintext elements. Assuming the scheme is perfectly correct, these nodes form a complete DAG, with the encryption of 1 at the beginning and the encryption of t at the end. Therefore, $\mathcal{G}$ must contain many complete DAGs on t nodes.

Moreover, security imparts additional structure on $\mathcal{G}$. Security says, roughly, that the encryptions of any two polynomial-length sequences of ordered messages must be indistinguishable. If we insist on *perfect* security, we have the following. For a given key k, consider the set T of encryptions of $1, \ldots, p$ for some

---

[5] In reality, we would want the number of plaintexts to be exponential, but our impossibility rules out even superpolynomial message spaces.

polynomial p. Then by security, there must be some key k' such that T are the encryptions under k' of $2, \ldots, p+1$. Therefore, the encryption of 1 under k' will have an edge to each of the nodes in T. Notice that this property must hold *for any* set T that can be represented as the encryptions of $1, \ldots, p$ for some key k.

The situation above is reminiscent of a problem studied by Erdös [15]. He asked the question: suppose every set of p nodes is *dominated* by another node; that is, for every set T of p nodes, there is a node u such that u has an edge to each node in T. He showed that the number of nodes in any tournament graph satisfying this property must be exponential in p. The proof is by induction: for any graph $\mathcal{G}$ satisfying the property for p, there is a graph on half as many nodes that satisfies the property for $p-1$. Continuing until the base case $p=1$, we see that there must be a graph $\mathcal{G}'$ that is exponentially smaller than $\mathcal{G}$, meaning $\mathcal{G}$ must be exponentially-large.

We prove an analog of Erdös's proof in our setting. Namely, we show that for any polynomial p, the number of nodes s in $\mathcal{G}$ must be exponential in p. Since s is exponential in any polynomial, then $\log s$ must larger than any polynomial, a contradiction. Our proof is inspired by Erdös's proof, except complicated in several ways:

- Our structure, while superficially similar, has several key differences. For example, there will be sets T that do not correspond to encryptions of $1, \ldots, p$ under one key. For example, T may be formed by encrypting $1, \ldots, p/2$ under k_1 and $1, \ldots, p/2$ under k_2.
- We do not insist on perfect security, but instead on statistical security. This means, for example, that the dominating property may not hold for all sets T that are encryptions of $1, \ldots, p$.

Nonetheless, we show an inductive argument that resolves these difficulties, and proves that s must be exponential in p for any polynomial p. Hence, $\log s$ must be larger than any polynomial, as desired.

The above discussion assumed that the scheme was perfectly correct. However, looking ahead, we would like to prove the impossibility for even partially correct schemes, where the output of Comp may be incorrect, but is biased toward the right answer. We show how to compile such a partially correct scheme into one that is perfectly correct. Then invoking the impossibility above, we see that even a partially correct scheme is impossible. The compilation is simple: first we run multiple instances of the scheme in parallel to boost correctness arbitrarily high, but still not necessarily perfect. However, we argue that we can boost correctness high enough so that, with high probability over the key, Comp will produce the right answer for all ciphertexts. Then we just change the scheme so that the key is chosen randomly from the set of "good" keys. This only negligibly affects security (since the key is "good" with high probability anyway). Verifying that a key is "good" will of course take exponential time since one must verify that it outputs the right answer for any possible pair of messages; however, this is fine since we do not place any computational restrictions.

Comparison to Boldyreva et al. [3]. Order *preserving* encryption is the special case of ORE where the entire ciphertext graph is actually one large DAG. Boldyreva et al.'s impossibility can be interpreted as a special case of our proof above where the graph is restricted to DAG. Our proof is much stronger, as it applies to much less structured graphs—any structure we use is solely a function of the correctness and security requirements, and no additional structure is assumed.

Compiling Schemes Where Comp Does Not Make Queries to $\mathcal{M}$. We show that if Comp does not make queries to $\mathcal{M}$, then it can be compiled into an information-theoretic scheme, and then we can apply the above impossibility to rule out the original scheme. Our compilation process works even if the starting scheme was only partially correct; since the impossibility above works with partially-correct schemes, we can still rule out partially correct schemes where Comp makes no oracle queries.

The process is simple. Since Comp does not make any queries to $\mathcal{M}$, the model is not needed outside of encryption. This means, in particular, that it makes sense to restrict the adversary from querying $\mathcal{M}$. Doing so only enhances security.

Next, we can simply have the secret key holder construct the oracle $\mathcal{M}$ for himself, and include it as part of the secret key. The description of the oracle might be exponential in size, but this is acceptable since we do not place any bounds on the key size or running time of the honest users. The result is a scheme which makes no reference to an idealized model.

Removing Oracle Queries From Comp. The final step is to remove oracle queries from Comp. This is the only part that is specific to the model $\mathcal{M}$ being considered. This step can be seen as an ORE analog of several recent results showing black box impossibilities for constructing obfuscation from simple objects. We note however, as expanded on below, that there are some crucial differences from obfuscation that make our proofs significantly different.

The Random Oracle Model. This first model $\mathcal{M}$ we consider is the random oracle model. Here, $\mathcal{M}$ just implements a random function $\mathcal{O}$. At a very high level, our compilation is conceptually similar to Canetti et al.'s [10] analogous compilation for program obfuscation. They show how to compile out a random oracle from the evaluation of an obfuscation scheme. Roughly, the idea is that evaluation of the obfuscated program will be "sensitive" only to the query points that were queried during the obfuscation; all other points will be independent of the obfuscated code, and hence can be answered randomly. Therefore, the obfuscator can just give the (polynomially-many) sensitive query answers out as part of the obfuscated code, and now the evaluator can answer any oracle query without actually making a call to the oracle.

In more detail, the sensitive queries can be split into two classes: "heavy" queries that are somewhat likely to be queried when evaluating the program on a random input, and "light" queries that are unlikely to be queried. Canetti et al. first run the obfuscated code on a handful of random "test" points, and collect the random oracle queries and responses. By setting the number of test queries to be sufficiently large, they guarantee that all heavy queries will make it into the list of query/response pairs. Then they just output this list as part of the obfuscated code. Since an adversary could always run the code on random inputs and make the oracle queries, this cannot impact the security of the obfuscator. However now the evaluator, on a random input, will usually not need to make any oracle queries. Indeed, on a random input, the evaluator will likely only need to query on heavy inputs (or non-sensitive inputs, which can be answered randomly), which it already has included as a part of the obfuscated code.

The straightforward attempt at translating this approach to our setting is to first encrypt a handful of random test plaintexts, run the comparison procedure between each pair of test ciphertexts, and collect all of the oracle queries made. Then hand out the list of query/response pairs as part of the public key.

Unfortunately, this strategy does not work, for at least three reasons:

- First, the test ciphertexts will allow one to learn the approximate difference between points, violating ORE security. In particular, using the ORE comparison procedure, one can compute the fraction of test ciphertexts lying between any two given ciphertexts. This fraction, scaled up by the size of the plaintext space, will approximately equal the difference between the plaintexts.
- Second, the notion of "sensitive" and "heavy" queries are specific to each individual plaintext, and not a global property of the encryption scheme. For example, it could be that to encrypt a message m, the oracle is queried on m. m will be a sensitive and heavy query point only for the message m. Therefore, as we increase the number of test ciphertexts, we also increase the number of sensitive and heavy queries, making it more difficult to ensure that we eventually capture all heavy queries for each ciphertext in question.
- Third, correctness will only hold for a plaintext drawn from the same distribution as the test points—namely random plaintexts—whereas our steps above require correctness to hold for *any* plaintexts.

To overcome the first limitation, we will simply set our test ciphertexts to be the smallest and largest several elements of the plaintext space. Now for any two ciphertexts not at the extremes of the domain, there will be no test ciphertexts between; we can therefore restrict the domain of actual ciphertexts to a smaller interval so as to not collide with the test ciphertexts. This change unfortunately makes the third limitation even worse: the test elements now are the extreme elements in the plaintext space, but we need correctness to hold for all possible points in between.

To remedy the second limitation, we further modify the compiled scheme so that in addition to comparing all pairs of test ciphertexts, any new ciphertext is also compared to all of the test ciphertexts. If we set the number of test ciphertexts to be much larger than the number of heavy queries for a ciphertext, then hopefully these comparisons will generate all heavy queries. Indeed, each comparison will generate heavy queries for one of the two ciphertexts being compared. Note, however, that at this point in the discussion, it could be the case that the comparisons only generate heavy queries for the test ciphertexts, which would be useless for establishing the correctness of the scheme.

To overcome this issue, as well as the third limitation above, we will invoke ORE security to switch back and forth between points in the middle of the plaintext space and the extreme points at the ends of the plaintext space. Using security (as opposed to an information-theoretic argument) means that the proof has to be phrased as a reduction, which requires a delicate analysis. For example, an adversary cannot necessarily test whether a query is sensitive or heavy, so our reduction cannot know if it learned all of the important queries for a particular ciphertext. We give the full details in Sect. 5.

The Generic Group Model. Next, we consider the generic group model. Here, there is a cyclic group $\mathbb{G}$. We will consider the group represented additively. Each group element is associated with a handle (that is, a bit string), and only the model $\mathcal{M}$ has access to the mapping. Everyone can query $\mathcal{M}$ on a group element g to get a handle h, and can also query $\mathcal{M}$ on two handles h_1, h_2, receiving the handle for the sum of corresponding group elements. However, it is not possible to query $\mathcal{M}$ on a handle h and recover the original group element g.

An equivalent formulation is the following. Instead of being able to query on two handles h_1, h_2 to get the handle for the sum, only the following is possible: query on a vector $\mathbf{h} = (h_1, \ldots, h_i)$ of handles corresponding to group elements $\mathbf{g} = (g_1, \ldots, g_i)$, and a vector $\mathbf{v} = (v_1, \ldots, v_i)$ of integers. The response will be a single bit: 0 if $\sum_j v_j g_j = 0$, and 1 otherwise. We call these queries *zero test* queries.

Our high-level proof strategy will be conceptually similar to Pass and Shelat [24], which show how to remove generic groups from obfuscation constructions[6]. However, our setting faces similar complications as to the random oracle setting above, requiring a much more delicate proof.

During encryption of a message m, Enc will query the generic group on several new group elements $g_1^{(m)}, \ldots, g_t^{(m)}$, obtaining handles. Now, when comparing two ciphertexts, Comp will make several zero test queries on various handles coming from m_0, m_1. Whenever Comp gets a 0 in response, it learns a linear constraint on the unknown g elements. Suppose the probability of getting a 0 in comparison is μ. We will assume that μ is noticeably large, since otherwise the zero test queries would be useless, as one could simulate them reasonably accurately just by always answering 1.

If the adversary sees q ciphertexts, the total number of constraints she can find will be $O(\mu q^2)$. And yet, the total number of unknown variables is only qt. For large enough q, this is much smaller than the number of constraints. The constraints are then necessarily linearly dependent. This means that, analogous to the random oracle case above, the adversary will be able to answer zero test queries for herself based on the results of previous queries. We show using a

---

[6] We note that Mahmoody et al. [22] extend the Pass and Shelat result to any (even non-commutative) finite ring; we leave extending our impossibility to the non-commutative setting as an interesting open problem.

similar strategy to the random oracle setting how to compile the ORE scheme in a way that preserves security and correctness, while removing the generic group oracle queries from Comp. Of course, formalizing this intuition is non-trivial, and we give the details in Sect. 6.

Difficulties for Extending to Bilinear and Multilinear Maps. Pass and Shelat's [24] proof naturally extends to bilinear maps and more generally constant-degree multilinear maps. A natural question is whether or not our techniques can be extended to these settings as well. Roughly, a bilinear map allows for zero-test queries that are degree 2 polynomials, and a multilinear map allows for even higher degree.

Pass and Shelat's proof, as well as ours, inherently relies on linear algebra, so does not immediately extend to non-linear settings. Indeed, their proofs and ours cannot possibly work for general multilinear maps, as there do exist black box constructions of obfuscation [8] and ORE [5] from polynomial-degree multilinear maps.

Nonetheless, Pass and Shelat show how to extend their result to *constant degree* multilinear maps. Essentially, the idea is to linearize the constant-degree polynomials by describing them as linear combinations of monomials. Then using similar arguments as in the generic group case, they show how to remove oracle queries from obfuscation.

Unfortunately, such linearization will not work in our setting, even in the bilinear map case. Once we linearize, the total number of variables grows $O((qt)^2)$, while the number of constraints is still only $O(\mu q^2)$. Since both grow with q^2, the number of variables always remains large than the number of constraints, so there is no linear dependence amongst the constraints. Without this linear dependence the proof falls apart. Another perspective for why the linearization does not work: in the bilinear group model, Enc(m) will query the generic group on new group elements $g_1^{(m)}, \ldots, g_t^{(m)}$, while the comparison on Enc(m_0), Enc(m_1) learns a degree-2 constraint on the variables, containing monomials such as $g_1^{(m_0)} \cdot g_1^{(m_1)}$. However, note that this monomial *only* appears in constraints obtained when comparing encryptions of m_0 and m_1; any other pair of messages will give different monomials. Hence, the constraints for different pairs of ciphertexts are linearly independent, making it difficult (if not impossible) to argue that the results of certain comparisons will help us answer other comparisons. We leave it as an interesting open question whether our impossibility can be extended to, say, the bilinear map setting, and if not, giving a black-box construction of ORE from bilinear maps.

1.3 Discussion

In light of our impossibility, it is natural to ask: *now what?* Here, we briefly discuss possible other directions.

Weaker Notions of Security. One possibility is to consider weaker notions of security, where more than just the order is revealed. For example, [12] give a construction of ORE where the position of the most significant differing bit of two plaintexts is revealed, but nothing else (put another way, the difference is revealed, rounded to a power of two). Their construction is efficient, using only PRFs (which can in turn be built from one-way functions). [11] give a still-practical construction using bilinear maps which reveals even less, though still more than the ideal security notion. [19] give a notion of functional revealing encryption and build an efficient ORE under the standard DLIN assumption, while it leaks no less than [11].

An interesting direction is to extend our impossibility result to other leakage profiles, perhaps showing that the leakage profile of [12] is optimal for constructions based on one-way functions. Such an impossibility would require reworking several parts of our proof, since we use the ideal ORE leakage in several parts, including the impossibility of information-theoretic ORE, as well as the step removing random oracle queries from Comp.

Non-Black-Box Constructions. Another option is to resort to non-black-box construction. We do not know if such a construction is possible. However, non-black-box techniques tend to result in inefficient schemes, as such a non-black-box construction is likely to be inefficient.

Other Cryptographic Tools. We only rule out black-box constructions from certain building blocks; other building blocks are still possible. For example, it may be possible to build ORE from the Learning With Errors (LWE) assumption, RSA or integer factorization, or bilinear/multilinear maps. Indeed, using multilinear maps of polynomial degree, it is possible to build ORE with ideal leakage, as shown by Boneh et al. [5]. However, many of the tools not covered by our impossibility, including polynomial-degree multilinear maps or learning with errors, involve large parameter sizes, likely resulting in somewhat impractical schemes. Nonetheless, we believe that constructing ideal ORE from weaker tools including LWE or bilinear maps, or providing black-box separations for these tools by building on our techniques, are fascinating open questions.

2   Background

NOTATION. For $n, n_1, n_2 \in \mathbb{N}$, let $[n] := \{1, \ldots, n\}, [n_1, n_2] := \{n_1, \ldots, n_2\}$. Throughout this paper, $\lambda \in \mathbb{N}$ denote the security parameter. For a finite set $\mathcal{S}$, we denote $s \leftarrow \mathcal{S}$ the process of sampling s uniformly from $\mathcal{S}$. For a probabilistic algorithm A, we denote $y \leftarrow A(x; R)$ the process of running A on input x and randomness R, and assigning y the result. We let $\mathcal{R}_A$ denote the randomness space of A; we require $\mathcal{R}_A$ to be the form $\mathcal{R}_A = \{0,1\}^r$. We write $y \leftarrow A(x)$ for $y \leftarrow A(x, R)$ with uniformly chosen $R \in \mathcal{R}_A$, and we write $y_1, \ldots, y_m \leftarrow A(x)$ for $y_1 \leftarrow A(x), \ldots, y_m \leftarrow A(x)$ with fresh randomness in each execution. If A's running time is polynomial in λ, then A is called probabilistic polynomial-time (PPT).

We say a function $\mu(n)$ is negligible if $\mu \in o(n^{-\omega(1)})$, and is non-negligible otherwise. We let negl(n) denote an arbitrary negligible function. If we say some

$p(n)$ is poly, we mean that there is some polynomial q such that for all sufficiently large n, $p(n) \leq q(n)$. We say a function $\rho(n)$ is noticeable if the inverse $1/\rho(n)$ is poly. We use boldface to denote vector, i.e. $\boldsymbol{m}$; we denote $\boldsymbol{m}_i$ as the i-th component of $\boldsymbol{m}$ and $|\boldsymbol{m}|$ as the length of $\boldsymbol{m}$. The statistical distance of two random variables X and Y over some countable domain S is defined as $\mathsf{SD}(X;Y) = \frac{1}{2}\sum_{s \in S} |\Pr[X = s] - \Pr[Y = s]|$. We write $X \overset{d}{\approx} Y$ for $\mathsf{SD}(X;Y) \leq d$, and $X \overset{\mathsf{stat}}{\approx} Y$ for $\mathsf{SD}(X;Y) \leq 2^{-\lambda}$.

ORE. The following definition of syntax for order-revealing encryption makes explicit that comparison may use helper information (e.g. a description of a particular group) by incorporating a *public key*, denote pk.

Definition 3 *(ORE). An ORE scheme with message space $[N]$ is a tuple of algorithms $\Pi = \mathsf{Gen}, \mathsf{Enc}, \mathsf{Comp}$ with the following syntax.*

- *The key generation algorithm Gen is randomized, takes inputs $(1^\lambda, N)$, and always emits two outputs $(\mathsf{pk}, \mathsf{sk})$. We refer to the first output pk as the* public key *and the second output sk as the* secret key.
- *The encryption algorithm Enc takes inputs (sk, m) where $m \in [N]$, and always emits a single output c, that we refer to as a* ciphertext.
- *The comparison algorithm Comp takes inputs (pk, c_1, c_2), and emits "¡", "="* or *"¿", which indicates the order of the underlying plaintexts.*

If Comp is simple integer comparison (i.e., if $\mathsf{Comp}(\mathsf{pk}, c_1, c_2)$ is a canonical algorithm that treats its the ciphertexts and binary representations of integers and tests which is greater) then the scheme is said to be an order-preserving encryption (OPE) *scheme.*

Correctness for ORE. Intuitively, an ORE scheme is correct if the comparison algorithm can output the order of the underlying plaintexts. For any two message pair (m_0, m_1), let $\mathsf{Comp}(m_0, m_1)$ be the order of (m_0, m_1), where:

$$\mathsf{Comp}(m_0, m_1) = \begin{cases} \text{"} < \text{"} & m_0 < m_1 \\ \text{"} = \text{"} & m_0 = m_1 \\ \text{"} > \text{"} & m_0 > m_1 \end{cases}$$

we consider four notions of correctness:

- **Perfect Correctness.** For any message pair (m_0, m_1), we have

  $\Pr[\mathsf{Comp}(\mathsf{pk}, C_0, C_1) = \mathsf{Comp}(m_0, m_1) : (\mathsf{pk}, \mathsf{sk}) \leftarrow \mathsf{Gen}(), C_b = \mathsf{Enc}(\mathsf{sk}, m_b)] = 1$

- **Almost Perfect Correctness.** There is a negligible function $\mu = \mathsf{negl}(\lambda)$ such that

  $\Pr[\exists (m_0, m_1), \mathsf{Comp}(\mathsf{pk}, C_{m_0}, C_{m_1}) \neq \mathsf{Comp}(m_0, m_1) : C_b = \mathsf{Enc}(\mathsf{sk}, m_b)] \leq \mu$

  where the probability is taken over the choice of $(\mathsf{pk}, \mathsf{sk}) \leftarrow \mathsf{Gen}()$.

- **Statistical Correctness.** There is a negligible function $\mu = \mathsf{negl}(\lambda)$ such that for any (m_1, m_2)

$$\Pr[\mathsf{Comp}(\mathsf{pk}, C_0, C_1) - \mathsf{Comp}(m_0, m_1) : C_b = \mathsf{Enc}(\mathsf{sk}, m_b)] \geq 1 - \mu$$

where the probability is taken over the choice of $(\mathsf{pk}, \mathsf{sk}) \leftarrow \mathsf{Gen}()$.
- **Partial Correctness.** There is a noticeable function $\rho(\lambda)$ such that, for any (m_1, m_2),

$$\Pr[\mathsf{Comp}(\mathsf{pk}, C_0, C_1) = \mathsf{Comp}(m_0, m_1) : (\mathsf{pk}, \mathsf{sk}) \leftarrow \mathsf{Gen}()] \geq \frac{1}{2} + \rho$$

In this work, we also consider ORE in idealized models, where the scheme's algorithms have access to an oracle.

Definition 4 *(Idealized Model). An idealized model is a deterministic function $\mathcal{M}$. $\mathcal{M}$ takes two inputs: a string k which is the seed for the model, and a query q. Unless otherwise stated, we allow all players—the honest parties, the protocol algorithms, and the adversary—to query $\mathcal{M}$. In a query to $\mathcal{M}$:*

- *Any player sends q to $\mathcal{M}$;*
- *The player receives $\mathcal{M}(k, q)$ in return.*

We will denote an ORE scheme Π in an idealized model $\mathcal{M}$ as $\Pi^{\mathcal{M}} = (\mathsf{Gen}^{\mathcal{M}}, \mathsf{Enc}^{\mathcal{M}}, \mathsf{Comp}^{\mathcal{M}})$. This notation means that key generation, encryption, and comparison have access to $\mathcal{M}$ and the outputs also depend on $\mathcal{M}$'s response. Our definitions of security and correctness for ORE easily extend to the idealized model, where the probabilities are over the random seed k that generates $\mathcal{M}$.

Efficiency for ORE. Typically in the literature, ORE is defined as having computationally efficient algorithms:

Definition 5. *Let $\Pi = (\mathsf{Gen}, \mathsf{Enc}, \mathsf{Comp})$ be an ORE scheme with respect to the message space $[N]$. We say Π is computationally efficient if $\mathsf{Gen}, \mathsf{Enc}, \mathsf{Comp}$ run in time polynomial in $(\log N, \lambda)$. If Π is a scheme in an idealized model $\mathcal{M}$, we additionally require that the algorithms only make a polynomial number of queries to $\mathcal{M}$.*

Here, we will generally not impose any such restrictions, and allow for computationally inefficient algorithms. We only impose two efficiency constraints. First, if the scheme is an ideal-model scheme, we still require the number of queries to be polynomial.

Definition 6. *Let $\Pi^{\mathcal{M}} = (\mathsf{Gen}^{\mathcal{M}}, \mathsf{Enc}^{\mathcal{M}}, \mathsf{Comp}^{\mathcal{M}})$ be an ORE scheme in an idealized model $\mathcal{M}$. We say Π is query efficient if $\mathsf{Gen}, \mathsf{Enc}, \mathsf{Comp}$ only make a number of queries that is polynomial in $(\log N, \lambda)$.*

The second efficiency requirement (for both idealized model schemes and standard model schemes) is that the ciphertexts produced by the scheme are polynomial sized.

Definition 7. *Let Π (resp. $\Pi^{\mathcal{M}}$) be an ORE with respect to the message space $[N]$ (resp. in idealized model). We say Π ($\Pi^{\mathcal{M}}$) has succinct ciphertexts if the ciphertext length is polynomial in $(\log N, \lambda)$.*

We call a scheme for which there is no idealized model but which still has succinct ciphertexts an *information-theoretic* scheme.

Security for ORE. An ORE scheme leaks the order of the underlying plaintexts, so the ideal security notion for ORE is that *only* the order is revealed. Roughly speaking, given two sequences of message $\boldsymbol{m}, \boldsymbol{m}'$ such that $\mathsf{Comp}(\boldsymbol{m}_i, \boldsymbol{m}_j) = \mathsf{Comp}(\boldsymbol{m}_i', \boldsymbol{m}_j'), \forall i, j \in |\boldsymbol{m}|$, the distribution of $\mathsf{Enc}(\boldsymbol{m})$ and $\mathsf{Enc}(\boldsymbol{m}')$ are statistically indistinguishable. We firstly consider a weak version, which we call t-time secure, with the restriction that $|\boldsymbol{m}| = |\boldsymbol{m}'| \leq t$, then we define an interactive game with an unbounded adversary in the following:

$t\text{-SIND}(\mathcal{A})$:
$(\mathsf{pk}, \mathsf{sk}) \leftarrow \mathsf{Gen}(N, 1^\lambda); \ m_1 < \ldots < m_t, m_1' < \ldots < m_t' \leftarrow \mathcal{A}(\mathsf{pk}, N, 1^\lambda);$
$C_0 = (\mathsf{pk}, \mathsf{Enc}(\mathsf{sk}, m_1), \ldots, \mathsf{Enc}(\mathsf{sk}, m_t)); C_1 = (\mathsf{pk}, \mathsf{Enc}(\mathsf{sk}, m_1'), \ldots, \mathsf{Enc}(\mathsf{sk}, m_t'));$
$b' \leftarrow \mathcal{A}(C_b); \text{Return } (b \overset{?}{=} b')$

Fig. 1. t-time static indistinguishable game

Definition 8. *Let $\Pi = (\mathsf{Gen}, \mathsf{Enc}, \mathsf{Comp})$ be an ORE scheme with respect to the message space $[N]$. For any PPT (resp. unbounded) adversary $\mathcal{A}$ we define the game* $t\text{-SIND}(\mathcal{A})$ *in Fig. 1. The advantage of $\mathcal{A}$ for the t-time static indistinguishable game is defined to be:*

$$\mathsf{Adv}_{\mathcal{A}}^{t\text{-SIND}}(1^\lambda) = 2Pr[t\text{-SIND}(\mathcal{A})] - 1$$

We say that Π is t-time computationally (resp. statistically) secure if for any PPT (resp. unbounded) adversary $\mathcal{A}$, $\mathsf{Adv}_{\mathcal{A}}^{t\text{-SIND}}(1^\lambda)$ is negligible. And we say Π is fully (computationally/statistically) secure if Π is t-time (computationally/statistically) secure for any polynomial $t = poly(logN, \lambda)$.

If Π is an ORE scheme in the idealized model $\mathcal{M}$, we extend the security notions above by allowing $\mathcal{A}$ to make a polynomial number of queries to $\mathcal{M}$, and all probabilities are taken over the seed for $\mathcal{M}$.

3   Impossibility of Information-Theoretic ORE

In this section, we show that for information-theoretic ORE, full statistical security is impossible if the message space is super-polynomial. Note that this is qualitatively tight, as [20][7] shows how to construct information-theoretic ORE where the ciphertext size is polynomial in the size of the message space.

---

[7] Here we treat the PRFs and PRPs in [20] as real random functions and permutations, which achieving statistical security, rather than only computational security.

Note that our impossibility applies to schemes where the public/secret key are allowed to be arbitrarily (e.g., exponentially) large, the running time of Enc, Comp are allowed to be arbitrary. However, the following restrictions must hold: (1) the size of ciphertexts must be polynomially bounded, (2) the security must hold for arbitrary adversaries (even for unbound adversary), (3) the adversary sees only a polynomial number of ciphertexts. Now, we prove our theorem.

Theorem 9. *In standard model, there does not exist a fully statistically secure ORE Π such that*

- *Π is partially correct;*
- *Π's message space is super-polynomial;*
- *Π has succinct ciphertexts.*

Roughly speaking, our proof strategy is: (1) prove the result in the simpler setting where we insist on *perfect* correctness, and then (2) show how to convert any partially correct information-theoretic ORE into a perfectly correct one.

3.1   Impossibility for Perfect Correct ORE

In this part, we consider the ORE scheme in the perfectly correct setting.

Theorem 10. *In standard model, there does not exist a statistically secure ORE Π such that*

- *Π is perfectly correct;*
- *Π's message space is super-polynomial;*
- *Π has succinct ciphertexts.*

Firstly, we give a brief description of our proof strategy. Let Π be an ORE scheme on message space $[t + 1]$, where $t = \mathsf{poly}(\lambda)$, such that Π is perfectly correct and statistically secure. We immediately observe that Π is t-time secure, next we show, for any such an ORE, there exists an exponential lower bound on the size of the ciphertext space (roughly $O(2^{t/2})$), which means the size of ciphertext is at least $\mathsf{poly}(t)$. Based on that, it's trivial to note that, for any ORE with super-polynomial message space, the ciphertext size is at least $\mathsf{poly}(t)$(for arbitrary $t = \mathsf{poly}(\lambda)$). Then we set t to be sufficiently large to contradict the theorem statement.

The core technique we use is inspired by Erdös [15]. Roughly, for any Π with plaintext space $[t + 1]$, we interpret its ciphertext space as a graph G_{t+1}, which has a similar structure to the graphs studied in [15]. Then we sample a sequence of sub-graphs such that $G_{t+1} \supseteq G_{t-1} \supseteq \ldots G_1$[8] in a specific way (based on our ORE). After that, we prove for any adjacent pair, we have $\mathbb{E}[\log |G_i|] \geq \mathbb{E}[\log |G_{i-2}|] + \log(1.6), \forall i \in \{t + 1, t - 1, \ldots, 3\}$, which means $\mathbb{E}[\log |G_{t+1}|] \geq \lfloor \frac{t-1}{2} \rfloor \log 1.6$. More precisely:

---

[8] Here we assume t is even.

Lemma 11. *In standard model, let Π be a perfectly correct t-time secure ORE on message space $[t+1]$, then Π requires ciphertexts of size at least $\lfloor \frac{t-1}{2} \rfloor \log 1.6$.*

Proof. This proof applies a similar spirit to a proof technique used by Erdös [15].

Let $\Pi_{t+1} = (\mathsf{Gen}, \mathsf{Enc}, \mathsf{Comp})$ be a perfect correct t-time secure ORE, with respect to message space $[t+1]$ and ciphertext space $\mathcal{C}$. We construct a new ORE Π_{t+1}^* as follows. The public key for Π_{t+1} defines a graph G_{t+1}, where the nodes of G_{t+1} represent the ciphertexts in $\mathcal{C}$. We set the edges for G_{t+1} as:

- If $\mathsf{Comp}(C_0, C_1) = $ "$<$", then there is a directed edge from C_0 to C_1
- Otherwise, we arbitrarily assign a single directed edge between the two nodes.

By perfect correctness of Π_{t+1}, we note that there is at most one directed edge between any two nodes, and if C_0 and C_1 are not simultaneously valid ciphertexts under the same secret key (we can view this as $C_0 = \mathsf{Enc}(\mathsf{sk}_0, i), C_1 = \mathsf{Enc}(\mathsf{sk}_1, j)$, and in such a case they are the ciphertexts encrypted under distinct secret keys), we set an arbitrary edge for these two nodes. Hence G_{t+1} is a "tournament" graph. Now we define $\Pi_{t+1}^* = (\mathsf{Gen}_{t+1}^*, \mathsf{Enc}_{t+1}^*, \mathsf{Comp}_{t+1}^*)$:

- $\mathsf{Gen}^*()$ Runs $(pk, sk) \leftarrow \mathsf{Gen}()$, computes G_{t+1} as above, and outputs $pk^* = (pk, G_{t+1}), sk^* = sk$;
- $\mathsf{Enc}^*(sk^*, m)$ It runs $C = \mathsf{Enc}(sk^*, m)$, and outputs $C^* = C$;
- $\mathsf{Comp}^*(pk^*, C_0^*, C_1^*)$ If $C_0^* = C_1^*$, outputs "$=$", else outputs "$<$" if there is directed edge from C_0^* to C_1^* in G_{t+1}, and "$>$" otherwise.

The only difference between Π_{t+1} and Π_{t+1}^* is adding G_{t+1} to the public key, which only affects the efficiency of Gen and Comp, while perfect correctness and t-time security are preserved.

Then, we sample the sub-graphs $G_{t-1} \supseteq \ldots \supseteq G_1$(assume t is even). For any $j \in \{2, 4, \ldots, t\}$, graph G_{t+1-j} is sampled as:

- Run $(pk^*, sk^*) \leftarrow \mathsf{Gen}_{t+1}^*$, compute $C_L^i = \mathsf{Enc}(sk^*, i), C_R^i = \mathsf{Enc}(sk^*, t+1-i)$ for $i \in [j/2]$;
- Set G_{t+1-j} be the sub-graph of G_{t+1} consisting of all nodes v dominated by $\{C_L^1, \ldots, C_L^{j/2}\}$ (that is, there is an edge from C_L^i to v for all i) and dominate $\{C_R^1, \ldots, C_R^{j/2}\}$ (that is, there is an edge from v to C_R^i for all i).

Clearly, $|G_1| \geq 1$, therefore it's sufficient to prove that for $j \in \{2, 4 \ldots, t\}$,

$$\mathbb{E}(\log |G_{t+3-j}|) \geq \mathbb{E}(\log |G_{t+1-j}|) + \log 1.6$$

First, recall that Π^* is t-time secure, implying the distribution of the encryptions for M_0 and M_1 are statistically close, over the probability $(pk^*, sk^*) \leftarrow \mathsf{Gen}_{t+1}^*$, where,

$$M_0 = (1, 2, \ldots, j/2, j/2+1, t+1-j/2, \ldots, t+1)$$
$$M_1 = (1, 2, \ldots, j/2, t-j/2, t+1-j/2, \ldots, t+1)$$

Then, let f_L, f_R be the expected fraction of nodes in G_{t+3-j} that are dominated by $\mathsf{Enc}(j/2 + 1), \mathsf{Enc}(t - j/2)$, respectively. Due to security, we have

$$(\mathsf{pk}^*, \mathsf{Enc}(M_0)) \overset{\text{stat}}{\approx} (\mathsf{pk}^*, \mathsf{Enc}(M_1)) \Rightarrow |f_L - f_R| \leq \mathsf{negl} \leq 1/4$$

Besides, G_{t+3-j} is also tournament, which indicates the expected fraction of nodes in G_{t+3-j} that dominate $\mathsf{Enc}(t - j/2)$ is

$$1 - f_R \leq 1 - f_L + 1/4$$

Moreover, G_{t+1-j} is the intersection of the nodes in G_{t+3-j} which dominate $\mathsf{Enc}(t - j/2)$ and which are dominated by $\mathsf{Enc}(j/2 + 1)$, the ratio $|G_{t+1-j}|/|G_{t+3-j}|$ is at most the minimum of:

- The fraction of nodes in G_{t+3-j} which dominate $\mathsf{Enc}(t - j/2)$
- The fraction of nodes in G_{t+3-j} dominated by $\mathsf{Enc}(j/2 + 1)$.

Now, we can upper bound $\mathbb{E}[\log |G_{t+1-j}|]$ as:

$$
\begin{aligned}
\mathbb{E}[\log |G_{t+1-j}|] &= \mathbb{E}[\log |G_{t+3-j}|] + \mathbb{E}[\log \frac{|G_{t+1-j}|}{|G_{t+3-j}|}] \\
&\leq \mathbb{E}[\log |G_{t+3-j}|] + \log \mathbb{E}[\frac{|G_{t+1-j}|}{|G_{t+3-j}|}] \quad \text{Jensen's inequality} \\
&\leq \mathbb{E}[\log |G_{t+3-j}|] + \log \min(f_L, 1 - f_L + 1/4) \\
&\leq \mathbb{E}[\log |G_{t+3-j}|] + \log \frac{1 + 1/4}{2} = \mathbb{E}[\log |G_{t+3-j}|] - \log 1.6
\end{aligned}
$$

For the last line, we used the fact that for any f_L, $\min(f_L, c - f_L) \leq \frac{c}{2}$. Putting everything together, we have

$$\mathbb{E}[\log |G_{t+1}|] \geq \mathbb{E}[\log |G_1|] + \lfloor \frac{t-1}{2} \rfloor \log 1.6$$

In addition, applying exactly the same technique, the theorem also holds when t is odd. $\qquad \square$

Now, we complete the entire proof for Theorem 10. Suppose Π is an ORE such that: (1) Π is perfect correct and statistically secure; (2) Π's message space is $[N]$, where N is super-polynomial; (3) Π has succinct ciphertexts, which is bounded by $r = \mathsf{poly}(\lambda, \log N)$. Then, let $t = 4r$ (t is still polynomial here), we know that Π is t-time secure. According to Lemma 11, $r \geq \lfloor \frac{t-1}{2} \rfloor \cdot \log 1.6 > r$, a contradiction. $\qquad \square$

3.2 Boosting to Perfect Correctness

To strengthen our result, we also consider ORE scheme that is only partially correct, and in this part, we show how to boost any partially correct scheme to a perfectly correct one.

Theorem 12. *If there exists partially correct and statistically secure ORE in the standard model that has succinct ciphertexts and super-polynomial message space, then statistically secure ORE in standard model with succinct ciphertexts and perfect correctness on the same message space exists.*

Proof. Let $\Pi = (\mathsf{Gen}, \mathsf{Enc}, \mathsf{Comp})$ be an ORE in the standard model such that

1. Π is $\frac{1}{2} + \rho$ correct, where ρ is noticeable;
2. Π's message space is $[N]$, where N is super-polynomial;
3. Π^* has succinct ciphertexts, which is bounded by $r = \mathrm{poly}(\lambda, \log N)$.

Then we construct a new ORE $\Pi' = (\mathsf{Gen}', \mathsf{Enc}', \mathsf{Comp}')$ that is statistically correct. More precisely, let $s = \frac{2}{\rho^2} \log N^2 \lambda$, we define Π' as

- $\mathsf{Gen}'(\rho, \log N, \lambda)$ runs $(\mathsf{pk}_i, \mathsf{sk}_i)_{i=1}^s \leftarrow \mathsf{Gen}()$, and outputs $\mathsf{pk}' = (\mathsf{pk}_i)_{i=1}^s; \mathsf{sk}' = (\mathsf{sk}_i)_{i=1}^s$;
- $\mathsf{Enc}'(\mathsf{sk}', m)$ runs $C_i = \mathsf{Enc}(\mathsf{sk}_i, m), i \in [s]$ Outputs $\boldsymbol{C} = (C_1, \ldots, C_s)$;
- $\mathsf{Comp}'(\mathsf{pk}', \boldsymbol{C_0}, \boldsymbol{C_1})$ let $\boldsymbol{C_0} = (C_1^0, \ldots, C_s^0), \boldsymbol{C_1} = (C_1^1, \ldots, C_s^1)$, outputs the majority of $(\mathsf{Comp}(pk_i, C_i^0, C_i^1))_{i=1}^s$.

We immediately observe that Π' also has succinct ciphertexts, and by hybrid argument, it's easy to have that Π' is statistically secure. Now, applying Chernoff Bound, we have

$$\Pr[\Pi' \text{ is correct}] \geq 1 - e^{-\frac{1}{1+2\rho} s \rho^2} \geq 1 - \frac{1}{N^2} e^{-\lambda}$$

We note Π' is statistically correct such that: within overwhelming probability over the choice of $(\mathsf{pk}', \mathsf{sk}')$, the comparison is correct for all message pairs. Then we construct the perfectly correct ORE $\Pi^* = (\mathsf{Gen}^*, \mathsf{Enc}^*, \mathsf{Comp}^*)$, same as Π' except we modify Gen^*: it draws $(\mathsf{pk}^*, \mathsf{sk}^*)$, conditioned on correctness holding for all message pairs. As $\Pi' \overset{\text{stat}}{\approx} \Pi^*$, this only negligibly changes the distribution of keys, Π^* is also statistically secure. Notice that Gen^* is no longer efficient even if Gen was. Fortunately, our notion in standard model allows us to have inefficient Gen. Thus, statistically secure ORE in standard model with succinct ciphertexts and perfect correctness on the same message space exists.

$\square$

Combing Theorems 10 and 12, we establish Theorem 9.

4   Impossibility of Statistically Secure ORE in Idealized Models

In this section, we begin our investigation of ORE in idealized models, where the algorithms of ORE have access to the model $\mathcal{M}$ ($\mathcal{M}$ is deterministic and computable). We give a unified strategy to help answer prove statements of the form:

For some particular idealized model $\mathcal{M}$, there does not exist randomized, partially correct and statistically secure ORE that has succinct ciphertexts with super-poly message space

Roughly speaking, our strategy is consist of four steps:

- Convert a randomized, partially correct and statistically secure ORE in an idealized model into a deterministic, partially correct and statistically secure ORE in the same model;
- Compile the scheme to remove the oracle queries from the comparison procedures;
- Remove the model from ORE completely;
- Invoke Theorem 9 to finish the impossibility.

In this section, we show that step 1 and 3 is achievable for any deterministic and computable model $\mathcal{M}$, and we note that when achieving step 3, it indicates the existence of partially correct and statistically secure ORE in standard model, which conflicts our result in Theorem 9. Hence the only step that depends on the exact model in question is step 2, removing the oracle query access from the comparison while still preserving the partial correctness and statistical security. In later sections, we will show how to do this for the random oracle model and generic group model.

Theorem 13. *If there exists a randomized partially correct and statistically secure ORE in idealized model $\mathcal{M}$ that has succinct ciphertexts and super-polynomial message space, then deterministic, partially correct and statistically secure ORE in the same model $\mathcal{M}$ with succinct ciphertexts on the same message space exists.*

Proof. ORE typically allows for randomized encryption. We may even allow for randomized comparison. However, we will show how to convert such a scheme into a deterministic one.

To handle a randomized comparison, we simply add a sequence of random coins to the secret key and every individual ciphertext. These random coins will be used for any run of Comp. While in the original scheme, each run of Comp uses independent randomness, here we use the same randomness every time. However, since the experiment defining correctness only considers a single run of Comp, the correctness probability is not affected by this change.

To handle a randomized encryption, we just generate the random coins r_m for every message m, and include r_m in the secret key. When encrypting a message m, encrypt using the random coins r_m. Notice that this blows up the secret key size. However, note that for this work we do not care about the size of the secret key; it can be exponential in size, and still our impossibility will hold. We note that another approach is to have r_m be the output of a PRF evaluated on m; suitable PRFs can be built from most interesting models, including the random oracle and generic group models we consider. This prevents the secret key length from exploding. However, this is unnecessary for our purposes.

Suppose $\Pi = (\mathsf{Gen}^{\mathcal{M}}, \mathsf{Enc}^{\mathcal{M}}, \mathsf{Comp}^{\mathcal{M}})$ be a randomized ORE where encryption and comparison procedures are both randomized, then we construct Π^* as:

- Gen^* runs $(\mathsf{pk}, \mathsf{sk}) \leftarrow \mathsf{Gen}$, samples $N + 1$ randomness $(r, r_1, \ldots, r_N)$, and outputs $\mathsf{pk}^* = \mathsf{pk}, \mathsf{sk}^* = (\mathsf{sk}, r, r_1, \ldots, r_N)$;
- $\mathsf{Enc}^*(\mathsf{sk}^*, m)$ runs $C = \mathsf{Enc}^{\mathcal{M}}(\mathsf{sk}, m, r_m)$ and outputs $C^* = (C \| r)$;
- $\mathsf{Comp}^*(\mathsf{pk}^*, C_0^*, C_1^*)$ outputs $\mathsf{Comp}^{\mathcal{M}}(\mathsf{pk}, C_0, C_1, r)$.

We note that Π^* is a deterministic ORE now, both in encryption and comparison. Moreover, ignoring r for ciphertexts, as long as we do not encrypt the same message twice, the distribution of the ciphertext in Π^* is exactly the same as Π's. We note that the correctness is well preserved. In fact, according to the partial correctness definition, the randomness used in Comp is uniform just as in the original scheme.

For statistical security, we see that the adversary only additionally learns a random string (r, used for Comp) after it submits the message sequence, and the random string is independent of the message sequence, hence the adversary does not gain more information than in Π. Thus, statistical security is also preserved.

From now on, we treat ORE scheme as deterministic encryption and the message space is super-polynomial, unless otherwise specified.

Theorem 14. *If there exists partially correct and statistically secure ORE in idealized model that makes no query to $\mathcal{M}$ in comparison procedure and has succinct ciphertext, then partially correct and statistically secure ORE in standard model exists that has succinct ciphertexts.*

Proof. This proof is very straightforward. Since there is no access to $\mathcal{M}$ during the comparison procedure, there is no need for the idealized model to be public. Instead, we set $\mathcal{M}$ as part of the secret key and only the encrypter has access to it. Not giving the adversary access to $\mathcal{M}$ only helps security. Of course, in such a setting, the secret key is now exponentially large, and encryption is no longer efficient. However, our notion of ORE in standard model allows such large key and inefficiencies of encryption, which completes the proof.

The only remaining part is step 2, which is model-specific and non-trivial. We need to remove $\mathcal{M}$ from comparison procedures, while the input of Comp only includes the public key and ciphertext, and we cannot just absorb the model to the public key as we did in Theorem 14. Otherwise, the adversary would have the complete access to the oracle, indicating that it gains more information than it has in t-time statistical security game, and might break the game. Hence, we need to find ways to simulate the model while still preserving the statistical security. In the next two sections, we present our methods on two specific models: random oracle model and generic group model.

5   The Random Oracle Model

In this section, we finish the separation result in the case that $\mathcal{M}$ is a random oracle, which we denote by $\mathcal{O}$. Using the results of Sects. 3 and 4, it remains to show that the random oracle model can be removed from the comparison procedure of an ORE scheme. Our proof is inspired by [10], which shows how to remove random oracles from obfuscation schemes. However, for reason's outlined in the introduction, the technical details of our proof will be substantially different.

We first observe the following. Consider running $\mathsf{Comp}^{\mathcal{O}}(C_0, C_1)$ where C_0, C_1 encrypt m_0, m_1 respectively. Consider an oracle query x made by Comp. If x was not a query made during encryption $(\mathsf{Enc}^{\mathcal{O}}(m_0), \mathsf{Enc}^{\mathcal{O}}(m_1))$, then we claim Comp must output the right answer, even if it is given the incorrect query response. Indeed, for any possible response y', there is an oracle $\mathcal{O}'$ that is consistent with $\mathcal{O}$ on the points queried during encryption of m_0, m_1, but where $\mathcal{O}'(x) = y'$. Therefore, any potentially incorrect query answer can be "explained" by an oracle $\mathcal{O}'$, and correctness of the scheme says that Comp must still output the right value in this case.

For a particular run of Comp on encryptions of m_0, m_1, we therefore call the oracle queries made during encryption "sensitive" queries. Comp only needs access to $\mathcal{O}$ on sensitive queries; for all others, it can answer randomly. The difficulty, then, is (1) allowing Comp to figure out the sensitive queries, and (2) giving it the right oracle answers in this case.

For simplicity, consider two extremes. On the one end, suppose none of Comp's queries are ever sensitive. In this case, Comp can just ignore its oracle entirely, simulating the responses with random answers. In this case, we are already done. In the other extreme, suppose all of Comp's queries are always sensitive. In this case, if the adversary sees ℓ ciphertexts, she expects to make at least $\Omega(\ell^2)$ oracle queries on sensitive queries. However, there are only $q\ell$ possible query values, where q is the number of queries made during each encryption. Therefore, heuristically, we may expect to eventually pick of all of the sensitive queries made during encryption by setting ℓ large enough (namely, bigger than q). Even so, security must hold. Therefore, we can construct a modified scheme where Enc simply outputs all the queries it makes and the corresponding answers along with the ciphertext. Then all the sensitive queries Comp needs are provided as input, and it does not need to make any oracle queries.

To formalize the above sketch, we must show how to handle cases between the two extremes, where some of Comp's queries are sensitive, and others are not, and we cannot necessarily tell which is the case. Moreover, we need to deal with the fact that we may not actually get all of the sensitive queries if there are sufficiently many collisions. In this case, handing out all of the queries made during encryption could actually hurt security (for example, if a query is made on the message itself). Nonetheless, we now prove the following theorem:

Theorem 15. *If there exists partially correct and statistically secure ORE in random oracle model that has succinct ciphertexts, then there exists partially* *correct and statistically secure ORE with succinct ciphertexts such that the comparison procedures makes no queries to the random oracle.*

Proof. Let $\Pi^0 = (\mathsf{Gen}_0, \mathsf{Enc}_0^{\mathcal{O}}, \mathsf{Comp}_0^{\mathcal{O}})$ be a statistically secure ORE in the random oracle model with plaintext space $[N]$. Here, we assume Gen_0 makes no queries to $\mathcal{O}$. This is actually without loss of generality: since $\mathcal{O}$ is a deterministic oracle, we can always treat sk as the random coins inputted to Gen_0, and run Gen_0 every time we encrypt a message.

For convenience, we denote $\Pr[\Pi^0]$ as the lower bound on the correctness probability:

$$\Pr[\Pi^0] = \min_{m_0, m_1} \Pr[\mathsf{Comp}_0^{\mathcal{O}}(\mathsf{pk}, C_0, C_1) = \mathsf{Comp}(m_0, m_1) : (\mathsf{pk}, \mathsf{sk}) \leftarrow \mathsf{Gen}_0(); C_b \leftarrow \mathsf{Enc}_0^{\mathcal{O}}(\mathsf{sk}, m_b)]$$

We assume that $\mathsf{Comp}_0(\mathsf{pk}_0, C_0, C_1)$ does not query the same point twice; since $\mathcal{O}$ is deterministic, Comp_0 can always store a table of query/response pairs already seen, and use this table to answer subsequent queries on the same point.

Here we specify some parameters:

1. $\Pr[\Pi^0] \geq \frac{1}{2} + 2\rho$, where ρ is noticeable; $q, u = \mathsf{poly}(\lambda)$ by query efficiency; $s := \frac{110u^4 \cdot q^2}{\rho^3}; s_i := \frac{110u^3 \cdot q^2 \cdot i}{\rho^3}, i \in [u]$.
2. $\mathsf{Enc}_0^{\mathcal{O}}$ makes q queries to the oracle $\mathcal{O}$. Let $Q_{\mathsf{sk}, m}$ be the set of query-answer pairs made when encrypting m under key sk. Notice that the set $Q_{\mathsf{sk}, m}$ is fully determined by sk and m since Enc and $\mathcal{O}$ are deterministic.
3. $\mathsf{Comp}_0^{\mathcal{O}}$ makes u queries to the oracle $\mathcal{O}$. Let $S_{\mathsf{pk}, m_0, m_1}$ be the set of query-answer pairs made when comparing the encryptions of (m_0, m_1) under key pk. Again, $S_{\mathsf{pk}, m_0, m_1}$ is fully determined by $\mathsf{pk}, \mathsf{sk}, m_0, m_1$.
4. $D := [s] \cup [N - s + 1, N]; D_i := [s_i] \cup [N - s_i + 1, N], i \in [u]$.
5. $T_i = [i] \cup [N - i + 1, N], i \in [N]$.

Next we construct a new ORE $\Pi^* = (\mathsf{Gen}, \mathsf{Enc}^{\mathcal{O}}, \mathsf{Comp})$ with plaintext space $[s + 1, N - s]$ as:

– $\mathsf{Gen}()$ runs $(\mathsf{pk}_0, \mathsf{sk}_0) \leftarrow \mathsf{Gen}_0()$, computes $C_i = \mathsf{Enc}_0^{\mathcal{O}}(\mathsf{sk}_0, i), i \in D$ and outputs $\mathsf{pk} = \mathsf{pk}_0, \mathsf{sk} = (\mathsf{sk}_0, \{C_i\}_{i \in D})$;
– $\mathsf{Enc}^{\mathcal{O}}(\mathsf{sk}, m)$ runs $C \leftarrow \mathsf{Enc}_0^{\mathcal{O}}(\mathsf{sk}_0, m)$. Then it runs $\mathsf{Comp}_0^{\mathcal{O}}(\mathsf{pk}_0, C_i, C)$ for all $i \in D$, recording all query-answer pairs $S_{\mathsf{pk}, m} = \cup_{i \in D} S_{\mathsf{pk}, m, i}$. Then it outputs $C^* = (C, S_{\mathsf{pk}, m})$;
– $\mathsf{Comp}(\mathsf{pk}, C_0^*, C_1^*)$: let $C_0^* = (C_0, S_0), C_1^* = (C_1, S_1)$. Run $\mathsf{Comp}_0^{\mathcal{O}}(\mathsf{pk}_0, C_0, C_1)$, except that when querying the oracle with input x, do the following:
    1. If there is a pair (x, y) in $S_0 \cup S_1$, Comp responds to the query with y;
    2. Otherwise, returns a random string.

We note that in the comparison procedure of Π^*, we remove the oracle access, so it remains to show that Π^* is statistically secure and partially correct.

Lemma 16. *If Π^0 is $t + 2s$ statically secure, then Π^* is t-time statically secure.*

Proof. The entire view of the adversary $\mathcal{A}$ in the t-time experiment for Π^* can be simulated by a $t + 2s$-time adversary $\mathcal{B}$ for Π^0: the lists of messages are those produced by $\mathcal{A}$, plus all the messages in D. Then, the lists S associated with ciphertext C can be constructed by comparing C to each of the C_i for $i \in D$. $\square$

It's obvious that Lemma 16 holds for any $t = \mathsf{poly}(\log N, \lambda)$, which means Π^* is statistically secure. And what's more interesting is that Π^*'s partial correctness. In the following, we prove that Π^* also preserves partial correctness, though there is some loss in the concrete correctness parameter.

Lemma 17. $\Pr[\Pi^*] \geq \frac{1}{2} + \rho$.

Proof. We establish our proof by hybrid argument, and define u alternative ORE schemes $\Pi_j = (\mathsf{Gen}_j, \mathsf{Enc}_j^{\mathcal{O}}, \mathsf{Comp}_j^{\mathcal{O}}), j \in [u]$ on message space $[s_j + 1, N - s_j]$:

- $\mathsf{Gen}_j()$ runs $(\mathsf{pk}_0, \mathsf{sk}_0) \leftarrow \mathsf{Gen}_0()$, computes $C_i = \mathsf{Enc}_0^{\mathcal{O}}(\mathsf{sk}_0, i)$ for $i \in D_j$ and outputs $\mathsf{pk}_j = \mathsf{pk}_0, \mathsf{sk}_j = (\mathsf{sk}_0, \{C_i\}_{i \in D_j})$;
- $\mathsf{Enc}_j^{\mathcal{O}}(\mathsf{sk}_j, m)$ runs $C \leftarrow \mathsf{Enc}_0^{\mathcal{O}}(\mathsf{sk}_0, m)$ and $\mathsf{Comp}_0^{\mathcal{O}}(\mathsf{pk}_0, C_i, C)$ for $i \in D_j$, records all query-answer pairs $S_{\mathsf{pk},m} = \cup_{i \in D_j} S_{\mathsf{pk},m,i}$ and outputs $C^* = (C, S_{\mathsf{pk},m})$;
- $\mathsf{Comp}_j^{\mathcal{O}}(\mathsf{pk}_j, C_0^*, C_1^*)$: let $C_0^* = (C_0, S_0), C_1^* = (C_1, S_1)$. It runs $\mathsf{Comp}_0^{\mathcal{O}}(\mathsf{pk}_j, C_0, C_1)$, except that when querying $\mathcal{O}$ with input x, it does the following:
  1. If x is one of the first $u - j$ queries, make a query to $\mathcal{O}$ as usual.
  2. If x is one of the final j queries and there is a pair $(x, y) \in S_0 \cup S_1$, then respond with y.
  3. Otherwise, returns a random string.

We observe that $\Pi_u = \Pi^*$, hence it suffices to prove the following lemma,

Lemma 18.
$$\Pr[\Pi_j] \geq \Pr[\Pi_{j-1}] - \frac{\rho}{u}, \forall j \in [u]$$

We here only prove the case $j = 1$, the rest can be handled analogously. Specifically, we show $\Pr[\Pi_1] \geq \frac{1}{2} + 2\rho - \frac{\rho}{u}$.

According to the definition, we see that Comp_1 works the same as Comp_0, except for the final query x to $\mathcal{O}$ in which we use the list of oracle outputs provided with the ciphertext to answer the oracle query. We prove that the response made by Π_1 for x does not significantly harm the ability of Comp_1 to output the correct answer. To do so, we introduce yet another sequence of s_1 ORE schemes $\Pi_{1,j}, j \in [s_1]$ on message space $[j + 1, N - j]$. The only difference between $\Pi_{1,j}$ and Π_1 is the number of test ciphertexts that are generated.

- $\mathsf{Gen}_{1,j}()$ runs $(\mathsf{pk}_0, \mathsf{sk}_0) \leftarrow \mathsf{Gen}_0()$, computes $C_i = \mathsf{Enc}_0^{\mathcal{O}}(\mathsf{sk}_0, i)$ for $i \in T_j$ and outputs $\mathsf{pk}_{1,j} = \mathsf{pk}_0, \mathsf{sk} = (\mathsf{sk}_0, \{C_i\}_{i \in T_j})$;
- $\mathsf{Enc}_{1,j}^{\mathcal{O}}(\mathsf{sk}_{1,j}, m)$ runs $C \leftarrow \mathsf{Enc}_0^{\mathcal{O}}(\mathsf{sk}_0, m)$ and $\mathsf{Comp}_0^{\mathcal{O}}(\mathsf{pk}_0, C_i, C)$ for $i \in T_j$, records all query-answer pairs $S_{\mathsf{pk},m}^{(j)} = \cup_i S_{\mathsf{pk},m,i}$ and outputs $C^* = (C, S_{\mathsf{pk},m}^{(j)})$;

- $\mathsf{Comp}_{1,j}^{\mathcal{O}}(\mathsf{pk}_{1,j}, C_0^*, C_1^*)$: let $C_0^* = (C_0, S_0), C_1^* = (C_1, S_1)$. It runs $\mathsf{Comp}_0^{\mathcal{O}}(\mathsf{pk}_{1,j}, C_0, C_1)$, except that when querying $\mathcal{O}$ with input x, it does the following:
  1. If x is one of the first $u - 1$ queries, make a query to $\mathcal{O}$ as usual.
  2. If x is the final query and there is a pair $(x, y) \in S_0 \cup S_1$, then respond with y.
  3. Otherwise, returns a random string.

We note that $\Pi_1 = \Pi_{1,s_1}$. We now claim that increasing j must improve the correctness of the scheme:

Claim. If $\Pr[\Pi_{1,j}] < \frac{1}{2} + 2\rho - \frac{\ell}{u}$, then $\Pr[\Pi_{1,j+1}] \geq \Pr[\Pi_{1,j}] + \frac{\rho^3}{110u^3 \cdot q^2}$.

Notice that this means as j increases, $\Pr[\Pi_{1,j}]$ must increase by increments of at least $\frac{1}{s_1} = \frac{\rho^3}{110u^3 \cdot q^2}$ until $\Pr[\Pi_{1,j}] \geq \frac{1}{2} + 2\rho - \frac{\ell}{u}$. Therefore, by setting $j = s_1$, we get that $\Pr[\Pi_1] = \Pr[\Pi_{1,s_1}] \geq \frac{1}{2} + 2\rho - \frac{\ell}{u}$ as desired. It remains to prove the claim.

Assuming $\Pr[\Pi_{1,j}] < \frac{1}{2} + 2\rho - \frac{\ell}{u}$, there are two messages m_0^*, m_1^* minimizing the correctness probability; that is, the comparison procedure on encryptions of m_0^*, m_1^* outputs the correct answer with probability less than $\frac{1}{2} + 2\rho - \frac{\ell}{u}$. Since comparison succeeding is a detectable event, we can invoke the security of ORE to conclude that, for *any* m_0, m_1, comparison must output the correct answer with probability at most $\frac{1}{2} + 2\rho - \frac{\ell}{u} + \mathsf{negl} < \frac{1}{2} + 2\rho - \frac{2\rho}{3u}$.

Fix two messages $m_0, m_1 \in [s_1 + 1, N - s_1]$. We denote $S^{(j)} := S_{\mathsf{pk},m_0}^{(j)} \cup S_{\mathsf{pk},m_1}^{(j)}$; $Q := Q_{\mathsf{sk},m_0} \cup Q_{\mathsf{sk},m_1}$. Let x be the final query made when comparing the encryptions of m_0, m_1.

Define the event Bad_j where the following happens:

- $x \in Q \setminus S^{(j)}$, so that x was queried during the encryption of m_0 or m_1, but not during any of the comparisons to the test ciphertexts.
- $\mathsf{Comp}_0^{\mathcal{O}}$ outputs the correct answer on encryptions of m_0, m_1.
- $\mathsf{Comp}_{1,j}^{\mathcal{O}}$ outputs the incorrect answer on encryptions of m_0, m_1.

We consider four cases:

- $x \in S^{(j)}$ In this case, Π_1 answers the same as $\Pi_{1,j}$ since it has access to $\mathcal{O}(x)$.
- $x \notin Q$ Then the ciphertexts components C_0, C_1 under Π_0 are independent of $\mathcal{O}(x)$, meaning that during the correctness experiment, $\mathcal{O}(x)$ in Π_0 is a random string. Hence Π_1 answers the query with the correct distribution.
- $x \in Q \setminus S^{(j)}$, but Bad_j does not occur. Here, we must have that Comp_0 either produced the incorrect answer, or $\mathsf{Comp}_{1,j}$ produced the correct answer.
- Bad_j occurs In this case, C_0, C_1 will depend on $\mathcal{O}(x)$, while $\Pi_{1,j}$ cannot find it in $S^{(j)}$. Hence, $\Pi_{1,j}$ will answer randomly, but Comp may expect an answer correlated with C_0, C_1. Moreover, we know that by answering randomly, $\mathsf{Comp}_{1,j}$ goes from outputting the correct answer to the incorrect answer.

We note in the first three cases above, the expected correctness probability does not decrease relative to $\Pi_{1,j}$. Indeed, in the first and third cases, $\Pi_{1,j}$ is at least as correct as Π_0, and in the second case, $\Pi_{1,j}$ in expectation has the same correctness as Π_0. Only in the final case might answering randomly decrease the probability of correctness. Therefore, since comparison in $\Pi_{1,j}$ outputs the correct answer with probability less than $\frac{1}{2}+2\rho-\frac{2\rho}{3u}$, we must have $\Pr[\mathsf{Bad}_j] > \frac{2\rho}{3u}$.

We consider two sub-events of Bad_j, denoted $\mathsf{Bad}_j^{(b)}$, corresponding to $x \in Q_{\mathsf{sk},m_b}/S$. Notice that $\Pr[\mathsf{Bad}_j] \leq \Pr[\mathsf{Bad}_j^{(0)}] + \Pr[\mathsf{Bad}_j^{(1)}]$. By our assumption above, we have $\max\{\Pr[\mathsf{Bad}_j^{(0)}], \Pr[\mathsf{Bad}_j^{(1)}]\} > \frac{\rho}{3u}$. We will assume that $\Pr[\mathsf{Bad}_j^{(0)}] > \frac{\rho}{3u}$, the other case handled analogously.

Next we split the message space into two parts: $[j+1, \frac{N}{2}]$ and $[\frac{N}{2}+1, N-j]$, and sample $w \leftarrow [j+1, \frac{N}{2}]$ and $z_1, \ldots, z_\ell \leftarrow [\frac{N}{2}+1, N-j]$, where $\ell = \frac{6u \cdot q}{\rho}$. Let t_i be the indicator as:

$$t_i = \begin{cases} 1 \text{ if } \mathsf{Bad}_j^{(0)} \text{ occurs for message pair } (w, z_i) \\ 0 \text{ Otherwise} \end{cases}$$

and T be the event that $\sum_{i=1}^{\ell} t_i > q$, we must have that:

$$\Pr[T] \cdot \ell + q \cdot (1 - \Pr[T]) \geq \mathbb{E}(\sum_{i=1}^{\ell} t_i) > 2q \Rightarrow \Pr[T] > \frac{\rho}{6u}$$

as $\Pr[t_i = 1] > \frac{\rho}{3u}$, which refers $\mathbb{E}\left[\sum_{i=1}^{\ell} t_i\right] > \ell \cdot \frac{\rho}{3u} > 2q$.

For three messages m_0, m_1, m_2, $m_0 < m_1 < m_2$, we define the event Collision as the following: the final queries x_1, x_2 when comparing encryptions of m_0 to m_1 and respectively m_0 to m_2 satisfy: (1) $\mathsf{Bad}_j^{(0)}$ occurs simultaneously for both (m_0, m_1) and (m_0, m_2), and (2) $x_1 = x_2$.

We observe that if T occurs, there are at least $q + 1$ index such that $t_i = 1$. Moreover, in $\mathsf{Enc}_{1,j}^{\mathcal{O}}(w)$, there are at most q distinct queries. This means there is some $z_{i_1} < z_{i_2}$ such that $\mathsf{Bad}_j^{(0)}$ occurs for both (w, z_{i_1}) and (w, z_{i_2}) and moreover the final query in both comparisons is identical. This in particular means that Collision happens for (w, z_{i_1}, z_{i_2}).

Now we bound the probability of Collision for a random message w in $[j+1, \frac{N}{2}]$ and random distinct z_1^*, z_2^* in $[\frac{N}{2}+1, N-j]$. One way to sample random w, z_1^*, z_2^* is to sample w at random in $[j+1, \frac{N}{2}]$, and sample ℓ random distinct z_i in $[\frac{N}{2}+1, N-j]$. Then we choose two random indices i_1, i_2, and set $z_b^* = z_{i_b}$. The above analysis shows that with probability at least $\rho/6u$, there some Collision among the z_i. Since z_b^* are chosen as a random pair from this set, there is a collision in z_1^*, z_2^* with probability at least

$$\Pr[\text{ Collision for random } (w, z_1^*, z_2^*)]\} \geq \frac{1}{\binom{\ell}{2}} \cdot \Pr[T] > \frac{\rho^3}{108u^3 \cdot q^2}$$

Now, we would like to use security of ORE to show that Collision happens for arbitrary fixed triples m_0, m_1, m_2. Unfortunately, Collision is not necessarily detectable by an adversary, since an adversary does not know Q. Instead, we define a slightly different event Collision'. Collision' is the same as Collision except that it removes the requirement that the common query x is in Q for either w, z_1^* or w, z_2^*. Since Collision implies Colision', we must have that Collision' happens with probability at least $\frac{\rho^3}{108u^3 \cdot q^2}$ for a random w, z_1^*, z_2^*.

Now, Collision' *is* an event that can be detected by an adversary, thus by statistical security, we have that for *arbitrary* $(m_0, m_1, m_2) \in [j+1, N-j]$,

$$\Pr[\text{ Collision' for } (m_0, m_1, m_2)] \geq \frac{\rho^3}{108u^3 \cdot q^2} - \text{negl} > \frac{\rho^3}{110u^3 \cdot q^2}$$

Specifically, let $m_2 = N - j$, we see that for any $(m_0, m_1) \in [j+2, N-j-1]$, if we move to $\Pi_{1,j+1}$, m_2 is included in the test queries for the scheme. Notice that Collision' means that in $\Pi_{1,j}$, comparing m_0, m_1 would have been incorrect (since the final query is answered randomly), but in $\Pi_{1,j+1}$ comparing m_0, m_1 would be correct due to the additional queries provided from comparing m_0, m_2 (since comparing m_0, m_2 would add the missing query x to the list of queries included in the encryption of m_0). Thus:

$$\Pr[\Pi_{1,j+1}] \geq \Pr[\Pi_{1,j}] + \frac{\rho^3}{110u^3 \cdot q^2} \Rightarrow \Pr[\Pi_1] \geq \Pr[\Pi_0] - \frac{\rho}{u}$$

Now we have shown that $\Pr[\Pi_1] \geq \Pr[\Pi_0] - \frac{\rho}{u}$. This handles the case of Π_1. However, note that at this point, what use to be the second-to-last query is now the last query (since the last query is no longer made). Therefore, we can apply the exact same techniques as above to handle the general case of Π_j, giving

$$\Pr[\Pi_{j+1}] \geq \Pr[\Pi_j] - \frac{\rho}{u}$$

Combing together, we get

$$\Pr[\Pi^*] \geq \frac{1}{2} + \rho$$

which completes the entire proof.   □

6   The Generic Group Model

In this section, we finish the separation result in generic group model, which we denote by $\mathcal{G}$. It remains to show that the generic group oracle model can be removed from the comparison procedure of any ORE scheme. Our strategy is inspired by [24], which shows how to remove constant graded encoding from obfuscation schemes. Before we illustrate the main idea of our proof, we recall a simple variant of the generic group model, which is equivalent to the usual generic group model [26]:

Definition 19. *(Variant Generic Group Model) Let $(G, \odot)$ be any group of size N and let S be any set of size at least N. The generic group oracle $\mathcal{G} : G \mapsto S$. At first an injective random function $\sigma : G \mapsto S$ is chosen, and two type of queries are answered as:*

- *Type 1: **Labeling queries.** Given $g \in G$, oracle returns handle $h = \sigma(g)$;*
- *Type 2: **Zero-test queries.** Given $\boldsymbol{h} = (h_1, \ldots h_n) \in S$, a vector $\boldsymbol{v} = (v_0, \ldots, v_n)$ of integers, oracle returns a single bit: 0 if there exists $g_1, \ldots, g_n \in G$ such that $h_i = \sigma(g_i)$ and $v_0 + \odot_j v_j g_j = 0$; 1 otherwise.*

WLOG, we can assume that the ORE scheme $\Pi = (\mathsf{Gen}, \mathsf{Enc}^{\mathcal{G}}, \mathsf{Comp}^{\mathcal{G}})$ satisfies the following:

- Gen makes no queries to $\mathcal{G}$.
- Enc has the access of both labeling and zero-test query, while Comp only makes zero-test queries. This is because Comp gains no advantage by making labeling queries; it can always keep track of any group element it would have made a labeling query on, and adjust the v_0 term in a zero-test query to compensate.
- Let $\boldsymbol{h}_m$ be the vector of handles returned by the labeling queries during the encryption of m. We will assume the comparison procedure, when comparing encryptions of m_0, m_1, only makes zero-test queries using handles derived during the encryption. In other words, it will always have the form $(\boldsymbol{h}_{m_0}, \boldsymbol{h}_{m_1}, \boldsymbol{v})$. We can assume this as $\mathsf{Comp}'s$ view only depends on those labels; if it queried the zero-test on other labels, then it would somehow be guessing labels it never saw before, which is statistically unlikely.
- For any m, $|\boldsymbol{h}_m| = |\boldsymbol{g}_m| = q$, where $q = \mathsf{poly}(\lambda)$ is a fixed integer.

Then we present a brief description of our strategy. Similar to our random oracle proof, given an ORE scheme $\Pi = (\mathsf{Gen}, \mathsf{Enc}^{\mathcal{G}}, \mathsf{Comp}^{\mathcal{G}})$ on message space $[N]$ with partial correctness $\frac{1}{2} + 2\rho$, we construct an new ORE $\Pi^* = (\mathsf{Gen}^*, \mathsf{Enc}^*, \mathsf{Comp}^*)$ on message space $[s+1, N-d](s, d = \mathsf{poly}(\log N, \lambda))$ with correctness $\frac{1}{2} + \rho$, where we remove $\mathcal{G}$ from Comp^*. In the key generation procedure, Π^* additionally outputs the encryption of $i, i \in [s] \cup [N - d + 1, N]$.

Next, $\mathsf{Enc}(k, m)$ runs $\mathsf{Enc}(k, m)$, $\mathsf{Comp}(\mathsf{Enc}(k, m), \mathsf{Enc}(k, i))$, $\mathsf{Comp}(\mathsf{Enc}(k, i), \mathsf{Enc}(k, j)), i, j \in [s] \cup [N - d + 1, N]$. It collects all of the zero test queries and responses produced during the comparisons. It deletes all queries that outputted 1. It is left with a set of linear constraints on the $g_1, \ldots, g_s, g_m, g_{N-d+1}, \ldots, g_N$ terms. It therefore produces a set S_m of linearly independent constrains over these variables. It finally outputs $(\mathsf{Enc}(m), S_m)$.

Meanwhile, $\mathsf{Comp}^*(C_{m_0}, C_{m_1})$, runs Comp on the two Π-ciphertexts contained in C_{m_0}, C_{m_1}. Whenever $\mathsf{Comp}_{1,j}$ tries to make a zero-test query, $\mathsf{Comp}^*_{1,j}$ intercepts, and answers using the sets S_{m_0}, S_{m_1} as follows. It determines if the zero test query is linearly dependent on the constraints in $S_{m_0} \cup S_{m_1}$. If so, it knows that the answer to the zero test query is 0. Otherwise, it guesses that the zero test query answer is non-zero.

We claim that this modified comparison procedure answers all zero test queries right except with small probability. Roughly, the idea is that Comp only needs to learn the constraint space when restricted to g_{m_0}, g_{m_1}, and does so using the constraints it obtains through the test ciphertexts. Notice that the number of constraints we obtain grows quadratically with the number of test ciphertexts computed, while the dimension of the space of constraints only grows linearly. Therefore, by using enough test elements, we "should" exhaust all linear constraints and recover the entire constraints space. Indeed, we show that with sufficiently large s, d, $S_{m_0} \cup S_{m_1}$ has either recovered the full basis of the space (which allows one to correctly answer all remaining zero-test queries), or it's very unlikely that a new constraint appears, which in turn means that Comp^* simulates the oracle itself properly except with a small probability. We now prove the following theorem:

Theorem 20. *If there exists partially correct and statistically secure ORE in generic group model that has succinct ciphertexts, then partially correct and statistically secure ORE with succinct ciphertexts that makes no query to generic group oracle in comparison procedures exists.*

Due to the space limit, we skip the rigorous proof here, and refer the whole proof in our full version [28].

Acknowledgments. Mark Zhandry is supported by NSF. Cong Zhang is partially supported by DARPA and SSC Pacific under contract N66001-15-C-4070. Any opinions, findings, and conclusions or recommendations expressed in this material are those of the author(s) and do not necessarily reflect the views of NSF, DARPA or SSC Pacific.

References

1. Agrawal, R., Kiernan, J., Srikant, R., Xu, Y.: Order preserving encryption for numeric data. In: Proceedings of the 2004 ACM SIGMOD International Conference on Management of Data, SIGMOD 2004, pp. 563–574. ACM (2004)
2. Arasu, A., et al.: Orthogonal security with cipherbase. In: 6th Biennial Conference on Innovative Data Systems Research (CIDR 2013), January 2013
3. Boldyreva, A., Chenette, N., Lee, Y., O'Neill, A.: Order-preserving symmetric encryption. In: Joux, A. (ed.) EUROCRYPT 2009. LNCS, vol. 5479, pp. 224–241. Springer, Heidelberg (2009). https://doi.org/10.1007/978-3-642-01001-9_13
4. Boldyreva, A., Chenette, N., O'Neill, A.: Order-preserving encryption revisited: improved security analysis and alternative solutions. In: Rogaway, P. (ed.) CRYPTO 2011. LNCS, vol. 6841, pp. 578–595. Springer, Heidelberg (2011). https://doi.org/10.1007/978-3-642-22792-9_33
5. Boneh, D., Lewi, K., Raykova, M., Sahai, A., Zhandry, M., Zimmerman, J.: Semantically secure order-revealing encryption: multi-input functional encryption without obfuscation. In: Oswald, E., Fischlin, M. (eds.) EUROCRYPT 2015. LNCS, vol. 9057, pp. 563–594. Springer, Heidelberg (2015). https://doi.org/10.1007/978-3-662-46803-6_19
6. Boneh, D., Sahai, A., Waters, B.: Fully collusion resistant traitor tracing with short ciphertexts and private keys. In: Vaudenay, S. (ed.) EUROCRYPT 2006. LNCS, vol. 4004, pp. 573–592. Springer, Heidelberg (2006). https://doi.org/10.1007/11761679_34

7. Boneh, D., Silverberg, A.: Applications of multilinear forms to cryptography. Contemp. Math. **324**(1), 71–90 (2003)
8. Brakerski, Z., Rothblum, G.N.: Virtual black-box obfuscation for all circuits via generic graded encoding. In: Lindell, Y. (ed.) TCC 2014. LNCS, vol. 8349, pp. 1–25. Springer, Heidelberg (2014). https://doi.org/10.1007/978-3-642-54242-8_1
9. Brakerski, Z., Segev, G.: Function-private functional encryption in the private-key setting. In: Dodis, Y., Nielsen, J.B. (eds.) TCC 2015. LNCS, vol. 9015, pp. 306–324. Springer, Heidelberg (2015). https://doi.org/10.1007/978-3-662-46497-7_12
10. Canetti, R., Kalai, Y.T., Paneth, O.: On obfuscation with random oracles. In: Dodis, Y., Nielsen, J.B. (eds.) TCC 2015. LNCS, vol. 9015, pp. 456–467. Springer, Heidelberg (2015). https://doi.org/10.1007/978-3-662-46497-7_18
11. Cash, D., Liu, F.-H., O'Neill, A., Zhang, C.: Reducing the leakage in practical order-revealing encryption. Technical report, Cryptology ePrint Archive, Report 2016/661 (2016)
12. Chenette, N., Lewi, K., Weis, S.A., Wu, D.J.: Practical order-revealing encryption with limited leakage. In: Peyrin, T. (ed.) FSE 2016. LNCS, vol. 9783, pp. 474–493. Springer, Heidelberg (2016). https://doi.org/10.1007/978-3-662-52993-5_24
13. Coron, J.-S., Lepoint, T., Tibouchi, M.: Practical multilinear maps over the integers. In: Canetti, R., Garay, J.A. (eds.) CRYPTO 2013. LNCS, vol. 8042, pp. 476–493. Springer, Heidelberg (2013). https://doi.org/10.1007/978-3-642-40041-4_26
14. Durak, F.B., DuBuisson, T.M., Cash, D.: What else is revealed by order-revealing encryption? In: Proceedings of the 2016 ACM SIGSAC Conference on Computer and Communications Security, pp. 1155–1166. ACM (2016)
15. Erdős, P., Sós, V.: On a problem of graph theory
16. Garg, S., Gentry, C., Halevi, S.: Candidate multilinear maps from ideal lattices. In: Johansson, T., Nguyen, P.Q. (eds.) EUROCRYPT 2013. LNCS, vol. 7881, pp. 1–17. Springer, Heidelberg (2013). https://doi.org/10.1007/978-3-642-38348-9_1
17. Gentry, C., Lewko, A., Waters, B.: Witness encryption from instance independent assumptions. In: Garay, J.A., Gennaro, R. (eds.) CRYPTO 2014. LNCS, vol. 8616, pp. 426–443. Springer, Heidelberg (2014). https://doi.org/10.1007/978-3-662-44371-2_24
18. Grubbs, P., Sekniqi, K., Bindschaedler, V., Naveed, M., Ristenpart, T.: Leakage-abuse attacks against order-revealing encryption. In: 2017 IEEE Symposium on Security and Privacy (SP), pp. 655–672. IEEE (2017)
19. Joye, M., Passelègue, A.: Function-revealing encryption. In: Catalano, D., De Prisco, R. (eds.) SCN 2018. LNCS, vol. 11035, pp. 527–543. Springer, Cham (2018). https://doi.org/10.1007/978-3-319-98113-0_28
20. Lewi, K., Wu, D.J.: Order-revealing encryption: new constructions, applications, and lower bounds. In: Proceedings of the 2016 ACM SIGSAC Conference on Computer and Communications Security, CCS 2016, pp. 1167–1178. ACM, New York (2016)
21. Lu, W., Varna, A.L., Wu, M.: Security analysis for privacy preserving search of multimedia. In: 2010 IEEE International Conference on Image Processing, pp. 2093–2096, September 2010
22. Mahmoody, M., Mohammed, A., Nematihaji, S.: On the impossibility of virtual black-box obfuscation in idealized models. In: Kushilevitz, E., Malkin, T. (eds.) TCC 2016. LNCS, vol. 9562, pp. 18–48. Springer, Heidelberg (2016). https://doi.org/10.1007/978-3-662-49096-9_2

23. Naveed, M., Kamara, S., Wright, C.V.: Inference attacks on property-preserving encrypted databases. In: Proceedings of the 22nd ACM SIGSAC Conference on Computer and Communications Security, pp. 644–655. ACM (2015)
24. Pass, R., Shelat, A.: Impossibility of VBB obfuscation with ideal constant-degree graded encodings. In: Kushilevitz, E., Malkin, T. (eds.) TCC 2016. LNCS, vol. 9562, pp. 3–17. Springer, Heidelberg (2016). https://doi.org/10.1007/978-3-662-49096-9_1
25. Popa, R.A., Redfield, C.M.S., Zeldovich, N., Balakrishnan, H.: CryptDB: protecting confidentiality with encrypted query processing. In: Proceedings of the 23rd ACM Symposium on Operating Systems Principles 2011, SOSP 2011, Cascais, Portugal, 23–26 October 2011, pp. 85–100 (2011)
26. Shoup, V.: Lower bounds for discrete logarithms and related problems. In: Fumy, W. (ed.) EUROCRYPT 1997. LNCS, vol. 1233, pp. 256–266. Springer, Heidelberg (1997). https://doi.org/10.1007/3-540-69053-0_18
27. Wang, C., Cao, N., Li, J., Ren, K., Lou, W.: Secure ranked keyword search over encrypted cloud data. In: 2010 IEEE 30th International Conference on Distributed Computing Systems (ICDCS), pp. 253–262, June 2010
28. Zhandry, M., Zhang, C.: Impossibility of order-revealing encryption in idealized models. Cryptology ePrint Archive, Report 2017/1001 (2017). https://eprint.iacr.org/2017/1001

A Ciphertext-Size Lower Bound
for Order-Preserving Encryption
with Limited Leakage

David Cash[1(✉)] and Cong Zhang[2]

[1] Department of Computer Science, University of Chicago, Chicago, USA
davidcash@uchicago.edu
[2] Department of Computer Science, Rutgers University, New Brunswick, USA
congresearch@gmail.com

Abstract. We consider a security definition of Chenette, Lewi, Weis, and
Wu for order-revealing encryption (ORE) and order-preserving encryption (OPE) (FSE 2016). Their definition says that the comparison of two
ciphertexts should only leak the index of the most significant bit on which
they differ. While their work could achieve order-revealing encryption
with short ciphertexts that expand the plaintext by a factor ≈ 1.58, it
could only find order-*preserving* encryption with longer ciphertexts that
expanded the plaintext by a security-parameter factor. We give evidence
that this gap between ORE and OPE is inherent, by proving that *any* OPE
meeting the information-theoretic version of their security definition (for
instance, in the random oracle model) must have ciphertext length close
to that of their constructions. We extend our result to identify an abstract
security property of any OPE that will result in the same lower bound.

Keywords: Symmetric encryption · Searchable encryption
Lower bound

1 Introduction

To enable fast operations on encrypted databases, several variants of encryption
have been suggested that trade security or efficiency for processing functionality on the server. Amongst the suggested constructions, *order-revealing encryption (ORE)* and its special case *order-preserving encryption (OPE)* [1,3,4] have
seen deployments in products[1] and usage in applied research [12,13,15]. ORE
schemes are symmetric key encryption schemes $\mathcal{E}$ such that, given ciphertexts
$\mathcal{E}_K(x), \mathcal{E}_K(y)$ for messages x, y, one can decide if $x < y$ or not without the decryption key. OPE schemes are the subset of ORE schemes for which the ciphertexts
themselves are numbers that can be compared (so $\mathcal{E}_K(x) < \mathcal{E}_K(y) \iff x < y$).

---

[1] e.g. https://www.skyhighnetworks.com, https://www.ciphercloud.com/, SAP's
SEEED https://www.sics.se/sites/default/files/pub/andreasschaad.pdf, https://
www.bluecoat.com/ and Cipherbase [2].

© International Association for Cryptologic Research 2018
A. Beimel and S. Dziembowski (Eds.): TCC 2018, LNCS 11240, pp. 159–176, 2018.
https://doi.org/10.1007/978-3-030-03810-6_6

A typical application of ORE is in databases, where one party encrypts numeric columns of a database table. Later, to issue a range query on the column, that party encrypts the endpoints of the range and requests all ciphertexts between them, an operation that can be processed by anyone who holds the encrypted column. In these settings, OPE is preferable because it can more easily be added to a database application, as the server can be oblivious to the fact that encryption is used at all. With more general ORE schemes, one needs to implement the specialized comparison operation in the database, which can be inconvenient (e.g. in a slow SQL implementation) or impossible, for instance when adding encryption to legacy systems.

This work studies the *ciphertext length* of any OPE construction achieving a certain new security notion recently given by a recent work of Chenette et al. [6] (we refer to this work as CLWW below). This notion is currently the best known security property for OPE that can be implemented and deployed. In particular, it results in strictly better security when combined with prior OPE via double-encryption. It seems likely that deployments using OPE (like those mentioned above) will be extended to use CLWW OPE if possible. And although recent attacks have shown that existing OPE is insecure in many contexts [8,11], it will likely continue to be used in practice in scenarios where the attacks do not apply.

CLWW constructed ORE with their security notion that has ciphertext length $\log_2(3)m \approx 1.58m$ bits, where m is the plaintext length, and showed how to convert their scheme to the more convenient OPE, but at the cost of increasing the ciphertext length to λm, where λ is the security parameter. This means that achieving OPE comes at a cost of increasing storage of the column by a factor typically in the range of 80 to 256, compared to the 1.58 expansion of ORE. Achieving smaller OPE ciphertexts with the same security would be highly desirable if possible, as large plaintext data sizes are often the motivating factor for outsourcing data to untrusted server in the first place. (We note that a different, incomparable ORE security notion of [3] can be achieved with $\approx m$ bit ciphertexts, although this fact will not be used in our work below.)

Below we give evidence that the large ciphertext size of the OPE in CLWW is inherent, by proving that any scheme meeting the information-theoretic version of their security notion must have ciphertexts of length

$$\lambda m - m \log m + m \log e,$$

where again m is the message length, logarithms are base 2, and e is the base of the natural logarithm. This bound shows that CLWW has almost optimal ciphertext size, as it has leading term λm instead of $(\lambda - \log m)m$.

In the remainder of this section we describe the prior work on ORE in more detail, and then sketch our results.

ORE SECURITY. It is immediate that an ORE scheme cannot be semantically secure against passive attacks, because one can compute information about plaintexts. But meaningful and formally-defined security targets for ORE have been suggested, starting with the work of [3]. This work defined two notions, one of which was a *ideal* ORE security that requires all plaintext information except order to be hidden. They also showed that no efficient OPE scheme (in particular, one with poly(λ, m)-size ciphertexts) could achieve ideal security. However, it was later shown [5] that ideal security for ORE is achievable using cryptographic multilinear pairings [9] or indistinguishability obfuscation [10]. This was apparently the first separation of OPE and ORE as primitives.

Motivated by the lack of a practical ideal construction, Boldyreva et al. [3] investigated a particular weaker notion called ROPF[2]. It was later shown [4] that ROPF-secure ciphers allow a passive adversary to compute the most-significant half of the bits of a random message with high probability, which may be too weak for some applications. The notion was however instantiated with fast blockcipher-based constructions under standard assumptions.

The recent CLWW work [6] introduced a different notion of security for ORE and demonstrated that it is stronger than ROPF-security by certain measures. In particular, that work gave a construction of ORE that could provably hide all but a logarithmic number of bits of a random plaintext. Moreover, the construction is simple to implement and uses only a blockcipher and standard assumptions. The CLWW security notion allows an adversary, given ciphertexts $\mathcal{E}_K(x), \mathcal{E}_K(y)$, to learn the index of the most significant bit on which x and y differ. As mentioned above, the ORE version of their construction has ciphertext size $\approx 1.58m$ while the OPE version has ciphertext size λm.

OUR RESULT. For technical reasons discussed below, we consider an information theoretic version of CLWW security, which requires the same security but against unbounded adversaries. The CLWW construction achieves this notion in the random oracle model, and we show that their construction is essentially optimal in terms of ciphertext length. Thus their large overhead in converting their construction from ORE to OPE is inherent, and should OPE with lower storage overhead be required, one will have to investigate other security notions for OPE.

We also generalize our lower bound to apply to any OPE with a new security notion that we call *inner-distance indistinguishability*. While not necessarily interesting as a security goal on its own (one would prefer something stronger), it encapsulates a property that must be avoided in order to build OPE with $O(m)$ size ciphertexts.

Our techniques start from first principles regarding when relations between random variables force their distributions to have large statistical distance. We sketch our proof in Sect. 4. We note that the *big-jump* attack of Boldyreva et al. [4] proves an exponential lower bound on ideal OPE, and bears some resemblance to our attack. But our attack treats a different and weaker security notion and obtains a fine-grained, polynomial lower bound.

---

[2] We will not need this definition in this paper. Roughly, ROPF security requires that a deterministic cipher be indistinguishable from a *random order preserving function* with the same domain and range.

INFORMATION-THEORETIC VERSUS COMPUTATIONAL SECURITY. We attempted to prove our result for any computationally-CLWW-secure ORE scheme, but our techniques do not seem suited to this case. An information-theoretic bound, however, applies to any construction secure in the random-oracle model and includes the CLWW construction. Moreover, if a scheme uses a PRF as its only cryptographic component, then our lower bound applies to a version of that scheme that uses a random-oracle in place of the PRF and thus to the original as well. We are unaware of any technique for building computationally-CLWW-secure OPE that circumvents our bound, and we conjecture that a ciphertext length lower bound also holds in the computational case.

COMPARISON TO CONCURRENT WORK. Recently, Segev and Shahaf [14] extend our result to computational security level, and our lower bound and their lower bound are identical in terms of the attacker's success probability, which implies the ciphertext expansion is inherent. Concretely, Segev and Shahaf prove their lower bound by presenting a non-uniform polynomial-time adversary, whereas we prove it via analyzing the statistical distance between ciphertexts distribution, which requires unbounded adversary. In their proof, Segev and Shahaf show that, if the lower bound N does not hold, then there exists a value $t \in [N]$ and ciphertexts $(c_0, c_1) = \{(\mathcal{E}(0), \mathcal{E}(2^{j+1} - 1), (\mathcal{E}(2^j - 1), \mathcal{E}(2^j))\}, 1 \leq j \leq m - 1$, such that the test $c_1 - c_1 \geq t$ can distinguish the two cases. We note that the two cases have the same leakage profile, which refers the evidence that there exists a non-uniform polynomial-time adversary.

WHY IT'S HARD FOR UNIFORM ADVERSARY? Our result only allows unbounded adversary, and Segev and Shahaf just improve the result to non-uniform computational setting[3], it would be nicer if we can have a tight lower bound be proved via a uniform polynomial adversary. According to our observation, we note that in both our result and [14], the distinguishing/testing algorithm is a simply comparison: $\mathbf{1}(c_1 - c_0 \geq t)$, and locating "$t$" is a super-poly algorithm. One hope might be extracting a more involved but still polynomial-time testing algorithm, and we leave it as an open problem.

ORGANIZATION. In Sect. 2 we recall definitions for ORE/OPE syntax and security and in Sect. 3 we recall the specific security notion that we study. In Sect. 4 we state our lower bound and sketch its proof, which is given in Sects. 5, 6 and 7. Finally in Sect. 8 we show how to generalize our result to an abstract security property.

2   Preliminaries

NOTATION AND BASIC RESULTS. We always use λ to denote the security parameter. For non-negative integers $a \leq b$ we write $[a, b]$ for the set $\{a, a + 1, \ldots, b\}$, $[n]$ for the set $\{1, \ldots, n\}$, and $[n]'$ for the set $\{0, 1, \ldots, n\}$. We use boldface to

---

[3] Also utilizing non-uniformity (or even unbounded computational power) in impossibility proofs is rather fair.

denote vector, i.e. $\boldsymbol{m}$; we denote $\boldsymbol{m}[i]$ as the i-th component of $\boldsymbol{m}$. If X_1, X_2 are r.v.s, we let

$$\Delta(X_1, X_2) = \frac{1}{2} \sum_k |\Pr[X_1 = k] - \Pr[X_2 = k]|$$

denote their statistical distance. We will use the following well-known *data processing lemma* (c.f. [7]) in our proof.

Lemma 1. *Let X and Y be r.v.s, and f be any function that includes the support of X and Y in its domain. Then $\Delta(f(X), f(Y)) \leq \Delta(X, Y)$.*

For a randomized algorithm $\mathcal{A}$ we write $y \xleftarrow{\$} \mathcal{A}(w)$ to denote running $\mathcal{A}$ on input w, and letting y be the random variable denoting its output. If $\mathcal{A}$ is deterministic, we denote $y \leftarrow \mathcal{A}(w)$ to denote running $\mathcal{A}$ and letting y be its output.

We write $\mathbf{1}(x < y)$ to mean 1 if $x < y$ and 0 otherwise.

ORE AND OPE. An *ORE scheme* Π is a tuple of algorithms $(\mathcal{K}, \mathcal{E}, \mathcal{C})$ for key generation, encryption, and comparison respectively, and always has an associated message space $\{0,1\}^m$ and ciphertext space $\{0,1\}^n$. The key generation algorithm $\mathcal{K}$ is randomized, and on input 1^λ, outputs a key K. The encryption algorithm $\mathcal{E}$ is deterministic and takes as input a key K and message $x \in \{0,1\}^m$ and outputs a ciphertext $c \leftarrow \mathcal{E}_K(x)$. The comparison algorithm takes as input two ciphertexts c_1, c_2 generated with the same K on messages x_1, x_2 and outputs a bit b.

We assume that all ORE schemes in this paper are *correct*, meaning that for all λ, keys K in the support of $\mathcal{K}(1^\lambda)$, and all $x, y \in \{0,1\}^m$, $\mathcal{C}(\mathcal{E}_K(x), \mathcal{E}_K(y))$ outputs $\mathbf{1}(x < y)$. Note that this allows testing if $x = y$ by running the comparison algorithm twice.

When an ORE scheme Π has a canonical comparison algorithm $\mathcal{C}$ that directly compares its inputs as numbers in $[2^n - 1]'$, we say that the scheme is an *order-preserving encryption (OPE)* scheme. In this case we omit the comparison algorithm and write $\Pi = (\mathcal{K}, \mathcal{E})$.

ORE SECURITY. Chenette et al. [6] gave a simulation-based definition for ORE security that used a leakage profile $\mathcal{L}$ as a parameter, where $\mathcal{L}$ is an efficient algorithm. We will use a weaker non-interactive indistinguishability-based version of their definition for our lower bounds (which makes our result stronger).

For an ORE scheme $\Pi = (\mathcal{K}, \mathcal{E}, \mathcal{C})$, leakage profile $\mathcal{L}$, and adversary $\mathcal{A}$ we consider the following game:

Game $\text{ORE}_{\Pi, \mathcal{L}, \mathcal{A}}(\lambda)$:

$K \xleftarrow{\$} \mathcal{K}(1^\lambda)$

$(\mathbf{m}_0, \mathbf{m}_1, s) \xleftarrow{\$} \mathcal{A}(\lambda)$

If $\mathcal{L}(\mathbf{m}_0) \neq \mathcal{L}(\mathbf{m}_1)$ then output 0.

For $i = 1, \ldots q$: $\mathbf{c}[i] \leftarrow \mathcal{E}_K(\mathbf{m}_b[i])$

$b' \xleftarrow{\$} \mathcal{A}(s, \mathbf{c})$

If $b' = b$ then output 1, Else output 0,

We define the $\mathcal{L}$-*advantage of* $\mathcal{A}$ *against* Π to be

$$\mathbf{Adv}^{\mathrm{ore}}_{\Pi,\mathcal{L},\mathcal{A}}(\lambda) = 2\Pr[\mathrm{ORE}_{\Pi,\mathcal{L},\mathcal{A}}(\lambda) = 1] - 1.$$

We say that Π is $\mathcal{L}$-*computationally secure* if for all efficient $\mathcal{A}$, $\mathbf{Adv}^{\mathrm{ore}}_{\Pi,\mathcal{L},\mathcal{A}}(\lambda)$ is a negligible function i.e. is $o(1/\mathrm{poly}(\lambda))$. We say that Π is $\mathcal{L}$-*statistically-secure* if the same condition holds for all (unbounded, wlog deterministic) adversaries $\mathcal{A}$; more specifically, we say Π is 2^{λ}-$\mathcal{L}$-*statistically-secure* if for all unbounded adversaries, the advantage is at least 2^{λ}.

We recall, as an example, that the *ideal* leakage profile only leaks order. Formally, this is

$$\mathcal{L}_{\mathrm{ideal}}(m_1,\ldots,m_q) = \{(i,j,\mathbf{1}(m_i < m_j)) \ : \ 1 \le i < j \le q\}.$$

3   CLWW Security and Constructions

In this section we recall and discuss the CLWW leakage profile and constructions.

CLWW LEAKAGE. CLWW considered the following leakage profile $\mathcal{L}_{\mathrm{clww}}$. On input $\mathbf{x} = (x_1,\ldots,x_q) \in (\{0,1\}^m)^q$, the leakage profile is defined by

$$\mathcal{L}_{\mathrm{clww}}(x_1,\ldots,x_q) := \{(i,j,\mathsf{ind}_{\mathrm{diff}}(x_i,x_j),\mathbf{1}(x_i < x_j)) \ : \ 1 \le i < j \le q\},$$

where $\mathsf{ind}_{\mathrm{diff}}(x_i,x_j) \in \{1,\ldots,m+1\}$ is the left-most bit on which x_i and x_j differ, or $m+1$ if they are equal. Compared to the ideal profile, only the $\mathsf{ind}_{\mathrm{diff}}(x_i,x_j)$ indices are extra leakage.

The intuition for the leakage is that, when comparing two numbers, an adversary will learn the length of the longest common prefix, and also which is larger. This information combines to reveal one bit of each of the plaintexts.

THE CLWW ORE AND OPE CONSTRUCTIONS. Our results will not need the CLWW construction, but it provides intuition for the lower bound and we recall it now, starting with a basic ORE construction $\Pi_{\mathrm{clww\text{-}ore}}$ and then describing an ORE variant with shorter ciphertexts, and how to build OPE $\Pi_{\mathrm{clww\text{-}ope}}$. We recall a version that is slightly different from theirs in that it is *perfectly* correct.

The scheme $\Pi_{\mathrm{clww\text{-}ore}} = (\mathcal{K}^{\mathrm{ore}}, \mathcal{E}^{\mathrm{ore}}, \mathcal{C}^{\mathrm{ore}})$ uses a PRF

$$F : \{0,1\}^{\lambda} \times ([m] \times \{0,1\}^m) \to (\{0,1\}^{\lambda} \setminus \{1^{\lambda}\}).$$

Thus the input domain of F is $[m] \times \{0,1\}^m$, and it outputs a λ-bit string that is assumed to never be 1^{λ} (of course we can modify any PRF so that this is true without affecting asymptotic security).

- Key generation $\mathcal{K}^{\mathrm{ore}}(1^{\lambda})$ outputs a random PRF key $K \xleftarrow{\$} \{0,1\}^{\lambda}$.
- Encryption $\mathcal{E}^{\mathrm{ore}}_K(x)$, on input a message $x \in \{0,1\}^m$, the algorithm computes for each $i = 1,\ldots,m$ the value

$$u_i = F(K, i \,\|\, x[1,\ldots,i-1] \,\|\, 0^{m-i+1}) + x[i], \tag{1}$$

where the addition is done by interpreting the bitstrings as members of $\{0,\ldots,2^{\lambda}-1\}$. Encryption outputs $(u_1,\ldots,u_m)$.

- The comparison algorithm $C^{\text{ore}}((u_1, \ldots, u_m), (u_1', \ldots, u_m'))$ takes as input two ciphertexts. It finds the smallest i such that $u_i \neq u_i'$, and it outputs 1 if $\mathbf{1}(u_i < u_i')$.

Correctness follows by observing that the u_i will be equal until the u_i, u_i' corresponding to the first differing bit in the plaintexts. At that position, u_i and u_i' will differ by 1 (additively) and the smaller plaintext has the smaller value. CLWW proved that $\Pi_{\text{clww-ore}}$ (and the variants below) are $\mathcal{L}_{\text{clww}}$-secure, assuming that F is a PRF. It is straightforward to derive from their proof that $\Pi_{\text{clww-ore}}$ is also statistically-secure with the same leakage profile in the random-oracle model.

CONVERSION TO OPE. Chenette et al. showed how to convert this construction to an OPE scheme $\Pi_{\text{clww-ope}}$ by simply concatenating the members of a ciphertext to form a bitstring in $\{0,1\}^{\lambda m}$ that is interpreted as a number for comparison. This scheme is perfectly correct because of our assumption that F never outputs the all-ones string, and thus the addition in (1) will never wrap modulo 2^λ.

COMPRESSING ORE CIPHERTEXTS. Chenette et al. showed that one can modify $\Pi_{\text{clww-ore}}$ to a new ORE scheme which has shorter ciphertext. More precisely, the new scheme use a PRF F' with range only $\{0,1,2\}$ instead of F, where

$$F' : \{0,1\}^\lambda \times ([m] \times \{0,1\}^m) \to \{0,1,2\}.$$

Now encryption uses F', and for $i = 1, \ldots, m$ computes

$$u_i = F'(K, i \parallel x[1, \ldots, i-1] \parallel 0^{m-i+1}) + x[i] \mod 3 \qquad (2)$$

It outputs the vector $(u_1, \ldots, u_n) \in \{0,1,2\}^m$.

Comparison now takes as input $(u_1, \ldots, u_m)$ $(u_1', \ldots, u_m')$. As before, it finds the first i such that $u_i \neq u_i'$. But now it outputs 1 if $u_i' = u_i + 1 \mod 3$, and otherwise it outputs 0.

A ciphertext for an m-bit input is now a vector in $\{0,1,2\}^m$, which can be represented using $log_2(3)m + O(1) \approx 1.58m$ bits.

4   Lower Bound Statement and Proof Sketch

We can now state our lower bound formally.

Theorem 2. *Suppose $\Pi = (\mathcal{K}, \mathcal{E}, \mathcal{C})$ is an order-preserving encryption scheme with associated message space $\{0,1\}^m$ and ciphertext space $\{0,1\}^n$, and that Π is $2^{-\lambda}$-$\mathcal{L}_{\text{clww}}$-statistically-secure. Then we have*

$$n \geq \lambda m - m \log m + m \log e$$

In any practical OPE scenario we are aware of, we have $\log m - \log e < \lambda$ and thus our bound is nontrivial. For example, considering the message space is 40 bytes, $\log m - \log e = \log 320/e < 7$, while in real world encryption, the secure parameter is always set to be 80 or larger.

NOTATION FOR THE PROOF. To explain why this theorem is true we start with a change of notation that is more convenient for the underlying statistical problem. We will freely treat a string $i \in \{0, 1\}^m$ as a member of $[2^m - 1]' = \{0, \ldots, 2^m - 1\}$ when convenient (and similarly for strings in $\{0, 1\}^n$). For each $i \in \{0, 1\}^m$ we define a random variable X_i by $X_i = \mathcal{E}_K(i)$, where $K \xleftarrow{\$} \mathcal{K}(1^\lambda)$. These random variables are dependent, and perfect correctness implies that $X_0 < X_1 < \cdots < X_{2^m - 1}$ with probability one (here we are treating the X_i as numbers).

Now we consider what the ϵ-$\mathcal{L}_{\mathrm{clww}}$-statistical security implies about our r.v.s $X_0, \ldots, X_{2^m - 1}$. For every possible pair of vectors of messages $\mathbf{m}_0, \mathbf{m}_1$ that does not automatically lose the game because of the leakage requirement, we get a condition about the statistical distance of the distributions of two tuples of random variables. For instance, if the adversary requests singleton vectors $\mathbf{m}_0 = i$ or $\mathbf{m}_1 = j \in \{0, 1\}^m$ then the leakage $\mathcal{L}_{\mathrm{clww}}(i) = \mathcal{L}_{\mathrm{clww}}(j) = \emptyset$, so we must have that

$$\Delta(X_i, X_j) \leq \varepsilon$$

for every i, j. More generally, for any two vectors $\mathbf{i} = (i_1, \ldots, i_q)$ and $\mathbf{j} = (j_1, \ldots, j_q)$ in $(\{0, 1\}^m)^q$ with $\mathcal{L}_{\mathrm{clww}}(\mathbf{i}) = \mathcal{L}_{\mathrm{clww}}(\mathbf{j})$, we must have

$$\Delta((X_{i_1}, \ldots, X_{i_q}), (X_{j_1}, \ldots, X_{j_q})) \leq \epsilon.$$

Thus we need to understand which $\mathbf{i}, \mathbf{j}$ satisfy $\mathcal{L}_{\mathrm{clww}}(\mathbf{i}) = \mathcal{L}_{\mathrm{clww}}(\mathbf{j})$. Fortunately, our proof will only require inputs of a particular structure. We observe that the following qualify for $t = 0, \ldots, m - 1$:

$$\mathbf{i} = (0, 2^{t+1} - 1) \quad \text{and} \quad \mathbf{j} = (2^t - 1, 2^t).$$

In binary, $\mathbf{i}$ is $(0^m, 0^{m-t-1}1^{t+1})$ and $\mathbf{j}$ is $(0^{m-t}1^t, 0^{m-t-1}10^t)$. In both cases, the most significant differing bit is in the $t + 1$-st least significant position (and the messages are in the same order), so the leakage in the same.

But why should this choice be useful? It represents the most extreme cases of two "distant" plaintexts and two "close" plaintexts that must appear indistinguishable. At a very high level, the scheme must "waste" a lot of its ciphertext space in order to make pairs like this appear indistinguishable. This is because the $\mathbf{i}$ side must have ciphertexts that are far apart (by roughly 2^{t+1}) simply because correctness forces many ciphertexts to be between X_0 and $X_{2^{t+1}-1}$, namely $X_1, X_2, \ldots, X_{2^{t+1}-2}$. In order to appear indistinguishable, X_{2^t-1} and X_{2^t} must also be far apart, with no other ciphertexts between them (again by correctness). Moreover, as t grows we get a *nested* sequence of pairs, where the space wasted by the previous pair force the next to waste even more.

Our proof will argue that this wasted space grows to the quoted bound. We consider the nested sequence of these tuples above, and then proceed by induction to show that a large ciphertext-space is needed for security. The key

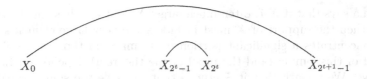

X_0 $\qquad\qquad\qquad\qquad X_{2^t-1}$ X_{2^t} $\qquad\qquad X_{2^{t+1}-1}$

Fig. 1. Two pairs of r.v.s that are required to be indistinguishable by the security definition. The top arc represents the gap G_1 and the bottom arc represents the gap G_2.

step in our induction is that, since the tuples $(X_0, X_{2^{t+1}-1})$ and (X_{2^t-1}, X_{2^t}) must have statistical distance at most ϵ, then their *gaps*

$$G_1 = X_{2^{t+1}-1} - X_0 \quad \text{and} \quad G_2 = X_{2^t} - X_{2^t-1}$$

must also satisfy $\Delta(G_1, G_2) \leq \epsilon$ by the data processing inequality. But the gap measured by G_2 is a subset of the gap measured by G_1, so $G_2 < G_1$. In fact, as we show via induction on t, G_2 must often be much less than G_1 (since G_1 contains the gap from X_{2^t-1} and X_0, which is the previous step of the induction). Using this fact, we apply the following lemma that is proved in Sect. 6 (Fig. 1).

Lemma 3. *For any two variables $X \geq Y \in [N-1]'$, and distinct positive integers $d_1, \ldots, d_k$ such that $Pr[X = Y + d_i] = p_i$, we have*

$$\Delta(X, Y) \geq \frac{\sum_{i=1}^{k} p_i \cdot d_i}{N-1}.$$

Intuitively, this lemma says that if one of the random variables is often much bigger than the other, then they must have large statistical distance.

CONTRAST WITH BIG JUMP. The *big jump* attack of [4] gave a ciphertext-size lower bound for any ideal OPE. With ideal ORE, *every* pair of two random variables $X_{i_1} < X_{i_2}$ and $X_{j_1} < X_{j_2}$ must be indistinguishable, which gives the attack more flexibility and results in an exponential bound (without resorting to recursion). Instead our bound works with a particular nested set of m pairs, with each step using a pair to increase the bound by roughly λ bits.

5   Proof of Theorem 2

We start with an additional technical lemma (proved in Sect. 7), and then give the proof.

Lemma 4. *Let $X > Y \in [N-1]'$ be random variables such that $\Delta(X, Y) \leq \delta$. Let $i \geq 1$ and assume that for all $q \in [0,1]$, $Pr[X > Y + \frac{(1-q)^i}{\delta^i \cdot i!}] \geq q$. Then for all $q \in [0,1]$ we have*

$$Pr[X > \frac{(1-q)^{i+1}}{\delta^{i+1}(i+1)!}] \geq q.$$

This lemma says that if X is often much larger Y, but also has small statistical distance, then the support of X must include some very large elements, and in fact X concentrates a significant portion of its mass on those large elements. The proof of this lemma (and the proof of the theorem) depends on Lemma 3 from above. We remark that it is crucial that we have the same probability q in the lemma assumption and conclusion, and achieving this requires a delicate argument. A weaker conclusion, where q changes, is more easily achieved using a Markov-type argument (and indeed earlier versions of this paper did exactly this, resulting in a weaker bound).

5.1   Proof

Let $\Pi = (\mathcal{K}, \mathcal{E})$ be an OPE scheme with associated message space $\{0,1\}^m$ and ciphertext space $\{0,1\}^n$, and assume Π is $2^{-\lambda}$-$\mathcal{L}_{\text{clww}}$-statistically-secure.

Below, for $i \in [2^m - 1]'$, we let $X_i = \mathcal{E}_K(i)$ where $K \xleftarrow{\$} \mathcal{K}(1^\lambda)$ as in the proof sketch. That is, the X_i are dependent random variables that represent the encryption of message i under a random key. Note that $X_0 < X_1 < \cdots < X_{2^m-1}$.

We will prove the theorem using following claim. Here, we let $\varepsilon = 2^{-\lambda}$.

Lemma 5. *For $i \in [2^m - 1]'$, let X_i be defined as above. Then for $1 \le j \le m$ and $q \in [0,1]$,*

$$\Pr[X_{2^j-1} - X_0 \ge \frac{(1-q)^{j-1}}{\varepsilon^{j-1} \cdot (j-1)!}] \ge q$$

Proof (of Lemma 5). The proof is by induction on j.

CASE $j = 1$. This case reduces to $\Pr[X_1 - X_0 \ge 1] = 1$, which is true by the correctness of the scheme.

CASE $j \implies j + 1$. We need to show that for any $q \in [0,1]$

$$\Pr[X_{2^{j+1}-1} - X_0 \ge \frac{(1-q)^j}{\varepsilon^j \cdot (j)!}] \ge q.$$

By the correctness of the scheme, we have that

$$X_{2^{j+1}-1} - X_0 \ge (X_{2^j} - X_{2^j-1}) + (X_{2^j-1} - X_0) + 1 \tag{3}$$

Now define "gap" random variables $G_1 = X_{2^{j+1}-1} - X_0$ and $G_2 = (X_{2^j} - X_{2^j-1})$. By induction we know that for any $q \in [0,1]$

$$\Pr[X_{2^j-1} - X_0 \ge \frac{(1-q)^{j-1}}{\varepsilon^{j-1} \cdot (j-1)!}] \ge q.$$

Plugging this, and the definitions of G_1, G_2 into (3), we have

$$\Pr[G_1 > G_2 + \frac{(1-q)^{j-1}}{\varepsilon^{j-1} \cdot (j-1)!}] \ge q.$$

Moreover, we know by the ε-$\mathcal{L}_{\mathrm{clww}}$-statistical security of Π and Lemma 1 that $\Delta(G_1, G_2) \leq \varepsilon$.

We now want to apply Lemma 4 to G_1 and G_2, to show that G_1 must be large and then conclude the induction. In the lemma, we set $G_1 = X, G_2 = Y, i = j$, and $\delta = \varepsilon$. The lemma gives

$$\Pr[G_1 > \frac{(1-q)^j}{\varepsilon^j \cdot (j)!}] \geq q,$$

obtaining the induction step.

We can now complete the proof of Theorem 2. The above lemma with $j = m$ tells us that for any $q \in [0, 1]$

$$\Pr[X_{2^m-1} > X_0 + \frac{(1-q)^{m-1}}{\varepsilon^{m-1} \cdot (m-1)!}] \geq q,$$

and thus for any $j \leq D = 1/\varepsilon^{m-1}(m-1)!$,

$$\Pr[X_{2^m-1} > X_0 + j] \geq 1 - ((m-1)! \cdot j)^{1/m-1}\varepsilon$$

and

$$\sum_{\ell=1}^{j} \Pr[X_{2^m-1} = X_0 + \ell] \leq ((m-1)! \cdot j)^{1/m-1}\varepsilon.$$

Besides, we claim $D \leq N - 1$, if not, then there exists $q > 0$ such that

$$N - 1 = \frac{(1-q)^{m-1}}{\varepsilon^{m-1} \cdot (m-1)!}$$

referring to

$$\Pr[X_{2^m-1} > X_0 + N - 1] \geq q > 0$$

which contradicts $X_i \in [N-1]'$.

Now we denote $p_\ell = \Pr[X_{2^m-1} = X_0 + \ell]$, and according to Lemma 3, we get that

$$\varepsilon \geq \Delta(X_{2^m-1}, X_0) \geq \frac{\sum_{\ell=1}^{N-1} p_\ell \cdot \ell}{N-1} \tag{4}$$

and

$$\sum_{\ell=1}^{N-1} p_\ell \cdot \ell = (p_1 + \cdots + p_{N-1}) + (p_2 + \cdots + p_{N-1}) + \cdots + p_{N-1}$$

$$\geq 1 + (1 - p_1) + (1 - p_1 - p_2) + \cdots + (1 - p_1 - \cdots - p_{D-1})$$

$$\geq 1 + \sum_{\ell=1}^{D-1} (1 - ((m-1)!\ell)^{\frac{1}{m-1}} \cdot \varepsilon)$$

$$= D - (m-1)!^{\frac{1}{m-1}} \cdot \varepsilon \sum_{\ell=1}^{D-1} \ell^{\frac{1}{m-1}}$$

$$\geq D - (m-1)!^{\frac{1}{m-1}} \cdot \varepsilon \cdot \int_0^D x^{\frac{1}{m-1}} \, dx$$

$$= \frac{1}{\varepsilon^{m-1}(m-1)!} \cdot \frac{1}{m} = \frac{1}{\varepsilon^{m-1} m!}.$$

Returning to (4), we have

$$N - 1 \geq 1/\varepsilon^m m!.$$

By setting $\varepsilon = 2^{-\lambda}$, we get

$$n \geq \lambda m - \log(m!) \geq \lambda m - \log((m/e)^m) = \lambda m - m \log m + m \log e.$$

$\square$

6   Proof of Lemma 3

We recall the lemma.

Lemma 3. *For any two variables* $X \geq Y \in [N-1]'$, *and distinct positive integers* $d_1, \ldots, d_k$ *such that* $\Pr[X = Y + d_i] = p_i$, *we have*

$$\Delta(X, Y) \geq \frac{\sum_{i=1}^k p_i \cdot d_i}{N - 1}.$$

Proof. We will show that one of the distinguishers $\mathcal{D}_i$, $i \in [N-1]$, has the needed advantage, where $\mathcal{D}_i$ is defined as follows: Given input $T \in [N-1]'$, $\mathcal{D}_i$ outputs 1 if and only if $T \geq i$.

The advantage of $\mathcal{D}_i$ is $\delta_i = \Pr[X \geq i] - \Pr[Y \geq i]$. We have that

$$
\begin{aligned}
\sum_{i=1}^{N-1} \delta_i &= \sum_{i=1}^{N-1} \Pr[X \geq i] - \sum_{i=1}^{N-1} \Pr[Y \geq i] \\
&= \sum_{i=0}^{N-1} \Pr[X \geq i] - \sum_{i=0}^{N-1} \Pr[Y \geq i] = E(X - Y) \geq \sum_{i=1}^{k} p_i d_i.
\end{aligned}
$$

Thus some δ_i must be at least this sum divided by $N - 1$. $\qquad\square$

7   Proof of Lemma 4

We first recall the lemma.

Lemma 4. *Let $X > Y \in [N - 1]'$ be random variables such that $\Delta(X, Y) \leq \delta$. Let $i \geq 1$ and assume that for all $q \in [0, 1]$, $\Pr[X > Y + \frac{(1-q)^i}{\delta^i, i!}] \geq q$. Then for all $q \in [0, 1]$ we have*

$$
\Pr[X > \frac{(1 - q)^{i+1}}{\delta^{i+1}(i + 1)!}] \geq q.
$$

Proof. Suppose for contradiction that there exists $q^* \in [0, 1]$ such that

$$
\hat{q} := \Pr[X > t] < q^*,
$$

where $t = (1 - q^*)^{i+1}/\delta^{i+1}(i + 1)!$.

We will show that $\Delta(X, Y) > \delta$, violating the assumption in the lemma. We will prove this by showing the following "truncated" r.v.s W, Z satisfy $\Delta(X, Y) \geq \Delta(W, Z) > \delta$, where W, Z are defined via the joint distribution

$$
\Pr[W = a, Z = b] = \begin{cases} \Pr[X = a, Y = b] & \text{if } (a, b) \in [t]^2 \setminus (0, 0), \\ \hat{q} & \text{if } (a, b) = (0, 0) \\ 0 & \text{otherwise} \end{cases}.
$$

According to the definition of (W, Z), we show $\Delta(X, Y) \geq \Delta(W, Z)$. For simplifying, we denote

$$
p_{i,j} = \Pr[X = i, Y = j]; \quad p_j = \sum_{k=0}^{t} p_{k,j}; \quad p_j^* = \sum_{k=t+1}^{N-1} p_{k,j}; \quad \forall i, j \in [t]
$$

and it's obvious to note that for $j \in [t]$: (1) $\Pr[X = j] = \Pr[W = j]$; (2) $\Pr[Z = j] = p_j$; (3) $\Pr[Y = j] = p_j + p_j^*$; (4) $\sum_{k=0}^{t} p_j^* = \sum_{k=t+1}^{N-1} (\Pr[X = k] - \Pr[Y = k])$.

Hence:

$$2\Delta(X,Y) = \sum_{j=0}^{N-1} |\Pr[X=j] - \Pr[Y=j]|$$

$$= \sum_{j=0}^{t} |\Pr[X=j] - \Pr[Y=j]| + \sum_{j=t+1}^{N-1} |\Pr[X=j] - \Pr[Y=j]|$$

$$\geq \sum_{j=0}^{t} |\Pr[X=j] - \Pr[Y=j]| + \sum_{j=t+1}^{N-1} (\Pr[X=j] - \Pr[Y=j])$$

$$= \sum_{j=0}^{t} |\Pr[X=j] - \Pr[Y=j]| + \sum_{j=0}^{t} p_j^*$$

$$= \sum_{j=0}^{t} |\Pr[W=j] - \Pr[Z=j] - p_j^*| + \sum_{j=0}^{t} p_j^*$$

$$\geq \sum_{j=0}^{t} |\Pr[W=j] - \Pr[Z=j]| = 2\Delta(W,Z)$$

In the following, it suffices to show that $\Delta(W,Z) > \delta$. We denote $d_j = \Pr[W = Z + j]$. Applying Lemma 3,

$$\Delta(W,Z) \geq \frac{\sum_{\ell=1}^{t} d_\ell \cdot \ell}{t}.$$

We now show that $\sum_{\ell=1}^{t} d_\ell \cdot \ell > \delta t$, completing the proof. Below we use the following technical claim, which we establish below:

Claim. In the notation of the proof, we have the following:

1. $\sum_{\ell=1}^{t} d_\ell = 1 - \hat{q}$,
2. For each j, $\sum_{\ell=1}^{j} d_\ell \leq (i! \cdot j)^{1/i}\delta$,
3. $t \geq \hat{t}$, where $\hat{t} = (1 - \hat{q})^i / \delta^i i!$.

Using the claim, we have

$$\sum_{\ell=1}^{t} d_\ell \cdot \ell \geq \sum_{\ell=1}^{\hat{t}} d_\ell \cdot \ell = (d_1 + \ldots + d_{\hat{t}}) + (d_2 + \ldots + d_{\hat{t}}) + \ldots + (d_{\hat{t}})$$

$$\geq (1-\hat{q}) + ((1-\hat{q}) - d_1) + ((1-\hat{q}) - d_1 - d_2) + \ldots + ((1-\hat{q}) - d_1 - \ldots - d_{\hat{t}-1})$$

$$\geq (1-\hat{q})\hat{t} - \sum_{\ell=1}^{\hat{t}-1} (\ell i!)^{1/i}\delta$$

$$\geq (1-\hat{q})\hat{t} - (i!)^{1/i}\delta \int_0^{\hat{t}} x^{1/i}dx$$

$$= (1-\hat{q})^{i+1}\hat{t} - (i!)^{1/i}\delta \cdot \frac{i}{i+1}\hat{t}^{\frac{i+1}{i}} = \frac{(1-\hat{q})^{i+1}}{\delta^i(i+1)!} > \delta t.$$

We now prove the claim. The first part follows easily from the definition of W, Z. For the second part, we have

$$\sum_{\ell=1}^{j} d_\ell \leq \sum_{\ell=1}^{j} \Pr[X = Y + \ell] = 1 - \Pr[X > Y + j] \leq (i!j)^{1/i}\delta,$$

where the last inequality follows since $\Pr[X > Y + (1-q)^i/\delta^i i!] \geq q$ holds for all $q \in [0,1]$, and particular $q = 1 - (i!j)^{1/i}\delta$.

For the third part of the claim, suppose for contradiction that $t < \hat{t}$. Then

$$\Pr[X > t] \geq \Pr[X > Y + t] \geq 1 - (i!t)^{1/i}\delta > 1 - (i!\hat{t})^{1/i}\delta = \hat{q}.$$

(The second inequality is another application of the condition in the lemma, similar to the proof of the second part.) But this contradicts the definition $\hat{q} = \Pr[X > t]$ and proves the third part of the claim. $\qquad\square$

8   Extensions of the Lower Bound

Our lower bound applies to the specific definition achieved by Chenette et al., and it is possible to circumvent the bound by targeting a different, but hopefully satisfactory, notion of security. In this section we identify an abstract property, which we term *inner-distance-indistinguishablity*, for which a similar lower bound applies. Thus, to avoid the bound for OPE with another definition, one must avoid this property, and the authors are not aware of an approach for doing so.

We also show how to apply our proof technique to give an essentially-tight lower bound on the ciphertext length of the "base-d" OPE variants suggested by Chenette et al., which achieve a weakened version of security with shorter ciphertexts.

INNER-DISTANCE-INDISTINGUISHABLITY. The following property seems mostly useful as a tool for understanding and generalizing the lower bound, and not as a stand-alone target for OPE security in practice.

Definition 6. *Let $\Pi = (\mathcal{K}, \mathcal{E}, \mathcal{C})$ be an OPE scheme with associated message space M, $d \geq 1$ be an integer, and $\varepsilon > 0$. We say that Π is (statistically) ε- inner-distance-indistinguishable for width d (denoted ε-IDI_d) if for all $i < j \in M$ such that $j - i > d$, there exist $k, \ell \in M$ such that*

1. $i \leq k < \ell \leq j$
2. $\ell - k \leq d$
3. $\Delta(D_1, D_2) \leq \varepsilon$, where $D_1 = \mathcal{E}_K(j) - \mathcal{E}_K(i)$ and $D_2 = \mathcal{E}_K(k) - \mathcal{E}_K(\ell)$ and K is random key.

Intuitively, ε-IDI_d says that the distance between every encrypted pair of messages must be indistinguishable from the gap between two encrypted messages which both lie between them, and moreover the latter gap is required to be small, namely d or less.

The CLWW notion implies ε-IDI$_1$ security. That is, for every pair $i < j$, $\mathcal{E}_K(j) - \mathcal{E}_K(i)$ is distinguishable from $\mathcal{E}_K(k+1) - \mathcal{E}_K(k)$ for some k between i and j (when $d = 1$, we must have $\ell = k+1$ in the definition).

To see this, fix some i, j, with $j > i+1$, and consider their binary expansions. We may write i in the form $p \| 0 \| x$ and j in the form $p \| 1 \| y$, where p is the longest common prefix and i and j, and $x, y \in \{0,1\}^L$ for some $L \geq 1$. Then consider

$$k = p \| 0 \| 1^L \quad \text{and} \quad \ell = p \| 1 \| 0^L.$$

We have that $\ell = k+1$ (treating ℓ, k as numbers), and that either $k \neq i$ or $\ell \neq j$. Moreover the CLWW security notion ensures that the condition of IDI$_1$ security holds for this choice of k, ℓ.

The following theorem generalizes Theorem 2.

Theorem 7. *Suppose $\Pi = (\mathcal{K}, \mathcal{E}, \mathcal{C})$ is an order-preserving encryption scheme with security parameter λ and associated message space $\{0,1\}^m$ and ciphertext space $\{0,1\}^n$, and Π is $2^{-\lambda}$-IDI$_d$ secure for some $d \geq 1$. Let $m' = m - \lceil \log d \rceil$. Then we have*

$$n \geq \lambda m' - m' \log m' + m' \log e$$

Proof. Let $\Pi = (\mathcal{K}, \mathcal{E}, \mathcal{C})$ be an OPE scheme with the syntax and conditions in the theorem. Below, for $i \in \{0,1\}^m$, we write $X_i = \mathcal{E}_K(i)$, and let m' be as defined in the theorem.

We will show how to carry out the same strategy used in the proof of Theorem 2. We will prove a version of Lemma 5 for a different nested sequence of pairs of messages $(i_j^L, i_j^R)_{j=1}^{m'}$ that we define inductively from m' down to 1 now.

- Base: $i_{m'}^L = 0, i_{m'}^R = 2^m - 1$.
- Step: Given (i_j^L, i_j^R), let $k < \ell$ be the pair between i_j^L and i_j^R guaranteed by IDI$_d$ security. We distinguish two cases:
  1. If $k - i_j^L > i_j^R - \ell$ then set (i_{j-1}^L, i_{j-1}^R) to be (i_j^L, k).
  2. Otherwise, set (i_{j-1}^L, i_{j-1}^R) to (ℓ, i_j^R).

Intuitively, we use the IDI$_d$ security property to find a nested sequence by moving to the "larger" gap at each step, and this continues for at least m' steps. Using this sequence, the rest of the proof of Lemma 5 can be carried out. Finally, the rest of the proof of Theorem 2 can be applied exactly as before. ☐

EXTENSION TO OPE VARIANTS. We can also extend our proof of Theorem 2 to the "d-ary" variants of Chenette et al. That construction saved a modest amount of space over the main CLWW construction via additional leakage, which is described via the following leakage profile $\mathcal{L}_{\text{clww}}^d$:

$$\mathcal{L}_{\text{clww}}^d(x_1, \ldots, x_q) := \{(i, j, \text{ind}_{\text{diff}}^{(d)}(x_i, x_j), \mathbf{1}(x_i < x_j)) : 1 \leq i < j \leq q\},$$

where $\mathrm{ind}_{\mathrm{diff}}^{(d)}(a,b)$ writes its inputs in base d as $a = (a[1],\ldots,a[m])$ and $b = (b[1],\ldots,b[m])$, and outputs $(k,|b[k]-a[k]|)$, where k is the smallest index such that $b[k] \neq a[k]$. If there is not such index (i.e. $a = b$) then it outputs $(m+1,0)$.

Intuitively, this leakage outputs the index of the first base-d digit where each pair of messages differ, and additionally outputs the absolute difference in that digit. (When $d = 2$ the additional output is trivial, since it is always 1.)

We will show how to carry out the same strategy used in the proof of Theorem 2. Here we denote $m^* = m/\log d - 1$, and we will prove a version of Lemma 5 for a different nested sequence of pairs of messages $(i_j^L, i_j^R)_{j=1}^{m^*}$ that we define as follows:

$$i_j^L = 0, \quad i_j^R = 0^{m^*-j}||1||(d-1)^j$$

And we define the pair $\hat{i}_j^L, \hat{i}_j^R$ as:

$$\hat{i}_j^L = 0^{m^*-j}||0||(d-1)^j, \quad \hat{i}_j^R = 0^{m^*-j}||1||0^j$$

According to the leakage profile, we have $(\mathcal{E}_K(i_j^L), \mathcal{E}_K(i_j^R))$ and $(\mathcal{E}_K(\hat{i}_j^L), \mathcal{E}_K(\hat{i}_j^R))$ are statistical indistinguishable. Using the sequence $(i_j^L, i_j^R)_{j=1}^{m^*}$, the rest of the proof of Lemma 5 can be carried out. Finally, the rest of the proof of Theorem 2 can be applied exactly as before. Hence we have the lower bound:

$$n \geq \lambda(m/\log d) - (m/\log d)\log(m/\log d)$$

referring to d-ary CLWW is also almost optimal.

Acknowledgments. We'd like to thank Yevgeniy Dodis and Daniel Wichs for their insightful remarks and suggestions, which inspire us simplify the proof in this work. David Cash is supported by NSF CNS-1453132. David Cash and Cong Zhang are partially supported by DARPA and SSC Pacific under contract N66001-15-C-4070. Any opinions, findings, and conclusions or recommendations expressed in this material are those of the author(s) and do not necessarily reflect the views of NSF, DARPA or SSC Pacific.

References

1. Agrawal, R., Kiernan, J., Srikant, R., Xu, Y.: Order preserving encryption for numeric data. In: Proceedings of the 2004 ACM SIGMOD International Conference on Management of Data, SIGMOD 2004, pp. 563–574. ACM (2004)
2. Arasu, A., et al.: Orthogonal security with cipherbase. In: 6th Biennial Conference on Innovative Data Systems Research (CIDR 2013), January 2013
3. Boldyreva, A., Chenette, N., Lee, Y., O'Neill, A.: Order-preserving symmetric encryption. In: Joux, A. (ed.) EUROCRYPT 2009. LNCS, vol. 5479, pp. 224–241. Springer, Heidelberg (2009). https://doi.org/10.1007/978-3-642-01001-9_13
4. Boldyreva, A., Chenette, N., O'Neill, A.: Order-preserving encryption revisited: improved security analysis and alternative solutions. In: Rogaway, P. (ed.) CRYPTO 2011. LNCS, vol. 6841, pp. 578–595. Springer, Heidelberg (2011). https://doi.org/10.1007/978-3-642-22792-9_33

5. Boneh, D., Lewi, K., Raykova, M., Sahai, A., Zhandry, M., Zimmerman, J.: Semantically secure order-revealing encryption: multi-input functional encryption without obfuscation. In: Oswald, E., Fischlin, M. (eds.) EUROCRYPT 2015. LNCS, vol. 9057, pp. 563–594. Springer, Heidelberg (2015). https://doi.org/10.1007/978-3-662-46803-6_19

6. Chenette, N., Lewi, K., Weis, S.A., Wu, D.J.: Practical order-revealing encryption with limited leakage. In: Peyrin, T. (ed.) FSE 2016. LNCS, vol. 9783, pp. 474–493. Springer, Heidelberg (2016). https://doi.org/10.1007/978-3-662-52993-5_24

7. Cover, T.M., Thomas, J.A.: Elements of Information Theory (Wiley Series in Telecommunications and Signal Processing). Wiley, Hoboken (2006)

8. Durak, F.B., DuBuisson, T.M., Cash, D.: What else is revealed by order-revealing encryption? In: ACM CCS (2016)

9. Garg, S., Gentry, C., Halevi, S.: Candidate multilinear maps from ideal lattices. In: Johansson, T., Nguyen, P.Q. (eds.) EUROCRYPT 2013. LNCS, vol. 7881, pp. 1–17. Springer, Heidelberg (2013). https://doi.org/10.1007/978-3-642-38348-9_1

10. Garg, S., Gentry, C., Halevi, S., Raykova, M., Sahai, A., Waters, B.: Candidate indistinguishability obfuscation and functional encryption for all circuits. SIAM J. Comput. 45(3), 882–929 (2016)

11. Grubbs, P., Sekniqi, K., Bindschaedler, V., Naveed, M., Ristenpart, T.: Leakage-abuse attacks against order-revealing encryption. Cryptology ePrint Archive, Report 2016/895 (2016). http://eprint.iacr.org/2016/895

12. Lu, W., Varna, A.L., Wu, M.: Security analysis for privacy preserving search of multimedia. In: 2010 IEEE International Conference on Image Processing, pp. 2093–2096, September 2010

13. Popa, R.A., Redfield, C.M.S., Zeldovich, N., Balakrishnan, H.: CryptDB: protecting confidentiality with encrypted query processing. In: Proceedings of the 23rd ACM Symposium on Operating Systems Principles 2011, SOSP 2011, Cascais, Portugal, 23–26 October 2011, pp. 85–100 (2011)

14. Segev, G., Shahaf, I.: Ciphertext expansion in limited-leakage order-preserving encryption: a tight computational lower bound. To appear in Proceeding of the 16th Theory of Cryptography Conference (2018). https://eprint.iacr.org/2018/521

15. Wang, C., Cao, N., Li, J., Ren, K., Lou, W.: Secure ranked keyword search over encrypted cloud data. In: 2010 IEEE 30th International Conference on Distributed Computing Systems (ICDCS), pp. 253–262, June 2010

Ciphertext Expansion in Limited-Leakage Order-Preserving Encryption: A Tight Computational Lower Bound

Gil Segev[✉] and Ido Shahaf

School of Computer Science and Engineering, Hebrew University of Jerusalem,
Jerusalem 91904, Israel
{segev,ido.shahaf}@cs.huji.ac.il

Abstract. Order-preserving encryption emerged as a key ingredient underlying the security of practical database management systems. Boldyreva et al. (EUROCRYPT '09) initiated the study of its security by introducing two natural notions of security. They proved that their first notion, a "best-possible" relaxation of semantic security allowing ciphertexts to reveal the ordering of their corresponding plaintexts, is not realizable. Later on Boldyreva et al. (CRYPTO '11) proved that any scheme satisfying their second notion, indistinguishability from a random order-preserving function, leaks about half of the bits of a random plaintext.

This unsettling state of affairs was recently changed by Chenette et al. (FSE '16), who relaxed the above "best-possible" notion and constructed a scheme satisfying it based on any pseudorandom function. In addition to revealing the ordering of any two encrypted plaintexts, ciphertexts in their scheme reveal only the position of the most significant bit on which the plaintexts differ. A significant drawback of their scheme, however, is its substantial ciphertext expansion: Encrypting plaintexts of length m bits results in ciphertexts of length $m \cdot \ell$ bits, where ℓ determines the level of security (e.g., $\ell = 80$ in practice).

In this work we prove a lower bound on the ciphertext expansion of any order-preserving encryption scheme satisfying the "limited-leakage" notion of Chenette et al. with respect to non-uniform polynomial-time adversaries, matching the ciphertext expansion of their scheme up to lower-order terms. This improves a recent result of Cash and Zhang (TCC '18), who proved such a lower bound for schemes satisfying this notion with respect to *computationally-unbounded* adversaries (capturing, for example, schemes whose security can be proved in the random-oracle model without relying on cryptographic assumptions). Our lower bound applies, in particular, to schemes whose security is proved in the standard model.

G. Segev and I. Shahaf—Supported by the European Union's Horizon 2020 Framework Program (H2020) via an ERC Grant (Grant No. 714253), by the Israel Science Foundation (Grant No. 483/13), by the Israeli Centers of Research Excellence (I-CORE) Program (Center No. 4/11), and by the US-Israel Binational Science Foundation (Grant No. 2014632).

A. Beimel and S. Dziembowski (Eds.): TCC 2018, LNCS 11240, pp. 177–191, 2018.
https://doi.org/10.1007/978-3-030-03810-6_7

1   Introduction

An order-preserving encryption (OPE) scheme is a private-key encryption scheme whose ciphertexts preserve the numerical ordering of their corresponding plaintexts. Such schemes were introduced in the database community by Agrawal et al. [2] for enabling efficient indexing of encrypted data and efficient range queries over encrypted databases. By now, order-preserving encryption has become a key cryptographic ingredient underlying the security of database management systems (see [17] for a long list of OPE-based commercial systems).

The Security of OPE. Given that the ciphertexts of any order-preserving encryption scheme reveal the numerical ordering of their corresponding plaintexts, such schemes clearly cannot satisfy the standard notion of semantic security. This motivated Boldyreva, Chenette, Lee and O'Neill [3,4] to initiate a foundational study of the security of order-preserving encryption. They introduced two notions of security for such schemes. Their first notion is a "best-possible" relaxation of the standard semantic security notion, allowing ciphertexts to reveal only the numerical ordering of their corresponding plaintexts. Informally, their notion asks that the encryptions of any two sequences of plaintexts should be indistinguishable as long as the two sequences share the same order pattern. Unfortunately, Boldyreva et al. then proved that such a notion cannot be satisfied.

Their second notion asks that an order-preserving encryption scheme should be indistinguishable from a random order-preserving function (similarly to the standard notion of pseudorandomness for pseudorandom functions). Boldyreva et al. provided an efficient scheme that satisfies this notion, but it was later on demonstrated by Boldyreva, Chenette and O'Neill [5,6] that a random order-preserving function may in fact reveal substantial information on its input (specifically, about half of the bits of a random message) – and thus this notion may not be sufficiently strong for most applications.

Limited-Leakage OPE. The absence of a strong (and realizable) notion of security has somewhat questioned our confidence in the potential security guarantees of order-preserving encryption. This state of affairs, however, has recently changed due to the work of Chenette, Lewi, Weis and Wu [13]. They rigorously relaxed the "best-possible" notion introduced by Boldyreva et al. [3,4] to allow a *limited amount of well-defined "leakage"* [11], and constructed a practical scheme that satisfies it, based on pseudorandom functions. Concretely, in addition to revealing the relative ordering of any two encrypted plaintexts, ciphertexts in their scheme reveal the position of the most significant bit on which they differ – but no additional information is revealed. We refer to this specific leakage as "CLWW-leakage", and to schemes that satisfy their notion as $\mathcal{L}_{\mathsf{CLWW}}$-secure schemes.

Drawback: Ciphertext Expansion. Incorporating the limited-leakage scheme of Chenette et al. in practical OPE-based systems finally enables to rigorously reason about their security. However, a significant drawback of their scheme is its ciphertext expansion. Roughly speaking, encrypting plaintexts of length m bits using their scheme results in ciphertexts of length $m \cdot \ell$ bits, where ℓ determines the level of security (i.e., "ℓ bits of security" – we discuss the relation between the ciphertext expansion and the security of their scheme in more detail in Sect. 1.1).

In fact, Chenette et al. first constructed an *order-revealing* encryption scheme [5,9] with ciphertexts of length only $\lceil \log_2 3 \cdot m \rceil$ bits, and then showed that the main ideas underlying their scheme can be used to construct an order-preserving encryption scheme – but with significantly longer ciphertexts (see Sect. 1.2 for more details on the less-strict notion of order-revealing encryption). Given the practical importance of order-preserving encryption, this poses the question of whether or not such a significant expansion is inherent.

Initial evidence indicating that such an expansion is inherent was recently provided by Cash and Zhang [14]. They introduced an *information-theoretic* variant of the limited-leakage notion of security considered by Chenette et al. (that is, a notion of security with respect to computationally-unbounded adversaries and CLWW-leakage), and showed that any scheme satisfying it must suffer from a significant ciphertext expansion, matching the ciphertext expansion in the scheme of Chenette et al. up to lower-order terms.

As discussed by Cash and Zhang, although no scheme can satisfy their information-theoretic notion in the standard model, they nevertheless capture schemes whose security can be proved in the random-oracle model without relying on any cryptographic assumption. They do not capture, however, schemes whose security is proved in the standard model based on cryptographic assumptions (such as the existence of pseudorandom functions, and specific number-theoretic or combinatorial assumptions).

1.1   Our Contributions

In this paper we prove a tight lower bound on the ciphertext expansion of any order-preserving encryption scheme that satisfies the "limited-leakage" notion of security considered by Chenette et al. [13]. In its weakest form, this notion asks that the encryptions of any two sequences of plaintexts should be indistinguishable as long as the two sequences share the same CLWW-leakage, as discussed above (see Sect. 2 for the formal definition). We prove the following theorem:

Theorem (informal). *Let Π be an order-preserving encryption scheme with m-bit plaintexts and n-bit ciphertexts. Then, there exists a non-uniform polynomial-time adversary $\mathcal{A}$ that breaks the $\mathcal{L}_{\mathsf{CLWW}}$-security of the scheme with probability at least $2^{-n/m} \cdot m^{-1}$.*

Under the minimal requirement that the success probability of any efficient adversary in breaking the $\mathcal{L}_{\mathsf{CLWW}}$-security of the scheme should be negligible, our theorem implies that ciphertexts must be of length at least $n = m \cdot \omega(\log \lambda)$ bits, where $\lambda \in \mathbb{N}$ is the security parameter. Practically, when aiming at (say) 80 bits of security (and focusing, for simplicity, on the significant $2^{-n/m}$ term), this implies that ciphertexts must be of length at least roughly $n = 80m$ bits.

Comparison to the Cash-Zhang Lower Bound. When compared to the lower bound proved by Cash and Zhang [14], our lower bound and their lower bound are identical in terms of the attacker's success probability (and, thus, in terms of the implications on the ciphertext expansion). As discussed above, however, their lower bound applies to an information-theoretic variant of the notion of security to which our lower bound applies. Concretely, Cash and Zhang prove their lower bound by analyzing the statistical distance between ciphertext distributions (which translates into a *computationally-unbounded* adversary), whereas we prove our lower bound by presenting a non-uniform *polynomial-time* adversary[1]. Thus, our lower bound applies to any $\mathcal{L}_{\mathsf{CLWW}}$-secure order-preserving encryption scheme, and most notably to such schemes whose security is proved in the standard model.

The Tightness of Our Lower Bound. Looking into the security of the scheme provided by Chenette et al. [13] (when adapted to offer perfect correctness as suggested by Cash and Zhang), we observe that our lower bound is in fact tight up to low-order terms. Specifically, their scheme is based on the existence of any pseudorandom function F mapping inputs of length at most $m = m(\lambda)$ bits to outputs of length $\ell = \ell(\lambda)$ bits, and encrypting plaintexts of length m bits using their scheme results in ciphertexts of length $n = m \cdot \ell$ bits. An analysis of the security of their construction shows that the advantage $\mathsf{Adv}^{\mathsf{OPE}}_{\Pi,\mathcal{L}_{\mathsf{CLWW}},\mathcal{A}}$ of any adversary $\mathcal{A}$ in breaking the $\mathcal{L}_{\mathsf{CLWW}}$-security of their scheme can be upper bounded as

$$\mathsf{Adv}^{\mathsf{OPE}}_{\Pi,\mathcal{L}_{\mathsf{CLWW}},\mathcal{A}} \leq \mathsf{Adv}^{\mathsf{PRF}}_{\mathsf{F},\mathcal{B}} + \frac{m \cdot q}{2^\ell},$$

where $q = q(\lambda)$ denotes the number of encryption queries made by $\mathcal{A}$, $\mathsf{Adv}^{\mathsf{PRF}}_{\mathsf{F},\mathcal{B}}$ denotes the advantage of an algorithm $\mathcal{B}$ (efficiently derived from $\mathcal{A}$) in breaking the pseudorandomness of F, and recall that $\ell = n/m$. The above theorem provides a lower bound on the advantage of our specific adversary (which issues only $q = 2$ encryption queries), and this yields

$$\frac{1}{2^{n/m} \cdot m} \leq \mathsf{Adv}^{\mathsf{OPE}}_{\Pi,\mathcal{L}_{\mathsf{CLWW}},\mathcal{A}}(\lambda) \leq \mathsf{Adv}^{\mathsf{PRF}}_{\mathsf{F},\mathcal{B}}(\lambda) + \frac{m \cdot 2}{2^{n/m}}.$$

Up to the lower-order terms in the above expression[2], our lower bound and the security of the scheme constructed by Chenette et al. match.

---

[1] Although utilizing non-uniformity in cryptographic constructions, reductions, and impossibility proofs is rather standard [19,20,22] (e.g., given the practical benefits of preprocessing-based attacks [8,10,12,16,23]), an interesting open question is whether or not the above theorem can even be proved via a *uniform* polynomial-time adversary.

[2] Assuming, in addition, that the security of the pseudorandom function is not the main bottleneck (for example, by choosing a sufficiently large security parameter, or by using AES in practice).

1.2   Related Work

Boldyreva, Chenette and O'Neill [5] introduced the notion of an order-revealing encryption (ORE) scheme, which is a less-strict variant of order-preserving encryption scheme[3]. Such schemes allow to compare plaintexts by invoking a publicly-computable comparison algorithm on their ciphertexts (no secret key is required), and can be viewed as a specific form of multi-input functional encryption [1,7,18,24]. The notion of order-preserving encryption is then obtained by requiring, in addition, that the comparison algorithm is simply a numerical comparison. Based on assumptions involving multi-linear maps, Boneh et al. [9] presented a (rather theoretical) construction of an ORE scheme that satisfies the aforementioned "best-possible" security notion of Boldyreva et al. [3]. This stands in contrast to the impossibility of Boldyreva et al. for constructing an order-preserving encryption scheme satisfying the same "best-possible" security notion.

As for ORE schemes that satisfy weaker notions of security, as mentioned above Chenette et al. [13] constructed an efficient $\mathcal{L}_{\mathsf{CLWW}}$-secure ORE scheme that has ciphertexts of length only $\lceil \log_2 3 \cdot m \rceil$, where m is the length of their corresponding plaintexts, and their construction is based on pseudorandom functions.

Finally, when dealing with encryption schemes that inherently leak non-trivial information, one should always pay attention to potential attacks that may be enabled by such leakage. Indeed, such attacks on order-revealing encryption are known in some specific settings (e.g., [15,21]), but this does not rule out their deployment in other settings.

1.3   Overview of Our Approach

In this section we provide a brief overview of the main ideas underlying the proof of our lower bound. In what follows, let $\Pi = (\mathsf{KeyGen}, \mathsf{Enc})$ be an order-preserving encryption scheme with plaintexts of length m bits and ciphertexts of length n bits (both m and n may be functions of the security parameter $\lambda \in \mathbb{N}$ – see Sect. 2 for the formal definition of such a scheme). For any plaintext $i \in \{0,1\}^m$, viewed an integer $0 \leq i \leq 2^m - 1$, we denote by $X_i = \mathsf{Enc}_K(i)$ the random variable corresponding to an encryption of i with respect to a randomly-generated key $K \leftarrow \mathsf{KeyGen}(1^\lambda)$. Each such random variable X_i is distributed over $\{0,1\}^n$, and is viewed as an integer $0 \leq X_i \leq 2^n - 1$. In addition, we let $\epsilon = 2^{-n/m} \cdot m^{-1}$ (note that this is the success probability stated by our theorem), and let $\Delta(X,Y)$ denote the statistical distance between the distributions X and Y.

The Proof of Cash and Zhang. Cash and Zhang [14] observed that for every $1 \leq j \leq m-1$ it holds that $\mathcal{L}_{\mathsf{CLWW}}(0, 2^{j+1} - 1) = \mathcal{L}_{\mathsf{CLWW}}(2^j - 1, 2^j)$, where

---

[3] Boldyreva et al. referred to such schemes as *efficiently-orderable encryption* schemes.

$\mathcal{L}_{\mathsf{CLWW}}$ is the CLWW-leakage as discussed above[4]. Assuming towards a contradiction that a scheme Π is $\mathcal{L}_{\mathsf{CLWW}}$-secure in the *statistical* sense that no computationally-unbounded adversary has advantage larger than ϵ, then the distributions $(\mathsf{Enc}_K(0), \mathsf{Enc}_K(2^{j+1} - 1))$ and $(\mathsf{Enc}_K(2^j - 1), \mathsf{Enc}_K(2^j))$ must be statistically close, as both $(0, 2^{j+1} - 1)$ and $(2^j - 1, 2^j)$ have the same CLWW-leakage. That is, it must hold that

$$\Delta((X_0, X_{2^{j+1}-1}), (X_{2^j-1}, X_{2^j})) \leq \epsilon.$$

Therefore, denoting $G_1^j = X_{2^{j+1}-1} - X_0$ and $G_2^j = X_{2^j} - X_{2^j-1}$, and noting that applying the same function to two distributions cannot increase their statistical distance, it also holds that $\Delta(G_1^j, G_2^j) \leq \epsilon$. By the order-preserving property of the scheme, it holds that $G_1^j \geq 0$, $G_2^j \geq 0$, and that

$$G_1^j = X_{2^{j+1}-1} - X_0 \geq (X_{2^j} - X_{2^j-1}) + (X_{2^j-1} - X_0) = G_2^j + G_1^{j-1}.$$

This shows that G_1^j is ϵ-statistically-close to G_2^j, and that G_1^j is larger than G_2^j by at least G_1^{j-1}. Equipped with this observation, Cash and Zhang inductively proved that the support of G_1^{j-1} must contain "large" values, and that the support of G_1^j must contain even larger values. As a final step, note that $X_{2^m-1} = X_0 + G_1^{m-1}$ and also $\Delta(X_0, X_{2^m-1}) \leq \epsilon$ as it trivially holds that $\mathcal{L}_{\mathsf{CLWW}}(0) = \mathcal{L}_{\mathsf{CLWW}}(2^m - 1)$. Using their reasoning once again, they deduced that the support of X_{2^m-1} must contain values larger than $2^n - 1$, which contradicts the definition of X_{2^m-1} as an integer in the range $\{0, \ldots, 2^n - 1\}$.

Our Approach: A Non-uniform Polynomial-Time Adversary. When considering schemes that are $\mathcal{L}_{\mathsf{CLWW}}$-secure in the standard *computational* sense, we cannot take advantage of the fact that $\Delta(G_1^j, G_2^j) \leq \epsilon$ and apply the reasoning of Cash and Zhang. Instead, we show that if the *consequence* of the reasoning of Cash and Zhang does not hold (specifically, if the support of G_1^j does not contain large values), then there exists a polynomial-time test that distinguishes between G_1^j and G_2^j: Given a sample y from either G_1^j or G_2^j, our distinguisher checks whether $y \leq t$ for some fixed threshold value $0 \leq t \leq 2^n - 1$.

Then, assuming that the consequence of the reasoning of Cash and Zhang does hold for every step $1 \leq j \leq m - 1$, we can then prove via an additional step that either there is a threshold test for distinguishing between X_0 and X_{2^m-1}, or it holds that support of X_{2^m-1} contains values larger than $2^n - 1$. Since the second case contradicts the definition of X_{2^m-1} as an integer in the range $\{0, \ldots, 2^n - 1\}$, it must be that the first case holds.

As a result, either there exist $1 \leq j \leq m - 1$ and $0 \leq t \leq 2^n - 1$ such that given ciphertexts $(c_1, c_2) \in \{(X_0, X_{2^{j+1}-1}), (X_{2^j-1}, X_{2^j})\}$, the test $c_1 - c_2 \leq t$

---

[4] Specifically, for any distinct two plaintexts m_i and m_j it holds that $\mathcal{L}_{\mathsf{CLWW}}(m_i, m_j) = (\mathsf{ind}_{\mathsf{diff}}(m_i, m_j), \mathbf{1}(m_i < m_j))$, where $\mathsf{ind}_{\mathsf{diff}}(m_i, m_j) \in \{1, \ldots, m, \perp\}$ is the index of the most significant bit on which m_i and m_j differ, and $\mathbf{1}(m_i < m_j) \in \{0, 1\}$ indicates whether or not $m_i < m_j$. For the full definition of $\mathcal{L}_{\mathsf{CLWW}}$, which takes input an arbitrary number of messages, see Sect. 2.

distinguishes between the two cases, or there exists $0 \leq t \leq 2^n - 1$ such that given a ciphertext $c \in \{X_0, X_{2^m-1}\}$, the test $c \leq t$ distinguishes between the two cases. This translates into a non-uniform polynomial-time adversary that breaks the $\mathcal{L}_{\mathsf{CLWW}}$-security of any given scheme with probability at least ϵ, where the non-uniform advice specifies which test out of the m possible tests to perform, as well as which threshold value $0 \leq t \leq 2^n - 1$ to use. We refer the reader to Sect. 3 for our proof.

2 Preliminaries

In this section we present the notation and definitions that are used in this work. We denote by $\lambda \in \mathbb{N}$ the security parameter. For a distribution X we denote by $x \leftarrow X$ the process of sampling a value x from the distribution X. Similarly, for a set $\mathcal{X}$ we denote by $x \leftarrow \mathcal{X}$ the process of sampling a value x from the uniform distribution over $\mathcal{X}$. A function $\mathsf{negl} : \mathbb{N} \to \mathbb{R}_{\geq 0}$ is *negligible* if for every constant $c > 0$ there exists an integer N_c such that $\mathsf{negl}(n) < n^{-c}$ for all $n > N_c$. All logarithms in this paper are to the base of 2. The *statistical distance* between two random variables X and Y over a finite domain Ω is $\Delta(X,Y) = \frac{1}{2} \sum_{\omega \in \Omega} |\Pr[X = \omega] - \Pr[Y = \omega]|$.

Order-Preserving Encryption [2,3]. An order-preserving encryption scheme Π is a pair (KeyGen, Enc) of probabilistic polynomial-time algorithms satisfying the following requirements for parameters $m = m(\lambda)$ and $n = n(\lambda)$:

- The key-generation algorithm KeyGen takes as input the security parameter $\lambda \in \mathbb{N}$ in unary representation and outputs a secret key K.
- The encryption algorithm Enc takes as input a secret key K and a plaintext $x \in \{0,1\}^m$ interpreted as a numerical value $0 \leq x \leq 2^m - 1$, and outputs ciphertext $c \in \{0,1\}^n$ interpreted as a numerical value $0 \leq c \leq 2^n - 1$.

Note that a decryption algorithm is not required by this definition. We say that Π is *correct* if for all $\lambda \in \mathbb{N}$ and $0 \leq i < j \leq 2^{m(\lambda)} - 1$ it holds that $\Pr[\mathsf{Enc}_K(i) < \mathsf{Enc}_K(j)] = 1$, where $K \leftarrow \mathsf{KeyGen}(1^\lambda)$.

Remark. It is also possible to consider a relaxed game-based correctness notion, where a probabilistic polynomial-time adversary (without explicit access to the secret key) should not be able to come up with plaintexts $0 \leq i < j \leq 2^{m(\lambda)} - 1$ such that $\mathsf{Enc}_K(i) \geq \mathsf{Enc}_K(j)$, expect with a negligible probability. In Sect. 3, we discuss the effect of such a relaxation on our lower bound.

Security. We prove our lower bound for any scheme that satisfies the following non-adaptive indistinguishability-based security notion. This notion is (tightly) implied by its (stronger) adaptive and/or simulation-based variants, and thus our lower bound applies to those as well.

More concretely, given a scheme $\Pi = (\mathsf{KeyGen}, \mathsf{Enc})$, a leakage function $\mathcal{L}$, an algorithm $\mathcal{A}$, a bit $b \in \{0, 1\}$, and a security parameter λ, we consider the following experiment.

The experiment $\mathsf{Ind}^{\mathsf{OPE}}_{\Pi, \mathcal{L}, \mathcal{A}, b}(\lambda)$

1. $K \leftarrow \mathsf{KeyGen}(1^\lambda)$.
2. $(\mathbf{m}_0, \mathbf{m}_1, \mathsf{state}) \leftarrow \mathcal{A}(1^\lambda)$, where $\mathbf{m}_0$ and $\mathbf{m}_1$ are plaintext vectors of the same length (which we denote by q).
3. $\mathbf{c} = (c_1, \ldots, c_q)$, where $c_i \leftarrow \mathsf{Enc}_K(\mathbf{m}_b[i])$ for every $1 \leq i \leq q$.
4. $b' \leftarrow \mathcal{A}(\mathsf{state}, \mathbf{c})$.
5. If $\mathcal{L}(\mathbf{m}_0) = \mathcal{L}(\mathbf{m}_1)$ then the experiment outputs b', and otherwise it outputs 0.

The advantage of $\mathcal{A}$ is defined as

$$\mathsf{Adv}^{\mathsf{OPE}}_{\Pi, \mathcal{L}, \mathcal{A}}(\lambda) = \left| \Pr[\mathsf{Ind}^{\mathsf{OPE}}_{\Pi, \mathcal{L}, \mathcal{A}, 1}(\lambda) = 1] - \Pr[\mathsf{Ind}^{\mathsf{OPE}}_{\Pi, \mathcal{L}, \mathcal{A}, 0}(\lambda) = 1] \right|.$$

As discussed above, in this paper we consider security with respect to non-uniform polynomial-time adversaries, captured by the following definition:

Definition 2.1. *An order-preserving encryption scheme Π is $\mathcal{L}$-secure if for every non-uniform polynomial-time algorithm $\mathcal{A}$ it holds that $\mathsf{Adv}^{\mathsf{OPE}}_{\Pi, \mathcal{L}, \mathcal{A}}(\lambda)$ is negligible.*

In this work we consider the leakage function introduced by Chenette et al. [13]:

$$\mathcal{L}_{\mathsf{CLWW}}(x_1, \ldots, x_q) = \{(i, j, \mathsf{ind}_{\mathsf{diff}}(x_i, x_j), \mathbf{1}(x_i < x_j)) : 1 \leq i < j \leq q\},$$

where $\mathsf{ind}_{\mathsf{diff}}(x_i, x_j) \in \{1, \ldots, m, \bot\}$ is the index of the most significant bit on which x_i and x_j differ (and is set to $\bot$ if $x_i = x_j$), and $\mathbf{1}(x_i < x_j) \in \{0, 1\}$ indicates whether or not $x_i < x_j$.

3   Our Lower Bound

In this section we prove the following theorem, and then show that it can be extended to schemes without perfect correctness.

Theorem 3.1. *Let Π be an order-preserving encryption scheme with plaintext length $m = m(\lambda)$ bits and ciphertext length $n = n(\lambda)$ bits, where $\lambda \in \mathbb{N}$ is the security parameter. Then, there exists a non-uniform polynomial-time adversary $\mathcal{A}$ such that $\mathsf{Adv}^{\mathsf{OPE}}_{\Pi, \mathcal{L}_{\mathsf{CLWW}}, \mathcal{A}}(\lambda) \geq 2^{-n/m} \cdot m^{-1}$ for all $\lambda \in \mathbb{N}$.*

Proof. For any $1 \leq j(\lambda) \leq m(\lambda) - 1$ and $0 \leq t(\lambda) \leq 2^{n(\lambda)} - 1$, we define an adversary $\mathcal{A}_{j,t}$ that participates in the experiment $\mathsf{Ind}_{\Pi,\mathcal{L},\mathcal{A},b}^{\mathsf{OPE}}(\lambda)$ (see Sect. 2) as follows:

The adversary $\mathcal{A}_{j,t}$:

- Given a security parameter 1^λ as input, $\mathcal{A}_{j,t}$ outputs $(\mathbf{m}_0, \mathbf{m}_1, \mathsf{state}) = ((0, 2^{j+1} - 1), (2^j - 1, 2^j), \perp)$.
- Given a state $\mathsf{state} = \perp$ and ciphertexts $\mathbf{c} = (c_1, c_2)$ as input, $\mathcal{A}_{j,t}$ outputs 1 if $c_2 - c_1 \leq t$ and 0 otherwise.

Additionally, we define an adversary $\mathcal{B}_t$ as follows:

The adversary $\mathcal{B}_t$:

- Given a security parameter 1^λ as input, $\mathcal{B}_t$ outputs $(\mathbf{m}_0, \mathbf{m}_1, \mathsf{state}) = ((2^m - 1), (0), \perp)$.
- Given a state $\mathsf{state} = \perp$ and a single ciphertext $\mathbf{c} = (c_1)$ as input, $\mathcal{B}_t$ outputs 1 if $c_1 \leq t$ and 0 otherwise.

It is easy to verify that both $\mathcal{A}_{j,t}$ and $\mathcal{B}_t$ output plaintext vectors with the same CLWW-leakage, and thus these are valid adversaries.

From this point on we fix a security parameter $\lambda \in \mathbb{N}$ and omit it for ease of notation. Denoting $\epsilon = 2^{-n/m} \cdot m^{-1}$, we show that either there exist $1 \leq j \leq m-1$ and $0 \leq t \leq 2^n - 1$ such that $\mathsf{Adv}_{\Pi,\mathcal{L}_{\mathsf{CLWW}},\mathcal{A}_{j,t}}^{\mathsf{OPE}} \geq \epsilon$ or there exists $0 \leq t \leq 2^n - 1$ such that $\mathsf{Adv}_{\Pi,\mathcal{L}_{\mathsf{CLWW}},\mathcal{B}_t}^{\mathsf{OPE}} \geq \epsilon$. This guarantees that the following non-uniform polynomial-time adversary $\mathcal{A}$ satisfies $\mathsf{Adv}_{\Pi,\mathcal{L}_{\mathsf{CLWW}},\mathcal{A}}^{\mathsf{OPE}} \geq \epsilon$ as claimed: Given a non-uniform advise $j \in \{1, \ldots, m-1, \perp\}$ and $0 \leq t \leq 2^n - 1$, if $j \neq \perp$ then $\mathcal{A}$ invokes $\mathcal{A}_{j,m}$, and if $j = \perp$ it invokes $\mathcal{B}_t$.

For any $0 \leq i \leq 2^m - 1$ let $X_i = \mathsf{Enc}_K(i)$ where $K \leftarrow \mathsf{KeyGen}(1^\lambda)$. Then, by the definition of the above adversaries it holds that

$$\mathsf{Adv}_{\Pi,\mathcal{L}_{\mathsf{CLWW}},\mathcal{A}_{j,t}}^{\mathsf{OPE}} = |\Pr[X_{2^j} - X_{2^j-1} \leq t] - \Pr[X_{2^{j+1}-1} - X_0 \leq t]|$$

and

$$\mathsf{Adv}_{\Pi,\mathcal{L}_{\mathsf{CLWW}},\mathcal{B}_t}^{\mathsf{OPE}} = |\Pr[X_0 \leq t] - \Pr[X_{2^m-1} \leq t]|.$$

For a parameter $1 \leq j \leq m - 1$, consider the following property:

Property(j): For each $t \in \mathbb{N}$ it holds that

$$\Pr[X_{2^{j+1}-1} \leq X_0 + t] \leq (t \cdot j!)^{1/j} \cdot \epsilon$$

We proceed to consider three cases, according to what values $1 \leq j \leq m-1$ (if any) satisfy Property(j).

Case I: Property(1) does not hold. In this case we rely on the following lemma, which we prove in Sect. 4.

Lemma 3.2. *Let (X, Y) be jointly distributed random variables, taking values in $\mathbb{Z}_{\geq 0}$, such that $X > Y$, and let $\epsilon \geq 0$. Then, at least one of the following must hold:*

1. *For every $t \in \mathbb{Z}_{\geq 0}$ it holds that $\Pr[X \leq t] \leq t \cdot \epsilon$.*
2. *There exists $t \in \mathbb{Z}_{\geq 0}$ such that $\Pr[Y \leq t] - \Pr[X \leq t] \geq \epsilon$.*

Observing that $X_3 - X_0 > X_2 - X_1$ and applying Lemma 3.2 for $X = X_3 - X_0$ and $Y = X_2 - X_1$, since Property(1) does not hold the second case of the lemma must hold. That is, there exists $t \in \mathbb{Z}_{\geq 0}$ such that $\Pr[X_2 - X_1 \leq t] - \Pr[X_3 - X_0 \leq t] \geq \epsilon$, and so $\mathcal{A}_{1,t}$ is an adversary with an advantage of at least ϵ.

Case II: Property($m-1$) holds. In this case we rely on the following lemma, which we prove in Sect. 4.

Lemma 3.3. *Let (X, Y) be jointly distributed random variables, taking values in $\mathbb{Z}_{\geq 0}$, such that $X \geq Y$. Suppose there exist $i \in \mathbb{N}$ and $\epsilon \geq 0$ such that for every $k \in \mathbb{Z}_{\geq 0}$ it holds that $\Pr[X \leq Y + k] \leq (k \cdot i!)^{1/i} \cdot \epsilon$. Then, at least one of the following must hold:*

1. *For every $t \in \mathbb{Z}_{\geq 0}$ it holds that $\Pr[X \leq t] \leq (t \cdot (i+1)!)^{1/(i+1)} \cdot \epsilon$.*
2. *There exists $t \in \mathbb{Z}_{\geq 0}$ such that $\Pr[Y \leq t] - \Pr[X \leq t] \geq \epsilon$.*

Applying Lemma 3.3 for $X = X_{2^m-1}$ and $Y = X_0$, the conditions hold since $X_{2^m-1} \geq X_0$ and Property($m-1$) holds, and we obtain that either there exists $t \in \mathbb{Z}_{\geq 0}$ such that $\Pr[X_0 \leq t] - \Pr[X_{2^m-1} \leq t] \geq \epsilon$, or for every $t \in \mathbb{Z}_{\geq 0}$ it holds that $\Pr[X_{2^m-1} \leq t] \leq (t \cdot m!)^{1/m} \cdot \epsilon$. In the first case we get that $\mathcal{B}_t$ is an adversary with an advantage of at least ϵ. In the second case, for $t = 2^n - 1$ we get that $1 = \Pr[X_{2^m-1} \leq 2^n - 1] < (2^n \cdot m!)^{1/m} \cdot \epsilon$. But then, using the bound $m! \leq m^m$ which holds for every positive m, we obtain that

$$\epsilon > 2^{-n/m} \cdot (m!)^{-1/m}$$
$$\geq 2^{-n/m} \cdot m^{-1},$$

which contradicts our definition of ϵ.

Case III: Property(1) holds but Property($m-1$) does not hold. In this case let $2 \leq j \leq m-1$ be the smallest j for which Property(j) does not hold. Observing that $X_{2^{j+1}-1} - X_0 \geq (X_{2^j} - X_{2^j-1}) + (X_{2^j-1} - X_0)$ and applying Lemma 3.3 for $X = X_{2^{j+1}-1} - X_0$ and $Y = X_{2^j} - X_{2^j-1}$, the conditions hold since Property($j-1$) holds, and we obtain that since Property(j) does not hold then the second case of the lemma must hold. That is, there exists $t \in \mathbb{Z}_{\geq 0}$ such that $\Pr[Y \leq t] - \Pr[X \leq t] \geq \epsilon$, so $\mathcal{A}_{j,t}$ is an adversary with advantage of at least ϵ. ∎

Extending the Proof to Schemes Without Prefect Correctness. We note that our lower bound is only based on the correctness of the scheme with respect to a polynomial number of pairs of plaintexts, that is, all pairs of plaintexts from the set $\{2^j : 1 \leq j \leq m - 1(\lambda)\} \cup \{2^j - 1 : 0 \leq j \leq m(\lambda)\}$. Therefore, even for a scheme that satisfies a relaxed game-based correctness notion, it must hold that the scheme is correct for all those pairs of plaintexts with probability $1 - \mathsf{negl}(\lambda)$, where negl is a fixed negligible function. Hence, similarly to Theorem 3.1, there must exist a non-uniform polynomial-time adversary $\mathcal{A}$ such that $\mathsf{Adv}^{\mathsf{OPE}}_{\Pi, \mathcal{L}_{\mathsf{CLWW}}, \mathcal{A}}(\lambda) \geq 2^{-n/m} \cdot m^{-1} - \mathsf{negl}(\lambda)$ for all $\lambda \in \mathbb{N}$.

4 Proofs of Lemma 3.2 and Lemma 3.3

We restate and prove Lemma 3.2.

Lemma 3.2. *Let (X, Y) be jointly distributed random variables, taking values in $\mathbb{Z}_{\geq 0}$, such that $X > Y$, and let $\epsilon \geq 0$. Then, at least one of the following must hold:*

1. *For every $t \in \mathbb{Z}_{\geq 0}$ it holds that $\Pr[X \leq t] \leq t \cdot \epsilon$.*
2. *There exists $t \in \mathbb{Z}_{\geq 0}$ such that $\Pr[Y \leq t] - \Pr[X \leq t] \geq \epsilon$.*

Proof. Assume that there exists $t \in \mathbb{N}$ such that $\Pr[X \leq t] > t \cdot \epsilon$ (the case $t - 0$ is impossible since then $Y < 0$), and let t_0 be the first such t. Then, it holds that $\Pr[X \leq t_0 - 1] \leq (t_0 - 1) \cdot \epsilon$, but $\Pr[Y \leq t_0 - 1] \geq \Pr[X \leq t_0] > t_0 \cdot \epsilon$, so it holds that $\Pr[Y \leq t_0 - 1] - \Pr[X \leq t_0 - 1] \geq \epsilon$. ∎

Next, we restate and prove Lemma 3.3.

Lemma 3.3. *Let (X, Y) be jointly distributed random variables, taking values in $\mathbb{Z}_{\geq 0}$, such that $X \geq Y$. Suppose there exist $i \in \mathbb{N}$ and $\epsilon \geq 0$ such that for every $k \in \mathbb{Z}_{\geq 0}$ it holds that $\Pr[X \leq Y + k] \leq (k \cdot i!)^{1/i} \cdot \epsilon$. Then, at least one of the following must hold:*

1. *For every $t \in \mathbb{Z}_{\geq 0}$ it holds that $\Pr[X \leq t] \leq (t \cdot (i + 1)!)^{1/(i+1)} \cdot \epsilon$.*
2. *There exists $t \in \mathbb{Z}_{\geq 0}$ such that $\Pr[Y \leq t] - \Pr[X \leq t] \geq \epsilon$.*

Proof. We make use of the following lemma.

Lemma 4.1. *Let (X, Y) be jointly distributed random variables, taking values in $\mathbb{Z}_{\geq 0}$, such that $X \geq Y$, and let $\epsilon \geq 0$. Then, at least one of the following must hold:*

1. *For every $t \in \mathbb{Z}_{\geq 0}$ and (possibly non-integer) $s > 0$ it holds that*

$$\Pr[X \leq t] \leq \frac{t}{s} \cdot \epsilon + \frac{1}{s} \int_0^s \Pr[X \leq Y + k] dk.$$

2. *There exists $t \in \mathbb{Z}_{\geq 0}$ such that $\Pr[Y \leq t] - \Pr[X \leq t] \geq \epsilon$.*

Assume for now the correctness of Lemma 4.1. We obtain that either there exists $t \in \mathbb{Z}_{\geq 0}$ such that $\Pr[Y \leq t] - \Pr[X \leq t] \geq \epsilon$, or that for every $t \in \mathbb{Z}_{\geq 0}$ it holds that

$$
\Pr[X \leq t] \leq \frac{t}{s} \cdot \epsilon + \frac{1}{s} \int_0^s \Pr[X \leq Y + k] dk
$$

$$
\leq \frac{t}{s} \cdot \epsilon + \frac{1}{s} \int_0^s (k \cdot i!)^{1/i} \cdot \epsilon dk
$$

$$
= \left(\frac{t}{s} + \frac{i}{i+1} (s \cdot i!)^{1/i} \right) \cdot \epsilon,
$$

and by choosing $s = (i+1)/(i+1)!^{1/(i+1)} \cdot t^{i/(i+1)}$ (which minimizes the above term), we obtain that $\Pr[X \leq t] \leq (t \cdot (i+1)!)^{1/(i+1)} \cdot \epsilon$ as claimed. ∎

We now prove Lemma 4.1.

Proof of Lemma 4.1. First, for $t = 0$ it always holds that

$$
\Pr[X \leq 0] \leq \Pr[X \leq Y]
$$

$$
= \frac{1}{s} \int_0^s \Pr[X \leq Y] dk
$$

$$
\leq \frac{1}{s} \int_0^s \Pr[X \leq Y + k] dk.
$$

Now, for every $t \in \mathbb{N}$ we show that either it holds that

$$
\Pr[X \leq t] \leq \frac{t}{s} \cdot \epsilon + \frac{1}{s} \int_0^s \Pr[X \leq Y + k] dk,
$$

or there exists $0 \leq k < t$ such that $\Pr[Y \leq k] - \Pr[X \leq k] \geq \epsilon$. We define the random variables (W, Z) as follows

$$
(W, Z) = \begin{cases} (X, Y) & X \leq t \\ (0, 0) & X > t. \end{cases}
$$

We bound $\mathbb{E}(W - Z)$ both from above and below. For the lower bound, it holds that

$$\mathbb{E}(W - Z) = \sum_{k=0}^{t} k \cdot \Pr[X = Y + k, X \leq t]$$

$$\geq s \cdot \sum_{k=0}^{t} \Pr[X = Y + k, X \leq t] - \sum_{k=0}^{\lfloor s \rfloor}(s - k) \cdot \Pr[X = Y + k, X \leq t]$$

$$\geq s \cdot \Pr[X \leq t] - \sum_{k=0}^{\lfloor s \rfloor}(s - k) \cdot \Pr[X = Y + k]$$

$$= s \cdot \Pr[X \leq t] - \int_{0}^{s} \Pr[X \leq Y + \lfloor k \rfloor] dk$$

$$= s \cdot \Pr[X \leq t] - \int_{0}^{s} \Pr[X \leq Y + k] dk.$$

For the upper bound, we make use of the following lemma (a similar lemma appears in [14]).

Lemma 4.2. *Let (W, Z) be jointly distributed random variables, taking values in $\{0, \ldots, t\}$. Then, there exists $0 \leq k < t$ such that $\Pr[Z \leq k] - \Pr[W \leq k] \geq \mathbb{E}(W - Z)/t$.*

Assume for now the correctness of Lemma 4.2. We obtain that there exists $0 \leq k < t$ such that $\Pr[Z \leq k] - \Pr[W \leq k] \geq \mathbb{E}(W - Z)/t$. Note that

$$\Pr[Z \leq k] - \Pr[W \leq k] = \Pr[Y \leq k, X \leq t] - \Pr[X \leq k] \leq \Pr[Y \leq k] - \Pr[X \leq k].$$

If $\Pr[Y \leq k] - \Pr[X \leq k] \geq \epsilon$ then we are done. Otherwise, it holds that

$$t \cdot \epsilon > s \cdot \Pr[X \leq t] - \int_{0}^{s} \Pr[X \leq Y + k] dk,$$

and the lemma follows. ∎

We finish by proving Lemma 4.2.

Proof of Lemma 4.2. It holds that

$$\mathbb{E}(W - Z) = \mathbb{E}W - \mathbb{E}Z$$

$$= \sum_{k=1}^{t} \Pr[W \geq k] - \sum_{k=1}^{t} \Pr[Z \geq k]$$

$$= \sum_{k=1}^{t} (1 - \Pr[W < k]) - \sum_{k=1}^{t} (1 - \Pr[Z < k])$$

$$= \sum_{k=0}^{t-1} (\Pr[Z \leq k] - \Pr[W \leq k]).$$

Hence, there exists $0 \le k < t$ such that $\Pr[Z \le k] - \Pr[W \le k] \ge \mathbb{E}(W - Z)/t$ as claimed.

Acknowledgments. We thank Gili Schul-Ganz and the anonymous referees for various useful comments.

References

1. Ananth, P., Jain, A.: Indistinguishability obfuscation from compact functional encryption. In: Gennaro, R., Robshaw, M. (eds.) CRYPTO 2015. LNCS, vol. 9215, pp. 308–326. Springer, Heidelberg (2015). https://doi.org/10.1007/978-3-662-47989-6_15
2. Agrawal, R., Kiernan, J., Srikant, R., Xu, Y.: Order-preserving encryption for numeric data. In: Proceedings of the ACM SIGMOD International Conference on Management of Data, pp. 563–574 (2004)
3. Boldyreva, A., Chenette, N., Lee, Y., O'Neill, A.: Order-preserving symmetric encryption. In: Joux, A. (ed.) EUROCRYPT 2009. LNCS, vol. 5479, pp. 224–241. Springer, Heidelberg (2009). https://doi.org/10.1007/978-3-642-01001-9_13
4. Boldyreva, A., Chenette, N., Lee, Y., O'Neill, A.: Order-preserving symmetric encryption. Cryptology ePrint Archive, Report 2012/624 (2012)
5. Boldyreva, A., Chenette, N., O'Neill, A.: Order-preserving encryption revisited: improved security analysis and alternative solutions. In: Rogaway, P. (ed.) CRYPTO 2011. LNCS, vol. 6841, pp. 578–595. Springer, Heidelberg (2011). https://doi.org/10.1007/978-3-642-22792-9_33
6. Boldyreva, A., Chenette, N., O'Neill, A.: Order-preserving encryption revisited: improved security analysis and alternative solutions. Cryptology ePrint Archive, Report 2012/625 (2012)
7. Brakerski, Z., Komargodski, I., Segev, G.: Multi-input functional encryption in the private-key setting: stronger security from weaker assumptions. In: Fischlin, M., Coron, J.-S. (eds.) EUROCRYPT 2016. LNCS, vol. 9666, pp. 852–880. Springer, Heidelberg (2016). https://doi.org/10.1007/978-3-662-49896-5_30
8. Bernstein, D.J., Lange, T.: Non-uniform cracks in the concrete: the power of free precomputation. In: Sako, K., Sarkar, P. (eds.) ASIACRYPT 2013. LNCS, vol. 8270, pp. 321–340. Springer, Heidelberg (2013). https://doi.org/10.1007/978-3-642-42045-0_17
9. Boneh, D., Lewi, K., Raykova, M., Sahai, A., Zhandry, M., Zimmerman, J.: Semantically secure order-revealing encryption: multi-input functional encryption without obfuscation. In: Oswald, E., Fischlin, M. (eds.) EUROCRYPT 2015. LNCS, vol. 9057, pp. 563–594. Springer, Heidelberg (2015). https://doi.org/10.1007/978-3-662-46803-6_19
10. Coretti, S., Dodis, Y., Guo, S., Steinberger, J.P.: Random Oracles and non-uniformity. In: Nielsen, J.B., Rijmen, V. (eds.) EUROCRYPT 2018. LNCS, vol. 10820, pp. 227–258. Springer, Cham (2018). https://doi.org/10.1007/978-3-319-78381-9_9
11. Chase, M., Kamara, S.: Structured encryption and controlled disclosure. In: Abe, M. (ed.) ASIACRYPT 2010. LNCS, vol. 6477, pp. 577–594. Springer, Heidelberg (2010). https://doi.org/10.1007/978-3-642-17373-8_33
12. Corrigan-Gibbs, H., Kogan, D.: The discrete-logarithm problem with preprocessing. In: Nielsen, J.B., Rijmen, V. (eds.) EUROCRYPT 2018. LNCS, vol. 10821, pp. 415–447. Springer, Cham (2018). https://doi.org/10.1007/978-3-319-78375-8_14

13. Chenette, N., Lewi, K., Weis, S.A., Wu, D.J.: Practical order-revealing encryption with limited leakage. In: Peyrin, T. (ed.) FSE 2016. LNCS, vol. 9783, pp. 474–493. Springer, Heidelberg (2016). https://doi.org/10.1007/978-3-662-52993-5_24
14. Cash, D., Zhang, C.: A ciphertext-size lower bound for order-preserving encryption with limited leakage. In: Proceedings of the 16th Theory of Cryptography Conference (2018, to appear)
15. Durak, F.B., DuBuisson, T.M., Cash, D.: What else is revealed by order-revealing encryption? In: Proceedings of the 2016 ACM Conference on Computer and Communications Security, pp. 1155–1166 (2016)
16. Fiat, A., Naor, M.: Rigorous time/space trade-offs for inverting functions. SIAM J. Comput. **29**(3), 790–803 (1999)
17. Fuller, B., et al.: SoK: cryptographically protected database search. In: Proceedings of the 38th IEEE Symposium on Security and Privacy, pp. 172–191 (2017)
18. Goldwasser, S., et al.: Multi-input functional encryption. In: Nguyen, P.Q., Oswald, E. (eds.) EUROCRYPT 2014. LNCS, vol. 8441, pp. 578–602. Springer, Heidelberg (2014). https://doi.org/10.1007/978-3-642-55220-5_32
19. Goldwasser, S., Kalai, Y.T.: Cryptographic assumptions: a position paper. In: Proceedings of the 13th Theory of Cryptography Conference, pp. 505–522 (2016)
20. Goldreich, O.: Foundations of Cryptography - Volume 2: Basic Applications. Cambridge University Press, Cambridge (2004)
21. Grubbs, P., Sekniqi, K., Bindschaedler, V., Naveed, M., Ristenpart, T.: Leakage-abuse attacks against order-revealing encryption. In: Proceedings of the 38th IEEE Symposium on Security and Privacy, pp. 655–672 (2017)
22. Gentry, C., Wichs, D.: Separating succinct non-interactive arguments from all falsifiable assumptions. In: Proceedings of the 43rd ACM Annual Symposium on Theory of Computing, pp. 99–108 (2011)
23. Hellman, M.E.: A cryptanalytic time-memory trade-off. IEEE Trans. Inf. Theor. **26**(4), 401–406 (1980)
24. Komargodski, I., Segev, G.: From minicrypt to obfustopia via private-key functional encryption. In: Coron, J.-S., Nielsen, J.B. (eds.) EUROCRYPT 2017. LNCS, vol. 10210, pp. 122–151. Springer, Cham (2017). https://doi.org/10.1007/978-3-319-56620-7_5

Towards Tight Security of Cascaded LRW2

Bart Mennink[✉]

Digital Security Group, Radboud University, Nijmegen, The Netherlands
b.mennink@cs.ru.nl

Abstract. The Cascaded LRW2 tweakable block cipher was introduced by Landecker et al. at CRYPTO 2012, and proven secure up to $2^{2n/3}$ queries. There has not been any attack on the construction faster than the generic attack in 2^n queries. In this work we initiate the quest towards a tight bound. We first present a distinguishing attack in $2n^{1/2}2^{3n/4}$ queries against a generalized version of the scheme. The attack is supported with an experimental verification and a formal success probability analysis. We subsequently discuss non-trivial bottlenecks in proving tight security, most importantly the distinguisher's freedom in choosing the tweak values. Finally, we prove that if every tweak value occurs at most $2^{n/4}$ times, Cascaded LRW2 is secure up to $2^{3n/4}$ queries.

Keywords: LRW2 · Cascaded LRW2 · Tweakable block cipher Tightness

1 Introduction

A block cipher is a family of permutations that is indexed via a secret key. While block ciphers are omnipresent in cryptographic permutations, they inherently lack flexibility and many applications of block ciphers are either implicitly or explicitly designed from a tweakable block cipher: a function $\widetilde{E} : \mathcal{K} \times \mathcal{T} \times \mathcal{M} \to \mathcal{M}$ that is a family of permutations indexed by secret key $k \in \mathcal{K}$ and public tweak $t \in \mathcal{T}$. Tweakable block ciphers were formalized by Liskov, Rivest, and Wagner [19] and find a broad range of applications, most notably in the direction of authenticated encryption (such as OCB [15,32,33], COPA [1], AEZ [11], and Deoxys [13,29]) and in XTS disk encryption [9].

This work centers around a generic tweakable block cipher design that was introduced in Liskov et al.'s original paper [19]. It internally uses a block cipher E, and is defined as follows:

$$\text{LRW2}((k, h), t, m) = E(k, m \oplus h(t)) \oplus h(t), \tag{1}$$

where k is a block cipher key and h an XOR universal hash function. The construction is strongly related with Rogaway's XEX [32] (in turn used in OCB1, OCB2, OCB3, and XTS disk encryption), and extensions by Chakraborty and

© International Association for Cryptologic Research 2018
A. Beimel and S. Dziembowski (Eds.): TCC 2018, LNCS 11240, pp. 192–222, 2018.
https://doi.org/10.1007/978-3-030-03810-6_8

Sarkar [3], Minematsu [21], and Granger et al. [10]. The LRW2 tweakable block cipher is proven to achieve security up to approximately $2^{n/2}$ queries. This bound is tight: for any two queries $(t, m), (t', m')$ with $m \oplus h(t) - m' \oplus h(t')$, the corresponding ciphertexts satisfy $c \oplus c' = h(t) \oplus h(t') = m \oplus m'$, and such a collision can be found in approximately $2^{n/2}$ queries.

A notable approach towards beyond birthday bound secure tweakable block ciphers is by Landecker et al. [17], who suggested to cascade two independent evaluations of LRW2:

$$\text{CLRW2}((k_1, k_2, h_1, h_2), t, m) = \text{LRW2}((k_2, h_2), t, \text{LRW2}((k_1, h_1), t, m)),$$
$$= E_{k_2}(E_{k_1}(m \oplus h_1(t)) \oplus h_1(t) \oplus h_2(t)) \oplus h_2(t),$$

where k_1, k_2 are two block cipher keys and h_1, h_2 XOR universal hash functions. They proved that this construction is indistinguishable from random up to approximately $2^{2n/3}$ queries. This proof was very technical, and Procter [30] pointed out that it was, in fact, flawed. The proof was subsequently fixed by both Landecker et al. and Procter, but it does not generalize to higher security, either for the construction as is or for a generalization to multiple cascades. So far, there has never been any attack justifying tightness of the bound; the best attack so far is a generic one in 2^n queries.

The state of affairs stands in sharp contrast with that of two rounds of Tweakable Even-Mansour, LRW2's sibling based on public permutations [6]:

$$\text{CTEM}((h_1, h_2), t, m) = p_2(p_1(m \oplus h_1(t)) \oplus h_1(t) \oplus h_2(t)) \oplus h_2(t),$$

where p_1, p_2 are two permutations and h_1, h_2 uniform and XOR universal hash functions. Cogliati et al. [6] proved that CTEM is indistinguishable from random up to approximately $2^{2n/3}$ queries, and this bound is tight: keeping the tweak constant reduces the scheme to a key alternating cipher for which Bogdanov et al. [2] derived an attack in query complexity approximately $2^{2n/3}$. This attack uses availability of the public permutations and is therefore not applicable to CLRW2.

1.1 Attack on Generalized Cascaded LRW2

We consider a generalized version of Cascaded LRW2, for brevity called "GCL:"

$$\text{GCL}^{f_1, f_2, f_3}((k_1, k_2, k_f), t, m) = E(k_2, E(k_1, m \oplus f_1(t)) \oplus f_2(t)) \oplus f_3(t), \quad (2)$$

where k_1, k_2 are two block cipher keys and k_f a key to the masking functions (f_1, f_2, f_3) (for ease of presentation, the key input to the f_i's is left implicit throughout). $\text{GCL}^{f_1, f_2, f_3}$ is depicted in Fig. 1. If h_1, h_2 are two XOR universal hash functions, then $\text{GCL}^{h_1, h_1 \oplus h_2, h_2}$ matches CLRW2 (where we set $k_f = (h_1, h_2)$).

We derive a generic attack against $\text{GCL}^{f_1, f_2, f_3}$ with arbitrary masking in $2n^{1/2}2^{3n/4}$ evaluations. The information-theoretic attack is given in Sect. 3 and relies on a boomerang-style observation on the mode, based on the observation

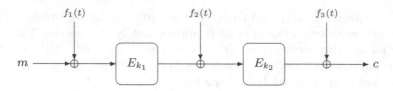

Fig. 1. Depiction of GCL^{f_1,f_2,f_3}.

that if there exist four queries where the first and second collide on the input to E_{k_1}, the second and third on the output of E_{k_2}, and the third and fourth on the input to E_{k_1}, then the first and fourth collide at the output of E_{k_2} with probability 1 if the tweak values are selected delicately.

In support of its correctness, the attack is backed up with a formal success probability computation in Sect. 3.3 as well as an implementation in Sect. 3.4. The formal success analysis demonstrates that for $n \geq 27$, the distinguisher's success probability is at least $1/2$. The small-scale implementation demonstrates that for GCL^{f_1,f_2,f_3} based on random permutations on $n = 16, 20, 24$ bits, the special collisions as searched for in the attack indeed appear more often than usual. The gap between the accuracy in n of the experimental verification and the security proof is caused by the fact that some loose probability bounds had to be used in the rather conservative proof.

The attack is independent of the masking functions f_1, f_2, f_3. It implies that GCL^{f_1,f_2,f_3} cannot achieve optimal security, regardless of the choice of masking. The attack particularly applies to CLRW2, therewith improving the best known attack to date.

1.2 Towards Tight Security?

In Sect. 4 we approach the attack from a more theoretical perspective, and describe the main limitations in proving security of GCL^{f_1,f_2,f_3} beyond $2^{2n/3}$. The quasi-formal discussion relies on equating executions of GCL^{f_1,f_2,f_3} with a bipartite graph, and by drawing a parallel with Patarin's mirror theory [20,22,26,28] we indicate various issues in trying to prove security beyond $2^{2n/3}$. The most notable one of these, namely the potential existence of four queries which alternatively collide on the input of E_{k_1} or output of E_{k_2} is precisely the one exploited in our attack in $2n^{1/2}2^{3n/4}$ queries. We also pinpoint where and how the current gap between a security lower bound of $2^{2n/3}$ and an attack upper bound of $2^{3n/4}$ arises. Most importantly, as the distinguisher can *freely choose* the value of the tweak for every query, it can set a certain distinguishing event with a significant probability.

1.3 Improved Security of Cascaded LRW2 Under Tweak Limits

In Sect. 5 we use these insights obtained in our quest towards tight security. We return to CLRW2, or equivalently $GCL^{h_1,h_1 \oplus h_2,h_2}$, and prove that if (i) h_1

and h_2 are 4-wise independent XOR universal hash functions and (ii) every tweak value occurs at most $q^{1/3}$ times, where q is the total amount of queries, then Cascaded LRW2 is secure up to $2^{3n/4}$ queries. In Sect. 2.2 we describe two possibilities of designing 4-wise independent XOR universal hash functions. The condition on the occurrence of the tweak seems restrictive, but many modes of operation based on a tweakable block cipher query their primitives for tweaks that are constituted of a nonce or random number concatenated with a counter value [10,12,15,29]: in a nonce-respecting setting, every nonce appears at most $1 + q_f$ times, where q_f is the amount of forgery attempts.

The proof relies on Patarin's mirror theory up to the first recursion, i.e., up to $3n/4$-bit security. It shares ideas with the analysis of Mennink and Neves [20] on Encrypted Davies-Meyer [7], namely that an evaluation (t, m, c) of CLRW2 can be rewritten as a sum of permutations "in the middle." Adversarial power to choose tweak values, however, precludes optimal security, and security up to $2^{3n/4}$ is the best possible bound.

1.4   Longer Cascades?

Lampe and Seurin [16] suggested the cascade of $\rho \geq 1$ evaluations of LRW2, and proved that for even ρ this construction is secure up to approximately $2^{\rho n/(\rho+2)}$ queries. Lee et al. [18] proved that if the universal hash functions are replaced by random functions, security up to $2^{\rho n/(\rho+1)}$ is achieved. It is generally conjectured that the security of the cascade of ρ LRW2's is $2^{\rho n/(\rho+1)}$ [16–18], but also for this larger cascade, nothing is known on the attack side, besides the trivial attack in 2^n queries. Unfortunately, it does not seem possible to generalize the attack of Sect. 3 nor the security proof of Sect. 5 to larger cascades. As before, it is noteworthy that a cascade of $\rho \geq 1$ evaluations of TEM can be attacked in approximately $2^{\rho n/(\rho+1)}$ queries [2].

2   Preliminaries

For $n \in \mathbb{N}$, $\{0,1\}^n$ denotes the set of bit strings of length n, and $\mathsf{perm}(n)$ the set of all permutations on $\{0,1\}^n$. Extending notation, for $\kappa \in \mathbb{N}$, we denote by $\mathsf{iperm}(\kappa, n)$ the set of all "indexed permutations," families of permutations $p_k \in \mathsf{perm}(n)$, indexed by $k \in \{0,1\}^\kappa$. We additionally denote by $\mathsf{iperm}(\kappa, \tau, n)$ for $\tau \in \mathbb{N}$ the set of all indexed permutations where the index consists of two elements $(k, t) \in \{0,1\}^\kappa \times \{0,1\}^\tau$. For $m, n \in \mathbb{N}$ such that $m \geq n$, the falling factorial is defined as $(m)_n = m(m-1) \cdots (m-n+1) = m!/(m-n)!$. For $n \in \mathbb{N}$ and $m \in \{0, \ldots, 2^{n-1}\}$, we denote by $\langle m \rangle_n$ the encoding of m as an n-bit string. If $\mathcal{X}$ is a finite set, $x \xleftarrow{\$} \mathcal{X}$ denotes the event of uniformly randomly drawing x from $\mathcal{X}$.

2.1   Block Ciphers and Tweakable Block Ciphers

A block cipher with key size κ and state size n is a function $E \in \mathsf{iperm}(\kappa, n)$. For fixed key $k \in \{0,1\}^\kappa$ we denote $E_k(\cdot) = E(k, \cdot)$, and its inverse is denoted

$E_k^{-1}(\cdot)$. A tweakable block cipher with key size κ, tweak size τ, and state size n is a function $\widetilde{E} \in \mathsf{iperm}(\kappa, \tau, n)$. For fixed key $k \in \{0,1\}^\kappa$ and $t \in \{0,1\}^\tau$ we denote $\widetilde{E}_k(t, \cdot) = \widetilde{E}(k, t, \cdot)$, and its inverse is denoted $\widetilde{E}_k^{-1}(t, \cdot)$.

Let $\kappa, n \in \mathbb{N}$ and let $E \in \mathsf{iperm}(\kappa, n)$ be a block cipher. The advantage of a distinguisher $\mathcal{D}$ in breaking the SPRP (strong pseudorandom permutation) security of E is defined as

$$\mathbf{Adv}_E^{\mathrm{sprp}}(\mathcal{D}) = \mathbf{Pr}\left(\mathcal{D}^{E_k^\pm} = 1\right) - \mathbf{Pr}\left(\mathcal{D}^{p^\pm} = 1\right), \tag{3}$$

where the probabilities are taken over the random drawing of $k \xleftarrow{\$} \{0,1\}^\kappa$, $p \xleftarrow{\$} \mathsf{perm}(n)$, and the randomness used by $\mathcal{D}$. The resources that $\mathcal{D}$ may use are typically expressed in terms of query complexity (to the oracle) and time complexity (for offline computations).

As block ciphers are a special case of tweakable block ciphers with tweak space of size 1 ($\tau = 0$), the security definition straightforwardly generalizes to the latter. Let $\kappa, \tau, n \in \mathbb{N}$ and let $\widetilde{E} \in \mathsf{iperm}(\kappa, \tau, n)$ be a tweakable block cipher. The advantage of a distinguisher $\mathcal{D}$ in breaking the STPRP (strong tweakable pseudorandom permutation) security of $\widetilde{E}$ is defined as

$$\mathbf{Adv}_{\widetilde{E}}^{\mathrm{stprp}}(\mathcal{D}) = \mathbf{Pr}\left(\mathcal{D}^{\widetilde{E}_k^\pm} = 1\right) - \mathbf{Pr}\left(\mathcal{D}^{\widetilde{p}^\pm} = 1\right), \tag{4}$$

where the probabilities are taken over the random drawing of $k \xleftarrow{\$} \{0,1\}^\kappa$, $\widetilde{p} \xleftarrow{\$} \mathsf{iperm}(\tau, n)$, and the randomness used by $\mathcal{D}$. The resources that $\mathcal{D}$ may use are typically bounded as before.

2.2   XOR Universal Hash Functions

We use the notion of ℓ-wise independent XOR universal hash functions, a slight adaptation of the original definition of Wegman and Carter [34]. For two non-empty sets $\mathcal{X}, \mathcal{Y}$, a hash function family $H = \{h : \mathcal{X} \to \mathcal{Y}\}$ is called ℓ-wise independent almost XOR universal up to bound ε, denoted ε-AXU_ℓ, if for any $j \in \{2, \dots, \ell\}$, any distinct $x_1, \dots, x_j \in \mathcal{X}$ and (not necessarily distinct) $y_2, \dots, y_j \in \mathcal{Y}$,

$$\mathbf{Pr}\left(h \xleftarrow{\$} H : h(x_1) \oplus h(x_2) = y_2, \dots, h(x_1) \oplus h(x_j) = y_j\right) \leq \varepsilon^{j-1}.$$

For $\mathcal{X} = \mathcal{Y} = \{0,1\}^n$, a 2^{-n}-AXU_2 hash function family can be defined using finite field multiplication with respect to some irreducible polynomial to represent the field, i.e., $h(x) := h \otimes x$. It is not ε-AXU_ℓ for $\ell > 2$. Defining the hash function family as

$$\mathbf{h}(x) := \bigoplus_{i=1}^{\ell-1} h_i \otimes x^i$$

for $\mathbf{h} = (h_1, \dots, h_{\ell-1})$ gives a 2^{-n}-AXU_ℓ hash function family for any $\ell \geq 2$. One can alternatively obtain a $(2^n - (\ell - 1))^{-1}$-AXU_ℓ by defining the hash function family using an ideal cipher or a family of random permutations.

3   Generic Attack

We present a generic attack against GCL^{f_1,f_2,f_3} in $2n^{1/2}2^{3n/4}$ queries. The attack is generic in nature, it does not exploit any weaknesses in the underlying cipher, and as such we simply assume that $E \xleftarrow{\$} iperm(\kappa, n)$ is an ideal cipher. It is fair to assume that the success probability of the attack simply *improves* if E is less than ideal, except for degenerate cases, e.g., if E_{k_1} and E_{k_2} are almost perfect nonlinear permutations (APNPs, cf., [8,23,24]). Throughout the attack, we simply denote $p_1 = E_{k_1}$ and $p_2 = E_{k_2}$ for brevity.

An informal rationale of our attack is given in Sect. 3.1, and the formal distinguisher in Sect. 3.2. Its advantage is lower bounded in Sect. 3.3, and the analysis is backed up with experimental verification in Sect. 3.4.

3.1   Informal Rationale of Attack

Suppose a distinguisher obtains four queries (t, m_1, c_1), (t', m'_2, c'_2), (t, m_3, c_3), and (t', m'_4, c'_4) of GCL^{f_1,f_2,f_3} such that

$$
\begin{aligned}
m_1 \oplus f_1(t) &= m'_2 \oplus f_1(t')\,, \\
c'_2 \oplus f_3(t') &= c_3 \oplus f_3(t)\,, \\
m_3 \oplus f_1(t) &= m'_4 \oplus f_1(t')\,.
\end{aligned}
\tag{5}
$$

In other words, the first and second query collide at the input to E_{k_1}, the second and third at the output of E_{k_2}, and the third and fourth at the input to E_{k_1}. As the four queries are performed using only two tweak values, each occurring twice, we have $f_2(t) \oplus f_2(t') \oplus f_2(t) \oplus f_2(t') = 0$, and from a simple inspection of the scheme (see also Fig. 2) one can conclude that, necessarily,

$$
c_1 \oplus f_3(t) = c'_4 \oplus f_3(t')\,.
\tag{6}
$$

Stated differently, under the assumption that (5) is satisfied, (6) is implied, and therefore the four equations combine to

$$
\begin{aligned}
m_1 \oplus m'_2 &= m_3 \oplus m'_4 = f_1(t) \oplus f_1(t')\,, \\
c'_2 \oplus c_3 &= c_1 \oplus c'_4 = f_3(t) \oplus f_3(t')\,.
\end{aligned}
$$

Unfortunately, the distinguisher does not know $f_1(t) \oplus f_1(t')$ and $f_3(t) \oplus f_3(t')$, but if we ignore these two values in above equations, we obtain

$$
\begin{aligned}
m_1 \oplus m'_2 &= m_3 \oplus m'_4\,, \\
c'_2 \oplus c_3 &= c_1 \oplus c'_4\,,
\end{aligned}
\tag{7}
$$

which *necessarily* holds if $m_1 \oplus m'_2 = f_1(t) \oplus f_1(t')$ and $c'_2 \oplus c_3 = f_3(t) \oplus f_3(t')$, but may hold by accident as well. Stated differently, if for some $d \in \{0,1\}^n$, there are about 2^n choices for the four queries such that

$$
m_1 \oplus m'_2 = m_3 \oplus m'_4 = d\,,
\tag{8}
$$

the expected number of solutions to (7) is close to 2 if $d = f_1(t) \oplus f_1(t')$ but close to 1 if $d \neq f_1(t) \oplus f_1(t')$. For an ideal permutation, the expected number of solutions is always close to 1 for any $d \in \{0,1\}^n$. By making approximately $2^{3n/4}$ queries, the distinguisher can ensure that there are about 2^n solutions to (8) for all d, including $d = f_1(t) \oplus f_1(t')$.

This almost allows for a distinguishing attack, but not quite: as the distinguisher does not actually know $f_1(t) \oplus f_1(t')$, it must simply hope that for some d there is a significant difference, but d may take 2^n values and false positives are likely to occur. By extending the number of queries slightly, i.e., by making about $n^{1/2} \cdot 2^{3n/4}$ queries, the case of $f_1(t) \oplus f_1(t')$ will stand out.

We remark that the attack is effectively an XOR subkey recovery attack, as the distinguisher learns $f_1(t) \oplus f_1(t')$ and $f_3(t) \oplus f_3(t')$. In case of Cascaded LRW2, where $f_1 = h_1$, $f_2 = h_1 \oplus h_2$, and $f_3 = h_2$ for two XOR universal hash functions h_1, h_2, this immediately gives $f_2(t) \oplus f_2(t')$, and potentially more, depending on the specific hash functions.

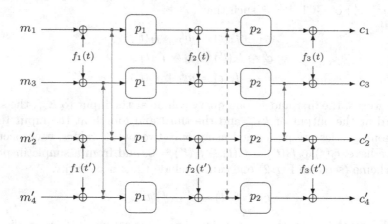

Fig. 2. Attack idea: the red (solid) collisions are targeted, the blue (dashed) one is implied by the red ones. (Color figure online)

3.2 Formal Description of Distinguisher

Let $\epsilon = \log_2(n)/2$ (assumed to be integral), and consider the following distinguisher $\mathcal{D}$ making $q = 2^{3n/4+\epsilon}$ queries.

(i) Fix arbitrary distinct $t, t' \in \{0,1\}^\tau$;
(ii) For $i = 0, \ldots, 2^{3n/4+\epsilon} - 1$, put $m_i = 0^{n/4-\epsilon} \| \langle i \rangle_{3n/4+\epsilon}$ and query (t, m_i) to obtain c_i;
(iii) For $i = 0, \ldots, 2^{3n/4+\epsilon} - 1$, put $m_i' = \langle i \rangle_{3n/4+\epsilon} \| 0^{n/4-\epsilon}$ and query (t', m_i') to obtain c_i';

(iv) For $d \in \{0,1\}^n$, define $I_d = \{(i,j) \mid m_i \oplus m'_j = d\}$. Note that $|I_d| = 2^{n/2+2\epsilon}$ for all $d \in \{0,1\}^n$, and define $q' := 2^{n/2+2\epsilon}$;

(v) For all $d \in \{0,1\}^n$ do:
  - Define $N_d = 0$;
  - For all distinct $(i,j), (k,l) \in I_d$: if $c_i \oplus c'_l = c'_j \oplus c_k$, put $N_d = N_d + 1$;

(vi) Briefly looking forward, for a random tweakable block cipher we have $\mathbf{Ex}(N_d) = \binom{q'}{2}/(2^n - 1)$ for any $d \in \{0,1\}^n$, whereas for $\mathrm{GCL}^{f_1, f_2, f_3}$, $\mathbf{Ex}(N_{f_1(t) \oplus f_1(t')}) \geq 2\binom{q'}{2}/2^n$. Inspired by this, define

$$\beta := \frac{3}{2}\binom{q'}{2}/2^n.$$

If there exists a $d \in \{0,1\}^n$ such that $N_d \geq \beta$, output 1. Otherwise, output 0.

3.3 Analysis of Distinguisher Advantage

A formal analysis confirms that the distinguisher succeeds with non-negligible probability.

Theorem 1. *Let $\kappa, \tau, n \in \mathbb{N}$ with $n \geq 16$, let $E \xleftarrow{\$} \mathrm{iperm}(\kappa, n)$, denote the size of the key space of (f_1, f_2, f_3) by κ_f, and consider $\mathrm{GCL}^{f_1, f_2, f_3} : \{0,1\}^{2\kappa} \times \{0,1\}^{\kappa_f} \times \{0,1\}^\tau \times \{0,1\}^n \to \{0,1\}^n$. Distinguisher $\mathcal{D}$ of Sect. 3.2 with query complexity $2n^{1/2} \cdot 2^{3n/4}$ has advantage*

$$\mathbf{Adv}^{\mathrm{stprp}}_{\mathrm{GCL}^{f_1, f_2, f_3}}(\mathcal{D}) \geq 1 - \frac{32}{n^2} - \frac{80}{n2^{n/2}} - 5 \cdot 2^n \left(\frac{10}{n}\right)^{3/100 \cdot n^2} - \frac{n^7}{2^{3n/2}}. \quad (9)$$

One can verify that the lower bound of (9) is at least $1/2$ for $n \geq 27$. This theorem is not the core contribution of the article (which is Theorem 2), and its proof is given Appendix A.

Note that the attack is de facto a TPRP-attack, only requiring forward access to the scheme. In addition, it is information-theoretical: the distinguisher's complexity is solely measured in its number of queries. The offline complexity is around $2^{3n/2}$.

3.4 Experimental Verification

We have implemented the distinguisher of Sect. 3.2 on a small scale, for $n = 16, 20, 24$ and with p_1, p_2, f_1, f_2, f_3 instantiated as independent uniform random permutations, noting that a uniform random permutation is a $(2^n - 1)^{-1}$-AXU$_2$ hash function (see Sect. 2.2). In each case, two distinct tweaks t, t' are evaluated for $q = 2^{3n/4+\epsilon}$ queries, with $\epsilon = 0, 1, 2$ (note that $2 \lesssim \log_2(n)/2$ for $n = 16, 20, 24$). The average values N_d for both the real and ideal world and both $d = f_1(t) \oplus f_1(t')$ and random d are summarized in Table 1. The computations confirm soundness of the rationale of Sect. 3.1 and the expected values of Sect. 3.2.

In more detail, the expected values given in Sect. 3.2 suggest that $N_d \approx 2^{4\epsilon}$ for $d = f_1(t) \oplus f_1(t')$ in the real world and $N_d \approx 2^{4\epsilon-1}$ in any other case (real or ideal world), and the statistics in Table 1 reasonably accurately match these numbers.

Note that, in particular, for $\epsilon = 0$ the value $N_{f_1(t) \oplus f_1(t')}$ already shows a small peak in the real world (for each of $n = 16, 20, 24$), but outliers in N_d for $d \neq f_1(t) \oplus f_1(t')$ are hidden by the statistics. For increasing ϵ, the gap becomes more significant and the success probability increases.

Table 1. Number of elements in N_d for the real and ideal world, for $d = f_1(t) \oplus f_1(t')$ and for random d. For the cases $n = 16, 20$, the numbers are averaged over 32 attacks; for $n = 24$ the numbers are averaged over 8 attacks.

n	ϵ	q	N_d in real world for $d =$		N_d in ideal world for $d =$	
			$f_1(t) \oplus f_1(t')$	random	$f_1(t) \oplus f_1(t')$	random
16	0	$1 \cdot 2^{12}$	0.843750	0.437500	0.343750	0.687500
	1	$2 \cdot 2^{12}$	16.343750	6.656250	7.625000	8.500000
	2	$4 \cdot 2^{12}$	256.593750	129.781250	127.093750	127.375000
20	0	$1 \cdot 2^{15}$	0.968750	0.500000	0.687500	0.593750
	1	$2 \cdot 2^{15}$	17.156250	7.593750	8.343750	8.187500
	2	$4 \cdot 2^{15}$	265.531250	133.312500	125.625000	128.750000
24	0	$1 \cdot 2^{18}$	1.125000	0.875000	0.250000	0.125000
	1	$2 \cdot 2^{18}$	16.375000	7.625000	8.375000	7.125000
	2	$4 \cdot 2^{18}$	246.750000	131.375000	120.625000	129.875000

4   Towards Tight Security?

Consider a simplification of GCL^{f_1,f_2,f_3} with its two block ciphers replaced by random permutations p_1, p_2 (this is a typical hybrid argument in security proofs performed at the cost of $2\mathbf{Adv}_E^{\text{sprp}}(\mathcal{D}')$ for some distinguisher $\mathcal{D}'$). For simplicity, assume that f_2 is injective (the scheme turns out to be significantly weakened if f_2 is non-injective). For an evaluation $\text{GCL}^{f_1,f_2,f_3}(t, m) = c$, denote

$$x = p_1(m \oplus f_1(t)),$$
$$y = p_2^{-1}(c \oplus f_3(t)),$$

in such a way that $x \oplus y = f_2(t)$.

Intuitively, one may think of a proof going "fine" if there is always some randomness available. For example, consider just a single forward query (t, m) to GCL^{f_1,f_2,f_3}. The value $m \oplus f_1(t)$ has never been evaluated by p_1, hence the value x will look uniformly randomly drawn from $\{0,1\}^n$; the value y satisfies $y = x \oplus f_2(t)$, and also y has never been evaluated by p_2 so the value $c \oplus f_3(t)$ is uniformly randomly drawn from $\{0,1\}^n$.

A more complicated case appears if there exist two distinct queries (m_1, t_1) and (m_2, t_2) such that $m_1 \oplus f_1(t_1) = m_2 \oplus f_1(t_2)$. The first query is handled as before, rendering fresh x_1 and $c_1 \oplus f_3(t_1)$. The second query satisfies $m_1 \oplus f_1(t_1) = m_2 \oplus f_1(t_2)$, meaning that $x_2 = x_1$. However, as the two queries are distinct, this equation implies that $t_1 \neq t_2$. As f_2 is injective, we subsequently have $f_2(t_1) \neq f_2(t_2)$ and thus $y_2 \neq y_1$. The evaluation of p_2 on y_2 yields a value uniformly drawn from $\{0, 1\}^n \backslash \{c_1 \oplus f_3(t_1)\}$.

Likewise, two queries could also collide at the right side, i.e., $c_1 \oplus f_3(t_1) = c_2 \oplus f_3(t_2)$. It is unlikely, though, that two queries collide at *both* the left and right side, at least if f_1 and f_3 are two randomized functions (as is the case in CLRW2), and we will ignore this case. If more than two queries are involved, one could visualize queries as a bipartite graph $G = (U, V, E)$. $U = \{0, 1\}^n$ corresponds to the input values to p_1, $V = \{0, 1\}^n$ to the output values of p_2, and for every query tuple (t_i, m_i, c_i), the edge $(m_i \oplus f_1(t_i), c_i \oplus f_3(t_i))$ with label $f_2(t_i)$ from U to V is added to E. An example graph G is depicted in Fig. 3.

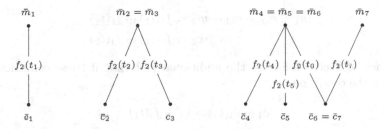

Fig. 3. Example of a bipartite graph G representing seven evaluations of GCL^{f_1, f_2, f_3}. For brevity, we denote $\bar{m}_i = m_i \oplus f_1(t_i)$ and $\bar{c}_i = c_i \oplus f_3(t_i)$. Graph view rotated for economical reasons.

What the above comprises is an informal introduction to a potential use of Patarin's mirror theory [20, 22, 26, 28], a powerful approach towards counting the number of solutions to a system of equations of the form $x \oplus y = \lambda$, where λ is known. If, in above graph, two queries touch on the left, i.e., $m_1 \oplus f_1(t_1) = m_2 \oplus f_1(t_2)$, they share the same $x_1 = x_2$ but have different y_1, y_2.

Unfortunately, the mirror theory does not turn out to be particularly suited here, most importantly as it is tailored towards comparing systems to random functions and we aim to compare our scheme to a family of permutations. Yet, closer inspection of the theory reveals that it puts two conditions on the graph that are "reasonably easily" violated:

(i) The graph should not contain a path of even length whose labels sum to 0;
(ii) The graph should not contain a circle.

The first condition prevents that there are two different inputs to p_1 with the same output (or two different outputs of p_2 with the same input). The second condition prevents that there exists a query with "no randomness." Both conditions are harmful for any possible even length, in the sense that Patarin's mirror theorem cannot be applied.

The attack of Sect. 3 relies on the fact that condition (i) can be violated easier than expected. Note that there cannot exist a path of length 2 whose labels sum to 0 (as f_2 is injective). A path of length 4 whose labels sum to 0 requires the existence of four queries $(t_1, m_1, c_1), \ldots, (t_4, m_4, c_4)$ such that

$$
\begin{aligned}
m_1 \oplus f_1(t_1) &= m_2 \oplus f_1(t_2), \\
c_2 \oplus f_3(t_2) &= c_3 \oplus f_3(t_3), \\
m_3 \oplus f_1(t_3) &= m_4 \oplus f_1(t_4), \\
f_2(t_1) \oplus f_2(t_2) \oplus f_2(t_3) \oplus f_2(t_4) &= 0.
\end{aligned}
\tag{10}
$$

As the four queries are distinct, the path may only appear if $t_1 \neq t_2 \neq t_3 \neq t_4$. However, it may be that $t_1 = t_3$ and $t_2 = t_4$, and this is how the attack of Sect. 3 exploits a path: in this case, the fourth equation of (10) is satisfied by design and the remaining three can be rewritten as

$$
\begin{aligned}
m_1 \oplus m_2 = m_3 \oplus m_4 &= f_1(t_1) \oplus f_1(t_2), \\
c_2 \oplus c_3 &= f_3(t_1) \oplus f_3(t_2).
\end{aligned}
\tag{11}
$$

The attack of Sect. 3 relies on the additional fact that if these conditions are met, then the condition

$$
c_4 \oplus f_3(t_2) = c_1 \oplus f_3(t_1)
\tag{12}
$$

holds with probability 1 in the real world (i.e., there is a circle as depicted in Fig. 4, violating condition (ii)), but with negligible probability in the ideal world. This property (that (11) implies (12)) gives a *clean and well-verifiable distinguishing event*.

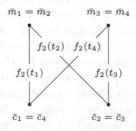

Fig. 4. A circle in bipartite graph G with $f_2(t_1) \oplus f_2(t_2) \oplus f_2(t_3) \oplus f_2(t_4) = 0$, as exploited in the attack of Sect. 3. We use the same convention as in Fig. 3.

A distinguisher can choose the m_i's smartly to make sure that $m_1 \oplus m_2 = m_3 \oplus m_4$ is satisfied. Consider a distinguisher that makes queries for at most two tweaks t, t', each queried q times, say for queries $(m_0, c_0), \ldots, (m_{q-1}, c_{q-1})$ and $(m'_0, c'_0), \ldots, (m'_{q-1}, c'_{q-1})$. Inspired by Sect. 3, denote

$$I_d = \{(i,j) \in \{0, \ldots, q-1\}^2 \mid m_i \oplus m'_j = d\}.$$

The probability that there exist four queries $(i, j) \neq (i', j')$ that comply with the equations of (11), denoted X, is

$$\mathbf{Pr}\,(X) = \sum_{d \in \{0,1\}^n} \mathbf{Pr}\,(X \mid f_1(t_1) \oplus f_1(t_2) = d) \cdot \mathbf{Pr}\,(f_1(t_1) \oplus f_1(t_2) = d)$$

$$\approx \sum_{d \in \{0,1\}^n} \frac{\binom{|I_d|}{2}}{2^n} \cdot \mathbf{Pr}\,(f_1(t_1) \oplus f_1(t_2) = d)$$

$$\approx \sum_{d \in \{0,1\}^n} \frac{\binom{|I_d|}{2}}{2^n} \cdot \frac{1}{2^n}, \tag{13}$$

where the first approximation assumes independence of events and that the c_i's are generated using a random function (for simplicity of reasoning), and the second approximation assumes that f_1 is close to a 2^{-n}-AXU$_2$ hash function. The two extremes in selecting the m_i's are the following:

- Choose the m_i's and m'_i's such that $|I_d| = q$ for q values of d and $|I_d| = 0$ for the remaining $2^n - q$ values. This is achieved by setting $m_i = m'_i = 0^{n - \log_2(q)} \| \langle i \rangle_{\log_2(q)}$ for $i = 0, \ldots, q - 1$. In this case, we obtain for (13):

$$(13) = q \cdot \binom{q}{2} / 2^{2n} \approx q^3 / 2^{2n};$$

- Choose the m_i's and m'_i's such that $|I_d| = q^2 / 2^n$ for all values of d, i.e., I_d is equally large for all d. This is achieved by setting $m_i = 0^{n - \log_2(q)} \| \langle i \rangle_{\log_2(q)}$ and $m'_i = \langle i \rangle_{\log_2(q)} \| 0^{n - \log_2(q)}$ for $i = 0, \ldots, q - 1$ (as in the attack of Sect. 3). In this case, we obtain for (13):

$$(13) = 2^n \cdot \binom{q^2 / 2^n}{2} / 2^{2n} \approx q^4 / 2^{3n}.$$

A security analysis, i.e., an upper bound on the distinguisher's success probability, would have to take into account any possible distinguisher, and it therefore seems such analysis caps at around $q^3 / 2^{2n}$. Yet, if the attack of Sect. 3 would have been based on the former strategy instead of the latter, it would have succeeded *only* if $|I_{f_1(t_1) \oplus f_1(t_2)}| \neq 0$, and the attack should have been evaluated $2^n / q$ times to succeed (resulting in total complexity of about 2^n). By making $2^{3n/4}$ queries, the distinguisher makes sure that $|I_d|$ is equally large for all d's and that way spreads its chances, but unfortunately, we see little opportunities in improving the attack.

It is important to remark that the attack of Sect. 3 and the discussion on the distinguishing event (11) consider the case where the distinguisher can *choose* the tweak values. This implies that an improved security bound can be achieved if the maximum number of queries for each tweak is fixed.

We explicitly remark that this limitation is *not a necessary condition*. In particular, above reasoning is informal and only included for intuitive reasons, and we cannot draw any formal conclusion from it. However, even for this limited scenario, improved security of CLRW2 is still a non-trivial open problem. We elaborate on the possibility of releasing the tweak usage limitation in Sect. 5.7. A final condition that the mirror theory puts on the graph, in addition to (i) and (ii) above, is the following:

(iii) The graph should not contain an excessively large tree.

This is a merely technical requirement to make the proof argument of the mirror theory work, and it is not clear how a violation of condition (iii) may break the scheme. That said, also condition (iii) can be easily violated, depending on the mixing functions in use. For example, if $f_1(t) = f_1 \otimes t$ (i.e., the example AXU$_2$ hash function of Sect. 2), a collision of the form

$$m_1 \oplus f_1(m_1) = m_2 \oplus f_1(m_2),$$

for $m_1, m_2 \neq 0$ implies that also

$$m_2 \oplus f_1(m_2) = m_1^{-1}m_2^2 \oplus f_1(m_1^{-1}m_2^2) = \cdots = m_1^{-\lambda}m_2^{\lambda+1} \oplus f_1(m_1^{-\lambda}m_2^{\lambda+1}),$$

for any $\lambda \geq 0$, potentially rendering an excessively large tree. The issue can be resolved by resorting to 4-wise independent XOR universal hash functions (see Sect. 2.2).

5   Improved Security of Cascaded LRW2 Under Tweak Limits

Based on the two conclusions from Sect. 4, we prove that if h_1 and h_2 are two 4-wise independent XOR universal hash functions and every tweak occurs at most $q^{1/3}$ times, the Cascaded LRW2 construction $\mathrm{GCL}^{h_1,h_1 \oplus h_2,h_2}$ of (2) achieves security up to complexity approximately $2^{3n/4}$.

Theorem 2. *Let $\kappa, \tau, n \in \mathbb{N}$, let $E \in \mathrm{iperm}(\kappa, n)$, H be an ε-AXU$_4$ hash function family, and consider $\mathrm{GCL}^{h_1,h_1 \oplus h_2,h_2} : \{0,1\}^{2\kappa} \times H^2 \times \{0,1\}^\tau \times \{0,1\}^n \to \{0,1\}^n$. Let $\gamma \in \mathbb{N}$ such that $2 \leq \gamma \leq q/4$ be a threshold. For any distinguisher $\mathcal{D}$ with query complexity at most $q \leq 2^n/1600$ that queries each tweak at most γ times, there exists a distinguisher $\mathcal{D}'$ that makes at most q queries such that*

$$\mathbf{Adv}_{\mathrm{GCL}^{h_1,h_1 \oplus h_2,h_2}}^{\mathrm{stprp}}(\mathcal{D}) \leq 6\binom{q}{4}2^n\varepsilon^4 + \binom{q}{2}(2\gamma+1)\varepsilon^2 + \frac{(\gamma+3)q}{2^n} + 2\mathbf{Adv}_E^{\mathrm{sprp}}(\mathcal{D}').$$

$$\tag{14}$$

Putting $\gamma = q^{1/3}$, the bound of (14) yields security up to $q \leq 2^{3n/4}$ queries. The limitation γ on the number of tweak repeats sounds restrictive, but it is not. In practical applications [10,12,29], the tweak is constituted of a random value concatenated with a counter.

The proof of Theorem 2 is based on Patarin's mirror theory [22,26,28], which found popularization in the work of Mennink and Neves on Encrypted Davies-Meyer and its dual [20]. Although the mirror theory is quite simple to understand and apply, its proof is heavy and the recursive argument underneath it is debated by some. In this work, however, we will only use the mirror theory up to $3n/4$-bit security, i.e., rely on the first recursion in the mirror theory proof only.

The security proof is comparable to that of EDM [20], and in particular also relies on the observation that any evaluation of $c = \mathrm{GCL}^{h_1, h_1 \oplus h_2, h_2}(\mathbf{k}, t, m)$ for $\mathbf{k} = (k_1, k_2, h_1, h_2)$ can be rewritten as

$$E_{k_1}(m \oplus h_1(t)) \oplus E_{k_2}^{-1}(c \oplus h_2(t)) = h_1(t) \oplus h_2(t). \qquad (15)$$

Differences in the analysis occur due to the possibility of the adversary to choose the tweak and the fact that the tweak occurs in all three parts of the equation (input to E_{k_1}, to $E_{k_2}^{-1}$, and in the right hand side $h_1(t) \oplus h_2(t)$). These differences cause that only security up to $2^{3n/4}$ is achievable. However, the differences compared with the analysis in [20] mostly affect description of oracle views and analysis of bad views; the application of the mirror theory is fairly the same. Therefore, we discard much of the details on mirror theory from the proof and include it in Appendix B; the proof is fully intelligible without this appendix.

The proof is given in Sects. 5.1–5.6. We discuss the possibility of releasing the limitation γ on the tweak usage in Sect. 5.7.

5.1 H-Coefficient Technique

We will use Patarin's H-coefficient technique [25,27], for which we follow the description by Chen and Steinberger [5]. Consider two oracles $\mathcal{O}$ and $\mathcal{P}$ with identical interfaces, and a deterministic distinguisher $\mathcal{D}$ with query complexity q and unbounded computational power that tries to distinguish both oracles. Denote its success probability by $\Delta_{\mathcal{D}}(\mathcal{O}; \mathcal{P})$. Let $X_{\mathcal{O}}$ denote the probability distribution of views when $\mathcal{D}$ is interacting with $\mathcal{O}$, and similarly $X_{\mathcal{P}}$ the distribution of views for interaction with $\mathcal{P}$. A view ν is called "attainable" if $\mathbf{Pr}(X_{\mathcal{P}} = \nu) > 0$, and denote by $\mathcal{V}$ the set of all attainable views. The H-coefficient technique states the following:

Lemma 1 (H-coefficient technique). *Let $\mathcal{D}$ be a deterministic distinguisher, and consider a partition $\mathcal{V} = \mathcal{V}_{\mathrm{bad}} \cup \mathcal{V}_{\mathrm{good}}$ of the set of attainable views. Let $\delta, \epsilon \in [0, 1]$ be such that $\mathbf{Pr}(X_{\mathcal{P}} \in \mathcal{V}_{\mathrm{bad}}) \leq \delta$, and $\dfrac{\mathbf{Pr}(X_{\mathcal{O}} = \nu)}{\mathbf{Pr}(X_{\mathcal{P}} = \nu)} \geq 1 - \epsilon$ for all $\nu \in \mathcal{V}_{\mathrm{good}}$. Then, the distinguishing advantage satisfies $\Delta_{\mathcal{D}}(\mathcal{O}; \mathcal{P}) \leq \delta + \epsilon$.*

A proof of the technique is given among others in [4,5,20].

For view $\nu = \{(x_1, y_1), \ldots, (x_q, y_q)\}$ consisting of q input/output tuples, an oracle $\mathcal{O}$ is said to *extend* ν, denoted $\mathcal{O} \vdash \nu$, if $\mathcal{O}(x_i) = y_i$ for all $i = \{1, \ldots, q\}$.

5.2   General Setting and Views

Let $\widetilde{p} \xleftarrow{\$} \mathrm{iperm}(\tau, n)$, $\mathbf{k} \xleftarrow{\$} \{0,1\}^{2\kappa} \times H^2$, and $p_1, p_2 \xleftarrow{\$} \mathrm{perm}(n)$. Consider any distinguisher $\mathcal{D}$ whose goal is to distinguish $\mathrm{GCL}_{\mathbf{k}}^{h_1, h_1 \oplus h_2, h_2}$ from $\widetilde{p}$.

As a first step, we replace (E_{k_1}, E_{k_2}) by (p_1, p_2^{-1}) at the cost of $2\mathbf{Adv}_E^{\mathrm{sprp}}(\mathcal{D}')$, where $\mathcal{D}'$ is some distinguisher with the same query complexity q as $\mathcal{D}$. (Note that we replaced E_{k_2} by *the inverse* of p_2 for simplicity of further analysis.) Denote the resulting scheme with F for brevity; it remains to bound the advantage of $\mathcal{D}$ in distinguishing $\mathcal{O} = F$ (the real world) from $\mathcal{P} = \widetilde{p}$ (the ideal world). As of now, we give the distinguisher unbounded computational power, and its complexity will only be measured by the number of oracle queries it makes. Without loss of generality, we can consider it to be deterministic, and will apply the H-coefficient technique of Lemma 1.

$\mathcal{D}$ makes q construction queries which are recorded in view $\nu' = \{(t_1, m_1, c_1), \ldots, (t_q, m_q, c_q)\}$. After $\mathcal{D}$'s interaction with its oracle, but before it outputs its decision bit, its oracle will reveal the subkeys h_1, h_2. In the real world, these are the XOR universal hash functions used in F, whereas in the ideal world these are dummy functions randomly drawn from H. We denote the complete view by

$$\nu = (\nu', h_1, h_2). \tag{16}$$

Without loss of generality, we assume that $\mathcal{D}$ never repeats queries, and hence that $(t_i, m_i) \neq (t_j, m_j)$ and $(t_i, c_i) \neq (t_j, c_j)$ for any $i \neq j$.

5.3   Attainable Index Mappings

In the real world $\mathcal{O}$, each tuple $(t_i, m_i, c_i) \in \nu'$ corresponds to an evaluation of F and satisfies

$$p_1(m_i \oplus h_1(t_i)) \oplus p_2(c_i \oplus h_2(t_i)) = h_1(t_i) \oplus h_2(t_i),$$

where we recall that E_{k_2} was replaced with p_2^{-1}. Writing $P_{a_i} := p_1(m_i \oplus h_1(t_i))$ and $P_{b_i} := p_2(c_i \oplus h_2(t_i))$, view ν defines the following q equations:

$$\begin{aligned}
P_{a_1} \oplus P_{b_1} &= h_1(t_1) \oplus h_2(t_1), \\
P_{a_2} \oplus P_{b_2} &= h_1(t_2) \oplus h_2(t_2), \\
&\vdots \\
P_{a_q} \oplus P_{b_q} &= h_1(t_q) \oplus h_2(t_q).
\end{aligned} \tag{17}$$

Here, some of the unknowns may be equal to each other. We have that $P_{a_i} \neq P_{a_j}$ if and only if $m_i \oplus h_1(t_i) \neq m_j \oplus h_1(t_j)$, and $P_{b_i} \neq P_{b_j}$ if and only if $c_i \oplus h_2(t_i) \neq c_j \oplus h_2(t_j)$. No condition a priori holds for P_{a_i} versus P_{b_j}, as these are defined by independent permutations. We have

$$r = |\{m_i \oplus h_1(t_i) \mid i \in \{1, \ldots, q\}\}| + |\{c_i \oplus h_2(t_i) \mid i \in \{1, \ldots, q\}\}| \tag{18}$$

unknowns.

5.4 Bad Views

Inspired by the discussion in Sect. 4, we associate a bipartite graph $G(\nu) = (U, V, E(\nu))$ with the view ν. $U = \{0,1\}^n$ corresponds to the input values to p_1, $V = \{0,1\}^n$ to the output values of p_2^{-1}, and for every $(t_i, m_i, c_i) \in \nu'$, the edge $(m_i \oplus h_1(t_i), c_i \oplus h_2(t_i))$ with label $h_1(t_i) \oplus h_2(t_i)$ from U to V is added to $E(\nu)$. The example graph of Fig. 3 still applies, be it with $f_1 = h_1$, $f_2 = h_1 \oplus h_2$, and $f_3 = h_2$.

In Sect. 4, we already informally discussed what problems could occur in such a graph, i.e., what properties would make the mirror theory inapplicable: it should not contain a path of even length whose labels sum to 0, a circle, or an excessively large tree. The latter is informal, it is often based on a pre-defined threshold on the maximum size of the tree. As our security analysis will cap on $3n/4$-bit security anyway, we can keep it simple, and put as one of the bad events that $G(\nu)$ should not contain a subgraph of ≥ 4 edges. This would imply the non-existence of an excessively large tree, as well as circles and paths of length ≥ 4. We still have to rule out the existence of a path of length 2 whose labels sum to 0 and a circle of length 2.

Formally, we say that a view ν is a *bad view* if its corresponding tree $G(\nu)$ contains

 (i) a path of length 2 whose labels sum to 0;
 (ii) a circle of length 2;
 (iii) a subgraph of ≥ 4 edges.

5.5 Probability of Bad Views (δ)

By Lemma 1, we have to analyze the probability that a view generated in the ideal world is bad, and the analysis will rely on the fact that h_1 and h_2 are 4-wise independent universal hash functions. We have

$$\mathbf{Pr}\left(X_{\widetilde{p}} \in \mathcal{V}_{\mathrm{bad}}\right) \leq \mathbf{Pr}\left(\mathrm{path}\right) + \mathbf{Pr}\left(\mathrm{circle}\right) + \mathbf{Pr}\left(\mathrm{subgraph}\right), \tag{19}$$

where the sizes of the path, circle, and subgraph, are left implicit.

(i) a path. Consider any two distinct queries $(t_i, m_i, c_i), (t_j, m_j, c_j)$. They yield a 0-label-sum path if either

$$m_i \oplus h_1(t_i) = m_j \oplus h_1(t_j) \text{ and } h_1(t_i) \oplus h_2(t_i) = h_1(t_j) \oplus h_2(t_j),$$

or

$$c_i \oplus h_2(t_i) = c_j \oplus h_2(t_j) \text{ and } h_1(t_i) \oplus h_2(t_i) = h_1(t_j) \oplus h_2(t_j).$$

If $t_i = t_j$, then necessarily $m_i \neq m_j$ and $c_i \neq c_j$ (as the two queries are distinct) and the conditions happen with probability 0. Otherwise, as h_1 and h_2 are ε-AXU$_4$, both conditions happen with probability at most ε^2. Thus,

$$\mathbf{Pr}\left(\mathrm{path}\right) \leq 2\binom{q}{2}\varepsilon^2. \tag{20}$$

(ii) a circle. Consider any two distinct queries $(t_i, m_i, c_i), (t_j, m_j, c_j)$. They yield a circle if

$$m_i \oplus h_1(t_i) = m_j \oplus h_1(t_j) \text{ and } c_i \oplus h_2(t_i) = c_j \oplus h_2(t_j),$$

which, as before, happens with probability at most ε^2. Thus,

$$\mathbf{Pr}\,(\text{circle}) \le \binom{q}{2}\varepsilon^2. \tag{21}$$

(iii) a subgraph. Consider any four distinct queries $(t_{i_1}, m_{i_1}, c_{i_1}), \ldots,$ $(t_{i_4}, m_{i_4}, c_{i_4})$ to yield a subgraph. We can consider six possible configurations, as described in Fig. 5. In these configurations, only collisions are explicitly indicated; two nodes that are different in the configuration may or may not collide. We treat all configurations independently, where we will rely on the fact that h_1 and h_2 are ε-AXU$_4$.

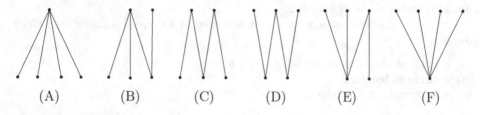

| (A) | (B) | (C) | (D) | (E) | (F) |

Fig. 5. Possible configurations of subgraphs of 4 edges. Upper shore is U, lower shore is V, and labels are omitted for brevity. Two nodes in the same shore may or may not be equal.

(A) Configuration (A) happens only if

$$m_{i_1} \oplus h_1(t_{i_1}) = m_{i_2} \oplus h_1(t_{i_2}) = m_{i_3} \oplus h_1(t_{i_3}) = m_{i_4} \oplus h_1(t_{i_4}).$$

If the tweaks are not all distinct, the condition is satisfied with probability 0. On the other hand, if $t_{i_1}, t_{i_2}, t_{i_3}, t_{i_4}$ are all distinct, the condition is satisfied with probability at most ε^3. There are at most $\binom{q}{4}$ possible choices of queries that satisfy this condition on the tweaks;

(B) Configuration (B) happens only if

$$m_{i_1} \oplus h_1(t_{i_1}) = m_{i_2} \oplus h_1(t_{i_2}) = m_{i_3} \oplus h_1(t_{i_3}),$$
$$c_{i_3} \oplus h_2(t_{i_3}) = c_{i_4} \oplus h_2(t_{i_4}).$$

Further analysis depends on the values of the tweaks.

– If $t_{i_1}, t_{i_2}, t_{i_3}, t_{i_4}$ are all distinct, the condition is satisfied with probability at most ε^3. There are at most $\binom{q}{4}$ possible choices of queries that satisfy this condition on the tweaks;

- If $t_{i_1} = t_{i_2}$, $t_{i_1} = t_{i_3}$, $t_{i_2} = t_{i_3}$, or $t_{i_3} = t_{i_4}$, the condition is satisfied with probability 0;
- If $t_{i_1} = t_{i_4}$, but $t_{i_1}, t_{i_2}, t_{i_3}$ are all distinct, the condition is satisfied with probability at most ε^3. There are at most $\binom{q}{3} \cdot (\gamma - 1)$ possible choices of queries that satisfy this condition on the tweaks, noting that every tweak occurs at most γ times;
- If $t_{i_2} = t_{i_4}$, but $t_{i_1}, t_{i_2}, t_{i_3}$ are all distinct, a similar reasoning applies.

Overall, configuration (B) is satisfied with probability at most

$$\max\left\{ \binom{q}{4}\varepsilon^3, \binom{q}{3}(\gamma - 1)\varepsilon^3 \right\} \leq \binom{q}{4}\varepsilon^3,$$

for $\gamma \leq q/4$;

(C) Configuration (C) happens only if

$$m_{i_1} \oplus h_1(t_{i_1}) = m_{i_2} \oplus h_1(t_{i_2}),$$
$$c_{i_2} \oplus h_2(t_{i_2}) = c_{i_3} \oplus h_2(t_{i_3}),$$
$$m_{i_3} \oplus h_1(t_{i_3}) = m_{i_4} \oplus h_1(t_{i_4}).$$

Further analysis depends on the values of the tweaks.

- If $t_{i_1}, t_{i_2}, t_{i_3}, t_{i_4}$ are all distinct, the condition is satisfied with probability at most $2^n \varepsilon^4$ (obtained by summing over all possible connections between the first and third equation, and then applying the ε-AXU$_4$ bound). There are at most $\binom{q}{4}$ possible choices of queries that satisfy this condition on the tweaks;
- If $t_{i_1} = t_{i_2}$, $t_{i_2} = t_{i_3}$, or $t_{i_3} = t_{i_4}$, the condition is satisfied with probability 0;
- If $t_{i_1} = t_{i_3}$, but $t_{i_1}, t_{i_2}, t_{i_4}$ are all distinct, the condition is satisfied with probability at most ε^3. There are at most $\binom{q}{3} \cdot (\gamma - 1)$ possible choices of queries that satisfy this condition on the tweaks, noting that every tweak occurs at most γ times;
- If $t_{i_2} = t_{i_4}$, but $t_{i_1}, t_{i_2}, t_{i_3}$ are all distinct, a similar reasoning applies;
- If $t_{i_1} = t_{i_4}$, but $t_{i_1}, t_{i_2}, t_{i_3}$ are all distinct, a similar reasoning applies;
- If $t_{i_1} = t_{i_3}$ and $t_{i_2} = t_{i_4}$ but t_{i_1}, t_{i_2} are distinct, the condition is satisfied with probability at most ε^2. There are at most $\binom{q}{2} \cdot (\gamma - 1)$ possible choices of queries that satisfy this condition on the tweaks, noting that every tweak occurs at most γ times and that there is at most one option for $(t_{i_4}, m_{i_4}, c_{i_4})$ once the other three queries are fixed.

Overall, configuration (C) is satisfied with probability at most

$$\max\left\{ \binom{q}{4}2^n\varepsilon^4, \binom{q}{3}(\gamma - 1)\varepsilon^3, \binom{q}{2}(\gamma - 1)\varepsilon^2 \right\} \leq \binom{q}{4}2^n\varepsilon^4 + \binom{q}{2}(\gamma - 1)\varepsilon^2,$$

for $\gamma \leq q/4$ and $2^n\varepsilon \geq 1$;

(D) Configuration (D) is symmetrical to configuration (C);
(E) Configuration (E) is symmetrical to configuration (B);
(F) Configuration (F) is symmetrical to configuration (A).

Thus,

$$\mathbf{Pr}\,(\text{subgraph}) \le 4\binom{q}{4}\varepsilon^3 + 2\binom{q}{4}2^n\varepsilon^4 + 2\binom{q}{2}(\gamma - 1)\varepsilon^2$$

$$\le 6\binom{q}{4}2^n\varepsilon^4 + 2\binom{q}{2}(\gamma - 1)\varepsilon^2\,. \tag{22}$$

Conclusion for bad events. From (19) and the individual probabilities of (20), (21), and (22), we obtain

$$\mathbf{Pr}\,(X_{\widetilde{p}} \in \mathcal{V}_{\text{bad}}) \le 3\binom{q}{2}\varepsilon^2 + 6\binom{q}{4}2^n\varepsilon^4 + 2\binom{q}{2}(\gamma - 1)\varepsilon^2$$

$$\le 6\binom{q}{4}2^n\varepsilon^4 + \binom{q}{2}(2\gamma + 1)\varepsilon^2\,,$$

for $\gamma \ge 2$.

5.6   Ratio for Good Views (ϵ)

Consider a given view $\nu = (\nu', h_1, h_2)$ where $\nu = \{(t_1, m_1, c_1), \ldots, (t_q, m_q, c_q)\}$. Define

$$r_1 = |\{m_i \oplus h_1(t_i) \mid i \in \{1, \ldots, q\}\}|, \tag{23}$$
$$r_2 = |\{c_i \oplus h_2(t_i) \mid i \in \{1, \ldots, q\}\}|. \tag{24}$$

Note that $r_1 + r_2$ is equal to the number of unknowns in the system of equations (see (18)). For any $t \in \{0,1\}^\tau$, we denote $u_t = |\{i \in \{1, \ldots, q\} \mid t_i = t\}|$.

For the ideal world $\widetilde{p}$, we have

$$\mathbf{Pr}\,(X_{\widetilde{p}} = \nu) = \mathbf{Pr}\,\left(\widetilde{p} \xleftarrow{\$} \mathrm{iperm}(\tau, n) \;:\; \widetilde{p} \vdash \nu'\right) \cdot \mathbf{Pr}\,\left((h_1, h_2) = (h_1', h_2') \xleftarrow{\$} H^2\right)$$

$$= \frac{1}{\prod_{t \in \{0,1\}^\tau} (2^n)_{u_t}} \cdot \frac{1}{|H|^2}\,, \tag{25}$$

where for the first probability we use that $\widetilde{p}$ is a family of permutations and for every $t \in \{0,1\}^\tau$ the view defines u_t values.

For the real world F, recall that it is built from two permutations p_1, p_2^{-1}. We have

$$\mathbf{Pr}\,(X_F = \nu) = \mathbf{Pr}\,\left(p_1, p_2^{-1} \xleftarrow{\$} \mathrm{perm}(n) \;:\; F \vdash \nu' \mid h_1, h_2\right) \cdot \mathbf{Pr}\,\left((h_1, h_2) = (h_1', h_2') \xleftarrow{\$} H^2\right)$$

$$= \mathbf{Pr}\,\left(p_1, p_2^{-1} \xleftarrow{\$} \mathrm{perm}(n) \;:\; F \vdash \nu' \mid h_1, h_2\right) \cdot \frac{1}{|H|^2}\,. \tag{26}$$

As has become clear from (17), $\nu = (\nu', h_1, h_2)$ fixes exactly q equations on r_1 unknowns for p_1 and r_2 unknowns for p_2^{-1}, where the inputs to p_1 and p_2^{-1} are fixed. We rely on the following lemma that is based on Patarin's mirror theory.

Lemma 2. *Consider good view* $\nu = (\nu', h_1, h_2)$ *whose system of* q *equations (17) has no subgraph of* ≥ 4 *edges, has no path of length 2 whose labels sum to 0, and no circle of length 2. As long as* $5^2 \cdot q \leq 2^n/64$, *the number of solutions to the* $r_1 + r_2$ *unknowns is at least*

$$\frac{(2^n)_{r_1}(2^n - 4)_{r_2}}{2^{nq}}.$$

The proof of Lemma 2 is omitted: it is very similar to the reasoning on EDM in [20] and follows straightforwardly from Patarin's mirror theory as reviewed in Appendix B. The side condition $5^2 \cdot q \leq 2^n/64$ is slightly different from that in [20], as we have adopted the bound from Nachef, Patarin, and Volte [22].

Every such solution defines r_1 evaluations of p_1, and r_2 evaluations of p_2, and hence the remaining probability in (26) satisfies

$$\mathbf{Pr}\left(p_1, p_2^{-1} \xleftarrow{\$} \mathsf{perm}(n) : F \vdash \nu' \mid h_1, h_2\right) \geq \frac{(2^n)_{r_1}(2^n - 4)_{r_2}}{2^{nq} \cdot (2^n)_{r_1}(2^n)_{r_2}}.$$

We obtain for the ratio:

$$\frac{\mathbf{Pr}\left(X_F = \nu\right)}{\mathbf{Pr}\left(X_{\widetilde{p}} = \nu\right)} \geq \frac{\prod_{t \in \{0,1\}^\tau}(2^n)_{u_t} \cdot |H|^2}{1} \cdot \frac{(2^n)_{r_1}(2^n - 4)_{r_2}}{2^{nq} \cdot (2^n)_{r_1}(2^n)_{r_2} \cdot |H|^2}$$

$$= \frac{\prod_{t \in \{0,1\}^\tau}(2^n)_{u_t} \cdot (2^n - 4)_{r_2}}{2^{nq} \cdot (2^n)_{r_2}}. \tag{27}$$

Using that for all t, $u_t \leq \gamma$, and that $\sum_{t \in \{0,1\}^\tau} u_t = q$:

$$(27) \geq \frac{\prod_{t \in \{0,1\}^\tau}(2^n - (\gamma - 1))^{u_t} \cdot (2^n - 4)_{r_2}}{2^{nq} \cdot (2^n)_{r_2}}$$

$$= \left(\frac{2^n - (\gamma - 1)}{2^n}\right)^q \cdot \prod_{i=0}^{3}\left(1 - \frac{r_2}{2^n - i}\right). \tag{28}$$

Using that $r_2 \leq q - 1$, and by simple algebra for $q \leq 2^n/3$:

$$(28) \geq 1 - \left(\frac{(\gamma - 1)q}{2^n} + \frac{q - 1}{2^n} + \frac{q - 1}{2^n - 1} + \frac{q - 1}{2^n - 2} + \frac{q - 1}{2^n - 3}\right)$$

$$\geq 1 - \frac{(\gamma + 3)q}{2^n}.$$

We have obtained $\epsilon = \frac{(\gamma + 3)q}{2^n}$, provided $5^2 \cdot q \leq 2^n/64$.

5.7 Releasing Tweak Usage Limitation

The limitation on the tweak usage, namely that the distinguisher can query each tweak at most γ times, is used at two places in the proof.

The first place is the last case of configuration (C) in Sect. 5.5, namely the case where $t_{i_1} = t_{i_3}$ and $t_{i_2} = t_{i_4}$. For upper bounding the number of choices for the four queries without relying on parameter γ, one may take into account that $m_{i_1} \oplus m_{i_2} = m_{i_3} \oplus m_{i_4}$ is necessarily needed. This value needs to be equal to the random value $h_1(t_{i_1}) \oplus h_2(t_{i_2})$. However, we see no possibility for deriving a formal bound here.

The second place is in the application of the mirror theory in Sect. 5.6. Our approach to achieve improved $3n/4$-bit security relies on Patarin's mirror theory, which is specifically developed to work well if a scheme is compared with a random function. Obviously, evaluations of CLRW2 under the same tweak will always give distinct responses. In particular, if a distinguisher uses the same tweak for all queries, all responses will be distinct, and the scheme can be distinguished from a random function with probability about $\binom{q}{2}/2^n$. More generally, if every tweak is evaluated at most γ times, the scheme can be distinguished from a random function with probability at most around $\gamma q/2^n$. Resolving the γ limitation here requires improving Patarin's mirror theory or employing a different proof technique.

Acknowledgments. Bart Mennink is supported by a postdoctoral fellowship from the Netherlands Organisation for Scientific Research (NWO) under Veni grant 016.Veni.173.017. The author would like to thank Mridul Nandi and Samuel Neves, and anonymous reviewers for their comments and suggestions.

A   A Proof of Theorem 1

Consider the distinguisher of Sect. 3.2 for any $\epsilon \geq 0$. Its success advantage satisfies

$$\mathbf{Adv}^{\text{stprp}}_{\text{GCL}^{f_1,f_2,f_3}}(\mathcal{D}) = \mathbf{Pr}\left(\mathcal{D}^{\text{GCL}^{f_1,f_2,f_3}} = 1\right) - \mathbf{Pr}\left(\mathcal{D}^{\widetilde{p}} = 1\right)$$

$$= 1 - \mathbf{Pr}\left(\mathcal{D}^{\text{GCL}^{f_1,f_2,f_3}} = 0\right) - \mathbf{Pr}\left(\mathcal{D}^{\widetilde{p}} = 1\right). \qquad (29)$$

The derivation relies on the following two lemmas, the proofs of which are in Sects. A.1 and A.2.

Lemma 3. *Provided $n \geq 6$,* $\mathbf{Pr}\left(\mathcal{D}^{\text{GCL}^{f_1,f_2,f_3}} = 0\right) \leq \frac{32}{2^{4\epsilon}} + \frac{80}{2^{n/2+2\epsilon}}.$

Lemma 4. *For any integral $1 \leq \alpha \leq \sqrt{\beta} - 1$, provided $n \geq 16$,* $\mathbf{Pr}\left(\mathcal{D}^{\widetilde{p}} = 1\right) \leq$ $\alpha 2^n \left(\frac{2\alpha}{2^{2\epsilon}}\right)^{3/(4\alpha^2)\cdot 2^{4\epsilon}} + \frac{2^{(\alpha+2)2\epsilon}}{2^{(\alpha-2)n/2}}.$

Putting $\epsilon = \log_2(n)/2$, we derive from (29) and Lemmas 3 and 4 that

$$\mathbf{Adv}^{\text{stprp}}_{\text{GCL}^{f_1,f_2,f_3}}(\mathcal{D}) \geq 1 - \frac{32}{n^2} - \frac{80}{n2^{n/2}} - \alpha 2^n \left(\frac{2\alpha}{n}\right)^{3/(4\alpha^2)\cdot n^2} - \frac{n^{(\alpha+2)}}{2^{(\alpha-2)n/2}},$$

provided $n \geq 16$, and for any integral $1 \leq \alpha \leq \sqrt{3/8}n - 1$. Clearly, the bound is meaningless for $\alpha = 1, 2$. Computer verification yields optimal choice $\alpha = 5$.

A.1   Proof of Lemma 3

Putting $d^* = f_1(t) \oplus f_1(t')$, we have

$$\mathbf{Pr}\left(\mathcal{D}^{\mathrm{GCL}^{f_1,f_2,f_3}} = 0\right) = \mathbf{Pr}\left(\forall_{d \in \{0,1\}^n} N_d < \beta\right) \leq \mathbf{Pr}\left(N_{d^*} < \beta\right). \qquad (30)$$

Clearly, if $f_2(t) \oplus f_2(t') = 0$, then $c_i \oplus c'_j = f_3(t) \oplus f_3(t')$ for all $(i,j) \in I_{d^*}$ and thus $N_{d^*} = \binom{q'}{2} > \beta$, implying $\mathbf{Pr}\left(N_{d^*} < \beta\right) = 0$. Henceforth, assume that $d^{**} := f_2(t) \oplus f_2(t') \neq 0$.

By Chebychev's inequality:

$$\begin{aligned}
\mathbf{Pr}\left(N_{d^*} < \beta\right) &= \mathbf{Pr}\left(N_{d^*} - \mathbf{Ex}\left(N_{d^*}\right) < \beta - \mathbf{Ex}\left(N_{d^*}\right)\right) \\
&\leq \mathbf{Pr}\left(\left|N_{d^*} - \mathbf{Ex}\left(N_{d^*}\right)\right| \geq \mathbf{Ex}\left(N_{d^*}\right) - \beta\right) \\
&\leq \frac{\mathbf{Var}\left(N_{d^*}\right)}{\left(\mathbf{Ex}\left(N_{d^*}\right) - \beta\right)^2} \\
&= \frac{\mathbf{Ex}\left(\left(N_{d^*}\right)^2\right) - \left(\mathbf{Ex}\left(N_{d^*}\right)\right)^2}{\left(\mathbf{Ex}\left(N_{d^*}\right) - \beta\right)^2}. \qquad (31)
\end{aligned}$$

For distinct $(i,j), (k,l) \in I_{d^*}$, define

$$N_{d^*}^{(i,j),(k,l)} = \begin{cases} 1, & \text{if } c_i \oplus c'_j = c_k \oplus c'_l, \\ 0, & \text{otherwise}, \end{cases} \qquad (32)$$

such that

$$N_{d^*} = \sum_{\substack{(i,j),(k,l) \in I_{d^*} \\ (i,j) \neq (k,l)}} N_{d^*}^{(i,j),(k,l)}. \qquad (33)$$

We have

$$\mathbf{Ex}\left(N_{d^*}\right) = \sum_{\substack{(i,j),(k,l) \in I_{d^*} \\ (i,j) \neq (k,l)}} \mathbf{Pr}\left(c_i \oplus c'_j = c_k \oplus c'_l\right), \qquad (34)$$

and

$$\begin{aligned}
\mathbf{Ex}\left(\left(N_{d^*}\right)^2\right) &= \mathbf{Ex}\left(\sum_{\substack{(i,j),(k,l) \in I_{d^*} \\ (i,j) \neq (k,l)}} \sum_{\substack{(i',j'),(k',l') \in I_{d^*} \\ (i',j') \neq (k',l')}} N_{d^*}^{(i,j),(k,l)} N_{d^*}^{(i',j'),(k',l')}\right) \\
&= \sum_{\substack{(i,j),(k,l) \in I_{d^*} \\ (i,j) \neq (k,l)}} \sum_{\substack{(i',j'),(k',l') \in I_{d^*} \\ (i',j') \neq (k',l')}} \mathbf{Pr}\left(c_i \oplus c'_j = c_k \oplus c'_l, \; c_{i'} \oplus c'_{j'} = c_{k'} \oplus c'_{l'}\right).
\end{aligned}$$

$$(35)$$

Above summation consists of $\binom{q'}{2}^2$ terms of independent probabilities, but their values differ depending on overlaps in the two sets $\{(i,j),(k,l)\}$, $\{(i',j'),(k',l')\}$. For any *distinct* $(i_1,j_1),(i_2,j_2),(i_3,j_3),(i_4,j_4) \in I_{d^*}$, define

$$\mathbf{P}_2 := \mathbf{Pr}\left(c_{i_1} \oplus c'_{j_1} = c_{i_2} \oplus c'_{j_2}\right),$$
$$\mathbf{P}_3 := \mathbf{Pr}\left(c_{i_1} \oplus c'_{j_1} = c_{i_2} \oplus c'_{j_2} = c_{i_3} \oplus c'_{j_3}\right),$$
$$\mathbf{P}_4 := \mathbf{Pr}\left(c_{i_1} \oplus c'_{j_1} = c_{i_2} \oplus c'_{j_2}, \ c_{i_3} \oplus c'_{j_3} = c_{i_4} \oplus c'_{j_4}\right).$$

We can observe that the sum in (35) consists of exactly $\binom{q'}{2}$ terms satisfying $\left|\{(i,j),(k,l)\} \cup \{(i',j'),(k',l')\}\right| = 2$, in which case the corresponding probability is of the form $\mathbf{P}_2$, exactly $\binom{q'}{2}2\binom{q'-2}{1}$ terms satisfying $\left|\{(i,j),(k,l)\} \cup \{(i',j'),(k',l')\}\right| = 3$, in which case the corresponding probability is of the form $\mathbf{P}_3$, and exactly $\binom{q'}{2}\binom{q'-2}{2}$ terms satisfying $\left|\{(i,j),(k,l)\} \cup \{(i',j'),(k',l')\}\right| = 4$, in which case the corresponding probability is of the form $\mathbf{P}_4$. We obtain (using independence of the probabilities)

$$\mathbf{Ex}\left((N_{d^*})^2\right) = \binom{q'}{2}\cdot\mathbf{P}_2 + \binom{q'}{2}2\binom{q'-2}{1}\cdot\mathbf{P}_3 + \binom{q'}{2}\binom{q'-2}{2}\cdot\mathbf{P}_4.$$

We likewise have $\mathbf{Ex}\left(N_{d^*}\right) = \binom{q'}{2}\cdot\mathbf{P}_2$, and using that $\beta = \frac{3}{2}\binom{q'}{2}/2^n$, we obtain for (30–31):

$$\mathbf{Pr}\left(\mathcal{D}^{\mathrm{GCL}^{f_1,f_2,f_3}} = 0\right) \leq \frac{\binom{q'}{2}\cdot\mathbf{P}_2 + \binom{q'}{2}2\binom{q'-2}{1}\cdot\mathbf{P}_3 + \binom{q'}{2}\binom{q'-2}{2}\cdot\mathbf{P}_4 - \left(\binom{q'}{2}\cdot\mathbf{P}_2\right)^2}{(\binom{q'}{2}\cdot\mathbf{P}_2 - \frac{3}{2}\binom{q'}{2}/2^n)^2}$$
$$= \frac{\mathbf{P}_2 + 2\binom{q'-2}{1}\cdot\mathbf{P}_3 + \binom{q'-2}{2}\cdot\mathbf{P}_4 - \binom{q'}{2}\cdot\mathbf{P}_2^2}{\binom{q'}{2}(\mathbf{P}_2 - \frac{3}{2}/2^n)^2}. \tag{36}$$

We can derive the following bounds on $\mathbf{P}_2, \mathbf{P}_3, \mathbf{P}_4$.

Claim. Provided $n \geq 6$, $\mathbf{P}_2 \geq 2/2^n$, $\mathbf{P}_3 \leq 5/2^{2n}$, and $\mathbf{P}_4 \leq \frac{4}{(2^n-6)(2^n-7)}$.

Proof (proof of claim). Before bounding the probabilities separately, note that in general for any distinct $(i,j),(k,l) \in I_{d^*}$, we have $i \neq k$ and $j \neq l$. Write

$$x_{i_1} = p_1(m_{i_1} \oplus f_1(t)) = p_1(m'_{j_1} \oplus f_1(t')),$$
$$x_{i_2} = p_1(m_{i_2} \oplus f_1(t)) = p_1(m'_{j_2} \oplus f_1(t')),$$
$$x_{i_3} = p_1(m_{i_3} \oplus f_1(t)) = p_1(m'_{j_3} \oplus f_1(t')),$$
$$x_{i_4} = p_1(m_{i_4} \oplus f_1(t)) = p_1(m'_{j_4} \oplus f_1(t')),$$

where we recall that $d^* = f_1(t) \oplus f_1(t') = m_{i_1} \oplus m'_{j_1} = \cdots = m_{i_4} \oplus m'_{j_4}$. Above values $x_{i_1}, x_{i_2}, x_{i_3}, x_{i_4}$ are pairwise distinct as $m_{i_1}, m_{i_2}, m_{i_3}, m_{i_4}$ are pairwise distinct as i_1, i_2, i_3, i_4 are. Furthermore, write

$$y_{i_1} = p_2^{-1}(c_{i_1} \oplus f_3(t)) = x_{i_1} \oplus f_2(t),$$
$$y'_{j_1} = p_2^{-1}(c'_{j_1} \oplus f_3(t')) = x_{i_1} \oplus f_2(t'),$$
$$y_{i_2} = p_2^{-1}(c_{i_2} \oplus f_3(t)) = x_{i_2} \oplus f_2(t),$$
$$y'_{j_2} = p_2^{-1}(c'_{j_2} \oplus f_3(t')) = x_{i_2} \oplus f_2(t'),$$
$$y_{i_3} = p_2^{-1}(c_{i_3} \oplus f_3(t)) = x_{i_3} \oplus f_2(t),$$
$$y'_{j_3} = p_2^{-1}(c'_{j_3} \oplus f_3(t')) = x_{i_3} \oplus f_2(t'),$$
$$y_{i_4} = p_2^{-1}(c_{i_4} \oplus f_3(t)) = x_{i_4} \oplus f_2(t),$$
$$y'_{j_4} = p_2^{-1}(c'_{j_4} \oplus f_3(t')) = x_{i_4} \oplus f_2(t').$$

Recall that $d^{**} := f_2(t) \oplus f_2(t') \neq 0$.

We start with bounding $\mathbf{P}_2$:

$$\mathbf{P}_2 = \mathbf{Pr}\left(c_{i_1} \oplus c'_{j_1} = c_{i_2} \oplus c'_{j_2}\right)$$
$$= \mathbf{Pr}\left(c_{i_1} \oplus c'_{j_1} = c_{i_2} \oplus c'_{j_2} \mid x_{i_1} \oplus x_{i_2} = d^{**}\right) \mathbf{Pr}\left(x_{i_1} \oplus x_{i_2} = d^{**}\right)$$
$$+ \mathbf{Pr}\left(c_{i_1} \oplus c'_{j_1} = c_{i_2} \oplus c'_{j_2} \mid x_{i_1} \oplus x_{i_2} \neq d^{**}\right) \mathbf{Pr}\left(x_{i_1} \oplus x_{i_2} \neq d^{**}\right).$$

Given that $x_{i_1} \neq x_{i_2}$, we have

$$\mathbf{Pr}\left(x_{i_1} \oplus x_{i_2} = d^{**}\right) = \frac{1}{2^n - 1}.$$

Conditioned on $x_{i_1} \oplus x_{i_2} = d^{**}$, we have $y_{i_1} = y'_{j_2}$ and $y'_{j_1} = y_{i_2}$, and $c_{i_1} \oplus c'_{j_1} = c_{i_2} \oplus c'_{j_2}$ holds with probability 1. Conditioned on $x_{i_1} \oplus x_{i_2} \neq d^{**}$ and using that $d^{**} \neq 0$, the values $y_{i_1}, y'_{j_1}, y_{i_2}, y'_{j_2}$ are pairwise distinct and

$$\mathbf{Pr}\left(p_2(y_{i_1}) \oplus p_2(y'_{j_1}) = p_2(y_{i_2}) \oplus p_2(y'_{j_2}) \mid x_{i_1} \oplus x_{i_2} \neq d^{**}\right) \leq \frac{1}{2^n - 3}.$$

We therefore obtain

$$\mathbf{P}_2 = \frac{1}{2^n - 1} + \frac{1}{2^n - 3}\left(1 - \frac{1}{2^n - 1}\right) = \frac{2 \cdot 2^n - 5}{(2^n - 1)(2^n - 3)} \geq \frac{2}{2^n}.$$

We next bound $\mathbf{P}_3$:

$$\mathbf{P}_3 = \mathbf{Pr}\left(c_{i_1} \oplus c'_{j_1} = c_{i_2} \oplus c'_{j_2} = c_{i_3} \oplus c'_{j_3}\right)$$
$$= \mathbf{Pr}\left(c_{i_1} \oplus c'_{j_1} = c_{i_2} \oplus c'_{j_2} = c_{i_3} \oplus c'_{j_3} \mid x_{i_1} \oplus x_{i_2} = d^{**}\right) \mathbf{Pr}\left(x_{i_1} \oplus x_{i_2} = d^{**}\right)$$
$$+ \mathbf{Pr}\left(c_{i_1} \oplus c'_{j_1} = c_{i_2} \oplus c'_{j_2} = c_{i_3} \oplus c'_{j_3} \mid x_{i_1} \oplus x_{i_3} = d^{**}\right) \mathbf{Pr}\left(x_{i_1} \oplus x_{i_3} = d^{**}\right)$$
$$+ \mathbf{Pr}\left(c_{i_1} \oplus c'_{j_1} = c_{i_2} \oplus c'_{j_2} = c_{i_3} \oplus c'_{j_3} \mid x_{i_2} \oplus x_{i_3} = d^{**}\right) \mathbf{Pr}\left(x_{i_2} \oplus x_{i_3} = d^{**}\right)$$
$$+ \mathbf{Pr}\left(c_{i_1} \oplus c'_{j_1} = c_{i_2} \oplus c'_{j_2} = c_{i_3} \oplus c'_{j_3} \mid x_{i_1} \oplus x_{i_2}, x_{i_1} \oplus x_{i_3}, x_{i_2} \oplus x_{i_3} \neq d^{**}\right)$$
$$\cdot \mathbf{Pr}\left(x_{i_1} \oplus x_{i_2}, x_{i_1} \oplus x_{i_3}, x_{i_2} \oplus x_{i_3} \neq d^{**}\right),$$

using that no two or more of the events "$x_{i_1} \oplus x_{i_2} = d^{**}$," "$x_{i_1} \oplus x_{i_3} = d^{**}$," and "$x_{i_2} \oplus x_{i_3} = d^{**}$" can hold simultaneously. Starting with the first line, as before we have

$$\mathbf{Pr}\left(x_{i_1} \oplus x_{i_2} = d^{**}\right) = \frac{1}{2^n - 1}.$$

Conditioned on $x_{i_1} \oplus x_{i_2} = d^{**}$, we have $y_{i_1} = y'_{j_2}$ and $y'_{j_1} = y_{i_2}$, and $c_{i_1} \oplus c'_{j_1} = c_{i_2} \oplus c'_{j_2}$ holds with probability 1. On the other hand, $x_{i_1} \oplus x_{i_3} \neq d^{**}$, and thus, the values $y_{i_1}, y'_{j_1}, y_{i_3}, y'_{j_3}$ are pairwise distinct and

$$\mathbf{Pr}\left(c_{i_1} \oplus c'_{j_1} = c_{i_2} \oplus c'_{j_2} = c_{i_3} \oplus c'_{j_3} \mid x_{i_1} \oplus x_{i_2} = d^{**}\right) \leq \frac{1}{2^n - 3}$$

(we now need to consider an upper bound, as the probability may be 0 if the targeted value is already sampled).

The second and third line go identically. For the fourth line, conditioned on the fact that $x_{i_1} \oplus x_{i_2}, x_{i_1} \oplus x_{i_3}, x_{i_2} \oplus x_{i_3} \neq d^{**}$ and using that $d^{**} \neq 0$, the values $y_{i_1}, y'_{j_1}, y_{i_2}, y'_{j_2}, y_{i_3}, y'_{j_3}$ are pairwise distinct and

$$\mathbf{Pr}\left(c_{i_1} \oplus c'_{j_1} = c_{i_2} \oplus c'_{j_2} = c_{i_3} \oplus c'_{j_3} \mid x_{i_1} \oplus x_{i_2}, x_{i_1} \oplus x_{i_3}, x_{i_2} \oplus x_{i_3} \neq d^{**}\right) \leq \frac{1}{(2^n - 4)(2^n - 5)}.$$

We therefore obtain

$$\mathbf{P}_3 \leq \frac{3}{(2^n - 1)(2^n - 3)} + \frac{1}{(2^n - 4)(2^n - 5)} \leq \frac{4}{(2^n - 4)(2^n - 5)} \leq \frac{5}{2^{2n}},$$

provided $2^n \geq 45$.

We finally bound $\mathbf{P}_4$:

$$\mathbf{P}_4 = \mathbf{Pr}\left(c_{i_1} \oplus c'_{j_1} = c_{i_2} \oplus c'_{j_2}, \ c_{i_3} \oplus c'_{j_3} = c_{i_4} \oplus c'_{j_4}\right)$$
$$= \mathbf{Pr}\left(c_{i_1} \oplus c'_{j_1} = c_{i_2} \oplus c'_{j_2}, \ c_{i_3} \oplus c'_{j_3} = c_{i_4} \oplus c'_{j_4} \mid x_{i_1} \oplus x_{i_2} = d^{**} \wedge x_{i_3} \oplus x_{i_4} = d^{**}\right)$$
$$\cdot \mathbf{Pr}\left(x_{i_1} \oplus x_{i_2} = d^{**} \wedge x_{i_3} \oplus x_{i_4} = d^{**}\right)$$
$$+ \mathbf{Pr}\left(c_{i_1} \oplus c'_{j_1} = c_{i_2} \oplus c'_{j_2}, \ c_{i_3} \oplus c'_{j_3} = c_{i_4} \oplus c'_{j_4} \mid x_{i_1} \oplus x_{i_2} = d^{**} \wedge x_{i_3} \oplus x_{i_4} \neq d^{**}\right)$$
$$\cdot \mathbf{Pr}\left(x_{i_1} \oplus x_{i_2} = d^{**} \wedge x_{i_3} \oplus x_{i_4} \neq d^{**}\right)$$
$$+ \mathbf{Pr}\left(c_{i_1} \oplus c'_{j_1} = c_{i_2} \oplus c'_{j_2}, \ c_{i_3} \oplus c'_{j_3} = c_{i_4} \oplus c'_{j_4} \mid x_{i_1} \oplus x_{i_2} \neq d^{**} \wedge x_{i_3} \oplus x_{i_4} = d^{**}\right)$$
$$\cdot \mathbf{Pr}\left(x_{i_1} \oplus x_{i_2} \neq d^{**} \wedge x_{i_3} \oplus x_{i_4} = d^{**}\right)$$
$$+ \mathbf{Pr}\left(c_{i_1} \oplus c'_{j_1} = c_{i_2} \oplus c'_{j_2}, \ c_{i_3} \oplus c'_{j_3} = c_{i_4} \oplus c'_{j_4} \mid x_{i_1} \oplus x_{i_2} \neq d^{**} \wedge x_{i_3} \oplus x_{i_4} \neq d^{**}\right)$$
$$\cdot \mathbf{Pr}\left(x_{i_1} \oplus x_{i_2} \neq d^{**} \wedge x_{i_3} \oplus x_{i_4} \neq d^{**}\right),$$

For the first line, the event $x_{i_1} \oplus x_{i_2} = d^{**} \wedge x_{i_3} \oplus x_{i_4} = d^{**}$ holds with probability $1/(2^n - 2)(2^n - 3)$, and conditioned on $x_{i_1} \oplus x_{i_2} = d^{**} \wedge x_{i_3} \oplus x_{i_4} = d^{**}$, the equations $c_{i_1} \oplus c'_{j_1} = c_{i_2} \oplus c'_{j_2}$ and $c_{i_3} \oplus c'_{j_3} = c_{i_4} \oplus c'_{j_4}$ hold with probability 1 (see the analysis of $\mathbf{P}_2$). The second and third line go as in the analysis of $\mathbf{P}_3$, giving

$$\mathbf{Pr}\left(x_{i_1} \oplus x_{i_2} = d^{**} \wedge x_{i_3} \oplus x_{i_4} \neq d^{**}\right) \leq \frac{1}{2^n - 1},$$

and

$$\mathbf{Pr}\left(c_{i_1} \oplus c'_{j_1} = c_{i_2} \oplus c'_{j_2} , \; c_{i_3} \oplus c'_{j_3} = c_{i_4} \oplus c'_{j_4} \mid x_{i_1} \oplus x_{i_2} = d^{**} \wedge x_{i_3} \oplus x_{i_4} \neq d^{**}\right) \leq \frac{1}{2^n - 3} .$$

For the fourth line, conditioned on the fact that $x_{i_1} \oplus x_{i_2} \neq d^{**} \wedge x_{i_3} \oplus x_{i_4} \neq d^{**}$ and using that $d^{**} \neq 0$, the values $y_{i_1}, y'_{j_1}, y_{i_2}, y'_{j_2}$ are pairwise distinct and so are $y_{i_3}, y'_{j_3}, y_{i_4}, y'_{j_4}$, and in addition, $y_{i_1}, y_{i_2}, y_{i_3}, y_{i_4}$ are pairwise distinct and $y'_{j_1}, y'_{j_2}, y'_{j_3}, y'_{j_4}$ are. We obtain

$$\mathbf{Pr}\left(c_{i_1} \oplus c'_{j_1} = c_{i_2} \oplus c'_{j_2} , \; c_{i_3} \oplus c'_{j_3} = c_{i_4} \oplus c'_{j_4} \mid x_{i_1} \oplus x_{i_2}, x_{i_3} \oplus x_{i_4} \neq d^{**}\right) \leq \frac{1}{(2^n - 6)(2^n - 7)} .$$

We therefore obtain

$$\mathbf{P}_4 \leq \frac{1}{(2^n - 2)(2^n - 3)} + \frac{2}{(2^n - 1)(2^n - 3)} + \frac{1}{(2^n - 6)(2^n - 7)} \leq \frac{4}{(2^n - 6)(2^n - 7)} .$$

$\square$

To suit further analysis of (36), we claim that the $\mathbf{P}_4$-term cancels out to the $\mathbf{P}_2^2$-term.

Claim. Provided $6q' \leq 2^n$, $\binom{q'-2}{2} \cdot \mathbf{P}_4 \leq \binom{q'}{2} \cdot \mathbf{P}_2^2$.

Proof (proof of claim). By above claim, $\mathbf{P}_4 \leq \frac{4}{(2^n - 6)(2^n - 7)}$ and $\mathbf{P}_2 \geq 2/2^n$, and it remains to prove that

$$\frac{(q' - 2)(q' - 3)}{(2^n - 6)(2^n - 7)} \leq \frac{q'(q' - 1)}{2^{2n}} .$$

This in turn follows from the fact that

$$\frac{q' - 3}{2^n - 7} \leq \frac{q' - 2}{2^n - 6} \leq \frac{q' - 1}{2^n} ,$$

as $6q' \leq 2^n$. $\square$

From (36) and the bounds of above two claims, we directly obtain

$$\mathbf{Pr}\left(\mathcal{D}^{\mathrm{GCL}^{f_1, f_2, f_3}} = 0\right) \overset{a}{\leq} \frac{\mathbf{P}_2 + 2\binom{q'-2}{1} \cdot \mathbf{P}_3}{\binom{q'}{2}(\mathbf{P}_2 - \frac{3}{2}/2^n)^2}$$

$$\overset{b}{\leq} \frac{2/2^n + 2\binom{q'-2}{1} \cdot 5/2^{2n}}{\binom{q'}{2}(2/2^n - \frac{3}{2}/2^n)^2}$$

$$= \frac{8 \cdot 2^n + 40(q' - 2)}{\binom{q'}{2}}$$

$$\overset{c}{\leq} \frac{32}{2^{4\epsilon}} + \frac{80}{2^{n/2 + 2\epsilon}} ,$$

where $\overset{a}{\leq}$ holds due to the second claim, $\overset{b}{\leq}$ holds as $\mathbf{P}_2 \geq 2/2^n$ and $\mathbf{P}_3 \leq 5/2^{2n}$ (note that a lower bound on $\mathbf{P}_2$ suffices for both the numerator and denominator as $A/(A - C) \leq B/(B - C)$ for $A \geq B > C > 0$), and $\overset{c}{\leq}$ holds as $\binom{q'}{2} \geq (q')^2/4$ and $q' = 2^{n/2 + 2\epsilon}$.

A.2   Proof of Lemma 4

For any $d \in \{0,1\}^n$, recall that N_d counts the number of collisions $c_i \oplus c_j' = c_k \oplus c_l'$ for distinct $(i,j), (k,l)$. There could be multi-collisions; for $\lambda \geq 2$ we say that $(i_1, j_1), \ldots, (i_\lambda, j_\lambda) \in I_d$ form a λ-collision if $c_{i_1} \oplus c_{j_1}' = \cdots = c_{i_5} \oplus c_{j_5}'$. Denote by N_d^λ the number of λ-collisions that are *not part of* a $(\lambda+1)$-collision. Denote by $N_d^{\geq \lambda}$ the number of λ-collisions (that may be part of a $(\lambda+1)$-collision).

Fix any $1 \leq \alpha \leq \sqrt{\beta} - 1$. By basic probability theory,[1]

$$
\mathbf{Pr}\left(\mathcal{D}^{\widetilde{p}} = 1\right) \leq \sum_{d \in \{0,1\}^n} \mathbf{Pr}\left(N_d \geq \beta\right)
$$

$$
\leq \sum_{d \in \{0,1\}^n} \mathbf{Pr}\left(N_d \geq \beta \mid N_d^{\geq \alpha+2} = 0\right) + \mathbf{Pr}\left(N_d^{\geq \alpha+2} \geq 1\right)
$$

$$
\leq \sum_{d \in \{0,1\}^n} \mathbf{Pr}\left(N_d \geq \beta \mid N_d^{\geq \alpha+2} = 0\right) + \binom{q'}{\alpha+2} \frac{1}{(2^n)_{\alpha+1}}. \quad (37)
$$

Conditioned on the fact that there is no $(\alpha+2)$-collision, by the pigeonhole principle, $N_d \geq \beta$ only if the number of collisions arising from either 2-collisions, 3-collisions, ..., or $(\alpha+1)$-collisions is at least β/α. Clearly, a 2-collision contributes 1 to N_d, a 3-collision contributes 3 to N_d, and generally, an i-collision contributes $\binom{i}{2}$ to N_d. Therefore, denoting $\mathbf{Pr}^\star(X) = \mathbf{Pr}\left(X \mid N_d^{\geq \alpha+2} = 0\right)$ for brevity,

$$
\mathbf{Pr}^\star(N_d \geq \beta) \leq \sum_{i=2}^{\alpha+1} \mathbf{Pr}^\star\left(N_d^i \geq \beta/\alpha\right)
$$

$$
\leq \sum_{i=2}^{\alpha+1} \binom{q'}{i \cdot \beta/(\alpha\binom{i}{2})} \frac{1}{(2^n)_{(i-1)\cdot\beta/(\alpha\binom{i}{2})}}. \quad (38)
$$

As $\alpha \leq \sqrt{\beta} - 1$, we particularly have $(i-1) \cdot \beta/(\alpha\binom{i}{2}) \geq 2$ for all i, and we obtain

$$
\binom{q'}{i \cdot \beta/(\alpha\binom{i}{2})} \frac{1}{(2^n)_{(i-1)\cdot\beta/(\alpha\binom{i}{2})}} \overset{a}{\leq} \frac{(q')_{(i-1)\cdot\beta/(\alpha\binom{i}{2})} \cdot (q'-2)^{\beta/(\alpha\binom{i}{2})}}{(2^n)_{(i-1)\cdot\beta/(\alpha\binom{i}{2})}} \cdot \left(\frac{e}{i \cdot \beta/(\alpha\binom{i}{2})}\right)^{i \cdot \beta/(\alpha\binom{i}{2})}
$$

$$
\overset{b}{\leq} \left(\left(\frac{e\alpha(i-1)}{2}\right)^i \cdot \frac{(q')^{i-1}(q'-2)}{2^{(i-1)n}} \cdot \frac{1}{\beta^i}\right)^{\beta/(\alpha\binom{i}{2})}
$$

$$
\overset{c}{\leq} \left(\left(\frac{2e\alpha}{3}\right)^i \cdot \frac{(i-1)^i}{2^{4\epsilon}(2^{n/2+2\epsilon} - 1)^{i-2}}\right)^{(3\cdot 2^{4\epsilon})/(8\alpha\binom{i}{2})}
$$

$$
\overset{d}{\leq} \left(\frac{2\alpha}{2^{2\epsilon}}\right)^{3/(4\alpha(i-1))\cdot 2^{4\epsilon}},
$$

---

[1] Note that a plain Markov bound or Chebychev's inequality do not help, as we have to sum over all possible $d \in \{0,1\}^n$.

where $\overset{a}{\leq}$ holds as $\binom{A}{B} \leq (A)_B \cdot (e/B)^B$ by Stirling's approximation, $\overset{b}{\leq}$ holds as $(A)_m/(B)_m \leq (A/B)^m$ if $A \leq B$, $\overset{c}{\leq}$ uses $\beta = \frac{3}{2}\binom{q'}{2}/2^n$, $q'(q'-2) \leq (q'-1)^2$, and $q' = 2^{n/2+2\epsilon}$, and, finally $\overset{d}{\leq}$ holds as $(i-1)^i \leq (2^{n/2-1})^{i-2}$ is satisfied for all i, provided that $n \geq 16$.

We obtain for (38):

$$\mathbf{Pr}^\star(N_d \geq \beta) \leq \sum_{i=2}^{\alpha+1} \left(\frac{2\alpha}{2^{2\epsilon}}\right)^{3/(4\alpha(i-1))\cdot 2^{4\epsilon}} \leq \alpha \left(\frac{2\alpha}{2^{2\epsilon}}\right)^{3/(4\alpha^2)\cdot 2^{4\epsilon}},$$

and for (37):

$$\mathbf{Pr}\left(\mathcal{D}^{\widetilde{p}} = 1\right) \leq \alpha 2^n \left(\frac{2\alpha}{2^{2\epsilon}}\right)^{3/(4\alpha^2)\cdot 2^{4\epsilon}} + \frac{2^{(\alpha+2)2\epsilon}}{2^{(\alpha-2)n/2}},$$

again using that $(A)_m/(B)_m \leq (A/B)^m$ if $A \leq B$. This bound holds for all $1 \leq \alpha < \sqrt{\beta} - 1$.

B   Mirror Theory

We will follow the description of Patarin's mirror theory [22,26,28] by Mennink and Neves [20]. We will restrict ourselves to the simplified setting where the equations are of the form $P_a \oplus P_b = \lambda$, where the P_a's and P_b's come from independent permutations, and we will use the theory for $3n/4$-bit security at most.

B.1   System of Equations

Consider a system of $q \geq 1$ equations

$$\mathcal{E} = \{P_{\varphi(a_1)} \oplus P_{\varphi(b_1)} = \lambda_1, \cdots, P_{\varphi(a_q)} \oplus P_{\varphi(b_q)} = \lambda_q\} \tag{39}$$

over $r \geq 1$ unknowns $\mathcal{P} = \{P_1, \ldots, P_r\}$, where φ is some surjective index mapping

$$\varphi : \{a_1, b_1, \ldots, a_q, b_q\} \to \{1, \ldots, r\}.$$

In our work we consider the case that the P_a's and P_b's come from independent permutations, hence $\varphi(a_i) \neq \varphi(b_j)$ for any i, j. We write $\mathcal{I}_1 = \{\varphi(a_i) \mid i \in \{1, \ldots, q\}\}$ and $\mathcal{I}_2 = \{\varphi(b_i) \mid i \in \{1, \ldots, q\}\}$, such that $\{1, \ldots, r\} = \mathcal{I}_1 \cup \mathcal{I}_2$ is a partition. For a subset $I \subseteq \{1, \ldots, q\}$, define the multiset $\mathcal{M}_I$ as

$$\mathcal{M}_I = \bigcup_{i \in I} \{\varphi(a_i), \varphi(b_i)\}.$$

We give three definitions with respect to the system of equations $\mathcal{E}$.

Definition 1 (circle-freeness). *For any* $I \subseteq \{1, \ldots, q\}$, $\mathcal{M}_I$ *has an element of odd multiplicity.*

Definition 2 (ξ-block-maximality). *There is a partition* $\{1, \ldots, r\} = \mathcal{R}_1 \cup \cdots \cup \mathcal{R}_s$ *of the* r *indices, all of size at most* ξ, *such that for any* $i \in \{1, \ldots, q\}$ *there is an* $\ell \in \{1, \ldots, s\}$ *such that* $\{\varphi(a_i), \varphi(b_i)\} \subseteq \mathcal{R}_\ell$.

Definition 3 (non-degeneracy). *For any* $I \subseteq \{1, \ldots, q\}$ *such that* $\mathcal{M}_I$ *has exactly two odd multiplicity element from either* $\mathcal{I}_1$ *or* $\mathcal{I}_2$, *it satisfies* $\bigoplus_{i \in I} \lambda_i \neq 0$.

Circle-freeness implies that there is no linear combination of the equations $\mathcal{E}$ that is independent of the unknowns, ξ-block maximality implies that there are not too many unknowns that are jointly related, and non-degeneracy implies that there is no linear combination of the equations $\mathcal{E}$ that implies equality of two distinct unknowns from either $\mathcal{I}_1$ or $\mathcal{I}_2$.

B.2   Main Result

The main theorem of Patarin's mirror theory, tailored to the case where we have a partition of the unknowns into two disjoint sets, is given below. We follow [20], with the side condition on $2^n/64$ from [22].

Theorem 3 (mirror theorem). *Let* $\{1, \ldots, r\} = \mathcal{I}_1 \cup \mathcal{I}_2$ *be a partition of the indices. Let* $\mathcal{E}$ *be a system of equations over the unknowns* $\mathcal{P}$ *that is (i) circle-free, (ii) ξ-block-maximal, and (iii) non-degenerate. Then, as long as* $\xi^2 \cdot \max\{|\mathcal{I}_1|, |\mathcal{I}_2|\} \leq 2^n/64$, *the number of solutions for* $\mathcal{P}$ *such that* $P_i \neq P_j$ *for all* $i, j \in \mathcal{I}_\ell$ *($\ell = 1, 2$) is at least*

$$\frac{\mathrm{NonEq}(\mathcal{I}_1, \mathcal{I}_2; \mathcal{E})}{2^{nq}},$$

where $\mathrm{NonEq}(\mathcal{I}_1, \mathcal{I}_2; \mathcal{E})$ *denotes the number of solutions to* $\mathcal{P}$ *that satisfy* $P_i \neq P_j$ *for all* $i, j \in \mathcal{I}_\ell$ *($\ell = 1, 2$) as well as the inequalities imposed by* $\mathcal{E}$ *(but the equalities themselves released).*

A lower bound on the technical quantity $\mathrm{NonEq}(\mathcal{I}_1, \mathcal{I}_2; \mathcal{E})$ can be derived as follows. Every equation $P_{\varphi(a)} \oplus P_{\varphi(b)} = \lambda \neq 0$ in $\mathcal{E}$ imposes $P_{\varphi(a)} \neq P_{\varphi(b)}$. As $\varphi(a) \in \mathcal{I}_1$ and $\varphi(b) \in \mathcal{I}_2$ are in distinct index sets, this inequality $P_{\varphi(a)} \neq P_{\varphi(b)}$ imposes an *extra* inequality over the ones suggested by $\mathcal{I}_1, \mathcal{I}_2$. An obvious lower bound thus is

$$\mathrm{NonEq}(\mathcal{I}_1, \mathcal{I}_2; \mathcal{E}) \geq (2^n)_{|\mathcal{I}_1|}(2^n - (\xi - 1))_{|\mathcal{I}_2|},$$

because every unknown of $\mathcal{I}_2$ is in exactly one block, and connects with at most $\xi - 1$ unknowns of $\mathcal{I}_1$ (as the system is ξ-block-maximal).

References

1. Andreeva, E., Bogdanov, A., Luykx, A., Mennink, B., Tischhauser, E., Yasuda, K.: Parallelizable and authenticated online ciphers. In: Sako, K., Sarkar, P. (eds.) ASIACRYPT 2013. LNCS, vol. 8269, pp. 424–443. Springer, Heidelberg (2013). https://doi.org/10.1007/978-3-642-42033-7_22
2. Bogdanov, A., Knudsen, L.R., Leander, G., Standaert, F.-X., Steinberger, J., Tischhauser, E.: Key-alternating ciphers in a provable setting: encryption using a small number of public permutations. In: Pointcheval, D., Johansson, T. (eds.) EUROCRYPT 2012. LNCS, vol. 7237, pp. 45–62. Springer, Heidelberg (2012). https://doi.org/10.1007/978-3-642-29011-4_5
3. Chakraborty, D., Sarkar, P.: A general construction of tweakable block ciphers and different modes of operations. In: Lipmaa, H., Yung, M., Lin, D. (eds.) Inscrypt 2006. LNCS, vol. 4318, pp. 88–102. Springer, Heidelberg (2006). https://doi.org/10.1007/11937807_8
4. Chen, S., Lampe, R., Lee, J., Seurin, Y., Steinberger, J.: Minimizing the two-round even-mansour cipher. In: Garay, J.A., Gennaro, R. (eds.) CRYPTO 2014. LNCS, vol. 8616, pp. 39–56. Springer, Heidelberg (2014). https://doi.org/10.1007/978-3-662-44371-2_3
5. Chen, S., Steinberger, J.: Tight security bounds for key-alternating ciphers. In: Nguyen, P.Q., Oswald, E. (eds.) EUROCRYPT 2014. LNCS, vol. 8441, pp. 327–350. Springer, Heidelberg (2014). https://doi.org/10.1007/978-3-642-55220-5_19
6. Cogliati, B., Lampe, R., Seurin, Y.: Tweaking even-mansour ciphers. In: Gennaro, R., Robshaw, M. (eds.) CRYPTO 2015. LNCS, vol. 9215, pp. 189–208. Springer, Heidelberg (2015). https://doi.org/10.1007/978-3-662-47989-6_9
7. Cogliati, B., Seurin, Y.: EWCDM: an efficient, beyond-birthday secure, nonce-misuse resistant MAC. In: Robshaw and Katz [31], pp. 121–149
8. Dunkelman, O., Keller, N.: A new criterion for nonlinearity of block ciphers. IEEE Trans. Inf. Theor. 53(11), 3944–3957 (2007)
9. Dworkin, M.: NIST SP 800–38E: Recommendation for Block Cipher Modes of Operation: The XTS-AES Mode for Confidentiality on Storage Devices (2010)
10. Granger, R., Jovanovic, P., Mennink, B., Neves, S.: Improved masking for tweakable blockciphers with applications to authenticated encryption. In: Fischlin, M., Coron, J.-S. (eds.) EUROCRYPT 2016. LNCS, vol. 9665, pp. 263–293. Springer, Heidelberg (2016). https://doi.org/10.1007/978-3-662-49890-3_11
11. Hoang, V.T., Krovetz, T., Rogaway, P.: Robust authenticated-encryption AEZ and the problem that it solves. In: Oswald, E., Fischlin, M. (eds.) EUROCRYPT 2015. LNCS, vol. 9056, pp. 15–44. Springer, Heidelberg (2015). https://doi.org/10.1007/978-3-662-46800-5_2
12. Iwata, T., Minematsu, K., Peyrin, T., Seurin, Y.: ZMAC: a fast tweakable block cipher mode for highly secure message authentication. In: Katz and Shacham [14], pp. 34–65
13. Jean, J., Nikolić, I., Peyrin, T., Seurin, Y.: Deoxys v1.41 (2016). submission to CAESAR competition
14. Katz, J., Shacham, H. (eds.): CRYPTO 2017. LNCS, vol. 10403. Springer, Cham (2017). https://doi.org/10.1007/978-3-319-63697-9
15. Krovetz, T., Rogaway, P.: The software performance of authenticated-encryption modes. In: Joux, A. (ed.) FSE 2011. LNCS, vol. 6733, pp. 306–327. Springer, Heidelberg (2011). https://doi.org/10.1007/978-3-642-21702-9_18

16. Lampe, R., Seurin, Y.: Tweakable blockciphers with asymptotically optimal security. In: Moriai, S. (ed.) FSE 2013. LNCS, vol. 8424, pp. 133–151. Springer, Heidelberg (2014). https://doi.org/10.1007/978-3-662-43933-3_8
17. Landecker, W., Shrimpton, T., Terashima, R.S.: Tweakable Blockciphers with Beyond Birthday-Bound Security. In: Safavi-Naini, R., Canetti, R. (eds.) CRYPTO 2012. LNCS, vol. 7417, pp. 14–30. Springer, Heidelberg (2012). https://doi.org/10.1007/978-3-642-32009-5_2
18. Lee, J., Luykx, A., Mennink, B., Minematsu, K.: Connecting tweakable and multi-key blockcipher security. Des. Codes Cryptogr. **86**(3), 623–640 (2018)
19. Liskov, M., Rivest, R.L., Wagner, D.: Tweakable block ciphers. In: Yung, M. (ed.) CRYPTO 2002. LNCS, vol. 2442, pp. 31–46. Springer, Heidelberg (2002). https://doi.org/10.1007/3-540-45708-9_3
20. Mennink, B., Neves, S.: Encrypted davies-meyer and its dual: towards optimal security using mirror theory. In: Katz and Shacham [14], pp. 556–583
21. Minematsu, K.: Improved security analysis of XEX and LRW modes. In: Biham, E., Youssef, A.M. (eds.) SAC 2006. LNCS, vol. 4356, pp. 96–113. Springer, Heidelberg (2007). https://doi.org/10.1007/978-3-540-74462-7_8
22. Nachef, V., Patarin, J., Volte, E.: Feistel Ciphers. Springer, Cham (2017). https://doi.org/10.1007/978-3-319-49530-9
23. Nyberg, K.: Perfect nonlinear S-boxes. In: Davies, D.W. (ed.) EUROCRYPT 1991. LNCS, vol. 547, pp. 378–386. Springer, Heidelberg (1991). https://doi.org/10.1007/3-540-46416-6_32
24. Nyberg, K., Knudsen, L.R.: Provable security against differential cryptanalysis. In: Brickell, E.F. (ed.) CRYPTO 1992. LNCS, vol. 740, pp. 566–574. Springer, Heidelberg (1993). https://doi.org/10.1007/3-540-48071-4_41
25. Patarin, J.: Étude des Générateurs de Permutations Basés sur le Schéma du D.E.S. Ph.D. thesis, Université Paris 6, Paris, France, November 1991
26. Patarin, J.: On linear systems of equations with distinct variables and small block size. In: Won, D.H., Kim, S. (eds.) ICISC 2005. LNCS, vol. 3935, pp. 299–321. Springer, Heidelberg (2006). https://doi.org/10.1007/11734727_25
27. Patarin, J.: The "Coefficients H" technique. In: Avanzi, R.M., Keliher, L., Sica, F. (eds.) SAC 2008. LNCS, vol. 5381, pp. 328–345. Springer, Heidelberg (2009). https://doi.org/10.1007/978-3-642-04159-4_21
28. Patarin, J.: Introduction to Mirror Theory: Analysis of Systems of Linear Equalities and Linear Non Equalities for Cryptography. Cryptology ePrint Archive, Report 2010/287 (2010)
29. Peyrin, T., Seurin, Y.: Counter-in-tweak: authenticated encryption modes for tweakable block ciphers. In: Robshaw and Katz [31], pp. 33–63
30. Procter, G.: A Note on the CLRW2 Tweakable Block Cipher Construction. Cryptology ePrint Archive, Report 2014/111 (2014)
31. Robshaw, M., Katz, J. (eds.): CRYPTO 2016. LNCS, vol. 9814. Springer, Heidelberg (2016). https://doi.org/10.1007/978-3-662-53018-4
32. Rogaway, P.: Efficient instantiations of tweakable blockciphers and refinements to modes OCB and PMAC. In: Lee, P.J. (ed.) ASIACRYPT 2004. LNCS, vol. 3329, pp. 16–31. Springer, Heidelberg (2004). https://doi.org/10.1007/978-3-540-30539-2_2
33. Rogaway, P., Bellare, M., Black, J., Krovetz, T.: OCB: a block-cipher mode of operation for efficient authenticated encryption. In: Reiter, M.K., Samarati, P. (eds.) ACM CCS 2001, pp. 196–205. ACM (2001)
34. Wegman, M.N., Carter, L.: New hash functions and their use in authentication and set equality. J. Comput. Syst. Sci. **22**(3), 265–279 (1981)

Information-Theoretic Cryptography II and Quantum Cryptography

Continuous NMC Secure Against Permutations and Overwrites, with Applications to CCA Secure Commitments

Ivan Damgård[1], Tomasz Kazana[2], Maciej Obremski[1(✉)], Varun Raj[3], and Luisa Siniscalchi[4]

[1] Aarhus University, Aarhus, Denmark
obremski@cs.au.dk
[2] Institute of Informatics, University of Warsaw, Warsaw, Poland
[3] Oracle America Inc., Redwood City, USA
[4] University of Salerno, Fisciano, Italy
luisa.siniscalchi88@gmail.com

Abstract. Non-Malleable Codes (NMC) were introduced by Dziembowski, Pietrzak and Wichs in ICS 2010 as a relaxation of error correcting codes and error detecting codes. Faust, Mukherjee, Nielsen, and Venturi in TCC 2014 introduced an even stronger notion of non-malleable codes called continuous non-malleable codes where security is achieved against continuous tampering of a single codeword *without* re-encoding.

We construct information theoretically secure CNMC resilient to bit permutations and overwrites, this is the first Continuous NMC constructed outside of the split-state model.

In this work we also study relations between the CNMC and parallel CCA commitments. We show that the CNMC can be used to bootstrap a Self-destruct parallel CCA bit commitment to a Self-destruct parallel CCA string commitment, where Self-destruct parallel CCA is a weak form of parallel CCA security. Then we can get rid of the Self-destruct limitation obtaining a parallel CCA commitment, requiring only one-way functions.

1 Introduction

In this paper, we study the interesting relationship between the notions of non-malleable codes and non-malleable commitments, and advance state of art for both of them. Before giving our results, we introduce the notions.

I. Damgård and M. Obremski—This work was supported by MPCPRO, ERC project nr. 669255.
T. Kazana—Supported by Polish National Science Centre (NCN) SONATA GRANT UMO-2014/13/D/ST6/03252.
L. Siniscalchi—This research received funding from: COST Action IC1306; "GNCS - INdAM". The work of 5th author has been done in part while visiting Aarhus University, Denmark.

A. Beimel and S. Dziembowski (Eds.): TCC 2018, LNCS 11240, pp. 225–254, 2018.
https://doi.org/10.1007/978-3-030-03810-6_9

1.1   Introduction to Non-malleable Codes

Non-Malleable Codes (NMC) were introduced by Dziembowski, Pietrzak and Wichs [27] as a relaxation of error correcting codes and error detecting codes. An NMC takes a message m and encodes it as a possibly longer and randomized codeword $c \leftarrow \mathsf{Enc}(m)$. The adversary chooses and submits a tampering function Tamper, that is applied to the code word to yield $c' = \mathsf{Tamper}(c)$. Applying the decoding algorithm yields a message $m' = \mathsf{Dec}(c')$. The security guarantee for an NMC now is that the decoded message m' is either identical to the original message m or, in case of a decoding error, a message *unrelated* to m. Correspondingly, the adversary is given either m' or a symbol "same" indicating that decoding was successful. Technically, we require that if $m' \neq m$, then m' can be simulated using just the tampering function Tamper, but without knowing anything about the tampered codeword c'.

It is generally impossible to give any meaningful guarantees if the tampering function is unrestricted (the tamper function could decode, and then encode a modified message). Therefore, the tampering function Tamper is always assumed to come from some class $\mathbb{T}$ of functions. An immediate example application of NM codes is for tamper resilient cryptography: if a secret key is stored in a hardware device, the adversary could try to tamper with the device and observe its behavior after the modification. But if the key is encoded with an NM code, the security guarantees immediately imply that either the tampering had no effect or the effect can be simulated without the device.

Continuous Non-Malleable Codes (CNMC). As mentioned in [37], non-malleable codes can provide protection against these kind of attacks if the device is allowed to freshly re-encode its state after each invocation to make sure that the tampering is applied to a fresh codeword at each step. After each execution the entire content of the memory is erased. While such perfect erasures may be feasible in some settings, they are rather problematic in the presence of tampering. Due to this reason, Faust et al. [28] introduced an even stronger notion of non-malleable codes called continuous non-malleable codes where security is achieved against continuous tampering of a single codeword *without* re-encoding. In this model the adversary can iteratively submit tampering functions Tamper_i and learn $m_i = \mathsf{Dec}(\mathsf{Tamper}_i(c))$. We call this the *continuous tampering model*. This stronger security notion is needed in many setting, for instance when using NMCs to make tamper resilient computations on von Neumann architectures [29].

Some additional restrictions are, however, necessary in the continuous tampering model. If the adversary was given an unlimited budget of tampering queries, then, given that the class of tampering functions is sufficiently expressive (e.g. it allows to overwrite single bits of the codeword), the adversary can efficiently learn the entire message just by observing whether tampering queries leave the codeword unmodified or lead to decoding errors, see e.g. [31].

To overcome this general issue, [28] assume a *self-destruct* mechanism which is triggered by decoding errors. In particular, once the decoder outputs a special symbol $\bot$ the device *self-destructs* and the adversary loses access to his tampering oracle. This model still allows an adversary many tamper attempts, as long as his attack remains covert. Jafargholi and Wichs [37] considered four variants of continuous non-malleable codes depending on

- Whether tampering is *persistent* in the sense that the tampering is always applied to the current version of the tampered codeword, and all previous versions of the codeword are lost. The alternative definition considers non-persistent tampering where the device resets after each tampering, and the tampering always occurs on the original codeword.
- Whether tampering to an invalid codeword (i.e., when the decoder outputs $\perp$) causes a *"self-destruct"* and the experiment stops and the attacker cannot gain any additional information, or alternatively whether the attacker can always continue to tamper and gain information.

A long line of research has tried to optimize the performance of NM codes with respect to the number of allowed tampering queries and the class of allowed tampering functions (see the related work section for details). In this paper we will be concerned with the case of CNMCs where there is no a priori bound on the number of queries. This model must include a *self-destruct* mechanism. Further we will be concerned with information theoretic NM codes where security holds for an unbounded adversary, and we will look at the single state model, where the tampering function is allowed to access the entire codeword. This is in contrast to the split-state model where the tamper function must consider disjoint parts of the codeword separately.

1.2   NMC- Our Result

We give a construction of a *self-destruct, non-persistent* continuous NMC (see Corollary 1 of Theorem 1) unconditionally secure against *bit permutations* composed with *bit overwrites*.

[5] gives a *one time* Non-Malleable Code resilient against *bit permutations* composed with *bit-wise tampering*. In [22] they construct a CNMC secure against *bitwise tampering* (but permutations are not allowed).

Unconditionally secure Continuous Non-Malleable Codes are notoriously hard to construct. Very little progress was made since CNMC were proposed in 2015:

- [22] authors construct a CNMC secure against *bitwise tampering* which is the variant of split-state model.
- [14] authors achieve a so-called many-many non-malleable code in the 2-split state model. Their construction achieves non-malleability as long as the number of rounds of tampering is at most n^γ for some constant $\gamma < 1$, where n is the length of the codeword.
- [4] authors give the *persistent* continuous NMC construction for 2–split state.
- [3] gives Continuous NMC against 8–split state tampering (optimal number of states would be 3).

This makes our result the first known unconditionally secure construction of CNMC outside of split-state model.

1.3   NMC- Related Work

In [27] the authors construct an efficient code which is non-malleable with respect to bit-wise tampering, i.e., tampering functions that modify each bit of the codeword arbitrarily but independently of the value of the other bits of the codeword. Later works [2,15,17,26,42] provided stronger results by considering a model where the codeword is split into s parts called *states*, which can each be tampered arbitrarily but independently of the other states. explicit constructions were later given in [16,30]. Other works considered tampering via permutations and perturbations [6], which are not captured in the split-state model. In [7] authors show how to construct efficient, unconditionally secure non-malleable codes for bounded output locality (i.e. when every bit of tampering output can depend on at most some n^δ bits of input for $\delta < 1$).

The definition in [27] allows the adversary to be computationally unbounded. We call this an *information theoretic* NMC. Later works considered a notion of *computational* NMC where the adversary and tampering functions are restricted to efficient computations, see for instance [1,8,18,46]. The definition in [27] allows the adversary to tamper the codeword *only once*. We call this *one-shot* tampering. Faust *et al.* [28] consider a stronger model where the adversary can iteratively submit tampering functions Tamper_i and learn $m_i = \mathsf{Dec}(\mathsf{Tamper}_i(c))$. We call this the *continuous tampering model*. This stronger security notion is needed in many setting, for instance when using NMCs to make tamper resilient computations on von Neumann architectures [29]. Some additional restrictions are, however, necessary in the continuous tampering model. If the adversary was given an unlimited budget of tampering queries, then, given that the class of tampering functions is sufficiently expressive (e.g. it allows to overwrite single bits of the codeword), the adversary can efficiently learn the entire message just by observing whether tampering queries leave the codeword unmodified or lead to decoding errors, see e.g. [31].

To overcome this general issue, [28] assume a *self-destruct* mechanism which is triggered by decoding errors. In particular, once the decoder outputs a special symbol $\bot$ the device *self-destructs* and the adversary loses access to his tampering oracle. This model still allows an adversary many tamper attempts, as long as his attack remains covert. Jafargholi and Wichs [37] provide a general study of when CNMCs can be built assuming a self-destruct mechanism.

Faust et al. [28] constructed a CNMC in the 2-state model which is secure against computationally bounded adversaries. It was shown in the same work that it is *impossible* to construct an information theoretic CNMC for the 2-state model.

Information-theoretic results for CNMC. In [22] authors construct a CNMC secure against *bitwise tampering* which is the simplest variant of split-state model. In [4] authors give the first information theoretic *persistent* continuous NMC construction for 2–split state. Finally in [3] authors give the first information theoretic construction of CNMC in 8–split state. Before [3] the only known result that achieves some sort of non-malleable codes secure against *non-persistent* continuous tampering was the result by Chattopadhyay, Goyal, and

Li [14]. They achieve this by constructing a so-called many-many non-malleable code in the 2-split state model. Their construction achieves non-malleability as long as the number of rounds of tampering is at most n^γ for some constant $\gamma < 1$, where n is the length of the codeword.

1.4 Application to Commitment Schemes

Commitment Schemes. The notion of commitment is perhaps the most fundamental concept in cryptographic protocol design. The idea is that a sender binds herself to a choice of a message m by exchanging some information with a receiver. The commitment should be *hiding*, i.e., the verifier does not learn the committed message. Later, the sender can choose to open the commitment, i.e., release more information allowing the receiver to determine m. The commitment should be *binding*, i.e., the sender cannot make the receiver output a message different from the one she had in mind at commit time.

The strongest possible security notion for commitment schemes is UC security, which intuitively asks that using the scheme is equivalent to giving m to a trusted party who will only release it on request from the committer. This is much stronger than simply asking for hiding and binding, e.g., we get security under general composition. But unfortunately, we know that UC security cannot be achieved without set-up assumptions. So a long line of research has been aimed at achieving weaker but meaningful security guarantees without set-up.

An important example of this is the notion of non-malleable (NM) commitments [24]. Here we consider an adversarial Man-in-the-middle (MiM), who on side receives a commitment from an honest sender to message m (the "left session") and on the other side sends a commitment to an honest receiver (the "right session"), containing m'. The MiM wins if he succeeds in forming a new commitment on the right such that m' has some non-trivial relation to m. The NM property does not follow from hiding and binding and is very important, for instance in making auctions where committed bid is fair, or towards implementing secure coin-flipping. Technically the NM property is captured by requiring a simulator that will simulate the left session without knowing m and still the MiM wins with essentially the same probability.

The strongest form of NM commitment security is concurrent NM commitments. Here, the MiM is allowed to start any number of left sessions and right sessions and can schedule them as he likes. One can also consider restricted versions of this, for instance a 1–1 NM commitment is secure if only 1 left and 1 right session is allowed. A restriction that we want to consider is self-destruct (SD) concurrent non-malleable commitment. In this version, once the MiM makes an invalid commitment in a right session, all commitment computed after that session are considered invalid and cannot be used to win the game. This notion is close in spirit to the one of the weak non-malleable commitments, which has been applied in multiple works.

An even stronger notion of commitment security is CCA security ([12]): we consider again a MiM, but he is now given an oracle that he can query on input a commitment from (one of) the right session(s), as long as it is not a copy of something from a left session. The requirement is that hiding holds for the left session(s), even in presence of the oracle. Intuitively, a CCA secure commitment is also NM secure, all other things being equal: if the MiM could break NM security and come up with a new commitment on the right side that is related to one from the left, he could submit it to the oracle in the CCA game and use the reply to break hiding on the left side. One restriction on CCA commitments that has been considered is parallel CCA security, where the MiM can ask only one query that may, however, contain an unbounded number of commitments. Another restriction is that of self-destruct (SD)-CCA, where the oracle stops working if the MiM submits an invalid commitment.

Parallel CCA Commitments from CNMC. In this second part we investigate possible applications our CNMC. In particular, we will show a bridge between (unconditionally secure) CNMC and (computational) cryptographic primitives secure in the concurrent setting.

For the stand-alone setting the result of [5] shows how to use a bit parallel CCA commitment[1] to construct a *1-1* string non-malleable commitment relying on stand-alone NM code. In particular, constructing string commitment from the corresponding 1-bit primitive, they first encode the input message with an NM code and then apply a 1-bit commitment scheme.

Following the same approach of [5] but using a CNMC (resilient to the same class of tampering functions of [5]) we are asking which flavor of non-malleability w.r.t. commitment we can achieve. In particular, is it enough to plug-in our CNMC in the construction of [5] to obtain a concurrent NM string commitment? The answer is only partially yes, due to the self-destruct limitation of CNMC. Indeed, a MiM adversary of NM commitments can compute multiple invalid commitments. Then, we show how to bypass this limitations requiring only OWFs.

In more details, we obtain a compiler that takes a CCA bit commitment and constructs an SD concurrent NM commitment. Due to the adaptiveness of our NM code we actually achieve a stronger security notion, namely a string SD-CCA commitment scheme. Furthermore we can relax the requirements on the CCA bit commitment: it just needs to be SD-CCA-secure instead of CCA-secure.

Summarizing, we show a compiler that on input a (non-tag based) SD-CCA bit commitment scheme and a continuous non-malleable code resilient against permutations and bit overwrites, outputs a (non-tag based) SD-CCA string commitment scheme. Our construction, like the one of [5], preserves the round complexity of the bit commitment scheme and does not require any additional

---

[1] Note that a particular accent is placed on the fact that the compiler requires as input a possible (non-tag based) n-parallel bounding CCA bit commitment because. The reduction is non-trivial only because they are working in the standard non-tag based setting. Otherwise, in case of tags, one can simply sign the entire transcript using the tags and obtain a non-malleable string commitment. In case of bit commitments, tag-based non-malleability is a stronger requirement than the standard (non-tag-based) non-malleability. Pass and Rosen [47] argue that for string commitments, the two notions are equivalent since one can simply commit the tag as part of the string, if there are no tags. Since we only have bit commitments, this does not work.

assumption. Finally, we show that a SD-parallel CCA string commitment scheme can be upgraded to a parallel string commitment scheme without self-destruct, assuming only one-way functions. The construction is non-trivial (it requires very recent developed tecniques) and adds only two rounds of interaction.

Together with our compiler described above, this implies the first construction that exploit the CNMC property to obtain a parallel CCA commitment. Furthermore, parallel CCA commitment founds multiple applications like [10,41]. Observe that parallel CCA commitment is not implied by parallel NM commitment (see [11]).

Previous Work on NMCs and NM Commitments. The literature presents works that exploit the properties of the non-malleable code to construct non-malleable commitments. Goyal et al. [35] use non-malleable codes in the split-state model to realize a 3-round one-one non-malleable commitment relying on one way permutations secure against a quasi-polynomial time adversary. Chandran et al. [13] show that block non-malleable codes with t blocks imply non-malleable commitments of $t - 1$ rounds. As we discuss above, Agrawal et al. [5] showed that is possible to construct a one-one non-malleable commitment relying on a non-malleable code and a bounded parallel CCA bit commitment. However, no one before uses non-malleable codes to construct a parallel CCA commitment scheme. The aim of this second part is to build bridges between different notions of non-malleability, and to not construct a new NM commitment or a CCA commitment that are already available in literature. Indeed, there is a long line of research that tries to reduce the round complexity of NM commitment (e.g. [9,19,20,24,32,33,35,36,38,39,43,45,47–49]). Several constructions of CCA commitment are also available in literature (e.g. [12,34,40,44]).

1.5   Technical Overview of Our CNMC Secure Against Permutations-and-Overwrites

Construction of Continuous Non-Malleable Code. Our code consists of an amalgamation of two different layers of encoding schemes.

The top layer is a Reed-Solomon code used here as a sharing scheme. We take a message m, append a random suffix and then encode it using Reed-Solomon to receive a codeword consisting of N blocks that may be seen as shares of $\lfloor \frac{N}{3} \rfloor$-out-of-$N$ secret sharing scheme. The intuition behind this scheme is that the adversary needs to learn at least $\frac{N}{3}$ shares to learn anything about the initial message.

The bottom layer is using a Two-Split State Super Strong Non-Malleable Code (instantiated either by [4] or [42]). Each share s_i from the above secret sharing scheme is converted into $(s_i \| i)$ and then encoded using the two-split state code to get two shares (L_i, R_i) (We also expect the bit-parity of L_i to be 0 and the bit-parity of R_i to be 1). The final code is $(L_1, R_1, ..., R_N, L_N)$.

To prove that the just described code is actually continuous non-malleable code, we first redefine the experiment in the definition of continuous codes. The new definition is obviously stronger, so it is sufficient to work with it. In the new definition, whenever an adversary tampers with a block (L_i, R_i) with non-constant functions and succeeds in creating valid (from the point of view of Super Strong NMC decoder) output blocks (L'_i, R'_i) (In particular, the parities of all (L'_i, R'_i) must be correct), we will reveal blocks (L_i, R_i) to the adversary.

As observed earlier, the adversary's necessary task is to learn at least $\lfloor \frac{N}{3} \rfloor$ blocks of the underlying s_i shares.

Since the adversary can only tamper bitwise and permute bits we can prove that if the adversary doesn't *know* $\frac{N}{3}$ blocks and he tries to modify the codeword he will either get detected with probability exponentially close to 1, or he can attempt to learn some small amount information about the codeword (i.e. tamper with few blocks L_i, R_i with non-constant function). However, using the bottom layer, we show that every attempt to learn even the smallest information about the codeword (i.e. by overwriting all but only few bits) yields some probability of detection which amplifies with amount of information adversary is trying to learn. We will therefore show that adversary can not (i.e. the probability is negligable) breach $\lfloor \frac{N}{3} \rfloor$ blocks threshold.

The argument consists of two main technical observations:

- If the adversary applies any non-constant functions f, g to single block L_i, R_i then, due to combination of super strong nmc properties and parity requirements we have placed on L_i, R_i, adversary risks close to $\frac{1}{2}$ detection probability.
- If the adversary decides to mix bits between different blocks (L_i, R_i) he has to risk violation of parity requirements on these blocks. This lemma is inspired by similar lemma for unary schemes from [6].

Using these ideas we can claim that if adversary tampers with k blocks using non-constant functions he also gets detected with a probability $1 - p^{-k}$. The proof of this fact is more involved because we have to deal with minute cases. For example if we prove that mixing of bits will make the parity unpredictable for each block it still may happen that the events of error are correlated so not obviously amplify the error rate. *Example 1.* Assume adversary tampers only with L_1 and L_2, if he permutes bits in a way that output L'_1 contains first halfs of vectors L_1, L_2, L'_2 contains second halfs of L_1, L_2. Then parity of L'_1 is correct if and only if parity of L'_2 is correct. We handle this by picking only largest possible subset of independent parity checks. In this case we would focus only on parity of L'_1 and discard any other checks generated by L_1, L_2, R_1, R_2.

Example 2. Consider a tampering function which takes one bit from some blocks (L_i, R_i) and permutes them to the last block (L'_N, R'_N) while fixing all other (L_i, R_i) to some constants. If (L'_N, R'_N) has a correct parity and valid Super-Strong NMC decoding then we will reveal, to adversary, all blocks that 'donated' bits to (L'_N, R'_N). Notice however that this will not reveal more bits then $|L_N| + |R_N|$ blocks.

Above examples illustrate how we bound number of blocks adversary can learn for each independent validity check he has to create.

1.6 Technical Overview of Our Self-destruct CCA Commitment and Parallel CCA Commitment

The Self-destruct CCA commitment scheme. We want to show that given a Self-destruct CCA bit commitment scheme (non-tag based), committing to each bit of the codeword individually, results in a Self-destruct CCA string commitment scheme. The security proof is based on the following high-level idea: if the adversary of the Self-destruct CCA string commitment is mauling, then, the attack on the commitment level can be "translated" into an attack on the non-malleable code. In other word, we can show an adversary $\mathcal{A}_{\mathsf{NMCode}}$ that breaks the security of the non-malleable code using the adversary $\mathcal{A}$ on the commitment level that distinguish a commitment of message m_0 from a commitment of message m_1. $\mathcal{A}_{\mathsf{NMCode}}$ will act as the sender in the left session with $\mathcal{A}$. Instead in the k-th right session (for $k = 1, \ldots, \mathtt{poly}(\lambda)$) $\mathcal{A}_{\mathsf{NMCode}}$ will act as a receiver of the string commitment. Then he needs to emulate the oracle $\mathcal{O}$ of the string commitment computing the following steps: (1) define a tamper function f_k based on value v committed in the right session (note that he can obtain v querying the oracle of the bit commitment $\mathcal{O}^{\mathsf{bit}2}$) (2) send back to $\mathcal{A}$ the decoding of $f_k(\mathsf{enc}_{m_b})$, where enc_{m_b} is an encoding of m_b (received from the challenger of the non-malleable code game). At the end, $\mathcal{A}_{\mathsf{NMCode}}$ will output what $\mathcal{A}$ outputs. However we notice that the adversary that we described is not yet an adversary against the non-malleable code since the tamper functions can be dependent on what is committed on the left. We can demonstrate that the hiding of the Self-destruct CCA bit commitment ensures that the distribution of the tamper functions is computational independent from the message committed by the sender. Therefore the final adversary against the non-malleable code will simply commits to a random message on the left session. Finally, we crucially need that the non-malleable code is information theoretic secure since we have no guarantee that $\mathcal{O}^{\mathsf{bit}}$ works in polynomial time.

Upgrade SD-PCCA Commitment Scheme to PCCA Commitment Scheme. At a very high level our PCCA string commitment scheme works as follows. The sender interacts with the receiver in order to compute a commitment τ of m using a Self-destruct PCCA string commitment. Furthermore, the receiver engages with the sender a protocol to allow the extraction of a trapdoor. We use the "trapdoor protocol" described in [20] where the trapdoor is represented by the knowledge of two signatures under a verification key sent by receiver in the 4th last round. In order to allow the extraction of the trapdoor, the receiver sends a signature of a randomly chosen message in the 3rd last round by the sender. Then, the sender executes a special witness-indistinguishable proof of knowledge (WIPoK) with the receiver in order to prove that he computed a valid commitment of m or that he knows a trapdoor.

Observe that if we use a 3-round WIPoK it is not clear how the proof of security will proceed. In particular, in the security proof there are some hybrids were we simulate the oracle of the parallel CCA commitment in polynomial time

---

[2] The definition of the tamper function is more complicated, see Sect. 4 for the details.

extracting the committed messages from the WIPoKs. Let us consider the hybrid were we switch the witness in one of the WIPoK. In the reduction to the WI we have to emulate the oracle of the parallel CCA commitments, since the reduction has to work in polynomial time. As we said, our hope to emulate the oracle is to extract the committed messages from the WIPoKs, however the extraction procedure rewinds also the challenger of the WI.

To overcome this problem we adopt the approach proposed in [20] relying on non-interactive primitives instead of 3-rounds WIPoK.

Therefore, similarly to [20], we construct this WIPoK relying on: instance-dependent trapdoor commitments (IDTC) and special honest-verifier zero knowledge (SHVZK).

In more details, let $(\mathsf{ls}^1_{\mathsf{trap}}, \mathsf{ls}^2_{\mathsf{trap}}, \mathsf{ls}^3_{\mathsf{trap}}, \mathsf{ls}^4_{\mathsf{trap}})$ be the transcript of a 4-round special HVZK delayed-input[3] proof of knowledge (PoK). The transcript $(\mathsf{ls}^1_{\mathsf{trap}}, \mathsf{ls}^2_{\mathsf{trap}}, \mathsf{ls}^3_{\mathsf{trap}}, \mathsf{ls}^4_{\mathsf{trap}})$ is used to prove knowledge of two signatures of two different message w.r.t. a verification key sent by the receiver. The transcript $(\mathsf{ls}^1_{\mathsf{trap}}, \mathsf{ls}^2_{\mathsf{trap}}, \mathsf{ls}^3_{\mathsf{trap}}, \mathsf{ls}^4_{\mathsf{trap}})$ is used to prove the knowledge of the trapdoor.

At the 4th last round the sender sends an equivocal com obtained running IDTC. At last round the sender will equivocate com in order to send as opening $(\mathsf{dec}, \mathsf{ls}^2_{\mathsf{trap}})$. In the last round also $\mathsf{ls}^4_{\mathsf{trap}}$ is sent. The instance used for the IDTC is τ, this means that the commitment com (computed using IDTC) can be opened to any value because τ is a well-formed commitment.

In the opening phase the sender sends the opening of the Self-destruct PCCA string commitment.

Note that the first two rounds of the "trapdoor protocol" can be run with the last two rounds of the Self-destruct commitment. Therefore the described construction has $t+2$ rounds (where t is the number of rounds of the Self-destruct PCCA string commitment).

Overview of the Security Proof. In the 1st experiment (the real game RG_0) the sender commits to m_0. We observe that due to the security of the signature scheme we can demonstrate that in the real game $\mathcal{A}$ is committing to a well-formed commitments in all parallel right sessions with non-negligible probability. Symmetrically there is the experiment RG_1 where the sender commits to m_1 and $\mathcal{A}$ is committing to a well-formed commitment in all parallel right sessions. Then we consider a hybrid game $\mathcal{H}^0_b$, for $b \in \{0,1\}$, where the sender commits to m_b and the oracle is emulated extracting the committed values from the special WIPoK. Note that $\mathcal{H}^0_b$ is distributed statistically close to RG_b until $\mathcal{A}$ receives the committed values, therefore we are ensured that we can extract the values committed in the right sessions. The 2nd hybrid game that we consider is $\mathcal{H}^1_b$ in which we switch the witness used to compute the transcript of the special WIPoK in the left sessions (i.e. we are using the trapdoor that is extracted by rewinding $\mathcal{A}$ in the left session). Using techniques that are similar to the one showed in [20] we are able to demonstrate that also in $\mathcal{H}^1_b$ we can extract the committed values in all parallel right sessions with non-negligible probability.

---

[3] By *delayed-input* we mean that the witness and the instance are needed only to play the last round.

Moreover, we can demonstrate that the distribution of the commitment values along with the view of $\mathcal{A}$ is indistinguishable between $\mathcal{H}_b^0$ and $\mathcal{H}_b^1$, for $b \in \{0,1\}$. Indeed, both in $\mathcal{H}_0^1$ and in $\mathcal{H}_1^1$ we are guaranteed that $\mathcal{A}$ is committing to a well-formed commitment in all parallel right sessions with non-negligible probability. Summing up, a detectable deviation from $\mathcal{H}_0^1$ and $\mathcal{H}_1^1$ implies a contradiction of the Self-destruct PCCA security of the underlining commitment. Finally we observe that the extraction procedure of the signatures does not interfere with the reductions since in the parallel right sessions the commitment phase made by $\mathcal{A}$ ends in the third last round. This observation concludes the high-level overview of the security proof.

2   Preliminaries

We denote the security parameter by λ and use "$||$" as concatenation operator (i.e., if a and b are two strings then by $a||b$ we denote the concatenation of a and b). We use the abbreviation PPT that stands for probabilistic polynomial time. We use $\texttt{poly}(\cdot)$ to indicate a generic polynomial function and $\mathbb{N}$ to denote the set of positive integer.

A *polynomial-time relation* Rel (or *polynomial relation*, in short) is a subset of $\{0,1\}^* \times \{0,1\}^*$ such that membership of (x,w) in Rel can be decided in time polynomial in $|x|$. For $(x,w) \in$ Rel, we call x the *instance* and w a *witness* for x. For a polynomial-time relation Rel, we define the $\mathcal{NP}$-language L_{Rel} as $L_{\mathsf{Rel}} = \{x | \exists w : (x,w) \in \mathsf{Rel}\}$. Analogously, unless otherwise specified, for an $\mathcal{NP}$-language L we denote by Rel_L the corresponding polynomial-time relation (that is, Rel_L is such that $L = L_{\mathsf{Rel}_L}$). We denote by $\hat{L}$ the language that includes both L and all well formed instances that do not have a witness. Moreover we require that membership in $\hat{L}$ can be tested in polynomial time. We implicitly assume that a PPT algorithm that is supposed to receive an instance in $\hat{L}$ will abort immediately if the instance does not belong to $\hat{L}$. Let A and B be two interactive probabilistic algorithms. We denote by $\langle A(\alpha), B(\beta) \rangle(\gamma)$ the distribution of B's output after running on private input β with A using private input α, both running on common input γ. Typically, one of the two algorithms receives 1^λ as input. A *transcript* of $\langle A(\alpha), B(\beta) \rangle(\gamma)$ consists of the messages exchanged during an execution where A receives a private input α, B receives a private input β and both A and B receive a common input γ. Moreover, we will refer to the *view* of A (resp. B) as the messages it received during the execution of $\langle A(\alpha), B(\beta) \rangle(\gamma)$, along with its randomness and its input. We say that a protocol (A, B) is public coin if B sends to A random bits only.

If $\mathcal{Z}$ is a set then $Z \leftarrow \mathcal{Z}$ will denote a random variable sampled uniformly from $\mathcal{Z}$. We start with some standard definitions and lemmas about the statistical distance. Recall that if X and X' are random variables over the same set $\mathcal{X}$ then the *statistical distance between X and X'* is denoted by $\Delta(X; X')$, and defined as $\Delta(X; X') = \frac{1}{2} \sum_{x \in \mathcal{X}} | \Pr X = x - \Pr X' = x |$. If the variables X and X' are such that $\Delta(X; X') \leq \epsilon$ then we say that X is ϵ-close to X', and write $X \approx_\epsilon X'$. If $\mathcal{E}, \mathcal{E}'$ are some events then by $\Delta(X|\mathcal{E} \ ; \ X'|\mathcal{E}')$ we will denote the distance between variables $\tilde{X}$ and $\tilde{X}'$, distributed according to the conditional distributions $P_{X|\mathcal{E}}$ and $P_{X'|\mathcal{E}'}$.

If $U_{\mathcal{X}}$ is the uniform distribution over $\mathcal{X}$ then $d(X|\mathcal{E}) := \Delta(X|\mathcal{E}; U_{\mathcal{X}})$ is called *statistical distance of X from uniform given the event $\mathcal{E}$.* Moreover, if Y is independent from X then $d(X|Y) := \Delta((X,Y); (U_{\mathcal{X}}, Y))$ is called *statistical distance of X from uniform given the variable Y.* More generally, if $\mathcal{E}$ is an event then $d(X|Y, \mathcal{E}) := \Delta((X,Y)|\mathcal{E}; (U_{\mathcal{X}}, Y)|\mathcal{E})$. It is easy to see that $d(X|Y)$ is equal to the average $\sum_y \Pr(Y = y) \cdot d(X|Y = y) = \mathbb{E}_y(d(X|Y = y))$.

Definition 1 ((Average-) Min-Entropy). *Let X have finite support $\mathcal{X}$. The min-entropy $\mathbf{H}_\infty(X)$ of X is defined by*

$$\mathbf{H}_\infty(X) = -\log \max_{x \in \mathcal{X}} \Pr(X = x).$$

For an event $\mathcal{E}$, the conditional min-entropy $\mathbf{H}_\infty(X|\mathcal{E})$ of X given $\mathcal{E}$ is defined by

$$\mathbf{H}_\infty(X|\mathcal{E}) = -\log \max_{x \in \mathcal{X}} \Pr(X = x|\mathcal{E}).$$

For an event $\mathcal{E}$ and a random variable Y with finite support $\mathcal{Y}$, the average min-entropy $\tilde{\mathbf{H}}_\infty(X|Y, \mathcal{E})$ of X given Y and $\mathcal{E}$ is defined by

$$\tilde{\mathbf{H}}_\infty(X|Y, \mathcal{E}) = -\log \mathbb{E}_y \max_{x \in \mathcal{X}} \Pr(X = x|Y = y, \mathcal{E}).$$

Randomness extractors will be the workhorses of our non-malleable code constructions.

Definition 2 (Flexible Two-Source Extractors). *A function $\mathsf{Ext} : \mathcal{X}_1 \times \mathcal{X}_2 \to \mathcal{Z}$ is called a flexible (ϵ, δ)-two-source extractor, if it holds for all tuples $((X_1, Y_1), (X_2.Y_2))$ for which (X_1, Y_1) is independent of (X_2, Y_2) and $\tilde{\mathbf{H}}_\infty(X_1|Y_1) + \tilde{\mathbf{H}}_\infty(X_2|Y_2) \geq \log(|\mathcal{X}|) + \log(|\mathcal{Y}|) - \delta$ that*

$$d(\mathsf{Ext}(X_1, X_2)|Y_1, Y_2) \leq \epsilon.$$

A well known example of a flexible two-source extractor is the Hadamard extractor or inner-product-extractor.

Lemma 1 (Hadamard Extractor [2]). *The function $\mathsf{Ext} : \mathbb{F}_q^n \times \mathbb{F}_q^n \to \mathbb{F}_q$ given by $\mathsf{Ext}(x, y) = \langle x, y \rangle$ is a flexible (ϵ, δ) extractor for $\delta \leq (n-1)\log(q) - 2\log(1/\epsilon)$.*

Lemma 2 (Entropy-preservation of inner-product for correlated distributions). *Let X be random variable over $\mathcal{X}^l$, let C be random variable such that for every c we have $\mathbf{H}_\infty(X|C = c) \geq l \cdot \log|\mathcal{X}| - d$, where $d < \log|\mathcal{X}|$. Then for any non-zero $v \in \mathcal{X}^l$*

$$\mathbf{H}_\infty(\langle X, v \rangle_{\mathcal{X}} \mid C = c) \geq \log|\mathcal{X}| - d$$

for every c in $\mathsf{supp}(C)$.

We will now assemble a few basic technical lemmata that we will need for our proofs.

Lemma 3 (Bayes' rule for statistical distance [26]). *Let* $(X, Y) \in \mathcal{X} \times \mathcal{Y}$ *be a random variables, such that* $d(X|Y) \leq \epsilon$. *Then for every* $x \in \mathcal{X}$ *we have*

$$\Delta(Y|X = x \; ; \; Y) \leq 2|\mathcal{X}|\epsilon.$$

Also if $\mathcal{A}$ *is a random event such that* $d(X|Y, \mathcal{A}) \leq \epsilon$, *we have:*

$$\Delta(Y|X = x, \mathcal{A} \; ; \; Y|\mathcal{A}) \leq 2|\mathcal{X}|\epsilon.$$

Lemma 4 ([25]). *Let* X, T *be any arbitrarily correlated random variables and let* $\mathcal{E}$ *be random event then*

$$\widetilde{\mathbf{H}}_\infty(X|T, \mathcal{E}) \geq \widetilde{\mathbf{H}}_\infty(X|T) - \log \frac{1}{\Pr(\mathcal{E})}.$$

In the Appendix A the reader can find a series of standard definitions used in the rest of the paper.

2.1 Definitions Related to Non-Malleable Codes

Definition 3 (Coding Schemes). *A coding scheme is a pair* (Enc, Dec), *where* Enc : $\mathcal{M} \to \mathcal{C}$ *is a randomized function and* Dec $\cdot \mathcal{C} \to \mathcal{M} \cup \{\bot\}$ *is a deterministic function, such that it holds for all* $M \in \mathcal{M}$ *that* Dec(Enc(M)) = M.

Definition 4 (Two-State Code). *A coding scheme* (Enc, Dec) *where the counterdomain of* Enc *has the form* $\mathcal{C} = \{0, 1\}^k \times \{0, 1\}^k$ *is called a* two-state *code.*

Definition 5 (Paritied Two-State Code). *Let* (Enc, Dec) *(where* Enc : $\mathcal{M} \to \mathcal{C} = \mathcal{C}_1 \times \mathcal{C}_2 = \{0, 1\}^k \times \{0, 1\}^k$*) be a two-state code. Now let* Enc^{par} : $\mathcal{M} \to \mathcal{C}$ *be a randomized function restricted to a condition that* $parity(\text{Enc}(m)_1) = 0$ *and* $parity(\text{Enc}(m)_2) = 1$, *where parity is a function calculating the parity of number of ones in a given vector (i.e.* $parity(0101011) = 0$ *and* $parity(011111) = 1$*).*

More formally, the procedure computing Enc$^{par}(m)$ *can be described as follows: we run in a loop the encoding procudure* $(c_1, c_2) \leftarrow$ Enc(m) *until* $parity(c_1) = 0$ *and* $parity(c_2) = 1$.

Similarily, let Dec^{par} : $\mathcal{C} \to \mathcal{M} \cup \{\bot\}$ *be defined as follows: for* $c = (c_1, c_2) \in \mathcal{C}$, *if* $parity(c_1) \neq 0$ *or* $parity(c_2) \neq 1$ *then* Dec$^{par}(c) := \bot$, *otherwise* Dec$^{par}(c) :=$ Dec(c).

Now, the coding scheme (Enc^{par}, Dec^{par}) *is called a* paritied *two-state code.*

We will now define the continuous tampering experiment. Our definition is a weaker version of [37]: instead of Super Strong Tampering experiment we will use the standard tamper experiment from [27].

Definition 6 ((Continuous-) Tampering Experiment). *We will define continuous non-persistent self-destruct non-malleable codes using [4] experiment, which is equivalent to original [27] experiment. Fix a coding scheme* (Enc, Dec) *with message space $\mathcal{M}$ and codeword space $\mathcal{C}$. Also fix a family of functions $\mathcal{F} : \mathcal{C} \to \mathcal{C}$. Let $\mathcal{D} = \{\mathcal{D}_C^f\}_{f \in \mathcal{F}, C \in \mathcal{C}}$ be some family of distributions over $\{0, 1\}$, indexed by tampering function f and a codeword C. We will first define the tampering oracle* $\mathsf{Tamper}_{C,\mathcal{D}}^{\mathsf{state}}(f)$, *for which initially* state = alive. *For a tampering function $f \in \mathcal{F}$ and a codeword $C \in \mathcal{C}$ define the tampering oracle by*

$\mathsf{Tamper}_{C,\mathcal{D}}^{\mathsf{state}}(f)$:
    If state = dead *output* $\perp$
    $C' \leftarrow f(C)$
    If $\mathsf{Dec}(C') = \mathsf{Dec}(C)$ *and* $\mathcal{D}_C^f = 0$ *output* same
    $M' \leftarrow \mathsf{Dec}(C')$
    If $M' = \perp$ *set* state $\leftarrow$ dead *and output* $\perp$
    Otherwise output C'

Fix a tampering adversary $\mathcal{A}$ and a codeword $C \in \mathcal{C}$. We define the continuous tampering experiment $\mathsf{CT}_{C,\mathcal{D}}(\mathcal{A})$ *by*

$\mathsf{CT}_{C,\mathcal{D}}(\mathcal{A})$:
    state $\leftarrow$ alive
    $v \leftarrow \mathcal{A}^{\mathsf{Tamper}_{C,\mathcal{D}}^{\mathsf{state}}(\cdot)}$
    Output v

Definition 7. *Let* (Enc, Dec) *be a coding scheme and* CT *be its corresponding continuous tampering experiment for a class $\mathcal{F}$ of tampering functions. We say that* (Enc, Dec) *is an ϵ-secure continuously non-malleable code against $\mathcal{F}$, if there exists a family of distributions $\mathcal{D} = \{\mathcal{D}_C^f\}_{f \in \mathcal{F}, C \in \mathcal{C}}$ over $\{0, 1\}$ such that for all tampering adversaries $\mathcal{A}$ and all pairs of messages $M_0, M_1 \in \mathcal{M}$ that*

$$\mathsf{CT}_{C_0,\mathcal{D}}(\mathcal{A}) \approx_\epsilon \mathsf{CT}_{C_1,\mathcal{D}}(\mathcal{A}),$$

where $C_0 \leftarrow \mathsf{Enc}(M_0)$ and $C_1 \leftarrow \mathsf{Enc}(M_1)$.

3   Continuous Non-Malleable Code Against Permutations-With-Overwrites

In this section we define a coding scheme $(\mathsf{Enc}_c, \mathsf{Dec}_c)$ and prove it is a continuous non-malleable code against a class PermOver of permutations-with-overwrites (the actual definition will follow).

3.1   Coding Scheme

Let $\mathcal{M} = \{0, 1\}^n$ and $\mathcal{C} = \mathcal{C}_1 \times \cdots \times \mathcal{C}_N$, where each $\mathcal{C}_i = \{0, 1\}^{k_1} \times \{0, 1\}^{k_1}$. Let also $(\mathsf{Enc}_2, \mathsf{Dec}_2)$ denote a two-state code (actually we need a two-state strong non-malleable code here, however the specific instantiation will be given later) and h_N denote a $\lfloor N/3 \rfloor$-out-of-N secret sharing scheme (again, the specific instantiation will be given later). Now we are ready to introduce the (randomized) function (procedure) $\mathsf{Enc}_c : \mathcal{M} \to \mathcal{C}$:

For $m \in \mathcal{M}$ and a random $r \in \{0,1\}^n$, let $(d_1, \ldots, d_N) \leftarrow h_N(m\|r)$ where $(d_1, \ldots, d_N) \in (\{0,1\}^{k_2})^N$ are shares for $(m\|r)$. Now, for each d_i let $(L_i, R_i) \leftarrow \mathsf{Enc}_2^{par}(d_i\|i)$.

Finally, we state $c_i \leftarrow (L_i, R_i)$ and $\mathsf{Enc}_s(m)$ outputs $(c_1, \ldots, c_N)$.

The definition of Dec_c is simple and straightforward (forced by the definition of a coding scheme).

Remark 1. The above construction is not tight for a given message length n since it also depends on the choice of parameters (N, k_1, k_2) and the specific definitions of both: the two-state code $(\mathsf{Enc}_2, \mathsf{Dec}_2)$ and the secret sharing scheme h_N. However, before we pick adequate parameters and schemes, we need one definition more:

Definition 8. *We call a two-split code $(\mathsf{Enc}_2, \mathsf{Dec}_2)$ ϵ-admissible if the scheme $(\mathsf{Enc}_2^{par}, \mathsf{Dec}_2^{par})$ fulfills the following requirements:*

1. *[Canonical encoding procedure:] $\mathsf{Enc}_2^{par}(m)$ is uniform in $\{c : \mathsf{Dec}_2^{par}(c) = m\}$.*
2. *[Detection of close to bijective tampering:] For any message m, if $\mathsf{Enc}_2^{par}(m) = (X, Y)$ then for any functions $f, g : \{0,1\}^{k_1} \to \{0,1\}^{k_1}$ such that $\mathbf{H}_\infty(f(X)), \mathbf{H}_\infty(g(Y)) \geq 2/3 \cdot k_1 - 1$ and (for any x or y) $f(x) \neq x$ or $g(y) \neq y$ it holds:*

$$\Pr(\mathsf{Dec}_2^{par}(f(X), g(Y)) = \bot) \geq 1 - \epsilon.$$

3. *[Detection of complete overwrite of one part:] For any constant $c \in \{0,1\}^{k_1}$, and any uniform $X, Y \in \{0,1\}^{k_1}$, such that parity of X is 0 and parity of Y is 1 we get,*

$$\Pr(\mathsf{Dec}_2(X, c) = \bot) \geq 1 - \epsilon,$$
$$\Pr(\mathsf{Dec}_2(c, Y) = \bot) \geq 1 - \epsilon$$

4. *[Leakage resilient storage:] For any message m, if $\mathsf{Enc}_2^{par}(m) = (X, Y)$ then for any functions $f, g : \{0,1\}^{k_1} \to \{0,1\}^{k_1}$ such that $\widetilde{\mathbf{H}}_\infty(X|f(X)) \geq 1/3 \cdot k_1$ and $\widetilde{\mathbf{H}}_\infty(Y|f(Y)) \geq 1/3 \cdot k_1$ we get*

$$\Delta\left[(f(X), Y) ; (f(U_0), U_1)\right] \leq \epsilon ,$$
$$\Delta\left[(X, g(Y)) ; (U_0, g(U_1))\right] \leq \epsilon ,$$

where U_0, U_1 are independent uniformly distributed over $\{0,1\}^{k_1}$, such that parity of U_i is equal i.

In the full version of the paper [23], we discuss possible instantiations (for an appropriate ϵ_c) of Definition 8:

with [4]: $\mathsf{Enc}_{\mathsf{AKO}} : \{0,1\}^m \to \left(\{0,1\}^{O(m^6)}\right)^2$ is $2^{-O(m)}-$ admissible,

with [42]:$\mathsf{Enc}_{\mathsf{Li}} : \{0,1\}^m \to \left(\{0,1\}^{O(m \cdot \log m)}\right)^2$ is $2^{-O(m)}-$ admissible.

(Of course the second code of the above gives better parameters. However we argue for both above statements.)

Through the rest of the paper we always refer to the second of the above specific two-state code and the specific error probability when notation $(\mathsf{Enc}_2, \mathsf{Dec}_2)$ and ϵ_c is used.

3.2   Definition of the Class of Tampering Functions

Here we define the class $\mathsf{PermOver}$ of tampering functions. Through this paper functions from this class $\mathsf{PermOver}$ are called permutations-with-overwrites.

Let us consider a set $\{0,1\}^q$ of vectors of q bits (q-vectors, for short). Now, let denote Π_q the class of permutations of bits of q-vectors. Denote also O_q the class of functions $f : \{0,1\}^q \to \{0,1\}^q$, such that:

for all i, either $f(x)_i = x_i$ or $f(x)_i = b_i$ for a fixed b_i.

Loosely speaking: any function from O_q, independently for each bit, either leaves it unchanged or sets it into a fixed value (i.e. overwrites it).

Now we simply define the class $\mathsf{PermOver}_q = O_q \circ \Pi_q$. For our application we will equate $\mathcal{C} = (\{0,1\}^{k_1} \times \{0,1\}^{k_1})^N$ with $\{0,1\}^{2k_1 N}$ and consider $\mathsf{PermOver} = \mathsf{PermOver}_{2k_1 N}$ as a tampering class for $\mathcal{C}$.

The above description of course finishes the definition of our class of tampering functions, however we want a few further related definitions.

Related definitions. Let us fix a tampering function $t \in \mathsf{PermOver}$. As mentioned above we will think of t as a function from $\mathcal{C}_1 \times \cdots \times \mathcal{C}_N$ to $\mathcal{C}_1 \times \cdots \times \mathcal{C}_N$. Now, for each $i \in \{1, \ldots, N\}$ we say that t either *leaves* or *overwrites* or *modifies* the i-th *block*. These phrases stand for the following:

If $t(c)_i = c_i$ then t leaves the i-th block. If $t(c)_i = a$ for some a independent of c then t overwrites the i-th block. Finally, if none of the previous occurs, then we say that t modifies the i-th block.

If t overwrites i-th block, two cases are possible. Either c_i is independent of $f(c)$ or some bits of c_i are moved to some modified blocks. In the first case we say that t strong-overwrites i-th block and in the second case, it weak-overwrites.

Touched blocks are blocks either modified or weak-overwritten. In that case we say that t *touches* these blocks.

For a function $t \in \mathsf{PermOver}$ and a codeword $c \in \mathcal{C}$ we denote $touch(t, c)$ the set of all touched blocks and its indices, more formally: $touch(t, c) = \{(c_i, i) | t \text{ touches } c_i\}$.

Example. The above definitions may look a little bit obscure at first sight, so – to make things clearer – we give an example.

Let $N = 4$ and each $\mathcal{C}_i = \{0,1\}^6$. Now let us consider:

$$t\left((b_1^1, b_2^1, b_3^1, b_4^1, b_5^1, b_6^1), (b_1^2, b_2^2, b_3^2, b_4^2, b_5^2, b_6^2), (b_1^3, b_2^3, b_3^3, b_4^3, b_5^3, b_6^3), (b_1^4, b_2^4, b_3^4, b_4^4, b_5^4, b_6^4)\right) =$$

$$\left((0,0,0,1,1,1), (b_1^2, b_2^2, b_3^2, b_4^2, b_5^2, b_6^2), (0,1,0,1,0,1), (0, b_5^1, b_4^4, 1, b_2^4, b_1^1)\right).$$

Obviously $t \in$ PermOver and we have that: t leaves the second block, overwrites the first and the 3-rd block and modifies the 4-th block. The first block is weak-overwritten (because the 5-th block gets one bit from the first block) and the 3-rd block is strongly overwritten. Function t touches the blocks of the indices 1 and 4 so, for exemplary

$$c = ((0,0,1,1,0,0),(0,0,1,1,1,1),(1,1,1,1,0,0),(1,0,0,0,0,1)),$$

we have:

$$touch(t,c) = \{((0,0,1,1,0,0),1),((1,0,0,0,0,1),4)\}.$$

3.3 Statement and Proof

The main statements for the whole Sect. 3 are the following:

Theorem 1. *The coding scheme* $(\mathsf{Enc}_c, \mathsf{Dec}_c)$ *is an* $(\alpha + 2\epsilon_c)^{\lfloor N/3 \rfloor}$*-secure continuous non-malleable code against* PermOver *for* $\alpha = (0.5)^{\frac{1}{8 \cdot k_1}}$.

Corollary 1. *Instantiation for the above code with* $(N, k_2, k_1) = (6\lceil n^{2/3} \rceil, \lceil n^{1/3} \rceil, c\lceil n^{1/3} \rceil \log \lceil n^{1/3} \rceil)$, *with* $(\mathsf{Enc}_2, \mathsf{Dec}_2) = (\mathsf{Enc}_{\mathsf{Li}}, \mathsf{Dec}_{\mathsf{Li}})$ *(see the end of Sect. 3.1) and* $h_N = RS_N$ *(see Appendix B) gives us a continuous non-malleable code against* PermOver *such that:*

- *the code rate is* $O(\log n)$, *and*
- *the error rate is* $O(2^{-\Omega(n^{1/3})})$.

Proof. The message length is n and the codeword length is $N \cdot 2 \cdot k_1 \approx 6n^{2/3} \cdot 2 \cdot cn^{1/3} \frac{1}{3} \log n = 4cn \log n$, so the code rate is approximately $4c \log n = O(\log n)$. (Remark: c is a constant from $\mathsf{Enc}_{\mathsf{Li}}$ rate.) The error rate is:

$$(\alpha + 2\epsilon_c)^{\lfloor N/3 \rfloor} = ((0.5)^{\frac{1}{8 \cdot k_1}} + 2\epsilon_c)^{\lfloor N/3 \rfloor} \leq (2^{-O\left(\frac{1}{n^{1/3} \log n}\right)} + 2^{-O(n)})^{n^{2/3}+1} = 2^{-O(n^{1/3})}.$$

Before the actual proof of Theorem 1 we want to introduce a slightly modified version of continuous tampering experiment for $(\mathsf{Enc}_c, \mathsf{Dec}_c)$ and PermOver and a definition of a specific type of distribution that we call block-wise distribution.

The described below experiment is obviously stronger (from adversary's point of view) then the original one so it is sufficient to prove that our coding scheme is secure against PermOver for the modified experiment:

Definition 9 ((Modified) Continuous Tampering Experiment). *Let us consider a tampering oracle* $\mathsf{ModTamp}_C^{\mathsf{state}}(t)$, *for which initially* state = alive. *For a tampering function* $t \in$ PermOver *and a codeword* $C \in \mathcal{C}$ *define the tampering oracle by*

$\mathsf{ModTamp}_C^{\mathsf{state}}(t)$:
    If state = dead *output* $\perp$
    $C' \leftarrow t(C)$
    If $\mathsf{Dec}_c(C') = \mathsf{Dec}_c(C)$ *output* (same, $touch(t,c)$)
    $M' \leftarrow \mathsf{Dec}_c(C')$
    If $M' = \perp$ *set* state $\leftarrow$ dead *and output* $\perp$
    Otherwise output C'

Fix a tampering adversary $\mathcal{A}$ and a codeword $C \in \mathcal{C}$. We define the (modified) continuous tampering experiment $\mathsf{MCT}_C(\mathcal{A})$ *by*

$\mathsf{MCT}_C(\mathcal{A}):$
    state $\leftarrow$ alive
    $v \leftarrow \mathcal{A}^{\mathsf{ModTamp}_C^{\text{state}}(\cdot)}$
    Output v

Remark 2. The main difference of the above experiment and the original one is the output of the oracle when $\mathsf{Dec}_c(C') = \mathsf{Dec}_c(C)$. In this case in our definition we give the adversary additionally all touched blocks.

Definition 10 (Block-wise Distribution). *For $\mathcal{C} = \mathcal{C}_1 \times \ldots \times \mathcal{C}_N$ the distribution D over $\mathcal{C}$ is a* block-wise distribution *if (informally speaking) each block $\mathcal{C}_i$ is either fixed or uniform and independent of the other blocks.*

Formally, we say that D is a block-wise distribution if there exists a set of indices $I \subset [1, 2, \ldots, N]$ such that for all $i \in I$ there exists $c_i \in \mathcal{C}_i$ such that:
$P_D(\mathcal{C}_i = c_i) = 1$, and
the conditional distribution $(D|\mathcal{C}_i = c_i$ for all $i)$ is uniform.

Remark 3. If $|I| = l$ in the above definition, then we will sometimes say that D *has l constant blocks or that the adversary* knows l blocks.

Proof sketch for Theorem 1. Our key observation is that after each oracle call in the tampering experiment, the distribution of the codewords (from the perspective of the adversary) is almost always block-wise. Moreover, to increase the number of known (constant) blocks, the adversary must take a risk of receiving $\perp$. This idea is expressed in the following Lemma 5. Notice, that from basic properties of secret sharing schemes, the tampering experiment is independent from the message m while the number of known blocks is smaller then $\lfloor N/3 \rfloor$. So, the only way for the adversary to distinguish between two different messages is to learn at least $\lfloor N/3 \rfloor$ blocks. However (from Lemma 5) this happens with probability at most $(\alpha + 2\epsilon_c)^{\lfloor N/3 \rfloor}$ (for $\alpha = (0.5)^{\frac{1}{8 \cdot k_1}}$) so this observation finishes the proof for Theorem 1. $\qquad\qquad\square$

Before the statement of the key Lemma 5, we need one definition more:

Definition 11. *For a block-wise distribution D and a tampering function $t \in$ PermOver we say that t* freshly-touches *the i-th block if t touches this block and this block is not known in context of D.*

Lemma 5. *Let $\alpha = (0.5)^{\frac{1}{8 \cdot k_1}}$, let $l_1, l_2 \in \mathbb{N}$ such that $l_1 + l_2 < \lfloor N/3 \rfloor$, and let D be a block-wise distribution over C with l_1 constant blocks and let $t \in$ PermOver be a tampering function freshly-touching l_2 blocks. Then, with probability at least $(1 - (\alpha + 2\epsilon_c)^{l_2})$ a call $\mathsf{ModTamp}_C^{\text{state}}(t)$ will return $\perp$. Moreover – with probability at least $(1 - 2^{-n})$ – the distribution D conditioned on the answer from the oracle will be block-wise with $l_1 + l_2$ constant blocks.*

The formal proof can be found in the full version of the paper [23].

4 SD-CCA Commitment Scheme

4.1 Definition of CCA Secure Commitment Schemes

We assuming that the reader has familiarity with the standard definition of commitment scheme and proof system.

Self-destruct CCA Secure Commitment Schemes. Let $\Pi = (\mathsf{Sen}, \mathsf{Rec})$ be a commitment scheme. The Self-destruct CCA-oracle $\mathcal{O}^{\mathsf{sdcca}}$ for $\Pi = (\mathsf{Sen}, \mathsf{Rec})$ acts as follows in an interaction with an adversary $\mathcal{A}$: it participates with $\mathcal{A}$ in polynomially many sessions of the commit phase of Π as an honest receiver. At the end of each session, if the session is valid, the oracle returns the unique value m committed in the interaction. The oracle outputs $\perp$ and implements the Self-destruct mode, (i.e. the oracle will respond with $\perp$ for all subsequent commitment queries) if one of the following cases happen: (1) a session has multiple valid committed values[4]; (2) the commitment is invalid; (3) if the committed value m is equal to a special Self-destruct symbol $\perp$.

More precisely, let us consider the following probabilistic experiment $\mathsf{IND}_b^{\mathsf{sdcca}}(\Pi = (\mathsf{Sen}, \mathsf{Rec}), \lambda, z, \mathcal{A})$. Let $\mathcal{O}^{\mathsf{sdcca}}$ be the SD CCA-oracle for Π. The adversary has access to $\mathcal{O}^{\mathsf{sdcca}}$ during the entire course of the experiment. On input 1^λ, and $z \in \{0,1\}^*$ the adversary $\mathcal{A}^{\mathcal{O}^{\mathsf{sdcca}}}$ sends two strings m_0 and m_1 with $|m_0| = |m_1|$ to the experiment. The experiment randomly selects a bit $b \leftarrow \{0,1\}$ and commits to m_b to $\mathcal{A}^{\mathcal{O}^{\mathsf{sdcca}}}$. Note that if $\mathcal{A}$ queries the oracle with a commitment of m s.t. $m \in \{m_0, m_1\}$[5] then, the oracle returns the special symbol **same**. Finally $\mathcal{A}^{\mathcal{O}^{\mathsf{sdcca}}}$ sends a bit y to the experiment. The output of the experiment is replaced by $\perp$ if $\mathcal{A}^{\mathcal{O}^{\mathsf{sdcca}}}$ sends a commitment to $\mathcal{O}^{\mathsf{sdcca}}$ whose transcript is identical to the one computed on the left. Otherwise, the output of the experiment is y. Let $\mathsf{IND}_b^{\mathsf{sdcca}}(\Pi = (\mathsf{Sen}, \mathsf{Rec}), \lambda, z, \mathcal{A})$ denote the output of the experiment described above.

Definition 12 (Self-destructCCA (SD-CCA) secure string commitment scheme). *Let $\Pi(\mathsf{Sen}, \mathsf{Rec})$ be a commitment scheme and $\mathcal{O}^{\mathsf{sdcca}}$ be the Self-destruct CCA-oracle for Π_{sdcca}. We say that Π_{sdcca} is Self-destruct CCA-secure (w.r.t. the committed-value oracle), if for every ppt-adversary $\mathcal{A}$ and all $z \in \{0,1\}^*$ it holds that:*

$$\{\mathsf{IND}_0^{\mathsf{sdcca}}(\Pi = (\mathsf{Sen}, \mathsf{Rec}), \lambda, z, \mathcal{A})\} \approx \{\mathsf{IND}_1^{\mathsf{sdcca}}(\Pi = (\mathsf{Sen}, \mathsf{Rec}), \lambda, z, \mathcal{A})\}$$

Definition 13 (Self-destruct parallel CCA (SD-PCCA) secure string commitment scheme). *The Self-destruct parallel CCA oracle is defined like the Self-destruct CCA-oracle, except that the adversary is restricted to a parallel*

---

[4] The statistical binding property guarantees that this happens with only negligible probability.

[5] As noted in [5], following [24], this definition allows MIM to commit to the same value. It is easy to prevent MIM from committing the same value generically in case of string commitments: convert the scheme to tag based by appending the tag with v, and then sign the whole transcript using the tag.

query, i.e., the adversary can only send a single query that may contain multiple commitments sent in parallel. Let $\text{IND}_b^{\text{sdpcca}}(\Pi = (\text{Sen}, \text{Rec}), \lambda, z, \mathcal{A})$ *define the output of the security game for Self-destruct parallel CCA security. The formal definition is then analogous to the definition of SD-CCA security.*

Note that any SD-CCA commitment scheme is also a SD-PCCA commitment scheme.

Definition 14 (Parallel CCA secure (PCCA) string commitment scheme [11,41]). *The parallel CCA oracle is defined like Self-destruct parallel CCA-oracle, except that the oracle does not implement the Self-destruct mode. In more details, when a commitment is not valid, or a session has multiple valid committed values the oracle returns* $\perp$, *and the committed messages (or the symbol* **same***) in all the other cases. Let* $\text{IND}_b^{\text{sdpcca}}(\Pi = (\text{Sen}, \text{Rec}), \lambda, z, \mathcal{A})$ *define the output of the security game for parallel CCA security (PCCA). The formal definition is then analogous to the definition of SD-PCCA security.*

In this paper we also consider a Self-destruct (parallel) CCA secure bit commitment scheme that is defined as in Definition 12 (13), except that the message space is $\{0, 1\}$ and the oracle never returns **same**.

In all the paper we denote by $\tilde{\delta}$ a value associated with the right session (where the adversary $\mathcal{A}$ plays with the oracle) where δ is the corresponding value in the left session. For example, the sender commits to v in the left session while $\mathcal{A}$ commits to $\tilde{v}$ in the right session.

4.2   SD-CCA Commitment Scheme from NMCode

In this subsection we describe our $\Pi_{\text{sdcca}} = (\text{Sen}_{\text{sdcca}}, \text{Rec}_{\text{sdcca}})$ a t-round (non-tag based) Self-destruct CCA string commitment scheme, that makes use of the following tools.

1. $\Pi_{\text{sdcca}}^{\text{bit}} = (\text{Com}_{\text{sdcca}}^{\text{bit}}, \text{Dec}_{\text{sdcca}}^{\text{bit}})$ is a t-round (non-tag based) Self-destruct CCA bit commitment scheme.
2. $\Pi_{\text{NMCode}} = (\text{Enc}, \text{Dec})$ is a continuos non-malleable code resilient against PermOver. The procedure Enc outputs a codeword that is n-bits long.

Our SD-CCA commitment scheme is described in Fig. 1.

Theorem 2. *If* $\Pi_{\text{sdcca}}^{\text{bit}} = (\text{Com}_{\text{sdcca}}^{\text{bit}}, \text{Dec}_{\text{sdcca}}^{\text{bit}})$ *is a t-round (non-tag based) Self-destruct CCA bit commitment scheme and* $\Pi_{\text{NMCode}} = (\text{Enc}, \text{Dec})$ *is a continuous non-malleable code resilient against PermOver, then* $\Pi_{\text{sdcca}} = (\text{Sen}_{\text{sdcca}}, \text{Rec}_{\text{sdcca}})$ *is a a t-round (non-tag based) Self-destruct CCA string commitment scheme.*

The formal proof can be found in the full version of the paper [23].

Common input: security parameter λ.

Input to $\mathsf{Sen_{sdcca}}$: $m \in \{0, 1\}^\lambda$.

Commitment phase:

1. $\mathsf{Sen_{sdcca}}$:
   1. Run $\mathsf{enc}^m \leftarrow \mathsf{Enc}(1^\lambda, m)$.
2. $\mathsf{Sen_{sdcca}} \leftrightarrow \mathsf{Rec_{sdcca}}$:
   1. For $i = 1, \ldots, n$, $\mathsf{Sen_{sdcca}}$ on input enc_i^m interacts with $\mathsf{Rec_{sdcca}}$ and computes the commitment phase τ_i of $\mathsf{Com_{sdcca}^{bit}}$ obtaining the i-th decommitment information dec_i^{sdcca} [a].
3. $\mathsf{Rec_{sdcca}}$: accepted the commitment iff the following conditions are satisfied.
   1. For $i = 1, \ldots, n$ τ_i is accepting.
   2. For $i, j = 1, \ldots, n$ and $i \neq j$ τ_i is not identical to τ_j.

Decomittment phase:

1. $\mathsf{Sen_{sdcca}} \rightarrow \mathsf{Rec_{sdcca}}$
   1. Send $(m, \mathsf{dec}_1^{sdcca}, \ldots, \mathsf{dec}_n^{sdcca})$ to $\mathsf{Rec_{sdcca}}$.
   2. $\mathsf{Rec_{sdcca}}$: For $i = 1, \ldots, n$ if dec_i^{sdcca} is not a valid decommitment of τ_i then abort, otherwise continue as follow.
      1. Run $(\mathsf{enc}_i^{m'}) \leftarrow \mathsf{Dec_{sdcca}^{bit}}(\tau_i, \mathsf{dec}_i^{sdcca})$.
      2. Set $\mathsf{enc}^{m'} = \mathsf{enc}_1^{m'} || \ldots || \mathsf{enc}_n^{m'}$ and run $m' \leftarrow \mathsf{Dec}(\mathsf{enc}^m)$.
      3. If $m \neq m'$ abort, otherwise output 1.

---

[a] The n commitment phases are computed in parallel.

Fig. 1. Description of our SD-CCA string commitment scheme.

4.3 Parallel CCA Commitment Scheme from SD-PCCA Commitment Scheme

In this subsection we describe our $\Pi_{\mathsf{pcca}} = (\mathsf{Sen_{pcca}}, \mathsf{Rec_{pcca}})$ a $t + 2$-round (non-tag based) PCCA string commitment scheme, that makes use of the following tools.

1. $\Pi_{\mathsf{sdpcca}} = (\mathsf{Sen_{sdcca}}, \mathsf{Rec_{sdcca}})$ is a t-round (non-tag based) SD-PCCA string commitment scheme.
2. a 2-round IDTC scheme $\Pi = (\mathsf{Sen}, \mathsf{Rec}, \mathsf{TFake})$ for the following $\mathcal{NP}$-language $L = \{\tau_{\mathsf{sdcca}} : (m, \mathsf{dec_{sdcca}})$ s.t. $\mathsf{Rec_{sdcca}}$ on input $(m, \mathsf{dec_{sdcca}})$ accepts m as a decommitment of $\tau_{\mathsf{sdcca}}\}$.
3. $\Pi_{\mathsf{sign}} = (\mathsf{Gen}, \mathsf{Sign}, \mathsf{Verify})$ is a signature scheme.
4. A 4-round delayed-input public coin $\mathsf{LS_{trap}} = (\mathcal{P}_{\mathsf{trap}}, \mathcal{V}_{\mathsf{trap}})$ with SHVZK simulator S_{trap}. $\mathsf{LS_{trap}} = (\mathcal{P}_{\mathsf{trap}}, \mathcal{V}_{\mathsf{trap}})$ is adaptive-input PoK for the $\mathcal{NP}$-relation $\mathsf{Rel}_{L_{\mathsf{trap}}}$ where $L_{\mathsf{trap}} = \{(\mathsf{vk} : \exists (\sigma_1, \mathsf{msg}_1, \sigma_2, \mathsf{msg}_2)$ s.t. $\mathsf{Verify}(\mathsf{vk}, \mathsf{msg}_1, \sigma_1) = 1$ AND $\mathsf{Verify}(\mathsf{vk}, \mathsf{msg}_2, \sigma_2) = 1$ AND $\mathsf{msg}_1 \neq \mathsf{msg}_2\}$. We denote with ℓ_{trap} the dimension of the instances belonging to $\mathsf{LS_{trap}}$.

Our $\Pi_{\mathsf{pcca}} = (\mathsf{Sen_{pcca}}, \mathsf{Rec_{pcca}})$ is described in Fig. 2.

Theorem 3. *If* $\Pi_{\mathsf{sdpcca}} = (\mathsf{Sen_{sdpcca}}, \mathsf{Rec_{sdpcca}})$ *is a t-round (non-tag based) Self-destruct PCCA string commitment scheme and OWFs exists, then* $\Pi^{\mathsf{sdcca}} = (\mathsf{Sen_{pcca}}, \mathsf{Rec_{pcca}})$ *is a a t + 2-round (non-tag based) PCCA string commitment scheme.*

Common input: security parameter λ, instances length: $\ell, \ell_{\mathsf{trap}}$.
Input to $\mathsf{Sen}_{\mathsf{pcca}}$: $m \in \{0,1\}^{\lambda}$.
Commitment phase:
1. $\mathsf{Sen}_{\mathsf{pcca}} \leftrightarrow \mathsf{Rec}_{\mathsf{pcca}}$:
   1. $\mathsf{Sen}_{\mathsf{pcca}}$ on input m interacts with $\mathsf{Rec}_{\mathsf{pcca}}$ and compute the commitment phase τ_{sdpcca} of $\mathsf{Sen}_{\mathsf{sdpcca}}$ obtaining the decommitment information $\mathsf{dec}_{\mathsf{sdpcca}}$.
   2. $\mathsf{Sen}_{\mathsf{pcca}}$ interacts with $\mathsf{Rec}_{\mathsf{pcca}}$ in order to prove that he computes a well-formed commitment of m [a]:
      a. $\mathsf{Rec}_{\mathsf{pcca}}$ runs the following algorithms: $(\mathsf{sk}, \mathsf{vk}) \leftarrow \mathsf{Gen}(1^{\lambda})$, $\rho \leftarrow \mathsf{Rec}(1^{\lambda}, \ell)$, $\mathsf{ls}^{1}_{\mathsf{trap}} \leftarrow \mathcal{V}_{\mathsf{trap}}(1^{\lambda}, \ell_{\mathsf{trap}})$. Then, he sends $(\mathsf{vk}, \rho, \mathsf{ls}^{1}_{\mathsf{trap}})$ to $\mathsf{Rec}_{\mathsf{pcca}}$.
      b. $\mathsf{Sen}_{\mathsf{pcca}}$ picks $\mathsf{msg}, \mathsf{ls}^{2}_{\mathsf{trap}} \leftarrow \{0,1\}^{\lambda}$, and runs the following algorithms: $\mathsf{ls}^{3}_{\mathsf{trap}} \leftarrow \mathcal{S}_{\mathsf{trap}}(1^{\lambda}, \ell_{\mathsf{trap}}, \mathsf{ls}^{3}_{\mathsf{trap}}; r_{\mathsf{trap}})$, $\mathsf{com}, \mathsf{aux} \leftarrow \mathsf{TFake}(1^{\lambda}, \rho, \tau_{\mathsf{sdpcca}})$. Then, he sends $(\mathsf{com}, \mathsf{msg})$ to $\mathsf{Rec}_{\mathsf{pcca}}$.
      c. $\mathsf{Rec}_{\mathsf{pcca}}$ picks $\mathsf{ls}^{3}_{\mathsf{trap}} \leftarrow \{0,1\}^{\lambda}$ and runs $\sigma \leftarrow \mathsf{Sign}(\mathsf{sk}, \mathsf{msg})$. Then, he sends (c, σ) to $\mathsf{Sen}_{\mathsf{pcca}}$.
      d. $\mathsf{Sen}_{\mathsf{pcca}}$ If $\mathsf{Verify}(\mathsf{vk}, \mathsf{msg}, \sigma) \neq 1$ then aborts, otherwise continues as follow. Runs $\mathsf{ls}^{4}_{\mathsf{trap}} \leftarrow \mathcal{S}_{\mathsf{trap}}(\mathsf{vk}, r_{\mathsf{trap}})$. Furthermore, he sets $x = (\tau_{\mathsf{sdpcca}})$ and $w = (m, \mathsf{dec}_{\mathsf{sdpcca}})$ then runs $\mathsf{dec} \leftarrow \mathsf{TFake}(x, w, \rho, \mathsf{ls}^{2}_{\mathsf{trap}}, \mathsf{aux})$. Then, he sends $(\mathsf{dec}, \mathsf{ls}^{3}_{\mathsf{trap}}, \mathsf{ls}^{4}_{\mathsf{trap}})$ to $\mathsf{Rec}_{\mathsf{pcca}}$.
1. $\mathsf{Rec}_{\mathsf{sdcca}}$: accept the commitment iff the following conditions are satisfied.
   1. $\mathsf{Rec}(\rho, x, \mathsf{com}, \mathsf{ls}^{2}_{\mathsf{trap}}, \mathsf{dec}) = 1$.
   2. $\mathcal{V}_{\mathsf{trap}}(\mathsf{vk}, \mathsf{ls}^{1}_{\mathsf{trap}}, \mathsf{ls}^{2}_{\mathsf{trap}}, \mathsf{ls}^{3}_{\mathsf{trap}}, \mathsf{ls}^{4}_{\mathsf{trap}}) = 1$
   3. If $\mathsf{Rec}_{\mathsf{sdpcca}}$ accepts the commitment τ_{sdpcca}.
Decomittment phase:
1. $\mathsf{Sen}_{\mathsf{pcca}} \to \mathsf{Rec}_{\mathsf{pcca}}$: send $(m', \mathsf{dec}_{\mathsf{sdcca}})$ to $\mathsf{Rec}_{\mathsf{pcca}}$.
2. $\mathsf{Rec}_{\mathsf{sdcca}}$: If $\mathsf{dec}_{\mathsf{sdcca}}$ is not a valid decommitment of τ_{sdpcca} then abort, otherwise runs $\mathsf{Rec}_{\mathsf{sdpcca}}$ on input $(\tau_{\mathsf{sdpcca}}, \mathsf{dec}_{\mathsf{sdpcca}})$ obtaining m. If $m = m'$ output 1 and 0 otherwise.

---

[a] The rounds a. and b. can be run in parallel with the last two rounds of the commitment phase of Π_{sdpcca}.

Fig. 2. Description of our Parallel CCA string commitment scheme.

The formal proof can be found in the full version of the paper [23].

Acknowledgments. We thank Michele Ciampi for several discussions on the applications of our CNMC.

A   Definition and Tools

Definition 15 (One-way function (OWF)). *A function* $f : \{0,1\}^{\star} \to \{0,1\}^{\star}$ *is called one way if the following two conditions hold:*

- *there exists a deterministic polynomial-time algorithm that on input y in the domain of f outputs $f(y)$;*
- *for every PPT algorithm $\mathcal{A}$ there exists a negligible function ν, such that for every auxiliary input $z \in \{0,1\}^{\mathtt{poly}(\lambda)}$:*

$$\mathrm{Prob}[y \leftarrow \{0,1\}^{\star} : \mathcal{A}(f(y), z) \in f^{-1}(f(y))] < \nu(\lambda).$$

Definition 16 (Following the notation of [50]**).** *A triple of* PPT *algorithms* (Gen, Sign, Verify) *is called a* signature scheme *if it satisfies the following properties.*

Validity: *For every pair* $(s, v) \leftarrow \mathsf{Gen}(1^\lambda)$, *and every* $m \in \{0, 1\}^\lambda$, *we have that*

$$\mathsf{Verify}(v, m, \mathsf{Sign}(s, m)) = 1.$$

Security: *For every* PPT $\mathcal{A}$, *there exists a negligible function* ν, *such that for all auxiliary input* $z \in \{0, 1\}^*$ *it holds that:*

$$\Pr[(s, v) \leftarrow \mathsf{Gen}(1^\lambda); (m, \sigma) \leftarrow \mathcal{A}^{\mathsf{Sign}(s, \cdot)}(z, v) \wedge \mathsf{Verify}(v, m, \sigma) = 1 \wedge m \notin Q] < \nu(\lambda)$$

where Q *denotes the set of messages whose signatures were requested by* $\mathcal{A}$ *to the oracle* $\mathsf{Sign}(s, \cdot)$.

Definition 17 (Proof/argument system). *A pair of* PPT *interactive algorithms* $\Pi = (\mathcal{P}, \mathcal{V})$ *constitute a* proof system *(resp., an* argument system*) for an* $\mathcal{NP}$*-language* L, *if the following conditions hold:*

Completeness: *For every* $x \in L$ *and* w *such that* $(x, w) \in \mathsf{Rel}_L$, *it holds that:*

$$\Pr[\, \langle \mathcal{P}(w), \mathcal{V} \rangle (x) = 1 \,] = 1.$$

Soundness: *For every interactive (resp.,* PPT *interactive) algorithm* $\mathcal{P}^*$, *there exists a negligible function* ν *such that for every* $x \notin L$ *and every* z:

$$\Pr[\, \langle \mathcal{P}^*(z), \mathcal{V} \rangle (x) = 1 \,] < \nu(|x|).$$

A proof/argument system $\Pi = (\mathcal{P}, \mathcal{V})$ for an $\mathcal{NP}$-language L, enjoys *delayed-input* completeness if $\mathcal{P}$ needs x and w only to compute the last round and $\mathcal{V}$ needs x only to compute the output. Before that, $\mathcal{P}$ and $\mathcal{V}$ run having as input only the size of x. The notion of delayed-input completeness was defined in [21]. An interactive protocol $\Pi = (\mathcal{P}, \mathcal{V})$ is *public coin* if, at every round, $\mathcal{V}$ simply tosses a predetermined number of coins (i.e. a random challenge) and sends the outcome to the prover. Moreover we say that the transcript τ of an execution $b = \langle \mathcal{P}(z), \mathcal{V} \rangle (x)$ is *accepting* if $b = 1$.

Definition 18 (Proof of Knowledge [43]**).** *A protocol* $\Pi = (\mathcal{P}, \mathcal{V})$ *that enjoys completeness is a* proof of knowledge *(PoK) for the relation* Rel_L *if there exists a probabilistic expected polynomial-time machine* Ext, *called the extractor, such that for every algorithm* $\mathcal{P}^*$, *there exists a negligible function* ν, *every statement* $x \in \{0, 1\}^\lambda$, *every randomness* $r \in \{0, 1\}^*$ *and every auxiliary input* $z \in \{0, 1\}^*$,

$$\Pr[\, \langle \mathcal{P}_r^*(z), \mathcal{V} \rangle (x) = 1 \,] \leq \Pr\left[\, w \leftarrow \mathsf{Ext}^{\mathcal{P}_r^*(z)}(x) : (x, w) \in \mathsf{Rel}_L \,\right] + \nu(\lambda).$$

We also say that an argument system Π *is a* argument of knowledge *(AoK) if the above condition holds w.r.t. any* PPT $\mathcal{P}^*$.

In this paper we also consider the *adaptive-input* PoK/AoK property for all the protocols that enjoy delayed-input completeness. Adaptive-input PoK/AoK ensures that the PoK/AoK property still holds when a malicious prover can choose the statement adaptively at the last round.

A *3-round protocol* $\Pi = (\mathcal{P}, \mathcal{V})$ for a relation Rel_L is an interactive protocol played between a prover $\mathcal{P}$ and a verifier $\mathcal{V}$ on common input x and private input w of $\mathcal{P}$ s.t. $(x, w) \in \mathsf{Rel}_L$. In a 3-round protocol the first message a and the third message z are sent by $\mathcal{P}$ and the second messages c is played by $\mathcal{V}$. At the end of the protocol $\mathcal{V}$ decides to accept or reject based on the data that he has seen, i.e. x, a, c, z.

We usually denote the message c sent by $\mathcal{V}$ as a *challenge*, and as *challenge length* the number of bit of c.

Definition 19 (Σ-Protocol). *A 3-round public-coin protocol $\Pi = (\mathcal{P}, \mathcal{V})$ for a relation Rel_L is a Σ-Protocol if the following properties hold:*

- *Completeness: if $(\mathcal{P}, \mathcal{V})$ follow the protocol on input x and private input w to $\mathcal{P}$ s.t. $(x, w) \in \mathsf{Rel}_L$, $\mathcal{V}$ always accepts.*
- *Special soundness: if there exists a polynomial time algorithm such that, for any pair of accepting transcripts on input x, $(a, c_1, z_1), (a, c_2, z_2)$ where $c_1 \neq c_2$, outputs witness w such that $(x, w) \in \mathsf{Rel}_L$.*
- *Special Honest Verifier Zero-knowledge (Special HVZK): there exists a PPT simulator algorithm $\mathcal{S}$ that for any $x \in L$, security parameter λ and any challenge c works as follow: $(a, z) \leftarrow \mathcal{S}(1^\lambda, x, c)$. Furthermore, the distribution of the output of $\mathcal{S}$ is computationally indistinguishable from the distribution of a transcript obtained when $\mathcal{V}$ sends c as challenge and $\mathcal{P}$ runs on common input x and any w such that $(x, w) \in \mathsf{Rel}_L$.*

A.1 2-Round Instance-Dependent Trapdoor Commitments

Here we define a special commitment scheme based on an $\mathcal{NP}$-language L where sender and receiver also receive as input an instance x. While correctness and computational hiding hold for any x, we require that statistical binding holds for $x \notin L$ and knowledge of a witness for $x \in L$ allows to equivocate. Finally, we require that a commitment along with two different openings allows to compute the witness for $x \in L$. We recall that $\hat{L}$ denotes the language that includes L and all well formed instances that are not in L.

Definition 20. *Let 1^λ be the security parameter, L be an $\mathcal{NP}$-language and Rel_L be the corresponding $\mathcal{NP}$-relation. A triple of PPT algorithms $\Pi = (\mathsf{Sen}, \mathsf{Rec}, \mathsf{Sen})$ is a 2-Round Instance-Dependent Trapdoor Commitment scheme if the following properties hold.*

Correctness. *In the 1st round, Rec on input 1^λ and $x \in \hat{L}$ outputs ρ. In the 2nd round Sen on input the message m, 1^λ, ρ and $x \in L$ outputs $(\mathsf{com}, \mathsf{dec})$. We will refer to the pair (ρ, com) as the commitment of m. Moreover we will refer to the execution of the above two rounds including the exchange of the* *corresponding two messages as the commitment phase. Then* Rec *on input m, x,* com, dec *and the private coins used to generate ρ in the commitment phase outputs 1. We will refer to the execution of this last round including the exchange of* dec *as the decommitment phase. Notice that an adversarial sender* Sen* *could deviate from the behavior of* Sen *when computing and sending* com *and* dec *for an instance $x \in \hat{L}$. As a consequence* Rec *could output 0 in the decommitment phase. We will say that* dec *is a valid decommitment of (ρ,* com*) to m for an instance $x \in \hat{L}$, if* Rec *outputs 1.*

Hiding. *Given a* PPT *adversary $\mathcal{A}$, consider the following hiding experiment* $\mathsf{ExpHiding}^b_{\mathcal{A},\Pi}(\lambda, x)$ *for $b = 0, 1$ and $x \in \hat{L}_R$:*

- *On input 1^λ and x, $\mathcal{A}$ outputs a message m, along with ρ.*
- *The challenger on input x, m, ρ, b works as follows: if $b = 0$ then it runs* Sen *on input m, x and ρ, obtaining a pair (*com, dec*), otherwise it runs* TFake *on input x and ρ, obtaining a pair (*com, aux*). The challenger outputs* com.
- *$\mathcal{A}$ on input* com *outputs a bit b' and this is the output of the experiment.*

We say that hiding *holds if for any* PPT *adversary $\mathcal{A}$ there exist a negligible function ν, s.t.:*

$$\left| \mathrm{Prob}\left[\mathsf{ExpHiding}^0_{\mathcal{A},\Pi}(\lambda, x) = 1 \right] - \mathrm{Prob}\left[\mathsf{ExpHiding}^1_{\mathcal{A},\Pi}(\lambda, x) = 1 \right] \right| < \nu(\lambda)$$

Special Binding. *There exists a* PPT *algorithm* Ext *that on input a commitment (ρ,* com*), the private coins used by* Rec *to compute ρ, and two valid decommitments (*dec, dec'*) of (ρ,* com*) to two different messages m and m' w.r.t. an instance $x \in L$, outputs w s.t. $(x, w) \in \mathsf{Rel}_L$ with overwhelming probability.*

Trapdoorness. *For any* PPT *adversary $\mathcal{A}$ there exist a negligible function ν, s.t. for all $x \in L$ it holds that:* $\left| \mathrm{Prob}\left[\mathsf{ExpCom}_{\mathcal{A},\Pi}(\lambda, x) = 1 \right] - \right.$

$\left. \mathrm{Prob}\left[\mathsf{ExpTrapdoor}_{\mathcal{A},\Pi}(\lambda, x) = 1 \right] \right| < \nu(\lambda)$ *where* $\mathsf{ExpCom}_{\mathcal{A},\Pi}(\lambda, x)$ *and* $\mathsf{ExpTrapdoor}_{\mathcal{A},\Pi}(\lambda, x)$ *are defined below[6].*

$\mathsf{ExpCom}_{\mathcal{A},\Pi}(\lambda, x)$:	$\mathsf{ExpTrapdoor}_{\mathcal{A},\Pi}(\lambda, x)$:
-On input 1^λ and x, $\mathcal{A}$ outputs (ρ, m).	*-On input 1^λ and x, $\mathcal{A}$ outputs (ρ, m).*
*-*Sen *on input 1^λ, x, m and ρ, outputs (*com, dec*).*	*-*TFake *on input 1^λ, x and ρ, outputs (*com, aux*).*
	*-*TFake *on input* tk *s.t. $(x,$ tk$) \in$* Rel_L, *x, ρ,* com, aux *and m outputs* dec.
*-$\mathcal{A}$ on input (*com, dec*) outputs a bit b and this is the output of the experiment.*	*-$\mathcal{A}$ on input (*com, dec*) outputs a bit b and this is the output of the experiment.*

---

[6] We assume w.l.o.g. that $\mathcal{A}$ is stateful.

B   Instantiation of a Secret Sharing Scheme

In this section we aim for a coding scheme $RS_N : \{0,1\}^{2n} \to (\{0,1\}^{k_2})^N$ that holds the $\lfloor N/3 \rfloor$-out-of-N secret sharing property. We show such construction for all parameters such that $\lfloor N/3 \rfloor \cdot k_2 \geq 2n$.

It turns out that the only we need for this purpose is the Reed-Solomon error correcting code c with following parameters:

- alphabet size $= 2^{k_2}$,
- block length $= N$,
- message length $M = 2 \cdot \lceil \frac{2n}{k_2} \rceil$.

Now our coding scheme may be defined as: $RS_N(m) = c(m||x)$, where x is a randomness of the same size as m.

We omit the simple proof that the above code actually holds the $\lfloor N/3 \rfloor$-out-of-N secret sharing property.

References

1. Aggarwal, D., Agrawal, S., Gupta, D., Maji, H.K., Pandey, O., Prabhakaran, M.: Optimal computational split-state non-malleable codes. In: Kushilevitz, E., Malkin, T. (eds.) TCC 2016, Part II. LNCS, vol. 9563, pp. 393–417. Springer, Heidelberg (2016). https://doi.org/10.1007/978-3-662-49099-0_15
2. Aggarwal, D., Dodis, Y., Lovett, S.: Non-malleable codes from additive combinatorics. In: STOC. ACM (2014)
3. Aggarwal, D., Döttling, N., Nielsen, J.B., Obremski, M., Purwanto, E.: Information theoretic continuously non-malleable codes in the constant split-state model. In: Presented at IMS Workshop on Information Theoretic Cryptography in NUS, Singapore (2016). Unpublished Manuscript, available on eprint
4. Aggarwal, D., Kazana, T., Obremski, M.: Inception makes non-malleable codes stronger. In: Kalai, Y., Reyzin, L. (eds.) TCC 2017. LNCS, vol. 10678, pp. 319–343. Springer, Cham (2017). https://doi.org/10.1007/978-3-319-70503-3_10
5. Agrawal, S., Gupta, D., Maji, H.K., Pandey, O., Prabhakaran, M.: Explicit non-malleable codes against bit-wise tampering and permutations. In: Gennaro, R., Robshaw, M. (eds.) CRYPTO 2015. LNCS, vol. 9215, pp. 538–557. Springer, Heidelberg (2015). https://doi.org/10.1007/978-3-662-47989-6_26
6. Agrawal, S., Gupta, D., Maji, H.K., Pandey, O., Prabhakaran, M.: A rate-optimizing compiler for non-malleable codes against bit-wise tampering and permutations. In: Dodis, Y., Nielsen, J.B. (eds.) TCC 2015. LNCS, vol. 9014, pp. 375–397. Springer, Heidelberg (2015). https://doi.org/10.1007/978-3-662-46494-6_16
7. Ball, M., Dachman-Soled, D., Kulkarni, M., Malkin, T.: Non-malleable codes for bounded depth, bounded fan-in circuits. Cryptology ePrint Archive, Report 2016/307 (2016). https://eprint.iacr.org/2016/307
8. Ball, M., Dachman-Soled, D., Kulkarni, M., Malkin, T.: Non-malleable codes from average-case hardness: Ac0, decision trees, and streaming space-bounded tampering. Cryptology ePrint Archive, Report 2017/1061 (2017). https://eprint.iacr.org/2017/1061

9. Barak, B.: Constant-round coin-tossing with a man in the middle or realizing the shared random string model. In: 43rd Symposium on Foundations of Computer Science (FOCS 2002), 16–19 November 2002, Vancouver, BC, Canada, Proceedings, pp. 345–355 (2002)

10. Broadnax, B., Döttling, N., Hartung, G., Müller-Quade, J., Nagel, M.: Concurrently composable security with shielded super-polynomial simulators. In: Coron, J.-S., Nielsen, J.B. (eds.) EUROCRYPT 2017. LNCS, vol. 10210, pp. 351–381. Springer, Cham (2017). https://doi.org/10.1007/978-3-319-56620-7_13

11. Broadnax, B., Fetzer, V., Müller-Quade, J., Rupp, A.: Non-malleability vs. CCA-security: the case of commitments. In: Abdalla, M., Dahab, R. (eds.) PKC 2018. LNCS, vol. 10770, pp. 312–337. Springer, Cham (2018). https://doi.org/10.1007/978-3-319-76581-5_11

12. Canetti, R., Lin, H., Pass, R.: Adaptive hardness and composable security in the plain model from standard assumptions. In: 51th Annual IEEE Symposium on Foundations of Computer Science, FOCS 2010, 23–26 October 2010, Las Vegas, Nevada, USA, pp. 541–550. IEEE Computer Society (2010)

13. Chandran, N., Goyal, V., Mukherjee, P., Pandey, O., Upadhyay, J.: Block-wise non-malleable codes. In: Chatzigiannakis, I., Mitzenmacher, M., Rabani, Y., Sangiorgi, D. (eds.) 43rd International Colloquium on Automata, Languages, and Programming, ICALP 2016, 11–15 July 2016, Rome, Italy, LIPIcs, vol. 55, pp. 31:1–31:14. Schloss Dagstuhl - Leibniz-Zentrum fuer Informatik (2016)

14. Chattopadhyay, E., Goyal, V., Li, X.: Non-malleable extractors and codes, with their many tampered extensions. In: Proceedings of the Forty-Eighth Annual ACM Symposium on Theory of Computing, pp. 285–298. ACM (2016)

15. Chattopadhyay, E., Zuckerman, D.: Non-malleable codes in the constant split-state model. iN: FOCS (2014)

16. Cheraghchi, M., Guruswami, V.: Capacity of non-malleable codes. In: Naor, M. (ed.) Innovations in Theoretical Computer Science, ITCS 2014, Princeton, NJ, USA, 12–14 January 2014, pp. 155–168. ACM (2014). https://doi.org/10.1145/2554797.2554814

17. Cheraghchi, M., Guruswami, V.: Non-malleable coding against bit-wise and split-state tampering. In: Lindell, Y. (ed.) TCC 2014. LNCS, vol. 8349, pp. 440–464. Springer, Heidelberg (2014). https://doi.org/10.1007/978-3-642-54242-8_19

18. Choi, S.G., Kiayias, A., Malkin, T.: BiTR: built-in tamper resilience. In: Lee, D.H., Wang, X. (eds.) ASIACRYPT 2011. LNCS, vol. 7073, pp. 740–758. Springer, Heidelberg (2011). https://doi.org/10.1007/978-3-642-25385-0_40

19. Ciampi, M., Ostrovsky, R., Siniscalchi, L., Visconti, I.: Concurrent non-malleable commitments (and More) in 3 rounds. In: Robshaw, M., Katz, J. (eds.) CRYPTO 2016. LNCS, vol. 9816, pp. 270–299. Springer, Heidelberg (2016). https://doi.org/10.1007/978-3-662-53015-3_10

20. Ciampi, M., Ostrovsky, R., Siniscalchi, L., Visconti, I.: Four-round concurrent non-malleable commitments from one-way functions. In: Katz, J., Shacham, H. (eds.) CRYPTO 2017. LNCS, vol. 10402, pp. 127–157. Springer, Cham (2017). https://doi.org/10.1007/978-3-319-63715-0_5

21. Ciampi, M., Persiano, G., Scafuro, A., Siniscalchi, L., Visconti, I.: Improved OR-composition of sigma-protocols. In: Kushilevitz, E., Malkin, T. (eds.) TCC 2016. LNCS, vol. 9563, pp. 112–141. Springer, Heidelberg (2016). https://doi.org/10.1007/978-3-662-49099-0_5

22. Coretti, S., Maurer, U., Tackmann, B., Venturi, D.: From single-bit to multi-bit public-key encryption via non-malleable codes. In: Dodis, Y., Nielsen, J.B. (eds.) TCC 2015. LNCS, vol. 9014, pp. 532–560. Springer, Heidelberg (2015). https://doi.org/10.1007/978-3-662-46494-6_22

23. Damgård, I., Kazana, T., Obremski, M., Raj, V., Siniscalchi, L.: Continuous NMC secure against permutations and overwrites, with applications to CCA secure commitments. Cryptology ePrint Archive, Report 2018/596 (2018). https://eprint.iacr.org/2018/596

24. Dolev, D., Dwork, C., Naor, M.: Non-malleable cryptography (extended abstract). In: Proceedings of the 23rd Annual ACM Symposium on Theory of Computing, 5–8 May 1991, New Orleans, Louisiana, USA, pp. 542–552 (1991)

25. Döttling, N., Nielsen, J.B., Obremski, M.: Information theoretic continuously non-malleable codes in the constant split-state model. iN: Presented at IMS Workshop on Information Theoretic Cryptography in NUS, Singapore (2016). Unpublished Manuscript, available on eprint

26. Dziembowski, S., Kazana, T., Obremski, M.: Non-malleable codes from two-source extractors. In: Canetti, R., Garay, J.A. (eds.) CRYPTO 2013. LNCS, vol. 8043, pp. 239–257. Springer, Heidelberg (2013). https://doi.org/10.1007/978-3-642-40084-1_14

27. Dziembowski, S., Pietrzak, K., Wichs, D.: Non-malleable codes. In: ICS, pp. 434–452. Tsinghua University Press (2010)

28. Faust, S., Mukherjee, P., Nielsen, J.B., Venturi, D.: Continuous non-malleable codes. In: Lindell, Y. (ed.) TCC 2014. LNCS, vol. 8349, pp. 465–488. Springer, Heidelberg (2014). https://doi.org/10.1007/978-3-642-54242-8_20

29. Faust, S., Mukherjee, P., Nielsen, J.B., Venturi, D.: A tamper and leakage resilient von neumann architecture. In: Katz, J. (ed.) PKC 2015. LNCS, vol. 9020, pp. 579–603. Springer, Heidelberg (2015). https://doi.org/10.1007/978-3-662-46447-2_26

30. Faust, S., Mukherjee, P., Venturi, D., Wichs, D.: Efficient non-malleable codes and key-derivation for poly-size tampering circuits. In: Nguyen, P.Q., Oswald, E. (eds.) EUROCRYPT 2014. LNCS, vol. 8441, pp. 111–128. Springer, Heidelberg (2014). https://doi.org/10.1007/978-3-642-55220-5_7

31. Gennaro, R., Lysyanskaya, A., Malkin, T., Micali, S., Rabin, T.: Algorithmic tamper-proof (ATP) security: theoretical foundations for security against hardware tampering. In: Naor, M. (ed.) TCC 2004. LNCS, vol. 2951, pp. 258–277. Springer, Heidelberg (2004). https://doi.org/10.1007/978-3-540-24638-1_15

32. Goyal, V.: Constant round non-malleable protocols using one way functions. In: Proceedings of the 43rd ACM Symposium on Theory of Computing, STOC 2011, San Jose, CA, USA, 6–8 June 2011, pp. 695–704 (2011)

33. Goyal, V., Lee, C., Ostrovsky, R., Visconti, I.: Constructing non-malleable commitments: A black-box approach. In: 53rd Annual IEEE Symposium on Foundations of Computer Science, FOCS 2012, New Brunswick, NJ, USA, 20–23 October 2012, pp. 51–60 (2012)

34. Goyal, V., Lin, H., Pandey, O., Pass, R., Sahai, A.: Round-efficient concurrently composable secure computation via a robust extraction lemma. In: Dodis, Y., Nielsen, J.B. (eds.) TCC 2015. LNCS, vol. 9014, pp. 260–289. Springer, Heidelberg (2015). https://doi.org/10.1007/978-3-662-46494-6_12

35. Goyal, V., Pandey, O., Richelson, S.: Textbook non-malleable commitments. In: Wichs, D., Mansour, Y. (eds.) Proceedings of the 48th Annual ACM SIGACT Symposium on Theory of Computing, STOC 2016, Cambridge, MA, USA, 18–21 June 2016, pp. 1128–1141. ACM (2016)

36. Goyal, V., Richelson, S., Rosen, A., Vald, M.: An algebraic approach to non-malleability. In: 55th IEEE Annual Symposium on Foundations of Computer Science, FOCS 2014, Philadelphia, PA, USA, 18–21 October 2014, pp. 41–50 (2014)
37. Jafargholi, Z., Wichs, D.: Tamper detection and continuous non-malleable codes. In: Dodis, Y., Nielsen, J.B. (eds.) TCC 2015. LNCS, vol. 9014, pp. 451–480. Springer, Heidelberg (2015). https://doi.org/10.1007/978-3-662-46494-6_19
38. Khurana, D.: Round optimal concurrent non-malleability from polynomial hardness. In: Kalai, Y., Reyzin, L. (eds.) TCC 2017. LNCS, vol. 10678, pp. 139–171. Springer, Cham (2017). https://doi.org/10.1007/978-3-319-70503-3_5
39. Khurana, D., Sahai, A.: How to achieve non-malleability in one or two rounds. In: Umans, C. (ed.) 58th IEEE Annual Symposium on Foundations of Computer Science, FOCS 2017, Berkeley, CA, USA, 15–17 October 2017, pp. 564–575. IEEE Computer Society (2017)
40. Kiyoshima, S.: Round-efficient black-box construction of composable multi-party computation. In: Garay, J.A., Gennaro, R. (eds.) CRYPTO 2014. LNCS, vol. 8617, pp. 351–368. Springer, Heidelberg (2014). https://doi.org/10.1007/978-3-662-44381-1_20
41. Kiyoshima, S.: Statistical concurrent non-malleable zero-knowledge from one-way functions. In: Gennaro, R., Robshaw, M. (eds.) CRYPTO 2015. LNCS, vol. 9216, pp. 85–106. Springer, Heidelberg (2015). https://doi.org/10.1007/978-3-662-48000-7_5
42. Li, X.: Improved non-malleable extractors, non-malleable codes and independent source extractors. In: STOC (2017) https://arxiv.org
43. Lin, H., Pass, R.: Constant-round non-malleable commitments from any one-way function. In: Fortnow, L., Vadhan, S.P. (eds.) Proceedings of the 43rd ACM Symposium on Theory of Computing, STOC 2011, San Jose, CA, USA, 6–8 June 2011, pp. 705–714. ACM (2011)
44. Lin, H., Pass, R.: Black-box constructions of composable protocols without set-up. In: Safavi-Naini, R., Canetti, R. (eds.) CRYPTO 2012. LNCS, vol. 7417, pp. 461–478. Springer, Heidelberg (2012). https://doi.org/10.1007/978-3-642-32009-5_27
45. Lin, H., Pass, R., Soni, P.: Two-round and non-interactive concurrent non-malleable commitments from time-lock puzzles. In: Umans, C. (ed.) 58th IEEE Annual Symposium on Foundations of Computer Science, FOCS 2017, Berkeley, CA, USA, 15–17 October 2017, pp. 576–587. IEEE Computer Society (2017)
46. Liu, F.-H., Lysyanskaya, A.: Tamper and leakage resilience in the split-state model. In: Safavi-Naini, R., Canetti, R. (eds.) CRYPTO 2012. LNCS, vol. 7417, pp. 517–532. Springer, Heidelberg (2012). https://doi.org/10.1007/978-3-642-32009-5_30
47. Pass, R., Rosen, A.: New and improved constructions of non-malleable cryptographic protocols. In: Gabow, H.N., Fagin, R. (eds.) Proceedings of the 37th Annual ACM Symposium on Theory of Computing, Baltimore, MD, USA, 22–24 May 2005, pp. 533–542. ACM (2005)
48. Pass, R., Wee, H.: Constant-round non-malleable commitments from sub-exponential one-way functions. In: Gilbert, H. (ed.) EUROCRYPT 2010. LNCS, vol. 6110, pp. 638–655. Springer, Heidelberg (2010). https://doi.org/10.1007/978-3-642-13190-5_32

49. Wee, H.: Black-box, round-efficient secure computation via non-malleability ampli-fication. In: 51th Annual IEEE Symposium on Foundations of Computer Science, FOCS 2010, 23–26 October 2010, Las Vegas, Nevada, USA, pp. 531–540. IEEE Computer Society (2010)
50. Chung, K.-M., Pass, R., Seth, K.: Non-black-box simulation from one-way functions and applications to resettable security. In: Boneh, D., Roughgarden, T., Feigenbaum, J. (eds.) Symposium on Theory of Computing Conference, STOC 2013, Palo Alto, CA, USA, 1–4 June 2013, pp. 231–240. ACM (2013). https://doi.org/10.1145/2488608.2488638

Best Possible Information-Theoretic MPC

Shai Halevi[1], Yuval Ishai[2], Eyal Kushilevitz[2], and Tal Rabin[1(✉)]

[1] IBM Research, Yorktown Heights, USA
shaih@alum.mit.edu, talr@us.ibm.com
[2] Technion, Haifa, Israel
{yuvali,eyalk}@cs.technion.ac.il

Abstract. We reconsider the security guarantee that can be achieved by general protocols for secure multiparty computation in the most basic of settings: information-theoretic security against a semi-honest adversary. Since the 1980s, we have elegant solutions to this problem that offer full security, as long as the adversary controls a minority of the parties, but fail completely when that threshold is crossed. In this work, we revisit this problem, questioning the optimality of the standard notion of security. We put forward a new notion of information-theoretic security which is strictly stronger than the standard one, and which we argue to be "best possible." This notion still requires full security against dishonest minority in the usual sense, and adds a meaningful notion of information-theoretic security even against dishonest majority.

We present protocols for useful classes of functions that satisfy this new notion of security. Our protocols have the unique feature of combining the efficiency benefits of protocols for an honest majority and (most of) the security benefits of protocols for dishonest majority. We further extend some of the solutions to the malicious setting.

Keywords: Information-theoretic security ·
Secure multiparty computation

1 Introduction

In this work we revisit a question that seemed to be well understood since the 1980s: What is the best security guarantee that can be achieved by general protocols for secure multiparty computation in the simplest of all models? We put forward and study a new notion of information-theoretic security that provides a strictly stronger security guarantee than the standard notion. This security

S. Halevi and T. Rabin—Supported by the Defense Advanced Research Projects Agency (DARPA) and Army Research Office (ARO) under Contract No. W911NF-15-C-0236.
Y. Ishai and E. Kushilevitz—Supported by ISF grant 1709/14, NSF-BSF grant 2015782, and a grant from the Ministry of Science and Technology, Israel and Department of Science and Technology, Government of India. Ishai was also supported by ERC grant 742754 (project NTSC).

© International Association for Cryptologic Research 2018
A. Beimel and S. Dziembowski (Eds.): TCC 2018, LNCS 11240, pp. 255–281, 2018.
https://doi.org/10.1007/978-3-030-03810-6_10

guarantee is in a sense the best possible. Before defining and motivating our new notion, we give some relevant background.

Protocols for secure multiparty computation (MPC) can be divided into two broad categories: *information-theoretic* MPC protocols, which offer unconditional security against computationally unbounded adversaries, and *computational* MPC protocols, which offer security against computationally bounded adversaries under standard cryptographic assumptions.

Information-theoretic MPC protocols not only provide unconditional security guarantees, but they are also typically simpler and have better concrete communication and computation costs than their computational counterparts. The efficiency gap can even grow with the number of parties by using efficient "packed secret-sharing" techniques [3,17,20], which divide the communication and computation costs between the parties (at the expense of slightly lowering the number of corruptions that can be tolerated).

A significant drawback of most information-theoretic MPC protocols, however, is that their security guarantees completely break down in the presence of a dishonest majority. Standard protocols, such as the so-called "BGW protocol" and its variants [6,11,34], allow a dishonest majority to learn the secret inputs of all parties. This is in contrast to computational protocols that can offer security even when all but one of the parties are dishonest. The above state of affairs gives rise to the following natural question:

Can we achieve the standard notion of information-theoretic security in the presence of an honest majority, while hiding the inputs of honest parties from a computationally unbounded dishonest majority?

Classical negative results rule out information-theoretic protocols with the standard notion of security in the presence of a dishonest majority, even for a function as simple as the OR of n input bits [6,13]. Unfortunately, these results further suggest that the answer to the question above may be negative. However, we observe that this *does not imply* that all inputs of the minority parties must be compromised, as is the case for existing protocols. This raises the possibility of finding a middle ground where only partial information about the inputs of honest parties is exposed.

Consider the following simple protocol for the OR function. Let G be a finite Abelian group, and let each party P_i locally map its input bit x_i to the group element $y_i = 0$ if $x_i = 0$ and to a uniformly random element $y_i \in G$ if $x_i = 1$. Now the parties run a secure addition protocol that computes the sum $Y = \sum_{i=1}^{n} y_i$ without revealing additional information to any subset of parties (even to a dishonest majority). Such addition protocol is easy to implement in the information-theoretic setting using the homomorphic property of additive secret sharing [7]. If $Y = 0$, then the parties output 0 and otherwise they output 1.

It is easy to see that the above protocol produces the correct output (i.e., the disjunction of the n inputs) except with $1/|G|$ error probability, which can be made arbitrarily small by choosing a large enough G. A key feature of this protocol is that even an adversary who corrupts a majority of the parties only learns limited information about the inputs of the uncorrupted parties, namely the OR of their input bits. This can provide in many cases a reasonable security guarantee. For instance, if the OR function is used to make a veto decision, then the adversary can only learn whether *at least one* of the uncorrupted parties decided to veto, without learning additional information about the number or identity of parties who vetoed. This provides deniability even in the case where all but two of the parties are corrupted.

However, the above protocol fails to meet the standard security requirement for information-theoretic MPC in the presence of a dishonest minority, i.e. that a minority adversary learns nothing about the inputs of the uncorrupted parties as long as at least one of the adversary's inputs is $x_i = 1$. In this case, the (semi-honest) adversary can both learn the OR of the honest parties' inputs and force the output to be 1. Thus, there is room to do better.

1.1   Our Contribution

In this work we initiate a systematic study of the "best-possible information-theoretic security" for MPC protocols, when the adversary can corrupt an arbitrary number of parties. For the case of passive (semi-honest) adversary, we characterize the information that *must* be leaked to a dishonest majority. Then, restricting the adversary to learn *only* that amount of information would yield the best possible security that can be obtained in this setting. For some interesting functions, we also design information theoretic protocols that achieve this notion, namely provide standard security for honest majority, and leak only the necessary information to a dishonest majority.[1] We now give a more detailed account of our results.

New Notion of Security. We formally define our new notion of Best-possible Information-Theoretic MPC (BIT-MPC) as one that offers the standard notion of security against a corruption of a minority of parties and, additionally, offers the following kind of *residual security* against an adversary who corrupts a majority of the parties: the adversary cannot learn anything more than the *residual function* of the honest parties' inputs. By this, we mean that the adversary is allowed to learn only the value of the function on the inputs of the honest parties combined with *every choice of inputs* for the corrupted parties. In the case of OR from the above example (and similarly for the dual case of AND), this means that the adversary can only learn the OR of uncorrupted inputs, because the output for any choice of corrupted inputs can be derived from this information. As another example, consider the maximum function; in this case a dishonest majority can only learn the maximum of the honest parties' inputs.

Positive Results. For some special functions of interest, we design protocols that realize the notion of BIT-MPC. This includes protocols for AND/OR, for deciding whether the inputs x_i satisfy a linear system of equations $Ax = b$ over a finite

---

[1] Our notion of best-possible security, as well as both positive and negative results, apply not only in the threshold case but also to general adversary structures, replacing "honest majority" by any Q2 structure [28].

field, and for computing functions like the maximum/minimum of the inputs, where the inputs come from a finite domain. While these functions are simple, they are useful for natural application scenarios. For instance, securely computing many parallel instances of AND can be useful for realizing multi-party instances of secure set intersection where sets come from a universe of bounded size. This in turn can be helpful for many real-world scenarios (consider a secure Doodle poll as a concrete example). Our protocols for these functions, especially when combined with other optimizations such as share-packing [17,20] and pseudo-random secret sharing [14], lead to protocols that retain the efficiency advantages of honest-majority MPC and additionally offer a very meaningful protection against corrupted majorities. We expect such protocols to be attractive for implementations. See Sect. 6 for discussion of applications and concrete efficiency. Finally, most (but not all) of our results are easy to extend to the setting of security against *malicious* adversaries. This extension is discussed in Sect. 7.

Our BIT-MPC protocols build on protocols for non-interactive MPC (NIMPC) in the model of [4]. We rely on a restricted type of NIMPC protocols in which the correlated randomness is sampled uniformly from a linear vector space. We design such protocols for the above functions and show how to generally transform any such restricted NIMPC protocol into a BIT-MPC protocol.

Our results on NIMPC are independently motivated by the goal of making correlated randomness in NIMPC reusable or replacing it by a PKI setup under standard assumptions. It was previously known that both goals can be achieved for *general* functions by using indistinguishability obfuscation (see [25] and [24] respectively). Our work gives the first nontrivial examples for functions that admit NIMPC protocols with these useful features under weaker assumptions: one-way functions for reusability, and non-interactive key exchange (NIKE) for PKI setup.

Negative Results. We complement our positive results by several negative results. First, by strengthening known results about characterizations of two-party secure computation (e.g., [5,6,12,32]) and applying *partition arguments* (e.g., [12]), we show that our notion of BIT-MPC, indeed provides the best possible security. Namely, we prove that, for every (non-trivial) function f and for any coalition T, if standard security holds against the set of parties $\overline{T}$, then the parties in T must learn the corresponding residual function and, therefore, residual security is the best one can hope for.

Contrary to the general feasibility results for the standard notion of security, e.g. [6,11], for our notion we rule out the possibility of *efficient* BIT-MPC protocols for all efficiently computable functions. More precisely, we show that such a positive result would imply that the polynomial hierarchy collapses. The proof of this fact is similar to the analogous negative result for best-possible indistinguishability obfuscation [23] (and implicitly in the context of instance hiding [1]). Our results do not rule out the possibility that *every* function f admits a BIT-MPC protocol if one does not take computational complexity into account. This is the main question left open by our work. We do provide a first step towards resolving this question, by showing that such protocols exist for all 4-input functions (see Sect. 4.4).

Finally, we show a negative result that applies to a restricted class of protocols that captures most of our positives results. When considering Boolean functions f (outputting a single bit), protocols that have a certain "bilinear" structure over a finite field $\mathbb{F}$ are limited to only functions $f(x)$ that can be expressed as a linear test "$Ax = b$?" over $\mathbb{F}$. This relies on analogous results on the power of degree-2 randomized encodings of functions [30].

1.2 Related Work

Several prior works, including the works of Chaum [10], Ishai et al. [31], and Hirt et al. [27], provide a hybrid security guarantee of information-theoretic security for honest majority but need to switch to computational security against dishonest majority. This is contrasted with our work, where in both cases security is information-theoretic. Beyond the fact that we manage to preserve the information-theoretic setting, our results enjoy the efficiency benefits of this setting while the protocols in the hybrid model do not and, in fact, are even less efficient than their purely computational counterparts.

The problem of MPC with "residual security," extending the NIMPC model from [4] to the interactive setting, was recently considered in an independent work of Agarwal et al. [2]. Like our work, they show that residual security is the best possible in the presence of a corrupted majority. Furthermore, they give a combinatorial characterization for the class of functions for which residual security is *equivalent* to standard security. Similarly to our work, they also suggest a compiler from NIMPC to MPC, but their compiler is more restrictive than ours in that it does not allow interaction for emulating the NIMPC evaluator. Unlike our work, they do not consider the question of combining standard security for dishonest minority with residual security for dishonest majority, nor do they consider the class of functions to which our positive results apply.

2 Definitions

Notation. For a vector $v = (v_1, ... v_n)$ and $T = \{i_1, \ldots, i_{n'}\} \subseteq [n]$ a subset of size n' we define v_T to be $(v_{i_1}, ... v_{i_{n'}})$.

Our notion of Best-possible Information-Theoretically-secure MPC protocols (BIT-MPC) begins with the standard notion of secure protocols that only provides security against some sets of corrupted parties, but not other (e.g., only against a corrupted minority).[2] We augment the standard notion by requiring that even corrupted sets for which it is impossible to guarantee standard security, do not learn anything more than the *residual function* of the honest parties'

---

[2] We note that in the pure information-theoretic setting we consider, the standard definitions below are equivalent to the definitions using a (computationally unbounded) simulator.

inputs (which we later show is necessary). We start by recalling the definition of the residual function.

Definition 2.1 (Residual Function [26]). *Consider a fixed n-input function $f : (\{0,1\}^*)^n \to \{0,1\}^*$, let $x = (x_1,\ldots,x_n)$ be an input to f, and let $T = \{i_1,\ldots,i_{n'}\} \subseteq [n]$ be a subset of size n'. The residual function for T and x is an n'-input function $f_{T,x} : (\{0,1\}^*)^{n'} \to \{0,1\}^*$, obtained from f by restricting the input variables indexed by $[n]\setminus T$ to their values in x. That is, $f_{T,x}(y_1,\ldots,y_{n'}) = f(z_1,\ldots,z_n)$, where for $\ell \notin T$ we have $z_\ell = x_\ell$, while for $\ell = i_j \in T$ we have $z_\ell = y_j$.*

Definition 2.2 (Standard and Residual Security). *Let f be an n-input function, let $\Pi[\kappa]$ be an n-party protocol, for parties $P_1,\ldots,P_n$, that depends on a parameter κ, and fix some subset of parties $T \subseteq [n]$. Define $\mathsf{View}_{P_i}(x)$ as the local view of party P_i (including its randomness and the messages it received) during the execution of $\Pi(x)$.*

Standard Security. *Π provides standard security against T if for any two inputs x, x' such that $x_T = x'_T$ and $f(x) = f(x')$, the two views $\mathsf{View}_T(x) = \{\{\mathsf{View}_{P_i}(x)\}_{i\in T}, f(x)\}$ and $\mathsf{View}_T(x') = \{\{\mathsf{View}_{P_i}(x')\}_{i\in T}, f(x')\}$ are statistically close, upto a distance of at most $2^{-\kappa}$.*

Residual Security. *Π provides residual security against T if for any two inputs x, x' such that $x_T = x'_T$ and the residual function, $f_{T,x} \equiv f_{T,x'}$, the two views $\mathsf{View}_T(x) = \{\{\mathsf{View}_{P_i}(x)\}_{i\in T}, f_{T,x}\}$ and $\mathsf{View}_T(x') = \{\{\mathsf{View}_{P_i}(x')\}_{i\in T}, f_{T,x'}\}$ are statistically close, upto a distance of at most $2^{-\kappa}$.*

Definition 2.3 (BIT-MPC). *Let f be an n-input function, let $\Pi[\kappa]$ be an n-party protocol that depends on parameter κ, and consider some threshold $t \leq n$. We say that Π is a t-private, best-possible, information-theoretic protocol for f (t-BIT-MPC) if the following conditions hold:*

- *Correctness: For all $x \in (\{0,1\}^*)^n$ it holds that $\Pi[\kappa](x) = f(x)$ with all but probability $2^{-\kappa}$ (taken over the randomness of Π).*
- *For any set $T \subseteq [n], |T| \leq t$, Π provides standard security against T.*
- *For any set $T \subseteq [n], |T| > t$, Π provides residual security against T.*

We note that the definitions above were written in terms of an n-input/1-output function, but they extend naturally also to n-input/n-output functions (and later in this paper we sometimes need that extension). The only difference is that when considering a set $T \subseteq [n]$ we only look at the outputs of parties in the set T (i.e. $f(x)_T$). Hence, the residual function for T and x will be an n'-input/n'-output function, and the standard security notion will refer to every x, x' such that $f(x)_T = f(x')_T$ (even if $f(x) \neq f(x')$ when considering also the outputs outside T).

We also note that there is nothing special about threshold, and Definition 2.3 extends to any adversary structure (so, rather than considering t-BIT-MPC, we can talk about $\mathcal{T}$-BIT-MPC for an arbitrary adversary structure $\mathcal{T}$).

3   NIMPC with Restricted Correlated Randomness

The main technical tool that we use for our positive results on BIT-MPC are non-interactive MPC (NIMPC) protocols [4,19], where parties cannot interact with each other. To provide security in this setting, the parties are provided with some *correlated randomness*, which is chosen ahead of time, independently of the secret inputs. With this setup in hand, each party simply announces a single message to all parties and the output of the function is computed locally (possibly by all parties) on these messages.

Definition 3.1 (Non-interactive MPC (NIMPC)). *A non-interactive MPC protocol $\Pi[\kappa]$ for n parties, $P_1, \ldots, P_n$, holding inputs $x = (x_1, \ldots, x_n)$ resp. (and parameter κ) is comprised of three parts:*

(1) randomness generation, $(r_1, \ldots, r_n) \leftarrow \mathsf{Gen}(\kappa)$, generating n random but correlated variables;

(2) local message functions, $\mathsf{Msg} = (\mathsf{Msg}_1, \ldots, \mathsf{Msg}_n)$, with Msg_i taking randomness r_i and local input x_i and outputting a message $m_i \leftarrow \mathsf{Msg}_i(x_i, r_i)$;

(3) evaluation function, $y \leftarrow \mathsf{Eval}(m_1, \ldots, m_n)$, taking n messages $\{m_i\}_i$ and computing the output y.

We define the view *of a subset $T \subseteq [n]$ in the execution of $\Pi[\kappa](x)$ as consisting of their own input and randomness, as well as everyone's messages,*

$$\mathsf{View}_T(x) = \{(x_i, r_i) | i \in T\} \cup \{m_1, \ldots, m_n\}.$$

We say that Π is a private non-interactive MPC protocol *for an n-input function $f(x_1, \ldots, x_n)$ if the following conditions hold.*

Correctness. *For any $x \in (\{0, 1\}^*)^n$ it holds that $\Pi[\kappa](x) = f(x)$ with all but probability $2^{-\kappa}$ (taken over the randomness of Π).*

Privacy. *Π provides residual security against any subset. That is, for any set $T \subset [n]$ and any two inputs x, x' such that $x_T = x'_T$ and $f_{T,x} \equiv f_{T,x'}$, the two views $\mathsf{View}_T(x)$ and $\mathsf{View}_T(x')$ are statistically close, upto distance of at most $2^{-\kappa}$.*

When using an NIMPC protocol Π as a tool in our interactive setting, we must address the issues of how to generate the randomness, how messages are announced, and how to compute the output. It will be helpful to consider the following hierarchy of correlated randomness setups. Each level in the hierarchy has features that are useful independently of our main goal of constructing interactive BIT-MPC protocols.

1. **Unrestricted correlation:** Here the joint distribution of $(r_1, \ldots, r_n)$ output by Gen is arbitrary. This setting enables the strongest known results for NIMPC. In particular, every finite function f has a perfectly secure NIMPC protocol (as per Definition 3.1) in which the length of the messages is comparable to the truth-table size of f, and symmetric functions over $\{0, 1\}^n$ have protocols in which the message length is quasi-polynomial in n [8].

2. **Linear correlation:** This is the type of setup most relevant to our work. A *linear correlation* is one that is uniform over some vector space $V \subset \mathbb{F}^m$ (for some $m \geq n$). More concretely, Gen is defined by a $k \times m$ matrix G over $\mathbb{F}$ and a partition of the m column indices of G into n sets S_i. The algorithm Gen proceeds by computing $r = sG$ for a random vector $s \in \mathbb{F}^k$ and letting r_i be r restricted to its S_i-entries. We will often let $m = n$ so that each r_i is a single field element.

3. **Replicated correlation:** This is a special case of linear correlation obtained by picking N random and independent field elements s_i and distributing each s_i to a fixed subset S_i of parties. An advantage of replicated correlations is that many copies of them can be generated by using a pseudo-random function. Thus, NIMPC with correlated randomness can be made *reusable* by using only a one-way function, or fast symmetric cryptography in practice. Using the share conversion technique from [14,21], any n-party NIMPC protocol that uses a linear correlation setup can be compiled into one that uses the weaker replicated correlation setup, at the cost of increasing the size of the correlated randomness by at most a factor of 2^n.

4. **Pairwise-replicated correlation:** This is a special case of replicated correlation where each S_i is of size 2. Namely, each pair of parties share some secret randomness, independent of the randomness of other pairs. An advantage of this setup is that it can be implemented with a public-key infrastructure (PKI), using any 2-party non-interactive key agreement (NIKE) (which can be based on standard assumptions such as DDH). In contrast, replacing more general types of correlated or even replicated randomness by PKI is only known under stronger primitives such as multilinear maps or indistinguishability obfuscation [24].

Our BIT-MPC protocols will employ NIMPC protocols with linear correlations, which can be reduced to replicated correlations. Some useful special cases can be even based on NIMPC with pairwise correlations. Such special NIMPC protocols are independently motivated by the features discussed above.

4   Protocols

4.1   Compiler from NIMPC to BIT-MPC

Our main positive result is a compiler, that starts with an NIMPC protocol for a function f, and constructs a BIT-MPC protocol for f. In more detail, the ingredients for our compiler are protocols for parties $P_1, ..., P_n$:

- An n-party NIMPC protocol $\Pi = \{\mathsf{Gen}, \mathsf{Msg}, \mathsf{Eval}\}$ for an n-input function f;
- An n-party interactive MPC protocol Ψ_{Gen} for the randomized Gen function of Π.
- An n-party interactive MPC protocol Ψ_{Eval} for the Eval function of Π.

Given these protocols, the resulting interactive protocol $\Phi = \mathsf{Compile}(\Pi, \Psi_{\mathsf{Gen}}, \Psi_{\mathsf{Eval}})$ is as follows. On inputs $x_1, \ldots, x_n$ held by $P_1, \ldots, P_n$ resp.:

1. The parties run Ψ_{Gen} to evaluate Gen; r_i is the output of party P_i;
2. Each party P_i computes locally $m_i = \mathsf{Msg}_i(x_i, r_i)$;
3. The parties run Ψ_{Eval} each using m_i as its input to the protocol, to get $y = \mathsf{Eval}(m_1, \ldots, m_n)$.

Lemma 4.1. *Let f be an n-input function, Π a private NIMPC protocol for f, and let $\Psi_{\mathsf{Gen}}, \Psi_{\mathsf{Eval}}$, and the resulting $\Phi = \mathsf{Compile}(\Pi, \Psi_{\mathsf{Gen}}, \Psi_{\mathsf{Eval}})$ be as above.*

Correctness. *If Ψ_{Gen} and Ψ_{Eval}, are correct then Φ is a correct protocol for f.*

Security. *For any subset $T \subseteq [n]$, the following holds:*

Residual Security. *If Ψ_{Gen} is correct and provides standard security against T, then Φ provides (at least) residual security against T.*

Standard Security. *If Ψ_{Gen} is correct and Ψ_{Eval} is correct and provides standard security against T then the resulting Φ also provides standard security against T.*

Proof. Correctness can be verified by inspection. It remains to show security.

Residual Security. The argument here is that, due to the security of Ψ_{Gen}, we are essentially in the world of NIMPC where members of T see only their own randomness and everyone's messages, hence we get (at least) residual security.

In more detail, since Ψ_{Gen} provides standard security against T, and as Gen has no secret inputs, then the transcript of Ψ_{Gen} does not reveal to the parties in T anything beyond their collective outputs, namely the (correlated) random values, $\{r_i : i \in T\}$.

Moreover, the transcript of Ψ_{Eval} is a randomized function of the inputs of that protocol, namely the m_i's, so at worst it reveals these m_i's to the parties in T. Hence, at worst, the view of the parties in T in the protocol $\Phi(x)$ consists of their own x_i, r_i's, and all the m_i's, which is exactly $\mathsf{View}_T(x)$ in Π, as defined in Definition 3.1. Similarly their view in $\Phi(x')$ is, at worst, $\mathsf{View}_T(x')$ in Π.

By the NIMPC security of Π, the views $\mathsf{View}_T(x)$ and $\mathsf{View}_T(x')$ are statistically close for any two x, x' with $x_T = x'_T$ and the same residual function relative to T, $f_{T,x} \equiv f_{T,x'}$.

Standard Security. Here the argument is that (a) Gen is independent of the inputs, and (b) the transcript of Ψ_{Eval} does not leak to T anything about the inputs other than the function value.

Fix x, x' such that $x_T = x'_T$ and $f(x) = f(x')$, and denote the messages that the parties compute on these inputs by $m = (m_1, \ldots, m_n)$ and $m' = (m'_1, \ldots, m'_n)$, respectively (i.e., $m_i = \mathsf{Msg}_i(x_i, r_i)$ and $m'_i = \mathsf{Msg}_i(x'_i, r_i)$). By correctness, we have that $\mathsf{Eval}(m) = \mathsf{Eval}(m')$ except with exponentially small probability. Since, by the locality of the messages in NIMPC protocols, we have $m_T = m'_T$, and as $\mathsf{Eval}(m) = \mathsf{Eval}(m')$, then the standard security against T of Ψ_{Eval} implies that the views of T in the executions $\Psi_{\mathsf{Eval}}(m)$ and $\Psi_{\mathsf{Eval}}(m')$ are statistically close.

Together with the fact that the protocol Ψ_{Gen} is independent of the inputs x, x', we conclude that the views of T in the executions $\Psi_{\mathsf{Eval}}(x)$ and $\Psi_{\mathsf{Eval}}(x')$ are also statistically close. $\qquad\square$

Using Lemma 4.1, we can deliver Best-possible Information-Theoretic MPC protocols in many interesting cases. Consider attempting a t-BIT-MPC for some function f, with a threshold $t < n/2$. By the lemma, all we need is some NIMPC protocol Π for f, together with:

- A protocol Ψ_{Eval} providing standard security against dishonest minority; and
- A protocol Ψ_{Gen} that provides complete privacy, even against dishonest majority, but only for the input-less function Gen.[3]

If we find an NIMPC protocol Π with a simple enough randomness generation function Gen, then we could hope to find a protocol Ψ_{Gen} with complete privacy. Adding a standard protocol for Eval (e.g., using the BGW construction), we would have standard security against dishonest minority, and residual security against dishonest majority, as needed. If we are willing to settle for a smaller threshold (say $t < 2n/5$), then we can use even more efficient protocols for Ψ_{Eval} (see, e.g., [17,20]). This could give truly practical protocols, that provide meaningful (residual) security, no matter how many parties are corrupted.

Theorem 4.1. *Let $f(\cdot)$ be an n-input function. If there exists a private NIMPC protocol for f, $\Pi = \{\mathsf{Gen}, \mathsf{Msg}, \mathsf{Eval}\}$, and a protocol Ψ_{Gen} that computes Gen with standard security for all $T \subset [n]$ then, for any threshold $t < n/2$, there exists a t-private BIT-MPC protocol for f.* □

We remark again that there is nothing special about threshold, and an analogous theorem holds for any realizable adversary structure.

The main condition in Theorem 4.1 is that we have a protocol Ψ_{Gen} for the randomness-generation function with complete privacy. As discussed in Sect. 3, there is a hierarchy of correlated-randomness types that can enable the computation of different functions of increasing complexity. In the following, we examine various correlations that can be generated with complete privacy. The ideas behind some of the schemes that follow have been previously suggested but are presented here for self-containment and, even more so, because they are good examples for the application of our BIT-MPC theorem.

4.2 BIT-MPC from NIMPC with Pairwise Shared Randomness

One class of correlated randomness that can be generated with complete privacy (i.e., standard security against any set $T \subset [n]$), is pairwise shared randomness. The protocol Ψ_{Gen} is obvious: For $i < j$, party P_i sends to party P_j a random value $r_{i,j} \in \mathbb{Z}_p$, and the randomness of each P_i is set as $\{r_{k,i} : k < i\} \cup \{r_{i,k} : i < k\}$. It can easily be verified that this $\binom{n}{2}$-message protocol offers the desired security guarantees: Every party P_i sees only the values $r_{i,j}$ that it sent and $r_{j,i}$ that it received, and any value shared between two honest parties is not known to the attacker. Below, we examine some functions that can be computed using such pairwise shared randomness.

---

[3] We sometimes use the term *complete privacy* to refer to protocols that provide standard security against every subset $T \subseteq [n]$.

Shares of Zero. Pairwise shared randomness can be easily converted into a correlated sharing of 0, just using local computation [9,14]: Each party P_i sets its share to $r_i = \sum_{k<i} r_{k,i} - \sum_{i<k} r_{i,k}$. It can be easily verified that, for any set of parties T, the only information revealed about the shares of the parties in $\overline{T}$ is their sum (and otherwise the shares of $\overline{T}$ are random).

Sum of Inputs. Shares of zero are used in the following simple private NIMPC protocol for computing the sum [9,14] in a finite Abelian group.

Parties: $P_1, \ldots, P_n$
Input: $x_i \in G$ held by P_i
Output: $\sum_{i=1}^{n} x_i \in G$
Protocol:
    Gen: Correlated sharing of 0; P_i has randomness r_i.
    $\text{Msg}_i(x_i, r_i)$: Output $m_i = x_i + r_i \in G$.
    $\text{Eval}(m_1, \ldots, m_n)$: Output $\sum_{i=1}^{n} m_i \in G$.

Fig. 1. Sum of Parties' Inputs in a finite Abelian group G

We remark that applying our BIT-MPC compiler to the NIMPC protocol in Fig. 1 is pointless, since the output of the SUM function by itself always exposes the residual function (i.e. the sum of the inputs of the honest parties), even to a dishonest minority. However, this NIMPC protocol will be a useful tool in compiling other functions into BIT-MPC.

Bitwise OR. Beimel et al. [4] present a private NIMPC for computing the OR function, assuming a (correlated randomness) sharing of 0. Each party chooses a new random value if its bit is 1 and uses the randomness from the zero-sharing if its input bit is 0. Then, the parties run the sum protocol on these values. If all the original bits are 0 then each party entered the randomness from the zero-sharing and thus the sum will be zero, and otherwise the sum will be nonzero with high probability. The parties output 0 if the sum is zero, and 1 otherwise. See Fig. 2.

The above protocol exemplifies nicely how applying our BIT-MPC compiler and Theorem 4.1 adds privacy to the inputs of the parties. Observe that this protocol by itself reveals the OR of the honest parties' bits to the adversary, regardless of the number of corrupted parties and their inputs. (For example, a single corrupted P_j can check the equality $r_j \overset{?}{=} -\sum_{i \neq j} m_i$.) Applying our compiler, we improve security by ensuring that the sum of m_i's is never exposed to any minority group. In particular a single adversarial P_i with input value 1 learns nothing about the inputs of the other parties.

Computing the Maximum. To compute $MAX(x_1, \ldots, x_n)$ (with the x_i's taken from $[p]$ for some $p \in \mathbb{Z}$), each party i with input x_i locally computes the p bits

Parties: $P_1, \ldots, P_n$
Input: $x_i \in \{0, 1\}$ held by P_i
Output: $OR_{i=1}^n x_i$
Protocol:
    Gen: Correlated sharing of 0, providing P_i with r_i.
    $\mathsf{Msg}_i(x_i, r_i)$: Output: $m_i = \begin{cases} r_i & \text{if } x_i = 0 \\ R_i \in_R \mathbb{Z}_p & \text{otherwise} \end{cases}$
    $\mathsf{Eval}(m_1, \ldots, m_n)$: $Output = \begin{cases} 0 & \text{if } \sum_{i=1}^n m_i = 0 \bmod p \\ 1 & \text{otherwise} \end{cases}$

Fig. 2. NIMPC protocol for the OR of Parties' Inputs

$\chi_{i,\ell} := (x_i \geq \ell)$, for all $\ell \in [p]$. Then, the parties run p copies of the OR protocol, computing $\psi_\ell := OR_{i \in [n]} \chi_{i,\ell}$, for all ℓ. The maximum value is the largest index ℓ for which $\psi_\ell = 1$. See Fig. 3.

Parties: $P_1, \ldots, P_n$
Input: $x_i \in \mathbb{Z}_p$ held by P_i
Output: $x^* = \max_i x_i$

Protocol:
    Gen : generate p independent sharings of 0. The randomness of P_i is all its
        shares $r_i = \big(r_i[\ell]\big)_{\ell \in [p]}$.

    $\mathsf{Msg}_i(x_i, r_i)$: 1. For each $\ell \in [p]$ compute the bit $\chi_{i,\ell} = \begin{cases} 1 & \text{if } x_i \geq \ell \\ 0 & \text{otherwise} \end{cases}$

        2. Run p instances of the Msg function of the OR protocol, setting
        $\forall \ell \in [p]$, $m_i[\ell] = \mathsf{Msg}^{OR}\big(\chi_{i,\ell}, \, r_i[\ell]\big)$.

        3. Concatenate $m_i = \big(m_i[\ell]\big)_{\ell \in [p]}$.
    $\mathsf{Eval}(m_1, \ldots, m_n)$: for each $\ell \in [p]$ set $\psi_\ell = \mathsf{Eval}^{OR}\big(m_1[\ell], \ldots, m_n[\ell]\big)$.
        Output the largest ℓ such that $\psi_\ell = 1$.

Fig. 3. NIMPC protocol for MAX, Maximum of Parties' Inputs

Lemma 4.2. *The protocol from Fig. 3 is a private NIMPC protocol for computing the maximum value of the inputs of the parties.* $\qquad\square$

We remark that since we are dealing with semi-honest parties, then we do not have issues of consistency between the inputs in the different OR instances. The protocol from Fig. 3, though constant round, is inefficient for large p as it requires p invocations of the OR protocol and thus pn messages over all. This means that also the BIT-MPC protocol that we get by compiling it will be inefficient.

Although we do not know of a more efficient non-interactive MPC protocol from pairwise shared randomness, we are able to get a more efficient interactive BIT-MPC protocol for MAX. In the interactive setting, we can run the multiple copies of the OR protocol sequentially, rather than all at once, hence using binary search to get only $\log p$ invocations of the underlying OR protocol. See Fig. 4. Note that the bits ψ_j that are exposed by the protocol from Fig. 4 are actually implied by the output value $\max_i x_i$. We get:

Parties: $P_1, \ldots, P_n$
Input: $x_i \in \mathbb{Z}_p$ held by P_i
Output: $x^* = \max_i x_i$
Protocol:

The parties first run in parallel $\lceil \log p \rceil$ executions of a random sharing of zero. The randomness of P_i is all its shares $r_i = \left(r_i[\ell] \right)_{\ell \in \lceil \log p \rceil}$. Then, each party P_i does the following:

1. Set $min := 0, max := p - 1$.
2. For $j = 1, \ldots, \lceil \log p \rceil$ do the following:
3.   Set $mid := \lceil (min + max)/2 \rceil$ and $\chi_{i,j} := (x_i \geq? mid)$.
4.   Run Msg_i of the OR protocol, broadcasting $m_{i,j} := \mathsf{Msg}_i^{OR}\left(\chi_{i,j}; r_i[j] \right)$.
5.   Execute $\Psi_{\mathsf{Eval}}^{OR}(m_{i,j})$ to get $\psi_j := \mathsf{Eval}^{OR}\left(m_{1,j}, \ldots, m_{n,j} \right)$.
6.   If $\psi_j = 1$ then $min := mid$, otherwise $max := mid - 1$.
7. End-for
8. Output min.

Fig. 4. A more efficient interactive BIT-MPC protocol for MAX

Lemma 4.3. *For any threshold $t \leq n/2$, if $\Psi_{\mathsf{Eval}}^{OR}(m_{i,j})$ from Fig. 4 provides standard security against sets of size up to t, then the protocol from Fig. 4 is an interactive t-BIT-MPC for computing the MAX function.* ☐

4.3 BIT-MPC Based on Linearly-Correlated Randomness

As stated earlier, linear correlation is a powerful class of correlated randomness that can handle many interesting functions. The simplest format of linear correlation has each party P_i holds a piece of randomness r_i, where the vector $r = (r_1, \ldots, r_n)$ was chosen at random in some known linear subspace in $\mathbb{F}^n$. Namely $r = s \cdot A$, where A is a fixed, public $k \times n$ matrix that defines the linear space, and s is a uniformly random vector in $\mathbb{F}^k$.

This class generalizes the secret-sharing of zero that we used above, and we can compute the randomness generation for it with complete privacy, using similar techniques as for zero-sharing [7,16]. Specifically, each party P_i chooses a random vector s_i and computes $t_i = s_i \times A$, then sends the entry $t_i[j]$ to P_j (for every j). The correlated-randomness element of each P_j is then set as $r_j = \sum_i t_i[j] = ((\sum_i s_i) \times A)[j]$.

To show complete privacy, fix a set $T \subset [n]$ of corrupted parties and note that the values $\{t_i[T] : i \notin T\}$ seen by the parties in T determine the s_i's only upto the solution of the system $(s_{\overline{T}} \times A)[T] = t_{\overline{T}}[T]$ (with $s_{\overline{T}}[T] = \sum_{i \notin T} s_i[T]$, $t_{\overline{T}}[T] = \sum_{i \notin T} t_i[T]$), which are exactly all the inputs with the same output at T.

We also note that using the share conversion technique from [14,21], we can localy convert "replicated correlated randomness" to linearly correlated randomness. In a little more detail, by giving every subset $T \subset [n]$ a different random seed for a PRG/PRF, the parties can locally generate unbounded number of pseudo-random vectors in the range of $f_A(s) = s \cdot A$, without any interaction. This means that every party must keep 2^{n-1} seeds, but for small values of n this still yields a very practical way of generating linearly-correlated (pseudo)randomness, which can then be used in the protocols that we describe below.

Testing for Membership in an Affine Space. We next show that linear correlations allow us to compute, for any matrix A, the function that determines whether an input vector belongs to the kernel of the rows of A. Namely

$$\mathsf{Affine}_{A,0}(x) = \begin{cases} 1 & \text{if } Ax = 0 \\ 0 & \text{otherwise} \end{cases}.$$

Since the parties have the vector $r = sA$ which is uniform in the columns space of A, it is sufficient to check if the inner product of x and r is zero. Hence each party computes $y_i = x_i r_i$, and the parties then run the SUM protocol from Fig. 1.

This protocol can be modified to compute the function $\mathsf{Affine}_{A,b}(x)$, i.e., to check whether $Ax = b$ for a matrix A, as before, and a known vector b (rather than equality to zero). This is done by fixing a known vector w such that $Aw = b$ and having each party set $y_i = (x_i - w_i)r_i$ and run the SUM protocol. The resulting protocol is described in Fig. 5.

Parties: $P_1, \ldots, P_n$
Parameter: Publicly known $A \in \mathbb{F}^{k \times n}$, $b \in \mathbb{F}^k$, and $w \in \mathbb{F}^n$ s.t. $Aw = b$.
Input: $x = (x_1, \ldots, x_n)$, $x_i \in \mathbb{F}$ held by P_i
Output: check whether $Ax = b$
Protocol:
  Gen:
      1. Linearly correlated randomness, $r = sA$ for a uniform $s \in \mathbb{F}^k$; P_i has r_i
      2. Correlated sharing of 0, providing P_i with ρ_i. Let $R_i = (r_i, \rho_i)$.
  Msg$_i$(x_i, R_i): Output $m_i = (x_i - w_i)r_i + \rho_i$

  Eval($m_1, \ldots, m_n$): Set $y = \Sigma_{i=1}^n m_i$, Output $= \begin{cases} 1 & \text{if } y = 0 \\ 0 & \text{otherwise} \end{cases}$

Fig. 5. NIMPC protocol for affine space membership, testing whether $Ax = b$ for public A, b,

Lemma 4.4. *The protocol from Fig. 5 is a private NIMPC protocol for affine space membership. Moreover, there exists a completely private protocol Π_{Gen} for computing the randomness generation function, with standard privacy against any set $T \subset [n]$.*

Proof. For correctness, note that $y = \langle r, x - w \rangle = sA(x - w) = \langle s, Ax - b \rangle$. Hence $y = 0$ with probability one when $Ax = b$, and $y \neq 0$ whp when $Ax \neq b$.

For privacy of the NIMPC protocol, we show that for any set $T \subset [n]$ and any two inputs x, x' such that $x_T = x'_T$ and $f_{T,x} \equiv f_{T,x'}$, the views of T on x and x' are distributed identically. It is convenient to first consider the case $b = 0$ (and thus w.l.o.g. $w = 0$). These views consist of (the public A and)

$$r_T = \{r_i : i \in T\}, \ \rho_T = \{\rho_i : i \in T\}, \ x_T = \{x_i : i \in T\} \text{ or } x'_T = \{x'_i : i \in T\}, \text{and}$$
$$m_{\overline{T}} = \{m_i = x_i r_i + \rho_i : i \notin T\} \text{ or } m' = \{m'_i = x'_i r_i + \rho_i : i \notin T\}, \text{respectively.}$$

Since the ρ_i's are a random n-out-of-n sharing of zero, then the m_i's (or m'_i are uniformly random subject to their sum, regardless of r_T, ρ_T, x_T. It is thus enough to show that for any fixed r, we have $\sum_{i \notin T} m_i = \sum_{i \notin T} m'_i$ iff $f_{T,x} \equiv f_{T,x'}$.

To see this, notice that $f_{T,x} \equiv f_{T,x'}$ iff $A_{\overline{T}} x_{\overline{T}} = A_{\overline{T}} x'_{\overline{T}}$, where $A_{\overline{T}} x_{\overline{T}}$ is the sum of the columns of A corresponding to $i \notin T$, each multiplied by the corresponding x_i's (and similarly for $A_{\overline{T}} x'_{\overline{T}}$). Namely $A_{\overline{T}} x_{\overline{T}} =: \sum_{i \notin T} x_i A_i$ and $A_T =: \sum_{i \notin T} x_i A_i$. This is true since, for any x^*_T, we have $f_{T,x}(x^*_T) = A_{\overline{T}} x_{\overline{T}} + A_T x^*_T$ and $f_{T,x'}(x^*_T) = A_{\overline{T}} x'_{\overline{T}} + A_T x^*_T$.

Consider therefore x, x' such that $A_{\overline{T}} x_{\overline{T}} = A_{\overline{T}} x'_{\overline{T}}$, and fix r and ρ. Then

$$\sum_{i \notin T} m_i - \sum_{i \notin T} \rho_i = \langle r_{\overline{T}}, x_{\overline{T}} \rangle = (sA)_{\overline{T}} x_{\overline{T}} = sA_{\overline{T}} x_{\overline{T}}$$

$$= sA_{\overline{T}} x'_{\overline{T}} = (sA)_{\overline{T}} x'_{\overline{T}} = \langle r_{\overline{T}}, x'_{\overline{T}} \rangle = \sum_{i \notin T} m'_i - \sum_{i \notin T} \rho_i,$$

and therefore $\sum_{i \notin T} m_i = \sum_{i \notin T} m'_i$. This completes the proof of privacy for the NIMPC protocol from Fig. 5 for the case of $b = 0$. The case of arbitrary b is similar (except that in the last equality we have another term $A_{\overline{T}} w_{\overline{T}}$ which is independent of x, x').

Finally, we note that the shared randomness in this protocol consists of $r = sA$ and a sharing of zero ρ, both of which can be computed with perfect privacy as we explained earlier.   □

Corollary 4.1 (Affine Membership Over A Field). *For any fixed $A \in \mathbb{F}^{k \times n}$ and $b \in \mathbb{F}^k$, there is a $n/2$-BIT-MPC protocols for checking $Ax = b$ over $\mathbb{F}$.*   □

Some Applications of the Affine Membership Protocol. Computing affine membership is more useful than it may seem. In particular, it captures most functions considered in the previous section as special cases, as well as additional useful functions. For example, the AND function can be realized utilizing the identity matrix $A = I$ and checking $Ax = b$ for $b = (1, \dots, 1)$. The OR function is identical to AND up to relabeling of inputs and outputs, but can be realized directly using any invertible matrix A and $b = 0$, since $Ax = 0$ holds if and only if all the x_i's are 0. Affine membership can also be used to check equality of all inputs, namely the function $\mathsf{AllEq}(x_1, \ldots, x_n)$ which outputs 1 if $x_1 = x_2 = \ldots = x_n$ and 0 otherwise. Here we use a matrix $A \in \mathbb{F}^{(n-1) \times n}$ that reflects the equations $x_1 - x_2 = 0$, $x_2 - x_3 = 0$, $\ldots$, $x_{n-1} - x_n = 0$, namely, the rows of A are all of the form $(0, \ldots, 0, 1, -1, 0, \ldots, 0)$. For this matrix A, the function $\mathsf{Affine}_{A,0}(x)$ is exactly $\mathsf{AllEq}(x)$.

4.4 Four-Input Functions

A somewhat surprising corollary of the per-subset nature of Lemma 4.1 is that any 4-input function can be computed with BIT-security against dishonest minority. Namely, we get standard security for a single corrupted party, and (at least) residual security for two or more corrupted parties.

Theorem 4.2. *For every 4-input function f, there is a 1-BIT-MPC interactive protocol for computing f.*

Proof. (Sketch) Let $\Pi = (\mathsf{Gen}, \mathsf{Msg}, \mathsf{Eval})$ be an NIMPC protocol for f with general correlated randomness (e.g., from [4]), and we describe interactive protocols for $\mathsf{Gen}, \mathsf{Eval}$ as needed.

- For Ψ_{Gen}, we use a 1-of-3 BGW protocol, run by P_2, P_3, P_4, to generate the needed correlated randomness.
- For Ψ_{Eval}, we use a 2-of-5 BGW protocol for evaluation, where P_2, P_3, P_4 each play a single party, and P_1 plays the role of two parties.

The reason that this construction works is that if there are three corruptions then the corrupted parties are allowed to learn the input of the honest party, so there is no security requirement. If there is only one corruption then the BGW protocols ensure standard security (even if the corrupted party is P_1 who plays a double role in the second BGW invocation).

It remains to show that we get (at least) residual security when two parties are corrupted. If the corrupted parties do not include P_1 then the 2-of-5 BGW protocol actually gives standard security. If P_1 is corrupted then two of P_2, P_3, P_4 are honest, hence we get standard security for the randomness generation step and therefore residual security for the combined protocol. □

5   Negative Results

5.1   When "Best-Possible" Is the Best Possible

The first negative result justifies the term "best-possible" security, showing that in the information-theoretical regime, the security requirement against majority sets typically cannot be further strengthened. We start by considering two-party protocols and strengthen standard impossibility results for this setting (e.g., [5, 6, 12, 32]). Specifically, we show that in a two-party protocol between Alice and Bob to compute a function $f(x, y)$, standard information-theoretic security against Bob (i.e. if Bob learns the output and nothing else), implies that Alice necessarily learns Bob's input y. More concretely:

Lemma 5.1. *Let $f(x, y)$ be a boolean function and assume that each y is distinct; namely, for all $y \neq y'$ there exists an x such that $f(x, y) \neq f(x, y')$ (this is without loss of generality as otherwise Bob can pick one y from each "equivalence class"). Let $\mathcal{P}$ be any protocol where Bob learns $f(x, y)$ (with prob. 1) but no other information about x, then Alice can always identify y.*

Proof. Assume not. Then, for some pair of Bob inputs y, y' there is an Alice input x on which she cannot distinguish y from y'. Namely Alice's view (which consists of the transcript, as well as her input and randomness) on $(x, y), (x, y')$ is identically distributed and, in particular, it follows that $f(x, y) = f(x, y') = v$, for some $v \in \{0, 1\}$. Since y, y' are "distinct" then, for some other Alice input x', we have $f(x', y) \neq f(x', y')$. Since f is boolean then, without loss of generality, $f(x', y) = v$. Since Bob is assumed to learn nothing beyond the output, his distribution of views on (x, y) and on (x', y) (in particular, the distribution of transcripts) is the same. By a standard "corners lemma" (see, e.g., [12,32]), it follows that the transcript on (x', y') is also distributed in the same way, contradicting the correctness of the protocol $\mathcal{P}$.   □

Extensions. As stated, Lemma 5.1 assumes perfect correctness and perfect privacy. This however need not be the case and indeed some of the above papers (e.g., [12]) show that the same holds even when allowing ε-error and δ-privacy (i.e., where the statistical distance between the corresponding distributions is bounded by δ). The same modification applies in our case.

Another important extension is to deal with non-boolean functions f. Here, rather than asking for distinctness of the y's, we need a slightly more demanding (but still quite simple) richness requirement. Specifically, we ask that for any pair of Bob inputs y, y' that are not trivially distinguishable by Alice (i.e., where for some Alice input x we have $f(x, y) = f(x, y') = v$), there must also exists another Alice input x' for which $f(x', y) \neq f(x', y')$ and that one of these two values is equal to v. To illustrate this condition, consider the function $\min(x, y)$ (over some interval), where for all $y < y'$ the above condition holds with $x = y$ and $x' = y'$. This condition is a generalization of the distinctness property for boolean functions, used above; if this property holds then we will refer to the function f as being *non-trivial*. One can readily verify that the proof of Lemma 5.1 still holds for all non-trivial functions f (boolean or non-boolean).

Next, we deal with the case of n-input functions f, by applying a standard *partition argument*. It shows that, for any subset of parties T, if a protocol $\mathcal{P}$ satisfies standard security against a corrupted $\overline{T}$ then it can do no better than offering residual security against a corrupted T. (We usually think of T as a majority set, where it is always possible to ensure standard security against a corrupted $\overline{T}$, but the statement holds for any set T and this is important for generalizing the negative result to non-threshold access structures.) Formally,

Theorem 5.1. *Let f be an n-input function. Let $T \subset [n]$ be a subset of parties. Define the corresponding induced 2-argument function $f^T(\{x_i\}_{i \in T}, \{x_i\}_{i \notin T}) =: f(x_1, \ldots, x_n)$ and assume that f^T is non-trivial. Let $\mathcal{P}$ be any protocol where the parties in $\overline{T}$ learn $f(x_1, \ldots, x_n)$ but no other information about the input (information theoretically). Then, the parties in T learn the residual function $f_{T,x}$.*

Proof. Consider the two-party protocol $\mathcal{P}_T$ derived from $\mathcal{P}$ by Alice simulating the parties in T, Bob simulating the parties in $\overline{T}$ and together they compute the value $f^T(\{x_i\}_{i \in T}, \{x_i\}_{i \notin T})$. By the assumption on $\mathcal{P}$, Bob learns the output of f^T but nothing else. Hence, by Lemma 5.1 (and the following discussion), Alice learns Bob's input. In the terminology of the n-party protocol $\mathcal{P}$, this means that the view of the parties in T necessarily identifies the residual function $f_{T,x}$ (note that if two n-argument inputs x, x' induce the same residual function, i.e. $f_{T,x} = f_{T,x'}$, then they are mapped to equivalent inputs for the two-input function f^T). □

5.2 Efficient BIT-MPC Protocols Are Rare

Our next goal is to show that *computationally efficient* BIT-MPC protocols are unlikely to exist even for simple families of functions. (Specifically, their existence would imply the collapse of the polynomial hierarchy.) We mimic similar results in the context of obfuscation [23] showing that if, for example, the family of 3-CNF formulas has efficient statistical-indistinguishability obfuscation, then the Polynomial Hierarchy collapses to its second level. This, in particular, relies on the following claim (implicit in [23]; see also [1] for a similar proof in the context of instance-hiding schemes):

Lemma 5.2. *Let $\mathcal{C}$ be a family of circuits where checking equivalence is co-NP complete (e.g., a simple family such as the family of all 3CNF formulae satisfies this). Assume that there exists a probabilistic polynomial time machine $\mathcal{S}$ that is given a circuit $C \in \mathcal{C}$ as its input and that its output is a probability distribution satisfying the following properties:*

- *If $C_1 \equiv C_2$ then $\mathcal{S}(C_1) \approx \mathcal{S}(C_2)$ (i.e., the statistical distance between $\mathcal{S}(C_1), \mathcal{S}(C_2)$ is bounded by some constant, say $1/3$).*
- *If $C_1 \not\equiv C_2$ then $\mathcal{S}(C_1)$ and $\mathcal{S}(C_2)$ are far (i.e., the statistical distance between $\mathcal{S}(C_1), \mathcal{S}(C_2)$ is bounded from below by some constant, say $2/3$).*

Then, the polynomial hierarchy collapses.

Consider the 3-input universal function $U_{\mathcal{C}}(C, x, \perp)$, where C is a boolean circuit from a family of circuits $\mathcal{C}$, as above, x is an input for the circuit C (and $\perp$ indicates that the third party has no input). We argue that there is no efficient BIT-MPC protocol for this function.

Theorem 5.2. *If there is a computationally efficient 3-party BIT-MPC protocol $\mathcal{P}$ for $U_{\mathcal{C}}$, then the polynomial hierarchy collapses.*

Proof. We use the protocol $\mathcal{P}$ to construct a machine $\mathcal{S}$, as required by Lemma 5.2. Doing so, the theorem follows.

We first turn $\mathcal{P}$ into a two-party protocol $\mathcal{P}'$ for computing the two-argument function $f(x, C) = U_C(C, x, \bot)$, with Bob simulating the party in $\mathcal{P}$ holding the circuit C (i.e., a minority among the 3 parties) and Alice simulating the two others (i.e., the majority). By the best possible security of $\mathcal{P}$, Alice learns the function f_C and only this function (note that now the inputs of Bob are not distinct, as there may be several circuits that compute the same function f_C; an argument similar to that of Lemma 5.1 shows that Alice indeed learns f_C with any input x she may have).

We now construct $\mathcal{S}(C)$ as follows. Run $\mathcal{P}'$ on inputs (x_0, C), where x_0 is an arbitrary (fixed) input for Alice, and output her view in the protocol. On one hand, if $C_1 \equiv C_2$ then $f_{C_1} \equiv f_{C_2}$ and so Alice's view in both cases is identically distributed. On the other hand, if $C_1 \not\equiv C_2$, then Alice's view in the two cases is far apart. □

5.3   Simple BIT-MPC Protocols Have Limited Reach

Our last negative result shows that a natural class of "bilinear" NIMPC protocols, which captures most of our positive results, is limited in power. A *bilinear* NIMPC protocol over a finite field $\mathbb{F}$ is one in which the randomness $r_1, \ldots, r_n$ is linearly correlated, i.e., generated by applying a linear transformation A to a vector of random elements $(\rho_1, \ldots, \rho_m)$, and where each message m_i can be computed using a bilinear function $\mathsf{Msg}_i(x, r)$. That is, Msg_i is linear in both x (the inputs) and r (the randomness). Our goal is to show that "bilinear" protocols and, more generally, protocols where messages are computed as degree-2 polynomials in x and r, are limited in power. This negative result relies on a negative result for degree-2 randomizing polynomials from [30]. Concretely, [30] proved the following:

Lemma 5.3. *Suppose $f : \{0,1\}^n \to \{0,1\}$ admits a degree-2 randomized encoding over a finite field $\mathbb{F}$. Then, either of the following holds:*

- *f or its negation test a linear condition over $\mathbb{F}$; namely, are of the form $f_{A,b}(x) = 1$ iff $Ax = b$, for some $A \in \mathbb{F}^{\ell \times n}, b \in \mathbb{F}^\ell$; or*
- *f is a (deterministic) degree-2 polynomial.*

We observe that a bilinear protocol for a function f gives rise to a randomized degree-2 representation of f (of the first type). The degree is bounded by 2 because each message m_i is computed via a bilinear function $\mathsf{Msg}_i(x, r)$ and because r itself is a linear function of the underlying vector $(\rho_1, \ldots, \rho_m)$. The correctness and full robustness of the protocol imply that $m_1, \ldots, m_n$ encode $f(x)$ but give no other information about x. Thus, using Lemma 5.3, we get:

Theorem 5.3. *Let $f : \{0,1\}^n \to \{0,1\}$ be a boolean function that has a bilinear NIMPC protocol over a finite field $\mathbb{F}$. Then, f or its negation test a linear condition over $\mathbb{F}$ (as defined above).*

6   Concrete Efficiency

In this section we make the case that our protocols, while restricted in the class of functionalities they apply to, can be useful for improving the concrete efficiency of natural secure computation tasks. We start by recalling some functions for which we present BIT-MPC protocols and discuss their relevance to natural secure computation tasks that can be motivated by real-world applications.

- AND/OR: Bitwise AND of long vectors of inputs can be used to realize multi-party Private Set Intersection (PSI) of sets over a universe of size $[N]$, where the input of each party is the length-N characteristic vector of its set. PSI has many real-world applications. One example is a secure Doodle poll, where the universe includes possible date and time slots, and each party's input is the subset of these slots in which he or she are available. See, e.g., [33] and references therein for pointers on existing PSI protocols and their applications. Many of these applications are relevant even with feasible domain size, and even in the multiparty case.
- MIN/MAX: This is generally useful for auctions. Note that the variant in which the identity of the winner is revealed is reducible to the plain variant by encoding the identity of the owner of each input in the least significant bits of the input.
- Multiparty equality: Deciding whether all inputs are equal can be useful for checking whether there is agreement on the same candidate, whether different copies of the same information are identical, etc. In some of these cases, it is important to hide the identity of the outliers. See [18] for applications of secure two-party equality computation, some of which are relevant also in the multi-party case.

In all of the above cases, the residual security guarantee that we get in the presence of a dishonest majority is meaningful. In particular, it only reveals a very small amount of joint information about the inputs of honest parties, and moreover this information can typically be obtained in the ideal model via an adversarial choice of the input.

We now discuss the asymptotic and concrete efficiency features of optimized variants of our BIT-MPC protocols that make them more attractive than standard protocols for MPC with no honest majority. For concreteness we focus on the AND function, but similar optimizations apply to the other functions as well. We exclude from the discussion protocols based on fully homomorphic encryption (let alone general-purpose obfuscation) that do not seem to offer a competitive alternative for such simple computational tasks.

Existing "GMW-style" protocols for n-party AND that remain secure in the presence of an arbitrary number of (semi-honest) corrupted parties require $O(n^3)$ instances of oblivious transfer. This makes the total communication complexity $O(kn^3)$, where k is a computational security parameter. While some optimizations are possible using pseudo-random secret sharing (PRSS) [14], we are not aware of an OT-based protocol whose communication complexity is below $O(kn^2)$. In particular, even for a small number of parties such as $n = 10$, each party should communicate thousands of bits for a single AND computation. The main barrier is the use of oblivious transfers: the protocol consumes many of them, and efficient OT extension techniques [29] still require a significant amount of communication per OT instance.

Our BIT-MPC protocols replace OT with linear secret sharing, whose efficiency can be amortized via PRSS and/or share packing [20]. We note that the PRSS technique, when applied to threshold secret sharing schemes, incurs a computational cost (e.g., number of PRG invocations) that grows exponentially with the number of parties. Thus, this optimization can only be applied in practice when the number of parties is not too big.

Concretely, given a PRSS setup of replicated PRG seeds, our BIT-MPC protocol for AND of n input bits with 2^{-s} error probability needs only two rounds of interaction, where each party broadcasts $s + 1$ bits in each round (or sends a total of $(n - 1)(s + 1)$ bits over point-to-point channels). The computational complexity is dominated by roughly $\binom{n}{n/2}$ PRG calls (that can be implemented in practice via AES) per party. We do not know how to get MPC protocols that achieve a similar level of efficiency in the setting of standard MPC with no honest majority. Note that these efficiency advantages become very relevant when computing a large number N of instances. This case is motivated by some of the applications discussed above.

When the number of parties n is big, the PRSS technique no longer applies, but can be replaced by the use of packed secret sharing. This gives an amortized communication cost of $O(s)$ bits of point-to-point communication per AND computation per party, at the price of a slightly reduced (full) security threshold. Here one does not need any setup nor a direct implementation of broadcast to get this level of efficiency.

7 BIT-MPC with Security Against Malicious Parties

Our main focus in this paper is on BIT-MPC in the presence of a semi-honest (i.e., passive) adversary, who does not modify the messages sent by corrupted parties. In this section, we briefly discuss an extension of our notion of BIT-MPC and some of our results to the setting of a malicious (i.e., active) adversary.

We start by discussing the modified security definition for this case. In the case of security against a malicious adversary, we need to replace the direct definitions of standard and residual security, from Definition 2.2, by a simulation-based definition that compares the real-world execution of the protocol in the presence of a malicious adversary to an ideal-world execution in the presence of a simulator. Moreover, whereas in the case of an honest majority one can achieve full security (either when $t < n/3$ over secure point-to-point channels [6,11] or with $t < n/2$ if broadcast is additionally available [34]), for the case of a dishonest majority we generally need to settle for "security with abort."

7.1 Defining BIT-MPC with a Malicious Adversary

At a high level, we modify the standard security definition of MPC (see [22]) by changing the ideal model experiment so that the adversary gets an explicit description of the residual function.[4]

For a set T of parties, we can consider four "types" of security that a protocol can offer against a corrupted T: ensuring either standard or residual security, and either guaranteed output delivery or security with abort. For simplicity, the definition below only deals with two types of sets, "minority sets" against which we have full security with guaranteed output delivery, and "majority sets" against which we can only ensure residual security with abort. (Dealing with four different "types" is of course possible, but cumbersome.) Also for simplicity we only deal with the threashold variants of the definition (rather than arbitrary access structures). Hence, below we have a single threshold t upto which we ensure *full security* with guaranteed output delivery, whereas for more than t corrupted parties we settle for *residual security with abort*. The typical threshold t is $t < n/3$, for protocols over secure point-to-point channels, or $t < n/2$ with broadcast.

Definition 7.1. *Let f be an n-input function. let $\Pi[\kappa]$ be an n-party protocol that depends on parameter κ, and consider some threshold $t \leq n$. We say that Π is a t-secure, best-possible, information-theoretic protocol for f in the presence of malicious adversaries (or malicious t-BIT-MPC) if for every (malicious, static, computationally unbounded) adversary $\mathcal{A}$ attacking $\Pi[\kappa]$ there exists a simulator S, with $2^{-\kappa}$ simulation error, that corrupts the same set of parties in the following ideal model:*

- **Standard security for up to t corruptions:** *If $\mathcal{A}$ corrupts at most t parties, the ideal model is as in the original definition from [22] for MPC with full security: each party sends its input to the trusted party (where the simulator S can change inputs of corrupted parties), the trusted party computes f and delivers the outputs to all parties.*
- **Residual security with abort beyond t corruptions:** *If $\mathcal{A}$ corrupts more than t parties, the ideal model is defined as follows: (1) each party sends its input to the trusted party; (2) the trusted party sends a description of the residual function of f (defined by the inputs of uncorrupted parties) to S; (3) S decides whether to abort or to have the trusted party deliver the outputs of uncorrupted parties.*

7.2 BIT-MPC Protocols with Malicious Adversaries

In this section, we discuss the possibility of applying variants of the protocols from Sect. 4 in the presence of malicious adversaries. For this, we need to examine

---

[4] Clearly, this definition can only be satisfied with efficient simulation for functions whose residual function has a small description, such as functions on a small input domain or symmetric functions. Our negative results suggest that this restriction is inevitable.

the effect of malicious behavior in all three components: the generation of the correlated randomness, the local computation of the NIMPC messages, and the distributed NIMPC evaluation. We discuss each of these components separately.

Correlated Randomness Generation. In the semi-honest case, we could generate any *linear correlation* n-securely using a simple information-theoretic protocol based on additive secret sharing. This protocol fails to be secure against malicious parties. In fact, the impossibility of information-theoretic coin-tossing with dishonest majority means that this insecurity is inherent. To get around this impossibility, we consider the following "semi-malicious" relaxation of NIMPC with *replicated* correlation: when considering security against a collusion of the evaluator and a set of parties T, all of the random inputs involving T can be chosen adversarially (independently of the random inputs that are owned only by uncorrupted parties) but they are restricted to satisfy the prescribed replication pattern. It is easy to check that all of the previous protocols in this model remain secure even in this slightly more adversarial setting. Intuitively, this follows from the fact that even in the semi-honest model, the security of the uncorrupted parties is only protected by the random inputs that are unknown to the adversary. Finally, we observe that in the special case of *pairwise-replicated correlation*, we can generate the randomness in the straightforward way by making one of each pair of parties P_i, P_j pick the common randomness $r_{i,j}$ and send it to the other. Here the effect of a malicious adversary is equivalent to that of a semi-malicious adversary who can pick the random inputs adversarially but otherwise behaves honestly. Note that this is not the case for general replicated randomness, where the adversary can make replicated randomness owned by different honest parties inconsistent. From here on, we focus on BIT-MPC protocols that are obtained via NIMPC with pairwise-replicated randomness. This captures most of the examples from the previous section, including AND/OR and AllEq.

Local Computation of NIMPC Messages. Here we need to ensure that any malicious strategy of picking NIMPC messages by the adversary (independently of the honest parties' NIMPC messages) can be simulated by an honest strategy. Consider for example the direct protocol for the OR function. Here each party first maps a 0 input to 0 or a 1 input to a random nonzero group element, and then adds the correlated randomness (obtained via pairwise-replicated randomness). Note that for any fixed choice of the correlated randomness, every group element is a valid message, and moreover it is easy for the simulator to extract the input from the correlated randomness and the message (namely, the input is 0 if the two values are equal and 1 otherwise). One can check that the same is true for the more general NIMPC protocol for affine space membership. Here each party multiplies its (shifted) input by the correlated randomness r_i. Unless $r_i = 0$, which occurs with negligible probability, the simulator can extract an effective input from r_i and the NIMPC message.

Distributed NIMPC Evaluation. This is the easiest part to handle, since we can simply apply off-the-shelf information-theoretic protocols that provide security against malicious adversaries. Depending on the setting, we can either use protocols such as [6,11] for perfect t-security over secure point-to-point channels when $t < n/3$, or alternatively protocols such as [34] for statistical security over secure point-to-point channels and broadcast when $t < n/2$.

Beyond Affine Space Membership. Using the above methodology, we can get BIT-MPC protocols for affine space membership whenever the correlated randomness can be obtained via pairwise-replicated correlation. This captures the most useful examples of AND/OR and AllEq, but does not directly capture applications that build on top of them, such as the protocols for the MAX function. Recall that the MAX function computes the maximum of n integers in $\mathbb{Z}_p$. We presented two BIT-MPC protocols for MAX in Figs. 3 and 4. The first has constant round complexity but high communication complexity (linear in p), while the second uses binary search and multiple rounds to make the communication complexity grow only logarithmically with p. Both of these protocols use a BIT-MPC protocol for OR as a subroutine. However, they are both insecure against a malicious adversary even if the underlying OR protocol is fully secure against a malicious adversary. The attack is the same in both cases: even a single malicious party chooses its inputs for the OR protocol non-monotonically it can both simultaneously "win" (i.e., determine the output) and learn the maximum of the honest parties' inputs. This contradicts the full security requirement for the case of dishonest minority.

We propose two solutions to overcome the above attack and obtain a BIT-MPC protocol for MAX with security against malicious adversaries. The first solution is a sequential version of the protocol from Fig. 3, where in round ℓ the input for the OR function of party P_i is a bit $\chi_{i,\ell}$ which equals 1 if its input is at least $p - \ell$ and 0 otherwise. The protocol terminates with output $p - \ell_0$ after the first round ℓ_0 in which the OR-output is 1. In the protocol, the only degree of freedom the adversary has is to choose the first round in which one of its inputs is 1 (assuming that the protocol did not terminate before this round), and this choice can be simulated by an honest strategy. Finally, we note that it is also possible to get a constant-round protocol for MAX via a non-interactive reduction to secure modular addition that uses the nested subgroup technique from [15]. The idea is that MAX of inputs in $[m]$ can be reduced to addition in the group $\mathbb{Z}_{q^m}$ (where q is a prime of size $> 2^\kappa$) in the following way. Each input x_i is locally encoded as a random multiple of q^{m-x_i} in $\mathbb{Z}_{q^m}$, and then the n encoded inputs x_i' are added via a BIT-MPC protocol for addition in $\mathbb{Z}_{q^m}$. Due to the nested subgroup structure, the maximal multiple of q which divides the output will reveal the MAX value except with $1/q$ probability. Moreover, in this protocol a malicious adversary has no cheating space, as every possible choice of the encoded input x_i' in $\mathbb{Z}_{q^m}$ corresponds to an honest input. We leave open the question of obtaining a BIT-MPC protocol for MAX, with security against a malicious adversary, where the communication complexity grows logarithmically with m.

References

1. Abadi, M., Feigenbaum, J., Kilian, J.: On hiding information from an oracle (extended abstract). In: Aho, A. (ed.) 19th ACM STOC, pp. 195–203. ACM Press, May 1987
2. Agarwal, N., Anand, S., Prabhakaran, M.: Brief announcement: on secure m-party computation, commuting permutation systems and unassisted non-interactive MPC. In: 45th International Colloquium on Automata, Languages, and Programming, ICALP 2018, 9–13 July 2018, Prague, Czech Republic, pp. 103:1–103:4 (2018). https://doi.org/10.4230/LIPIcs.ICALP.2018.103
3. Ames, S., Hazay, C., Ishai, Y., Venkitasubramaniam, M.: Ligero: lightweight sublinear arguments without a trusted setup. In: CCS, pp. 2087–2104. ACM (2017)
4. Beimel, A., Gabizon, A., Ishai, Y., Kushilevitz, E., Meldgaard, S., Paskin-Cherniavsky, A.: Non-interactive secure multiparty computation. In: Garay, J.A., Gennaro, R. (eds.) CRYPTO 2014. LNCS, vol. 8617, pp. 387–404. Springer, Heidelberg (2014). https://doi.org/10.1007/978-3-662-44381-1_22
5. Beimel, A., Malkin, T., Micali, S.: The all-or-nothing nature of two-party secure computation. In: Wiener, M. (ed.) CRYPTO 1999. LNCS, vol. 1666, pp. 80–97. Springer, Heidelberg (1999). https://doi.org/10.1007/3-540-48405-1_6
6. Ben-Or, M., Goldwasser, S., Wigderson, A.: Completeness theorems for non-cryptographic fault-tolerant distributed computation (extended abstract). In: 20th ACM STOC, pp. 1–10. ACM Press, May 1988
7. Benaloh, J.C.: Secret sharing homomorphisms: keeping shares of a secret sharing. In: Odlyzko, A.M. (ed.) CRYPTO 1986. LNCS, vol. 263, pp. 251–260. Springer, Heidelberg (1987). https://doi.org/10.1007/3-540-47721-7_19
8. Benhamouda, F., Krawczyk, H., Rabin, T.: Robust non-interactive multiparty computation against constant-size collusion. In: Katz, J., Shacham, H. (eds.) CRYPTO 2017. LNCS, vol. 10401, pp. 391–419. Springer, Cham (2017). https://doi.org/10.1007/978-3-319-63688-7_13
9. Chaum, D.: The dining cryptographers problem: unconditional sender and recipient untraceability. J. Cryptol. 1(1), 65–75 (1988)
10. Chaum, D.: The spymasters double-agent problem. In: Brassard, G. (ed.) CRYPTO 1989. LNCS, vol. 435, pp. 591–602. Springer, New York (1990). https://doi.org/10.1007/0-387-34805-0_52
11. Chaum, D., Crépeau, C., Damgård, I.: Multiparty unconditionally secure protocols (extended abstract). In: 20th ACM STOC, pp. 11–19. ACM Press, May 1988
12. Chor, B., Kushilevitz, E.: A zero-one law for Boolean privacy (extended abstract). In: 21st ACM STOC, pp. 62–72. ACM Press, May 1989
13. Chor, B., Kushilevitz, E.: A zero-one law for Boolean privacy. SIAM J. Discrete Math. 4, 36–47 (1991)
14. Cramer, R., Damgård, I., Ishai, Y.: Share conversion, pseudorandom secret-sharing and applications to secure computation. In: Kilian, J. (ed.) TCC 2005. LNCS, vol. 3378, pp. 342–362. Springer, Heidelberg (2005). https://doi.org/10.1007/978-3-540-30576-7_19
15. Cramer, R., Fehr, S., Ishai, Y., Kushilevitz, E.: Efficient multi-party computation over rings. In: Biham, E. (ed.) EUROCRYPT 2003. LNCS, vol. 2656, pp. 596–613. Springer, Heidelberg (2003). https://doi.org/10.1007/3-540-39200-9_37
16. Damgård, I., Ishai, Y.: Constant-round multiparty computation using a black-box pseudorandom generator. In: Shoup, V. (ed.) CRYPTO 2005. LNCS, vol. 3621, pp. 378–394. Springer, Heidelberg (2005). https://doi.org/10.1007/11535218_23

17. Damgård, I., Ishai, Y.: Scalable secure multiparty computation. In: Dwork, C. (ed.) CRYPTO 2006. LNCS, vol. 4117, pp. 501–520. Springer, Heidelberg (2006). https://doi.org/10.1007/11818175_30

18. Fagin, R., Naor, M., Winkler, P.: Comparing information without leaking it. Commun. ACM **39**(5), 77–85 (1996). https://doi.org/10.1145/229459.229469

19. Feige, U., Kilian, J., Naor, M.: A minimal model for secure computation (extended abstract). In: 26th ACM STOC, pp. 554–563. ACM Press, May 1994

20. Franklin, M.K., Yung, M.: Communication complexity of secure computation (extended abstract). In: 24th ACM STOC, pp. 699–710. ACM Press, May 1992

21. Gilboa, N., Ishai, Y.: Compressing cryptographic resources. In: Wiener, M. (ed.) CRYPTO 1999. LNCS, vol. 1666, pp. 591–608. Springer, Heidelberg (1999). https://doi.org/10.1007/3-540-48405-1_37

22. Goldreich, O.: Foundations of Cryptography: Basic Applications. Cambridge University Press, New York (2004)

23. Goldwasser, S., Rothblum, G.N.: On best-possible obfuscation. In: Vadhan, S.P. (ed.) TCC 2007. LNCS, vol. 4392, pp. 194–213. Springer, Heidelberg (2007). https://doi.org/10.1007/978-3-540-70936-7_11

24. Halevi, S., Ishai, Y., Jain, A., Komargodski, I., Sahai, A., Yogev, E.: Non-interactive multiparty computation without correlated randomness. In: Takagi, T., Peyrin, T. (eds.) ASIACRYPT 2017. LNCS, vol. 10626, pp. 181–211. Springer, Cham (2017). https://doi.org/10.1007/978-3-319-70700-6_7

25. Halevi, S., Ishai, Y., Jain, A., Kushilevitz, E., Rabin, T.: Secure multiparty computation with general interaction patterns. In: Proceedings of the 2016 ACM Conference on Innovations in Theoretical Computer Science, Cambridge, MA, USA, 14–16 January 2016, pp. 157–168 (2016). https://doi.org/10.1145/2840728.2840760

26. Halevi, S., Lindell, Y., Pinkas, B.: Secure computation on the web: computing without simultaneous interaction. In: Rogaway, P. (ed.) CRYPTO 2011. LNCS, vol. 6841, pp. 132–150. Springer, Heidelberg (2011). https://doi.org/10.1007/978-3-642-22792-9_8

27. Hirt, M., Lucas, C., Maurer, U., Raub, D.: Graceful degradation in multi-party computation (extended abstract). In: Fehr, S. (ed.) ICITS 2011. LNCS, vol. 6673, pp. 163–180. Springer, Heidelberg (2011). https://doi.org/10.1007/978-3-642-20728-0_15

28. Hirt, M., Maurer, U.M.: Player simulation and general adversary structures in perfect multiparty computation. J. Cryptol. **13**(1), 31–60 (2000)

29. Ishai, Y., Kilian, J., Nissim, K., Petrank, E.: Extending oblivious transfers efficiently. In: Boneh, D. (ed.) CRYPTO 2003. LNCS, vol. 2729, pp. 145–161. Springer, Heidelberg (2003). https://doi.org/10.1007/978-3-540-45146-4_9

30. Ishai, Y., Kushilevitz, E.: Randomizing polynomials: a new representation with applications to round-efficient secure computation. In: 41st FOCS, pp. 294–304. IEEE Computer Society Press, November 2000

31. Ishai, Y., Kushilevitz, E., Lindell, Y., Petrank, E.: Black-box constructions for secure computation. In: Kleinberg, J.M. (ed.) 38th ACM STOC, pp. 99–108. ACM Press, May 2006

32. Kushilevitz, E.: Privacy and communication complexity. In: 30th FOCS, pp. 416–421. IEEE Computer Society Press, October/November 1989

33. Pinkas, B., Schneider, T., Weinert, C., Wieder, U.: Efficient circuit-based PSI via cuckoo hashing. In: Nielsen, J.B., Rijmen, V. (eds.) EUROCRYPT 2018. LNCS, vol. 10822, pp. 125–157. Springer, Cham (2018). https://doi.org/10.1007/978-3-319-78372-7_5

34. Rabin, T., Ben-Or, M.: Verifiable secret sharing and multiparty protocols with honest majority (extended abstract). In: 21st ACM STOC, pp. 73–85. ACM Press, May 1989

Secure Certification of Mixed Quantum States with Application to Two-Party Randomness Generation

Frédéric Dupuis[3,4]([✉]), Serge Fehr[1,2], Philippe Lamontagne[5], and Louis Salvail[5]

[1] Centrum Wiskunde & Informatica (CWI), Amsterdam, The Netherlands
serge.fehr@cwi.nl
[2] Mathematical Institute, Leiden University, Leiden, The Netherlands
[3] Université de Lorraine, CNRS, Inria, LORIA, 54000 Nancy, France
frederic.dupuis@loria.fr
[4] Faculty of Informatics, Masaryk University, Brno, Czech Republic
[5] Université de Montréal (DIRO), Montréal, Canada
{lamontph,salvail}@iro.umontreal.ca

Abstract. We investigate sampling procedures that certify that an arbitrary quantum state on n subsystems is close to an ideal mixed state $\varphi^{\otimes n}$ for a given reference state φ, up to errors on a few positions. This task makes no sense classically: it would correspond to certifying that a given bitstring was generated according to some desired probability distribution. However, in the quantum case, this is possible if one has access to a prover who can supply a purification of the mixed state.

In this work, we introduce the concept of mixed-state certification, and we show that a natural sampling protocol offers secure certification in the presence of a possibly dishonest prover: if the verifier accepts then he can be almost certain that the state in question has been correctly prepared, up to a small number of errors.

We then apply this result to two-party quantum coin-tossing. Given that strong coin tossing is impossible, it is natural to ask "how close can we get". This question has been well studied and is nowadays well understood from the perspective of the bias of individual coin tosses. We approach and answer this question from a different—and somewhat orthogonal—perspective, where we do not look at individual coin tosses but at the global entropy instead. We show how two distrusting parties can produce a common high-entropy source, where the entropy is an arbitrarily small fraction below the maximum.

1 Introduction

1.1 Background and Motivation

Certifying correctness by means of cut-and-choose techniques is at the core of many – classical and quantum – cryptographic protocols. This goes back as far as Yao's garbled circuits, introduced in the 80s, where cut-and-choose is the

A. Beimel and S. Dziembowski (Eds.): TCC 2018, LNCS 11240, pp. 282–314, 2018.
https://doi.org/10.1007/978-3-030-03810-6_11

main technique used to obtain active security. Even more so, cut-and-choose is at the very heart of essentially any quantum-cryptographic protocol, where participants are often asked to prepare states that agree with some specification. Certifying that quantum states satisfy this specification is essential to proving the security of these protocols.

Underlying these techniques is one of the most fundamental tasks in statistics: sampling. It allows one to infer facts about a large set of data by only looking at a small subset of it. For example, one can estimate the number of zeros in an n-bit string with very high accuracy by looking only at a small, randomly selected subset of the bits. This is also true in quantum mechanics: given an n-qubit system, one can infer that it is almost entirely contained in a subspace span$\{|s\rangle : s$ is a bitstring with $(\delta \pm \epsilon)n$ 1's$\}$ by measuring a small subset of the qubits and observing that a fraction δ of the bits are ones [6].

One thing that a classical sampling procedure *cannot* do, however, is to infer the probability distribution from which the bitstring was generated. While a sampling procedure might be able to tell us that a bitstring contains roughly $n/2$ zeros and $n/2$ ones, that does not mean that it originally came from n fair coin flips—for all we know, it might be a fixed string that happens to have the right number of zeros and ones. If we were somehow able to do this, it would have interesting consequences for cryptography: for instance, we could get a coin-flipping protocol by getting one party to generate the coin flips, send them to the other party, and have the other party perform this hypothetical sampling procedure to certify that most of the bits indeed came from fair coin flips.

While this is clearly impossible in the classical case, it turns out that, perhaps surprisingly, this makes sense in the quantum scenario. This is due to the phenomenon of *purification*: given a mixed quantum state ρ_A on system A (which corresponds to a probability distribution on quantum states), it is possible to define a bipartite *pure* (i.e. deterministic) state $|\psi\rangle_{AR}$ which is in the same mixed state as ρ_A when looking at A only. Hence, one can *certify* that A is in the mixed state ρ_A by asking someone to produce the purifying system R and measuring that the combined system AR is indeed in state $|\psi\rangle_{AR}$. To give a more concrete example, suppose ρ_A is a uniformly random qubit, i.e. $\rho_A = \frac{1}{2}|0\rangle\langle0| + \frac{1}{2}|1\rangle\langle1|$. Then, the pure state $|\Phi\rangle_{AR} = \frac{1}{\sqrt{2}}(|00\rangle + |11\rangle)$ purifies it, and checking that AR is in state $|\Phi\rangle$ certifies that A was uniformly distributed in the first place. Note also that one does not need to trust the party who gives us the purification, making this suitable for an adversarial setting.

This leads to the following natural sampling protocol. Consider a sampler Sam who holds an arbitrary quantum state ρ_{A^n} on n subsystems, prepared by a possibly dishonest prover Paul. Sam would like to certify that this state is close to the ideal mixed state $\varphi^{\otimes n}$, possibly with errors on a small number of positions, for a given reference state φ. To do this, he selects a small subset of k positions at random, and he asks the distrusted prover Paul to deliver the purifying systems R^k for these positions. He then measures the POVM $\{|\varphi\rangle\langle\varphi|_{AR}, \mathbb{1} - |\varphi\rangle\langle\varphi|_{AR}\}$ on each of the selected systems in the sample to ensure that all of them are in the state $|\varphi\rangle_{AR}$ which purifies φ_A. He rejects if any errors are detected.

We emphasize that for verifying a *mixed* reference state, interaction with a prover is necessary, as there is no local measurement on Sam's side that can distinguish between the correct state $\varphi^{\otimes n}$ and a state that consists of the eigenvectors of φ in the correct proportions (given by the eigenvalues).

1.2 Our Contribution

In this paper, we investigate this type of sampling procedure in detail. Several challenges arise in the analysis of this protocol. First, defining what we mean when we say that the sampling works is not trivial. In the case of regular quantum sampling, we usually want to say that the state has a very small probability of being outside of a low-error subspace that corresponds to the statistics that we have observed. For mixed states, this definition fails completely: every subspace contains *pure* states, which we would want to exclude since they are very far from the ideal *mixed* state. We might then be tempted to include the purifying systems in the definition of the low-error subspace, but then we have no guarantee that an adversarial prover will respect the structure we want to impose on his part of the state—we don't even know that it consists of n subsystems. A second difficulty comes from the fact that the prover might not necessarily want to provide the state that gives him the best chance of passing the test, even if he has it. If we again look at the case of certifying uniformly random qubits, even if Sam has the ideal state before the sampling begins, Paul might want to bias the outcome, for example by passing the test if he measures $|0\rangle$ on all of the non-sampled qubits, and failing on purpose otherwise. Because of these difficulties, our main result does not follow from traditional sampling theorems.

We overcome these challenges and present a general class of mixed state certification protocols which contains the natural protocol described above. We show that any protocol that fits this class, and that satisfies the simple criteria of being invariant under permutations and performing well on i.i.d. states, allows us to control the post-sampling state in a meaningful way. A positive consequence of this modular analysis is that previous results on *pure state* certification also fit our framework, and thus fall under a special case of our analysis – just as pure states are a special case of mixed states. Because pure state certification has already found many applications in cryptography [6,10–12,29], the fact that we recover it as a special case positions our result as a powerful tool for quantum cryptography.

Another part of the paper is devoted to applying this result to coin tossing—or *randomness generation*. Given that strong coin tossing is known to be impossible, it is natural to ask "how close can we get?". This question has been well studied and is nowadays well understood from the perspective of the bias of individual coin tosses (see Sect. 1.3 below). We approach and answer this question from a different—and somewhat orthogonal—perspective, where we do not optimize individual coin tosses but the global entropy instead. From this entropic perspective, we show that "the next best" after strong coin tossing is possible. We show that the coin-flipping protocol loosely described above allows two distrusting parties to produce a common high-entropy source, where the entropy is an arbitrarily small fraction below the maximum (except with negligible probability).

Our protocol for the task of two party randomness generation outperforms any classical protocol in the information theoretical setting. The trivial classical protocol—where each party tosses $n/2$ unbiased coins and the output is the result of the n tosses—is optimal for this task [15].

The paper is organized as follows. First, in the next subsections, we discuss some previous work in the area and the relevance of our work for cryptography. In Sect. 2, we introduce the notation and recall some useful facts. Section 3 presents the main result in more detail. The coin-flipping protocol described above is presented in Sect. 4, and the proof of our main result then follows in Sect. 5.

1.3 Previous Work

Classical sampling results have been around since the foundations of modern probability theory, dating back to the work of Bernstein, Hoeffding and Chernoff on concentration of measure in the 1920s and 1930s. More recently, several quantum generalizations of these classics have been proven. These generalizations include, for instance, Ahlswede and Winter's operator Chernoff bound [1] and the quantum Chernoff bound of [4]. However, these generalizations are not easily amenable to giving results about sampling, unlike their classical counterparts. Other quantum results can be used to analyze sampling in certain contexts, such as quantum de Finetti theorems for quantum key distribution [9,23,24].

But perhaps the most direct analogues of the classical sampling results are those of [6]. There, the authors give a generic way to transpose classical sampling procedures to the quantum case. Roughly speaking, they show that if a classical sampling protocol says that a string of random variables $X_1, \cdots, X_n$ is contained in some "good" subset $\mathcal{X}_{good}$ except with negligible probability, then the quantum version of the same sampling procedure (defined in a precise way in [6]) would say that the final state $\rho_{X_1,\ldots,X_n}$ is almost entirely contained in the good subspace $\text{span}\{|x_1\rangle \otimes \cdots \otimes |x_n\rangle : x_1, \cdots, x_n \in \mathcal{X}_{good}\}$, except with negligible probability. This "good" set would normally correspond to strings that are consistent with what was observed in the sample. Our main result can be viewed as extending this to the case of mixed state sampling.

Our main application, coin flipping, also has a long history. The basic task was first defined in 1981 by Manuel Blum [5]. Since the early 2000's, it has received a lot of attention in the quantum cryptography community, as it is one of the most natural tasks for which quantum protocols can perform something that is impossible classically. There are two versions of coin flipping: *strong* coin flipping, in which we require the protocol to be equivalent to a black box that produces the coin flip and distributes the result, and *weak* coin flipping, in which each participant has a known preferred outcome and must be prevented from biasing the outcome in that direction. Several quantum protocols for strong coin flipping have been developed with various biases [3,27], but a fundamental lower bound of $(\frac{1}{\sqrt{2}} - \frac{1}{2})$ on the bias of such protocols was proven in [17] (see also [13]). Finally, a protocol with a bias matching the lower bound was proven in [7]. For weak coin flipping, we have had several protocols [16,18,19,28], again with various biases, but this time culminating in a protocol with arbitrarily small bias [20]. Quantum coin flipping has even been implemented in the lab [22]. Here, we go in a somewhat different direction: we show that even though strong coin flipping with negligible bias is impossible without assumptions, two distrustful parties can produce a common string of min-entropy arbitrarily close to maximum.

A strong quantum coin tossing protocol using ideas similar to that of the protocol described in Sect. 4 has been previously considered by Høyer and Salvail (unpublished) for achieving in a slightly simpler way the same $\frac{1}{4}$ bias than the one in [2]. Alice prepares two EPR pairs and sends one half of each to Bob. Bob picks at random one qubit out of the two and verifies that Alice holds the corresponding purification register of an EPR pair by asking her to measure it in a random BB84 basis before comparing the result with his own. If this test succeeds, Bob gets some evidence that the remaining pair of qubits can be used as a coin toss after measuring it in the canonical basis. Our protocol extends this test to a random sample of a population of N qubits, increasing the confidence that Bob has about the remaining qubits being "close" to ideal coin tosses when the test is successful.

1.4 Applications to Cryptography

Sampling with a Pure Reference State. Previous results on sampling from a quantum population have dealt with *pure* reference states. In this case, the sampler can choose its sample and perform local measurements on the sampled positions without any help from the prover. This setting allows for standard classical tools such as Hoeffding's inequality to be used to derive the probability that the sampled positions' proximity to the reference state is not a good indicator for the unsampled positions' proximity to the same reference state.

Since pure states are a special case of mixed states, a natural property that we would want for our mixed state sampling result is to recover a statement similar to the one for pure state sampling in the framework of [6]. This is indeed the case when we restrict our attention to the task of certification, i.e. when we do not tolerate any error in the sample. Although our results do not use the same tools, and are expressed in terms of a *post-selected* operator instead of in terms of proximity to an ideal state (see Sect. 3), we recover a statement equivalent to that of [6], albeit with slightly worse parameters, when we apply our results to pure reference states. Since most applications [6,11,12,29] of pure state sampling has been in the setting of certification, our results can also be used to prove those applications.

Sampling with a Distributed Pure Reference State. Our mixed state sampling result is also applicable to an instance of pure state certification that falls outside the framework of [6] and which was presented and analyzed in an ad hoc way in [10]. Their sampling algorithm was used as part of a protocol for leakage resilient computation.

The sampling task considered in [10] is as follows: spacially separated Alice and Bob want to certify that their joint registers – which was prepared by an untrusted third party – is of the form $|\varphi\rangle_{AB}^{\otimes n}$ for some entangled state $|\varphi\rangle$ where Alice holds the A part of each of the n states and Bob the B part. The fact that the state is distributed between Alice and Bob means that the techniques of [6] do not apply: the two samplers cannot perform a projective measurement to check that their shared registers are in the reference state $|\varphi\rangle_{AB}$.

Our results of Sect. 5 only requires that the sampling protocol's verification procedures is invariant under the permutation of the quantum population, and that it aborts when performed on an *obviously bad* state. Since the pure state certification protocol of [10] satisfies these properties, our techniques readily apply and can be used to analyze their protocol.

Application to Two-Party Computation. In [26], the power of quantum communication for secure unconditional two-party computation is investigated. Among other results, it was shown that *correct* quantum implementations of two-party classical cryptographic primitives must leak at least some minimal amount of information to one of the parties. For example, randomized variants[1] of one-out-of-two OT and secure AND sharing must leak at least $\frac{1}{2}$ bit on average. Protocols exist in the quantum honest-but-curious model that minimize the amount of leakage for a given primitive. The simplest such protocol consists of an adversary preparing and distributing an *embedding* of the primitive. An embedding of a cryptographic primitive is a pure state that yields the correct outcomes when measured in the computational basis, i.e. from each party's point of view, the state shared before the final measurement is a purification of the probability distribution for this party's output.

A protocol that achieves minimal leakage against *active* adversaries under the sole assumption that the parties have access to strong coin-tosses is easily obtained from mixed-state certification. One of the parties would generate many copies of the embedding of the primitive that minimizes leakage and the other party certifies correctness using our sampling procedure. They then choose one of the remaining embeddings, the target embedding, and measure it; the outcome acts as the output of the protocol. If the sampling succeeds, the unsampled positions are close to ideal embeddings from the sampler's perspective and randomly picking the target embedding would then have close to minimal leakage with good probability. However, without additional resources, an adversary (the sampler say) could measure its part of a few embeddings before choosing the target embedding as one that produces the output the adversary wants to see. Coin-tosses are therefore required to pick the target embedding without bias.

---

[1] Variants where the primitives considered are applied to random inputs.

2 Preliminaries

2.1 Notation

Let $\mathcal{H}_A, \mathcal{H}_B$ be two Hilbert spaces, we write $L(\mathcal{H}_A, \mathcal{H}_B)$ for the set of linear operators from $\mathcal{H}_A$ to $\mathcal{H}_B$ and we write $L(\mathcal{H}_A)$ for $L(\mathcal{H}_A, \mathcal{H}_A)$. Let $\mathcal{D}_\leq(\mathcal{H})$ be the set of positive semi-definite operators with trace less than or equal to 1, and let $\mathcal{D}(\mathcal{H})$ be the set of density operators on $\mathcal{H}$. The set of isometries from $\mathcal{H}_A$ to $\mathcal{H}_B$ is denoted $U(\mathcal{H}_A, \mathcal{H}_B)$. We use the notation $U_{A\to B}$ to illustrate that $U_{A\to B} \in U(\mathcal{H}_A, \mathcal{H}_B)$. When there is no ambiguity from doing so, we write U_A instead of $U_{A\to B}$. For an arbitrary isometry U, we sometimes write $[U](\rho)$ as shorthand for $U\rho U^\dagger$. For a pure state $|\psi\rangle$, we write ψ as shorthand for $|\psi\rangle\langle\psi|$ when this creates no ambiguity. For a linear operator A, $\|A\|_1 := \mathrm{tr}(\sqrt{A^\dagger A})$ denotes the *trace norm*. We denote $\mathbb{1}_A$ as the identity operator on $\mathcal{H}_A$ and id_A as the CPTP map that acts trivially on register A.

We let $[n] := \{1, \ldots, n\}$ denote the set of the first n positive integers for $n \in \mathbb{N}$. For a fixed finite set Y and any subset $X \subseteq Y$, $\bar{X}$ denotes the complement of X in Y, i.e. $\bar{X} = Y \setminus X$. Let $h(p) := -p\log_2(p) - (1-p)\log_2(1-p)$ be the binary entropy function; we make use of the fact that $\binom{n}{\beta n} \leq 2^{h(\beta)n}$ for $0 < \beta < 1$.

Let A be a quantum register, we use the notation A^n to denote n identical copies of A and label them $A_1, \ldots, A_n$ when the need arises to distinguish individual registers. For $t \subseteq [n]$, we write A_t as the composite register containing registers A_i for each $i \in t$.

2.2 Permutation Invariance and the Symmetric Subspace

Let $\mathcal{S}_n$ denote the symmetric group on n elements and let $A_1, \ldots, A_n$ be n quantum registers with identical state space $\mathcal{H}$. For $\pi \in \mathcal{S}_n$, we use the same symbol to denote the unitary operation that acts on $\mathcal{H}^{\otimes n}$ by

$$\pi(|\phi_1\rangle_{A_1} \otimes \cdots \otimes |\phi_n\rangle_{A_n}) = |\phi_{\pi^{-1}(1)}\rangle_{A_1} \otimes \cdots \otimes |\phi_{\pi^{-1}(n)}\rangle_{A_n}. \tag{1}$$

Definition 1. *The symmetric subspace of $\mathcal{H}^{\otimes n}$, denoted $\mathrm{Sym}^n(\mathcal{H})$, is the space spanned by all vectors $|\phi\rangle \in \mathcal{H}^{\otimes n}$ with $\pi|\phi\rangle = |\phi\rangle$ for any $\pi \in \mathcal{S}_n$. A pure state $|\phi\rangle \in \mathrm{Sym}^n(\mathcal{H})$ is referred to as a* symmetric state.

A density operator $\rho \in \mathcal{D}(\mathcal{H}^{\otimes n})$ is called permutation invariant *if $\pi\rho\pi^\dagger = \rho$ for all $\pi \in \mathcal{S}_n$.*

Remark 1 ([8,23]). Although not all permutation invariant operators have support in the symmetric subspace, the next lemma asserts that they have a purification that does: for any permutation invariant density operator ρ_{A^n} on $\mathcal{H}_A^{\otimes n}$ there exists a pure state $|\rho_{A^n B^n}\rangle \in \mathrm{Sym}^n(\mathcal{H}_A \otimes \mathcal{H}_B)$ where $\mathcal{H}_A \simeq \mathcal{H}_B$, such that $\mathrm{tr}_{B^n}(\rho_{A^n B^n}) = \rho_{A^n}$.

Remark 2 ([23,25]). Let $\mathcal{H}$ be a d-dimensional Hilbert space. The projector onto the symmetric subspace $\mathrm{Sym}^n(\mathcal{H})$ can be expressed as

$$c_{n,d} \int |\theta\rangle\langle\theta|^{\otimes n} d|\theta\rangle$$

where $d|\theta\rangle$ is the measure on the set of pure states of $\mathcal{H}$ induced by the Haar measure on the set of unitaries acting on $\mathcal{H}$ and where $c_{n,d} := \binom{n+d-1}{n} \leq (n+1)^{d-1}$ is the dimension of $\mathrm{Sym}^n(\mathcal{H})$.

2.3   Mathematical Tools and Definitions

We say that an operator $\tilde{\rho}_B$ is *post-selected* from register A of ρ_{AB} if there exists a POVM element $0 \leq E_A \leq \mathbb{1}_A$ such that $\tilde{\rho}_B = \mathrm{tr}_A((E_A \otimes \mathbb{1}_B)\rho_{AB})$. The following remark on relation between the reduced operator of a joint system before and after a post-selected measurement takes place will be useful.

Remark 3. Let ρ_{AB} be an arbitrary positive semi-definite operator on registers AB. Let $0 \leq E_A \leq \mathbb{1}_A$ be a positive semidefinite operator acting on register A. Then it holds that

$$\mathrm{tr}_A\left((E_A \otimes \mathbb{1}_B)\rho_{AB}\right) \leq \mathrm{tr}_A\left(\rho_{AB}\right).$$

The following observation shows that there is a strong relation between post-selected operators and upper-bounded operators.

Proposition 1. *Let $c \geq 0$ and let ρ_Q, σ_Q be two positive semi-definite operators. Then $\rho_Q \leq c \cdot \sigma_Q$ if and only if for any purification $|\sigma_{R_1 Q}\rangle$ of σ_Q and $|\rho_{R_2 Q}\rangle$ of ρ_Q, there exists a linear operator $A_{R_1 \to R_2}$ such that $A_{R_1}^\dagger A_{R_1} \leq \mathbb{1}_{R_1}$ and*

$$|\rho_{R_2 Q}\rangle = \sqrt{c} \cdot (A_{R_1 \to R_2} \otimes \mathbb{1}_Q)|\sigma_{R_1 Q}\rangle. \tag{2}$$

Proof. Let's start with the easier direction of the proof. Let $|\sigma_{R_1 Q}\rangle$ be a purification of σ_Q, let $|\rho_{R_2 Q}\rangle$ be a purification of ρ_Q and let $A_{R_1 \to R_2}$ be as in (2). Then by Remark 3, ρ_Q is equal to

$$\mathrm{tr}_{R_2}\left(\rho_{R_2 Q}\right) = c \cdot \mathrm{tr}_{R_1}\left((A_{R_1 \to R_2}^\dagger A_{R_1 \to R_2} \otimes \mathbb{1}_Q)\sigma_{R_1 Q}\right) \leq c \cdot \mathrm{tr}_{R_1}\left(\sigma_{R_1 Q}\right) = c \cdot \sigma_Q.$$

For the other direction, write σ_Q as $\sigma_Q = \frac{1}{c}(\rho_Q + \tilde{\sigma}_Q)$ where $\tilde{\sigma}_Q := c \cdot \sigma_Q - \rho_Q \geq 0$. Let $|\rho_{R_2 Q}\rangle$ be an arbitrary purification of ρ_Q and let $|\tilde{\sigma}_{R_2 Q}\rangle$ be a purification of $\tilde{\sigma}_Q$ that lives in the same space. Then consider the following purification of σ_Q: $|\sigma_{R' R_2 Q}\rangle := \sqrt{\frac{1}{c}}(|0\rangle_{R'}|\rho_{R_2 Q}\rangle + |1\rangle_{R'}|\tilde{\sigma}_{R_2 Q}\rangle)$. Let $|\sigma_{R_1 Q}\rangle$ be an arbitrary purification of σ_Q and let $A_{R_1 \to R_2} := (\langle 0|_{R'} \otimes \mathbb{1}_{R_2})V_{R_1 \to R' R_2}$ where $V_{R_1 \to R' R_2}$ is an isometry that maps $|\sigma_{R_1 Q}\rangle$ to $|\sigma_{R' R_2 Q}\rangle$. Then

$$(A_{R_1 \to R_2} \otimes \mathbb{1}_Q)|\sigma_{R_1 Q}\rangle = (\langle 0|_{R'} \otimes \mathbb{1}_R)|\sigma_{R' R_2 Q}\rangle = \sqrt{\frac{1}{c}}|\rho_{R_2 Q}\rangle.$$

$\square$

The following proposition is a simple corollary of the *pinching inequality* [14, Lemma 9]. A direct consequence of this is that a superposition of a few states can be *approximated* by a mixture of the same few states.

Proposition 2. *Let $\{|\psi_i\rangle\}_{i\in\mathcal{J}}$ be a family of vectors living on a Hilbert space $\mathcal{H}$ indexed by some finite set $\mathcal{J}$. Define operators*

$$\rho = \sum_{i,j\in\mathcal{J}} |\psi_i\rangle\langle\psi_j| \ \text{and } \rho^{\mathrm{mix}} = \sum_{i\in\mathcal{J}} |\psi_i\rangle\langle\psi_i|.$$

Then, $\rho \leq |\mathcal{J}| \cdot \rho^{\mathrm{mix}}$.

Definition 2 (Quantum "Hamming Ball"). *Let $|\Psi\rangle \in \mathcal{H}^{\otimes n}$ for $n \in \mathbb{N}$ and let $r \in [n]$. We define the quantum Hamming ball of radius r around $|\Psi\rangle$, denoted $\Delta_r(|\Psi\rangle)$, as the space spanned by all vectors of the form $U|\Psi\rangle$ where U is a unitary that acts as the identity on at least $n - r$ subsystems.*

For the special case where $|\Psi\rangle = |\nu\rangle^{\otimes n}$,

$$\Delta_r(|\nu\rangle^{\otimes n}) = \mathrm{span}\{\pi(|\nu\rangle^{\otimes n-r} \otimes |u\rangle) \ : \ |u\rangle \in \mathcal{B}, \pi \in \mathcal{S}_n\}$$

where $\mathcal{B}$ is an orthonormal basis of $\mathcal{H}^{\otimes r}$.

The projector onto the quantum Hamming ball of radius r around an i.i.d. state $|\nu\rangle^{\otimes n} \in \mathcal{H}_{A_1} \otimes \cdots \otimes \mathcal{H}_{A_n}$ can be written as

$$\mathbb{P}_{A^n}^{r,|\nu\rangle} = \sum_{E\subseteq[n]\ :\ |E|\leq r} \left(\bigotimes_{i\in E}(\mathbb{1} - |\nu\rangle\langle\nu|)_{A_i} \bigotimes_{i\notin E} |\nu\rangle\langle\nu|_{A_i} \right).$$

The following Lemma says that n i.i.d. copies of a state close to $|\nu\rangle$ is almost entirely contained in a Hamming ball around $|\nu\rangle^{\otimes n}$.

Lemma 1. *Let $|\nu\rangle, |\theta\rangle \in \mathcal{H}$ be such that $|\langle\theta|\nu\rangle|^2 \geq 1 - \epsilon$. Then, for any $\alpha > 0$,*

$$\mathrm{tr}\left(\mathbb{P}^{r,|\nu\rangle} \cdot |\theta\rangle\langle\theta|^{\otimes n}\right) \geq 1 - \exp(-2\alpha^2 n)$$

where $\mathbb{P}^{r,|\nu\rangle}$ is the projector onto $\Delta_r(|\nu\rangle^{\otimes n})$ for $r = (\epsilon + \alpha)n$.

Proof. Observe that

$$\mathrm{tr}\left(\mathbb{P}^{r,|\nu\rangle}|\theta\rangle\langle\theta|^{\otimes n}\right) = \Pr[wt(X_\theta) \leq r] = \Pr[wt(X_\theta) - \epsilon n \leq \alpha n]$$

where X_θ is a random variable obtained by measuring n copies of $|\theta\rangle$ with observables $M_0 = |\nu\rangle\langle\nu|$ and $M_1 = \mathbb{1} - |\nu\rangle\langle\nu|$ and where $wt(\cdot)$ is the Hamming weight function, i.e. the number of ones. Since X_θ consists of n i.i.d. Bernoulli trials with parameter $1 - F(\nu, \theta)^2 \leq \epsilon$, Hoeffding's inequality allows us to lower-bound the above quantity: $\mathrm{tr}(\mathbb{P}^{r,|\nu\rangle} |\theta\rangle\langle\theta|^{\otimes n}) \geq 1 - \exp(-2\alpha^2 n)$. $\square$

3   Certification of Mixed States

The task we analyze can be understood as an interactive game between two participants: a *prover* Paul, and a *sampler* Sam. Paul is supposed to prepare multiple copies of some *reference state* φ before sending them to Sam, and the purpose of the game is for Sam to detect when the state produced by Paul is (close to) what it is supposed to be, no matter how maliciously Paul behaves. Here, the reference state φ may be an arbitrary but known *mixed* state. A canonical example of such a quantum sampling protocol is depicted in Fig. 1. It consists of Sam asking Paul to deliver the purification registers of k randomly chosen positions. Sam then measures these purifications in order to learn if they were in the right state.[2]

Purification-Based Sampling

1. Paul prepares N copies of the purification $|\psi_{PS}\rangle$ of φ_S, he sends N registers in state φ_S labeled S_1 to S_N to Sam and keeps the corresponding purification registers P_1 to P_N.
2. Sam picks a subset $t \subseteq [N]$ of size k uniformly at random.
3. Sam sends t to Paul and asks him to send him the purification registers P_i for $i \in t$.
4. Sam measures each register P_iS_i for $i \in t$ using projective measurement $\{|\varphi\rangle\langle\varphi|_{PS}, \mathbb{1}_{PS} - |\varphi\rangle\langle\varphi|_{PS}\}$. Sam accepts if he observed $|\varphi\rangle\langle\varphi|^{\otimes k}$, otherwise, he rejects.

Fig. 1. The purification-based mixed state quantum sampling protocol with reference state φ_S. Paul and Sam need to have previously agreed on a purification $|\varphi_{PS}\rangle$ of φ_S.

In the extreme case of a reference state that is empty on Paul's side, and thus pure on Sam's side (and so there is no purification for Paul to provide in step 2), the sampling protocol of Fig. 1 pretty much coincides with the pure-state sampling procedure considered and analyzed in [6]. For a true mixed reference state, however, it is significantly harder to prove that the sampling protocol "does its job" because of the additional freedom that Paul has in preparing the purification registers that may depend on the choice of t. This very much renders the techniques from [6] useless. Indeed, the idea of the analysis in [6] was to assume, for the sake of the argument, that the positions outside of t are measured as well, and then to delay the choice of t to after the measurement so as to reduce to a classical sampling procedure. Because of Paul's freedom in choosing the purifications dependent on t, it makes no sense to speak about the

---

[2] Note that there is no loss in generality in announcing the positions that Sam wants to check *in one go* as is done in Fig. 1, compared to announcing them *one-by-one*; doing it the latter way only makes it harder for Paul.

outcome of the reference measurement $\{|\varphi\rangle\langle\varphi|, \mathbb{1} - |\varphi\rangle\langle\varphi|\}$ *before* t is chosen, or about the measurement being applied to a position *outside* of t. As such, we need an entirely different approach.

Before worrying about analyzing the mixed-state sampling protocol of Fig. 1, we first need to specify what it should actually mean for it to "do its job"; this is not entirely obvious. Intuitively, we want that after the sampling, if Sam accepts then his part of the state should be "somehow close" to what it is supposed to be, namely $\varphi^{\otimes n}$ where we set $n = N - k$. However, Paul can obviously cheat in a small number of positions, i.e., start off with a state that consists of i.i.d. copies of $|\varphi\rangle$ except for a small number of positions where the state may deviate arbitrarily, and he still has a fair chance of not being caught. Of course, the same holds for a mixture of such states, and therefore, by purification, also for a superposition of such states. This motivates the definition below of an "ideal state", which captures the best we can hope for. The formal statement of what the sampling protocol of Fig. 1 achieves is then in terms of controlling Sam's part of the state after the protocol by means of Sam's part of such an ideal state. This is somewhat similar in spirit as the approach in [6] for pure-state sampling, though there are some technical differences.

Definition 3 (Ideal States). *For $\epsilon > 0$, a state $\psi_{S^n} \in \mathcal{D}_{\leq}(\mathcal{H}_S^{\otimes n})$ is said to be ϵ-ideal if there exists a purification $|\psi_{RP^n S^n}\rangle$ of ψ_{S^n} such that*

$$|\psi\rangle_{RP^n S^n} \in \mathcal{H}_R \otimes \Delta_{\epsilon n}(|\varphi\rangle_{P^n S^n}^{\otimes n}).$$

We loosely say that ψ_{S^n} is ideal when it is ϵ-ideal for small ϵ.

This basically means that an ideal state is one where Paul could transform his system into one where he holds n systems P^n and an additional purifying R system, and where the $P^n S^n$ part of the state lives in a low-error subspace.

Our analysis of the sampling protocol described in Fig. 1 (and some variants of it) preserves many aspects of the operational interpretation provided in [6] when sampling with respect to a pure reference state. We establish that Sam's *subnormalized* final state of register S^n upon acceptance can be controlled by an ideal state. The subnormalized state is simply the state Sam is left with when he accepts scaled down by the probability of acceptance (i.e. its trace corresponds to the probability for Sam to accept). Let $d := \dim(\mathcal{H}_S)$ be the size of the register holding φ_S and let $\epsilon > 0$ be a parameter. Informally, our main theorem (Theorem 2 and Corollary 2) establishes that Sam's subnormalized final state upon acceptance $\rho_{S^n}^{\mathrm{acc}} \in \mathcal{D}_{\leq}(\mathcal{H}_S^{\otimes n})$ is such that

$$\rho_{S^n}^{\mathrm{acc}} \leq (N+1)^{d^2-1} \psi_{S^n} + \sigma_{S^n}, \tag{3}$$

where ψ_{S^n} is ideal and $\|\sigma_{S^n}\|_1$ is negligible in N.

Any state $\rho_{S^n}^{\mathrm{acc}}$ that satisfies (3) can be considered to be an ideal state in many applications. Let $\mathcal{Q}$ be a completely positive trace non-increasing super-operator modelling a task that we would like to apply upon $\rho_{S^n}^{\mathrm{acc}}$. Suppose that $\mathcal{Q}$ behaves nicely when it is executed from an ideal state ψ_{S^n}. That is, the bad event represented by a POVM element E_{bad} has negligible probability on the ideal state $p_{\text{bad}}^{\text{id}} := \text{tr}(E_{\text{bad}}\mathcal{Q}(\psi_{S^n})) \leq 2^{-\alpha N}$ for $\alpha > 0$. Running $\mathcal{Q}$ upon $\rho_{S^n}^{\text{acc}}$ instead produces the state $\mathcal{Q}(\rho_{S^n}^{\text{acc}}) \leq \mathcal{Q}((N+1)^{d^2-1}\psi_{S^n} + \sigma_{S^n})$. We then have that the probability of the bad event in the real case is $p_{\text{bad}}^{\text{real}} := \text{tr}(E_{\text{bad}}\mathcal{Q}(\rho_{S^n}^{\text{acc}})) \leq (N+1)^{d^2-1}p_{\text{bad}}^{\text{id}} + \|\sigma_{S^n}\|_1$, which remains negligible when $p_{\text{bad}}^{\text{id}}$ is negligible and d is small enough (i.e. a constant). In other words, any negligible upper bound on the probability of some "bad" event occurring when processing the ideal state translates to a negligible upper bound on the "bad" event when processing the real state instead. In these cases, it is good enough to analyze the ideal state, for which an analysis is typically simpler because of the specific form of the state as given by Definition 3.

Our main result can also be interpreted as a statement about Paul and Sam's joint state when Sam accepts. To do so, we invoke Proposition 1 upon (3). For the sake of simplicity, assume that $\rho_{S^n}^{\text{acc}} \leq c \cdot \psi_{S^n}$, which is essentially what (3) means for $c := (N+1)^{d^2-1}$. Proposition 1 then establishes the existence of a linear operator A acting upon registers RP^n for which $A^\dagger A \leq \mathbb{1}$ such that

$$|\rho^{\text{acc}}\rangle_{RP^n S^n} = \sqrt{c}(A \otimes \mathbb{1}_{S^n})|\psi\rangle_{RP^n S^n}, \tag{4}$$

where $|\rho^{\text{acc}}\rangle_{RP^n S^n}$ and $|\psi\rangle_{RP^n S^n}$ are purifications of $\rho_{S^n}^{\text{acc}}$ and ψ_{S^n}, respectively. The operator $E := AA^\dagger$ can be viewed as the outcome of a POVM applied upon registers RP^n implemented by the detection operator A. It follows from (4) that $\rho_{RP^n S^n}^{\text{acc}}$ can be obtained with a non-negligible probability of success $1/c$ by applying a measurement upon an ideal state $\psi_{RP^n S^n}$. Therefore, any application having a negligible probability for Paul to generate a *bad* shared state from an ideal one has also a negligible probability to generate a *bad* shared state from the real one.

We now state our main result in the special case of the basic protocol given in Fig. 1. To do so, we define $\mathcal{E}_{RS^N \to S^n}^{\text{acc}}$ as a completely positive, trace non-increasing map that represents the execution of the protocol in the accepting case, meaning that given an initial state ρ_{RS^n}, $\mathcal{E}_{RS^N \to S^n}^{\text{acc}}(\rho_{RS^n})$ will be a subnormalized density matrix representing the output given that the verifier accepted, and $\text{tr}[\mathcal{E}_{RS^N \to S^n}^{\text{acc}}(\rho)]$ will be the probability of acceptance on that input state. The statement is the following:

Theorem 1. Let $\mathcal{E}_{RS^N \to S^n}^{\text{acc}}$ be defined as above, and let $\rho_{RS^N} \in \mathcal{D}(\mathcal{H}_R \otimes \mathcal{H}_S^{\otimes N})$ be an arbitrary input state. For any $\epsilon > 0$, there exist a subnormalized ϵ-ideal operator $\psi_{S^n} \in \mathcal{D}_{\leq}(\mathcal{H}_S^{\otimes n})$ and σ_{S^n} such that

$$\mathcal{E}_{RS^N \to S^n}^{\text{acc}}(\rho_{RS^N}) \leq c_{N,d^2} \cdot \psi_{S^n} + \sigma_{S^n}$$

where $\|\sigma_{S^n}\|_1 \leq \exp(-\Omega(N))$.

The proof is deferred to Sect. 5 (Theorem 2 and Corollary 2), where it will be a corollary of a more general statement.

3.1 Sampling Protocol Using LOCC only

Our analysis of mixed state sampling protocols is not limited to the protocol of Fig. 1. In Sect. 5, we show that any sampling protocol that satisfy certain criteria can be analyzed using our techniques. One such protocol is the one depicted in Fig. 2. It is a protocol for certifying that Paul prepares—and purifies—halves of EPR pairs that requires only local operations and classical communication (LOCC) after the initial state preparation and distribution phase. EPR pairs are states of the form $|\Phi^+\rangle = \frac{1}{\sqrt{2}}(|00\rangle + |11\rangle)$ that have the unique property that measurements in both the computational and diagonal bases are perfectly correlated. The protocol exploits this fact in the following way: for each position in the sample, Sam asks Paul for the result of measuring his purifying register in a random basis, and checks that this result corresponds to his own measurement in the same basis.

EPR-LOCC Sampling

1. Paul prepares N EPR pairs and sends half of each to Sam.
2. Sam chooses a sample $t \subset [N]$ of size k and a basis $c \in \{+, \times\}^k$ both uniformly at random, and sends both to Paul.
3. Upon reception of t and c, Paul measures each qubit of the sample in the corresponding basis c_i. He sends the outcome $\hat{X} \in \{0, 1\}^k$ back to Sam.
4. Sam measures each of his sampled qubit in the corresponding basis c_i, let $X \in \{0, 1\}^k$ be the outcome. He rejects if $\hat{X} \neq X$.

Fig. 2. The sampling protocol with local measurements for sampling halves of EPR pairs, i.e. with reference state $\varphi = \frac{1}{2}$.

4   Two-Party Randomness Generation

Before we prove our main result, we first apply the protocol in Fig. 1 to a two-party randomness generation problem.

4.1   The Protocol

The protocol for randomness generation is depicted in Fig. 3. The protocol works as follows: Alice first has to generate N EPR pairs and send half of each to Bob. Bob then uses our sampling protocol of Fig. 1 to certify that the state Alice sent him is (close to) the prescribed state. If Bob's check succeeds, then our quantum sampling result says that Alice basically prepared the right state, up to a few errors. Bob's measurement outcome will then have very high min-entropy (arbitrarily close to the maximum n).

1. Alice prepares the state $|\Phi^+\rangle^{\otimes N}_{A^N B^N}$ for $|\Phi^+\rangle := \frac{1}{\sqrt{2}}(|00\rangle + |11\rangle)$ and sends the system B^N to Bob.
2. Alice and Bob perform protocol **Purification-Based Sampling** from Fig. 1 with Alice as the prover and Bob as the sampler and with $k = \beta N$ for $\beta > 0$ such that βN is an integer. Let $\rho_{A^n B^n} \in \mathcal{D}((\mathcal{H}_2 \otimes \mathcal{H}_2)^{\otimes n})$ be the resulting normalized joint state of $n = N - k$ pairs of qubits.
3. Alice and Bob respectively measure their n qubits in the computational basis and output their respective measurement outcomes X_A and X_B.

Fig. 3. The randomness generation protocol. N is the security parameter, β determines the size of the sample.

4.2 Entropy of Alice and Bob's Outputs

Since Alice is the preparer of the N EPR pairs, her output will have high min-entropy. The tricky part of the following proof is showing that Bob's freedom in choosing t and accepting or refusing the sampling outcome cannot influence too much the distribution of Alice's measurement outcome.

Lemma 2 (Entropy of Alice's output). *If Alice follows the protocol, then for any $\gamma > 0$, her output $X_A \in \{0,1\}^n$ satisfies*

$$\mathrm{H}_\infty(X_A) \geq (1 - \gamma)n,$$

except with probability negligible in n.

Proof. Let $\rho_{A^N B^N}$ be the joint state of Alice and Bob before the sampling phase. As the preparer of the quantum state, Alice prepares N perfect EPR pairs (i.e. $\rho_{A^N B^N} = |\Phi^+\rangle\langle\Phi^+|^{\otimes N}$), so her measurement outcome would have maximal min-entropy for the n remaining qubits were it not for Bob's actions. Bob can bias the outcome of Alice's measurement in two possible ways: (1) he can measure his register B^N *before* choosing t and make t depend on this measurement outcome and (2) he can make the sampling abort even though Alice was honest. We analyze both possibilities separately, showing that each cannot reduce the min-entropy by more than a small linear amount, except with negligible probability.

For (1), suppose Bob performs some measurement on his register B^N that yields sample choice $t \subset [N]$ with probability p_t and results in the reduced density operator $\rho^t_{A^N}$ on Alice's side. Suppose also that Alice was to measure her whole state at this point, resulting in a measurement outcome $X_A \in \{0,1\}^N$. Observe that by the law of total probability,

$$2^{-N} = 2^{-\mathrm{H}_\infty(X_A)_\rho} = \sum_t p_t \cdot 2^{-\mathrm{H}_\infty(X_A|T=t)_{\rho^t}},$$

where $2^{-H_\infty(X_A|T=t)_{\rho^t}}$ gives the maximal probability of guessing X_A given $T = t$ when X_A was obtained by measuring $\rho^t_{A^N}$. It holds by Markov's inequality that

$$\sum_t p_t \cdot [H_\infty(X_A \mid T = t)_{\rho^t} \leq N - (\alpha N)] \leq 2^{-\alpha N}$$

where $[\cdot]$ is the Iverson bracket which evaluates to 1 if the contents is true and to 0 otherwise. In other words, the values of t for which $H_\infty(X_A \mid T = t)_{\rho^t}$ is less than $(1 - \alpha)N$ have combined probability less than $2^{-\alpha N}$. Now, Alice does not measure her whole state, but instead only those positions that do not belong to t, so let $X_A^{\bar{t}}$ be the outcome of measuring the qubits outside of t and let X_A^t be the outcome for the positions in t. The following holds except with negligible probability over the choice of t:

$$H_\infty(X_A^{\bar{t}} \mid T = t) \geq H_\infty(X_A \mid T = t, X_A^t) \geq (1 - \alpha - \beta)N \tag{5}$$

where the last inequality follows from the chain rule for the min-entropy with $H_0(X_A^t) = \beta N$.

To deal with (2), observe that

$$2^{-H_\infty(X_A^{\bar{t}}|T=t,\mathrm{acc})} \leq 2^{-H_\infty(X_A^{\bar{t}}|T=t)} / \Pr[\mathrm{acc}] \leq 2^{-H_\infty(X_A^{\bar{t}}|T=t)+\alpha N} \tag{6}$$

whenever $\Pr[\mathrm{acc}] \geq 2^{-\alpha N}$.

We can conclude that, except with negligible probability upper bounded by $2 \cdot 2^{-\alpha N}$, the min-entropy of Alice's output is

$$H_\infty(X_A^{\bar{t}} \mid T = t, \mathrm{acc}) \geq (1 - 2\alpha - \beta)N$$

by combining the bounds (5) and (6) and the respective probabilities that these bounds hold. The statement is satisfied by choosing α and β such that $\gamma = 2\alpha + \beta$ and noting that $N > n$. □

We rely on the next Lemma to lower-bound the amount of min-entropy in the measurement outcome of Bob. It says that if the joint state of Alice and Bob lives in a quantum Hamming ball of small radius around n copies of an EPR pair, then Bob's reduced density operator has high min-entropy.

Lemma 3. *Let $\epsilon > 0$ and $|\sigma_{RP^n S^n}\rangle \in \mathcal{H}_R \otimes \Delta_{\epsilon n}(|\Phi^+\rangle^{\otimes n}_{P^n S^n})$. It holds that*

$$H_\infty(S^n)_\sigma \geq (1 - \epsilon - h(\epsilon))n.$$

Proof. Let $\Pi_\epsilon = \{E \subseteq [n] : |E| \leq \epsilon n\}$ and let $\mathbb{P}^{\epsilon n, |\Phi^+\rangle}_{P^n S^n} = \sum_{E \in \Pi_\epsilon} \mathbb{P}^E_{P^n S^n}$ be the projector onto $\Delta_{\epsilon n}(|\Phi^+\rangle^{\otimes n}_{P^n S^n})$ where

$$\mathbb{P}^E_{P^n S^n} = \bigotimes_{i \in E}(\mathbb{1} - |\Phi^+\rangle\langle\Phi^+|)_{P_i S_i} \bigotimes_{i \notin E} |\Phi^+\rangle\langle\Phi^+|_{P_i S_i}.$$

Define $|\tilde{\sigma}^E_{RP^nS^n}\rangle = (\mathbb{1}_R \otimes \mathbb{P}^E_{P^nS^n})|\sigma_{RP^nS^n}\rangle$ for each $E \in \Pi_\epsilon$. It holds by Proposition 2 that

$$\sigma_{RP^nS^n} = \sum_{E,E' \in \Pi_\epsilon} |\tilde{\sigma}^E_{RP^nS^n}\rangle\langle\tilde{\sigma}^{E'}_{RP^nS^n}| \leq 2^{h(\epsilon)n} \sum_{E \in \Pi_\epsilon} |\tilde{\sigma}^E_{RP^nS^n}\rangle\langle\tilde{\sigma}^E_{RP^nS^n}|$$

because the set Π_ϵ contains at most $2^{h(\epsilon)n}$ elements. Furthermore, we know by the definition of $|\tilde{\sigma}^E_{RP^nS^n}\rangle$ that

$$\frac{\tilde{\sigma}^E_{S^n}}{\|\tilde{\sigma}^E_{S^n}\|_1} = \left(\bigotimes_{i \notin E} \frac{\mathbb{1}_{S_i}}{2}\right) \otimes \psi_{S_E} \leq 2^{-n+|E|}\mathbb{1}_{S^n}$$

for some normalized state ψ_{S_E} living on register $S_E = \bigotimes_{i \in E} S_i$. Since $|E| \leq \epsilon n$, it directly follows that

$$\sigma_{S^n} \leq 2^{h(\epsilon)n} \sum_{E \in \Pi_\epsilon} \tilde{\sigma}^E_{S^n} \leq 2^{-(1-\epsilon-h(\epsilon))n}\mathbb{1}_{S^n}$$

and we can thus conclude that $H_\infty(S^n)_\sigma \geq (1 - \epsilon - h(\epsilon))n$. $\square$

Lower-bounding Bob's output min-entropy is essentially applying Lemma 3 to Bob's state after the sampling step of protocol of Fig. 3 which can be approximated by an ideal state by means of our main result (Theorem 1).

Lemma 4 (Entropy of Bob's output). *If Bob follows the protocol, for any $\gamma > 0$, his output $X_B \in \{0,1\}^n$ satisfies*

$$H_\infty(X_B) \geq (1 - \gamma)n,$$

except with probability negligible in n.

Proof. The security of the protocol against dishonest Alice is almost a direct consequence of our quantum sampling result (Theorem 1). Let $\rho_{B^n} \in \mathcal{D}(\mathcal{H}_2^{\otimes n})$ be the normalized state of Bob after step 2 of the protocol of Fig. 3 given that Bob did not reject and let P_{acc} be the probability that he did not reject the sampling. By Theorem 1, it holds that for any $\epsilon > 0$ there exists an ideal ψ_{B^n} and an operator σ_{B^n} with negligible norm such that

$$\rho_{B^n} \leq P_{acc}^{-1}(c_{N,d^2}\psi_{B^n} + \sigma_{B^n}). \tag{7}$$

Let $\tilde{\psi}_{B^n} = \frac{c_{N,d^2}}{P_{acc}} \cdot \psi_{B^n}$. Then

$$\left\|\frac{c_{N,d^2}}{P_{acc}}(\psi_{B^n} + \sigma_{B^n}) - \tilde{\psi}_{B^n}\right\|_1 = \frac{1}{P_{acc}}\|\sigma_{B^n}\|_1,$$

which is negligible in N whenever P_{acc} is non-negligible. It follows that except with negligible probability, the right-hand side of (7) will behave exactly like

$\tilde{\psi}_{B^n}$, in which case their min-entropy will be equal. This min-entropy is bounded below by

$$\mathrm{H}_{\infty}(\tilde{\psi}_{B^n}) = \mathrm{H}_{\infty}(\psi_{B^n}) - \log \frac{c_{N,d^2}}{P_{\mathrm{acc}}} \geq (1 - \epsilon - h(\epsilon))n - \log \frac{c_{N,d^2}}{P_{\mathrm{acc}}} \tag{8}$$

by Lemma 3.

Using the bound of (8), we can claim that the min-entropy of ρ_{B^n} is lower-bounded by

$$(1 - \epsilon - h(\epsilon) - \alpha)n$$

unless one of two negligible probability events occurred. The first event is that ρ_{B^n} behaves like σ_{B^n} instead of $\tilde{\psi}_{B^n}$ and the second event is that Bob accepted the outcome of a sampling that had probability $P_{\mathrm{acc}} \leq c_{N,d^2} \cdot 2^{-\alpha n}$ of being accepted. We can conclude that the result X_B of measuring ρ_{B^n} in the computational basis will have min-entropy at least $(1 - \epsilon - h(\epsilon) - \alpha)n$, except with negligible probability. The statement follows by choosing ϵ and α in the above such that $\gamma = \epsilon + h(\epsilon) + \alpha$. □

5   Proof of Our Main Result

We now turn to the proof of our main result. In this section, we present the techniques that allow to analyze sampling protocols similar to that of Fig. 1. The key property of the sampling protocol that makes the tools of this section applicable is that it is invariant under the permutation of the sampler's register, up to an adjustment of the adversary's attack and of the output state. In order to make this more explicit, we actually consider and analyze a general class of sampling protocols that are permutation invariant and perform well on i.i.d. states, and we then show (1) that the protocol of Fig. 1 falls into that class and (2) that any protocol from that class allows us to control the post-sampling state the way we want. As an additional bonus of this modular analysis is that we can then easily extend our results to other sampling protocols. For instance, the sampling protocol of Fig. 2 for certifying EPR pairs presented in Sect. 3.1 also falls into the class of protocols that we consider. In that protocol, Paul is not asked to provide his respective parts of the EPR pairs from within the sampled subset, but he is instead asked to provide the *measurement outcome* of those, when measured in a random basis chosen and announced by Sam, and Sam compares with the corresponding measurement outcomes on his side.

5.1   Mixed State Sampling Protocols and Permutation Invariance

The general form of the sampling protocols we consider is depicted in Fig. 4. For simplicity, we assume that the protocol always outputs the same number of qudits $n = N - k$, i.e. that it lives in the Hilbert space $\mathcal{H}_S^{\otimes n}$. Note that this means that there is no freedom in the way we choose the sample t; the only permutation invariant probability distribution on the subsets of $[N]$ of size k is the uniform distribution. We also assume that k is of the order of N.

General Mixed State Sampling Protocol

1. Paul prepares $\rho_{RS^N} \in \mathcal{D}(\mathcal{H}_R \otimes \mathcal{H}_S^{\otimes N})$ and sends register S^N to Sam.
2. Sam chooses a sample $t \subset [N]$ of size k uniformly at random and a challenge c and sends both to Paul.
3. Upon reception of t and c, Paul sends back a quantum register Q.
4. Sam performs a binary outcome measurement that depends on c and t on the joint system of registers Q and S_i for $i \in t$, and accepts or rejects based on the outcome.

Fig. 4. The general form of a mixed state sampling protocol for sampling a mixed reference state φ.

The obvious example instantiation of such a sampling protocol is the sampling protocol of Fig. 1, where c is empty and Sam's measurement consists of projecting onto $|\varphi\rangle\langle\varphi|^{\otimes k}$. Another example is the one we discuss in Sect. 3.1 for certifying EPR pairs, where c then is a randomly chosen sequence of bases that specifies how Paul is supposed to measure his parts of the EPR pairs.

Clearly, for a given instantiation of the general protocol of Fig. 4, the adversary's attack strategy consists of the choice of ρ_{RS^N} and of the quantum operation (that depends on t and c) that produces Q in step 3.

We now define the notion of permutation invariance that sampling strategies must satisfy for our techniques to apply.

Definition 4 (Permutation Invariance for Sampling Protocols). *A sampling protocol that implements the framework of Fig. 4 is invariant under the permutation of the sampler's register if for any adversarial strategy for Paul, the completely positive trace non-increasing map $\mathcal{E}^{\text{acc}}_{RS^N \to S^n}$, which represents the output state of the sampler when he accepts, satisfies*

1. for any input $\rho_{RS^N} \in \mathcal{D}(\mathcal{H}_R \otimes \mathcal{H}_S^{\otimes N})$ there exists $\bar{\mathcal{E}}^{\text{acc}}_{P^N S^N \to \Pi S^n}$ such that

$$\frac{1}{n!} \sum_{\pi \in \mathcal{S}_n} |\pi\rangle\langle\pi|_\Pi \otimes \pi_{S^n} \mathcal{E}^{\text{acc}}_{RS^N \to S^n}(\rho_{RS^N}) \pi^\dagger_{S^n} = \bar{\mathcal{E}}^{\text{acc}}_{P^N S^N \to \Pi S^n}(\bar{\rho}_{P^N S^N}) \quad (9)$$

for some symmetric purification $|\bar{\rho}_{P^N S^N}\rangle \in \text{Sym}^N(\mathcal{H}_P \otimes \mathcal{H}_S)$ of $\frac{1}{N!} \sum_{\pi \in \mathcal{S}_N} \pi_{S^N} \rho_{S^N} \pi^\dagger_{S^N}$,

2. for any $\epsilon > 0$, $\|\bar{\mathcal{E}}^{\text{acc}}_{P^N S^N \to \Pi S^n}(|\theta\rangle\langle\theta|^{\otimes N})\|_1 \leq \exp(-\Omega(N))$ whenever $F(\theta_S, \varphi_S)^2 < 1 - \epsilon$, and

3. $\bar{\mathcal{E}}^{\text{acc}}_{P^N S^N \to \Pi S^n}$ acts trivially on the unsampled systems, up to reordering. Formally, $\bar{\mathcal{E}}^{\text{acc}}_{P^N S^N \to \Pi S^n}$ satisfies

$$\text{tr}_\Pi \left(\bar{\mathcal{E}}^{\text{acc}}_{P^N S^N \to \Pi S^n}(|\theta\rangle\langle\theta|^{\otimes N}_{PS}) \right) \leq \theta_S^{\otimes n}.$$

The first criterion effectively requires that any attack against the sampling protocol of Fig. 4 can be transformed into an *equivalent* attack on a symmetric state—up to a random reordering of the positions. The second criterion demands that Bob rejects with overwhelming probability in case of an "obviously bad" state, i.e., in case of i.i.d. copies of a state that is far from the reference state φ. The third criterion simply asks that the sampling protocol (and the corresponding symmetrized map $\mathcal{E}^{\mathrm{acc}}_{P^N S^N \to \Pi S^n}$) does not measure registers outside the sample.

From a technical perspective, the first criterion allows us to apply the observations from Sect. 2.2 to the promised symmetric state, so that we can upper bound the latter by a convex linear combination of i.i.d. states, and the second criterion then allows us to control the "bad part" of this convex linear combination (see Sect. 5.3). What then still turns out to be cumbersome to deal with is the random permutation, which got introduced by the first criterion, and to get a bound on the actual state $\mathcal{E}^{\mathrm{acc}}_{RS^N \to S^n}(\rho_{RS^N})$ instead; we show how to do this in Sect. 5.4.

We point out that the "cheap" way to deal with the random permutation would be to simply modify the sampling protocol by *really* permuting the registers at the end of the protocol, so that the permuted state *is* the final state after the sampling protocol. Besides being esthetically less appealing, because it would mean a less natural and more complicated sampling protocol than really necessary, this would also give more freedom to the party who chooses the permutation in choosing it adversarially. For instance, in our application in Sect. 4, where the final state is used to produce a high min-entropy source, we cannot allow that either player can rearrange the registers and so, say, move the zero-outputs into the positions he wants them to be.

5.2 Permutation Invariance of Our Sampling Protocols

As a first step in analyzing the sampling protocol **Purification-Based Sampling** of Fig. 1, we show that it satisfies the above definition of permutation invariance. Given that Sam's actions are obviously symmetric with respect to permuting his registers, this is probably not very surprising; spelling out the details though still turns out to be somewhat cumbersome. We therefore move the proof to Appendix A.1 and simply give a high-level proof sketch below.

Proposition 3. *The protocol* **Purification-Based Sampling** *of Fig. 1 satisfies Definition 4.*

Proof (sketch). For the first criterion, we need to argue that any adversary against the real sampling protocol can be adapted into an adversary against a symmetrized version of the protocol that will yield the same output state, up to a random permutation.

We first observe that when sampling from a permutation invariant operator, it doesn't matter which registers we sample from since the reduced density operator of any subset of k registers is the same, i.e. $\rho_{S_t} = \rho_{S_{t'}}$ for any $t, t' \subseteq [N]$ of size k. Therefore we can make the simplifying assumption that we always sample from the first k registers of S^N.

We construct the symmetric adversary: from the symmetric state $\bar\rho_{P^N S^N}$ from the first criterion of Definition 4, the adversary will compute the permutation $\pi \in \mathcal{S}_N$ applied on S^N. This permutation defines the set $t_\pi \subset [N]$ of positions to which π sends positions $1, \ldots, k$. The symmetric adversary will then simulate the real adversary on this sample t_π and will permute the output according to π before sending it to Sam (such that each register sent by the adversary aligns with the corresponding register on Sam's side).

The second criterion follows from the observation that the maximal probability of measuring $|\varphi\rangle\langle\varphi|^{\otimes k}$ in the sampling protocol on input $|\theta\rangle\langle\theta|^{\otimes N}$ is the fidelity between $\theta^{\otimes k}$ and $\varphi^{\otimes k}$ which is negligible in k when $F(\theta_S, \varphi_S)^2 < 1 - \epsilon$.

The third criterion follows from the fact that the unsampled positions are untouched in both the real and the symmetrized protocols.   □

The following proposition allows us to apply the techniques of this section to the LOCC sampling protocol presented in Fig. 2. Its proof can be found in Appendix A.2.

Proposition 4. *The sampling protocol* **EPR-LOCC Sampling** *from Fig. 2 satisfies Definition 4.*

Proof (sketch). We need to argue that the protocol is permutation invariant in the sense of Definition 4, and that it performs well on i.i.d. states. The first part follows from the permutation invariance of the choice of t and c and of the measurement on the sampler's qubits. Suppose Sam was to permute his register with $\pi \in \mathcal{S}_N$ before performing the sampling. Then we can modify the adversary such that it attacks the sampling protocol with this new ordering of Sam's register: if Sam chooses sample t, announce $\pi(t)$ to Paul instead, the same goes for c. Let x be Paul's message to Sam, then permute x such that it aligns correctly with the corresponding qubits on Sam's register. The probability of accepting is exactly the same and the output of the protocol will be shuffled according to π's action on the unsampled qubits.

The second criterion follows from the fact that the only state that is perfectly correlated in both the computational and the diagonal bases is the EPR pair $|\Phi^+\rangle$. Therefore if all of Paul and Sam's measurement outcomes are perfectly correlated in the randomly chosen basis, it should hold that they shared states close to perfect EPR pairs. More precisely, if they share a state $|\theta\rangle^{\otimes N}$ where each θ has fidelity at most $1 - \epsilon$ with $|\Phi^+\rangle$, then their outputs cannot be perfectly correlated in at least one of the bases, except with negligible probability. The third criterion follows trivially from the fact that the unsampled qubits are not measured or acted upon.   □

5.3   Proof of Sampling Against Symmetric Adversaries

By considering sampling protocols that are permutation invariant in the sense of Definition 4, we can use the specific properties of symmetric states to upper-bound the failure probability of such protocols for symmetric adversaries (adversaries which prepare a state $|\bar\rho_{P^N S^N}\rangle$ that lives in the symmetric subspace $\mathrm{Sym}^N(\mathcal{H}_P \otimes \mathcal{H}_S)$).

Lemma 5 below shows that since symmetric states are approximated by a mixture of i.i.d. states, then the output of the sampling executed on such a mixture is approximated by a mixture of states i.i.d. in states that are close to the reference state φ.

Lemma 5. *Let $\mathcal{E}^{\mathrm{acc}}_{RS^N \to S^n}$ be the output of a sampling protocol that satisfies Definition 4 and let $\rho_{RS^N} \in \mathcal{D}(\mathcal{H}_R \otimes \mathcal{H}_S^{\otimes N})$. For any $\epsilon > 0$ there exists a subnormalized measure $d\theta_S$ on the set of mixed states $\theta_S \in \mathcal{D}(\mathcal{H}_S)$ which satisfy $F(\theta_S, \varphi_S)^2 \geq 1 - \epsilon$ and an operator $\tilde{\sigma}_{S^n}$ such that*

$$\frac{1}{n!} \sum_{\pi \in \mathcal{S}_n} \pi_{S^n} \mathcal{E}^{\mathrm{acc}}_{RS^N \to S^n} (\rho_{RS^N}) \pi^{\dagger}_{S^n} \leq c_{N,d^2} \cdot \int \theta_{S^n}^{\otimes n} d\theta_S + \tilde{\sigma}_{S^n} \tag{10}$$

and $\|\tilde{\sigma}_{S^n}\|_1 \leq \exp(-\Omega(N))$, where c_{N,d^2} is the dimension of $\mathrm{Sym}^N(\mathcal{H}_P \otimes \mathcal{H}_S)$.

Proof. By Definition 4, there exists $\bar{\mathcal{E}}^{\mathrm{acc}}_{P^N S^N \to \Pi S^n}$ and $\bar{\rho}_{P^N S^N} \in \mathrm{Sym}^N(\mathcal{H}_P \otimes \mathcal{H}_S)$ such that

$$\frac{1}{n!} \sum_{\pi \in \mathcal{S}_n} |\pi\rangle\langle\pi|_{\Pi} \otimes \pi_{S^n} \mathcal{E}^{\mathrm{acc}}_{RS^N \to S^n} (\rho_{RS^N}) \pi^{\dagger}_{S^n} = \bar{\mathcal{E}}^{\mathrm{acc}}_{P^N S^N \to \Pi S^n} (\bar{\rho}_{P^N S^N}). \tag{11}$$

Therefore it suffices to prove the statement for $\bar{\mathcal{E}}^{\mathrm{acc}}_{P^N S^N \to S^n}$ obtained by tracing out the register Π from the output of $\bar{\mathcal{E}}^{\mathrm{acc}}_{P^N S^N \to \Pi S^n}$.

Since $|\bar{\rho}_{P^N S^N}\rangle \in \mathrm{Sym}^N(\mathcal{H}_P \otimes \mathcal{H}_S)$, it holds by Remark 2 that $\bar{\rho}_{P^N S^N} \leq c_{N,d^2} \cdot \int |\theta\rangle\langle\theta|^{\otimes N}_{P^N S^N} d|\theta_{PS}\rangle$ where $d|\theta_{PS}\rangle$ is the normalized Haar measure on the set of pure states on $\mathcal{H}_P \otimes \mathcal{H}_S$. It follows that

$$\bar{\mathcal{E}}^{\mathrm{acc}}_{P^N S^N \to S^n} (\bar{\rho}_{P^N S^N}) \leq \bar{\mathcal{E}}^{\mathrm{acc}}_{P^N S^N \to S^n} \left(c_{N,d^2} \cdot \int |\theta\rangle\langle\theta|^{\otimes N}_{P^N S^N} d|\theta\rangle \right)$$

$$= c_{N,d^2} \cdot \bar{\mathcal{E}}^{\mathrm{acc}}_{P^N S^N \to S^n} \left(\int_{\theta_S \approx^{\epsilon} \varphi_S} |\theta\rangle\langle\theta|^{\otimes N}_{P^N S^N} d|\theta\rangle \right.$$

$$\left. + \int_{\theta_S \not\approx^{\epsilon} \varphi_S} |\theta\rangle\langle\theta|^{\otimes N}_{P^N S^N} d|\theta\rangle \right)$$

$$\leq c_{N,d^2} \cdot \int_{\theta_S \approx^{\epsilon} \varphi_S} \theta_{S^n}^{\otimes n} d\theta_S + \tilde{\sigma}_{S^n}$$

where $\theta_S \approx^{\epsilon} \varphi_S$ means that $F(\theta_S, \varphi_S)^2 \geq 1 - \epsilon$ and where the operator $\tilde{\sigma}_{S^n} := c_{N,d^2} \cdot \bar{\mathcal{E}}^{\mathrm{acc}}_{P^N S^N \to S^n} \left(\int_{\theta_S \not\approx^{\epsilon} \varphi} |\theta\rangle\langle\theta|^{\otimes N} d|\theta\rangle \right)$ satisfies $\|\tilde{\sigma}_{S^n}\|_1 \leq \exp(-\Omega(N))$ by the second criterion of Definition 4. The last inequality of the above follows from the third criterion of Definition 4 and from Remark 3: since the trace non-increasing map $\bar{\mathcal{E}}^{\mathrm{acc}}_{P^N S^N \to S^n}$ does not act on the unsampled qubits, the state of S^n *after* the application of this map is upper-bounded by the state of the unsampled qubits *before* its application.

Finally, the measure $d\theta_S$ is obtained by taking the partial trace over P on the measure $d|\theta_{PS}\rangle$ on the restricted set of $|\theta_{PS}\rangle$ where $F(\theta_S, \varphi_S)^2 \geq 1 - \epsilon$. This corresponds to a measure proportional to the Hilbert-Schmidt measure [25,31] over density operators on $\mathcal{H}_S$ which have fidelity squared at least $1 - \epsilon$ with φ_S. $\qquad \square$

From the above Lemma, we can conclude that the *permuted* output of the sampling protocol is upper bounded by an ideal state in the spirit of (3).

Corollary 1. *Let $\mathcal{E}^{\mathrm{acc}}_{RS^N \to S^n}$ be the output of a sampling protocol that satisfies Definition 4 and let $\rho_{RS^N} \in \mathcal{D}(\mathcal{H}_R \otimes \mathcal{H}_S^{\otimes N})$. For any $\epsilon > 0$, there exist a subnormalized ϵ-ideal operator $\psi_{S^n} \in \mathcal{D}_{\leq}(\mathcal{H}_S^{\otimes n})$ and σ_{S^n} such that*

$$\frac{1}{n!} \sum_{\pi \in \mathcal{S}_n} \pi_{S^n} \mathcal{E}^{\mathrm{acc}}_{RS^N \to S^n}(\rho_{RS^N}) \pi^{\dagger}_{S^n} \leq c_{N,d^2} \cdot \psi_{S^n} + \sigma_{S^n} \tag{12}$$

where $\|\sigma_{S^n}\|_1 \leq \exp(-\Omega(N))$.

Proof. Fix $\beta = \epsilon/2$ and let $d\theta_S$ and $\tilde{\sigma}_{S^n}$ be as in Lemma 5 for parameter β, i.e. such that

$$\frac{1}{n!} \sum_{\pi \in \mathcal{S}_n} \pi_{S^n} \mathcal{E}^{\mathrm{acc}}_{RS^N \to S^n}(\rho_{RS^N}) \pi^{\dagger}_{S^n} \leq c_{N,d^2} \cdot \int \theta_{S^n}^{\otimes n} d\theta_S + \tilde{\sigma}_{S^n} \tag{13}$$

where $d\theta_S$ is a subnormalized measure on the set of mixed states which satisfy $F(\theta_S, \varphi_S)^2 \geq 1 - \beta$ and where $\tilde{\sigma}_{S^n}$ has negligible norm.

Let $\tau_{P^n S^n} := \int |\theta\rangle\langle\theta|^{\otimes n}_{P^n S^n} d\theta_S$ be an extension of $\int \theta_{S^n}^{\otimes n} d\theta_S$ where each $|\theta_{PS}\rangle$ is such that $|\langle\theta_{PS}|\varphi_{PS}\rangle|^2 = F(\theta_S, \varphi_S)^2 \geq 1 - \beta$ and let $\tilde{\sigma}_{P^n S^n}$ be an extension of $\tilde{\sigma}_{S^n}$. Then from Lemma 1, we have

$$\mathrm{tr}\left((\mathbb{1} - \mathbb{P}^{2\beta n, |\varphi\rangle}_{P^n S^n})(\tau_{P^n S^n})\right) \leq \exp(-2\beta^2 n). \tag{14}$$

Choose $\psi_{S^n} = \mathrm{tr}_{P^n}(\mathbb{P}^{2\beta n, |\varphi\rangle}_{P^n S^n} \tau_{P^n S^n} \mathbb{P}^{2\beta n, |\varphi\rangle}_{P^n S^n})$. Then, using (13), we have

$$\frac{1}{n!} \sum_{\pi \in \mathcal{S}_n} \pi_{S^n} \mathcal{E}^{\mathrm{acc}}_{RS^N \to S^n}(\rho_{RS^N}) \pi^{\dagger}_{S^n} \leq c_{N,d^2} \cdot \int \theta_{S^n}^{\otimes n} d\theta_S + \tilde{\sigma}_{S^n}$$

$$= \mathrm{tr}_{P^n}\left(c_{N,d^2} \cdot \tau_{P^n S^n} + \tilde{\sigma}_{P^n S^n}\right) = c_{N,d^2} \cdot \psi_{S^n} + \sigma_{S^n}$$

where $\sigma_{S^n} := \mathrm{tr}_{P^n}(c_{N,d^2}(\tau_{P^n S^n} - \mathbb{P}^{2\beta n, |\varphi\rangle}_{P^n S^n} \tau_{P^n S^n} \mathbb{P}^{2\beta n, |\varphi\rangle}) + \tilde{\sigma}_{P^n S^n})$ has norm upper bounded by

$$\|\sigma_{P^n S^n}\|_1 \leq c_{N,d^2} \|\tau_{P^n S^n} - \mathbb{P}^{2\beta n, |\varphi\rangle}_{P^n S^n} \tau_{P^n S^n} \, \mathbb{P}^{2\beta n, |\varphi\rangle}_{P^n S^n}\|_1 + \|\tilde{\sigma}_{P^n S^n}\|_1 \leq \exp(-\Omega(N))$$

by first applying the triangle inequality and then the Gentle Measurement's Lemma [21,30] with the bound of (14).   □

It should be noted that the operator σ_{S^n} from the above Corollary is not positive semidefinite in general, but since its norm is negligible, this shouldn't matter because it can simply be ignored for most applications.

5.4   Proof Against Arbitrary Adversaries: Unpermuting the Output

In order to conclude that the sampling protocol works as intended on an arbitrary input state and adversarial strategy, we need to argue that if we remove the permutation from the contents of (12), then the left-hand side, which becomes the post-sampling state, is still approximated by a state having a purification in a low-error subspace. It turns out that the intuitive statement "if the permuted output is ideal then the non-permuted output is also ideal" that we want to show is quite tricky to prove. We stress that this step is necessary if we want to keep the permutation "under the hood" and have a statement that doesn't require to physically shuffle the systems, which would lead to unnatural sampling protocols.

Lemma 6 below is the first step in this proof, it shows that the property of having a purification in a low-error subspace, i.e. of being *ideal*, does indeed persist after "unpermutation" of the registers.

Lemma 6. *Let $\epsilon > 0$ and let $\sigma_{S^n} \in \mathcal{D}(\mathcal{H}_S^{\otimes n})$ be such that $\frac{1}{n!} \sum_{\pi \in \mathcal{S}_n} \pi_{S^n} \sigma_{S^n} \pi_{S^n}^\dagger$ is ϵ-ideal, then σ_{S^n} is also ϵ-ideal.*

Proof. Let $r = \epsilon n$. We need to show that if $\bar{\sigma}_{S^n} := \frac{1}{n!} \sum_{\pi \in \mathcal{S}_n} \pi_{S^n} \sigma_{S^n} \pi_{S^n}^\dagger$ has a purification in $\mathcal{H}_R \otimes \Delta_r(|\varphi\rangle_{P^n S^n}^{\otimes n})$ for some register R, then σ_{S^n} also has a purification in $\mathcal{H}_R \otimes \Delta_r(|\varphi\rangle_{P^n S^n}^{\otimes n})$. Let $|\bar{\sigma}_{RP^n S^n}\rangle \in \mathcal{H}_R \otimes \Delta_r(|\varphi\rangle_{P^n S^n}^{\otimes n})$ be the purification of $\bar{\sigma}_{S^n}$ that exists by assumption and let $\sum_i p_i |i_{S^n}\rangle\langle i_{S^n}|$ be the spectral decomposition of σ_{S^n}. Define the pure state

$$|\bar{\sigma}_{\Pi P^n S^n}\rangle = \sqrt{\frac{1}{n!}} \sum_{\pi \in \mathcal{S}_n} |\pi\rangle_\Pi \otimes \left(\sum_i \sqrt{p_i} |i_{P^n}\rangle \otimes \pi_{S^n} |i_{S^n}\rangle \right)$$

where $\{|i_{P^n}\rangle\}_i$ is an orthonormal basis of $\mathcal{H}_{P^n}$. Note that this state is a purification of $\bar{\sigma}_{S^n}$, so there exists an isometry $V_{\Pi P^n \to RP^n}$ such that $V_{\Pi P^n \to RP^n} |\bar{\sigma}_{\Pi P^n S^n}\rangle = |\bar{\sigma}_{RP^n S^n}\rangle \in \mathcal{H}_R \otimes \Delta_r(|\varphi\rangle_{P^n S^n}^{\otimes n})$. We can express $|\bar{\sigma}_{RP^n S^n}\rangle$ as:

$$|\bar{\sigma}_{RP^n S^n}\rangle = (V_{\Pi P^n \to RP^n} \otimes \mathbb{1}_{S^n}) |\sigma_{\Pi P^n S^n}\rangle$$
$$= \sum_{\pi, i} \sqrt{\frac{p_i}{n!}} V_{\Pi P^n \to RP^n} |\pi\rangle_\Pi |i_{P^n}\rangle \otimes \pi_{S^n} |i_{S^n}\rangle = \sum_{\pi, i} \sqrt{\frac{p_i}{n!}} |\xi_{\pi,i}\rangle_{RP^n} \otimes \pi_{S^n} |i_{S^n}\rangle$$

where the vectors $|\xi_{\pi,i}\rangle_{RP^n} := V_{\Pi P^n \to RP^n} |\pi\rangle_\Pi |i_{P^n}\rangle$ are orthogonal to each other. Then by acting on this state with an isometry that extracts π from registers RP^n and that undoes π on registers P^n and S^n, we get

$$\sum_{\pi, i} \sqrt{\frac{p_i}{n!}} (\mathbb{1}_R \otimes \pi_{P^n}^{-1}) |\xi_{\pi,i}\rangle_{RP^n} \otimes |i_{S^n}\rangle$$

Note that both before and after this isometry is applied, the state of registers P^n and S^n has support in $\Delta_r(|\varphi\rangle_{P^n S^n}^{\otimes n})$ because this subspace is invariant under permutation of these registers. The proof is then completed since the above state is a purification of σ_{S^n} that lies in $\mathcal{H}_R \otimes \Delta_r(|\varphi\rangle_{P^n S^n}^{\otimes n})$. $\qquad\square$

We now have all the tools we need to prove our main result, Theorem 2 below. Its proof combines the above lemma with Lemmas 1 and 5 to show that the output of the sampling is negligibly close to a state that is post-selected from a purification of an ideal state.

Theorem 2 (Main Result). *Let $\mathcal{E}^{acc}_{RS^N \to S^n}$ be the output of a sampling protocol that satisfies Definition 4 and let $\rho_{RS^N} \in \mathcal{D}(\mathcal{H}_R \otimes \mathcal{H}_S^{\otimes N})$. For any $\epsilon > 0$, there exists a non-normalized vector*

$$\left| \tilde{\psi}_{R'P^nS^n} \right\rangle \in \mathcal{H}_{R'} \otimes \Delta_{\epsilon n}(|\varphi\rangle^{\otimes n}_{P^nS^n})$$

and a completely positive trace non-increasing superoperator $\tilde{\mathcal{K}}_{R'P^n \to \mathbb{C}}$ such that

$$\left\| \mathcal{E}^{acc}_{RS^N \to S^n}(\rho_{RS^N}) - c_{N,d^2}(\tilde{\mathcal{K}}_{R'P^n} \otimes \mathrm{id}_{S^n})(\tilde{\psi}_{R'P^nS^n}) \right\|_1 \leq \exp(-\Omega(N))$$

By means of Proposition 1 and Remark 3, we can express the statement of Theorem 2 in terms of an operator inequality as suggested in (3), rather than by means of post-selection.

Corollary 2. *Let $\mathcal{E}^{acc}_{RS^N \to S^n}$ be the output of a sampling protocol that satisfies Definition 4 and let $\rho_{RS^N} \in \mathcal{D}(\mathcal{H}_R \otimes \mathcal{H}_S^{\otimes N})$. For any $\epsilon > 0$, there exist a subnormalized ϵ-ideal operator $\psi_{S^n} \in \mathcal{D}_{\leq}(\mathcal{H}_S^{\otimes n})$ and σ_{S^n} such that*

$$\mathcal{E}^{acc}_{RS^N \to S^n}(\rho_{RS^N}) \leq c_{N,d^2} \cdot \psi_{S^n} + \sigma_{S^n}$$

where $\|\sigma_{S^n}\|_1 \leq \exp(-\Omega(N))$.

Proof (of Theorem 2). Let ψ_{S^n} and σ_{S^n} be as in the statement of Corollary 1, i.e. such that

$$\frac{1}{n!} \sum_{\pi \in \mathcal{S}_n} \pi_{S^n} \mathcal{E}^{acc}_{RS^N \to S^n}(\rho_{RS^N}) \pi^\dagger_{S^n} \leq c_{N,d^2} \cdot \psi_{S^n} + \sigma_{S^n} \qquad (15)$$

and define $\tau_{S^n} := \psi_{S^n} + c^{-1}_{N,d^2} \cdot \sigma_{S^n}$. Since ψ_{S^n} is ϵ-ideal, let $|\psi_{R'P^nS^n}\rangle$ be the purification of ψ_{S^n} that lives in the low error subset $\mathcal{H}_{R'} \otimes \Delta_{\epsilon n}(|\varphi\rangle^{\otimes n}_{P^nS^n})$. Let $|\tau_{R'P^nS^n}\rangle$ be a purification[3] of τ_{S^n} such that $\|\psi_{R'P^nS^n} - \tau_{R'P^nS^n}\|_1 \leq \exp(-\Omega(N))$. From (15) and Proposition 1 we can show that there exists a trace non-increasing completely positive map $\mathcal{K}_{R'P^n \to \Pi}$ that produces a classical register Π from purification registers $R'P^n$ with the property that

$$\frac{1}{n!} \sum_{\pi \in \mathcal{S}_n} |\pi\rangle\langle\pi|_\Pi \otimes \pi_{S^n} \mathcal{E}^{acc}_{RS^N \to S^n}(\rho_{RS^N}) \pi^\dagger_{S^n} = c_{N,d^2}(\mathcal{K}_{R'P^n \to \Pi} \otimes \mathrm{id}_{S^n})(\tau_{R'P^nS^n}).$$

---

[3] The existence of a purification of τ_{S^n} with this property can be argued by using Uhlmann's Theorem: since τ_{S^n} is close in fidelity to ψ_{S^n}, for any purification $|\psi_{R'P^nS^n}\rangle$ of ψ_{S^n}, there exists a purification $|\tau_{R'P^nS^n}\rangle$ that is also close to $|\psi_{R'P^nS^n}\rangle$.

Suppose now we were to submit both sides of the above equality to the following quantum operation: measure register Π and undo the observed permutation on register S^n. The left-hand side of the above would become $\mathcal{E}^{\mathrm{acc}}_{RS^N \to S^n}(\rho_{RS^N})$ whereas the right-hand side becomes

$$c_{N,d^2} \cdot \sum_{\pi \in \mathcal{S}_n} ((\langle \pi |_{\Pi} \otimes \pi^{-1}_{S^n})(\mathcal{K}_{R'P^n \to \Pi} \otimes \mathrm{id}_{S^n})(\tau_{R'P^n S^n})(|\pi\rangle_{\Pi} \otimes (\pi^{-1}_{S^n})^{\dagger}).$$

We now show how to represent this operator in a way that corresponds to the statement we need to prove, i.e. as post-selected from a rank-one operator living almost entirely in the low-error subspace. To this end, define[4] an isometry $U_{R'P^n \to Z\Pi}$ that purifies the action of $\mathcal{K}_{R'P^n \to \Pi}$, i.e. such that for any $\nu_{R'P^n}$,

$$\mathcal{K}_{R'P^n \to \Pi}(\nu_{R'P^n}) := \mathrm{tr}_Z \left((\mathbb{P}_Z \otimes \mathbb{1}_{\Pi}) \cdot U_{R'P^n \to Z\Pi} \cdot \nu_{R'P^n} \cdot (U_{R'P^n \to Z\Pi})^{\dagger} \right)$$

for some projector $\mathbb{P}_Z$. Using this representation, the post-sampling operator can be expressed as

$$\mathcal{E}^{\mathrm{acc}}_{RS^N \to S^n}(\rho_{RS^N}) = c_{N,d^2} \cdot \mathrm{tr}_Z \left((\mathbb{P}_Z \otimes \mathbb{1}_{S^n}) \cdot \sum_{\pi \in \mathcal{S}_n} [U^{\pi}_{R'P^n \to Z} \otimes \pi^{-1}_{S^n}](\tau_{R'P^n S^n}) \right)$$

$$\tag{16}$$

where $U^{\pi}_{R'P^n \to Z} := (\mathbb{1}_Z \otimes \langle \pi |_{\Pi}) \cdot U_{R'P^n \to Z\Pi}$ and where $[U](\rho)$ is short for $U\rho U^{\dagger}$.
Define the operator

$$\tilde{\psi}_{ZS^n} := \sum_{\pi \in \mathcal{S}_n} (U^{\pi}_{R'P^n \to Z} \otimes \pi^{-1}_{S^n})\psi_{R'P^n S^n}(U^{\pi}_{R'P^n \to Z} \otimes \pi^{-1}_{S^n})^{\dagger}.$$

where $\psi_{R'P^n S^n}$ is the purification of ψ_{S^n} defined earlier. It isn't too hard to show that $\tilde{\psi}_{S^n}$ is such that $\psi_{S^n} = \frac{1}{n!} \sum_{\pi \in \mathcal{S}_n} \pi_{S^n} \tilde{\psi}_{S^n} \pi^{\dagger}_{S^n}$. Since ψ_{S^n} has a purification in the low-error subspace, Lemma 6 implies that $\tilde{\psi}_{S^n}$ itself admits a purification in this subspace. Let $|\tilde{\psi}_{R'P^n S^n}\rangle$ be this purification and let $\tilde{\mathcal{K}}_{R'P^n \to C}$ be the superoperator that first maps $|\tilde{\psi}_{R'P^n S^n}\rangle$ to $\tilde{\psi}_{ZS^n}$ and then applies $\sigma_Z \mapsto \mathrm{tr}_Z(\mathbb{P}_Z \sigma_Z)$ to register Z. Then, using the definition of $\tilde{\psi}_{R'P^n S^n}$ and $\tilde{\mathcal{K}}_{R'P^n}$, and since completely positive trace non-increasing maps cannot increase the trace distance,

---

[4] It is always possible to define such an isometry and projector for any trace non-increasing completely positive superoperator $\mathcal{E}_{A \to B}$. To see this, let $\mathcal{E}(\sigma_A) = \sum_k E_k \sigma_A E_k^{\dagger}$ where $E_k \in L(\mathcal{H}_A, \mathcal{H}_B)$ are the Kraus operators of $\mathcal{E}$ and define the isometry $U_{A \to BZ}$ as mapping an arbitrary state $|\psi\rangle_A$ to $\sum_k E_k |\psi\rangle_A |k\rangle_Z + \sqrt{1 - \sum_k E_k^{\dagger} E_k} |\psi\rangle_A |\perp\rangle_Z$ where $|\perp\rangle_Z$ is orthogonal to $|k\rangle_Z$ for every k. Then $\mathbb{P}_Z = \sum_k |k\rangle\langle k|_Z$ suffices as the required projector since $\mathrm{tr}_Z((\mathbb{1}_B \otimes \mathbb{P}_Z)U_{A \to BZ}\sigma_A U^{\dagger}_{A \to BZ}) = \sum_k E_k \sigma_A E_k^{\dagger} = \mathcal{E}_{A \to B}(\sigma_A)$.

$$\|\mathcal{E}^{\mathrm{acc}}_{RS^N \to S^n}(\rho_{RS^N}) - c_{N,d^2}(\tilde{\mathcal{K}}_{R'P^n} \otimes \mathrm{id}_{S^n})(\tilde{\psi}_{R'P^nS^n})\|_1$$

$$= \left\| c_{N,d^2} \cdot \mathrm{tr}_Z \left(\mathbb{P}_Z \otimes \mathbb{1}_{S^n} \cdot \right. \right.$$

$$\left. \left. \sum_{\pi \in \mathcal{S}_n} [U^\pi_{R'P^n \to Z} \otimes \pi^{-1}_{S^n}] \left(\tau_{R'P^nS^n} - \psi_{R'P^nS^n} \right) \right) \right\|_1$$

$$\leq c_{N,d^2} \cdot \|\tau_{R'P^nS^n} - \psi_{R'P^nS^n}\|_1$$

$$\leq \exp(-\Omega(N))$$

where in the first inequality $\mathcal{E}^{\mathrm{acc}}_{RS^N \to S^n}(\rho_{RS^N})$ is replaced with (16) and the last inequality follows from our choice of $|\tau_{R'P^nS^n}\rangle$. $\square$

6   Conclusion and Open Questions

Statistical sampling is a natural task that is well understood from a classical perspective. Classical tools such as Hoeffding's inequality, Azuma's inequality and other results on concentration of measure that are used to analyze classical sampling (and quantum sampling to a certain degree [6]) are of no use when trying to sample from quantum data with a *mixed* reference state. The tools of symmetric invariance can substitute the classical tools up to a certain degree when analyzing fully quantum sampling protocols. We have introduced a framework for sampling mixed states by presenting a general sampling protocol and we have shown that if an instantiation of that general protocol respects simple criteria, then it can be used to certify that a quantum population is close to an n-fold tensor product of a reference state φ in an adversarial setting.

We have also shown that this result can be applied to yield a two-party randomness generation protocol. While perfect coin tossing is impossible without assumptions, we can achieve the "next best thing" by producing a string that has an almost-maximal min-entropy from the point of view of both participants.

Sampling of a quantum population is a new concept and many questions are left unanswered, especially when sampling with a mixed reference state where the usual (classical) tools do not apply. Precisely, future directions for this work include:

1. A formulation of our results where a conclusion can be made when an error rate significantly larger than 0 has been observed. From an observed error rate of $\delta > 0$ within the sample, we would want to conclude that the state of the remaining positions can be controlled by means of an $(\varepsilon + \delta)$-ideal state for small $\varepsilon > 0$.
2. An extension of our results to multiple reference states for the same population instead of a fixed reference state φ, e.g. with reference states φ_0, φ_1 where register i of the population is tested against φ_{x_i} for $x \in \{0,1\}^n$. While sampling according to an arbitrary (pure) reference state is given "for free" for pure state sampling (since all pure states are related by a unitary transformation on the sampler's register), it requires more work in the case of mixed state sampling.

3. On top of the previous point, it is often useful for quantum sampling applications to have a statement in terms of an *adaptive* sampling protocol where the reference states (i.e. the bits of x) are chosen adaptively by the adversary based on what positions were sampled. Such an extension would have applications in two-party cryptography where sampling is done in a sequential manner using a 1- or 2-bit cryptographic primitive, such as cut-and-choose. In fact, if our results were extended in such a way, it would allow to certify states with a 2-bit description (such as the BB84 encoding) using a 1-bit cut-and-choose, a task that is not known to be possible relying on existing sampling tools. The pure-state sampling framework of [6] was shown to apply in the adaptive setting in [12].

Acknowledgments. FD acknowledges funding from GAČR grant GA16-22211S, and LS is funded by NSERC discovery and acceleration to discovery grants.

A   Permutation Invariance of Sampling Protocols

A.1   Proof of Proposition 3

We can assume w.l.o.g. that the state $\rho_{RS^N} \in \mathcal{D}(\mathcal{H}_R \otimes \mathcal{H}_S^{\otimes N})$ is pure and that adversarial strategies against the protocol depicted in Fig. 1 is described by a family of isometries of the form $U_{R \to R'P^k}^t$ for $t \subseteq [N]$ of size k, where P^k represents the register sent to Sam and supposed to contain the purifications of φ_S, and R' is a register kept by Paul.

For convenience, define the isometry $V_{S^N \to S^n S^k}^t$ that, for any $t \subseteq [N]$, maps subsystems S_i for $i \in t$ into the last k subsystems (denoted S^k) and subsystems S_i for $i \notin t$ into the first $n = N - k$ subsystems (denoted S^n). In other words, isometry V_S^t simply groups together the registers to be sampled.

For an adversarial strategy as described above, the completely positive trace non-increasing map $\mathcal{E}_{RS^N \to S^n}^{\mathrm{acc}}$ that maps the input state ρ_{RS^N} to the sampler's conditional output is defined by

$$\mathcal{E}_{RS^N \to S^n}^{\mathrm{acc}}(\rho_{RS^N}) := \frac{1}{\binom{N}{k}} \sum_{t \subseteq [N]} \mathrm{tr}_{R'} \left(\langle \varphi |_{P^k S^k}^{\otimes k} \cdot [U_R^t \otimes V_{S^N}^t](\rho_{PS}) \cdot |\varphi\rangle_{P^k S^k}^{\otimes k} \right) .$$

where we left the identity operator acting on $R'S^n$ implicit and where $[U](\rho)$ is short for $U\rho U^\dagger$ for any isometry U.

The following property of $V_{S^N \to S^n S^k}^t$ will be useful for proving Lemma 7 below.

Remark 4. Let $\pi \in \mathcal{S}_N$, and let $t_\pi = \{\pi^{-1}(i) \mid i \in [k]\}$. There exist $\tau^\pi \in \mathcal{S}_k$ and $\bar{\tau}^\pi \in \mathcal{S}_n$ such that $V_{S^N \to S^n S^k}^{[k]} \cdot \pi_S = (\bar{\tau}_{S^n}^\pi \otimes \tau_{S^k}^\pi) \cdot V_{S^N \to S^n S^k}^{t_\pi}$. Furthermore, there is a one-to-one correspondence between permutations $\pi \in \mathcal{S}_N$ and triplets $(t_\pi, \tau^\pi, \bar{\tau}^\pi)$.

Lemma 7. *Protocol* **Purification-Based Sampling** *from Fig. 1 satisfies the first criterion of Definition 4.*

Proof. We need to show the existence of a completely positive trace non-increasing map $\bar{\mathcal{E}}^{\text{acc}}_{P^N S^N \to \Pi S^n}$ such that for any ρ_{RS^N},

$$\frac{1}{n!} \sum_{\pi \in \mathcal{S}_n} |\pi\rangle\langle\pi|_{\Pi} \otimes \pi_{S'} \mathcal{E}^{\text{acc}}_{RS^N \to S^n}(\rho_{RS^N}) \pi^{\dagger}_{S'} = \bar{\mathcal{E}}^{\text{acc}}_{P^N S^N \to \Pi S^n}(\bar{\rho}_{P^N S^N}) \qquad (17)$$

for some symmetric purification $|\bar{\rho}_{P^N S^N}\rangle$ of $\frac{1}{N!}\sum_{\pi \in \mathcal{S}_N} \pi_{S^N} \rho_{S^N} \pi^{\dagger}_{S^N}$ where $\mathcal{E}^{\text{acc}}_{RS^N \to S^n}$ is defined earlier in this section.

Let $|\bar{\rho}_{P^N S^N}\rangle \in \text{Sym}^N(\mathcal{H}_P \otimes \mathcal{H}_S)$ be an arbitrary purification of $\frac{1}{N!}\sum_{\pi \in \mathcal{S}_N} \pi_{S^N} \rho_{S^N} \pi^{\dagger}_{S^N}$. Since all purifications are equivalent up to an isometry on the purifying register, there exists an isometry $W_{P^N \to R\bar{\Pi}}$ such that

$$(W_{P^N} \otimes \mathbb{1}_{S^N})|\bar{\rho}_{P^N S^N}\rangle = \frac{1}{\sqrt{N!}} \sum_{\pi \in \mathcal{S}_N} (\mathbb{1}_R \otimes \pi_{S^N})|\rho_{RS^N}\rangle \otimes |\pi\rangle_{\bar{\Pi}}.$$

Let $\bar{U}_{P^N \to \bar{R}P^k}$ be the isometry that performs the following actions unitarily on register P^N of $|\bar{\rho}_{P^N S^N}\rangle$:

1. Apply W_{P^N}, producing registers R and $\bar{\Pi}$.
2. From permutation $\pi \in \mathcal{S}_N$ held in register $\bar{\Pi}$, compute t_{π}, $\tau^{\pi} \in \mathcal{S}_k$ and $\bar{\tau}^{\pi} \in \mathcal{S}_n$ as in Remark 4, i.e. such that $V^{[k]}_{S^N \to S^n S^k} \cdot \pi_S = (\tau^{\pi}_{\hat{S}} \otimes \bar{\tau}^{\pi}_{S'}) \cdot V^{t_{\pi}}_{S^N \to S^n S^k}$.
3. Apply attack $U^{t_{\pi}}_{R \to R'P^k}$ on register R, producing registers R' and P^k and reorder register P^k using permutation τ^{π} so that each P_l aligns with the right sampled S_i.
4. Let register $\bar{R}$ be composed of registers R', $\bar{\Pi}$. Output registers P^k, $\bar{R}$ and register Π containing the permutation $\bar{\tau}^{\pi}$ that acts on the output S^n (i.e. on the unsampled registers).

From the definition of the above isometry,

$$(\bar{U}_{P^N \to \bar{R}P^k} \otimes V^{[k]}_{S^N \to S^n S^k})|\bar{\rho}_{P^N S^N}\rangle$$
$$= \frac{1}{\sqrt{N!}} \sum_{\pi \in \mathcal{S}_N} (\tau^{\pi}_{P^k} \otimes \tau^{\pi}_{S^k} \otimes \bar{\tau}^{\pi}_{S^n})(U^{t_{\pi}}_{R \to R'P^k} \otimes V^{t_{\pi}}_{S^N \to S^n S^k})|\rho_{RS^N}\rangle |\pi\rangle_{\bar{\Pi}} |\bar{\tau}^{\pi}\rangle_{\Pi}$$

Tracing out register $\bar{\Pi}$ from the above and using the one-to-one correspondence between π and $(t_{\pi}, \tau^{\pi}, \bar{\tau}^{\pi})$ to break the sum over π into sums over t, τ and $\bar{\tau}$, we get

$$\frac{1}{N!} \sum_{\pi \in \mathcal{S}_N} [(\tau^{\pi}_{P^k} \otimes \tau^{\pi}_{S^k} \otimes \mathbb{1}_{R'} \otimes \bar{\tau}^{\pi}_{S^n})(U^{t_{\pi}}_{R \to R'P^k} \otimes V^{t_{\pi}}_{S^N \to S^n S^k})](\rho_{RS^N}) \otimes |\bar{\tau}^{\pi}\rangle\langle\bar{\tau}^{\pi}|_{\Pi}$$

$$= \frac{1}{n!} \frac{1}{k!} \frac{1}{\binom{N}{k}} \sum_{\bar{\tau} \in \mathcal{S}_n} \bar{\tau}_{S^n} \left(\sum_{\substack{\tau \in \mathcal{S}_k \\ t \subseteq [N]:|t|=k}} [(\tau_{P^k} \otimes \tau_{S^k})(U^t_R \otimes V^t_{S^N})](\rho_{RS^N}) \right) (\bar{\tau}_{S^n})^{\dagger} \otimes |\bar{\tau}^{\pi}\rangle\langle\bar{\tau}^{\pi}|_{\Pi}$$

Taking the partial inner product with $|\varphi\rangle^{\otimes k}_{P^k S^k}$ and tracing out R' leaves us with

$$\frac{1}{n!\binom{N}{k}} \sum_{\bar{\tau} \in \mathcal{S}_n} \bar{\tau}_{S^n} \left(\sum_t \mathrm{tr}_{R'} \left(\langle\varphi|^{\otimes k}_{P^k S^k} \cdot [U^t_R \otimes V^t_{SN}](\rho_{RSN}) \cdot |\varphi\rangle^{\otimes k}_{P^k S^k} \right) \right) (\bar{\tau}_{S^n})^\dagger \otimes |\bar{\tau}^\pi\rangle\langle\bar{\tau}^\pi|_\Pi$$

$$= \frac{1}{n!} \sum_{\bar{\tau} \in \mathcal{S}_n} \bar{\tau}_{S^n} \mathcal{E}^{\mathrm{acc}}_{RS^N \to S^n}(\rho_{RS^N}) \bar{\tau}^\dagger_{S^n} \otimes |\bar{\tau}^\pi\rangle\langle\bar{\tau}^\pi|_\Pi$$

where the sum over τ disappeared because $|\varphi\rangle^{\otimes k}_{P^k S^k}$ is invariant under permutation. Then $\bar{\mathcal{E}}^{\mathrm{acc}}_{P^N S^N \to \Pi S^n}$ defined as

$$\bar{\mathcal{E}}^{\mathrm{acc}}_{P^N S^N \to \Pi S^n}(\bar{\rho}_{P^N S^N}) := \mathrm{tr}_{\bar{R}} \left(\langle\varphi|^{\otimes k}_{P^k S^k} \cdot [\bar{U}_{P^N} \otimes V^{[k]}_{S^N}](\bar{\rho}_{P^N S^N}) \cdot |\varphi\rangle^{\otimes k}_{P^k S^k} \right).$$

satisfies (17). $\hfill \square$

Lemma 8. *Protocol* **Purification-Based Sampling** *from Fig. 1 satisfies the second criterion of Definition 4.*

Proof. We need to show that for any $\epsilon > 0$, $\|\bar{\mathcal{E}}^{\mathrm{acc}}_{P^N S^N \to \Pi S^n}(|\theta\rangle\langle\theta|^{\otimes N}_{P^N S^N})\|_1 \leq \exp(-\Omega(N))$ whenever $F(\theta_S, \varphi_S)^2 < 1 - \epsilon$ where

$$\bar{\mathcal{E}}^{\mathrm{acc}}_{P^N S^N \to \Pi S^n}(\bar{\rho}_{P^N S^N}) := \mathrm{tr}_{\bar{R}} \left(\langle\varphi|^{\otimes k}_{P^k S^k} \cdot [\bar{U}_{P^N} \otimes V^{[k]}_{S^N}](\bar{\rho}_{P^N S^N}) \cdot |\varphi\rangle^{\otimes k}_{P^k S^k} \right).$$

The proof is based on the simple observation that the isometry $\bar{U}$ that maximizes the probability of observing $|\varphi\rangle^{\otimes k}$ on registers $P^k S^k$ is the one that matches the fidelity with $\varphi^{\otimes k}$ by the fact that the fidelity is monotonous. Therefore it holds that, since the fidelity is multiplicative for product states,

$$\|\bar{\mathcal{E}}^{\mathrm{acc}}_{P^N S^N \to \Pi S^n} \left(|\theta\rangle\langle\theta|^{\otimes N}_{P^N S^N} \right) \|_1 \leq F(\theta^{\otimes k}_{S^k}, \varphi^{\otimes k}_{S^k})^2 \leq (1 - \epsilon)^{2k} \leq \exp(-2\epsilon k)$$

whenever $F(\theta_S, \varphi_S)^2 < 1 - \epsilon$. $\hfill \square$

The third criterion of Definition 4 follows trivially from the observation that neither $\mathcal{E}^{\mathrm{acc}}_{RS^N \to S^n}$ nor $\bar{\mathcal{E}}^{\mathrm{acc}}_{P^N S^N \to \Pi S^n}$ acts on the unsampled qubits other than by rearranging them.

A.2   Proof of Proposition 4

As in Appendix A.1, let us establish that the protocol satisfies the each criterion of Definition 4.

Lemma 9 (First criterion). *Let* $\mathcal{E}^{\mathrm{acc}}_{RS^N \to S^n}$ *be the output of the sampling protocol* **EPR-LOCC Sampling** *from Fig. 2. For any* $\rho_{RS^N} \in \mathcal{D}(\mathcal{H}_R \otimes \mathcal{H}^{\otimes N}_S)$ *there exists* $\bar{\mathcal{E}}^{\mathrm{acc}}_{P^N S^N \to \Pi S^n}$ *such that*

$$\frac{1}{n!} \sum_{\pi \in \mathcal{S}_n} |\pi\rangle\langle\pi|_\Pi \otimes \pi_{S^n} \mathcal{E}^{\mathrm{acc}}_{RS^N \to S^n}(\rho_{RS^N}) \pi^\dagger_{S^n} = \bar{\mathcal{E}}^{\mathrm{acc}}_{P^N S^N \to \Pi S^n}(\bar{\rho}_{P^N S^N}) \qquad (18)$$

for some symmetric purification $|\bar{\rho}_{P^N S^N}\rangle$ *of* $\frac{1}{N!} \sum_{\pi \in \mathcal{S}_N} \pi_{S^N} \rho_{S^N} \pi^\dagger_{S^N}$.

Proof. Recall the linear operator $V_{S^N \to S^n S^k}^t$ from Appendix A.1 that maps S_t to S^k and $S_{\bar{t}}$ to S^n (where S^k is understood to represent the last k registers). The completely positive trace non-increasing map $\mathcal{E}_{RS^N \to S^n}^{acc}$ that models the action of the protocol on the state ρ_{RS^N} when Sam accepts can be represented as

$$2^{-k} \binom{N}{k}^{-1} \sum_{t,c,x} \mathrm{tr}_{RS^k} \left((E_x^{t,c} \otimes \mathbb{P}_{S^k}^{x,c}) V_{S^N \to S^n S^k}^t \rho_{RS^N} V_{S^N \to S^n S^k}^t \right)$$

where the sum is over $t \subset [N]$ such that $|t| = k$, $c \in \{+, \times\}^k$ and $x \in \{0,1\}^k$ and where, for t and c sent by Sam, $E^{t,c} = \{E_x^{t,c}\}_{x \in \{0,1\}^k}$ is the POVM measurement on R that produces x and $\mathbb{P}_{S^k}^{x,c} := H^{\otimes c}|x\rangle\langle x|H^{\otimes c}$ is the projector onto x in basis c.

Let $\bar{\rho}_{P^N S^N}$ be an arbitrary purification of $\frac{1}{N!} \sum_{\pi \in \mathcal{S}_N} \pi_{S^N} \rho_{S^N} \pi_{S^N}^\dagger$. Define the map $\bar{\mathcal{E}}_{P^N S^N \to \Pi S^n}^{acc}$ as follows:

1. Map state $\bar{\rho}_{P^N S^N}$ to $\frac{1}{N!} \sum_{\pi \in \mathcal{S}_N} |\pi\rangle\langle\pi|_{\bar{\Pi}} \otimes (\mathbb{1}_R \otimes \pi_{S^N})\rho_{RS^N}(\mathbb{1}_R \otimes \pi_{S^N}^\dagger)$.
2. From permutation $\pi \in \mathcal{S}_N$ held in register R, compute t_π, $\tau^\pi \in \mathcal{S}_k$ and $\bar{\tau}^\pi \in \mathcal{S}_n$ as in Remark 4.
3. Apply $V_{S^N \to S^n S^k}^{[k]}$ on S^N, choose $c \in \{+, \times\}^k$ at random and apply POVM $E^{t_\pi, c}$ on R producing output x.
4. Measure the sampled registers S^k by projecting on $H^{\otimes \tau^\pi(c)}|\tau^\pi(x)\rangle_{S^k} = \tau^\pi H^{\otimes c}|x\rangle_{S^k}$.
5. Output $\bar{\tau}^\pi$ in register Π and register S^n.

The output of $\bar{\mathcal{E}}_{P^N S^N \to \Pi S^n}^{acc}$ applied on $\bar{\rho}_{P^N S^N}$ is

$$\frac{2^{-k}}{N!} \sum_{\pi,c,x} \mathrm{tr}_{RS^k} \left((E_x^{t_\pi,c} \otimes \tau_{S^k}^\pi \mathbb{P}_{S^k}^{x,c}(\tau_{S^k}^\pi)^\dagger) \cdot [V_{S^N \to S^n S^k}^{[k]} \pi_{S^N}](\rho_{RS^N}) \right) \otimes |\bar{\tau}^\pi\rangle\langle\bar{\tau}^\pi|_\Pi$$

$$= \frac{2^{-k}}{N!} \sum_{\pi,c,x} \bar{\tau}_{S^n}^\pi \, \mathrm{tr}_{RS^k} \left(E_x^{t_\pi,c} \otimes \mathbb{P}_{S^k}^{x,c})[V_{S^N \to S^n S^k}^{t_\pi}](\rho_{RS^N}) \right) \bar{\tau}_{S^n}^\pi \otimes |\bar{\tau}^\pi\rangle\langle\bar{\tau}^\pi|_\Pi$$

$$= \frac{2^{-k}}{n!} \binom{N}{k}^{-1} \sum_{\bar{\tau}^\pi \in \mathcal{S}_n} [\bar{\tau}_{S^n}^\pi] \left(\sum_{t,c,x} \mathrm{tr}_{RS^k} \left((E_x^{t,c} \otimes \mathbb{P}_{S^k}^{x,c})[V_{S^N}^t](\rho_{RS^N}) \right) \right) \otimes |\bar{\tau}^\pi\rangle\langle\bar{\tau}^\pi|_\Pi$$

$$= \frac{1}{n!} \sum_{\bar{\tau}^\pi \in \mathcal{S}_n} \bar{\tau}_{S^n}^\pi \mathcal{E}_{RS^N \to S^n}^{acc}(\rho_{RS^N}) \bar{\tau}_{S^n}^\pi \otimes |\bar{\tau}^\pi\rangle\langle\bar{\tau}^\pi|_\Pi$$

where the second equality uses Remark 4.   □

Lemma 10 (Second criterion). *Let $\bar{\mathcal{E}}_{P^N S^N \to \Pi S^n}^{acc}$ be as in the proof of Lemma 9. For any $\epsilon > 0$, $\|\bar{\mathcal{E}}_{P^N S^N \to \Pi S^n}^{acc}(|\theta\rangle\langle\theta|_{P^N S^N}^{\otimes N})\|_1 \le \exp(-\Omega(N))$ whenever $F(\theta_S, \varphi_S)^2 < 1 - \epsilon$.*

Proof. For any $c \in \{+, \times\}^k$, let $\bar{E}_x^c$ be the POVM element on P^N that gives the probability of x being outputted in Step 3 of $\bar{\mathcal{E}}_{P^N S^N \to \Pi S^n}^{acc}$ when c is chosen in the same step. In essence, $\bar{E}_x^c$ is to $\bar{\mathcal{E}}_{P^N S^N \to \Pi S^n}^{acc}$ what $E^{t_\pi,c}$ is to $\mathcal{E}_{RS^N \to S^n}^{acc}$; it gives the probability of observing x when the following measurement is done on

P^N: produce registers $\bar{\varPi}R$ from P^N, measure π from register $\bar{\varPi}$, compute the corresponding sample t_π, and apply the measurement corresponding to POVM $E^{t_\pi,c}$.

Using these POVM operators $\bar{E}_x^c$, we can express the norm we wish to upper-bound as

$$\|\bar{\mathcal{E}}_{P^N S^N \to \varPi S^n}^{\mathrm{acc}}(|\theta\rangle\langle\theta|_{P^N S^N}^{\otimes N})\|_1 = 2^{-k} \sum_{c,x} \mathrm{tr}\left((\bar{E}_x^c \otimes \mathbb{P}_{S^k}^{x,c} \otimes \mathbb{1}_{S^n})|\theta\rangle\langle\theta|_{P^N S^N}^{\otimes N}\right) \quad (19)$$

where $\mathbb{P}_{S^k}^{x,c}$ is the projector onto x in basis c. Note that the right-hand side of (19) can be interpreted as the probability of guessing the outcome of measuring register S^k in a known but random basis c by observing the reduced operator of register P^N. We now analyze this guessing probability to provide an upper-bound on (19).

Since each measurement on S^k is independent of each other and since the joint state is in an i.i.d. form, the probability of Paul guessing outcome x is of the form γ^k where γ corresponds to the probability of guessing a single bit of x. This probability is given by the expression

$$\gamma = \frac{1}{2}\Pr(\text{guess } X \mid C = +) + \frac{1}{2}\Pr(\text{guess } X \mid C = \times)$$

We show that at least one of the above conditional term is bounded above by a constant strictly smaller than 1 when $F(\theta_S, \varphi_S) < 1 - \epsilon$, which means that γ^k is negligible in k.

The maximum probability of guessing X when $C = +$ is given by the probability of distinguishing states

$$|\theta_P^0\rangle = (\mathbb{1}_p \otimes \langle 0|_S)|\theta_{PS}\rangle \text{ and } |\theta_P^1\rangle = (\mathbb{1}_p \otimes \langle 1|_S)|\theta_{PS}\rangle$$

and the same holds when $C = \times$ for similarly defined $|\theta_P^+\rangle$ and $|\theta_P^-\rangle$. Let

$$\sqrt{\lambda_0}|f_0\rangle_P|e_0\rangle_S + \sqrt{\lambda_1}|f_1\rangle_P|e_1\rangle_S$$

be the Schmidt decomposition of $|\theta_{PS}\rangle$ and consider the quantity

$$|\langle\theta_P^0|\theta_P^1\rangle| + |\langle\theta_P^+|\theta_P^-\rangle| \geq |\langle\theta_P^0|\theta_P^1\rangle + \langle\theta_P^+|\theta_P^-\rangle|$$
$$= |\langle\theta_{PS}|(\mathbb{1}_P \otimes |0\rangle\langle 1|_S)|\theta_{PS}\rangle + \langle\theta_{PS}|(\mathbb{1}_P \otimes |+\rangle\langle-|_S)|\theta_{PS}\rangle|$$
$$= \frac{1}{2}|\langle\theta_{PS}|(\mathbb{1}_P \otimes H_S)|\theta_{PS}\rangle| = \frac{1}{2}|\lambda_0\langle e_0|_S H_S|e_0\rangle_S + \lambda_1\langle e_1|_S H_S|e_1\rangle_S|$$
$$= \frac{1}{2}|\lambda_0 - \lambda_1|$$

where $H_S = \begin{pmatrix} 1 & 1 \\ 1 & -1 \end{pmatrix}$, the only inequality above is the triangle inequality and the last equality follows from the fact that $\langle e_0|_S H_S|e_0\rangle_S = -\langle e_1|_S H_S|e_1\rangle_S$ for any two orthogonal vectors $|e_0\rangle_S$ and $|e_1\rangle_S$. The last term from the above equation can be bounded above by ϵ since

$$|\lambda_0 - \lambda_1| = \left|\lambda_0 - \frac{1}{2}\right| + \left|\lambda_1 - \frac{1}{2}\right| = \left\|\theta_S - \frac{\mathbb{1}_S}{2}\right\|_1 \geq 2(1 - F(\theta_S, \frac{\mathbb{1}_S}{2})) \geq 2\epsilon$$

Suppose that $|\langle\theta_P^0|\theta_P^1\rangle| \geq \epsilon/2$ (otherwise, $|\langle\theta_P^+|\theta_P^-\rangle| \geq \epsilon/2$ and the same argument holds for those two states), this means that Paul cannot distinguish between the two reduced states $|\theta_P^0\rangle$ and $|\theta_P^1\rangle$ with probability better than one minus some constant (that depends on ϵ). We conclude that γ is bounded above by a constant strictly less than 1 and that the probability γ^k of guessing all measurement outcomes correctly declines exponentially fast in k. $\square$

The third criterion of Definition 4 follows trivially from the observation that neither $\mathcal{E}_{RS^N \to S^n}^{\mathrm{acc}}$ nor $\bar{\mathcal{E}}_{PN\,S^N \to \Pi S^n}^{\mathrm{acc}}$ acts on the unsampled qubits other than by relabeling them.

References

1. Ahlswede, R., Winter, A.: Strong converse for identification via quantum channels. IEEE Trans. Inf. Theory **48**(3), 569–579 (2002)
2. Ambainis, A.: A new protocol and lower bounds for quantum coin flipping. In: Proceedings of the Thirty-third Annual ACM Symposium on Theory of Computing, STOC 2001, pp. 134–142. ACM, New York (2001)
3. Ambainis, A.: A new protocol and lower bounds for quantum coin flipping. J. Comput. Syst. Sci. **68**(2), 398–416 (2004)
4. Koenraad, M.R., et al.: Discriminating states: the quantum Chernoff bound. Phys. Rev. Lett. **98**(16), 160501 (2007)
5. Blum, M.: Coin-flipping by telephone. In: Proceedings of CRYPTO 1991, pp. 11–15 (1981)
6. Bouman, N.J., Fehr, S.: Sampling in a quantum population, and applications. In: Rabin, T. (ed.) CRYPTO 2010. LNCS, vol. 6223, pp. 724–741. Springer, Heidelberg (2010). https://doi.org/10.1007/978-3-642-14623-7_39
7. Chailloux, A., Kerenidis, I.: Optimal quantum strong coin flipping. In: Proceedings of FOCS 2009, pp. 527–533 (2009)
8. Christandl, M., König, R., Mitchison, G., Renner, R.: One-and-a-half quantum de Finetti theorems. Commun. Math. Phys. **273**(2), 473–498 (2007)
9. Christandl, M., König, R., Renner, R.: Postselection technique for quantum channels with applications to quantum cryptography. Phys. Rev. Lett. **102**, 020504 (2009)
10. Damgård, I., Dupuis, F., Nielsen, J.B.: On the orthogonal vector problem and the feasibility of unconditionally secure leakage-resilient computation. In: Lehmann, A., Wolf, S. (eds.) ICITS 2015. LNCS, vol. 9063, pp. 87–104. Springer, Cham (2015). https://doi.org/10.1007/978-3-319-17470-9_6
11. Dupuis, F., Fehr, S., Lamontagne, P., Salvail, L.: Adaptive versus non-adaptive strategies in the quantum setting with applications. In: Robshaw, M., Katz, J. (eds.) CRYPTO 2016. LNCS, vol. 9816, pp. 33–59. Springer, Heidelberg (2016). https://doi.org/10.1007/978-3-662-53015-3_2
12. Fehr, S., Katz, J., Song, F., Zhou, H.-S., Zikas, V.: Feasibility and completeness of cryptographic tasks in the quantum world. In: Sahai, A. (ed.) TCC 2013. LNCS, vol. 7785, pp. 281–296. Springer, Heidelberg (2013). https://doi.org/10.1007/978-3-642-36594-2_16
13. Gutoski, G., Watrous, J.: Toward a general theory of quantum games. In: Proceedings of STOC 2007, pp. 565–574. ACM, New York (2007)

14. Hayashi, M.: Optimal sequence of quantum measurements in the sense of Stein's lemma in quantum hypothesis testing. J. Phys. A Math. Gen. **35**(50), 10759–10773 (2002)

15. Hofheinz, D., Müller-Quade, J., Unruh, D.: On the (Im-)possibility of extending coin toss. In: Vaudenay, S. (ed.) EUROCRYPT 2006. LNCS, vol. 4004, pp. 504–521. Springer, Heidelberg (2006). https://doi.org/10.1007/11761679_30

16. Kerenidis, I., Nayak, A.: Weak coin flipping with small bias. Inf. Process. Lett. **89**(333), 131–135 (2004)

17. Kitaev, A.: Quantum coin-flipping. Presentation at the 6th Workshop on Quantum Information Processing (QIP 2003) (2003)

18. Mochon, C.: Quantum weak coin-flipping with bias of 0.192. In: Proceedings of FOCS 2004, pp. 2–11 (2004)

19. Mochon, C.: Large family of quantum weak coin-flipping protocols. Phys. Rev. A **72**(2), 022341 (2005)

20. Mochon C.: Quantum weak coin flipping with arbitrarily small bias (2007)

21. Ogawa, T., Nagaoka, H.: A new proof of the channel coding theorem via hypothesis testing in quantum information theory. In: IEEE International Symposium on Information Theory, p. 73 (2002)

22. Pappa, A., et al.: Experimental plug and play quantum coin flipping. Nature Commun. **5**, 3717 (2014)

23. Renner, R.: Security of quantum key distribution. Ph.D. thesis, ETH Zürich (2005)

24. Renner, R.: Symmetry of large physical systems implies independence of subsystems. Nature Phys. **3**, 645–649 (2007)

25. Renner, R.: Simplifying information-theoretic arguments by post-selection. Quantum Cryptogr. Comput. **26**, 66–75 (2010)

26. Salvail, L., Schaffner, C., Sotáková, M.: Quantifying the leakage of quantum protocols for classical two-party cryptography. Int. J. Quantum Inf. **13**(04), 1450041 (2015)

27. Spekkens, R.W., Rudolph, T.: Degrees of concealment and bindingness in quantum bit commitment protocols. Phys. Rev. A **65**(1), 012310 (2001)

28. Spekkens, R.W., Rudolph, T.: Quantum protocol for cheat-sensitive weak coin flipping. Phys. Rev. Lett. **89**(22), 227901 (2002)

29. Winkler, S., Wullschleger, J.: On the efficiency of classical and quantum secure function evaluation. IEEE Trans. Inf. Theory **60**(6), 3123–3143 (2014)

30. Winter, A.: Coding theorem and strong converse for quantum channels. IEEE Trans. Inf. Theory **45**(7), 2481–2485 (1999)

31. Zyczkowski, K., Sommers, H.-J.: Induced measures in the space of mixed quantum states. J. Phys. A Math. Gen. **34**(35), 7111 (2001)

Classical Proofs for the Quantum Collapsing Property of Classical Hash Functions

Serge Fehr[1,2(✉)]

[1] CWI, Amsterdam, The Netherlands
serge.fehr@cwi.nl
[2] Mathematical Institute, Leiden University, Leiden, The Netherlands

Abstract. Hash functions are of fundamental importance in theoretical and in practical cryptography, and with the threat of quantum computers possibly emerging in the future, it is an urgent objective to understand the security of hash functions in the light of potential future quantum attacks. To this end, we reconsider the *collapsing property* of hash functions, as introduced by Unruh, which replaces the notion of *collision resistance* when considering quantum attacks. Our contribution is a formalism and a framework that offers significantly simpler proofs for the collapsing property of hash functions. With our framework, we can prove the collapsing property for hash domain extension constructions entirely by means of decomposing the iteration function into suitable elementary composition operations. In particular, given our framework, one can argue *purely classically* about the quantum-security of hash functions; this is in contrast to previous proofs which are in terms of sophisticated quantum-information-theoretic and quantum-algorithmic reasoning.

1 Introduction

Background. Given the threat of possible future quantum computing capabilities, it is an important and urgent objective to evaluate the security of classical cryptographic schemes against quantum attacks. There are different places where security can break down when using quantum computing techniques to attack a cryptographic scheme that was designed to withstand standard classical attacks. The most prominent place is the computational hardness *assumption*, which is typically well justified to hold for classical models of computation but may be false with respect to quantum computation. Another place is the security *proof*, which may use techniques that fail to work in the context of a quantum attacker, like proofs that rely on rewinding techniques. Finally, another place where things can go wrong is the security *definition*, which may not capture anymore what it is supposed to capture when allowing quantum attacks.

An example of the latter is the computational binding property of a commitment scheme. Our intuitive understanding of what a commitment should achieve is that once a commitment is "on the table" there should be no freedom left for the (computationally bounded) committer in choosing the value to which he can

© International Association for Cryptologic Research 2018
A. Beimel and S. Dziembowski (Eds.): TCC 2018, LNCS 11240, pp. 315–338, 2018.
https://doi.org/10.1007/978-3-030-03810-6_12

open the commitment. The formal definition of the binding property expresses this requirement by demanding that no (computationally bounded) dishonest committer should be able to open a commitment in two distinct ways. While for classical committers this captures precisely what we want, it fails to do so for quantum committers. Indeed, a quantum committer can potentially open a commitment to *one* value that he *freely chooses* after he has put the commitment "on the table", without contradicting the requirement of being unable to produce *two* distinct openings; this is because producing the opening information may involve a destructive quantum measurement that can only be applied once.

We stress that being able to open a given commitment to an arbitrary value that one can freely choose renders a commitment scheme useless in essentially all applications. So, when considering the security of commitment schemes against quantum attacks, it is essential that one uses a *stronger notion of security* than the standard computational binding property extended to quantum attackers.

A similar and related example is the collision resistance of hash functions. Also here, in the presence of a quantum attacker, the standard formal requirement that it should be computationally hard to produce two colliding inputs does not capture our intuitive understanding of a hash value as acting as a "fingerprint" that removes any freedom in the message to which it fits. As such, also here, when considering security against quantum attacks, the standard security notion, i.e. collision resistance, needs to be replaced by something stronger.

The Collapsing Property. Unruh [5] proposed the notion of *collapsing*; in the context of commitment schemes as a counterpart for the computational binding property when considering quantum attacks, and in the context of hash functions as a counterpart for collision resistance. In essence, for hash functions, the collapsing property requires that for any computationally bounded adversary that output a hash value together with a *quantum superposition* of corresponding preimages, he should not be able to tell if the superposition gets measured or not. The details of the notion, and why it indeed restores the right security properties when considering quantum attacks, are not so important for the discussion here. In terms of achievability, Unruh proved that the random oracle is collapsing as a hash function, and thus that simple hash-function-based commitment schemes are collapsing in the random oracle model. In the context of hash functions, he proved in a follow-up work [6] that the *Merkle-Damgård* construction for hash functions is collapsing (under some mild restriction on the padding) if the underlying compression function is. Given that the random oracle is collapsing, this in particular implies that the Merkle-Damgård construction is collapsing in the random oracle model, and thus gives heuristic evidence that certain practical hash functions like SHA-2 are collapsing. Recently, Czajkowski *et al.* [2] showed a similar result for the *Sponge* construction [1], which for instance underlies the hash function standard SHA-3: the Sponge construction is collapsing if both parts of the underlying round function, i.e., the so-called *inner* and *outer* parts, are collapsing, and if the inner part is "zero-preimage resistant".[1]

Our Contribution. In this work, we introduce a new *formalism* and a new *framework* for arguing about the collapsing property of (hash) functions. The advantage of our new approach is that it allows for significantly simper proofs compared to the previous work above.

At the heart of our new *formalism* is a pseudo-metric that abstracts away computational aspects, and which allows for an "algebraic" formulation of the collapsing property. This in turn allows for simple proofs of basic *composability results* for the collapsing property. Some of those have already been claimed and proven in the work mentioned above; however, our proofs are much simpler. For instance, proving that the collapsing property is preserved under nested composition takes 2 full pages in [5] (see Lemma 27 in the full version of [5]), with various quantum circuits depicted; our proof (see Lemma 5) is a few lines. The main reason for this difference lies in the "algebraic" nature of our formulation, compared to the "algorithmic" approach used in prior work. This means that instead of specifying quantum reduction algorithms and arguing that they "do the job", our proofs are almost entirely by means of *term-manipulations*, where we manipulate the terms of interest by using a small set of basic rules that come along with our formalism. This not only results in very compact proofs, these proofs are also mathematically very clean in that in every term-manipulation step we can—and typically do—specify what basic rule was used.

These composability results for the collapsing property, together with a couple of basic features when "disallowing" certain inputs, form what we call our *framework*. With this framework, proving the collapsing property of hash domain extensions boils down to decomposing the iteration function under consideration into a few simple composition operations.

We demonstrate this new proof methodology on various examples. Applied to Merkle-Damgård, we obtain a proof of the collapsing property without any restriction on the padding as in [6], but with the additional assumption on the compression function to be "*iv*-preimage resistant" (which is satisfied in the random oracle model). We can also recover Unruh's original result, which requires a restriction on the padding but avoids the "*iv*-preimage resistance". By adding a counter and "salt" to the compression function but otherwise using the same kind of reasoning, we get a proof of the collapsing property of *HAIFA* [3], as proposed by Biham and Dunkelman. Applied to the *Sponge* construction, we recover the result from [2] up to an insignificant difference in the exact parameter.

The distinguishing feature of our proofs lies in their conceptual simplicity and low technical complexity. Our proofs are entirely in terms of decomposing the iteration function into elementary composition operations that are ensured to preserve the collapsing property. In particular, our proofs are purely classical. In contrast, the proofs provided in [2,6] are in terms of lengthy hybrid arguments

---

[1] This again implies security in the random oracle model, but a subtle issue here is that if the round function is efficiently invertible then the assumptions on the two parts are not satisfied. Hence, this is not so strong evidence yet that e.g. SHA-3 is collapsing.

that consider sequences of "quantum games" and in terms of quantum information theoretic arguments and quantum reduction algorithms for reasoning that
every game in the sequence behaves similarly to its predecessor.

As such, even though the collapsing property of HAIFA is new, we consider
our main contribution more in terms of offering a simple understanding of *why*
certain hash function are collapsing, and in providing a tool to *easily* check if
similar results also hold for other hash functions (as we demonstrate on HAIFA).

The Framework in Action. To give a better idea, we illustrate here on the
various examples how our framework enables to argue for the collapsing property by means of decomposing the iteration function into suitable elementary
decomposition operations, and thus in particular by means of purely classical
reasoning. We challenge the reader to compare our proofs with those in [2,6].

Merkle-Damgård. The Merkle-Damgård hash of a message $x_1, \ldots, x_i$, consisting of i blocks, is given by $IH_i(x_1, \ldots, x_i)$, where IH_i is iteratively defined as

$$IH_i(x_1, \ldots, x_i) := f\big(IH_{i-1}(x_1, \ldots, x_{i-1}), x_i\big)$$

with $IH_0() = iv$. The round function f is assumed to be collapsing. We observe
that IH_i is the *nested composition* of f with the *concurrent composition* of IH_{i-1}
with the identity $x_i \mapsto x_i$. Our framework ensures that these compositions preserve the collapsing property; thus, by recursive application, given that IH_0 is
trivially collapsing, we get that IH_L is collapsing for every *fixed* L, and hence
the Merkle-Damgård hash is collapsing when restricted to inputs of *fixed* size.

In order to deal with messages of variable size, we allow in the definition of
$IH_i(x_1, \ldots, x_i)$ the left-most message blocks to be "empty", i.e., x_1 up to some
x_j may be $\perp$, and we set $IH_i(\perp, \ldots, \perp) := iv$ (for any i) and keep to recursive
definition above if $x_i \neq \perp$. This extended version of IH_i is then the *disjoint union*
of the trivial function $\{\perp^i\} \to \{iv\}$ and the restriction of IH_i to inputs different
than $\perp^i$, *if* we "disallow" non-$\perp^i$ inputs that are mapped to iv.[2] Thus, as long
as we "disallow" such inputs (which is something our framework can capture),
we still have that the recursive definition of IH_i decomposes into composition
operations that are covered by our framework, and thus we can conclude that
IH_L is collapsing for every fixed L, but now for inputs that may have $\perp$-prefixes,
i.e., variable length. Finally, by the assumed "*iv*-preimage resistant" of f, inputs
$(\neq \perp^i)$ that IH_i maps to iv are hard to find, and therefore "disallowing" those
has no noticeable effect.

HAIFA. The HAFIA hash function is a variant of Merkle-Damgård that
includes a counter in the iteration function, and it uses a "salt" (which we
though treat as ordinary input). Formally,

$$IH_i(salt, x_1, \ldots, x_i) := f\big(salt, IH_{i-1}(salt, x_1, \ldots, x_{i-1}), x_i, i\big).$$

Here, we can reason exactly as above, except that now the iteration function is
a *nested composition* of the function $f(\cdot, \cdot, \cdot, i)$, which is collapsing if f is, with

---

[2] The latter is because (our notion of) the disjoint union of two functions requires not
only the two respective domains but also the two respective ranges to be disjoint.

the *parallel composition* of the projection function $(salt, x_1, \ldots, x_i) \mapsto salt$ with the *concurrent composition* of IH_{i-1} with the identity function $x_i \mapsto x_i$. All these composition operations are covered by our framework, and so the collapsing property follows as for the original Merkle-Damgård construction, assuming again that f is "*iv*-preimage resistance" in case of arbitrary length messages.

Sponge. The Sponge hash[3] of a message $x_1, \ldots, x_i$ of i blocks is given by $S_i^0(x_1, \ldots, x_i)$, where S_i^b is iteratively defined as

$$S_i^b(x_1, \ldots, x_i) := f^b\big(S_{i-1}^0(x_1, \ldots, x_{i-1}) \oplus x_i, S_{i-1}^1(x_1, \ldots, x_{i-1})\big)$$

for $b \in \{0, 1\}$, with $S_0^0() = 0 = S_0^1()$, and it is assumed that both components of the round function $f = (f^0, f^1)$ are collapsing. Here, S_i^b is the *nested composition* of f^b with a function that is yet another *composition* of the functions S_{i-1}^0 and S_{i-1}^1, and our framework immediately ensures that S_i^0 and S_i^1 stay collapsing as long as S_{i-1}^1 is. Thus, again, the iteration function decomposes into composition operations that are ensured to preserve the collapsing property, and so by recursive application we get that $S_1^1, \ldots, S_{L-1}^1$ and eventually S_L^0 are collapsing. The only difference to above is that here, we have to set $S_i^b(\perp, \ldots, \perp) := S_0^b() = 0$ to ensure that S_L^0 acts correctly on messages of smaller block size, i.e., that $S_j^b(x_1, \ldots, x_j) = S_L^b(\perp, \ldots, \perp, x_1, \ldots, x_j)$. As a consequence, for the recursive reasoning, to have S_i^1 be the disjoint union of the trivial function $\{\perp^i\} \to \{0\}$ and the restriction of S_i^1 to non-$\perp^i$ inputs, we need to "disallow" inputs $(\neq \perp^i)$ which S_i^1 maps to 0; this has no noticeable effect though if f^1 is "zero-preimage resistant".

2 Preliminaries

2.1 Basic Quantum Formalism

Knowledge of basic concepts of quantum information science is necessary in order to prove "correctness" of our framework (but not to apply the framework); we fix here some notation and conventions, which both are not fully standard.

Typically, the *state* of a quantum system with state space $\mathcal{H}$ is given by a density matrix ρ, i.e., by a trace-1 positive-semidefinite matrix that acts on $\mathcal{H}$, and a *quantum operation* is expressed by a CPTP map $\mathbb{T}$ which maps a state ρ to a new state $\mathbb{T}(\rho)$ over a possibly different state space. In this work, for technical reasons, we allow states to be *subnormalized*, and we consider the more general notion of completely-positive *trace-nonincreasing* (CPTN) maps, which are of the form $\mathbb{T} = \sum_i \mathbb{T}_i$ with $\mathbb{T}_i : \rho \mapsto T_i \rho T_i^\dagger$ and $\sum_i T_i^\dagger T_i \leq I$ (the identity on $\mathcal{H}$).[4]

For the purpose of this work, a *measurement* is a CPTN map $\mathbb{P} = \sum_i \mathbb{P}_i$ with $\mathbb{P}_i : \rho \mapsto P_i \rho P_i^\dagger$ as above, but with the restriction that the P_i's are mutually

---

[3] For simplicity, we consider *one* block of output only; multiple output blocks are argued by means of composition too.

[4] This can be understood in that quantum operations may "abort", and the trace $\mathrm{tr}(\rho) \leq 1$ expresses the probability that the process that produces ρ does not abort.

orthogonal Hermitian *projections* on $\mathcal{H}$. If $\mathbb{P}$ is in fact a CPTP map, i.e., $\sum_i P_i = I$, then we speak of a *total* measurement, and otherwise of a *partial* measurement. The individual "components" $\mathbb{P}_i$ of such a (partial or total) measurement are sometimes also referred to as *measurements with post-selection*.

We write $\Pr[\mathbb{P}(\rho) = i]$ for $\mathrm{tr} \circ \mathbb{P}_i(\rho) = \mathrm{tr}(P_i \rho P_i)$, i.e., the probability that "outcome i is observed". An elementary property of any (*projective*, as considered here) measurement $\mathbb{P}$, is Winter's "gentle-measurement lemma" [7], which captures that the measurement does not disturb the state much if the outcome is almost certain. Formally,[5] for any state ρ and any $\beta \geq 0$:

$$\exists i : \Pr[\mathbb{P}(\rho) = i] \geq \mathrm{tr}(\rho) - \beta \implies \delta(\mathbb{P}(\rho), \rho) \leq \sqrt{\beta} + \beta. \tag{1}$$

where δ is the *trace distance*, given by $\delta(\rho, \sigma) := \frac{1}{2}\|\rho - \sigma\|_{tr}$.

Different quantum systems are identified by means of "labels" X, Y etc., and we write ρ_X for the state of system X and $\mathcal{H}_X$ for its state space, etc. For a CPTN map $\mathbb{T}$, we may write $\mathbb{T}_X$ to emphasize that it acts on system X, and $\mathbb{T}_{X \to X'}$ to additionally emphasize that it maps into system X'. For simplicity, we tend to write $\rho_{\mathbb{T}(X)Y}$ rather than $(\mathbb{T}_X \otimes \mathbb{I}_Y)(\rho_{XY})$.

For any state space we consider a fixed orthonormal basis, referred to as the *computational* basis. For state spaces $\mathcal{H}_X$ and $\mathcal{H}_Y$ with respective computational bases $\{|x\rangle\}_{x \in \mathcal{X}}$ and $\{|y\rangle\}_{y \in \mathcal{Y}}$, we associate to any function $f : \mathcal{X} \to \mathcal{Y}$ the CPTP "evaluation" map $\mathbb{E}[f]_{X \to XY} : \rho \mapsto V[f] \rho V[f]^\dagger$ given by the isometry $V[f] : |x\rangle \mapsto |x\rangle|f(x)\rangle$. Here, we also write $\rho_{Xf(X)Z}$ instead of $\rho_{\mathbb{E}[f](X)Z}$.[6] We note that $\mathbb{E}[f]$ admits a *left inverse*, i.e., a CPTP map $\mathbb{E}^{inv}[f]_{XY \to X}$ such that $\mathbb{E}^{inv}[f] \circ \mathbb{E}[f] = \mathbb{I}_X$.

The composition $\mathrm{tr}_Y \circ \mathbb{E}[f]_{X \to XY}$ of a CPTP evaluation map with the partial trace tr_Y equals the measurement $\mathbb{M}[f] = \sum_y \mathbb{M}[f = y]$, where $\mathbb{M}[f = y]$ is the CPTN map given by the projection into the span of $\{|x\rangle \mid f(x) = y\}$. To simplify notation, we may also write $\rho_{X^f Z}$ instead of $\rho_{\mathbb{M}[f](X)Z}$, and, similarly, $\rho_{X^f = y Z}$ instead of $\rho_{\mathbb{M}[f = y](X)Z}$.

The usual "measurement in the computational basis", given by the projections $|x\rangle\langle x|$, is simply denoted by $\mathbb{M}$. For lighter notation, we often use $\overline{(\cdot)}$ instead of $\mathbb{M}$ and write $\rho_{\bar{X}Y}$ instead of $\rho_{\mathbb{M}(X)Y}$. A quantum system X of a (possibly) joint state ρ_{XY} is called *classical* if $\rho_{\bar{X}Y} = \rho_{XY}$.

When the state is clear from the context, then we may do the "arithmetic" on the labels. For instance, using this convention, we can then say that any state ρ_{XZ} satisfies

$$\bar{X}f(X)Z = \bar{X}f(\bar{X})Z = \bar{X}\overline{f(\bar{X})}Z = \bar{X}\overline{f(X)}Z, \tag{2}$$

to express that $\mathbb{M}_X$ and $\mathbb{E}[f]_X$ commute, and that $f(\bar{X})$ is classical given that $\bar{X}$ is. Similarly, we may then write $\Pr[\mathbb{M}[f](X) = y] = \Pr[\mathbb{M}(f(X)) = y] = \Pr[f(\bar{X}) = y]$, which may be interpreted differently but coincide.

---

[5] This bound can e.g. be derived from [8]. [2] claims the bound $\sqrt{\beta}$, but their proof has a small flaw; fixing it gives $\sqrt{2\beta}$ instead (but only works for *total* measurements). .

[6] A subtle issue with this notation is that $\mathrm{tr}_Y(\rho_{Xf(X)Z}) \neq \rho_{XZ}$, but rather $= \rho_{\mathbb{M}[f](X)Z}$ (see below).

2.2 Randomized Functions and States, and Their Complexity

In Appendix A, we offer a formal discussion of *randomized functions, randomized CPTN maps,* and *randomized quantum states.* As one would expect, these are simply functions, CPTN maps and states that depend on some *global randomness* r, which is randomly chosen once and for all from some finite set $\mathcal{R}$.

Informally, when considering randomized functions, one can make the following distinction. In one case, r is given as input to the function f (or to the algorithm that computes f, if you prefer); one then typically speaks of *keyed* or *seeded* functions. In the other case, f makes queries to an *oracle* that computes every reply dependent on r, in which case one refers to f as an *oracle function.* A similar distinction can be made for randomized CPTN maps, and thus for randomized states, which are simply randomized CPTN maps that act on the trivial state space $\mathbb{C}$.

Formally, the way the two variants differ is by the way *complexity* is captured: for keyed functions one consider the *computational complexity* of computing the function whereas for oracle functions one considers the *query complexity.*

Our results apply to both variants in that we consider an *abstract* complexity measure c that assigns to every randomized function f a non-negative integer $\mathsf{c}(f)$, also denoted c_f, and similarly for randomized CPTN maps, and which satisfies natural properties that one would expect from a complexity measure. The details of this are given in Appendix B. The computational complexity and the query complexity are then just specific instantiations.

2.3 The Distinguishing Advantage

The following parameterized indistinguishability measure, and our understanding of it as an abstract metric, is one of the central notions of our formalism.

Definition 1. *For randomized states ρ_X and ρ_Y (with randomness r) over a common Hilbert space $\mathcal{H}_X = \mathcal{H}_Y$, and for any non-negative integer q, we set*

$$
\delta_q(\rho_X, \rho_Y) := \sup_{\mathbb{T}} \frac{1}{|\mathcal{R}|} \sum_r \big| \Pr\big[\mathsf{M}(\mathbb{T}(X)) = 0\big] - \Pr\big[\mathsf{M}(\mathbb{T}(Y)) = 0\big] \big|
$$

$$
= \sup_{\mathbb{T}} \frac{1}{|\mathcal{R}|} \sum_r \delta\big(\mathsf{M} \circ \mathbb{T}(\rho_X), \mathsf{M} \circ \mathbb{T}(\rho_Y)\big),
$$

where the supremum is over all randomized CPTN maps $\mathbb{T}$ (with randomness r) that map into the two-dimensional qubit state space and have complexity $\mathsf{c}(\mathbb{T}) \leq q$ and, by convention, M is the measurement in the computational basis.

Following the convention of doing the "arithmetic" on the labels, we typically write $\delta_q(X, Y)$ instead of $\delta_q(\rho_X, \rho_Y)$. Also, we write $\delta_q(X, Y|Z)$ as a short hand for $\delta_q(\rho_{XZ}, \rho_{YZ})$.

We emphasize that δ_q is a *pseudometric*: it is non-negative, symmetric, and satisfies triangle inequality, but it may potentially vanish for non-identical states.

Furthermore, δ_q is upper bounded by the trace distance δ, and it coincides with δ in case $q = \infty$, i.e., there is no restriction on $\mathfrak{c}(\mathbb{T})$. Finally, δ_q inherits several properties from the ordinary trace distance, which can easily be verified. For instance, it is *monotone* under randomized CPTN maps as

$$\delta_q\big(\mathbb{T}(X), \mathbb{T}(Y)\big) \le \delta_{q+\mathfrak{c}(\mathbb{T})}(X, Y),$$

and for any randomized CPTN map $\mathbb{T} = \sum_i \mathbb{T}_i$, we have *subadditivity* as

$$\delta_q\big(\mathbb{T}(X), \mathbb{T}(Y)\big) \le \sum_i \delta_q\big(\mathbb{T}_i(X), \mathbb{T}_i(Y)\big).$$

To simplify terminology, from now on we drop on the word "randomized" and take it as understood that functions, CPTN maps and states may be randomized, either in the form of keyed functions or as oracle functions, etc.

3   The Collapsing Property

We state here (a slight variation of) the definition of the collapsing property of functions, as proposed by Unruh [5], but using the formalism introduced above. In Sect. 3.2 we then discuss the straightforward extension to *partial* functions, which will turn out to be useful, and in Sect. 3.3 we show that the collapsing property behaves nicely under various composition operations. These composability results are all rather natural, and—with our formalism!—have simple short proofs. All together, this section then stands as "the framework" that we propose for arguing about the collapsing property of hash functions.

3.1   The Definition

The original formulation of the collapsing property for a function h is by means of two "games", where an "adversary" produces a (normalized) state ρ_{XYE} of a certain form, namely Y must be classical and equal to $h(X)$, and then in one game X is measured in the computation basis whereas in the other game it is left untouched instead, and the definition requires that it should be hard for any "distinguisher" to distinguish between the two games.

As for the notion of collision resistance, the collapsing property is meaningful only for randomized functions h.[7] In case of a *keyed* variant of such a function, one can aim for *conditional* results that state that h is collapsing (against computationally bounded adversaries) under some computational hardness assumption. In case of an *oracle* function and aiming for *unconditional* results, there is no exploitable effect in restricting the computational power of the parties, as long as the query complexity is limited. Our approach of using an abstract complexity notion allows us to cover *both* these settings simultaneously.

Our formal definition of the collapsing property is given below. Compared to the original definition by Unruh (which comes in a couple of different flavors,

---

[7] See the discussion in Appendix C for an exception to the rule.

which we discuss in Appendix C), we use a somewhat different terminology and formalism. For instance we do not explicitly speak of "games", and instead of quantifying over the possible adversaries we quantify over the states that may possibly be prepared by an adversary, and the quantification over the distinguishers is absorbed into the pseudometric δ_q. These modifications to the mathematical language have obviously no effect on the notion. There are a few more differences compared to the definition proposed by Unruh, but they all have no more than a small quantitative effect, as we discuss below.

Definition 2. *A function $h : \mathcal{X} \to \mathcal{Y}$ is called $\varepsilon(q)$-collapsing if*

$$\mathsf{cAdv}[h](q) := \sup_{\rho_{XYE}} \delta_q(X, \bar{X} \mid \bar{Y}E) \leq \varepsilon(q)$$

for all q, where the supremum is over all states[8] $\rho_{XYE} = \rho_{Xh(X)E}$ with complexity $\mathsf{c}(\rho_{XYE}) \leq q$. The measure $\mathsf{cAdv}[h]$ is called the collapsing advantage *of h.*

Beyond the change in mathematical language, another difference is that in the original definition the system Y of the state ρ_{XYE}, as produced by the adversary, is required to be classical, whereas in Definition 2 we allow it to be non-classical but then "make it classical" by measuring it; this is obviously equivalent (given that measuring has zero complexity). A slightly more substantial difference is that we allow the state ρ_{XYE} to be *subnormalized*; i.e., we allow the adversary to abort. However, the collapsing advantage $\delta_q(X, \bar{X} \mid \bar{Y}E)$ of any subnormalized state ρ_{XYE} is the same as of the normalized state $\tilde{\rho}_{XYE} := \rho_{XYE} + (1 - \mathrm{tr}(\rho_{XYE}))|x_\circ\rangle\langle x_\circ| \otimes |h(x_\circ)\rangle\langle h(x_\circ)| \otimes |0\rangle\langle 0|$ for an arbitrary choice of $x_\circ \in \mathcal{X}$ on which h is defined. Since $\mathsf{c}(\tilde{\rho}_{XYE}) \leq \mathsf{c}(\rho_{XYE}) + \mathsf{c}(h)$, this has only a small quantitative effect that is insignificant if $\mathsf{c}(h)$ is insignificant compared to q. In other words, we can easily transform an adversary that aborts into one that does not abort but outputs $x_\circ$ and $y_\circ = h(x_\circ)$ instead.

Finally, in the original definition, the complexity of the adversary and the distinguisher *together* is bounded (by q), whereas we bound the individual complexities (both by q). This is merely for simplicity, and has only a factor-2 quantitative effect.

3.2 *Partial* versus *Total* Functions

In Definition 2, we implicitly considered the function $h : \mathcal{X} \to \mathcal{Y}$ to be a *total* function, i.e., a function that is defined on its entire domain $\mathcal{X}$. However, it will be useful to extend the definition to *partial* functions, which are defined only on a subset $\mathcal{X}_{\mathrm{eff}} \subseteq \mathcal{X}$ of the domain.[9] In the context of *randomized* functions, as considered here, we allow $\mathcal{X}_{\mathrm{eff}}$ to depend on the global randomness r; this is

---

[8] We recall that the requirement $\rho_{XYE} = \rho_{Xh(X)E}$ is a shorthand for asking ρ_{XYE} to be equal to a state obtained by applying $\mathbb{E}[h]$ to system X.

[9] This may be understood in that the computation of h "fails" on inputs not in $\mathcal{X}_{\mathrm{eff}}$.

what distinguishes such a partial function from a total function with a smaller domain, since the domain $\mathcal{X}$ of a function is declared fixed and independent of r.

Definition 2 applies directly to such partial functions as well, given that the definition of the evaluation map $\mathbb{E}[h]$ is naturally extended to partial functions h by having the defining operator $V[h]$ map $|x\rangle$ to 0 for any $x \notin \mathcal{X}_{\text{eff}}$. The effect of this is that the requirement $\rho_{XYE} = \rho_{Xh(X)E}$ enforces X to contain no inputs from outside of $\mathcal{X}_{\text{eff}}$. Hence, considering partial functions in Definition 2 serves as a convenient way to "disallow" certain inputs.

Formally, consider a function $h : \mathcal{X} \to \mathcal{Y}$ (which may be partial but let us think of it as a total function for now), and let $\pi : \mathcal{X} \to \{0,1\}$ be a predicate, which will always be understood to be a total function. Then, we define $h|_\pi$ to be the partial function $h|_\pi : \mathcal{X} \to \mathcal{Y}$ that is undefined for $x \in \mathcal{X}$ with $\pi(x) = 0$, and that coincides with h for the remaining $x \in \mathcal{X}$. The collapsing advantage of $h|_\pi$ then coincides with the collapsing advantage of h modified in that the quantification over ρ_{XYE} is restricted to states for which $\Pr[\pi(\bar{X}) = 0] = 0$.

Below, in Lemmas 1 and 2, we show how $\mathsf{cAdv}[h]$ and $\mathsf{cAdv}[h|_\pi]$ relate to each other. Lemma 1 follows trivially from the above observation, i.e., that $\rho_{Xh|_\pi(X)E}$ implies $\rho_{XYE} = \rho_{Xh(X)E}$.

Lemma 1. *If h is $\varepsilon(q)$-collapsing then so is $h|_\pi$, i.e., $\mathsf{cAdv}[h|_\pi] \leq \mathsf{cAdv}[h]$.*

Applied to h of the form $h|_\tau$, and noting that $(h|_\tau)|_\pi = h|_{\pi \wedge \tau}$, we get the following, which captures that disallowing more inputs can only decrease the collapsing advantage.

Corollary 1. *For any predicates π and τ, it holds that $\mathsf{cAdv}[h|_{\pi \wedge \tau}] \leq \mathsf{cAdv}[h|_\tau]$. In particular, if π implies τ, i.e. $\pi(x) = 1 \Rightarrow \tau(x) = 1$, then $\mathsf{cAdv}[h|_\pi] \leq \mathsf{cAdv}[h|_\tau]$.*

For the other direction, disallowing some inputs has little effect if those are hard to find. For the formal statement, we need the following definition.

Definition 3. *A predicate $\pi : \mathcal{X} \to \{0,1\}$ is called $\beta(q)$-almost-certain if it holds that $\Pr[\pi(\bar{X}) = 0] \leq \beta(q)$ for any state ρ_X with complexity q.*

Lemma 2. *If π is $\beta(q)$-almost-certain then*

$$\mathsf{cAdv}[h](q) \leq \mathsf{cAdv}[h|_\pi](q + \mathfrak{c}_\pi) + \sqrt{\beta(q)} \cdot \min\{\sqrt{2}, 1 + \sqrt{\beta(q)}\}.$$

Proof. Let $\rho_{XYZ} = \rho_{Xh(X)E}$ be with complexity q. Consider the measurement $\mathbb{P} = \mathbb{P}_0 + \mathbb{P}_1$ given by $\mathbb{P}_0 := \mathbb{M} \circ \mathbb{M}[\pi = 0]$ and $\mathbb{P}_1 := \mathbb{M}[\pi = 1]$.[10] By triangle inequality and since $\mathbb{M} = \mathbb{P} \circ \mathbb{M}$, we have

$$\delta_q(X, \bar{X} \mid \bar{Y}E) \leq \delta_q(X, \mathbb{P}(X) \mid \bar{Y}E) + \delta_q(\mathbb{P}(X), \mathbb{P}(\bar{X}) \mid \bar{Y}E)$$
$$\leq \delta(X, \mathbb{P}(X) \mid \bar{Y}E) + \delta_q(X^{\pi=1}, \bar{X}^{\pi=1} \mid \bar{Y}E) + \delta_q(\bar{X}^{\pi=0}, \bar{X}^{\pi=0} \mid \bar{Y}E)$$
$$\leq \sqrt{\beta(q)} + \beta(q) + \mathsf{cAdv}[h|_\pi](q + \mathfrak{c}_\pi),$$

---

[10] I.e., $\mathbb{P}$ first performs the measurement $\mathbb{M}[\pi]$, and then measures the resulting state in the computation basis if (and only if) the measurement outcome was 0.

where the second inequality is because $\delta_q \leq \delta$, and by subadditivity and choice of $\mathbb{P}$, and the last inequality is by the "gentle-measurement lemma" (1), plus footnote 5, given that $\Pr\big[\mathbb{P}(X) = 1\big] = \Pr\big[\pi(\bar{X}) = 1\big] \geq \mathrm{tr}(\rho_X) - \beta(q)$, plus the observation that $\rho_{X^{\pi=1}YE}$ has complexity $q + \mathfrak{c}_\pi$. $\square$

We conclude with the following simple observation, which follows from the fact that under the given assumptions, $\Pr[\tau(\bar{X}) = 0] \leq \Pr[\pi \circ \lambda(\bar{X}) = 0] \leq \beta(q + \mathfrak{c}(\lambda))$ for any state ρ_X with complexity q.

Lemma 3. *Consider predicates $\pi : \mathcal{X}' \to \{0,1\}$ and $\tau : \mathcal{X} \to \{0,1\}$ and a total function $\lambda : \mathcal{X}' \to \mathcal{X}$ such that $\pi \circ \lambda$ implies τ, i.e., $\pi(\lambda(x)) = 1 \Rightarrow \tau(x) = 1$. If π is $\beta(q)$-almost-certain then τ is $\beta(q + \mathfrak{c}(\lambda))$-almost-certain.*

3.3 Composability Properties

We show composability of the collapsing property under different means of composing functions. In one or another form, some of these composability properties are also present in previous work (see e.g. Lemma 27 in the full version of [5] for the corresponding claim on nested composition); we cover them here for completeness and since our notion differs in minor ways, but also in order to demonstrate how succinctly these composability properties can be *phrased* and *proven* using our formalism.

We take it as understood that for partial functions g and h, the considered composition is defined whenever g and h are both defined on their respective inputs.

Lemma 4 (Concurrent composition). *For $g : \mathcal{X} \to \mathcal{Y}$ and $h : \mathcal{W} \to \mathcal{Z}$, the concurrent composition $g \| h : \mathcal{X} \times \mathcal{W} \to \mathcal{Y} \times \mathcal{Z}$, $(x, w) \mapsto (g(x), h(w))$ satisfies*

$$\mathsf{cAdv}[g \| h] \leq \mathsf{cAdv}[g] + \mathsf{cAdv}[h].$$

Proof. Let $\rho_{XWYZE} = \rho_{XWg(X)h(W)E}$ be with complexity q. Then, by triangle inequality,

$$\begin{aligned}
\delta_q(XW, \bar{X}\bar{W} | \bar{Y}\bar{Z}E) &\leq \delta_q(XW, X\bar{W} | \bar{Y}\bar{Z}E) + \delta_q(XW, \bar{X}\bar{W} | \bar{Y}\bar{Z}E) \\
&= \delta_q(W, \bar{W} | \bar{Z}XYE) + \delta_q(X, \bar{X} | \bar{Y}W\bar{Z}E) \\
&\leq \mathsf{cAdv}[g](q) + \mathsf{cAdv}[h](q).
\end{aligned}$$
$\square$

Lemma 5 (Nested composition). *For $g : \mathcal{X} \to \mathcal{Y}$ and $h : \mathcal{Y} \to \mathcal{Z}$, the nested (or sequential) composition $h \circ g : \mathcal{X} \to \mathcal{Z}$, $x \mapsto h\big(g(x)\big)$ satisfies*

$$\mathsf{cAdv}[h \circ g](q) \leq \mathsf{cAdv}[g](q + \mathfrak{c}_g) + \mathsf{cAdv}[h](q + \mathfrak{c}_g).$$

Proof. Let $\rho_{XZE} = \rho_{X(h\circ g)(X)E}$ be with complexity q. Then, $\rho_{XYZE} = \rho_{Xg(X)ZE}$ has complexity at most $q + c_g$. Recalling that ρ_{XZE} is recovered from ρ_{XYZE} by applying $\mathbb{E}^{inv}[g]_{XY\to X}$, we get

$$\delta_q(X, \bar{X}|\bar{Z}E) \leq \delta_{q+c_g}(XY, \bar{X}Y|\bar{Z}E) \qquad \text{(monotonicity)}$$
$$\leq \delta_{q+c_g}(XY, X\bar{Y}|\bar{Z}E) + \delta_{q+c_g}(X\bar{Y}, \bar{X}Y|\bar{Z}E) \quad (\triangle \text{ inequality})$$
$$\leq \delta_{q+c_g}(Y, \bar{Y}|\bar{Z}XE) + \delta_{q+c_g}(X, \bar{X}|\bar{Y}\bar{Z}E) \qquad (\bar{X}Y = \bar{X}\bar{Y} \text{ by (2)})$$
$$\leq \mathsf{cAdv}[g](q + c_g) + \mathsf{cAdv}[h](q + c_g). \qquad \qquad \square$$

Lemma 6. *For $g : \mathcal{X} \to \mathcal{Y}$ and $h : \mathcal{W} \times \mathcal{X} \to \mathcal{Z}$, where the latter function is such that $h(\cdot, x)$ is injective for any $x \in \mathcal{X}$, the composition $f : \mathcal{W} \times \mathcal{X} \to \mathcal{Y} \times \mathcal{Z}$, $(w, x) \mapsto \big(g(x), h(w, x)\big)$ satisfies*

$$\mathsf{cAdv}[f] \leq \mathsf{cAdv}[g].$$

We emphasize that the statement includes the special case where $\mathcal{W}$ is empty, i.e., $h : \mathcal{X} \to \mathcal{Z}$, in which case the the injectivity requirement becomes void, so that in particular the following holds.

Corollary 2 (Parallel composition). *For $g : \mathcal{X} \to \mathcal{Y}$ and $h : \mathcal{X} \to \mathcal{Z}$, the parallel composition $(g, h) : \mathcal{X} \to \mathcal{Y} \times \mathcal{Z}$, $x \mapsto \big(g(x), h(x)\big)$ satisfies*

$$\mathsf{cAdv}[(g, h)] \leq \min\{\mathsf{cAdv}[g], \mathsf{cAdv}[h]\}.$$

Proof (of Lemma 6). Let $\rho_{WXYZE} = \rho_{Wg(X)h(W,X)E}$ be with complexity q. Then, using that $\bar{W}\bar{X}\bar{Z} = W\bar{X}\bar{Z}$, which holds by (2) because w is a function of x and $z = h(w, x)$,

$$\delta_q(WX, \bar{W}\bar{X}|\bar{Y}\bar{Z}E) = \delta_q(X, \bar{X}|\bar{Y}\bar{Z}WE) \leq \mathsf{cAdv}[g](q). \qquad \square$$

Lemma 7 (Disjoint union). *For $g : \mathcal{X} \to \mathcal{Y}$ and $h : \mathcal{W} \to \mathcal{Z}$ with disjoint domains and images, the disjoint union $g \sqcup h : \mathcal{X} \cup \mathcal{W} \to \mathcal{Y} \cup \mathcal{Z}$, which maps $x \in \mathcal{X}$ to $g(x)$ and $w \in \mathcal{W}$ to $h(w)$, satisfies*

$$\mathsf{cAdv}[g \sqcup h] \leq \mathsf{cAdv}[g] + \mathsf{cAdv}[h].$$

Proof. Let $\rho_{UVE} = \rho_{U(g\sqcup h)(U)E}$, and consider the "distinguishing function" $dis : \mathcal{X} \cup \mathcal{W} \to \{0, 1\}$ that maps $x \in \mathcal{X}$ to 1 and $w \in \mathcal{W}$ to 0. By our convention on function domains being recognizable, dis has zero complexity. Furthermore, $\rho_{U^{dis}VE} = \rho_{\mathbb{M}[dis](U)VE}$ is of the form

$$\rho_{U^{dis}VE} = \rho_{U^{dis=0}VE} + \rho_{U^{dis=1}VE} = \rho_{Xg(X)E} + \rho_{Wh(W)E}$$

and, by the disjointness of the images, $\rho_{U\bar{V}E} = \rho_{U^{dis}\bar{V}E}$, and so it follows from subadditivity that

$$\delta_q(U, \bar{U}|\bar{V}E) = \delta_q(U^{dis}, \bar{U}^{dis}|\bar{V}E) \leq \delta_q(X, \bar{X}|\bar{Y}E) + \delta_q(W, \bar{W}|\bar{Z}E)$$

which is bounded by $\mathsf{cAdv}[g] + \mathsf{cAdv}[h]$. $\qquad \square$

4 Application I: Merkle-Damgård and HAIFA

We demonstrate the usefulness of our framework. Here, we do so by (re)proving the collapsing property Merkle-Damgård, and by showing that the proof trivially translates to the HAIFA variation [3]. In the subsequent section we analyze the Sponge construction [1]. Our proofs argue entirely by means of decomposing the iteration function under consideration into a few composition operations.

Here and in the remainder, for $b \in \{0, 1, \bot\}$ and positive integer $i \in \mathbb{N}$, we write $b^i \in \{0, 1, \bot\}^i$ for the i-fold concatenation $(b, \ldots, b)$ of b with itself.

4.1 The Construction

Let $f : \{0,1\}^c \times \{0,1\}^r \to \{0,1\}^c$ be a (total) function, which will act as the round function in the Merkle-Damgård construction. For any positive integer i, we consider the function $IH_i : \left(\{0,1\}^r\right)^i \to \{0,1\}^c$ given recursively by

$$IH_i(x_1, \ldots, x_i) := f\big(IH_{i-1}(x_1, \ldots, x_{i-1}), x_i\big) \tag{3}$$

with $IH_0() := iv$, some fixed string in $\{0,1\}^c$ called the *initialization vector*. The Merkle-Damgård hash function is then formally given by[11]

$$MD : \left(\{0,1\}^r\right)^* \to \{0,1\}^c, \ (x_1, \ldots, x_i) \mapsto IH_i(x_1, \ldots, x_i).$$

For technical reasons, we extend the domain of IH_i above to

$$\mathcal{X}_i := \left\{ (x_1, \ldots, x_i) \in \left(\{\bot\} \cup \{0,1\}^r\right)^i \,\middle|\, x_j = \bot \Rightarrow x_1 = \cdots = x_j = \bot \right\}$$

by setting $IH_i(\bot, \ldots, \bot) := iv$ and keeping the recursive definition (3) for $x_i \neq \bot$. We can now apply IH_L to messages of size $i < L$ blocks by pre-padding it with $\bot$'s: $IH_i(x_1, \ldots, x_i) = IH_{i+1}(\bot, x_1, \ldots, x_i) = \cdots = IH_L(\bot, \ldots, \bot, x_1, \ldots, x_i)$, and thus the restriction of MD to messages of block size $0 \leq i \leq L$ can be expressed as $MD^{\leq L}(x_1, \ldots, x_i) = IH_L(\bot, \ldots, \bot, x_1, \ldots, x_i)$.

4.2 The Analysis

Using our framework, we will now prove the following security statement for Merkle-Damgård. The assumption on $\mathfrak{c}(f)$ is simply for normalization, and for f to be β-*iv-preimage-resistant* means, by definition, that the predicate $1_{f(y) \neq iv}$, which is 1 if y satisfies $f(y) \neq iv$ and 0 otherwise, is β-almost-certain.

Theorem 1. *If f has complexity $\mathfrak{c}(f) = 1$, is ε-collapsing and β-iv-preimage-resistant, then, for any integer $L \geq 0$, the function $MD^{\leq L}$ is γ-collapsing with*

$$\gamma(q) = L \cdot \varepsilon\big(q + \tfrac{1}{2}L(L+1)\big) + \sqrt{2\beta(q + L)}.$$

---

[11] Since the bit size of the input to MD must be an integer multiple of r, the Merkle-Damgård construction usually comes with a *padding* that maps a string of arbitrary size into a sequence of blocks of bit size r. We can safely ignore this since any injective padding preserves the collapsing property by Lemma 5.

For the purpose of the proof, we define for any i the predicate $\pi_i : \mathcal{X}_i \to \{0,1\}$ as

$$\pi_i(x_1, \ldots, x_i) = 1 \iff \forall j \in \{1, \ldots, i\} : x_j = \bot \vee IH_j(x_1, \ldots, x_j) \neq iv,$$

i.e., the bit is set unless the input is a non-trivial iv-preimage of some IH_j. In particular, if $\pi_i(x_1, \ldots, x_i) = 0$ then it must be that $IH_j(x_1, \ldots, x_j) = iv$ for some j with $x_j \neq \bot$, and thus $y := \big(IH_{j-1}(x_1, \ldots, x_{j-1}), x_j\big)$ satisfies $f(y) = IH_j(x_1, \ldots, x_j) = iv$ by (3). So, by Lemma 3, the following holds.

Lemma 8. *If f is β-iv-preimage-resistant then π_i is $\beta(q + c_{IH_{i-1}})$-almost-certain.*

Recall that $IH_i|_{\pi_i}$ is the partial function that is defined only for the inputs which satisfy π_i. The heart of the proof of Theorem 2 is the following recursive statement, which ensures that if $IH_{i-1}|_{\pi_{i-1}}$ is collapsing then so is $IH_i|_{\pi_i}$. By repeated application, we then get that $IH_L|_{\pi_L}$ is collapsing, and since π_L is almost-certain, IH_L is collapsing as well (by Lemma 2).

Proposition 1. *For any positive integer i:*

$$\mathsf{cAdv}\big[IH_i|_{\pi_i}\big](q) \leq \mathsf{cAdv}\big[IH_{i-1}|_{\pi_{i-1}}\big]\big(q + c_{IH_{i-1}}\big) + \varepsilon\big(q + c_{IH_{i-1}}\big).$$

Proof. We let $\dot{IH}_i$ and $\dot{\pi}_i$ be the respective restrictions of IH_i and π_i to the domain $\dot{\mathcal{X}}_i := \mathcal{X}_i \setminus \{\bot^i\}$. Then, we see that $IH_i|_{\pi_i}$ is the disjoint union of the trivial function $\{\bot^i\} \to \{iv\}$ and $\dot{IH}_i|_{\dot{\pi}_i}$; the crucial observation here is that the image of $\dot{IH}_i|_{\dot{\pi}_i}$ is disjoint with $\{iv\}$. Therefore, by Lemma 7,

$$\mathsf{cAdv}\big[IH_i|_{\pi_i}\big](q) \leq \mathsf{cAdv}\big[\dot{IH}_i|_{\dot{\pi}_i}\big](q) \leq \mathsf{cAdv}\big[\dot{IH}_i|_{\pi_{i-1}}\big](q),$$

where the latter inequality is by Lemma 1, given that $\dot{\pi}_i$ implies π_{i-1}.[12] Furthermore, since

$$\dot{IH}_i(x_1, \ldots, x_i) = f\big(IH_{i-1}(x_1, \ldots, x_{i-1}), x_i\big)$$

on its domain $\dot{\mathcal{X}}_i$, i.e., it is the nested composition of f with the concurrent composition of IH_{i-1} and the identity function $x_i \mapsto x_i$, Lemma 4 and 5 imply

$$\mathsf{cAdv}\big[\dot{IH}_i|_{\pi_{i-1}}\big](q) \leq \mathsf{cAdv}\big[IH_{i-1}|_{\pi_{i-1}}\big]\big(q + c_{IH_{i-1}}\big) + \mathsf{cAdv}\big[f\big]\big(q + c_{IH_{i-1}}\big),$$

which completes the proof. $\qquad\square$

Proof (of Theorem 1). $IH_0|_{\pi_0} = IH_0$ is trivially 0-collapsing. For convenience, we let n_i be the sum of integers $n_i := 1 + 2 + \cdots i = \frac{1}{2}i(i+1)$. Assuming by induction that $\mathsf{cAdv}[IH_i|_{\pi_i}](q) \leq i \cdot \varepsilon(q + n_{i-1})$, we get from Proposition 1 that

$$\mathsf{cAdv}\big[IH_{i+1}^1|_{\pi_{i+1}}\big](q) \leq \varepsilon(q + i) + i \cdot \varepsilon(q + n_{i-1} + i) \leq (i+1) \cdot \varepsilon(q + n_i),$$

using that $c_{IH_i} = i \cdot c_f = i$ and $n_{i-1} + i = n_i$. Hence, the induction assumption holds for all i, and

$$\mathsf{cAdv}\big[IH_L\big](q) \leq \mathsf{cAdv}\big[IH_L|_{\pi_L}\big](q + L) + \sqrt{2\beta(q + L)} \qquad \text{(Lemma 2 \& 8)}$$

$$\leq L \cdot \varepsilon\big(q + L + n_{L-1}\big) + \sqrt{2\beta(q + L)}. \qquad\qquad \square$$

---

[12] Here, we understand π_{i-1} as $\pi_{i-1} : \dot{\mathcal{X}}_i \to \{0,1\}$, $(x_1, \ldots, x_i) \mapsto \pi_{i-1}(x_1, \ldots, x_{i-1})$.

4.3   Instantiation with a Random Oracle

If f is a *random oracle*, which formally means that we consider the oracle O that is a uniformly random function $\{0,1\}^c \times \{0,1\}^r \rightarrow \{0,1\}^c$ and f is the trivial oracle function that outputs whatever O outputs on the given input, then, as shown by Unruh in [5], f is $O(\sqrt{q^3/2^c})$-collapsing.[13] Furthermore, by the results on the hardness of quantum search from [4, Theorem 1], applied to the oracle function $F : \{0,1\}^c \times \{0,1\}^r \rightarrow \{0,1\}$ given by $F(y) = 1$ if and only if $f(y) = iv$, we immediately get that f is $8(q+1)^2/2^c$-*iv*-preimage-resistant. As such, we obtain that for messages of block-size at most L, the Merkle-Damgård hash function $MD^{\leq L}$ is ε-collapsing with

$$\varepsilon(q) = O\left(L\sqrt{(q+L^2)^3/2^c}\right).$$

As far as we understand, the results of [6] imply a collapsing advantage of $O(L\sqrt{(q+L)^3/2^c})$, which is slightly better because of the L^2 that we have in our bound, but this is insignificant in typical settings where $q \gg L$.

4.4   HAIFA

Along the very same lines as for the original Merkle-Damgård construction, we can easily show that also HAIFA, a variant proposed by Biham and Dunkelmann [3], is collapsing, under the same assumptions. HAIFA works similarly to Merkle-Damgård except that

$$IH_i(salt, x_1, \ldots, x_i) := f\left(salt, IH_{i-1}(salt, x_1, \ldots, x_{i-1}), x_i, i\right)$$

i.e., the round function takes as additional inputs the round number i and some salt (that is the same for every round).[14] Proposition 1 immediately extends to HAIFA; the only thing that changes in the proof is that f becomes $f_i = f(\cdot, \cdot, \cdot, i)$, which is collapsing if f is, and we also have to use Corollary 2 to argue that the parallel composition of $(salt, x_1, \ldots, x_i) \mapsto salt$ with the concurrent composition of IH_{i-1} and $x_i \mapsto x_i$ stays collapsing. The collapsing property of HAIFA then follows easily by inductively applying this variation of Proposition 1 as in the proof of Theorem 1.

4.5   Merkle-Damgård Without iv-Preimage-Resistance

We can also recover Unruh's original result on MD, which does not require f to be *iv*-preimage-resistant but instead restricts the set of inputs to be *suffix-free*.

---

[13] Even though our definition of the collapsing property differs slightly from the definition in [5], these differences disappear in such asymptotic statements, as discussed in Sect. 3. See also Appendix C.

[14] For the purpose of collisions and the collapsing property, we can think of the salt simply as part of the input: we do not want collisions even for different choices of the salt.

For that, given a fixed integer $L > 0$ and arbitrary $0 \le i \le L$, consider the map IH_i^* given by

$$IH_i^* : (x_1, \ldots, x_L) \mapsto \big(IH_i(x_1, \ldots, x_i), x_{i+1}, \ldots, x_L\big),$$

defined on the considered suffix-free inputs of size at most L blocks, left-padded with $\perp$'s, and we argue the following variant of Proposition 1: if $IH_i^*|_{x_i \ne \perp}$ is collapsing then $IH_{i+1}^*|_{x_{i+1} \ne \perp}$ is collapsing too (for $i < L$). This variant of Proposition 1 follows from the observation that the latter is obtained as the nested composition $IH_{i+1}^*|_{x_{i+1} \ne \perp} = (f \| id) \circ IH_i^*|_{x_{i+1} \ne \perp}$ of $IH_i^*|_{x_{i+1} \ne \perp}$ with the concurrent composition of f and the identity id acting on $x_{i+2}, \ldots, x_L$. Furthermore,

$$IH_i^*|_{x_{i+1} \ne \perp}(x_1,\ldots,x_L) = \begin{cases} IH_i^*|_{x_i \ne \perp}(x_1,\ldots,x_L) = \big(IH_i(x_1,\ldots,x_i), x_{i+1},\ldots,x_L\big) & \text{if } x_i \ne \perp \\ (iv, x_{i+1}, x_{i+2},\ldots,x_L) & \text{if } x_i = \perp \end{cases}$$

and therefore $IH_i^*|_{x_{i+1} \ne \perp}$ is the disjoint union of $IH_i^*|_{x_i \ne \perp}$ and the function $(\perp^i, x_{i+1}, \ldots, x_L) \mapsto (iv, x_{i+1}, x_{i+2}, \ldots, x_L)$. Here, we are using the suffix-freeness of the considered inputs $x_1, \ldots, x_L$; this ensures that not only the domains but also the images of the two functions are disjoint: if $(\perp^i, x_{i+1}, \ldots, x_L)$ is "allowed" then $(x_1, \ldots, x_L)$ is not unless x_1 up to x_i are all $\perp$. The above variant of Proposition 1 then follows from the preservation of the collapsing property under the different compositions, and then, by inductively applying this variant of Proposition 1, we obtain that $IH_L^*|_{x_L \ne \perp}$ is collapsing, and thus $MD^{\le L}$ is, given that the input is from a suffix-free set.

5   Application II: The Sponge

Here, we apply our framework to the Sponge construction [1]. As one can see, we follow the exact same blueprint as in Sect. 4.

5.1   The Construction

Let $f = (f^0, f^1) : \{0,1\}^r \times \{0,1\}^c \to \{0,1\}^r \times \{0,1\}^c$ be a (total) function, which will act as the round function in the Sponge construction. For any positive integer i, consider the function

$$S_i = (S_i^0, S_i^1) : \big(\{0,1\}^r\big)^i \to \{0,1\}^r \times \{0,1\}^c$$

given recursively by

$$S_i(x_1, \ldots, x_i) := f\big(S_{i-1}^0(x_1, \ldots, x_{i-1}) \oplus x_i, S_{i-1}^1(x_1, \ldots, x_{i-1})\big) \tag{4}$$

with $S_0() := 0$. The sponge function (with s rounds of "squeezing") is then formally given by[15]

$$Sponge[s] : (\{0,1\}^r)^* \to (\{0,1\}^r)^s$$
$$(x_1,\ldots,x_i) \mapsto \big(S_i^0(x_1,\ldots,x_i), S_{i+1}^0(x_1,\ldots,x_i,0^r),\ldots, S_{i+s-1}^0(x_1,\ldots,x_i,0^r,\ldots,0^r)\big).$$

---

[15]   Like for Merkle-Damgård, we can safely ignore the padding here.

For technical reasons, we extend the domain of S_i above to

$$\mathcal{X}_i := \left\{ (x_1, \ldots, x_i) \in \left(\{\bot\} \cup \{0,1\}^r \right)^i \mid x_j = \bot \Rightarrow x_1 = \cdots = x_j = \bot \right\}$$

i.e., to strings that may have $\bot$-prefixes. We do so by setting

$$S_i(\bot, \ldots, \bot) := 0^{r+c}$$

and keeping the recursive definition (4) for $x_i \neq \bot$. This extension allows us to apply S_L to messages $(x_1, \ldots, x_i) \in (\{0,1\}^r)^i$ of size $i < L$ blocks by pre-padding it with $\bot$'s: $S_i(x_1, \ldots, x_i) = S_{i+1}(\bot, x_1, \ldots, x_i) = \cdots = S_L(\bot, \ldots, \bot, x_1, \ldots, x_i)$, and thus the restriction of $Sponge[s]$ to messages of block size $1 \leq i \leq L$ can be expressed as:

$$Sponge[s]^{\leq L}(x_1, \ldots, x_i) = \left(S_L^0(\bot^{L-i}, x_1, \ldots, x_i), S_{L+1}^0(\bot^{L-i}, x_1, \ldots, x_i, 0^r), \ldots \right) \quad (5)$$

where we note that we insist here on $i \geq 1$, i.e., the message is non-empty.

5.2   The Analysis

Here, we prove the following. Also here, the assumption on $c(f)$ is simply for normalization, and for f^1 to be β-zero-preimage-resistant means, by definition, that the predicate $1_{f^1(y) \neq 0^c}$ is β-almost-certain.

Theorem 2. *If f has complexity 1, and f^0 and f^1 are ε^0- and ε^1-collapsing, and f^1 is β-zero-preimage-resistant, then, for any integer $L \geq 0$, the Sponge function $Sponge[s]^{\leq L}$ is γ-collapsing with*

$$\gamma(q) \leq \varepsilon^0(q + 2L - 1) + (L-1) \cdot \varepsilon^1 \left(q + \tfrac{1}{2}L(L+1) \right) + \sqrt{2\beta(q+L)}.$$

For the purpose of the proof, we define for any i the predicate $\pi_i : \mathcal{X}_i \to \{0,1\}$ as

$$\pi_i(x_1, \ldots, x_i) = 1 \iff \forall j \in \{1, \ldots, i\} : x_j = \bot \lor S_j^1(x_1, \ldots, x_j) \neq 0^c,$$

i.e., the bit is set unless the input is a non-trivial zero-preimage of some S_j^1. In particular, if $\pi_i(x_1, \ldots, x_i) = 0$ then $S_j^1(x_1, \ldots, x_j) = 0^c$ for some j with $x_j \neq \bot$, and thus $y := \left(S_{j-1}^0(x_1, \ldots, x_{j-1}) \oplus x_j, S_{j-1}^1(x_1, \ldots, x_{j-1}) \right)$ satisfies $f^1(y) = S_j^1(x_1, \ldots, x_j) = 0^c$ by (4). Thus, by Lemma 3, the following holds.

Lemma 9. *If f^1 is β-zero-preimage-resistant then π_i is $\beta(q + c_{S_{i-1}})$-almost-certain, and the same holds for $\dot{\pi}_i$, defined as below.*

For any i, let $\dot{S}_i^b$ and $\dot{\pi}_i$ be the respective restrictions of S_i^b and π_i to the domain $\dot{\mathcal{X}}_i := \mathcal{X}_i \setminus \{\bot^i\}$. The heart of the proof of Theorem 2 is the following recursive statement, which ensures that if $S_{i-1}^1|_{\pi_{i-1}}$ is collapsing then so are $\dot{S}_i^0|_{\dot{\pi}_i}$ and $S_i^1|_{\pi_i}$. By repeated application, we then get that $\dot{S}_L^0|_{\dot{\pi}_L}$ is collapsing, and since $\dot{\pi}_L$ is almost-certain, $\dot{S}_L^0$ is collapsing as well (by Lemma 2).

Proposition 2. *For any positive integer* i:

$$\mathsf{cAdv}\big[\dot{S}_i^0|_{\dot{\pi}_i}\big](q), \mathsf{cAdv}\big[S_i^1|_{\pi_i}\big](q) \le \mathsf{cAdv}\big[S_{i-1}^1|_{\pi_{i-1}}\big]\big(q + \mathfrak{c}_{S_{i-1}}\big) + \varepsilon^b\big(q + \mathfrak{c}_{S_{i-1}}\big).$$

Proof. We note that $S_i^1|_{\pi_i}$ is the disjoint union of the trivial function $\{\perp^i\} \to \{0^c\}$ and $\dot{S}_i^1|_{\dot{\pi}_i}$; the crucial observation here is that the image of $\dot{S}_i^1$ does not contain 0^c. Therefore, by Lemma 7,

$$\mathsf{cAdv}\big[S_i^1|_{\pi_i}\big](q) \le \mathsf{cAdv}\big[\dot{S}_i^1|_{\dot{\pi}_i}\big](q) \le \mathsf{cAdv}\big[\dot{S}_i^1|_{\pi_{i-1}}\big](q).$$

where the latter inequality is by Lemma 1, given that $\dot{\pi}_i$ implies π_{i-1}.[16] Furthermore, since

$$\dot{S}_i^1(x_1, \dots, x_i) = f^1\big(S_{i-1}^0(x_1, \dots, x_{i-1}) \oplus x_i, S_{i-1}^1(x_1, \dots, x_{i-1})\big)$$

on its domain $\dot{\mathcal{X}}_i$, i.e., it is a nested composition of f^1 with a function that is obtained as a composition as considered in Lemma 6, Lemmas 5 and 6 imply that

$$\mathsf{cAdv}\big[\dot{S}_i^1|_{\pi_{i-1}}\big](q) \le \mathsf{cAdv}\big[S_{i-1}^1|_{\pi_{i-1}}\big]\big(q + \mathfrak{c}_{S_{i-1}}\big) + \mathsf{cAdv}\big[f^b\big]\big(q + \mathfrak{c}_{S_{i-1}}\big),$$

which was to be proven. The reasoning for $\dot{S}_i^0|_{\dot{\pi}_i}$ is exactly as for $\dot{S}_i^1|_{\dot{\pi}_i}$ above. □

Proof (of Theorem 2). $S_0^1|_{\pi_0} = S_0^1$ is trivially 0-collapsing. For convenience, we let n_i be the sum of integers $n_i := 1 + 2 + \cdots i = \frac{1}{2}i(i+1)$. Assuming by induction that $\mathsf{cAdv}[S_i^1|_{\pi_i}](q) \le i \cdot \varepsilon^1(q + n_{i-1})$, we get from Proposition 2 that

$$\mathsf{cAdv}\big[S_{i+1}^1|_{\pi_{i+1}}\big](q) \le \varepsilon^1(q + i) + i \cdot \varepsilon^1(q + n_{i-1} + i) \le (i+1) \cdot \varepsilon^1(q + n_i),$$

using that $\mathfrak{c}_{S_i} = i \cdot \mathfrak{c}_f = i$ and $n_{i-1} + i = n_i$. Hence, the induction assumption holds for all i, and

$$\begin{aligned}
\mathsf{cAdv}\big[\dot{S}_L^0\big](q) &\le \mathsf{cAdv}\big[\dot{S}_L^0|_{\dot{\pi}_L}\big](q + L) + \sqrt{\beta(q + L)} \\
&\le \varepsilon^0(q + 2L - 1) + \mathsf{cAdv}\big[S_{L-1}^1|_{\pi_{L-1}}\big](q + 2L - 1) + \sqrt{2\beta(q + L)} \\
&\le \varepsilon^0(q + 2L - 1) + (L - 1) \cdot \varepsilon^1(q + n_L) + \sqrt{2\beta(q + L)}.
\end{aligned}$$

where the first inequality is by Lemmas 2 and 9, and the second by Proposition 2. The claim on $Sponge[s]^{\le L}$ follows now from (5) and Corollary 2. □

5.3   Instantiation with a Random Oracle

If $f = (f^0, f^1)$ is a *random oracle*, then it follows easily from the work of Unruh in [5] on the collapsing property of the random oracle that f^0 and f^1 are respectively $O(\sqrt{q^3/2^r})$- and $O(\sqrt{q^3/2^c})$-collapsing. Furthermore, as pointed out in [2], by the results on the hardness of quantum search from [4, Theorem 1] to the oracle function $F : \{0,1\}^r \times \{0,1\}^c \to \{0,1\}$ given by $F(y) = 1$ if and

---

[16] Here, we understand π_{i-1} as $\pi_{i-1} : \dot{\mathcal{X}}_i \to \{0,1\}$, $(x_1, \dots, x_i) \mapsto \pi_{i-1}(x_1, \dots, x_{i-1})$.

only if $f^1(y) = 0^c$, we immediately get that the function f^1 is $8(q+1)^2/2^c$-zero-preimage-resistant. Therefore, we get that for messages of block-size at most L, the sponge function $Sponge[s]^{\leq L}$, with the round function modeled by a random oracle, is ε-collapsing with

$$\varepsilon(q) = O\left(\sqrt{(q+L)^3/2^r} + L\sqrt{(q+L^2)^3/2^c}\right).$$

This matches with single-execution-variant (i.e. $t = 1$) of Theorem 33 of [2], except for the square in the L^2 term. When considering a t-fold parallel composition $Sponge[s]^{\leq L} \| \cdots \| Sponge[s]^{\leq L}$, it follows immediately from Lemma 6 that the collapsing parameter grows linearly with t, i.e., as

$$O\left(t\sqrt{(q+L)^3/2^r} + tL\sqrt{(q+L^2)^3/2^c}\right),$$

which is comparable to Theorem 33 of [2] with a general t, which states a collapsing advantage of

$$O\left(t\sqrt{(q+tL)^3/2^r} + tL\sqrt{(q+tL)^3/2^c}\right).$$

6   Conclusion

We consider the quantum *collapsing* property of classical hash functions, which replaces the notion of *collision resistance* in the presence of quantum attacks, and we propose a formalism and a framework that enables to argue about the collapsing property of hash domain extension constructions simply by means of decomposing the iteration function under consideration into elementary composition operations. In particular, our framework allows us to argue by purely classical means that hash functions are secure against quantum attacks.

We demonstrate this proof methodology on several examples. For Merkle-Damgård and the Sponge construction, we recover what has already been proven in [2,6], up to insignificant differences, whereas our result for HAIFA is, strictly speaking, new. It is well possible that the respective proof provided in [6] extends to HAIFA as well; however, this is cumbersome to verify (we challenge the reader to do so). With our approach, on the other hand, it is *trivial* to see that our proof for Merkle-Damgård extends to this variation: the only thing that needs to be verified is that the modified iteration function still decomposes into composition operations that are covered by our framework.

We think it is fair to say that, compared to previous work which proves that some hash domain extension constructions *are* collapsing, our approach gives much more insight into *why* they are collapsing. Furthermore, our framework should be a helpful tool when designing new hash functions that are meant to withstand quantum attacks.

Last but not least, from a conceptual perspective, we find it particularly interesting to see that our simplified proofs are the result of departing from the common methodology of proving a conditional security statement by means of an algorithmic reduction. Instead of assuming an attack against the construction and then building an attack against the underlying component, we argue *directly*—and in some sense "algebraically"—that if the underlying component is secure then so is the construction.

A   Randomized Functions and CPTN Maps

In this work, we will consider two variants of the notion of a *randomized function*, and our techniques will apply to both. Formally, a randomized function is a function $f : \mathcal{R} \times \mathcal{X} \to \mathcal{Y}$ for a fixed choice of the (finite) set $\mathcal{R}$, and it is understood that $r \in \mathcal{R}$ is chosen uniformly at random once-and-for-all. Informally, we think of such a randomized function as a function $f : \mathcal{X} \to \mathcal{Y}$ that produces its output $f(x) = f(r, x)$ for any input x dependent on some "global randomness" r, which is the same for all inputs and all randomized functions considered at a time.

Informally, the two variants we consider in this work differ in the way the randomness r is accessed by the function. In one case, r is *explicitly* given as input to the function f (or to the algorithm that computes f, if you prefer); one then typically speaks of *keyed* (or *seeded*) functions. In the other case, r is not explicitly given to f but instead, f makes *oracle queries* to a designated randomized function $\mathcal{O}$, called the *oracle*, which computes every reply dependent on r. This latter case is typically referred to as an *oracle function*.

We point out that from a mathematical perspective, there is no distinction yet between a keyed and an oracle function, in that both are merely functions that additionally act on some global randomness r. The way the two variants differ formally is by the way we capture *complexity*: for keyed functions we consider the *computational complexity* whereas for oracle functions we consider the *query complexity*.[17] We address this in more detail in the subsequent section.

In line with the above, we can also consider the notion of a *randomized CPTN map* $\mathbb{T}$, which is a CPTN map whose action on a quantum state depends on the global randomness r, and we can distinguish between *keyed* CPTN maps that have *direct* access to r, and *oracle* CPTN maps that have *quantum oracle access* to a designated randomized function $\mathcal{O} : \mathcal{R} \times \mathcal{U} \to \mathcal{V}$. Here, "quantum oracle access" means that $\mathbb{T}$ can query $\mathcal{O}$ in superposition, i.e., it may ask to have the unitary $|u\rangle|v\rangle \mapsto |u\rangle|v + \mathcal{O}(r, u)\rangle$ applied to any state (of appropriate dimension). Again, the formal distinction between the two variants is in terms of the complexity measure.

We point out that by considering randomized CPTN maps $\mathbb{T}$ (of either flavor) that act on the empty system with trivial one-dimensional state space, we may also speak of *randomized states* (of either flavor) as the states ρ produced as $\rho = \mathbb{T}(1)$ for such a randomized CPTN map. We take it as understood here that the description of such a randomized state includes the dependency on the randomness r.

---

[17] For the latter, one could actually consider both simultaneously.

B   Complexity

We introduce here the abstract notion of *complexity* that we consider in this work and discuss below the two main instantiations that are relevant for us. In the context of randomized functions $f : \mathcal{X} \to \mathcal{Y}$, we consider a map that assigns to any such function a non-negative integer $c(f)$, called the *complexity* of f, which is meant to express how hard it is to "compute" f. We assume that our abstract notion satisfies natural properties, like that the identity function on any set has zero complexity, and that it behaves well under composition, so that

$$c(g \circ f) \leq c(f) + c(g) \qquad \text{and} \qquad c(f \| g) \leq c(f) + c(g)$$

for any f and g with appropriate domain/range, where $g \circ f : x \mapsto g(f(x))$ and $f \| g : (x, w) \mapsto \big(f(x), g(w)\big)$. For simplicity, we additionally assume that certain "simple" functions have zero complexity. These are: constants, copying, deleting, swapping, checking equality, as well as bit-wise XOR. Also, to avoid certain technical complications, once c is fixed we only consider randomized functions $f : \mathcal{X} \to \mathcal{Y}$ for which $\mathcal{X}$ can be recognized with zero complexity.[18] For lighter notation, we may also write c_f instead of $c(f)$.

We also consider a notion of complexity for randomized CPTN maps, which, as above, assigns a non-negative integer $c(\mathbb{T})$ to any randomized CPTN map $\mathbb{T}$. Similarly to above, we assume that the identity $\mathbb{I}$ has zero complexity, that

$$c(\mathbb{S} \circ \mathbb{T}) \leq c(\mathbb{T}) + c(\mathbb{S}) \qquad \text{and} \qquad c(\mathbb{T} \otimes \mathbb{S}) \leq c(\mathbb{T}) + c(\mathbb{S}),$$

and that certain "simple" maps have zero complexity, namely: the preparation of states in the computational basis, measurements (with or without post-selection) in the computational basis, partial traces, and swapping registers. On top, we assume the complexity notion for CPTN maps to be consistent with that of functions, in that we require that

$$c\big(\mathbb{E}[f]\big), c\big(\mathbb{E}^{inv}[f]\big), c\big(\mathbb{M}[f]\big), c\big(\mathbb{M}[f{=}y]\big) \leq c(f)$$

where the latter two actually follow from the first, given that partial traces and measurements in the computational basis are "for free".

Given such a notion of complexity (for randomized CPTN maps), we can define the complexity of a randomized state ρ as $c(\rho) := c(\mathbb{T})$ where $\mathbb{T}$ is the randomized CPTN map with minimal complexity that produces ρ as $\rho = \mathbb{T}(1)$. It obviously holds that $c\big(\mathbb{T}(\rho)\big) \leq c(\rho) + c(\mathbb{T})$ for any randomized CPTN map. A last requirement we pose onto our abstract complexity measure c is that $c\big(\rho + (1 - \mathrm{tr}(\rho))\sigma\big) \leq c(\rho) + c(\sigma)$ for all randomized states.[19]

---

[18] Meaning that for any $\mathcal{X}' \supset \mathcal{X}$, the function $\mathcal{X}' \to \{0, 1\}$ that maps $x \in \mathcal{X}$ to 1 and $x \in \mathcal{X}' \setminus \mathcal{X}$ to 0 has zero complexity. This is trivially satisfied for *any* function f in case of c^{query} (given in Example 2).

[19] This is in line with our interpretation of $\mathrm{tr}(\rho) < 1$ as capturing an "abort" of the preparation process.

Example 1. An important class of examples for such a complexity measure arises by considering keyed functions and keyed CPTN maps and writing them as *circuits* that get the global randomness as additional input. The complexity can then be specified to be the minimal number of gates (of certain types) of any such circuit representation. For instance, writing any randomized function f as a binary circuit with AND and XOR gates, one may define $c^{comp}(f)$ to be the minimal necessary number of AND gates.[20] Similarly for randomized CPTN maps, where one could for instance count the number of gates (or the number of non-Clifford gates) with respect to a fixed universal set of gates. These kinds of notions of complexity are referred to as *computational complexity*.

Example 2. Another example that is relevant for us is the *query complexity* c^{query} for oracle functions and oracle CPTN maps, which counts the number of (quantum) oracle queries that the function or CPTN map makes to the oracle $\mathcal{O}$.

We note that this abstract treatment of complexity allows us to *explicitly* cover computational complexity and query complexity in one go, using one language. Also, all results expressed using this language do *explicitly* not depend on the technical details of any model of computation. Related to the latter, this approach allows us to reason about *functions* (and *CPTN* maps etc.), which are unambiguously defined objects that do not depend on any model of computation.

C   On the Definitions of the Collapsing Property in [5,6]

As already mentioned in Sect. 3, the definition of the collapsing property introduced by Unruh comes in a few different variations in [5,6], which we want to briefly recall here, and we discuss how they compare to our definition. Some differences (like allowing non-normalized states), which have some minor quantitative impact, have already been discussed in Sect. 3; here, we focus on some technical differences that are orthogonal to those.

The definition originally proposed in [5, Definition 20] (respectively Definition 23 in the full version) is of asymptotic nature and for a deterministic function h (that depends on a security parameter κ): it requires that every (uniform) quantum-polynomial time adversary has a negligible collapsing advantage. Note that it makes sense to consider a *deterministic* hash function h in this case since a *uniform* model of computation is considered, i.e., the adversary that has a collision hard-wired into its code (for any κ) is not allowed. In the formal statement on the collapsing property of a random oracle [5, Theorem 31], which bounds the advantage by $O(q^3/\text{size of the range})$, an obvious variation (in terms of oracle algorithms, and with the randomness also over the oracle's random choices) of this definition is then (implicitly) considered. It also remains implicit that the bound (and in particular the hidden constant) is independent of the running time of the adversary; indeed, the proof considers "q-query adversaries", which have bounded query complexity but (possibly) unbounded running time. As such, the

---

[20] Remember that we want XOR's to be "for free".

bound $O(q^3/\text{size of the range})$ carries over to our non-asymptotic definition of the collapsing property (with the complexity measure being the query complexity), with the understanding that the bound includes a hidden constant and only applies for a large enough range of h (compared to q).

In terms of comparing Unruh's original definition [5, Definition 20] with our Definition 2, though being similar in spirit (up small differences as discussed in Sect. 3), they are technically incomparable: an asymptotic definition as [5, Definition 20] makes no meaningful statement about a fixed instance, while, on the other hand, our non-asymptotic definition is meaningless for a deterministic hash function, for instance. If we consider an asymptotic variant of our Definition 2, which would ask $\mathsf{cAdv}[h_\kappa](q(\kappa))$ to be negligible in the security parameter κ for any polynomially bounded function q, we get a *non-uniform* (and thus stronger) variant of [5, Definition 20]. It is easy to see that all our results directly carry over to such an asymptotic variant.

In [6, Definition 8], Unruh also considers a non-asymptotic "concrete security" variant of his original definition, which considers a *keyed* hash function (using our terminology) and defines the "collapsing advantage" of an arbitrary but fixed adversary in the obvious way, as the advantage of this adversary distinguishing the two games.[21] For a function h being $\varepsilon(q)$-collapsing according to our definition thus immediately implies that the "collapsing advantage" according to [6, Definition 8] is bounded by $\varepsilon(q)$ (up to a small constant factor, as explained in Sect. 3) for any adversary that is bounded by q, and vice versa. In that sense, our Definition 2 and Unruh's "concrete security" variant [6, Definition 8] are *equivalent* (again, up to negligible quantitative differences).

However, formalized as in [6], i.e., not as a security property of h but as a property of an arbitrary but fixed adversary that is attacking h, security statements are bound to be in reductionistic form. Indeed, all the concrete-security statements in [6] are like:

> "Let A be a q-time (or query) adversary with collapsing advantage ε against function h, then there exists a $2q$-time (or query) adversary A' with collapsing advantage ε^2 against h'"

where we consider concrete example functions for the "security loss". On the other hand, our definition allows us to express such a statement simply as:

> "If the function h' is $\varepsilon'(q')$-collapsing then h is $\sqrt{\varepsilon'(2q)}$-collapsing"

or even more compactly as

$$\mathsf{cAdv}[h](q) \leq \sqrt{\mathsf{cAdv}[h](2q)}\,.$$

Again, these statements are *equivalent* (up to the minor quantitative differences discussed in Sect. 3), so it is merely a matter of taste what sort of language one prefers.

---

[21] As a matter of fact, [6, Definition 8] considers a t-fold parallel repetition of the game, where t is an additional parameter of the definition. We ignore this for the discussion here, recalling that we obtain immediately a similar variant of our definition by means of concurrent composition.

A more crucial difference is that we not only can state but also *prove* these kinds of security claims "in the forward direction", i.e., not via the counter position of assuming an attacker A that breaks the target primitive and turning it into an attacker A' that breaks something else. Indeed, we have "algebraic" proofs that avoid reasoning about algorithms altogether. On the other hand, the proofs in [2,5,6] are typically constructive, in that the adversary A' is *explicitly* constructed from the adversary A. One can then for instance easily check that A' does not rely on any non-uniform auxiliary information, and thus that the reductions are *uniform*. Our proofs do not spell out the reductions; however, if desired, they could still be extracted by backtracking the proofs all the way down to the basic properties of the pseudometric δ_q upon which the proofs rely, and which all have simple—uniform—reduction proofs. This ensures that also our implicitly defined reductions are uniform.

References

1. Bertoni, G., Daemen, J., Peeters, M., Van Assche, G.: On the indifferentiability of the sponge construction. In: Smart, N. (ed.) EUROCRYPT 2008. LNCS, vol. 4965, pp. 181–197. Springer, Heidelberg (2008). https://doi.org/10.1007/978-3-540-78967-3_11

2. Czajkowski, J., Groot Bruinderink, L., Hülsing, A., Schaffner, C., Unruh, D.: Post-quantum security of the sponge construction. In: Lange, T., Steinwandt, R. (eds.) PQCrypto 2018. LNCS, vol. 10786, pp. 185–204. Springer, Cham (2018). https://doi.org/10.1007/978-3-319-79063-3_9

3. Biham, E., Dunkelman, O.: A framework for iterative hash functions – HAIFA. In: Second NIST Cryptographic Hash Workshop (2006). https://eprint.iacr.org/2007/278.pdf

4. Hülsing, A., Rijneveld, J., Song, F.: Mitigating multi-target attacks in hash-based signatures. In: Cheng, C.-M., Chung, K.-M., Persiano, G., Yang, B.-Y. (eds.) PKC 2016. LNCS, vol. 9614, pp. 387–416. Springer, Heidelberg (2016). https://doi.org/10.1007/978-3-662-49384-7_15

5. Unruh, D.: Computationally binding quantum commitments. In: Fischlin, M., Coron, J.-S. (eds.) EUROCRYPT 2016. LNCS, vol. 9666, pp. 497–527. Springer, Heidelberg (2016). https://doi.org/10.1007/978-3-662-49896-5_18

6. Unruh, D.: Collapse-binding quantum commitments without random oracles. In: Cheon, J.H., Takagi, T. (eds.) ASIACRYPT 2016. LNCS, vol. 10032, pp. 166–195. Springer, Heidelberg (2016). https://doi.org/10.1007/978-3-662-53890-6_6

7. Winter, A.: Coding theorem and strong converse for quantum channels. IEEE Trans. Inf. Theory **45**(7), 2481–2485 (1999). https://arxiv.org/abs/1409.2536

8. Wilde, M.: From Classical to Quantum Shannon Theory, 2nd edn. (2016). https://arxiv.org/abs/1106.1445. Manuscript

LWE-Based Cryptography

Traitor-Tracing from LWE Made Simple and Attribute-Based

Yilei Chen[1](✉), Vinod Vaikuntanathan[2], Brent Waters[3], Hoeteck Wee[4], and Daniel Wichs[5]

[1] Visa Research, Palo Alto, USA
yilchen@visa.com
[2] MIT, Cambridge, USA
vinodv@csail.mit.edu
[3] The University of Texas at Austin, Austin, USA
bwaters@cs.utexas.edu
[4] CNRS, ENS, PSL, Paris, France
wee@di.ens.fr
[5] Northeastern University, Boston, USA
wichs@ccs.neu.edu

Abstract. A traitor tracing scheme is a public key encryption scheme for which there are many secret decryption keys. Any of these keys can decrypt a ciphertext; moreover, even if a coalition of users collude, put together their decryption keys and attempt to create a new decryption key, there is an efficient algorithm to trace the new key to at least one the colluders.

Recently, Goyal, Koppula and Waters (GKW, STOC 18) provided the first traitor tracing scheme from LWE with ciphertext and secret key sizes that grow polynomially in $\log n$, where n is the number of users. The main technical building block in their construction is a strengthening of (bounded collusion secure) secret-key functional encryption which they refer to as mixed functional encryption (FE).

In this work, we improve upon and extend the GKW traitor tracing scheme:
- We provide simpler constructions of mixed FE schemes based on the LWE assumption. Our constructions improve upon the GKW construction in terms of expressiveness, modularity, and security.
- We provide a construction of attribute-based traitor tracing for all circuits based on the LWE assumption.

1 Introduction

A traitor tracing scheme [14] is a public key encryption scheme for which there are many secret decryption keys, so that any of these keys could decrypt the ciphertext. In addition, if a coalition of users collude to create a new decryption key, then there is an efficient algorithm to trace the new key to (at least one of) its creators.

A. Beimel and S. Dziembowski (Eds.): TCC 2018, LNCS 11240, pp. 341–369, 2018.
https://doi.org/10.1007/978-3-030-03810-6_13

Recently, Goyal, Koppula and Waters (GKW) [20] constructed the first traitor tracing scheme from standard assumptions with ciphertext and secret key sizes that grow polynomially in $\log n$, where n is the number of users. The security of the scheme relies on the polynomial hardness of the LWE assumption with sub-exponential modulus-to-noise ratio. The main technical building block in their construction is a strengthening of bounded-collusion-secure secret-key functional encryption which they refer to as *mixed functional encryption* (mixed FE), and the bulk of the paper (over 60 pages) is dedicated to constructing mixed FE for branching programs.

Mixed FE. A functional encryption (FE) scheme allows us to encrypt a program f and create secret keys for inputs x, so that given an encryption of f and a key for x, we learn $f(x)$ and nothing else about f. In this work, we focus on secret-key FE schemes where encryption requires the master secret key, and security is guaranteed for an *a-priori bounded number of ciphertexts*, but an unbounded number of secret keys. A mixed FE scheme is a secret-key FE scheme with an additional "restricted" public-key encryption algorithm that enables encrypting only the "all accept" program; roughly speaking, we can obliviously sample encryptions of the "all accept" programs without knowing the master secret key.

This Work. In this work, we improve upon and extend the GKW traitor tracing scheme:

- We provide simpler and more modular constructions of mixed FE schemes based on the LWE assumption. Our constructions improve upon the GKW construction in terms of both expressiveness and security. Our first construction obtains mixed FE for all circuits and with adaptive security, whereas the prior construction [20] only achieves selective security for branching programs. Our second construction achieves selective security for all circuits with tighter overhead growth for the number of secret key ciphertexts generated.
- We provide a construction of attribute-based traitor tracing schemes for all circuits based on the LWE assumption.

1.1   Technical Overview

In the technical overview, we focus on our simpler constructions of mixed FE schemes. See Fig. 1 for a brief summary. In addition to the algorithms (Setup, SKGen, SK-Enc, Dec) in a standard secret-key FE scheme, a mixed FE scheme has an additional PK-Enc algorithm that is able to encrypt "all-1" program without knowing the master secret key.

Both of our new constructions work for any arbitrary polynomial bound t on the number of ciphertexts. The GKW construction focused on the setting

Construction	Function class	blow-up	security
[20]	NC^1	$O(t^2)$	selective
Lockable obfuscation + [18]	poly-size circuits	$O(t^4)$	adaptive
Lockable obfuscation + [4]	poly-size circuits	$O(t^2)$	selective
Key-homomorphic PCPRF	poly-size circuits	$O(t)$	selective

Fig. 1. Summary of our t-CT mixed FE schemes. PCPRF refers to private constrained PRF. Here, selective means that all t ciphertexts queries come before the (unbounded) secret key queries, whereas adaptive allows arbitrary interweaving of these queries. Note that "FULL-SIM security" in [4] correspond to selective security here (in Definition 2.2 for FULL-SIM in the paper, secret keys in the security game correspond to ciphertexts in our setting). As noted earlier, the work of [20] proved security for the case of $t = 2$ and the more general case with $O(t^2)$ blowup was only sketched.

$t = 2$ which already suffices for traitor-tracing, and provided a brief sketch for extending the construction to arbitrary t but without any analysis.[1]

We provide two constructions achieving incomparable guarantees, based on two natural and complementary approaches:

1. The first construction shows how to generically transform a t-CT secret-key functional encryption (SKFE) into a t-CT mixed FE using lockable obfuscation (a.k.a. "compute-and-compare obfuscator") [19,28], which can be based on LWE. This construction extends the coverage of mixed FE in [20] from branching programs to all circuits. It also carries over the adaptivity achieved by the underlying t-CT SKFE schemes (e.g. in [2,4,18][2]) to the final mixed FE scheme. A t-CT SKFE schemes can be constructed from any one-way function [18,27]; thus, this construction shows how to leverage lockable obfuscation to add a "restricted public-key mode" to any t-CT SKFE scheme and give us a mixed-FE scheme. The construction and proof fit in a little over a page.

2. The second construction starts from the observation that the LWE-based private-constrained PRFs in [11–13] already give a 1-CT mixed FE scheme. Furthermore, we show how to construct a t-CT mixed FE in a natural way leveraging the key-homomorphic property of the private constrained PRFs. Therefore we get a construction of t-CT mixed FE for circuits for which security follows directly from the key-homomorphic PCPRF.

---

[1] In this work we use a simulation based definition of security where t refers to the (maximum) total number of ciphertexts seen by the attacker. The work of [20] uses an indistinguishability notion of security where they refer to the number of encryption oracle queries given to the attacker in addition to the challenge ciphertext. Roughly, a t ciphertext scheme in our definition corresponds to a $t - 1$ query scheme in [20].

[2] These prior works construct 1-CT t-SK public-key FE scheme, which implies a many-CT t-SK public-key FE scheme, and therefore a many-CT, t-SK secret-key FE scheme. By flipping the ciphertexts and secret keys, we obtain a t-CT, many-SK SKFE.

The blow-up of our t-CT mixed-FE is only $O(t)$. Previously for simulation-secure secret-key FE with bounded collusion, the blow-up is at least $O(t^2)$ [2,4] (let us remark that these constructions are public-key FE schemes). We sketch this construction and proof later in the introduction, again in a little over a page.

1.2   Mixed FE from Lockable Obfuscation

Our first construction adds lockable obfuscation on top of a plain t-CT SKFE to produce the public-key ciphertext, i.e. let the public-key ciphertext be the dummy obfuscated programs that always evaluate to "$\perp$".

In more detail, we construct the mixed-FE scheme as follows:

- Setup: Choose a master secret key (msk) for the SKFE.
- SKGen(msk, x): use the SKFE msk to generate sk_x.
- SK-Enc(msk, f): sample a random "lock" α, then run the SKFE secret-key encryption for a function $H_{\alpha,f}$ which computes the following multiple-output-bit functionality

$$H_{\alpha,f}(x) = \begin{cases} \alpha & \text{if } f(x) = 0 \\ 0 & \text{else} \end{cases}.$$

  Then, produce the lockable obfuscation $\mathsf{Obf}[P_{\mathsf{FE.ct}_H}, \alpha]$ as the ciphertext, where $P_{\mathsf{FE.ct}_H}(Y)$ parses Y as a SKFE secret key and computes the SKFE decryption functionality.
- PK-Enc: Use the simulator of lockable obfuscation to get a dummy obfuscated program of appropriate size. The program outputs "$\perp$" on every input.
- Dec: Run the obfuscated program, if it outputs "$\perp$" then output 1, else output 0.

We need mixed-FE to satisfy two security conditions. First, an adversary's view given polynomially many secret keys for inputs x, and at most t (secret key) ciphertexts for functions $f_1, \ldots, f_t$ can be simulated given only the function evaluations $f_i(x)$ for all x. This property, called functional indistinguishability, follows directly from the security of the SKFE. Indeed, we do not rely on obfuscation security here. The second security property, called secret/public mode indistinguishability, says that a public-key encryption and a secret key encryption of the trivial branching program f (which outputs 1 on all inputs) are computationally indistinguishable. Furthermore, this should hold even given polynomially many SKFE keys and $t - 1$ SKFE ciphertexts for arbitrary functions. This property follows from a combination of symmetric-FE security and lockable obfuscation, by first changing the symmetric-FE ciphertext from $H_{\alpha,f}$ to the "all $\perp$" function, then changing real obfuscation to simulated using the lockable obfuscation security.

1.3   Mixed FE from Private Constrained PRFs

A constrained PRF is a standard PRF with the additional property that given a program M and a PRF key K, we can create a constrained key that allows someone to evaluate the PRF at inputs x where $M(x) = 0$ while randomizing the outputs of all other inputs. A private constrained PRF (PCPRF) satisfies the additional requirement that the constrained key hides M (in the appropriate sense). We will work with a strengthening of this requirement, which says that given M along with a sequence of inputs $\{x_i\}$ such that $M(x_i) = 1$, the joint distribution of the constrained key for M along with the PRF evaluations at $\{x_i\}$ are pseudorandom.

We show how to construct a 1-CT mixed-FE scheme starting from any PCPRF. We then show how to "boost" this basic construction to a t-CT mixed-FE, assuming that the underlying PCPRF is also key-homomorphic [5], namely for all K, K', x, we have $\mathsf{PRF}_{K+K'}(x) \approx \mathsf{PRF}_K(x) + \mathsf{PRF}_{K'}(x)$. Our schemes achieve simulation-based security, and support functions computable by polynomial-size circuits.

1-CT Scheme. We observe that a PCPRF scheme already gives a 1-CT mixed FE scheme:

- Setup: Choose a master secret key msk for the PCPRF.
- SKGen(msk, x): A secret key for x is a PRF evaluation at x;
- SK-Enc(msk, M): An encryption of a program M is a constrained key for M;
- PK-Enc: Use the simulator of the PCPRF to produce a simulated constrained key.
- Dec: To decrypt, we compare the constrained evaluation at x with the PRF evaluation at x; if they are equal, we output 0, and otherwise, we output 1.

The existing security proofs show that, if for all x_i we have $M(x_i) = 1$, then the constrained key for the program is computationally indistinguishable from a random key that is independent of the PRF evaluations. This means that we can *obliviously* sample encryptions of the "always-1" program by sampling a random ciphertext.

From 1-CT to 2-CT. We provide an almost generic transformation from a 1-CT to a 2-CT scheme, assuming that the underlying scheme is key-homomorphic, and also satisfies a natural distribution requirement. Namely, we require that for $\mathsf{msk}_1, \mathsf{msk}_2, \mathsf{msk}'$ that are correctly generated from the 1-CT mixed FE scheme, the distributions of $\mathsf{msk}_1 + \mathsf{msk}_2$, $\mathsf{msk}_1 - \mathsf{msk}_2$, and msk' are identical. In addition, for all x, we have

$$\mathsf{skGen}(\mathsf{msk}_1, x) + \mathsf{skGen}(\mathsf{msk}_2, x) = \mathsf{skGen}(\mathsf{msk}_1 + \mathsf{msk}_2, x)$$

When the 1-CT mixed FE schemes are instantiated by the PCPRFs in [11–13], they satisfy an approximate notion of key-homomorphism, which suffices for the purpose of constructing collusion resistant mixed FE. In the rest of the introduction we assume the underlying PCPRFs are exact key-homomorphic for simplicity, and leave the instantiations from the approximate ones in the main body.

Our 2-CT mixed FE scheme works as follows:

- Setup: choose λ pairs of $\mathsf{msk}_{i,b}$ as the master secret keys for the 1-CT scheme;
- SKGen(msk, x): The secret key for x runs the secret-key generation algorithm for the 1-CT scheme over all the λ pairs of $\mathsf{msk}_{i,b}$, outputs $\{\mathsf{skGen}(\mathsf{msk}_{i,b}, x)\}_{i \in [\lambda], b \in \{0,1\}}$;
- SK-Enc(msk, M): To encrypt a program M, we pick a random $\mathbf{z} \in \{0,1\}^{\lambda}$, output $\mathbf{z}$ and the 1-CT encryption SK-Enc($\mathsf{msk}_{\mathbf{z}}, M$) as the ciphertext, where $\mathsf{msk}_{\mathbf{z}} := \mathsf{msk}_{1,z_1} + \cdots + \mathsf{msk}_{\lambda,z_\lambda}$;
- PK-Enc: pick a random $\mathbf{z} \in \{0,1\}^{\lambda}$, then run the PK-Enc mode of the 1-CT scheme.
- Dec: To decrypt, first derive $\mathsf{skGen}(\mathsf{msk}_{\mathbf{z}}, x) = \sum_{i=1}^{\lambda} \mathsf{skGen}(\mathsf{msk}_{i,z_i}, x)$ and then run the 1-CT decryption algorithm.

Next, we sketch a proof of security by constructing a simulator for the 2-CT scheme, starting from that for the 1-CT scheme. Suppose we want to simulate encryptions of two programs M^1, M^2 under tags $\mathbf{z}^1, \mathbf{z}^2$. The only property we need from $\mathbf{z}^1, \mathbf{z}^2$ is that they differ in one bit position, which happens with probability $1 - 2^{-\lambda}$. For notational simplicity, assume that

$$\mathbf{z}^1 = 00\cdots0, \mathbf{z}^2 = 10\cdots0$$

Now, using the simulator for the 1-CT scheme (and a hybrid argument), we can simulate the 1-CT encryptions SK-Enc($\widetilde{\mathsf{msk}}_1, M^1$), SK-Enc($\widetilde{\mathsf{msk}}_2, M^2$) for two random $\widetilde{\mathsf{msk}}_1, \widetilde{\mathsf{msk}}_2$, along with $\mathsf{skGen}(\widetilde{\mathsf{msk}}_1, x)$ and $\mathsf{skGen}(\widetilde{\mathsf{msk}}_2, x)$ for arbitrarily many x's.

To construct a simulator for the 2-CT scheme, we follow the natural simulation strategy where we pick $\mathsf{msk}_{i,b}$ and program

$$\mathsf{msk}_{\mathbf{z}^1} = \widetilde{\mathsf{msk}}_1, \mathsf{msk}_{\mathbf{z}^2} = \widetilde{\mathsf{msk}}_2$$

as follows:

- We sample $(\mathsf{msk}_{i,0}, \mathsf{msk}_{i,1}), i = 2, \ldots, \lambda$ ourselves;
- We implicitly program

$$\mathsf{msk}_{1,0} = \widetilde{\mathsf{msk}}_1 - \sum_{i=2}^{\lambda} \mathsf{msk}_{i,0}, \mathsf{msk}_{1,1} = \widetilde{\mathsf{msk}}_2 - \sum_{i=2}^{\lambda} \mathsf{msk}_{i,0}$$

Simulating the ciphertexts is straight-forward. To simulate a key $\{\mathsf{skGen}(\mathsf{msk}_{i,b}, x)\}$ for x,

- We can compute $\mathsf{skGen}(\mathsf{msk}_{i,0}, x), \mathsf{skGen}(\mathsf{msk}_{i,1}, x), i = 2, \ldots, \lambda$ ourselves since we know $\mathsf{msk}_{i,0}, \mathsf{msk}_{i,1}$;

– We can compute $\mathsf{skGen}(\mathsf{msk}_{1,0}, x)$ using the key-homomorphic property via

$$\mathsf{skGen}(\mathsf{msk}_{1,0}, x) = \mathsf{skGen}(\widetilde{\mathsf{msk}}_1, x) - \sum_{i=2}^{\lambda} \mathsf{skGen}(\mathsf{msk}_{i,0}, x)$$

We can similarly compute $\mathsf{skGen}(\mathsf{msk}_{1,1}, x)$.

From 2-CT to t-CT. To obtain a scheme that is secure for t ciphertexts, we follow [20, Remark 8.1] and sample each entry of the tag $\mathbf{z}$ from a larger alphabet. The natural extension of the previous argument is to require that with high probability over $\mathbf{z}^{(1)}, \ldots, \mathbf{z}^{(t)}$, there exists $j^* \in [\lambda]$ such that $z_{j^*}^{(1)}, \ldots, z_{j^*}^{(t)}$ are all distinct. This would require an alphabet of size $\Omega(t^2)$. Instead, we observe that it suffices that there exists $j_1^*, \ldots, j_t^* \in [\lambda]$ such that the t pairs $(j_1^*, z_{j_1^*}^{(1)}), \ldots, (j_t^*, z_{j_t^*}^{(t)})$ are distinct (the natural extension corresponds to the special case $j_1^* = \cdots = j_t^* = j^*$); this relaxation allows us to work with an alphabet of size $O(t)$. In the security proof, we will receive ciphertexts and secret keys corresponding to t independent $\widetilde{\mathsf{msk}}_1, \ldots, \widetilde{\mathsf{msk}}_t$, which we "embed" into $\mathsf{msk}_{j_1^*, z_{j_1^*}^{(1)}}, \ldots, \mathsf{msk}_{j_t^*, z_{j_t^*}^{(t)}}$.

We proceed to describe our construction in a bit more detail. We replace λ pairs of master secret keys $\{\mathsf{msk}_{j,d}\}_{j \in [\lambda], d \in \{0,1\}}$ (in the 2-CT scheme) with λ many $(2t-2)$-tuples of $\{\mathsf{msk}_{j,d}\}_{j \in [\lambda], d \in [2t-2]}$, and sample the tag $\mathbf{z}$ from $[2t-2]^\lambda$. For each tag $\mathbf{z}^{(i)}$, $i \in [t]$, the probability that the jth coordinate of $\mathbf{z}^{(i)}$ does not show up in the other $t-1$ tags is $\geq \frac{(2t-2)-(t-1)}{2t-2} = \frac{1}{2}$, therefore the probability that one of the coordinate of $\mathbf{z}^{(i)}$ is unique is at least $1 - 2^{-\lambda}$ (this unique coordinate corresponds to j_i^*). By a union bound, with probability at least $1 - t \cdot 2^{-\lambda}$, all the tags has one unique coordinate.

1.4 Attribute-Based Traitor Tracing

Finally, we very briefly describe our results on attribute-based traitor tracing. An attribute-based traitor-tracing (AB-TT) scheme is like an ABE with tracing capabilities. The key generation algorithm gives out secret keys $\mathsf{sk}_{f,i}$ for functions f with respect to some identity i. The encryption procedure encrypts a message m with respect to an attribute x and the resulting ciphertext can be correctly decrypted by $\mathsf{sk}_{f,i}$ if $f(x) = 1$. The identity i is completely irrelevant from the point of view of ABE correctness/security. The tracing algorithm is given a decoder D which is able to distinguish between the encryptions of some two messages m_0, m_1 with respect to some attribute x. The goal is to recover some traitor i whose key $\mathsf{sk}_{f,i}$ was used in the creation of the decoder *and* who is qualified to decrypt meaning that $f(x) = 1$. Note that there may be many other traitors that participate in the creation of the decoder and who are not qualified to decrypt (e.g., have keys $\mathsf{sk}_{g,j}$ for some g such that $g(x) = 0$) but the tracing algorithm must find a traitor who is qualified to decrypt.

We argue that catching a qualified user is the correct definition for tracing. For example, imagine that a system is setup such that for a certain attribute x corresponds to extremely sensitive information that only highly positioned individuals can access. By the ABE security properties, if a decoder D were discovered that could decrypt such ciphertexts it must be the case that such a highly positioned user contributed to it. It would be rather unsatisfying if a tracing algorithm were only able to finger a lower level individual that contributed to it. We note that such tracing definitions were considered in prior works [1, 21–23], however, any black box tracing in such works required a $\sqrt{n}$ factor of ciphertext blowup for n users which was inherited from [7, 8]. We improve this to $\mathsf{polylog}(n)$, by constructing AB-TT from attribute-based mixed FE, which can be obtained from ABE and mixed-FE for all polynomial-time computations. For more details, we refer the reader to Sect. 5.

Additional Related Work on Tracing. Our work and comparisons focus on tracing schemes that are collusion resistant. Starting with [14] there existed many cryptosystems that would be collusion resistant up to t corrupted users where t was some parameter of system setup. See [3] and the references therein for further discussion of collusion bounded systems. Boneh, Sahai and Waters [7] gave the first collusion resistant tracing schemes with ciphertext size that was sublinear in the number of users n. They achieved ciphertext growth proportional to $\sqrt{n}$ using composite order bilinear groups. Later variants [8, 15, 16] achieved similar ciphertext size under improved bilinear assumptions. Several years later Boneh and Zhandry [9] utilized indistinguishability obfuscation to achieve the ideal case where ciphertexts grow polynomially in $\log(n)$ and λ. However, indistinguishability obfuscation is not known from standard assumptions.

2   Preliminaries

Notations and Terminology. In cryptography, the security parameter (denoted as λ) is a variable that is used to parameterize the computational complexity of the cryptographic algorithm or protocol, and the adversary's probability of breaking security. An algorithm is "efficient" if it runs in (probabilistic) polynomial time over λ.

When a variable v is drawn randomly from the set S we denote as $v \xleftarrow{\$} S$ or $v \leftarrow U(S)$, sometimes abbreviated as v when the context is clear. We use $\approx_s$ and $\approx_c$ as the abbreviation for statistically close and computationally indistinguishable.

Let $\mathbb{R}, \mathbb{Z}, \mathbb{N}$ be the set of real numbers, integers and positive integers. Denote $\mathbb{Z}/(q\mathbb{Z})$ by $\mathbb{Z}_q$. For $n \in \mathbb{N}$, $[n] := \{1, ..., n\}$. A vector in $\mathbb{R}^n$ (represented in column form by default) is written as a bold lower-case letter, e.g. $\mathbf{v}$. For a vector $\mathbf{v}$, the ith component of $\mathbf{v}$ will be denoted by v_i. A matrix is written as a bold capital letter, e.g. $\mathbf{A}$. The ith column vector of $\mathbf{A}$ is denoted $\mathbf{a}_i$. The length of a vector is the ℓ_p-norm $\|\mathbf{v}\|_p = (\sum v_i^p)^{1/p}$. The length of a matrix is the norm of its longest column: $\|\mathbf{A}\|_p = \max_i \|\mathbf{a}_i\|_p$. By default we use ℓ_2-norm unless explicitly mentioned. When a vector or matrix is called "small", we refer to its norm.

2.1   Learning with Errors

We recall the learning with errors problem.

Definition 2.1 (Decisional learning with errors (LWE) [26]**).** *For $n, m \in \mathbb{N}$ and modulus $q \geq 2$, distributions for secret vectors, public matrices, and error vectors $\theta, \pi, \chi \subseteq \mathbb{Z}_q$. An LWE sample is obtained from sampling $\mathbf{s} \leftarrow \theta^n$, $\mathbf{A} \leftarrow \pi^{n \times m}$, $\mathbf{e} \leftarrow \chi^m$, and outputting $(\mathbf{A}, \mathbf{s}^T \mathbf{A} + \mathbf{e}^T \mod q)$.*

We say that an algorithm solves $\mathsf{LWE}_{n,m,q,\theta,\pi,\chi}$ if it distinguishes the LWE sample from a random sample distributed as $\pi^{n \times m} \times U(\mathbb{Z}_q^{1 \times m})$ with probability bigger than $1/2$ plus non-negligible.

Lemma 2.2 (Standard form [10,24–26]**).** *Given $n \in \mathbb{N}$, for any $m = \mathrm{poly}(n)$, $q \leq 2^{\mathrm{poly}(n)}$. Let $\theta = \pi = U(\mathbb{Z}_q)$, $\chi = D_{\mathbb{Z},\sigma}$ where $\sigma \geq 2\sqrt{n}$. If there exists an efficient (possibly quantum) algorithm that breaks $\mathsf{LWE}_{n,m,q,\theta,\pi,\chi}$, then there exists an efficient (possibly quantum) algorithm for approximating SIVP and GapSVP in the ℓ_2 norm, in the worst case, to within $\tilde{O}(nq/\sigma)$ factors.*

We drop the subscripts of LWE when referring to standard form of LWE with the parameters specified in Lemma 2.2.

2.2   Secret-Key and Mixed Functional Encryption

t-CT SKFE. We begin with the definition for SKFE:

Definition 2.3 (Secret-key functional encryption (SKFE)). *A secret-key functional encryption scheme for a class of functions $\mathcal{F}_\mu = \{f : \{0,1\}^\mu \to \{0,1\}\}$ is a tuple of probabilistic polynomial time (p.p.t) algorithms (Setup, skGen, skEnc, Dec) such that:*

- *Setup(1^λ) takes as input the security parameter 1^λ, and outputs the master secret key msk and the public parameters pp.*
- *skGen(msk, m) takes as input msk and a message $m \in \{0,1\}^\mu$, and outputs a decryption key sk_m.*
- *skEnc(msk, f) takes as input msk and a function $f \in \mathcal{F}_\mu$, and outputs a ciphertext ct.*
- *Dec(sk_m, ct) takes as input sk_m and ct, and outputs a single bit.*

Correctness. For every message $m \in \{0,1\}^\mu$ and function $f \in \mathcal{F}_\mu$ we have:

$$\Pr[\mathsf{msk} \leftarrow \mathsf{Setup}(1^\lambda);\ \mathsf{sk}_m \leftarrow \mathsf{skGen}(\mathsf{msk}, m) :$$
$$\mathsf{Dec}(\mathsf{sk}_m, \mathsf{skEnc}(\mathsf{msk}, f)) = f(m)] = 1 - \mathrm{negl}(\lambda),$$

where the probability is taken over the randomness of the algorithms Setup, skGen, skEnc, Dec.

Function-Hiding Security. For all p.p.t stateful algorithms Adv, there is a p.p.t. stateful algorithm Sim such that:

$$\left\{ \text{Experiment REAL}_{\mathsf{Adv}}(1^\lambda) \right\}_{\lambda \in \mathbb{N}} \approx_c \left\{ \text{Experiment IDEAL}_{\mathsf{Adv},\mathsf{Sim}}(1^\lambda) \right\}_{\lambda \in \mathbb{N}}$$

where the real and ideal experiments of stateful algorithms Adv, Sim are as follows:

Experiment $\text{REAL}_{\text{Adv}}(1^\lambda)$

$\text{msk} \leftarrow \text{Gen}(1^\lambda)$,

For $i \in [t]$:

$\text{Adv} \rightarrow f^{[i]}$;

  $\text{Adv} \leftarrow \text{ct}^{[i]} = \text{skEnc}(\text{pp}, \text{msk}, f^{[i]})$;

Repeat polynomially many times:

  $\text{Adv} \rightarrow m$; $\text{Adv} \leftarrow \text{skGen}(\text{pp}, \text{msk}, m)$

$\text{Adv} \rightarrow b$; Output b

Experiment $\text{IDEAL}_{\text{Adv}, \text{Sim}}(1^\lambda)$

$\text{Sim} \leftarrow 1^\lambda$

For $i \in [t]$:

$\text{Adv} \rightarrow f^{[i]}$;

  $\text{Adv} \leftarrow \text{ct}^{[i]} = \text{Sim}(1^{|f^{[i]}|})$;

Repeat polynomially many times:

  $\text{Adv} \rightarrow m$; $\text{Adv} \leftarrow \text{Sim}(m, \{f^{[i]}(m)\}_{i \in [t]})$

$\text{Adv} \rightarrow b$; Output b

In the experiments, the adversary Adv can ask for t ciphertexts followed by polynomially many decryption key queries. Once Adv makes a ciphertext query for a function $f \in \mathcal{F}_\lambda$, in the real experiment Adv obtains the ciphertext generated by the secret-key encryption algorithm; in the ideal experiment Adv obtains the ciphertext generated by Sim given only the (circuit) size of f. Once Adv makes a message query m, in the real experiment Adv obtains sk_m from the decryption key generation algorithm; in the ideal experiment, Adv obtains the decryption key generated by the simulator who is given m, and $\{f^{[i]}(m)\}_{i \in [t]}$. The output of the experiment is the final output bit of Adv.

Remark 2.4 (adaptive security). A t-CT SKFE scheme is called adaptively secure if the function and ciphertext queries can be made adaptively in any order. Some constructions achieve partially adaptive security and we will explicitly mention the restrictions.

t-CT Mixed FE. We provide a simulation-based definition for t-ciphertext (t-CT) mixed-FE, which is same as the definition in [20, Sect. 5] where it is referred to as $(t - 1)$-bounded mixed-FE.

Definition 2.5 (Mixed functional encryption). *A mixed functional encryption scheme for a class of functions $\mathcal{F}_\mu = \{f : \{0, 1\}^\mu \rightarrow \{0, 1\}\}$ is a tuple of probabilistic polynomial time (p.p.t) algorithms* (Setup, skGen, skEnc, Dec, pkEnc) *such that:*

- (Setup, skGen, skEnc, Dec) *are the same as SKFE.*
- pkEnc(pp) *takes as input* pp, *and outputs a ciphertext* ct.

Correctness and Function-Hiding Security. *Same as SKFE.*

Public/Secret-Key Mode Indistinguishability. *In addition to the security requirement above for a normal secret-key functional encryption, a mixed-FE further requires that for a function f queried to the encryption oracle, if for all message m queried by the adversary, $f(m) = 1$ (the other potential $t - 1$ functions does not have to satisfy this requirement), then the secret-key ciphertext* skEnc(msk, f) *is indistinguishable from a sample from* pkEnc(pp). *Formally, we* *require that for all p.p.t stateful algorithms* Adv, *the following two experiments produce indistinguishable outputs:*

$$\left\{ \text{Experiment } SKEXP_{\mathsf{Adv}}(1^\lambda) \right\}_{\lambda \in \mathbb{N}} \approx_c \left\{ \text{Experiment } PKEXP_{\mathsf{Adv}}(1^\lambda) \right\}_{\lambda \in \mathbb{N}}$$

The experiments are as follows:

Experiment $SKEXP_{\mathsf{Adv}}(1^\lambda)$	Experiment $PKEXP_{\mathsf{Adv}}(1^\lambda)$
$\mathsf{pp}, \mathsf{msk} \leftarrow \mathsf{Gen}(1^\lambda),$	$\mathsf{pp}, \mathsf{msk} \leftarrow \mathsf{Gen}(1^\lambda),$
For i in $[i^* - 1]$:	*For i in $[i^* - 1]$:*
$\mathsf{Adv} \rightarrow f^{[i]};$	$\mathsf{Adv} \rightarrow f^{[i]};$
$\mathsf{Adv} \leftarrow \mathsf{ct}^{[i]} = \mathsf{skEnc}(\mathsf{msk}, f^{[i]});$	$\mathsf{Adv} \leftarrow \mathsf{ct}^{[i]} = \mathsf{skEnc}(\mathsf{msk}, f^{[i]});$
$\mathsf{Adv} \rightarrow f^{[i^*]};$	$\mathsf{Adv} \rightarrow f^{[i^*]};$
$\mathsf{Adv} \leftarrow \mathsf{ct}^{[i^*]} = \mathsf{skEnc}(\mathsf{msk}, f^{[i^*]});$	$\mathsf{Adv} \leftarrow \mathsf{ct}^{[i^*]} = \mathsf{pkEnc}(\mathsf{pp});$
For i in $[i^* + 1, t]$:	*For i in $[i^* + 1, t]$:*
$\mathsf{Adv} \rightarrow f^{[i]};$	$\mathsf{Adv} \rightarrow f^{[i]};$
$\mathsf{Adv} \leftarrow \mathsf{ct}^{[i]} = \mathsf{skEnc}(\mathsf{msk}, f^{[i]});$	$\mathsf{Adv} \leftarrow \mathsf{ct}^{[i]} = \mathsf{skEnc}(\mathsf{msk}, f^{[i]});$
Repeat polynomially many times:	*Repeat polynomially many times:*
$\mathsf{Adv} \rightarrow m; \ \mathsf{Adv} \leftarrow \mathsf{skGen}(\mathsf{msk}, m)$	$\mathsf{Adv} \rightarrow m; \ \mathsf{Adv} \leftarrow \mathsf{skGen}(\mathsf{msk}, m)$
$\mathsf{Adv} \rightarrow b; \ \textit{Output } b$	$\mathsf{Adv} \rightarrow b; \ \textit{Output } b$

Remark 2.6 (comparison with [20]). What we call a t-CT mixed FE is referred as a $(t - 1)$-query mixed FE in [20]. In the latter, security is formalized using a indistinguishability-based paradigm. For the public/secret-key mode indistinguishability, they require that the two ciphertexts are indistinguishable given honestly generated secret keys from skGen.

3 t-CT Mixed-FE from Lockable Obfuscation and t-CT SKFE

In this section, we present a construction of t-ciphertext mixed-FE for the class of all poly-time computable functions from any lockable obfuscation for all poly-time computable functions and t-ciphertext secret key functional encryption for all poly-time computable functions. Thus, our construction shows how to use lockable obfuscation to generically add a public-key oblivious sampling mode to a SKFE.

3.1 Lockable Obfuscation

Recall the definition of lockable obfuscation from [19,28].

Definition 3.1 (Lockable (or compute-and-compare) obfuscation).
Consider a family of functions $\mathcal{F} = \{\mathcal{F}_\lambda\}_{\lambda \in \mathbb{N}}$ *where* $\mathcal{F}_\lambda = \{f : \{0,1\}^{\ell(\lambda)} \rightarrow \{0,1\}^{\nu(\lambda)}\}$, $\nu(\lambda) = \omega(\log \lambda)$. *A lockable obfuscator takes a function* $f \in \mathcal{F}$ *and a target* $\alpha \in \{0,1\}^\nu$, *outputs an obfuscated program* $\mathsf{Obf}[f, \alpha]$ *which satisfies the following properties:*

Functionality. $\mathsf{Obf}[f, \alpha]$ *takes an input* $x \in \{0,1\}^\ell$, *output 1 if* $f(x) = \alpha$; $\perp$ *otherwise.*

Virtual Black-Box Security. *A lockable obfuscator is said to satisfy virtual black-box security if there is a p.p.t. simulator* S *such that for all* $f \in \mathcal{F}$,

$$\mathsf{Obf}[f, \alpha] \approx_c S(1^\lambda, 1^{|f|})$$

over $\alpha \xleftarrow{\$} \{0,1\}^\nu$ *and the randomness of the obfuscator and* S.

3.2 The Mixed-FE Construction

Construction 3.2. *Given a t-CT SKFE* $\mathsf{FE} = (\mathsf{FE.Gen}, \mathsf{FE.skGen}, \mathsf{FE.skEnc}, \mathsf{FE.Dec})$ *and a lockable obfuscator* Obf, *construct a t-CT mixed-FE as follows.*

- $\mathsf{Setup}(1^\lambda)$ *runs* $\mathsf{FE.msk} \leftarrow \mathsf{FE.Gen}(1^\lambda)$, *and treat it as the master secret key.*
- $\mathsf{skGen}(\mathsf{msk}, x)$ *outputs* $\mathsf{FE.sk}_x \leftarrow \mathsf{FE.skGen}(\mathsf{FE.msk}, x)$.
- $\mathsf{pkEnc}(\mathsf{pp})$ *outputs the simulated code for the lockable obfuscation* $\mathsf{Obf}.S(1^\lambda, 1^{\mathrm{poly}(|f|)})$.
- $\mathsf{skEnc}(\mathsf{msk}, f)$ *samples a random string* $\alpha \leftarrow \{0,1\}^\lambda$, *runs* $\mathsf{FE.ct}_H \leftarrow \mathsf{FE.skEnc}(\mathsf{msk}, H_{\alpha,f})$ *where* $H_{\alpha,f}$ *computes the following multiple-output-bit functionality*

$$H_{\alpha,f}(x) = \begin{cases} \alpha & \text{if } f(x) = 0 \\ 0 & \text{else} \end{cases}.$$

  Then, produce the lockable obfuscation $\mathsf{Obf}[P_{\mathsf{FE.ct}_H}, \alpha]$ *as the ciphertext, where* $P_{\mathsf{FE.ct}_H}(Y)$ *computes* $\mathsf{FE.Dec}(\mathsf{FE.ct}_H, Y)$.
- $\mathsf{Dec}(\mathsf{sk}_x, \mathsf{ct})$ *parses* sk_x *as* $\mathsf{FE.sk}_x$, *and* ct *as* $\mathsf{Obf}[P_{\mathsf{FE.ct}_H}, \alpha]$, *outputs* $\mathsf{Obf}[P_{\mathsf{FE.ct}_H}, \alpha](\mathsf{FE.sk}_x)$.

3.3 The Security Analysis

Theorem 3.3. *Construction 3.2 is a t-CT mixed-FE assuming the underlying obfuscator* Obf *is a lockable obfuscation and* FE *is a t-CT secure secret-key FE.*

The only additional property (compared to a normal SKFE) is the indistinguishability of the public-key and the secret-key ciphertext for a function f s.t. for all x queried in the game, $f(x) = 1$. The intuition is that in that case, the α in the SKFE ciphertexts is hidden following the plain SKFE security. Therefore the α in the lockable obfuscation target is random and independent, and we can trigger the simulation security of the lockable obfuscation.

Proof. We prove the indistinguishability of the public and secret-key modes.

Consider the following intermediate distribution for the t-CT mixed-FE experiment. Once Adv makes a ciphertext query for a function $f^{(i)} \in \mathcal{F}_\lambda$, $i \in [t]$, the challenger responds by sampling a random string $\alpha^{(i)} \leftarrow \{0,1\}^\lambda$, runs $\mathsf{FE.ct}_H \leftarrow \mathsf{FE.Sim}(1^{\mathrm{poly}\,|H_{f^{(i)}}|})$. Then produces the lockable obfuscation $\mathsf{Obf}[P_{\mathsf{FE.ct}_H}, \alpha^{(i)}]$ as the ciphertext, where $P_{\mathsf{FE.ct}_H}(Y)$ computes $\mathsf{FE.Dec}(\mathsf{FE.ct}_H, Y)$. Once Adv makes a message query m, the challenger responds with a decryption key $\mathsf{FE.sk}_m \leftarrow \mathsf{FE.Sim}(m, \{1^{(i)}\}_{i \in [t]})$.

So if there is an adversary that distinguishes the real distribution and the intermediate distribution, then there is an adversary that breaks the simulation security for the t-CT SKFE. If there is an adversary that distinguishes the intermediate distribution from the public key mode, then we build an adversary that breaks the lockable obfuscation, due to the fact that the $P_{\mathsf{FE.ct}_H}$ in the intermediate distribution does not depend on $\alpha^{(i)}$.

4 t-CT Mixed-FE from Key-Homomorphic Private Constrained PRF

In this section we present a construction of mixed-FE from key-homomorphic PCPRF.

4.1   Background of Key-Homomorphic Private Constrained PRFs

We first give the definition of a key-homomorphic private constrained PRF, which literally combines key-homomorphism [5] with private constrained PRFs [6,12]. For the purpose of this paper we work with the KHPCPRFs that satisfy the simulation-based definition given one constrained key and many input queries. We then explain that the PCPRF constructions in [11–13] satisfy an approximate version of key-homomorphism, which suffices for constructing mixed-FE.

Definition 4.1 (Key-homomorphic   private   constrained   PRF (KHPCPRF)). *Consider a family of functions $\mathcal{F} = \{\mathcal{F}_\lambda\}_{\lambda \in \mathbb{N}}$ where $\mathcal{F}_\lambda = \{F_k : D_\lambda \to R_\lambda\}$, along with a tuple of efficient functions (ppGen, skGen, Constrain, Eval, Constrain.Eval). For a constraint family $\mathcal{C} = \{\mathcal{C}_\lambda = \{C : D_\lambda \to \{0,1\}\}\}_{\lambda \in \mathbb{N}}$,*

- *The public parameter generation algorithm $\mathsf{ppGen}(1^\lambda, \mathcal{F}_\lambda)$ takes the security parameter λ and the description of the constraint class $\mathcal{F}_\lambda$, generates the public parameter pp.*
- *The secret key generation algorithm $\mathsf{skGen}(1^\lambda, \mathsf{pp})$ takes the security parameter λ, and the public parameter pp, generates the secret key sk.*
- *The evaluation algorithm $\mathsf{Eval}(\mathsf{sk}, x)$ takes sk, an input x, outputs $F_{\mathsf{sk}}(x)$.*
- *The constraining algorithm $\mathsf{Constrain}(1^\lambda, \mathsf{pp}, \mathsf{sk}, C)$ takes sk, a constraint $C \in \mathcal{C}_\lambda$, outputs the constrained key ck_C.*

– *The constrained evaluation algorithm* Constrain.Eval(ck_C, x) *takes a constrained key* ck_C, *an input* x, *outputs* $F_{ck_C}(x)$.

$\mathcal{F}$ *is called a family of* key-homomorphic private constrained PRF *for* $\mathcal{C}$ *if it satisfies the following properties:*
Functionality preservation for $C(x) = 0$. *For any constraint* $C \in \mathcal{C}_\lambda$, *any input* $x \in D_\lambda$ *s.t.* $C(x) = 0$,

$$\Pr[\mathsf{Eval}(sk, x) = \mathsf{Constrain.Eval}(ck_C, x)] \geq 1 - \mathrm{negl}(\lambda),$$

where the probability is taken over the randomness in algorithms ppGen, skGen *and* Constrain.

Pseudorandomness and Constraint-Hiding. *For any polynomial time algorithm* Adv, *there is a polynomial time algorithm* Sim *such that:*

$$\left\{ Experiment\ REAL_{\mathsf{Adv}}(1^\lambda) \right\}_{\lambda \in \mathbb{N}} \approx_c \left\{ Experiment\ IDEAL_{\mathsf{Adv},\mathsf{Sim}}(1^\lambda) \right\}_{\lambda \in \mathbb{N}}.$$

where the ideal and real experiments are defined as follows. In the experiments the adversary can ask a single constraint query followed by polynomially many input queries. Once Adv *makes the constraint query* $C \in \mathcal{C}_\lambda$, *in the real experiment* Adv *obtains the constrained key generated by the constraining algorithm; in the ideal experiment* Adv *obtains a key generated by* Sim, *whereas* Sim *is given only the size of* C. *Once* Adv *makes an input query* x, Adv *is expected to provide a bit* d_x *indicating the value of* $C(x)$. *In the real experiment* Adv *obtains the unconstrained function value at* x. *In the ideal experiment* Sim *learns the indicator bit* d_x; *if* $d_x = 0$ *then* Adv *gets a value generated by* Sim, *and if* $d_x = 1$ *then* Adv *obtains a random value from the range* R *of the function. The output of the experiment is the final output bit of* Adv.

$Experiment\ REAL_{\mathsf{Adv}}(1^\lambda)$	$Experiment\ IDEAL_{\mathsf{Adv},\mathsf{Sim}}(1^\lambda)$
pp $\leftarrow$ ppGen(1^λ),	Sim $\leftarrow 1^\lambda$
sk $\leftarrow$ skGen(1^λ, pp),	Sim $\leftarrow 1^\lambda$
Adv $\rightarrow C$;	Adv $\rightarrow C$;
Adv $\leftarrow$ Constrain(pp, sk, C)	Adv $\leftarrow$ Sim($1^{|C|}$)
Repeat :	*Repeat* :
Adv $\rightarrow x$; $y = $ Eval(sk, x)	Adv $\rightarrow x$; $y = $ Sim(x, d_x)
Adv $\leftarrow y$	if $d_x = 1$ then $y = U(R)$; Adv $\leftarrow y$
Adv $\rightarrow b$; *Output* b	Adv $\rightarrow b$; *Output* b

Key-Homomorphism for the SK. *Let* $\circ$ *denote the group operation. For* pp $\leftarrow$ ppGen($1^\lambda, \mathcal{F}_\lambda$), $sk_1, sk_2 \leftarrow$ skGen(1^λ, pp), *and any input* $x \in D_\lambda$.

$$\Pr[\mathsf{Eval}(sk_1 \circ sk_2, x) = \mathsf{Eval}(sk_1, x) \circ \mathsf{Eval}(sk_2, x)] \geq 1 - \mathrm{negl}(\lambda).$$

The Distribution Requirement on the Secret Keys. Let $\circ$ denote the group operation. We additionally require that for $\mathsf{pp} \leftarrow \mathsf{ppGen}(1^\lambda, \mathcal{F}_\lambda)$, for $\mathsf{sk}_1, \mathsf{sk}_2, \mathsf{sk}'$ sampled from $\mathsf{skGen}(1^\lambda, \mathsf{pp})$ with independent randomness, $\mathsf{sk}_1 \circ \mathsf{sk}_2$, $\mathsf{sk}_1 \circ (-\mathsf{sk}_2)$, and sk' are from the same distribution.

Almost Key-Homomorphic PCPRF and the LWE-Based Constructions. The existing LWE-based PCPRFs satisfies the notion of almost-key-homomorphism. For simplicity we focus on the case where the range of the PRF is $\mathbb{Z}_p^n$ for $n, p \in \mathbb{N}$, and let the operation be $+$, which is what the LWE-based PCPRFs work with.

Definition 4.2 (Almost-Key-Homomorphism). *For $B, p, n \in \mathbb{N}$ such that $B < p$. Let $+$ be the group operation. A family of PRFs $\mathcal{F} = \{\mathcal{F}_\lambda\}_{\lambda \in \mathbb{N}}$ with domain D_λ and range $\mathbb{Z}_p^n$ is called B-almost-key-homomorphic if for $\mathsf{pp} \leftarrow \mathsf{ppGen}(1^\lambda, \mathcal{F}_\lambda)$, $\mathsf{sk}_1, \mathsf{sk}_2 \leftarrow \mathsf{skGen}(1^\lambda, \mathsf{pp})$, and any input $x \in D_\lambda$.*

$$\|\mathsf{Eval}(\mathsf{sk}_1, x) + \mathsf{Eval}(\mathsf{sk}_2, x) - \mathsf{Eval}(\mathsf{sk}_1 \circ \mathsf{sk}_2, x)\|_\infty \leq B$$

Next we briefly explain how to set the parameters for the existing lattice-based PCPRFs to achieve almost-key-homomorphism.

Let $q > p \geq 2$ be the moduli. In all the LWE-based PCPRF constructions, the evaluation algorithms first work entirely over $\mathbb{Z}_q^n$, then finalize by applying a (coordinate-wise) rounding operation $\lfloor a \rceil_p : \mathbb{Z}_q \to \mathbb{Z}_p$ by multiplying a by p/q and rounding the result to the nearest integer. For any $a, b \in \mathbb{Z}_q$, we have

$$| \lfloor a \rceil_p + \lfloor b \rceil_p - \lfloor a + b \rceil_p | \leq 1$$

For the two PCPRF constructions [12,13] for branching programs from the GGH15 approach [17]. Let h be the length of the branching program (i.e. the number of indexes), ℓ be the bit-length of the input, and π be the index-to-input mapping. Recall that the (secret-key) evaluation algorithm takes as input a sequence of matrices $\{\mathbf{S}_{i,b} \in Z_q^{n \times n}\}_{i \in [h], b}$ and a vector $\mathbf{a}$ sampled uniformly random from $\mathbb{Z}_q^n$, computes the output on $x \in \{0,1\}^\ell$ as

$$\mathbf{y} = \left\lfloor \prod_{i \in [h]} \mathbf{S}_{i, x_{\pi(i)}} \cdot \mathbf{a} \right\rceil_p$$

By treating $\mathbf{a}$ as the secret key, the matrices in $\{\mathbf{S}_{i,b} \in Z_q^{n \times n}\}_{i \in [h], b}$ as the public parameters (which is explicit proved in [13] and generalizable to the setting in [12]), we have 1-almost-key-homomorphism since for all $x \in \{0,1\}^\ell$,

$$\left\lfloor \prod_{i \in [h]} \mathbf{S}_{i, x_{\pi(i)}} \cdot \mathbf{a}_1 \right\rceil_p + \left\lfloor \prod_{i \in [h]} \mathbf{S}_{i, x_{\pi(i)}} \cdot \mathbf{a}_2 \right\rceil_p \in \left\lfloor \prod_{i \in [h]} \mathbf{S}_{i, x_{\pi(i)}} \cdot (\mathbf{a}_1 + \mathbf{a}_2) \right\rceil_p + \{-1, 0, 1\}$$

So setting p to be a bit larger than the appropriated number of key addition suffices for achieving a meaningful key-homomorphism. The distribution property holds since the secret key is sampled uniformly random from $\mathbb{Z}_q^n$.

For the PCPRF constructions for all poly-size circuits in [11], the first construction [11, Sect. 4] satisfies almost-key homomorphism and the distribution requirement. Very briefly, the construction uses a secret key $\mathbf{s}$ sampled uniformly random from $\mathbb{Z}_q^n$, and a set of matrices in the public parameter pp. The evaluator takes an input x and pp, derives a matrix $\mathsf{pp}(x)$ which is independent of the secret key, then computes $\lfloor \mathbf{s}^T \cdot \mathsf{pp}(x) \rceil_p$. The approximate-key homomorphism and the distribution property follow immediately.

Remark 4.3. One can also define key-homomorphism for the constrained keys in the natural way, although it is not used in this paper. Let us remark that the constrained keys of the PCPRFs from [12,13] are also key-homomorphic.

4.2 Constructing t-CT Mixed-FE from KHPCPRF

Next we construct a t-CT secure mixed-FE from key-homomorphic PCPRF. The construction achieves t-CT security with a $O(t)$ blow-up in the size of the functional decryption key, which is smaller than the other existing secret-key functional encryptions with bounded collusion.

We first describe the construction of a mixed-FE from a PCPRF with exact key-homomorphism, then explain how to modify the construction and security analysis slightly to work with the LWE-based almost-key-homomorphic PCPRFs.

Let us remark that the construction and security analysis for a 1-CT secure mixed-FE from PCPRF (even without key-homomorphism) is implicit in [12, Sect. 6] and is explained in the introduction. So we deal with the case of $2 \leq t \leq \mathrm{poly}(\lambda)$ directly.

Let $\mathcal{T} = \{1, 2, ..., 2t - 2\}$. The idea is to pick $\lambda \times (2t - 2)$ independently sampled secret keys for the KHPCPRF scheme, denote each of them as $\mathsf{sk}_{j,d}$, $j \in [\lambda]$, $d \in \mathcal{T}$. To generate a ciphertext for a function f, pick a random vector $\mathbf{z} \in \mathcal{T}^\lambda$, and encrypt the function f in the constrained key derived from the secret key $\sum_{j \in [\lambda]} \mathsf{sk}_{j,z_j}$. We then prove each encryption is a constrained key derived from an independently generated master secret key with overwhelming probability.

Construction 4.4. *Given a key-homomorphic PCPRF* F *with group operation* $+$, *domain* D *and range* R, *construct a t-CT secure mixed-FE* MFE *as follows.*

- MFE.Setup(1^λ) *runs* F.ppGen(1^λ) *to generate* F.pp. *Then runs* F.skGen(1^λ, pp) *for* $\lambda \cdot (2t - 2)$ *times with independent randomness, denote the resulting set of secret keys as* $\{\mathsf{F.sk}_{j,d}\}_{j \in [\lambda], d \in \mathcal{T}}$. *Let* MFE.msk $:=$ F.pp, $\{\mathsf{F.sk}_{j,d}\}_{j \in [\lambda], d \in \mathcal{T}}$, *let* MFE.pp $:=$ F.pp.

- MFE.skGen(MFE.msk, x) *takes a message* $x \in D_\lambda$, *outputs*

$$\mathsf{sk}_x = x, \{\mathsf{F.Eval}(\mathsf{F.sk}_{j,d}, x)\}_{j \in [\lambda], d \in \mathcal{T}}.$$

- MFE.skEnc(MFE.msk, f) *samples* $\mathbf{z} \xleftarrow{\$} \mathcal{T}^\lambda$. *Then let* $\mathsf{F.sk}_f = \sum_{j \in [\lambda]} \mathsf{F.sk}_{j,z_j}$. *Outputs*

$$\mathsf{ct}_f = \mathbf{z}, \mathsf{F.Constrain}(\mathsf{F.pp}, \mathsf{F.sk}_f, f).$$

- MFE.pkEnc(MFE.pp) *runs the simulator of* F *on the size of the maximum constraint* $1^{|C_\lambda|}$ *to generate a simulated constrained key* F.Sim.ck, *outputs*

$$\text{ct}_f = \mathbf{z} \xleftarrow{\$} T^\lambda, \text{F.Sim.ck}$$

- MFE.Dec(sk$_x$, ct$_f$) *parses* sk$_x$ *as* $x, \{y_{j,d}\}_{j\in[\lambda], d\in T}$ *and* ct$_f$ *as* $\mathbf{z}$, ck$_f$, *outputs*

$$\begin{cases} 0 & \textit{if } \text{F.Constrain.Eval}(\text{ck}_f, x) = \sum_{j\in[\lambda]} y_{j,z_j} \\ 1 & \textit{else} \end{cases}.$$

Correctness. For f and x such that $f(x) = 0$, then

$$\text{F.Constrain.Eval}(\text{ck}_f, x) = \text{F.Eval}(\text{F.sk}_f, x) = \sum_{j\in[\lambda]} \text{F.Eval}(\text{F.sk}_{j,z_j}, x),$$

where the first equality follows the correctness of the PCPRF, the second equality follows the exact key-homomorphism.

For f and x such that $f(x) = 1$, by the pseudorandomness of the PRF evaluations on x such that $f(x) = 1$, F.Eval(F.sk$_f$, x) looks random, and is therefore unlikely to be equal to F.Constrain.Eval(ck$_f$, x) as long as the range R is super-polynomially large.

Theorem 4.5. *Assuming* F *is a key-homomorphic PCPRF, Construction 4.4 gives a t-CT secure mixed-FE.*

Proof. We construct the mixed-FE simulator MFE.Sim(1^λ) as follows:

1. Preprocessing: Sample a set of tags $\left\{\mathbf{z}^{[i]} \xleftarrow{\$} T^\lambda\right\}_{i\in[t]}$. We define $t+1$ sets $\mathcal{H}^{[i]}$, for $i \in [t]$, and $\mathcal{G}$ w.r.t. the tags, where $\mathcal{H}^{[i]}$ contains the coordinates that only appear in $\mathbf{z}^{[i]}$; $\mathcal{G}$ contains the indexes that either appear in the tags for more than once, or never appear in the tags. Later we will prove that w.h.p. all the sets $\mathcal{H}^{[i]}$, $i \in [t]$, are non-empty.

   Formally, first initialize all the sets as empty sets. Then for $(j, d) \in [\lambda] \times T$:
   - If there exists an $i^* \in [t]$ such that $\mathbf{z}_j^{[i^*]} = d$ and $\forall i \neq i^*$, $\mathbf{z}_j^{[i^*]} \neq d$, then add (j, d) in $\mathcal{H}^{[i^*]}$.
   - Else, add (j, d) in $\mathcal{G}$.

2. Given the ith ciphertext query, MFE.Sim(1^λ) calls for F.Sim.ck$^{[i]} \leftarrow$ F.Sim($1^{|C|}$), outputs $\mathbf{z}^{[i]}$, F.Sim.ck$^{[i]}$ as the simulated ciphertext ct$^{[i]}$.

3. Given a decryption key query on the input x with the indicators $\left\{f^{[i]}(x)\right\}_{i\in[t]}$, the mixed-FE simulator MFE.Sim($1^\lambda, x, \left\{f^{[i]}(x)\right\}_{i\in[t]}$) outputs x and $\{y_{x,j,d}\}_{j\in[\lambda], d\in T}$, where each $y_{x,j,d}$ is computed in the following way:

   - First go over all $(j, d) \in \mathcal{G}$, and let $y_{x,j,d} \xleftarrow{\$} R_\lambda$, where R_λ is the range of the KHPCPRF.

- Then, for each $i \in [t]$, let $p^{[i]} := |\mathcal{H}^{[i]}|$.

  For the first $p - 1$ indexes $(j, d) \in \mathcal{H}^{[i]}$, let $y_{x,j,d} \xleftarrow{\$} R_\lambda$.

  For the last index $(j^*, d^*) \in \mathcal{H}^{[i]}$, let

$$
y_{x,j^*,d^*} := \begin{cases} \mathsf{F.Constrain.Eval}(\mathsf{F.Sim.ck}^{[i]}, x) - \sum_{j \in [\lambda], j \neq j^*} y_{x,j,z_j^{[i]}} & \text{if } f^{[i]}(x) = 0 \\ U(R_\lambda) & \text{if } f^{[i]}(x) = 1 \end{cases}.
$$
(1)

We first prove that with all but negligible probability, all the sets $\mathcal{H}^{[i]}$, $i \in [t]$, are non-empty.

Lemma 4.6. *With probability greater or equal to $1 - t \cdot 2^{-\lambda}$, $|\mathcal{H}^{[i]}| \geq 1$ for all $i \in [t]$.*

Proof. For each tag $\mathbf{z}^{[i]}$, $i \in [t]$, the probability that the jth coordinate of $\mathbf{z}^{[i]}$ does not show up in the other $t - 1$ tags is $\geq \frac{(2t-2)-(t-1)}{2t-2} = \frac{1}{2}$. Therefore the probability that $|\mathcal{H}^{[i]}| \geq 1$ is $1 - 2^{-\lambda}$. Therefore with probability greater or equal to $1 - t \cdot 2^{-\lambda}$, $|\mathcal{H}^{[i]}| \geq 1$ for all $i \in [t]$.

Next we reduce the simulation security of the KHPCPRF (with the same public parameter and many independent secret keys) to the indistinguishability of the real experiment and the simulated one for the mixed-FE scheme. Suppose there is a p.p.t. adversary A that breaks the t-CT secure mixed-FE MFE with non-negligible probability η, we build a p.p.t. adversary A' for the KHPCPRF F. A' goes through the following stages.

1. Preprocessing: A' sample a set of tags $\left\{ \mathbf{z}^{[i]} \xleftarrow{\$} \mathcal{T}^\lambda \right\}_{i \in [t]}$. Define the sets $\mathcal{H}^{[i]}$, for $i \in [t]$, and $\mathcal{G}$ w.r.t. the tags in the same way as was defined for the MFE simulator.

2. The mixed-FE ciphertext queries: Once the mixed-FE adversary A makes the encryption queries for $\left\{ f^{[i]} \right\}_{i \in [t]}$, A' then forwards the t functions as the KHPCPRF constrained key queries. A' gets back t constrained keys $\left\{ \mathsf{ck}^{[i]} \right\}_{i \in [t]}$, each of them is either a real constrained key $\mathsf{ck}^{[i]} \leftarrow \mathsf{F.Constrain}(\mathsf{F.pp}, \mathsf{F.sk}^{[i]}, f^{[i]})$ derived from some secret key $\mathsf{F.sk}^{[i]}$, or a simulated constrained key $\mathsf{ck}^{[i]} \leftarrow \mathsf{F.Sim}(1^{|C|})$.
   A' then responses $\mathbf{z}^{[i]}, \mathsf{ck}^{[i]}$ to A as the ciphertext $\mathsf{ct}^{[i]}$, for $i \in [t]$.

3. The mixed-FE decryption key queries: Once the mixed-FE adversary A makes a functional decryption key query on x, A' forwards x with the indicators $\left\{ f^{[i]}(x) \right\}_{i \in [t]}$ as a KHPCPRF evaluation query. A' gets back t evaluations $\left\{ y^{[i]} \right\}_{i \in [t]}$, each of them is either the real evaluation $y^{[i]} = \mathsf{F.Eval}(\mathsf{F.sk}^{[i]}, x)$ on some secret key $\mathsf{F.sk}^{[i]}$, or a simulated evaluation $y^{[i]} = \mathsf{F.Sim}(x, f^{[i]}(x))$. A' then produces the set $\{y_{x,j,d}\}_{j \in [\lambda], d \in \mathcal{T}}$ as follows:

   - First go over all $(j, d) \in \mathcal{G}$, and let $y_{x,j,d} \xleftarrow{\$} R_\lambda$, where R_λ is the range of the KHPCPRF.

– Then, for each $i \in [t]$, let $p^{[i]} := |\mathcal{H}^{[i]}|$.

For the first $p - 1$ indexes $(j, d) \in \mathcal{H}^{[i]}$, let $y_{x,j,d} \xleftarrow{\$} R_\lambda$.

For the last index $(j^*, d^*) \in \mathcal{H}^{[i]}$, let $y_{x,j^*,d^*} = y^{[i]} - \sum_{j \in [\lambda], j \neq j^*} y_{x,j,z_j^{[i]}}$.

A' then responses $x, \{y_{x,j,d}\}_{j \in [\lambda], d \in \mathcal{T}}$ to A as the functional decryption key for x.

4. Finally A' forwards the answer of A on whether the scheme is real or simulated.

We justify that the distributions produced by A' are computationally close to the desired distributions in the mixed-FE security game. Recall that all the sets $\mathcal{H}^{[i]}$, for $i \in [t]$, are non-empty with probability $\geq 1 - t \cdot 2^{-\lambda}$ due to Lemma 4.6. If the KHPCPRF samples A' received are from the real distribution, then

– The correct distribution of a mixed-FE ciphertext is

$$U(\mathcal{T}^\lambda), \mathsf{F.Constrain}(\mathsf{F.pp}, \mathsf{F.sk}_f, f), \text{ where } \mathsf{F.sk}_f = \sum_{j \in [\lambda]} \mathsf{F.sk}_{j,z_j}.$$

The distribution of the mixed-FE ciphertext produced by A' is

$$U(\mathcal{T}^\lambda), \mathsf{F.Constrain}(\mathsf{F.pp}, \mathsf{F.sk}, f), \text{ with some correctly generated secret key } \mathsf{F.sk}.$$

These two distributions are the same due to the distribution requirement for the correctly generated secret keys for F. Recall that for $\mathsf{sk}_1, \mathsf{sk}_2, \mathsf{sk}'$ sampled from $\mathsf{F.skGen}(1^\lambda, \mathsf{pp})$ with independent randomness, $\mathsf{sk}_1 + \mathsf{sk}_2$ and sk' are required to be from the same distribution. This immediately implies that the sum of many correctly generated secret keys distributes the same as a single secret key.

– The correct mixed-FE functional decryption key for x is $\mathsf{sk}_x = x, \{\mathsf{F.Eval}(\mathsf{F.sk}_{j,d}, x)\}_{j \in [\lambda], d \in \mathcal{T}}$. We argue that the mixed-FE functional decryption key for x produced by A' is computationally indistinguishable to the real one due to the pseudorandomness of the PRF evaluations w.r.t. the secret keys whose constrained keys are not giving out.

• For all $(j, d) \in \mathcal{G}$, the PRF secret keys on these indexes are independent from the constrained keys that are given out, so the PRF evaluations on these indexes are indistinguishable from random.

• For each $i \in [t]$, pick an index $(j^*, d^*) \in \mathcal{H}^{[i]}$, the real PRF evaluation y_{x,j^*,d^*} can be re-written following the key-homomorphism as

$$\mathsf{F.Eval}(\mathsf{F.sk}_f, x) - \sum_{j \in [\lambda], j \neq j^*} \mathsf{F.Eval}(\mathsf{F.sk}_{j,z_j^{[i]}}, x) = \mathsf{F.Eval}((\mathsf{F.sk}_f - \sum_{j \in [\lambda], j \neq j^*} \mathsf{F.sk}_{j,z_j^{[i]}}), x).$$

Therefore, y_{x,j^*,d^*} distributes correctly due to the distribution requirement of the KHPCPRF secret keys. The PRF evaluations on the rest of the indexes in $\mathcal{H}^{[i]}$ are using independent PRF secret keys, so these evaluations are pseudorandom.

If the KHPCPRF samples A' received are from the simulated distribution, then

- The correct simulated distribution of the mixed-FE ciphertexts is $U(\mathcal{T}^\lambda), \mathsf{F.Sim}(1^{|C|})$, which is exactly what A' produces.
- For the simulated mixed-FE functional decryption key for x. Observe that the constrained PRF simulator outputs $U(R_\lambda)$ if $f(x) = 1$, outputs $\mathsf{F.Constrain.Eval}(\mathsf{F.Sim.ck}, x)$ if $f(x) = 0$. So the functional decryption key produced by A' follows the correct distribution.

Hence A' wins with $\eta - \mathrm{negl}(\lambda)$ advantage in the KHPCPRF simulation security game.

Finally we verify the public/secret-key mode indistinguishability. It follows from observing that if $f^{[i]}(x) = 1$ for all x being queried, the simulated ciphertext is independent from the simulated functional decryption keys, and has the same distribution as the public-key mode.

The Instantiation from the LWE-Based Almost-Key-Homomorphic PCPRFs. We provide the details for instantiating the mixed-FE from the LWE-based 1-almost-key-homomorphic PCPRFs. Note that the maximum number of key addition is λ in both the construction and the analysis, so we can choose the modulus p to be $\geq 4\lambda$, the range R as $\mathbb{Z}_p^n$ where $n = \Omega(\lambda)$, and the rest of the parameters under the restrictions mentioned in the original PCPRF construction.

In the construction of the mixed-FE, we change the decryption algorithm as: $\mathsf{MFE.Dec}(\mathsf{sk}_x, \mathsf{ct}_f)$ parses sk_x as $x, \{y_{j,d}\}_{j\in[\lambda], d\in\mathcal{T}}$ and ct_f as $\mathbf{z}, \mathsf{ck}_f$, outputs

$$\begin{cases} 0 & \text{if } \left\| \mathsf{F.Constrain.Eval}(\mathsf{ck}_f, x) - \left(\sum_{j\in[\lambda]} y_{j,z_j}\right) \right\|_\infty \leq \lambda \\ 1 & \text{else} \end{cases}.$$

In the simulation, we change one piece in the simulated functional decryption key for each $i \in [t]$. That is, for the last index $(j^*, d^*) \in \mathcal{H}^{[i]}$, we let

$$y_{x,j^*,d^*} := \begin{cases} \mathsf{F.Constrain.Eval}(\mathsf{F.Sim.ck}^{[i]}, x) + N(\lambda) - \sum_{j\in[\lambda], j\neq j^*} y_{x,j,z_j}^{[i]} & \text{if } f^{[i]}(x) = 0 \\ U(R_\lambda) & \text{if } f^{[i]}(x) = 1 \end{cases} \tag{2}$$

where $N(\lambda)$ is a noise factor added to compensate the error caused by the almost-hey-homomorphism. The distribution of $N(\lambda)$ is efficiently sampleable and identical to the distribution of

$$\sum_{j\in[\lambda]} \mathsf{F.Eval}(\mathsf{F.sk}_j, x) - \mathsf{F.Eval}(\mathsf{F.sk}_\Sigma, x)$$

where $\left\{\mathsf{F.sk}_j \leftarrow \mathsf{F.skGen}(1^\lambda, \mathsf{F.pp})\right\}_{j\in[\lambda]}$ and $\mathsf{F.sk}_\Sigma = \sum_{j\in[\lambda]} \mathsf{F.sk}_j$.

5   Attribute-Based Traitor Tracing

5.1   Definition of Attribute-Based Traitor Tracing

Definition 5.1 (Attribute-Based   Traitor   Tracing   (AB-TT)). *An attribute-based traitor-tracing (AB-TT) scheme for a class of functions $\mathcal{F}_\mu = \{f : \{0,1\}^\mu \to \{0,1\}\}$ and a message length ℓ (where μ, ℓ are functions of the security parameter λ) is a tuple of p.p.t. algorithms* (Setup, skGen, Enc, Dec, Trace) *such that:*

- Setup(1^λ) *takes as input the security parameter 1^λ, outputs the master secret key* msk *and the public parameter* pp.
- skGen(msk, f, i) *takes* msk, *a function $f \in \mathcal{F}_\mu$ and an identity $i \in [2^\lambda]$ and outputs a decryption key* $\mathsf{sk}_{f,i}$.
- Enc(pp, x, m) *takes as input* pp, *the attribute $x \in \{0,1\}^\mu$ and a message $m \in \{0,1\}^\ell$ and outputs a ciphertext* ct.
- Dec($\mathsf{sk}_{f,i}$, ct) *takes $\mathsf{sk}_{f,i}$ and* ct, *outputs the message m or $\perp$.*
- Trace^D(msk, $1^n, 1^h, x, m_0, m_1$) *takes as input* msk *the number of identities $n \in \mathbb{Z}$, a correctness parameter h, an attribute $x \in \{0,1\}^\mu$ and two messages m_0, m_1 as well as oracle-access to a "decoder" D. Outputs an identity $t \in [2^\lambda]$ or $\perp$ to indicate that no identity was traced.*

The scheme satisfies the following properties:

- *Correctness: This is the same as in standard ABE if we ignore the index i (allow it to be arbitrary).*
- *ABE Security: This is the same as in standard ABE if we ignore the index i (allow the adversary to choose it arbitrarily).*
- *Tracing Security: For any $\varepsilon(\lambda) = 1/\operatorname{poly}(\lambda)$. We define the following experiment between an adversary* A *and a challenger:*
  1. $1^n \leftarrow A(1^\lambda)$.
  2. (mpk, msk) $\leftarrow$ Setup(1^λ)
  3. $(D, x, m_0, m_1) \leftarrow A^{\mathsf{skGen}(\mathsf{msk}, \cdot, \cdot)}(\mathsf{pp})$: $x \in \{0,1\}^\mu, m \in \{0,1\}^\ell$ *and oracle queries (f, t) must satisfy $f \in \mathcal{F}_\mu$ and $t \in [n]$.*
  4. $t \leftarrow$ Trace^D(msk, $1^n, 1^{\lceil 1/\varepsilon \rceil}, x, m_0, m_1$)

  Within the above experiment, define the event GoodDecoder *to occur if*

  $$\Pr[D(\mathsf{ct}) = b \ : \ b \leftarrow \{0,1\}, \mathsf{ct} \leftarrow \mathsf{Enc}(\mathsf{pp}, x, m_b)] \geq 1/2 + \varepsilon(\lambda)$$

  where D, x, m_0, m_1 are defined in step 3 of the experiment. Define the event BadTrace *to occur if, for the t output by the trace algorithm in step 4, the adversary never made a* skGen *query of the form (f, t) where $f(x) = 1$. We require that $\Pr[\mathsf{GoodDecoder} \wedge \mathsf{BadTrace}] \leq \operatorname{negl}(\lambda)$.*

We make several remarks about the above definition. Firstly, while syntactically the scheme allows the identities i to come from a large space $[2^\lambda]$, for tracing security we assume that the range of identities $[n]$ is polynomially sized where the polynomial can be chosen arbitrarily by the adversary. Secondly, we think of the identities i as corresponding to users but each user can get several different keys $\mathsf{sk}_{f,i}$ for different functions f.

5.2   Tool: Attribute-Based Mixed FE

An attribute-based Mixed FE (AB-MFE) combines aspects of MFE and ABE. In particular, like in ABE, a secret key is associated with an ABE function f and a (public-key) ciphertext is associated with an ABE attribute x and a message m and decryption works if $f(x) = 1$. However, like in MFE, the secret key is also associated with an MFE function g. The MFE function is irrelevant when decrypting public-key ciphertexts. But there is also a secret-key encryption algorithm that additionally associates a ciphertext with an MFE attribute y. A secret-key ciphertext decrypts correctly if $f(x) = 1$ and $g(y) = 1$. The security requirements are a combination of MFE and ABE security.

(Note that, from the point of view of MFE, we switched the role of attributes and functions from the original definition by associating secret keys with functions and ciphertexts with attributes. This change is essentially cosmetic to better fit the connection with ABE and one can convert back and forth easily using universal circuits).

Definition 5.2 (Attribute-Based Mixed FE). *An* attribute-based mixed-FE *(AB-MFE) scheme for a class of ABE functions* $\mathcal{F}_\mu = \{f : \{0,1\}^\mu \to \{0,1\}\}$, *MFE functions* $\mathcal{G}_\nu = \{g : \{0,1\}^\nu \to \{0,1\}\}$ *and message length* ℓ *(where* μ, ν, ℓ *are functions of the security parameter* λ*) is a tuple of p.p.t. algorithms* (Setup, skGen, pkEnc, skEnc, Dec) *such that:*

- Setup(1^λ) *takes as input the security parameter* 1^λ, *outputs the master secret key* msk *and the public parameter* pp.
- skGen(msk, f, g) *takes* msk, *an ABE function* $f \in \mathcal{F}_\mu$, *a MFE function* $g \in \mathcal{G}_\nu$ *and outputs a decryption key* $\mathsf{sk}_{f,g}$.
- pkEnc(pp, x, m) *takes as input* pp, *the ABE attribute* $x \in \{0,1\}^\mu$ *and a message* $m \in \{0,1\}^\ell$ *and outputs a ciphertext* ct.
- skEnc(msk, x, y, m) *takes as input* pp, *the ABE attribute* $x \in \{0,1\}^\mu$ *the MFE attribute* $y \in \{0,1\}^\nu$ *and a message* $m \in \{0,1\}^\ell$ *and outputs a ciphertext* ct.
- Dec($\mathsf{sk}_{f,g}$, ct) *takes* $\mathsf{sk}_{f,g}$ *and* ct, *outputs a message* m *or* $\perp$.

The scheme is q-query secure for some polynomial $q = q(\lambda)$ *if it satisfies the following properties:*

- **Correctness:** *For all* $f \in \mathcal{F}_\mu$ *and all* $x \in \{0,1\}^\mu$ *such that* $f(x) = 1$, *for all* $g \in \mathcal{G}_\nu$ *and all* $m \in \{0,1\}^\ell$ *it holds that*

$$\Pr\left[\mathsf{Dec}(\mathsf{sk}_{f,g}, \mathsf{ct}) = m \; : \; \begin{array}{l} (\mathsf{pp}, \mathsf{msk}) \leftarrow \mathsf{Setup}(1^\lambda), \\ \mathsf{sk}_{f,g} \leftarrow \mathsf{skGen}(\mathsf{msk}, f, g), \\ \mathsf{ct} \leftarrow \mathsf{pkEnc}(\mathsf{pp}, x, m) \end{array}\right] \geq 1 - \mathsf{negl}(\lambda)$$

Furthermore, for all f, x, m *as above and all* $y \in \{0,1\}^\nu$ *such that* $g(y) = 1$ *it holds that:*

$$\Pr\left[\mathsf{Dec}(\mathsf{sk}_{f,g}, \mathsf{ct}) = m \; : \; \begin{array}{l} (\mathsf{pp}, \mathsf{msk}) \leftarrow \mathsf{Setup}(1^\lambda), \\ \mathsf{sk}_{f,g} \leftarrow \mathsf{skGen}(\mathsf{msk}, f, g), \\ \mathsf{ct} \leftarrow \mathsf{skEnc}(\mathsf{pp}, x, y, m) \end{array}\right] \geq 1 - \mathsf{negl}(\lambda)$$

- **ABE Security:** *The algorithms* (Setup, skGen, pkEnc, Dec) *satisfy ABE security if we ignore the g part of* skGen.
- **Public/Secret Hiding:** *Consider the following experiment with an adversary* A
  1. $(\mathsf{mpk}, \mathsf{msk}) \leftarrow \mathsf{Setup}(1^\lambda)$
  2. $(x^*, y^*, m^*) \leftarrow \mathsf{A}^{\mathsf{skGen}(\mathsf{msk}, \cdot, \cdot), \mathsf{skEnc}(\mathsf{msk}, \cdot, \cdot, \cdot)}(\mathsf{mpk})$
  3. $b \leftarrow \{0, 1\}$. *If* $b = 0$ *then set* $\mathsf{ct} \leftarrow \mathsf{pkEnc}(\mathsf{pp}, x^*, m^*)$ *else if* $b = 1$ *set* $\mathsf{ct} \leftarrow \mathsf{skEnc}(\mathsf{msk}, x^*, y^*, m^*)$.
  4. $b' \leftarrow \mathsf{A}(\mathsf{ct})$.

  An adversary A *in the above experiment is* legal *if (a) it makes at most* q *queries to the* skEnc *oracle, and (b) every query* (f, g) *made to the* skGen *oracle satisfies* $g(y^*) = 1$, *meaning that the MFE component is always qualified to decrypt. We require that for any legal* A *in the above game we have* $\Pr[b' = b] \leq \frac{1}{2} + \mathrm{negl}(\lambda)$.

- **MFE Attribute Hiding:** *Consider the following experiment with an adversary* A
  1. $(\mathsf{mpk}, \mathsf{msk}) \leftarrow \mathsf{Setup}(1^\lambda)$
  2. $(x^*, m^*, y_0, y_1) \leftarrow \mathsf{A}^{\mathsf{skGen}(\mathsf{msk}, \cdot, \cdot), \mathsf{skEnc}(\mathsf{msk}, \cdot, \cdot, \cdot)}(\mathsf{mpk})$
  3. $b \leftarrow \{0, 1\}$, $\mathsf{ct} \leftarrow \mathsf{skEnc}(\mathsf{msk}, x^*, y_b, m^*)$.
  4. $b' \leftarrow \mathsf{A}(\mathsf{ct})$.

  An adversary A *in the above experiment is* legal *if (a) it makes at most* q *queries to the* skEnc *oracle, and (b) every query* (f, g) *made to the* skGen *oracle satisfies* $g(y_0) = g(y_1)$. *We require that for any legal* A *in the above game we have* $\Pr[b' = b] \leq \frac{1}{2} + \mathrm{negl}(\lambda)$.

- **Message Hiding:** *Consider the following experiment with an adversary* A
  1. $(\mathsf{mpk}, \mathsf{msk}) \leftarrow \mathsf{Setup}(1^\lambda)$
  2. $(x^*, y^*, m_0, m_1) \leftarrow \mathsf{A}^{\mathsf{skGen}(\mathsf{msk}, \cdot, \cdot), \mathsf{skEnc}(\mathsf{msk}, \cdot, \cdot, \cdot)}(\mathsf{mpk})$
  3. $b \leftarrow \{0, 1\}$, $\mathsf{ct} \leftarrow \mathsf{skEnc}(\mathsf{msk}, x^*, y^*, m_b)$.
  4. $b' \leftarrow \mathsf{A}(\mathsf{ct})$.

  An adversary A *in the above experiment is* legal *if (a) it makes at most* q *queries to the* skEnc *oracle, and (b) every query* (f, g) *made to the* skGen *oracle satisfies* $g(y^*) = 0$ *or* $f(x^*) = 0$. *We require that for any legal* A *in the above game we have* $\Pr[b' = b] \leq \frac{1}{2} + \mathrm{negl}(\lambda)$.

Decoder-Based Security. In the above definition of AB-MFE security we considered three security properties each of which consists of a 4-step experiment. For each of them, the adversary can make at most q queries to $\mathsf{skEnc}(\mathsf{msk}, \cdot)$ oracle during the experiment and at the end of the experiment gets as input a ciphertext ct and outputs a bit b. We now consider a variant of the three security properties which we call *decoder-based security*. Firstly, the adversary loses access to the $\mathsf{skEnc}(\mathsf{msk}, \cdot)$ oracle entirely in each of the experiments. Secondly, in step 2 of each of the experiments the adversary additionally outputs a decoder circuit D and the experiment ends. For some $\varepsilon = \varepsilon(\lambda)$, we say that the decoder is ε-good if $\Pr[D(\mathsf{ct}) = b] \geq 1/2 + \varepsilon$ where b and ct are sampled as in step 3 of each of the original experiments. For decoder-based security we will require that in each of the experiments, for any legal adversary A and for any $\varepsilon(\lambda) = 1/\operatorname{poly}(\lambda)$ it holds that

$$\Pr[D \text{ is } \varepsilon(\lambda)\text{-good}] \leq \operatorname{negl}(\lambda)$$

where D is the output of the adversary in step 2 of the experiment.

The reason for defining both standard and decoder-based security properties is that the standard definitions are more natural to target when constructing Attribute-Based Mixed-FE, while the decoder definitions are directly compatible with tracing definitions. The lemma below connects them, allowing us to get the best of both worlds.

Lemma 5.3. *An AB-MFE with $(q = 1)$-query security also satisfies decoder-based security.*

A variant of the above lemma for MFE was given in [20] (Sect. 4). The proof of our lemma for AB-MFE is identical, up to minor syntactic changes needed to account for the expanded ABE syntax.

5.3   From Attribute-Based Mixed-FE to Attribute-Based Traitor Tracing

We now move on to building Attribute-Based Traitor Tracing from Attribute-Based Mixed-FE using the decoder-based security properties. We begin with some high level intuition. Suppose an attacker produces a decoder D that can decrypt ciphertexts associated with some attribute x. A natural approach would be to follow [20] using the Mixed-FE piece to remove each user one index at a time until we reach an index i where the decryption probability between encryptions to index i and $i+1$ differ. At this point we can finger user i as having contributed to creating the box D. However, the problem with this strategy is that the decoder algorithm might catch (and only catch) a user i who was not qualified to decrypt the ABE ciphertext to begin with. As argued earlier a meaningful trace will catch a user with a private key for f where $f(x) = 1$.

For that reason the MixedFE component will be used to gradually remove *only* qualified decryptors one index at a time. That is the function g will be of the form if $f(x) = 0$ or $j \geq i$. So a user with index i and $f(x) = 0$ will always have the Mixed-FE component output 1 even if $j \geq i$. Therefore if there is some index i where the decoding probability differs between encryptions to index $i - 1$ and i it must be the case that user i was a contributor and was qualified to decrypt. This is perhaps slightly counterintuitive as our tracing strategy explicitly always allows non-qualified users to pass the Mixed-FE portion.

We observe that for any good decoder box there must be some such i. The public/secret hiding property guarantees that any good decryptor box for the public key encryption will still decrypt well on index $i = 0$. The Message hiding property guarantees that when encrypting to index $i = n$ that no user will be able to decrypt. This is either because $f(x) = 0$ or due to the way g was selected. Thus there must exists some i where the decoder has a non-negligible gap in decrypting.

A formal description of the tracing system appears below.

Let $\mathcal{F}_\mu = \{f : \{0,1\}^\mu \to \{0,1\}\}$ be a function family. Define the family $\mathcal{G}_\nu = \{g : \{0,1\}^\nu \to \{0,1\}\}$ consisting of functions

$$g_{f,i}(x,j) = \begin{cases} 1 & \text{if } f(x) = 0 \text{ or } j \geq i \\ 0 & \text{otherwise} \end{cases}$$

where $i \in [2^\lambda]$, $j \in [2^\lambda] \cup \{0\}$ and $f \in \mathcal{F}_\mu$.

Assume that $\mathsf{ABMFE} = (\mathsf{Setup}, \mathsf{skGen}, \mathsf{pkEnc}, \mathsf{skEnc}, \mathsf{Dec})$ is an AB-MFE for the class of ABE functions $\mathcal{F}_\mu$ and the class of MFE functions $\mathcal{G}_\nu$. Further assume that ABMFE satisfies decoder-based security.

We show how to construct an AB-TT scheme $\mathsf{ABTT} = (\mathsf{Setup}', \mathsf{skGen}', \mathsf{Enc}', \mathsf{Dec}', \mathsf{Trace})$ for the function class $\mathcal{F}_\mu = \{f : \{0,1\}^\mu \to \{0,1\}\}$ as follows.

- Setup' is the same as Setup.
- $\mathsf{skGen}'(\mathsf{msk}, f, i)$: Construct $g_{f,i} \in \mathcal{G}_\nu$ and let $\mathsf{sk}_{f,i} \leftarrow \mathsf{skGen}(\mathsf{msk}, f, g_{f,i})$.
- Enc' is the same as pkEnc.
- Dec' is the same as Dec.
- $\mathsf{Trace}^D(\mathsf{msk}, 1^n, 1^h, x, m_0, m_1)$: Let $\varepsilon = 1/h$ and $W = \lambda \cdot (n \cdot h)^2$. For $i = 0$ to n, the trace algorithm does the following:
  1. It first sets $c_i := 0$. For $j = 1$ to W, it does the following:
     (a) It chooses $b_{i,j} \leftarrow \{0,1\}$, sets $\mathsf{ct}_{i,j} \leftarrow \mathsf{skEnc}(\mathsf{msk}, x, (x,i), m_{b_{i,j}})$. If $D(\mathsf{ct}_{i,j}) = b_{i,j}$, it sets $c_i = c_i + 1$.
  2. It sets $\hat{p}_i = c_i/W$.

  The trace algorithm outputs the first index $i \in \{1, 2, \ldots, n\}$ such that $\hat{p}_{i-1} - \hat{p}_i \geq \varepsilon/4n$. If no such index exists output $\bot$.

Theorem 5.4. *For any $\mathcal{F}_\mu$ with a corresponding $\mathcal{G}_\nu$, if ABMFE is a secure AB-MFE for the ABE class $\mathcal{F}_\mu$ and the MFE class $\mathcal{G}_\nu$ satisfying decoder-based security then the scheme ABTT is a secure attribute-based traitor tracing scheme (AB-TT).*

A variant of the above theorem showing that (non attribute-based) MFE implies traitor-tracing was given in [20] (Sect. 4.2.2). The proof of our theorem for AB-MFE is essentially identical. We give a high level proof below.

Proof. Assume that, in the tracing game, the adversary outputs a good decoder D meaning that the event $\mathsf{GoodDecoder}$ occurs. This means D can find b given $\mathsf{pkEnc}(\mathsf{pp}, x, m_b)$ with some noticeable advantage ε.

- By (decoder-based) public/secret hiding, it must be the case that D can find b given $\mathsf{skEnc}(\mathsf{msk}, x, (x,0), m_b)$ with advantage $\varepsilon - \mathsf{negl}(\lambda)$. Otherwise D could distinguish between $\mathsf{pkEnc}(\mathsf{pp}, x, m_b)$ and $\mathsf{skEnc}(\mathsf{msk}, x, (x,0), m_b)$ even though for all f, i we have $g_{f,i}(x,0) = 1$.
- By (decoder-based) message hiding, D can only have negligible advantage in finding b given $\mathsf{skEnc}(\mathsf{msk}, x, (x, n+1), m_b)$. Not that for every AB-MFE secret key obtained by the adversary associated with functions $(f, g_{f,i})$ we have that either $f(x) = 0$ or $g_{f,i}(x, n+1) = \neg f(x) = 0$.

- Combining the above two points, there must be at least one index j such that the advantage of D in finding b given $\mathsf{skEnc}(\mathsf{msk}, x, (x, j), m_b)$ is at least $(\varepsilon - \mathrm{negl}(\lambda))/n \geq \varepsilon/(2n)$ larger for j versus $j + 1$. We can use the Chernoff bound to argue that, with overwhelming probability, the tracing algorithm outputs some t for which the difference in advantage is at least $\varepsilon'/8n$. For this t there must be at least one $b \in \{0, 1\}$ such that the decoder D can distinguish between $\mathsf{skEnc}(\mathsf{msk}, x, (x, t), m_b)$ and $\mathsf{skEnc}(\mathsf{msk}, x, (x, t + 1), m_b)$ with noticeable advantage.
- By (decoder-based) attribute-hiding security, the above can only happen if the adversary got an AB-MFE secret key for the functions $(f, g_{f,j})$ such that $g_{f,j}(x, t) \neq g_{f,j}(x, t + 1)$, which can only happen if $f(x) = 1$ and $j = t$. This means that the adversary must have queried an AB-TT secret key for the function f such that $f(x) = 1$ with the identity t. Therefore the tracing algorithm succeeds in finding a valid traitor t and the event $\mathsf{BadTrace}$ does not occur whenever $\mathsf{GoodDecoder}$ occurs as we wanted to show.

5.4   From Mixed-FE to Attribute-Based Mixed-FE

Let $\mathsf{ABE} = (\mathsf{ABE.Setup}, \mathsf{ABE.skGen}, \mathsf{ABE.Enc}, \mathsf{ABE.Dec})$ be an ABE scheme for all circuits. Let $\mathsf{MFE} = (\mathsf{MFE.Setup}, \mathsf{MFE.skGen}, \mathsf{MFE.pkEnc}, \mathsf{MFE.skEnc}, \mathsf{MFE.Dec})$ be an MFE scheme (without a message) for some function class $\mathcal{F}_\mu = \{f : \{0, 1\}^\mu \to \{0, 1\}\}$; for simplicity we switch the roles of attribute/function and associate keys with functions and ciphertexts with attributes. We construct and AB-MFE scheme $\mathsf{ABMFE} = (\mathsf{Setup}, \mathsf{skGen}, \mathsf{pkEnc}, \mathsf{skEnc}, \mathsf{Dec})$ as follows:

- Setup: Run $(\mathsf{ABE.pp}, \mathsf{ABE.msk}) \leftarrow \mathsf{ABE.Setup}(1^\lambda)$ and $(\mathsf{MFE.pp}, \mathsf{MFE.msk}) \leftarrow \mathsf{MFE.Setup}(1^\lambda)$. Output $\mathsf{pp} = (\mathsf{ABE.pp}, \mathsf{MFE.pp})$ and $\mathsf{msk} = (\mathsf{ABE.msk}, \mathsf{MFE.msk})$.
- $\mathsf{skGen}(\mathsf{msk}, f, g)$: Let $\mathsf{MFE.sk}_g \leftarrow \mathsf{MFE.skGen}(\mathsf{MFE.msk}, g)$. Let C be a circuit which has $f, \mathsf{MFE.sk}_g$ hard-coded inside it, takes as input $x, \mathsf{MFE.ct}$ and outputs 1 if $f(x) = 1$ and $\mathsf{MFE.Dec}(\mathsf{MFE.sk}_g, \mathsf{ct}) = 1$. Output $\mathsf{sk}_{f,g} \leftarrow \mathsf{ABE.skGen}(\mathsf{ABE.msk}, C)$.
- $\mathsf{pkEnc}(\mathsf{pp}, x, m)$: Let $\mathsf{MFE.ct} \leftarrow \mathsf{MFE.pkEnc}(\mathsf{MFE.pp})$. Output $\mathsf{ct} \leftarrow \mathsf{ABE.Enc}(\mathsf{ABE.pp}, (x, \mathsf{MFE.ct}), m)$.
- $\mathsf{skEnc}(\mathsf{msk}, x, y, m)$: Let $\mathsf{MFE.ct} \leftarrow \mathsf{MFE.skEnc}(\mathsf{MFE.msk}, y)$. Output $\mathsf{ct} \leftarrow \mathsf{ABE.Enc}(\mathsf{ABE.pp}, (x, \mathsf{MFE.ct}), m)$.
- $\mathsf{Dec}(\mathsf{sk}_{f,g}, \mathsf{ct})$: Output $\mathsf{ABE.Dec}(\mathsf{sk}_{f,g}, \mathsf{ct})$.

Theorem 5.5. *If* ABE *is a secure ABE scheme and* MFE *is a secure MFE scheme then* ABMFE *is a secure AB-MFE scheme.*

Proof. The correctness of the AB-MFE follows directly from that of the ABE and MFE schemes. The ABE security of the AB-MFE follows directly from the ABE security of the ABE. The "public/secret hiding" security of the AB-MFE follows directly from that of the MFE. The "attribute-hiding" security of the AB-MFE follows directly from the "attribute-hiding" security of the MFE (previously we called this "function hiding" but since we switched the roles of attributes and functions this is now "attribute hiding"). Lastly for message-hiding security of the AB-MFE we rely on the security of the ABE. In particular, the adversary gets as a challenge an ABE ciphertext with attribute $(x^*, \mathsf{MFE.ct} = \mathsf{MFE.skEnc}(\mathsf{MFE.msk}, y^*))$ but only has ABE keys for circuits C such that $C(x, \mathsf{MFE.ct}) = 1$ if $f(x^*) = 1$ and $\mathsf{MFE.Dec}(\mathsf{MFE.sk}_g, \mathsf{ct}) = 1 \Leftrightarrow g(y^*) = 1$. Therefore if one of $f(x^*) = 0$ or $g(y^*) = 0$ always holds, it must mean that none of the ABE secret keys are qualified to decrypt the challenge ciphertext.

Acknowledgments. The research of Yilei Chen was conducted at Boston University supported by the NSF MACS project and NSF grant CNS-1422965. Vinod Vaikuntanathan is supported in part by NSF Grants CNS-1350619 and CNS-1414119, Alfred P. Sloan Research Fellowship, Microsoft Faculty Fellowship, the NEC Corporation and a Steven and Renee Finn Career Development Chair from MIT. This work was also sponsored in part by the Defense Advanced Research Projects Agency (DARPA) and the U.S. Army Research Office under contracts W911NF-15-C-0226 and W911NF-15-C-0236. Brent Waters is supported by NSF CNS-1414082, DARPA SafeWare, Microsoft Faculty Fellowship, and Packard Foundation Fellowship. Hoeteck Wee is supported by ERC Project aSCEND (H2020 639554). Daniel Wichs is supported by NSF grants CNS-1314722, CNS-1413964.

References

1. Abdalla, M., Dent, A.W., Malone-Lee, J., Neven, G., Phan, D.H., Smart, N.P.: Identity-based traitor tracing. In: Okamoto, T., Wang, X. (eds.) PKC 2007. LNCS, vol. 4450, pp. 361–376. Springer, Heidelberg (2007). https://doi.org/10.1007/978-3-540-71677-8_24

2. Agrawal, S.: Stronger security for reusable garbled circuits, general definitions and attacks. In: Katz, J., Shacham, H. (eds.) CRYPTO 2017. LNCS, vol. 10401, pp. 3–35. Springer, Cham (2017). https://doi.org/10.1007/978-3-319-63688-7_1

3. Agrawal, S., Bhattacherjee, S., Phan, D.H., Stehlé, D., Yamada, S.: Efficient public trace and revoke from standard assumptions: extended abstract. In: Proceedings of the 2017 ACM SIGSAC Conference on Computer and Communications Security, CCS 2017, Dallas, TX, USA, October 30–November 03 2017, pp. 2277–2293 (2017)

4. Agrawal, S., Rosen, A.: Functional encryption for bounded collusions, revisited. In: Kalai, Y., Reyzin, L. (eds.) TCC 2017. LNCS, vol. 10677, pp. 173–205. Springer, Cham (2017). https://doi.org/10.1007/978-3-319-70500-2_7

5. Boneh, D., Lewi, K., Montgomery, H., Raghunathan, A.: Key homomorphic PRFs and their applications. In: Canetti, R., Garay, J.A. (eds.) CRYPTO 2013. LNCS, vol. 8042, pp. 410–428. Springer, Heidelberg (2013). https://doi.org/10.1007/978-3-642-40041-4_23

6. Boneh, D., Lewi, K., Wu, D.J.: Constraining pseudorandom functions privately. In: Fehr, S. (ed.) PKC 2017. LNCS, vol. 10175, pp. 494–524. Springer, Heidelberg (2017). https://doi.org/10.1007/978-3-662-54388-7_17

7. Boneh, D., Sahai, A., Waters, B.: Fully collusion resistant traitor tracing with short ciphertexts and private keys. In: Vaudenay, S. (ed.) EUROCRYPT 2006. LNCS, vol. 4004, pp. 573–592. Springer, Heidelberg (2006). https://doi.org/10.1007/11761679_34

8. Boneh, D., Waters, B.: A fully collusion resistant broadcast, trace, and revoke system. In: Proceedings of the 13th ACM Conference on Computer and Communications Security, CCS 2006, Alexandria, VA, USA, I October 30–November 3 2006, pp. 211–220 (2006)

9. Boneh, D., Zhandry, M.: Multiparty key exchange, efficient traitor tracing, and more from indistinguishability obfuscation. In: Garay, J.A., Gennaro, R. (eds.) CRYPTO 2014. LNCS, vol. 8616, pp. 480–499. Springer, Heidelberg (2014). https://doi.org/10.1007/978-3-662-44371-2_27

10. Brakerski, Z., Langlois, A., Peikert, C., Regev, O., Stehlé, D.: Classical hardness of learning with errors. In: Proceedings of the Forty-Fifth Annual ACM Symposium on Theory of Computing, pp. 575–584. ACM (2013)

11. Brakerski, Z., Tsabary, R., Vaikuntanathan, V., Wee, H.: Private constrained PRFs (and More) from LWE. In: Kalai, Y., Reyzin, L. (eds.) TCC 2017. LNCS, vol. 10677, pp. 264–302. Springer, Cham (2017). https://doi.org/10.1007/978-3-319-70500-2_10

12. Canetti, R., Chen, Y.: Constraint-hiding constrained PRFs for NC^1 from LWE. In: Coron, J.-S., Nielsen, J.B. (eds.) EUROCRYPT 2017. LNCS, vol. 10210, pp. 446–476. Springer, Cham (2017). https://doi.org/10.1007/978-3-319-56620-7_16

13. Chen, Y., Vaikuntanathan, V., Wee, H.: GGH15 beyond permutation branching programs: proofs, attacks, and candidates. In: Shacham, H., Boldyreva, A. (eds.) CRYPTO 2018. LNCS, vol. 10992, pp. 577–607. Springer, Cham (2018). https://doi.org/10.1007/978-3-319-96881-0_20

14. Chor, B., Fiat, A., Naor, M.: Tracing traitors. In: Desmedt, Y.G. (ed.) CRYPTO 1994. LNCS, vol. 839, pp. 257–270. Springer, Heidelberg (1994). https://doi.org/10.1007/3-540-48658-5_25

15. Freeman, D.M.: Converting pairing-based cryptosystems from composite-order groups to prime-order groups. In: Gilbert, H. (ed.) EUROCRYPT 2010. LNCS, vol. 6110, pp. 44–61. Springer, Heidelberg (2010). https://doi.org/10.1007/978-3-642-13190-5_3

16. Garg, S., Kumarasubramanian, A., Sahai, A., Waters, B.: Building efficient fully collusion-resilient traitor tracing and revocation schemes. In: Proceedings of the 17th ACM Conference on Computer and Communications Security, CCS 2010, pp. 121–130 (2010)

17. Gentry, C., Gorbunov, S., Halevi, S.: Graph-induced multilinear maps from lattices. In: Dodis, Y., Nielsen, J.B. (eds.) TCC 2015. LNCS, vol. 9015, pp. 498–527. Springer, Heidelberg (2015). https://doi.org/10.1007/978-3-662-46497-7_20

18. Gorbunov, S., Vaikuntanathan, V., Wee, H.: Functional encryption with bounded collusions via multi-party computation. In: Safavi-Naini, R., Canetti, R. (eds.) CRYPTO 2012. LNCS, vol. 7417, pp. 162–179. Springer, Heidelberg (2012). https://doi.org/10.1007/978-3-642-32009-5_11

19. Goyal, R., Koppula, V., Waters, B.: Lockable obfuscation. In: FOCS, pp. 612–621 (2017)

20. Goyal, R., Koppula, V., Waters, B.: Collusion resistant traitor tracing from learning with errors. In: STOC (2018)

21. Katz, J., Schröder, D.: Bootstrapping obfuscators via fast pseudorandom functions. In: Annual Conference of the ITA (ACITA) (2011)

22. Liu, Z., Cao, Z., Wong, D.S.: Blackbox traceable CP-ABE: how to catch people leaking their keys by selling decryption devices on eBay. In: 2013 ACM SIGSAC Conference on Computer and Communications Security, CCS 2013, Berlin, Germany, 4–8 November 2013, pp. 475–486 (2013)

23. Liu, Z., Wong, D.S.: Practical ciphertext-policy attribute-based encryption: traitor tracing, revocation, and large universe. In: Malkin, T., Kolesnikov, V., Lewko, A.B., Polychronakis, M. (eds.) ACNS 2015. LNCS, vol. 9092, pp. 127–146. Springer, Cham (2015). https://doi.org/10.1007/978-3-319-28166-7_7
24. Peikert, C.: Public-key cryptosystems from the worst-case shortest vector problem: extended abstract. In: STOC, pp. 333–342 (2009)
25. Peikert, C., Regev, O., Stephens-Davidowitz, N.: Pseudorandomness of Ring-LWE for any ring and modulus. In: STOC, pp. 461–473. ACM (2017)
26. Regev, O.: On lattices, learning with errors, random linear codes, and cryptography. J. ACM **56**(6), 1–40 (2009)
27. Sahai, A., Seyalioglu, H.: Worry-free encryption: functional encryption with public keys. In: Al-Shaer, E., Keromytis, A.D., Shmatikov, V. (eds.) Proceedings of the 17th ACM Conference on Computer and Communications Security, CCS 2010, Chicago, Illinois, USA, 4–8 October 2010, pp. 463–472. ACM (2010)
28. Wichs, D., Zirdelis, G.: Obfuscating compute-and-compare programs under LWE. In: FOCS, pp. 600–611 (2017)

Two-Message Statistically Sender-Private OT from LWE

Zvika Brakerski[1]([✉]) and Nico Döttling[2]

[1] Weizmann Institute of Science, Rehovot, Israel
zvika.brakerski@weizmann.ac.il
[2] CISPA Helmholtz Center, Saarbrücken, Germany
doettling@cispa.saarland

Abstract. We construct a two-message oblivious transfer (OT) proto-col without setup that guarantees statistical privacy for the sender even against malicious receivers. Receiver privacy is game based and relies on the hardness of learning with errors (LWE). This flavor of OT has been a central building block for minimizing the round complexity of witness indistinguishable and zero knowledge proof systems, non-malleable com-mitment schemes and multi-party computation protocols, as well as for achieving circuit privacy for homomorphic encryption in the malicious setting. Prior to this work, all candidates in the literature from stan-dard assumptions relied on number theoretic assumptions and were thus insecure in the post-quantum setting. This work provides the first (pre-sumed) post-quantum secure candidate and thus allows to instantiate the aforementioned applications in a post-quantum secure manner.

Technically, we rely on the transference principle: Either a lattice or its dual must have short vectors. Short vectors, in turn, can be trans-lated to information loss in encryption. Thus encrypting one message with respect to the lattice and one with respect to its dual guarantees that at least one of them will be statistically hidden.

1 Introduction

Oblivious transfer (OT), introduced by Rabin [32], is one of the most fundamen-tal cryptographic tasks. A sender (S) holds two values μ_0, μ_1 and a receiver (R) holds a bit β. The functionality should allow the receiver to learn μ_β and noth-ing else, the sender should learn nothing. OT has been a fundamental building block for many cryptographic applications, in particular ones related to secure multi-party computation (MPC), starting with [15,35].

A central measure for the complexity of a protocol or a proof system is its round complexity. One could imagine a protocol implementing the OT function-ality with only two messages: a first message from the receiver to the sender, and

The full version of this paper is available at https://eprint.iacr.org/2018/530.

Z. Brakerski—Supported by the Israel Science Foundation (Grant No. 468/14), Bina-tional Science Foundation (Grants No. 2016726, 2014276), and by the European Union Horizon 2020 Research and Innovation Program via ERC Project REACT (Grant 756482) and via Project PROMETHEUS (Grant 780701).

A. Beimel and S. Dziembowski (Eds.): TCC 2018, LNCS 11240, pp. 370–390, 2018.
https://doi.org/10.1007/978-3-030-03810-6_14

a second message from the sender to the receiver. Indeed, in the semi-honest setting, where parties are assumed to follow the protocol, this can be achieved based on a variety of concrete cryptographic assumptions (Decisional Diffie-Hellman, Quadratic Residuosity, Decisional Composite Residuosity, Learning with Errors, to name a few), as well as based on generic assumptions such as trapdoor permutations, additively homomorphic encryption and public key encryption with oblivious public key generation (e.g. [7,13]).

In the malicious setting, where an adversarial party might deviate from the designated protocol, the ultimate simulation based security notion cannot be achieved in a two message protocol (without assuming setup such as a common random string or a random oracle) [16]. The standard security notion in this setting, which originated from the works of Naor and Pinkas [27] and Aiello et al. [1], and was further studied in [3,18,21], provides a meaningful relaxation of the standard (simulation-based) security notion. This definition requires that the receiver's only message is computationally indistinguishable between the cases of $\beta = 0$ and $\beta = 1$[1], and that regardless of the receiver's first message, the sender's message statistically hides at least one of μ_0, μ_1. Alternative equivalent formulations are simulation using a computationally unbounded (or exponential time) simulator, or the existence of a computationally unbounded (or exponential time) extractor, that can extract a β value from any receiver message.

With the aforementioned connection to secure MPC, it is not surprising that this notion of malicious statistical sender-private OT (SSP-OT) found numerous applications. In particular in recent years as the round complexity of MPC and related objects is taken to the necessary minimum. Badrinarayanan et al. [3], Jain et al. [19] and Kalai et al. [22] used it to construct two-message witness indistinguishable proof systems, and even restricted forms of zero-knowledge proof systems.

Badrinarayanan et al. [4] used similar techniques to present malicious MPC with minimal round complexity (4-rounds). In particular, their building blocks are SSP-OT and a 3-round semi-malicious MPC protocol (a comparable result was achieved by Halevi et al. [17] using different techniques, in particular requiring NIZK/ZAP). Khurana and Sahai [24] used SSP-OT to construct two-message non-malleable commitment schemes (with respect to the commitment), and Khurana [23] used it (together with ZAPs) to achieve 3-round non-malleable commitments from polynomial assumptions. Badrinarayanan et al. [5] relied on SSP-OT to construct 3-round concurrent MPC.

Ostrovsky, Paskin-Cherniavsky and Paskin-Cherniavsky [28] used SSP-OT to show that any fully homomorphic encryption scheme (FHE) can be converted to one that is statistically circuit private even against maliciously generated public keys and ciphertexts.

Our Results and Applications. Prior to this work it was only known how to construct SSP-OT from number theoretic assumptions such as DDH [1,27], QR and DCR [18]. If setup is allowed, specifically a common random string,

---

[1] Notice that it is impossible to achieve statistical indistinguishability in this setting, at least against non-uniform malicious receivers.

then an LWE-based construction by Peikert, Vaikuntanathan and Waters [31] achieves strong simulation security (even in the UC model). However, the afore-mentioned applications require a construction without setup and could therefore not be instantiated in a post-quantum secure manner. In this work, we construct SSP-OT from the learning with errors (LWE) assumption [33], with polyno-mial noise-ratio, which translates to the hardness of polynomially approximating short-vector problems (such as SIVP or GapSVP) to within a polynomial factor. Currently, no polynomial time quantum algorithm is known for these problems, and thus they serve as a major candidate for constructing post-quantum secure cryptography.

Relying on our construction, it is possible for the first time, to instantiate the works of [3,5,19,22,24] from LWE, i.e. in a post-quantum secure manner, and obtain proof systems with witness-indistinguishable or (limited) zero-knowledge properties, as well as non-malleable commitment schemes and concurrent MPC protocols. It is also possible to construct a round-optimal malicious MPC from LWE by applying the result of [4] using our SSP-OT and the LWE-based 3-round semi-malicious MPC of Brakerski et al. [8]. Lastly, our result allows to achieve malicious circuit private FHE from LWE by instantiating the [28] result with our LWE-based SSP-OT and relying on the numerous existing LWE-based FHE schemes. We stress that none of these applications had prior post-quantum secure candidates.

1.1   Technical Overview

Our construction relies on some fundamental properties of lattices. For our pur-poses we will only consider the so called q-ary lattices that can be described as follows. Given a matrix $\mathbf{A} \in \mathbb{Z}_q^{n \times m}$ for some modulus q and $m \geq n$, we can define $\Lambda_q(\mathbf{A}) = \{\mathbf{y} \in \mathbb{Z}^m : \mathbf{y} = \mathbf{sA} \pmod{q}\}$ which is the lattice defined by the row-span of $\mathbf{A}$, and $\Lambda_q^\perp(\mathbf{A}) = \{\mathbf{x} \in \mathbb{Z}^m : \mathbf{Ax} = \mathbf{0} \pmod{q}\}$ which is the lattice defined by the kernel of $\mathbf{A}$. Note that both lattices have rank m over the integers, i.e. they contain a set of m linearly independent vectors over the integers (but not modulo q), since they contain $q \cdot \mathbb{Z}^m$. There is a duality relation between these two lattices, both induced by the matrix $\mathbf{A}$, and this relation will be instrumental for our methods.

An important fact about lattices is that a good basis implies decoding. Specif-ically, if $\Lambda_q^\perp(\mathbf{A})$ contains m linearly independent vectors (over the integers) of length at most ℓ, then it is possible to decode vectors of the form $\mathbf{sA}+\mathbf{e} \pmod{q}$, if $\|\mathbf{e}\|$ is sufficiently smaller than q/ℓ. Namely, to recover $\mathbf{s}, \mathbf{e}$. Such a short basis is sometimes called a trapdoor for $\mathbf{A}$.[2]

Consider sampling $\mathbf{s}$ uniformly in $\mathbb{Z}_q^n$ and $\mathbf{e}$ from a Gaussian s.t. $\|\mathbf{e}\|$ is slightly below the decoding capability q/ℓ. Then if $\Lambda_q^\perp(\mathbf{A})$ indeed has an ℓ-basis then $\mathbf{s}, \mathbf{e}$ can be recovered from $\mathbf{sA} + \mathbf{e} \pmod{q}$. However, a critical observation for us is

---

[2] While the form $\mathbf{sA}+\mathbf{e} \pmod{q}$ bears resemblance to an instance of the LWE problem (to be discussed below), the matrix $\mathbf{A}$ in our setting might be chosen by a malicious party and therefore cannot be assumed to be close to uniform.

that this encoding becomes *lossy* if the lattice $\Lambda_q(\mathbf{A})$ contains a vector of norm $\ll q/\ell$. That is, in this case it is information theoretically impossible to recover the original $\mathbf{s}$. This is because the component of $\mathbf{sA}$ that is in the direction of the short vector is masked by the noise $\mathbf{e}$ (which is Gaussian and thus has a component in every direction). This property was also used by Goldreich and Goldwasser [14] to show that some lattice problems are in **coAM**.

To utilize this structure for our purposes, we specify the OT receiver message to be a matrix $\mathbf{A}$. Then the OT sender generates $\mathbf{sA} + \mathbf{e}$ (mod q) and encodes one of its inputs, say μ_1 using entropy from the vector $\mathbf{s}$ (e.g. using a randomness extractor). We get that this value is recoverable if $\mathbf{A}$ has ℓ-basis and information-theoretically hidden if $\Lambda_q(\mathbf{A})$ has a short vector. If the receiver's choice bit is 1, all it needs to do is generate $\mathbf{A}$ that has an ℓ-trapdoor, for which there are many well known methods to generate such $\mathbf{A}$'s that are statistically indistinguishable from uniform (starting from [2] with numerous followups). In order to complete the OT functionality we need to find a way to encode μ_0 in a way that is *lossy* if $\Lambda_q(\mathbf{A})$ has no short vector. This will guarantee that regardless of the (possibly malicious) choice of matrix $\mathbf{A}$, either μ_0 or μ_1 are information theoretically hidden.

Let us examine the case where all vectors in $\Lambda_q(\mathbf{A})$ are of length $\gg t$ for some parameter t. Then the duality relations expressed in Banaszczyk's transference theorems [6] guarantees that $\Lambda_q^\perp(\mathbf{A})$ has a basis of length $\ll q/t$. In such case we can use the *smoothing* principle to conclude that if $\mathbf{x}$ is a discrete Gaussian with parameter q/t then $\mathbf{Ax}$ (mod q) is statistically close to uniform. We can thus instruct the sender to compute $\mathbf{Ax}+\mathbf{d}$ (mod q) for some vector $\mathbf{d}$, and encode μ_1 using entropy extracted from $\mathbf{d}$. This guarantees lossiness if $\Lambda_q(\mathbf{A})$ has no short vectors as required. Furthermore, it is possible to generate a pseudorandom $\mathbf{A}$ (under the LWE assumption) and specify $\mathbf{d}$ such that $\mathbf{d}$ is recoverable (this $\mathbf{A}$ corresponds to the public key in Regev's original encryption scheme [33]).

All that is left is to set the relation between ℓ, t, q so as to make sure that if one mode of the OT is decodable then the other is lossy. One may be suspicious whether there is a valid setting of parameters, but in fact there is quite some slackness in the choice of parameters. We can start by setting ℓ, t to be some fixed polynomial in n that is sufficient to guarantee correct recovery in the respective cases. This can be done regardless of the value of q. We will set the parameter q to ensure that if μ_1 is recoverable then μ_0 is not, which is sufficient to guarantee statistical sender privacy against malicious receiver. Specifically, if μ_1 is recoverable then $\Lambda_q(\mathbf{A})$ does not have vectors of length $q/(k\ell)$, where k is some polynomial in n (that does not depend on q), and thus $\Lambda_q^\perp(\mathbf{A})$ has a $k\ell$ basis. We therefore require that $q/t \gg k\ell$, or equivalently $q \gg k\ell t$, which guarantees that μ_0 is not recoverable in this case. Since k, ℓ, t are fixed polynomials in n, it is sufficient to choose q to be a sufficiently larger polynomial than the product $k\ell t$ to guarantee security. Receiver privacy is guaranteed since $\mathbf{A}$ is either statistically indistinguishable from uniform if the choice bit β is 1, or computationally indistinguishable from uniform if $\beta = 0$.

Disadvantages of the Basic Solution, and Our Actual Improved Scheme. The proposal above can indeed be used to implement an SSP-OT. However, when actual parameters are assigned, it becomes apparent that the argument about the lossiness of $\mathbf{s}$ given $\mathbf{sA} + \mathbf{e}$ (mod q) when $\Lambda_q(\mathbf{A})$ has some short vector does not produce sufficient randomness to allow extraction. This can be resolved by repetition (many $\mathbf{s}$ values with the same $\mathbf{A}$). However, the lossiness argument for $\mathbf{d}$ guarantees much more and in fact allows to extract random bits from $\mathbf{d}$ deterministically. The consequence is an unnecessarily inefficient scheme. In particular, the information rate is inverse polynomial in the security parameter of the scheme.

The scheme we actually introduce and analyze is therefore a balanced version of the above outline, where we "pay" in weakening the lossiness in $\mathbf{d}$ in exchange for strengthening the lossiness for $\mathbf{s}$, which leads to a scheme with information rate $\widetilde{\Omega}(1)$ (achieving constant information rate while preserving statistical security remains an intriguing question). Towards this end, we introduce refinements of known lattice tools that may be of independent interest.

The idea is to improve the lossiness in $\mathbf{s}$ by considering the case where $\Lambda_q(\mathbf{A})$ has multiple short vectors, instead of just one. Intuitively, this will introduce entropy into additional components of $\mathbf{s}$, thus increasing the lossiness. We formalize this by considering the Gaussian measure of $\Lambda_q(\mathbf{A})$. A high Gaussian measure translates (at least intuitively) to the existence of a multitude of short vectors, formally it characterizes the potency of $\mathbf{e}$ to hide information about $\mathbf{s}$. The formal argument goes through the optimal Voronoi cell decoder, see Sect. 3 for formal statement and additional details.

Of course the lossiness in $\mathbf{s}$ needs to be complemented by lossiness in $\mathbf{d}$ if the Gaussian measure of $\Lambda_q(\mathbf{A})$ is small, which translates to having few independent short vectors in $\Lambda_q(\mathbf{A})$. We show that in this case we can derive *partial smoothing* where for a Gaussian $\mathbf{x}$, the value $\mathbf{Ax}$ (mod q) is no longer uniform, but rather is uniform over some subspace modulo q. If the dimension of this subspace is large enough, we can get lossiness for the vector $\mathbf{d}$ and complete the security proof. Partial smoothing and implications are discussed in Sect. 4.

To apply these principles we need to slightly modify the definition of the vector $\mathbf{d}$ and the matrix $\mathbf{A}$ in the case of $\beta = 0$. Now $\mathbf{A}$ will no longer correspond to the public key of the Regev scheme but rather, interestingly, to the public key of the batched scheme introduced in [31] (which is also concerned with constructing OT, but allowing setup). The complete construction and analysis can be found in Sect. 5.

2   Preliminaries

2.1   Statistical Sender-Private Two-Message Oblivious Transfer

We now define the object of main interest in this work, namely SSP-OT. We only define the two-message perfect-correctness variant since this is what we achieve in this work. A two-message oblivious transfer protocol consists of a tuple PPT algorithms (OTR, OTS, OTD) with the following syntax.

- $\mathsf{OTR}(1^\lambda, \beta)$ takes the security parameter λ and a selection bit β and outputs a message ot_1 and secret state st.
- $\mathsf{OTS}(1^\lambda, (\mu_0, \mu_1), \mathsf{ot}_1)$ takes the security parameter λ, two inputs $(\mu_0, \mu_1) \in \{0,1\}^{\mathsf{len}}$ (where len is a parameter of the scheme) and a message ot_1. It outputs a message ot_2.
- $\mathsf{OTD}(1^\lambda, \beta, \mathsf{st}, \mathsf{ot}_2)$ takes the security parameter, the bit β, secret state st and message ot_2 and outputs $\mu' \in \{0,1\}^{\mathsf{len}}$.

Correctness and security are defined as follows.

Definition 2.1. *A tuple* $(\mathsf{OTR}, \mathsf{OTS}, \mathsf{OTD})$ *is a SSP-OT scheme if the following hold.*

- **Correctness.** *For all* $\lambda, \beta, \mu_0, \mu_1$, *letting* $(\mathsf{ot}_1, \mathsf{st}) = \mathsf{OTR}(1^\lambda, \beta)$, $\mathsf{ot}_2 = \mathsf{OTS}(1^\lambda, (\mu_0, \mu_1), \mathsf{ot}_1)$, $\mu' = \mathsf{OTD}(1^\lambda, \beta, \mathsf{st}, \mathsf{ot}_2)$, *it holds that* $\mu' = \mu_\beta$ *with probability* 1.
- **Receiver Privacy.** *Consider the distribution* $\mathcal{D}_\beta(\lambda)$ *defined by running* $(\mathsf{ot}_1, \mathsf{st}) = \mathsf{OTR}(1^\lambda, \beta)$ *and outputting* ot_1. *Then* $\mathcal{D}_0, \mathcal{D}_1$ *are computationally indistinguishable.*
- **Statistical Sender Privacy.** *There exists an extractor* OTExt *(possibly computationally unbounded) s.t. for any sequence of messages* $\mathsf{ot}_1 = \mathsf{ot}_1(\lambda)$ *and inputs* $(\mu_0, \mu_1) = (\mu_0(\lambda), \mu_1(\lambda))$, *the distribution ensembles* $\mathsf{OTS}(1^\lambda, (\mu_0, \mu_1), \mathsf{ot}_1)$ *and* $\mathsf{OTS}(1^\lambda, (\mu_{\beta'}, \mu_{\beta'}), \mathsf{ot}_1)$, *where* $\beta' = \mathsf{OTExt}(\mathsf{ot}_1)$, *are statistically indistinguishable.*

2.2   Linear Algebra, Min-Entropy and Extractors

Random Matrices: The probability that a uniformly random matrix $\mathbf{A} \xleftarrow{\$} \mathbb{Z}_2^{n \times m}$ (with $m \geq n$) has full rank is given by

$$\Pr_{\mathbf{A}}[\mathrm{rank}(\mathbf{A}) < n] = 1 - \prod_{i=0}^{n-1}(1 - 2^{i-m}) \leq \sum_{i=0}^{n-1} 2^{i-m} \leq 2^{n-m},$$

where the first inequality follows from the union-bound.

Average Conditional Min-Entropy. Let X be a random-variable supported on a finite set $\mathcal{X}$ and let Z be a (possibly correlated) random variable supported on a finite set $\mathcal{Z}$. The average-conditional min-entropy $\tilde{H}_\infty(X|Z)$ of X given Z is defined as

$$\tilde{H}_\infty(X|Z) = -\log\left(\mathsf{E}_z\left[\max_{x \in \mathcal{X}} \Pr[X = x | Z = z]\right]\right).$$

We will use the following easy-to-establish fact about uniform distributions on binary vector-spaces: If $\mathsf{U}, \mathsf{V} \subseteq \mathbb{Z}_2^n$ are sub-vectorspaces of $\mathbb{Z}_2^n$, and if $\mathbf{u} \xleftarrow{\$} \mathsf{U}$ and $\mathbf{v} \xleftarrow{\$} \mathsf{V}$, then it holds that

$$\tilde{H}_\infty(\mathbf{u}|\mathbf{u} + \mathbf{v}) = \dim(\mathsf{U} \cap \mathsf{V}).$$

Extractors. A function $\mathsf{Ext} : \{0,1\}^d \times \mathcal{X} \to \{0,1\}^\ell$ is called a *seeded strong average-case (k,ϵ)-extractor*, if it holds for all random variables X with support $\mathcal{X}$ and Z defined on some finite support that if $\tilde{H}_\infty(X|Z) \geq k$, then it holds that

$$(\mathsf{s}, \mathsf{Ext}(\mathsf{s}, X), Z) \approx_\epsilon (\mathsf{s}, U, Z),$$

where $\mathsf{s} \xleftarrow{\$} \{0,1\}^d$ and $U \xleftarrow{\$} \{0,1\}^\ell$. Such extractors can be constructed from universal hash functions [11,12]. In fact, any extractor is an average-case extractor for slightly worse parameters by the averaging principle[3].

2.3   Lattices

We recall the standard facts about lattices. A lattice $\Lambda \subseteq \mathbb{R}^m$ is the set of all integer-linear combinations of a set of linearly independent basis-vectors, i.e. for every lattice Λ there exists a full-rank matrix $\mathbf{B} \in \mathbb{R}^{k \times m}$ such that $\Lambda = \Lambda(\mathbf{B}) = \{\mathbf{z} \cdot \mathbf{B} \mid \mathbf{z} \in \mathbb{Z}^k\}$. We call k the rank of Λ and $\mathbf{B}$ a basis of Λ. More generally, for a set $S \subseteq \Lambda$ we denote by $\Lambda(S)$ the smallest sub-lattice of Λ which contains S. Moreover, we will write $\mathsf{rank}(S)$ to denote $\mathsf{rank}((\Lambda(S))$.

The dual-lattice $\Lambda^* = \Lambda^*(\Lambda)$ of a lattice Λ is defined by $\Lambda^*(\Lambda) = \{\mathbf{x} \in \mathbb{R}^n \mid \forall \mathbf{y} \in \Lambda : \langle \mathbf{x}, \mathbf{y} \rangle \in \mathbb{Z}\}$. Note that it holds that $(\Lambda^*)^* = \Lambda$. The determinant of a lattice Λ is defined by $\det \Lambda = \sqrt{\det(\mathbf{B} \cdot \mathbf{B}^\top)}$ where $\mathbf{B}$ is any basis of Λ. It holds that $\det \Lambda^* = 1/\det \Lambda$. If $\Lambda = \Lambda(\mathbf{B})$ and the norm of each row of $\mathbf{B}$ is at most ℓ, then an argument using Gram-Schmidt orthogonalization establishes $\det \mathbf{B} \leq \ell^k$.

For a basis $\mathbf{B} \in \mathbb{R}^{k \times m}$ of Λ, we define the parallel-epiped of $\mathbf{B}$ by $\mathcal{P}(\mathbf{B}) = \{\mathbf{x} \cdot \mathbf{B} \mid \mathbf{x} \in [-1/2, 1/2)^k\}$. In abuse of notation we write $\mathcal{P}(\Lambda)$ to denote $\mathcal{P}(\mathbf{B})$ for some canonic basis $\mathbf{B}$ of Λ (such as e.g. a Hermite basis). For lattices $\Lambda \subseteq \Lambda_0$, we will use $\mathcal{P}(\Lambda) \cap \Lambda_0$ as a system of (unique) representatives for the quotient group Λ_0/Λ.

We say that a lattice is q-ary if $(q\mathbb{Z})^m \subseteq \Lambda \subseteq \mathbb{Z}^m$. In particular, for every q-ary lattice Λ there exists a matrix $\mathbf{A} \in \mathbb{Z}_q^{k \times m}$ such that $\Lambda = \Lambda_q(\mathbf{A}) = \{\mathbf{y} \in \mathbb{Z}^m \mid \exists \mathbf{x} \in \mathbb{Z}_q^k : \mathbf{y} = \mathbf{x} \cdot \mathbf{A}(\bmod q)\}$. We also define the lattice $\Lambda_q^\perp(\mathbf{A}) = \{\mathbf{y} \in \mathbb{Z}_q^m \mid \mathbf{A} \cdot \mathbf{y} = 0(\bmod q)\}$. It holds that $(\Lambda_q(\mathbf{A}))^* = \frac{1}{q}\Lambda_q^\perp(\mathbf{A})$.

Gaussians. The Gaussian function $\rho_\sigma : \mathbb{R}^m \to \mathbb{R}$ is defined by

$$\rho_\sigma(\mathbf{x}) = e^{-\pi \cdot \frac{\|\mathbf{x}\|^2}{\sigma^2}}.$$

For a lattice $\Lambda \subseteq \mathbb{R}^m$ and a parameter $\sigma > 0$, we define the *discrete Gaussian distribution* $D_{\Lambda,\sigma}$ on Λ as the distribution with probability-mass function $\Pr[\mathbf{x} = \mathbf{x}'] = \rho_\sigma(\mathbf{x}')/\rho_\sigma(\Lambda)$ for all $\mathbf{x}' \in \Lambda$. Let in the following $\mathcal{B} = \{\mathbf{x} \in \mathbb{R}^m \mid \|\mathbf{x}\| \leq 1\}$ be the closed ball of radius 1 in $\mathbb{R}^m$. A standard concentration inequality for discrete gaussians on general lattices is provided by Banaszczyk's Theorem.

---

[3] I.e. a simple application of Markov's inequality.

Theorem 2.2 ([6]). *For any lattice $\Lambda \in \mathbb{R}^m$, parameter $\sigma > 0$ and $u \geq 1/\sqrt{2\pi}$ it holds that*

$$\rho_\sigma(\Lambda \setminus u\sigma\sqrt{m}\mathcal{B}) \leq 2^{-c_u \cdot m} \cdot \rho_\sigma(\Lambda),$$

where $c_u = -\log(\sqrt{2\pi e}u \cdot e^{-\pi u^2})$.

Setting $\Lambda = \mathbb{Z}^m$ and $u = 1$ in Theorem 2.2 we obtain the following corollary.

Corollary 2.3. *Let $\sigma > 0$ and $\mathbf{x} \xleftarrow{\$} D_{\mathbb{Z}^m,\sigma}$. Then it holds that $\|\mathbf{x}\| \leq \sigma \cdot \sqrt{m}$, except with probability 2^{-m}.*

Uniform Matrix Distributions with Decoding Trapdoor. For our construction we will need an efficiently samplable ensemble of matrices which is statistically close to uniform and is equipped with an efficient bounded-distance-decoder. Such an ensemble was first constructed by Ajtai [2] for q-ary lattices with prime q. We use a more efficient ensemble due to Micciancio and Peikert [25] which works for arbitrary modulus.

Lemma 2.4 ([25]). *Let $\kappa(n) = \omega(\sqrt{\log(n)})$ be any function that grows faster than $\sqrt{\log(n)}$ and τ be a sufficiently large constant. There exists a pair of algorithms* (SampleWithTrapdoor, Decode) *such that if* $(\mathbf{A}, \mathrm{td}) \leftarrow$ SampleWithTrapdoor(q, n), *then $\mathbf{A}$ is of size $n \times m$ with $m = m(q, n) = O(n \cdot \log(q))$ and $\mathbf{A}$ is 2^{-n} close to uniform. For any $\mathbf{s} \in \mathbb{Z}_q^m$ and $\boldsymbol{\eta} \in \mathbb{Z}_q^m$ with $\|\boldsymbol{\eta}\| < \frac{q}{\sqrt{m} \cdot \kappa(n)}$ the algorithm* Decode *on input* td *and $\mathbf{s} \cdot \mathbf{A} + \boldsymbol{\eta}$ will output $\mathbf{s}$.*

2.4 Learning with Errors

The learning with errors (LWE) problem was defined by Regev [33]. In this work we exclusively use the decisional version. The $\mathrm{LWE}_{n,m,q,\chi}$ problem, for $n, m, q \in \mathbb{N}$ and for a distribution χ supported over $\mathbb{Z}$ is to distinguish between the distributions $(\mathbf{A}, \mathbf{s}\mathbf{A} + \mathbf{e} \pmod{q})$ and $(\mathbf{A}, \mathbf{u})$, where $\mathbf{A}$ is uniform in $\mathbb{Z}_q^{n \times m}$, $\mathbf{s}$ is a uniform row vector in $\mathbb{Z}_q^n$, $\mathbf{e}$ is a uniform row vector drawn from χ^m, and $\mathbf{u}$ is a uniform vector in $\mathbb{Z}_q^m$. Often we consider the hardness of solving LWE for *any* $m = \mathrm{poly}(n \log q)$. This problem is denoted $\mathrm{LWE}_{n,q,\chi}$. The matrix version of this problem asks to distinguish $(\mathbf{A}, \mathbf{S} \cdot \mathbf{A} + \mathbf{E})$ from $(\mathbf{A}, \mathbf{U})$, where $\mathbf{S} \xleftarrow{\$} \mathbb{Z}_q^{k \times n}$, $\mathbf{E} \xleftarrow{\$} \chi^{k \times m}$ and $\mathbf{U} \leftarrow \mathbb{Z}_q^{k \times m}$. The hardness of the matrix version for any $k = \mathrm{poly}(n)$ can be established from $\mathrm{LWE}_{n,m,q,\chi}$ via a routine hybrid-argument.

As shown in [30,33], the $\mathrm{LWE}_{n,q,\chi}$ problem with χ being the discrete Gaussian distribution with parameter $\sigma = \alpha q \geq 2\sqrt{n}$ (i.e. the distribution over $\mathbb{Z}$ where the probability of x is proportional to $e^{-\pi(|x|/\sigma)^2}$, see more details below), is at least as hard as approximating the shortest independent vector problem (SIVP) to within a factor of $\gamma = \tilde{O}(n/\alpha)$ in *worst case* dimension n lattices. This is proven using a quantum reduction. Classical reductions (to a slightly different problem) exist as well [9,29] but with somewhat worse parameters.

The best known (classical or quantum) algorithms for these problems run in time $2^{\tilde{O}(n/\log\gamma)}$, and in particular they are conjectured to be intractable for $\gamma = \text{poly}(n)$.

3   Lossy Modes for q-Ary Lattices

The following lemmata borrow techniques of the proofs of two lemmata by Chung et al. [10] (Lemmas 3.3 and 3.4), but are not directly implied by these lemmata. In this section and Sect. 4, it will be instructive to think of Λ_0 as $\mathbb{Z}^n$, which will be the case in our application in Sect. 5.

Lemma 3.1. *Let $\Lambda \subseteq \Lambda_0 \subseteq \mathbb{R}^m$ be full rank lattices and let $T \subseteq \Lambda_0$ be a system of coset representatives of Λ_0/Λ, i.e. we can write every $\mathbf{x} \in \Lambda_0$ as $\mathbf{x} = \mathbf{t} + \mathbf{z}$ for unique $\mathbf{t} \in T$ and $\mathbf{z} \in \Lambda$. Then it holds for any parameter $\sigma > 0$ that*

$$\frac{\rho_\sigma(T)}{\rho_\sigma(\Lambda_0)} \leq \frac{1}{\rho_\sigma(\Lambda)}.$$

Proof. As the $T + \mathbf{y}$ cover Λ_0 it holds that

$$\rho_\sigma(\Lambda_0) = \sum_{\mathbf{y} \in \Lambda} \frac{1}{2}(\rho_\sigma(T + \mathbf{y}) + \rho_\sigma(T - \mathbf{y}))$$

$$= \sum_{\mathbf{y} \in \Lambda} \sum_{\mathbf{t} \in T} \frac{1}{2}(\rho_\sigma(\mathbf{t} + \mathbf{y}) + \rho_\sigma(\mathbf{t} - \mathbf{y}))$$

$$= \sum_{\mathbf{y} \in \Lambda} \sum_{\mathbf{t} \in T} \rho_\sigma(\mathbf{y}) \cdot \rho_\sigma(\mathbf{t}) \cdot \underbrace{\frac{1}{2}(e^{-2\pi\langle \mathbf{t},\mathbf{y}\rangle/\sigma^2} + e^{2\pi\langle \mathbf{t},\mathbf{y}\rangle/\sigma^2})}_{\geq 1}$$

$$\geq \sum_{\mathbf{y} \in \Lambda} \rho_\sigma(\mathbf{y}) \sum_{\mathbf{t} \in T} \rho_\sigma(\mathbf{t})$$

$$= \rho_\sigma(\Lambda) \cdot \rho_\sigma(T),$$

where the first equality follows from the fact that $\sum_{\mathbf{y} \in \Lambda} \rho_\sigma(T + \mathbf{y}) = \sum_{\mathbf{y} \in \Lambda} \rho_\sigma(T - \mathbf{y}) = \rho_\sigma(\Lambda_0)$. The claim follows immediately.

Lemma 3.2. *Fix a matrix $\mathbf{A} \in \mathbb{Z}_q^{n \times m}$ with $m = O(n\log(q))$ and a parameter $0 < \sigma < \frac{q}{2\sqrt{m}}$. Let $\mathbf{s} \xleftarrow{\$} \mathbb{Z}_q^n$ and $\mathbf{e} \xleftarrow{\$} D_{\mathbb{Z}^m,\sigma}$. Then it holds that $\tilde{H}_\infty(\mathbf{s}|\mathbf{s}\mathbf{A} + \mathbf{e} \bmod q) \geq -\log\left(\frac{1}{\rho_\sigma(\Lambda_q(\mathbf{A}))} + 2^{-m}\right).$*

Proof. Given arbitrary $\mathbf{A}$ and $\mathbf{y}$, we would like to find an $\mathbf{s}^*$ that maximizes the probability $\Pr[\mathbf{s} = \mathbf{s}^* | \mathbf{y} = \mathbf{s}\mathbf{A} + \mathbf{e}]$. By Bayes' rule, it holds that

$$
\begin{aligned}
\Pr[\mathbf{s} = \mathbf{s}^* | \mathbf{y} = \mathbf{s}\mathbf{A} + \mathbf{e}] &= \Pr[\mathbf{y} = \mathbf{s}\mathbf{A} + \mathbf{e} | \mathbf{s} = \mathbf{s}^*] \cdot \frac{\Pr[\mathbf{s} = \mathbf{s}^*]}{\Pr[\mathbf{y} = \mathbf{s}\mathbf{A} + \mathbf{e}]} \\
&= \Pr[\mathbf{e} = \mathbf{y} - \mathbf{s}^*\mathbf{A}] \cdot \frac{\Pr[\mathbf{s} = \mathbf{s}^*]}{\sum_{\mathbf{s}'} \Pr[\mathbf{y} = \mathbf{s}\mathbf{A} + \mathbf{e} | \mathbf{s} = \mathbf{s}'] \Pr[\mathbf{s} = \mathbf{s}']} \\
&= \Pr[\mathbf{e} = \mathbf{y} - \mathbf{s}^*\mathbf{A}] \cdot \frac{q^{-n}}{\sum_{\mathbf{s}'} \Pr[\mathbf{e} = \mathbf{y} - \mathbf{s}'\mathbf{A}] q^{-n}} \\
&= \frac{\Pr[\mathbf{e} = \mathbf{y} - \mathbf{s}^*\mathbf{A}]}{\sum_{\mathbf{s}'} \Pr[\mathbf{e} = \mathbf{y} - \mathbf{s}'\mathbf{A}]}.
\end{aligned}
$$

As the denominator $\sum_{\mathbf{s}'} \Pr[\mathbf{e} = \mathbf{y} - \mathbf{s}'\mathbf{A}]$ is independent of $\mathbf{s}^*$, it suffices to maximize the numerator $\Pr[\mathbf{e} = \mathbf{y} - \mathbf{s}^*\mathbf{A}]$ with respect to $\mathbf{s}^*$. As $\Pr[\mathbf{e} = \mathbf{y} - \mathbf{s}^*\mathbf{A}] = \frac{\rho_\sigma(y - s^*\mathbf{A})}{\rho_\sigma(\mathbb{Z}^m)}$ is monotonically decreasing in $\|y - s^*\mathbf{A}\|$, this probability is maximal for the $\mathbf{s}^*$ that minimizes $\|\mathbf{y} - \mathbf{s}^*\mathbf{A}\|$.

Let $V \subseteq \mathbb{Z}^n$ be the *discretized Voronoi-cell* of $\Lambda_q(\mathbf{A})$, that is V consists of all the points in $\mathbb{Z}^m$ that are (strictly) closer to 0 than to any other point in Λ and, for any point $\mathbf{x} \in \mathbb{Z}^m$ that is equi-distant to several lattice-points $\mathbf{z}_1, \ldots, \mathbf{z}_\ell$ (where $\mathbf{z}_1 = 0$), assume that there is some tie-breaking rule $\mathbf{x} \mapsto i(\mathbf{x})$, such that $\mathbf{x} - \mathbf{z}_{i(\mathbf{x})} \subset V$, but for all $j \in [\ell] \setminus \{i(\mathbf{x})\}$ it holds that $\mathbf{x} - \mathbf{z}_j \notin V$. By construction, V is a system of coset representatives of $\mathbb{Z}^m / \Lambda_q(\mathbf{A})$.

Moreover, for the maximum-likelihood $\mathbf{s}^*$ it holds that $\Pr[\mathbf{s} = \mathbf{s}^* | \mathbf{y} = \mathbf{s}\mathbf{A} + \mathbf{e}] = \Pr[\mathbf{e} \bmod q \in V]$. By Corollary 2.3 it holds that $\|\mathbf{e}\| \le \sigma \cdot \sqrt{m} < q/2$, except with probability 2^{-m}. Moreover, conditioned on $\|\mathbf{e}\| < q/2$ the events $\mathbf{e} \bmod q \in V$ and $\mathbf{e} \in V$ are equivalent. We can therefore bound $\Pr[\mathbf{e} \bmod q \in V] \le \Pr[\mathbf{e} \in V] + 2^{-m}$. By Lemma 3.1 we obtain $\Pr[\mathbf{e} \in V] \le \frac{\rho_\sigma(V)}{\rho_\sigma(\mathbb{Z}^m)} \le \frac{1}{\rho_\sigma(\Lambda_q(\mathbf{A}))}$ and therefore $\Pr[\mathbf{e} \bmod q \in V] \le \frac{1}{\rho_\sigma(\Lambda_q(\mathbf{A}))} + 2^{-m}$

We conclude that $\max_{\mathbf{s}^* \in \mathbb{Z}_q^n} \Pr[\mathbf{s} = \mathbf{s}^* | \mathbf{y} = \mathbf{s}\mathbf{A} + \mathbf{e}] = \Pr[\mathbf{e} \bmod q \in V] \le \frac{1}{\rho_\sigma(\Lambda_q(\mathbf{A}))} + 2^{-m}$. Thus, it holds that

$$
\begin{aligned}
\tilde{H}_\infty(\mathbf{s} | \mathbf{s}\mathbf{A} + \mathbf{e}) &= -\log\left(\mathsf{E}_\mathbf{y}\left[\max_{\mathbf{s}^*} \Pr_{\mathbf{s}, \mathbf{e}}[\mathbf{s} = \mathbf{s}^* | \mathbf{y} = \mathbf{s}\mathbf{A} + \mathbf{e}]\right]\right) \\
&= -\log(\mathsf{E}_\mathbf{y}[\Pr[\mathbf{e} \bmod q \in V]]) \\
&= -\log(\Pr[\mathbf{e} \bmod q \in V]) \\
&\ge -\log\left(\frac{1}{\rho_\sigma(\Lambda_q(\mathbf{A}))} + 2^{-m}\right)
\end{aligned}
$$

4   Partial Smoothing

In this section we will state a variant of the smoothing lemma of Micciancio and Regev [26]. Consider a discrete gaussian $D_{\Lambda_0, \sigma}$ on a lattice Λ_0. As in the setting of the smoothing Lemma of [26], we want to analyze what happens to the distribution of this Gaussian when we reduce it modulo a sublattice $\Lambda \subseteq \Lambda_0$. The new lemma states that if the mass of the Fourier-transform of the probability-mass function of $D_{\Lambda_0,\sigma}$ mod Λ is concentrated on short vectors of the dual lattice Λ^*, then $D_{\Lambda_0,\sigma}$ mod Λ will be uniform on a certain sublattice Λ_1 with $\Lambda_0 \subseteq \Lambda_1 \subseteq \Lambda$.

Lemma 4.1. *Let $\sigma > 0$ and let $\Lambda \subseteq \Lambda_0 \subseteq \mathbb{R}^n$ be full-rank lattices where $\det(\Lambda_0) = 1$. Furthermore, let $\gamma > 0$. Define $\Lambda_1 = \{\mathbf{z} \in \Lambda_0 \mid \forall \mathbf{y} \in \Lambda^* \cap \gamma \mathcal{B} : \langle \mathbf{y}, \mathbf{z} \rangle \in \mathbb{Z}\}$. Given that $\rho_{1/\sigma}(\Lambda^* \backslash \gamma \mathcal{B}) \leq \epsilon$, it holds that*

$$\mathbf{x} \bmod \Lambda \approx_\epsilon (\mathbf{x} + \mathbf{u}) \bmod \Lambda,$$

where $\mathbf{x} \overset{\$}{\leftarrow} D_{\Lambda_0,\sigma}$ and $\mathbf{u} \overset{\$}{\leftarrow} \mathcal{P}(\Lambda) \cap \Lambda_1$.

Notice that for the case of $\Lambda^* \cap \gamma \mathcal{B} = \{0\}$ we recover the standard smoothing lemma of [26]. The proof of Lemma 4.1 uses standard Fourier-analytic techniques akin to [26] and is deferred to Appendix A. We will make use of the following consequence of Lemma 4.1.

Corollary 4.2. *Let $q > 0$ be an integer and let $\gamma > 0$. Let $\mathbf{A} \in \mathbb{Z}_q^{m \times n}$ and let $\sigma > 0$ and $\epsilon > 0$ be such that $\rho_{q/\sigma}(\Lambda_q(\mathbf{A}) \backslash \gamma \mathcal{B}) \leq \epsilon$. Let $\mathbf{D} \in \mathbb{Z}_q^{k \times m}$ be a full-rank (and therefore minimal) matrix with $\Lambda_q^\perp(\mathbf{D}) = \{\mathbf{x} \in \mathbb{Z}^m \mid \forall \mathbf{y} \in \Lambda_q(\mathbf{A}) \cap \gamma \mathcal{B} : \langle \mathbf{x}, \mathbf{y} \rangle = 0 \pmod q\}$. Let $\mathbf{x} \overset{\$}{\leftarrow} D_{\mathbb{Z}^m,\sigma}$ and $\mathbf{u} \overset{\$}{\leftarrow} \Lambda_q^\perp(\mathbf{D})$ mod q. Then it holds that*

$$\mathbf{A}\mathbf{x} \bmod q \approx_\epsilon \mathbf{A} \cdot (\mathbf{x} + \mathbf{u}) \bmod q.$$

Proof. Setting $\Lambda_0 = \mathbb{Z}^n$, $\Lambda = \Lambda_q^\perp(\mathbf{A})$ and $\gamma' = \gamma/q$, it holds that $\Lambda^* = \frac{1}{q}\Lambda_q(\mathbf{A})$ and

$$\epsilon \geq \rho_{q/\sigma}(\Lambda_q(\mathbf{A}) \backslash \gamma \mathcal{B}) = \rho_{1/\sigma}\left(\frac{1}{q}\Lambda_q(\mathbf{A}) \backslash \frac{\gamma}{q}\mathcal{B}\right) = \rho_{1/\sigma}(\Lambda^* \backslash \gamma' \mathcal{B}).$$

Therefore, we can set

$$\begin{aligned}
\Lambda_1 &= \{\mathbf{x} \in \mathbb{Z}^m \mid \forall \mathbf{y} \in \Lambda^* \cap \gamma' \mathcal{B} : \langle \mathbf{x}, \mathbf{y} \rangle \in \mathbb{Z}\} \\
&= \{\mathbf{x} \in \mathbb{Z}^m \mid \forall \mathbf{y} \in \Lambda_q(\mathbf{A}) \cap \gamma \mathcal{B} : \langle \mathbf{x}, \mathbf{y} \rangle = 0(\bmod q)\} \\
&= \Lambda_q^\perp(\mathbf{D}).
\end{aligned}$$

Now it holds by Lemma 4.1 as $\mathbf{u} \overset{\$}{\leftarrow} \Lambda_q^\perp(\mathbf{D})$ that $\mathbf{x} \bmod \Lambda_q^\perp(\mathbf{A}) \approx_\epsilon (\mathbf{x} + \mathbf{u}) \bmod \Lambda_q^\perp(\mathbf{A})$. Write $\mathbf{y}_1 = \mathbf{x} \bmod \Lambda_q^\perp(\mathbf{A})$ as $\mathbf{y}_1 = \mathbf{x} + \mathbf{z}_1 \bmod q$ for a suitable $\mathbf{z}_1 \in \Lambda_q^\perp(\mathbf{A})$. Likewise, we can write $\mathbf{y}_2 = \mathbf{x} + \mathbf{u} \bmod \Lambda_q^\perp(\mathbf{A})$ as $\mathbf{y}_2 = \mathbf{x} + \mathbf{u} + \mathbf{z}_2 \bmod q$ for a suitable $\mathbf{z}_2$. Thus it holds that

$$\mathbf{A}\mathbf{x} = \mathbf{A}(\mathbf{x} + \mathbf{z}_1) \approx_\epsilon \mathbf{A}(\mathbf{x} + \mathbf{u} + \mathbf{z}_2) = \mathbf{A}(\mathbf{x} + \mathbf{u}) \ (\bmod q).$$

We will also use the following lower bound on the gaussian measure of lattices that have many short linearly independent vectors. The proof of Lemma 4.3 is technically similar to the proof of the transference theorem in [6].

Lemma 4.3. *Let $\Lambda \in \mathbb{R}^m$, $\sigma > 0$ and $\gamma > 0$ be such that $\Lambda \cap \gamma\mathcal{B}$ contains at least k linearly independent vectors. Then it holds that $\rho_\sigma(\Lambda) \geq (\sigma/\gamma)^k$.*

Proof. Let $\Lambda' \subseteq$ be the sublattice generated by the vectors in $\Lambda \cap \gamma\mathcal{B}$. Let k be the dimension of the span of Λ'. As $\Lambda' \subseteq \Lambda$, it holds that $\rho_\sigma(\Lambda) \geq \rho_\sigma(\Lambda')$. As Λ' has a basis of length at most γ, we we have that $\det(\Lambda') \leq \gamma^k$ and conclude $\det((\Lambda')^*) = 1/\det(\Lambda') \geq \frac{1}{\gamma^k}$. By the Poisson-summation formula, we get that

$$\rho_\sigma(\Lambda') = \sigma^k \cdot \det((\Lambda')^*) \cdot \rho_{1/\sigma}((\Lambda')^*)$$
$$\geq (\sigma/\gamma)^k,$$

as $\rho_{1/\sigma}((\Lambda')^*) \geq 1$. Thus we conclude that $\rho_\sigma(\Lambda) \geq (\sigma/\gamma)^k$.

5 Our Oblivious Transfer Protocol

We are now ready to provide our statistically sender private oblivious transfer protocol. In the following, let $q, n, \ell = \text{poly}(\lambda)$ and assume that q is of the form $q = 2p$ for an odd p. Let (SampleWithTrapdoor, Decode) be the pair of algorithms provided in Lemma 2.4 and let $m = m(q,n)$ be such that the matrices $\mathbf{A}$ generated by SampleWithTrapdoor$(q, 2n)$ are elements of $\mathbb{Z}^{2n \times m}$. Let $\text{Ext}_0 : \{0,1\}^d \times \{0,1\}^n \to \{0,1\}^\ell$ and $\text{Ext}_1 : \{0,1\}^d \times \mathbb{Z}_q^{2n} \to \{0,1\}^\ell$ be seeded extractors, both with seed-length d and ℓ bits of output. Finally, let $\sigma_0, \sigma_1 > 0$ be parameters for discrete Gaussians and χ be an LWE error-distribution.

The protocol $\text{OT} = (\text{OTR}, \text{OTS}, \text{OTD})$ is given as follows.

- OTR$(1^\lambda, \beta \in \{0,1\})$:
  - If $\beta = 0$, choose a matrix $\mathbf{A}_1 \xleftarrow{\$} \mathbb{Z}_q^{n \times m}$, a matrix $\mathbf{S} \leftarrow \mathbb{Z}_q^{n \times n}$, $\mathbf{E} \xleftarrow{\$} \chi^{n \times m}$. Set $\mathbf{A}_2 \leftarrow \mathbf{S} \cdot \mathbf{A}_1 + \mathbf{E}$ and $\mathbf{A} \leftarrow \begin{bmatrix} \mathbf{A}_1 \\ \mathbf{A}_2 \end{bmatrix}$. Repeat this step until $\mathbf{A}$ mod 2 has full rank.
    Output $ot_1 \leftarrow \mathbf{A}$ and $st \leftarrow \mathbf{S}$.
  - If $\beta = 1$, sample $(\mathbf{A}, td) \xleftarrow{\$} \text{SampleWithTrapdoor}(q, 2n)$. Repeat this step until $\mathbf{A}$ mod 2 has full rank. Output $ot_1 \leftarrow \mathbf{A}$ and $st \leftarrow td$.
- OTS$(1^\lambda, (\mu_0, \mu_1) \in (\{0,1\}^\ell)^2, ot_1 = \mathbf{A})$:
  - Check if $\mathbf{A}$ mod 2 has full rank, if not output $\bot$.
  - Parse $\mathbf{A} = \begin{bmatrix} \mathbf{A}_1 \\ \mathbf{A}_2 \end{bmatrix}$. Sample and reject a discrete Gaussian $\mathbf{x} \xleftarrow{\$} D_{\mathbb{Z}^m, \sigma_0}$ until $\|\mathbf{x}\| < \sigma_0\sqrt{m}$. Choose a uniformly random $\mathbf{r} \leftarrow \{0,1\}^n$ and choose a random seed $s_0 \xleftarrow{\$} \{0,1\}^d$ for the extractor Ext_0. Compute $\mathbf{y}_1 \leftarrow \mathbf{A}_1\mathbf{x}$ and $\mathbf{y}_2 \leftarrow \mathbf{A}_2\mathbf{x} + \frac{q}{2} \cdot \mathbf{r}$. Set $c_0 \leftarrow (\mathbf{y}_1, \mathbf{y}_2, s_0, \text{Ext}_0(s_0, \mathbf{r}) \oplus \mu_0)$.
  - Sample and reject $\boldsymbol{\eta} \xleftarrow{\$} D_{\mathbb{Z}^m, \sigma_1}$ until $\|\boldsymbol{\eta}\| < \sigma_1\sqrt{m}$. Choose a uniformly random $\mathbf{t} \xleftarrow{\$} \mathbb{Z}_q^{2n}$ and a seed $s_1 \xleftarrow{\$} \{0,1\}^d$ for the extractor Ext_1. Compute $\mathbf{y} \leftarrow \mathbf{t} \cdot \mathbf{A} + \boldsymbol{\eta}$ set $c_1 \leftarrow (\mathbf{y}, s_1, \text{Ext}_1(s_1, \mathbf{t}) \oplus \mu_1)$.
  - Output $ot_2 \leftarrow (c_0, c_1)$.
- OTD$(\beta, st, ot_2 = (c_0, c))$
  - If $\beta = 0$: Parse $st = \mathbf{S}$ and $c_0 = (\mathbf{y}_1, \mathbf{y}_2, s_0, \tau)$. Compute $\mathbf{r}' \leftarrow \lfloor \mathbf{y}_2 - \mathbf{S} \cdot \mathbf{y}_1 \rceil_{q/2}$ and output $\mu_0' \leftarrow \text{Ext}_0(s_0, \mathbf{r}') \oplus \tau$.

- If $\beta = 1$: Parse st = td and $c_1 = (y, s_1, \tau)$. Compute $t' \leftarrow$ Decode(td, y) and output $\mu_1' \leftarrow \mathsf{Ext}_1(s_1, t') \oplus \tau$.

We will first show correctness of our protocol.

Lemma 5.1 (Correctness). *Assume that the distribution χ is a B-bounded. Provided that $\sigma_0 \leq \frac{q}{4B \cdot m}$ and $\sigma_1 \leq \frac{q}{m \cdot \kappa(n)}$ (where $\kappa(n) = \omega(\sqrt{\log(n)})$ as in Lemma 2.4), the protocol OT is perfectly correct.*

Proof. First note that as $m \geq n \cdot \log(q)$, it holds for a uniformly random $\mathbf{A} \xleftarrow{\$} \mathbb{Z}_q^{2n \times m}$ that $\mathbf{A}$ mod 2 has full rank, except with negligible probability 2^{n-m} (as detailed in Sect. 2.2). Moreover for $\mathbf{x} \leftarrow D_{\mathbb{Z}^m, \sigma_0}$ and $\boldsymbol{\eta} \xleftarrow{\$} D_{\mathbb{Z}^m, \sigma_1}$ it holds by Corollary 2.3 that $\|\mathbf{x}\| < \sigma_0 \sqrt{m}$ and $\|\boldsymbol{\eta}\| < \sigma_1 \sqrt{m}$, except with negligible probability. Thus, rejection in OTR and OTS happens only with negligible probability.

In the case of $\beta = 0$, it holds that

$$\mathbf{y}_2 - \mathbf{S} \cdot \mathbf{y}_1 = (\mathbf{S}\mathbf{A}_1 + \mathbf{E})\mathbf{x} + \frac{q}{2}\mathbf{r} - \mathbf{S}\mathbf{A}_1\mathbf{x}$$

$$= \mathbf{E} \cdot \mathbf{x} + \frac{q}{2} \cdot \mathbf{r}.$$

By the Cauchy-Schwarz inequality it holds for each row $\mathbf{e}_i$ of $\mathbf{E}$ that $|\langle \mathbf{e}_i, \mathbf{x} \rangle| \leq \|\mathbf{e}_i\| \cdot \|\mathbf{x}\|$. As the entries of $\mathbf{e}_i$ are chosen according to χ, we can bound $\|\mathbf{e}_i\|$ by $\|\mathbf{e}_i\| \leq B \cdot \sqrt{m}$. As $\|\mathbf{x}\| < \sigma_0 \cdot \sqrt{m}$, we have that

$$|\langle \mathbf{e}_i, \mathbf{x} \rangle| \leq B \cdot \sigma_0 \cdot m < \frac{q}{4}$$

as $\sigma_0 \leq \frac{q}{4B \cdot m}$. We conclude that $\mathbf{r}' = \lfloor \mathbf{y}_2 - \mathbf{S} \cdot \mathbf{y}_1 \rceil_{q/2}$ is identical to the vector $\mathbf{r}$ used during encryption. Consequently, it holds that $\mu_0' = \mathsf{Ext}_0(s_0, \mathbf{r}') \oplus \tau = \mathsf{Ext}_0(s_0, \mathbf{r}') \oplus \mathsf{Ext}_0(s_0, \mathbf{r}) \oplus \mu_0 = \mu_0$.

For the case of $\beta = 1$, as $\|\boldsymbol{\eta}\| < \sigma_1 \sqrt{m} \leq \frac{q}{\sqrt{m} \cdot \kappa(n)}$ it holds by Lemma 2.4 that Decode(td, $\mathbf{y}_1$) outputs the correct $t' = t$. We conclude that $\mu_1' = \mathsf{Ext}_1(s_1, t') \oplus \tau = \mathsf{Ext}_1(s_1, t') \oplus \mathsf{Ext}_1(s_1, t) \oplus \mu = \mu_1$.

We now show that OT has computational receiver privacy under the decisional matrix LWE assumption.

Lemma 5.2 (Computational Receiver Security). *Given that the decisional $LWE_{n,q,\chi}$-assumption holds, the protocol OT = (OTR, OTS, OTD) has receiver privacy.*

Proof. Let $(\mathbf{A}, \mathsf{st}_0) \leftarrow \mathsf{OTR}(1^\lambda, 0)$ and $(\mathbf{A}', \mathsf{st}_1) \leftarrow \mathsf{OTR}(1^\lambda, 1)$. Assume towards contradiction that there exists a PPT-distinguisher $\mathcal{D}$ which distinguishes $\mathbf{A}$ and $\mathbf{A}'$ with non-negligible advantage ϵ. We can immediately use $\mathcal{D}$ to distinguish decisional matrix LWE. Decomposing $\mathbf{A} = \begin{bmatrix} \mathbf{A}_1 \\ \mathbf{A}_2 \end{bmatrix}$, it holds that $\mathbf{A}_1$ is uniformly random and $\mathbf{A}_2 = \mathbf{S} \cdot \mathbf{A}_1 + \mathbf{E}$, i.e. $(\mathbf{A}_1, \mathbf{A}_2)$ is a sample of the matrix LWE distribution. On the other hand, due to the uniformity property of SampleWithTrapdoor (provided in Lemma 2.4) it holds that $\mathbf{A}' \approx_s \mathbf{A}^*$ for a uniformly random $\mathbf{A}^* \xleftarrow{\$} \mathbb{Z}_q^{2n \times m}$. Consequently

$$
\begin{aligned}
\mathsf{Adv}_{LWE}(\mathcal{D}) &= |\Pr[\mathcal{D}(\mathbf{A}) = 1] - \Pr[\mathcal{D}(\mathbf{A}^*) = 1]| \\
&\geq |\Pr[\mathcal{D}(\mathbf{A}) = 1] - \Pr[\mathcal{D}(\mathbf{A}') = 1]| - |\Pr[\mathcal{D}(\mathbf{A}^*) = 1] - \Pr[\mathcal{D}(\mathbf{A}') = 1]| \\
&\geq \epsilon - \mathsf{negl},
\end{aligned}
$$

which contradicts the hardness of decisional matrix LWE.

We will now show that OT is statistically sender-private.

Theorem 5.3. (Statistical Sender Security). *Let $q = 2p$ for an odd p. Given that $\sigma_0 \cdot \sigma_1 \geq 4\sqrt{m} \cdot q$, $\sigma_1 < \frac{q}{2\sqrt{m}}$ and both Ext_0 and Ext_1 are strong average-case $(n/2, \mathsf{negl})$-extractors, then the above scheme enjoys statistical sender security.*

Proof. Fix a maliciously generated ot_1-message $\mathsf{ot}_1 = \mathbf{A}$. Let in the following $\gamma := \sqrt{m} \cdot \frac{q}{\sigma_0}$. Consider the following two cases.

1. $\rho_{q/\sigma_0}(\Lambda_q(\mathbf{A})) > 2^{n/2+1}$ or $\mathsf{rank}(\Lambda_q(\mathbf{A}) \cap \gamma \mathcal{B})) > n/2$.
2. $\rho_{q/\sigma_0}(\Lambda_q(\mathbf{A})) \leq 2^{n/2+2}$ and $\mathsf{rank}(\Lambda_q(\mathbf{A}) \cap \gamma \mathcal{B}) \leq n/2$.

First notices that the two cases are slightly overlapping, but for any choice of $\mathbf{A}$ one of the two cases must be true.

The unbounded message extractor OTExt takes input $\mathbf{A}$ and decides if item 1 or item 2 holds. If item 1 holds it outputs 0, otherwise 1. Note that $\mathsf{rank}(\Lambda_q(\mathbf{A}) \cap \gamma \mathcal{B})$ can be computed exactly. On the other hand, it is sufficient approximate $\rho_{q/\sigma_0}(\Lambda_q(\mathbf{A}))$ to a certain precision to determine which case holds.

We will now show that in case 1 the sender-message μ_1 is statistically hidden, whereas in case 2 the sender-message μ_0 is statistically hidden.

Case 1. We will start with the (easier) first case. We will show that either statement implies $\rho_{\sigma_1}(\Lambda_q(\mathbf{A})) \geq 2^{n/2+1}$. If it holds that $\rho_{q/\sigma_0}(\Lambda_q(\mathbf{A})) > 2^{n/2+1}$, we can directly conclude that

$$
\rho_{\sigma_1}(\Lambda_q(\mathbf{A})) \geq \rho_{4\sqrt{m} \cdot \frac{q}{\sigma_0}}(\Lambda_q(\mathbf{A})) \geq \rho_{\frac{q}{\sigma_0}}(\Lambda_q(\mathbf{A})) > 2^{n/2+1}.
$$

If the second statement $\mathsf{rank}(\Lambda_q(\mathbf{A}) \cap \gamma \mathcal{B})) > n/2$ holds, Lemma 4.3 implies

$$
\rho_{\sigma_1}(\Lambda_q(\mathbf{A})) \geq (\sigma_1/\gamma)^{n/2+1} \geq 2^{n+2} \geq 2^{n/2+1},
$$

as $\sigma_1 \geq 4\gamma$.

Now let $\mathsf{c}_1 = (\mathbf{y}, \mathsf{s}_1, \tau)$, where $\mathbf{y} \leftarrow \mathbf{t} \cdot \mathbf{A} + \boldsymbol{\eta}$. Note that we can switch to a hybrid in which the distribution of $\boldsymbol{\eta}$ is $D_{\mathbb{Z}^m, \sigma_1}$ instead of the truncated version while only incurring a negligible statistical error.

As $\rho_{\sigma_1}(\Lambda_q(\mathbf{A})) \geq 2^{n/2+1}$ and $\sigma_1 < \frac{q}{2\sqrt{m}}$, Lemma 3.2 implies that

$$
\tilde{H}_\infty(\mathbf{t}|\mathbf{y}) \geq -\log(1/\rho_{\sigma_1}(\Lambda_q(\mathbf{A})) + 2^{-m}) \geq -\log(2^{-n/2-1} + 2^{-m}) \geq n/2
$$

Thus, as Ext_1 is a strong $(n/2, \mathrm{negl})$-extractor, we get that $\mathsf{Ext}_1(\mathbf{s}_1, \mathbf{t})$ is statistically close to uniform given $\mathbf{y}$. Consequently, $\tau = \mathsf{Ext}_1(\mathbf{s}_1, \mathbf{t}) \oplus \mu_1$ is statistically close to uniform given $\mathbf{s}_1$ and $\mathbf{y}$, which concludes the first case.

Case 2. We will now turn to the second case, i.e. it holds that $\rho_{q/\sigma_0}(\Lambda_q(\mathbf{A})) \le 2^{n/2+2}$ and $\mathrm{rank}(\Lambda_q(\mathbf{A}) \cap \gamma \mathcal{B})) \le n/2$. Theorem 2.2 yields that

$$\rho_{q/\sigma_0}(\Lambda_q(\mathbf{A}) \backslash \gamma \mathcal{B}) = \rho_{q/\sigma_0}\left(\Lambda_q(\mathbf{A}) \backslash \frac{\sqrt{m} \cdot q}{\sigma_0} \mathcal{B}\right)$$
$$\le 2^{-C \cdot m} \cdot \rho_{q/\sigma_0}(\Lambda_q(\mathbf{A}))$$
$$\le 2^{-C \cdot m} \cdot 2^{n/2+2} = 2^{n/2+2-C \cdot m}$$

where $C > 0$ is a constant. This expression is negligible as $m \ge n \cdot \log(q)$. Consequently, the precondition $\rho_{q/\sigma_0}(\Lambda_q(\mathbf{A}) \backslash \gamma \mathcal{B}) \le \mathrm{negl}$ of Corollary 4.2 is fulfilled.

Now let $\mathbf{D} \in \mathbb{Z}_q^{k \times m}$ be a full-rank matrix with $\Lambda_q^\perp(\mathbf{D}) = \{\mathbf{z} \in \mathbb{Z}^m \mid \forall \mathbf{v} \in \Lambda_q(\mathbf{A}) \cap \gamma \mathcal{B} : \langle \mathbf{z}, \mathbf{v} \rangle = 0 (\bmod q))\}$. Thus it holds that $\Lambda_q(\mathbf{A}) \cap \gamma \mathcal{B} \subset \Lambda_q(\mathbf{D})$ and there is no matrix with fewer than k rows with this property. As $\mathrm{rank}(\Lambda_q(\mathbf{A}) \cap \gamma \mathcal{B}) \le n/2$, it holds that $k \le n/2$.

Decompose the matrix $\mathbf{A}$ into $\mathbf{A} = \begin{bmatrix} \mathbf{A}_1 \\ \mathbf{A}_2 \end{bmatrix}$ with $\mathbf{A}_1 \in \mathbb{Z}_q^{n \times m}$ and $\mathbf{A}_2 \in \mathbb{Z}_q^{n \times m}$. Let $\mathbf{c}_0 = (\mathbf{y}_1, \mathbf{y}_2, \mathbf{s}_0, \tau)$, where $\mathbf{y}_1 = \mathbf{A}_1 \mathbf{x}$ and $\mathbf{y}_2 = \mathbf{A}_2 \mathbf{x} + \frac{q}{2} \mathbf{r}$ with $\mathbf{x} \xleftarrow{\$} D_{\mathbb{Z}^m, \sigma_0}$ and $\mathbf{r} \xleftarrow{\$} \{0,1\}^n$. As $\rho_{q/\sigma_0}(\Lambda_q(\mathbf{A}) \backslash \gamma \mathcal{B}) \le \epsilon$, Corollary 4.2 implies that

$$(\mathbf{y}_1, \mathbf{y}_2) = \left(\mathbf{A}_1 \mathbf{x}, \mathbf{A}_2 \mathbf{x} + \frac{q}{2} \mathbf{r}\right) \approx_\epsilon \left(\mathbf{A}_1(\mathbf{x} + \mathbf{u}), \mathbf{A}_2(\mathbf{x} + \mathbf{u}) + \frac{q}{2} \mathbf{r}\right) =: (\mathbf{y}_1', \mathbf{y}_2')$$

where $\mathbf{u} \xleftarrow{\$} \Lambda_q^\perp(\mathbf{D})$. We can therefore switch to a hybrid experiment in which we replace $\mathbf{x}$ with $\mathbf{x} + \mathbf{u}$ while only incurring negligible statistical distance. We will now show that $\tilde{H}_\infty(\mathbf{r} | \mathbf{y}_1', \mathbf{y}_2') \ge n/2$.

As $q = 2p$ and p is odd, it holds by the Chinese remainder theorem that

$$\mathbf{y}_1' \equiv (\mathbf{A}_1(\mathbf{x} + \mathbf{u}) \bmod 2, \mathbf{A}_1(\mathbf{x} + \mathbf{u}) \bmod p)$$
$$\mathbf{y}_2' \equiv (\mathbf{A}_2(\mathbf{x} + \mathbf{u}) + \mathbf{r} \bmod 2, \mathbf{A}_1(\mathbf{x} + \mathbf{u}) \bmod p)$$

Note that $\mathbf{u} \bmod 2$ and $\mathbf{u} \bmod p$ are independent. As the $\bmod p$ part does not depend on $\mathbf{r}$, we only need to consider the $\bmod 2$ part. Let in the following variables with a hat denote this variable is reduced modulo 2, e.g. $\hat{\mathbf{x}} = \mathbf{x} \bmod 2$. It holds that $\hat{\mathbf{u}}$ is chosen uniformly from $\ker(\hat{\mathbf{D}}) = \{\mathbf{w} \in \mathbb{Z}_2^m \mid \hat{\mathbf{D}} \cdot \mathbf{w} = 0\}$. The dimension of $\ker(\hat{\mathbf{D}})$ is at least $m - k \ge m - n/2$. Let $\hat{\mathbf{B}} \in \mathbb{Z}_2^{m \times m}$ be a basis of $\ker(\hat{\mathbf{D}})$. As $\hat{\mathbf{A}}$ has full rank and therefore $\mathrm{rank}(\ker(\hat{\mathbf{A}})) = m - 2n$, it holds that $\mathrm{rank}(\hat{\mathbf{A}} \cdot \hat{\mathbf{B}}) \ge \frac{3}{2}n$. Therefore $\hat{\mathbf{A}} \cdot \hat{\mathbf{u}}$ is uniformly random in an $\frac{3}{2}n$ dimensional subspace. But this means that $(\hat{\mathbf{y}}_1', \hat{\mathbf{y}}_2') = (\hat{\mathbf{A}}_1 \hat{\mathbf{x}} + \hat{\mathbf{A}}_1 \hat{\mathbf{u}}, \hat{\mathbf{A}}_2 \hat{\mathbf{x}} + \hat{\mathbf{A}}_2 \hat{\mathbf{u}} + \mathbf{r})$ loses at least $n/2$ bits of information about $\mathbf{r}$ (c.f. Sect. 2.2). Consequently, it holds that $\tilde{H}_\infty(\mathbf{r} | \mathbf{y}_1', \mathbf{y}_2') \ge n/2$. Therefore, as Ext_0 is a strong $(n/2, \mathrm{negl})$-extractor, we get that $\mathsf{Ext}_0(\mathbf{s}_0, \mathbf{r})$ is statistically close to uniform given $\mathbf{y}_1', \mathbf{y}_2'$. Finally, $\tau = \mathsf{Ext}_0(\mathbf{s}_0, \mathbf{r}) \oplus \mu_0$ is statistically close to uniform given $\mathbf{s}_0$ and $\mathbf{y}_1', \mathbf{y}_2'$, which concludes the second case.

5.1 Setting the Parameters

We will now show that the parameters of the scheme can be chosen such that correctness, statistical sender privacy and computational receiver privacy hold.

- By Lemma 5.1, OT is correct if $\sigma_0 \leq \frac{q}{4B \cdot m}$ and $\sigma_1 \leq \frac{q}{m \cdot \kappa(n)}$ (where $\kappa(n) = \omega(\sqrt{\log(n)})$).
- By Theorem 5.3, OT is statistically sender private if $\sigma_0 \cdot \sigma_1 \geq 4\sqrt{m} \cdot q$ and $\sigma_1 < \frac{q}{2\sqrt{m}}$.

These requirements can be met if

$$\frac{q^2}{4\kappa(n)Bm^2} \geq 4\sqrt{m} \cdot q,$$

which is equivalent to

$$q \geq 16\kappa(n) \cdot B \cdot m^{2.5}. \tag{1}$$

If χ is a discrete Gaussian on $\mathbb{Z}$ with parameter αq, i.e. $\chi = D_{\mathbb{Z},\alpha q}$, then, given that $\alpha q \geq \eta_\epsilon(\mathbb{Z}) = \omega(\sqrt{\log(n)})$ it holds that χ is αq bounded, i.e. $B \leq \alpha q$ (with overwhelming probability). This means that

$$\alpha \leq \frac{1}{16 \cdot \kappa(n)m^{2.5}} = \tilde{O}(n^{-2.5})$$

implies inequality (1). Thus, we get a worst-case approximation factor $\tilde{O}(n/\alpha) = \tilde{O}(n^{3.5})$ for SIVP (compared to $\tilde{O}(n^{1.5})$ for primal Regev encryption). With this choice of α, we can choose $q = \tilde{O}(n^3)$, $\sigma_0 = \tilde{O}(n^{2.5})$ and $\sigma_1 = \tilde{O}(n)$.

Acknowledgement. We would like to thank the anonymous TCC 2018 reviewers for insightful comments that helped to improve the presentation of the paper.

A Appendix

In this Section we will provide the proof for Lemma 4.1. We will first provide some additional preliminaries.

A.1 Additional Preliminaries

Fourier Transforms. We now recall a few basic facts about Fourier-transforms on lattices. Let $f : \mathbb{R}^m \to \mathbb{C}$ and Λ be a lattice, if it exists, we will write $f(\Lambda) := \sum_{\mathbf{x} \in \Lambda} f(\mathbf{x})$. For a *nice enough*[4] function $f : \mathbb{R}^m \to \mathbb{C}$, we define the continuous Fourier-transform $\hat{f} : \mathbb{R}^m \to \mathbb{C}$ by $\hat{f}(\omega) = \int_{\mathbf{x} \in \mathbb{R}^m} f(x) \cdot e^{-2\pi i \cdot \langle \omega, \mathbf{x} \rangle} d\mathbf{x}$.

---

[4] Where *nice enough* means that $\int_{\mathbf{x} \in \mathbb{R}^m} |f(\mathbf{x})| d\mathbf{x}$ is finite.

The Poisson summation formula states that $f(\Lambda) = \det(\Lambda^*) \cdot \hat{f}(\Lambda^*)$. The Fourier-transform of the Gaussian function $\rho_\sigma(\mathbf{x})$ is $\sigma^m \cdot \rho_{1/\sigma}(\boldsymbol{\omega})$. Consequently, we get by the Poisson summation formula that

$$\rho_\sigma(\Lambda) = \sigma^m \cdot \det(\Lambda^*) \cdot \rho_{1/\sigma}(\Lambda^*).$$

Fix a full-rank lattice $\Lambda_0 \subseteq \mathbb{R}^m$ and assume henceforth that $\Lambda \subseteq \Lambda_0$. We say a function $f : \Lambda_0 \to \mathbb{C}$ is Λ-periodic if it holds for all $\mathbf{x} \in \Lambda_0$ and all $\mathbf{z} \in \Lambda$ that $f(\mathbf{x} + \mathbf{z}) = f(\mathbf{x})$. Now let $f : \Lambda_0 \to \mathbb{C}$ be a Λ-periodic function. We define the discrete Fourier transform $\hat{f} : \Lambda^* \to \mathbb{C}$ of f by

$$\hat{f}(\boldsymbol{\omega}) = \sum_{\mathbf{x} \in \mathcal{P}(\Lambda) \cap \Lambda_0} f(\mathbf{x}) \cdot e^{-2\pi i \langle \mathbf{x}, \boldsymbol{\omega} \rangle}.$$

Here, $\mathcal{P}(\Lambda) \cap \Lambda_0$ can be replaced by any system of representatives for the quotient group Λ_0/Λ. Using Fourier-inversion, we can express f as

$$f(\mathbf{x}) = \frac{\det \Lambda_0}{\det \Lambda} \cdot \sum_{\boldsymbol{\omega} \in \mathcal{P}(\Lambda_0^*) \cap \Lambda^*} \hat{f}(\boldsymbol{\omega}) \cdot e^{2\pi i \langle \boldsymbol{\omega}, \mathbf{x} \rangle}.$$

Note that $\hat{f}$ is Λ_0^* periodic.

Let $\mathbf{x}$ and $\mathbf{y}$ be random variables defined on Λ_0/Λ. Let the probability-mass function of the distribution of $\mathbf{x}$ be given by a Λ-periodic function $X : \Lambda_0 \to \mathbb{R}$, and let the probability-mass function of $\mathbf{y}$ be given by a Λ-periodic function $Y : \Lambda_0 \to \mathbb{R}$. Finally, let $Z : \Lambda_0 \to \mathbb{R}$ be the probability mass function of $\mathbf{x} + \mathbf{y}$. The convolution theorem states that it holds that

$$\hat{Z}(\boldsymbol{\omega}) = \hat{X}(\boldsymbol{\omega}) \cdot \hat{Y}(\boldsymbol{\omega}),$$

for all $\boldsymbol{\omega} \in \Lambda^*$.

If $\mathbf{x}$ is distributed according to a discrete Gaussian $D_{\Lambda_0,\sigma}$ and $\Lambda \subseteq \Lambda_0$, then $\mathbf{x} \bmod \Lambda$ has the probability-mass function of a periodic gaussian given by

$$\psi_\sigma(\mathbf{x}') = \Pr[\mathbf{x} = \mathbf{x}'] = \frac{1}{\rho_\sigma(\Lambda_0)} \cdot \sum_{\mathbf{z} \in \Lambda} \rho_\sigma(\mathbf{x}' + \mathbf{z})$$

and it holds that

$$\widehat{\psi_\sigma}(\boldsymbol{\omega}) = \frac{1}{\det(\Lambda_0^*) \cdot \rho_{1/\sigma}(\Lambda_0^*)} \cdot \sum_{\boldsymbol{\xi} \in \Lambda_0^*} \rho_{1/\sigma}(\boldsymbol{\omega} + \boldsymbol{\xi})$$

for $\boldsymbol{\omega} \in \Lambda^*$.

We define the Dirac-function $\delta : \Lambda_0 \to \mathbb{R}$ as $\delta(0) = 1$ and $\delta(\mathbf{x}) = 0$ for $\mathbf{x} \neq 0$. If $\Lambda \subseteq \Lambda_1 \subset \Lambda_0$ and $\mathbf{u}$ is distributed uniformly random on $\mathcal{P}(\Lambda) \cap \Lambda_1$, then $\mathbf{u}$ has the probability-mass function

$$U(\mathbf{x}) = \frac{\det \Lambda_1}{\det \Lambda} \sum_{\mathbf{y} \in \Lambda_1} \delta(\mathbf{x} + \mathbf{y})$$

and the Fourier-transform

$$\hat{U}(\boldsymbol{\omega}) = \sum_{\boldsymbol{\xi} \in \Lambda_1^*} \delta(\boldsymbol{\omega} + \boldsymbol{\xi}).$$

A.2   Proof of the Partial Smoothing Lemma

Lemma A.1. *Let $\sigma > 0$ and let $\Lambda \subseteq \Lambda_0 \subseteq \mathbb{R}^n$ be full-rank lattices where $\det(\Lambda_0) = 1$. Furthermore, let $\gamma > 0$. Define $\Lambda_1 = \{\mathbf{z} \in \Lambda_0 \mid \forall \mathbf{y} \in \Lambda^* \cap \gamma\mathcal{B} : \langle \mathbf{y}, \mathbf{z} \rangle \in \mathbb{Z}\}$. Given that $\rho_{1/\sigma}(\Lambda^* \backslash \gamma\mathcal{B}) \leq \epsilon$, it holds that*

$$\mathbf{y} \bmod \Lambda \approx_\epsilon (\mathbf{y} + \mathbf{u}) \bmod \Lambda,$$

where $\mathbf{y} \xleftarrow{\$} D_{\Lambda_0, \sigma}$ and $\mathbf{u} \xleftarrow{\$} \mathcal{P}(\Lambda) \cap \Lambda_1$.

Proof. First notice that $\Lambda \subseteq \Lambda_1 \subseteq \Lambda_0$ and $\Lambda^* \cap \gamma\mathcal{B} \subseteq \Lambda_1^*$. The probability-mass function of $\mathbf{y}$ is given by

$$Y(\mathbf{x}) = \frac{1}{\rho_\sigma(\Lambda_0)} \sum_{\mathbf{z} \in \Lambda} \rho_\sigma(\mathbf{x} + \mathbf{z})$$

for $\mathbf{x} \in \mathcal{P}(\Lambda) \cap \Lambda_0$. The Fourier-transform of Y is

$$\hat{Y}(\boldsymbol{\omega}) = \frac{1}{\det(\Lambda_0^*) \cdot \rho_{1/\sigma}(\Lambda_0^*)} \cdot \sum_{\boldsymbol{\xi} \in \Lambda_0^*} \rho_{1/\sigma}(\boldsymbol{\omega} + \boldsymbol{\xi}) = \frac{1}{\rho_{1/\sigma}(\Lambda_0^*)} \cdot \sum_{\boldsymbol{\xi} \in \Lambda_0^*} \rho_{1/\sigma}(\boldsymbol{\omega} + \boldsymbol{\xi})$$

for $\boldsymbol{\omega} \in \mathcal{P}(\Lambda_0^*) \cap \Lambda^*$.

The probability-mass function of $\mathbf{u}$ is

$$U(\mathbf{x}) = \frac{\det \Lambda_1}{\det \Lambda} \sum_{\mathbf{y} \in \Lambda_1} \delta(\mathbf{x} + \mathbf{y})$$

for $\mathbf{x} \in \mathcal{P}(\Lambda) \cap \Lambda_0$.

Note that $U(\mathbf{x})$ is Λ-periodic as $\Lambda \subseteq \Lambda_1$. We can therefore compute the Fourier-transform of U and obtain

$$\hat{U}(\boldsymbol{\omega}) = \sum_{\boldsymbol{\xi} \in \Lambda_1^*} \delta(\boldsymbol{\omega} + \boldsymbol{\xi}),$$

i.e. $\hat{U}(\boldsymbol{\omega})$ is constant 1 on $\mathcal{P}(\Lambda_0^*) \cap \Lambda_1^\top$ and 0 everywhere else.

By the convolution theorem, the Fourier-transform of the probability mass function of $\mathbf{r} = \mathbf{y} + \mathbf{u} \bmod \Lambda$ is

$$R(\boldsymbol{\omega}) = \hat{Y}(\boldsymbol{\omega}) \cdot \hat{U}(\boldsymbol{\omega})$$

for $\boldsymbol{\omega} \in \mathcal{P}(\Lambda_0^*) \cap \Lambda^*$.

Consequently, we can bound the statistical distance between $\mathbf{y}$ and $\mathbf{r}$ by

$$2 \cdot \Delta(\mathbf{y}, \mathbf{r}) = \sum_{\mathbf{x} \in \mathcal{P}(\Lambda) \cap \Lambda_0} |Y(\mathbf{x}) - R(\mathbf{x})|$$

$$\leq \frac{\det \Lambda}{\det \Lambda_0} \cdot \max_{\mathbf{x} \in \mathcal{P}(\Lambda) \cap \Lambda_0} |Y(\mathbf{x}) - R(\mathbf{x})|$$

$$= \frac{\det \Lambda}{\det \Lambda_0} \cdot \max_{\mathbf{x} \in \mathcal{P}(\Lambda) \cap \Lambda_0} \left| \frac{\det \Lambda_0}{\det \Lambda} \cdot \sum_{\boldsymbol{\omega} \in \mathcal{P}(\Lambda_0^*) \cap \Lambda^*} \hat{Y}(\boldsymbol{\omega})(1 - \hat{U}(\boldsymbol{\omega}))e^{2\pi i \langle \boldsymbol{\omega}, \mathbf{x} \rangle} \right|$$

$$= \max_{\mathbf{x} \in \mathcal{P}(\Lambda) \cap \Lambda_0} \left| \sum_{\boldsymbol{\omega} \in \mathcal{P}(\Lambda_0^*) \cap \Lambda^* \setminus \Lambda_1^*} \hat{Y}(\boldsymbol{\omega})e^{2\pi i \langle \boldsymbol{\omega}, \mathbf{x} \rangle} \right|$$

$$= \max_{\mathbf{x} \in \mathcal{P}(\Lambda) \cap \Lambda_0} \left| \sum_{\boldsymbol{\omega} \in \mathcal{P}(\Lambda_0^*) \cap \Lambda^* \setminus \Lambda_1^*} \frac{1}{\rho_{1/\sigma}(\Lambda_0^*)} \sum_{\boldsymbol{\xi} \in \Lambda_0^*} \rho_{1/\sigma}(\boldsymbol{\omega} + \boldsymbol{\xi})e^{2\pi i \langle \boldsymbol{\omega}, \mathbf{x} \rangle} \right|$$

$$\leq \max_{\mathbf{x} \in \mathcal{P}(\Lambda) \cap \Lambda_0} \left| \sum_{\boldsymbol{\omega} \in \Lambda^* \setminus \Lambda_1^*} \rho_{1/\sigma}(\boldsymbol{\omega})e^{2\pi i \langle \boldsymbol{\omega}, \mathbf{x} \rangle} \right|$$

$$\leq \max_{\mathbf{x} \in \mathcal{P}(\Lambda) \cap \Lambda_0} \sum_{\boldsymbol{\omega} \in \Lambda^* \setminus \Lambda_1^*} |\rho_{1/\sigma}(\boldsymbol{\omega})e^{2\pi i \langle \boldsymbol{\omega}, \mathbf{x} \rangle}|$$

$$= \sum_{\boldsymbol{\omega} \in \Lambda^* \setminus \Lambda_1^*} \rho_{1/\sigma}(\boldsymbol{\omega}) = \rho_{1/\sigma}(\Lambda^* \setminus \Lambda_1^*) \leq \rho_{1/\sigma}(\Lambda^* \setminus \gamma \mathcal{B}) \leq \epsilon$$

The second inequality holds as $\frac{1}{\rho_{1/\sigma}(\Lambda_0^*)} \leq 1$ and the third inequality is an application of the triangle inequality.

References

1. Aiello, B., Ishai, Y., Reingold, O.: Priced oblivious transfer: how to sell digital goods. In: Pfitzmann, B. (ed.) EUROCRYPT 2001. LNCS, vol. 2045, pp. 119–135. Springer, Heidelberg (2001). https://doi.org/10.1007/3-540-44987-6_8
2. Ajtai, M.: Generating hard instances of the short basis problem. In: Wiedermann, J., van Emde Boas, P., Nielsen, M. (eds.) ICALP 1999. LNCS, vol. 1644, pp. 1–9. Springer, Heidelberg (1999). https://doi.org/10.1007/3-540-48523-6_1
3. Badrinarayanan, S., Garg, S., Ishai, Y., Sahai, A., Wadia, A.: Two-message witness indistinguishability and secure computation in the plain model from new assumptions. In: Takagi, T., Peyrin, T. (eds.) ASIACRYPT 2017. LNCS, vol. 10626, pp. 275–303. Springer, Cham (2017). https://doi.org/10.1007/978-3-319-70700-6_10
4. Badrinarayanan, S., Goyal, V., Jain, A., Kalai, Y.T., Khurana, D., Sahai, A.: Promise zero knowledge and its applications to round optimal MPC. IACR Cryptology ePrint Archive 2017, 1088 (2017). http://eprint.iacr.org/2017/1088
5. Badrinarayanan, S., Goyal, V., Jain, A., Khurana, D., Sahai, A.: Round optimal concurrent MPC via strong simulation. In: Kalai and Reyzin [20], pp. 743–775. https://doi.org/10.1007/978-3-319-70500-2_25
6. Banaszczyk, W.: New bounds in some transference theorems in the geometry of numbers. Math. Ann. **296**(1), 625–635 (1993)

7. Bellare, M., Micali, S.: Non-interactive oblivious transfer and applications. In: Brassard, G. (ed.) CRYPTO 1989. LNCS, vol. 435, pp. 547–557. Springer, New York (1990). https://doi.org/10.1007/0-387-34805-0_48

8. Brakerski, Z., Halevi, S., Polychroniadou, A.: Four round secure computation without setup. In: Kalai and Reyzin [20], pp. 645–677. https://doi.org/10.1007/978-3-319-70500-2_22

9. Brakerski, Z., Langlois, A., Peikert, C., Regev, O., Stehlé, D.: Classical hardness of learning with errors. In: Boneh, D., Roughgarden, T., Feigenbaum, J. (eds.) Symposium on Theory of Computing Conference, STOC 2013, Palo Alto, CA, USA, 1–4 June 2013, pp. 575–584. ACM (2013). http://doi.acm.org/10.1145/2488608.2488680

10. Chung, K., Dadush, D., Liu, F., Peikert, C.: On the lattice smoothing parameter problem. In: IEEE Conference on Computational Complexity, pp. 230–241. IEEE Computer Society (2013)

11. Dodis, Y., Ostrovsky, R., Reyzin, L., Smith, A.D.: Fuzzy extractors: how to generate strong keys from biometrics and other noisy data. SIAM J. Comput. $38(1)$, 97–139 (2008)

12. Dodis, Y., Reyzin, L., Smith, A.: Fuzzy extractors: how to generate strong keys from biometrics and other noisy data. In: Cachin, C., Camenisch, J.L. (eds.) EUROCRYPT 2004. LNCS, vol. 3027, pp. 523–540. Springer, Heidelberg (2004). https://doi.org/10.1007/978-3-540-24676-3_31

13. Gertner, Y., Kannan, S., Malkin, T., Reingold, O., Viswanathan, M.: The relationship between public key encryption and oblivious transfer. In: FOCS, pp. 325–335. IEEE Computer Society (2000)

14. Goldreich, O., Goldwasser, S.: On the limits of non-approximability of lattice problems. In: Vitter, J.S. (ed.) Proceedings of the Thirtieth Annual ACM Symposium on the Theory of Computing, Dallas, Texas, USA, 23–26 May 1998, pp. 1–9. ACM (1998). http://doi.acm.org/10.1145/276698.276704

15. Goldreich, O., Micali, S., Wigderson, A.: How to play any mental game or a completeness theorem for protocols with honest majority. In: Aho, A.V. (ed.) Proceedings of the 19th Annual ACM Symposium on Theory of Computing, 1987, New York, New York, USA, pp. 218–229. ACM (1987). http://doi.acm.org/10.1145/28395.28420

16. Goldreich, O., Oren, Y.: Definitions and properties of zero-knowledge proof systems. J. Cryptol. $7(1)$, 1–32 (1994)

17. Halevi, S., Hazay, C., Polychroniadou, A., Venkitasubramaniam, M.: Round-optimal secure multi-party computation. IACR Cryptology ePrint Archive 2017, 1056 (2017). http://eprint.iacr.org/2017/1056

18. Halevi, S., Kalai, Y.T.: Smooth projective hashing and two-message oblivious transfer. J. Cryptol. $25(1)$, 158–193 (2012). https://doi.org/10.1007/s00145-010-9092-8

19. Jain, A., Kalai, Y.T., Khurana, D., Rothblum, R.: Distinguisher-dependent simulation in two rounds and its applications. In: Katz, J., Shacham, H. (eds.) CRYPTO 2017. LNCS, vol. 10402, pp. 158–189. Springer, Cham (2017). https://doi.org/10.1007/978-3-319-63715-0_6

20. Kalai, Y., Reyzin, L. (eds.): TCC 2017. LNCS, vol. 10677. Springer, Cham (2017). https://doi.org/10.1007/978-3-319-70500-2

21. Kalai, Y.T.: Smooth projective hashing and two-message oblivious transfer. In: Cramer, R. (ed.) EUROCRYPT 2005. LNCS, vol. 3494, pp. 78–95. Springer, Heidelberg (2005). https://doi.org/10.1007/11426639_5

22. Kalai, Y.T., Khurana, D., Sahai, A.: Statistical witness indistinguishability (and more) in two messages. In: Nielsen, J.B., Rijmen, V. (eds.) EUROCRYPT 2018. LNCS, vol. 10822, pp. 34–65. Springer, Cham (2018). https://doi.org/10.1007/978-3-319-78372-7_2

23. Khurana, D.: Round optimal concurrent non-malleability from polynomial hardness. In: Kalai, Y., Reyzin, L. (eds.) TCC 2017. LNCS, vol. 10678, pp. 139–171. Springer, Cham (2017). https://doi.org/10.1007/978-3-319-70503-3_5

24. Khurana, D., Sahai, A.: How to achieve non-malleability in one or two rounds. In: Umans, C. (ed.) 58th IEEE Annual Symposium on Foundations of Computer Science, FOCS 2017, Berkeley, CA, USA, 15–17 October 2017, pp. 564–575. IEEE Computer Society (2017). https://doi.org/10.1109/FOCS.2017.58

25. Micciancio, D., Peikert, C.: Trapdoors for lattices: simpler, tighter, faster, smaller. In: Pointcheval, D., Johansson, T. (eds.) EUROCRYPT 2012. LNCS, vol. 7237, pp. 700–718. Springer, Heidelberg (2012). https://doi.org/10.1007/978-3-642-29011-4_41

26. Micciancio, D., Regev, O.: Worst-case to average-case reductions based on Gaussian measures. SIAM J. Comput. **37**(1), 267–302 (2007)

27. Naor, M., Pinkas, B.: Efficient oblivious transfer protocols. In: Kosaraju, S.R. (ed.) Proceedings of the Twelfth Annual Symposium on Discrete Algorithms, 7–9 January 2001, Washington, DC, USA, pp. 448–457. ACM/SIAM (2001). http://dl.acm.org/citation.cfm?id=365411.365502

28. Ostrovsky, R., Paskin-Cherniavsky, A., Paskin-Cherniavsky, B.: Maliciously circuit-private FHE. In: Garay, J.A., Gennaro, R. (eds.) CRYPTO 2014. LNCS, vol. 8616, pp. 536–553. Springer, Heidelberg (2014). https://doi.org/10.1007/978-3-662-44371-2_30

29. Peikert, C.: Public-key cryptosystems from the worst-case shortest vector problem: extended abstract. In: Mitzenmacher, M. (ed.) STOC, pp. 333–342. ACM (2009)

30. Peikert, C., Regev, O., Stephens-Davidowitz, N.: Pseudorandomness of Ring-LWE for any ring and modulus. In: Hatami, H., McKenzie, P., King, V. (eds.) Proceedings of the 49th Annual ACM SIGACT Symposium on Theory of Computing, STOC 2017, Montreal, QC, Canada, 19–23 June 2017, pp. 461–473. ACM (2017). http://doi.acm.org/10.1145/3055399.3055489

31. Peikert, C., Vaikuntanathan, V., Waters, B.: A framework for efficient and composable oblivious transfer. In: Wagner, D. (ed.) CRYPTO 2008. LNCS, vol. 5157, pp. 554–571. Springer, Heidelberg (2008). https://doi.org/10.1007/978-3-540-85174-5_31

32. Rabin, M.O.: How to exchange secrets with oblivious transfer. Harvard University Technical Report (1981). http://eprint.iacr.org/2005/187

33. Regev, O.: On lattices, learning with errors, random linear codes, and cryptography. In: Gabow, H.N., Fagin, R. (eds.) STOC, pp. 84–93. ACM (2005). Full version in [34]

34. Regev, O.: On lattices, learning with errors, random linear codes, and cryptography. J. ACM **56**(6), 34 (2009)

35. Yao, A.C.C.: How to generate and exchange secrets (extended abstract). In: FOCS, pp. 162–167 (1986)

Adaptively Secure Distributed PRFs
from LWE

Benoît Libert[1,2]([⊠]), Damien Stehlé[2], and Radu Titiu[2,3]

[1] CNRS, Laboratoire LIP, Lyon, France
benoit.libert@ens-lyon.fr
[2] ENS de Lyon, Laboratoire LIP (U. Lyon, CNRS, ENSL, INRIA, UCBL),
Lyon, France
[3] Bitdefender, Bucharest, Romania

Abstract. In distributed pseudorandom functions (DPRFs), a PRF secret key SK is secret shared among N servers so that each server can locally compute a partial evaluation of the PRF on some input X. A combiner that collects t partial evaluations can then reconstruct the evaluation $F(SK, X)$ of the PRF under the initial secret key. So far, all non-interactive constructions in the standard model are based on lattice assumptions. One caveat is that they are only known to be secure in the static corruption setting, where the adversary chooses the servers to corrupt at the very beginning of the game, before any evaluation query. In this work, we construct the first fully non-interactive adaptively secure DPRF in the standard model. Our construction is proved secure under the LWE assumption against adversaries that may adaptively decide which servers they want to corrupt. We also extend our construction in order to achieve robustness against malicious adversaries.

Keywords: LWE · Pseudorandom functions · Distributed PRFs Threshold cryptography · Adaptive security

1 Introduction

A pseudorandom function (PRF) family [35] is a set $\mathcal{F}$ of keyed functions with common domain Dom and range Rng such that no ppt adversary can distinguish a real experiment, where it has oracle access to a random member $f \hookleftarrow \mathcal{F}$ of the PRF family, from an ideal experiment where it is interacting with a truly random function $R : \text{Dom} \to \text{Rng}$. To be useful, a PRF should be efficiently computable – meaning that $F_\mathbf{s}(x)$ must be deterministically computable in polynomial time given the key $\mathbf{s}$ and the input $x \in \text{Dom}$ – and the key size must be polynomial.

Pseudorandom functions are fundamental objects in cryptography as most central tasks of symmetric cryptography (like secret-key encryption, message authentication or identification) can be efficiently realized from a secure PRF family. Beyond their use for cryptographic purposes, they can also be used to prove circuit lower bounds [56] and they are strongly connected to the hardness of certain tasks in learning theory [62].

© International Association for Cryptologic Research 2018
A. Beimel and S. Dziembowski (Eds.): TCC 2018, LNCS 11240, pp. 391–421, 2018.
https://doi.org/10.1007/978-3-030-03810-6_15

Goldreich, Goldwasser and Micali (GGM) [35] showed how to build a PRF from any length-doubling pseudorandom generator (PRG). In turn, PRGs are known [39] to exist under the sole assumption that one-way functions exist. However, much more efficient constructions can be obtained by relying on specific number theoretic assumptions like the Decision Diffie-Hellman assumption [51] and related variants [17,21,28,44] or the hardness of factoring [51,52].

In the context of lattice-based cryptography, the noisy nature of hard-on-average problems, like Learning-With-Errors (LWE) [57], makes it challenging to design efficient PRF families. The LWE assumption for a modulus q states that, given a random matrix $\mathbf{A} \in \mathbb{Z}_q^{m \times n}$ with $m > n$, the vector $\mathbf{A} \cdot \mathbf{s} + \mathbf{e}$ is computationally indistinguishable from a uniform vector over $\mathbb{Z}_q^m$ when $\mathbf{s} \in \mathbb{Z}_q^n$ is uniformly chosen in $\mathbb{Z}_q^n$ and $\mathbf{e} \in \mathbb{Z}^m$ is a small-norm noise vector sampled from a Gaussian distribution. In order to design PRFs with small-depth evaluation circuits, several works [7,8,16] rely on the Learning-With-Rounding (LWR) technique [8], which is a "de-randomization" of LWE where noisy vectors $\mathbf{A} \cdot \mathbf{s} + \mathbf{e}$ are replaced by rounded vectors $\lfloor (p/q) \cdot (\mathbf{A} \cdot \mathbf{s}) \rceil \in \mathbb{Z}_p^m$ for a smaller modulus $p < q$.

An appealing advantage of lattice-based techniques is that they enable the design of *key-homomorphic* PRF families [7,16]. Namely, assuming that their range and key space form an additive group, for any input x and keys $\mathbf{s}, \mathbf{t}$, we have $F_{\mathbf{s}+\mathbf{t}}(x) \approx F_{\mathbf{s}}(x) + F_{\mathbf{t}}(x)$. In turn, key-homomorphic PRFs provide simple and non-interactive constructions of distributed pseudorandom functions [50]. In a (threshold) distributed PRF (DPRF), secret keys are broken into N shares $\mathbf{s}_1, \ldots, \mathbf{s}_N$, each of which is given to a different server. Using its secret key share $\mathbf{s}_i$, the i-th server can locally compute a partial evaluation $F_{\mathbf{s}_i}(x)$ of the function. A dedicated server can then gather at least $t \leq N$ correct partial evaluations $F_{\mathbf{s}_{i_1}}(x), \ldots, F_{\mathbf{s}_{i_t}}(x)$ and reconstruct the evaluation $F_{\mathbf{s}}(x)$ for the long-term key $\mathbf{s}$. As such, threshold PRFs inherit the usual benefits of threshold cryptography [25]. First, setting $t < N$ allows for fault-tolerant systems that can keep running when some server crashes. Second, the adversary is forced to break into t servers to compromise the security of the whole scheme. Ideally, servers should be able to generate their partial evaluations without interacting with one another.

Boneh *et al.* [16] gave a generic construction of non-interactive DPRF from any almost key homomorphic PRF (where "almost" means that $F_{\mathbf{s}+\mathbf{t}}(x)$ only needs to be sufficiently "close" to $F_{\mathbf{s}}(x) + F_{\mathbf{t}}(x)$). Their construction, however, is only proved to be secure under *static* corruptions. Namely, the adversary has to choose the corrupted servers all-at-once and before making any evaluation query.

CONTRIBUTION. We consider the problem of proving security in the stronger *adaptive* corruption model, where the adversary chooses which servers it wants to corrupt based on the previously obtained information. In particular, an adaptive adversary is allowed to obtain partial evaluations before corrupting any server.

In this stronger adversarial model, we provide the first realization of non-interactive distributed pseudorandom function with a security proof under a polynomial reduction. We prove the security of our construction in the standard model under the Learning-With-Errors (LWE) assumption [57] with super-polynomial approximation factors.

In its basic version, our DPRF is only secure against passive adversaries. However, robustness against malicious adversaries can be readily achieved using leveled homomorphic signatures [37], as was suggested by earlier works on threshold lattice-based cryptography [14,15]. To our knowledge, we thus obtain the first DPRF candidate which is simultaneously: (i) secure under adaptive corruptions in the standard model under a well-studied assumption; (ii) robust against malicious adversaries; (iii) non-interactive (i.e., each server only sends one message to the combiner that reconstructs the final output of the PRF).

TECHNIQUES. For a polynomial N and when $t \approx N/2$, proving adaptive security is considerably more challenging as a trivial complexity leveraging argument (i.e., guessing the set of corrupted servers upfront) makes the reduction super-polynomial. Moreover, we show that allowing a *single* partial evaluation query before the first corruption query already results in a definition which is strictly stronger than that of static security. In the adaptive corruption setting, the difficulty is that, by making N partial evaluation queries before corrupting any server, the adversary basically commits the challenger to all secret key shares. Hence, a reduction that only knows $t - 1 \approx N/2$ shares is unlikely to work as it would have to make up its mind on which set of $t - 1$ shares it wants to know at the outset of the game. In particular, this hinders a generic reduction from the security of an underlying key-homomorphic PRF. This suggests to find a reduction that knows all shares of the secret key, making it easier to consistently answer adaptive corruption queries.

To this end, we turn to lossy trapdoor functions [54], which are function families that contain both injective and lossy functions with computationally indistinguishable evaluation keys. We rely on the fact that the LWE function and its deterministic LWR variant [8] are both lossy trapdoor functions (as shown in [6,9,36]). Namely, the function that maps $\mathbf{s} \in \mathbb{Z}^n$ to $\lfloor \mathbf{A} \cdot \mathbf{s} \rfloor_p$ is injective when $\mathbf{A} \in \mathbb{Z}_q^{m \times n}$ is a random matrix and becomes lossy when $\mathbf{A}$ is of the form $\bar{\mathbf{A}} \cdot \mathbf{C} + \mathbf{E}$, where $\bar{\mathbf{A}} \in \mathbb{Z}_q^{m \times n'}$, $\mathbf{C} \in \mathbb{Z}_q^{n' \times n}$ are uniformly random and $\mathbf{E} \in \mathbb{Z}^{m \times n}$ is a small-norm matrix. Our idea is to first construct a PRF which maps an input x to $\lfloor \mathbf{A}(x) \cdot \mathbf{s} \rfloor_p$, where $\mathbf{s} \in \mathbb{Z}^n$ is the secret key and $\mathbf{A}(x) \in \mathbb{Z}_q^{m \times n}$ is derived from public matrices. We thus evaluate a lossy trapdoor function on an input consisting of the secret key using a matrix that depends on the input. In the security proof, we use admissible hash functions [13] and techniques from fully homomorphic encryption [33] to "program" $\mathbf{A}(x)$ in such a way that, with non-negligible probability, it induces a lossy function in all evaluation queries and an injective function in the challenge phase.[1] (We note that this use of lossy trapdoor functions is somewhat unusual since their injective mode is usually used to handle adversarial queries while the lossy mode comes into play in the challenge phase.) By choosing a large enough ratio q/p, we can make sure that

---

[1] We use a "find-then-guess" security game where the adversary obtains correct evaluation for inputs of its choice before trying to distinguish a real function evaluation from a random element of the range.

evaluation queries always reveal the same information about the secret s. Since $\lfloor \mathbf{A}(x^\star) \cdot \mathbf{s} \rfloor_p$ is an injective function in the challenge phase, we can argue that it has high min-entropy, even conditionally on responses to evaluation queries. At this point, we can extract statistically uniform bits from $\lfloor \mathbf{A}(x^\star) \cdot \mathbf{s} \rfloor_p$ using a deterministic randomness extractor: analogously to the deterministic encryption case [55], we need to handle a source that may be correlated with the seed.

We note that the above approach bears resemblance with key-homomorphic PRFs [7,16] which also evaluate functions of the form $\lfloor \mathbf{A}(x) \cdot \mathbf{s} \rfloor_p$. However, our proof method is very different in that it relies on the lossy mode of LWE and the homomorphic encryption scheme of [33]. The advantage of our approach is that the challenger knows the secret key s at all steps of the security proof. In the distributed setting, this makes it easier to handle adaptive adversaries because the reduction can always correctly answer corruption queries. In order to share the secret key s among N servers, we rely on the Linear Integer Secret Sharing (LISS) schemes of Damgård and Thorbek [24], which nicely fit the requirements of our security proof. Among other properties, they allow secret key shares to remain small with respect to the modulus, which helps us making sure that partial evaluations – as lossy functions of their share – always reveal the same information about uncorrupted shares. Moreover, they also enable small reconstruction constants: the secret s can be recovered as a linear combination of authorized shares with coefficients in $\{-1, 0, 1\}$, which is useful to avoid blowing up error terms when partial evaluations are combined together. A notable difference with [24] is that our DPRF uses a LISS scheme with Gaussian entries (instead of uniform ones), which makes it easier to analyze the remaining entropy of the key in the final step of the proof.

RELATED WORK. Distributed pseudorandom functions were initially suggested by Micali and Sidney [47] and received a lot of attention since then [27,29,50,51, 53]. They are motivated by the construction of distributed symmetric encryption schemes, distributed key distribution centers [50], or distributed coin tossing and asynchronous byzantine agreement protocols [18]. They also provide a distributed source of random coins that allows removing interaction from threshold decryption mechanisms, such as the one of Canetti and Goldwasser [20].

As mentioned in [16], the early DPRF realizations [47] were only efficient when the threshold t was very small or very large with respect to N. Before 2010, other solutions [27,29,50,51,53] either required random oracles [50] or multiple rounds of interaction [27,29,51,53]. Boneh, Lewi, Montgomery and Raghunathan [16] (BLMR) suggested a generic construction of non-interactive DPRF from key-homomorphic PRFs. They also put forth the first key-homomorphic PRF in the standard model assuming the hardness of LWE. Banerjee and Peikert [7] generalized the BLMR construction and obtained more efficient constructions under weaker LWE assumptions. Boneh et al. [14,15] described another generic DPRF construction from a general "universal thresholdizer" tool, which allows distributing many cryptographic functionalities. So far, none of these solutions is known to provide security under adaptive corruptions.

In the context of threshold cryptography, adaptive security has been addressed in a large body of work [1,5,19,30,42,46]. These techniques, however, require interaction (except in some cases when all players always correctly provide their contribution to the computation) and none of them is known to be compatible with existing non-interactive DPRFs. While lattice-based threshold protocols were studied by Bendlin et al. back in 2010 [11,12], they focused on distributing decryption operations or sharing lattice trapdoors and it is not clear how to apply them in our setting. Boneh et al. [14,15] showed how to generically compile cryptographic functionalities into threshold functionalities using distributed FHE. However, they do not consider adaptive corruptions and proceed by generically evaluating the circuit of the functionality at hand. While we follow their approach of using fully homomorphic signatures to acquire robustness, our basic PRF is a direct and more efficient construction.

To our knowledge, the approach of using lossy trapdoor functions to construct advanced PRFs was never considered before. In spirit, our construction is somewhat similar to a random-oracle-based threshold signature proposed in [45], which also relies on the idea of always revealing the same information about the key in all evaluation queries. This DDH-based threshold signature can be turned into an adaptively secure DPRF in the random oracle model (like a variant of the Naor-Pinkas-Reingold DPRF [50]) but it has no standard-model counterpart.

The idea of using randomness extraction as part of the security proof of a PRF appears in [38, Sect. 6.2], where the function only needs to be secure in a model without evaluation queries. Here, we have to handle a different setting which prevents us from using the standard Leftover Hash Lemma.

ORGANIZATION. Sect. 2 recalls some relevant material about lattices, pseudorandom functions and integer secret sharing. A centralized version of our DPRF is presented in Sect. 3 as a warm-up. We describe its distributed variant in Sect. 4. In the full version of the paper, we explain how the techniques of [14,15] apply to obtain robustness without using interaction nor random oracles.

2   Background

For any $q \geq 2$, we let $\mathbb{Z}_q$ denote the ring of integers with addition and multiplication modulo q. We always set q as a prime integer. For $2 \leq p < q$ and $x \in \mathbb{Z}_q$, we define $\lfloor x \rceil_p := \lfloor (p/q) \cdot x \rceil \in \mathbb{Z}_p$. This notation is readily extended to vectors over $\mathbb{Z}_p$. If $\mathbf{x}$ is a vector over $\mathbb{R}$, then $\|\mathbf{x}\|$ denotes its Euclidean norm. If $\mathbf{M}$ is a matrix over $\mathbb{R}$, then $\|\mathbf{M}\|$ denotes its induced norm. We let $\sigma_n(\mathbf{M})$ denote the least singular value of $\mathbf{M}$, where n is the rank of $\mathbf{M}$. For a finite set S, we let $U(S)$ denote the uniform distribution over S. If X is a random variable over a countable domain, the min-entropy of X is defined as $H_\infty(X) = \min_x(-\log_2 \Pr[X = x])$. If X and Y are distributions over the same domain, then $\Delta(X, Y)$ denotes their statistical distance.

2.1 Lattices

Let $\Sigma \in \mathbb{R}^{n \times n}$ be a symmetric positive definite matrix, and $\mathbf{c} \in \mathbb{R}^n$. We define the Gaussian function on $\mathbb{R}^n$ by $\rho_{\Sigma,\mathbf{c}}(\mathbf{x}) = \exp(-\pi(\mathbf{x}-\mathbf{c})^\top \Sigma^{-1}(\mathbf{x}-\mathbf{c}))$ and if $\Sigma = \sigma^2 \cdot \mathbf{I}_n$ and $\mathbf{c} = \mathbf{0}$ we denote it by ρ_σ.

For a lattice Λ, we define $\eta_\varepsilon(\Lambda)$ as the smallest $r > 0$ such that $\rho_{1/r}(\widehat{\Lambda} \setminus \mathbf{0}) \leq \varepsilon$ with $\widehat{\Lambda}$ denoting the dual of Λ, for any $\varepsilon \in (0,1)$. In particular, we have $\eta_{2^{-n}}(\mathbb{Z}^n) \leq O(\sqrt{n})$. We define $\lambda_1^\infty(\Lambda) = \min(\|\mathbf{x}\|_\infty : \mathbf{x} \in \Lambda \setminus \mathbf{0})$.

For a matrix $\mathbf{A} \in \mathbb{Z}_q^{n \times m}$, we define the lattices $\Lambda^\perp(\mathbf{A}) = \{\mathbf{x} \in \mathbb{Z}^m : \mathbf{A} \cdot \mathbf{x} = \mathbf{0} \bmod q\}$ and $\Lambda(\mathbf{A}) = \mathbf{A}^\top \cdot \mathbb{Z}^n + q\mathbb{Z}^m$.

Lemma 2.1 ([32, Lemma 5.3]). *Let $m \geq 2n \cdot \log q$ and $q \geq 2$ prime and let $\mathbf{A} \hookleftarrow U(\mathbb{Z}_q^{n \times m})$. With probability $\geq 1 - 2^{-\Omega(n)}$, we have $\lambda_1^\infty(\Lambda(\mathbf{A})) \geq q/4$.*

Lemma 2.2 (Adapted from [49, Lemma 4.4]**).** *For any n-dimensional lattice Λ, $\mathbf{x}', \mathbf{c} \in \mathbb{R}^n$ and symmetric positive definite $\Sigma \in \mathbb{R}^{n \times n}$ satisfying $\sigma_n(\sqrt{\Sigma}) \geq \eta_{2^{-n}}(\Lambda)$, we have*

$$\rho_{\Sigma,\mathbf{c}}(\Lambda + \mathbf{x}') \in [1 - 2^{-n}, 1 + 2^{-n}] \cdot \det(\Sigma)^{1/2}/\det(\Lambda).$$

Lemma 2.3. *For $c \in \mathbb{R}$ and $\sigma > 0$ such that $\sigma \geq \sqrt{\ln 2(1 + 1/\epsilon)/\pi}$, we have*

$$H_\infty(D_{\mathbb{Z},\sigma,c}) \geq \log(\sigma) + \log(1 + 2e^{-\pi\sigma^2}) - \log\left(1 + \frac{2\epsilon}{1-\epsilon}\right)$$

Proof. From [49, Lemma 3.3] we know that $\eta_\epsilon(\mathbb{Z}) \leq \sqrt{\ln 2(1 + 1/\epsilon)/\pi}$. So $\sigma \geq \eta_\epsilon(\mathbb{Z})$. By [48, Lemma 2.5], this implies that $\frac{1-\epsilon}{1+\epsilon} \cdot \rho_\sigma(\mathbb{Z}) \leq \rho_{\sigma,c}(\mathbb{Z})$, which translates into

$$H_\infty(D_{\mathbb{Z},\sigma,c}) \geq H_\infty(D_{\mathbb{Z},\sigma}) - \log\left(\frac{1+\epsilon}{1-\epsilon}\right)$$

From [58, Claim 8.1], we have $\rho_\sigma(\mathbb{Z}) \geq \sigma \cdot (1 + 2e^{-\pi\sigma^2})$, so

$$H_\infty(D_{\mathbb{Z},\sigma}) \geq \log \sigma + \log(1 + 2e^{-\pi\sigma^2})$$

$\square$

Remark 2.4. For $\sigma = \Omega(\sqrt{n})$, we get $H_\infty(D_{\mathbb{Z},\sigma,c}) \geq \log(\sigma) - 2^{-n}$.

Definition 2.5 (LWE). *Let $m \geq n \geq 1$, $q \geq 2$ and $\alpha \in (0,1)$ be functions of a security parameter λ. The LWE problem consists in distinguishing between the distributions $(\mathbf{A}, \mathbf{As} + \mathbf{e})$ and $U(\mathbb{Z}_q^{m \times n} \times \mathbb{Z}_q^m)$, where $\mathbf{A} \sim U(\mathbb{Z}_q^{m \times n})$, $\mathbf{s} \sim U(\mathbb{Z}_q^n)$ and $\mathbf{e} \sim D_{\mathbb{Z}^m, \alpha q}$. For an algorithm $\mathcal{A} : \mathbb{Z}_q^{m \times n} \times \mathbb{Z}_q^m \to \{0,1\}$, we define:*

$$\mathbf{Adv}_{q,m,n,\alpha}^{\mathsf{LWE}}(\mathcal{A}) = |\Pr[\mathcal{A}(\mathbf{A}, \mathbf{As} + \mathbf{e}) = 1] - \Pr[\mathcal{A}(\mathbf{A}, \mathbf{u}) = 1]|,$$

where the probabilities are over $\mathbf{A} \sim U(\mathbb{Z}_q^{m \times n})$, $\mathbf{s} \sim U(\mathbb{Z}_q^n)$, $\mathbf{u} \sim U(\mathbb{Z}_q^m)$ and $\mathbf{e} \sim D_{\mathbb{Z}^m, \alpha q}$ and the internal randomness of $\mathcal{A}$. We say that $\mathsf{LWE}_{q,m,n,\alpha}$ is hard if for all ppt algorithm $\mathcal{A}$, the advantage $\mathbf{Adv}_{q,m,n,\alpha}^{\mathsf{LWE}}(\mathcal{A})$ is negligible.

Micciancio and Peikert [48] described a trapdoor mechanism for LWE. Their technique uses a "gadget" matrix $\mathbf{G} \in \mathbb{Z}_q^{n \times m}$ for which anyone can publicly sample short vectors $\mathbf{x} \in \mathbb{Z}^m$ such that $\mathbf{G} \cdot \mathbf{x} = \mathbf{0}$. As in [48], we call $\mathbf{R} \in \mathbb{Z}^{m \times m}$ a $\mathbf{G}$-trapdoor for a matrix $\mathbf{A} \in \mathbb{Z}_q^{n \times 2m}$ if $\mathbf{A} \cdot [\mathbf{R}^\top \mid \mathbf{I}_m]^\top = \mathbf{H} \cdot \mathbf{G}$ for some invertible matrix $\mathbf{H} \in \mathbb{Z}_q^{n \times n}$ which is referred to as the trapdoor tag. If $\mathbf{H} = \mathbf{0}$, then $\mathbf{R}$ is called a "punctured" trapdoor for $\mathbf{A}$.

Lemma 2.6 ([48, Section 5]). *Assume that $m \geq 2n \log q$. There exists a ppt algorithm* GenTrap *that takes as inputs matrices* $\bar{\mathbf{A}} \in \mathbb{Z}_q^{n \times m}$, $\mathbf{H} \in \mathbb{Z}_q^{n \times n}$ *and outputs matrices* $\mathbf{R} \in \{-1, 1\}^{m \times m}$ *and*

$$\mathbf{A} = [\bar{\mathbf{A}} \mid -\bar{\mathbf{A}}\mathbf{R} + \mathbf{H}\mathbf{G}] \in \mathbb{Z}_q^{n \times 2m}$$

such that if $\mathbf{H} \in \mathbb{Z}_q^{n \times n}$ *is invertible, then* $\mathbf{R}$ *is a* $\mathbf{G}$*-trapdoor for* $\mathbf{A}$ *with tag* $\mathbf{H}$*; and if* $\mathbf{H} = \mathbf{0}$*, then* $\mathbf{R}$ *is a punctured trapdoor.*

Further, in case of a $\mathbf{G}$*-trapdoor, one can efficiently compute from* $\mathbf{A}, \mathbf{R}$ *and* $\mathbf{H}$ *a basis* $(\mathbf{b}_i)_{i \leq 2m}$ *of* $\Lambda^\perp(\mathbf{A})$ *such that* $\max_i \|\mathbf{b}_i\| \leq O(m^{3/2})$.

Micciancio and Peikert also showed that a $\mathbf{G}$-trapdoor for $\mathbf{A} \in \mathbb{Z}_q^{n \times 2m}$ can be used to invert the LWE function $(\mathbf{s}, \mathbf{e}) \mapsto \mathbf{A}^\top \cdot \mathbf{s} + \mathbf{e}$, for any $\mathbf{s} \in \mathbb{Z}_q^n$ and any sufficiently short $\mathbf{e} \in \mathbb{Z}^{2m}$.

2.2   Admissible Hash Functions

Admissible hash functions were introduced by Boneh and Boyen [13] as a combinatorial tool for partitioning-based security proofs for which Freire *et al.* [31] gave a simplified definition. Jager [41] considered the following generalization in order to simplify the analysis of reductions under decisional assumption.

Definition 2.7 ([41]). *Let* $\ell(\lambda), L(\lambda) \in \mathbb{N}$ *be functions of a security parameter* $\lambda \in \mathbb{N}$. *Let* AHF $: \{0,1\}^\ell \to \{0,1\}^L$ *be an efficiently computable function. For every* $K \in \{0, 1, \perp\}^L$, *let the partitioning function* $P_K : \{0,1\}^\ell \to \{0,1\}$ *be defined as*

$$P_K(X) := \begin{cases} 0 & if \quad \forall i \in [L] \quad (\mathsf{AHF}(X)_i = K_i) \ \vee \ (K_i = \perp) \\ 1 & otherwise \end{cases}$$

We say that AHF *is a* **balanced admissible hash function** *if there exists an efficient algorithm* AdmSmp$(1^\lambda, Q, \delta)$ *that takes as input* $Q \in \mathsf{poly}(\lambda)$ *and a non-negligible* $\delta(\lambda) \in (0, 1]$ *and outputs a key* $K \in \{0, 1, \perp\}^L$ *such that, for all* $X^{(1)}, \ldots, X^{(Q)}, X^\star \in \{0,1\}^\ell$ *such that* $X^\star \notin \{X^{(1)}, \ldots, X^{(Q)}\}$, *we have*

$$\gamma_{\max}(\lambda) \geq \Pr_K \left[P_K(X^{(1)}) = \cdots = P_K(X^{(Q)}) = 1 \ \wedge \ P_K(X^\star) = 0 \right] \geq \gamma_{\min}(\lambda),$$

where $\gamma_{\max}(\lambda)$ *and* $\gamma_{\min}(\lambda)$ *are functions such that*

$$\tau(\lambda) = \gamma_{\min}(\lambda) \cdot \delta(\lambda) - \frac{\gamma_{\max}(\lambda) - \gamma_{\min}(\lambda)}{2}$$

is a non-negligible function of λ.

Intuitively, the condition that $\tau(\lambda)$ be non-negligible requires $\gamma_{\min}(\lambda)$ to be noticeable and the difference of $\gamma_{\max}(\lambda) - \gamma_{\min}(\lambda)$ to be small.

It is known [41] that balanced admissible hash functions exist for $\ell, L = \Theta(\lambda)$.

Theorem 2.8 ([41, Theorem 1]). *Let $(C_\ell)_{\ell \in \mathbb{N}}$ be a family of codes $C_\ell :$ $\{0,1\}^\ell \to \{0,1\}^L$ with minimal distance $c \cdot L$ for some constant $c \in (0, 1/2)$. Then, $(C_\ell)_{\ell \in \mathbb{N}}$ is a family of balanced admissible hash functions. Furthermore, $\mathsf{AdmSmp}(1^\lambda, Q, \delta)$ outputs a key $K \in \{0, 1, \perp\}^L$ for which $\eta = \lfloor \frac{\ln(2Q + Q/\delta)}{-\ln((1-c))} \rfloor$ components are not $\perp$ and*

$$\gamma_{\max} = 2^{-\eta}, \qquad \gamma_{\min} = (1 - Q(1-c))^\eta \cdot 2^{-\eta},$$

so that $\tau = (2\delta - (2\delta + 1) \cdot Q \cdot (1-c)^\eta)/2^{\eta+1}$ is a non-negligible function of λ.

Lemma 2.9 ([43, Lemma 8], [2, Lemma 28]). *Let an input space $\mathcal{X}$ and consider a mapping γ that maps a $(Q+1)$-tuple of elements $(X^\star, X_1, \ldots, X_Q)$ in $\mathcal{X}$ to a probability value in $[0,1]$. We consider the following experiment where we first execute the PRF security game, in which the adversary eventually outputs a guess $\hat{b} \in \{0,1\}$ of the challenger's bit $b \in \{0,1\}$ and wins with advantage ε. We denote by $X^\star \in \mathcal{X}$ the challenge input and $X_1, \ldots, X_Q \in \mathcal{X}$ the evaluation queries. At the end of the game, we flip a fair random coin $b'' \hookleftarrow U(\{0,1\})$. With probability $\gamma = \gamma(X^\star, X_1, \ldots, X_Q)$, we define $b' = \hat{b}$ and, with probability, $1 - \gamma$, we define $b' = b''$. Then, we have*

$$|\Pr[b' = b] - 1/2| \geq \gamma_{\min} \cdot \varepsilon - \frac{\gamma_{\max} - \gamma_{\min}}{2},$$

where $\gamma_{\min}$ and $\gamma_{\max}$ are the maximum and minimum of $\gamma(\mathbb{X})$ for any $\mathbb{X} \in \mathcal{X}^{Q+1}$.

2.3   (Deterministic) Randomness Extractors

A consequence of the Leftover Hash Lemma was used by Agrawal *et al.* [2] to re-randomize matrices over $\mathbb{Z}_q$ by multiplying them with small-norm matrices. We also rely on the following generalization of [2, Lemma 13].

Lemma 2.10. *Let integers m, n, ℓ such that $m > 2(n + \ell) \cdot \log q$, for some prime $q > 2$. Let $\mathbf{B}, \widetilde{\mathbf{B}} \hookleftarrow U(\mathbb{Z}_q^{m \times \ell})$ and $\mathbf{R} \hookleftarrow U(\{-1,1\}^{m \times m})$. For any matrix $\mathbf{F} \in \mathbb{Z}_q^{m \times n}$, the distributions $(\mathbf{B}, \mathbf{R} \cdot \mathbf{B}, \mathbf{R} \cdot \mathbf{F})$ and $(\mathbf{B}, \widetilde{\mathbf{B}}, \mathbf{R} \cdot \mathbf{F})$ are within $2^{-\Omega(n)}$ statistical distance.*

In our security proof, we will need to extract statistically uniform bits from a high-entropy source. Here, we cannot just apply the Leftover Hash Lemma since the source may not be independent of the seed. For this reason, we will apply techniques from deterministic extraction [26,60] and seeded extractors with seed-dependent sources [55]. In particular, we will apply a result of Dodis [26] which extends techniques due to Trevisan and Vadhan [60] to show that, for a sufficiently large $\xi > 0$, a fixed ξ-wise-independent functions can be used to deterministically extract statistically uniform bits.

Lemma 2.11 ([26, Corollary 3]). *Fix any integers $\bar{n}$, m, M, any real $\epsilon < 1$ and any collection $\mathcal{X}$ of M distributions over $\{0,1\}^{\bar{m}}$ of min-entropy $\bar{n}$ each. Define*

$$\xi = \bar{n} + \log M, \qquad \bar{k} = \bar{n} - \left(2\log\frac{1}{\epsilon} + \log\log M + \log\bar{n} + O(1)\right),$$

and let $\mathcal{F}$ be any family of ξ-wise independent functions from $\bar{m}$ bits to $\bar{k}$ bits. With probability at least $(1-1/M)$, a random function $f \hookleftarrow U(\mathcal{F})$ is a good deterministic extractor for the collection $\mathcal{X}$. Namely, $f(X)$ is ϵ-close to $U(\{0,1\}^{\bar{k}})$ for any distribution $X \in \mathcal{X}$.

It is well-known that ξ-wise independent function can be obtained by choosing random polynomials of degree $\xi - 1$ over $GF(2^{\bar{m}})$ (which cost $O(\xi\bar{m})$ bits to describe) and truncating their evaluations to their first $\bar{k}$ bits.

2.4 Linear Integer Secret Sharing

This section recalls the concept of linear integer secret sharing (LISS), as defined by Damgård and Thorbek [24]. The definitions below are taken from [59] where the secret to be shared lives in an interval $[-2^l, 2^l]$ centered in 0, for some $l \in \mathbb{N}$.

Definition 2.12. *A monotone access structure on $[N]$ is a non-empty collection $\mathbb{A}$ of sets $A \subseteq [N]$ such that $\emptyset \notin \mathbb{A}$ and, for all $A \in \mathbb{A}$ and all sets B such that $A \subseteq B \subseteq [N]$, we have $B \in \mathbb{A}$. For an integer $t \in [N]$, the threshold-t access structure $T_{t,N}$ is the collection of sets $A \subseteq [N]$ such that $|A| \geq t$.*

Let $P = [N]$ be a set of shareholders. In a LISS scheme, a dealer D wants to share a secret s in a publicly known interval $[-2^l, 2^l]$. To this end, D uses a share generating matrix $M \in \mathbb{Z}^{d \times e}$ and a random vector $\boldsymbol{\rho} = (s, \rho_2, \ldots, \rho_e)^\top$, where s is the secret to be shared $\{\rho_i\}_{i=2}^e$ are chosen uniformly in $[-2^{l_0+\lambda}, 2^{l_0+\lambda}]^e$, for a large enough $l_0 \in \mathbb{N}$. The dealer D computes a vector $\boldsymbol{s} = (s_1, \ldots, s_d)^\top$ of share units as

$$\boldsymbol{s} = (s_1, \ldots, s_d)^\top = M \cdot \boldsymbol{\rho} \in \mathbb{Z}^d.$$

Each party in $P = \{1, \ldots, N\}$ is assigned a set of share units. Letting $\psi : \{1, \ldots, d\} \rightarrow P$ be a surjective function, the i-th share unit s_i is assigned to the shareholder $\psi(i) \in P$, in which case player $\psi(i)$ is said to own the i-th row of M. If $A \subseteq P$ is a set of shareholders, $M_A \in \mathbb{Z}^{d_A \times e}$ denotes the set of rows jointly owned by A. Likewise, $\boldsymbol{s}_A \in \mathbb{Z}^{d_A}$ denotes the restriction of $\boldsymbol{s} \in \mathbb{Z}^d$ to the coordinates jointly owned by the parties in A. The j-th shareholder's share consists of $\boldsymbol{s}_{\psi^{-1}(j)} \in \mathbb{Z}^{d_j}$, so that it receives $d_j = |\psi^{-1}(j)|$ out of the $d = \sum_{j=1}^n d_j$ share units. The *expansion rate* $\mu = d/N$ is defined to be the average number of share units per player. Sets $A \in \mathbb{A}$ are called *qualified* and $A \notin \mathbb{A}$ are called *forbidden*.

Definition 2.13. *A LISS scheme is private if, for any two secrets s, s', any independent random coins $\boldsymbol{\rho} = (s, \rho_2, \ldots, \rho_e)$, $\boldsymbol{\rho}' = (s', \rho_2', \ldots, \rho_e')$ and any forbidden set A of shareholders, the distributions $\{s_i(s, \boldsymbol{\rho}) = M_i \cdot \boldsymbol{\rho} \mid i \in A\}$ and $\{s_i(s', \boldsymbol{\rho}') = M_i \cdot \boldsymbol{\rho}' \mid i \in A\}$ are $2^{-\Omega(\lambda)}$ apart in terms of statistical distance.*

Damgård and Thorbek [24] showed how to build LISS scheme from integer span programs [23].

Definition 2.14 ([23]). *An integer span program (ISP) is a tuple* $\mathcal{M} = (M, \psi, \varepsilon)$, *where* $M \in \mathbb{Z}^{d \times e}$ *is an integer matrix whose rows are labeled by a surjective function* $\psi : \{1, \ldots, d\} \rightarrow \{1, \ldots, N\}$ *and* $\varepsilon = (1, 0, \ldots, 0)$ *is called target vector. The size of* $\mathcal{M}$ *is the number of rows* d *in* M.

Definition 2.15. *Let* Γ *be a monotone access structure and let* $\mathcal{M} = (M, \psi, \varepsilon)$ *an integer span program. Then,* $\mathcal{M}$ *is an ISP for* Γ *if it computes* Γ: *namely, for all* $A \subseteq \{1, \ldots, N\}$, *the following conditions hold:*

1. *If* $A \in \Gamma$, *there exists a reconstruction vector* $\boldsymbol{\lambda} \in \mathbb{Z}^{d_A}$ *such that* $\boldsymbol{\lambda}^{\top} \cdot M_A = \varepsilon^{\top}$.
2. *If* $A \notin \Gamma$, *there exists* $\boldsymbol{\kappa} = (\kappa_1, \ldots, \kappa_e)^{\top} \in \mathbb{Z}^e$ *such that* $M_A \cdot \boldsymbol{\kappa} = \mathbf{0} \in \mathbb{Z}^d$ *and* $\boldsymbol{\kappa}^{\top} \cdot \varepsilon = 1$ *(i.e.,* $\kappa_1 = 1$*). In this case,* $\boldsymbol{\kappa}$ *is called a sweeping vector for* A.

We also define $\kappa_{\max} = \max\{|a| \mid a$ *is an entry in some sweeping vector*$\}$.

Damgård and Thorbek showed [24] that, if we have an ISP $\mathcal{M} = (M, \psi, \varepsilon)$ that computes the access structure Γ, a statistically private LISS scheme for Γ can be obtained by using M as the share generating matrix and setting $l_0 = l + \lceil \log_2(\kappa_{\max}(e-1)) \rceil + 1$, where l is the length of the secret.

A LISS scheme $\mathcal{L} = (\mathcal{M} = (M, \psi, \varepsilon), \Gamma, \mathcal{R}, \mathcal{K})$ is thus specified by an ISP for the access structure Γ, a space $\mathcal{R}$ of reconstruction vectors satisfying Condition 1 of Definition 2.15, and a space $\mathcal{K}$ of sweeping vectors satisfying Condition 2.

Lemma 2.16 ([59, Lemma 3.1]). *Let* $l_0 = l + \lceil \log_2(\kappa_{\max}(e-1)) \rceil + 1$. *If* $s \in [-2^l, 2^l]$ *is the secret to be shared and* $\boldsymbol{\rho}$ *is randomly sampled from* $[-2^{l_0+\lambda}, 2^{l_0+\lambda}]^e$ *conditionally on* $\langle \boldsymbol{\rho}, \varepsilon \rangle = s$, *the LISS scheme derived from* $\mathcal{M}$ *is private. For any arbitrary* $s, s' \in [-2^l, 2^l]$ *and any forbidden set of shareholders* $A \subset [N]$, *the two distributions* $\{s_A = M_A \cdot \boldsymbol{\rho} \mid \boldsymbol{\rho} \hookleftarrow U([-2^{l_0+\lambda}, 2^{l_0+\lambda}]^e)$ *s.t.* $\langle \boldsymbol{\rho}, \varepsilon \rangle = s\}$, *and* $\{s'_A = M_A \cdot \boldsymbol{\rho} \mid \boldsymbol{\rho} \hookleftarrow U([-2^{l_0+\lambda}, 2^{l_0+\lambda}]^e)$ *s.t.* $\langle \boldsymbol{\rho}, \varepsilon \rangle = s'\}$ *are within statistical distance* $2^{-\lambda}$.

In the following, we do not rely on the result of Lemma 2.16 as we will share vectors sampled from Gaussian (instead of uniform) distributions using Gaussian random coins. We also depart from Lemma 2.16 in that the random coins $(\rho_2, \ldots, \rho_e)$ are not sampled from a wider distribution than the secret: the standard deviation of $(\rho_2, \ldots, \rho_e)$ will be the same as that of s. While this choice does not guarantee the LISS to be private in general, we will show that it suffices in our setting because we only need the secret to have sufficient min-entropy conditionally on the shares observed by the adversary. Aside from the distribution of secrets and random coins, we rely on the technique of Damgård and Thorbek [24] for building share generating matrices.

It was shown in [24] that LISS schemes can be obtained from [10,23]. While the Benaloh-Leichter (BL) secret sharing [10] was initially designed to work over finite groups, Damgård and Thorbek generalized it [24] so as to share integers using access structures consisting of any monotone Boolean formula. In turn, this implies a LISS scheme for any threshold access structure by applying a result of Valiant [34,61]. Their LISS scheme built upon Benaloh-Leichter [10] comes in handy for our purposes because the reconstruction coefficients and the sweeping vectors are small: as can be observed from [24, Lemmas 4], the entries of $\boldsymbol{\lambda}$ live in $\{-1, 0, 1\}$ and [24, Lemma 5] shows that $\kappa_{\max} = 1$. For a monotone Boolean f, the BL-based technique allows binary share distribution matrices $M \in \{0, 1\}^{d \times e}$ such that $d, e = O(\mathrm{size}(f))$ and which have at most $\mathrm{depth}(f) + 1$ non-zero entries, so that each share unit s_i has magnitude $O(2^{l_0 + \lambda} \cdot \mathrm{depth}(f))$.

Valiant's result [61] implies the existence of a monotone Boolean formula of the threshold-t function $T_{t,N}$, which has size $d = O(N^{5.3})$ and depth $O(\log N)$. Since each player receives d/N rows of M on average, the average share size is thus $O(N^{4.3} \cdot (l_0 + \lambda + \log \log N))$ bits. Valiant's construction was improved by Hoory et al. [40] who give a monotone formula of size $O(N^{1+\sqrt{2}})$ and depth $O(\log N)$ for the majority function.[2] This reduces the average share size to $O(N^{\sqrt{2}} \cdot (l_0 + \lambda + \log \log N))$ bits.

2.5 Some Useful Lemmas

Lemma 2.17 ([49, Lemma 4.4]). *For $\sigma = \omega(\sqrt{\log n})$ there is a negligible function $\epsilon = \epsilon(n)$ such that:*

$$\Pr_{\mathbf{x} \sim D_{\mathbb{Z}^n, \sigma}} [\|\mathbf{x}\| > \sigma \sqrt{n}] \leq \frac{1 + \epsilon}{1 - \epsilon} \cdot 2^{-n}$$

Lemma 2.18 ([6, Lemma 2.7]). *Let p, q be positive integers such that $p < q$. Given $R > 0$ an integer, the probability that there exists $e \in [-R, R]$ such that $\lfloor y \rfloor_p \neq \lfloor y + e \rfloor_p$, when $y \hookleftarrow U(\mathbb{Z}_q)$, is smaller than $\frac{2Rp}{q}$.*

Lemma 2.19. *If q is prime and $\mathcal{M}$ be a distribution over $\mathbb{Z}_q^{m \times n}$, and V a distribution over $\mathbb{Z}_q^n$ such that $\Delta\left(\mathcal{M}, U(\mathbb{Z}_q^{m \times n})\right) \leq \epsilon$. We have $\Delta\left(\mathcal{M} \cdot V, U(\mathbb{Z}_q^m)\right) \leq \epsilon + \alpha \cdot \left(1 - \frac{1}{q^m}\right)$, where $\alpha := \Pr[V = \mathbf{0}]$.*

2.6 (Distributed) Pseudorandom Functions

A pseudorandom function family is specified by efficient algorithms (Keygen, Eval), where Keygen a randomized key generation algorithm that takes in a security parameter 1^λ and outputs a random key $K \hookleftarrow \mathcal{K}$ from a key space $\mathcal{K}$. Eval is a deterministic evaluation algorithm, which takes in a key $K \in \mathcal{K}$ and an input X in a domain $\mathcal{D} = \{0, 1\}^\ell$ and evaluates a function $F(K, X)$ in a range $\mathcal{R} = \{0, 1\}^\mu$. The standard security definitions for PRFs are recalled in the full version of the paper.

---

[2] Note that a threshold-t function can be obtained from the majority function by fixing the desired number of input bits, so that we need a majority function of size $\leq 2N$ to construct a threshold function $T_{t,N}$.

A distributed pseudorandom function (DPRF) is a tuple of algorithms (Setup, Share, PEval, Eval, Combine) of efficient algorithms with the following specification. Setup takes as input a security parameter 1^λ, a number of servers 1^N, a threshold 1^t and a desired input length 1^ℓ and outputs public parameters pp. The key sharing algorithm Share : $\mathcal{K} \to \mathcal{K}^N$ inputs a random master secret key $SK_0 \in \mathcal{K}$ and outputs a tuple of shares $(SK_1, \ldots, SK_N) \in \mathcal{K}^N$, which form a (t, N)-threshold secret sharing of SK_0. The partial evaluation algorithm Eval : $\mathcal{K} \times \mathcal{D} \to \mathcal{R}$ takes as input a key share SK_i and an input X and outputs a partial evaluation $Y_i = \mathsf{PEval}(SK_i, X) \in \mathcal{R}$. Algorithm Combine : $\mathcal{S} \times \mathcal{R}^t \to \mathcal{R}$ takes in a t-subset $\mathcal{S} \subset [N]$ together with t partial evaluations $\{Y_i\}_{i \in \mathcal{S}}$, where $Y_i \in \mathcal{R}$ for all $i \in \mathcal{S}$, and outputs a value $Y \in \mathcal{R}$. The centralized evaluation algorithm Eval : $\mathcal{K} \times \mathcal{D} \to \mathcal{R}$ operates as in a ordinary PRF and outputs a value $Y = \mathsf{Eval}(SK_0, X) \in \mathcal{R}$ on input of $X \in \mathcal{D}$ and a key $SK_0 \in \mathcal{K}$.

CONSISTENCY. A DPRF is consistent if, for any pp $\leftarrow \mathsf{Setup}(1^\lambda, 1^\ell, 1^t, 1^N)$, any master key $SK_0 \hookleftarrow \mathcal{K}$ shared according to $(SK_1, \ldots, SK_N) \leftarrow \mathsf{Share}(SK_0)$, any t-subset $\mathcal{S} = \{i_1, \ldots, i_t\} \subset [N]$ and any input $X \in \mathcal{D}$, if $Y_{i_j} = \mathsf{PEval}(SK_{i_j}, X)$ for each $j \in [t]$, then we have $\mathsf{Eval}(SK_0, X) = \mathsf{Combine}(\mathcal{S}, (Y_{i_1}, \ldots, Y_{i_t}))$ with overwhelming probability over the random coins of Setup and Share.

We say that a DPRF provides adaptive security if it remains secure against an adversary that can adaptively choose which servers it wants to corrupt. In particular, the adversary can arbitrarily interleave evaluation and corruption queries as long as they do not allow it to trivially win.

Definition 2.20 (Adaptive DPRF security). *Let λ be a security parameter and let integers $t, N \in \mathsf{poly}(\lambda)$. We say that a (t, N)-DPRF is pseudorandom under adaptive corruptions if no PPT adversary has non-negligible advantage in the following game:*

1. *The challenger generates* pp $\leftarrow \mathsf{Setup}(1^\lambda, 1^\ell, 1^t, 1^N)$ *and chooses a random key $SK_0 \hookleftarrow \mathcal{K}$, which is broken into N shares $(SK_1, \ldots, SK_N) \leftarrow \mathsf{Share}(SK_0)$. It also initializes an empty set $\mathcal{C} \leftarrow \emptyset$ and flips a random coin $b \hookleftarrow U(\{0,1\})$.*
2. *The adversary $\mathcal{A}$ adaptively interleaves the following kinds of queries.*

   Corruption: *$\mathcal{A}$ chooses an index $i \in [N]\backslash\mathcal{C}$. The challenger returns SK_i to $\mathcal{A}$ and sets $\mathcal{C} := \mathcal{C} \cup \{i\}$.*
   Evaluation: *$\mathcal{A}$ chooses a pair $(i, X) \in [N] \times \mathcal{D}$ and the challenger returns $Y_i = \mathsf{PEval}(SK_i, X)$.*
3. *The adversary chooses an input $X^\star$. At this point, the challenger randomly samples $Y_0 \hookleftarrow U(\{0,1\}^\mu)$ and computes $Y_1 = \mathsf{Eval}(SK_0, X^\star)$. Then, it returns Y_b to the adversary.*
4. *The adversary $\mathcal{A}$ adaptively makes more queries as in Stage 2 under the restriction that, at any time, we should have $|\mathcal{C} \cup \mathcal{E}| < t$, where $\mathcal{E} \subset [N]$ denotes the set of indexes for which an evaluation query of the form $(i, X^\star)$ was made in Stage 2 or in Stage 4.*
5. *$\mathcal{A}$ outputs a bit $\hat{b} \in \{0, 1\}$ and wins if $\hat{b} = b$. Its advantage is defined to be $\mathbf{Adv}_{\mathcal{A}}^{\mathrm{DPRF}}(\lambda) := |\Pr[\hat{b} = b] - 1/2|$.*

Definition 2.20 is a game based definition, which may not imply security in the sense of simulation-based definitions. Still, we show it is strictly stronger than the definition of static security used in [16]. It is well-known that static security does not imply adaptive security in distributed threshold protocols (see, e.g., [22]). In the case of DPRFs, we show in the full version of the paper that allowing even a *single* evaluation query before any corruption query already gives a stronger game-based definition than the game-based security definition of static security.

Theorem 2.21. *For any $t, N \in \mathsf{poly}(\lambda)$ such that $t < N/2$, there is a DPRF family which is secure in the sense of Definition A.1 (in Appendix A) but insecure in the sense of Definition 2.20.*

Note that the above separation still holds for small non-constant values of t and N if we assume polynomial or slightly super-polynomial adversaries.

3   A Variant of the BLMR PRF

Before describing our distributed PRF, we present its centralized version which can be seen as a variant of the key-homomorphic PRFs described by Boneh et al. [16] and Banerjee-Peikert PRFs [7]. However, the security proof is very different in that it does not use a hybrid argument over the input bits. Instead, it applies the strategy of partitioning the input space into disjoint subspaces (analogously to proof techniques for, e.g., identity-based encryption [63]) and builds on the lossy mode of LWE [36].

In [7,16], a PRF evaluation of an input x is of the form $\mathbf{y} = \lfloor \mathbf{A}(x)^\top \cdot \mathbf{s} \rfloor_p \in \mathbb{Z}_p^m$, where $\mathbf{s} \in \mathbb{Z}_q^n$ is the secret key and $\mathbf{A}(X) \in \mathbb{Z}_q^{n \times m}$ is an input-dependent matrix obtained from public matrices $\mathbf{A}_0, \mathbf{A}_1 \in \mathbb{Z}_q^{n \times m}$. Our variant is similar at a high level, with two differences. First, we derive $\mathbf{A}(x)$ from a set of $2L$ public matrices $\{\mathbf{A}_{i,0}, \mathbf{A}_{i,1}\}_{i=1}^L$. Second, $\lfloor \mathbf{A}(x)^\top \cdot \mathbf{s} \rfloor_p$ is not quite our PRF evaluation. Instead, we obtain the PRF value by using $\lfloor \mathbf{A}(x)^\top \cdot \mathbf{s} \rfloor_p$ as a source of entropy for a deterministic randomness extractor.

The security proof departs from [7,16] by exploiting the connection between the schemes and the Gentry-Sahai-Waters FHE [33]. For each $i \in [L]$ and $b \in \{0,1\}$, we interpret $\mathbf{A}_{i,b} \in \mathbb{Z}_q^{n \times m}$ as a GSW ciphertext $\mathbf{A}_{i,b} = \mathbf{A} \cdot \mathbf{R}_{i,b} + \mu_{i,b} \cdot \mathbf{G}$, where $\mathbf{R}_{i,b} \in \{-1,1\}^{m \times m}$, $\mu_{i,b} \in \{0,1\}$ and $\mathbf{G} \in \mathbb{Z}_q^{n \times m}$ is the gadget matrix of [48]. Before evaluating the PRF on an input X, we encode $X \in \{0,1\}^\ell$ into $x \in \{0,1\}^L$ using an admissible hash function. Then, we homomorphically derive $\mathbf{A}(x)$ as a GSW ciphertext $\mathbf{A}(x) = \mathbf{A} \cdot \mathbf{R}_x + (\prod_{i=1}^L \mu_{i,x[i]}) \cdot \mathbf{G}$, for some small-norm $\mathbf{R}_x \in \mathbb{Z}^{m \times m}$. By carefully choosing $\{\mu_{i,b}\}_{i \in [L], b \in \{0,1\}}$, the properties of admissible hash functions ensure that the product $\prod_{i=1}^L \mu_{i,x[i]}$ cancels out in all evaluation queries but evaluates to 1 on the challenge input $X^\star$.

In the next step of the proof, we move to a modified experiment where the random matrix $\mathbf{A} \in \mathbb{Z}_q^{n \times m}$ is replaced by a lossy matrix $\mathbf{A}^\top = \bar{\mathbf{A}}^\top \cdot \mathbf{C} + \mathbf{E}$, where $\bar{\mathbf{A}} \hookleftarrow U(\mathbb{Z}_q^{n' \times m})$, $\mathbf{C} \hookleftarrow U(\mathbb{Z}_q^{n' \times n})$ and $\mathbf{E} \in \mathbb{Z}^{m \times n}$ is a short Gaussian matrix. This modification has the consequence of turning $\lfloor \mathbf{A}(x)^\top \cdot \mathbf{s} \rfloor_p$ into a lossy function of $\mathbf{s}$ on all inputs X for which $\prod_{i=1}^{L} \mu_{i,x[i]} = 0$. At the same time, the function remains injective whenever $\prod_{i=1}^{L} \mu_{i,x[i]} = 1$. Using the properties of admissible hash functions, we still have a noticeable probability that the function be lossy in all evaluation queries and injective in the challenge phase. Moreover, by using a small-norm secret $\mathbf{s} \in \mathbb{Z}^n$ and setting the ratio q/p large enough, we can actually make sure that evaluation queries always reveal the same information (namely, the product $\mathbf{C} \cdot \mathbf{s}$) about $\mathbf{s}$. As long as we have $\prod_{i=1}^{L} \mu_{i,x^*[i]} = 1$ for the challenge input X^*, the value $\tilde{\mathbf{z}} = \lfloor \mathbf{A}(x^*)^\top \cdot \mathbf{s} \rfloor_p = \lfloor (\mathbf{A} \cdot \mathbf{R}_{x^*} + \mathbf{G})^\top \cdot \mathbf{s} \rfloor_p$ is guaranteed to have a lot of entropy as an injective function of an unpredictable $\mathbf{s}$. At this point, we can extract statistically uniform bits from the source $\tilde{\mathbf{z}}$. Since the latter depends on x^* (which can be correlated with the seed included in public parameters), we need an extractor that can operate on seed-dependent sources. Fortunately, deterministic extractors come in handy for this purpose.

3.1 Decomposing Random Matrices into Invertible Binary Matrices

In the following, we set $k = n\lceil \log q \rceil$ and $m = 2k$ and define

$$\mathbf{G} = [\, \mathbf{I}_n \otimes (1, 2, 4, \ldots, 2^{\lceil \log q \rceil - 1}) \mid \mathbf{I}_n \otimes (1, 2, 4, \ldots, 2^{\lceil \log q \rceil - 1})\,] \in \mathbb{Z}_q^{n \times m}$$

which is a variant of the gadget matrix of [48]. We also define $\mathbf{G}^{-1} : \mathbb{Z}_q^{n \times m} \rightarrow \mathbb{Z}^{m \times m}$ to be a deterministic algorithm that inputs $\mathbf{A} \in \mathbb{Z}_q^{n \times m}$ and outputs a binary matrix $\mathbf{G}^{-1}(\mathbf{A}) \in \{0,1\}^{m \times m}$ such that $\mathbf{G} \cdot \mathbf{G}^{-1}(\mathbf{A}) = \mathbf{A}$. We will require that, for any $\mathbf{A} \in \mathbb{Z}_q^{n \times m}$, $\mathbf{G}^{-1}(\mathbf{A})$ be invertible over $\mathbb{Z}_q$ with sufficiently high probability. The next lemma shows a function $\mathbf{G}^{-1}(\cdot)$ satisfying this condition.

Lemma 3.1 (Adapted from [16, Lemma A.3]). *Let $k = n\lceil \log q \rceil$. If $q \geq 2^{k/n} \cdot (1 - \frac{1}{2n})$, there exists an efficient algorithm that samples a statistically uniform matrix $\mathbf{A} \hookleftarrow U(\mathbb{Z}_q^{n \times m})$ such that $\mathbf{G}^{-1}(\mathbf{A}) \in \{0,1\}^{m \times m}$ is $\mathbb{Z}_q$-invertible.*

Proof. We first show how to sample a sequence of $k = n\lceil \log q \rceil$ uniform vectors over $\mathbb{Z}_q^n$ whose binary decompositions form a full-rank binary matrix over $\mathbb{Z}_q$. In turn, this will allow us to sample a random $\mathbf{A} \hookleftarrow U(\mathbb{Z}_q^{n \times m})$, where $m = 2k$, such that $\mathbf{G}^{-1}(\mathbf{A}) \in \{0,1\}^{m \times m}$ is invertible. As in the proof of [16, Lemma A.3], we use the observation that, for any i linearly independent vectors $\mathbf{v}_1, \ldots, \mathbf{v}_i \in \mathbb{Z}_q^k$ over $\mathbb{Z}_q$, if $V = \text{span}_{\mathbb{Z}_q}(\mathbf{v}_1, \ldots, \mathbf{v}_i)$, we have $|V \cap \{0,1\}^k| \leq 2^i$.

For an index $i \in [k-1]$, suppose that we have chosen $\mathbb{Z}_q$-independent vectors $\mathbf{b}_1, \ldots, \mathbf{b}_i \in \{0,1\}^k$ and that $\mathbf{b}_{i+1} \in \{0,1\}^k$ is obtained as the binary decomposition of a random $\mathbf{a}_{i+1} \hookleftarrow U(\mathbb{Z}_q^n)$. The probability that $\mathbf{b}_{i+1}$ is independent of $\mathbf{b}_1, \ldots, \mathbf{b}_i$ is $\geq (q^n - 2^i)/q^n$. If we sample $\mathbf{a}_1, \ldots, \mathbf{a}_k \hookleftarrow U(\mathbb{Z}_q^n)$, the probability that their binary decompositions are linearly independent over $\mathbb{Z}_q$ is

$$\prod_{i=0}^{k-1} \Pr[\mathbf{b}_{i+1} \notin \text{span}_{\mathbb{Z}_q}(\mathbf{b}_1, \ldots, \mathbf{b}_i)] = \prod_{i=0}^{k-1} \frac{q^n - 2^i}{q^n} \tag{1}$$

Note that the factors the right-hand side member of (1) are all positive: indeed, we have $2^{k/n} \cdot (1 - \frac{1}{2n}) \leq q \leq 2^{k/n}$. Since $(1 - \frac{1}{2n})^n \approx \exp(-1/2)$ for large values

of n, this implies $2^k/\sqrt{\exp(1)} \leq q^n \leq 2^k$ and thus $2^{k-1}/q^n \leq \sqrt{\exp(1)}/2 < 1$.
We now proceed to bound (1) as

$$\prod_{i=0}^{k-1}\left(1 - \frac{2^i}{q^n}\right) = \exp\left(\sum_{i=0}^{k-1}\ln\left(1 - \frac{2^i}{q^n}\right)\right)$$

$$\geq \exp\left(-\frac{3}{q^n} \cdot \sum_{i=0}^{k-1} 2^i\right) = \exp\left(-\frac{3}{q^n} \cdot 2^k\right) = \exp(-3 \cdot \sqrt{\exp(1)}),$$

where the inequality holds because $\ln(1 - x) \geq -3x$ for all $x \in \left(0, \sqrt{\exp(1)}/2\right)$.

Hence, if we sample $141 \cdot k > k/\exp(-3 \cdot \sqrt{\exp(1)})$ vectors $\mathbf{a}_i \hookleftarrow U(\mathbb{Z}_q^n)$ and stack up the binary decompositions of $\mathbf{a}_i^\top$, the probability that the resulting matrix contains a $\mathbb{Z}_q$-invertible sub-matrix over $\{0,1\}^k$ is at least $1 - 2^{-\Omega(k)}$.

We can thus sample a random matrix $\mathbf{A} = [\mathbf{A}_L | \mathbf{A}_R] \hookleftarrow U(\mathbb{Z}_q^{n \times m})$ that satisfies the required conditions by defining $\mathbf{G}^{-1}(\mathbf{A}) \in \{0,1\}^{m \times m}$ so that it contains the binary decomposition $\mathsf{BD}(\mathbf{A}_L) \subset \{0,1\}^{k \times k}$ in its upper-left corner and $\mathsf{BD}(\mathbf{A}_R) \in \{0,1\}^{k \times k}$ in its lower-right corner. □

3.2   A Centralized Construction

Let λ be a security parameter and let $\ell \in \Theta(\lambda)$, $L \in \Theta(\lambda)$. We use parameters consisting of prime moduli p and q such that $q/p > 2^{L+\lambda} \cdot r$, dimensions $n, m, k \in \mathrm{poly}(\lambda)$ such that $m \geq 2n \cdot \lceil \log q \rceil$, an integer $\beta > 0$, $\alpha > 0$ and $r = m^{L+2} \cdot n \cdot \beta \cdot \alpha q$. We rely on the following ingredients.

- A balanced admissible hash function $\mathsf{AHF} : \{0,1\}^\ell \to \{0,1\}^L$.
- A family Π_λ of ξ-wise independent hash functions $\pi_i : \mathbb{Z}_p^m \to \mathbb{Z}_p^k$ for a suitable $\xi > 0$ that will be determined later on. Let a random member π of Π_λ. For example, the function π can be a random polynomial $\pi(Z) \in GF(p^m)[Z]$ of degree $\xi - 1$ with outputs truncated to their k first coordinates.

We also choose a Gaussian parameter $\sigma > 0$, which will specify an interval $[-\beta, \beta] = [-\sigma\sqrt{n}, \sigma\sqrt{n}]$ where the coordinates of the secret will be confined (with probability exponentially close to 1). We also need a rounding parameter $r > 0$, set as indicated above.

The pseudorandom function family assumes the availability of public parameters

$$\mathsf{pp} := \left(q, \pi, \mathbf{A}_0, \{\mathbf{A}_{i,0}, \mathbf{A}_{i,1} \in \mathbb{Z}_q^{n \times m}\}_{i=1}^L, \mathsf{AHF}, r, \sigma\right),$$

where $\mathbf{A}_0 \sim U(\mathbb{Z}_q^{n \times m})$ and $\mathbf{A}_{i,0}, \mathbf{A}_{i,1} \sim U(\mathbb{Z}_q^{n \times m})$ for each $i \in [L]$. Importantly, $\{\mathbf{A}_{i,0}, \mathbf{A}_{i,1}\}_{i=1}^L$ should be chosen in such a way that $\mathbf{G}^{-1}(\mathbf{A}_{i,b}) \in \mathbb{Z}^{m \times m}$ is $\mathbb{Z}_q$-invertible for all $i \in [L]$ and $b \in \{0,1\}$.

Keygen(pp): Given pp, sample a vector $\mathbf{s} \hookleftarrow D_{\mathbb{Z}^n, \sigma}$ so that $\|\mathbf{s}\|_\infty < \beta = \sigma\sqrt{n}$ with overwhelming probability. The secret key is $SK := \mathbf{s} \in [-\beta, \beta]^n$.

Eval(pp, SK, X): Given $SK = \mathbf{s} \in \mathbb{Z}^n$ and an input $X \in \{0,1\}^\ell$,

1. Compute $x = \mathsf{AHF}(X) \in \{0,1\}^L$ and parse it as $x = x_1 \ldots x_L$.
2. Compute

$$\mathbf{z} = \left\lfloor \left(\mathbf{A}(x)\right)^\top \cdot \mathbf{s} \right\rceil_p \in \mathbb{Z}_p^m, \tag{2}$$

where

$$\mathbf{A}(x) = \mathbf{A}_0 \cdot \prod_{i=1}^{L} \mathbf{G}^{-1}\left(\mathbf{A}_{i,x_i}\right),$$

and output $\mathbf{y} = \pi(\mathbf{z}) \in \mathbb{Z}_p^k$.

We remark that the way to compute $\mathbf{z} \in \mathbb{Z}_p^m$ in (2) is reminiscent of the key-homomorphic PRFs of [7,16]. Unlike [7,16], our security proof requires the secret $\mathbf{s}$ to have small entries. Also, our PRF is not key-homomorphic as the output is $\mathbf{y} = \pi(\mathbf{z}) \in \mathbb{Z}_p^k$ instead of $\mathbf{z} \in \mathbb{Z}_p^m$. Fortunately, losing the key-homomorphic property does not prevent us from building a DPRF since the randomness extraction step is only applied to the result of combining t partial evaluations.

Theorem 3.2. *Set an entropy lower bound* $\bar{n} = \lfloor n \cdot \log \sigma - n' \cdot \log q \rfloor - 1$ *as* $\Omega(\lambda)$. *If we choose the output length* $\bar{k} = k \cdot \log p$ *in such a way that*

$$\xi = \bar{n} + \ell, \qquad \bar{k} = \bar{n} - 2 \cdot (\lambda + \log \ell + \log \bar{n}),$$

then the construction above is a secure PRF family under the $\mathsf{LWE}_{q,m,n',\alpha}$ *assumption.*

The proof is given in the full version of the paper. It may be inferred as a sub-proof of the security proof of the upcoming DPRF construction.

4   The DPRF Construction

We design the distributed PRF by using a LISS inside the PRF construction of Sect. 3. As mentioned earlier, the latter is well-suited to our purposes because, in the security proof, the secret key is known to the challenger at any time. When the secret key $\mathbf{s}$ is shared using a LISS, the challenger is always able to consistently answer corruption queries because it has all shares at disposal.

In the construction, we rely on the specific LISS construction of Damgård and Thorbek [24], which is based on the Benaloh-Leichter secret sharing [10]. This particular LISS scheme is well-suited to our needs for several reasons. First, it has binary share generating matrices, which allows obtaining relatively short shares of $\mathbf{s} \in \mathbb{Z}^n$: in the security proof, this is necessary to ensure that the adversary always obtains the same information about uncorrupted shares in partial evaluation queries. Another advantage of the Benaloh-Leichter-based LISS is that its reconstruction constants live in $\{-1, 0, 1\}$, which avoids blowing up the homomorphism errors when partial evaluations are combined together. Finally, its sweeping vectors also have their coordinates in $\{-1, 0, 1\}$ (whereas they may be exponentially large in the number N of servers in the construction based on Cramer-Fehr [23]) and we precisely need sweeping vectors $\boldsymbol{\kappa}$ to be small in the proof of our Lemma 4.4.

4.1 Description

Setup$(1^\lambda, 1^\ell, 1^t, 1^N)$: On input of a security parameter λ, a number of servers N, a threshold $t \in [1, N]$ and an input length $\ell \in \Theta(\lambda)$, set $d, e = O(N^{1+\sqrt{2}})$. Then, choose a real $\alpha > 0$, a Gaussian parameter $\sigma = \sqrt{e} \cdot \Omega(\sqrt{n})$, which will specify an interval $[-\beta, \beta] = [-\sigma\sqrt{n}, \sigma\sqrt{n}]$ where the coordinates of the secret will live (with probability exponentially close to 1). Next, do the following.

1. Choose prime moduli p, q and u such that $p/u > d \cdot 2^{\lambda+L}$ and $q/p > 2^{L+\lambda} \cdot r$, where dimensions $n, m, k \subset \mathrm{poly}(\lambda)$ such that $m \geq 2n \cdot \lceil \log q \rceil$, and $r = m^{L+2} \cdot n \cdot \beta^* \cdot \alpha q$ with $\beta^* = O(\beta \cdot \log N)$.
2. Choose a balanced admissible hash function $\mathsf{AHF} : \{0,1\}^\ell \to \{0,1\}^L$, for a suitable $L \subset O(\lambda)$. Choose a family Π_λ of ξ-wise independent hash functions $\pi_i : \mathbb{Z}_u^m \to \mathbb{Z}_u^k$, for a suitable integer $\xi > 0$, with $\pi \hookleftarrow U(\Pi_\lambda)$.
3. Choose random matrices $\mathbf{A}_0 \hookleftarrow U(\mathbb{Z}_q^{n \times m})$ and $\mathbf{A}_{i,b} \hookleftarrow U(\mathbb{Z}_q^{n \times m})$, for each $i \in [L]$, $b \in \{0, 1\}$, subject to the constraint that $\mathbf{G}^{-1}(\mathbf{A}_{i,b}) \in \mathbb{Z}^{m \times m}$ be $\mathbb{Z}_q$-invertible for all $i \subset [L]$ and $b \in \{0, 1\}$.

Output

$$\mathsf{pp} := \Big(q, \ p, \ u, \ \pi, \ \mathbf{A}_0, \ \{\mathbf{A}_{i,0}, \mathbf{A}_{i,1} \ \in \mathbb{Z}_q^{n \times m}\}_{i=1}^L, \ \mathsf{AHF}\Big),$$

Share(pp, SK_0): Given pp and a key $SK_0 = \mathbf{s}$ consisting of an integer vector $\mathbf{s}$ sampled from the Gaussian distribution $D_{\mathbb{Z}^n, \sigma}$, return $\perp$ if $\mathbf{s} \notin [-\beta, \beta]^n$, where $\beta = \sigma\sqrt{n}$. Otherwise, generate a LISS of $\mathbf{s}$ as follows.

1. Using the BL-based LISS scheme, construct the matrix $M \in \{0, 1\}^{d \times e}$ that computes the Boolean formula associated with the $T_{t,N}$ threshold function. By using [40], we obtain a matrix $M \in \{0,1\}^{d \times e}$, so that each row of M contains $O(\log N)$ non-zero entries.
2. For each $k \in [n]$, generate a LISS of the k-th coordinate s_k of $\mathbf{s} \in \mathbb{Z}^n$. To this end, define a vector $\boldsymbol{\rho}_k = (s_k, \rho_{k,2}, \ldots, \rho_{k,e})^\top$, with Gaussian entries $\rho_{k,2}, \ldots, \rho_{k,e} \hookleftarrow D_{\mathbb{Z}, \sigma}$, and compute

$$\mathbf{s}_k = (s_{k,1}, \ldots, s_{k,d})^\top = M \cdot \boldsymbol{\rho}_k \ \in \mathbb{Z}^d,$$

   whose entries are smaller than $\|\mathbf{s}_k\|_\infty \leq \beta^* = O(\beta \cdot \log N)$.
3. Define the matrix $\mathbf{S} = [\mathbf{s}_1 \mid \ldots \mid \mathbf{s}_n] \in \mathbb{Z}^{d \times n}$. For each $j \in [N]$, define the share of server P_j to be the sub-matrix $\mathbf{S}_{I_j} = M_{I_j} \cdot [\boldsymbol{\rho}_1 \mid \ldots \mid \boldsymbol{\rho}_n] \in \mathbb{Z}^{d_j \times n}$, where $I_j = \psi^{-1}(j) \subset \{1, \ldots, d\}$ is the set of indexes such that P_j owns the sub-matrix $M_{I_j} \in \{0, 1\}^{d_j \times e}$.

For each $j \in [N]$, the share $SK_j = \mathbf{S}_{I_j} \in \mathbb{Z}^{d_j \times n}$ is privately sent to P_j.

PEval(pp, SK_j, X): Given $SK_j = \mathbf{S}_{I_j} \in \mathbb{Z}^{d_j \times n}$ and an input $X \in \{0,1\}^\ell$,

1. Compute $x = \mathsf{AHF}(X) \in \{0,1\}^L$ and parse it as $x = x_1 \ldots x_L$.
2. Parse $\mathbf{S}_{I_j}^\top = [\boldsymbol{\rho}_1 \mid \ldots \mid \boldsymbol{\rho}_n]^\top \cdot M_{I_j}^\top \in \mathbb{Z}^{n \times d_j}$ as $[\bar{\mathbf{s}}_{j,1} \mid \ldots \mid \bar{\mathbf{s}}_{j,d_j}]$. For each $\theta \in \{1, \ldots, d_j\}$, compute

$$\mathbf{z}_{j,\theta} = \left\lfloor \left(\mathbf{A}(x)\right)^\top \cdot \bar{\mathbf{s}}_{j,\theta} \right\rfloor_p \in \mathbb{Z}_p^m, \qquad (3)$$

where

$$\mathbf{A}(x) = \mathbf{A}_0 \cdot \prod_{i=1}^{L} \mathbf{G}^{-1}(\mathbf{A}_{i,x_i}),$$

and output the partial evaluation $\mathbf{Y}_j = [\mathbf{z}_{j,1} \mid \ldots \mid \mathbf{z}_{j,d_j}] \in \mathbb{Z}_p^{m \times d_j}$.

Eval(pp, SK_0, X): Given $SK_0 = \mathbf{s} \in \mathbb{Z}^n$ and an input $X \in \{0,1\}^\ell$,

1. Compute $x = \mathsf{AHF}(X) \in \{0,1\}^L$ and write it as $x = x_1 \ldots x_L$.
2. Compute

$$\tilde{\mathbf{z}} = \left\lfloor \left(\mathbf{A}(x)\right)^\top \cdot \mathbf{s} \right\rfloor_p \in \mathbb{Z}_p^m,$$

where $\mathbf{A}(x) = \mathbf{A}_0 \cdot \prod_{i=1}^{L} \mathbf{G}^{-1}(\mathbf{A}_{i,x_i})$, and output $\mathbf{y} = \pi(\lfloor \tilde{\mathbf{z}} \rfloor_u) \in \mathbb{Z}_u^k$.

Combine$(\mathcal{S}, (\mathbf{Y}_{j_1}, \ldots, \mathbf{Y}_{j_t}))$: Write $\mathcal{S} = \{j_1, \ldots, j_t\}$ and parse each $\mathbf{Y}_{j_\kappa} \in \mathbb{Z}_p^{m \times d_{j_\kappa}}$ as $[\mathbf{z}_{j_\kappa,1} \mid \ldots \mid \mathbf{z}_{j_\kappa,d_{j_\kappa}}]$ for all $\kappa \in [t]$.

1. Determine the vector $\boldsymbol{\lambda}_{\mathcal{S}} \in \{-1,0,1\}^{d_{\mathcal{S}}}$ such that $\boldsymbol{\lambda}_{\mathcal{S}}^\top \cdot M_{\mathcal{S}} = (1,0,\ldots,0)^\top$, where $M_{\mathcal{S}} \in \{0,1\}^{d_{\mathcal{S}} \times e}$ is the sub-matrix of M owned by the parties in $\mathcal{S}$ and $d_{\mathcal{S}} = \sum_{\kappa=1}^{t} d_{j_\kappa}$ with $d_{j_\kappa} = |\psi^{-1}(j_\kappa)|$ for all $\kappa \in [t]$. Then, parse $\boldsymbol{\lambda}_{\mathcal{S}}$ as $[\boldsymbol{\lambda}_{j_1}^\top \mid \ldots \mid \boldsymbol{\lambda}_{j_t}^\top]^\top$, where $\boldsymbol{\lambda}_{j_\kappa} \in \{-1,0,1\}^{d_{j_\kappa}}$ for all $\kappa \in [t]$.
2. Compute $\tilde{\mathbf{z}} = \sum_{\kappa=1}^{t} \mathbf{Y}_{j_\kappa} \cdot \boldsymbol{\lambda}_{j_\kappa} \in \mathbb{Z}_p^m$, which equals

$$\tilde{\mathbf{z}} = \left\lfloor \left(\mathbf{A}(x)\right)^\top \cdot \mathbf{s} \right\rfloor_p + \mathbf{e}_z \in \mathbb{Z}_p^m,$$

for some $\mathbf{e}_z \in \{-2d_{\mathcal{S}}, \ldots, 2d_{\mathcal{S}}\}^m$.
3. Compute $\mathbf{z} = \lfloor \tilde{\mathbf{z}} \rfloor_u \in \mathbb{Z}_u^m$, which equals

$$\mathbf{z} = \left\lfloor \left\lfloor \left(\mathbf{A}(x)\right)^\top \cdot \mathbf{s} \right\rfloor_p \right\rfloor_u \in \mathbb{Z}_u^m$$

with overwhelming probability. Finally, output $\mathbf{y} = \pi(\mathbf{z}) \in \mathbb{Z}_u^k$.

By setting $\sigma = \sqrt{e \cdot n} = O(N^{\frac{1+\sqrt{2}}{2}}) \cdot \sqrt{n}$ as allowed by [40], we have share units of magnitude $\beta^* = \Theta(\sigma\sqrt{n}\log N) = O\left(N^{\frac{1+\sqrt{2}}{2}}\log N\right) \cdot n$. Since $d = O(N^{1+\sqrt{2}})$, the average share size amounts to $\frac{d \cdot n \cdot \log \beta^*}{N} = n \cdot N^{\sqrt{2}} \cdot (\log n + O(\log N))$ bits.

Regarding the parameters, Theorem 4.2 allows us to rely on the presumed hardness of $\mathsf{LWE}_{q,m,n',\alpha}$ for n' which may be set as $\Theta(n(\log Nn)/(\log q))$ if $n(\log Nn) = \Omega(\lambda)$. To make sure that the best known attacks on LWE require 2^λ bit operations, it suffices that $\alpha q = \Omega(\sqrt{n'})$ and $n' \log q / \log^2 \alpha = \Omega(\lambda/\log\lambda)$. We may set $n = \mathsf{poly}(\lambda)$ (for a small degree polynomial) and $q = 2^{\Omega(\lambda\log\lambda)}$ since r contains a term $m^L = \mathsf{poly}(\lambda)^{\Theta(\lambda)} = 2^{O(\lambda\log\lambda)}$.

We remark that our modulus q is exponential in the input length L, but not in the number of servers N. In contrast, the DPRF of [16] requires an exponential modulus in N incurred by the use of Shamir's secret sharing and the technique of clearing out the denominators [3].

4.2 Security and Correctness

We now show that the construction provides statistical consistency.

Lemma 4.1. *Let* $\mathsf{pp} \leftarrow \mathsf{Setup}(1^\lambda, 1^\ell, 1^t, 1^N)$ *and let a secret key* $SK_0 = s \leftarrow D_{\mathbb{Z}^n,\sigma}$, *which is shared as* $(SK_1, \ldots, SK_N) \leftarrow \mathsf{Share}(\mathsf{pp}, SK_0)$. *For any* t*-subset* $S = \{j_1, \ldots, j_t\} \subset [N]$ *and input* $X \in \{0,1\}^\ell$, *if* $Y_{j_k} = \mathsf{PEval}(\mathsf{pp}, SK_{j_k}, X)$ *for all* $\kappa \in [t]$, *we have*

$$\mathsf{Combine}(S, (Y_{j_1}, \ldots, Y_{j_t})) = \mathsf{Eval}(\mathsf{pp}, SK_0, X)$$

with probability exponentially close to 1.

Proof. Let $\boldsymbol{\lambda}_S \in \{-1,0,1\}^{d_S}$ such that $\boldsymbol{\lambda}_S^\top \cdot M_S = (1, 0, \ldots, 0) \in \mathbb{Z}^e$. If we parse $\boldsymbol{\lambda}_S$ as $[\boldsymbol{\lambda}_{j_1}^\top \mid \ldots \mid \boldsymbol{\lambda}_{j_t}^\top]^\top$ we have

$$\mathbf{s} = [\boldsymbol{\rho}_1 \mid \cdots \mid \boldsymbol{\rho}_n]^\top \cdot M_S^\top \cdot \boldsymbol{\lambda}_S = \sum_{k=1}^{t} \mathbf{S}_{I_{j_k}}^\top \cdot \boldsymbol{\lambda}_{j_k}.$$

In turn, this implies

$$\lfloor \mathbf{A}(x)^\top \cdot \mathbf{s} \rfloor_p = \left\lfloor \sum_{k=1}^{t} \mathbf{A}(x)^\top \cdot \mathbf{S}_{I_{j_k}}^\top \cdot \boldsymbol{\lambda}_{j_k} \right\rfloor_p = \sum_{k=1}^{t} \left\lfloor \mathbf{A}(x)^\top \cdot \mathbf{S}_{I_{j_k}}^\top \right\rfloor_p \cdot \boldsymbol{\lambda}_{j_k} + e, \quad (4)$$

where the last equality of (4) stems from fact that, for any two vectors $\boldsymbol{v}_1, \boldsymbol{v}_2 \in \mathbb{Z}_q^m$, we have $\lfloor \boldsymbol{v}_1 + \boldsymbol{v}_2 \rfloor_p = \lfloor \boldsymbol{v}_1 \rfloor_p + \lfloor \boldsymbol{v}_2 \rfloor_p + \boldsymbol{e}^+$, for some vector $\boldsymbol{e}^+ \in \{0,1\}^m$, and $\lfloor \boldsymbol{v}_1 - \boldsymbol{v}_2 \rfloor_p = \lfloor \boldsymbol{v}_1 \rfloor_p - \lfloor \boldsymbol{v}_2 \rfloor_p + \boldsymbol{e}^-$, where $\boldsymbol{e}^- \in \{-1,0\}^m$. The error vector $\boldsymbol{e}$ of (4) thus lives in $\{-d_S, \ldots, d_S\}^m$. By the definition of $Y_{j_k} = \lfloor \mathbf{A}(x)^\top \cdot \mathbf{S}_{I_{j_k}}^\top \rfloor_p$, if we define $\tilde{\mathbf{z}} := \sum_{k=1}^{t} Y_{j_k} \cdot \boldsymbol{\lambda}_{j_k}$ and $\boldsymbol{e}_z := -\boldsymbol{e} \in \{-d_S, \ldots, d_S\}^m$, we have

$$\tilde{\mathbf{z}} = \left\lfloor (\mathbf{A}(x))^\top \cdot \mathbf{s} \right\rfloor_p + \boldsymbol{e}_z \in \mathbb{Z}_p^m.$$

Then, we observe that $\mathbf{A}(x)^\top \cdot \mathbf{s}$ is of the form $\mathbf{T}_q \cdot \mathbf{A}_0^\top \cdot \mathbf{s}$, for some matrix $\mathbf{T}_q = (\prod_{i=1}^{L} \mathbf{G}^{-1}(\mathbf{A}_{i,x_i}))^\top$ which is a product of $\mathbb{Z}_q$-invertible matrices. By Lemma 2.19, $\mathbf{A}_0^\top \cdot \mathbf{s}$ is statistically close to the uniform distribution $U(\mathbb{Z}_q^m)$. Since $\mathbf{T}_q$ is invertible, the vector $\mathbf{A}(x)^\top \cdot \mathbf{s}$ is itself statistically close to $U(\mathbb{Z}_q^m)$. Hence, the vector $\lfloor \mathbf{A}(x)^\top \cdot \mathbf{s} \rfloor_p$ is statistically close to $U(\mathbb{Z}_p^m)$ since the statistical distance between $\lfloor U(\mathbb{Z}_q^m) \rfloor_p$ and $U(\mathbb{Z}_p^m)$ is at most $m \cdot (p/q)$. Therefore we can apply Lemma 2.18, which implies that

$$\left\lfloor \lfloor \mathbf{A}(x)^\top \cdot \mathbf{s} \rfloor_p \right\rfloor_u = \left\lfloor \lfloor \mathbf{A}(x)^\top \cdot \mathbf{s} \rfloor_p + e_z \right\rfloor_u$$

except with probability $2^L \cdot m \cdot \frac{4ds \cdot u}{p} \leq 2^L \cdot m \cdot \frac{4d \cdot u}{p} \leq m \cdot 2^{-\lambda}$.

This shows that the equality $\lfloor \tilde{\mathbf{z}} \rfloor_u = \left\lfloor \lfloor \mathbf{A}(x)^\top \cdot \mathbf{s} \rfloor_p \right\rfloor_u$ holds with overwhelming probability if the vector $\tilde{\mathbf{z}} := \sum_{k=1}^{t} \mathbf{Y}_{j_k} \cdot \boldsymbol{\lambda}_{j_k}$ in the left-hand-side member is computed by the Combine algorithm and the right-hand-side member is the $\lfloor \tilde{\mathbf{z}} \rfloor_u$ computed by Eval. $\qquad\square$

Theorem 4.2. *Assume that an entropy lower bound $\bar{n} = \lfloor n \cdot \log \sigma - \frac{n}{2} \cdot \log e - n' \cdot \log q \rfloor - 1$ is $\Omega(\lambda)$. If we set the output length $\bar{k} = k \cdot \log u$ so as to have*

$$\xi = \bar{n} + \ell, \qquad \bar{k} = \bar{n} - 2 \cdot (\lambda + \log \ell + \log \bar{n}),$$

then the construction above is an adaptively secure DPRF family under the $\mathsf{LWE}_{q,m,n',\alpha}$ assumption.

Proof. The proof considers a sequence of hybrid games. In each game, we call W_i the event that $b' = b$.

Game$_0$: This is the experiment, as described by Definition 2.20. Namely, the challenger initially samples a secret Gaussian vector $SK_0 = \mathbf{s} \hookleftarrow D_{\mathbb{Z}^n, \sigma}$, which is shared by computing

$$\mathbf{S}_{I_j} = M_{I_j} \cdot [\boldsymbol{\rho}_1 \mid \ldots \mid \boldsymbol{\rho}_n] = M_{I_j} \cdot \boldsymbol{\Gamma} \quad \in \mathbb{Z}^{d_j \times n} \qquad \forall j \in [N],$$

where

$$\boldsymbol{\Gamma} = [\boldsymbol{\rho}_1 \mid \ldots \mid \boldsymbol{\rho}_n] = \begin{bmatrix} \mathbf{s}^\top \\ \hline \rho_{1,2} \cdots \rho_{n,2} \\ \vdots \ddots \vdots \\ \rho_{1,e} \cdots \rho_{n,e} \end{bmatrix} \in \mathbb{Z}^{e \times n},$$

with $\rho_{k,\nu} \hookleftarrow D_{\mathbb{Z},\sigma}$ for all $(k,\nu) \in [1,n] \times [2,e]$. At each partial evaluation query $(j, X^{(i)}) \in [N] \times \{0,1\}^\ell$, the adversary $\mathcal{A}$ obtains

$$\mathbf{Y}_j = \left\lfloor (\mathbf{A}(x))^\top \cdot \mathbf{S}_{I_j}^\top \right\rfloor_p \in \mathbb{Z}_p^{m \times d_j}. \tag{5}$$

In the challenge phase, the adversary chooses an input $X^\star \in \{0,1\}^\ell$. It obtains a random vector $\mathbf{y}^\star \hookleftarrow U(\mathbb{Z}_u^k)$ if the challenger's bit is $b = 0$. If $b = 1$, it obtains the real evaluation $\mathbf{y}^\star = \pi(\lfloor \tilde{\mathbf{z}}^\star \rfloor_u) \in \mathbb{Z}_u^k$, where

$$\tilde{\mathbf{z}}^\star = \left\lfloor (\mathbf{A}(x^\star))^\top \cdot \mathbf{s} \right\rfloor_p \in \mathbb{Z}_p^m,$$

with $\mathbf{A}(x^\star) = \mathbf{A}_0 \cdot \prod_{i=1}^{L} \mathbf{G}^{-1}(\mathbf{A}_{i,x_i^\star})$ and $x^\star = \mathsf{AHF}(X^\star) \in \{0,1\}^L$. At the end of the game, we define $\mathcal{C}^\star \subset [N]$ to the set of servers that were corrupted by $\mathcal{A}$ or such that an evaluation query of the form $(i, X^\star)$ was made. By hypothesis, we have $|\mathcal{C}^\star| < t$. When the adversary halts, it outputs $\hat{b} \in \{0,1\}$ and the challenger defines $b' := \hat{b}$. The adversary's advantage is $\mathbf{Adv}(\mathcal{A}) := |\Pr[W_0] - 1/2|$, where W_0 is event that $b' = b$.

Game$_1$: This game is identical to Game$_0$ with the following changes. First, the challenger runs $K \leftarrow \mathsf{AdmSmp}(1^\lambda, Q, \delta)$ to generate a key $K \in \{0,1,\perp\}^L$ for a balanced admissible hash function $\mathsf{AHF} : \{0,1\}^\ell \to \{0,1\}^L$, with $\delta := \mathbf{Adv}(\mathcal{A})$ and Q is an upper bound on the number of queries that the adversary makes. When the adversary halts and outputs $\hat{b} \in \{0,1\}$, the challenger checks if the conditions

$$P_K(X^{(1)}) = \cdots = P_K(X^{(Q)}) = 1 \quad \wedge \quad P_K(X^\star) = 0 \qquad (6)$$

are satisfied, where $X^\star$ is the challenge input and $X^{(1)}, \ldots, X^{(Q)}$ are the adversarial queries. If these conditions do not hold, the challenger ignores $\mathcal{A}$'s output $\hat{b} \in \{0,1\}$ and overwrites it with a random bit $b'' \leftarrow \{0,1\}$ to define $b' = b''$. If conditions (6) are satisfied, the challenger sets $b' = \hat{b}$. By Lemma 2.9, we have

$$|\Pr[W_1] - 1/2| = |\Pr[b' = b] - 1/2|$$
$$\geq \gamma_{\min} \cdot \mathbf{Adv}(\mathcal{A}) - \frac{1}{2} \cdot (\gamma_{\max} - \gamma_{\min}) = \tau,$$

where $\tau(\lambda)$ is a noticeable function.

Game$_2$: In this game, we modify the generation of pp in the following way. Initially, the challenger samples a uniformly random matrix $\mathbf{A} \leftarrow U(\mathbb{Z}_q^{n \times m})$. Next, for each $i \in [L]$, it samples $\mathbf{R}_{i,0}, \mathbf{R}_{i,1} \leftarrow U(\{-1,1\})^{m \times m}$ and defines $\{\mathbf{A}_{i,0}, \mathbf{A}_{i,1}\}_{i=1}^{L}$ as follows for all $i \in [L]$ and $j \in \{0,1\}$:

$$\mathbf{A}_{i,j} := \begin{cases} \mathbf{A} \cdot \mathbf{R}_{i,j} & \text{if } (j \neq K_i) \wedge (K_i \neq \perp) \\ \mathbf{A} \cdot \mathbf{R}_{i,j} + \mathbf{G} & \text{if } (j = K_i) \vee (K_i = \perp) \end{cases} \qquad (7)$$

It also defines $\mathbf{A}_0 = \mathbf{A} \cdot \mathbf{R}_0 + \mathbf{G}$ for a randomly sampled $\mathbf{R}_0 \leftarrow U(\{-1,1\}^{m \times m})$. Since $\mathbf{A} \in \mathbb{Z}_q^{n \times m}$ was chosen uniformly, the Leftover Hash Lemma ensures that $\{\mathbf{A}_{i,0}, \mathbf{A}_{i,1}\}_{i=1}^{L}$ are statistically independent and uniformly distributed over $\mathbb{Z}_q^{n \times m}$. It follows that $|\Pr[W_2] - \Pr[W_1]| \leq L \cdot 2^{-\lambda}$ since the distribution of pp is statistically unchanged.

We note that, at each query X, we can view $\mathbf{A}(x)$ as a GSW encryption

$$\mathbf{A}(x) = \mathbf{A} \cdot \mathbf{R}_x + \left(\prod_{i=1}^{n} \mu_i\right) \cdot \mathbf{G},$$

for some small norm $\mathbf{R}_x \in \mathbb{Z}^{m \times m}$, where

$$\mu_i := \begin{cases} 0 & \text{if } (\mathsf{AHF}(X)_i \neq K_i) \wedge (K_i \neq \perp) \\ 1 & \text{if } (\mathsf{AHF}(X)_i = K_i) \vee (K_i = \perp) \end{cases}$$

If conditions (6) are satisfied, at each query $X^{(i)}$, the admissible hash function ensures that $x^{(i)} = \mathsf{AHF}(X^{(i)})$ satisfies

$$\mathbf{A}(x^{(i)}) = \mathbf{A} \cdot \mathbf{R}_{x^{(i)}}, \tag{8}$$

for some small norm $\mathbf{R}_{x^{(i)}} \in \mathbb{Z}^{m \times m}$. Moreover, the admissible hash function maps the challenge input $X^\star$ to an L-bit string $x^\star = \mathsf{AHF}(X^\star)$ such that

$$\mathbf{A}(x^\star) = \mathbf{A} \cdot \mathbf{R}_{x^\star} + \mathbf{G}. \tag{9}$$

Game$_3$: In this game, we modify the distribution of pp and replace the uniform matrix $\mathbf{A} \in \mathbb{Z}_q^{n \times m}$ by a lossy matrix such that

$$\mathbf{A}^\top = \bar{\mathbf{A}}^\top \cdot \mathbf{C} + \mathbf{E} \ \in \mathbb{Z}_q^{m \times n}, \tag{10}$$

where $\bar{\mathbf{A}} \hookleftarrow U(\mathbb{Z}_q^{n' \times m})$, $\mathbf{C} \hookleftarrow U(\mathbb{Z}_q^{n' \times n})$ and $\mathbf{E} \hookleftarrow D_{\mathbb{Z}^{m \times n}, \alpha q}$, for n' significantly smaller than n. The matrix in (10) is thus "computationally close" to a matrix $\bar{\mathbf{A}}^\top \cdot \mathbf{C}$ of much lower rank than n. Under the LWE assumption with in dimension n', this change should not significantly alter $\mathcal{A}$'s behavior and a straightforward reduction $\mathcal{B}$ shows that $|\Pr[W_3] - \Pr[W_2]| \leq n \cdot \mathbf{Adv}_{\mathcal{B}}^{\mathsf{LWE}_{q,m,n',\alpha}}(\lambda)$, where the factor n comes from the use of an LWE assumption with n secrets.

The modification introduced in Game$_3$ has the following consequence. Assuming that conditions (6) are satisfied, for each partial evaluation query $X^{(i)}$ such that $X^{(i)} \neq X^\star$, the response is of the form $\mathbf{Y}_j = [\mathbf{z}_{j,1} \mid \ldots \mid \mathbf{z}_{j,d_j}] \in \mathbb{Z}_p^{m \times d_j}$, where

$$\begin{aligned} \mathbf{z}_{j,\theta} &= \lfloor (\mathbf{A} \cdot \mathbf{R}_{x^{(i)}})^\top \cdot \bar{\mathbf{s}}_{j,\theta} \rfloor_p \\ &= \lfloor (\mathbf{R}_{x^{(i)}}^\top \cdot \bar{\mathbf{A}}^\top \cdot \mathbf{C} + \mathbf{R}_{x^{(i)}}^\top \cdot \mathbf{E}) \cdot \bar{\mathbf{s}}_{j,\theta} \rfloor_p \qquad \forall \theta \in [d_j]. \end{aligned}$$

Game$_4$: In this game, we modify the evaluation oracle and introduce a bad event. We define BAD to be the event that the adversary makes a partial evaluation query (j, X) such that the AHF-encoded input $x = \mathsf{AHF}(X) \in \{0,1\}^L$ corresponds to a matrix $\mathbf{A}(x) = \mathbf{A} \cdot \mathbf{R}_x$, for some small-norm $\mathbf{R}_x \in \mathbb{Z}^{m \times m}$, such that we have

$$\mathbf{z}_{j,\theta} = \lfloor (\mathbf{A} \cdot \mathbf{R}_x)^\top \cdot \bar{\mathbf{s}}_{j,\theta} \rfloor_p \neq \lfloor (\mathbf{R}_x^\top \cdot \bar{\mathbf{A}}^\top \cdot \mathbf{C}) \cdot \bar{\mathbf{s}}_{j,\theta} \rfloor_p. \tag{11}$$

for some $\theta \in [d_j]$. Note that the challenger can detect this event since it knows $\bar{\mathbf{A}} \in \mathbb{Z}_q^{n' \times m}$, $\mathbf{C} \in \mathbb{Z}_q^{n' \times n}$ and $\mathbf{E} \in \mathbb{Z}^{m \times n}$ satisfying (10). If BAD occurs, the challenger overwrites $\mathcal{A}$'s output $\hat{b}$ with a random bit $b'' \hookleftarrow \{0,1\}$ and sets $b' = b''$ (otherwise, it sets $b' = \hat{b}$ as before). Lemma 4.3 shows that we have the inequality $|\Pr[W_4] - \Pr[W_3]| \leq \Pr[\mathsf{BAD}] \leq 2^{-\Omega(\lambda)}$.

We note that, if BAD does not occur, we have

$$\left\lfloor (\mathbf{A} \cdot \mathbf{R}_{x^{(i)}})^\top \cdot \bar{\mathbf{s}}_{j,\theta} \right\rfloor_p = \left\lfloor (\mathbf{R}_{x^{(i)}}^\top \cdot \bar{\mathbf{A}}^\top \cdot \mathbf{C}) \cdot \bar{\mathbf{s}}_{j,\theta} \right\rfloor_p \qquad \forall (j,\theta) \in [N] \times [d_j] \tag{12}$$

at each query $(j, X^{(i)})$ for which $X^{(i)} \neq X^\star$. We note that the right-hand-side member of (12) is fully determined by $\mathbf{R}_{x^{(i)}}^\top \cdot \bar{\mathbf{A}}^\top$ and the product $\mathbf{C} \cdot \bar{\mathbf{s}}_{j,\theta} \in \mathbb{Z}_q^{n'}$. This means that partial evaluation queries $(j, X^{(i)})$ such that $X^{(i)} \neq X^\star$ always reveal the same information (namely, $\mathbf{C} \cdot \bar{\mathbf{s}}_{j,\theta} \in \mathbb{Z}_q^{n'}$) about $\bar{\mathbf{s}}_{j,\theta} \in \mathbb{Z}^n$.

Conversely, the right-hand-side member of (12) uniquely determines $\mathbf{C} \cdot \bar{\mathbf{s}}_{j,\theta}$ with high probability: observe that $\mathbf{R}_{x^{(i)}}^\top \cdot \bar{\mathbf{A}}^\top$ is statistically uniform over $\mathbb{Z}_q^{m \times n'}$, so by Lemma 2.1, the quantity $\lfloor \mathbf{R}_{x^{(i)}}^\top \cdot \bar{\mathbf{A}}^\top \cdot (\mathbf{C} \cdot \mathbf{s}) \rfloor_p$ is an injective function of $\mathbf{C} \cdot \mathbf{s} \bmod q$. It comes that partial evaluation queries information-theoretically reveal $\mathbf{C} \cdot \mathbf{s} \bmod q$, but we will show that $\mathbf{s}$ still retains high entropy in $\mathcal{A}$'s view.

Game₅: In this game, we modify the challenge value for which, if $b = 1$, the adversary is given a random $\mathbf{y}^\star \hookleftarrow U(\mathbb{Z}_u^k)$. Clearly, we have $\Pr[W_5] = 1/2$ since the distribution of the challenge value does not depend on $b \in \{0, 1\}$. Moreover, we will show that $|\Pr[W_5] - \Pr[W_4]| \leq 2^{-\Omega(\lambda)}$.

Indeed, we claim that, conditionally on $\mathcal{A}$'s view, the vector $\mathbf{y}^\star$ is already statistically uniform over $\mathbb{Z}_u^k$ in Game₄. Indeed, the source $\lfloor \tilde{\mathbf{z}}^\star \rfloor_u$ depends on an injective function $\mathbf{G}^\top \cdot \mathbf{s} \in \mathbb{Z}_q^m$ of the vector $\mathbf{s}$. In Lemma 4.4, we show that this vector has high min-entropy if BAD does not occur.

We observe that the source $\lfloor \tilde{\mathbf{z}}^\star \rfloor_u$ can be written

$$\lfloor \tilde{\mathbf{z}}^\star \rfloor_u = \left\lfloor \lfloor (\mathbf{A} \cdot \mathbf{R}_{x^\star} + \mathbf{G})^\top \mid \mathbf{0} \rfloor_p \right\rfloor_u \tag{13}$$

$$= \lfloor (\mathbf{A} \cdot \mathbf{R}_{x^\star} + \mathbf{G})^\top \cdot \mathbf{s} \rfloor_u + \mathbf{e}_{s,x,u} \qquad \text{with } \mathbf{o}_{s,x,u} \subset \{-1, 0\}^m$$

$$= \lfloor \mathbf{R}_{x^\star}^\top \cdot \mathbf{A}^\top \cdot \mathbf{s} \rfloor_u + \lfloor \mathbf{G}^\top \cdot \mathbf{s} \rfloor_u + \mathbf{e}_{s,x,u} + \mathbf{e}_{s,x}, \text{ with } \mathbf{e}_{s,x} \in \{0, 1\}^m$$

$$= \lfloor \mathbf{R}_{x^\star}^\top \cdot \mathbf{A}^\top \cdot \mathbf{s} \rfloor_u + \lfloor \mathbf{G}^\top \cdot \mathbf{s} \rfloor_u + \mathbf{e}'_{s,x}, \qquad \text{with } \mathbf{e}'_{s,x} \in \{-1, 0, 1\}^m. \tag{14}$$

The proof of Lemma 4.3 (see also the proof of the claim in Game 4 in the proof of Theorem 3.2) implies that $\lfloor \mathbf{R}_{x^\star}^\top \cdot \mathbf{A}^\top \cdot \mathbf{s} \rfloor_p = \lfloor \mathbf{R}_{x^\star}^\top \cdot \bar{\mathbf{A}}^\top \cdot \mathbf{C} \cdot \mathbf{s} \rfloor_p$ with overwhelming probability. In turn, this implies $H_\infty(\lfloor \mathbf{R}_{x^\star}^\top \cdot \mathbf{A}^\top \cdot \mathbf{s} \rfloor_u \mid \mathbf{C} \cdot \mathbf{s}) = 0$ with high probability. In the expression of $\tilde{\mathbf{z}}^\star$ in (14), we also remark that $\lfloor \mathbf{G}^\top \cdot \mathbf{s} \rfloor_u + \mathbf{e}'_{s,x}$ is an injective function of $\mathbf{s} \in \mathbb{Z}^n$. To see this, observe that

$$\lfloor \mathbf{G}^\top \cdot \mathbf{s} \rfloor_u + \mathbf{e}'_{s,x} = (u/q) \cdot \mathbf{G}^\top \cdot \mathbf{s}' - \mathbf{t}_{s,x} + \mathbf{e}'_{s,x}$$

for some $\mathbf{t}_{s,x} \in (0, 1)^m$, so that

$$(q/u) \cdot (\lfloor \mathbf{G}^\top \cdot \mathbf{s} \rfloor_u + \mathbf{e}'_{s,x}) = \mathbf{G}^\top \cdot \mathbf{s} + \mathbf{e}''_{s,x} \tag{15}$$

for some $\mathbf{e}''_{s,x} \in (-q/u, 2 \cdot q/u)^m$. The vector $\mathbf{s}$ is thus uniquely determined by (15) using the public trapdoor of $\mathbf{G}$ so long as $q/u \ll q$.

Consider the entropy of $\tilde{\mathbf{z}}^\star$ conditionally on $\mathcal{A}$'s view. We have

$$H_\infty(\lfloor \tilde{\mathbf{z}}^\star \rfloor_u \mid \mathbf{C} \cdot \mathbf{\Gamma}^\top, \{\mathbf{S}_{I_j}\}_{j \in \mathcal{C}^\star})$$

$$= H_\infty(\lfloor \mathbf{R}_{x^\star}^\top \cdot \mathbf{A}^\top \cdot \mathbf{s} \rfloor_u + \lfloor \mathbf{G}^\top \cdot \mathbf{s} \rfloor_u + \mathbf{e}'_{s,x} \mid \mathbf{C} \cdot \mathbf{\Gamma}^\top, \{\mathbf{S}_{I_j}\}_{j \in \mathcal{C}^\star})$$

$$= H_\infty(\lfloor \mathbf{G}^\top \cdot \mathbf{s} \rfloor_u + \mathbf{e}'_{s,x} \mid \mathbf{C} \cdot \mathbf{\Gamma}^\top, \{\mathbf{S}_{I_j}\}_{j \in \mathcal{C}^\star})$$

$$= H_\infty(\mathbf{s} \mid \mathbf{C} \cdot \mathbf{\Gamma}^\top, \{\mathbf{S}_{I_j}\}_{j \in \mathcal{C}^\star}) \geq n \cdot \log \sigma - \frac{n}{2} \cdot \log e - n' \cdot \log q - 1.$$

Here, the last inequality is given by Lemma 4.4. The second equality follows from the fact that, for any random variables X, Y, Z defined over an additive group, we have $H_\infty(Y + Z \mid X) = H_\infty(Z|X)$ if $H_\infty(Y|X) = 0$.

In order to extract statistically random bits from $\tilde{\mathbf{z}}^\star$, we must take into account that it possibly depends on $x^\star$ which may depend on pp. As long as $P_K(X^\star) = 0$, the source $\tilde{\mathbf{z}}^\star$ is taken from a distribution determined by the challenge input $X^\star \in \{0,1\}^\ell$ within a collection of less than 2^ℓ distributions (namely, those inputs X for which $P_K(X) = 0$), which all have min-entropy $\bar{n} \geq n \log \sigma - \frac{n}{2} \cdot \log e - n' \log q - 1$. By applying Lemma 2.11 with $\epsilon = 2^{-\lambda}$ for a collection $\mathcal{X}$ of at most $M = 2^\ell$ distributions, we obtain that the distribution of $\pi(\lfloor \tilde{\mathbf{z}}^\star \rfloor_u)$ is $2^{-\Omega(\lambda)}$-close to the uniform distribution over $\mathbb{Z}_u^k$. $\square$

Lemma 4.3. *Assume that $q/p > 2^{L+\lambda} \cdot r$, where $r = m^{L+2} \cdot n \cdot \beta^\star \cdot \alpha q$ with $\beta^\star = O(\beta \cdot \log N)$. Then, we have the inequality*

$$| \Pr[W_4] - \Pr[W_3]| \leq \Pr[\mathsf{BAD}] \leq 2^{-\Omega(\lambda)}.$$

(The proof is given in the full version of the paper.)

Lemma 4.4. *In Game_4, the min-entropy of $\mathbf{s}$ conditionally on $\mathcal{A}$'s view is at least $n \cdot \log \sigma - \frac{n}{2} \cdot \log e - n' \cdot \log q - \frac{n}{2^n}$.*

Proof. Let us assume that BAD does not occur in Game_4 since, if it does, the challenger replaces the adversary's output with a random bit, in which case both games have the same outcome. We show that, assuming $\neg\mathsf{BAD}$, the shared secret vector $\mathbf{s}$ retains high min-entropy conditionally on the adversary's view.

Let us first recap what the adversary can see in Game_4. For each partial evaluation query $(j, X^\star)$, the response $\lfloor (\mathbf{A} \cdot \mathbf{R}_{x^\star} + \mathbf{G})^\top \cdot \mathbf{S}_{I_j}^\top \rfloor_p$ consists of non-lossy functions of $\mathbf{S}_{I_j}^\top \in \mathbb{Z}^{n \times d_j}$. We thus consider partial evaluation queries of the form $(j, X^\star)$ as if they were corruption queries and assume that they information-theoretically reveal $\mathbf{S}_{I_j}$ (we thus merge the two sets $\mathcal{C}$ and $\mathcal{E}$ of Definition 2.20 into one set $\mathcal{C}^\star$). As for uncorrupted shares $\{\mathbf{S}_{I_j}\}_{j\in[N]\backslash\mathcal{C}^\star}$, partial evaluation queries $(j, X^{(i)})$ for which $X^{(i)} \neq X^\star$ only reveal the information $\{\mathbf{C} \cdot \mathbf{S}_{I_j}^\top\}_{j\in[N]\backslash\mathcal{C}^\star}$. More precisely, those partial evaluations $\{\mathbf{Y}_j\}_{j\in[N]\backslash\mathcal{C}^\star}$ can be written

$$\mathbf{Y}_j = \left\lfloor (\mathbf{A}(x^{(i)}))^\top \cdot \mathbf{S}_{I_j}^\top \right\rfloor_p = \left\lfloor (\mathbf{R}_{x^{(i)}} \cdot \bar{\mathbf{A}}^\top \cdot \mathbf{C}) \cdot \mathbf{S}_{I_j}^\top \right\rfloor_p \tag{16}$$

where

$$\mathbf{S}_{I_j}^\top = \begin{bmatrix} \boldsymbol{\rho}_1^\top \\ \vdots \\ \boldsymbol{\rho}_n^\top \end{bmatrix} \cdot M_{I_j}^\top \in \mathbb{Z}^{n \times d_j}$$

is a product of $M_{I_j}^\top$ with the matrix $[\boldsymbol{\rho}_1 \mid \dots \mid \boldsymbol{\rho}_n]^\top \in \mathbb{Z}^{n \times e}$ whose first column is the secret $SK_0 = \mathbf{s} \in \mathbb{Z}^n$. Hence, the information revealed by (16) for $j \in [N]\backslash\mathcal{C}^\star$ is only a lossy function $\mathbf{C} \cdot \mathbf{S}_{I_j}^\top$ of the share $\mathbf{S}_{I_j}$: namely,

$$\mathbf{C} \cdot \begin{bmatrix} \boldsymbol{\rho}_1^\top \\ \vdots \\ \boldsymbol{\rho}_n^\top \end{bmatrix} \cdot M_{I_j}^\top = \left[\ \mathbf{C} \cdot \mathbf{s} \ \middle| \ \mathbf{C} \cdot \begin{pmatrix} \rho_{2,2} \\ \vdots \\ \rho_{n,2} \end{pmatrix} \ \middle| \ \cdots \ \middle| \ \mathbf{C} \cdot \begin{pmatrix} \rho_{2,e} \\ \vdots \\ \rho_{n,e} \end{pmatrix} \right] \cdot M_{I_j}^\top, \quad (17)$$

$$= \mathbf{C} \cdot \boldsymbol{\Gamma}^\top \cdot M_{I_j}^\top,$$

where

$$\boldsymbol{\Gamma} = [\boldsymbol{\rho}_1 \mid \cdots \mid \boldsymbol{\rho}_n] = \begin{bmatrix} \mathbf{s}^\top \\ \hline \rho_{2,2} \cdots \rho_{n,2} \\ \vdots \ \ddots \ \vdots \\ \rho_{2,e} \cdots \rho_{n,e} \end{bmatrix} \in \mathbb{Z}^{e \times n}$$

is the matrix of Gaussian entries which is used to compute secret key shares

$$\mathbf{S}_{I_j} = M_{I_j} \cdot \boldsymbol{\Gamma} \qquad \forall j \in [N].$$

The information revealed by exposed shares $\{\mathbf{S}_{I_j}\}_{j \in \mathcal{C}^\star}$ can thus be written

$$\mathbf{S}_{I_j} = [\mathbf{s}_{I_j,1} \mid \cdots \mid \mathbf{s}_{I_j,n}] = M_{I_j} \cdot \boldsymbol{\Gamma} \ \in \mathbb{Z}^{d_j \times n} \qquad \forall j \in \mathcal{C}^\star. \qquad (18)$$

At this stage, we see that proving the following fact on distributions is sufficient to complete the proof of the lemma.

Fact. *Let $M_{\mathcal{C}^\star}$ to be the sub-matrix of M obtained by stacking up the rows assigned to corrupted parties $j \in \mathcal{C}^\star$. Conditionally on*

$$(\mathbf{C}, \ \mathbf{C} \cdot \boldsymbol{\Gamma}^\top \cdot M^\top, \ M_{\mathcal{C}^\star}, \ M_{\mathcal{C}^\star} \cdot \boldsymbol{\Gamma}), \qquad (19)$$

the vector $\mathbf{s}^\top = (1, 0, \ldots, 0)^\top \cdot \boldsymbol{\Gamma}$ has min-entropy at least

$$n \cdot \log \sigma - \frac{n}{2} \cdot \log e - n' \cdot \log q - \frac{n}{2^n}.$$

To prove this statement, we apply arguments inspired from [4, Lemma 1]. First, we observe that conditioning on (19) is the same as conditioning on $(\mathbf{C}, \mathbf{C} \cdot \boldsymbol{\Gamma}^\top \cdot M_{[N] \setminus \mathcal{C}^\star}^\top, M_{\mathcal{C}^\star}, M_{\mathcal{C}^\star} \cdot \boldsymbol{\Gamma})$ since $M_{\mathcal{C}^\star} \cdot \boldsymbol{\Gamma}$ and $\mathbf{C}$ are given. In fact, it is sufficient to prove the result when conditioning on

$$(\mathbf{C}, \mathbf{C} \cdot \boldsymbol{\Gamma}^\top, M_{\mathcal{C}^\star}, M_{\mathcal{C}^\star} \cdot \boldsymbol{\Gamma}),$$

as $\mathbf{C} \cdot \boldsymbol{\Gamma}^\top \cdot M_{[N] \setminus \mathcal{C}^\star}^\top$ is computable from $\mathbf{C} \cdot \boldsymbol{\Gamma}^\top$. By the definition of an Integer Span Program, we know that there exists a sweeping vector $\boldsymbol{\kappa} \in \mathbb{Z}^e$ whose first coordinate is $\kappa_1 = 1$ and such that $M_{\mathcal{C}^\star} \cdot \boldsymbol{\kappa} = \mathbf{0}$. The rows of $M_{\mathcal{C}^\star}$ thus live in the lattice $\mathcal{L}_{\mathcal{C}^\star} = \{\mathbf{m} \in \mathbb{Z}^e : \langle \mathbf{m}, \boldsymbol{\kappa} \rangle = 0\}$. Hence, if we define a matrix $L_{\mathcal{C}^\star} \in \mathbb{Z}^{(e-1) \times e}$ whose rows form a basis of $\mathcal{L}_{\mathcal{C}^\star}$, we may prove the min-entropy lower bound conditioned on

$$(\mathbf{C}, \mathbf{C} \cdot \boldsymbol{\Gamma}^\top, L_{\mathcal{C}^\star}, L_{\mathcal{C}^\star} \cdot \boldsymbol{\Gamma}).$$

This is because $L_{\mathcal{C}^\star} \cdot \boldsymbol{\Gamma}$ provides at least as much information as $M_{\mathcal{C}^\star} \cdot \boldsymbol{\Gamma}$.

We first consider the distribution of Γ, conditioned on $(L_{\mathcal{C}^*}, L_{\mathcal{C}^*} \cdot \Gamma)$. Since the columns of Γ are statistically independent, we may look at them individually. For each $i \in [n]$, we let $\rho_i^* \in \mathbb{Z}^e$ be an arbitrary solution of $L_{\mathcal{C}^*} \cdot \rho_i^* = L_{\mathcal{C}^*} \cdot \rho_i \in \mathbb{Z}_q^{e-1}$. The distribution of $\rho_i \in \mathbb{Z}^e$ conditionally on $(L_{\mathcal{C}^*}, L_{\mathcal{C}^*} \cdot \rho_i)$ is $\rho_i^* + D_{\Lambda, \sigma, -\rho_i^*}$, where $\Lambda = \{\boldsymbol{x} \in \mathbb{Z}^e \mid L_{\mathcal{C}^*} \cdot \boldsymbol{x} = \boldsymbol{0}\}$ is the 1-dimensional lattice $\Lambda = \boldsymbol{\kappa} \cdot \mathbb{Z}$.

At this stage, we know that conditioned on $(L_{\mathcal{C}^*}, L_{\mathcal{C}^*} \cdot \Gamma)$, each row $\rho_i = (s_i, \rho_{i,2}, \ldots, \rho_{i,e})^\top$ of $\Gamma^\top$ is Gaussian over an affine line. We use this observation to show that conditioning on $(\mathbf{C}, \mathbf{C} \cdot \Gamma^\top, L_{\mathcal{C}^*}, L_{\mathcal{C}^*} \cdot \Gamma)$ is the same as conditioning on $(\mathbf{C}, \mathbf{C} \cdot \mathbf{s}, L_{\mathcal{C}^*}, L_{\mathcal{C}^*} \cdot \Gamma)$.[3] In fact, we claim that, conditioned on $(L_{\mathcal{C}^*}, L_{\mathcal{C}^*} \cdot \Gamma)$, the last $e - 1$ columns of $\Gamma^\top$ do not reveal any more information than its first column. Indeed, conditioned on $(L_{\mathcal{C}^*}, L_{\mathcal{C}^*} \cdot \Gamma)$, each ρ_i can be written $\rho_i = \xi_i \cdot \boldsymbol{\kappa} + \rho_i^*$ for some integer $\xi_i \in \mathbb{Z}$. We may assume that the shifting vector $\rho_i^* = (\rho_{i,1}^*, \ldots, \rho_{i,e}^*)^\top \in \mathbb{Z}_q^e$ is known to $\mathcal{A}$ as it can be obtained from $L_{\mathcal{C}^*} \cdot \rho_i$ via de-randomized Gaussian elimination. Writing $\boldsymbol{\kappa} = (\kappa_1, \ldots, \kappa_e)$, the j-th column $(\Gamma^\top)_j$ of $\Gamma^\top$ is

$$(\Gamma^\top)_j = \kappa_j \cdot \begin{pmatrix} \xi_1 \\ \vdots \\ \xi_n \end{pmatrix} + \begin{pmatrix} \rho_{1,j}^* \\ \vdots \\ \rho_{n,j}^* \end{pmatrix} \qquad \forall j \in [e].$$

As $\kappa_1 = 1$, we have

$$(\Gamma^\top)_j = \kappa_j \cdot (\Gamma^\top)_1 - \kappa_j \cdot \begin{pmatrix} \rho_{1,1}^* \\ \vdots \\ \rho_{n,1}^* \end{pmatrix} + \begin{pmatrix} \rho_{1,j}^* \\ \vdots \\ \rho_{n,j}^* \end{pmatrix} \qquad \forall j \in [e].$$

In the latter, the last two terms are information-theoretically known to $\mathcal{A}$ (once we have conditioned on $(L_{\mathcal{C}^*}, L_{\mathcal{C}^*} \cdot \Gamma)$) and so is κ_j.

We now study the distribution of $\mathbf{s} = (\Gamma^\top)_1$ conditioned on $(L_{\mathcal{C}^*}, L_{\mathcal{C}^*} \cdot \Gamma)$. By statistical independence, we may consider each coordinate $s_i = (1, 0, \ldots, 0)^\top \cdot \rho_i$ of $\mathbf{s}$ individually. Recall that, conditioned on $(L_{\mathcal{C}^*}, L_{\mathcal{C}^*} \cdot \Gamma)$, each ρ_i is distributed as $\rho_i^* + D_{\kappa \mathbb{Z}, \sigma, -\rho_i^*}$. Write $\rho_i^* = y \cdot \boldsymbol{\kappa} + (\rho_i^*)^\perp$, with $y \in \mathbb{R}$ and $(\rho_i^*)^\perp$ orthogonal to $\boldsymbol{\kappa}$. Then,

$$\rho_i^* + D_{\kappa \mathbb{Z}, \sigma, -\rho_i^*} = (\rho_i^*)^\perp + y \cdot \boldsymbol{\kappa} + D_{\kappa \mathbb{Z}, \sigma, -y \cdot \boldsymbol{\kappa} - (\rho_i^*)^\perp}$$
$$= (\rho_i^*)^\perp + y \cdot \boldsymbol{\kappa} + \boldsymbol{\kappa} \cdot D_{\mathbb{Z}, \sigma/\|\kappa\|, -y}.$$

We now take the inner product with $(1, 0, \ldots, 0)$ and use the fact that $\kappa_1 = 1$ to obtain that, conditioned on $(L_{\mathcal{C}^*}, L_{\mathcal{C}^*} \cdot \Gamma)$, the coordinate s_i is distributed as $(\rho_i^*)_1^\perp + y + D_{\mathbb{Z}, \sigma/\|\kappa\|, -y}$. As $\boldsymbol{\kappa} \in \{-1, 0, 1\}^e$ with the Benaloh-Leichter-based LISS scheme of [24], and by our choice of σ, we have that $\sigma/\|\kappa\| = \Omega(\sqrt{n})$. Using Lemma 2.3 (Remark 2.4), this implies that each s_i has min-entropy $\geq$

---

[3] Note that conditioned on $(L_{\mathcal{C}^*}, L_{\mathcal{C}^*} \cdot \Gamma)$, the *rows* of $\Gamma^\top$ are Gaussian on affine lines, but a *column* of $\Gamma^\top$ is an inner product of unit vector with all these rows.

$\log{(\sigma/\|\boldsymbol{\kappa}\|)} - 2^{-n} \geq \log{\sigma} - \frac{1}{2}\log{e} - 2^{-n}$. Overall, we obtain

$$H_\infty\left(\mathbf{s} \mid L_{\mathcal{C}^\star}, L_{\mathcal{C}^\star} \cdot \boldsymbol{\Gamma}\right) \geq n \cdot \log{\sigma} - \frac{n}{2} \cdot \log{e} - \frac{n}{2^n}.$$

We are now ready to conclude. By the above, to prove the fact (and hence the lemma), it suffices to obtain a lower bound on the min-entropy of $\mathbf{s}$ conditioned on $(\mathbf{C}, \mathbf{C} \cdot \mathbf{s}, L_{\mathcal{C}^\star}, L_{\mathcal{C}^\star} \cdot \boldsymbol{\Gamma})$. We then use the above min-entropy lower bound on $\mathbf{s}$ conditioned on $(L_{\mathcal{C}^\star}, L_{\mathcal{C}^\star} \cdot \boldsymbol{\Gamma})$ and the fact that given $\mathbf{C}$, the quantity $\mathbf{C} \cdot \mathbf{s} \in \mathbb{Z}_q^{n'}$ reveals at most $n' \log{q}$ bits. □

Acknowledgements. We thank Javier Herranz for his suggestion to use linear integer secret sharing schemes. Part of this research was funded by the French ANR ALAMBIC project (ANR-16-CE39-0006) and by BPI-France in the context of the national project RISQ (P141580). This work was also supported in part by the European Union PROMETHEUS project (Horizon 2020 Research and Innovation Program, grant 780701). The second author was supported by ERC Starting Grant ERC-2013-StG-335086-LATTAC.

A   Definition of Static DPRF Security

In this section, we recall the definition of static security used in [16].

Definition A.1. *Let λ be a security parameter and let integers $t, N \in \mathsf{poly}(\lambda)$. A (t, N)-DPRF is pseudorandom under static corruptions if no PPT adversary has non-negligible advantage in the following game:*

1. *The challenger generates $\mathsf{pp} \leftarrow \mathsf{Setup}(1^\lambda, 1^\ell, 1^t, 1^N)$ and chooses a random key $SK_0 \hookleftarrow \mathcal{K}$, which is broken into N shares $(SK_1, \ldots, SK_N) \leftarrow \mathsf{Share}(SK_0)$. It also initializes empty sets $\mathcal{C}, \mathcal{V} \leftarrow \emptyset$ and flip a random coin $b \hookleftarrow U(\{0,1\})$.*
2. *The adversary $\mathcal{A}$ chooses a set $S^\star = \{i_1, \ldots, i_{t-1}\}$ and the challenger returns the secret key shares $\{SK_{i_1}, \ldots, SK_{i_{t-1}}\}$.*
3. *The adversary $\mathcal{A}$ adaptively interleaves the following kinds of queries.*

   Evaluation: *$\mathcal{A}$ chooses an input $X \in \mathcal{D}$. The challenger replies by returning $\{Y_i = \mathsf{PEval}(SK_i, X)\}_{i \in [N] \setminus S^\star}$ and updating $\mathcal{V} := \mathcal{V} \cup \{X\}$.*
   Challenge: *$\mathcal{A}$ chooses an input $X \in \mathcal{D}$. If X previously occurred in a challenge query, the challenger returns the same output as before. Otherwise, it randomly chooses $Y_{X,0} \hookleftarrow U(\{0,1\}^\mu)$ and computes $Y_{X,1} = \mathsf{Eval}(SK_0, X)$. It returns $Y_{X,b}$ and updates $\mathcal{C} := \mathcal{C} \cup \{X\}$.*

   It is required that $\mathcal{C} \cap \mathcal{V} = \emptyset$ at any time.
4. *The adversary $\mathcal{A}$ outputs a bit $\hat{b} \in \{0,1\}$ and wins if $\hat{b} = b$. Its advantage is defined to be $\mathbf{Adv}_{\mathcal{A}}^{\mathrm{DPRF}}(\lambda) := |\Pr[\hat{b} = b] - 1/2|$.*

We may assume w.l.o.g. that the adversary only makes one challenge query in the experiment of Definition A.1. Indeed, a standard hybrid argument allows showing that security in the single-challenge sense implies security when polynomially-many queries are allowed.

References

1. Abe, M., Fehr, S.: Adaptively secure Feldman VSS and applications to universally-composable threshold cryptography. In: Franklin, M. (ed.) CRYPTO 2004. LNCS, vol. 3152, pp. 317–334. Springer, Heidelberg (2004). https://doi.org/10.1007/978-3-540-28628-8_20

2. Agrawal, S., Boneh, D., Boyen, X.: Efficient lattice (H)IBE in the standard model. In: Gilbert, H. (ed.) EUROCRYPT 2010. LNCS, vol. 6110, pp. 553–572. Springer, Heidelberg (2010). https://doi.org/10.1007/978-3-642-13190-5_28

3. Agrawal, S., Boyen, X., Vaikuntanathan, V., Voulgaris, P., Wee, H.: Functional encryption for threshold functions (or Fuzzy IBE) from lattices. In: Fischlin, M., Buchmann, J., Manulis, M. (eds.) PKC 2012. LNCS, vol. 7293, pp. 280–297. Springer, Heidelberg (2012). https://doi.org/10.1007/978-3-642-30057-8_17

4. Agrawal, S., Libert, B., Stehlé, D.: Fully Secure Functional Encryption for Inner Products, from Standard Assumptions. In: Robshaw, M., Katz, J. (eds.) CRYPTO 2016. LNCS, vol. 9816, pp. 333–362. Springer, Heidelberg (2016). https://doi.org/10.1007/978-3-662-53015-3_12

5. Almansa, J.F., Damgård, I., Nielsen, J.B.: Simplified threshold RSA with adaptive and proactive security. In: Vaudenay, S. (ed.) EUROCRYPT 2006. LNCS, vol. 4004, pp. 593–611. Springer, Heidelberg (2006). https://doi.org/10.1007/11761679_35

6. Alwen, J., Krenn, S., Pietrzak, K., Wichs, D.: Learning with rounding, revisited. In: Canetti, R., Garay, J.A. (eds.) CRYPTO 2013. LNCS, vol. 8042, pp. 57–74. Springer, Heidelberg (2013). https://doi.org/10.1007/978-3-642-40041-4_4

7. Banerjee, A., Peikert, C.: New and improved key-homomorphic pseudorandom functions. In: Garay, J.A., Gennaro, R. (eds.) CRYPTO 2014. LNCS, vol. 8616, pp. 353–370. Springer, Heidelberg (2014). https://doi.org/10.1007/978-3-662-44371-2_20

8. Banerjee, A., Peikert, C., Rosen, A.: Pseudorandom functions and lattices. In: Pointcheval, D., Johansson, T. (eds.) EUROCRYPT 2012. LNCS, vol. 7237, pp. 719–737. Springer, Heidelberg (2012). https://doi.org/10.1007/978-3-642-29011-4_42

9. Bellare, M., Kiltz, E., Peikert, C., Waters, B.: Identity-based (Lossy) trapdoor functions and applications. In: Pointcheval, D., Johansson, T. (eds.) EUROCRYPT 2012. LNCS, vol. 7237, pp. 228–245. Springer, Heidelberg (2012). https://doi.org/10.1007/978-3-642-29011-4_15

10. Benaloh, J., Leichter, J.: Generalized secret sharing and monotone functions. In: Goldwasser, S. (ed.) CRYPTO 1988. LNCS, vol. 403, pp. 27–35. Springer, New York (1990). https://doi.org/10.1007/0-387-34799-2_3

11. Bendlin, R., Damgård, I.: Threshold decryption and zero-knowledge proofs for lattice-based cryptosystems. In: Micciancio, D. (ed.) TCC 2010. LNCS, vol. 5978, pp. 201–218. Springer, Heidelberg (2010). https://doi.org/10.1007/978-3-642-11799-2_13

12. Bendlin, R., Krehbiel, S., Peikert, C.: How to share a lattice trapdoor: threshold protocols for signatures and (H)IBE. In: Jacobson, M., Locasto, M., Mohassel, P., Safavi-Naini, R. (eds.) ACNS 2013. LNCS, vol. 7954, pp. 218–236. Springer, Heidelberg (2013). https://doi.org/10.1007/978-3-642-38980-1_14

13. Boneh, D., Boyen, X.: Secure identity based encryption without random oracles. In: Franklin, M. (ed.) CRYPTO 2004. LNCS, vol. 3152, pp. 443–459. Springer, Heidelberg (2004). https://doi.org/10.1007/978-3-540-28628-8_27

14. Boneh, D., et al.: Threshold cryptosystems from threshold fully homomorphic encryption. In: Shacham, H., Boldyreva, A. (eds.) CRYPTO 2018. LNCS, vol. 10991, pp. 565–596. Springer, Cham (2018). https://doi.org/10.1007/978-3-319-96884-1_19

15. Boneh, D., Gennaro, R., Goldfeder, S., Kim, S.: A lattice-based universal thresholdizer for cryptographic systems. Cryptology ePrint Archive: Report 2017/251, September 2017

16. Boneh, D., Lewi, K., Montgomery, H., Raghunathan, A.: Key homomorphic PRFs and their applications. In: Canetti, R., Garay, J.A. (eds.) CRYPTO 2013. LNCS, vol. 8042, pp. 410–428. Springer, Heidelberg (2013). https://doi.org/10.1007/978-3-642-40041-4_23

17. Boneh, D., Montogomery, H., Raghunathan, A.: Algebraic pseudorandom functions with improved efficiency from the augmented cascade. In: ACM-CCS (2010)

18. Cachin, C., Kursawe, K., Shoup, V.: Random oracles in constantinople: practical asynchronous byzantine agreement using cryptography. In: PODC (2000)

19. Canetti, R., Gennaro, R., Jarecki, S., Krawczyk, H., Rabin, T.: Adaptive security for threshold cryptosystems. In: Wiener, M. (ed.) CRYPTO 1999. LNCS, vol. 1666, pp. 98–116. Springer, Heidelberg (1999). https://doi.org/10.1007/3-540-48405-1_7

20. Canetti, R., Goldwasser, S.: An efficient threshold public key cryptosystem secure against adaptive chosen ciphertext attack (Extended Abstract). In: Stern, J. (ed.) EUROCRYPT 1999. LNCS, vol. 1592, pp. 90–106. Springer, Heidelberg (1999). https://doi.org/10.1007/3-540-48910-X_7

21. Chase, M., Meiklejohn, S.: Déjà Q: using dual systems to revisit q-type assumptions. In: Nguyen, P.Q., Oswald, E. (eds.) EUROCRYPT 2014. LNCS, vol. 8441, pp. 622–639. Springer, Heidelberg (2014). https://doi.org/10.1007/978-3-642-55220-5_34

22. Cramer, R., Damgård, I., Dziembowski, S., Hirt, M., Rabin, T.: Efficient multiparty computations secure against an adaptive adversary. In: Stern, J. (ed.) EUROCRYPT 1999. LNCS, vol. 1592, pp. 311–326. Springer, Heidelberg (1999). https://doi.org/10.1007/3-540-48910-X_22

23. Cramer, R., Fehr, S.: Optimal black-box secret sharing over arbitrary abelian groups. In: Yung, M. (ed.) CRYPTO 2002. LNCS, vol. 2442, pp. 272–287. Springer, Heidelberg (2002). https://doi.org/10.1007/3-540-45708-9_18

24. Damgård, I., Thorbek, R.: Linear integer secret sharing and distributed exponentiation. In: Yung, M., Dodis, Y., Kiayias, A., Malkin, T. (eds.) PKC 2006. LNCS, vol. 3958, pp. 75–90. Springer, Heidelberg (2006). https://doi.org/10.1007/11745853_6

25. Desmedt, Y., Frankel, Y.: Threshold cryptosystems. In: Brassard, G. (ed.) CRYPTO 1989. LNCS, vol. 435, pp. 307–315. Springer, New York (1990). https://doi.org/10.1007/0-387-34805-0_28

26. Dodis, Y.: Exposure-Resilient Cryptography. Ph.D. thesis, MIT (2000)

27. Dodis, Y.: Efficient construction of (distributed) verifiable random functions. In: Desmedt, Y.G. (ed.) PKC 2003. LNCS, vol. 2567, pp. 1–17. Springer, Heidelberg (2003). https://doi.org/10.1007/3-540-36288-6_1

28. Dodis, Y., Yampolskiy, A.: A verifiable random function with short proofs and keys. In: Vaudenay, S. (ed.) PKC 2005. LNCS, vol. 3386, pp. 416–431. Springer, Heidelberg (2005). https://doi.org/10.1007/978-3-540-30580-4_28

29. Dodis, Y., Yampolskiy, A., Yung, M.: Threshold and proactive pseudo-random permutations. In: Halevi, S., Rabin, T. (eds.) TCC 2006. LNCS, vol. 3876, pp. 542–560. Springer, Heidelberg (2006). https://doi.org/10.1007/11681878_28

30. Frankel, Y., MacKenzie, P., Yung, M.: Adaptively-secure distributed public-key systems. In: Nešetřil, J. (ed.) ESA 1999. LNCS, vol. 1643, pp. 4–27. Springer, Heidelberg (1999). https://doi.org/10.1007/3-540-48481-7_2

31. Freire, E.S.V., Hofheinz, D., Paterson, K.G., Striecks, C.: Programmable hash functions in the multilinear setting. In: Canetti, R., Garay, J.A. (eds.) CRYPTO 2013. LNCS, vol. 8042, pp. 513–530. Springer, Heidelberg (2013). https://doi.org/10.1007/978-3-642-40041-4_28

32. Gentry, C., Peikert, C., Vaikuntanathan, V.: Trapdoors for hard lattices and new cryptographic constructions. In: Proceedings of STOC, pp. 197–206. ACM (2008)

33. Gentry, C., Sahai, A., Waters, B.: Homomorphic encryption from learning with errors: conceptually-simpler, asymptotically-faster, attribute-based. In: Canetti, R., Garay, J.A. (eds.) CRYPTO 2013. LNCS, vol. 8042, pp. 75–92. Springer, Heidelberg (2013). https://doi.org/10.1007/978-3-642-40041-4_5

34. Goldreich, O.: Valiant's polynomial-size monotone formula for majority (2014)

35. Goldreich, O., Goldwasser, S., Micali, S.: How to construct random functions. J. ACM **33**, 792 (1986)

36. Goldwasser, S., Kalai, Y., Peikert, C., Vaikuntanathan, V.: Robustness of the learning with errors assumption. In: ICS (2010)

37. Gorbunov, S., Vaikuntanathan, V., Wichs, D.: Leveled fully homomorphic signatures from standard lattices. In: STOC (2015)

38. Goyal, R., Hohenberger, S., Koppula, V., Waters, B.: A generic approach to constructing and proving verifiable random functions. In: Kalai, Y., Reyzin, L. (eds.) TCC 2017. LNCS, vol. 10678, pp. 537–566. Springer, Cham (2017). https://doi.org/10.1007/978-3-319-70503-3_18

39. Hastad, J., Impagliazzo, R., Levin, L., Luby, M.: A pseudorandom generator from any one-way function. SIAM J. Comput. **8**(4), 1364–1396 (1999)

40. Hoory, S., Magen, A., Pitassi, T.: Monotone circuits for the majority function. In: Díaz, J., Jansen, K., Rolim, J.D.P., Zwick, U. (eds.) APPROX/RANDOM -2006. LNCS, vol. 4110, pp. 410–425. Springer, Heidelberg (2006). https://doi.org/10.1007/11830924_38

41. Jager, T.: Verifiable random functions from weaker assumptions. In: Dodis, Y., Nielsen, J.B. (eds.) TCC 2015. LNCS, vol. 9015, pp. 121–143. Springer, Heidelberg (2015). https://doi.org/10.1007/978-3-662-46497-7_5

42. Jarecki, S., Lysyanskaya, A.: Adaptively secure threshold cryptography: introducing concurrency, removing erasures. In: Preneel, B. (ed.) EUROCRYPT 2000. LNCS, vol. 1807, pp. 221–242. Springer, Heidelberg (2000). https://doi.org/10.1007/3-540-45539-6_16

43. Katsumata, S., Yamada, S.: Partitioning via non-linear polynomial functions: more compact IBEs from ideal lattices and bilinear maps. In: Cheon, J.H., Takagi, T. (eds.) ASIACRYPT 2016. LNCS, vol. 10032, pp. 682–712. Springer, Heidelberg (2016). https://doi.org/10.1007/978-3-662-53890-6_23

44. Lewko, A., Waters, B.: Efficient pseudorandom functions from the decisional linear assumption and weaker variants. In: ACM-CCS (2009)

45. Libert, B., Joye, M., Yung, M.: Born and raised distributively: fully distributed non-interactive adaptively secure threshold signatures with short shares. In: PODC (2014)

46. Lysyanskaya, A., Peikert, C.: Adaptive security in the threshold setting: from cryptosystems to signature schemes. In: Boyd, C. (ed.) ASIACRYPT 2001. LNCS, vol. 2248, pp. 331–350. Springer, Heidelberg (2001). https://doi.org/10.1007/3-540-45682-1_20

47. Micali, S., Sidney, R.: A simple method for generating and sharing pseudo-random functions, with applications to clipper-like key escrow systems. In: Coppersmith, D. (ed.) CRYPTO 1995. LNCS, vol. 963, pp. 185–196. Springer, Heidelberg (1995). https://doi.org/10.1007/3-540-44750-4_15

48. Micciancio, D., Peikert, C.: Trapdoors for lattices: simpler, tighter, faster, smaller. In: Pointcheval, D., Johansson, T. (eds.) EUROCRYPT 2012. LNCS, vol. 7237, pp. 700–718. Springer, Heidelberg (2012). https://doi.org/10.1007/978-3-642-29011-4_41

49. Micciancio, D., Regev, O.: Worst-case to average-case reductions based on Gaussian measures. SIAM J. Comput. **37**(1), 267–302 (2007)

50. Naor, M., Pinkas, B., Reingold, O.: Distributed pseudo-random functions and KDCs. In: Stern, J. (ed.) EUROCRYPT 1999. LNCS, vol. 1592, pp. 327–346. Springer, Heidelberg (1999). https://doi.org/10.1007/3-540-48910-X_23

51. Naor, M., Reingold, O.: Number-theoretic constructions of efficient pseudo-random functions. In: FOCS (1997)

52. Naor, M., Reingold, O., Rosen, A.: Pseudo-random functions and factoring. In: STOC (2000)

53. Nielsen, J.B.: A threshold pseudorandom function construction and its applications. In: Yung, M. (ed.) CRYPTO 2002. LNCS, vol. 2442, pp. 401–416. Springer, Heidelberg (2002). https://doi.org/10.1007/3-540-45708-9_26

54. Peikert, C., Waters, B.: Lossy trapdoor functions and their applications. In: STOC, pp. 187–196. ACM (2008)

55. Raghunathan, A., Segev, G., Vadhan, S.: Deterministic public-key encryption for adaptively chosen plaintext distributions. In: Johansson, T., Nguyen, P.Q. (eds.) EUROCRYPT 2013. LNCS, vol. 7881, pp. 93–110. Springer, Heidelberg (2013). https://doi.org/10.1007/978-3-642-38348-9_6

56. Razborov, A., Rudich, S.: Natural proofs. J. Comput. Syst. Sci. **55**(1), 24–35 (1987)

57. Regev, O.: On lattices, learning with errors, random linear codes, and cryptography. In: STOC (2005)

58. Regev, O., Stephens-Davidowitz, S.: A reverse Minkowski theorem. In: STOC (2017)

59. Thorbek, R.: Linear integer secret sharing. Ph.D. thesis, Department of Computer Science - University of Arhus (2009)

60. Trevisan, L., Vadhan, S.: Extracting randomness from samplable distributions. In: FOCS (2000)

61. Valiant, L.: Short monotone formulae for the majority function. J. Alg. **5**(3), 363 (1984)

62. Valiant, L.: A theory of the learnable. Commun. ACM 27(11), 1134 (1984)

63. Waters, B.: Efficient identity-based encryption without random oracles. In: Cramer, R. (ed.) EUROCRYPT 2005. LNCS, vol. 3494, pp. 114–127. Springer, Heidelberg (2005). https://doi.org/10.1007/11426639_7

iO and Authentication

A Simple Construction of iO for Turing Machines

Sanjam Garg$^{(\boxtimes)}$ and Akshayaram Srinivasan

University of California, Berkeley, USA
{sanjamg,akshayaram}@berkeley.edu

Abstract. We give a simple construction of indistinguishability obfuscation for Turing machines where the time to obfuscate grows only with the description size of the machine and otherwise, independent of the running time and the space used. While this result is already known [Koppula, Lewko, and Waters, STOC 2015] from $i\mathcal{O}$ for circuits and injective pseudorandom generators, our construction and its analysis are conceptually much simpler. In particular, the main technical component in the proof of our construction is a simple combinatorial pebbling argument [Garg and Srinivasan, EUROCRYPT 2018]. Our construction makes use of indistinguishability obfuscation for circuits and somewhere statistically binding hash functions.

1 Introduction

Indistinguishability Obfuscation ($i\mathcal{O}$) [BGI+12, GGH+13] is a central primitive in cryptography giving rise to new and powerful cryptographic applications [SW14, GGHR14]. $i\mathcal{O}$ requires that for any two circuits C_0 and C_1 computing the exact same functionality, obfuscation of C_0 is computationally indistinguishable from the obfuscation of C_1. While circuits are powerful enough to simulate other models of computation such as Turing machines or RAM programs [PF79], a drawback of using them is that size of the circuit (and hence the size of obfuscation) grows with both the running time and the space of the computation. In a beautiful work Koppula, Lewko and Waters [KLW15] (building on prior work [BGL+15, CHJV15]) showed a method for removing this limitation by giving a construction of succinct $i\mathcal{O}$ for Turing machines from $i\mathcal{O}$ for circuits and injective pseudorandom generators. By succinct, we mean that the time to obfuscate a machine grows only with its description size and is otherwise independent of its running time and its space complexity.

Our Contribution. In this paper, we give a *simple* construction of succinct indistinguishability obfuscation for Turing machines from sub-exponentially

Research supported in part from 2017 AFOSR YIP Award, DARPA/ARL SAFEWARE Award W911NF15C0210, AFOSR Award FA9550-15-1-0274, and research grants by the Okawa Foundation, Visa Inc., and Center for Long-Term Cybersecurity (CLTC, UC Berkeley). The views expressed are those of the author and do not reflect the official policy or position of the funding agencies.

© International Association for Cryptologic Research 2018
A. Beimel and S. Dziembowski (Eds.): TCC 2018, LNCS 11240, pp. 425–454, 2018.
https://doi.org/10.1007/978-3-030-03810-6_16

secure $i\mathcal{O}$ for circuits and sub-exponentially secure somewhere statistically binding hash functions [HW15, KLW15]. Our new construction is simple to describe and its analysis is much simpler than the previous works. Inspired by [GS18a], the main technical component in our security proof is a simple combinatorial pebbling argument.

In a bit more detail, we achieve the above new result by first giving a new construction of *succinct randomized encoding* [AIK04, CHJV15, BGL+15, App17] from polynomially hard indistinguishability obfuscation for circuits and laconic oblivious transfer [CDG+17, DG17, BLSV18, DGHM18].[1] A randomized encoding allows to encode a Turing machine M, an input x and a time bound t to $\widehat{M}_{x,t}$. Given $\widehat{M}_{x,t}$, the decoding procedure recovers $M(x)$ which is the output of M on input x obtained in time t. The security property requires that the distribution of $\widehat{M}_{x,t}$ does not leak anything about x except $M(x)$. A randomized encoding is said to be *succinct* if the encoding procedure runs in time that is polynomial in the security parameter, the machine description size and the input size and is otherwise independent of the time and space complexity of M. Next, to construct succinct $i\mathcal{O}$ for Turing machines, we use a transformation from any succinct randomized encoding (with sub-exponential security) to succinct $i\mathcal{O}$ for Turing machines given in the works of [CHJV15, BGL+15]. This yields the desired result.

1.1 Overview

In this section, we give a high level overview of our construction of succinct randomized encodings and the security proof.

Starting Point. The starting point of our work is the construction of *semi-succinct* randomized encodings for Turing machines in [CHJV15, BGL+15] based on $i\mathcal{O}$ for circuits and Yao's garbling scheme. Semi-succinct randomized encodings require that the time to encode a machine to be independent of its running time but could depend on the space complexity of the computation. In particular, it is a weaker requirement when compared to full succinctness wherein we also require the time to encode a machine to be independent of the space complexity. Below we start by recalling this construction and explain why it achieves only semi-succinctness when compared to full succinctness.

The encoding procedure is given as input a Turing machine M, an input x and a time bound t and it has to output a randomized encoding $\widehat{M}_{x,t}$. The first step in the above works is to reduce the machine M to a "succinctly describable" circuit C that computes the same function as that of M. We say that a circuit is succinctly describable if there exists a "small" circuit C_{sc} that on

---

[1] Note that [CDG+17] also described a construction of laconic oblivious transfer from witness encryption [GGSW13] and somewhere statistically binding hash functions. Since witness encryption can be instantiated from $i\mathcal{O}$ for circuits and one-way functions (which is implied by somewhere statistically binding hash functions), we obtain our main result from $i\mathcal{O}$ for circuits and somewhere statistically binding hash functions.

input any gate index, outputs the binary function computed by that gate along with the description of its input and output wires. Next, these works observed that Yao's garbling procedure is highly "local", meaning that given only the local information about a gate (which includes its input, output wires and the functionality computed by it), Yao's garbling procedure can output the garbled encryption table corresponding to that gate. Now, these two ideas are combined in an elegant way to obtain a randomized encoding of a Turing machine. To give more details, the encoding consists of an obfuscated circuit that on input any gate index, outputs the garbled encryption table corresponding to that gate. Specifically, this circuit uses the succinct description to obtain the binary logic computed by the gate along with the description of the input and output wires. It uses a (puncturable) PRF key to obtain the labels corresponding to the input and the output wires and outputs the Yao's garbled table corresponding to that gate (using randomness derived from the puncturable PRF key). The encoding procedure outputs this obfuscation along with the labels corresponding to the input x. The decoding procedure evaluates this obfuscation on every gate index to obtain the garbled tables corresponding to every gate and then evaluates the garbled circuit to obtain the output.

Let us now describe the simulator for the above construction. Recall that the simulator on input $M(x)$ must output a randomized encoding such that the distribution of the simulator's output is computationally indistinguishable to the distribution of an honestly generated encoding. The simulator in these works obfuscates a circuit that on input any gate number, outputs the simulated Yao's garbled table. Intuitively, it should follow from the security of Yao's garbled circuit construction that the real garbled tables are computationally indistinguishable to the simulated garbled tables. However, for the proof to go through, these works cannot change the distribution of all the garbled gates from the real to simulated in one shot. Rather, they use a careful hybrid argument wherein they change the distribution of the garbled tables from the real to simulated for one gate at a time and this where the succinctness takes a hit. Let us now explain this in more detail.

Recall from the proof of Yao's garbled circuit construction [LP09], that each hybrid corresponds to a particular distribution of garbled encryption tables (also called as configurations in [HJO+16]). In a particular configuration, a garbled gate can either be in three modes: the real mode, or the input dependent simulation mode, or the simulated mode. The real mode is one where in the garbled encryption tables are distributed exactly as in the construction. In the input dependent simulation mode, all the entries of the garbled encryption table encrypt a single label and this label corresponds to the output of that gate. In the simulated mode, every entry of the garbled encryption table encrypts a single label and this label corresponds to the bit 0. The real world distribution corresponds to a configuration wherein each garbled gate is in the real mode and the simulated configuration is one in which each garbled gate is in the simulated mode. In order to go from the real world distribution to the simulated distribution, we need to go over a sequence of hybrids. Each hybrid change corresponds to changing the configuration of a particular gate. These changes can be made according to the following two rules:

- **Rule A:** A garbled gate can be changed from the real mode to input dependent simulation mode if all its fan-in gates are in input dependent simulation mode.
- **Rule B:** A garbled gate can be changed from an input dependent simulation mode to the simulated mode if all its fan-out gates are in input dependent simulation mode.

A direct consequence of such a hybrid argument is that the obfuscated circuit (in the construction of succinct randomized encoding) in a particular hybrid must somehow encode the outputs of all the gates that are in the input dependent simulation mode. Notice that in general, the fan-out of a gate could be as large as the space of the computation (denoted by s). Thus, to change one garbled gate from input dependent simulation mode to the simulated mode, we must encode the outputs of at most s gates in the obfuscated circuit. Thus, the size of the obfuscated circuit in this intermediate hybrids grows with s. Thus, to use $i\mathcal{O}$ security, the real world obfuscation must also be padded to the size of the circuit in the intermediate hybrid and hence, these works could only achieve semi-succinctness. Because of the above-mentioned challenges, this approach seemed insufficient for realizing full succinctness. Thus, Koppula, Lewko and Waters [KLW15] gave a very different approach for realizing full succinctness. However, unfortunately, their realization is rather involved.

Our Approach. In this work, we start with the above-mentioned approach followed in the realization of semi-succinct iO constructions but employ a crucial technique to achieve full succinctness. Specifically, to achieve full succinctness, we use a *linearized garbling scheme* (introduced in the work of Garg and Srinivasan [GS18a]) in place of Yao's garbling scheme. Informally, a linearized garbled circuit helps in "flattening" the underlying circuit which may have large width into a circuit with width 1. Intuitively, such a flattening would be helpful as the size of intermediate obfuscations may not have to grow with the width of the circuit (which is proportional to the space complexity). In the rest of the overview, we give an informal description of the linearlized garbled circuit, state its properties and explain the combinatorial pebbling game that forms the main crux of the proof. This approach allows us to achieve a simpler construction than Koppula, Lewko and Waters [KLW15].

Linearized Garbled Circuits. To understand the concept of a linearized garbled circuits[2], it is best to view the circuit C as a *sequence of step circuits*. In more details, we will consider C as a sequence of step circuits along with a database/memory D. The i-th step circuit implements the i-th gate (with some topological ordering of the gates) in the circuit C. The database D is initially loaded with the input x and contents of the database represent the state of the computation. That is, the snapshot of the database before the evaluation of the

---

[2] This paragraph is taken verbatim from [GS18a].

i-th step circuit contains the output of every gate $g < i$ in the execution of C on input x. The i-th step circuit reads contents from two pre-determined locations in the database and writes a bit to location i. The bits that are read correspond to the values in the input wires for the i-th gate. The output of the circuit is easily derived from the contents of the database at the end of the computation.

To garble a circuit C, we must garble each of the step circuits and the database D. To draw a parallel with the Yao's garbling scheme, the garbled encryption tables are now replaced with garbled step circuits. As in the of Yao's garbling procedure, the task of garbling the step circuits has the desired locality property, meaning that given only the locations accessed by the step circuit and the functionality computed by it, we can computed the garbled version of that particular step circuit. Furthermore, we can think of the distributions wherein a step circuit is in real mode, or in input dependent simulation mode, or in simulated mode as natural extensions of the same notions for a garbled gate. For the sake of keeping things simple in the introduction, we wouldn't be going into the exact details of the actual distributions in these three modes.

Now we are ready to state the properties of a linearized garbled circuit. We say a garbling scheme to be linearized if it satisfies the following two properties:

1. **Rule A:** A step circuit can be changed from the real mode to an input dependent simulation mode (or, vice-versa) if the previous step circuit is in input dependent simulation mode. This restriction however, does not apply to the first step circuit i.e., it can always be changed from real to input dependent simulation mode (or, vice-versa).
2. **Rule B:** A step circuit can be changed from input dependent simulation mode to the simulated mode if the previous step circuit is in input dependent simulation mode and all the subsequent step circuits are in simulated mode. This rule must be contrasted with the corresponding rule for Yao's garbled circuits wherein we must maintain all the gates which fan-out from this particular gate in input dependent simulation mode.

Garg and Srinivasan [GS18a] constructed such a linearized garbling scheme from laconic oblivious transfer [CDG+17].[3] We will now show that how this linearized garbling structure is helpful in obtaining a fully succinct randomized encoding scheme.

Pebbling Game. Now, let us explain how the concept of linearized garbled circuit helps us in achieving full succinctness. The simulator for our construction of succinct randomized encoding is exactly the same as in the previous constructions [CHJV15,BGL+15]. In particular, it obfuscates a circuit that on input any step circuit index, outputs the garbled version of that step circuit in the simulated mode. In the real world distribution, all the step circuits are garbled in the real mode whereas in the simulated distribution all the step circuits are garbled in the simulated mode. The goal is to change all the step circuits

---

[3] As mentioned in the introduction, a laconic oblivious transfer can be constructed from $i\mathcal{O}$ for circuits and somewhere statistically binding hash functions.

from the real mode to the simulated mode where in each step/hybrid, we can use either one of the above two rules to change the configuration of a particular gate. In order to keep the size of the intermediate obfuscations small, we need to minimize the number of step circuits that are present in the input dependent simulation mode. This is because for every step circuit that is present in the input dependent simulation mode, we must hardcode the output of the gate in the obfuscation and hence the size of the obfuscation grows with this number. These requirements can be abstractly modeled as the following pebbling game whose description is taken verbatim from [GS18a].

Consider the positive integer line $1, 2, \ldots, N$. We are given pebbles of two colors: gray and black . A black pebble corresponds to a step circuit in the simulated mode and a gray pebble corresponds to a step circuit in the input dependent simulation mode. A position without any pebble corresponds to real garbling. We can place the pebbles on this positive integer line according to the following two rules:

Rule A: We can place or remove a gray pebble in position i if and only if there is a gray pebble in position $i-1$. This restriction does not apply to position 1: we can always place or remove a gray pebble at position 1. This rule captures the first requirement of a linearized garbling scheme.

Rule B: We can replace a gray pebble in position i with a black pebble as long as all the positions $> i$ have black pebbles and there is a gray pebble in position $i - 1$ or if $i = 1$. This rule captures the second requirement of a linearized garbling scheme.

Optimization Goal of the Pebbling Game. The goal is to pebble the line $[1, N]$ such that every position has a black pebble while minimizing the number of gray pebbles that are present on the line at any point in time.

Any strategy for the above pebbling game that uses a maximum of ℓ gray pebbles gives a randomized encoding scheme where the time to encode grows with ℓ. We note that the same pebbling game was considered in the work of [GS18a] in the context of constructing adaptive garbled circuits with optimal online complexity. Using the pebbling strategy considered in their work (that uses $\log N$ gray pebbles), we give a construction of randomized encoding scheme where the time to encode grows only with $\mathsf{poly}(|M|, |x|, \lambda, \log T)$ where T is the running time of the computation. This gives us the desired succinctness.

1.2   Concurrent Work

In a concurrent and independent work, Ananth and Lombardi [AL18] gave a construction of succinct randomized encoding from polynomially hard compact functional encryption and laconic oblivious transfer. They defined an abstraction called as strong locally simulatable garbling schemes and then used it to construct a succinct randomized encoding. At a conceptual level, the notion of strong locally simulatable garbling scheme is similar to our notion of linearized garbling schemes and hence the underlying techniques used in both these papers are similar. We remark that even our construction can be instantiated from polynomially hard compact functional encryption using the works of [AJ15, BV15] as the size of the input to the obfuscation scheme is $O(\log \lambda)$ where λ is the security parameter.

2   Preliminaries

Let λ denote the security parameter. A function $\mu(\cdot) : \mathbb{N} \to \mathbb{R}^+$ is said to be negligible if for any polynomial $\mathsf{poly}(\cdot)$ there exists $\lambda_0 \in \mathbb{N}$ such that for all $\lambda > \lambda_0$ we have $\mu(\lambda) < \frac{1}{\mathsf{poly}(\lambda)}$. For a probabilistic algorithm A, we denote $A(x; r)$ to be the output of A on input x with the content of the random tape being r. When r is omitted, $A(x)$ denotes a distribution. For a finite set S, we denote $x \leftarrow S$ as the process of sampling x uniformly from the set S. We will use PPT to denote Probabilistic Polynomial Time. We denote $[a]$ to be the set $\{1, \dots, a\}$ and $[a, b]$ to be the set $\{a, a+1, \dots, b\}$ for $a \leq b$ and $a, b \in \mathbb{Z}$. For a binary string $x \in \{0, 1\}^n$, we will denote the ith bit of x by x_i. We assume without loss of generality that the length of the random tape used by all cryptographic algorithms is λ. We will use $\mathsf{negl}(\cdot)$ to denote an unspecified negligible function and $\mathsf{poly}(\cdot)$ to denote an unspecified polynomial function.

2.1   Succinct Circuits

We now recall the definition of succinct circuits. Most of this subsection is taken verbatim from [BGT14].

Definition 1 (Succinct Circuits). *Let $C : \{0, 1\}^n \to \{0, 1\}$ be a circuit with $N - n$ binary gates. The gates of the circuit are numbered as follows. The input gates are given the numbers $\{1, \dots, n\}$. The intermediate gates are numbered $\{n+1, n+2, \dots, N-1\}$ such that a gate that receives its input from gates i and j is given a number greater than i and j. The output gate is numbered N. Each gate $g \in [n+1, N]$ is described by a tuple $(i, j, f_g) \in [g-1]^2 \times \mathsf{GType}$ where outputs of gates i and j serves as inputs to gate g and f_g denotes the binary functionality computed by the gate. Here, GType denotes the set of all binary functions.*

We say that C is succinctly represented by a circuit C_{sc}, if C_{sc} given a gate label $g \in [n+1, N]$ gives out its description (i, j, f_g). Furthermore, $|C_{\mathsf{sc}}| < |C|$.

We now recall the lemma from [PF79] that converts any uniform Turing machine to a succinct circuit.

Lemma 1 ([PF79]). *Any Turing machine M, which for inputs of size n, requires a maximal running time $t(n)$ and space $s(n)$, can be converted in time $O(|M| + \log(t(n)))$ to a circuit C_{sc} that succinctly represents $C : \{0, 1\}^n \to \{0, 1\}$ where C computes the same function as M (for inputs of size n), and is of size $\tilde{O}(t(n) \cdot s(n))$.*

2.2   Succinct Randomized Encoding

We now recall the definition of succinct randomized encoding.

Definition 2 ([BGT14]). *A succinct randomized encoding (SRE) consists of two algorithms* (sRE.Enc, sRE.Dec) *with the following syntax:*

- $\widehat{M}_{x,t} \leftarrow$ sRE.Enc$(1^\lambda, M, x, t)$: *takes as input the security parameter λ, a machine M, input x, time bound (encoded in binary) t and outputs the randomized encoding $\widehat{M}_{x,t}$.*
- $y \leftarrow$ sRE.Dec$(M, \widehat{M}_{x,t})$: *takes as input the machine M and the randomized encoding $\widehat{M}_{x,t}$ and deterministically computes the output y.*

We require the scheme to satisfy the following three properties.

- **Correctness:** *For every x and M such that M halts on input x within t steps, it holds that $y = M(x)$ with probability 1 over the random coins of* sRE.Enc.
- **Security:** *there exists a PPT simulator* Sim *such that for any poly size adversary $\mathcal{A}$ there exists a negligible* negl$(\cdot)$ *such that for all $\lambda \in \mathbb{N}$, machine M, input x, and time bound t:*

$$\left| \Pr[\mathcal{A}(\widehat{M}_{x,t}) = 1] - \Pr[\mathcal{A}(\mathsf{Sim}(1^\lambda, y, M, t, 1^{|x|})) = 1] \right| \leq \mathsf{negl}(\lambda) \cdot p(t)$$

where $\widehat{M}_{x,t} \leftarrow$ sRE.Enc$(1^\lambda, M, x, t)$, y is the output of $M(x)$ after t steps and $p(\cdot)$ is a fixed polynomial that does not depend on (M, x, t).[4]
- **Succinctness:** *The running time of* sRE.Enc *and the size of the encoding $\widehat{M}_{x,t}$ are* poly$(|M|, |x|, \log t, \lambda)$. *The running time of* sRE.Dec *is* poly(t, λ).

Remark 1. We note that our definition of succinct randomized encoding differs from the original definition given in [BGT14] as the procedure sRE.Dec additionally takes in M as input. We note that this is without loss of generality as we can always set M to be the universal Turing machine and include the description of the machine that has to be encoded as part of the input.

2.3   Indistinguishability Obfuscation

We now define indistinguishability obfuscator from [BGI+12, GGH+13].

Definition 3. *A PPT algorithm $i\mathcal{O}$ is an indistinguishability obfuscator for a family of circuits $\{C_\lambda\}_\lambda$ that satisfies the following properties:*

- **Correctness:** *For all λ and for all $C \in C_\lambda$ and for all x,*

$$\Pr[i\mathcal{O}(C)(x) = C(x)] = 1$$

where the probability is over the random choices of $i\mathcal{O}$.

---

[4] When t bounded by a polynomial then RHS can just be negl(λ).

- **Security:** For all $C_0, C_1 \in C_\lambda$ such that for all x, $C_0(x) = C_1(x)$ and for all poly sized adversaries $\mathcal{A}$,

$$|\Pr[\mathcal{A}(i\mathcal{O}(C_0)) = 1] - \Pr[\mathcal{A}(i\mathcal{O}(C_1)) = 1]| \leq \mathsf{negl}(\lambda)$$

We now give the definition of a succinct indistinguishability obfuscation.

Definition 4 (Succinct Indistinguishability Obfuscator [BGL+15]). *A succinct indistinguishability obfuscator for a machine class $\{\mathcal{M}_\lambda\}_{\lambda \in \mathbb{N}}$ consists of a uniform PPT machine $i\mathcal{O}\mathsf{M}$ that works as follows:*

- *$i\mathcal{O}\mathsf{M}$ takes as input the security parameter 1^λ, the machine M to obfuscate, and an input length n and time bound t for M.*
- *$i\mathcal{O}\mathsf{M}$ outputs a machine $ob\mathsf{M}$ which is an obfuscation of M corresponding to input length n and time bound t. $ob\mathsf{M}$ takes as input $x \in \{0,1\}^n$ and $t' \leq t$.*

The scheme should satisfy the following three requirements.

- **Correctness:** *For all security parameters $\lambda \in \mathbb{N}$, for all $M \in \mathcal{M}_\lambda$, for all inputs $x \in \{0,1\}^n$, time bounds t and $t' \leq t$, let y be the output of M on t' steps, then we have that:*

$$\Pr[ob\mathsf{M}(x, t') = y : ob\mathsf{M} \leftarrow i\mathcal{O}\mathsf{M}(1^\lambda, 1^n, 1^{\log t}, M)] = 1$$

- **Security:** *For any (not necessarily uniform) PPT distinguisher D, there exists a negligible function α such that the following holds: For all security parameters $\lambda \in \mathbb{N}$, time bounds t, and pairs of machines $M_0, M_1 \in \mathcal{M}_\lambda$ of the same size such that for all running times $t' \leq t$ and for all inputs x, $M_0(x) = M_1(x)$ when M_0 and M_1 are executed for time t', we have that:*

$$\left| \Pr\left[D(i\mathcal{O}\mathsf{M}(1^\lambda, 1^n, 1^{\log t}, M_0)) = 1\right] - \Pr\left[D(i\mathcal{O}\mathsf{M}(1^\lambda, 1^n, 1^{\log t}, M_1)) = 1\right] \right| \leq \alpha(\lambda)$$

- **Efficiency and Succinctness:** *We require that the running time of $i\mathcal{O}\mathsf{M}$ and the length of its output, namely the obfuscated machine $ob\mathsf{M}$, is $\mathsf{poly}(|M|, \log t, n, \lambda)$. We also require that the obfuscated machine on input x and t' runs in time $\mathsf{poly}(|M|, t', n, \log t, \lambda)$ (or $\mathsf{poly}(t', \lambda)$ for short).*

2.4   Garbled Circuits

Below we recall the definition of garbling scheme for circuits [Yao82, Yao86, AIK04] with selective security (see Lindell and Pinkas [LP09] and Bellare et al. [BHR12] for a detailed proof and further discussion). A garbling scheme for circuits is a tuple of PPT algorithms (GarbleCkt, EvalCkt). Very roughly, GarbleCkt is the circuit garbling procedure and EvalCkt is the corresponding evaluation procedure. We use a formulation where input labels for a garbled circuit are provided as input to the garbling procedure rather than generated as output. (This simplifies the presentation of our construction.) More formally:

- $\widetilde{\mathsf{C}} \leftarrow$ GarbleCkt $\left(1^\lambda, C, \{\mathsf{lab}_{w,b}\}_{w\in x, b\in\{0,1\}}\right)$: GarbleCkt takes as input a security parameter λ, a circuit C, and input labels $\mathsf{lab}_{w,b}$ where $w \in x$ (x is the set of input wires to the circuit C) and $b \in \{0,1\}$. This procedure outputs a *garbled circuit* $\widetilde{\mathsf{C}}$. We assume that for each w, b, $\mathsf{lab}_{w,b}$ is chosen uniformly from $\{0,1\}^\lambda$.
- $y \leftarrow$ EvalCkt $\left(\widetilde{\mathsf{C}}, \{\mathsf{lab}_{w,x_w}\}_{w\in x}\right)$: Given a garbled circuit $\widetilde{\mathsf{C}}$ and a sequence of input labels $\{\mathsf{lab}_{w,x_w}\}_{w\in x}$ (referred to as the garbled input), EvalCkt outputs a string y.

Correctness. For correctness, we require that for any circuit C, input $x \in \{0,1\}^{|x|}$ and input labels $\{\mathsf{lab}_{w,b}\}_{w\in x, b\in\{0,1\}}$ we have that:

$$\Pr\left[C(x) = \mathsf{EvalCkt}\left(\widetilde{\mathsf{C}}, \{\mathsf{lab}_{w,x_w}\}_{w\in x}\right)\right] = 1$$

where $\widetilde{\mathsf{C}} \leftarrow$ GarbleCkt $\left(1^\lambda, C, \{\mathsf{lab}_{w,b}\}_{w\in x, b\in\{0,1\}}\right)$.

Selective Security. For security, we require that there exists a PPT simulator $\mathsf{Sim}_{\mathsf{Ckt}}$ such that for any circuit C and input $x \in \{0,1\}^{|x|}$, we have that

$$\left\{\widetilde{\mathsf{C}}, \{\mathsf{lab}_{w,x_w}\}_{w\in x}\right\} \stackrel{c}{\approx} \left\{\mathsf{Sim}_{\mathsf{Ckt}}\left(1^\lambda, 1^{|C|}, C(x), \{\mathsf{lab}_{w,x_w}\}_{w\in x}\right), \{\mathsf{lab}_{w,x_w}\}_{w\in x}\right\}$$

where $\widetilde{\mathsf{C}} \leftarrow$ GarbleCkt $\left(1^\lambda, C, \{\mathsf{lab}_{w,b}\}_{w\in x, b\in\{0,1\}}\right)$ and for each $w \in x$ and $b \in \{0,1\}$ we have $\mathsf{lab}_{w,b} \leftarrow \{0,1\}^\lambda$. Here $\stackrel{c}{\approx}$ denotes that the two distributions are computationally indistinguishable.

Theorem 1 ([Yao86,LP09]). *Assuming the existence of one-way functions, there exists a construction of garbling scheme for circuits.*

2.5 Updatable Laconic Oblivious Transfer

In this subsection, we recall the definition of updatable laconic oblivious transfer from [CDG+17].

Definition 5 ([CDG+17]). *An updatable laconic oblivious transfer consists of the following algorithms:*

- $\mathsf{crs} \leftarrow \mathsf{crsGen}(1^\lambda)$: *It takes as input the security parameter 1^λ (encoded in unary) and outputs a common reference string* crs.
- $(\mathsf{d}, \widehat{D}) \leftarrow \mathsf{Hash}(\mathsf{crs}, D)$: *It takes as input the common reference string* crs *and database $D \in \{0,1\}^*$ as input and outputs a digest d and a state $\widehat{D}$. We assume that the state $\widehat{D}$ also includes the database D.*
- $\mathsf{d}^* \leftarrow \mathsf{HashUpdate}(\mathsf{crs}, \mathsf{d}, (L, b), \mathsf{aux})$: *It takes as input the common reference string* crs, *a digest d, position $L \in N$, a bit b and some auxiliary information of size $\mathsf{poly}(\log|D|, \lambda)$ and outputs d^*.*

- $e \leftarrow$ Send(crs, d, L, m_0, m_1) : *It takes as input the common reference string* crs, *a digest* d, *a location* $L \in \mathbb{N}$ *and two messages* $m_0, m_1 \in \{0,1\}^{p(\lambda)}$ *and outputs a ciphertext* e.

- $m \leftarrow$ Receive$^{\widehat{D}}$(crs, e, L) : *This is a RAM algorithm with random read access to* $\widehat{D}$. *It takes as input a common reference string* crs, *a ciphertext* e, *and a database location* $L \in \mathbb{N}$ *and outputs a message* m.

- $e_w \leftarrow$ SendWrite(crs, d, $L, b, \{m_{j,0}, m_{j,1}\}_{j=1}^{|d|}$) : *It takes as input the common reference string* crs, *a digest* d, *a location* $L \in \mathbb{N}$, *a bit* $b \in \{0,1\}$ *to be written, and* $|d|$ *pairs of messages* $\{m_{j,0}, m_{j,1}\}_{j=1}^{|d|}$, *where each* $m_{j,c}$ *is of length* $p(\lambda)$ *and outputs a ciphertext* e_w.

- $\{m_j\}_{j=1}^{|d|} \leftarrow$ ReceiveWrite$^{\widehat{D}}$(crs, L, b, e_w) : *This is a RAM algorithm with random read/write access to* $\widehat{D}$. *It takes as input the common reference string* crs, *a location* L, *a bit* $b \in \{0,1\}$ *and a ciphertext* e_w. *It updates the state* $\widehat{D}$ *(such that* $D[L] = b$*) and outputs messages* $\{m_j\}_{j=1}^{|d|}$.

We require an updatable laconic oblivious transfer to satisfy the following properties.

Correctness: *We require that for any database* D *of size at most* $M = \mathsf{poly}(\lambda)$, *any memory location* $L \in [M]$, *any pair of messages* $(m_0, m_1) \subset \{0,1\}^{p(\lambda)}$ *where* $p(\cdot)$ *is a polynomial that*

$$\Pr\left[m = m_{D[L]} \,\middle|\, \begin{array}{rl} \mathsf{crs} & \leftarrow \mathsf{crsGen}(1^\lambda) \\ (\mathsf{d}, \widehat{D}) & \leftarrow \mathsf{Hash}(\mathsf{crs}, D) \\ e & \leftarrow \mathsf{Send}(\mathsf{crs}, \mathsf{d}, L, m_0, m_1) \\ m & \leftarrow \mathsf{Receive}^{\widehat{D}}(\mathsf{crs}, e, L) \end{array} \right] = 1,$$

Correctness of Hash Updates: *We require that for any database* D *of size* $M = \mathsf{poly}(\lambda)$, *any memory location* $L \in [M]$, *any bit* $b \in \{0,1\}$, *we require* HashUpdate(crs, d, (L, i), aux) *to be same as* Hash(crs, D^*) *where* D^* *is same as* D *except that* $D^*[L] = b$. *Here,* aux *corresponds to an auxiliary information that is specific to position* L.

Correctness of Writes: *Let database* D *be of size at most* $M = \mathsf{poly}(\lambda)$ *and let* $L \in [M]$ *be any memory location. Let* D^* *be a database that is identical to* D *except that* $D^*[L] = b$. *For any sequence of messages* $\{m_{j,0}, m_{j,1}\}_{j \in [\lambda]} \in \{0,1\}^{p(\lambda)}$ *we require that*

$$\Pr\left[\begin{array}{l} m'_j = m_{j,\mathsf{d}^*_j} \\ \forall j \in [|\mathsf{d}|] \end{array} \,\middle|\, \begin{array}{rl} \mathsf{crs} & \leftarrow \mathsf{crsGen}(1^\lambda) \\ (\mathsf{d}, \widehat{D}) & \leftarrow \mathsf{Hash}(\mathsf{crs}, D) \\ (\mathsf{d}^*, \widehat{D}^*) & \leftarrow \mathsf{Hash}(\mathsf{crs}, D^*) \\ e_w & \leftarrow \mathsf{SendWrite}\left(\mathsf{crs}, \mathsf{d}, L, b, \{m_{j,0}, m_{j,1}\}_{j=1}^{|\mathsf{d}|}\right) \\ \{m'_j\}_{j=1}^{|\mathsf{d}|} & \leftarrow \mathsf{ReceiveWrite}^{\widehat{D}}(\mathsf{crs}, L, b, e_w) \end{array} \right] = 1,$$

Sender Privacy: *There exists a PPT simulator* $\mathsf{Sim}_{\ell\mathsf{OT}}$ *such that the for any non-uniform PPT adversary* $\mathcal{A} = (\mathcal{A}_1, \mathcal{A}_2)$ *there exists a negligible function* negl($\cdot$) *s.t.*,

$$\left| \Pr[\mathsf{SenPrivExpt}^{\mathsf{real}}(1^\lambda, \mathcal{A}) = 1] - \Pr[\mathsf{SenPrivExpt}^{\mathsf{ideal}}(1^\lambda, \mathcal{A}) = 1] \right| \leq \mathsf{negl}(\lambda)$$

where $\mathsf{SenPrivExpt}^{\mathsf{real}}$ *and* $\mathsf{SenPrivExpt}^{\mathsf{ideal}}$ *are described in Fig. 1.*

Sender Privacy for Writes: *There exists a PPT simulator* $\mathsf{Sim}_{\ell\mathsf{OTW}}$ *such that the for any non-uniform PPT adversary* $\mathcal{A} = (\mathcal{A}_1, \mathcal{A}_2)$ *there exists a negligible function* negl($\cdot$) *s.t.*,

$$\left| \Pr[\mathsf{WriSenPrivExpt}^{\mathsf{real}}(1^\lambda, \mathcal{A}) = 1] - \Pr[\mathsf{WriSenPrivExpt}^{\mathsf{ideal}}(1^\lambda, \mathcal{A}) = 1] \right| \leq \mathsf{negl}(\lambda)$$

where $\mathsf{WriSenPrivExpt}^{\mathsf{real}}$ *and* $\mathsf{WriSenPrivExpt}^{\mathsf{ideal}}$ *are described in Fig. 2.*

Efficiency: *The algorithm Hash runs in time* $|D|\mathsf{poly}(\log|D|, \lambda)$. *The algorithms* HashUpdate, Send, SendWrite, Receive, ReceiveWrite *run in time* $\mathsf{poly}(\log|D|, \lambda)$.

$\mathsf{SenPrivExpt}^{\mathsf{real}}[1^\lambda, \mathcal{A}]$ $\qquad\qquad$ $\mathsf{SenPrivExpt}^{\mathsf{ideal}}[1^\lambda, \mathcal{A}]$

1. $\mathsf{crs} \leftarrow \mathsf{crsGen}(1^\lambda)$. $\qquad\qquad$ 1. $\mathsf{crs} \leftarrow \mathsf{crsGen}(1^\lambda)$.
2. $(D, L, m_0, m_1, \mathsf{st}) \leftarrow \mathcal{A}_1(\mathsf{crs})$. $\quad$ 2. $(D, L, m_0, m_1, \mathsf{st}) \leftarrow \mathcal{A}_1(\mathsf{crs})$.
3. $(\mathsf{d}, \widehat{D}) \leftarrow \mathsf{Hash}(\mathsf{crs}, D)$. $\qquad\quad$ 3. $(\mathsf{d}, \widehat{D}) \leftarrow \mathsf{Hash}(\mathsf{crs}, D)$.
4. Output $\qquad\qquad\qquad\qquad\qquad$ 4. Output $\mathcal{A}_2(\mathsf{st}, \mathsf{Sim}_{\ell\mathsf{OT}}(\mathsf{crs}, D, L, m_{D[L]}))$.
   $\mathcal{A}_2(\mathsf{st}, \mathsf{Send}(\mathsf{crs}, \mathsf{d}, L, m_0, m_1))$.

Fig. 1. Sender privacy security game

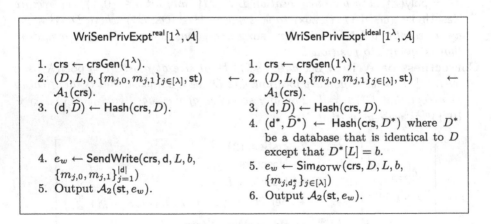

$\mathsf{WriSenPrivExpt}^{\mathsf{real}}[1^\lambda, \mathcal{A}]$ $\qquad\qquad$ $\mathsf{WriSenPrivExpt}^{\mathsf{ideal}}[1^\lambda, \mathcal{A}]$

1. $\mathsf{crs} \leftarrow \mathsf{crsGen}(1^\lambda)$. $\qquad\qquad\qquad$ 1. $\mathsf{crs} \leftarrow \mathsf{crsGen}(1^\lambda)$.
2. $(D, L, b, \{m_{j,0}, m_{j,1}\}_{j \in [\lambda]}, \mathsf{st}) \leftarrow$ $\quad$ 2. $(D, L, b, \{m_{j,0}, m_{j,1}\}_{j \in [\lambda]}, \mathsf{st}) \leftarrow$
   $\mathcal{A}_1(\mathsf{crs})$. $\qquad\qquad\qquad\qquad\qquad$ $\mathcal{A}_1(\mathsf{crs})$.
3. $(\mathsf{d}, \widehat{D}) \leftarrow \mathsf{Hash}(\mathsf{crs}, D)$. $\qquad\qquad$ 3. $(\mathsf{d}, \widehat{D}) \leftarrow \mathsf{Hash}(\mathsf{crs}, D)$.
   $\qquad\qquad\qquad\qquad\qquad\qquad\qquad$ 4. $(\mathsf{d}^*, \widehat{D}^*) \leftarrow \mathsf{Hash}(\mathsf{crs}, D^*)$ where D^*
   $\qquad\qquad\qquad\qquad\qquad\qquad\qquad$ be a database that is identical to D
   $\qquad\qquad\qquad\qquad\qquad\qquad\qquad$ except that $D^*[L] = b$.
4. $e_w \leftarrow \mathsf{SendWrite}(\mathsf{crs}, \mathsf{d}, L, b,$ $\quad$ 5. $e_w \leftarrow \mathsf{Sim}_{\ell\mathsf{OTW}}(\mathsf{crs}, D, L, b,$
   $\{m_{j,0}, m_{j,1}\}_{j=1}^{|\mathsf{d}|})$ $\qquad\qquad\qquad\quad$ $\{m_{j,\mathsf{d}_j^*}\}_{j \in [\lambda]})$
5. Output $\mathcal{A}_2(\mathsf{st}, e_w)$. $\qquad\qquad\qquad$ 6. Output $\mathcal{A}_2(\mathsf{st}, e_w)$.

Fig. 2. Sender privacy for writes security game

Theorem 2 ([CDG+17]). *Assuming iO for circuits and* somewhere statistically binding hash functions, *there exists a construction of updatable laconic oblivious transfer.*

Remark 2. We note that the security requirements given in Definition 5 is stronger than the one in [CDG+17] as we require the crs to be generated before the adversary provides the database D and the location L. However, the constructions given in [CDG+17] already satisfies this stronger definition and this was noted in [GS18a].

A Note on Hash Updates. The construction of updatable Laconic Oblivious Transfer given in [CDG+17] uses a Merkle Hash to hash the database. Thus, to compute the hash we need the contents of the entire database to be specified. But in our construction of succinct randomized encodings, we need a methodology to compute the Merkle tree "on the fly." More specifically, let us consider a scenario wherein we are not initially specified the entire database $D \in \{0,1\}^M$ but are only given the contents of the first n locations. We give a methodology to compute the Merkle hash which "binds" the first n locations, keeps the other locations to be unspecified and runs in time $\mathsf{poly}(n, \lambda, \log M)$. A similar trick has been used in [OPWW15].

Let us assume that we are given a hash function $H : \{0,1\}^{2\lambda} \to \{0,1\}^{\lambda}$. To store a database of size M, the Merkle tree consists of M leaves where each leaf stores a λ bit string which either corresponds to the bit 0, or the bit 1 or a special symbol $\perp$ (using some canonical encoding). We construct the Merkle tree in a bottom-up fashion by labeling all the internal nodes. The label of the root node gives the hash value. We label each internal node of the Merkle tree with children given labels lab_ℓ and lab_r as follows:

- If both lab_ℓ and lab_r are given labels $\perp$, then node is given $\perp$ as its label.
- Otherwise, the node is given $H(\mathsf{lab}_\ell \| \mathsf{lab}_r)$ as the label where $\|$ denotes concatenation.

Note that if all the locations are unspecified then the label of the root corresponds to $\perp$. For each additional location L that is specified, we just fix the auxiliary information aux to be labels of the all the nodes in the root to the leaf given by L along with their siblings. Note we only need to maintain the state of all labels which are not equal $\perp$ when performing an hash update. Given this information, we can easily recompute the label of the root. This gives the required methodology to update the hash value in time $\mathsf{poly}(n, \lambda, \log M)$ where n is the number of specified locations.

2.6 Puncturable Pseudorandom Function

We recall the notion of puncturable pseudorandom function from [SW14]. The construction of pseudorandom function given in [GGM86] satisfies the following definition [BW13, KPTZ13, BGI14].

Definition 6. *A punctured pseudorandom function* PPRF *is a tuple of PPT algorithms* (KeyGen$_{\text{PPRF}}$, PRF, Punc) *with the following properties:*

- *Efficiently Computable: For all λ and for all $S \leftarrow$ KeyGen$_{\text{PPRF}}(1^\lambda)$, PRF$_S$: $\{0,1\}^\lambda \rightarrow \{0,1\}^\lambda$ is polynomial time computable.*
- *Functionality is preserved under puncturing: For all λ, for all $y \in \{0,1\}^\lambda$ and $\forall x \neq y$,*

$$\Pr[\text{PRF}_{S\{y\}}(x) = \text{PRF}_S(x)] = 1$$

  where $S \leftarrow$ KeyGen$_{\text{PPRF}}(1^\lambda)$ and $S\{y\} \leftarrow$ Punc(S, y).
- *Pseudorandomness at punctured points: For all λ, for all $y \in \{0,1\}^\lambda$, and for all poly sized adversaries $\mathcal{A}$*

$$|\Pr[\mathcal{A}(\text{PRF}_S(y), S\{y\}) = 1] - \Pr[\mathcal{A}(U_\lambda, S\{y\}) = 1]| \leq \text{negl}(\lambda)$$

  where $S \leftarrow$ KeyGen$_{\text{PPRF}}(1^\lambda)$, $S\{y\} \leftarrow$ Punc(S, y) and U_λ denotes the uniform distribution over $\{0,1\}^\lambda$.

Remark 3. We can generalize the puncturing procedure to puncture at multiple points $y_1, \ldots, y_m$. The security requirement now is that even given the punctured key $S\{y_1, \ldots, y_m\}$, the PRF evaluations on inputs $y_1, \ldots, y_m$ are computationally indistinguishable to random. We note that in the case of multiple puncturings, the size of the punctured key $S\{y_1, \ldots, y_m\}$ grows polynomially in m and λ.

3   Construction of Succinct Randomized Encoding

In this section, we give a construction of succinct randomized encoding for succinctly describable Turing machines. More formally, we show that:

Theorem 3. *Assuming the existence of indistinguishability obfuscation and updatable laconic oblivious transfer, there exists a construction of succinct randomized encoding.*

As shown in [BGL+15], a succinct randomized encoding with sub-exponential security gives a construction of succinct $i\mathcal{O}$ for Turing machines. For completeness, we sketch the details of this transformation in the full version of our paper [GS18b]. We give the formal description of our construction of succinct randomized encodings in Fig. 3 and give an overview below.

Overview. Let us start with an overview of the encoding scheme. The encoding procedure takes as input a description of the Turing machine M and an input x on which the machine has to be evaluated. The procedure first reduces M to a circuit C_{sc} (as given in Lemma 1) that succinctly represents the circuit C which computes the same function as that of M. Let C consist of $N - n$ binary gates with N being the output gate. Each gate $g \in [n+1, N]$ is described by a tuple $(i, j, f_g) \in [g-1]^2 \times$ GType where outputs of gates i and j serves as inputs to gate g and f_g is the binary function computed by gate g. Given an input $g \in [n+1, N]$, the succinct circuit C_{sc} outputs (i, j, f_g).

For our construction, we consider an alternate view of the circuit C. We view the circuit C as a sequence of step circuits $SC_{n+1}, \ldots, SC_N$ along with a database D. The database is initially loaded with the input x and each step circuit writes a single bit to the database. More precisely, for each $g \in [n+1, N]$, the step circuit SC_g implements the functionality of the gate g and writes the output of that gate to position g in the database. Further, the step circuits access the database via an updatable laconic OT. Specifically, the step circuit SC_g takes as input the digest of the database where the first $g-1$ cells are filled appropriately and the rest of the positions being $\perp$. Using the digest, it reads the contents of the database in positions i and j (where (i, j) are the inputs to gate g) using the Send function of laconic OT. Once it has read the contents of those two locations, it applies the function f_g on those two bits and writes the output to the location g using the SendWrite function. It passes on the updated digest to the next circuit SC_{g+1}. Thus, each of the step circuits faithfully model the computation of the corresponding gate and the contents in location N of the database gives the output of the circuit C.

Let us now explain how the encoding procedure uses the above view of the circuit. The encoding procedure obfuscates the function Gate (formally described in Fig. 4). The function Gate on input $g \in [n+1, N]$, uses the succinct circuit C_{sc} to get the description of gate g. Next, it constructs the step circuit SC_g (formally described in Fig. 5) and garbles the circuit (the randomness and the labels are derived using a puncturable pseudorandom function). The Gate function finally outputs the garbled step circuit $\widetilde{SC}_g$. The output of the encoding function is this obfuscation along with the labels corresponding to the initial digest of the database (where the input is loaded).

Given an obfuscation of the function Gate, a decoder can run this obfuscation on every gate $g \in [n+1, N]$ to obtain the garbled step circuit $\widetilde{SC}_g$. Given the labels corresponding to the initial digest, the decoder evaluates each of the garbled step circuits from $n+1$ to N (labels corresponding to the gth step circuit are output by the $(g-1)^{th}$ circuit). At the end of the computation, the content of the database at location N gives the output.

However, there is one technical issue. Recall that the laconic OT is not guaranteed to hide the contents of the database. In order to hide the contents of the database, we use a one-time pad to mask each bit that is written. This one time pad is succinctly derived using a puncturable pseudorandom function.

Correctness. This argument is based on the correctness proof in [GS18a]. Let D_{g^*} be the contents of the database at the beginning of g^*-th iteration of the **for** loop in sRE.Dec. We first argue via an inductive argument that for each gate $g^* \in [1, N]$, $D_{g^*+1, g}$ is the output of gate g masked with r_g for every $g \in [1, g^*]$. Given this, the correctness follows by setting $g^* := N$ and observing that the $D_{N+1, N}$ is unmasked using r_N in Step 7 of sRE.Dec.

The base case is $g^* = n$ which is clearly true since in the beginning D_{n+1} is set as $(r_{[1,n]} \oplus x || \perp^{N-n})$. In order to prove the inductive step for a gate g^*

$\mathsf{sRE.Enc}(1^\lambda, M, x, t)$: On input a Turing machine M, an input $x \in \{0,1\}^n$ and a time bound t do:

1. Reduce M to a succinct circuit C_{sc} from Lemma 1 that describes the circuit $C : \{0,1\}^n \to \{0,1\}$ computing the same function as that of M. Let $N - n$ be the number of binary gates in C.

2. Sample $\mathsf{crs} \leftarrow \mathsf{crsGen}(1^\lambda)$ and three PRF keys $S, R, K \leftarrow \mathsf{KeyGen}_{\mathsf{PPRF}}(1^\lambda)$. We will truncate the output length of $\mathsf{PRF}_R(\cdot)$ to one bit.

3. For each $k \in [\lambda]$ and $b \in \{0,1\}$, compute $\mathsf{lab}^1_{k,b} = \mathsf{PRF}_K((1, k, b))$.

4. Compute $i\mathcal{O}(\mathsf{pad}_\ell(\mathsf{Gate}[C_{\mathsf{sc}}, \mathsf{crs}, S, R, K]))$ where the circuit Gate is described in Figure 4 and $\mathsf{pad}_\ell(\cdot)$ pads the circuit to size ℓ which will be specified in the proof.

5. For each $i \in [n]$, set $y_i = x_i \oplus \mathsf{PRF}_R(i)$.

6. Set $\mathsf{d} = \bot$ and for each $i \in [n]$,
   (a) Recompute $\mathsf{d} = \mathsf{HashUpdate}(\mathsf{crs}, \mathsf{d}, (i, y_i), \mathsf{aux})$ where aux is the auxiliary information for updating position i.

7. Compute $r_N = \mathsf{PRF}_R(N)$.

8. Output $\left(i\mathcal{O}(\mathsf{pad}_\ell(\mathsf{Gate}[C_{\mathsf{sc}}, \mathsf{crs}, S, R, K])), \{\mathsf{lab}^1_{k,\mathsf{d}_k}\}_{k \in [\lambda]}, \{y_i\}_{i \in [n]}, r_N \right)$.

$\mathsf{sRE.Dec}(M, \widehat{M}_{x,t})$: On input the machine M and the randomized encoding $\widehat{M}_{x,t}$ do:

1. Initialize the Merkle tree $\widehat{D}$ with the leaf node i storing bit y_i for every $i \in [n]$. Initialize all other leaves with special symbol $\bot$.

2. For each $g \in [n+1, N]$ do:
   (a) $\widetilde{\mathsf{SC}}_g := i\mathcal{O}(\mathsf{pad}_\ell(\mathsf{Gate}[C_{\mathsf{sc}}, \mathsf{crs}, S, R, K]))(g)$.

3. Set $\overline{\mathsf{lab}} = \{\mathsf{lab}^1_{k,\mathsf{d}_k}\}_{k \in [\lambda]}$.

4. **for** each g from $n+1$ to N **do:**
   (a) Let (i, j, f_g) be the description of gate g.
   (b) Compute $(\gamma, e) := \mathsf{Receive}^{\widehat{D}}(\mathsf{crs}, \mathsf{Receive}^{\widehat{D}}(\mathsf{crs}, \mathsf{EvalCkt}(\widetilde{\mathsf{SC}}_g, \overline{\mathsf{lab}}), i), j)$.
   (c) Set $\overline{\mathsf{lab}} := \mathsf{ReceiveWrite}^{\widehat{D}}(\mathsf{crs}, g, \gamma, e)$.

5. Recover the contents of the leaves D from the final state $\widehat{D}$.

6. Output $D_N \oplus r_N$.

Fig. 3. Succinct randomized encoding

(with description (i, j, f_{g^*})), we now argue that that the γ recovered in Step 4.(b) of $\mathsf{sRE.Dec}$ corresponds to $f_{g^*}(D_{g^*,i} \oplus r_i D_{g^*,j} \oplus r_j) \oplus r_{g^*}$ which by inductive hypothesis corresponds to output of the gate g^* masked with r_{g^*}. This is shown as follows.

$$(\gamma, e) := \mathsf{Receive}^{\widehat{D}}(\mathsf{crs}, \mathsf{Receive}^{\widehat{D}}(\mathsf{crs}, \mathsf{EvalCkt}(\widetilde{\mathsf{SC}}_g, \overline{\mathsf{lab}}), i), j)$$

$$= \mathsf{Receive}^{\widehat{D}}(\mathsf{crs}, \mathsf{Receive}^{\widehat{D}}(\mathsf{crs}, \mathsf{Send}(\mathsf{crs}, \mathsf{d}, i, c_0, c_1), i), j)$$

$$= \mathsf{Receive}^{\widehat{D}}(\mathsf{crs}, c_{D_{g^*,i}}, j)$$

$$= \mathsf{Receive}^{\widehat{D}}\left(\mathsf{crs}, \mathsf{Send}\left(\mathsf{crs}, \mathsf{d}, j, (\gamma(D_{g^*,i}, 0), e_{\gamma(D_{g^*,i}, 0)}), (\gamma(D_{g^*,i}, 1), e_{\gamma(D_{g^*,i}, 1)})\right), j\right)$$

$$= \left(\gamma(D_{g^*,i}, D_{g^*,j}), e_{\gamma(D_{g^*,i}, D_{g^*,j})}\right)$$

$$= \left(f_{g^*}(D_{g^*,i} \oplus r_i D_{g^*,j} \oplus r_j) \oplus r_{g^*}, e_{f_{g^*} D_{g^*,i} \oplus r_i D_{g^*,j} \oplus r_j \oplus r_{g^*}}\right)$$

Gate

Input: A gate $g \in [n+1, N]$.
Hardcoded: The circuit C_{sc}, common reference string crs, a triplet of PRF keys (S, R, K).

1. Run C_{sc} on input g to obtain (i, j, f_g).
2. Set $r_i = \mathsf{PRF}_R(i)$, $r_j = \mathsf{PRF}_R(j)$ and $r_g = \mathsf{PRF}_R(g)$.
3. Compute $\mathsf{lab}^g_{k,b} = \mathsf{PRF}_K(g, k, b)$ and $\mathsf{lab}^{g+1}_{k,b} = \mathsf{PRF}_K(g+1, k, b)$ for each $k \in [\lambda]$ and $b \in \{0, 1\}$. (We use $\{\mathsf{lab}^g_{k,b}\}$ to denote $\{\mathsf{lab}^g_{k,b}\}_{k \in [\lambda], b \in \{0,1\}}$.)
4. Compute (where the step-circuit SC is described in Figure 5)

$$\widetilde{\mathsf{SC}}_g \leftarrow \mathsf{GarbleCkt}\left(1^\lambda, \mathsf{SC}[\mathsf{crs}, (r_i, r_j, r_g), (i, j), f_g, \{\mathsf{lab}^{g+1}_{k,b}\}, 0], \{\mathsf{lab}^g_{k,b}\}; \mathsf{PRF}_S(g)\right).$$

5. Output $\widetilde{\mathsf{SC}}_g$.

Fig. 4. Description of Gate

Step Circuit SC

Input: A digest d.
Hardcoded: The common reference string crs, a triplet of masking bits (r_i, r_j, r_g), a description (i, j) of gate g, a binary function $f_g : \{0, 1\}^2 \rightarrow \{0, 1\}$, a set of labels $\{\mathsf{lab}_{k,b}\}$ and a bit τ ($\tau = 1$ case is only relevant for the proof).

1. Compute $e_b \leftarrow \mathsf{SendWrite}(\mathsf{crs}, \mathsf{d}, g, b, \{\mathsf{lab}_{k,0}, \mathsf{lab}_{k,1}\}_{k \in [\lambda]})$ for $b \in \{0, 1\}$.
2. Define for all $\alpha, \beta \in \{0, 1\}$, $\gamma(\alpha, \beta) := \begin{cases} f_g(\alpha \oplus r_i, \beta \oplus r_j) \oplus r_g & \text{if } \tau = 0 \\ r_g & \text{if } \tau = 1 \end{cases}$
3. Generate

$$c_0 \leftarrow \mathsf{Send}\left(\mathsf{crs}, \mathsf{d}, j, (\gamma(0, 0), e_{\gamma(0,0)}), (\gamma(0, 1), e_{\gamma(0,1)})\right),$$

$$c_1 \leftarrow \mathsf{Send}\left(\mathsf{crs}, \mathsf{d}, j, (\gamma(1, 0), e_{\gamma(1,0)}), (\gamma(1, 1), e_{\gamma(1,1)})\right).$$

4. Output $\mathsf{Send}(\mathsf{crs}, \mathsf{d}, i, c_0, c_1)$.

Fig. 5. Description of the step circuit

4   Security Proof

In this section, we prove that the construction presented in the Sect. 3 satisfies security property given in Definition 2. In Subsect. 4.1, we start by defining circuit configurations. Next, in Subsect. 4.2 we show that both the real world garbling procedure and the simulated distributions are special cases of this circuit configuration. Finally, in the rest of the subsection we show that the real garbling and the simulated distributions are indistinguishable.

4.1 Circuit Configuration

Our proof of security proceeds via a hybrid argument over different *circuit configurations* which we describe in this section. A circuit configuration denoted by $\mathsf{conf} = (I, i)$ consists of a set $I \subseteq [n + 1, N]$ and an index $i \in [n + 1, N]$. Intuitively, each circuit configuration defines a distribution of the randomized encoding $\widehat{M}_{x,t}^{\mathsf{conf}}$. Let us now explain the semantics of the set I and the index i.

Recall that from our construction described in Fig. 3, $i\mathcal{O}(\mathsf{pad}_\ell(\mathsf{Gate}))$ outputs $\widetilde{\mathsf{SC}}_g$ when given a gate $g \in [n + 1, N]$ as input. Intuitively, a configuration of a circuit defines a particular distribution of $\widetilde{\mathsf{SC}}_g$ for each $g \in [n + 1, N]$. In particular, for each gate g, the distribution of $\widetilde{\mathsf{SC}}_g$ can be in one of the three modes: White mode, Gray mode and the Black mode. We say that $\widetilde{\mathsf{SC}}_g$ is said to be in White mode if for the distribution of $\widetilde{\mathsf{SC}}_g$ is same as the honest garbling procedure given in Fig. 4. We say that $\widetilde{\mathsf{SC}}_g$ is in Gray mode if its distribution depends only on the output of the gate g when the circuit C is evaluated with input x. We say that $\widetilde{\mathsf{SC}}_g$ is in Black mode if its distribution is independent of the input x. Looking ahead, initially all the step circuits will be in White mode and the goal will be to convert all of them to Black in the simulation. We will achieve this in the reverse order i.e., we first change SC_N to Black mode and then change SC_{N-1} and so on. The index i (given as part of defining the circuit configuration) is such that for all $g > i$ the distribution of the garbled step circuit $\widetilde{\mathsf{SC}}_g$ is in Black mode. We can also extend the notion of Black mode to input gates $[1, n]$. So i can be any element in the set $[0, N]$. The subset I indicates the set of gates g such that the distribution of the garbled step circuit $\widetilde{\mathsf{SC}}_g$ is in Gray mode. The rest of the garbled step circuits $\widetilde{\mathsf{SC}}_g$ where $g \notin I$ and $g \leq i$ are generated in White mode. We say a configuration is valid if $I \cap [i + 1, N] = \emptyset$.

Simulation in a Valid Configuration. In Fig. 6, we describe the simulated encoding procedure SimsRE.Enc for any given configuration conf. Note that these simulated encoding function also takes x as input whereas the ideal world simulation does not. We describe our simulator functions with these additional inputs so that it captures simulation in all of our intermediate hybrids. We note that final ideal world simulation does not use these values.

4.2 Our Hybrids

For every circuit configuration $\mathsf{conf} = (I, i)$, we define $\mathsf{Hybrid}_{\mathsf{conf}}$ to be a distribution of $\widehat{M}_{x,t}$ as given in Fig. 6. We start by observing that both real world and ideal distribution from Definition 2 can be seen as instance of $\mathsf{Hybrid}_{\mathsf{conf}}$ where $\mathsf{conf} = (\emptyset, N)$ and $\mathsf{conf} = (\emptyset, 0)$, respectively. In other words, the real world distribution corresponds to having all gates in White mode and the ideal world

---

SimsRE.Enc$(1^\lambda, M, x, t)$: On input a Turing machine M, an input $x \in \{0,1\}^n$ and a time bound t do:

1. Reduce M to a succinct circuit C_{sc} from Lemma 1 that describes the circuit $C : \{0,1\}^n \to \{0,1\}$. Let $N - n$ be the number of binary gates in C.

2. Sample $crs \leftarrow crsGen(1^\lambda)$ and three PRF keys $S, R, K \leftarrow KeyGen_{PPRF}(1^\lambda)$. We will truncate the output length of $PRF_R(\cdot)$ to one bit.

3. **Notation:** For $g \in [n+1, N+1]$, we let D_g be such that

$$D_{g,w} = \begin{cases} x_w \oplus PRF_R(w) & w \leq n, \\ E_w \oplus PRF_R(w) & n+1 \leq w < g, \\ \bot & \text{otherwise,} \end{cases}$$

where E_w is the bit assigned to wire w of the circuit C computed on input x. Finally, we let d_g be the digest of D_g (i.e., $(d_g, \cdot) := Hash(crs, D_g)$) and $d_{g,k}$ be the kth bit of d_g.

4. For each $k \in [\lambda]$ and $b \in \{0,1\}$, compute $lab^1_{k,b} = PRF_K((1, k, b))$.

5. **for each** g from N down to $n+1$ such that $g \in I$:
   (a) Set $e \leftarrow Sim_{\ell OTW}(crs, D_g, g, D_{g+1,g}, \{lab^{g+1}_{k,d_{g+1,k}}\}_{k \in [\lambda]})$.
   (b) Set $out_g \leftarrow Sim_{\ell OT}(crs, D_g, i, Sim_{\ell OT}(crs, D_g, j, e))$

6. Compute $iO(pad_\ell(SimGate[C_{sc}, crs, S, R, K, (I, i), \{out_g, d_g\}_{g \in I}]))$ where the circuit SimGate is described in Figure 7 and $pad_\ell(\cdot)$ pads the circuit to size ℓ which will be specified later.

7. For each $w \in [n]$, set $y_w = PRF_R(w)$ if $w > i$ and $y_w = x_w \oplus PRF_R(w)$ otherwise.

8. Set $d = \bot$ and for each $w \in [n]$,
   (a) Recompute $d = HashUpdate(d, aux, w, y_w)$ where aux is the auxiliary information for updating position w.

9. If $i < N$ then compute $r'_N = PRF_R(N) \oplus M(x)$; else, compute $r'_N = PRF_R(N)$.

10. Output $(iO(pad_\ell(Gate[C_{sc}, S, R, K])), \{lab_{k,d_k}\}_{k \in [\lambda]}, \{y_i\}_{i \in [n]}, r'_N)$.

Fig. 6. Succinct randomized encoding in configuration $conf = (I, i)$.

distribution corresponds to having all gates in Black mode. The goal is to move from the real world distribution to the ideal world distribution while minimizing the maximum number of gates in the Gray mode in any intermediate hybrid.[5]

4.2.1 Rules of Indistinguishability

We will now describe the two rules (we call these rule A and rule B) to move from one valid circuit configuration conf to another valid configuration conf' such that Hybrid$_{conf}$ is computationally indistinguishable from Hybrid$_{conf'}$.

---

[5] This is because the number of gates in the Gray mode increases the circuit size of SimGate by a proportional factor.

SimGate

Input: A gate $g \in [n+1, N]$.
Hardcoded: The circuit C_{sc}, common reference string crs, a triplet of PRF keys (S, R, K), the configuration (I, i), $\{out_g\}_{g \in I}$ and $\{d_g\}_{g \in I}$.

1. Run C_{sc} on input g to obtain $f_g, (i, j)$.
2. Set $r_i = \mathsf{PRF}_R(i)$, $r_j = \mathsf{PRF}_R(j)$ and $r_g = \mathsf{PRF}_R(g)$.
3. Compute $\mathsf{lab}^g_{k,b} = \mathsf{PRF}_K(g, k, b)$ and $\mathsf{lab}^{g+1}_{k,b} = \mathsf{PRF}_K(g+1, k, b)$ for each $k \in [\lambda]$ and $b \in \{0, 1\}$. (We use $\{\mathsf{lab}^g_{k,b}\}$ to denote $\{\mathsf{lab}^g_{k,b}\}_{k \in [\lambda], b \in \{0,1\}}$.)
4. If $g \leq i$ and $g \notin I$ then compute (where the step-circuit SC is described in Figure 5)

$$\widetilde{\mathsf{SC}}_g \leftarrow \mathsf{GarbleCkt}\left(1^\lambda, \mathsf{SC}[\mathsf{crs}, (r_i, r_j, r_g), (i, j), f_g, \{\mathsf{lab}^{g+1}_{k,b}\}, 0], \{\mathsf{lab}^g_{k,b}\}; \mathsf{PRF}_S(g)\right).$$

5. Else if $g > i$, compute

$$\widetilde{\mathsf{SC}}_g \leftarrow \mathsf{GarbleCkt}\left(1^\lambda, \mathsf{SC}[\mathsf{crs}, (0, 0, r_g), (i, j), \{\mathsf{lab}^{g+1}_{k,b}\}, 1], \{\mathsf{lab}^g_{k,b}\}; \mathsf{PRF}_S(g)\right).$$

6. Else, compute $\widetilde{\mathsf{SC}}_g \leftarrow \mathsf{Sim}_{\mathsf{Ckt}}\left(1^\lambda, 1^{|\mathsf{SC}|}, out_g, \{\mathsf{lab}^g_{k,d_{g,k}}\}_{k \in [\lambda]}; \mathsf{PRF}_S(g)\right)$.
7. Output $\widetilde{\mathsf{SC}}_g$.

Fig. 7. Description of SimGate

Rule A: Rule A says that for any valid configuration conf we can indistinguishably change gate g^* in White mode to Gray mode if it is the first gate or if its predecessor is also in Gray mode. More formally, let $\mathsf{conf} = (I, i)$ and $\mathsf{conf}' = (I', i')$ be two valid circuit configurations and $g^* \in [n+1, N]$ be a gate such that:

- $i = i'$.
- $g^* \notin I$, $I' = I \cup \{g^*\}$ and $g^* \leq i$.
- Either $g^* = n+1$ or $g^* - 1 \in I$.

In Lemma 4, we will show that for two valid configurations conf, conf' satisfying the above constraints we have that $\mathsf{Hybrid}_{\mathsf{conf}} \overset{c}{\approx} \mathsf{Hybrid}_{\mathsf{conf}'}$. Note that we can also use this rule to move a gate g^* from Gray mode to White mode. We refer to those invocations of the rule as *inverse A rule*. Rule A is illustrated in Fig. 8.

Rule B: Rule B says that for any configuration for any valid configuration conf we can indistinguishably change gate g^* in Gray mode to Black mode if all gates subsequent to g^* is in Black mode and the predecessor is in Gray mode. More formally, let $\mathsf{conf} = (I, g^*)$ and $\mathsf{conf}' = (I', g')$ be two valid circuit configurations such that:

- $g^* = g' + 1$.
- $g^* \in I$, $I' = I \setminus \{g^*\}$.
- Either $g^* = n+1$ or $g^* - 1 \in I$.

In Lemma 5, we will show that for an valid configurations $\mathsf{conf}, \mathsf{conf}'$ satisfying the above constraints we have that $\mathsf{Hybrid}_{\mathsf{conf}} \overset{c}{\approx} \mathsf{Hybrid}_{\mathsf{conf}'}$. Rule B is illustrated in Fig. 9.

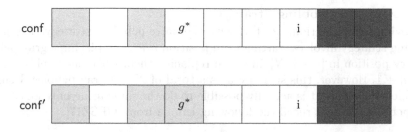

Fig. 8. Example of Rule A

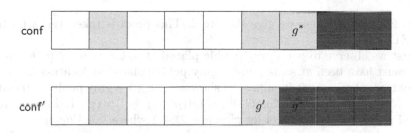

Fig. 9. Example of Rule B

4.2.2 Interpreting the Rules of Indistinguishability as a Pebbling Game

Sections 4.2.2 and 4.2.3 are taken verbatim from [GS18a]. Our sequence of hybrids from the real to the ideal world follow an optimal strategy for the following pebbling game. The two rules described above correspond to the rules of our pebbling game below.

Consider the positive integer line $n+1, n+2, \ldots N$. We are given pebbles of two colors: gray and black . A black pebble corresponds to a gate in the Black (i.e., input independent simulation) mode and a gray pebble corresponds to a gate in the Gray (i.e., input dependent simulation) mode. A position without any pebble corresponds to real garbling or in the White mode. We can place the pebbles on this positive integer line according to the following two rules:

Rule A: We can place or remove a gray pebble in position i if and only if there is a gray pebble in position $i-1$. This restriction does not apply to position $n+1$: we can always place or remove a gray pebble at position $n+1$.

Rule B: We can replace a gray pebble in position i with a black pebble as long as all the positions $> i$ have black pebbles and there is a gray pebble in position $i-1$ or if $i = n+1$.

Optimization Goal of the Pebbling Game. The goal is to pebble the line $[n + 1, N]$ such that every position has a black pebble while minimizing the number of gray pebbles that are present on the line at any point in time.

4.2.3   Optimal Pebbling Strategy

To provide some intuition, we start with the naïve pebbling strategy. The naïve pebbling strategy involves starting from position $n+1$ and placing a gray pebble at every position in $[n + 1, N]$ and then replacing them with black pebbles from N to $n + 1$. However, this strategy uses a total of $N - n$ gray pebbles. Using a more clever strategy, it is actually possible to do the same using only $\log(N - n)$ gray pebbles. We first recall the following lemma from [GPSZ17].

Lemma 2 ([GPSZ17]). *For any integer $n+1 \le p \le n+2^k - 1$, it is possible to make $O((p - n)^{\log_2 3}) \approx O((p - n)^{1.585})$ moves and get a gray pebble at position p using k gray pebbles.*

Proof. For completeness we give the proof. This proof is taken verbatim from [GPSZ17].

First we observe to get a gray pebble placed at p, for each $i \in [n + 1, p - 1]$ there must have been at some point a gray pebble placed at location i.

Next, we observe that it suffices to show we can get a gray pebble at position $p = n + 2^k - 1$ for every k using $O(3^k) = O((p - n)^{\log_2 3})$ steps. Indeed, for more general p, we run the protocol for $p' = n + 2^k - 1$ where $k = \lceil \log_2(p - n - 1) \rceil$, but stop the first time we get a gray pebble at position p. Since $p'/p \le 3$, the running time is at most $O((p - n)^{\log_2 3})$.

Now for the algorithm. The sequence of steps will create a fractal pattern, and we describe the steps recursively. We assume an algorithm A_{k-1} using $k-1$ gray pebbles that can get a gray pebble at position $n + 2^{k-1} - 1$. The steps are as follows:

- Run A_{k-1}. There is now a gray pebble at position $n + 2^{k-1} - 1$ on the line.
- Place the remaining gray pebble at position $n + 2^{k-1}$, which is allowed since there is a gray pebble at position $n + 2^{k-1} - 1$.
- Run A_{k-1} in reverse, recovering all of the $k - 1$ gray pebbles used by A. The result is that there is a single gray pebble on the line at position $n + 2^{k-1}$.
- Now associate the portion of the number line starting at $n + 2^{k-1} + 1$ with a new number line. That is, associate $n + 2^{k-1} + a$ on the original number line with $n' + a$ (where $n' = n + 2^{k-1}$) on the new number line. We now have $k - 1$ gray pebbles, and on this new number line, all of the same rules apply. In particular, we can always add or remove a gray pebble from the first position $n' + 1 = n + 2^{k-1} + 1$ since we have left a gray pebble at $n + 2^{k-1}$. Therefore, we can run A_{k+1} once more on the new number line starting at $n' + 1$. The end result is a pebble at position $n' + 2^{k-1} - 1 = n + 2^{k-1} + (2^{k-1} - 1) = n + 2^k - 1$.

It remains to analyze the running time. The algorithm makes 3 recursive calls to A_{k-1}, so by induction the overall running time is $O(3^k)$, as desired.

Using the above lemma, we now give an optimal strategy for our pebbling game.

Lemma 3 ([GS18a]). *For any $N \in \mathbb{N}$, there exists a strategy for pebbling the line graph $[n+1, N]$ according to rules A and B by using at most $\log N$ gray pebbles and making $\mathsf{poly}(N)$ moves.*

Proof. The proof is taken verbatim from [GS18a].

The strategy is given below. For each g from N down to $n+1$ **do**:

1. Use the strategy in Lemma 2 to place a gray pebble in position g. Note that there exists a gray pebble in position $g - 1$ as well.
2. Replace the gray pebble in position g with a black pebble. This replacement is allowed since all positions $> g$ have black pebbles and there is a gray pebble in position $g - 1$.
3. Recover all the gray pebbles by reversing the moves.

The correctness of this strategy follows by inspection and the number of moves is polynomial in N.

4.3   Proof of Indistinguishability for the Rules

In this subsection, we will use the security of underlying primitives to implement the two rules.

4.3.1   Implementing Rule A

Lemma 4 (Rule A). *Let* conf *and* conf$'$ *be two valid circuit configurations satisfying the constraints of rule A, then assuming the security of garbling scheme for circuits, updatable laconic oblivious transfer, indistinguishability obfuscation and puncturable PRFs we have that* Hybrid$_{\mathsf{conf}} \overset{c}{\approx}$ Hybrid$_{\mathsf{conf}'}$.

Proof. We prove this via a hybrid argument.

- Hybrid$_{\mathsf{conf}}$: This is our starting hybrid and is distributed as Hybrid$_{(I,i)}$.
- Hybrid$_1$: In this hybrid, instead of hardwiring the PPRF keys K and S in the circuit SimGate, we hardwire the key K that is punctured at (g^*, k, b) for every $k \in [\lambda], b \in \{0, 1\}$ and S punctured at g^*. We additionally hardwire $\{\mathsf{lab}_{k,b}^{g^*}\}_{k \in [\lambda], b \in \{0,1\}}$ and $\mathsf{PRF}_S(g^*)$. This blows up the size of the circuit by a factor $\mathsf{poly}(\lambda)$. On input $g^* - 1$ and g^*, the circuit now uses the hardwired labels/randomness instead of computing them using the PPRF.

  It can be noted that the SimGate circuits in both Hybrid$_{\mathsf{conf}}$ and Hybrid$_1$ computes the exact same functionality and hence the indistinguishability between Hybrid$_{\mathsf{conf}}$ and Hybrid$_1$ follows from the security of $i\mathcal{O}$.
- Hybrid$_2$: We make three changes to the SimGate.
  - By conditions of Rule A, we have that $g^* - 1 \in I$ (if $g^* \neq n+1$). Therefore, we note that all the input labels $\{\mathsf{lab}_{k,b}^{g^*}\}$ are not used in SimGate but only the labels corresponding to d_{g^*} i.e., $\{\mathsf{lab}_{k,d_{g^*,k}}^{g^*}\}_{k \in [\lambda]}$. We just hardwire these labels in SimGate.

- We also hardwire $\widetilde{\mathsf{SC}}_{g^*}$ (that is computed using randomness $\mathsf{PRF}_S(g^*)$) in SimGate instead of generating it inside SimGate.
- We remove the hardwired randomness $\mathsf{PRF}_S(g^*)$.

The computational indistinguishability between Hybrid_2 from Hybrid_1 follows from the security of $i\mathcal{O}$ since the function computed by SimGate in Hybrid_1 and Hybrid_2 is exactly the same.

- $\underline{\mathsf{Hybrid}_3}$: In this hybrid, we sample the labels $\{\mathsf{lab}_{k,d_{g^*,k}}\}_{k\in[\lambda]}$ and the randomness used in generating $\widetilde{\mathsf{SC}}_{g^*}$ uniformly at random instead of generating them as outputs of the puncturable PRF. The computational indistinguishability between Hybrid_2 and Hybrid_3 follows from the security of puncturable PRF.

- $\underline{\mathsf{Hybrid}_4}$: In this hybrid, we generate $\widetilde{\mathsf{SC}}_{g^*}$ (that is hardwired inside SimGate) from the simulated distribution. More formally, we generate

$$\widetilde{\mathsf{SC}}_{g^*} \leftarrow \mathsf{Sim}_{ckt}(1^\lambda, 1^{|\mathsf{SC}|}, \mathsf{out}, \{\mathsf{lab}_{k,d_{g^*,k}}^{g^*}\}_{k\in[\lambda]})$$

where $\mathsf{out} \leftarrow \mathsf{SC}[\mathsf{crs}, (r_i, r_j, r_g), (i, j, f_g), \{\mathsf{lab}_{k,b}^{g^*+1}\}, 0](d_{g^*})$.

The only change in hybrid Hybrid_3 from Hybrid_2 is in the generation of the garbled circuit $\widetilde{\mathsf{SC}}_{g^*}$ and the security follows directly from the selective security of the garbling scheme.

- $\underline{\mathsf{Hybrid}_5}$: In this hybrid, we change how the output value out hardwired in $\widetilde{\mathsf{SC}}_{g^*}$ is generated. Recall that in Hybrid_4 this value is generated by first computing c_0 and c_1 as in Fig. 5 and then generating out as $\mathsf{Send}\,(\mathsf{crs}, d, i, c_0, c_1)$. In this hybrid, we just generate $c_{D_{g^*,i}}$ and use the laconic OT simulator to generate out. More formally, out is generated as

$$\mathsf{out} \leftarrow \mathsf{Sim}_{\ell OT}\left(\mathsf{crs}, D_{g^*}, i, c_{D_{g^*,i}}\right).$$

Computational indistinguishability between hybrids Hybrid_4 and Hybrid_5 follows directly from the sender privacy of the laconic OT scheme.

- $\underline{\mathsf{Hybrid}_6}$: In this hybrid, we change how the value $c_{D_{g^*,i}}$ is generated. Recall from Fig. 5 that $c_{D_{g^*,i}}$ is set as $\mathsf{Send}(\mathsf{crs}, d, j, (\gamma(D_{g^*,i}, 0), e_{\gamma(D_{g^*,i},0)}), (\gamma(D_{g^*,i}, 1), e_{\gamma(D_{g^*,i},1)}))$. We change the distribution of $c_{D_{g^*,i}}$ to $\mathsf{Sim}_{\ell OT}(\mathsf{crs}, D_{g^*}, j, e_{D_{g^*+1,g^*}})$, where $e_{D_{g^*+1,g^*}}$ is sampled as in Fig. 5.

Computational indistinguishability between hybrids Hybrid_6 and Hybrid_5 follows directly from the sender privacy of the laconic OT scheme. The argument is analogous to the argument of indistinguishability between Hybrid_4 and Hybrid_5.

- $\underline{\mathsf{Hybrid}_7}$: In this hybrid, we change how $e_{D_{g^*+1,g^*}}$ is generated. More specifically, we generate it using the simulator $\mathsf{Sim}_{\ell OTW}$. In other words, $e_{D_{g^*+1,g}}$ is generated as

$$\mathsf{Sim}_{\ell OTW}(\mathsf{crs}, D_{g^*}, g^*, D_{g^*+1,g^*}, \{\mathsf{lab}_{k,d_{g^*+1,k}}^{g^*+1}\}_{k\in[\lambda]}).$$

Computational indistinguishability between hybrids Hybrid_6 and Hybrid_7 follows directly from the sender privacy for writes of the laconic OT scheme.

– $\mathsf{Hybrid}_8 - \mathsf{Hybrid}_{10}$: In this hybrid, we reverse the changes made in Hybrid_1 to Hybrid_3 except that we hardwire $\{\mathsf{out}_{g^*}, \mathsf{d}_{g^*}\}$ in SimGate and use it to generate $\widetilde{\mathsf{SC}}_{g^*}$. The indistinguishability between Hybrid_7 to Hybrid_{10} follows in analogous manner to the indistinguishability between $\mathsf{Hybrid}_{\mathsf{conf}}$ to Hybrid_3. Finally, observe that hybrid Hybrid_{10} is the same as $\mathsf{Hybrid}_{\mathsf{conf}'}$.

This completes the proof of the lemma. We additionally note that the above sequence of hybrids is reversible. This implies the inverse rule A.

4.3.2   Implementing Rule B

Lemma 5 (Rule B).   *Let* conf *and* conf' *be two valid circuit configurations satisfying the constraints of rule B, then assuming the security of somewhere equivocal encryption, garbling scheme for circuits and updatable laconic oblivious transfer, we have that* $\mathsf{Hybrid}_{\mathsf{conf}} \overset{c}{\approx} \mathsf{Hybrid}_{\mathsf{conf}'}$.

Proof. We prove this via a hybrid argument starting with $\mathsf{Hybrid}_{\mathsf{conf}'}$ and ending in hybrid $\mathsf{Hybrid}_{\mathsf{conf}}$. We follow this ordering of the hybrids as this keeps the proof very close to the proof of Lemma 4.

– $\mathsf{Hybrid}_{\mathsf{conf}'}$: This is our starting hybrid and is distributed as $\mathsf{Hybrid}_{(I', g')}$.
– Hybrid_1 : In this hybrid, instead of hardwiring the PPRF keys K, R and S in the circuit SimGate, we hardwire the key K that is punctured at (g^*, k, b) for every $k \in [\lambda], b \in \{0,1\}$, R and S are punctured at g^*. We additionally hardwire $\{\mathsf{lab}^{g^*}_{k,b}\}_{k\in[\lambda],b\in\{0,1\}}$, $(r_i, r_{j,g})$, $\mathsf{PRF}_R(g^*)$ and $\mathsf{PRF}_S(g^*)$. This blows up the size of the circuit by a factor $\mathsf{poly}(\lambda)$. On input $g^* - 1$ and g^*, the circuit now uses the hardwired labels/randomness instead of computing them using the PPRF. Note that by constraints on conf and conf', $\mathsf{PRF}_R(g^*)$ is only needed on input g^*. This is because all gates $g > g^*$ are in Black mode. It can be noted that the SimGate circuits in both $\mathsf{Hybrid}_{\mathsf{conf}}$ and Hybrid_1 computes the exact same functionality and hence the indistinguishability between $\mathsf{Hybrid}_{\mathsf{conf}}$ and Hybrid_1 follows from the security of $i\mathcal{O}$.
– Hybrid_2 : We make three changes to the SimGate.
  - By conditions of Rule A, we have that $g^* - 1 \in I$ (if $g^* \neq n+1$). Therefore, we note that all the input labels $\{\mathsf{lab}^{g^*}_{k,b}\}$ are not used in SimGate but only the labels corresponding to d_{g^*} i.e., $\{\mathsf{lab}^{g^*}_{k,\mathsf{d}_{g^*,k}}\}_{k\in[\lambda]}$. We just hardwire these labels in SimGate.
  - We also hardwire $\widetilde{\mathsf{SC}}_{g^*}$ (where SC_{g^*} has r_{g^*} hardwired and $\widetilde{\mathsf{SC}}_{g^*}$ is computed using randomness $\mathsf{PRF}_S(g^*)$) in SimGate instead of generating it inside SimGate.
  - We remove the hardwired randomness $\mathsf{PRF}_S(g^*)$ and $\mathsf{PRF}_R(g^*)$.
  The computational indistinguishability between Hybrid_2 from Hybrid_1 follows from the security of $i\mathcal{O}$ since the function computed by SimGate in Hybrid_1 and Hybrid_2 is exactly the same.
– Hybrid_3 : In this hybrid, we sample the labels $\{\mathsf{lab}_{k,\mathsf{d}_{g^*,k}}\}_{k\in[\lambda]}$, $\mathsf{PRF}_R(g^*)$ and the randomness used in generating $\widetilde{\mathsf{SC}}_{g^*}$ uniformly at random instead

of generating them as outputs of the puncturable PRF. The computational indistinguishability between Hybrid_2 and Hybrid_3 follows from the security of puncturable PRF.

- Hybrid_4 : In this hybrid, we generate $\widetilde{\mathsf{SC}}_{g^*}$ (that is hardwired inside $\mathsf{SimGate}$) from the simulated distribution. More formally, we generate

$$\widetilde{\mathsf{SC}}_{g^*} \leftarrow \mathsf{Sim}_{ckt}(1^\lambda, 1^{|\mathsf{SC}|}, \mathsf{out}, \{\mathsf{lab}^{g^*}_{k, d_{g^*,k}}\}_{k \in [\lambda]})$$

where $\mathsf{out} \leftarrow \mathsf{SC}[\mathsf{crs}, (0, 0, r_g), (i, j, f_g), \{\mathsf{lab}^{g^*+1}_{k,b}\}, 1](d_{g^*})$.

The only change in hybrid Hybrid_3 from Hybrid_4 is in the generation of the garbled circuit $\widetilde{\mathsf{SC}}_{g^*}$ and the security follows directly from the selective security of the garbling scheme.

- Hybrid_5 : In this hybrid, we set change how the output value out hardwired in $\widetilde{\mathsf{SC}}_{g^*}$ is generated. Recall that in hybrid Hybrid_4 this value is generated by first computing c_0 and c_1 as in Fig. 5 and then generating out as $\mathsf{Send}\,(\mathsf{crs}, \mathsf{d}, i, c_0, c_1)$. In this hybrid, we just generate $c_{D_{g^*,i}}$ and use the laconic OT simulator to generate out. More formally, out is generated as

$$\mathsf{out} \leftarrow \mathsf{Sim}_{\ell\mathsf{OT}}\left(\mathsf{crs}, D_{g^*}, i, c_{D_{g^*,i}}\right).$$

Computational indistinguishability between hybrids Hybrid_4 and Hybrid_5 follows directly from the sender privacy of the laconic OT scheme.

- Hybrid_6 : In this hybrid, we change how the how the value $c_{D_{g^*,i}}$ is generated in hybrid Hybrid_5. Recall from Fig. 5 that $c_{D_{g^*,i}}$ is set as $\mathsf{Send}\left(\mathsf{crs}, \mathsf{d}, j, e_{r_{g^*}}, e_{r_{g^*}}\right)$. We change the distribution of $c_{D_{g^*,i}}$ to $\mathsf{Sim}_{\ell\mathsf{OT}}\left(\mathsf{crs}, D_g, j, e_{r_{g^*}}\right)$, where $e_{r_{g^*}}$ is sampled as in Fig. 5.

Computational indistinguishability between hybrids Hybrid_5 and Hybrid_6 follows directly from the sender privacy of the laconic OT scheme. The argument is analogous to the argument of indistinguishability between Hybrid_4 and Hybrid_5.

- Hybrid_7 : In this hybrid, we change how $e_{r_{g^*}}$ is generated. More specifically, we generate it using the simulator $\mathsf{Sim}_{\ell\mathsf{OTW}}$. In other words, $e_{r_{g^*}}$ is generated as

$$\mathsf{Sim}_{\ell\mathsf{OTW}}(\mathsf{crs}, D_{g^*}, g^*, r_{g^*}, \{\mathsf{lab}^{g^*+1}_{k, d_{g^*+1,k}}\}_{k \in [\lambda]}).$$

Computational indistinguishability between hybrids Hybrid_6 and Hybrid_7 follows directly from the sender privacy for writes of the laconic OT scheme.

- Hybrid_8 : The only difference between Hybrid_7 and Hybrid_8 is how D_{g^*+1,g^*} is set. Namely, in Hybrid_7 this value is set to be r_{g^*} while in Hybrid_8 this value is set as $r_{g^*} \oplus f_{g^*}(D_{g^*,i} \oplus r_i, D_{g^*,j} \oplus r_j)$. We argue that the distributions Hybrid_7 and Hybrid_8 are identical. Two cases arise:
  - $g^* \leq N - 1$: In this case, note that since r_{g^*} is not hardwired anywhere else, we have that the distribution r_{g^*} and $r_{g^*} \oplus f_{g^*}(D_{g^*,i} \oplus r_i D_{g^*,j} \oplus r_j)$ are both uniform and identical.
  - $g^* = N$: In this case, we have that $r_{g^*} = M(x) \oplus r'_{g^*}$ which is again identical to the distribution of r_{g^*} in Hybrid_8.

– Hybrid_9 – Hybrid_{11} : In this hybrid, we reverse the changes made in Hybrid_1 to Hybrid_3 except that we hardwire $\{\mathsf{out}_{g^*}, \mathsf{d}_{g^*}\}$ in $\mathsf{SimGate}$ and use it to generate $\widetilde{\mathsf{SC}}_{g^*}$.. The indistinguishability between Hybrid_8 to Hybrid_{11} follows in analogous manner to the indistinguishability between $\mathsf{Hybrid}_{\mathsf{conf}'}$ to Hybrid_3. Observe that Hybrid_{11} is distributed identically to $\mathsf{Hybrid}_{\mathsf{conf}}$.

This completes the proof of the lemma.

4.3.3 Completing the Hybrids

The strategy given in Lemma 3 yields a sequence of configurations $\mathsf{conf}_0 \ldots \mathsf{conf}_m$ for an appropriate polynomial m with $\mathsf{conf}_0 = (\emptyset, N)$ and $\mathsf{conf}_m = (\emptyset, n)$, where $\mathsf{Hybrid}_{\mathsf{conf}_{i-1}} \overset{c}{\approx} \mathsf{Hybrid}_{\mathsf{conf}_i}$ either using rule A (i.e., Lemma 4) or using rule B (i.e., Lemma 5). We now show that $\mathsf{Hybrid}_{\mathsf{conf}_m}$ is computationally indistinguishable to the ideal world distribution given by $\mathsf{Hybrid}_{(\emptyset,0)}$. This is argued using the security property of puncturable PRF using the key R and the security of $i\mathcal{O}$ as follows.

– Hybrid_1 : In this hybrid, we puncture the PRF key R at points $\{1, \ldots, n\}$ and hardwire it in $\mathsf{SimGate}$. Note that in $\mathsf{Hybrid}_{(\emptyset,n)}$, the function $\mathsf{SimGate}$ never uses the PRF key on inputs $\{1, \ldots, n\}$ and hence the functionality computed by the $\mathsf{SimGate}$ is exactly the same in this hybrid and $\mathsf{Hybrid}_{(\emptyset,n)}$. The computational indistinguishability follows from the security of $i\mathcal{O}$.
– Hybrid_2 : In this hybrid, we replace y_w with a random bit r_w for each $w \in [n]$. The computational indistinguishability between Hybrid_1 and Hybrid_2 follows from the security of puncturable PRF.
– Hybrid_3 : In this hybrid, we replace y_w with $\mathsf{PRF}_R(w)$ for every $w \in [n]$. The computational indistinguishability between Hybrid_2 and Hybrid_3 follows from the security of puncturable PRF.
– Hybrid_4 : In this hybrid, we reverse the change made in Hybrid_1 and the indistinguishability follows from the security of $i\mathcal{O}$. Notice that Hybrid_4 is distributed identically to $\mathsf{Hybrid}_{(\emptyset,\phi)}$.

Finally, the padding size ℓ is set to be maximum over the sizes of $\mathsf{SimGate}$ in every intermediate hybrid in the proof of Lemmas 4 and 5 and in the proof of indistinguishability between $\mathsf{Hybrid}_{(\emptyset,n)}$ and $\mathsf{Hybrid}_{(\emptyset,0)}$. This is observed to be $\mathsf{poly}(|M|, \log N, \lambda, n)$. This completes the proof of security.

References

[AIK04] Applebaum, B., Ishai, Y., Kushilevitz E.: Cryptography in NC^0. In: 45th Annual Symposium on Foundations of Computer Science, pages 166–175, Rome, Italy, 17–19 October 2004. IEEE Computer Society Press (2004)

[AJ15] Ananth, P., Jain, A.: Indistinguishability obfuscation from compact functional encryption. In: Gennaro, R., Robshaw, M. (eds.) CRYPTO 2015. LNCS, vol. 9215, pp. 308–326. Springer, Heidelberg (2015). https://doi.org/10.1007/978-3-662-47989-6_15

[AL18]   Ananth, P., Lombardi, A.: Succinct garbling schemes from functional encryption through a local simulation paradigm (2018 to appear in TCC). https://eprint.iacr.org/2018/759

[App17] Applebaum, B.: Garbled circuits as randomized encodings of functions: a primer. Cryptology ePrint Archive, Report 2017/385 (2017). http://eprint.iacr.org/2017/385

[BGI+12] Barak, B., et al.: On the (im)possibility of obfuscating programs. J. ACM **59**(2), 6 (2012)

[BGI14] Boyle, E., Goldwasser, S., Ivan, I.: Functional signatures and pseudorandom functions. In: Krawczyk, H. (ed.) PKC 2014. LNCS, vol. 8383, pp. 501–519. Springer, Heidelberg (2014). https://doi.org/10.1007/978-3-642-54631-0_29

[BGL+15] Bitansky, N., Garg, S., Lin, H., Pass, R., Telang, S.: Succinct randomized encodings and their applications. In: Servedio, R.A., Rubinfeld, R. (eds.) 47th Annual ACM Symposium on Theory of Computing, pp. 439–448, Portland, OR, USA, 14–17 June 2015. ACM Press (2015)

[BGT14] Bitansky, N., Garg, S., Telang, S.: Succinct randomized encodings and their applications. Cryptology ePrint Archive, Report 2014/771 (2014). http://eprint.iacr.org/2014/771

[BHR12] Bellare, M., Hoang, V.T., Rogaway, P.: Foundations of garbled circuits. In: Yu, T., Danezis, G., Gligor, V.D. (eds.) ACM CCS 12: 19th Conference on Computer and Communications Security, pp. 784–796, Raleigh, NC, USA, 16–18 October 2012. ACM Press (2012)

[BLSV18] Brakerski, Z., Lombardi, A., Segev, G., Vaikuntanathan, V.: Anonymous IBE, leakage resilience and circular security from new assumptions. In: Nielsen, J.B., Rijmen, V. (eds.) EUROCRYPT 2018. LNCS, vol. 10820, pp. 535–564. Springer, Cham (2018). https://doi.org/10.1007/978-3-319-78381-9_20

[BV15]   Bitansky, N., Vaikuntanathan, V.: Indistinguishability obfuscation from functional encryption. In: Guruswami, V. (ed.) 56th Annual Symposium on Foundations of Computer Science, pp. 171–190, Berkeley, CA, USA, 17–20 October 2015. IEEE Computer Society Press (2015)

[BW13]   Boneh, D., Waters, B.: Constrained pseudorandom functions and their applications. In: Sako, K., Sarkar, P. (eds.) ASIACRYPT 2013. LNCS, vol. 8270, pp. 280–300. Springer, Heidelberg (2013). https://doi.org/10.1007/978-3-642-42045-0_15

[CDG+17] Cho, C., Döttling, N., Garg, S., Gupta, D., Miao, P., Polychroniadou, A.: Laconic receiver oblivious transfer and applications, 2017, to appear in Crypto

[CHJV15] Canetti, R., Holmgren, J., Jain, A., Vaikuntanathan, V.: Succinct garbling and indistinguishability obfuscation for RAM programs. In: Servedio, R.A., Rubinfeld, R., (eds.) 47th Annual ACM Symposium on Theory of Computing, pp. 429–437, Portland, OR, USA, 14–17 June 2015. ACM Press (2015)

[DG17]   Döttling, N., Garg, S.: Identity based encryption from diffie-hellman assumptions. 2017, to appear in Crypto

[DGHM18] Döttling, N., Garg, S., Hajiabadi, M., Masny, D.: New constructions of identity-based and key-dependent message secure encryption schemes. In: Abdalla, M., Dahab, R. (eds.) PKC 2018. LNCS, vol. 10769, pp. 3–31. Springer, Cham (2018). https://doi.org/10.1007/978-3-319-76578-5_1

[GGH+13] Garg, S., Gentry, C., Halevi, S., Raykova, M., Sahai, A., Waters, B.: Candidate indistinguishability obfuscation and functional encryption for all circuits. In: 54th Annual Symposium on Foundations of Computer Science, pp. 40–49, Berkeley, CA, USA, 26–29 October 2013. IEEE Computer Society Press (2013)

[GGHR14] Garg, S., Gentry, C., Halevi, S., Raykova, M.: Two-round secure MPC from indistinguishability obfuscation. In: Lindell, Y. (ed.) TCC 2014. LNCS, vol. 8349, pp. 74–94. Springer, Heidelberg (2014). https://doi.org/10.1007/978-3-642-54242-8_4

[GGM86] Goldreich, O., Goldwasser, S., Micali, S.: How to construct random functions. J. ACM **33**(4), 792–807 (1986)

[GGSW13] Garg, S., Gentry, C., Sahai, A., Waters, B.: Witness encryption and its applications. In: Boneh, D., Roughgarden, T., Feigenbaum, J. (eds.) 45th Annual ACM Symposium on Theory of Computing, pp. 467–476, Palo Alto, CA, USA, 1–4 June 2013. ACM Press (2013)

[GPSZ17] Garg, S., Pandey, O., Srinivasan, A., Zhandry, M.: Breaking the subexponential barrier in obfustopia. In: Coron, J.-S., Nielsen, J.B. (eds.) EUROCRYPT 2017. LNCS, vol. 10212, pp. 156–181. Springer, Cham (2017). https://doi.org/10.1007/978-3-319-56617-7_6

[GS18a] Garg, S., Srinivasan, A.: Adaptively secure garbling with near optimal online complexity. IACR Cryptology ePrint Archive 2018/151 (2018)

[GS18b] Garg, S., Srinivasan, A.: A simple construction of io for turing machines. Cryptology ePrint Archive, Report 2018/771 (2018). https://eprint.iacr.org/2018/771

[HJO+16] Hemenway, B., Jafargholi, Z., Ostrovsky, R., Scafuro, A., Wichs, D.: Adaptively secure garbled circuits from one-way functions. In: Robshaw, M., Katz, J. (eds.) CRYPTO 2016. LNCS, vol. 9816, pp. 149–178. Springer, Heidelberg (2016). https://doi.org/10.1007/978-3-662-53015-3_6

[HW15] Hubacek, P., Wichs, D.: On the communication complexity of secure function evaluation with long output. In: Roughgarden, T. (ed.) ITCS 2015: 6th Innovations in Theoretical Computer Science, pp. 163–172, Rehovot, Israel, 11–13 January 2015. Association for Computing Machinery (2015)

[KLW15] Koppula, V., Lewko, A.B., Waters, B.: Indistinguishability obfuscation for turing machines with unbounded memory. In: Servedio, R.A., Rubinfeld, R. (eds.) 47th Annual ACM Symposium on Theory of Computing, pp. 419–428, Portland, OR, USA, 14–17 June 2015. ACM Press (2015)

[KPTZ13] Kiayias, A., Papadopoulos, S., Triandopoulos, N., Zacharias, T.: Delegatable pseudorandom functions and applications. In: 2013 ACM SIGSAC Conference on Computer and Communications Security, CCS 2013, Berlin, Germany, 4–8 November 2013, pp. 669–684 (2013)

[LP09] Lindell, Y., Pinkas, B.: A proof of security of Yao's protocol for two-party computation. J. Cryptol. **22**(2), 161–188 (2009)

[OPWW15] Okamoto, T., Pietrzak, K., Waters, B., Wichs, D.: New realizations of somewhere statistically binding hashing and positional accumulators. In: Iwata, T., Cheon, J.H. (eds.) ASIACRYPT 2015. LNCS, vol. 9452, pp. 121–145. Springer, Heidelberg (2015). https://doi.org/10.1007/978-3-662-48797-6_6

[PF79] Pippenger, N., Fischer, M.J.: Relations among complexity measures. J. ACM **26**(2), 361–381 (1979)

[SW14] Sahai, A., Waters, B.: How to use indistinguishability obfuscation: deniable encryption, and more. In: Symposium on Theory of Computing, STOC 2014, New York, NY, USA, 31 May–03 June 2014, pp. 475–484 (2014)

[Yao82] Yao, A.C.-C.: Protocols for secure computations (extended abstract). In: 23rd Annual Symposium on Foundations of Computer Science, pp. 160–164, Chicago, Illinois, 3–5 November 1982. IEEE Computer Society Press (1982)

[Yao86] Yao, A.C.-C.: How to generate and exchange secrets (extended abstract). In: 27th Annual Symposium on Foundations of Computer Science, Toronto, Ontario, Canada, 27–29 October 1986, pp. 162–167. IEEE Computer Society Press (1986)

Succinct Garbling Schemes from Functional Encryption Through a Local Simulation Paradigm

Prabhanjan Ananth$^{(\boxtimes)}$ and Alex Lombardi

MIT, Cambridge, USA
prabhanjan@csail.mit.edu, alexjl@mit.edu

Abstract. We study a simulation paradigm, referred to as *local simulation*, in garbling schemes. This paradigm captures simulation proof strategies in which the simulator consists of many local simulators that generate different blocks of the garbled circuit. A useful property of such a simulation strategy is that only a few of these local simulators depend on the input, whereas the rest of the local simulators only depend on the circuit.

We formalize this notion by defining locally simulatable garbling schemes. By suitably realizing this notion, we give a new construction of succinct garbling schemes for Turing machines assuming the polynomial hardness of compact functional encryption and standard assumptions (such as either CDH or LWE). Prior constructions of succinct garbling schemes either assumed sub-exponential hardness of compact functional encryption or were designed only for small-space Turing machines.

We also show that a variant of locally simulatable garbling schemes can be used to generically obtain adaptively secure garbling schemes for circuits. All prior constructions of adaptively secure garbling that use somewhere equivocal encryption can be seen as instantiations of our construction.

1 Introduction

Garbling schemes are ubiquitous to cryptography. Their notable applications include secure computation on the web [GHV10, HLP11], constructions of functional encryption [SS10, GVW12, GKP+12], one-time programs [GKR08], delegation of computation [GGP10, AIK10], and garbled RAMs [GHL+14, GLOS15]. In fact, there are many more applications under the umbrella of randomized encodings, which are implied by garbling schemes. These applications include parallel cryptography [AIK04, AIK06], bootstrapping theorems in functional encryption and indistinguishability obfuscation [ABSV15, App14a], and key-dependent message security [BHHI10, App14b]. More recently, garbling schemes

---

The full version of this paper is available at https://eprint.iacr.org/2018/759.

© International Association for Cryptologic Research 2018
A. Beimel and S. Dziembowski (Eds.): TCC 2018, LNCS 11240, pp. 455–472, 2018.
https://doi.org/10.1007/978-3-030-03810-6_17

were also crucially used to solve two longstanding open problems in cryptography: achieving two-round passively secure MPC [GS17,BL18,GS18c] and identity-based encryption from weaker assumptions [DG17,BLSV18,DGHM18].

A garbling scheme allows for efficiently encoding a circuit C, represented by $\langle C \rangle$ (also referred to as *garbled circuit*), and separately encoding an input x, represented by $\langle x \rangle$. We require that given $\langle C \rangle$ and $\langle x \rangle$, it is possible to efficiently recover $C(x)$ and moreover, the encodings should not leak anything beyond $(C, C(x))$[1]. This notion was first introduced by Yao [Yao82, Yao86] as a technique to solve two-party secure computation (a full proof of this application was only given much later by Lindell and Pinkas [LP09]). More than three decades later, proposing new constructions of garbling schemes is still an active and fascinating research direction.

While the traditional notion of garbling schemes considers encoding circuits, this notion can be generalized for other models of computation. In particular, we consider garbling *Turing machines*; this notion is often referred to as succinct garbling schemes [BGL+15, CHJV15, KLW15]. The non-triviality in this setting is to encode both the Turing machine M and the input x in time independent of the runtime of M. In more detail, we require that the time to garble a Turing machine M should be polynomial in λ (security parameter) and $|M|$ while the time to encode an input x should be polynomial in λ and $|x|$. For decoding, we require that it should only take time polynomial in λ and t to recover $M(x)$, where t is the runtime of M on x.

Succinct garbling schemes have been used in many applications including time-lock puzzles [BGJ+16], concurrent zero-knowledge [CLP15], indistinguishability obfuscation for Turing machines [BGL+15, CHJV15, KLW15] and delegation for deterministic computations [BGL+15, CHJV15, KLW15]. In terms of constructions, the initial works of [BGL+15, CHJV15] proposed succinct garbling schemes with the caveat that the size of the garbled Turing machine grows with the maximum space taken by the Turing machine during its execution. Subsequently, Koppula et al. [KLW15] showed how to get rid of this caveat and presented a construction of succinct randomized encodings (a notion where M and x are encoded together) assuming indistinguishability obfuscation and one-way functions.

It is worth noting that the approach taken by [BGL+15] differs substantially from the approach taken by [CHJV15, KLW15] to obtain succinct randomized encodings. The construction of [BGL+15] is very simple to describe: they succinctly garble a Turing machine M (running in time at most T) by outputting an obfuscated program that on input $i \leq T$ outputs the ith garbled table of a Yao garbled circuit [Yao82, Yao86, LP09] associated to a circuit C representing M's computation. One might hope that this already yields a fully succinct garbling scheme, but the security proof of [BGL+15] requires hardwiring $O(s)$ bits

---

[1] In this work, we only consider the case of hiding the input x. To hide the circuit C being garbled, we can garble an universal circuit with an encryption of C hardwired inside it and produce an input encoding of x along with the decryption key.

of information in the obfuscated program when M requires space s, so this does not yield a fully succinct garbling scheme (which [KLW15] does achieve).

While the final result has an undesirable dependence on s, the [BGL+15] approach has the advantage of relying only on obfuscation for circuits of input length $\log(T) = O(\log(\lambda))$ and hence can be proved secure assuming the existence of polynomially secure functional encryption [AJ15, BV15, LZ17, LT17]. The approach of [CHJV15, KLW15] does not share this property, and indeed there is currently no known construction of fully succinct garbling from (poly-secure) FE. In general, there are a few primitives (such as trapdoor permutations and non-interactive key exchange) known to follow from FE [GPS16, GS16, GPSZ17, LZ17] while many others (such as NIZK [SW14, BP15], deniable encryption [SW14], and long output secure function evaluation [HW15]) we know only how to construct from IO (see [LZ17] for a more detailed discussion). One of our main goals is to understand whether constructing succinct garbling schemes requires the full power of IO in this sense.

Rather intriguingly, the progress on succinct randomized encodings followed a similar pattern to progress on the problem of constructing adaptively secure circuit garbling schemes. There is a simple transformation [BHR12] from selectively secure garbling schemes to adaptively secure garbling schemes in which the online complexity (that is, the size of the input encoding) grows with the circuit size. Subsequent to [BHR12], the work of [HJO+16] showed how to achieve adaptive schemes with online complexity that only depends on the width w of the circuit (from one-way functions) or depth d of the circuit (from $2^{-O(d)}$ secure one-way functions). Following [HJO+16], the works of [JW16, JSW17] present additional constructions of adaptive circuit garbling schemes. Finally, a beautiful work of Garg and Srinivasan [GS18a] showed how to achieve adaptive garbling schemes with online complexity $|x| + \text{poly}(\log(|C|, \lambda)$ assuming either the computational Diffie-Hellman (CDH) or learning with errors (LWE) assumption.

We note that the measure of width complexity in the case of circuits is related to the measure of space complexity in the case of Turing machines. Indeed, we can transform a Turing machine M that requires space s on inputs of length n into a circuit of width $O(n+s)$; similarly, a circuit of width w can be simulated by a Turing machine which takes space at most $O(w)$. Moreover, there are actually major similarities between the *security proofs* of [HJO+16] (for their width-dependent adaptive garbling scheme) and [BGL+15] (for their space-dependent succinct garbling scheme). At a high level, both require opening up the [LP09] proof of security for Yao's garbling scheme and make use of the fact that security is argued by a gate-by-gate hybrid argument.

These similarities present the possibility of transporting some of the techniques from the adaptive garbling literature in order to construct new and improved succinct garbling schemes. In particular, we ask: can the ideas from [GS18a] be used to construct succinct garbling?

1.1   Our Contributions

We give a new construction of succinct garbling schemes using the ideas of [GS18a]. Unlike the work of [KLW15][2] based on sub-exponentially secure compact functional encryption, our construction is based on polynomially secure compact functional encryption and polynomially secure CDH/LWE. As an added advantage, our construction is conceptually simpler. Instead of using IO/FE to compress a Yao garbled circuit as in [BGL+15], we compress an appropriately modified [GS18a] garbled circuit.

To prove security, we identify a property, termed as *local simulation*, of selectively secure garbling schemes for circuits that when combined with other tools yields succinct garbling schemes. To describe this property, we first recall the security experiment of garbling schemes. To prove that a given garbling scheme is secure, one needs to exhibit a simulator with the following property: given just the circuit C and the output $C(x)$, it can output a simulated garbled circuit and input encoding that is indistinguishable from an honest garbled circuit and input encoding. Typically this indistinguishability is shown by a sequence of hybrids: in every step, a hybrid simulator is defined to take an input C and x produces the simulated garbling and input encoding. The first hybrid defines the honest garbling of C and the honest encoding of x, while the final hybrid defines the simulated distribution. At a bare minimum, our notion of local simulation captures a class of such hybrid arguments wherein the simulation of garbled circuit is divided into blocks and in every hybrid, only a *small L_{sim}*-sized subset of blocks are simulated using C and x while the rest are simulated only using C. We observe that this seemingly artificial property is already satisfied by current known schemes [Yao86, GS18a].

To make the local simulation notion useful for applications, we need to consider strengthenings of this notion. We formalize the above informal description of local simulation and call this **weak** local simulation; correspondingly the garbling scheme will be called a weak locally simulatable garbling scheme (weak LSGS). We consider two strengthenings: (i) **strong** locally simulatable garbling schemes (strong LSGS) and (ii) **semi-adaptive** locally simulatable garbling schemes (semi-adaptive LSGS). Both the notions of semi-adaptive LSGS and strong LSGS imply weak LSGS and will be parameterized by (L_{sim}, L_{inp}), where L_{inp} refers to the online complexity of the garbling scheme.

We now state our results on succinct garbling.

SUCCINCT GARBLING. We prove the following theorem.

---

[2] We note that [KLW15] construct succinct randomized encodings scheme and not garbling schemes. However, their construction can be adapted to get succinct garbling schemes.

Theorem 1. *(Main Theorem) Assuming single-key compact[3] public-key functional encryption for circuits[4] and X, where $X \in \{$Computational Diffie-Hellman, Factoring, Learning with Errors$\}$, there exists a succinct garbling scheme for Turing machines.*

Previous constructions of succinct garbling schemes were based on indistinguishability obfuscation[5] (implied by *sub-exponentially* secure compact functional encryption) and one-way functions [KLW15]. This is the first work to show the feasibility of succinct garbling schemes from falsifiable assumptions. Moreover, [KLW15] is significantly more involved whereas our construction is conceptually simpler. We note that several works subsequent to [KLW15] use their construction to achieve various primitives including garbled RAM [CH16, CCC+16, CCHR16, ACC+16], constrained PRFs for Turing machines [DKW16], indistinguishability obfuscation for Turing machines with constant overhead [AJS17a], patchable indistinguishability obfuscation [AJS17b, GP17] and so on. We hope that our simpler construction will correspondingly yield simpler presentation of these applications as well.

One new consequence of the above theorem is that we obtain collusion-resistant functional encryption for Turing machines from collusion-resistant functional encryption for circuits and standard assumptions; this follows from [AS16].

We prove Theorem 1 in two steps. First, we prove the following proposition.

Proposition 1 (Informal). *Assuming strong $(L_{\text{sim}}, L_{\text{inp}})$-LSGS and compact functional encryption for circuits, there exists a succinct garbling scheme in which the complexity of garbling a Turing machine M is $\text{poly}(\lambda, |M|, L_{\text{sim}})$ and the complexity of encoding x is $L_{\text{inp}}(\lambda, |x|, m)$, where m is the output length of M.*

Once we prove the above proposition, we show how to instantiate strong LSGS from laconic oblivious transfer[6] to obtain our result.

Proposition 2 (Informal). *Assuming laconic oblivious transfer, there exists a strong $(L_{\text{sim}}, L_{\text{inp}})$-LSGS with $L_{\text{sim}} = \text{poly}(\lambda)$.*

---

[3] From prior works [BV15, AJS15], we can replace compact public-key FE with collusion-resistant FE in the theorem statement.

[4] A public-key functional encryption scheme is a public-key encryption scheme with the additional key generation procedure that takes as input circuit C and produces a functional key for C that can be used to decrypt an encryption of x to obtain $C(x)$. A **compact** functional encryption is a functional encryption scheme where the complexity to encrypt a message x is a fixed polynomial in $(\lambda, |x|)$ and in particular, the encryption complexity grows only with $\log(|C|)$. A functional encryption scheme is a **single-key scheme** if it satisfies $\{\text{PK}, \text{Enc}(\text{PK}, x_0), sk_C\} \cong_c \{\text{PK}, \text{Enc}(\text{PK}, x_1), sk_C\}$ for an adversarially chosen C and x and specifically, the adversary is only issued a single key in the security experiment.

[5] See the full version for a formal definition.

[6] We actually use the existentially equivalent notion of *appendable laconic OT*, which we define in the full version.

Since laconic oblivious transfer can be instantiated from CDH, factoring, LWE and other assumptions [CDG+17,DG17,BLSV18,DGHM18], this proves Theorem 1. In addition, we note (in full version) that laconic OT[7] can be constructed from IO and one-way functions; combined with the above propositions, this says that our succinct garbling scheme can also be instantiated from IO and OWFs alone (giving an alternative construction to [KLW15]).

We note that the garbling scheme of Yao [Yao86] also yields a strong $(L_{\mathsf{sim}}, L_{\mathsf{inp}})$-LSGS with L_{sim} proportional to the width of the circuit being garbled. Combining this with Proposition 1, we get a succinct garbling scheme for small space Turing machines; this is essentially the same scheme as that of [BGL+15].

ADAPTIVE CIRCUIT GARBLING. Next, we show how to construct adaptive circuit garbling schemes using our notion of (semi-adaptive) LSGS. First, we recall the definition of adaptive circuit garbling schemes. In the adaptive security experiment, an adversary can submit the circuit C and the input x in any order; specifically, it can choose the input as a function of the garbled circuit or vice versa. We show,

Theorem 2 (Informal). *Assuming semi-adaptive $(L_{\mathsf{sim}}, L_{\mathsf{inp}})$-LSGS and one-way functions, there exists an adaptively secure circuit garbling scheme with online complexity $L_{\mathsf{inp}} + \mathrm{poly}(\lambda, L_{\mathsf{sim}})$.*

This theorem can be seen as an abstraction of what the somewhere equivocal encryption-based technique of [HJO+16] can accomplish. For example, the semi-adaptive LSGS can be instantiated from laconic oblivious transfer, recovering the result of [GS18a]. The theorem below follows from a previous work [GS18a].

Theorem 3 ([GS18a]). *Assuming laconic oblivious transfer, there exists a semi-adaptive $(L_{\mathsf{sim}}, L_{\mathsf{inp}})$-LSGS scheme with online complexity $L_{\mathsf{inp}}(\lambda, n, m) = n+m+ \mathrm{poly}(\lambda)$ and $L_{\mathsf{sim}} = \mathrm{poly}(\lambda)$, where n and m denote the input and output lengths for the circuit.*

We note that Yao's garbling scheme is also a semi-adaptive $(L_{\mathsf{sim}}, L_{\mathsf{inp}})$-LSGS with L_{sim} being proportional to the width of the circuit and thus, combining the above two theorems we get an adaptively secure circuit garbling scheme with the online complexity proportional to the width of the circuit. This construction is essentially the same as the width-based construction of [HJO+16], with a more modular security proof.

We summarise the results in Fig. 1.

1.2 Concurrent Work

In concurrent and independent work, Garg and Srinivasan [GS18b] give a construction of succinct randomized encodings from IO (and laconic OT)

---

[7] We can only achieve laconic OT satisfying selective security, which suffices for Proposition 2.

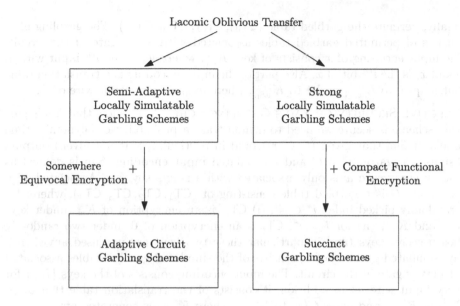

Fig. 1. Summary of results.

that implicitly relies on only IO for logarithmic length inputs, and hence polynomially-secure functional encryption. While their work is phrased differently from this work (in particular, they give a direct construction without considering the abstraction of local simulatability), the basic SRE constructions are essentially the same.

1.3 Technical Overview

We first recall the garbling scheme of Yao [Yao86] and describe an overview of its security proof. Yao's scheme will serve as a starting point to understanding the definition of locally simulatable garbling schemes.

Yao's Garbling Scheme [Yao86]. Consider a boolean circuit $C : \{0,1\}^\ell \to \{0,1\}$ comprising only of NAND gates. For ease of presentation, we assume that C is layered such that all gates that are at the same distance from the output gate belong to the same layer. Moreover, every intermediate wire in the circuit connects two gates in adjacent layers.

The first step in the garbling of a circuit C is to generate two wire keys K_w^0 and K_w^1 for every wire w in the circuit. Next, associate with every gate G a garbled table consisting of four entries $(\mathsf{CT}_{00}, \mathsf{CT}_{01}, \mathsf{CT}_{10}, \mathsf{CT}_{11})$. For $b_0, b_1 \in \{0,1\}$, $\mathsf{CT}_{b_0 b_1}$ is an encryption of $K_{w_c}^{\mathrm{NAND}(b_0, b_1)}$ under the two keys[8] $K_{w_a}^{b_0}$ and $K_{w_b}^{b_1}$. Wires w_a and w_b are input wires of G and w_c is the output wire of G.

---

[8] There are many ways of realizing an encryption scheme under two different secret keys. One convenient method is to secret share the message and encrypt the two shares using the two keys.

Finally, permute the garbled table $(\mathsf{CT}_{00}, \mathsf{CT}_{01}, \mathsf{CT}_{10}, \mathsf{CT}_{11})$. The garbling of C consists of permuted garbled tables associated with every gate in the circuit. The input encoding of x consists of keys $K_{w_i}^{x_i}$, where w_i is the ith input wire of C and x_i is the ith bit of x. Also part of the input encoding is a translation table that maps 0 to $K_{w_{\mathrm{out}}}^0$ and 1 to $K_{w_{\mathrm{out}}}^1$, where w_{out} is the output wire of C.

SELECTIVE SECURITY OF YAO'S GARBLING SCHEME: To show that Yao's garbling scheme is secure we need to demonstrate a probabilistic polynomial time simulator Sim that given $(C, C(x))$ (and in particular, x is not given) outputs a simulated garbling of C and a simulated input encoding. Sim is defined as follows: every wire w is only associated with a single key K_w. Associated with every gate G is a garbled table consisting of $(\mathsf{CT}_1, \mathsf{CT}_2, \mathsf{CT}_3, \mathsf{CT}_4)$, where: for a randomly picked index $i^* \in [4]$, (i) CT_{i^*} is an encryption of K_{w_c} under keys K_{w_a} and K_{w_b}, (ii) for $i \neq i^*$, CT_i is an encryption of 0 under two randomly chosen secret keys (and in particular these two keys are not used anywhere). The simulated garbling of C consists of the simulated garbled tables associated with every gate in the circuit. The input encoding consists of the keys $\{K_w\}$ for every input wire w. In addition, it consists of the translation table that maps $C(x)$ to $K_{w_{\mathrm{out}}}$ and maps $\overline{C(x)}$ to $K'_{w_{\mathrm{out}}}$, where $K'_{w_{\mathrm{out}}}$ is generated afresh.

The indistinguishability of the output of Sim from an honestly generated garbled circuit and input encoding can be argued by a hybrid argument explicitly described in [HJO+16]. This hybrid argument will be associated with a sequence of intermediate simulators $\mathsf{Sim}_1, \ldots, \mathsf{Sim}_q$. Except Sim_q, all the other simulators take as input circuit and the input; (C, x). The final simulator Sim_q takes as input $(C, C(x))$. Sim_1 computes the garbling of C and the input encoding of x as dictated by the scheme. The final intermediate simulator Sim_q is identical to Sim.

The ith intermediate simulator Sim_i works as follows: for every wire w such that w is the output wire of a jth layer for $j \geq i$, sample two keys K_w^0 and K_w^1. For any other wire w, sample a single wire key K_w. The simulator consists of two components:

- **Input-Dependent Simulation.** This component takes as input (C, x) and simulates all the garbled gates in the ith layer of C. For every gate G (with input wires w_a, w_b and output wire w_c) in the ith layer, generate a garbled table $(\mathsf{CT}_1, \mathsf{CT}_2, \mathsf{CT}_3, \mathsf{CT}_4)$, where for a randomly picked index $i^* \in [4]$, (i) CT_{i^*} is an encryption of $K_{w_c}^{\mathsf{val}(w_c)}$ under keys K_{w_a} and K_{w_b}, (ii) for $i \neq i^*$, CT_i is an encryption of 0 under two randomly chosen secret keys (and in particular these two keys are not used anywhere). Here, $\mathsf{val}(w_c)$ denotes the value assigned to the wire w_c during the evaluation of C on x.

- **Input-Independent Simulation.** This component only takes as input C and simulates the garbled gates in all the layers except the ith layer. There are two cases:
  - for a gate G in the jth layer, for $j < i$, the simulation of the garbled gate for G is performed according to Sim.
  - for a gate G in the jth layer, for $j > i$, the garbled gate for G is generated according to the scheme.

Once the computational indistinguishability of Sim_i and Sim_{i+1} is shown for every i, the security of the scheme follows.

Complexity of Input-Dependent Simulation. Observe that the output length of the input-dependent simulation component of every simulator Sim_i is only proportional to the width of the circuit (in other words, the maximum length of any layer in C). This observation has been crucially exploited in two lines of work:

- The work of [HJO+16] introduced the powerful tool of somewhere equivocal encryption (SEE) and showed how to combine it with the garbling scheme of Yao to obtain adaptive garbling schemes with online complexity that grows with the width of the circuit. Informally, somewhere equivocal encryption is used in conjunction with the above proof of security for Yao's scheme: in each step of a hybrid argument, the input-dependent simulated gates are equivocated in the online phase of the adaptive security game. Since the number of input-dependent simulated gates is bounded by the width w of the circuit, the online complexity of this garbling scheme is proportional to w. Alternative proof strategies for Yao's garbling scheme can be used instead of our sketch above to obtain, for example, the depth-based result of [HJO+16].
- The work of [BGL+15] showed how to combine indistinguishability obfuscation for circuits and the garbling scheme of Yao to obtain a succinct garbling scheme for small-space Turing machines. To garble a Turing machine M that has worst-case runtime T, they construct an obfuscation of a circuit that takes as input an index i and outputs the garbled table corresponding to the ith gate of C^9. Security is argued by sequentially invoking the simulators $(\mathsf{Sim}_1, \ldots, \mathsf{Sim}_q)$ of Yao's garbling scheme. Hardwiring the entire simulator's output in the obfuscated circuit would ruin the encoding complexity of the succinct garbling scheme. However, it turns out that security can be argued when only the *input-dependent* simulation component is hardwired. This is exactly the reason why the encoding complexity of this succinct garbling scheme grows with the maximum space complexity of the Turing machines.

Locally Simulatable Garbling Schemes. We introduce the notion of a locally simulatable garbling scheme as an abstraction that connects the above proofs of adaptive security and succinctness for garbling schemes. We give a brief overview of the security property associated with a locally simulatable garbling scheme. The security property is parameterized by an integer L_{sim} and a sequence of simulators $(\mathsf{Sim}_1, \ldots, \mathsf{Sim}_q)$ for some polynomial q. Every simulator Sim_i consists of an input-dependent component and an input-independent component.

- The input-dependent component of Sim_i takes as input circuit C and input x to be simulated. We require that this component of Sim_i is of size at most $L_{\mathsf{sim}} \cdot \mathsf{poly}(\lambda)$ for some fixed polynomial poly.
- The input-independent component of Sim_i takes as input only the circuit C.

---

[9] Their actual scheme instead outputs an entire layer of garbled tables at once, but this variant has the same efficiency and security proof.

We require that the output distribution of Sim_1 is computationally indistinguishable from an honest generated garbling of C and honestly generated encoding of x. The output distributions of Sim_i and Sim_{i+1} are required to be computationally indistinguishable. Finally, we require that the final simulator Sim_q does not have any input-dependent component and in particular, Sim_q can simulate the garbled circuit and input encoding on input $(C, C(x))$. We refer to this security property as *weak* local simulation security.

Note that Yao's garbling scheme, using the security proof given in our outline, is a particular instantiation of a locally simulatable garbling scheme with L_{sim} set to be the width of the circuit being garbled. The depth-based analysis of Yao's garbling scheme given in [HJO+16] can also be seen as an instantiation of weak local simulation, albeit with $q = 2^{O(d)}$ hybrids.

While the above security property captures the essence of local simulation, it does not suffice for either the application of adaptively secure garbling schemes or the application of succinct garbling schemes. To get around this, we strengthen the security definition in two ways, resulting in notions of **semi-adaptive** locally simulatable garbling schemes and **strong** locally simulatable garbling schemes.

Succinct Garbling from Strong LSGS. We define the notion of a strong locally simulatable garbling scheme and use it as an intermediate tool to construct a succinct garbling scheme. To motivate our definition, we will consider a candidate succinct garbling scheme (and proof strategy) from IO and a weak LSGS, and see what additional properties are required from the LSGS.

Generalizing the approach of [BGL+15], our candidate succinct garbling scheme is as follows: garbling a Turing machine M with a runtime bound T consists of computing an indistinguishability obfuscation of a circuit $H_{M,T,\mathsf{MSK}}$ with hardwired values M, T and a master secret key MSK. This circuit takes as input an index $i \leq T$, constructs the ith gate of C, where C is the circuit representing T steps of M's computation on inputs of length n, and then outputs a garbling of this gate computed with respect to MSK. Encoding x consists of computing the input encoding of x with respect to the LSGS. Decoding proceeds by evaluating the obfuscated circuit on all indices ranging from 1 to T to obtain the different gate encodings. These encodings are then decoded to obtain the result.

We are already implicitly assuming some properties of the underlying LSGS in order for the above construction to make any sense at all. Specifically,

- Our candidate implicitly assumes that a garbling of C is computed in a gate-by-gate fashion. To enable this, we introduce the notion of a local encoding of an LSGS, which guarantees that a garbling of C consists of components that are each computed in time independent of $|C|$; in particular, it must be computable from a small amount of information about C. In fact, we further require that this information about C is efficiently computable from M. In the case of Yao, this amounts to saying that an individual gate of C can be computed very efficiently from M.
- A priori, the master secret key MSK could be as large as $|C| = \mathrm{poly}(T)$. Strictly speaking, this means that the above candidate is not succinct. To

overcome this, we think of $\mathsf{MSK} = (sk_1, \ldots, sk_N)$ and define a *local key generation* procedure that takes as input an index j and only generates the local secret key sk_j. Then, the program H in our scheme takes as input an index i, determines the keys sk_j that are necessary to encode the ith component of C, and then computes the ith garbled component.

- To identify the subset of keys to be locally generated for the ith component, we define a *key list generation* procedure that takes as input i and outputs a list L_i. This allows us to compress the potentially large MSK using a pseudorandom function key.
- The size of the input encoding of the succinct garbling candidate is exactly the same as the online complexity of the underlying strong LSGS scheme. Thus, in order for our scheme to be succinct, the online complexity of the underling LSGS scheme will have to be independent of T.

By carefully defining the above notions, we can guarantee that the program H is sufficiently small (polynomial in λ) so that the candidate garbling scheme is succinct. What remains is to prove security in a way such that programs H' that are obfuscated in the security proof are also small. This is the most subtle step; in particular, this is the step where [BGL+15] is limited to achieving succinctness that depends on the space of the Turing machine.

To prove the security of the above scheme, a naive approach would be to hardwire the entire simulated garbled circuit inside the obfuscation of $H_{M,T,\mathsf{MSK}}$; however, this would violate succinctness. Instead, we want to leverage *local simulation* in the following way: in each of a sequence of hybrid circuits $(H_1, \ldots, H_q)$, only hardwire the *input-dependent* components of Sim_i, and instead include the code of the input-independent components of Sim_i (which naively contains all of MSK) inside H_i. We would then hope to argue using some combination of IO security and LSGS security that adjacent hybrid programs in this sequence are indistinguishable.

If the size of the input-dependent portion is small, meaning polynomial in λ, then we can hope to achieve succinctness using this proof strategy. This approach again implicitly assumes properties of the LSGS; namely, that the input-independent local simulators each require only a small portion of the master secret key (just as in the honest garbling case). This is required so that the hybrid circuit H_i is still small.

Unfortunately, the security argument above is flawed. The problem is that information about the master secret key MSK is contained within the obfuscated program $\tilde{H}$, so it is unclear how to argue that the input-dependent components of Sim_i and Sim_{i+1} (i.e. the components that are hardwired) are indistinguishable. Indeed, if the above strategy is not carefully implemented (e.g. if the program H_i actually reveals the entire MSK), they will be distinguishable.

To circumvent these issues, we require that the input-dependent portion of the garbled circuit output by Sim_i is indistinguishable from the corresponding input-dependent portion of the garbled circuit output by Sim_{i+1} *even in the presence of $\{sk_j\}_{j \in S}$, where S consists of all indices accessed by the* *input-independent portion of the garbled circuit.* In fact, we define a stronger property that allows the adversary to choose the keys $\{sk_j\}_{j \in S}$.

In order to complete the hybrid argument, our proof strategy then works in two steps: first switch the input-dependent components of the simulated circuit from Sim_i to Sim_{i+1} (using the above strong LSGS security), and then switch the input-independent components from Sim_i to Sim_{i+1}. Since we are actually including the code of these input-independent simulators within the obfuscated circuit, we must require that the input-independent components of Sim_i and Sim_{i+1} are functionally equivalent to invoke IO security.

To summarize, a strong LSGS must satisfy two main properties in order for the security of our succinct garbling scheme to be proved:

- The input-dependent components of Sim_i and Sim_{i+1} must be indistinguishable *even given* all of the local secret keys necessary to compute the input-independent components of Sim_i.
- The *algorithms* computing the input-independent components of Sim_i and Sim_{i+1} must be functionally equivalent.

Indeed, the security proof of [BGL+15] can be retroactively seen as invoking the above properties of Yao's garbling scheme. For completeness, we sketch a proof (see the full version) that Yao's garbling scheme satisfies this definition with L_{sim} proportional to the width of the circuit.

Constructing Strong LSGS from Laconic OT. In order to complete the proof of Theorem 1, we show that the garbling scheme of [GS18a] can be adapted to satisfy our strong LSGS notion with $L_{\mathsf{sim}} = \mathrm{poly}(\lambda)$. We begin by giving a high level description of the [GS18a] garbling scheme:

- An encoding of an input x consists of (1) a somewhere equivocal encryption secret key, (2) a one-time pad encryption $r \oplus x$ of x, (3) a hash value $h_0 = H(r \oplus x \| 0^{|C|-n})$ of an initial memory state for the computation, (4) a signature on h_0, and (5) the one-time pads corresponding to each output gate. The hash function H is associated to a laconic OT scheme (we omit a discussion of laconic OT from this overview).
- An encoding of a circuit C consists of $s = |C|$ "garbled programs" maintaining the following invariant: after executing i such programs, the evaluator will have obtained a one-time pad encryption of the first $n+i$ gates of C evaluated on the input x along with a hash of this one-time padded state and a signature on this hash value. The garbled programs are then jointly encrypted using a somewhere equivocal encryption scheme.
- Simulation security is argued by a sequence of hybrid simulators; in a hybrid simulator, each garbled program is either computed via an input-independent simulator or an input-dependent simulator, and moreover only $\mathrm{poly}(\lambda)$ garbled programs require input-dependent simulation. To prove adaptive security, the input-dependent simulated gates are equivocated as part of the input encoding.

We interpret the scheme of [GS18a] – after removing the somewhere equivocal encryption layer – as a LSGS by thinking of each garbled program above as one component of the LSGS. Indeed, we show that each garbled program in the [GS18a] scheme only requires a small amount of the garbling secret key and that the input-dependent components of Sim_i and Sim_{i+1} are indistinguishable even in the presence of adversarially chosen secret keys used for the other components. In fact, all but one of the properties of a strong LSGS as defined earlier can be demonstrated to hold for the [GS18a] scheme without modification.

The only problem with using the [GS18a] scheme as a strong LSGS is that computation of the initial hash value $H(r \oplus x || 0^{|C|-n})$ requires $O(|C|)$ time. Naively, this means that computing even the input encoding would take $O(|C|)$ time, but [GS18a] note that if H is computed via a Merkle tree, the computation of $H(0^{|C|-n})$ can be delegated to the garbled circuit and only $H(r \oplus x)$ need be computed during the input encoding. However, computing $H(0^{|C|-n})$ cannot be done locally (i.e. distributed in pieces to local components of the garbled circuit), which violates the local encoding property of a strong LSGS.

To circumvent this problem, we modify the [GS18a] scheme so that the initial hash value $h_0 = H(r \oplus x)$ is a hash of only an n-bit string, and we redesign the garbled programs so that each step updates the one-time padded computation state by *appending* the next value. Instantiating this corresponds to a new notion of *appendable laconic OT*, which we define and construct generically from laconic OT. The local simulators for our new scheme remain essentially the same, and our previous security proof carries over to this modified version. We note that the same modification could be made to the [GS18a] adaptive garbled circuit construction, with the advantage that the more complicated notion of *updatable laconic OT* is not required, and hence the [GS18a] scheme can be somewhat simplified.

Combining this construction of strong LSGS from laconic OT with our construction of succinct garbling from FE and strong LSGS, we obtain Theorem 1.

Adaptive Garbling from Semi-Adaptive LSGS. In order to construct adaptive garbling schemes, it turns out that the notion of strong LSGS does not capture the essence of the adaptive security proof. We define a notion of semi-adaptive LSGS and show that a semi-adaptive LSGS can be used to construct adaptive circuit garbling schemes. We define the notion below.

The semi-adaptive security property is associated with a sequence of simulators $(\mathsf{Sim}_1, \ldots, \mathsf{Sim}_q)$ for some polynomial $q = q(\lambda)$. As before, the output of Sim_i consists of an input-dependent component and an input-independent component. However, in this security definition, we allow the adversary to choose the input *after* he receives the input-*independent* component of the garbled circuit from the challenger. In particular, the adversary can choose the instance as a function of the input-independent component.

Our transformation from semi-adaptive LSGS to adaptive garbling is inspired by the work of [HJO+16]. In particular, our transformation abstracts out the usage of somewhere equivocal encryption in this and other prior works. In this transformation, the size of the input-dependent component (i.e. L_{sim}) determines the size of the secret key in a somewhere equivocal encryption scheme, and hence plays a role in determining the online complexity of the adaptive garbling scheme. The online complexity of the resulting adaptively secure garbling scheme is the sum of $\mathrm{poly}(\lambda, L_{\mathsf{sim}})$ and the online complexity L_{inp} of the semi-adaptive LSGS. This can be used to recover the result of [GS18a] (as well as that of [HJO+16]).

Acknowledgements. We thank Huijia Lin and Vinod Vaikuntanathan for useful discussions. We also thank the anonymous reviewers for their helpful feedback.

References

[ABSV15] Ananth, P., Brakerski, Z., Segev, G., Vaikuntanathan, V.: From selective to adaptive security in functional encryption. In: Gennaro, R., Robshaw, M. (eds.) CRYPTO 2015. LNCS, vol. 9216, pp. 657–677. Springer, Heidelberg (2015). https://doi.org/10.1007/978-3-662-48000-7_32

[ACC+16] Ananth, P., Chen, Y.-C., Chung, K.-M., Lin, H., Lin, W.-K.: Delegating RAM computations with adaptive soundness and privacy. In: Hirt, M., Smith, A. (eds.) TCC 2016. LNCS, vol. 9986, pp. 3–30. Springer, Heidelberg (2016). https://doi.org/10.1007/978-3-662-53644-5_1

[AIK04] Applebaum, B., Ishai, Y., Kushilevitz, E.: Cryptography in nc^0. In: Proceedings of 45th Symposium on Foundations of Computer Science (FOCS 2004), 17–19 October 2004, Rome, Italy, pp. 166–175 (2004)

[AIK06] Applebaum, B., Ishai, Y., Kushilevitz, E.: Computationally private randomizing polynomials and their applications. Comput. Complex. **15**(2), 115–162 (2006)

[AIK10] Applebaum, B., Ishai, Y., Kushilevitz, E.: From secrecy to soundness: efficient verification via secure computation. In: Abramsky, S., Gavoille, C., Kirchner, C., Meyer auf der Heide, F., Spirakis, P.G. (eds.) ICALP 2010. LNCS, vol. 6198, pp. 152–163. Springer, Heidelberg (2010). https://doi.org/10.1007/978-3-642-14165-2_14

[AJ15] Ananth, P., Jain, A.: Indistinguishability obfuscation from compact functional encryption. In: Gennaro, R., Robshaw, M. (eds.) CRYPTO 2015. LNCS, vol. 9215, pp. 308–326. Springer, Heidelberg (2015). https://doi.org/10.1007/978-3-662-47989-6_15

[AJS15] Ananth, P., Jain, A., Sahai, A.: Indistinguishability obfuscation from functional encryption for simple functions. Eprint **730**, 2015 (2015)

[AJS17a] Ananth, P., Jain, A., Sahai, A.: Indistinguishability obfuscation for turing machines: constant overhead and amortization. In: Katz, J., Shacham, H. (eds.) CRYPTO 2017. LNCS, vol. 10402, pp. 252–279. Springer, Cham (2017). https://doi.org/10.1007/978-3-319-63715-0_9

[AJS17b] Ananth, P., Jain, A., Sahai, A.: Patchable indistinguishability obfuscation: $i\mathcal{O}$ for evolving software. In: Coron, J.-S., Nielsen, J.B. (eds.) EUROCRYPT 2017. LNCS, vol. 10212, pp. 127–155. Springer, Cham (2017). https://doi.org/10.1007/978-3-319-56617-7_5

[App14a] Applebaum, B.: Bootstrapping obfuscators via fast pseudorandom functions. In: Sarkar, P., Iwata, T. (eds.) ASIACRYPT 2014. LNCS, vol. 8874, pp. 162–172. Springer, Heidelberg (2014). https://doi.org/10.1007/978-3-662-45608-8_9

[App14b] Applebaum, B.: Key-dependent message security: generic amplification and completeness. J. Cryptol. **27**(3), 429–451 (2014)

[AS16] Ananth, P., Sahai, A.: Functional encryption for turing machines. In: Kushilevitz, E., Malkin, T. (eds.) TCC 2016. LNCS, vol. 9562, pp. 125–153. Springer, Heidelberg (2016). https://doi.org/10.1007/978-3-662-49096-9_6

[BGJ+16] Bitansky, N., Goldwasser, S., Jain, A., Paneth, O., Vaikuntanathan, V., Waters, B.: Time-lock puzzles from randomized encodings. In: Proceedings of the 2016 ACM Conference on Innovations in Theoretical Computer Science, pp. 345–356. ACM (2016)

[BGL+15] Bitansky, N., Garg, S., Lin, H., Pass, R., Telang, S.: Succinct randomized encodings and their applications. In: STOC (2015)

[BHHI10] Barak, B., Haitner, I., Hofheinz, D., Ishai, Y.: Bounded key-dependent message security. In: Gilbert, H. (ed.) EUROCRYPT 2010. LNCS, vol. 6110, pp. 423–444. Springer, Heidelberg (2010). https://doi.org/10.1007/978-3-642-13190-5_22

[BHR12] Bellare, M., Hoang, V.T., Rogaway, P.: Foundations of garbled circuits. In: Proceedings of the 2012 ACM Conference on Computer and Communications Security, pp. 784–796. ACM (2012)

[BL18] Benhamouda, F., Lin, H.: k-round multiparty computation from k-round oblivious transfer via garbled interactive circuits. In: Nielsen, J.B., Rijmen, V. (eds.) EUROCRYPT 2018. LNCS, vol. 10821, pp. 500–532. Springer, Cham (2018). https://doi.org/10.1007/978-3-319-78375-8_17

[BLSV18] Brakerski, Z., Lombardi, A., Segev, G., Vaikuntanathan, V.: Anonymous IBE, leakage resilience and circular security from new assumptions. In: Nielsen, J.B., Rijmen, V. (eds.) EUROCRYPT 2018. LNCS, vol. 10820, pp. 535–564. Springer, Cham (2018). https://doi.org/10.1007/978-3-319-78381-9_20

[BP15] Bitansky, N., Paneth, O.: ZAPs and non-interactive witness indistinguishability from indistinguishability obfuscation. In: Dodis, Y., Nielsen, J.B. (eds.) TCC 2015. LNCS, vol. 9015, pp. 401–427. Springer, Heidelberg (2015). https://doi.org/10.1007/978-3-662-46497-7_16

[BV15] Bitansky, N., Vaikuntanathan, V.: Indistinguishability obfuscation from functional encryption. In: 2015 IEEE 56th Annual Symposium on Foundations of Computer Science (FOCS), pp. 171–190. IEEE (2015)

[CCC+16] Chen, Y.-C., Chow, S.S.M., Chung, K.-M., Lai, R.W.F., Lin, W.-K., Zhou, H.-S.: Cryptography for parallel ram from indistinguishability obfuscation. In: Proceedings of the 2016 ACM Conference on Innovations in Theoretical Computer Science, pp. 179–190. ACM (2016)

[CCHR16] Canetti, R., Chen, Y., Holmgren, J., Raykova, M.: Adaptive succinct garbled RAM or: how to delegate your database. In: Hirt, M., Smith, A. (eds.) TCC 2016. LNCS, vol. 9986, pp. 61–90. Springer, Heidelberg (2016). https://doi.org/10.1007/978-3-662-53644-5_3

[CDG+17] Cho, C., Döttling, N., Garg, S., Gupta, D., Miao, P., Polychroniadou, A.: Laconic oblivious transfer and its applications. In: Katz, J., Shacham, H. (eds.) CRYPTO 2017. LNCS, vol. 10402, pp. 33–65. Springer, Cham (2017). https://doi.org/10.1007/978-3-319-63715-0_2

[CH16] Canetti, R., Holmgren, J.: Fully succinct garbled ram. In: Proceedings of the 2016 ACM Conference on Innovations in Theoretical Computer Science, pp. 169–178. ACM (2016)

[CHJV15] Canetti, R., Holmgren, J., Jain, A., Vaikuntanathan, V.: Indistinguishability obfuscation of iterated circuits and RAM programs. In: STOC (2015)

[CLP15] Chung, K.-M., Lin, H., Pass, R.: Constant-round concurrent zero-knowledge from indistinguishability obfuscation. In: Gennaro, R., Robshaw, M. (eds.) CRYPTO 2015. LNCS, vol. 9215, pp. 287–307. Springer, Heidelberg (2015). https://doi.org/10.1007/978-3-662-47989-6_14

[DG17] Döttling, N., Garg, S.: Identity-based encryption from the diffie-hellman assumption. In: Katz, J., Shacham, H. (eds.) CRYPTO 2017. LNCS, vol. 10401, pp. 537–569. Springer, Cham (2017). https://doi.org/10.1007/978-3-319-63688-7_18

[DGHM18] Döttling, N., Garg, S., Hajiabadi, M., Masny, D.: New constructions of identity-based and key-dependent message secure encryption schemes. In: Abdalla, M., Dahab, R. (eds.) PKC 2018. LNCS, vol. 10769, pp. 3–31. Springer, Cham (2018). https://doi.org/10.1007/978-3-319-76578-5_1

[DKW16] Deshpande, A., Koppula, V., Waters, B.: Constrained pseudorandom functions for unconstrained inputs. In: Fischlin, M., Coron, J.-S. (eds.) EUROCRYPT 2016. LNCS, vol. 9666, pp. 124–153. Springer, Heidelberg (2016). https://doi.org/10.1007/978-3-662-49896-5_5

[GGP10] Gennaro, R., Gentry, C., Parno, B.: Non-interactive verifiable computing: outsourcing computation to untrusted workers. In: Rabin, T. (ed.) CRYPTO 2010. LNCS, vol. 6223, pp. 465–482. Springer, Heidelberg (2010). https://doi.org/10.1007/978-3-642-14623-7_25

[GHL+14] Gentry, C., Halevi, S., Lu, S., Ostrovsky, R., Raykova, M., Wichs, D.: Garbled RAM revisited. In: Nguyen, P.Q., Oswald, E. (eds.) EUROCRYPT 2014. LNCS, vol. 8441, pp. 405–422. Springer, Heidelberg (2014). https://doi.org/10.1007/978-3-642-55220-5_23

[GHV10] Gentry, C., Halevi, S., Vaikuntanathan, V.: i-hop homomorphic encryption and rerandomizable yao circuits. In: Rabin, T. (ed.) CRYPTO 2010. LNCS, vol. 6223, pp. 155–172. Springer, Heidelberg (2010). https://doi.org/10.1007/978-3-642-14623-7_9

[GKP+12] Goldwasser, S., Kalai, Y.T., Popa, R.A., Vaikuntanathan, V., Zeldovich, N.: Succinct functional encryption and applications: Reusable garbled circuits and beyond. IACR Cryptology ePrint Archive, 2012:733 (2012)

[GKR08] Goldwasser, S., Kalai, Y.T., Rothblum, G.N.: One-time programs. In: Wagner, D. (ed.) CRYPTO 2008. LNCS, vol. 5157, pp. 39–56. Springer, Heidelberg (2008). https://doi.org/10.1007/978-3-540-85174-5_3

[GLOS15] Garg, S., Lu, S., Ostrovsky, R., Scafuro, A.: Garbled ram from one-way functions. In: Proceedings of the Forty-Seventh Annual ACM on Symposium on Theory of Computing, pp. 449–458. ACM (2015)

[GP17] Garg, S., Pandey, O.: Incremental program obfuscation. In: Katz, J., Shacham, H. (eds.) CRYPTO 2017. LNCS, vol. 10402, pp. 193–223. Springer, Cham (2017). https://doi.org/10.1007/978-3-319-63715-0_7

[GPS16] Garg, S., Pandey, O., Srinivasan, A.: Revisiting the cryptographic hardness of finding a nash equilibrium. In: Robshaw, M., Katz, J. (eds.) CRYPTO 2016. LNCS, vol. 9815, pp. 579–604. Springer, Heidelberg (2016). https://doi.org/10.1007/978-3-662-53008-5_20

[GPSZ17] Garg, S., Pandey, O., Srinivasan, A., Zhandry, M.: Breaking the subexponential barrier in obfustopia. In: Coron, J.-S., Nielsen, J.B. (eds.) EUROCRYPT 2017. LNCS, vol. 10212, pp. 156–181. Springer, Cham (2017). https://doi.org/10.1007/978-3-319-56617-7_6

[GS16] Garg, S., Srinivasan, A.: Single-key to multi-key functional encryption with polynomial loss. In: Hirt, M., Smith, A. (eds.) TCC 2016. LNCS, vol. 9986, pp. 419–442. Springer, Heidelberg (2016). https://doi.org/10.1007/978-3-662-53644-5_16

[GS17] Garg, S., Srinivasan, A.: Garbled protocols and two-round MPC from bilinear maps. In: FOCS 2017 (2017)

[GS18a] Garg, S., Srinivasan, A.: Adaptively secure garbling with near optimal online complexity. In: Nielsen, J.B., Rijmen, V. (eds.) EUROCRYPT 2018. LNCS, vol. 10821, pp. 535–565. Springer, Cham (2018). https://doi.org/10.1007/978-3-319-78375-8_18

[GS18b] Garg, S., Srinivasan, A.: A simple construction of iO for turing machines. In: Beimel, A., Dziembowski, S. (eds.) TCC 2018. LNCS, vol. 11240, pp. 425–454. Springer, Cham (2018)

[GS18c] Garg, S., Srinivasan, A.: Two-round multiparty secure computation from minimal assumptions. In: Nielsen, J.B., Rijmen, V. (eds.) EUROCRYPT 2018. LNCS, vol. 10821, pp. 468–499. Springer, Cham (2018). https://doi.org/10.1007/978-3-319-78375-8_16

[GVW12] Gorbunov, S., Vaikuntanathan, V., Wee, H.: Functional encryption with bounded collusions via multi-party computation. In: Safavi-Naini, R., Canetti, R. (eds.) CRYPTO 2012. LNCS, vol. 7417, pp. 162–179. Springer, Heidelberg (2012). https://doi.org/10.1007/978-3-642-32009-5_11

[HJO+16] Hemenway, B., Jafargholi, Z., Ostrovsky, R., Scafuro, A., Wichs, D.: Adaptively secure garbled circuits from one-way functions. In: Robshaw, M., Katz, J. (eds.) CRYPTO 2016. LNCS, vol. 9816, pp. 149–178. Springer, Heidelberg (2016). https://doi.org/10.1007/978-3-662-53015-3_6

[IILP11] Halevi, S., Lindell, Y., Pinkas, B.: Secure computation on the web: computing without simultaneous interaction. In: Rogaway, P. (ed.) CRYPTO 2011. LNCS, vol. 6841, pp. 132–150. Springer, Heidelberg (2011). https://doi.org/10.1007/978-3-642-22792-9_8

[HW15] Hubacek, P., Wichs, D.: On the communication complexity of secure function evaluation with long output. In: Proceedings of the 2015 Conference on Innovations in Theoretical Computer Science, pp. 163–172. ACM (2015)

[JSW17] Jafargholi, Z., Scafuro, A., Wichs, D.: Adaptively indistinguishable garbled circuits. In: Kalai, Y., Reyzin, L. (eds.) TCC 2017. LNCS, vol. 10678, pp. 40–71. Springer, Cham (2017). https://doi.org/10.1007/978-3-319-70503-3_2

[JW16] Jafargholi, Z., Wichs, D.: Adaptive security of yao's garbled circuits. In: Hirt, M., Smith, A. (eds.) TCC 2016. LNCS, vol. 9985, pp. 433–458. Springer, Heidelberg (2016). https://doi.org/10.1007/978-3-662-53641-4_17

[KLW15] Koppula, V., Lewko, A.B., Waters, B.: Indistinguishability obfuscation for turing machines with unbounded memory. In: STOC (2015)

[LP09] Lindell, Y., Pinkas, B.: A proof of security of yao's protocol for two-party computation. J. Cryptol. 22(2), 161–188 (2009)

[LT17] Lin, H., Tessaro, S.: Indistinguishability obfuscation from trilinear maps and block-wise local PRGs. In: Katz, J., Shacham, H. (eds.) CRYPTO 2017. LNCS, vol. 10401, pp. 630–660. Springer, Cham (2017). https://doi.org/10.1007/978-3-319-63688-7_21

[LZ17] Liu, Q., Zhandry, M.: Exploding obfuscation: a framework for building applications of obfuscation from polynomial hardness. IACR Cryptology ePrint Archive 2017:209 (2017)

[SS10] Sahai, A., Seyalioglu, H.: Worry-free encryption: functional encryption with public keys. In: Proceedings of the 17th ACM Conference on Computer and Communications Security, pp. 463–472. ACM (2010)

[SW14] Sahai, A., Waters, B.: How to use indistinguishability obfuscation: deniable encryption, and more. In: Shmoys, D.B. (ed.) Symposium on Theory of Computing, STOC 2014, New York, NY, USA, May 31–June 03 2014, pp. 475–484. ACM (2014)

[Yao82] Yao, A.C.: Protocols for secure computations. In: 1982 23rd Annual Symposium on Foundations of Computer Science, SFCS 2008, pp. 160–164. IEEE (1982)

[Yao86] Yao, A.C.-C.: How to generate and exchange secrets (extended abstract). In: FOCS, pp. 162–167 (1986)

FE and iO for Turing Machines
from Minimal Assumptions

Shweta Agrawal[✉] and Monosij Maitra

IIT Madras, Chennai, India
shweta.a@cse.iitm.ac.in, monosij@cse.iitm.ac.in

Abstract. We construct Indistinguishability Obfuscation (iO) and
Functional Encryption (FE) schemes in the Turing machine model from
the minimal assumption of compact FE for circuits (CktFE). Our constructions overcome the barrier of sub-exponential loss incurred by all
prior work. Our contributions are:

1. We construct iO in the Turing machine model from the same assumptions as required in the circuit model, namely, sub-exponentially
   secure FE for circuits. The previous best constructions [6,41] require
   sub-exponentially secure iO for circuits, which in turn requires sub-
   exponentially secure FE for circuits [5,15].
2. We provide a new construction of single input FE for Turing machines
   with unbounded length inputs and optimal parameters from *polynomially* secure, compact FE for circuits. The previously best known
   construction by Ananth and Sahai [7] relies on iO for circuits, or
   equivalently, sub-exponentially secure FE for circuits.
3. We provide a new construction of multi-input FE for Turing
   machines. Our construction supports a fixed number of encryptors
   (say k), who may each encrypt a string $\mathbf{x}_i$ of *unbounded* length. We
   rely on sub-exponentially secure FE for circuits, while the only previous construction [10] relies on a strong knowledge type assumption,
   namely, public coin differing inputs obfuscation.

Our techniques are new and from first principles, and avoid usage of
sophisticated iO specific machinery such as positional accumulators and
splittable signatures that were used by all relevant prior work [6,7,41].

1 Introduction

The notion of indistinguishability obfuscation (iO) [11] seeks to garble programs
such that the obfuscations of any two functionally equivalent programs are indistinguishable. While non-obvious at first what such a guarantee is good for,
iO has emerged as a surprisingly powerful notion in cryptography, leading to
many advanced cryptographic applications that were previously out of reach
[12,14,22–24,26,27,41,44,46,50].

Functional encryption (FE) [16,48,49] is a generalization of public key encryption that enables fine grained access control on encrypted data. In FE, a secret
key corresponds to a function f and ciphertexts correspond to strings from the

© International Association for Cryptologic Research 2018
A. Beimel and S. Dziembowski (Eds.): TCC 2018, LNCS 11240, pp. 473–512, 2018.
https://doi.org/10.1007/978-3-030-03810-6_18

domain of f. Given a function key SK_f and a ciphertext $\mathsf{CT_x}$, the decryptor learns $f(\mathbf{x})$ and nothing else.

While an important primitive in its own right, FE has also been shown to imply iO, albeit with sub-exponential loss [5,15]. Over the last few years, both primitives have received significant attention, with a rich body of work that attempts to support more general models of computation [4,12,20–22,25,41], rely on weaker assumptions [8,13,19,30,37–40,42,43,45], achieve stronger security [3,19] and greater efficiency [6].

In this work, we make further progress towards the goal of basing iO and FE on minimal assumptions, in the Turing machine model of computation. This question has been studied extensively [4,6,7,12,20–22,25,34,41] – we refer the reader to [6,7] for a detailed discussion. Below, we summarize the state of art:

1. iO for Turing Machines with unbounded memory and bounded inputs are constructed in the works of Koppula et al. and Ananth et al. [6,41]. Both works rely on the existence of sub-exponentially secure iO for circuits along with other standard assumptions. We note that FE for circuits implies iO with sub-exponential loss, so when relying on FE for circuits, these works incur double sub-exponential loss.
2. For *single input* FE for Turing machines that accept unbounded length inputs and place no restriction on the description size or space complexity of the machine, the state of art is the work of Ananth and Sahai [7], which relies on the existence of iO for circuits.
3. For *multi-input* FE in the Turing machine model, the only known construction is [10], which relies on the existence of public coin differing inputs obfuscation (diO).

Our Results. We construct Indistinguishability Obfuscation (iO) and Functional Encryption (FE) schemes in the Turing machine model from the minimal assumption of compact FE for circuits (CktFE). Our constructions overcome the barrier of sub-exponential loss incurred by all prior work. Our contributions are:

1. We construct iO for Turing machines with bounded inputs and unbounded memory from the same assumptions as required by iO for circuits, namely, sub-exponentially secure FE for circuits. The previous best constructions [6, 41] require sub-exponentially secure iO for circuits, which in turn requires sub-exponentially secure FE for circuits [5,15], resulting in double sub-exponential loss.
2. We provide a new construction of single input FE for Turing machines with unbounded inputs, achieving optimal parameters from *polynomially* secure, compact FE for circuits. The previously best known construction by Ananth and Sahai [7] relies on iO for circuits, or equivalently, sub-exponentially secure FE for circuits. We note that iO for circuits implies decomposable compact FE for circuits [27] (please see the full version [1]), so our construction also implies FE for TMs from iO for circuits.

3. We provide a new construction of multi-input FE for Turing machines. Our construction supports a fixed number of encryptors (say k), who may each encrypt a string $\mathbf{x}_i$ of *unbounded* length. We rely on sub-exponentially secure FE for circuits, while the only previous construction [10] relies on a strong knowledge type assumption, namely, public coin differing inputs obfuscation. The arity k supported by our scheme depends on the underlying multi-input CktFE scheme, for instance using [40], we can support $k = \mathsf{polylog}(\lambda)$.

Our constructions make use of FE for circuits that satisfy a mild property called *decomposablity*, which in turn can be constructed generically from FE for circuits (please see Appendix A). Decomposable FE, analogously to decomposable randomized encodings [9], roughly posits that a long string be encrypted bit by bit using shared randomness across bits. This property is already satisfied by all known constructions of CktFE in the literature to the best of our knowledge.

Our techniques are new and from first principles, and avoid usage of sophisticated iO specific machinery such as positional accumulators and splittable signatures that were used by all prior work [6,7,41]. Our work leverages the security notion of distributional indistinguishability (DI) for CktFE which was first considered by [31], who provided a construction for single input FE satisfying DI security assuming the existence of iO. We strengthen this result by constructing DI secure CktFE from standard CktFE. Please see Fig. 1 for an overview of our results.

Additional Prior Work. Since iO is considered an inherently sub-exponential assumption and much stronger than the polynomial assumption of compact FE, replacing iO by FE in cryptographic constructions has already been studied extensively, for instance in the context of PPAD hardness [28], multi-input FE for circuits [19,40] as well as trapdoor one-way permutations and universal samplers [29]. We note that aside from reliance on weaker, better understood assumptions, avoiding sub-exponential loss results in significantly more efficient schemes. We refer the reader to [29] for a detailed discussion.

Distributional indistinguishability was also considered in the context of output compressing randomized encodings [44]; indeed, this work implies that achieving DI security for FE for Turing machines with *long* outputs is impossible in the plain model. We note that our construction sidesteps this lower bound by considering Turing machines with a single output bit.

iO for TMs with unbounded memory has been constructed by [6,41] as discussed above, other prior works were limited to bounded space constraints. We note that [6] additionally achieve constant overhead in the size of the obfuscated program as well as amortization, which we do not consider in this work. We also note that the work of [10] achieve miFE for TMs where the number of encrypting parties can be arbitrary, whereas we only support a-priori fixed, bounded number of parties.

The approach of using decomposable FE for circuits to construct FE for deterministic finite automata (DFA) in the *single key* setting was suggested by [2]. In this work we develop and significantly generalize their ideas. In particular, we handle the unbounded key setting in FE for TMs which necessitates dealing with the much more complex indistinguishability style definition, for which we develop new proof techniques which use a novel "sliding trapdoor" approach and leverage distributional indistinguishability. In contrast, since [2] use simulation security for single key FE, their proof must not contend with any of these challenges. Please see below for details.

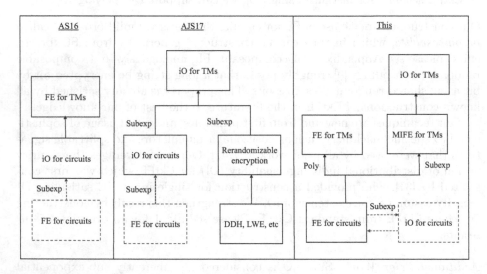

Fig. 1. Prior work and our results. The reductions with subexponential loss are specified, no specification implies standard polynomial loss. The dashed blue lines indicate primitives that are not actually used by the work in question; we add these to elucidate the relationship between primitives. We do not include [10] here since it relies on public coin diO.

Our Techniques. We describe an overview of our constructions, starting with single input FE, generalizing to multi-input FE and then building iO. All our constructions support the Turing machine model of computation. Our constructions rely on a single input FE scheme for *circuits*, denoted by CktFE, which satisfies *decomposability*. In Appendix A, we show that decomposable FE for circuits is implied by FE for circuits. Intuitively, decomposability means that the ciphertext CT_x for a multi-bit message $\mathbf{x}$ be decomposable into multiple ciphertext components CT_i for $i \in |\mathbf{x}|$, one for each bit x_i of the message. Moreover, the ciphertext components encoding individual bits of a single input are tied together by common randomness, that is $CT_i = \mathcal{E}(PK, r, x_i)$ where $\mathcal{E}$ is an encoding function and r is common randomness used for all $i \in |\mathbf{x}|$[1]. The notion of decomposability has been widely studied and used in the context of randomized encodings, which may be seen as a special case of functional encryption; please see [9] as an example.

---

[1] Encoding of each bit may also use additional independent randomness, which is not relevant to the discussion here, and hence omitted.

Single Input. TMFE. Recall that a Turing machine at any time step reads a symbol, state pair and produces a new symbol which is written to the work tape, a new state and a left or right head movement. By assuming the Turing machine is *oblivious*, the head movements of the TM may be fixed; thus, at any given time step when a work tape cell is read, we can compute the next time step when the same work tape cell will be accessed. This reduces the output at any time step t to a symbol, state pair, where the state is read in the next time step $t+1$ and the symbol is read at a future (fixed) time step $t' > t$.

Our construction uses two CktFE schemes, $1FE_1$ and $1FE_2$, where $1FE_2$ is decomposable. Intuitively, $1FE_1$ is used by the encryptor to encode the unbounded length input, while $1FE_2$ is used to mimic the computation of the Turing machine, as we describe next. The ciphertext of $1FE_2$ is divided into two parts, encoding input components (t, σ) and q respectively. Here, t is the current time step in the computation and σ, q are the current work-tape symbol and state respectively. We maintain the invariant that at any time step t in the computation, both components of the ciphertext have been computed using common randomness derived from $PRF_K((t\|salt))$, where salt is an input chosen by the key generator and the PRF key K is chosen by the encryptor.

Now, to mimic the TM computation, we provide a function key for the Next functionality, that stores the transition table, receives as input the current (symbol, state) pair, computes the symbol to be written on the work tape and the next state using the transition table, derives the randomness using the PRF for the appropriate time step and outputs the encodings of the new (symbol, state) pair. In more detail, say the encryptor provides encodings of each input symbol x_i, for $i \in [\|\mathbf{x}\|]$, in addition to an encoding for the first (fixed) state q_{st}, where the encodings of $(1, x_1)$ and q_{st} share the same randomness so that they may be concatenated to yield a complete ciphertext for $(1, x_1, q_{st})$. Now, the function key may read input $(1, x_1, q_{st})$, lookup the transition table and produce an encryption of the next state q_2 and the symbol to be written x_2'. The randomness used to encrypt q_2 is derived using a PRF as described above, and is the *same* as the randomness used by the encryptor to encode $(2, x_2)$. Hence, the two ciphertext components encoding $(2, x_2)$ and q_2 may be concatenated to yield a complete $1FE_2$ ciphertext which may be again decrypted using the function key.

Now consider how to support writing on tape. Say the symbol x_2' will be read at future fixed time step t'. Then the function key encodes the tuple (t', x_2') using randomness $PRF_K((t'\|salt))$. The state for time step t', say q' is computed at time step $t' - 1$, also using randomness $PRF_K((t'\|salt))$. Thus, encodings of (t', x_2') and q' may be joined together to yield a complete $1FE_2$ ciphertext which may be decrypted to propagate the computation.

A detail brushed away by the above description is that the encryptor, given input $\mathbf{x}$, cannot compute randomness generated by a PRF which has input a value salt chosen by the key generator. This is handled by making use of an additional scheme $1FE_1$, which re-encrypts ciphertexts provided by the encryptor via a ReRand functionality, using the requisite randomness. Note that we support inputs of unbounded length by leveraging the fact that CktFE schemes $1FE_1$, $1FE_2$

support encryption of unbounded *number* of inputs, even if each must be of bounded length. Thus, the encryptor provides an unbounded number of $1FE_1$ ciphertexts which are rerandomized and translated to ciphertexts under $1FE_2$ using the ReRand function key provided by the key generator.

Encoding the PRF key. The above informal description hides an important detail – for the function key to produce ciphertext components using a PRF, it must have the key of the PRF, chosen by the encryptor[2], passed to it as input. Thus the ciphertext must additionally encode the PRF key along with inputs (t, x, q). However, the ciphertext is constructed using randomness derived from the same PRF- resulting in circularity. We resolve this difficulty by using *constrained* PRFs [17,18,36], and having a ciphertext encode a PRF key that only allows computation of randomness for time steps *of the future*; this does not compromise its own security. For this constraint family, we provide a construction of cPRFs from standard assumptions. We believe this construction and the method of its application may be useful elsewhere[3].

More formally, our construction makes use of constrained, delegatable PRF for the function family $f_t : \{0,1\}^{2\cdot\lambda} \to \{0,1\}$ defined as follows.

$$f_t(x\|z) = 1 \quad if \ \ x \geq t$$
$$= 0 \quad otherwise$$

We denote the constrained PRF key K_{f_t} by K_t for brevity. By the delegation property of constrained PRFs, we have that if $t' \geq t$ then $K_{t'}$ can be derived from K_t. The proof requires the PRF to be punctured at a fixed point in each hybrid, we provide a construction of delegatable punctured PRF in the full version of the paper [1].

Proof Overview. While the above description of single input TMFE is natural and intuitive, the proof of indistinguishability based security is quite subtle and requires new techniques as we discuss next. For ease of exposition, we describe the proof overview for the case where the adversary makes a single key request corresponding to some TM M. We must argue that the challenge ciphertext, which is a sequence of $1FE_1$ ciphertexts, together with ReRand and Next keys corresponding to a TM M, do not distinguish the bit b.

As discussed above, the $1FE_1$ ciphertexts are decrypted using the ReRand key to produce a sequence of $1FE_2$ ciphertexts, each corresponding to a time step in the TM execution (when the encoded symbol is read), which are in turn decrypted by Next keys to compute new $1FE_2$ ciphertexts for future time steps. We may view the $1FE_2$ ciphertexts as forming a chain, with each link of the chain corresponding to a single step of the TM computation, and each ciphertext producing (via decryption) a new ciphertext for the next time step,

---

[2] Note that the PRF key must be encoded in the ciphertext rather than function key since it is required to be hidden.

[3] For instance, a similar situation w.r.t circularity arises in the original garbled RAM construction of Lu and Ostrovsky [47].

finally yielding the output when the TM halts (after T steps, say). Intuitively, since the output of the TM does not distinguish the bit b by admissibility of the TMFE adversary, we may argue by security of $1FE_2$ that the ciphertext at the penultimate step $T-1$ also does not distinguish b, which implies that the ciphertext at step $T-2$ hides b and so on, ultimately yielding indistinguishability of the entire chain, and hence of the $1FE_1$ challenge ciphertext.

Formalizing this intuitive argument is quite tricky. A natural approach would be to consider a sequence of hybrids, one corresponding to each link in the chain, and switch the $1FE_2$ ciphertexts one by one starting from the end of the chain. While intuitive, this idea is misleading – note that a naive implementation of this idea would lead to a chain which is "broken": namely, its first links correspond to $b=0$, and last links to $b=1$. Since the ciphertext at a given step is decrypted to compute the ciphertext at the next step, a ciphertext corresponding to $b=0$ cannot in general output a ciphertext for $b=1$.

A standard approach to deal with this difficulty is to embed a "trapdoor" mode within the functionality [3,5,19] which lets us "hardwire" the ciphertexts that must be output by decryption directly in the key, allowing decryption to yield an inconsistent chain. However, this approach also fails in our case, since the length of the chain is unbounded and there isn't sufficient space in the key to incorporate all its values.

Our Approach: "Sliding" Trapdoors. We deal with this difficulty by designing a novel "sliding-window" trapdoor approach which lets us hardwire the decryption chain "piece by piece". In more detail, we start with the last two time steps ($T, T-1$), program the key to produce the output corresponding to $b=1$ for time step T and $b=0$ for $T-1$, then transition to a world where the output corresponds to $b=1$ for both T and $T-1$. At this point, the hardwiring of the output for time step T is redundant, since the ciphertext output by the decryption process at time step $T-1$ automatically computes the output coresponding to $b=1$ at time step T. Thus, we may now *slide* the trapdoor to program to the next pair ($T-1, T-2$), switching the decryption output at time step $T-2$ to $b=1$ and so on, until the entire chain corresponds to $b=1$.

Intuitively, we are "programming" the decryption only for outputs at both ends of the "broken link", so that preceding links are generated using $b=0$ and subsequent links are generated using $b=1$. We leverage the fact that the chain links corresponding to future time-steps are encoded *implicitly* in a given time step – hence if we manage to hide the chain inconsistency at a certain position i, this implies that the remainder of the chain is constructed using the bit encoded at step i. Formalizing this argument requires a great deal of care, as we must keep track of the "target" time steps corresponding to the two ends of the broken link that are being programmed, the time steps at which the symbol and state ciphertexts are generated to be "consumed" at the target time-steps, the particular values that must be encoded in the symbol, state fields in both cases as well as the key that is being handled at a given time in the proof. For more details, please see Sect. 3.3.

Generalising to Multi-input FE for Turing Machines. For the k party setting, a natural idea is to have each party encrypt its own input $\mathbf{x}_i$, and use a k input CktFE scheme kFE [19,40], to "aggregate" these into the "input" ciphertext $\mathsf{CT}(\mathbf{x})$ for one long input $\mathbf{x} = (\mathbf{x}_1 \| \mathbf{x}_2 \| \dots \| \mathbf{x}_k)$, under a different CktFE scheme 1FE. Note that the length of $\mathbf{x}$ is unknown hence it may not be encoded "all at once" but must be encoded bit by bit as in the previous scheme. Now, by additionally providing the 1FE ciphertext encoding the start state of the Turing machine $\mathsf{CT}(\mathsf{q_{st}})$, and a function key to compute the transition table of the TM as in the previous scheme, we may proceed with the computation exactly as before.

Formalizing this idea must contend with several hurdles. In the multi-input setting, the ith encryptor may encode multiple inputs and functionality permits "mix and match" of ciphertexts in the sense that any input encoded by party i may be combined with any input encoded by parties $j \in [k]$, $j \neq i$. Therefore, if each of k parties encodes T ciphertexts, there are T^k valid input combinations that the TM may execute on. However, when the TM is executing on any input combination, we must ensure that it cannot mix and match symbol, state pairs across different input combinations. Moreover, an encryption for a symbol, state pair produced by some machine M_i should not be decryptable by any machine M_j for $j \neq i$. These issues are handled by careful design of the aggregate functionality to ensure that an execution thread of any input combination by any machine is separate from any other. The proof extends naturally from the single input case. Please see Sect. 4 for details.

Distributional Indistinguishability. As discussed above, our constructions rely on the security notion of *distributional indistinguishability* (DI) for functional encryption for circuits [31]. Intuitively, this notion says that if the outputs produced by a circuit on two input distributions are merely indistinguishable (as against exactly equal), then the ciphertexts encoding those inputs must also be indistinguishable. In the full version [1] we give a construction of DI secure single input FE from standard FE.

Indistinguishability Obfuscation. Constructing iO for TMs given miFE for TM is straightforward, and adapts the miFE to iO circuit compiler by [33] to the TM setting. As in the circuit case, an miFE for TM that supports two ciphertext queries and single key query suffices for this transformation. Please see Sect. 5 for details. Since our security proof for miFE for TM is tight, this compiler yields iO for TM from sub-exponentially secure FE for circuits rather than sub-exponentially secure iO for circuits.

Organization of the Paper. Definitions and preliminaries are provided in Sect. 2 as well as the full version [1]. In Sect. 3, we provide our construction for single input FE for Turing machines. In Sect. 4, we provide our construction for multi-input FE for Turing machines for any fixed arity k and in Sect. 5 we describe our iO for TMs for bounded inputs.

2 Preliminaries

In this section, we define some notation and preliminaries that we require.

Notation. We begin by defining the notation that we will use throughout the paper. We use bold letters to denote vectors and the notation $[a, b]$ to denote the set of integers $\{k \in \mathbb{N} \mid a \leq k \leq b\}$. We use $[n]$ to denote the set $[1, n]$. Concatenation is denoted by the symbol $\|$.

We say a function $f(n)$ is *negligible* if it is $O(n^{-c})$ for all $c > 0$, and we use $\mathrm{negl}(n)$ to denote a negligible function of n. We say $f(n)$ is *polynomial* if it is $O(n^c)$ for some $c > 0$, and we use $\mathrm{poly}(n)$ to denote a polynomial function of n. We use the abbreviation PPT for probabilistic polynomial-time. We say an event occurs with *overwhelming probability* if its probability is $1 - \mathrm{negl}(n)$. The function $\log x$ is the base 2 logarithm of x.

2.1 Definitions: FE for Circuits

In this section, we define functional encryption for circuits, in both the single and multi-input setting.

Single Input Functional Encryption for Circuits. Let $\mathcal{X} = \{\mathcal{X}_\lambda\}_{\lambda \in \mathbb{N}}$ and $\mathcal{Y} = \{\mathcal{Y}_\lambda\}_{\lambda \in \mathbb{N}}$ denote ensembles where each $\mathcal{X}_\lambda$ and $\mathcal{Y}_\lambda$ is a finite set. Let $\mathcal{F} = \{\mathcal{F}_\lambda\}_{\lambda \in \mathbb{N}}$ denote an ensemble where each $\mathcal{F}_\lambda$ is a finite collection of circuits, and each circuit $f \in \mathcal{F}_\lambda$ takes as input a string $\mathbf{x} \in \mathcal{X}_\lambda$ and outputs $f(\mathbf{x}) \in \mathcal{Y}_\lambda$.

A functional encryption scheme CktFE for $\mathcal{F}$ consists of four algorithms CktFE = (CktFE.Setup, CktFE.Keygen, CktFE.Enc, CktFE.Dec) defined as follows.

- CktFE.Setup(1^λ) is a PPT algorithm that takes as input the unary representation of the security parameter and outputs the master public and secret keys (PK, MSK). Sometimes, the CktFE.Setup algorithm may also accept as input a parameter 1^ℓ, denoting the length of the input. In this case, the input lives in domain $\mathcal{X}^\ell$.
- CktFE.Keygen(MSK, f) is a PPT algorithm that takes as input the master secret key MSK and a circuit $f \in \mathcal{F}_\lambda$ and outputs a corresponding secret key SK_f.
- CktFE.Enc(PK, $\mathbf{x}$) is a PPT algorithm that takes as input the master public key PK and an input message $\mathbf{x} \in \mathcal{X}_\lambda$ and outputs a ciphertext CT.
- CktFE.Dec(SK_f, $\mathsf{CT}_\mathbf{x}$) is an (a deterministic) algorithm that takes as input the secret key SK_f and a ciphertext $\mathsf{CT}_\mathbf{x}$ and outputs $f(\mathbf{x})$.

Definition 1 (Correctness). *A functional encryption scheme CktFE is correct if for all $\lambda \in \mathbb{N}$, all $f \in \mathcal{F}_\lambda$ and all $x \in \mathcal{X}_\lambda$,*

$$\Pr\left[\begin{array}{l}(\mathsf{PK}, \mathsf{MSK}) \leftarrow \mathsf{CktFE.Setup}(1^\lambda); \\ \mathsf{CktFE.Dec}\big(\mathsf{CktFE.Keygen}(\mathsf{MSK}, f), \mathsf{CktFE.Enc}(\mathsf{PK}, \mathbf{x})\big) \neq f(\mathbf{x})\end{array}\right] = \mathrm{negl}(\lambda)$$

where the probability is taken over the coins of CktFE.Setup, CktFE.Keygen, and CktFE.Enc.

Definition 2 (Compactness [5]). *A functional encryption scheme for circuits is said to be compact if for any input message* **x**, *the running time of the encryption algorithm is polynomial in the security parameter and the size of* **x**. *In particular, it does not depend on the circuit description size or the output length of any function f supported by the scheme.*

A weaker version of compactness, known as **succinct** or semi-compact FE, allows the run time of the encryption algorithm to depend on the output length of the functions. Equivalently, a semi-compact FE scheme is simply a compact FE scheme when we restrict our attention to functions with single-bit outputs.

Distributional Indistinguishability for Circuit FE. In this section we define the notion of distributional indistinguishability for functional encryption for circuits. The notion was first defined by [31, Sect. 3.4] in the context of reusable garbled circuits, i.e. single key functional encryption but may be generalized to the multi-key setting in a straightforward way. Intuitively, this notion says that if the outputs produced by a circuit on two input distributions are indistinguishable, then the ciphertexts encoding those inputs must also be indistinguishable.

Definition 3. *A functional encryption scheme $\mathcal{F}$ for a circuit family $\mathcal{G}$ is secure in the distributional indistinguishability game, if for all* PPT *adversaries $\mathcal{A}$, the advantage of $\mathcal{A}$ in the following experiment is negligible in the security parameter λ:*

1. *Public Key: Challenger returns* PK *to the adversary.*
2. *Pre-Challenge Key Queries: $\mathcal{A}$ may adaptively request keys for any circuits $g_i \in \mathcal{G}$. In response, $\mathcal{A}$ is given the corresponding keys SK_{g_i}. This step may be repeated any polynomial number of times by the attacker.*
3. *Challenge Declaration: $\mathcal{A}(1^\lambda, \mathsf{PK})$ outputs two ensembles of challenge distributions $\big(D_0(\lambda), D_1(\lambda)\big)^4$ to the challenger, subject to the restriction that for any $\mathbf{x}_0 \leftarrow D_0, \mathbf{x}_1 \leftarrow D_1$, it holds that $g_i(\mathbf{x}_0) \overset{c}{\approx} g_i(\mathbf{x}_1)$ for all i.*
4. *Challenge CT: $\mathcal{A}$ requests the challenge ciphertext, to which challenger chooses a random bit b, samples $\mathbf{x}_b \leftarrow D_b$ and returns the ciphertext $\mathsf{CT}_{\mathbf{x}_b}$.*
5. *Key Queries: The adversary may continue to request keys for additional functions g_i, subject to the same restriction that for any $\mathbf{x}_0 \leftarrow D_0, \mathbf{x}_1 \leftarrow D_1$, it holds that $g_i(\mathbf{x}_0) \overset{c}{\approx} g_i(\mathbf{x}_1)$ for all i.*
6. *$\mathcal{A}$ outputs a bit b', and succeeds if $b' = b$.*

The advantage of $\mathcal{A}$ is the absolute value of the difference between its success probability and $1/2$. In the selective game, the adversary is required to declare the challenge distributions in the very first step, without seeing the public key.

Comparison with Standard Indistinguishability. We note that the standard indistinguishably game is implied by the above by restricting the adversary to choose distributions D_0, D_1 above to simply be two messages $\mathbf{x}_0, \mathbf{x}_1$ with probability 1 and requesting keys that satisfy $g_i(\mathbf{x}_0) = g_i(\mathbf{x}_1)$ for all i, which is a special case of $g_i(\mathbf{x}_0) \overset{c}{\approx} g_i(\mathbf{x}_1)$.

---

[4] We omit the parameter λ in what follows for brevity of notation.

Decomposable Functional Encryption for Circuits. In this section, we recall the notion of *decomposable functional encryption* (DFE) defined by [2]. Decomposable functional encryption is analogous to the notion of decomposable randomized encodings [9]. Intuitively, decomposability requires that the public key PK and the ciphertext $CT_\mathbf{x}$ of a functional encryption scheme be decomposable into components PK_i and CT_i for $i \in [|\mathbf{x}|]$, where CT_i depends on a single deterministic bit x_i and the public key component PK_i. In addition, the ciphertext may contain components that are independent of the message and depend only on the randomness.

Formally, let $\mathbf{x} \in \{0,1\}^k$. A functional encryption scheme is said to be decomposable if there exists a deterministic function $\mathcal{E} : \mathcal{P} \times \{0,1\} \times \mathcal{R}_1 \times \mathcal{R}_2 \to \mathcal{C}$ such that:

1. The public key may be interpreted as $PK = (PK_1, \ldots, PK_k, PK_{\text{indpt}})$ where $PK_i \in \mathcal{P}$ for $i \in [k]$. The component $PK_{\text{indpt}} \in \mathcal{P}^j$ for some $j \in \mathbb{N}$.
2. The ciphertext may be interpreted as $CT_\mathbf{x} = (CT_1, \ldots, CT_k, CT_{\text{indpt}})$, where

$$CT_i = \mathcal{E}\left(PK_i, x_i, r, \hat{r}_i\right) \forall i \in [k] \quad \text{and} \quad CT_{\text{indpt}} = \mathcal{E}\left(PK_{\text{indpt}}, r, \hat{r}\right)$$

Here $r \in \mathcal{R}_1$ is common randomness used by all components of the encryption. Apart from the common randomness r, each CT_i may additionally make use of independent randomness $\hat{r}_i \in \mathcal{R}_2$.

We note that if a scheme is decomposable "bit by bit", i.e. into k components for inputs of size k, it is also decomposable into components corresponding to any partition of the interval $[k]$. Thus, we may decompose the public key and ciphertext into any $i \leq k$ components of length k_i each, such that $\sum k_i = k$. We will sometimes use $\bar{\mathcal{E}}(\mathbf{y})$ to denote the tuple of function values obtained by applying $\mathcal{E}$ to each component of a vector, i.e. $\bar{\mathcal{E}}(PK, \mathbf{y}, r) \triangleq \left(\mathcal{E}(PK_1, y_1, r, \hat{r}_1), \ldots, \mathcal{E}(PK_k, y_k, r, \hat{r}_k)\right)$, where $|\mathbf{y}| = k$. We assume that given the security parameter, the spaces $\mathcal{P}$, $\mathcal{R}_1$, $\mathcal{R}_2$, $\mathcal{C}$ are fixed, and the length of the message $|\mathbf{x}|$ can be any polynomial.

Multi-input Functional Encryption for Circuits. We define the notion of private-key t-input functional encryption for circuits here. Our definition follows that of [40].

Let $\forall i \in [t], \mathcal{X}_i = \{(\mathcal{X}_i)\}_{\lambda \in \mathbb{N}}$ and $\mathcal{Y} = \{\mathcal{Y}_\lambda\}_{\lambda \in \mathbb{N}}$ be ensembles of finite sets, and let $\mathcal{F} = \{\mathcal{F}_\lambda\}_{\lambda \in \mathbb{N}}$ be an ensemble of finite t-ary function families. For each $\lambda \in \mathbb{N}$, each function $f \in \mathcal{F}_\lambda$ takes as input t strings, $\mathbf{x}_1 \in (\mathcal{X}_1)_\lambda, \ldots, \mathbf{x}_t \in (\mathcal{X}_t)_\lambda$, and outputs a value $f(\mathbf{x}_1, \ldots, \mathbf{x}_t) \in \mathcal{Y}_\lambda$.

A private-key t-input functional encryption scheme t-CktFE for $\mathcal{F}$ consists of four algorithms t-CktFE $=$ (t-CktFE.Setup, t-CktFE.Keygen, t-CktFE.Enc, t-CktFE.Dec) defined as follows.

- t-CktFE.Setup(1^λ) is a PPT algorithm that takes as input the unary representation of the security parameter and outputs the master secret key MSK.
- t-CktFE.Keygen(MSK, f) is a PPT algorithm that takes as input the master secret key MSK and a circuit $f \in \mathcal{F}_\lambda$ and outputs a corresponding secret key SK_f.
- t-CktFE.Enc(MSK, $\mathbf{m}$, ind) is a PPT algorithm that takes as input the master secret key MSK, an input message $\mathbf{m} = \mathbf{x}_i \in (\mathcal{X}_i)_\lambda$ if ind $= i, i \in [t]$, and outputs a ciphertext $\mathsf{CT}_{\mathsf{ind}}$.
- t-CktFE.Dec(SK_f, ($\mathsf{CT}_1, \ldots, \mathsf{CT}_t$)) is an (a deterministic) algorithm that takes as input the secret key SK_f and t ciphertexts $\mathsf{CT}_1, \ldots, \mathsf{CT}_t$ and outputs a string $y \in \mathcal{Y}_\lambda \cup \perp$.

Definition 4 (Correctness). *A private-key t-input functional encryption scheme t-CktFE is correct if for all $\lambda \in \mathbb{N}$, $f \in \mathcal{F}_\lambda$ and all $(\mathbf{x}_1, \ldots, \mathbf{x}_t) \in (\mathcal{X}_1)_\lambda \times \ldots \times (\mathcal{X}_t)_\lambda$,*

$$\Pr\left[\begin{array}{l} t\text{-CktFE.Dec}\Big(t\text{-CktFE.Keygen(MSK}, f), \big(t\text{-CktFE.Enc(MSK}, \mathbf{x}_1, 1), \ldots, \\ t\text{-CktFE.Enc(MSK}, \mathbf{x}_t, t)\big)\Big) \neq f(\mathbf{x}_1, \ldots, \mathbf{x}_t) \end{array}\right] = \mathsf{negl}(\lambda)$$

Here, MSK $\leftarrow t$-CktFE.Setup(1^λ) and probability is taken over the random coins of t-CktFE.Setup, t-CktFE.Enc and t-CktFE.Keygen.

Distributional Indistinguishability. We define the notion of distributional indistinguishability for a t-input functional encryption scheme for circuits. To begin, we describe a valid t-input adversary.

Definition 5 (Valid t-Input Adversary). *A PPT algorithm $\mathcal{A}$ is a valid t-input adversary if for all private-key t-input functional encryption schemes over message space $(\mathcal{X}_1)_\lambda \times \ldots \times (\mathcal{X}_t)_\lambda$, and a circuit space $\mathcal{F}$, for any (f_0, f_1) queried by the adversary, and any t pairs of input distribution ensembles $(D_{01}(\lambda), D_{11}(\lambda)), \ldots, (D_{0t}(\lambda), D_{1t}(\lambda))$[5] output by the adversary such that D_{bj} is a distribution over $\mathcal{X}_j$ for $b \in \{0, 1\}$, $j \in [t]$, it holds that*

$$f_0(\mathbf{x}_{01}, \ldots, \mathbf{x}_{0t}) \stackrel{c}{\approx} f_1(\mathbf{x}_{11}, \ldots, \mathbf{x}_{1t}),$$

where $\mathbf{x}_{bj} \leftarrow D_{bj}$ for $b \in \{0, 1\}$, $j \in [t]$.

We define the following game between a challenger and an adversary:

1. **Key Queries.** $\mathcal{A}$ may adaptively submit key requests for pairs of functions $(f_0, f_1) \in \mathcal{F}$. In response, $\mathcal{A}$ is given the corresponding keys SK_{f_b} for some random bit b chosen by the challenger. This step may be repeated any polynomial number of times by the attacker.

---

[5] We omit the argument λ where it is implicit for notational brevity.

2. **Ciphertext Queries.** $\mathcal{A}(1^\lambda)$ submits ciphertext requests for pairs of challenge distribution ensembles $(D_{01}, D_{11}), \ldots, (D_{0t}, D_{1t})$ to the challenger. The challenger samples $\mathbf{x}_j \leftarrow D_{bj}$ for $j \in [t]$ and returns $t\text{-CktFE.Enc}(\text{MSK}, \mathbf{x}_j, j), \forall j \in [t]$. This step may be repeated any polynomial number of times by the attacker.
3. **Guess.** $\mathcal{A}$ outputs a bit b', and succeeds if $b' = b$.

In the above definition, ciphertext and key queries may be interspersed in any order. The *advantage* of $\mathcal{A}$ is the absolute value of the difference between its success probability and $1/2$. In the *selective* game, the adversary is required to declare the challenge ciphertext distributions in the very first step, without seeing the public key.

Definition 6. *A t-input functional encryption scheme t-CktFE for a circuit family $\mathcal{F}$ is secure in the distributional indistinguishability game, if for all valid PPT adversaries $\mathcal{A}$, the advantage of $\mathcal{A}$ in the above game is negligible in the security parameter λ.*

We note that the standard indistinguishability game is the special case where the adversary submits challenge messages rather than distributions and all queried functions must output exactly the same rather than indistinguishable values.

2.2 Definitions: FE for Turing Machines

In this section, we will define functional encryption for Turing Machines (TM). We denote the runtime (i.e. number of steps the head takes) by $\text{runtime}(M, \mathbf{w})$.

Let $\mathcal{M} = \{\mathcal{M}_\lambda\}_{\lambda \in \mathbb{N}}$ be a family of Turing machines with alphabet $\Sigma = \{\Sigma_\lambda\}_{\lambda \in \mathbb{N}}$ and the running time upper-bounded by a polynomial in λ. A functional encryption scheme TMFE for a Turing machine family $\mathcal{M}$ consists of four algorithms TMFE = (TMFE.Setup, TMFE.KeyGen, TMFE.Enc, TMFE.Dec) defined as follows.

- TMFE.Setup(1^λ) is a PPT algorithm that takes as input the unary representation of the security parameter and outputs the master public and secret keys (PK, MSK).
- TMFE.KeyGen(MSK, M) is a PPT algorithm that takes as input the master secret key MSK and a TM M and outputs a corresponding secret key SK_M.
- TMFE.Enc(PK, $\mathbf{x}$) is a PPT algorithm that takes as input the master public key PK, and an input message $\mathbf{x} \in \Sigma_\lambda^*$ of arbitrary length, outputs a ciphertext $\text{CT}_\mathbf{x}$.
- TMFE.Dec(SK_M, $\text{CT}_\mathbf{x}$) is an (a deterministic) algorithm that takes as input the secret key SK_M and a ciphertext $\text{CT}_\mathbf{x}$ and outputs a bit b.

Correctness is defined analogously to the circuit setting.

Efficiency [7]. The efficiency property of a public-key FE scheme for Turing machines says that the algorithm TMFE.Setup on input 1^λ should run in time polynomial in λ, TMFE.KeyGen on input the Turing machine M and the master key MSK should run in time polynomial in $(\lambda, |M|)$, TMFE.Enc on input a message $\mathbf{x}$ and the public key should run in time polynomial in $(\lambda, |\mathbf{x}|)$. Finally, TMFE.Dec on input a functional key of M and an encryption of $\mathbf{x}$ should run in time polynomial in $(\lambda, |M|, |\mathbf{x}|, \mathsf{runtime}(M, \mathbf{x}))$.

The multi-input case may be defined as in the circuit setting.

Indistinguishability Obfuscation for Turing Machines. As in prior work, we construct iO for Turing machines (TMs) in the setting where the input length is fixed a-priori. A uniform P.P.T machine iO is an indistinguishability obfuscator for a class of Turing machines $\{\mathcal{M}_\lambda\}_{\lambda \in \mathbb{N}}$ with input length L, if the following conditions are satisfied:

1. **Correctness.** For all security parameters $\lambda \in \mathbb{N}$, for any $M \in \mathcal{M}_\lambda$ and every input $\mathbf{x} \in \{0,1\}^{\leq L}$, we have that:

$$\Pr\left[M' \leftarrow \mathsf{iO}(1^\lambda, M, L) : M'(\mathbf{x}) = M(\mathbf{x})\right] = 1$$

   where the probability is taken over the coin-tosses of the obfuscator iO.

2. **Indistinguishability of Equivalent TMs.** For every ensemble of pairs of Turing machines $\{M_{0,\lambda}, M_{1,\lambda}\}_{\lambda \in \mathbb{N}}$, such that $M_{0,\lambda}(\mathbf{x}) = M_{1,\lambda}(\mathbf{x})$ for every $\mathbf{x} \in \{0,1\}^{\leq L}$ and $\mathsf{runtime}(M_{0,\lambda}, \mathbf{x}) = \mathsf{runtime}(M_{1,\lambda}, \mathbf{x})$, we have that the following ensembles of pairs of distributions are indistinguishable to any PPT Adv:

$$\left\{M_{0,\lambda}, M_{1,\lambda}, \mathsf{iO}(1^\lambda, M_{0,\lambda})\right\} \stackrel{c}{\approx} \left\{M_{0,\lambda}, M_{1,\lambda}, \mathsf{iO}(1^\lambda, M_{1,\lambda})\right\}$$

3. **Succinctness.** For all security parameters $\lambda \in \mathbb{N}$, for any $M \in \mathcal{M}_\lambda$, we have that the running time of $\mathsf{iO}(1^\lambda, M, L)$ is $\mathrm{poly}(\lambda, |M|, L)$ and the evaluation time of $\mathsf{iO}(M)$ on input $\mathbf{x}$ where $\mathbf{x} \in \{0,1\}^{\leq L}$, is $\mathrm{poly}(|M|, L, t)$ where $t = \mathsf{runtime}(M, \mathbf{x})$.

2.3   Constrained Pseudorandom Functions

Constrained pseudorandom functions (introduced concurrently by Boneh and Waters (CCS 2013), Boyle, Goldwasser, and Ivan (PKC 2014), and Kiayias, Papadopoulos, Triandopoulos, and Zacharias (CCS 2013)), are pseudorandom functions (PRFs) that allow the owner of the secret key K to compute a constrained key K_f, such that anyone who possesses K_f can compute the output of the PRF on any input x such that $f(x) = 1$ for some predicate f. The security requirement of constrained PRFs state that the PRF output must still look indistinguishable from random for any x such that $f(x) = 0$. We will also require the property of delegatability, formalized below.

Definition 7 ([17]). *Let* $F : \{0,1\}^{\mathsf{seed}(\lambda)} \times \{0,1\}^{\mathsf{in}(\lambda)} \to \{0,1\}^{\mathsf{out}(\lambda)}$ *be an efficient function, where* seed, in *and* out *are all polynomials in the security parameter* λ. *We say that* F *is a delegatable constrained pseudorandom function with respect to a set system* $\mathcal{S} \subseteq 2^{\{0,1\}^{\mathsf{in}(\lambda)}}$ *if there exist algorithms* (Setup, Constrain, Eval, KeyDel) *that satisfy the following:*

- Setup$(1^\lambda, 1^{\mathsf{in}(\lambda)})$ *outputs a pair of keys* pk, sk.
- Constrain(sk, S) *outputs a constrained key* K_S *which enables evaluation of* $F(\mathsf{sk}, \mathbf{x})$ *on all* $\mathbf{x} \in S$ *and no other* $\mathbf{x}$.
- KeyDel(K_S, S') *outputs a constrained key* $K_{S \cap S'}$ *which enables the evaluation of* $F(\mathsf{sk}, \mathbf{x})$ *for all* $\mathbf{x} \in S \cap S'$ *and no other* $\mathbf{x}$. *We note that in systems where* KeyDel *is supported, the* Constrain *algorithm above can be expressed as a special case of* KeyDel *by letting* sk *correspond to the set of all inputs, i.e.* $\mathsf{sk} = K_{\{0,1\}^{\mathsf{in}(\lambda)}}$.
- Eval$(K_S, \mathbf{x})$ *outputs* $F(\mathsf{sk}, \mathbf{x})$ *if* $\mathbf{x} \in S$, $\perp$ *otherwise*.

Please refer to the full version [1] for the definition of security.

3 Construction: Single Input FE for Turing Machines

In this section, we construct a single input functional encryption scheme for Turing machines, denoted by TMFE from the following ingredients:

1. Two compact functional encryption schemes for circuits, $\mathsf{1FE}_1$ and $\mathsf{1FE}_2$. We will assume that the scheme $\mathsf{1FE}_2$ is decomposable as defined in the preliminaries.
2. A symmetric encryption scheme SKE = (SKE.KeyGen, SKE.Enc, SKE.Dec).
3. A delegatable constrained pseudorandom function (cPRF), denoted by F which supports T delegations for the function family $f_t : \{0,1\}^{2\cdot\lambda} \to \{0,1\}$ defined as follows. Let x, t denote integers whose binary representations are $\mathbf{x}, \mathbf{t}$ of λ bits. Then,

$$f_t(\mathbf{x}\|\mathbf{z}) = 1, \text{ if } x \geq t \text{ and } 0 \text{ otherwise}$$

Intuitively, the function is parametrized by a value t and evaluates to 1 if the first half of its input, $x \geq t$. We will denote the constrained PRF key K_{f_t} corresponding to function f_t by K_t for ease of notation. By the delegation property of constrained PRFs, we have that if $t' \geq t$ then $\mathsf{K}_{t'}$ can be derived from K_t. In our construction the parameter t will represent the time step in the computation, which means that a PRF key of the current time step can be used to derive PRF keys for future time steps. We will denote a PRF for this functionality by F. The security proof makes use a punctured version of the above cPRF, please see the full version [1] for details.

3.1   Construction

Below we provide our construction for single input FE for Turing machines.

Notation. Note that since $1FE_2$ is decomposable, there exists an encoding function $\mathcal{E}$ which encodes each bit of the input and since it is compact, the output length of $\mathcal{E}$ is independent of the circuit class supported by $1FE_2$. Thus, by choosing the encoding function first, the CktFE scheme may support a circuit class that outputs its own ciphertext components. We denote by $\bar{\mathcal{E}}$ the encoding function $\mathcal{E}$ applied bitwise to a vector, i.e. $\bar{\mathcal{E}}(\mathbf{w}) = \mathcal{E}(w_1)\ldots\mathcal{E}(w_n)$.

TMFE.Setup(1^λ): Upon input the security parameter 1^λ, do the following:

1. Let $(1FE_2.PK, 1FE_2.MSK) \leftarrow 1FE_2.Setup(1^\lambda)$, where $1FE_2$ is a decomposable functional encryption scheme for the circuit family

$$\text{Next} : \Big(\big(\{\text{SYM}\} \times \{0,1\}^{4\lambda} \times \Sigma \times \text{Trap}\big) \times \big(\{\text{ST}\} \times \mathcal{Q}\big) \Big) \to \big(\mathcal{C}^{1FE_2}\big)^2 \cup \{\text{ACC}, \text{REJ}, \bot\}$$

Here, Σ and $\mathcal{Q}$ are the alphabet and state space respectively of the Turing machine family. The tokens SYM and ST are flags denoting a symbol and a state respectively. The set $\{0,1\}^{4\lambda}$ encodes in order, a random value key-id associated with a TM M, a cPRF key, the current time step in the computation and the length of the input string, each of λ bits. Here, Trap is a data structure of fixed polynomial length which will be used in the proof. Since we do not need it in the construction, we do not discuss it here, please see Fig. 6 for its definition. $\mathcal{C}^{1FE_2}$ denotes the ciphertext space of $1FE_2$, and ACC and REJ are bits indicating accepting and a rejecting states of a TM respectively.

2. Let $(1FE_1.PK, 1FE_1.MSK) \leftarrow 1FE_1.Setup(1^\lambda)$, where $1FE_1$ is a compact, public-key CktFE scheme for the circuit family

$$\text{ReRand} : \Big(\{0,1\}^{3\lambda} \times \Sigma \times \text{Trap}\Big) \to \mathcal{C}^{1FE_2} \times \big(\mathcal{C}^{1FE_2} \cup \{\bot\}\big)$$

Again, $\{0,1\}^{3\lambda}$ encodes in order, a root cPRF key, a time step and the length of the input string respectively, while Σ, Trap and $\mathcal{C}^{1FE_2}$ are as described above.

3. Output $PK = 1FE_1.PK$ and $MSK = (1FE_1.MSK, (1FE_2.PK, 1FE_2.MSK))$.

TMFE.Enc($PK, \mathbf{w}$): Upon input the public key PK, and message $\mathbf{w}$ of arbitrary length $\ell = |\mathbf{w}|$, do the following:

1. Sample the root key K_0 for function f_t where $t = 0$ for the cPRF F described above.
2. For $i \in [\ell]$, let $CT_i = 1FE_1.Enc(PK, (K_0, i, \ell, w_i, \text{Trap}))$, where Trap is a data structure which is only relevant in the proof. Here, all fields of Trap are set to $\bot$ except a flag Trap.mode-real $= 1$ which indicates that we are in the real world. Please see Fig. 6 for the definition of Trap.
3. Output $CT_\mathbf{w} = \{CT_i\}_{i \in [\ell]}$.

TMFE.KeyGen(MSK, M): Upon input the master secret key MSK and the description of a Turing machine M, do the following. We will assume, w.l.o.g. that the TM is oblivious (see [1] for a justification) and $q_{st} \in \mathcal{Q}$ is the start state of M.

1. Sample a random value salt $\leftarrow \{0,1\}^{\lambda}$.
2. Interpret MSK = (1FE$_1$.MSK, (1FE$_2$.PK, 1FE$_2$.MSK)).
3. Let SK$_{\mathsf{ReRand}}$ = 1FE$_1$.KeyGen(1FE$_1$.MSK, ReRand$_{1FE_2.PK,salt,q_{st},\perp,\perp}$) where Fig. 2 defines the circuit ReRand$_{1FE_2.PK,salt,q_{st},\perp,\perp}$.
4. Let SK$_{\mathsf{Next}}$ = 1FE$_2$.KeyGen(1FE$_2$.MSK, Next$_{1FE_2.PK,salt,M,\perp,\perp}$) where Fig. 4 defines the circuit Next$_{1FE_2.PK,salt,M,\perp,\perp}$.
5. Output SK$_M$ = (SK$_{\mathsf{ReRand}}$, SK$_{\mathsf{Next}}$).

TMFE.Dec(SK$_M$, CT$_\mathbf{w}$): Upon input secret key SK$_M$ and ciphertext CT$_\mathbf{w}$, do the following:

1. Interpret SK$_M$ = (SK$_{\mathsf{ReRand}}$, SK$_{\mathsf{Next}}$) and CT$_\mathbf{w}$ = (CT$_1$, ..., CT$_{|\mathbf{w}|}$).
2. For $i \in [|\mathbf{w}|]$, do the following:
   (a) If $i = 1$, invoke 1FE$_1$.Dec(SK$_{\mathsf{ReRand}}$, CT$_1$) to obtain (CT$_{\mathsf{sym},1}$, CT$_{\mathsf{st},1}$).
   (b) Else, invoke 1FE$_1$.Dec(SK$_{\mathsf{ReRand}}$, CT$_i$) to obtain (CT$_{\mathsf{sym},i}$, $\perp$).
3. Denote $\big((CT_{\mathsf{sym},1}, CT_{\mathsf{st},1}), CT_{\mathsf{sym},2}, \ldots, CT_{\mathsf{sym},|\mathbf{w}|}\big)$ as the new sequence of ciphertexts obtained under the Next scheme.
4. Let $t = 1$. While the Turing machine does not halt, do:
   (a) Invoke 1FE$_2$.Dec$\big($SK$_{\mathsf{Next}}$, (CT$_{\mathsf{sym},t}$, CT$_{\mathsf{st},t}$)$\big)$ to obtain:
      – ACC or REJ. In this case, output "Accept" or "Reject" respectively, and exit the loop.
      – $\big(CT_{\mathsf{sym},t'}, CT_{\mathsf{st},t+1}\big)$.
      Note that t' is the next time step that the work tape cell accessed at time step t will be accessed again.
   (b) Let $t = t + 1$ and go to start of loop.

3.2 Correctness and Efficiency of Single Input TMFE

We now argue that the above scheme is correct. The TMFE.Dec algorithm takes as input a secret key SK$_M$ = (SK$_{\mathsf{ReRand}}$, SK$_{\mathsf{Next}}$) and a ciphertext CT$_\mathbf{w}$ = (CT$_1$, ..., CT$_{|\mathbf{w}|}$) under the 1FE$_1$ scheme supporting the functionality ReRand := ReRand$_{1FE_2.PK,salt,q_{st},\mathcal{C}_2,\mathcal{C}_2}$. Firstly, note that given a secret key SK$_{\mathsf{ReRand}}$ along with a ciphertext CT$_\mathbf{w}$, we have as follows.

1. Since CT$_1$ encodes Trap with Trap.mode-real = 1, hence by the correctness of the 1FE$_1$ scheme, we get 1FE$_1$.Dec(SK$_{\mathsf{ReRand}}$, CT$_1$) = (CT$_{\mathsf{sym},1}$, CT$_{\mathsf{st},1}$) as output.
2. For $i \in [2, |\mathbf{w}|]$, since CT$_i$ encodes Trap with Trap.mode-real = 1, hence by the correctness of the 1FE$_1$ scheme, we get 1FE$_1$.Dec(SK$_{\mathsf{ReRand}}$, CT$_i$) = (CT$_{\mathsf{sym},i}$, $\perp$) as the correct output.

Function ReRand$_{1FE_2.PK,salt,q_{st},C_1,C_2}$ $\big((K_0, i, \ell, w_i, \text{Trap})\big)$

(a) **Initialization and Choosing Real or Trapdoor mode.**
  Initialize an input vector $\text{inp} = (w_i, q_{st})$. If Trap.mode-real $= 1$, set out $= (c_1, c_2)$, where $c_1 = c_2 = \bot$. If $i \neq 1$, set $\text{inp} = (w_i, \bot)$. Else invoke Trap-Mode$_{\text{ReRand}}\big(\text{Trap}, \text{inp}, \text{salt}, \ell, C_1, C_2, i\big)$ as described in Figure 3 to obtain ($\text{inp} = (u_1, u_2)$, out $= (c_1, c_2)$).

(b) **Computing Encrypted Symbols using randomness derived from cPRF.** If out.$c_1 = \bot$, do the following.
  i. Noting that $i > 0$, derive delegated cPRF key K_i from K_0 as $K_i = \text{F.KeyDel}(K_0, f_i)$. Compute randomness for encryption as $r_i = \text{F.Eval}(K_i, (i\|\text{salt}))$.
  ii. Derive delegated cPRF key $K_{i+1} = \text{F.KeyDel}(K_i, f_{i+1})$. Set key-id $= \text{salt}$.
  iii. Compute the $1FE_2$ ciphertext component encoding $w_i = \text{inp}.u_1$ for time step i as
  $$CT_{\text{sym},i} = \bar{\mathcal{E}}\big(1FE_2.PK_1, (SYM, \text{key-id}, K_{i+1}, i, \ell, w_i, \text{Trap}); r_i\big)$$
  iv. Set out.$c_1 = CT_{\text{sym},i}$.

(c) **Computing Encrypted State for First Time Step.** If $\big((\text{out}.c_2 = \bot) \wedge (i = 1)\big)$, do the following.
  i. Compute $1FE_2$ ciphertext component to encode the starting state $q_{st} = \text{inp}.u_2$ as
  $$CT_{\text{st},1} = \bar{\mathcal{E}}\big(1FE_2.PK_2, (ST, q_{st}); r_1\big)$$
  ii. Set out.$c_2 = CT_{\text{st},1}$.

(d) **Output.** If $i = 1$, output out $= (CT_{\text{sym},1}, CT_{\text{st},1})$, else output out $= (CT_{\text{sym},i}, \bot)$.

Fig. 2. This circuit re-randomizes the ciphertexts provided during encryption to use randomness derived from a cPRF. The seed for the cPRF is specified in the ciphertext and the input is specified by the key. This ensures that each ciphertext, key pair form a unique "thread" of execution.

Subroutine Trap-Mode$_{\text{ReRand}}\big(\text{Trap}, \text{inp}, \text{salt}, \ell, C_1, C_2, i\big)$

Interpret $\text{inp} = (u_1, u_2) = (w_i, q_{st})$ and initialize out $= (c_1, c_2)$, where $c_1 = c_2 = \bot$.

If Trap.key-id $=$ salt, do the following.

(a) If Trap.mode-trap$_3 = 1$, do the following:
  i. If $\big((\text{Trap.Sym TS} = i) \wedge (i \leq \ell)\big)$, compute the $1FE_2$ ciphertext $CT_{\text{sym},i} = \text{SKE.Dec}(\text{Trap.SKE.K}, C_1)$ and set out.$c_1 = CT_{\text{sym},i}$.

  ii. If $\big((\text{Trap.ST TS} = i) \wedge (i = 1)\big)$, compute the $1FE_2$ ciphertext $CT_{\text{st},i} = \text{SKE.Dec}(\text{Trap.SKE.K}, C_2)$ and set out.$c_2 = CT_{\text{st},1}$.

(b) If Trap.mode-trap$_1 = 1$, do the following:
  i. If $\big((\text{Trap.Sym TS}_1 = i) \wedge (i \leq \ell)\big)$, set $\text{inp}.u_1 = \text{Trap.Sym val}_1$ with the symbol to be encrypted and output at time step i.

  ii. If $\big((\text{Trap.ST TS}_1 = i) \wedge (i = 1)\big)$, set $\text{inp}.u_2 = \text{Trap.ST val}_1$ with the start state to be encrypted and output at time step 1.

(c) If Trap.mode-trap$_2 = 1$, do the following:
  i. If $\big((\text{Trap.Sym TS}_2 = i) \wedge (i \leq \ell)\big)$, set $\text{inp}.u_1 = \text{Trap.Sym val}_2$ with the symbol to be encrypted and output at time step i.

  ii. If $\big((\text{Trap.ST TS}_2 = i) \wedge (i = 1)\big)$, set $\text{inp}.u_2 = \text{Trap.ST val}_2$ with the start state to be encrypted and output at time step 1.

If Trap.key-id $\neq$ salt, do the following.

(a) If salt $>$ Trap.key-id set $b = 0$; else set $b = 1^a$.
(b) If $i \neq 1$, update $\text{inp} = (\text{Trap.val}_b, \bot)$; else update $\text{inp} = (\text{Trap.val}_b, q_{st})$.

Output. Return (inp, out).

---
^{a} We assume a lexicographic ordering on the salt values and a generalized comparison operator.

Fig. 3. Subroutine handling the trapdoor modes in ReRand. This is "active" only in the proof.

Function $\mathsf{Next}_{\mathsf{1FE_2.PK},\mathsf{salt},M,C_1,C_2}\big((\mathbf{z}_1,\mathbf{z}_2)\big)$

(a) **Reading Current (Symbol, State) Pair and Looking up Transition Table.**
   i. Interpret $\mathbf{z}_1 = (\mathsf{type},\mathsf{key\text{-}id},\mathsf{K}_{t+1},t,\ell,s,\mathsf{Trap})$, $\mathbf{z}_2 = (\mathsf{type},s)$. If $((\mathbf{z}_1.\mathsf{type} \neq \mathsf{SYM}) \vee (\mathbf{z}_2.\mathsf{type} \neq \mathsf{ST}) \vee (\mathbf{z}_1.\mathsf{key\text{-}id} \neq \mathsf{salt}))$, output $\perp$ and abort.
   ii. Interpret $(\mathbf{z}_1.s,\mathbf{z}_2.s) = (\sigma_t,\mathsf{q}_t)$ as the symbol, state pair for the current time step $t = \mathbf{z}_1.t$, input $\mathsf{K}_{t+1} = \mathbf{z}_1.\mathsf{K}_{t+1}$ as the constrained PRF key for future time steps. Denote $\mathsf{key\text{-}id} = \mathbf{z}_1.\mathsf{key\text{-}id}$, $\ell = \mathbf{z}_1.\ell$ and $\mathsf{Trap} = \mathbf{z}_1.\mathsf{Trap}$. Using the transition table of the machine M, look up the next state q_{t+1} as well as the symbol $\sigma_{t'}$ to be written on the work-tape, where t' is the time step the current work tape cell will next be read by M. If q_{t+1} is an accept or reject state, then output ACC or REJ and exit.
   iii. Initialize $\mathsf{inp} = (\sigma_{t'},\mathsf{q}_{t+1})$.
(b) **Choosing Real or Trapdoor mode.** If $\mathsf{Trap.mode\text{-}real} = 1$, initialize an output vector $\mathsf{out} = (c_1,c_2)$, where $c_1 = c_2 = \perp$. Else invoke $\mathsf{Trap\text{-}Mode}_{\mathsf{Next}}\big(\mathsf{Trap},\mathsf{inp},\mathsf{salt},\ell,C_1,C_2,t,t'\big)$ as described in Figure 5 to obtain $\big(\mathsf{inp} = (u_1,u_2),\mathsf{out} = (c_1,c_2)\big)$.
(c) **Computing Next Encrypted Symbol.** If $\mathsf{out}.c_1 = \perp$, do the following.
   i. Noting that $t' > t$, derive the randomness at time step t' using the delegated key K_{t+1} as $r_{t'} = \mathsf{F.Eval}(\mathsf{K}_{t+1},(t'\|\mathsf{salt}))$. Compute the delegated PRF key $\mathsf{K}_{t'+1} = \mathsf{F.KeyDel}(\mathsf{K}_{t+1},f_{t'+1})$.
   ii. Compute the $\mathsf{1FE}_2$ ciphertext component encoding the symbol $\sigma_{t'} = \mathsf{inp}.u_1$ for time step t' as

$$\mathsf{CT}_{\mathsf{sym},t'} = \bar{\mathcal{E}}\big(\mathsf{1FE}_2.\mathsf{PK}_1,(\mathsf{SYM},\mathsf{key\text{-}id},\mathsf{K}_{t'+1},t',\ell,\sigma_{t'},\mathsf{Trap});r_{t'}\big)$$

   iii. Set $\mathsf{out}.c_1 = \mathsf{CT}_{\mathsf{sym},t'}$.
(d) **Computing Next Encrypted State.** If $\mathsf{out}.c_2 = \perp$, do the following.
   i. Derive the randomness at time step $t + 1$ as $r_{t+1} = \mathsf{F.Eval}(\mathsf{K}_{t+1},(t+1\|\mathsf{salt}))$ and compute the $\mathsf{1FE}_2$ ciphertext component encoding the state $\mathsf{q}_{t+1} = \mathsf{inp}.u_2$ for time step $t + 1$ as

$$\mathsf{CT}_{\mathsf{st},t+1} = \bar{\mathcal{E}}\big(\mathsf{1FE}_2.\mathsf{PK}_2,(\mathsf{ST},\mathsf{q}_{t+1});r_{t+1}\big)$$

   ii. Set $\mathsf{out}.c_2 = \mathsf{CT}_{\mathsf{st},t+1}$.
(e) **Output :** $\mathsf{out} = \big(\mathsf{CT}_{\mathsf{sym},t'},\mathsf{CT}_{\mathsf{st},t+1}\big)$

Fig. 4. Function to mimic TM computation. It reads the current symbol, state pair and outputs an encryption of the new state and symbol to be written under the appropriate randomness generated using a cPRF.

Subroutine $\mathsf{Trap\text{-}Mode}_{\mathsf{Next}}\big(\mathsf{Trap},\mathsf{inp},\mathsf{salt},\ell,C_1,C_2,t,t'\big)$

Interpret the input vector $\mathsf{inp} = (u_1,u_2) = (\sigma_{t'},\mathsf{q}_{t+1})$ and initialize the output vector $\mathsf{out} = (c_2,c_2)$, where $c_1 = c_2 = \perp$.

(a) If $\big((\mathsf{Trap.key\text{-}id} = \mathsf{salt}) \wedge (\mathsf{Trap.mode\text{-}trap}_3 = 1)\big)$, do the following.
   i. If $\big((\mathsf{Trap.Sym\ TS} = t) \wedge (\mathsf{Trap.Target\ TS} = t') \wedge (t > \ell)\big)$, compute the $\mathsf{1FE}_2$ symbol ciphertext $\mathsf{CT}_{\mathsf{sym},t'} = \mathsf{SKE.Dec}(\mathsf{Trap.SKE.K},C_1)$ and set $\mathsf{out}.c_1 = \mathsf{CT}_{\mathsf{sym},t'}$.

   ii. If $\big((\mathsf{Trap.ST\ TS} = t) \wedge (\mathsf{Trap.Target\ TS} = t + 1) \wedge (t > 1)\big)$, compute the $\mathsf{1FE}_2$ state ciphertext $\mathsf{CT}_{\mathsf{st},t+1} = \mathsf{SKE.Dec}(\mathsf{Trap.SKE.K},C_2)$ and set $\mathsf{out}.c_2 = \mathsf{CT}_{\mathsf{st},t+1}$.
(b) If $\big((\mathsf{Trap.key\text{-}id} = \mathsf{salt}) \wedge (\mathsf{Trap.mode\text{-}trap}_1 = 1)\big)$, do the following:
   i. If $\big((\mathsf{Trap.Sym\ TS}_1 = t) \wedge (\mathsf{Trap.Target\ TS}_1 = t') \wedge (t > \ell)\big)$, set $\mathsf{inp}.u_1 = \mathsf{Trap.Sym\ val}_1$ with the symbol $\sigma_{t'} = \mathsf{Trap.Sym\ val}_1$ to be encrypted and given as output for time step t'.

   ii. If $\big((\mathsf{Trap.ST\ TS}_1 = t) \wedge (\mathsf{Trap.Target\ TS}_1 = t + 1) \wedge (t > 1)\big)$, set $\mathsf{inp}.u_2 = \mathsf{Trap.ST\ val}_1$ with the state $\mathsf{q}_{t+1} = \mathsf{Trap.ST\ val}_1$ to be encrypted and given as output for time step $t + 1$.
(c) If $\big((\mathsf{Trap.key\text{-}id} = \mathsf{salt}) \wedge (\mathsf{Trap.mode\text{-}trap}_2 = 1)\big)$, do the following:
   i. If $\big((\mathsf{Trap.Sym\ TS}_2 = t) \wedge (\mathsf{Trap.Target\ TS}_2 = t') \wedge (t > \ell)\big)$, set $\mathsf{inp}.u_1 = \mathsf{Trap.Sym\ val}_2$ with the symbol $\sigma_{t'} = \mathsf{Trap.Sym\ val}_2$ to be encrypted and given as output for time step t'.

   ii. If $\big((\mathsf{Trap.ST\ TS}_2 = t) \wedge (\mathsf{Trap.Target\ TS}_2 = t + 1) \wedge (t > 1)\big)$, set $\mathsf{inp}.u_2 = \mathsf{Trap.ST\ val}_2$ with the state $\mathsf{q}_{t+1} = \mathsf{Trap.ST\ val}_2$ to be encrypted and given as output for time step $t + 1$.
(d) Exit the subroutine returning $(\mathsf{inp},\mathsf{out})$.

Fig. 5. Subroutine handling the trapdoor modes in Next. This is "active" only in the proof.

The new sequence of $1FE_2$ ciphertexts output by ReRand are now sequenced as $((CT_{sym,1}, CT_{st,1}), CT_{sym,2}, \ldots, CT_{sym,|w|})$. The $1FE_2$ scheme supports the functionality Next $:=$ $Next_{1FE_2.PK,salt,M,\mathcal{C}_1,\mathcal{C}_2}$. Throughout the $1FE_2$ decryption, we maintain the invariant that at any time step t, apart from a secret key SK_{Next}, the input to the $1FE_2$.Dec algorithm is an entire $1FE_2$ ciphertext decomposed into two components corresponding to a symbol and a state ciphertext both of which are computed with the same randomness, which is computed as $F.Eval(K_0, (t\|salt))^6$.

We show that given a secret key SK_{Next} and the sequence of ciphertexts $((CT_{sym,1}, CT_{st,1}), CT_{sym,2}, \ldots, CT_{sym,|w|})$ generated from the outputs of the $1FE_1$.Dec algorithm, $1FE_2$.Dec correctly computes the decomposed ciphertext components of a symbol and a state that occur along the computation path and finally outputs the value of machine M on the sequenced input. Define $\tau = runtime(M, \mathbf{w})$. Formally, by the correctness of $1FE_2$ scheme, at any time step $t \in [\tau - 2]$, $1FE_2$.Dec$(SK_{Next}, (CT_{sym,t}, CT_{st,t}))$ correctly outputs either $(CT_{sym,t'}, CT_{st,t+1})$ with $t < t' \leq \tau - 1$. Further, for any time step $t \in [\tau - 2]$, we have:

1. Let $t \in [\tau - 2] \setminus [\ell]$. If the current work tape cell was accessed[7], at some time step $\tilde{t} < t$, then $CT_{sym,t}$ encoding $(SYM, key\text{-}id, K_{t+1}, t, \ell, \sigma_t, Trap)$ was constructed at time step $\tilde{t}$. Note that σ_t may be the blank symbol β. When $t \in [\ell]$, $CT_{sym,t}$ is constructed at time step t via the ReRand circuit.
2. The ciphertext component $CT_{st,t}$ encoding (ST, q_t) at time step t was constructed at time step $t - 1$ for $t > 1$ and at time step 1, when $t = 1$.
3. The randomness $r_t = F.Eval(K_{\tilde{t}+1}, (t\|salt)) = F.Eval(K_t, (t\|salt))$ binds the components $CT_{sym,t}$ and $CT_{st,t}$.

Thus, at any given time step $t \in [\tau - 2]$, we have a complete ciphertext of $1FE_2$ which may be fed again with SK_{Next} to $1FE_2$.Dec in order to proceed with the computation. Thus, the execution of $1FE_2$.Dec at the $(\tau-2)^{th}$ time step provides the complete pair $(CT_{sym,\tau-1}, CT_{st,\tau-1})$. By the correctness of $1FE_2$ scheme again, at time step $t = \tau - 1$, invoking $1FE_2$.Dec$(SK_{Next}, (CT_{sym,\tau-1}, CT_{st,\tau-1}))$ outputs either "Accept" or "Reject" by simulating the execution of M for the final time step τ inside the function Next, thus correctly outputting $M(\mathbf{w})$.

Efficiency. The TMFE construction described above inherits its efficiency from the underlying CktFE constructions. Note that the ciphertext is compact and is of size $poly(\lambda, |\mathbf{w}|)$. Also, the running time of the decryption procedure is input specific since it mimics the computation of M on $\mathbf{w}$ using secret key encoding M and ciphertext encoding all the intermediate states of the computation. Additionally, the public parameters are short $poly(\lambda)$, since these are just the public

---

[6] We do not explicitly construct ciphertext components corresponding to blank tape cells in the Next functionality for ease of exposition; we assume w.l.o.g that any non-input cell that is accessed by the OTM has been written to by the Next functionality in a previous step, thus generating the requisite symbol ciphertext.

[7] We assume that every time a cell is accessed, it is written to, by writing the same symbol again if no change is made.

parameters of a compact CktFE scheme. The function keys are also short, since they are CktFE function keys for circuits ReRand and Next which are of size $\text{poly}(\lambda)$ and $\text{poly}(|M|, \lambda)$ respectively.

3.3 Proof of Security for Single Input TMFE

Next, we prove that the above TMFE scheme satisfies distributional indistinguishability (DI) for single (or constant) length outputs, as long as the underlying CktFE scheme satisfies distributional indistinguishability for any output length. In the full version [1], we provide an instantiation of a CktFE scheme satisfying distributional indistinguishability.

Theorem 1. *Assume that the functional encryption schemes for circuits* 1FE_1 *and* 1FE_2 *are DI secure and that F is a secure cPRF for the function family defined above. Then, the construction of functional encryption for Turing machines TMFE is selective DI secure for single bit outputs.*

The Trapdoor Data Structure. To implement the approach discussed in Sect. 1, we will make use of a data-structure Trap that lets us store all the requisite trapdoor information needed for the security proof within the ciphertext. In our construction, decryption of a particular input by a particular function key results in a chain of ciphertexts, each of which contain the trapdoor data structure. In the real world, this information is not used but as we progress through the proof, different fields become relevant. The data structure is outlined in Fig. 6.

mode-real	key-id	val_0	val_1	SKE.K	$\perp$
mode-trap$_1$	Target TS$_1$	Sym TS$_1$	Sym val$_1$	ST TS$_1$	ST val$_1$
mode-trap$_2$	Target TS$_2$	Sym TS$_2$	Sym val$_2$	ST TS$_2$	ST val$_2$
mode-trap$_3$	Target TS	Sym TS	$\perp$	ST TS	$\perp$

Fig. 6. Data structure Trap used for proof

Row 1. Above, key-id refers to the particular function key being considered and we switch the execution chain from $b = 0$ to $b = 1$ key by key. All the ciphertexts in a given execution chain share the key-id value. We assume a lexicographic order on the key-id fields, this can be easily ensured by having a counter as part of the key-id field. We do not make this explicit below for notational brevity. If key-id* is the key identity programmed in a particular execution chain, then all keys with values smaller than key-id* will decrypt the chain using the input bit $b = 1$, and all keys with values larger than key-id* will use $b = 0$. Hence, the 1FE_1 ciphertexts provided by the encryptor must encode messages corresponding to both values of b, the fields val_0 and val_1 are designed for this purpose[8]. Note that 1FE_2 ciphertexts computed by

---

[8] For the knowledgeable reader, this is similar to what was done by [5].

decryption need not track messages corresponding to both values of b, since the "chain is extended" via decryption corresponding to exactly one of $b = 0$ or $b = 1$ depending on the relation between the key identities in the ciphertext and the function key. The field SKE.K refers to the key of a symmetric key encryption scheme, which is used to decrypt some encrypted value embedded in the function key. This is a standard trick when the key must hide something in the public key setting. The flag mode-real means the scheme operates in the real world mode and the trapdoor information is not used.

Rows 2 and 3. The fields Target TS_1 and Target TS_2 refer to the time steps corresponding to the "broken link" in the decryption chain, namely the two time steps for which the ciphertext and function key are being programmed so as to switch from $b = 0$ to $b = 1$. The fields Sym TS_1 and ST TS_1 are the time steps when the symbol and state ciphertexts for time step Target TS_1 are generated; for instance ST TS_1 = Target $TS_1 - 1$ since the state ciphertext for a given time step is always generated in the previous time step, while the symbol ciphertext for a given time step may be generated much earlier. Sym TS_2 and ST TS_2 are defined analogously. The fields Sym val_1 and ST val_1 contain the symbol and state values which will be encrypted in the hybrid at the time steps Sym TS_1 and ST TS_1 when mode-trap$_1$ is set; Sym val_2 and ST val_2 are defined analogously.

Row 4. When mode-trap$_3$ is set, the symbol and state values are set to $\perp$, and the values hard coded in the function key are used for the target time step. In more detail, the function key contains SKE encryptions of symbol and state ciphertexts corresponding to time step Target TS hard-coded within itself. If key-id* = key-id, where key-id* is the key identity programmed in a particular execution chain and key-id is the key identity of the function key in question, and mode-trap$_3 = 1$, then at time steps SYM TS and ST TS the SKE secret key in row 1 of the Trap data structure is used to decrypt the SKE encryptions and output the encrypted values.

The Hybrids. We now proceed to describe our hybrids. For simplicity we first describe the hybrids for a single function request, for some Turing machine M. We denote by T the time taken by M to run on the challenge messages. Since the proof is very involved, we describe it first for the weak selective game, where the adversary specifies the challenge vectors and machine at the same time. In the full version [1] we discuss how to remove this restriction.

$\mathcal{H}(0)$: This is the real world, when mode-real $= 1$ and mode-trap$_1$ = mode-trap$_2$ = mode-trap$_3 = \perp$.

$\mathcal{H}(1,1)$: In this world, all ciphertexts (constructed by the encryptor as well as function keys) have mode-real $= \perp$, mode-trap$_1 = 1$, mode-trap$_2 = 1$, mode-trap$_3 = \perp$. We program the last link in the decryption chain for switching bit b by setting:

$$\text{Target } TS_1 = T - 1, \text{Target } TS_2 = T - 2$$

The fields Sym TS_1 and ST TS_1 contain the time steps when the symbol and state ciphertext pieces are generated for time step $T - 1$, and the fields

Sym val_1 and ST val_1 contain the symbol and state values which must be encrypted by the function key in the above time steps when mode-trap$_1$ is set. Note that these fields exactly mimic the behaviour in the real world, namely the time steps and values are set to be exactly what the real world decryption would output. The fields corresponding to TS_2 are defined analogously.

Indistinguishability follows from security of $1FE_1$, since the decryption values in both hybrids are exactly the same.

$\mathcal{H}(1,2)$: Hardwire the key with an SKE encryption of symbol and state ciphertexts output at step $T-1$ for $b=0$. Use the same ciphertexts as would be generated in the previous hybrid.

Indistinguishability follows from security of SKE, since the only difference is the value of the message encrypted using SKE which is embedded in the key.

$\mathcal{H}(1,3)$: Set mode-trap$_1 = \perp$, mode-trap$_2 = 1$, mode-trap$_3 = 1$ and Target TS $= T-1$. In this hybrid the hardwired value in the key is used to be output as step $T-1$ ciphertext.

Indistinguishability follows from security of $1FE_1$, since the decryption values in both hybrids are exactly the same.

$\mathcal{H}(1,4)$: Change normal root key K_0 to punctured root key K_0^{T-1} which punctures all delegated keys at point $(T-1\|\text{key-id})$.

Indistinguishability follows from security of $1FE_1$. Note that we evaluate the cPRF at point $(T-1\|\text{key-id})$ only to construct the $1FE_2$ ciphertext output at time step $T-1$ identified with key-id. This ciphertext is currently hardwired in the function key, and is computed exactly the same way in both hybrids. Thus, the cPRF key is only required to compute randomness of points $\neq (T-1\|\text{key-id})$, for which the punctured key suffices, and which moreover evaluates to the same value as the normal key on all such points. Hence, we have that the decryption values in both hybrids are exactly the same. Note that the punctured key is not used to evaluate on the punctured points.

$\mathcal{H}(1,5)$: Switch the randomness in the $1FE_2$ ciphertexts for time step $T-1$ which are hardwired in the key to true randomness.

Indistinguishability follows from security of punctured cPRF for the aforementioned function family, since the remainder of the distribution only uses the punctured key.

$\mathcal{H}(1,6)$: Switch the value encoded in the $1FE_2$ ciphertexts for time step $T-1$ which are hardwired in the key to correspond to $b=1$.

Indistinguishability follows from security of $1FE_2$. Formally, we do a reduction which plays the security game against the $1FE_2$ challenger and simulates the TMFE adversary. The reduction simulates $1FE_1$ itself and receives the $1FE_2$ public and function keys from the challenger. The only difference between the two hybrids is the $1FE_2$ ciphertext for time step $T-1$ which is embedded in the function key as received from the $1FE_2$ challenger.

$\mathcal{H}(1,7)$: Switch randomness back to PRF randomness in the ciphertext hardwired in key, using the punctured key for all but the hardwired ciphertext.

Indistinguishability follows from security of cPRF as discussed above.

$\mathcal{H}(1,8)$: Switch the punctured root key to the normal root key.

Indistinguishability follows from security of $1FE_1$ as discussed above.

$\mathcal{H}(2,1)$: Switch ciphertext in slot 1 for target $T-1$ to be for $b = 1$. Slot 2 remains $b = 0$. Set mode-trap$_3 = \bot$ and mode-trap$_1$ = mode-trap$_2 = 1$.

Indistinguishability follows from security of 1FE$_1$, since the decryption values in both hybrids are exactly the same.

$\mathcal{H}(2,2)$: Hardwire key with SKE encryption of 1FE$_2$ ciphertext for time step $T-2$ and bit $b = 0$ (same as hybrid $(1,2)$ but for $T-2$).

Indistinguishability follows from security of SKE as above.

$\mathcal{H}(2,3)$: Set mode-trap$_1 = 1$ with target $T-1$, mode-trap$_2 = \bot$, and mode-trap$_3 = 1$ with target $T-2$.

Indistinguishability follows from security of 1FE$_1$, since the decryption values in both hybrids are exactly the same.

$\mathcal{H}(2,4)$: Switch normal root key to punctured key at point $(T-2\|$key-id$)$.

Indistinguishability follows from security of 1FE$_1$ as discussed above.

$\mathcal{H}(2,5)$: Switch randomness to true in the ciphertext hardwired in key.

Indistinguishability follows from security of cPRF as discussed above.

$\mathcal{H}(2,6)$: Switch hardwired 1FE$_2$ ciphertext for step $T-2$ to correspond to bit $b = 1$.

Indistinguishability follows from security of 1FE$_2$.

$\mathcal{H}(2,7)$: Switch randomness back to use the PRF in the ciphertext hardwired in key.

Indistinguishability follows from security of cPRF as discussed above.

$\mathcal{H}(2,8)$: Switch punctured root key to normal root key.

Indistinguishability follows from security of 1FE$_1$ as discussed above.

$\mathcal{H}(3,1)$: Intuitively, we slide the trapdoor left by one step, i.e. change target time-steps to $T-2$ and $T-3$ in the ciphertext. Now slot 1 for $T-2$ corresponds to $b = 1$ and slot 2 for $T-3$ to $b = 0$. Set mode-real = mode-trap$_3 = \bot$ and mode-trap$_1$ = mode-trap$_2 = 1$.

Indistinguishability follows from security of 1FE$_1$, since the decryption values in both hybrids are exactly the same. Note that now slot $T-1$ is redundant, since $T-2$ ciphertext is already switched to $b = 1$.

Hybrid $\mathcal{H}(3,i)$ will be analogous to $\mathcal{H}(2,i)$ for $i \in [8]$.

As we proceed left in the execution chain one step at a time, we reach step ℓ where $\ell = |\mathbf{w}|$, i.e. time steps for which 1FE$_1$ ciphertexts are provided by the encryptor. At this point we will hardwire the ReRand key with symbol ciphertexts for ℓ time steps, one at a time, and the Next key for the state ciphertexts[9]. Moreover, we must now add an additional hybrid in which the challenge 1FE$_1$ ciphertext at position ℓ contains the message bit corresponding to $b = 1$; intuitively, we must switch the bit before we slide the trapdoor since the ciphertext for this position is not generated by decrypting the previous ciphertext. In more detail, in $\mathcal{H}(T - \ell, 8)$, analogously to hybrid $(1, 8)$, the $T - (T - \ell) = \ell^{th}$ bit hard-wired in the trapdoor is changed to 1. We now add one more hybrid, namely:

---

[9] There is an exception at time step 1 when both the symbol ciphertext and the start state ciphertexts are hardwired in the ReRand key.

$\mathcal{H}(T - \ell, 9)$: In this hybrid, we modify the $1FE_1$ challenge ciphertext in position ℓ as follows: the encoded message is changed corresponding to $b = 1$ and flag mode-real $= 1$. The other flags mode-trap$_1$ $=$ mode-trap$_2$ $=$ mode-trap$_3$ $= \perp$. Note that all ciphertexts previous to time step ℓ remain unchanged, and output their corresponding symbol ciphertexts correctly. The Next circuit outputs the state ciphertext for time step ℓ corresponding to bit $b = 1$. The only difference between this hybrid and the previous one is that here we use the real mode to output the symbol ciphertext for $b = 1$ whereas previously we used the trapdoor mode to output the same symbol ciphertext. Hence, decryption values in both hybrids are exactly the same, and indistinguishability follows from security of $1FE_1$.

Finally in $\mathcal{H}(T - 1, 9)$, the entire chain has been replaced to use $b = 1$ and all the challenge $1FE_1$ ciphertexts have encoded messages corresponding to $b = 1$ with mode-real $= 1$.

$\mathcal{H}(T)$: In this hybrid, all the other fields in the trapdoor data structure, excepting mode-real are disabled and set to $\perp$. This is the real world with $b = 1$.

Since all the encoded messages use $b = 1$, decryption values are all exactly the same as in $\mathcal{H}(T - 1, 9)$, hence indistinguishability follows from security of $1FE_1$.

The formal reductions are provided in the full version [1].

Multiple Keys. We handle multiple keys by repeating the above set of hybrids key by key. Each key carries within it an identifier key-id, and if this is less than the key identifier encoded in the ciphertext, the bit $b = 1$ is used, if it is greater then the bit $b = 0$ is used and if it is equal, then the above sequence of hybrids is performed to switch from $b = 0$ to $b = 1$. To support this, the $1FE_1$ ciphertexts provided by the encryptor must encode messages corresponding to both values of b, the fields val$_0$ and val$_1$ in the trapdoor data structure of Fig. 6 are provided for this purpose. Security follows by a standard hybrid argument as in [5], we defer the formal description to the full version of the paper [1].

3.4 Constructing the cPRF

In the full version [1], we provide a construction for a cPRF F which supports puncturing and delegation as required; the T cPRFs F_i for $i \in [T]$ may each be constructed similarly. To begin, note that we require the root key of F to be punctured at a point i^* (say). The cPRF construction for punctured PRF [17,18,36] (which is in turn inherited from the standard PRG based GGM [32]) immediately satisfies this constraint, so we are left with the question of delegation.

Recall that we are required to delegate T times, where T is the (polynomial) runtime of the Turing machine on the encrypted input (please see preliminaries in [1]), and the jth delegated key must support evaluation of points $\{(k\|z) : z \in \{0,1\}^\lambda\}$ for $k \geq j$, *except* when $(k\|z) = i^*$. This may be viewed as the jth key being punctured on points $[1, j - 1] \cup i^*$. We show that the GGM based construction for puncturing a single point can be extended to puncturing an interval (plus an extra point). Intuitively, puncturing an interval corresponds to puncturing at most λ internal nodes in the GGM tree. In more detail, we show that regardless of the value of j, it suffices to puncture at most λ points in the GGM tree to achieve puncturing of the entire interval $[1, j-1]$. Please see the full version [1] for details.

4 Construction: Multi-input FE for Turing Machines

In this section we construct a multi-input functional encryption scheme for Turing machines. Our construction supports a fixed number of encryptors (say k), who may each encrypt a string $\mathbf{w}_i$ of *unbounded* length. Function keys may be provided for Turing machines, so that given k ciphertexts for $\mathbf{w}_i$ and a function key for TM M, decryption reveals $M(\mathbf{w}_1 \| \ldots \| \mathbf{w}_k)$ and nothing else. We use the following ingredients for our construction:

1. A compact, k-input functional encryption scheme for circuits, kFE and a compact, public-key functional encryption scheme 1FE. As before, we will assume that the scheme 1FE is decomposable as defined in the preliminaries.
2. A symmetric encryption scheme SKE = (SKE.KeyGen, SKE.Enc, SKE.Dec).
3. A delegatable constrained pseudorandom function (cPRF), denoted by F which supports T delegations for the function family $f_t : \{0,1\}^{(k+2)\cdot\lambda} \to \{0,1\}$ defined as follows. Let x, t denote integers whose binary representations are $\mathbf{x}, \mathbf{t}$ of λ bits. Then,

$$f_t(\mathbf{x}\|\mathbf{z}) = 1, \text{if } x \geq t \text{ and } 0 \text{ otherwise}$$

The functionalities supported by kFE and 1FE are called Agg and Next respectively, described next. Agg aggregates the inputs $\mathbf{w}_1, \ldots, \mathbf{w}_k$ of all k parties into one long "global" string $(\mathbf{w}_1 \| \ldots \| \mathbf{w}_k)$, encrypted under the scheme 1FE. Since the length of this aggregate string is unbounded, a single invocation of Agg produces an encryption of a single symbol in the string, and the function is invoked repeatedly to produce ciphertexts for the entire string. Each ciphertext output by the Agg scheme contains a symbol w_i as well as the position of the symbol within the global string. The encryption of the symbols (and the initial state) also contains a *global salt* which Agg computes from the random salts provided in the ciphertexts under the kFE scheme by the individual encryptors. The global salt identifies the particular input combination that is aggregated, and serves as input to the PRF in the Next functionality.

Our k-input CktFE scheme may be either private or public key, and will result in the corresponding notion for k-input TMFE. Since the multi input setting for FE is considered more interesting in the symmetric key setting (see [19] for a discussion), we present our construction in the symmetric key setting – the public key adaptation is straightforward.

We note that ciphertexts output by Agg, which are encryptions of the symbols in the aggregate string under the 1FE scheme, are exactly the same as the output of the ReRand function in the single input scheme of Sect. 3. Therefore, as before, we may have the functionality Next of the 1FE scheme mimic the computation of the Turing machine on the global string $(\mathbf{w}_1 \| \ldots \| \mathbf{w}_k)$. As in the previous construction, 1FE.Dec accepts as its inputs a ciphertext decomposed into two components encoding the current symbol on the worktape and the current state in the computation, both of which have been encrypted using the same randomness, and outputs a ciphertext component corresponding to the symbol written on the tape, as well as the next state. The global salt in the ciphertext, along with a random nonce chosen by KeyGen are used as input to a cPRF as before, to compute the randomness used to generate ciphertexts. This ensures that the execution of a given machine on a given input combination is maintained separate from any other execution, and thwarts "mix and match" attacks, where, for instance, an attacker may try to combine a state generated at some time step t in one execution with a symbol generated at time step t from a different execution.

If we instantiate the underlying multi-input CktFE by the construction of [40], we may let the arity k be poly-logarithmic in the security parameter. If we instantiate multi-input CktFE by the construction of [33], we may support fixed polynomial arity at the cost of worsening the assumption. Note that [33] rely on iO while [40] rely on compact FE. Note that [10] support unbounded polynomial arity, but from public coin DiO as discussed in Sect. 1.

4.1 Construction of Multi-input TMFE

In the following, we denote a k-input, private-key CktFE scheme by k-CktFE and a decomposable, public key CktFE scheme by 1FE. Since our scheme supports an a-priori fixed number of parties, say k, we assume that every user is pre-assigned an index ind $\in [k]$.

kTMFE.Setup($1^\lambda, 1^k$): Upon input the security parameter 1^λ and the bound 1^k, do the following:

1. **Choosing the functionality for 1FE.** Let 1FE be a decomposable, public-key CktFE for the following circuit family.

$$\text{Next}: \Big((\{\text{SYM}\} \times \{0,1\}^{(k+4)\lambda} \times \Sigma \times \text{Trap}) \times (\{\text{ST}\} \times \mathcal{Q} \times \{0,1\}^{k \cdot \lambda}) \Big) \rightarrow \Big(\mathcal{C}^{1\text{FE}} \Big)^2 \cup \{\text{ACC}, \text{REJ}, \bot\}$$

The tokens SYM and ST are flags denoting a symbol and a state respectively of a Turing machine M which has Σ and $\mathcal{Q}$ as the alphabet and state space respectively. The set $\{0,1\}^{(k+4)\lambda}$ encodes in order, a random value key-id associated with a TM M, a constrained PRF key, the current time step in the computation, the length of the input string, each of λ bits and a string of length $k \cdot \lambda$ bits encoding a random value gsalt. Here, Trap is a data structure of fixed polynomial length which will be used in the proof. Since we do not need it in the construction, we do not discuss it here, please see the full version [1] for its definition. The set $\{0,1\}^{k \cdot \lambda}$ encodes again a random value gsalt associated with the message component for state. $\mathcal{C}^{1\text{FE}}$ is the ciphertext space of 1FE. ACC and REJ denote tokens when M reaches an accepting state and a rejecting state respectively.

2. **Choosing the functionality for kFE.** Let kFE be a k-CktFE for the following circuit family.

$$\text{Agg} : (\{\text{SYM}, \text{SP}\} \times \{0,1\}^{4\lambda} \times [k] \times \Sigma \times \text{Trap})^k \to \mathcal{C}^{1\text{FE}} \times (\mathcal{C}^{1\text{FE}} \cup \{\perp\})$$

The special token SP denotes an encryption of the length of an input string corresponding to any user. The set $\{0,1\}^{4\lambda}$ encodes in order, a constrained PRF key, the time step of the current symbol, the input length and a random salt each of λ bits. Σ, Trap and $\mathcal{C}^{1\text{FE}}$ are as described above.

3. **Choosing keys for kFE and 1FE.**

Let $\text{kFE.MSK} \leftarrow \text{kFE.Setup}(1^\lambda, 1^k), (\text{1FE.PK}, \text{1FE.MSK}) \leftarrow \text{1FE.Setup}(1^\lambda, 1^k)$

4. Output $\text{MSK} = (\text{kFE.MSK}, (\text{1FE.PK}, \text{1FE.MSK}))$.

$\text{kTMFE.Enc}(\text{MSK}, \mathbf{w}_{\text{ind}}, \text{ind})$: Upon input the master key MSK, and message $\mathbf{w}_{\text{ind}}$ of arbitrary length ℓ_{ind} and an index $\text{ind} \in [k]$, do the following:

1. Interpret the input $\text{MSK} = (\text{kFE.MSK}, (\text{1FE.PK}, \text{1FE.MSK}))$.
2. Let $\mathbf{w}_{\text{ind}} = w_1 w_2 \ldots w_{\ell_{\text{ind}}}$. Sample $\text{salt}_{\text{ind}} \leftarrow \{0,1\}^\lambda$.
3. Construct the data structure Trap and set all its fields to $\perp$ except a flag Trap.mode-real $= 1$ which indicates that we are in the real world. The data structure Trap is only relevant in the proof. Please see [1] for the definition of Trap.
   - **Encoding Input String and Its Length**

4. If $\text{ind} = 1$, do the following:
   (a) Sample a root key for the constrained PRF F as $\text{K}_0 \leftarrow \text{F.Setup}(1^\lambda)$.
   (b) Construct the input message $\text{len}_1 = (\text{SP}, \text{K}_0, \perp, \ell_1, \text{salt}_1, 1, \perp, \text{Trap})$.
   (c) Encrypt ℓ_1 as a special ciphertext $\text{CT}_{1,\text{SP}} = \text{kFE.Enc}(\text{kFE.MSK}, \text{len})$.
   (d) For $i \in [\ell_1]$ do the following:
       i. Construct the input message $\mathbf{y}_{1,i} \stackrel{\cdot}{=} (\text{SYM}, \text{K}_0, i, \ell_1, \text{salt}_1, 1, w_i, \text{Trap})$.
       ii. Compute the ciphertext $\text{CT}_{1,\text{SYM},i} = \text{kFE.Enc}(\text{kFE.MSK}, \mathbf{y}_i)$.
5. If $\text{ind} \in [2, k]$, do the following:
   (a) Construct the input message $\text{len}_{\text{ind}} = (\text{SP}, \perp, \perp, \ell_{\text{ind}}, \text{salt}_{\text{ind}}, \text{ind}, \perp, \text{Trap})$.
   (b) Encrypt ℓ_{ind} as a special ciphertext $\text{CT}_{\text{ind},\text{SP}} = \text{kFE.Enc}(\text{kFE.MSK}, \text{len})$.
   (c) For $i \in [\ell_{\text{ind}}]$ do the following:
       i. Construct the input message $\mathbf{y}_{\text{ind},i} = (\text{SYM}, \perp, i, \ell_{\text{ind}}, \text{salt}_{\text{ind}}, \text{ind}, w_i, \text{Trap})$.
       ii. Compute the ciphertext $\text{CT}_{\text{ind},\text{SYM},i} = \text{kFE.Enc}(\text{kFE.MSK}, \mathbf{y}_i)$.
6. Output $\text{CT}_{\mathbf{w}_{\text{ind}}} = (\text{CT}_{\text{ind},\text{SP}}, \{\text{CT}_{\text{ind},\text{SYM},i}\}_{i \in [\ell_{\text{ind}}]})$.

kTMFE.KeyGen(MSK, M): Upon input the master secret key MSK and the description of a Turing machine M, do the following. We will assume, w.l.o.g. that the TM is oblivious (see [1] for a justification) and $q_{st} \in \mathcal{Q}$ is the start state of M.

1. Sample a random value rand $\leftarrow \{0,1\}^\lambda$.
2. Interpret MSK $=$ (kFE.MSK, (1FE.PK, 1FE.MSK)).
3. Let SK_{Agg} $=$ kFE.KeyGen(kFE.MSK, $Agg_{1FE.PK,rand,q_{st},\perp,\perp}$), where Fig. 7 defines the circuit $Agg_{1FE.PK,rand,q_{st},\perp,\perp}$.
4. Let SK_{Next} $=$ 1FE.KeyGen(1FE.MSK, $Next_{1FE.PK,rand,M,\perp,\perp}$), where Fig. 9 defines the circuit $Next_{1FE.PK,rand,M,\perp,\perp}$.
5. Output the secret key as $SK_M = (SK_{Agg}, SK_{Next})$.

kTMFE.Dec($SK_M, \{CT_{w_i}\}_{i\in[k]}$): Upon input secret key SK_M and k ciphertexts $CT_{w_1}, \ldots, CT_{w_k}$, do the following:

1. Interpret the secret key as $SK_M = (SK_{Agg}, SK_{Next})$.
2. Parse $CT_{w_{ind}} = (CT_{ind,SP}, (CT_{ind,SYM,1}, \ldots, CT_{ind,SYM,\ell_{ind}}))$ for all ind $\in [k]$.

- **Aggregate the ciphertexts of all users.**
3. For $i = 1$ to k, do the following:
   (a) For $j - 1$ to ℓ_i, do the following:
      i. If $((i = 1) \wedge (j = 1))$, invoke kFE.Dec $(SK_{Agg}, (CT_{1,SYM,1},$ $\{CT_{n,SP}\}_{n\in[k]\setminus\{1\}}))$ to obtain $(CT_{sym,1}, CT_{st,1})$.
      ii. If $((i = 1) \wedge (j > 1))$, invoke kFE.Dec $(SK_{Agg}, (CT_{1,SYM,j},$ $\{CT_{n,SP}\}_{n\in[k]\setminus\{1\}}))$ to obtain $(CT_{sym,j}, \perp)$.
      iii. Else, invoke kFE.Dec $(SK_{Agg}, (CT_{i,SYM,j}, \{CT_{n,SP}\}_{n\in[k]\setminus\{i\}}))$ to obtain $(CT_{sym,\widetilde{L_i}+j}, \perp)$, where $\widetilde{L_i} = \sum_{m=1}^{i-1} \ell_m$.
- **Execute the TM on aggregated input.**
4. The aggregated sequence of ciphertexts under the Next scheme, of length $L_k = \sum_{j=1}^{k} \ell_j$ computed above is expressed as:
$$((CT_{sym,1}, CT_{st,1}), CT_{sym,2}, \ldots, CT_{sym,\ell_1}, CT_{sym,\ell_1+1}, \ldots, CT_{sym,L_k}).$$
5. Let $t = 1$. While the Turing machine does not halt, do:
   (a) Invoke 1FE.Dec$(SK_{Next}, (CT_{sym,t}, CT_{st,t}))$ to obtain:
      - ACC or REJ. In this case, output "Accept" or "Reject" respectively, and exit the loop.
      - $(CT_{sym,t'}, CT_{st,t+1})$.
      Note that t' is the next time step that the work tape cell accessed at time step t will be accessed again.
   (b) Let $t = t + 1$ and go to start of loop.

Function $\text{Agg}_{1\text{FE.PK},\text{rand},\text{q}_{st},C_1,C_2}(x_1, x_2, \ldots, x_k)$

(a) Interpret $x_i = (\text{type}, K, t, \ell, \text{salt}, \text{ind}, s, \text{Trap})$, for $i \in [k]$ and set a flag $\text{proceed}_1 = \text{proceed}_2 = 0$.

(b) For all $i, j \in [k]$, if $x_i.\text{ind} \neq x_j.\text{ind}$ for $i \neq j$, set $\text{proceed} = 1$. If there exists *exactly* one $i \in [k]$ for which $x_i.\text{type} = \text{SYM}$ and $x_j.\text{type} = \text{SP}, \forall j \in [k] \setminus \{i\}$ and $\text{proceed}_1 = 1$, set $\text{proceed}_2 = 1$. If $\text{proceed}_2 = 0$, output $\perp$ and abort.

(c) **Initialization and Choosing Real or Trapdoor mode.**

Let $i \in [k]$ be such that $x_i.\text{type} = \text{SYM}$. Initialize an input vector $\text{inp} = (\sigma, \text{q}_{st})$, where $\sigma = x_i.s$. Let $\text{gsalt} = (x_1.\text{salt}\|x_2.\text{salt}\|\ldots\|x_k.\text{salt})$ and $\ell = \sum_{i=1}^{k} x_i.\ell$ denote the global salt and the aggregate input length respectively. Denote $\text{pos} = x_i.t$ and do the following:

   i. **Computing Global Symbol Position :** If $1 < x_i.\text{ind} \leq k$, compute the new position of the symbol as $\text{pos} = \text{pos} + \sum_{r \in S} x_r.\ell$, where the set $S = \{r \mid x_r.\text{ind} < x_i.\text{ind}\} \subset [k]$.

   ii. If $\text{Trap.mode-real} = 1$, set $\text{out} = (c_1, c_2)$, where $c_1 = c_2 = \perp$. If $\text{pos} \neq 1$, set $\text{inp} = (\sigma, \perp)$.

   iii. Else obtain $(\text{inp} = (u_1, u_2), \text{out} = (c_1, c_2)) = \text{Trap-Mode}_{\text{Agg}}(\text{Trap}, \text{inp}, \text{rand}, \text{gsalt}, \ell, C_1, C_2, \text{pos})$ as described in Figure 8.

(d) If $((\text{out}.c_1 = \perp) \vee (\text{out}.c_2 = \perp))$, do the following.

   i. Let $p \in [k]$ be such that $x_p.\text{ind} = 1$ and denote $K_0 = x_p.K$ as the root key for cPRF.

   ii. Derive the randomness for encryption at time step pos as $r_{\text{pos}} = \text{F.Eval}(K_0, (\text{pos}\|\text{rand}\|\text{gsalt}))$.

   iii. **Computing Encrypted Symbols using randomness derived from** cPRF. If $\text{out}.c_1 = \perp$, do the following.

     • Compute the delegated PRF key $K_{\text{pos}+1} = \text{F.KeyDel}(K_0, f_{\text{pos}+1})$. Set $\text{key-id} = \text{rand}$.

     • Compute the 1FE symbol ciphertext encoding $\sigma = \text{inp}.u_1$ as $\text{CT}_{\text{sym,pos}} = \bar{\mathcal{E}}(1\text{FE.PK}_1, y_1; r_{\text{pos}})$, where $y_1 = (\text{SYM}, \text{key-id}, K_{\text{pos}+1}, \text{pos}, \ell, \text{gsalt}, \sigma, \text{Trap})$.

   iv. **Computing Encrypted State for First Time Step.** If $((\text{out}.c_2 = \perp) \wedge (\text{pos} = 1))$, do the following.

     • Compute the 1FE state ciphertext encoding $\text{q}_{st} = \text{inp}.u_2$ as $\text{CT}_{st,1} = \bar{\mathcal{E}}(1\text{FE.PK}_2, y_2; r_1)$, where $y_2 = (\text{ST}, \text{q}_{st}, \text{gsalt})$. Set $\text{out}.c_2 = \text{CT}_{st,1}$.

(e) If $\text{pos} = 1$, output $\text{out} = (\text{CT}_{\text{sym},1}, \text{CT}_{st,1})$. Otherwise, output $\text{out} = (\text{CT}_{\text{sym,pos}}, \perp)$.

Fig. 7. This circuit aggregates and re-randomizes the ciphertexts provided during encryption to use randomness derived from a cPRF. The seed for the cPRF is specified in the ciphertext for first party and the input is specified by the key. This ensures that each ciphertext, key pair form a unique "thread" of execution.

Subroutine $\text{Trap-Mode}_{\text{Agg}}(\text{Trap}, \text{inp}, \text{rand}, \text{gsalt}, \ell, C_1, C_2, \text{pos})$

Interpret $\text{inp} = (u_1, u_2) = (w_i, \text{q}_{st})$ and initialize $\text{out} = (c_1, c_2)$, where $c_1 = c_2 = \perp$.

If $\text{Trap.key-id} = \text{rand},$ **do the following.**

(a) If $((\text{Trap.global-salt} = \text{gsalt}) \wedge (\text{Trap.mode-trap}_3 = 1))$, do the following:

   i. If $((\text{Trap.Sym TS} = \text{pos}) \wedge (\text{pos} \leq \ell))$, compute $\text{CT}_{\text{sym,pos}} = \text{SKE.Dec}(\text{Trap.SKE.K}, C_1)$ and set $\text{out}.c_1 = \text{CT}_{\text{sym,pos}}$.

   ii. If $(\text{Trap.ST TS} = \text{pos}) \wedge (\text{pos} = 1))$, compute $\text{CT}_{st,\text{pos}} = \text{SKE.Dec}(\text{Trap.SKE.K}, C_2)$ and set $\text{out}.c_2 = \text{CT}_{st,1}$.

(b) If $((\text{Trap.global-salt} = \text{gsalt}) \wedge (\text{Trap.mode-trap}_1 = 1))$, do the following:

   i. If $((\text{Trap.Sym TS}_1 = \text{pos}) \wedge (\text{pos} \leq \ell))$, set $\text{inp}.u_1 = \text{Trap.Sym val}_1$ with the symbol to be encrypted and output at time step pos.

   ii. If $((\text{Trap.ST TS}_1 = \text{pos}) \wedge (\text{pos} = 1))$, set $\text{inp}.u_2 = \text{Trap.ST val}_1$ with the start state to be encrypted and output at time step 1.

(c) If $((\text{Trap.global-salt} = \text{gsalt}) \wedge (\text{Trap.mode-trap}_2 = 1))$, do the following:

   i. If $((\text{Trap.Sym TS}_2 = \text{pos}) \wedge (\text{pos} \leq \ell))$, set $\text{inp}.u_1 = \text{Trap.Sym val}_2$ with the symbol to be encrypted and output at time step pos.

   ii. If $((\text{Trap.ST TS}_2 = \text{pos}) \wedge (\text{pos} = 1))$, set $\text{inp}.u_2 = \text{Trap.ST val}_2$ with the start state to be encrypted and output at time step 1.

(d) If $\text{Trap.global-salt} < \text{gsalt}$, set $b = 0$, if $\text{Trap.global-salt} > \text{gsalt}$, set $b = 1$.

   i. If $\text{pos} \neq 1$, update $\text{inp} = (\text{Trap.val}_b, \perp)$; else update $\text{inp} = (\text{Trap.val}_b, \text{q}_{st})$.

If $\text{Trap.key-id} > \text{rand},$ set $b = 1$, **if** $\text{Trap.key-id} < \text{rand}$ set $b = 0$.

(a) If $\text{pos} \neq 1$, update $\text{inp} = (\text{Trap.val}_b, \perp)$; else update $\text{inp} = (\text{Trap.val}_b, \text{q}_{st})$.

Output. Return (inp, out).

Fig. 8. Subroutine handling the trapdoor modes in Agg. This is "active" only in the proof.

4.2   Correctness of Multi-input TMFE

The proof of correctness is split into two parts. In the first part we argue that, given as input the secret key $\mathsf{SK_{Agg}}$ along with k ciphertexts under the kFE scheme, exactly one of which encodes a symbol and the other $(k-1)$ encode the individual input lengths, the kFE.Dec algorithm computes a 1FE ciphertext component of the symbol with its updated position in the global string. By repeating this process for all symbols encoded by all users, we obtain a sequence of 1FE ciphertext components, each containing its updated position in the aggregated string. Additionally, each of these ciphertext components contains a global/aggregate salt that is generated from concatenating each individual encryptor's randomly generated salts. This global salt identifies the particular input combination being aggregated.

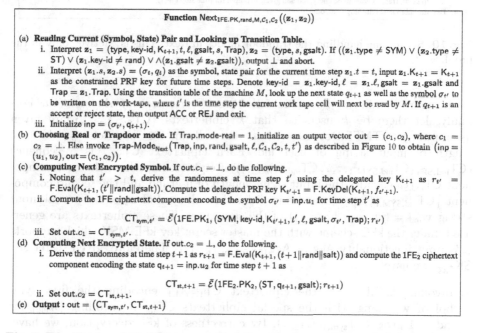

Function $\mathsf{Next}_{\mathsf{1FE.PK,rand},M,\mathcal{C}_1,\mathcal{C}_2}\big((\mathbf{z}_1,\mathbf{z}_2)\big)$

(a) **Reading Current (Symbol, State) Pair and Looking up Transition Table.**
  i. Interpret $\mathbf{z}_1 = (\text{type, key-id}, \mathsf{K}_{t+1}, t, \ell, \text{gsalt}, s, \text{Trap})$, $\mathbf{z}_2 = (\text{type}, s, \text{gsalt})$. If $((\mathbf{z}_1.\text{type} \neq \mathsf{SYM}) \vee (\mathbf{z}_2.\text{type} \neq$
     $\mathsf{ST}) \vee (\mathbf{z}_1.\text{key-id} \neq \text{rand}) \vee \wedge(\mathbf{z}_1.\text{gsalt} \neq \mathbf{z}_2.\text{gsalt}))$, output $\bot$ and abort.
  ii. Interpret $(\mathbf{z}_1.s, \mathbf{z}_2.s) = (\sigma_t, q_t)$ as the symbol, state pair for the current time step $\mathbf{z}_1.t = t$, input $\mathbf{z}_1.\mathsf{K}_{t+1} = \mathsf{K}_{t+1}$
     as the constrained PRF key for future time steps. Denote key-id $= \mathbf{z}_1.\text{key-id}$, $\ell = \mathbf{z}_1.\ell$, gsalt $= \mathbf{z}_1.\text{gsalt}$ and
     $\text{Trap} = \mathbf{z}_1.\text{Trap}$. Using the transition table of the machine M, look up the next state q_{t+1} as well as the symbol $\sigma_{t'}$ to
     be written on the work-tape, where t' is the time step the current work tape cell will next be read by M. If q_{t+1} is an
     accept or reject state, then output ACC or REJ and exit.
  iii. Initialize inp $= (\sigma_{t'}, q_{t+1})$.
(b) **Choosing Real or Trapdoor mode.** If $\text{Trap.mode-real} = 1$, initialize an output vector out $= (c_1, c_2)$, where $c_1 =$
  $c_2 = \bot$. Else invoke $\mathsf{Trap\text{-}Mode}_{\mathsf{Next}}\big(\text{Trap, inp, rand, gsalt}, \ell, \mathcal{C}_1, \mathcal{C}_2, t, t'\big)$ as described in Figure 10 to obtain $\big($inp $=$
  (u_1, u_2), out $=(c_1, c_2)\big)$.
(c) **Computing Next Encrypted Symbol.** If out.$c_1 = \bot$, do the following.
  i. Noting that $t' > t$, derive the randomness at time step t' using the delegated key K_{t+1} as $r_{t'} =$
     $\mathsf{F.Eval}(\mathsf{K}_{t+1}, (t'\|\text{rand}\|\text{gsalt}))$. Compute the delegated PRF key $\mathsf{K}_{t'+1} = \mathsf{F.KeyDel}(\mathsf{K}_{t+1}, f_{t'+1})$.
  ii. Compute the 1FE ciphertext component encoding the symbol $\sigma_{t'} = \text{inp}.u_1$ for time step t' as

$$\mathsf{CT}_{\text{sym},t'} = \bar{\mathcal{E}}\big(\mathsf{1FE.PK}_1, (\mathsf{SYM}, \text{key-id}, \mathsf{K}_{t'+1}, t', \ell, \text{gsalt}, \sigma_{t'}, \text{Trap}); r_{t'}\big)$$

  iii. Set out.$c_1 = \mathsf{CT}_{\text{sym},t'}$.
(d) **Computing Next Encrypted State.** If out.$c_2 = \bot$, do the following.
  i. Derive the randomness at time step $t+1$ as $r_{t+1} = \mathsf{F.Eval}(\mathsf{K}_{t+1}, (t+1\|\text{rand}\|\text{salt}))$ and compute the $\mathsf{1FE}_2$ ciphertext
     component encoding the state $q_{t+1} = \text{inp}.u_2$ for time step $t+1$ as

$$\mathsf{CT}_{\text{st},t+1} = \bar{\mathcal{E}}\big(\mathsf{1FE}_2.\mathsf{PK}_2, (\mathsf{ST}, q_{t+1}, \text{gsalt}); r_{t+1}\big)$$

  ii. Set out.$c_2 = \mathsf{CT}_{\text{st},t+1}$.
(e) **Output :** out $= \big(\mathsf{CT}_{\text{sym},t'}, \mathsf{CT}_{\text{st},t+1}\big)$

Fig. 9. Function to mimic TM computation. It reads the current symbol, state pair and outputs an encryption of the new state and symbol to be written under the appropriate randomness generated using a cPRF.

Correctness of the second part corresponds to the correct execution of the Turing machine on the aggregate sequence of ciphertexts, and this is exactly the same as in Sect. 3. As before, we maintain the invariant that at any time step t, the input to the 1FE.Dec algorithm is a complete 1FE ciphertext decomposed into two components corresponding to symbol and state (along with additional auxiliary inputs), both computed with the same randomness $\mathsf{F.Eval}(\mathsf{K}_0, (t\|\text{rand}\|\text{gsalt}))$.

Subroutine Trap-Mode$_{\text{Next}}$(Trap, inp, rand, gsalt, ℓ, $\mathcal{C}_1$, $\mathcal{C}_2$, t, t')

Interpret the input vector inp $= (u_1, u_2) = (\sigma_{t'}, q_{t+1})$ and initialize the output vector out $= (c_2, c_2)$, where $c_1 = c_2 = \perp$.

1. If $((\text{Trap.key-id} = \text{salt}) \wedge (\text{Trap.global-salt} = \text{gsalt}) \wedge (\text{Trap.mode-trap}_3 = 1))$, do the following.
    (a) If $((\text{Trap.Sym TS} = t) \wedge (\text{Trap.Target TS} = t') \wedge (t > \ell))$, compute the 1FE$_2$ symbol ciphertext $\text{CT}_{\text{sym},t'} = \text{SKE.Dec}(\text{Trap.SKE.K}, \mathcal{C}_1)$ and set out.$c_1 = \text{CT}_{\text{sym},t'}$.

    (b) If $((\text{Trap.ST TS} = t) \wedge (\text{Trap.Target TS} = t + 1) \wedge (t > 1))$, compute the 1FE$_2$ state ciphertext $\text{CT}_{\text{st},t+1} = \text{SKE.Dec}(\text{Trap.SKE.K}, \mathcal{C}_2)$ and set out.$c_2 = \text{CT}_{\text{st},t+1}$.
2. If $((\text{Trap.key-id} = \text{salt}) \wedge (\text{Trap.global-salt} = \text{gsalt}) \wedge (\text{Trap.mode-trap}_1 = 1))$, do the following:
    (a) If $((\text{Trap.Sym TS}_1 = t) \wedge (\text{Trap.Target TS}_1 = t') \wedge (t > \ell))$, set inp.$u_1 = \text{Trap.Sym val}_1$ with the symbol $\sigma_{t'} = \text{Trap.Sym val}_1$ to be encrypted and given as output for time step t'.

    (b) If $((\text{Trap.ST TS}_1 = t) \wedge (\text{Trap.Target TS}_1 = t + 1) \wedge (t > 1))$, set inp.$u_2 = \text{Trap.ST val}_1$ with the state $q_{t+1} = \text{Trap.ST val}_1$ to be encrypted and given as output for time step $t + 1$.
3. If $((\text{Trap.key-id} = \text{salt}) \wedge (\text{Trap.global-salt} = \text{gsalt}) \wedge (\text{Trap.mode-trap}_2 = 1))$, do the following:
    (a) If $((\text{Trap.Sym TS}_2 = t) \wedge (\text{Trap.Target TS}_2 = t') \wedge (t > \ell))$, set inp.$u_1 = \text{Trap.Sym val}_2$ with the symbol $\sigma_{t'} = \text{Trap.Sym val}_2$ to be encrypted and given as output for time step t'.

    (b) If $((\text{Trap.ST TS}_2 = t) \wedge (\text{Trap.Target TS}_2 = t + 1) \wedge (t > 1))$, set inp.$u_2 = \text{Trap.ST val}_2$ with the state $q_{t+1} = \text{Trap.ST val}_2$ to be encrypted and given as output for time step $t + 1$.
4. Exit the subroutine returning (inp, out).

Fig. 10. Subroutine handling the trapdoor modes in Next. This is "active" only in the proof.

In more detail, we have the following. *Correctness of Aggregation.* Formally, let there be k users so that k ciphertexts $\{\text{CT}_{\mathbf{w}_{\text{ind}}}\}_{\text{ind} \in [k]}$ are given as input to kTMFE.Dec algorithm. For all ind $\in [k]$, let ℓ_{ind} be the length of input string of user ind. Each ciphertext $\text{CT}_{\mathbf{w}_{\text{ind}}}$ is a sequence $(\text{CT}_{\text{ind},\text{SP}}, (\text{CT}_{\text{ind},\text{SYM},1}, \dots, \text{CT}_{\text{ind},\text{SYM},\ell_{\text{ind}}}))$ of ciphertexts, where the first component $\text{CT}_{\text{ind},\text{SP}}$ encodes the input string length of user ind and the second component $\{\text{CT}_{\text{ind},\text{SYM},i}\}_{i \in [\ell_{\text{ind}}]}$ encodes in order the i-th symbol w_i of the actual input string $\mathbf{w}_{\text{ind}} = (w_1, w_2, \dots, w_{\ell_{\text{ind}}})$ of the same user. These ciphertexts are generated under the kFE scheme with the master secret key kFE.MSK which supports a k-input functionality $\text{Agg} := \text{Agg}_{\text{1FE.PK},\text{rand},q_{\text{st}},\perp,\perp}$. Therefore, given secret key SK_{Agg}, we have:

1. Invoking kFE.Dec on the ciphertext $\text{CT}_{1,\text{SYM},1}$ encoding the first symbol of $\mathbf{w}_1$ along with the special ciphertexts $\text{CT}_{\text{ind},\text{SP}}$ encoding $|\mathbf{w}_{\text{ind}}|$ for ind $\neq 1$ gives $(\text{CT}_{\text{sym},1}, \text{CT}_{\text{st},1})$. By correctness of kFE decryption, we have: $\text{kFE.Dec}\big(\text{SK}_{\text{Agg}}, (\text{CT}_{1,\text{SYM},1}, \{\text{CT}_{\text{ind},\text{SP}}\}_{\text{ind} \in [k] \setminus \{1\}})\big) = (\text{CT}_{\text{sym},1}, \text{CT}_{\text{st},1})$.
2. Invoking kFE.Dec on the ciphertext $\text{CT}_{1,\text{SYM},j}$ encoding the jth symbol of $\mathbf{w}_1$ along with the special ciphertexts $\text{CT}_{\text{ind},\text{SP}}$ encoding $|\mathbf{w}_{\text{ind}}|$ for ind $\neq 1$ gives $(\text{CT}_{\text{sym},j}, \perp)$. By correctness of kFE decryption, we have: $\text{kFE.Dec}\big(\text{SK}_{\text{Agg}}, (\text{CT}_{1,\text{SYM},j}, \{\text{CT}_{\text{ind},\text{SP}}\}_{\text{ind} \in [k] \setminus \{1\}})\big) = (\text{CT}_{\text{sym},j}, \perp)$.
3. Finally, $\forall$ ind $\in [k] \setminus \{1\}$, invoking kFE.Dec on the ciphertext $\text{CT}_{\text{ind},\text{SYM},j}$ encoding the jth symbol of $\mathbf{w}_{\text{ind}}$ along with the special ciphertexts $\text{CT}_{\text{ind}',\text{SP}}$ encoding $|\mathbf{w}_{\text{ind}'}|$ for ind $\neq \text{ind}'$ computes the new global position of the symbol in the aggregated string and outputs $(\text{CT}_{\text{sym},\widetilde{L}_i+j}, \perp)$. By correctness of kFE decryption, we have: $\text{kFE.Dec}\big(\text{SK}_{\text{Agg}}, (\text{CT}_{\text{ind},\text{SYM},j}, \{\text{CT}_{\text{ind}',\text{SP}}\}_{\text{ind}' \in [k] \setminus \{\text{ind}\}})\big) = (\text{CT}_{\text{sym},\widetilde{L}_i+j}, \perp)$, where $\widetilde{L}_i = \sum_{m=1}^{\text{ind}-1} \ell_m$.

Note that $\mathsf{F.Eval}(\mathsf{K}_0, (\mathsf{pos}\|\mathsf{rand}\|\mathsf{gsalt}))$ is the randomness used to compute each of these ciphertext components, where pos refers to the global position specific to a symbol in the aggregate input string.

Correctness of TM Execution. The 1FE scheme supports the functionality $\mathsf{Next} := \mathsf{Next}_{\mathsf{1FE.PK},\mathsf{rand},M,\perp,\perp}$. Let the newly generated and organized sequence of ciphertexts based on time steps be as follows: $\big((\mathsf{CT}_{\mathsf{sym},1}, \mathsf{CT}_{\mathsf{st},1}), \{\mathsf{CT}_{\mathsf{sym},i}\}_{i\in[2,L_k]} \big)$ with $L_k = \sum_{i=1}^{k}\ell_i$. Let $\mathbf{w} = (w_1, w_2, \ldots, w_{\ell_1}, w_{\ell_1+1}, w_{\ell_1+2}, \ldots, w_{\ell_1+\ell_2}, \ldots, w_{L_k})$ be the aggregated input string and define $\tau = \mathsf{runtime}(M, \mathbf{w})$. For any time step $t \in [\tau - 2]$, we have

1. Let $t \in [\tau - 2] \setminus [\ell]$. If the current work tape cell was accessed[10], at some time step $\tilde{t} < t$, then $\mathsf{CT}_{\mathsf{sym},t}$ encoding $(\mathsf{SYM}, \mathsf{key\text{-}id}, \mathsf{K}_{t+1}, t, \ell, \mathsf{gsalt}, \sigma_t, \mathsf{Trap})$ was constructed at time step $\tilde{t}$. Note that σ_t may be the blank symbol β. When $t \in [\ell]$, $\mathsf{CT}_{\mathsf{sym},t}$ is constructed at time step t via the Agg circuit.
2. The ciphertext component $\mathsf{CT}_{\mathsf{st},t}$ encoding $(\mathsf{ST}, \mathsf{q}_t, \mathsf{gsalt})$ at time step t was constructed at time step $t - 1$ for $t > 1$ and at time step 1, when $t = 1$.
3. The randomness $r_t = \mathsf{F.Eval}(\mathsf{K}_{\tilde{t}+1}, (t\|\mathsf{rand}\|\mathsf{gsalt})) = \mathsf{F.Eval}(\mathsf{K}_t, (t\|\mathsf{rand}\|\mathsf{gsalt}))$ binds $\mathsf{CT}_{\mathsf{sym},t}$ and $\mathsf{CT}_{\mathsf{st},t}$ and both the encoded messages also share the same global salt.

Thus, at any given time step $t \in [\tau - 2]$, we have a complete ciphertext of 1FE which may be fed again with $\mathsf{SK}_{\mathsf{Next}}$ to 1FE.Dec in order to proceed with the computation. Thus, the execution of 1FE.Dec at the $(\tau - 2)^{\text{th}}$ time step provides the complete pair $(\mathsf{CT}_{\mathsf{sym},\tau-1}, \mathsf{CT}_{\mathsf{st},\tau-1})$. By the correctness of 1FE scheme again, at time step $t = \tau - 1$, invoking $\mathsf{1FE.Dec}(\mathsf{SK}_{\mathsf{Next}}, (\mathsf{CT}_{\mathsf{sym},\tau-1}, \mathsf{CT}_{\mathsf{st},\tau-1}))$ outputs either "Accept" or "Reject" by simulating the execution of M for the final time step τ inside the function Next, thus correctly outputting $M(\mathbf{w})$.

4.3   Proof of Security for Multi-input TMFE

Security of the above construction follows the same blueprint as the proof in Sect. 3 except that instead of single input functionality ReRand, we now use a k-input functionality Agg to aggregate and rerandomize the inputs. We emphasize that the outputs produced by the Agg functionality are *exactly the same* as the outputs produced by ReRand functionality in Sect. 3: namely a sequence of 1FE ciphertexts encoding the symbol and global position, computed using randomness derived from a cPRF. Hence, the chief new ingredient in the security proof is the security of Agg functionality, which is derived from the security of the kFE scheme.

---

[10] We assume that every time a cell is accessed, it is written to, by writing the same symbol again if no change is made.

Formally, we argue that:

Theorem 2. *Assume that the k input FE for circuits* kFE *satisfies standard indistinguishability, and the single input FE for circuits* 1FE *satisfies distributional indistinguishability. Assume that the* cPRF *is secure according to definition. Then, the above construction of k input* kTMFE *satisfies standard indistinguishability.*

The proof follows the outline of the single input case, except that now we must additionally keep track of multiple execution threads corresponding to various combinations of ciphertexts across multiple users, i.e. various "global salt" values. In more detail, if each of k users makes Q ciphertext requests, then we have Q^k total possible combinations of ciphertexts, each yielding a different execution thread per key. Note that each of the Q^k combinations is identified with a unique "global salt". We will assume w.l.o.g that there is a lexicographic ordering on all the global salt values; this can be easily ensured by associating a counter value with each random salt. We do not explicitly include this for notational brevity.

In the single input case, we replaced the execution chain of a machine over an input string from $b = 0$ to $b = 1$, step by step, and enumerated over all keys. Now, we again replace an execution chain step by step as in the single input case, but additionally enumerate over all Q^k combinations for each key, as well as over all keys as before. The number of hybrids grows multiplicatively by Q^k. Details are again deferred to in the full version [1].

5 Indistinguishability Obfuscation for Turing Machines

In this section we construct indistinguishability obfuscation for Turing machines with bounded length input, i.e. the input length $n = n(\lambda)$ is any fixed polynomial in the security parameter. To support inputs of length n, we need an $(n+1)$-ary miFE for Turing machines denoted as $(\mathsf{n+1})$-TMFE; we instantiate this with our construction from Sect. 4.

5.1 Construction

Let $\mathcal{M} = \{\mathcal{M}_\lambda\}_{\lambda \in \mathbb{N}}$ denote an ensemble of Turing machines with alphabet $\Sigma_\lambda = \{0,1\}$. Let $\mathsf{Encode} = \{\mathsf{Encode}_\lambda : \mathcal{M}_\lambda \to \Sigma_{\mathsf{enc}}^*\}_{\lambda \in \mathbb{N}}$ be an ensemble of encoding schemes for $\mathcal{M}$ on alphabet Σ_{enc} such that for any $M \in \mathcal{M}_\lambda, \mathsf{Encode}_\lambda(M) = \langle M \rangle$. Further, let $\mathcal{U} = \{\mathsf{U}_\lambda\}_{\lambda \in \mathbb{N}}$ denote the set of Universal Turing machines parameterized by the security parameter with alphabet $\Sigma_{\mathcal{U}} = \Sigma_{\mathsf{enc}} \cup \Sigma_\lambda$ such that for all $\lambda \in \mathbb{N}$, for any $M \in \mathcal{M}_\lambda$ and any $\mathbf{x} = (x_1, \ldots, x_n) \in \Sigma_\lambda^n$, $\mathsf{U}_\lambda(\mathbf{x}, \langle M \rangle)$ takes $\mathbf{x}$ and an encoding $\langle M \rangle$ of M, simulates M on $\mathbf{x}$ and outputs $M(\mathbf{x})$.

Let $(\mathsf{n+1})$-TMFE denote the $(n + 1)$-ary multi-input functional encryption scheme for Turing machines with alphabet $\Sigma_{\mathcal{U}}$. We construct an ensemble of indistinguishability obfuscators $\mathsf{iO} = \{\mathsf{iO}_\lambda\}_{\lambda \in \mathbb{N}}$ with $\mathsf{iO}_\lambda = (\mathsf{iO}.\mathsf{Obf}, \mathsf{iO}.\mathsf{Eval})$ for $\mathcal{M}_\lambda$ with inputs $\mathbf{x} \in \Sigma_\lambda^n$ as follows.

iO.Obf$(1^\lambda, 1^n, M)$: On input the security parameter λ, a bound $n \in \mathbb{N}$ and a Turing machine $M \in \mathcal{M}_\lambda$, do the following:

1. Compute the encoding of M as Encode$_\lambda$ $(M) = \langle M \rangle$.
2. Compute a master secret key MSK $\leftarrow$ (n+1)-TMFE.Setup $(1^\lambda, 1^{n+1})$.
3. Compute the secret key for machine U_λ as SK_U $\leftarrow$ (n+1)-TMFE.KeyGen(MSK, U_λ).
4. For $i \in [n]$, compute the encryptions $CT_i^b = $ (n+1)-TMFE.Enc(MSK, (b, i)), $b \in \Sigma_\lambda$.
5. Compute the encoding of M as $CT_{n+1} = $ (n+1)-TMFE.Enc(MSK, $(\langle M \rangle, n+1)$).
6. Output the obfuscated machine as $\widetilde{M}$ = $\Big(SK_U, \big(\{CT_i^b\}_{i \in \{1,\ldots,n\}, b \in \Sigma_\lambda}, CT_{n+1}\big)\Big)$.

iO.Eval$(\widetilde{M}, \mathbf{x})$: On input the obfuscated machine $\widetilde{M}$ and an input $\mathbf{x} \in \Sigma_\lambda^n$, do the following:

1. Parse $\widetilde{M} = \Big(SK_U, \big(\{CT_i^b\}_{i \in \{1,\ldots,n\}, b \in \Sigma_\lambda}, CT_{n+1}\big)\Big)$ and $\mathbf{x} = (x_1, \ldots, x_n)$.
2. Compute and output (n+1)-TMFE.Dec $(SK_U, (CT_1^{x_1}, \ldots, CT_n^{x_n}, CT_{n+1}))$.

Correctness is directly followed by the correctness of (n+1)-TMFE scheme. Since the (n+1)-TMFE we use is compact, the obfuscation size obtained by the above scheme is poly$(\lambda, |U|, |M|, n)$. In the full version [1], we show that our construction is secure:

Theorem 3. *Assume that* (n+1)-TMFE *is a 1-key, 2-ciphertext selectively secure* (n+1)-*ary multi-input functional encryption scheme for Turing machines which satisfies standard indistinguishability. Then the construction in Sect. 5.1 is a secure indistinguishability obfuscator for the Turing machines with bounded input length* n.

Acknowledgement. We thank Vinod Vaikuntanathan for suggesting the generic transformation from FE to decomposable FE.

A   Construction: Decomposable FE for Circuits

Given any single-input circuit FE scheme 1FE satisfying standard indistinguishability based security, a *projective* garbled circuit scheme GC = (GCirc, GInp, GEval) with indistinguishability based security [35] supporting a circuit class $\mathcal{C} = \{\mathcal{C}_\lambda\}_{\lambda \in \mathbb{N}}$ with n-bit inputs, a simple PRF F = (F.Setup, F.Eval) and a symmetric encryption scheme SYM, we can construct a single-input decomposable FE scheme DFE supporting the circuit class $\mathcal{C}$. We note that projective garbled circuit schemes satisfying indistinguishability based security are implied from one-way functions [35].

DFE.Setup$(1^\lambda, 1^n)$: On input the security parameter λ and input message size n, do the following:

1. Generate $(\mathsf{1FE.PK}, \mathsf{1FE.MSK}) \leftarrow \mathsf{1FE.Setup}(1^\lambda, 1^{2\lambda + \log n + 2})$.
2. Output $(\mathsf{PK}, \mathsf{MSK}) = (\mathsf{1FE.PK}, \mathsf{1FE.MSK})$.

$\mathsf{DFE.Enc}(\mathsf{PK}, \mathbf{x})$: On input the public key PK and a message $\mathbf{x} = (x_1, \ldots, x_n)$ of length $n = |\mathbf{x}|$, do the following:

1. Sample a PRF key $\mathsf{K} \leftarrow \mathsf{F.Setup}(1^\lambda)$ and set a flag mode $= 0$.
2. Compute $\mathsf{CT}_{x_i} = \mathsf{1FE.Enc}(\mathsf{PK}, (\mathsf{K}, \mathbf{0}, i, x_i, \mathsf{mode})), \forall i \in [n]$ and output $\mathsf{CT}_{\mathbf{x}} = \{\mathsf{CT}_{x_i}\}_{i \in [n]}$.

$\mathsf{DFE.KeyGen}(\mathsf{MSK}, C)$: On input the master secret key MSK and a circuit $C \in \mathcal{C}_\lambda$, do the following:

1. Sample a random salt $\leftarrow \{0,1\}^\lambda$, $\mathsf{CT}_i \leftarrow \{0,1\}^{\ell(\lambda)}, \forall i \in [0, n]$.
2. Output $\mathsf{SK}_{\widehat{C}} = \mathsf{1FE.KeyGen}(\mathsf{MSK}, \widehat{C}_{C,\mathsf{salt},\{\mathsf{CT}_i\}_{i \in [n]},\mathsf{CT}_0})$, where $\widehat{C}_{C,\mathsf{salt},}$ $\{\mathsf{SYM.CT}_i\}_{i \in [n]}, \mathsf{SYM.CT}_{\widetilde{C}}$ is a circuit described in Fig. 11.

$\mathsf{DFE.Dec}(\mathsf{SK}_{\widehat{C}}, \mathsf{CT}_{\mathbf{x}})$: On input a function key $\mathsf{SK}_{\widehat{C}}$ and a decomposed ciphertext $\mathsf{CT}_{\mathbf{x}} = \{\mathsf{CT}_{x_i}\}_{i \in [n]}$, do the following:

1. For $i = 1$, invoke $\mathsf{1FE.Dec}(\mathsf{SK}_{\widehat{C}}, \mathsf{CT}_{x_1})$ to obtain a pair $(\ell_{1,x_1}, \widetilde{C})$.
2. For all $i \in [2, n]$, invoke $\mathsf{1FE.Dec}(\mathsf{SK}_{\widehat{C}}, \mathsf{CT}_{x_i})$ to obtain $(\ell_{i,x_i}, \perp)$.
3. Note that $\widetilde{\mathbf{x}} = \{\ell_{i,x_i}\}_{i \in [n]}$ represents the labels corresponding to the garbled input underlying $\mathsf{CT}_{\mathbf{x}}$ generated as outputs of $\widehat{C}$, while $\widetilde{C}$ represents the garbled circuit for C.
4. Run $\mathsf{GEval}(\widetilde{C}, \widetilde{\mathbf{x}})$ to get $\mathbf{y}$.

Functionality $\widehat{C}_{C,\mathsf{salt},\{\mathsf{SYM.CT}_i\}_{i\in[n]},\mathsf{SYM.CT}_{\widetilde{C}}}(\mathsf{K}, \mathsf{SYM.K}, i, x_i, \mathsf{mode})$

(a) Initialize the vector out $= (c_1, c_2)$, where $c_j = \perp, \forall j \in [2]$.
(b) If mode $= 1$, do the following:
    i. Let out.$c_1 = \mathsf{SYM.Dec}(\mathsf{SYM.K}, \mathsf{SYM.CT}_i)$.
    ii. If $i = 1$, let out.$c_2 = \mathsf{SYM.Dec}(\mathsf{SYM.K}, \mathsf{SYM.CT}_{\widetilde{C}})$.
(c) If mode $= 0$, do the following:
    i. Compute randomness $r = \mathsf{F.Eval}(\mathsf{K}, \mathsf{salt})$.
    ii. Use randomness r to generate the garbled circuit for C as $(\widetilde{C}, \mathsf{sk}) = \mathsf{GCirc}(1^\lambda, C; r)$ as well as to generate the label corresponding to the ith input wire as $\ell_{i,x_i} = \mathsf{GInp}(\mathsf{sk}, (x_i, i); r)$.
    iii. Let out.$c_1 = \ell_{i,x_i}$. If $i = 1$, let out.$c_2 = \widetilde{C}$.
(d) **Output :** out.

Fig. 11. Functionality $\widehat{C}_{C,\mathsf{salt},\{\mathsf{SYM.CT}_i\}_{i\in[n]},\mathsf{SYM.CT}_{\widetilde{C}}}$

Correctness. We have by correctness of $\mathsf{1FE.Dec}$ that it outputs the garbled input $\widetilde{\mathbf{x}}$ and the garbled circuit $\widetilde{C}$ correctly. The correctness of GEval implies that decryption recovers $C(\mathbf{x})$ as desired.

The proof of security is provided in the full version [1].

References

1. Agrawal, S., Maitra, M.: FE and IO for turing machines from minimal assumptions. Cryptology ePrint Archive, Report 2018/ (2018). http://www.cse.iitm.ac.in/~shwetaag/research/tm-mife-full.pdf
2. Agrawal, S., Singh, I.P.: Reusable garbled deterministic finite automata from lWE. In: ICALP (2017)
3. Ananth, P., Brakerski, Z., Segev, G., Vaikuntanathan, V.: From selective to adaptive security in functional encryption. In: Gennaro, R., Robshaw, M. (eds.) CRYPTO 2015. LNCS, vol. 9216, pp. 657–677. Springer, Heidelberg (2015). https://doi.org/10.1007/978-3-662-48000-7_32
4. Ananth, P., Chen, Y.-C., Chung, K.-M., Lin, H., Lin, W.-K.: Delegating RAM computations with adaptive soundness and privacy. In: Hirt, M., Smith, A. (eds.) TCC 2016. LNCS, vol. 9986, pp. 3–30. Springer, Heidelberg (2016). https://doi.org/10.1007/978-3-662-53644-5_1
5. Ananth, P., Jain, A.: Indistinguishability obfuscation from compact functional encryption. In: Gennaro, R., Robshaw, M. (eds.) CRYPTO 2015. LNCS, vol. 9215, pp. 308–326. Springer, Heidelberg (2015). https://doi.org/10.1007/978-3-662-47989-6_15
6. Ananth, P., Jain, A., Sahai, A.: Indistinguishability obfuscation for turing machines: constant overhead and amortization. In: Katz, J., Shacham, H. (eds.) CRYPTO 2017. LNCS, vol. 10402, pp. 252–279. Springer, Cham (2017). https://doi.org/10.1007/978-3-319-63715-0_9
7. Ananth, P., Sahai, A.: Functional encryption for turing machines. In: Kushilevitz, E., Malkin, T. (eds.) TCC 2016. LNCS, vol. 9562, pp. 125–153. Springer, Heidelberg (2016). https://doi.org/10.1007/978-3-662-49096-9_6
8. Ananth, P., Sahai, A.: Projective arithmetic functional encryption and indistinguishability obfuscation from degree-5 multilinear maps. In: Coron, J.-S., Nielsen, J.B. (eds.) EUROCRYPT 2017. LNCS, vol. 10210, pp. 152–181. Springer, Cham (2017). https://doi.org/10.1007/978-3-319-56620-7_6
9. Applebaum, B., Ishai, Y., Kushilevitz, E.: How to garble arithmetic circuits. SIAM J. Comput. **43**(2), 905–929 (2014)
10. Badrinarayanan, S., Gupta, D., Jain, A., Sahai, A.: Multi-input functional encryption for unbounded arity functions. In: Iwata, T., Cheon, J.H. (eds.) ASIACRYPT 2015. LNCS, vol. 9452, pp. 27–51. Springer, Heidelberg (2015). https://doi.org/10.1007/978-3-662-48797-6_2
11. Barak, B., et al.: On the (Im)possibility of obfuscating programs. In: Kilian, J. (ed.) CRYPTO 2001. LNCS, vol. 2139, pp. 1–18. Springer, Heidelberg (2001). https://doi.org/10.1007/3-540-44647-8_1
12. Bitansky, N., Garg, S., Lin, H., Pass, R., Telang, S.: Succinct randomized encodings and their applications. In: STOC (2015)
13. Bitansky, N., Nishimaki, R., Passelègue, A., Wichs, D.: From cryptomania to obfustopia through secret-key functional encryption. In: Hirt, M., Smith, A. (eds.) TCC 2016. LNCS, vol. 9986, pp. 391–418. Springer, Heidelberg (2016). https://doi.org/10.1007/978-3-662-53644-5_15
14. Bitansky, N., Paneth, O., Rosen, A.: On the cryptographic hardness of finding a nash equilibrium. In: 2015 IEEE 56th Annual Symposium on Foundations of Computer Science (FOCS), pp. 1480–1498. IEEE (2015)
15. Bitansky, N., Vaikuntanathan, V.; Indistinguishability obfuscation from functional encryption. In: FOCS (2015)

16. Boneh, D., Sahai, A., Waters, B.: Functional encryption: definitions and challenges. In: Ishai, Y. (ed.) TCC 2011. LNCS, vol. 6597, pp. 253–273. Springer, Heidelberg (2011). https://doi.org/10.1007/978-3-642-19571-6_16

17. Boneh, D., Waters, B.: Constrained pseudorandom functions and their applications. In: Sako, K., Sarkar, P. (eds.) ASIACRYPT 2013. LNCS, vol. 8270, pp. 280–300. Springer, Heidelberg (2013). https://doi.org/10.1007/978-3-642-42045-0_15

18. Boyle, E., Goldwasser, S., Ivan, I.: Functional signatures and pseudorandom functions. In: Krawczyk, H. (ed.) PKC 2014. LNCS, vol. 8383, pp. 501–519. Springer, Heidelberg (2014). https://doi.org/10.1007/978-3-642-54631-0_29

19. Brakerski, Z., Komargodski, I., Segev, G.: Multi-input functional encryption in the private-key setting: stronger security from weaker assumptions. In: Fischlin, M., Coron, J.-S. (eds.) EUROCRYPT 2016. LNCS, vol. 9666, pp. 852–880. Springer, Heidelberg (2016). https://doi.org/10.1007/978-3-662-49896-5_30

20. Canetti, R., Chen, Y., Holmgren, J., Raykova, M.: Succinct adaptive garbled RAM. Cryptology ePrint Archive, Report 2015/1074 (2015). https://eprint.iacr.org/2015/1074

21. Canetti, R., Holmgren, J.: Fully succinct garbled RAM. In: Proceedings of the 2016 ACM Conference on Innovations in Theoretical Computer Science, pp. 169–178. ACM (2016)

22. Canetti, R., Holmgren, J., Jain, A., Vaikuntanathan, V.: Indistinguishability obfuscation of iterated circuits and RAM programs. In: Proceedings of the Forty-Seventh Annual ACM on Symposium on Theory of Computing, STOC 2015 (2015)

23. Canetti, R., Lin, H., Tessaro, S., Vaikuntanathan, V.: Obfuscation of probabilistic circuits and applications. In: Dodis, Y., Nielsen, J.B. (eds.) TCC 2015. LNCS, vol. 9015, pp. 468–497. Springer, Heidelberg (2015). https://doi.org/10.1007/978-3-662-46497-7_19

24. Carmer, B., Malozemoff, A.J., Raykova, M.: 5Gen-C: multi-input functional encryption and program obfuscation for arithmetic circuits. In: Proceedings of the 2017 ACM SIGSAC Conference on Computer and Communications Security, pp. 747–764. ACM (2017)

25. Chen, Y.C., Chow, S.S., Chung, K.M., Lai, R.W., Lin, W.K., Zhou, H.S.: Computation-trace indistinguishability obfuscation and its applications. IACR Cryptology ePrint Archive, 2015 (2015)

26. Cohen, A., Holmgren, J., Nishimaki, R., Vaikuntanathan, V., Wichs, D.: Watermarking cryptographic capabilities. In: Proceedings of the Forty-Eighth Annual ACM symposium on Theory of Computing, pp. 1115–1127. ACM (2016)

27. Garg, S., Gentry, C., Halevi, S., Raykova, M., Sahai, A., Waters, B.: Candidate indistinguishability obfuscation and functional encryption for all circuits. In: FOCS (2013). http://eprint.iacr.org/

28. Garg, S., Pandey, O., Srinivasan, A.: Revisiting the cryptographic hardness of finding a nash equilibrium. In: Robshaw, M., Katz, J. (eds.) CRYPTO 2016. LNCS, vol. 9815, pp. 579–604. Springer, Heidelberg (2016). https://doi.org/10.1007/978-3-662-53008-5_20

29. Garg, S., Pandey, O., Srinivasan, A., Zhandry, M.: Breaking the sub-exponential barrier in obfustopia. Technical report, Cryptology ePrint Archive, Report 2016/102 (2016). http://eprint.iacr.org/2016/102

30. Garg, S., Srinivasan, A.: Single-key to multi-key functional encryption with polynomial loss. In: Hirt, M., Smith, A. (eds.) TCC 2016. LNCS, vol. 9986, pp. 419–442. Springer, Heidelberg (2016). https://doi.org/10.1007/978-3-662-53644-5_16

31. Gentry, C., Halevi, S., Raykova, M., Wichs, D.: Outsourcing private RAM computation. In: 55th IEEE Annual Symposium on Foundations of Computer Science, FOCS (2014)

32. Goldreich, O., Goldwasser, S., Micali, S.: How to construct random functions. J. ACM **33**(4), 792–807 (1986)

33. Goldwasser, S., et al.: Multi-input functional encryption. In: Nguyen, P.Q., Oswald, E. (eds.) EUROCRYPT 2014. LNCS, vol. 8441, pp. 578–602. Springer, Heidelberg (2014). https://doi.org/10.1007/978-3-642-55220-5_32

34. Goldwasser, S., Kalai, Y.T., Popa, R.A., Vaikuntanathan, V., Zeldovich, N.: How to run turing machines on encrypted data. In: Canetti, R., Garay, J.A. (eds.) CRYPTO 2013, Part II. LNCS, vol. 8043, pp. 536–553. Springer, Heidelberg (2013). https://doi.org/10.1007/978-3-642-40084-1_30

35. Jafargholi, Z., Scafuro, A., Wichs, D.: Adaptively indistinguishable garbled circuits. In: Kalai, Y., Reyzin, L. (eds.) TCC 2017. LNCS, vol. 10678, pp. 40–71. Springer, Cham (2017). https://doi.org/10.1007/978-3-319-70503-3_2

36. Kiayias, A., Papadopoulos, S., Triandopoulos, N., Zacharias, T.: Delegatable pseudorandom functions and applications. In: Proceedings of the 2013 ACM SIGSAC Conference on Computer & #38; Communications Security, CCS 2013 (2013)

37. Kitagawa, F., Nishimaki, R., Tanaka, K.: Indistinguishability obfuscation for all circuits from secret-key functional encryption. IACR Cryptology ePrint Archive 2017, 361 (2017)

38. Kitagawa, F., Nishimaki, R., Tanaka, K.: Obfustopia built on secret-key functional encryption. In: Nielsen, J.B., Rijmen, V. (eds.) EUROCRYPT 2018. LNCS, vol. 10821, pp. 603–648. Springer, Cham (2018). https://doi.org/10.1007/978-3-319-78375-8_20

39. Kitagawa, F., Nishimaki, R., Tanaka, K.: Simple and generic constructions of succinct functional encryption. In: Abdalla, M., Dahab, R. (eds.) PKC 2018. LNCS, vol. 10770, pp. 187–217. Springer, Cham (2018). https://doi.org/10.1007/978-3-319-76581-5_7

40. Komargodski, I., Segev, G.: From minicrypt to obfustopia via private-key functional encryption. In: Coron, J.-S., Nielsen, J.B. (eds.) EUROCRYPT 2017. LNCS, vol. 10210, pp. 122–151. Springer, Cham (2017). https://doi.org/10.1007/978-3-319-56620-7_5

41. Koppula, V., Lewko, A.B., Waters,B.: Indistinguishability obfuscation for turing machines with unbounded memory. In: Proceedings of the Forty-Seventh Annual ACM on Symposium on Theory of Computing, STOC 2015 (2015)

42. Li, B., Micciancio, D.: Compactness vs collusion resistance in functional encryption. In: Hirt, M., Smith, A. (eds.) TCC 2016. LNCS, vol. 9986, pp. 443–468. Springer, Heidelberg (2016). https://doi.org/10.1007/978-3-662-53644-5_17

43. Lin, H.: Indistinguishability obfuscation from SXDH on 5-linear maps and locality-5 PRGs. In: Katz, J., Shacham, H. (eds.) CRYPTO 2017. LNCS, vol. 10401, pp. 599–629. Springer, Cham (2017). https://doi.org/10.1007/978-3-319-63688-7_20

44. Lin, H., Pass, R., Seth, K., Telang,S.: Output-compressing randomized encodings and applications. In: TCC-A (2016)

45. Lin, H., Tessaro, S.: Indistinguishability obfuscation from trilinear maps and blockwise local PRGs. In: Katz, J., Shacham, H. (eds.) CRYPTO 2017. LNCS, vol. 10401, pp. 630–660. Springer, Cham (2017). https://doi.org/10.1007/978-3-319-63688-7_21

46. Liu, Q., Zhandry, M.: Decomposable obfuscation: a framework for building applications of obfuscation from polynomial hardness. In: Kalai, Y., Reyzin, L. (eds.)

TCC 2017. LNCS, vol. 10677, pp. 138–169. Springer, Cham (2017). https://doi.org/10.1007/978-3-319-70500-2_6

47. Lu, S., Ostrovsky, R.: How to garble RAM programs? In: Johansson, T., Nguyen, P.Q. (eds.) EUROCRYPT 2013. LNCS, vol. 7881, pp. 719–734. Springer, Heidelberg (2013). https://doi.org/10.1007/978-3-642-38348-9_42

48. O'Neill, A.: Definitional issues in functional encryption. IACR Cryptology ePrint Archive 2010, 556 (2010)

49. Sahai, A., Waters, B.: Fuzzy identity-based encryption. In: Cramer, R. (ed.) EUROCRYPT 2005. LNCS, vol. 3494, pp. 457–473. Springer, Heidelberg (2005). https://doi.org/10.1007/11426639_27

50. Sahai, A., Waters, B.: How to use indistinguishability obfuscation: deniable encryption, and more. In: STOC (2014). http://eprint.iacr.org/2013/454.pdf

The MMap Strikes Back: Obfuscation and New Multilinear Maps Immune to CLT13 Zeroizing Attacks

Fermi Ma[✉] and Mark Zhandry

Princeton University, Princeton, USA
fermima1@gmail.com, mzhandry@princeton.edu

Abstract. All known multilinear map candidates have suffered from a class of attacks known as "zeroizing" attacks, which render them unusable for many applications. We provide a new construction of *polynomial-degree* multilinear maps and show that our scheme is provably immune to zeroizing attacks under a strengthening of the Branching Program Un-Annihilatability Assumption (Garg et al., TCC 2016-B).

Concretely, we build our scheme on top of the CLT13 multilinear maps (Coron et al., CRYPTO 2013). In order to justify the security of our new scheme, we devise a weak multilinear map model for CLT13 that captures zeroizing attacks and generalizations, reflecting *all known* classical polynomial-time attacks on CLT13. In our model, we show that our new multilinear map scheme achieves *ideal security*, meaning no known attacks apply to our scheme. Using our scheme, we give a new multiparty key agreement protocol that is several orders of magnitude more efficient that what was previously possible.

We also demonstrate the general applicability of our model by showing that several existing obfuscation and order-revealing encryption schemes, when instantiated with CLT13 maps, are secure against known attacks. These are schemes that are actually being implemented for experimentation, but until our work had no rigorous justification for security.

1 Introduction

Cryptographic multilinear maps have proven to be a revolutionary tool. Very roughly, a multilinear map is an encoding scheme where one can blindly compute polynomials over encoded elements, without any knowledge of the underlying elements. They have been used for numerous cutting-edge cryptographic applications, such as multiparty non-interactive key agreement [2], attribute-based encryption for circuits [3], asymptotically optimal broadcast encryption [4], witness encryption [5], functional encryption [6,7], and most notably mathematical program obfuscation [6]. In turn, obfuscation has been used to construct many more amazing applications [8–15] as well as establish interesting connections to other areas of computer science [16,17].

The full version of this paper is available on the IACR ePrint Archive [1].

ⓒ International Association for Cryptologic Research 2018
A. Beimel and S. Dziembowski (Eds.): TCC 2018, LNCS 11240, pp. 513–543, 2018.
https://doi.org/10.1007/978-3-030-03810-6_19

Unfortunately, all known multilinear maps for degree $d > 2$ [18–20] have suffered from devastating attacks known as "zeroizing" attacks [18,21–23]. These attacks have rendered most of the applications above insecure. In response, many authors introduced "fixes"; these fixes came in many forms, from tweaking how information is extracted from the map [24] to compiling the existing weak multilinear maps into new ones that were presumably stronger [7,25,26]. However, these fixes were largely ad hoc, and indeed it was quickly shown how to generalize the zeroizing attacks to circumvent the fixes [25–29].

Given the many attacks and the speed at which fixes were subsequently broken, researchers have begun attempting to build applications in a sound way using weak maps. The initial observation by Badrinarayanan, Miles, Sahai, and Zhandry [30] is that all (classical polynomial-time[1]) attacks require the ability to obtain an encoding of zero. Miles, Sahai, and Zhandry [36] observed moreover that all zeroizing attacks on the original GGH13 multilinear map have a very similar structure. They define an abstract attack model, called the "annihilating attack model," that encompasses and generalizes all existing zeroizing attacks on these specific maps. Since their initial publication, all subsequent attacks on GGH13 have either relied on quantum procedures [35] or on the specific setting of parameters [34]. On the other hand, zeroizing attacks are inherently *parameter-independent*, as they only depend on the functionality of the zero-testing procedure. It remains the case today that all classical, parameter-independent attacks on GGH13 fit in the "weak model" of Miles et al. [36]. Therefore, this annihilating model appears to be a fully general abstraction of the inherent vulnerabilities of the GGH13 multilinear maps.

Within the weak model, Badrinaryanan et al. [30] constructed a secure witness encryption scheme, while Garg, Miles, Mukherjee, Sahai, Srinivasan, and Zhandry [37] built secure obfuscation and order revealing encryption. Since these constructions have been proven secure in the weak model, they are secure against all known attacks on GGH13. To date, these are the only *direct* applications of multilinear maps that have been proved secure in the weak multilinear map model for GGH13.[2] Moreover, GGH13 is the only multilinear map for which an accurate weak model has been devised. This leads to the following goals:

Devise weak multilinear map models for other multilinear maps — such as CLT13 or GGH15 — that capture all known attack strategies on the maps.

Give new applications of multilinear maps that can be constructed and proven secure in weak multilinear map models.

---

[1] Sub-exponential [31–33], parameter-dependent [34], and quantum attacks [35] have been discovered on multilinear map candidates. In this work we will focus on classical adversaries, and will not consider quantum attacks. We will also not consider parameter-dependent or sub-exponential attacks as a break, since they can be defeated by increasing the security parameter.

[2] Most other applications are possible by using obfuscation as a building block.

A weak multilinear map model for CLT13 is especially important, as it is currently the most efficient multilinear map known [38], and therefore most likely to eventually become usable in practice.

In addition, the vulnerabilities of existing multilinear map candidates lead to a natural third goal:

Construct multilinear maps that are not vulnerable to zeroizing attacks.

There has been some initial progress toward this goal. Several authors [39, 40] have shown how to construct a version of multilinear maps from obfuscation, which can in turn be built from weak multilinear maps using the aforementioned constructions. This gives a compelling proof of concept that multilinear maps immune to zeroizing attacks should be possible. However, as obfuscation is currently incredibly inefficient, such multilinear map constructions are entirely impractical today. Moreover, obfuscation can be used to directly achieve most applications of multilinear maps, so adding a layer of multilinear maps between obfuscation and application will likely compound the efficiency limitations. Therefore, it is important to build multilinear maps without obfuscation.

1.1   Our Work: New Multilinear Maps

In this paper, we make additional progress on all three goals above. We revisit the idea of "fixing" multilinear maps by using weak maps to build strong maps. We do not use obfuscation, though our scheme is inspired by obfuscation techniques. Unlike the fixes discussed above that were quickly broken, we develop our fix in a methodical way that allows us to formally argue our fix is immune to generalizations of zeroizing attacks. Specifically, our results are the following:

Weak CLT13 Model. First, we need a framework in which to argue security against zeroizing attacks. Our first result is a new weak multilinear map model for CLT13 maps. We demonstrate that this model naturally captures all known attack strategies on CLT13. The model is somewhat different from the model for the GGH13 maps, owing to the somewhat different technical details of the attacks. Unlike the GGH13 case, where the common thread amongst all the attacks was rather explicit[3], the common features of CLT13 attacks are a bit more nebulous, and require additional effort to pull out and formalize.

Model Conversion Theorem. To aid the analysis of schemes in our model, we prove that an attack in the weak CLT13 model requires the existence of a certain type of "annihilating polynomial," analogous to the annihilating polynomials in the weak GGH13 model, but simpler. This "plain annihilating model" makes it very easy to test if a particular usage of CLT13 is safe. For example, it is immediate from known results that an *existing* class of obfuscation constructions [30, 41] is secure in our plain annihilating model, under the same algebraic complexity

---

[3] Namely, all attacks compute the ideal $\langle g \rangle$ generated by some element g.

assumption as in [37]. Hence, these schemes are also secure in our weak CLT13 model. This is the first rigorous argument for security of these schemes. We note that these obfuscation constructions are currently being implemented [38], so justifying their security is important.

Note that [30,41] are *not* secure in the weak GGH13 model, indicating that the weak CLT13 model may be somewhat more useful.

New Multilinear Map Scheme. Armed with a weak model for CLT13, we devise a new *polynomial-degree* multilinear map scheme built on top of CLT13. We then prove that within our weak CLT13 model, *there are no attacks on our new scheme* under a new "Vector-Input Branching Program Un-Annihilatability" Assumption. That is, under our new assumption, any attack at all on our scheme will yield an attack that does not fit in our CLT13 model, and hence gives a brand new attack technique on CLT13 maps. Our scheme is based on obfuscation techniques, but avoids building a full obfuscation scheme, making our scheme significantly more efficient than obfuscation-based multilinear maps, at least for simple settings.

Concretely, to implement a 4-Party Non-Interactive Key Exchange with 80 bits of security, our scheme requires approximately 2^{31} CLT13 encodings with degree 281. For comparison, the most efficient obfuscation-based approach requires at least 2^{44} CLT13 encodings from a much higher-degree map [42]. These estimates are derived in the full version of this paper [1].

The lack of a zeroizing attack means we can be more liberal in the types of encodings that are made public. This allows for greatly enhanced functionality compared to existing multilinear map schemes: for example, we can encode arbitrary ring elements and give out encodings of zero.

The notable limitation of our construction and analysis is that our security proof relies on the Vector-Input Branching Program Un-Annihilatability Assumption, a new algebraic complexity assumption about annihilating polynomials. The assumption is similar to the Branching Program Un-Annihilatability Assumption used in [37], though our new assumption is somewhat stronger and less justified than theirs.

While our scheme is far from practical, we believe this result is a proof of concept that multilinear maps without zeroizing attacks are possible without first building obfuscation. Hopefully, future work will be able to streamline our construction to obtain much more efficient multilinear maps.

Applications. Despite some minor functionality limitations, our multilinear maps can still be used to solve problems that were not previously possible without first building obfuscation. For example, we show how to use it for multiparty non-interactive key exchange (NIKE) for a polynomial number of users. This is the most efficient scheme for $n > 3$ users that is immune to known attacks. Hopefully, our maps can be used to make other applications much more efficient as well.

Ideal Multilinear Maps from GGH13. We note that our techniques for constructing multilinear maps from CLT13 can be combined with the techniques of Garg
et al. [37] to give new multilinear maps in the weak model for GGH13.

1.2   Techniques

Weak CLT13 Model. In CLT13, there is a composite modulus $N = \prod_i p_i$.[4]
An encoding s is an integer mod N. Let $s_i = s \bmod p_i$ be the vector of Chinese
Remainder Theorem components. Each component s_i encodes a component m_i
of the plaintext element. An element in the plaintext space can therefore be
interpreted as a vector of integers. Each encoding is associated to a level, which
is a subset of $\{1, \ldots, d\}$, where d is the multilinearity of the map. Encodings can
be added and multiplied, following certain level-restrictions, until a "top-level"
encoding is obtained, which is an encoding relative to the set $\{1, \ldots, d\}$. For
singleton sets, we drop the set notation and let level $\{i\}$ be denoted as level i.

In CLT13, if s is a top-level encoding of zero — meaning all components of
the plaintext are 0 — then one can obtain from it $t = \sum_i \gamma_i s_i$, where γ_i is a
rational number, and equality holds over the rationals. The γ_i are unknown, but
global constants determined by the parameters of the scheme. That is, for each
s, the derived t will use the same γ_i.

All known attacks on the CLT13 multilinear maps follow a particular form.
First, public encodings are combined to give top-level encodings, *using operations
explicitly allowed by the maps*. If these top-level encodings are zero, then one
obtains a t term. The next step in the attack is to solve a polynomial equation
Q where the coefficients are obtained from the t terms. In current attacks, the
polynomial equation is the characteristic polynomial of a matrix whose entries
are rational functions of the zeros.

The next step is to show that the solutions to Q isolate the various s_i components of the initial encodings. Then by performing some GCD computations,
one is then able to extract the prime factors p_i, which leads to a complete break
of the CLT13 scheme. We show how to capture this attack strategy, and in
fact much more general potential strategies, in a new abstract attack model for
CLT13. Our model is defined as follows:

- Denote the set of encodings provided to the adversary as $\langle s \rangle$, where each s
  encodes some plaintext element.
- The adversary is allowed to combine the encodings as explicitly allowed by the
  multilinear map. Operations are performed component-wise on the underlying
  plaintext elements.
- If the adversary ever gets a top-level encoding of zero — meaning that the
  plaintext element is zero in all coordinates — this zero is some polynomial p
  in the underlying plaintext elements. The adversary obtains a handle to the
  corresponding element $t = \sum_i \gamma_i p(\langle s \rangle_i)$. Here, $\langle s \rangle_i$ represents the collection
  of ith components of the various encodings provided.

---

[4] In [19], this modulus is referred to as x_0.

– The adversary then tries to construct a polynomial Q_i that isolates the ith component for some i. The way we model a successful isolation is that Q_i is a polynomial in two sets of variables: T variables — which correspond to the t terms obtained above — and S variables — which correspond to the ith components of the s encodings. The adversary's goal is to devise a polynomial Q_i such that Q evaluates to 0 when S is substituted for $\langle s \rangle_i$ and T is substituted for the set of t obtained above. We say the adversary wins if she finds such a Q.

In a real attack, roughly, the adversary takes Q, plugs in the values of t, and then solves over the rationals for $\langle s \rangle_i$. Then by taking $GCD(N, s - s_i)$ for some encoding s, she obtains the prime factor p_i. The real adversary does this for every i until she completely factors N. In general, solving Q for $\langle s \rangle_i$ is a computationally intractable task and may not yield unique solutions. The attacks in the literature build a specific Q that can be solved efficiently. In our model, we conservatively treat *any* Q the adversary can find, even ones that are intractable to solve, as a successful attack.

We note that the attacks described in the literature actually build a Q that is a rational function. However, such rational functions can readily be converted into polynomial functions. We indeed demonstrate that such a polynomial Q is implicit in all known attack strategies.

Next, we prove a "model conversion theorem" that implies any attack in our CLT13 model actually yields an attack in a much simpler model that we call the "plain annihilating model." Here, the adversary still constructs polynomials p of the underlying encodings, trying to find a top-level zero. However now, instead of trying to find a Q_i as above, the adversary simply tries to find a polynomial R that annihilates the p polynomials. That is, $R(\{p(\langle S \rangle)\}_p)$ is identically zero as a polynomial over $\langle S \rangle$, where $\langle S \rangle$ are now treated as formal variables.

With this simpler model in hand, we immediately obtain the VBB-security of existing obfuscation constructions [30,41] based on branching programs. Those works show that the only top-level zeros that can be obtained correspond to the evaluations of branching programs. Therefore, relying on the Branching Program Un-Annihilatability Assumption (BPUA) of [37], we find that it is impossible to find an annihilating polynomial R, and hence a polynomial Q_i. This gives security in our CLT13 model.

New Multilinear Maps. We now turn to developing a new multilinear map scheme that we can prove secure in our weak model for CLT13. Guided by our annihilation analysis, we design the scheme to only release encodings for which the successful zero-test polynomials cannot be annihilated by polynomial-size circuits; our model conversion theorem shows that such encodings will be secure in the weak CLT13 model.

In this work, we focus on building an asymmetric scheme, where levels are subsets of $\{1, \ldots, d\}$, and elements can only be multiplied if they belong to disjoint levels. It is straightforward to extend to symmetric multilinear maps. The scheme will be based heavily on obfuscation techniques, plus some new techniques that we develop; however, we will not build a full obfuscation scheme. Therefore, we expect that our multilinear maps will be much more efficient than those that can be built using obfuscation.

Our starting point is Garg, Gentry, Halevi, and Zhandry [7][5], which offered a potential fix to block zeroizing attacks that we call the GGHZ16 fix. The fix was quickly broken, but we show how to further develop the idea into a complete fix. Garg et al. define a level-i "meta-encoding" of x to be a matrix of level-i CLT13 encodings, obtained by encoding component-wise matrices of the form:

$$R \cdot \begin{pmatrix} x & 0 & \dots & 0 \\ 0 & \$ & \dots & \$ \\ \vdots & \vdots & \ddots & \vdots \\ 0 & \$ & \dots & \$ \end{pmatrix} \cdot R^{-1}$$

where $\$$ represent plaintexts drawn at random[6], and R is a random matrix of plaintext elements.

Such meta-encodings can be added and multiplied just like CLT13 encodings, since the matrices R cancel out. However, due to the R matrices, it is no longer possible to isolate the upper-left corner to perform a zero-test on x. Instead, also handed out are "bookend" vectors s, t which encode the plaintext vectors

$$\left(1 \ 0 \ \cdots \ 0 \right) \cdot R^{-1} \text{ and } R \cdot \left(1 \ 0 \ \cdots \ 0 \right)^T ,$$

respectively. Now by multiplying a meta-encoding by the bookend vectors on the left and right, one obtains a CLT13 encoding of the plaintext x, which can then be zero-tested.

Next, Garg et al. include with the public parameters meta-encodings of various powers of 2, as well as many meta-encodings of 0. Powers of 2 allow for anyone to encode arbitrary elements, and the encodings of 0 allow for re-randomizing encodings. Unfortunately, as shown in [27], this fix does not actually protect against zeroizing attacks: with a bit more work, the meta-encodings of 0 can be used just like regular encodings of zero in the attacks to break the scheme.

To help motivate our new scheme, think of the GGHZ16 fix as follows: arrange the matrices in a grid where the columns of the grid correspond to the levels, and the matrices for level i are listed out in column i in an arbitrary order. We will call a "monomial" the product of one meta-encoding from each level, in level order (e.g. the level-1 encoding comes first, then level-2, etc.). Such monomials correspond to an iterated matrix product that selects one matrix from each column. We re-interpret these monomials as evaluations of a certain branching program. In this branching program, there are t inputs, and each input is not a bit, but a digit from 0 to $k - 1$ where k is the number of matrices in each

---

[5] We actually need the version of [7] dated November 12, 2014 from https://eprint.iacr.org/eprint-bin/versions.pl?entry=2014/666. More recent versions and the proceedings version removed the CLT13 fix that we start from.

[6] Actually, in [7], some of the zeros are also set to be random elements, but the above form suffices for our discussion and more naturally leads to our construction.

column. Each input digit selects the matrix from the corresponding column, and the result of the computation is the result of the corresponding iterated matrix product.

Note that this branching program is *read-once*, and this is fundamentally why the fix does not succeed. One way to see this is through the lens of our model conversion theorem: a read-once branching program can be annihilated, in the sense that it is possible to construct a set of inputs and an annihilating polynomial Q such that Q always evaluates to zero on the set of branching program outputs. For example, one can partition the input bits into two sets, and select subsets S and T of partial inputs from each half of the input partition. Evaluate the branching program on all points in the combinatorial rectangle defined by S, T, and arrange as a matrix. The rank of this matrix is at most the width of the branching program. Therefore, as long as the number of partial inputs is larger than the width, this branching program will be annihilated by the determinant. This is true for arbitrary branching programs, not just the branching programs derived above.

One possible way to block the attack above is to make the branching program so wide that even if the adversary queries on the entire domain, the matrix obtained above is still full rank. While it is possible to do this to build a *constant degree* multilinear map over CLT13, the map will be of little use. Roughly, the reason is that the branching program is now so wide that adding a random subset-sum of zero encodings is insufficient to fully re-randomize.

Instead, we turn to Garg et al. [37]'s obfuscator, which blocks this annihilating attack for obfuscation by explicitly requiring the branching program being obfuscated to read each input many times. By reading each input multiple times, the rank of the matrix above grows exponentially in the number of reads, blocking determinant-style attacks. Moreover, under the assumption that there are PRFs that can be computed by branching programs, such read-many programs cannot be annihilated in general. Garg et al. therefore conjecture a branching program un-annihilatability assumption, which says that read-many branching programs cannot be annihilated. Under this assumption, Garg et al. prove security in the weak GGH13 model.

Inspired by this interpretation and by techniques used to prove security of obfuscation, we modify GGHZ16 to correspond to a read-many branching program. This will allow us to block determinant-style attacks without increasing the width, allowing for re-randomization. Toward that end, we associate each meta-level i with ℓ different CLT13 levels, interleaving the levels for different i. This means that for a d-level meta-multilinear map, we will need $d\ell + 2$ CLT13 levels (the extra 2 levels for the bookends). An encoding at level i will be a sequence of ℓ different matrices of encodings, where the ℓ matrices are encoded at the ℓ corresponding CLT13 levels. The matrices (in the 3×3 case) have the form:

$$R_{i-1} \begin{pmatrix} x & 0 & 0 \\ 0 & \$ & \$ \\ 0 & \$ & \$ \end{pmatrix} R_i^{-1}, R_{d+i-1} \begin{pmatrix} 0 & 0 & 0 \\ 0 & \$ & \$ \\ 0 & \$ & \$ \end{pmatrix} R_{d+i}^{-1}, \cdots, R_{(\ell-1)d+i-1} \begin{pmatrix} 0 & 0 & 0 \\ 0 & \$ & \$ \\ 0 & \$ & \$ \end{pmatrix} R_{(\ell-1)d+i}^{-1}$$

Essentially, each of our meta-encodings is a list of GGHZ16 meta-encodings, where the first meta-encoding encodes x, and the rest encode 0. Our bookend vectors have the form $\left(1 \ \$ \cdots \$ \right) \cdot R_0^{-1}$ and $R_{d\ell} \cdot \left(1 \ \$ \cdots \$ \right)^T$ and are encoded, respectively, in the two remaining CLT13 levels. Unlike GGHZ16, we will not have the $ terms be random, but instead chosen more carefully (details below). Note that we choose different randomizing matrices R in each position; this corresponds to the randomizing matrices used for Kilian [43] randomization of branching programs in obfuscation. Such randomization forces matrices to be multiplied in order as in a branching program.

Addition is component-wise. For this discussion, we will only allow a pairing operation that goes directly to the top level; this is the kind of multilinear map envisioned by [2]. We explain how to give intermediate levels below.

The pairing operation takes one meta-encoding for each meta-level, and arranges all the matrices in branching-program order. Then, roughly, it multiplies the matrices together, along with the bookends. The result is a single top-level CLT13 encoding, which can be zero-tested as in CLT13. We have to slightly tweak the procedure scheme for this to work, as multiplying all the matrices of a top-level encoding will always give an encoding of zero, owing to most of the GGHZ16 meta-encodings containing 0. Instead, we add an offset vector midway through the pairing operation to make the CLT13 encoding an encoding of the correct value; see Sect. 4 for details. For the purposes of this discussion, however, this tweak can be ignored.

The good news is that if one restricts to adding and pairing encodings as described, this blocks the zeroizing attack on GGH16 meta-encodings, assuming ℓ is large enough. We would now like to prove our scheme is actually secure, using the branching program un-annihilatability assumption as was done in obfuscation. Unfortunately, there are several difficulties here:

- First, we need to force the adversary to follow the prescribed pairing procedure. While the pairing operation is basically just a branching program evaluation, this ends up being quite different than in the setting of obfuscation. For example, in obfuscation, forcing input consistency can be done with the level structure of the underlying multilinear map. In our case, this appears impossible. The reason is that we want to be able to add two encodings at the same meta-level before pairing, meaning the underlying encodings must be at the same CLT13 level. In obfuscation, the different encodings for a particular input are encoded at different levels. There are other ways to force input consistency [6,44], but they appear to run into similar problems.
- Second, the ability to add encodings means we cannot quite interpret allowed operations as just evaluations of a branching program. For example, if one adds two meta-encodings, and then multiplies them by a third, the result is a linear combination of iterated matrix products containing *cross terms* of the branching program that mix inputs. This is a result of the degree of zero-testing being non-linear. Therefore, prior means of forcing input consistency will be too restrictive for our needs.

We overcome these issues by developing several new techniques:

- First, we prove a generalization of a lemma by Badrinarayanan et al. [30] which tightly characterizes the types of iterated matrix products that an adversary is allowed to create. Our lemma works in far more general settings so as to be applicable to our scheme.
- Second, we re-interpret the allowed operations not as branching program evaluations, but as *vector-input* branching program evaluations, a new notion we define. In a vector-input branching program, inputs are no longer digits, but a list of vectors. The vectors specify a linear combination. To evaluate, for each column apply the corresponding linear combination, and then multiply all the results together. By being able to take linear combinations of the input matrices, we now capture the ability of an adversary to add encodings.
- Finally, we introduce new "enforcing" matrices that we place in the $ entries. The goal of our enforcing matrices is to force the adversary's operations to correspond to vector-input branching program evaluations.

Using our enforcing matrices and our new analysis techniques, we show that the adversary is limited to producing linear combinations of vector-input branching program evaluations. Therefore, by our model conversion theorem, if the adversary can attack in our weak CLT13 model, it can find an annihilating polynomial for vector-input branching programs. We therefore formulate a concrete conjecture that, like regular branching programs, vector-input branching programs cannot be annihilated. Under this assumption, no zeroizing attacks exist on our scheme.

Discussion. We now discuss some limitations of our construction above.

- We do not know how to justify our vector-input branching program assumption based on PRFs, unlike the corresponding assumption for standard branching programs. The reasons are twofold:

  • Most importantly, we do not know of any PRFs that can be evaluated by vector-input branching programs.
  • In our analysis, the adversary can produce a linear combination of *exponentially many* vector-input branching program evaluations. Therefore, an annihilating polynomial annihilates exponentially-many inputs, and therefore would not correspond to a polynomial-time attack on a PRF, even if one were computable by vector-input branching programs. We note that, if we were to ignore the first issue, it is straightforward to overcome the second issue using a sub-exponentially secure PRF, since a sub-exponential time algorithm can potentially query a PRF on the entire domain and construct exponential-sized linear combinations. Furthermore, we hope that this second limitation arises from our analysis and is not a fundamental problem, leaving room for subsequent work.

We observe that if a sub-exponentially secure PRF can be computed by vector-input branching programs, it should be possible to prove our assumption based on the security of said PRF.

Even without a justification based on general hardness assumptions, the only efficient annihilating polynomials we could find for vector-input branching programs are determinant polynomials as described above. These are interestingly also the only annihilating polynomials we know of for plain branching programs. Therefore, it seems reasonable at this time to conjecture that determinants are the only annihilating polynomials. If this conjecture holds, then any annihilating polynomial will require circuits of size roughly w^ℓ, where w is the width of matrices in the branching program. By setting w^ℓ to be 2^λ for desired security parameter λ, this will block known attacks. In the full version of this work [1], we give some evidence for why this conjecture should hold in restricted settings.

– Our discussion above only allows for directly pairing to the top level. If we are willing to sacrifice polynomial degree for constant degree, we can define pairing operations for intermediate levels. Adjacent levels (say 1,2) can easily be paired by simply constructing ℓ matrices that are the pairwise products of the ℓ matrices in the two levels. Due to the different Kilian randomization matrices between each pair of levels, we cannot directly pair non-adjacent levels, such as 1 and 3. For non-adjacent levels, instead of matrix multiplications, we can *tensor* the encodings, generating all degree 2 monomials. This tensoring can also be extended to higher levels. Unfortunately, this greatly expands the size of encodings and thus can only be done when the degree is constant.

Alternatively, we note that the ability to only multiply adjacent levels corresponds to the "graph induced" multilinear map notion [20] for the line graph. Hence, we obtain a multilinear map for general line graphs. Such maps are sufficient for most applications. Moreover, such graphs can easily be used to build symmetric multilinear maps, by simply encoding at all possible singleton levels.

– Finally, it is not possible to multiply an encoding by scalar. One could try repeated doubling, but our scheme inherits the noisiness of CLT13, and this repeated doubling will cause the noise to increase too much. One potential solution is that an encoding of x actually consists of encodings of $x, 2x, 4x, 8x$, etc. Now instead of repeated doubling, multiplying by a scalar is just a subset sum. Of course, this operation "eats up" the powers of 2, so it can only be done a few times before one runs out of encodings.

Another potential option, depending on the application, is to introduce additional "dummy" levels. To multiply by a scalar, first encode it in the "dummy" level, and then pair with the element. This of course changes the level at which the element is encoded, but for some applications this is sufficient. Below, we show how to use this idea to give a multiparty NIKE protocol for a polynomial number of users.

Multiparty Non-interactive Key Exchange (NIKE). Here, we very briefly describe how to use our new multilinear maps to construct multiparty NIKE. The basic scheme shown by Boneh and Silverberg [2] will not work because (1) they need an symmetric multilinear map, and (2) they need to be able to multiply encodings by ring elements. We show how to tweak the scheme to work with an asymmetric map that does not allow multiplying encodings by ring elements. For d users, instantiate our scheme with d levels, one more than is needed by [2].

User i chooses a random ring element a_i, and then computes encodings $[a_i]_u$ of a_i at every singleton level u. User i publishes all the encodings (after re-randomization), *except* the encoding at level 1.

Upon receiving the encodings from all other users, user i arbitrarily assigns each of the other $d - 1$ users to the levels $2, \ldots, d$. Let u_j be the level assigned to user j. Then it pairs its private elements $[a_i]_1$ together with $[a_j]_{u_j}$ for each $j \neq i$. The result is an encoding of $\prod_j a_j$ at the top level. Everyone computes the same encoding, which can be extracted to get the shared secret key.

Meanwhile, an adversary, who never sees an encoding of a_i at level 1, cannot possibly construct an encoding of $\prod_j a_j$ without using the same level twice. Using a variant of the multilinear Diffie-Hellman assumption, this scheme can be proven secure. This assumption can be justified in the generic multilinear map model, and hence our scheme can be proven secure in the weak CLT13 model.

Concurrent Work: A Weak Model for GGH15. In a concurrent work, Bartusek, Guan, Ma, and Zhandry [45] propose a weak multilinear map model for the GGH15 maps [20]. They demonstrate that all known zeroizing attacks on the GGH15 construction are captured by their weak model, and they construct an obfuscation scheme that is provably secure in their weak model. We compare and contrast our models and results below.

– The CLT13 and GGH15 schemes are quite different, and the respective zeroizing attacks exploit different vulnerabilities. The security of CLT13 crucially depends on the secrecy of the primes p_i, for which there is no analogue in the GGH15 scheme. Thus, our weak model captures the adversary's ability to perform a certain step that all known attacks on CLT13 go through in order to recover the p_i's. The Bartusek et al. [45] weak model uses a different condition that captures an adversary's ability to learn non-trivial information about an encoded plaintext.

– Bartusek et al. [46] prove security against a slightly larger class of "arithmetic adversaries," initially considered by Miles, Sahai, and Weiss [47]. To achieve obfuscation secure against such adversaries, Bartusek et al. [45] rely on an additional p-Bounded Speedup Hypothesis of Miles et al. [47] (a strengthening of the Exponential Time Hypothesis).

– Our work proposes a candidate "fix" for the CLT13 multilinear maps that enables a direct Non-Interactive Key Exchange (NIKE) construction secure against zeroizing attacks under a new VBPUA assumption. Bartusek et al. do not propose a corresponding fix for the GGH15 maps.

- All of the constructions in this paper are trivially broken by quantum attacks that factor the public CLT13 modulus N.[7] In contrast, all currently known quantum attacks on GGH15 [49] fall under the class of zeroizing attacks, and as a result the obfuscation construction of Bartusek et al. resists all known classical and quantum attacks.

2   Preliminaries

2.1   Multilinear Maps and the Generic Model

A multilinear map (also known as a graded encoding scheme) with universe set $\mathbb{U}$ and a plaintext ring $\mathcal{R}_{\mathsf{ptxt}}$ supports encodings of plaintext elements in $\mathcal{R}_{\mathsf{ptxt}}$ at levels corresponding to subsets of $\mathbb{U}$. A plaintext element a encoded at $S \subseteq \mathbb{U}$ is denoted as $[a]_S$. Multilinear maps support some subset of the following operations on these encodings:

- (Encoding) Given an element $a \in \mathcal{R}_{\mathsf{ptxt}}$ and level set $S \in \mathbb{U}$, output $[a]_S$.
- (Addition) Two encodings at the same level $S \subseteq \mathbb{U}$ can be added / subtracted. Informally, $[a_1]_S \pm [a_2]_S = [a_1 \pm a_2]_S$.
- (Multiplication) An encoding at level $S_1 \subseteq \mathbb{U}$ can be multiplied with an encoding at level $S_2 \subseteq \mathbb{U}$, provided $S_1 \cap S_2 = \emptyset$. The product is an encoding at level $S_1 \cup S_2$. Informally: $[a_1]_{S_1} \cdot [a_2]_{S_2} = [a_1 \cdot a_2]_{S_1 \cup S_2}$.
- (Re-randomization) We will allow for schemes with non-unique encodings. In this case, we may want a re-randomization procedure, which takes as input an encoding of a potentially unknown element a, and outputs a "fresh" encoding of a, distributed statistically close to a direct encoding of a.
- (Zero-Testing) An encoding $[a]_\mathbb{U}$ at level $\mathbb{U}$ can be tested for whether $a = 0$.
- (Extraction) An encoding $[a]_\mathbb{U}$ at level $\mathbb{U}$ can be extracted, obtaining a string r. Different encodings of the same a must yield the same r.

Most multilinear map schemes, due to security vulnerabilities, only support addition, multiplication, and zero-testing/extraction, but do not support public re-randomization or encoding. Instead, encoding must be performed by a secret key holder.

2.2   Overview of the CLT13 Multilinear Maps

We give a brief overview of the CLT13 multilinear maps, adapted from text in [50]. For a full description of the scheme, see [19]. The CLT13 scheme relies on the Chinese Remainder Theorem (CRT) representation. For large secret primes p_k, let $N = \prod_{k=1}^{n} p_k$. Let $\mathsf{CRT}(s_1, s_2, \ldots, s_n)$ or $\mathsf{CRT}(s_k)_k$ denote the number $s \in \mathbb{Z}_N$ such that $s \equiv s_k \pmod{p_k}$ for all $k \in [n]$. The plaintext space of the CLT13 scheme is $\mathbb{Z}_{g_1} \times \mathbb{Z}_{g_2} \times \cdots \times \mathbb{Z}_{g_n}$ for small secret primes g_k. An encoding of a vector $m = (m_1, \ldots, m_n)$ at level set $S = \{i_0\}$ is an integer $\alpha \in \mathbb{Z}_N$ such

---

[7] Our work leaves open the problem of devising composite-order multilinear maps whose security does not rely on the hardness of factoring [48].

that $\alpha = \mathsf{CRT}(m_1 + g_1 r_1, \ldots, m_n + g_n r_n)/z_{i_0} \pmod{N}$ for small integers r_k, and where z_{i_0} is a secret mask in $\mathbb{Z}_N$ uniformly chosen during the parameters generation procedure of the multilinear map. To support κ-level multilinearity, κ distinct z_i's are used.

Additions between encodings in the same level set can be done by modular additions in $\mathbb{Z}_N$. Multiplication between encodings can be done by modular multiplication in $\mathbb{Z}_N$, only when those encodings are in disjoint level sets, and the resulting encoding level set is the union of the input level sets. At the top level set $[\kappa]$, an encoding can be tested for zero by multiplying it by the zero-test parameter $p_{zt} = \sum_{k=1}^{n} p_k^* h_k((\prod_{i \in [\kappa]} z_i) g_k^{-1} \bmod p_k) \pmod{N}$ in $\mathbb{Z}_N$ where $p_k^* = N/p_k$, and comparing the result to N. An encoding α can be expressed as $\frac{1}{\prod_{i=1}^{\kappa} z_i} \mathsf{CRT}(s_k)_k$ where s_k denotes the numerator of its kth CRT component. When α is an encoding of zero, it can be shown that

$$p_{zt}\alpha \pmod{N} = \sum_{k=1}^{n} \gamma_k s_k,$$

where $\gamma_k = p_k^* h_k g_k^{-1}$ are "smallish" global secret parameters that depend on the other CLT13 parameters. For encodings of zero, each s_k is "small", so $p_{zt}\alpha \pmod{N}$ is small relative to N. If α does not encode 0, then one heuristically expects $p_{zt}\alpha \pmod{N}$ to be large relative to N. Thus, we can zero test by determining if this quantity is small.[8] We can also extract a unique representation of any encoded element by computing $p_{zt}\alpha \pmod{N}$, and rounding appropriately.

2.3   Vector-input Branching Programs

We generalize matrix branching programs to vector-input branching programs, a new notion we define (for the formal definition of matrix branching programs we consider, see the full version [1]). Single-input branching programs consist of a sequence of pairs of matrices, where an input bit is read for each pair to select one of them. Our vector input generalization allows for selecting a *linear combination* of matrices. In addition, we replace pairs of matrices with sets of k matrices. Thus, a program input is a d-tuple of vectors of dimension k, each consisting of non-negative integers. We can stack these d column vectors into a matrix $(\mathbb{Z})^{k \times d}$, so for any input $x \in (\mathbb{Z})^{k \times d}$, $x_{i,j} \in \mathbb{Z}$ denotes the jth component of the ith vector.

These vector-input branching programs arise in the security proof of our new multilinear map construction in Sect. 5. Thus, we will only consider a restricted

---

[8] In the full CLT13 scheme, there is a vector of zero-testing elements created in a way to prove that the result is large for non-zero encodings. However, in practice this is far less efficient, so most implementations only use a single zero test vector as described here (see e.g. [38]). We stress that giving out fewer zero-testing parameters can only make the scheme more secure, and parameters can be set so that correctness of zero-testing still holds with overwhelming probability.

class of vector-input branching programs tailored to fit the requirements of our analysis. Specifically, we use read-ℓ programs, meaning that each vector in the input is read exactly ℓ times. These programs are single-input, so there are $d\ell$ sets of matrices. Furthermore, the input selection is fixed so that the ith input vector is read for matrix sets $i, d + i, \ldots, (\ell - 1)d + i$. In other words, the input selection function is simply $\mathsf{inp}(j) = j \pmod{d}$.

Definition 1. *A read-ℓ vector-input branching program over a ring $\mathcal{R}$ with input length n, vector dimension k, and matrix width w is given by a sequence*

$$VBP = \left(s, t, \{\boldsymbol{B}_{i,j}\}_{i \in [d\ell], j \in [k]}\right)$$

where each $\boldsymbol{B}_{i,j}$ is a $w \times w$ matrix, s is a w-dimensional row vector, and t is a w-dimensional column vector. All entries are elements in $\mathcal{R}$. Then $VBP :$ $(\mathbb{Z})^{k \times d} \to \mathcal{R}$ is computed as

$$VBP(x) = s \cdot \left(\prod_{i=1}^{d\ell} \left(\sum_{j=1}^{k} x_{i (mod\ d), j} \boldsymbol{B}_{i,j} \right) \right) \cdot t.$$

For further intuition and examples of vector-input branching programs, refer to the full version [1].

We remark that vector-input branching programs are reminiscent of arithmetic branching programs [51,52], where an input string specifies a set of accepting s-t paths in a weighted directed acyclic graph, and the output is a sum of the products of all edge weights on each accepting path. With some care, we can re-express vector-input branching programs as a certain type of arithmetic branching program. However, we use the vector-input formulation as it intuitively captures the structure of our multilinear map construction in Sect. 4.

2.4 Kilian Randomization of Matrix Sequences

Consider a collection of n columns of matrices, where each column may contain an arbitrary polynomial number of matrices. Denote the jth matrix in column i as $A_{i,j}$. Suppose the matrices within each column have the same dimensions, and across columns have compatible dimensions so that matrices in adjacent columns can be multiplied together, and multiplying one matrix from each column results in a scalar. Kilian [43] describes a method to partially randomize such branching programs. Randomly sample invertible square matrices R_i. Then matrix $A_{i,j}$ is left-multiplied by R_i^{-1} and right-multiplied by R_{i+1}. When performing an iterated matrix product selecting one matrix from each column, the R_i and R_i^{-1} cancel out, so the product is unchanged by this randomization.

3 The Model

In this section, we define two models. The first is the weak CLT13 model, intended to capture all known classical attacks on the CLT13 multilinear maps.

The second is the CLT13 annihilation model, a modification of the weak CLT13 model with different winning conditions. We justify our first model by demonstrating that it captures known attacks from the literature. The main theorem of this section is that an adversary in the weak CLT13 model implies the existence of an adversary in the CLT13 annihilation model. Combining this theorem with the Branching Program Un-Annihilatability Assumption of [37], we immediately obtain virtual black box (VBB) security of the obfuscator of Badrinarayanan et al. [30]. Additionally, this shows that the order-revealing encryption scheme of Boneh et al. [53] is secure in our model.

3.1   CLT13 Weak Multilinear Map Model

Notation. We will let uppercase letters such as M, S, Γ denote formal variables, and lower case letters such as m, s, γ denote actual values. Bold letters will be used to distinguish vectors from scalars. Let m_{ji} be a set of elements indexed by j and i. We introduce $\langle \mathbf{m} \rangle_i$ as shorthand for the set $\{m_{ji}\}_j$ of all elements with index i, and $\langle \mathbf{m} \rangle$ to denote the set $\{\langle \mathbf{m} \rangle_i\}_i$. For a set $M_{j,i}$ of formal variables indexed by j and i, define $\langle \mathbf{M} \rangle_i$ and $\langle \mathbf{M} \rangle$ analogously.

We now define our weak CLT13 model, with the following interfaces:

Initialize Parameters. At the beginning of the interaction with the model $\mathcal{M}$, $\mathcal{M}$ is initialized with the security parameter λ and the multilinearity parameter $\kappa \leq \mathsf{poly}(\lambda)$. We generate the necessary parameters of the CLT13 scheme (including the vector dimension n, the primes g_i, p_i for $i \in [n]$) according to the distributions suggested by Coron et al. [19]. Let $\mathcal{R}_{\mathsf{ptxt}} = \mathbb{Z}_{\prod_i g_i} = \otimes_i \mathbb{Z}_{g_i}$ be the plaintext ring. Let $\mathcal{R}_{\mathsf{ctxt}} = \mathbb{Z}_{\prod_i p_i} = \otimes_i \mathbb{Z}_{p_i}$. We will usually interpret elements in $\mathcal{R}_{\mathsf{ptxt}}$ and $\mathcal{R}_{\mathsf{ctxt}}$ as vectors of their Chinese Remaindering components.

Initialize Elements. Next, $\mathcal{M}$ is given a number of plaintext vectors $\mathbf{m}_j \in R$ as well as an encoding level S_j for each plaintext. $\mathcal{M}$ generates the CLT13 numerators $\mathbf{s}_j$ where $s_{ji} = m_{ji} + g_i r_{ji}$ as in the CLT13 encoding procedure. For each j, $\mathcal{M}$ stores the tuple $(\mathbf{m}_j, \mathbf{s}_j, S_j)$ in the a pre-zero test table.

Zero-testing. The adversary submits a polynomial p_u to $\mathcal{M}$, represented as a polynomial-size *level-respecting* algebraic circuit. Here, level-respecting means that all wires are associated with a level S, input wires are associated to the sets S_j, add gates must add wires with the same level and output a wire with the same level, multiply gates must multiply wires with sets $S_0 \cap S_1 = \emptyset$ and output a wire with the level $S_0 \cup S_1$, and the final output wire must have set $\{1, \ldots, \kappa\}$.

Next, $\mathcal{M}$ checks whether $p_u(\langle \mathbf{m} \rangle_i) = 0$ for all i. If the check fails for any i, $\mathcal{M}$ returns "fail". If the check passes for all i, $\mathcal{M}$ returns "success". We assume without loss of generality that the set $\{p_u\}$ of *successful* zero tests are linearly independent as polynomials (since otherwise a zero-test on one p_u can be derived from the result of a zero-test on several other p_u).

If we stop here, we recover the plain generic multilinear map model [44]. However, in our model, a successful zero test does more. If zero testing is successful, p_u corresponds to a valid construction of a top-level zero encoding. $\mathcal{M}$ then additionally returns a handle T_u to the value $t_u(\langle\boldsymbol{\gamma}\rangle,\langle\mathbf{s}\rangle) = \sum_i \gamma_i p_u(\langle\mathbf{s}\rangle_i)$, the result of the zero-test computation. Each handle T_u along with the corresponding the zero-test result is stored in a *zero-test table*.

Post-zero-test. Finally, the adversary submits a polynomial Q on the handles $\{T_u\}_u$ and the formal variables $\langle\mathbf{S}\rangle_i$ for some $i \in [n]$ (that $\mathcal{A}$ picks). This Q must be represented by a polynomial-sized algebraic circuit, and the degree must be at most $2^{o(\lambda)}$.[9] The model looks up each handle T_u in the zero-test table and plugs in the corresponding values t_u. The model outputs "WIN" if the following two conditions are satisfied.

1. $Q(\{t_u(\langle\boldsymbol{\gamma}\rangle,\langle\mathbf{s}\rangle)\}_u,\langle\mathbf{S}\rangle_i) \not\equiv 0$ as a polynomial over the formal variables $\langle\mathbf{S}\rangle_i$.
2. $Q(\{t_u(\langle\boldsymbol{\gamma}\rangle,\langle\mathbf{s}\rangle)\}_u,\langle\mathbf{s}\rangle_i) = 0$.

Intuitively, these conditions imply that Q is a polynomial with non-zero degree over the $\langle\mathbf{S}\rangle_i$ formal variables that is "solved" when the correct values $\langle\mathbf{s}\rangle_i$ are plugged in.

Plain Annihilation Model. We define a modification of the above CLT13 weak multilinear map model, which is identical except for post-zero-test queries:

Post-zero-test. $\mathcal{A}$ submits a polynomial Q' on a set of formal variables $\{P_u\}_u$, where P_u represents the successful zero test polynomial p_u. Again, this Q' must be represented by a polynomial-sized algebraic circuit, and the degree must be at most $2^{o(\lambda)}$. The model outputs "WIN" if the following conditions are satisfied.

1. $Q'(\{P_u\}_u)$ *is not* identically zero over the $\{P_u\}_u$ formal variables.
2. $Q'(\{p_u(\langle\mathbf{S}\rangle_i)\}_u)$ *is* identically zero over the $\langle\mathbf{S}\rangle_i$ formal variables.

In other words, $\mathcal{A}$ wins if it submits a Q' that annihilates the $\{p_u\}_u$ polynomials.

3.2 Classical Attacks in the Weak CLT13 Model

We first show that the original attack on the CLT13 multilinear maps by Cheon et al. fits into this framework [21].

Mounting this attack requires that the set of plaintext vectors $\{\mathbf{m}_j\}$ given to M can be divided into three distinct sets of vectors, A, B, C that satisfy certain properties. We can discard/ignore any other plaintext vectors. For ease of exposition, we relabel the vectors in these sets as:

$$A = \{\mathbf{m}_1^A, \ldots, \mathbf{m}_n^A\} \qquad B = \{\mathbf{m}_1^B, \mathbf{m}_2^B\} \qquad C = \{\mathbf{m}_1^C, \ldots, \mathbf{m}_n^C\}$$

These vectors can be encoded at arbitrary levels, as long as for any j, σ, k, $\mathbf{m}_j^A \cdot \mathbf{m}_\sigma^B \cdot \mathbf{m}_k^C$ is a plaintext of zeros at the top level. Accordingly, $\mathcal{A}$ submits polynomials $p_{j,\sigma,k}$ for all $j, k \in [n], \sigma \in [2]$ for zero-testing where

$$p_{j,\sigma,k}(m_1^A, \ldots, m_n^A, m_1^B, m_2^B, m_1^C, \ldots, m_n^C) = m_j^A \cdot m_\sigma^B \cdot m_k^C$$

---

[9] We note that these restrictions are analogous to restrictions made for annihilation attacks on GGH13 [37].

Each of these polynomials clearly gives a successful zero-test. In response to each query, $\mathcal{M}$ returns a handle $T_{j,\sigma,k}$ to the value

$$t_{j,\sigma,k} = \sum_{i=1}^{n} \gamma_i s_{j,i}^A \cdot s_{\sigma,i}^B \cdot s_{k,i}^C.$$

For $\sigma \in \{1,2\}$, define W_σ to be the $n \times n$ matrix whose (j,k)th entry is $T_{j,\sigma,k}$. In the real attack, the adversary computes the matrix $W_1 W_2^{-1}$, which Cheon et al. [21] show has eigenvalues $\frac{s_{1,i}^B}{s_{2,i}^B}$. The adversary solves the characteristic polynomial of $W_1 W_2^{-1}$ for these eigenvalues. In our model $\mathcal{A}$ cannot immediately submit this characteristic polynomial, as it involves rational functions of the handles T, and can only be solved for ratios of the s_{ji} values. However, we observe that the characteristic polynomial

$$\det\left(W_1 W_2^{-1} - \lambda I\right) = \det\left(W_1 W_2^{-1} - \left(\frac{S_{1,i}^B}{S_{2,i}^B}\right) I\right) = 0$$

can be re-written by substituting $W_2^{-1} = \frac{W_2^{adj}}{\det(W_2)}$. (where W_2^{adj} denotes the adjoint matrix of W_2). Applying properties of the determinant then gives

$$\det(W_1 W_2^{adj} S_{2,i}^B - S_{1,i}^B \det(W_2) I) = 0$$

$\mathcal{A}$ submits the left-hand side expression above as its polynomial Q in a post-zero-test query. Since the Cheon et al. attack is successful, we know Q is nonzero over the formal variables $\langle \mathbf{S} \rangle_i$ after the values associated with the handles T are plugged in. Additionally, plugging in the appropriate solutions $\langle \mathbf{s} \rangle_i$ satisfies the above expression, so both win conditions are satisfied. Thus, $\mathcal{A}$ wins in our model.

In the full version of this work [1], we show how the general attack framework of Coron et al. [27] can be expressed in our model.

3.3   Model Conversion Theorem

Theorem 1. *If there exists an adversary $\mathcal{A}$ that wins with non-negligible probability in the weak CLT13 multilinear map model, there exists an adversary $\mathcal{A}'$ that wins with non-negligible probability in the CLT13 annihilation model. $\mathcal{A}'$ is the same as $\mathcal{A}$ up to and including the zero-test queries, and only differs on the post-zero test queries.*

We give a brief outline of the proof strategy (for the whole proof, refer to the full version of this paper [1]). An adversary that wins in the weak CLT13 model produces a non-trivial polynomial Q that evaluates to 0 on the actual CLT13 parameters and the numerators of the encodings. Since the CLT13 parameters and encodings are sampled using randomness hidden from the adversary, we can use a generalization of the Schwartz-Zippel lemma to conclude that the polynomial must be identically zero over its formal variables. We can view this polynomial as being over the formal variables corresponding to the CLT13 parameters, where the remaining formal variables constitute "coefficients". Since the overall polynomial is identically zero, all coefficients must also be identically zero. To conclude, we use the fact that the polynomial is non-trivial to show that there must exist a coefficient which acts as an annihilating polynomial for the zero-test polynomials.

3.4 Secure Obfuscation and Order-revealing Encryption in the Weak CLT13 Model

Security in our weak CLT13 model means security in the plain generic multilinear map model, plus the inability to construct an annihilating polynomial. We observe that Badrinarayanan et al. [30] show for their obfuscator (which is a tweak of the obfuscator of Barak et al. [41]), the only successful zero tests an adversary can perform are linear combinations of honest obfuscation evaluations on some inputs. Moreover, the linear combinations can only have polynomial support. Recall that in [30], evaluation is just a branching program evaluation over the encoded values. Therefore, any annihilating polynomial in the plain annihilation model is actually an annihilating polynomial for branching programs. Therefore, using the branching program un-annihilatability assumption of Garg et al. [37], we immediately conclude that no such annihilating polynomial is possible. Thus, there is no weak CLT13 attack on this obfuscator.[10]

We similarly observe that in the order-revealing encryption (ORE) scheme of Boneh et al. [53], any successful zero is also a linear combination of polynomially-many branching program evaluations. Therefore, by a similar argument, we immediately obtain that Boneh et al.'s scheme is secure in our weak CLT13 model.

4 A New Multilinear Map Candidate

In this section, we give a candidate polynomial-degree multilinear map scheme. We show, given an assumption about annihilating vector-input branching programs, that this multilinear map is secure in the weak CLT13 model. Here, we discuss our basic scheme; in the full version of this work, we show how to leverage the "slotted" structure of CLT13 encodings to obtain efficiency improvements [1].

4.1 Construction Overview

The levels will be non-empty subsets of $[d]$ for some polynomial d. For simplicity, here we describe how to build a multilinear map that only allows a pairing

---

[10] The Garg et al. obfuscator is defined as a dual-input obfuscator, which is the version we consider. The dual-input requirement is crucial; a single-input variant of this obfuscator is insecure and was attacked by Coron et al. [54]. The key point is that the branching program un-annihilatability assumption only holds for branching programs with significant interleaving of input bits, which can be ensured by a dual-input requirement.

operation that takes d elements, one from each singleton set, directly to a top-level encoding. This is the style of multilinear map envisioned by Boneh and Silverberg [2].

Our construction is logically organized into $d\ell$ columns, numbered from 1 to $d\ell$. The columns are further partitioned into d groups numbered 1 through d of ℓ columns, where the columns in each group are interleaved: group u consists of columns $u, u+d, u+2d, \ldots, u+(\ell-1)d$. Each column will correspond to one level of the underlying CLT13 maps, and each group of columns will correspond to one meta-level of our scheme. We set the plaintext space of both the underlying CLT13 scheme and our scheme to be $\mathcal{R}_{\mathsf{ptxt}} = \mathbb{Z}_M$ where $M = \prod_i g_i$. Recall that in the CLT13 scheme, M is not public.

We first describe the format of a meta-encoding in our scheme. An encoding at singleton level u will consist of ℓ matrices of CLT13 encodings, one in each of the columns corresponding to column group u. We will denote by $A_i^{(u)}$ the ith matrix in the encoding for level u. To construct $A_i^{(u)}$, we first define the diagonal matrix $\widetilde{A_i^{(u)}}$, of the form

$$\mathrm{diag}(m_i, v_i, w_i, \xi_1 I, \ldots, \xi_{u-1} I, E_i^{(u)}, \xi_{u+1} I, \ldots, \xi_d I).$$

These components of the diagonal matrix work as follows:

- m_i is a plaintext element used for the actual plaintext encoding.
- v_i and w_i are freshly sampled uniformly random elements from the plaintext space $\mathbb{Z}_M$. Their sole purpose is to enforce a requirement called non-shortcutting, which will arise in the security proof. They are canceled out in valid products by 0's in the bookend vectors, defined later.
- The remainder of the diagonal consists of d block matrices, where $d-1$ blocks are essentially unused and set to random multiples of the identity, while the uth matrix is set to be an "enforcing matrix" $E_i^{(u)}$. Note that i corresponds to this being the ith matrix for encoding u. The purpose of these matrices is roughly to prevent an adversary from arbitrarily mixing and matching the matrices from different encodings. We defer the details of these matrices to Sect. 4.2.

Next, $d\ell + 1$ Kilian randomization matrices R_i are generated [43] to left and right multiply each of the $d\ell$ columns. All encodings will share the same Kilian matrices. Each $\widetilde{A_i^{(u)}}$ matrix at meta-level u is left- and right- multiplied by the appropriate Kilian matrices, giving

$$R_{u+(i-1)d-1}^{-1} \widetilde{A_i^{(u)}} R_{u+(i-1)d}.$$

Each element of this Kilian-randomized matrix is encoded in an asymmetric CLT13 multilinear map at level $\{u+(i-1)d\}_{CLT13}$ (we differentiate levels of the underlying CLT13 map with this subscript, to avoid confusion with the levels of our multilinear map) corresponding to the column it belongs to. The resulting matrix of CLT13 encodings is taken to be $A_i^{(u)}$.

For a matrix $A_i^{(u)}$, we refer to the underlying ring element m_i as the *matrix plaintext*. This is the only component of the matrix used for encoding actual plaintext elements. Therefore, as described so far, every meta-encoding in our scheme encodes a length-ℓ vector of ring elements.

We also give out "bookends" s, t, which are CLT13 encodings of the vectors

$$\hat{s} = (1,1,0,F_1,\ldots,F_d) \cdot R_0 \, , \quad \hat{t} = R_{d\ell}^{-1} \cdot (1,0,1,G_1,\ldots,G_d)^T \, .$$

For the sake of clarity, we defer discussing the F, G vectors until Sect. 4.2. The 1 in the first position is used to extract the matrix plaintexts. The 0 in the second position of $\hat{t}$ will zero-out the v_i terms, while the 0 in the third position of $\hat{s}$ will zero-out the w_i terms. s is encoded at CLT13 level 0, while t is encoded at level $d\ell + 1$.

A meta-encoding of $x \in \mathcal{R}_{\text{ptxt}} = \mathbb{Z}_M$ at singleton level $\{u\}$ is simply a sequence of matrices $(A_i^{(u)})_{i \in [\ell]}$ whose corresponding sequence of matrix plaintexts is $(x, 0, 0, \ldots, 0)$.

At instance generation, we generate and publish a set of initial public encodings.

- For each singleton level $\{u\} \subseteq [d]$, we publish encodings of $1, 2, 4, \ldots, 2^{\rho-1}$, where ρ is specified later.
- For each singleton level $\{u\} \subseteq [d]$, we publish τ encodings of zero, where τ is specified later.
- For the top level $[d]$, we publish a special *pre-zero-test encoding* that will have most of the structure of a valid top level encoding, except that it will not correctly encode an actual plaintext element. Its sequence of matrix plaintexts will be $(0, 1, 1, \ldots, 1)$, which differs from a normal encoding where the matrix plaintexts are all 0 after the first slot. The sole purpose of this encoding is to be added to any top level encoding we seek to zero test. Roughly, the element submitted for zero testing is the product of an encoding's matrix plaintexts, and without this step the product would always be zero.

To add/subtract two meta-encodings at the same singleton level $\{u\}$, which are two sequences of ℓ matrices, we line up the sequences of matrices and add/subtract the corresponding matrices component-wise. The resulting sequence of ℓ matrices is taken as the encoding of the sum. Intuitively, this works because adding these matrices also adds the sequence of matrix plaintexts. As we show in Sect. 4.2, the structure of the enforcing matrices is also preserved. If the input encodings have matrix plaintexts $(x_1, 0, \ldots, 0)$ and $(x_2, 0, \ldots, 0)$, the result of addition/subtraction has matrix plaintexts $(x_1 \pm x_2, 0, \ldots, 0)$.

To pair d meta-encodings, one from each singleton level, we do the following. For each $i \in [\ell]$, we line up the ith matrix from each encoding, in the order specified by the columns of our scheme, and multiply the matrices together. The resulting i matrices are then added to the corresponding i matrices from the pre-zero-test encoding. Based on the structure of our encoding scheme, the resulting i matrices have the matrix plaintext sequence $(\prod_u x_u, 1, \ldots, 1)$, where x_u was the value encoded at level $\{u\}$. Finally, we multiply all of these matrices together. The resulting matrix will have $\prod_u x_u$ in the upper-left corner. Finally, we multiply by the bookends s, t to obtain a single top-level CLT13 encoding. We set up the enforcing matrices in Sect. 4.2 to guarantee that this product becomes a CLT13 encoding of $\prod_u x_u$.

The remaining procedures work as follows.

Encode. To encode a plaintext $x \in \mathbb{Z}_{2^\rho}$ at a singleton level $\{u\}$, write the plaintext in base 2, and then sum the appropriate public encodings of powers of 2. We note that we do not publish a description of the plaintext ring $\mathcal{R}_{\text{ptxt}} = \mathbb{Z}_M$, where $M = \prod_i g_i$. Therefore, the input to the encoding procedure is some integer $x \in \mathbb{Z}_{2^\rho}$, and the output is an encoding of $x \bmod M$, where $\mathcal{R}_{\text{ptxt}} = \mathbb{Z}_M$. We set $\rho = M \times 2^\lambda$ for a security parameter λ so that a random $x \in \mathbb{Z}_{2^\rho}$ yields an element $x \bmod M$ that is statistically close to random in $\mathcal{R}_{\text{ptxt}}$.

Re-randomize. To re-randomize this encoding, add a random subset sum of the public encodings of zero available for the level. We choose the parameter τ, roughly, to be large enough so that the result is statistically close to a fresh random encoding. For further discussion, see the full version [1].

Zero-test and Extract. Zero testing and extraction on top-level encodings (which are just top-level CLT13 encodings) are performed exactly as in CLT13.

4.2   Enforcing Matrix Structure

We now describe the enforcing matrix structure used in the matrices of our scheme. Consider the ℓ matrices associated to an encoding at any singleton level $\{u\}$, which all have a block diagonal form. For each matrix, all the diagonal entries except the top left three entries are responsible for providing the enforcing structure. As described in Sect. 4.1, the rest of the diagonal entries are divided into d equally-sized diagonal matrices. The uth block is set to $E_i^{(u)}$, which provides the enforcing structure for level $\{u\}$, while the other $d-1$ blocks are set to random multiples of the identity to avoid interfering with the enforcing structure of the other singleton levels.

To construct $E_i^{(u)}$ for a new encoding, we sample a random vector α of dimension ℓ. Denote the ith component as α_i. The matrix $E_i^{(u)}$ is set to be the following diagonal matrix of width $2(\ell - 1)$:

$$E_i^{(u)} = \operatorname{diag}(\alpha_i, \alpha_{\sigma_{(12)}(i)}, \alpha_i, \alpha_{\sigma_{(23)}(i)}, \ldots, \alpha_i, \alpha_{\sigma_{(\ell-1,\ell)}(i)})$$

Here, $\sigma_{(ab)}$ denotes the transposition swapping a and b. We additionally have two bookend vectors F, G, used by all enforcing matrices for a particular singleton level. The left bookend vector F is simply the all 1's row vector of dimension $2(\ell - 1)$. The right bookend vector G is a column vector of dimension $2(\ell - 1)$. To set the entries of G, we sample $\ell - 1$ random values $\{\eta_i\}_{i \in [\ell-1]}$, and set the entry in position $2i-1$ to η_i, and the entry in position $2i$ to $-\eta_i$ for all $i \in [\ell-1]$.

Restrictions on Matrix Products. The sole purpose of the enforcing matrices is to ensure that the adversary respects the meta-encoding structure. For example, since each meta-encoding consists of ℓ separate matrices, an adversary may try to swap some of these matrices for matrices from other meta-encodings. We show that any attempt to do so will inevitably lead to a useless top-level encoding of a random plaintext.

Consider a setting where the adversary has access to dk meta-encodings of various matrix plaintext vectors, k in each singleton level. These encodings form a $k \times d\ell$ grid, with k matrices in each of the $d\ell$ columns. Since we have k encodings per singleton level, we modify our notation slightly; now $A_{i,j}^{(u)}$ will denote the jth encoding of the ith matrix for meta-level u. Furthermore, we can ignore the first three rows and columns of each $A_{i,j}^{(u)}$ matrix, as they play no role in the enforcing structure. Let $C_{i,j}^{(u)}$ be the width $2d(\ell - 1)$ diagonal matrix that remains.

To recap, $d - 1$ of the blocks of $C_{i,j}^{(u)}$ are set to be width-$2(\ell - 1)$ identity matrices (randomly scaled) and the uth block is set to $E_{i,j}^{(u)}$. For any meta-encoding j at level u, a fresh random set of $\{E_{i,j}^{(u)}\}_{i \in [\ell]}$ is generated. The bookends are formed by concatenating d independently generated instances of our $2(\ell - 1)$ dimensional bookends. The arrangement of the $C_{i,j}^{(u)}$ matrices (without the bookends) in the $k \times d\ell$ grid is shown below:

$$
\begin{array}{ccc|ccc|c|ccc}
C_{1,1}^{(1)} & C_{1,1}^{(2)} & \cdots & C_{1,1}^{(d)} & C_{2,1}^{(1)} & C_{2,1}^{(2)} & \cdots & C_{2,1}^{(d)} & & C_{\ell,1}^{(1)} & C_{\ell,1}^{(2)} & \cdots & C_{\ell,1}^{(d)} \\
C_{1,2}^{(1)} & C_{1,2}^{(2)} & \cdots & C_{1,2}^{(d)} & C_{2,2}^{(1)} & C_{2,2}^{(2)} & \cdots & C_{2,2}^{(d)} & \cdots & C_{\ell,2}^{(1)} & C_{\ell,2}^{(2)} & \cdots & C_{\ell,2}^{(d)} \\
\vdots & \vdots & & \vdots & \vdots & \vdots & & \vdots & & \vdots & \vdots & & \vdots \\
C_{1,k}^{(1)} & C_{1,k}^{(2)} & \cdots & C_{1,k}^{(d)} & C_{2,k}^{(1)} & C_{2,k}^{(2)} & \cdots & C_{2,k}^{(d)} & & C_{\ell,k}^{(1)} & C_{\ell,k}^{(2)} & \cdots & C_{\ell,k}^{(d)}
\end{array}
$$

The matrices are divided into ℓ groups, each consisting of k rows and d columns of matrices. Picking the matrix in row j and column u for each group gives the ℓ matrices that comprise the enforcing component of the jth meta-encoding at level u.

Notice that adding point-wise $C_{1,j_0}^{(u)}, \ldots, C_{\ell,j_0}^{(u)}$ to $C_{1,j_1}^{(u)}, \ldots, C_{\ell,j_1}^{(u)}$ or scaling $C_{1,j}^{(u)}, \ldots, C_{\ell,j}^{(u)}$ preserves the form of the matrices (though now the α's are different). Notice also that multiplying all the matrices in $C_{1,j}^{(u)}, \ldots, C_{\ell,j}^{(u)}$ together along with our bookend vectors gives 0. Therefore, we can take arbitrary linear combinations of meta-encodings, multiply them together, and still get 0. We will show that this is essentially the only way to combine different $C_{i,j}^{(u)}$ to get zero.

Applied to our construction, the matrices are the various meta-encodings of 0 and powers of 2 that the adversary is given in the public parameters. The adversary also has access to a pre-zero-test encoding, which does not fit this pattern. However, we can think of the pre-zero-test encoding as arising from d meta-encodings with matrix plaintext sequence $(0, 1, \ldots, 1)$, one encoding per singleton level. The actual pre-zero-test encoding is obtained by multiplying these encodings together.

While the CLT13 level structure allows an adversary to multiply together any collection of matrices that picks one from each column, our enforcing matrix structure will restrict the adversary to taking products of linear combinations of meta-encodings (or linear combinations of such products).

To formalize this notion, we first introduce the following definition.

Definition 2. *We define a valid monomial to be a polynomial representing a product of the $C_{i,j}^{(u)}$ matrices, so that exactly one matrix is taken from each column, in column order, along with the bookends.*

Next, we re-cast the $C_{i,j}^{(u)}$ matrices as the matrices of a read-ℓ vector-input branching program (an extension of matrix branching programs defined in Sect. 2.3) that takes inputs $x \in (\mathbb{Z})^{k \times d}$. The point of adopting the vector-input branching program (VBP) view is that read-ℓ VBP evaluations correspond exactly to valid manipulations of meta-encodings.

If we expand out any linear combination of read-ℓ VBP evaluations, the resulting polynomial is a linear combination of valid monomials. However, given an arbitrary linear combination of valid monomials, it is not immediately clear if it can be expressed as a linear combination of read-ℓ VBP evaluations (and hence a valid combination of meta-encodings). The following lemma characterizes precisely when this occurs.

Lemma 1. *Let Q be a linear combination of valid monomials. If Q evaluates to 0 as a polynomial over the underlying randomness of the $C_{i,j}^{(u)}$ matrices, Q is a linear combination of read-ℓ VBP evaluations, where the VBP is the one defined by the same $C_{i,j}^{(u)}$ matrices.*

For a more precise statement of this lemma and its proof, see the full version [1].

5   Security of Our Multilinear Map

Strategy Overview. To prove the security of our multilinear map construction within the CLT13 weak model, we define "real" and "ideal" experiments. Recall that an encoding of a plaintext in our scheme consists of numerous CLT13 plaintexts at different CLT13 levels. The "real" experiment allows the adversary to perform operations on any of these individual CLT13 encodings, and win through any of the victory conditions in the weak model. The "ideal" experiment provides the same interface to the adversary, but is run by a simulator that only has access to the vanilla generic multilinear map model. Intuitively, if there exists a simulator for which the adversary cannot distinguish between the two experiments, then no extra information is leaked in the real world and our multilinear map achieves ideal security.

Real and Ideal Experiments. Suppose the multilinear map is used to encode a sequence $m_1, \ldots, m_v$ of plaintexts at levels $S_1, \ldots, S_v$.

In the "real" world experiment, denoted EXP_{real}, the adversary interacts with our weak CLT13 model, whose plaintexts consist of all the elements of all the matrices output by our multilinear map encoding procedure as well as all the elements of the public parameter matrices. These plaintexts are encoded at the appropriate levels derived from $S_1, \ldots, S_v$. The adversary can submit level-respecting polynomials over these plaintexts as zero-test queries, and receives a handle to the result of the zero-test computation for successful queries. Then the adversary enters a post-zero test stage, and can win by submitting a polynomial Q that satisfies the win conditions of the CLT13 weak model.

In the "ideal" world experiment, denoted EXP_{ideal}, the adversary interacts with a simulator $\mathcal{S}$ that can interact with a vanilla generic multilinear map model. In this world, the model only stores the actual plaintexts $m_1, \ldots, m_v$ and levels $S_1, \ldots, S_v$. The adversary submits level-respecting polynomials over the plaintexts of the real world. The simulator $\mathcal{S}$ answers these queries using only queries to its model over the actual plaintexts. As in the real world, the adversary enters a post-zero test stage, which the simulator must respond to.

For any adversary $\mathcal{A}$, let $\text{EXP}_{real}(\mathcal{A})$ (respectively $\text{EXP}_{ideal}(\mathcal{S}, \mathcal{A})$) denote the probability that $\mathcal{A}$ can win in the "real" (respectively "ideal") world.

5.1 The Vector-input Branching Program Un-annihilatability (VBPUA) Assumption

The security of our multilinear map rests on a new assumption about annihilating vector-input branching programs (VBPs), defined in Sect. 2.3. Define a *generic* vector-input branching program (VBP) to be a VBP whose matrix entries are all distinct formal variables, instead of fixed ring elements. A generic VBP is evaluated just like a regular VBP, but the program output is a polynomial over formal variables. We refer to these outputs as generic VBP evaluation polynomials.

Note to the reader: The following is the simplest formal statement of our assumption. As the assumption relies on a number of newly introduced terms, it may be helpful to refer to the full version of this work [1] where we give concrete illustrations of our assumption for small cases.

We now define the polynomial-size arithmetic circuits A_r that will be necessary for the assumption statement. A_r takes the matrices of the vector-input branching program as input. The output of A_r is restricted to be a linear combination of vector-input branching program evaluations (though note that a polynomial-size arithmetic circuit can compute exponentially large linear combinations).

Assumption 1 (The (ℓ, w, k)-VBPUA Assumption). *Let $\ell = \text{poly}(d, \lambda)$, $w = \text{poly}(d, \lambda), k = \text{poly}(d, \lambda)$ be parameters, and let $f(x)$ for $(x_1, \ldots, x_d) \in (\mathbb{Z}^k)^d$ (where each input vector x_i is a k-dimensional integer vector) be a generic* *vector-input branching program that reads each input vector x_i ℓ times and consists of $w \times w$ matrices. For each $r = 1, \ldots, m$, let A_r be any arithmetic circuits satisfying the definition above, each with size $\mathsf{poly}(d, k, \lambda)$. The output of A_r is a polynomial over the formal variables of the generic vector-input branching program, and denote it by P_r. Suppose further that $P_1, \ldots, P_m$ are linearly independent as polynomials over the formal variables of the generic vector-input branching program. Then there does not exist any polynomial-sized circuit Q of degree at most $2^{o(\lambda)}$ such that $Q(\{P_r\}_r) \equiv 0$ as a polynomial over the formal variables of the generic VBP.*

Note that each pair of functions ℓ, w, k gives a distinct assumption. In general, increasing ℓ or w intuitively gives a harder problem (and therefore milder assumption), while increasing k gives a potentially easier problem (and therefore stronger assumption). Our construction is quite flexible, and can be tailored to work with multiple possible settings of ℓ, w, k. Importantly, however, we will usually need k to be substantially larger than $w^2\ell$. For more precise bounds on ℓ, w, k, refer to the full version [1].

We conjecture that the assumption is for any choices of ℓ, w, k provided w^ℓ is exponential in λ, d. We conjecture that determinant-style annihilating attacks (discussed in the full version [1]) give the lowest-complexity annihilating polynomials for VBPs, as this appears to be the case for matrix branching programs. w^ℓ lower bounds the size of such determinant-style annihilations. Verifying this would imply security for the choices of ℓ, w, k that we require.

This assumption is similar to the Branching Program Un-Annihilatability Assumption of Garg et al. [37], but we do not know how to base our assumption on PRFs. For a detailed comparison of the statements of these assumptions, refer to the full version [1].

Note that the assumption states that no polynomial-size circuits Q of degree at most $2^{o(\lambda)}$ can annihilate a non-trivial set of VBP evaluations (generated by polynomial-size circuits). As evidence that this assumption is not trivially false, we heuristically argue in the full version of this work [1] that there are no circuits Q that can annihilate VBP evaluations up to a certain polynomial degree, even if we allow Q to have exponential size.

5.2   Security Proof

Our multilinear map is secure as long as (1) the adversary can never create a successful polynomial Q in the real world, and (2) any information the adversary gets in the real world, the adversary can also obtain in the ideal world. Formally, this requires proving the existence of a simulator such that no PPT adversary can distinguish between the two worlds.

Let d be the desired asymmetric degree of the multilinear map. We instantiate the construction with the number of meta-encodings k released per level set large enough to support secure re-randomization of meta-encodings under the Leftover Hash Lemma, and the number of matrices per meta-encoding ℓ set large enough so that brute-force determinant attacks are blocked. The width w of each matrix is set to $3 + 2d(\ell - 1)$ to fit the construction. For further details on the recommended parameter choices, refer to the full version [1].

With this setting of ℓ, w, k, security of our construction follows from the (ℓ, w, k)-VBPUA assumption.

Theorem 2. *Under the (ℓ, w, k)-VBPUA Assumption, our construction with the above parameter choices is secure in the CLT13 weak model. That is, there exists a PPT simulator S such that for all PPT adversaries $\mathcal{A}$,*

$$\Pr[\text{EXP}_{real}(\mathcal{A}) = \text{EXP}_{ideal}(S, \mathcal{A})] = 1 - negl(\lambda)$$

Moreover, S always responds to post-zero test queries with 0.

Due to space restrictions, we give a high level overview of the major proof techniques and defer the full proof to [1].

Proof Sketch. We start with an application of Theorem 1, which states that if an adversary $\mathcal{A}$ can break our scheme in the weak CLT13 model, there exists an adversary $\mathcal{A}'$ in the CLT13 annihilating model. Recall that in the annihilating model, $\mathcal{A}'$ wins if it can annihilate the formal polynomials that correspond to successful zero-tests. Therefore, our first task is to show that the only successful zero-tests the adversary can compute are those that correspond to valid manipulations of our multilinear map meta-encodings. Then if we view the matrices in our scheme as the matrices of a read-ℓ vector-input branching program (VBP), a valid top-level meta-encoding corresponds to a linear combination of honest VBP evaluations. Given the VBPUA assumption, an adversary cannot successfully annihilate these evaluations.

Recall that the meta-encodings are themselves sequences of individual matrices. We must first show that the adversary must respect the structure of these individual matrices. We rely on an extension of Lemma 5.2 in [30], which we state and prove in the full version of this paper [1]. At a high level, our lemma shows that Kilian randomization matrices force the adversary to respect the original matrix structure; if the adversary attempts to pluck individual scalar entries out of these matrices and obtain zero-tests that do not correspond to products of matrices, then it will be unable to obtain successful zero-tests with any non-negligible probability. The next step is to show, roughly speaking, that an adversary cannot manipulate (i.e. add/multiply) one matrix from a meta-encoding without simultaneously performing the same operation on all of them. This follows from Lemma 1 (proven in the full version [1]), which implies that if the adversary does not respect the meta-encoding structure, our "enforcing matrices" will guarantee it does not obtain a successful zero-test except with negligible probability.

Taken together, these steps show that the adversary can never be successful in the post-zero-test stage of the CLT13 annihilating model. Therefore it can only distinguish the real experiment from the ideal experiment by making ordinary zero-test queries. In the full proof [1], we conclude by showing how a simulator S with access to an ideal implementation of our multilinear map can correctly simulate the 0/1 response to any zero-test query.

Acknowledgements. We thank Amit Sahai, Tancrède Lepoint, James Bartusek, and Leon Zhang for helpful discussions. We also thank the anonymous reviewers for feedback on prior versions of this work. Research supported in part from a DARPA SAFEWARE award and NSF. The views expressed are those of the author and do not reflect the official policy or position of the Department of Defense, the National Science Foundation, or the U.S. Government.

References

1. Ma, F., Zhandry, M.: The MMAP strikes back: obfuscation and new multilinear maps immune to CLT13 zeroizing attacks. Cryptology ePrint Archive, Report 2017/946 (2017). https://eprint.iacr.org/2017/946
2. Boneh, D., Silverberg, A.: Applications of multilinear forms to cryptography. Contemp. Math. **324**, 71–90 (2003)
3. Garg, S., Gentry, C., Halevi, S., Sahai, A., Waters, B.: Attribute-based encryption for circuits from multilinear maps. In: Canetti, R., Garay, J.A. (eds.) CRYPTO 2013. LNCS, vol. 8043, pp. 479–499. Springer, Heidelberg (2013). https://doi.org/10.1007/978-3-642-40084-1_27
4. Boneh, D., Waters, B., Zhandry, M.: Low overhead broadcast encryption from multilinear maps. In: Garay, J.A., Gennaro, R. (eds.) CRYPTO 2014. LNCS, vol. 8616, pp. 206–223. Springer, Heidelberg (2014). https://doi.org/10.1007/978-3-662-44371-2_12
5. Garg, S., Gentry, C., Sahai, A., Waters, B.: Witness encryption and its applications, pp. 467–476 (2013)
6. Garg, S., Gentry, C., Halevi, S., Raykova, M., Sahai, A., Waters, B.: Candidate indistinguishability obfuscation and functional encryption for all circuits, pp. 40–49 (2013)
7. Garg, S., Gentry, C., Halevi, S., Zhandry, M.: Functional encryption without obfuscation. In: Kushilevitz, E., Malkin, T. (eds.) TCC 2016. LNCS, vol. 9563, pp. 480–511. Springer, Heidelberg (2016). https://doi.org/10.1007/978-3-662-49099-0_18
8. Sahai, A., Waters, B.: How to use indistinguishability obfuscation: deniable encryption, and more, pp. 475–484 (2014)
9. Hohenberger, S., Sahai, A., Waters, B.: Replacing a random oracle: full domain hash from indistinguishability obfuscation. In: Nguyen, P.Q., Oswald, E. (eds.) EUROCRYPT 2014. LNCS, vol. 8441, pp. 201–220. Springer, Heidelberg (2014). https://doi.org/10.1007/978-3-642-55220-5_12
10. Boneh, D., Zhandry, M.: Multiparty key exchange, efficient traitor tracing, and more from indistinguishability obfuscation. In: Garay, J.A., Gennaro, R. (eds.) CRYPTO 2014. LNCS, vol. 8616, pp. 480–499. Springer, Heidelberg (2014). https://doi.org/10.1007/978-3-662-44371-2_27
11. Pandey, O., Prabhakaran, M., Sahai, A.: Obfuscation-based non-black-box simulation and four message concurrent zero knowledge for NP. In: Dodis, Y., Nielsen, J.B. (eds.) TCC 2015. LNCS, vol. 9015, pp. 638–667. Springer, Heidelberg (2015). https://doi.org/10.1007/978-3-662-46497-7_25
12. Chung, K.-M., Lin, H., Pass, R.: Constant-round concurrent zero-knowledge from indistinguishability obfuscation. In: Gennaro, R., Robshaw, M. (eds.) CRYPTO 2015. LNCS, vol. 9215, pp. 287–307. Springer, Heidelberg (2015). https://doi.org/10.1007/978-3-662-47989-6_14
13. Hubacek, P., Wichs, D.: On the communication complexity of secure function evaluation with long output, pp. 163–172 (2015)

14. Ananth, P., Sahai, A.: Functional encryption for turing machines. In: Kushilevitz, E., Malkin, T. (eds.) TCC 2016. LNCS, vol. 9562, pp. 125–153. Springer, Heidelberg (2016). https://doi.org/10.1007/978-3-662-49096-9_6

15. Bitansky, N., Paneth, O., Wichs, D.: Perfect structure on the edge of chaos. In: Kushilevitz, E., Malkin, T. (eds.) TCC 2016. LNCS, vol. 9562, pp. 474–502. Springer, Heidelberg (2016). https://doi.org/10.1007/978-3-662-49096-9_20

16. Bun, M., Zhandry, M.: Order-revealing encryption and the hardness of private learning. In: Kushilevitz, E., Malkin, T. (eds.) TCC 2016. LNCS, vol. 9562, pp. 176–206. Springer, Heidelberg (2016). https://doi.org/10.1007/978-3-662-49096-9_8

17. Bitansky, N., Paneth, O., Rosen, A.: On the cryptographic hardness of finding a Nash equilibrium, pp. 1480–1498 (2015)

18. Garg, S., Gentry, C., Halevi, S.: Candidate multilinear maps from ideal lattices. In: Johansson, T., Nguyen, P.Q. (eds.) EUROCRYPT 2013. LNCS, vol. 7881, pp. 1–17. Springer, Heidelberg (2013). https://doi.org/10.1007/978-3-642-38348-9_1

19. Coron, J.-S., Lepoint, T., Tibouchi, M.: Practical multilinear maps over the integers. In: Canetti, R., Garay, J.A. (eds.) CRYPTO 2013. LNCS, vol. 8042, pp. 476–493. Springer, Heidelberg (2013). https://doi.org/10.1007/978-3-642-40041-4_26

20. Gentry, C., Gorbunov, S., Halevi, S.: Graph-induced multilinear maps from lattices. In: Dodis, Y., Nielsen, J.B. (eds.) TCC 2015. LNCS, vol. 9015, pp. 498–527. Springer, Heidelberg (2015). https://doi.org/10.1007/978-3-662-46497-7_20

21. Cheon, J.H., Han, K., Lee, C., Ryu, H., Stehlé, D.: Cryptanalysis of the multilinear map over the integers. In: Oswald, E., Fischlin, M. (eds.) EUROCRYPT 2015. LNCS, vol. 9056, pp. 3–12. Springer, Heidelberg (2015). https://doi.org/10.1007/978-3-662-46800-5_1

22. Hu, Y., Jia, H.: Cryptanalysis of GGH map. In: Fischlin, M., Coron, J.-S. (eds.) EUROCRYPT 2016. LNCS, vol. 9665, pp. 537–565. Springer, Heidelberg (2016). https://doi.org/10.1007/978-3-662-49890-3_21

23. Coron, J.-S., Lee, M.S., Lepoint, T., Tibouchi, M.: Cryptanalysis of GGH15 multilinear maps. In: Robshaw, M., Katz, J. (eds.) CRYPTO 2016. LNCS, vol. 9815, pp. 607–628. Springer, Heidelberg (2016). https://doi.org/10.1007/978-3-662-53008-5_21

24. Coron, J.-S., Lepoint, T., Tibouchi, M.: New multilinear maps over the integers. In: Gennaro, R., Robshaw, M. (eds.) CRYPTO 2015. LNCS, vol. 9215, pp. 267–286. Springer, Heidelberg (2015). https://doi.org/10.1007/978-3-662-47989-6_13

25. Boneh, D., Wu, D.J., Zimmerman, J.: Immunizing multilinear maps against zeroizing attacks. Cryptology ePrint Archive, Report 2014/930 (2014). http://eprint.iacr.org/2014/930

26. Halevi, S.: Graded encoding, variations on a scheme. Cryptology ePrint Archive, Report 2015/866 (2015). http://eprint.iacr.org/2015/866

27. Coron, J.S., et al.: Zeroizing without low-level zeroes: new MMAP attacks and their limitations. In: Gennaro, R., Robshaw, M. (eds.) CRYPTO 2015. LNCS, vol. 9215, pp. 247–266. Springer, Heidelberg (2015). https://doi.org/10.1007/978-3-662-47989-6_12

28. Brakerski, Z., Gentry, C., Halevi, S., Lepoint, T., Sahai, A., Tibouchi, M.: Cryptanalysis of the quadratic zero-testing of GGH. Cryptology ePrint Archive, Report 2015/845 (2015). http://eprint.iacr.org/2015/845

29. Cheon, J.H., Fouque, P.-A., Lee, C., Minaud, B., Ryu, H.: Cryptanalysis of the new CLT multilinear map over the integers. In: Fischlin, M., Coron, J.-S. (eds.) EUROCRYPT 2016. LNCS, vol. 9665, pp. 509–536. Springer, Heidelberg (2016). https://doi.org/10.1007/978-3-662-49890-3_20

30. Badrinarayanan, S., Miles, E., Sahai, A., Zhandry, M.: Post-zeroizing obfuscation: new mathematical tools, and the case of evasive circuits. In: Fischlin, M., Coron, J.-S. (eds.) EUROCRYPT 2016. LNCS, vol. 9666, pp. 764–791. Springer, Heidelberg (2016). https://doi.org/10.1007/978-3-662-49896-5_27

31. Cramer, R., Ducas, L., Peikert, C., Regev, O.: Recovering short generators of principal ideals in cyclotomic rings. In: Fischlin, M., Coron, J.-S. (eds.) EUROCRYPT 2016. LNCS, vol. 9666, pp. 559–585. Springer, Heidelberg (2016). https://doi.org/10.1007/978-3-662-49896-5_20

32. Albrecht, M., Bai, S., Ducas, L.: A subfield lattice attack on overstretched NTRU assumptions. In: Robshaw, M., Katz, J. (eds.) CRYPTO 2016. LNCS, vol. 9814, pp. 153–178. Springer, Heidelberg (2016). https://doi.org/10.1007/978-3-662-53018-4_6

33. Cheon, J.H., Jeong, J., Lee, C.: An algorithm for NTRU problems and cryptanalysis of the GGH multilinear map without a low level encoding of zero. Cryptology ePrint Archive, Report 2016/139 (2016). http://eprint.iacr.org/2016/139

34. Cheon, J.H., Hhan, M., Kim, J., Lee, C.: Cryptanalyses of branching program obfuscations over GGH13 multilinear map from the NTRU problem. In: Shacham, H., Boldyreva, A. (eds.) CRYPTO 2018. LNCS, vol. 10993, pp. 184–210. Springer, Cham (2018). https://doi.org/10.1007/978-3-319-96878-0_7

35. Pellet-Mary, A.: Quantum attacks against indistinguishablility obfuscators proved secure in the weak multilinear map model. In: Shacham, H., Boldyreva, A. (eds.) CRYPTO 2018. LNCS, vol. 10993, pp. 153–183. Springer, Cham (2018). https://doi.org/10.1007/978-3-319-96878-0_6

36. Miles, E., Sahai, A., Zhandry, M.: Annihilation attacks for multilinear maps: cryptanalysis of indistinguishability obfuscation over GGH13. In: Robshaw, M., Katz, J. (eds.) CRYPTO 2016. LNCS, vol. 9815, pp. 629–658. Springer, Heidelberg (2016). https://doi.org/10.1007/978-3-662-53008-5_22

37. Garg, S., Miles, E., Mukherjee, P., Sahai, A., Srinivasan, A., Zhandry, M.: Secure obfuscation in a weak multilinear map model. In: Hirt, M., Smith, A. (eds.) TCC 2016. LNCS, vol. 9986, pp. 241–268. Springer, Heidelberg (2016). https://doi.org/10.1007/978-3-662-53644-5_10

38. Lewi, K., et al.: 5Gen: A framework for prototyping applications using multilinear maps and matrix branching programs, pp. 981–992 (2016)

39. Paneth, O., Sahai, A.: On the equivalence of obfuscation and multilinear maps. Cryptology ePrint Archive, Report 2015/791 (2015). http://eprint.iacr.org/2015/791

40. Albrecht, M.R., Farshim, P., Hofheinz, D., Larraia, E., Paterson, K.G.: Multilinear maps from obfuscation. In: Kushilevitz, E., Malkin, T. (eds.) TCC 2016. LNCS, vol. 9562, pp. 446–473. Springer, Heidelberg (2016). https://doi.org/10.1007/978-3-662-49096-9_19

41. Barak, B., Garg, S., Kalai, Y.T., Paneth, O., Sahai, A.: Protecting obfuscation against algebraic attacks. In: Nguyen, P.Q., Oswald, E. (eds.) EUROCRYPT 2014. LNCS, vol. 8441, pp. 221–238. Springer, Heidelberg (2014). https://doi.org/10.1007/978-3-642-55220-5_13

42. Boneh, D., Ishai, Y., Sahai, A., Wu, D.J.: Lattice-based SNARGs and their application to more efficient obfuscation. In: Coron, J.-S., Nielsen, J.B. (eds.) EUROCRYPT 2017. LNCS, vol. 10212, pp. 247–277. Springer, Cham (2017). https://doi.org/10.1007/978-3-319-56617-7_9
43. Kilian, J.: Founding cryptography on oblivious transfer, pp. 20–31 (1988)
44. Brakerski, Z., Rothblum, G.N.: Virtual black-box obfuscation for all circuits via generic graded encoding. In: Lindell, Y. (ed.) TCC 2014. LNCS, vol. 8349, pp. 1–25. Springer, Heidelberg (2014). https://doi.org/10.1007/978-3-642-54242-8_1
45. Bartusek, J., Guan, J., Ma, F., Zhandry, M.: Preventing zeroizing attacks on GGH15. Cryptology ePrint Archive, Report 2018/511 (2018). https://eprint.iacr.org/2018/511
46. Bartusek, J., Guan, J., Ma, F., Zhandry, M.: Return of GGH15: provable security against zeroizing attacks. In: TCC 2018 (2018)
47. Miles, E., Sahai, A., Weiss, M.: Protecting obfuscation against arithmetic attacks. Cryptology ePrint Archive, Report 2014/878 (2014). http://eprint.iacr.org/2014/878
48. Zimmerman, J.: How to obfuscate programs directly. In: Oswald, E., Fischlin, M. (eds.) EUROCRYPT 2015. LNCS, vol. 9057, pp. 439–467. Springer, Heidelberg (2015). https://doi.org/10.1007/978-3-662-46803-6_15
49. Chen, Y., Gentry, C., Halevi, S.: Cryptanalyses of candidate branching program obfuscators. In: Coron, J.-S., Nielsen, J.B. (eds.) EUROCRYPT 2017. LNCS, vol. 10212, pp. 278–307. Springer, Cham (2017). https://doi.org/10.1007/978-3-319-56617-7_10
50. Coron, J.S., Lee, M.S., Lepoint, T., Tibouchi, M.: Zeroizing attacks on indistinguishability obfuscation over CLT13. Cryptology ePrint Archive, Report 2016/1011 (2016). http://eprint.iacr.org/2016/1011
51. Beimel, A., Gál, A.: On arithmetic branching programs. J. Comput. Syst. Sci. 59(2), 195–220 (1999)
52. Ishai, Y., Kushilevitz, E.: Perfect constant-round secure computation via perfect randomizing polynomials. In: Widmayer, P., Eidenbenz, S., Triguero, F., Morales, R., Conejo, R., Hennessy, M. (eds.) ICALP 2002. LNCS, vol. 2380, pp. 244–256. Springer, Heidelberg (2002). https://doi.org/10.1007/3-540-45465-9_22
53. Boneh, D., Lewi, K., Raykova, M., Sahai, A., Zhandry, M., Zimmerman, J.: Semantically secure order-revealing encryption: multi-input functional encryption without obfuscation. In: Oswald, E., Fischlin, M. (eds.) EUROCRYPT 2015. LNCS, vol. 9057, pp. 563–594. Springer, Heidelberg (2015). https://doi.org/10.1007/978-3-662-46803-6_19
54. Coron, J.-S., Lee, M.S., Lepoint, T., Tibouchi, M.: Zeroizing attacks on indistinguishability obfuscation over CLT13. In: Fehr, S. (ed.) PKC 2017. LNCS, vol. 10174, pp. 41–58. Springer, Heidelberg (2017). https://doi.org/10.1007/978-3-662-54365-8_3

Return of GGH15: Provable Security Against Zeroizing Attacks

James Bartusek[✉], Jiaxin Guan, Fermi Ma, and Mark Zhandry

Princeton University, Princeton, USA
bartusek.james@gmail.com, jiaxin@guan.io, fermima1@gmail.com,
mzhandry@princeton.edu

Abstract. The GGH15 multilinear maps have served as the foundation for a number of cutting-edge cryptographic proposals. Unfortunately, many schemes built on GGH15 have been explicitly broken by so-called "zeroizing attacks," which exploit leakage from honest zero-test queries. The precise settings in which zeroizing attacks are possible have remained unclear. Most notably, none of the current indistinguishability obfuscation (iO) candidates from GGH15 have any formal security guarantees against zeroizing attacks.

In this work, we demonstrate that all known zeroizing attacks on GGH15 implicitly construct *algebraic relations* between the results of zero-testing and the encoded plaintext elements. We then propose a "GGH15 zeroizing model" as a new general framework which greatly generalizes known attacks.

Our second contribution is to describe a new GGH15 variant, which we formally analyze in our GGH15 zeroizing model. We then construct a new iO candidate using our multilinear map, which we prove secure in the GGH15 zeroizing model. This implies resistance to all known zeroizing strategies. The proof relies on the Branching Program Un-Annihilatability (BPUA) Assumption of Garg et al. [TCC 16-B] (which is implied by PRFs in NC^1 secure against P/poly) and the complexity-theoretic p-Bounded Speedup Hypothesis of Miles et al. [ePrint 14] (a strengthening of the Exponential Time Hypothesis).

1 Introduction

1.1 Motivation

Multilinear maps [2] are a powerful cryptographic tool that have enabled many cryptographic applications, ranging from multiparty key agreement [2] to extremely powerful indistinguishability obfuscation (iO) [3]. There are currently three families of multilinear maps: those of Garg, Gentry, and Halevi [4] (GGH13), those of Coron, Lepoint, and Tibouchi [5] (CLT13), and those of Gentry, Gorbunov, and Halevi [6] (GGH15).

The full version of this paper is available on the IACR ePrint Archive [1].

A. Beimel and S. Dziembowski (Eds.): TCC 2018, LNCS 11240, pp. 544–574, 2018.
https://doi.org/10.1007/978-3-030-03810-6_20

Each of these multilinear map families are based on fully homomorphic encryption (FHE) schemes. However, the FHE schemes are intentionally weakened by providing a broken secret key to allow useful information to be extracted from encrypted values. Because of these broken secret keys, extensive cryptanalysis is required before we can gain confidence that some security remains. In this work, we study the GGH15 multilinear maps. We believe these maps are particularly interesting for a couple reasons:

- In some cases, by specializing the GGH15 construction to certain settings, security can actually be proved based on the well-studied Learning with Errors (LWE) assumption [7]. Notably, the lockable obfuscation constructions of Wichs and Zirdelis [8], of Goyal, Koppula, and Waters [9], and of Chen, Vaikuntanathan, and Wee [10], and the private puncturable PRFs of Canetti and Chen [11] and Chen et al. [10], are all based in part on the GGH15 multilinear maps, and can be proved secure under LWE.[1] Therefore, the GGH15 multilinear maps seem to be the most promising route to achieving security based on LWE.
- The other two candidate multilinear maps, GGH13 and CLT13, have been shown vulnerable to quantum attacks [13–17]. In contrast, given the positive results above and the fact that LWE appears resistant to quantum attacks, it seems reasonable to expect that GGH15 is quantum immune, at least in certain settings. This leaves GGH15 as the main candidate multilinear map for the post-quantum era.

Despite the above positive results, there is still a large gap between what is provably secure under LWE and what the community hopes to achieve with multilinear maps, namely iO. On the positive side, "direct attacks" on the multilinear maps seem unlikely. Here "direct attacks" refer to attempts to attack the underlying FHE schemes, ignoring the extra information provided through the broken secret key.

Unfortunately, all multilinear map candidates have been subject to very strong "zeroizing" attacks [4,18,19] which exploit the broken secret key. These attacks have broken many of the applications which had not been proven secure. Since the original attacks, the field has seen a continual cycle of breaking schemes and fixing them. In the case of GGH15, these attacks [10,19,20] have broken many applications, including multiparty key agreement, and several of the iO candidates.

Given the importance of iO, it is important to study the security of multilinear maps even in the setting that lacks a security proof under well-studied assumptions. In order to break free from the cycle above, our aim is to develop a rigorous and formal justification for security, despite the lack of "provable" security.

---

[1] The lockable obfuscation constructions in [8] and [9] use ideas from prior work of Goyal, Koppula, and Waters [12] which introduced techniques for using GGH15 encodings to encrypt branching programs.

Recent works have shown how to break the attack-fix-repeat cycle for GGH13 [21] and CLT13 [22] multilinear maps by devising abstract "zeroizing" models that capture and generalize all known zeroizing attack strategies on the maps. These works formally prove security of applications in these models, demonstrating in a rigorous sense that the analyzed schemes are resistant to known zeroizing attacks. Since these works, all subsequent classical polynomial-time attacks have fit the proposed models, demonstrating that these models may reasonably reflect the security of the maps.

Our goal is to extend these works to the GGH15 setting, devising a model that captures and generalizes all known zeroizing attack strategies. For GGH15, however, there are unique challenges that make this task non-trivial:

- The underlying mathematics of the scheme differs from previous schemes, and the details of the attacks are quite different. As such, any attack model will be different.
- There does not appear to be a single unified GGH15 multilinear map in the literature, but instead many variants — the basic GGH15 map, a version with safeguards, a version with commutative plaintexts, etc. Moreover, many applications do not conform to the multilinear map interface, and are instead described directly on the GGH15 implementation. The many variants of GGH15 and applications are accompanied by similarly varied settings for the attacks.
- Additionally, there are some functional limitations of GGH15: plaintexts are required to be "short", by default plaintexts do not commute, and the level structure derives from graphs instead of sets. These present challenges in applying the standard multilinear map tools (such as Kilian randomizing branching programs, straddling sets, etc.) to the GGH15 setting. This breaks many of the analysis techniques that have been applied to other multilinear map candidates, and has also led to some ad hoc proposals, such as using diagonal matrices for the plaintexts, multiplying by random scalars to create levels, or Kilian randomizing using special types of matrices.

Therefore, our goal will be to:

Develop an abstract zeroizing attack model that captures all known zeroizing attacks on all variants of GGH15, and develop new techniques for proving security in this model.

Our Results. In this work we devise an abstract attack model that applies to all existing variants of GGH15 and applications built on top of GGH15. We demonstrate that our attack model captures and generalizes all zeroizing attacks.

We then describe a new variant of GGH15, based on several prior works in the area, which we can prove strong security statements about in our model. Our new scheme is flexible enough to support a simple obfuscation scheme which we can prove secure in our model. The result is a scheme that is provably resistant to zeroizing attacks. Before giving our results, we start with a very brief overview of the GGH15 maps and known attacks.

1.2   The GGH15 Multilinear Map

GGH15 is a "graph-induced" multilinear map, which departs somewhat from the usual multilinear map notions. Here, we have a connected directed acyclic graph $G = (V, E)$ of d nodes with a single source (labeled 1) and a single sink (labeled d). A "level" is a pair of vertices (u, v) for which there is a path from u to v; we will denote such levels by $u \rightsquigarrow v$ (different paths between u, v will be considered the same level). Plaintexts $\mathbf{S}$ are encoded relative to levels $u \rightsquigarrow v$, and we denote such an encoding as $[\mathbf{S}]_{u \rightsquigarrow v}$.

Given a handful of encodings, the following operations can be performed:

- **Addition:** Two encodings $[\mathbf{S}_0]_{u \rightsquigarrow v}, [\mathbf{S}_1]_{u \rightsquigarrow v}$ relative to the same pair of vertices can be added, obtaining the encoding of the sum $[\mathbf{S}_0 + \mathbf{S}_1]_{u \rightsquigarrow v}$ (relative to the same pair of vertices).
- **Multiplication:** Two encodings $[\mathbf{S}_0]_{u \rightsquigarrow v}, [\mathbf{S}_1]_{v \rightsquigarrow w}$ whose nodes form a path $u \rightsquigarrow v \rightsquigarrow w$ can be multiplied, obtaining an encoding $[\mathbf{S}_0 \cdot \mathbf{S}_1]_{u \rightsquigarrow w}$ of the product at the level corresponding to concatenating the paths.
- **Zero Testing:** Given an encoding $[\mathbf{S}]_{1 \rightsquigarrow d}$ between the unique source and sink, we can test whether or not $\mathbf{S}$ is equal to 0.

In GGH15, the "plaintexts" are also matrices, rather than scalars, meaning the multiplications above are non-commutative. Moreover, in GGH15, the plaintext matrices are required to be "short".

GGH15 works as follows. Associated to each node u is a matrix $\mathbf{A}_u$. An encoding of $\mathbf{S}$ at level $u \rightsquigarrow v$ is a matrix $\mathbf{D}$ that satisfies $\mathbf{A}_u \mathbf{D} = \mathbf{S} \mathbf{A}_v + \mathbf{E} \mod q$ where both $\mathbf{D}$ and $\mathbf{E}$ are "short". This encoding is generated using a lattice trapdoor.

Addition is straightforward to verify. For multiplication, suppose $\mathbf{A}_u \mathbf{D}_0 = \mathbf{S}_0 \mathbf{A}_v + \mathbf{E}_0 \mod q$ and $\mathbf{A}_v \mathbf{D}_1 = \mathbf{S}_1 \mathbf{A}_w + \mathbf{E}_1 \mod q$. Then $\mathbf{A}_u \mathbf{D}_0 \mathbf{D}_1 = \mathbf{S}_0 \mathbf{S}_1 \mathbf{A}_w + \mathbf{E}_0 \mathbf{D}_1 + \mathbf{S}_0 \mathbf{E}_1 \mod q$.

Since $\mathbf{S}_b$, $\mathbf{D}_b$ and $\mathbf{E}_b$ are short, we can define $\mathbf{E}_2 = \mathbf{E}_0 \mathbf{D}_1 + \mathbf{S}_0 \mathbf{E}_1$, which is also short, and we see that $\mathbf{D}_0 \mathbf{D}_1$ is an encoding of $\mathbf{S}_0 \mathbf{S}_1$ relative to the path $u \rightsquigarrow w$.

For zero-testing, we note that if we have an encoding $\mathbf{D}$ of $\mathbf{S}$ relative to $1 \rightsquigarrow d$ and we compute $\mathbf{A}_1 \mathbf{D} \mod q = \mathbf{S} \mathbf{A}_d + \mathbf{E} \mod q$, the resulting matrix will be "short" relative to q if $\mathbf{S} = 0$, and otherwise, we would expect the result to be large relative to q.

1.3   Zeroizing Attacks on GGH15

As with all current multilinear map candidates, GGH15 is vulnerable to "zeroizing" attacks. These attacks leverage the fact that any time a zero-test actually detects 0, the procedure also produces an equation that holds over the integers.

For GGH15, notice that zero-testing computes $\mathbf{A}_1 \mathbf{D} \mod q = \mathbf{S} \mathbf{A}_d + \mathbf{E} \mod q$. If $\mathbf{S} = 0$, the result is just $\mathbf{E} \mod q$, which equals $\mathbf{E}$ since $\mathbf{E}$ is guaranteed to be short relative to q. But recall from the GGH15 description that if $\mathbf{D}$ is the result of several multilinear map operations, $\mathbf{E}$ depends on not just the error terms of the original encodings, but also on the plaintext values **S**. Therefore, any successful zero-test will give an equation depending on the original plaintext values, and this equation holds over the integers. These equations can then potentially be manipulated to learn non-trivial information about the underlying plaintexts. This is the heart of all known zeroizing attacks on GGH15.

More abstractly, suppose that c plaintext matrices $\mathbf{S}_1, \ldots, \mathbf{S}_c$ are encoded relative to various edges, producing the corresponding encoding matrices $\mathbf{D}_1, \ldots, \mathbf{D}_c$. In all known zeroizing attacks, the adversary adds and multiplies the matrices $\{\mathbf{D}_i\}_i$ honestly (respecting the edge-constraints of the graph) to produce top-level encodings of zero.[2] Let $p_u(\{\mathbf{D}_i\}_i)$ denote the u-th top-level encoding of zero the adversary constructs. Each top-level zero $p_u(\{\mathbf{D}_i\}_i)$ is then zero-tested by multiplying on the left by $\mathbf{A}_1$, successfully obtaining a low-norm matrix of *zero-test results*, which we denote as T_u (in some constructions, T_u is simply a scalar). The current attacks all build a new matrix **W** whose entries are plucked from the various T_u matrices (or T_u itself in the case of a scalar). From this point, the known attacks differ in strategy from each other. But at a high level, all of them extract some piece of information from **W**, such as its kernel or its rank, and use this information to recover non-trivial information about the hidden plaintext matrices $\{\mathbf{S}_i\}_i$.

1.4   Our Zeroizing Model for GGH15

We make the following observation: all known attacks that recover information about the plaintexts $\{\mathbf{S}_i\}_i$ from the $\{T_u\}_u$ set up an *algebraic relation* between the two (we will often refer to this relation as a polynomial). More precisely, this means that implicit in all successful zeroizing attacks on GGH15, there is a non-trivial bounded-degree polynomial Q such that

$$Q(\{T_u\}_u, \{S_{i,j,k}\}_{i,j,k}) = 0$$

holds over the integers, where $S_{i,j,k}$ denotes the (j,k)-th entry of matrix $\mathbf{S}_i$. In known attacks, this Q depends on the matrix **W** in some way; however, anticipating potential new avenues for attack, we consider a much more general attack format which assumes as little as possible about the structure of the attacks. Hence, our general condition makes no reference to a matrix **W**.

While this condition seems simple, it is not a priori obvious that any of the GGH15 zeroizing attacks actually produce such a Q. In theory, an adversary might recover information about the plaintext matrix entries $\{S_{i,j,k}\}_{i,j,k}$ through *any* efficient algorithm taking $\{T_u\}_u$ as input. We certainly cannot hope to re-express any poly-time algorithm as a polynomial over its inputs and outputs. However, we are able to show that all known attacks can be recast as procedures that uncover a Q polynomial.

---

[2] Technically, the Coron et al. attack on key exchange does not compute top-level encodings of zero, but encodings of the same matrix relative to different source-to-sink paths [19]. However, by connecting a master source node to the original source nodes, we can assume that all GGH15 graphs have a single source. In this case, the Coron et al. attack indeed computes top-level encodings of zero.

Example: The CLLT16 Attack. In Coron et al. [19], the first step of the attack is to construct the matrix $\mathbf{W}$ as above, and then compute a vector $\mathbf{v}$ in the left kernel of $\mathbf{W}$. They show, using the algebraic structure of GGH15, that such a $\mathbf{v}$ in fact gives a relation amongst the plaintext elements only (no error terms). In particular, there is a vector $\mathbf{x}$ of fixed polynomials in the underlying plaintext elements such that $\mathbf{v}$ is orthogonal to $\mathbf{x}$. The attack then proceeds to use this relation amongst the plaintexts to break the scheme.

We observe that an equivalent view of their analysis is that $\mathbf{x}$ is in the column span of $\mathbf{W}$. This means that if we append the column vector $\mathbf{x}$ to $\mathbf{W}$, the rank will be unchanged. Suppose for the moment that $\mathbf{W}$ itself is full rank, and that it is one column shy of being square. Then we can capture the fact that the rank does not increase with a simple algebraic relation: the determinant of $[\,\mathbf{W}\mid\mathbf{x}\,]$ equals 0. Therefore, in this restricted setting where $\mathbf{W}$ is full rank and almost square, we see that the CLLT16 attack implicitly contains a polynomial Q as desired.

In the actual attack, $\mathbf{W}$ may not be full rank, meaning the determinant may trivially be 0 no matter what $\mathbf{x}$ is; this means Q does not give us a useful relation over the plaintexts. Moreover, $[\,\mathbf{W}\mid\mathbf{x}\,]$ may not be square, so the determinant may not be defined. With a bit more effort, we can see that a polynomial Q is nonetheless implicit in the attack for general $\mathbf{W}$. Basically, if we knew the rank r of $\mathbf{W}$, we could choose a "random" matrix $\mathbf{R}$ with $r+1$ rows, and a "random" matrix $\mathbf{S}$ with $r+1$ columns. If we compute $\mathbf{R}\cdot[\,\mathbf{W}\mid\mathbf{x}\,]\cdot\mathbf{S}$, we will obtain an $(r+1)\times(r+1)$ matrix whose rank is (with high probability) identical to the rank of $[\,\mathbf{W}\mid\mathbf{x}\,]$. Now we can take the determinant of $\mathbf{R}\cdot[\,\mathbf{W}\mid\mathbf{x}\,]\cdot\mathbf{S}$ to be our algebraic relation. In practice, we do not know r, but we can guess it correctly with non-negligible probability since r is polynomially bounded.

The GGH15 Zeroizing Model. With our observations above in hand, we can define a new zeroizing model for GGH15. Roughly, the model allows the attacker to perform multilinear map operations as explicitly allowed by the multilinear map interface (i.e. following edge constraints). Then, after performing a zero-test, if the encoding actually contained a zero, the adversary obtains a handle to the elements produced by zero-testing (the $\mathbf{E}$ matrix in the discussion above, but potentially a different quantity for different GGH15 variants). Next, the adversary tries to construct an algebraic relation Q between the zero-test results and the original plaintexts. The only restrictions we place on Q are that it must be computable by an efficient algebraic circuit, and that it must have degree that is not too large (e.g. sub-exponential). These restrictions are very conservative, as the known attacks are quite low degree and very efficiently computable.

In the full version, we also discuss how to relax the model even further in two different ways. In one, we allow the adversary to zero-test arbitrary (degree-bounded) polynomials over the encodings, which may not necessarily obey edge restrictions. In the other relaxed model (which is incomparable to the first relaxation), we allow the adversary to zero-test polynomials over handles to *elements* of encodings rather than over handles to the full matrices, as long as the polynomials still follow the edge constraints.

1.5   A New GGH15 Variant

For our next result, we describe a new GGH15 variant. Our goal with this variant is to add safeguards — some of which have been proposed in the literature — in a rigorous way that allows us to formally analyze the effectiveness of these safeguards. Our modifications to GGH15 are as follows:

Tensored Plaintexts. First, we will modify plaintexts as suggested in Chen et al. [10]. Plaintexts will still be matrices $\mathbf{M}$. However, before encoding, we will manipulate $\mathbf{M}$ as follows. First, we will tensor $\mathbf{M}$ with a random matrix $\mathbf{S}$. Then we will also append $\mathbf{S}$ as a block diagonal, obtaining the matrix

$$\mathbf{S}' = \begin{bmatrix} \mathbf{M} \otimes \mathbf{S} & \\ & \mathbf{S} \end{bmatrix}$$

Then we will encode $\mathbf{S}'$ as in plain GGH15. By performing this encoding, we can use the Chen et al. [10] proof to show that direct attacks (those that do not use the broken secret key) are provably impossible, assuming LWE.

Block Diagonal Ciphertexts. Next, after obtaining a plain GGH15 encoding $\mathbf{D}'$ of $\mathbf{S}'$, we append a block diagonal $\mathbf{B}$. Each matrix $\mathbf{B}$ will have "smallish" entries, and will be chosen independently for each encoding. These matrices will multiply independently of the encodings $\mathbf{D}'$. After multiplying to the top level, we will introduce bookend vectors which will combine the products of the $\mathbf{D}'$ and $\mathbf{B}$ matrices together. Since the $\mathbf{B}$ matrices are small, this will not affect zero-testing.

   These block diagonals are used to inject sufficient entropy into the encodings, which will be crucial for several parts of our analysis. In particular, these block diagonals will be used to prove that any attack in our zeroizing model will also lead to an attack in a much simpler "GGH15 Annihilation Model", discussed below in Sect. 1.6. Their role is similar to block diagonals introduced by Garg et al. [21], in the context of GGH13 multilinear maps. However, we note that their role here is somewhat different: our block diagonals are added to the ciphertexts, whereas in [21] they are added to the plaintexts before encoding.

Kilian Randomization. As described so far, the block diagonals $\mathbf{B}$ can simply be stripped off by the adversary, and therefore do not provide any real-world security, despite offering security in our model as discussed in Sect. 1.6. The reason for this inconsistency is that our model assumes the adversary treats the encoding matrices monolithically, only operating on whole encoding matrices. Such an adversary cannot decompose a block diagonal matrix into its blocks.

   We therefore employ the relaxation of our model discussed above, where the adversary can manipulate the individual components of an encoding independently (this is done in the full version [1]). This model captures any adversary's attempts to decompose a block matrix, and potentially much more. In order to maintain security even in this relaxed model, we Kilian-randomize the encodings, which is one of the suggested safeguards from the original GGH15 paper [6].

More precisely, we associate a random matrix $\mathbf{R}_u$ with each node u. Then, when encoding on an edge $u \leadsto v$, we left-multiply the block diagonal encoding from above by $\mathbf{R}_u^{-1}$, and right multiply by $\mathbf{R}_v$. Note that the inner $\mathbf{R}$ matrices cancel out when multiplying two compatible encodings. Moreover, we include $\mathbf{R}$'s in the bookend vectors to cancel out the outer matrices when zero-testing.

This randomization, intuitively, allows us to bind the matrices $\mathbf{B}$ to $\mathbf{D}'$. We formally prove in our relaxed model that the adversary learns nothing extra if it attempts to manipulate the individual matrix entries; therefore, the adversary might as well just operate monolithically on whole encodings. This allows our analysis from above to go through.

Asymmetric Levels. Finally, we introduce asymmetric levels. In an asymmetric multilinear map, plaintexts are encoded relative to subsets of $\{1, \ldots, \kappa\}$. Encodings relative to the same subset can be added, and encodings relative to disjoint subsets can be multiplied. Encodings relative to the "top" level $\{1, \ldots, \kappa\}$ can be zero-tested.

We do not quite obtain asymmetric multilinear maps from GGH15. Instead, we add the asymmetric level structure on top of the graph structure. That is, there is still a graph on d nodes as well as a set of asymmetric levels. Any plaintext is now encoded relative to a pair $(u \leadsto v, L)$, where $u \leadsto v$ is a path in the graph and L is a subset of $\{1, \ldots, \kappa\}$. Encodings can be added as long as both the graph-induced and asymmetric levels are identical, and encodings can be multiplied as long as both sets of levels are compatible. An element can be zero tested only if it is encoded relative to the source-to-sink path $1 \leadsto d$, and the "top" asymmetric level $\{1, \ldots, \kappa\}$. Asymmetric levels are useful for creating straddling sets [23] for proving the security of obfuscation.

To achieve this functionality, we use a technique suggested by Halevi [24]. Simply associate a random scalar to each asymmetric level, and divide an encoding by the corresponding subset of level scalars. We choose the level scalars so that they cancel out if and only if they are multiplied together, corresponding to a "top"-level encoding.

We note that it is possible for an adversary to combine elements that do not conform to the asymmetric level structure. For example, an adversary can multiply two encodings with the same asymmetric level. The point is that the adversary will not be able to successfully zero-test such an encoding.

However, the ability to combine illegal elements presents some difficulty for our analysis. Namely, the adversary could combine some illegal elements, and then cancel them out later at some point prior to zero-testing. Such a procedure will generate a valid zero-test, despite being composed of illegal operations. This breaks usual security proofs relying on asymmetric levels, which assume the ability to immediately reject any illegal operations. Essentially what we get then is an "arithmetic model" for the asymmetric levels, due to Miles, Sahai, and Weiss [25]. We will therefore use the techniques from their work in order to prove security in our model.

1.6   An Annihilation Model for Our Scheme

Next, we define a GGH15 Annihilation Model which is much simpler than the zeroizing model described above. This model makes it very easy to evaluate whether a set of plaintexts could possibly lead to an attack.

Up until successful zero-tests, this model is similar to the original model described above: the adversary can combine elements as long as they respect the edges in the underlying graph G. One key difference is that encodings are also associated with an asymmetric level structure. For the asymmetric level structure, we work with the arithmetic model, which allows the adversary to combine arbitrary elements, but any zero-test must be on elements which respect the asymmetric level structure (in addition to respecting the graph level structure).

After successful zero-tests, the model changes from above. Instead of trying to compute a polynomial relation Q, the adversary simply tries to compute an annihilating polynomial Q' for the set of zero-test polynomials previously submitted (where each is evaluated over matrices of formal variables). We show that any attack on our scheme in the GGH15 zeroizing model corresponds to an attack in the GGH15 annihilation model, allowing us to focus on proving the security of schemes in the simpler to reason about annihilation model.

1.7   Zeroizing-Proof Obfuscation

We now turn to constructing obfuscation secure against zeroizing attacks. With our new GGH15 construction and models in hand, the construction becomes quite simple. As with the original obfuscator of Garg et al. [3], our obfuscator works on matrix branching programs; such an obfuscator can be "bootstrapped" to a full obfuscator using now-standard techniques (e.g. using FHE as in [3]). Our obfuscator is essentially the obfuscation construction of [26], which in turn is based on [23]. We do have some simplifications, owing to the fact that our multilinear map directly works with matrices.

- We assume the branching program is given as a "dual-input" branching program, following the same restrictions as in [23].[3] Any branching program can be converted into such a dual-input program using simple transformations as described in [23].
- We instantiate our multilinear map with the single path graph G whose length matches the length ℓ of the branching program. We also use the version with asymmetric level structure, using ℓ asymmetric levels.
- We directly encode the branching program matrices. Each matrix is encoded at the asymmetric level corresponding to how it would be encoded in [26]. Its graph-induced level is chosen to be consistent with evaluation order; namely, the branching program matrices in column i are encoded at the i-th edge in G.

---

[3] Dual-input is necessary to invoke the p-Bounded Speedup Hypothesis for MAX 2-SAT. This arises in the proof of Lemma 7.

We can then easily prove our obfuscator is secure against zeroizing attacks. The following is a sketch of the proof: in our GGH15 annihilation model, following previous analysis of [25], we can show that under the p-Bounded Speedup Hypothesis, the only successful zero-tests the adversary can construct are linear combinations of polynomially many honest branching program evaluations. But then, any annihilation attack gives an annihilating polynomial for branching programs. We then rely on a non-uniform variant of the *Branching Program Un-Annihilatability* Assumption (BPUA) of [21], which conjectures that such annihilating polynomials are computationally intractable. This assumption can be proven true under the very mild assumption that PRFs secure against P/poly and computable by branching programs exist (in particular, PRFs computable by log-depth circuits suffice).[4]

1.8 Concurrent Work: A Weak Model for CLT13

Ma and Zhandry [28] propose a weak multilinear map model for the CLT13 multilinear maps [5], which they show captures all known zeroizing attacks on CLT13. They prove that an obfuscation scheme of Badrinarayanan, Miles, Sahai, and Zhandry [26] as well as an order revealing encryption construction of Boneh et al. [27] are secure against zeroizing attacks when instantiated with CLT13. They also give a polynomial-degree asymmetric multilinear map "fix" which they prove secure in their model under a new assumption they call the "Vector-Input Branching Program Un-Annihilatability Assumption," a strengthening of the BPUA Assumption.

Due to the substantial differences between the CLT13 and GGH15 multilinear maps, the techniques of Ma and Zhandry do not apply to the GGH15 setting. Most notably, their model captures an attacker's ability to perform a step that leads to factoring the CLT13 modulus. There is no composite modulus in the GGH15 scheme and thus the zeroizing attacks we consider are quite different.

2 Preliminaries

2.1 Notation

Throughout this paper we use capital bold letters to denote a matrix $\mathbf{M}$. Lowercase bold letters denote vectors $\mathbf{v}$. Occasionally, we will use $diag(\mathbf{M}_1, \ldots, \mathbf{M}_k)$ to denote a matrix with block diagonals $\mathbf{M}_1, \ldots, \mathbf{M}_k$. We will often need to distinguish between values and formal variables. For example, in a situation where the variable $x = 2$, it can be difficult to tell when x represents a formal variable or when it represents the number 2. Thus, whenever we want x to denote a formal variable, we explicitly write it as $\hat{x}$. When an expression over formal variables is identically 0, we write $\equiv$ (or $\not\equiv$ if it is not). Finally, we identify the ring $\mathbb{Z}_q$ with elements $[-q/2, q/2)$.

---

[4] Using similar arguments, we can adapt the order-revealing encryption (ORE) construction of [27] to our scheme, and prove security under BPUA, analogous to constructing ORE from GGH13 as in [21].

2.2 Background on Lattices

Here, we give a very brief background on lattices. A lattice Λ of dimension n is a discrete additive subgroup of $\mathbb{R}^n$ that is generated by n basis vectors denoted as $\{\mathbf{b}_1, \ldots, \mathbf{b}_n \in \mathbb{R}^n\}$. Specifically, we have $\Lambda = \{\sum_{i \in [n]} x_i \cdot \mathbf{b}_i\}$ for integer x_i's. We then have the following useful definitions and lemmas.

Definition 1 (Discrete Gaussian on Lattices). *First, define the Gaussian function on $\mathbb{R}^n$ with center $\mathbf{c} \in \mathbb{R}^n$ and width $\sigma > 0$ as*

$$\forall \mathbf{x} \in \mathbb{R}^n, \rho_{\sigma,\mathbf{c}}(\mathbf{x}) = e^{-\pi \|\mathbf{x}-\mathbf{c}\|^2/\sigma^2}.$$

Then, the discrete Gaussian distribution over an n-dimensional Λ with center $\mathbf{c} \in \mathbb{R}^n$ and width σ is defined as

$$\forall \mathbf{x} \in \Lambda, D_{\Lambda,\sigma,\mathbf{c}}(\mathbf{x}) = \frac{\rho_{\sigma,\mathbf{c}}(\mathbf{x})}{\sum_{\mathbf{y} \in \Lambda} \rho_{\sigma,\mathbf{c}}(\mathbf{y})}.$$

Note that we omit the subscript $\mathbf{c}$ when it is $\mathbf{0}$.

Definition 2 (Decisional Learning with Errors (LWE) [7]). *For $n, m \in \mathbb{N}$ and modulus $q \geq 2$, distributions for secret vectors, public matrices, and error vectors $\theta, \pi, \chi \subseteq \mathbb{Z}_q$, an LWE sample is defined as $(\mathbf{A}, \mathbf{s}^T\mathbf{A} + \mathbf{e}^T \mod q)$ with $\mathbf{s}, \mathbf{A}, \mathbf{e}$ sampled as $\mathbf{s} \leftarrow \theta^n$, $\mathbf{A} \leftarrow \pi^{m \times n}$, and $\mathbf{e} \leftarrow \chi^m$.*

An algorithm is said to solve $\mathsf{LWE}_{n,m,q,\theta,\pi,\chi}$ if it is able to distinguish the LWE sample from one that is uniformly sampled from $\pi^{m \times n} \times U(\mathbb{Z}_q^{m \times 1})$ with probability non-negligibly greater than $1/2$.

Lemma 1 (Hardness of LWE [7]). *Given $n \in \mathbb{N}$, for any $m = \mathsf{poly}(n), q \leq 2^{\mathsf{poly}(n)}$, let $\theta = \pi = U(\mathbb{Z}_q), \chi = D_{\mathbb{Z},\sigma}$ where $\sigma \geq 2\sqrt{n}$. If there exists an efficient (possible quantum) algorithm that breaks $\mathsf{LWE}_{n,m,q,\theta,\pi,\chi}$, then there exists an efficient (possible quantum) algorithm for approximating SIVP and GAPSVP in the ℓ_2 norm, in the worst case, to within $\tilde{O}(nq/\sigma)$ factors.*

Lemma 2 (LWE with Small Public Matrices [29]). *Given n, m, q, σ chosen as in Lemma 1, $\mathsf{LWE}_{n',m,q,U(\mathbb{Z}_q),D_{\mathbb{Z},\sigma},D_{\mathbb{Z},\sigma}}$ is as hard as $\mathsf{LWE}_{n,m,q,U(\mathbb{Z}_q),U(\mathbb{Z}_q),D_{\mathbb{Z},\sigma}}$ for $n' \geq 2n \log q$.*

Lemma 3 (Trapdoor Sampling [30]). *There exists a PPT algorithm called $\mathsf{TrapSam}(1^n, 1^m, q)$ that, given any integers $n \geq 1$, prime $q \geq 2$, and sufficiently large $m = O(n \log q)$, outputs $(\mathbf{A}, \tau)$ where $\mathbf{A}$ is statistically close to uniform over $\mathbb{Z}_q^{n \times m}$, and τ is a trapdoor for $\mathbf{A}$. Furthermore, there is another PPT algorithm $\mathsf{SampleD}(\mathbf{A}, \tau, \mathbf{y}, \sigma)$ that outputs a sample of vector $\mathbf{d}$ from $D_{\mathbb{Z}^m,\sigma}$ conditioned on $\mathbf{Ad} = \mathbf{y}$. For sufficiently large $\sigma = O(\sqrt{n \log q})$, with all but negligible probability, we have*

$$\{\mathbf{A}, \mathbf{d}, \mathbf{y} : \mathbf{y} \leftarrow U(\mathbb{Z}_q^n), \ \mathbf{d} \leftarrow \mathsf{SampleD}(\mathbf{A}, \tau, \mathbf{y}, \sigma)\}$$
$$\approx_s$$
$$\{\mathbf{A}, \mathbf{d}, \mathbf{y} : \mathbf{d} \leftarrow D_{\mathbb{Z}^m,\sigma}, \mathbf{y} = \mathbf{Ad}\}.$$

2.3   Matrix Branching Programs

We introduce dual-input matrix branching programs of the type considered in [31] but with one minor modification. Formally, a dual-input matrix branching program BP of length h, width w, and input length ℓ consists of an input selection function $\mathsf{inp} : [h] \to [\ell] \times [\ell]$ and $4h$ matrices

$$\{M_{i,b_1,b_2} \in \{0,1\}^{w \times w}\}_{i \in [h]; b_1, b_2 \in \{0,1\}}.$$

BP is evaluated on input $x \in \{0,1\}^\ell$ by checking whether or not

$$\prod_{i \in [h]} M_{i,x(i)} = 0^{w \times w}$$

where $x(i) := (x_{\mathsf{inp}(i)_1}, x_{\mathsf{inp}(i)_2})$. Note that the definition from [31] includes right and left bookend vectors that are multiplied on either side of the branching program product resulting in a scalar that is either zero or non-zero. We can simply turn each bookend into a matrix by repetition of rows/columns in order to recover the functionality described above. As noted in [31], branching programs of this type can be constructed from any NC^1 circuit with $h = \mathsf{poly}(n)$ and $w = 5$ by Barrington's theorem [32].

2.4   Straddling Sets

Our obfuscator uses the notion of straddling sets in order to enforce input consistency. Please refer to Barak et al. [23] for a simple construction.

Definition 3 (Straddling Set System). *A straddling set system with n entries is a universe set $\mathbb{U}$ and a collection of subsets $\mathbb{S} = \{S_{i,b} \subseteq \mathbb{U}\}_{i \in [n], b \in \{0,1\}}$ such that*

- $\bigcup_{i \in [n]} S_{i,0} = \bigcup_{i \in [n]} S_{i,1} = \mathbb{U}$
- *For any distinct $C, D \subseteq \mathbb{S}$ such that $\bigcup_{S \in C} S = \bigcup_{S \in D} S$, there exists $b \in \{0,1\}$ such that $C = \{S_{i,b}\}_{i \in [n]}$ and $C = \{S_{i,1-b}\}_{i \in [n]}$*

3   GGH15 Zeroizing Model

3.1   Graph-Induced Ideal Model

We discuss the syntax of graph-induced graded encoding schemes and describe an ideal model (also known as a generic multilinear map model) for the graph-induced setting. Note that this is completely analogous to the ideal model for symmetric/asymmetric multilinear maps, which itself is an extension of the generic group model to the multilinear map setting [3,4].

We consider directed acyclic graphs (DAGs) $G = (V, E)$ where $|V| = d$. We assume the graph has a single source and a single sink. We label the vertices from 1 to d according to some fixed topological ordering, so that all edges/paths in the graph can be written as $j \rightsquigarrow k$ where $j, k \in [d], j < k$. (Note that the precise distinction between paths and edges in graph-induced maps is not important, since the intermediate nodes on a path do not matter).

Formally, the graph-induced ideal model is instantiated with a DAG $G = (V, E)$, a plaintext ring R, and a set of plaintexts $\{M_i, u_i \rightsquigarrow v_i\}_i$. The plaintexts are indexed by i, and plaintext M_i comes with an associated path $u_i \rightsquigarrow v_i$, where $u_i, v_i \in [d], u_i < v_i$.

We describe the model as an interaction between an oracle $\mathcal{M}$ (the "model") and a user $\mathcal{A}$ (the "adversary").

– *Instance Generation.* The model $\mathcal{M}$ is instantiated with the graph G, plaintext ring R and the set $\{M_i, u_i \rightsquigarrow v_i\}_i$. For each i, the model $\mathcal{M}$ generates a handle $\widehat{C}_i$, stores a pointer from $\widehat{C}_i$ to M_i, and releases $(\widehat{C}_i, u_i \rightsquigarrow v_i)$ publicly.

$\mathcal{A}$ can only interact with the handles $\widehat{C}_i$, which in the ideal setting leak no information about M_i. The model provides the following interfaces for $\mathcal{A}$:

– *Addition.* Addition on two handles $\widehat{C}_i$, $\widehat{C}_j$ is permitted only if their corresponding paths $u_i \rightsquigarrow v_i$, $u_j \rightsquigarrow v_j$ are the same. The model $\mathcal{M}$ looks up the corresponding plaintexts M_i, M_j, and returns a newly generated handle $\widehat{C}_k$ to the sum $M_i + M_j$, along with the path $u_i \rightsquigarrow v_i$.
– *Multiplication.* Multiplication on two handles $\widehat{C}_i$, $\widehat{C}_j$ is permitted only if the path $u_i \rightsquigarrow v_i$ ends where path $u_j \rightsquigarrow v_j$ begins ($v_i = u_j$). The model $\mathcal{M}$ looks up the corresponding plaintexts M_i, M_j, and returns a newly generated handle $\widehat{C}_k$ to the product $M_i \cdot M_j$, along with the combined path $u_i \rightsquigarrow v_j$.
– *Zero-Test.* $\mathcal{A}$ can request a zero-test on a handle $\widehat{C}$. $\mathcal{M}$ responds with "zero" if the corresponding plaintext is 0, and the corresponding path is the source-to-sink path. Otherwise, the result is "not zero."

Implicit in this model is the assumption that the adversary cannot learn anything beyond what the interfaces explicitly allow. In particular, it can only learn the bits returned by zero-testing honestly generated source-to-sink encodings, and nothing more.

Zero-Test Circuits. Observe that addition, multiplication, and zero-testing can be handled in a single interface. Here, $\mathcal{A}$ simply submits an arithmetic circuit p that computes a polynomial over the handles $\{\widehat{C}_i\}_i$. Any handle that results in a successful zero-test in the above model can be represented as a polynomial-size circuit over $\{\widehat{C}_i\}_i$ where each arithmetic gate respects the addition and multiplication restrictions enforced by the graph structure.

However, we can relax the restriction on the arithmetic circuit so that the individual gates may not necessarily respect the graph constraints, but the resulting polynomial still computes a valid source-to-sink encoding (for example, if terms that violate graph constraints cancel out in the final evaluation). Looking ahead to our GGH15 Zeroizing Model, we will require this relaxed constraint on arithmetic circuits, which only makes the model more conservative.

3.2 GGH15 Variants

There are a number of GGH15 variants in the literature that modify the original GGH15 construction at a number of key points. We identify several points in which the various schemes differ, and establish standard notation before introducing our model.

Pre-Processing. In the original GGH15 construction [6], an encoding of a plaintext matrix $\mathbf{M}$ at path $u \rightsquigarrow v$ is the matrix $\mathbf{D}$ satisfying $\mathbf{A}_u \cdot \mathbf{D} = \mathbf{M} \cdot \mathbf{A}_v + \mathbf{E}$.

A number of works have proposed performing additional pre-processing to $\mathbf{M}$ before sampling the matrix $\mathbf{D}$. For example, the $\gamma_{\otimes\mathrm{diag}}$-GGH15 encodings of Chen et al. [10] encode a plaintext matrix $\mathbf{M}$ by first sampling a random $\mathbf{P}$ (in the notation of [10], this is the $\mathbf{S}_{i,b}$ matrix) and constructing the matrix $diag(\mathbf{M} \otimes \mathbf{P}, \mathbf{P})$ where $\otimes$ denotes the tensor product (Kronecker product).

Then the encoding $\mathbf{D}$ is the matrix satisfying

$$\mathbf{A}_u \cdot \mathbf{D} = \begin{bmatrix} \mathbf{M} \otimes \mathbf{P} \\ & \mathbf{P} \end{bmatrix} \cdot \mathbf{A}_v + \mathbf{E}.$$

As other GGH15 variants perform different pre-processing steps on the initial plaintext $\mathbf{M}$, we denote the result of pre-processing as $\mathbf{S}$. If there is no pre-processing step, then $\mathbf{S} = \mathbf{M}$. In the example above $\mathbf{S} = diag(\mathbf{M} \otimes \mathbf{P}, \mathbf{P})$.[5] The encoding is then computed as $\mathbf{A}_u \cdot \mathbf{D} = \mathbf{S} \cdot \mathbf{A}_v + \mathbf{E}$.

Post-Encoding. The original GGH15 paper [6] as well as Halevi [24] discuss various steps intended to safeguard the scheme against attacks (sometimes called "GGH15 with safeguards"). These steps essentially perform operations on the matrix $\mathbf{D}$ generated from the standard GGH15 encoding procedure to produce a "final" encoding $\mathbf{C}$. We will adopt this notation, and set $\mathbf{C}$ to be the result of the overall encoding process. If there is no post-encoding step, then $\mathbf{C} = \mathbf{D}$.

Zero-Testing. In the original GGH15 construction, zero-testing a source-to-sink encoding is done by computing a matrix from the public parameters and the encodings $\mathbf{C}$, and testing if this matrix is small. Ideally, only the bit of information (whether or not the result is small) is useful to the adversary. Of course, the zeroizing attacks on GGH15 show that this assumption is false, and that the actual matrix resulting from the zero-test can provide useful information to the adversary [10,19,20]. This matrix will be referred to as the "result" of zero-testing. To avoid confusion, the 0/1 bit learned from the zero-test will be referred to as a bit rather than the result.

In certain GGH15 variants, the result of zero-testing is not a matrix. For example in "GGH15 with safeguards" [6,24], the result of zero-testing is a scalar. We will use the letter T to generically denote the result of zero-testing (noting that T may represent a matrix depending on the scheme, even though it might not be written in bold).

---

[5] Essentially, $\mathbf{S}$ is the result of the γ functions in the notation of [10]. However, the $\mathbf{S}$ notation is more natural for our setting, especially when referring to entries of these matrices.

GGH15 Algorithms. Unlike the graph-induced ideal model, our GGH15 Zeroizing Model is defined with respect to a specific GGH15 scheme/variant in mind. For example, in the ideal setting, a zero-test is successful if and only if the product of the plaintexts is zero. In our GGH15 Zeroizing Model, the model explicitly maintains encodings corresponding to each plaintext, and whether a zero-test is successful is determined by performing computations on the encodings and public parameters corresponding to an actual GGH15 variant.

To specify our model, we let the scheme be denoted by G. For example, G may be the original GGH15 construction [6], the "GGH15 with safeguards" [24], etc. To be a valid GGH15 scheme, we require G to have the following algorithms (in the literature, PreProcess is usually implicit):

- G.KeyGen($1^\lambda, G, R,$ aux): Takes the security parameter, a description of a graph G with source 1 and sink d, a ring R, and potential auxiliary information aux, and produces public parameters pp and secret parameters sp.
- G.PreProcess(sp, $\mathbf{M}$): Converts the input plaintext $\mathbf{M}$ into a pre-encoding $\mathbf{S}$. For many schemes (including the original GGH15 construction), $\mathbf{S} = \mathbf{M}$.
- G.Enc(sp, $\mathbf{S}, u_i \rightsquigarrow v_i$): Encodes $\mathbf{S}$ on the path $u_i \rightsquigarrow v_i$.
- G.Add(pp, $\mathbf{C}_1, \mathbf{C}_2$): Takes an encoding $\mathbf{C}_1$ of $\mathbf{M}_1$ at path $u_1 \rightsquigarrow v_1$ and an encoding $\mathbf{C}_2$ of $\mathbf{M}_2$ at path $u_2 \rightsquigarrow v_2$. If $u_1 = u_2$ and $v_1 = v_2$, this produces an encoding $\mathbf{C}_3$ of $\mathbf{M}_1 + \mathbf{M}_2$ at path $u_1 \rightsquigarrow v_1$.
- G.Mult(pp, $\mathbf{C}_1, \mathbf{C}_2$): Takes an encoding $\mathbf{C}_1$ of $\mathbf{M}_1$ at path $u_1 \rightsquigarrow v_1$ and an encoding $\mathbf{C}_2$ of $\mathbf{M}_2$ at path $u_2 \rightsquigarrow v_2$. If $v_1 = u_2$, this produces an encoding $\mathbf{C}_3$ of $\mathbf{M}_1 \cdot \mathbf{M}_2$ at path $u_1 \rightsquigarrow v_2$.
- G.ZeroTest(pp, $\mathbf{C}$): Takes an encoding $\mathbf{C}$, computes a result T, and returns (T, b). If $\mathbf{C}$ is an encoding of 0 relative to path $1 \rightsquigarrow d$, then T is "small" and $b = 1$ (indicating successful zero-test). Otherwise, $b = 0$ with overwhelming probability.

3.3   GGH15 Zeroizing Model

Initialize Parameters. $\mathcal{M}$ is initialized with a security parameter λ, a graph $G = (V, E)$, a ring R, potential auxiliary information aux, and a graph-induced encoding scheme G. It runs G.KeyGen($1^\lambda, G, R,$ aux) to generate the public and secret parameters (pp, sp), which it stores.

Initialize Elements. $\mathcal{M}$ is given a set of initial plaintext elements $\{\mathbf{M}_i, u_i \rightsquigarrow v_i\}_i$ where each plaintext is indexed by i, and i-th plaintext $\mathbf{M}_i$ is associated with path $u_i \rightsquigarrow v_i$. The model applies a pre-processing procedure to the plaintext (recall in the standard GGH15 construction, this procedure does nothing):

$$\mathbf{S}_i \leftarrow \mathsf{G.PreProcess}(\mathsf{sp}, \mathbf{M}_i).$$

Then it computes the encoding $\mathbf{C}_i$ from the pre-encoding $\mathbf{S}_i$:

$$\mathbf{C}_i \leftarrow \mathsf{G.Enc}(\mathsf{sp}, \mathbf{S}_i, u_i \rightsquigarrow v_i).$$

Each tuple $(\mathbf{S}_i, \mathbf{C}_i, u_i \rightsquigarrow v_i)$ is stored in the *pre-zero-test table*. For each encoding $\mathbf{C}_i$, the model generates a corresponding handle $\widehat{C}_i$ that contains no information about $\mathbf{C}_i$ or $\mathbf{S}_i$. The handle is released, along with the corresponding encoding level $u_i \rightsquigarrow v_i$, and the model internally stores a mapping between the handle $\widehat{C}_i$ and the tuple $(\mathbf{S}_i, \mathbf{C}_i, u_i \rightsquigarrow v_i)$. While the encoding $\mathbf{C}_i$ is a matrix, the adversary is given a single handle $\widehat{C}_i$ to the entire matrix.

Zero-Testing. The adversary generates a polynomial p (represented as a $\mathsf{poly}(\lambda)$-size arithmetic circuit), over the handles $\widehat{C}_i$ and submits it to the model. Note that since the handles correspond to non-commutative encodings, p must be treated as a polynomial over non-commuting variables.

The model verifies that p computes an edge-respecting polynomial, meaning that each monomial is a product of encodings corresponding to a source-to-sink path. If p is not edge-respecting, the model returns $\perp$. If p is edge-respecting, the model $\mathcal{M}$ evaluates p on the encodings $\mathbf{C}_i$, producing a matrix $p(\{\mathbf{C}_i\}_i)$ that corresponds to a valid source-to-sink encoding (or a linear combination of source-to-sink encodings). Finally, $\mathcal{M}$ zero-tests $p(\{\mathbf{C}_i\}_i)$, obtaining $(T, b) \leftarrow$ $\mathsf{G.ZeroTest}(\mathsf{pp}, p(\{\mathbf{C}_i\}_i))$. If the zero-test is successful ($b = 1$), the model stores the value T (possibly a matrix, vector, or scalar) and generates a handle $\widehat{T}_\ell$ to each element of T. Otherwise, the model returns $\perp$.

We index the successful zero-tests by the letter u, so T_u will denote the result of the u-th successful zero-test, $\widehat{T}_u$ will be the corresponding handles, and p_u will be the polynomial submitted for the u-th successful zero-test.[6]

Post-Zero-Test. In the post-zero-test stage, the adversary submits a polynomial Q of degree at most $2^{o(\lambda)}$ over the handles $\{\widehat{T}_u\}_u$ and pre-encoding elements $\{\widehat{S}_{i,j,k}\}_{i,j,k}$ where $\widehat{S}_{i,j,k}$ is a handle to the (j, k)-th entry of the i-th pre-encoding matrix $\mathbf{S}_i$. For the sake of readability, we will frequently drop the outer subscripts and denote these sets as $\{\widehat{T}_u\}$ and $\{\widehat{S}_{i,j,k}\}$. The model $\mathcal{M}$ checks the following:

1. $Q(\{T_u\}, \{S_{i,j,k}\}) = 0$
2. $Q(\{T_u\}, \{\widehat{S}_{i,j,k}\}) \not\equiv 0$
3. $Q(\{\widehat{T}_u\}, \{S_{i,j,k}\}) \not\equiv 0$

If all three checks pass, the model returns "Win", and otherwise it returns $\perp$. In Sect. 3.4, we explain how we derive these conditions, and in Sect. 3.5 we justify how these conditions capture the known attacks. We note that $\mathcal{A}$ is free to submit as many polynomials Q as it wants as long as it remains polynomial time. If any such Q causes $\mathcal{M}$ to return "Win" then the adversary is successful.

Note that in reality, a zeroizing attack that succeeds with non-negligible probability is indeed considered successful. Thus, we will allow the adversary to be possibly randomized, and we define a successful adversary to be one that can obtain a "Win" with non-negligible probability (over the randomness of the model and the adversary).

---

[6] Although we denote each zero-test result as T_u, an adversary is not required to use T_u monolithically. For example, an adversary can extract a single entry of T_u in the case when T_u are matrices.

3.4   Deriving the Post-Zero-Test Win Condition

All known zeroizing attacks on GGH15 exclusively rely on the results of zero-tests to recover information about the hidden plaintexts [10, 19, 20]. In our model, this can be viewed as using the values $\{T_u\}$ to learn something about the values $\{S_{i,j,k}\}$. Furthermore, we claim that all attacks that do this recover information that can be expressed as an *algebraic relation* (we justify this claim in Sect. 3.5).

More precisely, underneath all successful zeroizing attacks on GGH15, there is a non-trivial bounded-degree polynomial Q (the algebraic relation) such that

$$Q(\{T_u\}, \{S_{i,j,k}\}) = 0$$

holds over the integers.

This corresponds to the intuition that in a zeroizing attack, the adversary can learn something about the pre-encoding entries $S_{i,j,k}$ by plugging the results of zero-testing $\{T_u\}$ into the above relation. While not every algebraic relation is solvable, we take the conservative route and model any non-trivial relation the adversary can construct as a win.

Now we formalize what it means for Q to be non-trivial. If the adversary can indeed plug in the results of zero-testing to learn something about the $S_{i,j,k}$, then the expression must not be identically zero over the $\widehat{S}_{i,j,k}$ terms (taken as formal variables), when the $\{T_u\}$ values are plugged in. Thus, we have the condition

$$Q(\{T_u\}, \{\widehat{S}_{i,j,k}\}) \not\equiv 0.$$

We also want to ensure that the zeroizing attack uncovers information about the pre-encodings beyond what the adversary can learn honestly. Note that if the adversary obtains a successful zero-test, it learns that some function of the pre-encoding entries $\widehat{S}_{i,j,k}$ evaluates to 0. As a simple example, if the adversary learns from an honest zero-test that matrix $\mathbf{S}_{i'}$ is the 0 matrix, then $\mathbf{S}_{i',j',k'} = 0$ for any choice of j', k'. The formal polynomial $Q = \widehat{S}_{i',j',k'}$ for any j', k' would then satisfy both of the above conditions. However, we should not consider this a successful zeroizing "attack," as it does not use the zero-test results to derive information about the pre-encodings.

To ensure that what the adversary learns about the pre-encodings relies on T_u in a non-trivial way, we enforce a third condition

$$Q(\{\widehat{T}_u\}, \{S_{i,j,k}\}) \not\equiv 0.$$

Roughly, this condition states that the relation is not always satisfied regardless of what the $\{T_u\}$ values are, and thus the attack "uses" the zero-test leakage.

3.5   Algebraic Relations in Known Attacks

We now describe in detail how in the Coron et al. [19] attack (henceforth CLLT16) on multiparty key exchange over GGH15, we can derive an algebraic relation Q satisfying our three win conditions with non-negligible probability.

For the analogous description of the other major zeroizing attacks [10,20], refer to the full version of this work [1], and for a review of the settings of these attacks, refer to the full version or the original papers [10,19,20].

Step 1: Compute Top-Level Encodings of Zero. The CLLT16 attack on GGH15 key exchange does not explicitly compute encodings of zero in the original exposition. Instead, the attack computes encodings of the same plaintext on two different source-to-sink paths (starting from different sources), and subtracts the encodings. In our setting we enforce without loss of generality that all graphs must have a single source, which can be generically achieved by connecting a "super" source node to the original source nodes of the graph, and encoding a 1 (or identity matrix) on edges leading into the original sources.

The encodings used in the key exchange are $\mathbf{C}_{i,0}$ for $1 \le i \le 3$ (which we introduce to connect the super source node) and $\mathbf{C}_{i,i',l}$ for $1 \le i,i' \le 3, 1 \le l \le N$ (for some large enough N). Then for $\{\mathbf{C}\} = \{\mathbf{C}_{i,0}\}_{i\in\{1,2,3\}} \cup \{\mathbf{C}_{i,i',l}\}_{i,i'\in\{1,2,3\},l\in[N]}$, the polynomial

$$p_{j,k}(\{\mathbf{C}\}) = \mathbf{C}_{2,0} \cdot \mathbf{C}_{2,1,1} \cdot \mathbf{C}_{2,2,j} \cdot \mathbf{C}_{2,3,k} - \mathbf{C}_{3,0} \cdot \mathbf{C}_{3,1,k} \cdot \mathbf{C}_{3,2,1} \cdot \mathbf{C}_{3,3,j}$$

is an encoding of $s_{3,1} \cdot s_{1,j} \cdot s_{2,k} - s_{2,k} \cdot s_{3,1} \cdot s_{1,j} = 0$ for all choices of $j \in [J], k \in [K]$, where for this attack $J = K = N$ (N is a parameter in the key exchange construction). Recall the key exchange construction uses a GGH15 variant that supports a commutative plaintext space, so this is always an encoding of 0.

Step 2: Zero-Test and Build W Matrix. Zero-test each of these top-level encodings, and let the result of zero-testing $p_{j,k}(\{\mathbf{C}\})$ be $T_{j,k}$. Construct a $J \times K$ matrix $\mathbf{W}$ where the (j, k)-th entry $W_{j,k}$ is derived from $T_{j,k}$. In all current attacks, the matrix $\mathbf{W}$ has the following properties:

– $\mathbf{W}$ factors into $\mathbf{X} \times \mathbf{Y}$ where the rows of $\mathbf{Y}$ are linearly independent over the integers (with high probability).
– There exists a column of $\mathbf{X}$ that is in the column space of a $J \times \eta$ dimensional matrix $\mathbf{M}$, for some η that we specify below for each attack. Each entry of $\mathbf{M}$ is a polynomial over the entries of pre-encoding matrices $\{\mathbf{S}\}$.

In the CLLT16 setting (augmented with our "super" source $\mathcal{S}$), we zero-test by multiplying $\mathbf{A}_{\mathcal{S}}$ with $p_{j,k}(\{C\})$ evaluated over the encodings. This gives a zero-test result $T_{j,k}$ as a vector. Coron et al. observe that the first element of this vector can be written as a dot product $\mathbf{x}_j \cdot \mathbf{y}_k$ where the entries of $\mathbf{x}_j$ depend only on the encodings corresponding to user 1 (and the fixed encodings) and the entries of $\mathbf{y}_k$ depend only on the encodings corresponding to user 2 (and the fixed encodings). Moreover, the first element of $\mathbf{x}_j$ is the pre-encoding $s_{1,j}$. Coron et al. also argue that arranging many column vectors $\mathbf{y}_k$ into a square matrix $\mathbf{Y}$ results in $\mathbf{Y}$ being invertible with high probability. Thus we take $W_{j,k}$ to be the first element of $T_{j,k}$, $\mathbf{X}$ to consist of the row vectors $\mathbf{x}_1, ..., \mathbf{x}_J$, and $\mathbf{M}$ to simply be the column vector $[s_{1,1} \ s_{1,2} \ \cdots \ s_{1,J}]^\top$ (of dimension $J \times \eta$ where $\eta = 1$).

Step 3: Deriving an Algebraic Relation. To show how the CLLT16 attack is captured by our model, we demonstrate that this $\mathbf{W}$ matrix is already sufficient to come up with a Q satisfying our post-zero-test win condition (with non-negligible probability). For this it suffices to give a polynomial-time procedure (the adversary) that extracts a Q satisfying our win condition.

To win in our model, the adversary will pick the parameter K so that $\mathbf{Y}$ turns out to be square and thus invertible and the parameter $J \geq K + \eta$ (where η is specified in step 2 by the setting we are in). $\mathbf{Y}$ being invertible implies that every column of $\mathbf{X}$ is in the column space of $\mathbf{W}$, so in particular we have a column of $\mathbf{X}$ that is in both the column space of $\mathbf{W}$ and the column space of $\mathbf{M}$. Intuitively, if we are able to combine the columns of $\mathbf{W}$ and $\mathbf{M}$ into a square matrix, we are guaranteed that the determinant of this matrix will be zero. We just have to ensure that the columns from $\mathbf{W}$ and the columns from $\mathbf{M}$ are each linearly independent so that the determinant polynomial is not identically zero when either set of variables is substituted in. The adversary mounts the attack as follows, where the parameter β is taken to be exponential in the security parameter λ that the underlying scheme was initialized with, and $\xleftarrow{\text{U}}$ denotes "drawing uniformly at random."

To start, the adversary forms the matrix $\mathbf{W}$ of handles to honest zero-test results and the matrix $\mathbf{M}$ of pre-encoding handles where $\mathbf{W} \in \mathbb{Z}^{J \times K}$ and $\mathbf{M} \in \mathbb{Z}^{J \times \eta}$. The adversary then guesses the ranks $r_\mathbf{M}$ of $\mathbf{M}$ and $r_\mathbf{W}$ of $\mathbf{W}$ uniformly at random. The adversary guesses the correct ranks with probability $1/(K\eta)$.

The adversary then draws four random matrices $\mathbf{U}, \mathbf{U}' \xleftarrow{\text{U}} \mathbb{Z}_\beta^{(r_\mathbf{M} + r_\mathbf{W}) \times J}$, $\mathbf{V} \xleftarrow{\text{U}} \mathbb{Z}_\beta^{\eta \times r_\mathbf{M}}$, $\mathbf{V}' \xleftarrow{\text{U}} \mathbb{Z}_\beta^{K \times r_\mathbf{W}}$, and constructs

$$\mathbf{M}' = \mathbf{U} \cdot \mathbf{M} \cdot \mathbf{V}, \text{ and } \mathbf{W}' = \mathbf{U}' \cdot \mathbf{W} \cdot \mathbf{V}'.$$

Note that $\mathbf{M}' \in \mathbb{Z}^{(r_\mathbf{M} + r_\mathbf{W}) \times r_\mathbf{M}}$, and $\mathbf{W}' \in \mathbb{Z}^{(r_\mathbf{M} + r_\mathbf{W}) \times r_\mathbf{W}}$. Lastly, the adversary constructs a square $(r_\mathbf{M} + r_\mathbf{W}) \times (r_\mathbf{M} + r_\mathbf{W})$ matrix $\mathbf{A} = [\ \mathbf{M}' \ | \ \mathbf{W}' \ ]$ by concatenating $\mathbf{M}'$ and $\mathbf{W}'$. Note that the entries of $\mathbf{A}$ are over handles to the zero-test results and the pre-encodings. The adversary takes the determinant polynomial Q of this matrix and submits Q as the post-zero-test polynomial.

Assume the adversary has guessed the two ranks correctly, which happens with non-negligible probability since $K, \eta = \mathsf{poly}(\lambda)$. We now show that Q will satisfy the following three win conditions in our model with non-negligible probability.

1. $Q(\{T_{j,k}\}, \{S_{i,j,k}\}) = 0$
2. $Q(\{T_{j,k}\}, \{\widehat{S}_{i,j,k}\}) \not\equiv 0$
3. $Q(\{\widehat{T}_{j,k}\}, \{S_{i,j,k}\}) \not\equiv 0$

First, $Q(\{T_{j,k}\}, \{S_{i,j,k}\}) = 0$ since we have explicitly introduced a linear dependency among the columns of $\mathbf{A}$. Now we argue that with high probability, $\mathbf{M}'$ has an $r_\mathbf{M} \times r_\mathbf{M}$ dimensional submatrix of rank $r_\mathbf{M}$ which implies that its columns are linearly independent and thus that $Q(\{\widehat{T}_{j,k}\}, \{S_{i,j,k}\}) \not\equiv 0$. The same argument applies to $\mathbf{W}'$ implying that $Q(\{T_{j,k}\}, \{\widehat{S}_{i,j,k}\}) \not\equiv 0$. This follows from an application of the following lemma (with proof in the full version [1]), noting that in our case, β is exponential in λ and the dimensions of $\mathbf{M}$ and $\mathbf{W}$ are polynomial in λ.

Lemma 4. *Suppose an* $M \in \mathbb{Z}_\beta^{n \times m}$ *has rank* r. *Draw uniformly random* $U \leftarrow \mathbb{Z}_\beta^{r \times n}, V \leftarrow \mathbb{Z}_\beta^{m \times r}$. *Then* $M' := U \cdot M \cdot V$ *is full rank with probability at least* $1 - \frac{2r}{\beta}$.

3.6 Limitations of Our Model

Our model does not permit a number of common operations that might arise in standard lattice cryptanalysis. For example, we naturally disallow any modular reductions or rounding on the results of zero-testing, since the relation would no longer be algebraic. This may at first appear problematic, since it means our model does not capture many simple attack strategies such as LLL [33].

We stress, however, that this is a common feature of many abstract attack models defined in the literature. For example, the random oracle model does not allow for differential cryptanalysis, despite it being a powerful way to attack hash functions. This is usually considered okay, since schemes are tuned (say, by increasing the number of rounds) to make such attacks useless. Similarly, the generic group model is often applied to elliptic curves, even though the model does not allow for known attacks such as the MOV attack [34]. Instead, these models capture things the adversary can do no matter how parameters are chosen.

Our setting is similar, as most lattice attacks can be defeated by tuning parameters. The most devastating attacks on schemes such as GGH15 are zeroizing attacks, as they are present *no matter how parameters are chosen*. Therefore, we devise a model that accurately captures how zeroizing attacks are performed, and tune parameters to block all other attacks.

4 Towards Zeroizing Resistance: New Models and Constructions

4.1 Section Overview

In this section we construct a graph-induced encoding scheme with two desirable properties.

Property 1: Asymmetric Levels. In asymmetric multilinear maps such as GGH13 and CLT13, plaintexts are encoded relative to subsets $\ell \subseteq [\kappa]$, where κ is a positive integer. Two encodings can be added if and only if they are encoded at the same level set and can be multiplied if and only if they are encoded at disjoint level sets. Only top level $[\kappa]$ encodings can be zero-tested. In certain settings such as obfuscation, it is desirable to enforce restrictions based on these asymmetric levels (for example, to implement straddling sets which prevent "mixed-input" attacks [23, 25]). Unfortunately, the GGH15 edge restrictions do not immediately give us the same capabilities of asymmetric level restrictions. Thus, we require a notion of "Graph-Induced Multilinear Maps with Asymmetric Levels", which simultaneously associates every encoding with a graph path $u_i \rightsquigarrow v_i$ as well as a level set $\ell \subseteq [\kappa]$ (first described by Halevi [24]). Addition, multiplication, and zero-test operations are only allowed as long as both the graph-induced restrictions and the asymmetric level set restrictions are satisfied.

We naturally redefine our GGH15 Zeroizing Model for this new notion, calling the resulting model the "Level-Restricted GGH15 Zeroizing Model". This model is identical to the GGH15 Zeroizing Model, except the adversary is now forced to additionally respect the asymmetric level restrictions when computing a top-level encoding of zero.

Property 2: Semantic Security of Encodings. Recent techniques of Chen et al. [10] show how to produce GGH15 encodings that achieve provable semantic security from LWE via a new construction they call "γ-GGH15 encodings". We give the formal security statement and show how to adapt their security proof to our setting in the full version [1]. Note that this semantic security guarantee is orthogonal to what our GGH15 Zeroizing Model captures. Semantically secure encodings ensure that the encodings themselves do not leak information, but only in the setting where successful zero-tests are computationally unachievable. On the other hand, our GGH15 Zeroizing Model captures adversaries who attack using the zero-test leakage but only under the idealized assumption that the encodings themselves leak nothing.

A New GGH15 Variant. We integrate these two new techniques into a new construction we call γ-GGH15-AL (γ-encodings and asymmetric levels). We enforce asymmetric levels using a simple trick of dividing by random scalars due to Halevi [24]. We show that security of our γ-GGH15-AL construction in the GGH15 Zeroizing Model implies security in a (more restrictive) Level-Restricted GGH15 Zeroizing Model. In other words, we prove that an attack on γ-GGH15-AL that is free to disobey the asymmetric level restrictions has no more power than an attack that obeys the asymmetric level restrictions. The proof proceeds from applications of the Schwartz-Zippel lemma, which allow us to argue that a top-level encoding that disobeys level restrictions will not give a successful zero-test (with overwhelming probability). To achieve semantic security guarantees, we incorporate the γ-GGH15 encoding strategy of [10] into our γ-GGH15-AL construction.

We note that semantic security is only a heuristic statement in our setting. The semantic security proofs of [10] hold when the adversary cannot successfully zero-test, but in our construction, zero-testing can be achieved using a right bookend vector. Thus, our construction only has semantic security when this bookend vector is hidden from the adversary. The intuition is that when the right bookend vector is not hidden, security is lost because of zeroizing attacks, at which point we appeal to our GGH15 Zeroizing Model.

At the end of this section, we introduce a third model we call the "GGH15 Annihilation Model." We show that any successful zeroizing attacks in the GGH15 Zeroizing Model on our γ-GGH15-AL construction imply the existence of a successful adversary in the GGH15 Annihilation Model (by first going through the Level-Restricted GGH15 Zeroizing Model). An adversary in the GGH15

Annihilation Model will correspond to a polynomial-complexity arithmetic circuit that *annihilates* the zero-test polynomials submitted by the adversary.

4.2   A Graph-Induced Encoding Scheme with Asymmetric Levels

Overview. To encode a plaintext matrix $\mathbf{M}$ on an edge $i \rightsquigarrow j$ with level set $L \subseteq [\kappa]$ we first generate a random matrix $\mathbf{P}$ in order to apply the $\gamma_{\otimes\mathrm{diag}}$ function of [10]. The resulting pre-encoding $diag(\mathbf{M} \otimes \mathbf{P}, \mathbf{P})$ is encoded via the ordinary GGH15 encoding procedure to obtain an encoding $\mathbf{D}$. The next step is to draw a random $k \times k$ matrix $\mathbf{B}$ and append it on along the diagonal. This matrix $\mathbf{B}$ ensures each final encoding matrix $\mathbf{C}$ has sufficient entropy (used in Lemma 5), and is crucial for Lemma 6. The next step is to multiply by Kilian-randomization matrices (drawn by KeyGen for each vertex), and then divide by level scalars $\prod_{\ell \in L} z_\ell$. The resulting encoding is

$$\mathbf{C} = (\prod_{\ell \in L} z_\ell)^{-1} \cdot \mathbf{R}_i^{-1} \cdot \begin{bmatrix} \mathbf{D} \\ & \mathbf{B} \end{bmatrix} \cdot \mathbf{R}_j.$$

To ensure that zero-testing works, we construct our right bookend vector $\mathbf{w}$ to contain the product $(\prod_{\ell \in [\kappa]} z_\ell)$, which cancels out the level scalars in the encoding as long as it is at the top level $[\kappa]$. The left and right bookends also contain Kilian-randomization matrices $\mathbf{R}_1$ and $\mathbf{R}_d^{-1}$ multiplied in to cancel out the Kilian-randomization on the encodings. The bookends contain additional components $\mathbf{b}_v$ and $\mathbf{b}_w^\top$ which multiply with the $\mathbf{B}$ random matrices during zero-testing. This has the effect of adding the products of random matrices (with two random bookends) to the result of any zero-test (this will be crucial for our obfuscation security proof, where it will have the effect of adding a random branching program evaluation). The remaining bookend components are essentially set to be the bookends required by the γ-GGH15 encodings. However, we also multiply them by randomly sampled vectors $\mathbf{v}'$ and $\mathbf{w}'$ to simplify dimensions.

Construction γ-GGH15-AL.KeyGen$(1^\lambda, G, R = \mathbb{Z}, \kappa, \beta, k)$:[7]

Parameter Generation

- Label the nodes of G in topological order as $1, \ldots, d$ where node 1 is the unique source and node d is the unique sink.
- Choose parameters $n, w, n', m, q, \sigma, \chi, B$ where $n = wn' + n'$ according to the remark below. All operations happen over $\mathbb{Z}_q$. Plaintexts have dimension $w \times w$ with entries bounded by β, pre-encodings have dimension $n \times n$ with entries bounded (with high probability) by $\beta \cdot \sigma \cdot \sqrt{n}$, and encodings have dimension $(m + k) \times (m + k)$ with entries bounded by $\nu = 2^\lambda$. We draw error matrices under distribution $(\chi)^{n \times m}$ and set B to be the zero-test bound.

---

[7] κ is the number of asymmetric levels, β is a bound on the size of plaintext entries, and k is the dimension of the block diagonal matrices we append during the encoding procedure.

Instance Generation

- (GGH15 matrices and trapdoors) For each vertex $i \in V$, sample $(\mathbf{A}_i, \tau_i) \leftarrow$ TrapSam$(1^n, 1^m, q)$.
- (Kilian-randomization matrices) For each vertex $i \in V$, sample a random invertible $\mathbf{R}_i \in \mathbb{Z}_q^{(m+k)\times(m+k)}$.
- (Asymmetric level scalars) For each level $\ell \in [\kappa]$, sample a random invertible $z_\ell \in \mathbb{Z}_q$.

Bookend Generation

- (Left bookend matrix from γ-GGH15 encodings) Sample a random $\mathbf{J}' \leftarrow \{0,1\}^{n' \times wn'}$ and define

$$\mathbf{J} := [\mathbf{J}' \mid \mathbf{I}^{n' \times n'}].$$

- (Encoding matrix used in right bookend) Sample a uniform $\mathbf{A}^* \leftarrow \mathbb{Z}_q^{n \times m}$, an error matrix $\mathbf{E}^* \leftarrow (\chi)^{n \times m}$, and compute

$$\mathbf{D}^* \leftarrow \mathsf{SampleD}(\mathbf{A}_d, \tau_d, \begin{bmatrix} \mathbf{I}^{wn' \times wn'} \\ \mathbf{0}^{n' \times n'} \end{bmatrix} \cdot \mathbf{A}^* + \mathbf{E}^*, \sigma)$$

This encoding serves to cancel out the lower random block diagonals on pre-encodings and enables zero-testing on the actual plaintexts.
- (Random bookend vectors) Sample $\mathbf{v}' \leftarrow D_{\mathbb{Z},\sigma}^{n'}, \mathbf{w}' \leftarrow D_{\mathbb{Z},\sigma}^m$.
- (Final bookend vectors) Sample uniform $\mathbf{b}_v \in \mathbb{Z}_\nu^k, \mathbf{b}_w \in \mathbb{Z}_\nu^k$ and compute the final bookends

$$\mathbf{v} = [\mathbf{v}' \cdot \mathbf{J} \cdot \mathbf{A}_1 | \mathbf{b}_v] \cdot \mathbf{R}_1, \quad \mathbf{w} = (\prod_{\ell \in [\kappa]} z_\ell) \cdot \mathbf{R}_d^{-1} \cdot \begin{bmatrix} \mathbf{D}^* \cdot \mathbf{w}'^\top \\ \mathbf{b}_w^\top \end{bmatrix}.$$

Output

- Public parameters $\mathsf{pp} = \{n, w, n', m, k, q, \sigma, \chi, B, \mathbf{v}, \mathbf{w}\}$
- Secret parameters $\mathsf{sp} = \{\mathbf{A}_i, \tau_i, \mathbf{R}_i\}_{i \in [d]}, \{z_\ell\}_{\ell \in [\kappa]}$

γ-GGH15-AL.Enc$(\mathsf{sp}, \mathbf{M} \in \mathbb{Z}_\beta^{w \times w}, i \rightsquigarrow j, L \subseteq [\kappa])$:

- Draw $\mathbf{P} \leftarrow D_{\mathbb{Z},\sigma}^{n' \times n'}$ and $\mathbf{E} \leftarrow (\chi)^{n \times m}$
- Compute $\mathbf{D} \leftarrow \mathsf{SampleD}(\mathbf{A}_i, \tau_i, \begin{bmatrix} \mathbf{M} \otimes \mathbf{P} \\ & \mathbf{P} \end{bmatrix} \cdot \mathbf{A}_j + \mathbf{E}, \sigma)$
- Draw uniform $\mathbf{B} \leftarrow \mathbb{Z}_\nu^{k \times k}$ and output the encoding

$$\mathbf{C} = (\prod_{\ell \in L} z_\ell)^{-1} \cdot \mathbf{R}_i^{-1} \cdot \begin{bmatrix} \mathbf{D} \\ & \mathbf{B} \end{bmatrix} \cdot \mathbf{R}_j$$

γ-GGH15-AL.ZeroTest$(\mathsf{pp}, \mathbf{C})$:

- Return zero if $|\mathbf{v} \cdot \mathbf{C} \cdot \mathbf{w}^\top| \leq B$, and not zero otherwise.

Parameters. First, we derive an additional security parameter $\lambda_{\text{LWE}} = \text{poly}(\lambda)$ which determines the hardness of LWE instances associated with the construction. We set the encoding bound $\nu = 2^\lambda$ and choose $n, w, n', m, q, \sigma, \chi = D_{\mathbb{Z},s}$ where $n = wn' + n'$, $m = \Theta(n \log q)$ and $\sigma = \Theta(\sqrt{n \log q})$ for trapdoor functionality and $n' = \Theta(\lambda_{\text{LWE}} \log q)$ and $s = \Omega(\sqrt{n'})$ for LWE security.[8] Set the zero-test bound $B := (m \cdot \beta \cdot \sigma \cdot \sqrt{n})^{d+1} + (k \cdot \nu)^{d+1}$ and choose $q \geq B \cdot \omega(\text{poly}(\lambda))$ such that $q \leq (\sigma/\lambda_{\text{LWE}}) \cdot (2^{\lambda_{\text{LWE}}})^{1-\epsilon}$ for some $\epsilon \in (0, 1)$.

In the full version of this paper, we show that these constraints can be satisfied with $\lambda_{\text{LWE}} = \text{poly}(\lambda)$, and furthermore that this setting of parameters satisfies correctness [1].

4.3   Level-Restricted GGH15 Zeroizing Model

In order to define this model, we need the following definition.

Definition 4 (Level-Respecting Encodings). *Fix a universe of levels $[\kappa]$. Let L_i be the set of levels associated with encoding $\mathbf{C}_i$. Let m be a monomial over encodings $\{\mathbf{C}_i\}$ which contains the j encodings $\mathbf{C}_1, ..., \mathbf{C}_j$. Then m is level-respecting if $L_1, ..., L_j$ are disjoint and $\bigcup_{i=1}^{j} L_i = [\kappa]$. A polynomial p over encodings $\{\mathbf{C}_i\}$ is level-respecting if and only if each of its monomials is.*

We only mention the differences between this model and the GGH15 Zeroizing Model. Here we expect that the GGH15 variant G that the model is initialized with supports asymmetric levels, namely that G.Enc additionally takes as input a level set $L \subseteq [\kappa]$.

Initialize Parameters. The model $\mathcal{M}$ in addition takes a parameter κ denoting the number of asymmetric levels.

Initialize Elements. $\mathcal{M}$ is additionally given a level set $L_i \subseteq [\kappa]$ along with each plaintext $\mathbf{M}_i$ and path $u_i \rightsquigarrow v_i$. $\mathcal{M}$ computes the corresponding pre-encoding $\mathbf{S}_i$ (from G.PreProcess), and computes the encoding

$$\mathbf{C}_i \leftarrow \text{G.Enc}(\text{sp}, \mathbf{S}_i, u_i \rightsquigarrow v_i, L_i).$$

$\mathcal{M}$ stores $(\mathbf{S}_i, \mathbf{C}_i, u_i \rightsquigarrow v_i, L_i)$ in a *pre-zero-test table*.

Zero-test. When the adversary submits a polynomial p, $\mathcal{M}$ additionally checks that it is level-respecting, and if it is not, $\mathcal{M}$ returns $\bot$.

Lemma 5. *Let $\mathcal{A}$ be a successful adversary in the GGH15 Zeroizing Model instantiated with γ-GGH15-AL. Then there exists a successful adversary $\mathcal{A}'$ in the Level-Restricted GGH15 Zeroizing Model instantiated with γ-GGH15-AL.*

See the full version [1] for a proof of the above lemma, which relies on a simple application of the Schwartz-Zippel lemma applied to polynomials over formal variables corresponding to the level scalars.

---

[8] Following Chen et al. [10].

4.4 GGH15 Annihilation Model

We turn to describing a new model which has properties that are much easier to reason about when proving security. Instead of requiring the adversary to find an algebraic relation in the post-zero-test stage, we instead require the adversary to find an annihilating polynomial for the set of successful zero-test polynomials it previously obtained. More specifically, this polynomial must annihilate the zero-test polynomials when evaluated on square matrices of formal variables of some dimension k. This k affects the difficulty of winning in the model, since matrices of larger dimension will be harder to annihilate. The advantage of having this model is that we have a notion of winning that corresponds more directly to the underlying plaintexts encoded with the scheme. Namely, if we are able to encode plaintexts (taking advantage of asymmetric levels) in such a way that annihilating successful zero-test polynomials is hard, we can immediately obtain security in this model.

We describe the differences between this model and the Level-Restricted GGH15 Zeroizing Model. First, there is no computational bound on the adversary — it can submit as many zero-test queries as it wants and can take as much computation as it wants in the post-zero-test stage. However, each post-zero-test polynomial it submits must be implemented with a polynomial size circuit. The other modifications are described below.

Initialize Parameters. The model $\mathcal{M}$ takes in an additional 'tuning' parameter k, which determines in some sense how strong the win condition will be.

Post-zero-test. At this point the adversary has submitted a set $\{p_u\}_u$ of successful zero-test polynomials which we associate with a set of formal variables $\{\widehat{p_u}\}_u$. The adversary now submits a *polynomial sized* circuit $\bar{C}$ that implements a polynomial $\bar{Q}(\{\widehat{p_u}\}_u)$ over these formal variables. The model $\mathcal{M}$ associates a set of $k \times k$ matrices $\{\widehat{\mathbf{C}}_i\}_i$ of formal variables with the set of encodings $\{\mathbf{C}_i\}_i$ and considers two additional k-dimensional vectors $\widehat{\mathbf{v}}$ and $\widehat{\mathbf{w}}$ of formal variables. Note that each individual entry of each of these matrices and vectors is a distinct formal variable. $\mathcal{M}$ returns "Win" if the following hold:

1. The degree of $\bar{Q}$ is $2^{o(\lambda)}$
2. $\bar{Q}(\{\widehat{p_u}\}_u) \not\equiv 0$
3. $\bar{Q}(\{\widehat{\mathbf{v}} \cdot p_u(\{\widehat{\mathbf{C}}_i\}_i) \cdot \widehat{\mathbf{w}}^\top\}_u) \equiv 0$

Lemma 6. *Fix any $k \in \mathbb{N}$. Let $\mathcal{A}$ be a successful adversary in the Level-Restricted GGH15 Zeroizing Model instantiated with γ-GGH15-AL where KeyGen receives the parameter k. Then there exists a successful adversary $\mathcal{A}'$ in the GGH15 Annihilation Model with tuning parameter k.*

A proof of the above can also be found in the full version [1]. It again relies on the Schwartz-Zippel lemma, this time applied to polynomials over formal variables corresponding to the elements of the block diagonals added during γ-GGH15-AL.Enc.

5   An iO Candidate with Zeroizing Resistance

We design our obfuscator to invoke the Branching Program Un-Annihilatability (BPUA) Assumption of Garg et al. [21]. Roughly, this assumption states that no polynomial-size circuit can annihilate the evaluations of every matrix branching program, provided we consider branching programs whose input bits are read many times and in interleaved layers.

Thus, the first step of our obfuscator is to pad the input branching program in order to satisfy the requirement of the BPUA Assumption. To facilitate this, one of the inputs to our obfuscator is the parameter $t = t(\ell, \lambda) \geq 4\ell^4$ which specifies the minimum number of layers required. Note that the resulting padded program may have length greater than t, so we use a separate variable d to denote the actual length of the branching program after padding. We also enforce that each *pair* of input bits is read together in many layers, which is required to invoke the p-Bounded Speedup Hypothesis of [25].

To encode the matrices with γ-GGH15-AL, we pick asymmetric level sets from a straddling set system. The sets are assigned precisely to enforce that evaluations respect the input read structure of the padded branching program. The encoding edges are picked so that the branching program evaluations are naturally computed by traversing a path graph.

5.1   Construction

Input. The input to the obfuscator is the security parameter λ and a dual-input branching program BP (defined in Sect. 2.3) of length h, width w, and input length ℓ. BP consists of the matrices $\{\mathbf{M}_{i,b_1,b_2}\}_{i \in [h], b_1, b_2 \in \{0,1\}}$ and input selection function $\mathsf{inp} : [h] \to [\ell] \times [\ell]$ which satisfies the following requirements:

– For each $i \in [h]$: $\mathsf{inp}(i)_1 \neq \mathsf{inp}(i)_2$, where $\mathsf{inp}(i)_1, \mathsf{inp}(i)_2$ denote the first and second slots of $\mathsf{inp}(i)$, respectively.
– For each pair $j \neq k \in [\ell]$, there exists $i \in [h]$ such that $\mathsf{inp}(i) \in \{(j,k), (k,j)\}$.

BP is evaluated on input $x \in \{0,1\}^\ell$ by checking whether

$$\prod_{i \in [h]} \mathbf{M}_{i,x(i)} = 0^{w \times w}$$

where we abbreviate $x(i) := (x_{\mathsf{inp}(i)_1}, x_{\mathsf{inp}(i)_2})$.

Step 1: Pad the branching program. We pad the branching program with identity matrices until it has $d \geq t$ layers to ensure the following conditions:

– Each pair of input bits (j, k) is read in at least $4\ell^2$ different layers.
– There exist layers $i_1 < i_2 < \cdots < i_t$ such that $\mathsf{inp}(i_1)_1, \ldots, \mathsf{inp}(i_t)_1$ cycles t/ℓ times through $[\ell]$.

Step 2: Form straddling sets. For each input index $i \in [\ell]$, let r_i be the number of layers in which the bit i is read, and create a straddling set system with universe $\mathbb{U}^{(i)}$ and subsets $\{S_{j,b}^{(i)}\}_{j \in [r_i], b \in \{0,1\}}$. Let $\mathbb{U} := \bigcup_{i \in [\ell]} \mathbb{U}^{(i)}$.

Step 3: Encode with γ-GGH15-AL. Let G be a path graph with $d + 1$ nodes $1, ..., d + 1$ and initialize the γ-GGH15-AL construction[9]

$$\mathsf{pp}, \mathsf{sp} \leftarrow \gamma\text{-GGH15-AL.KeyGen}(1^\lambda, G, \mathbb{Z}, |\mathbb{U}|, \max_{i,b_1,b_2}\{\|\mathbf{M}_{i,b_1,b_2}\|_\infty\}, k = 5).$$

For $i \in [d]$ and $b \in \{1, 2\}$, define $j_b(i)$ to be the number of times $\mathsf{inp}(i)_b$ has been read after reading i columns of the branching program, and compute

$$\mathbf{C}_{i,b_1,b_2} \leftarrow \gamma\text{-GGH15.Enc}(\mathsf{sp}, \mathbf{M}_{i,b_1,b_2}, i \rightsquigarrow i + 1, S_{j_1(i),b_1}^{\mathsf{inp}(i)_1} \cup S_{j_2(i),b_2}^{\mathsf{inp}(i)_2}).$$

5.2 Security

In order to state the p-Bounded speedup hypothesis, we recall the following definition of Miles et al. [25].

Definition 5 (X-Max-2-SAT Solver). *Consider a set $X \subseteq \{0, 1\}^\ell$. We say that an algorithm $\mathcal{A}$ is an X-Max-2-SAT solver if it solves the Max-2-SAT problem restricted to inputs in X. Namely given a 2-CNF formula ϕ on ℓ variables, $\mathcal{A}(\phi) = 1$ iff $\exists x \in X$ that satisfies at least a $7/10$ fraction of ϕ's clauses.*

Assumption 1. *(p-Bounded Speedup Hypothesis, introduced in [25]). Let $p : \mathbb{N} \to \mathbb{N}$. Then for any X-Max-2-SAT solver that has size $t(\ell)$, $|X| \leq p(\mathsf{poly}(t(\ell)))$.*

The assumption essentially states that the NP-complete problem Max-2-SAT is still hard even for restricted sets of variable assignments. This hardness is parameterized by p, and in its strongest form, p is taken to be a polynomial. In this form, the assumption states that no polynomial time algorithm can solve X-Max-2-SAT on an X of super-polynomial size. However, we can also take p to be $2^{\mathsf{polylog}(n)}$ and obtain meaningful results as we discuss in the full version of this work [1].

We now state a non-uniform variant of the BPUA, but first we need the following definition from [21].

Definition 6. *A matrix branching program BP is L-bounded for $L \in \mathbb{N}$ if every intermediate value computed when evaluating BP on any input is at most L. In particular all of BP's outputs and matrix entries are at most L.*

Assumption 2. *(Non-uniform variant of the BPUA assumption of [21]) Let $t = \mathsf{poly}(\ell, \lambda)$ and let $\mathcal{X} \subseteq \{0, 1\}^\ell$ have $\mathsf{poly}(\lambda)$ size and Q be a $\mathsf{poly}(\lambda)$-size $2^{o(\lambda)}$-degree polynomial over $\mathbb{Z}$. Then for all ℓ, sufficiently large λ, and all primes $2^\lambda < p < 2^{\mathsf{poly}(\lambda)}$, there exists a 2^λ-bounded dual-input matrix branching program $BP : \{0, 1\}^\ell \to [2^\lambda]$ of length t whose first input selection function (inp_1) iterates over the ℓ input bits t/ℓ times, such that $Q(\{BP(x)\}_{x \in \mathcal{X}}) \neq 0 \pmod{p}$.*

---

[9] We set $k = 5$ so that the dimension of the random block diagonals added during encoding match the dimension of matrix branching programs obtained from Barrington's theorem.

Note that this statement is a very mild strengthening of the original BPUA assumption stated in [21]. Their assumption is required to hold for any Q of bounded degree generated by a polynomial-time algorithm, whereas our assumption must hold for any Q of polynomial size and bounded degree. However, we note that Garg et al. [21] justify their assumption by showing it is implied by the existence of PRFs in NC^1 secure against $P/poly$. With a minor tweak to their proof, we can show our non-uniform BPUA is also implied by the existence of PRFs in NC^1 secure against $P/poly$. We simply modify the non-uniform adversary used in [Theorem 2, [21]] to take the polynomial-size Q as advice.

Finally, we use the following definition in our security proof.

Definition 7 (Input-Respecting Polynomial). *Given a branching program* $\{M_{i,b_1,b_2}\}_{i\in[h],b_1,b_2\in\{0,1\}}$ *with input selection function* $inp : [h] \rightarrow [\ell] \times [\ell]$, *a polynomial p over the matrices (or elements of matrices) is input-respecting if no monomial involves two encodings* $\{M_{i,b_1^{(i)},b_2^{(i)}}\}, \{M_{j,b_1^{(j)},b_2^{(j)}}\}$ *(or entries of encodings) such that* $inp(i)_1 = inp(j)_1$ *and* $b_1^{(i)} \neq b_1^{(j)}$ *or* $inp(i)_2 = inp(j)_2$ *and* $b_2^{(i)} \neq b_2^{(j)}$.

Theorem 1 (Main Theorem). *Assuming the p-Bounded Speedup Hypothesis and the non-uniform BPUA Assumption (implied by the existence of PRFs in NC^1 secure against $P/poly$), our obfuscator is secure in the GGH15 Zeroizing Model.*

Proof. It suffices to prove security in the GGH15 Annihilation Model with parameter 5 (since we set $k = 5$ in the obfuscation construction). Suppose an adversary $\mathcal{A}$ wins in this model instantiated with our obfuscator. We argue that every successful zero-test polynomial submitted by $\mathcal{A}$ is a linear combination of polynomially many branching program evaluations and thus that the existence of a Q used to win in the GGH15 Annihilation Model would violate Assumption 2. We know that every successful zero-test polynomial submitted by $\mathcal{A}$ in this model is level-respecting, so by construction of straddling sets, we can conclude that every polynomial is input-respecting. A polynomial that is both edge-respecting (so each monomial contains exactly one branching program matrix from each layer) and input-respecting, is a linear combination of branching program evaluations. However, we have no bound on the number of terms in the linear combination. We now rely on the analysis techniques of Miles, Sahai, and Weiss [25] to show that each polynomial is in fact a linear combination of polynomially many branching program evaluations, assuming the p-Bounded Speedup Hypothesis. A proof of the following lemma is available in the full version [1].

Lemma 7. *(adapted from [25]) Consider an adversary $\mathcal{A}$ interacting with our obfuscation candidate in the GGH15 Annihilating Model. Assuming the p-Bounded Speedup Hypothesis, any edge-respecting and input-respecting polynomial submitted by $\mathcal{A}$ is a linear combination of polynomially-many branching program evaluations.*

With this lemma in hand, we inspect the Q submitted by $\mathcal{A}$ that resulted in the model outputting "Win". Notice that the $\{\widehat{\mathbf{C}}_i\}_i$ are in the shape of a dual-input branching program of width 5 (without the bookends), so by Lemma 7, every $\widehat{\mathbf{v}} \cdot p_u(\{\widehat{\mathbf{C}}_i\}_i) \cdot \widehat{\mathbf{w}}^\top$ is actually a linear combination of polynomially many honest branching program evaluations. Since there are only polynomially many p_u's (since Q is implemented with a polynomial size circuit), and since Q is identically zero over these evaluations, Q contradicts Assumption 2, and we can conclude that $\mathcal{A}$ could not have won in the GGH15 Annihilation model and thus in the GGH15 Zeroizing Model except with negligible probability. $\square$

References

1. Bartusek, J., Guan, J., Ma, F., Zhandry, M.: Return of GGH15: Provable security against zeroizing attacks. Cryptology ePrint Archive, Report 2018/511 (2018). https://eprint.iacr.org/2018/511
2. Boneh, D., Silverberg, A.: Applications of multilinear forms to cryptography. Contemp. Math. **324**, 71–90 (2003)
3. Garg, S., Gentry, C., Halevi, S., Raykova, M., Sahai, A., Waters, B.: Candidate indistinguishability obfuscation and functional encryption for all circuits, pp. 40–49 (2013)
4. Garg, S., Gentry, C., Halevi, S.: Candidate multilinear maps from ideal lattices. In: Johansson, T., Nguyen, P.Q. (eds.) EUROCRYPT 2013. LNCS, vol. 7881, pp. 1–17. Springer, Heidelberg (2013). https://doi.org/10.1007/978-3-642-38348-9_1
5. Coron, J.-S., Lepoint, T., Tibouchi, M.: Practical multilinear maps over the integers. In: Canetti, R., Garay, J.A. (eds.) CRYPTO 2013. LNCS, vol. 8042, pp. 476–493. Springer, Heidelberg (2013). https://doi.org/10.1007/978-3-642-40041-4_26
6. Gentry, C., Gorbunov, S., Halevi, S.: Graph-induced multilinear maps from lattices. In: Dodis, Y., Nielsen, J.B. (eds.) TCC 2015. LNCS, vol. 9015, pp. 498–527. Springer, Heidelberg (2015). https://doi.org/10.1007/978-3-662-46497-7_20
7. Regev, O.: On lattices, learning with errors, random linear codes, and cryptography, pp. 84–93 (2005)
8. Wichs, D., Zirdelis, G.: Obfuscating compute-and-compare programs under LWE, pp. 600–611 (2017)
9. Goyal, R., Koppula, V., Waters, B.: Lockable obfuscation, pp. 612–621 (2017)
10. Chen, Y., Vaikuntanathan, V., Wee, H.: GGH15 beyond permutation branching programs: proofs, attacks, and candidates. In: Shacham, H., Boldyreva, A. (eds.) CRYPTO 2018. LNCS, vol. 10992, pp. 577–607. Springer, Cham (2018). https://doi.org/10.1007/978-3-319-96881-0_20
11. Canetti, R., Chen, Y.: Constraint-hiding constrained PRFs for NC^1 from LWE. In: Coron, J.-S., Nielsen, J.B. (eds.) EUROCRYPT 2017. LNCS, vol. 10210, pp. 446–476. Springer, Cham (2017). https://doi.org/10.1007/978-3-319-56620-7_16
12. Goyal, R., Koppula, V., Waters, B.: Separating semantic and circular security for symmetric-key bit encryption from the learning with errors assumption. In: Coron, J.-S., Nielsen, J.B. (eds.) EUROCRYPT 2017. LNCS, vol. 10211, pp. 528–557. Springer, Cham (2017). https://doi.org/10.1007/978-3-319-56614-6_18
13. Shor, P.W.: Algorithms for quantum computation: Discrete logarithms and factoring, pp. 124–134 (1994)

14. Albrecht, M., Bai, S., Ducas, L.: A subfield lattice attack on overstretched NTRU assumptions. In: Robshaw, M., Katz, J. (eds.) CRYPTO 2016. LNCS, vol. 9814, pp. 153–178. Springer, Heidelberg (2016). https://doi.org/10.1007/978-3-662-53018-4_6

15. Cramer, R., Ducas, L., Peikert, C., Regev, O.: Recovering short generators of principal ideals in cyclotomic rings. In: Fischlin, M., Coron, J.-S. (eds.) EUROCRYPT 2016. LNCS, vol. 9666, pp. 559–585. Springer, Heidelberg (2016). https://doi.org/10.1007/978-3-662-49896-5_20

16. Biasse, J.F., Song, F.: Efficient quantum algorithms for computing class groups and solving the principal ideal problem in arbitrary degree number fields, pp. 893–902 (2016)

17. Pellet-Mary, A.: Quantum attacks against indistinguishablility obfuscators proved secure in the weak multilinear map model. In: Shacham, H., Boldyreva, A. (eds.) CRYPTO 2018. LNCS, vol. 10993, pp. 153–183. Springer, Cham (2018). https://doi.org/10.1007/978-3-319-96878-0_6

18. Cheon, J.H., Han, K., Lee, C., Ryu, H., Stehlé, D.: Cryptanalysis of the multilinear map over the integers. In: Oswald, E., Fischlin, M. (eds.) EUROCRYPT 2015. LNCS, vol. 9056, pp. 3–12. Springer, Heidelberg (2015). https://doi.org/10.1007/978-3-662-46800-5_1

19. Coron, J.-S., Lee, M.S., Lepoint, T., Tibouchi, M.: Cryptanalysis of GGH15 multilinear maps. In: Robshaw, M., Katz, J. (eds.) CRYPTO 2016. LNCS, vol. 9815, pp. 607–628. Springer, Heidelberg (2016). https://doi.org/10.1007/978-3-662-53008-5_21

20. Chen, Y., Gentry, C., Halevi, S.: Cryptanalyses of candidate branching program obfuscators. In: Coron, J.-S., Nielsen, J.B. (eds.) EUROCRYPT 2017. LNCS, vol. 10212, pp. 278–307. Springer, Cham (2017). https://doi.org/10.1007/978-3-319-56617-7_10

21. Garg, S., Miles, E., Mukherjee, P., Sahai, A., Srinivasan, A., Zhandry, M.: Secure obfuscation in a weak multilinear map model. In: Hirt, M., Smith, A. (eds.) TCC 2016. LNCS, vol. 9986, pp. 241–268. Springer, Heidelberg (2016). https://doi.org/10.1007/978-3-662-53644-5_10

22. Ma, F., Zhandry, M.: New multilinear maps from CLT13 with provable security against zeroizing attacks. Cryptology ePrint Archive, Report 2017/946 (2017). http://eprint.iacr.org/2017/946

23. Barak, B., Garg, S., Kalai, Y.T., Paneth, O., Sahai, A.: Protecting obfuscation against algebraic attacks. In: Nguyen, P.Q., Oswald, E. (eds.) EUROCRYPT 2014. LNCS, vol. 8441, pp. 221–238. Springer, Heidelberg (2014). https://doi.org/10.1007/978-3-642-55220-5_13

24. Halevi, S.: Graded encoding, variations on a scheme. Cryptology ePrint Archive, Report 2015/866 (2015). http://eprint.iacr.org/2015/866

25. Miles, E., Sahai, A., Weiss, M.: Protecting obfuscation against arithmetic attacks. Cryptology ePrint Archive, Report 2014/878 (2014). http://eprint.iacr.org/2014/878

26. Badrinarayanan, S., Miles, E., Sahai, A., Zhandry, M.: Post-zeroizing obfuscation: new mathematical tools, and the case of evasive circuits. In: Fischlin, M., Coron, J.-S. (eds.) EUROCRYPT 2016. LNCS, vol. 9666, pp. 764–791. Springer, Heidelberg (2016). https://doi.org/10.1007/978-3-662-49896-5_27

27. Boneh, D., Lewi, K., Raykova, M., Sahai, A., Zhandry, M., Zimmerman, J.: Semantically secure order-revealing encryption: multi-input functional encryption without obfuscation. In: Oswald, E., Fischlin, M. (eds.) EUROCRYPT 2015. LNCS,

vol. 9057, pp. 563–594. Springer, Heidelberg (2015). https://doi.org/10.1007/978-3-662-46803-6_19

28. Ma, F., Zhandry, M.: The mmap strikes back: Obfuscation and new multilinear maps immune to CLT13 zeroizing attacks. In: Beimel, A., Dziembowski, S. (eds.) TCC 2018. LNCS, vol. 11240, pp. 513–543. Springer, Cham (2018)

29. Boneh, D., Lewi, K., Montgomery, H., Raghunathan, A.: Key homomorphic PRFs and their applications. In: Canetti, R., Garay, J.A. (eds.) CRYPTO 2013. LNCS, vol. 8042, pp. 410–428. Springer, Heidelberg (2013). https://doi.org/10.1007/978-3-642-40041-4_23

30. Gentry, C., Peikert, C., Vaikuntanathan, V.: Trapdoors for hard lattices and new cryptographic constructions. In: Proceedings of the Fortieth Annual ACM Symposium on Theory of Computing, pp. 197–206. ACM (2008)

31. Garg, S., Miles, E., Mukherjee, P., Sahai, A., Srinivasan, A., Zhandry, M.: Secure obfuscation in a weak multilinear map model. Cryptology ePrint Archive, Report 2016/817 (2016). http://eprint.iacr.org/2016/817

32. Barrington, D.A.M.: Bounded-width polynomial-size branching programs recognize exactly those languages in NC^1, pp. 1–5 (1986)

33. Lenstra, A.K., Lenstra, H.W., Lovász, L.: Factoring polynomials with rational coefficients. Mathematische Annalen $261(4)$, 515–534 (1982)

34. Menezes, A.J., Okamoto, T., Vanstone, S.A.: Reducing elliptic curve logarithms to logarithms in a finite field. IEEE Trans. Inf. Theory $39(5)$, 1639–1646 (1993)

The Security of Lazy Users in Out-of-Band Authentication

Moni Naor[1](✉), Lior Rotem[2], and Gil Segev[2]

[1] Department of Computer Science and Applied Mathematics,
Weizmann Institute of Science, 76100 Rehovot, Israel
moni.naor@weizmann.ac.il
[2] School of Computer Science and Engineering, Hebrew University of Jerusalem,
91904 Jerusalem, Israel
{lior.rotem,segev}@cs.huji.ac.il

Abstract. Faced with the threats posed by man-in-the-middle attacks, messaging platforms rely on "out-of-band" authentication, assuming that users have access to an external channel for authenticating one short value. For example, assuming that users recognizing each other's voice can authenticate a short value, Telegram and WhatApp ask their users to compare 288-bit and 200-bit values, respectively. The existing protocols, however, do not take into account the plausible behavior of users who may be "lazy" and only compare parts of these values (rather than their entirety).

Motivated by such a security-critical user behavior, we study the security of lazy users in out-of-band authentication. We start by showing that both the protocol implemented by WhatsApp and the statistically-optimal protocol of Naor, Segev and Smith (CRYPTO '06) are completely vulnerable to man-in-the-middle attacks when the users consider only a half of the out-of-band authenticated value. In this light, we put forward a framework that captures the behavior and security of lazy users. Our notions of security consider both statistical security and computational security, and for each flavor we derive a lower bound on the tradeoff between the number of positions that are considered by the lazy users and the adversary's forgery probability.

Within our framework we then provide two authentication protocols. First, in the statistical setting, we present a transformation that converts any out-of-band authentication protocol into one that is secure even when executed by lazy users. Instantiating our transformation with a new refinement of the protocol of Naor et al. results in a protocol whose tradeoff essentially matches our lower bound in the statistical setting.

M. Naor—Incumbent of the Judith Kleeman Professorial Chair. Supported in part by a grant from the Israel Science Foundation.

L. Rotem and G. Segev—Supported by the European Union's Horizon 2020 Framework Program (H2020) via an ERC Grant (Grant No. 714253), by the Israel Science Foundation (Grant No. 483/13), by the Israeli Centers of Research Excellence (I-CORE) Program (Center No. 4/11), and by the US-Israel Binational Science Foundation (Grant No. 2014632).

A. Beimel and S. Dziembowski (Eds.): TCC 2018, LNCS 11240, pp. 575–599, 2018.
https://doi.org/10.1007/978-3-030-03810-6_21

Then, in the computational setting, we show that the computationally-optimal protocol of Vaudenay (CRYPTO '05) is secure even when executed by lazy users – and its tradeoff matches our lower bound in the computational setting.

1   Introduction

Instant messaging platforms are gaining increased popularity and hold an overall user base of more than 1.5 billion active users (e.g., WhatsApp, Signal, Telegram and many more [Wik]). These platforms recognize user authentication and end-to-end encryption as key ingredients for ensuring secure communication within them, and extensive efforts are currently put into the security of messaging, both commercially (e.g., [PM16, Telb, Wha, Vib]) and academically (e.g., [FMB+16, BSJ+17, CCD+17, KBB17]). A key challenge in securing messaging platforms is that of protecting against man-in-the-middle attacks when setting up secure end-to-end channels. This is exacerbated by the ad-hoc nature of these platforms.

Out-of-Band Authentication. Faced with the threats posed by man-in-the-middle attacks, existing messaging platforms enable "out-of-band" authentication, assuming that users have access to an *external* channel for authenticating short values. These values are typically derived from the public keys of the users, or more generally from the transcript of any key-exchange protocol that the users execute for setting up a secure end-to-end channel.

For example, some messaging platforms offer users the ability to compare with each other a value that is displayed by their devices (see Telegram [Tela], WhatsApp [Wha], Viber [Vib] and more [Mem17]). This relies on the assumption two users can establish a *low-bandwidth authenticated channel* (e.g., by recognizing each other's voice): A man-on-the-middle adversary can view, delay or even remove any message sent over this channel, but cannot undetectably modify its content.

Such an authentication model that assumes a low-bandwidth authenticated channel was considered back in 1984 by Rivest and Shamir [RS84].[1] More recently, this model was formalized by Vaudenay [Vau05] in the computational setting (i.e., considering computationally-bounded adversaries) and extended by Naor et al. [NSS06, NSS08] to the statistical setting (i.e., considering computationally-unbounded adversaries) and by Rotem and Segev [RS18] to the group setting. The out-of-band message authentication problem considers a sender that would like to authenticate a message m to a receiver.[2] The

---

[1] Rivest and Shamir proposed the "Interlock" protocol which enables two users, who recognize each other's voice, to mutually authenticate their public keys in the absence of a trusted infrastructure. Potential attacks on the Interlock protocol were identified later on [BM94, Ell96].

[2] As mentioned above, for messaging platforms the message m typically corresponds to the public keys of the users or to the transcript of any key-exchange protocol that they execute.

users communicate over two channels: An insecure channel over which a man-in-the-middle adversary has complete control, and a low-bandwidth authenticated channel, enabling the sender to "out-of-band" authenticate one short value. The security requirement asks for an upper bound on any man-in-the-middle adversary's probability of fooling the receiver into accepting a fraudulent message.

An Effort vs. Security Tradeoff. Given that the out-of-band channel has only low bandwidth, research on out-of-band authentication has so far focused on constructing protocols that offer the best-possible tradeoff between the length of their out-of-band authenticated values (corresponding to the amount of effort required from the users) and their security (corresponding to the adversary's forgery probability). Vaudenay [Vau05], Naor et al. [NSS06] and Rotem and Segev [RS18] provided complete characterizations of this tradeoff in their above-mentioned respective settings, providing both lower bounds and protocols that match them. However, these protocols rely on the assumption that the *human users* indeed follow the protocol in its entirety. In particular, they rely on the assumption that the users out-of-band authenticate the *entire* value that the protocols instruct them to authenticate.

This assumption, however, may not always be realistic: The lengths of the out-of-band authenticated values offered by the existing messaging platforms may not align with the potential effort of different users. Specifically, existing messaging platforms ask their users to out-of-band authenticate values whose lengths range from roughly 200 bits (e.g., WhatsApp and Signal) to 288 bits (e.g., Telegram) – see Fig. 1. Given that the out-of-band channel in implemented in these platforms via a manual comparison operation, the security of such protocols must take into account users that may compare only a subset of the positions of these values. We refer to such users, who out-of-band authenticate only a substring of the protocol's out-of-band authenticated value, as "lazy users".

As repeatedly demonstrated by research on usable security and human-computer interaction, it is rather likely that a substantial part of the messaging platforms' user base may in fact be considered lazy (see, for example, [LS03, PLF03, BA04, Her09, HZF+14, AFJ15, DDB+16] and the references therein). This state of affairs, where a security-critical user behavior is not taken into account, is extremely bothering.

1.1 Our Contributions

Motivated by the above-described plausible and security-critical behavior of "lazy" users, we put forward a framework that captures the behavior and security of such users in out-of-band authentication. Within our framework we characterize the possible security guarantees for lazy users by presenting protocols together with essentially matching lower bounds both in the computational setting and in the statistical setting. Our main contributions are as follows.

The Insecurity of Existing Protocols. We strengthen our motivation by showing that the protocol implemented by WhatsApp [Wha] and the protocol of Naor et al. [NSS06] are completely vulnerable to man-in-the-middle attacks

Fig. 1. Out-of-band authentication in WhatsApp and Telegram. WhatApp and Telegram (as well as many other messaging platforms) implement the out-of-band channel by asking their users to manually compare two strings. WhatApp (on the right) asks its users to manually compare 60 decimal digits corresponding to an out-of-band authenticated value [Wha] of about 200 bits. Telegram (on the left) asks its users to manually compare 64 characters corresponding to a 288-bit out-of-band authenticated value [Telc]. The images are taken from [Mem17].

when the parties consider only a half (or fewer) of the characters of the out-of-band authenticated value. This demonstrates that it is not only the case that the existing protocols do not take security-critical user behavior into account, they may in fact become completely insecure when executed by lazy users. In the following section, we discuss the main underlying reason for these protocols' vulnerability, and how our constructions overcome it.

Modeling the Behavior and Security of Lazy Users. We put forward a framework that captures the behavior and security of lazy users. Our notions of security consider both computational security and statistical security, and for each flavor we derive a lower bound on the tradeoff between the number of positions that are considered by the lazy users out of the out-of-band authenticated value and the adversary's forgery probability. These lower bounds are summarized in Table 1, and we refer the reader to Sect. 1.3 for a more detailed overview.

Immunizing Statistically-Secure Protocols Against Lazy Users. Recall that the statistically-secure protocol of Naor et al. [NSS06] becomes completely insecure when executed by lazy users. Intuitively, this is the case because the

Table 1. Summary of our results – protocols vs. lower bounds. We denote by $\mathcal{I}$ the subset of positions of the out-of-band authenticated value that the users consider, by Σ the alphabet over which the out-of-band authenticated value is defined, and by n the length of the sender's input message. Our computationally-secure protocol relies on the existence of any one-way function (see Theorem 6.1), whereas our statistically-secure protocol and our two lower bounds do not rely on any computational assumptions (see Corollary 5.2, Theorem 7.1 and Corollary 7.3). Note that our upper bound and lower bound in the computational setting match within an additive 2^{-n} term (which is a significantly lower-order term for not-too-short input messages). In the statistical setting our bounds match within a constant factor (in addition to the additive 2^{-n} term).

	Our protocols		Our lower bounds
	Forgery probability	Alphabet size	
Computational security	$2^{-|\mathcal{I}|}$	2	$2^{-|\mathcal{I}|\cdot\log|\Sigma|} - 2^{-n}$
Statistical security	$2^{-|\mathcal{I}|}$	2^8	$2^{-|\mathcal{I}|\cdot\log|\Sigma|/2} - 2^{-n}$

influence of each bit of the sender's input message (i.e., the message to be authenticated) is not "well-spread" across the out-of-band authenticated value (see Sect. 4 for an in-depth discussion).

Addressing this property, we provide a transformation that converts any statistically-secure protocol (that does not necessarily provide any security for lazy users) into a protocol that is statistically-secure for lazy users. Instantiating our transformation with the protocol of Naor et al. results in a concrete statistically-secure protocol for lazy users. Moreover, in the full version of the paper [NRS18] we show that by refining the protocol of Naor et al. the resulting instantiation uses an alphabet whose size is as small as 2^8 – which nearly matches our above-mentioned lower bound in the statistical setting.[3] We stress that our transformation and the protocol resulted from applying it to the protocol of Naor et al. are oblivious to the subset $\mathcal{I}$ of positions that users eventually read or even to the number of positions they read. Meaning, we provide a *single* protocol that guarantees security for every possible subset $\mathcal{I}$. An interesting open question is whether a protocol which is statistically-secure for lazy users can be constructed over a binary alphabet.

In fact, our transformation can also be applied to any computationally-secure protocol that satisfies a natural parallel composability guarantee. However, as shown by our next result, this is somewhat unnecessary.

Matching the Optimal Tradeoff for Computationally-Secure Protocols. Whereas the statistically-optimal protocol of Naor et al. is completely insecure for lazy users, we show that the computationally-optimal protocol of

---

[3] As we discuss in more detail in Sect. 1.3, when moving to the setting of lazy users, the size of the alphabet over which the out-of-band authenticated value is defined becomes of great importance. This is in contrast to the traditional (non-lazy) setting, in which this has no impact on security.

Vaudenay [Vau05] is optimally secure for lazy users as well. Intuitively, this is due to the following observation: Even though the out-of-band authenticated value in this protocol is determined independently of the sender's input message (which is reminiscent of the protocol of Naor et al. in the statistical setting), the protocol "ties together" the message and the out-of-band authenticated value *in their entirety* using a non-malleable commitment scheme (which, in practice, can be replaced by a hash function modeled as a random oracle). Note that as in the statistical setting, the protocol is oblivious to the particular subset of positions that the users eventually consider.

Extensions. We also discuss possible extensions of our framework. First, in the full version [NRS18], we consider the notion of *adaptive laziness*, which gives the adversary the ability to choose the subset of positions to be considered by the users even *after* the out-of-band authenticated value is determined. Although we find this notion somewhat less motivated in the context of lazy users, we nevertheless extend our definitions and proofs of security to this stronger notion.

Second, we note that our notions of security, lower bounds and protocols naturally extend to the group setting considered by Rotem and Segev [RS18]. Specifically, in the computational setting the protocol of Rotem and Segev can be shown to be optimally-secure for lazy users; and in the statistical setting, our general transformation can be easily adapted to support group protocols (and can then be instantiated with the statistically-secure protocol of Rotem and Segev).

1.2   Related Work

Bounds for Out-of-Band Authentication. In the standard setting of out-of-band authentication (i.e., with non-lazy users), Vaudenay [Vau05] and Vaudenay and Pasini [PV06] established tight bounds for the tradeoff between the length of the (entire) out-of-band authenticated value and the adversary's forgery probability in the computational setting. They provided a protocol [Vau05] in which the forgery probability is bounded by $2^{-\ell}$, where ℓ is the bit-length of the out-of-band authenticated value, and a matching lower bound [PV06]. Naor et al. [NSS06] observed a gap between the computational and the statistical settings: They proved that the forgery probability in the statistical setting of any protocol is always at least $2^{-\ell/2}$, and provided a protocol that matches this lower bound within a constant factor. We refer the reader to Table 2 for a summary of these bounds, and note that our results provide a similar characterization for lazy users in both the computational and the statistical settings (recall Table 1).

The Security of Messaging Platforms. Many recent works addressed the goals of formalizing the security guarantees of messaging platforms, as well as analyzing the security of the protocols used by these platforms and identifying potential weaknesses within them – see, for example, [FMB+16, HL16, BSJ+17, CCD+17, CGCG+17, CGC17, KBB17, SKH17, RMS18, Gre18a, Gre18b] and the references therein. Throughout this extensive line of research, the security of

Table 2. Previous work – protocols vs. lower bounds. We denote by ℓ the length of the out-of-band authenticated value and by n the length of the sender's input message. The computationally-secure protocol of Vaudenay [Vau05] relies on the existence of any one-way function, whereas the statistically-secure protocol of Naor et al. [NSS06] and the two lower bounds [NSS06, PV06] do not rely on any computational assumptions.

	Protocols	Lower bounds
Computational security [Vau05, PV06]	$2^{-\ell}$	$2^{-\ell} - 2^{-n}$
Statistical security [NSS06]	$O\left(2^{-\ell/2}\right)$	$2^{-\ell/2} - 2^{-n}$

messaging protocols assumes an initial authentication phase for avoiding man-in-the-middle attacks. As mentioned in most of the afore-listed references, such an initial authentication phase is based on out-of-band authentication.

1.3 Overview of Our Contributions

We extend the existing framework for out-of-band authentication protocols [Vau05, PV06, NSS06, RS18] to accommodate the security-critical behavior of "lazy users", that may consider only a certain part of the out-of-band authenticated value (e.g., its left-most half, its right-most 10 characters, or a few randomly-chosen positions). We model this behavior by having the sender send only a substring of the out-of-band authenticated value, and requiring that for any such substring the man-in-the-middle attacker's forgery probability is bounded by some pre-defined parameter associated with it. That is, whereas a standard (i.e., "non-lazy") out-of-band authentication protocol is parameterized by an upper bound $\epsilon \in (0, 1)$ on the adversary's forgery probability, a protocol in our framework is parameterized by a function $\epsilon(\cdot)$ which maps every subset $\mathcal{I}$ of positions of the out-of-band authenticated value to an associated upper bound $\epsilon(\mathcal{I})$.[4]

In addition, our definitions also extend those of Vaudenay and Naor et al. by accounting for out-of-band authentication values over *non-binary* alphabets (indeed, in the existing real-world implementations of out-of-band authentication protocols, the out-of-band authenticated value is displayed to the users as a string over some non-binary alphabet – recall Fig. 1). When the users are assumed to consider the entire out-of-band authenticated value, the particular choice of alphabet (and alphabet size) is mainly a matter of providing a convenient user interface. In the presence of lazy users, however, the size of the alphabet of the out-of-band authenticated value plays an important role in what may be referred to as the "granularity" of the users' laziness.

---

[4] Note that protocols in our framework must explicitly address (in terms of both completeness and soundness) the case where only part of the out-of-band authenticated value is considered. This is the case, in particular, in our motivating example where verification is done by comparing the out-of-band authenticated string to a value that is computed by the receiver.

Let us consider for concreteness a pair of users that read some 32 bits out of a 64-bit out-of-band authenticated value. If the out-of-band authenticated value is simply a 64-bit string (i.e., over a binary alphabet), then the users may possibly read any of the $\binom{64}{32} > 1.83 \times 10^{18}$ many 32-bit substrings of it. On the other hand, if the alphabet is of larger size, say 8 characters, the users' ability to partially access the out-of-band authenticated value is more coarse-grained. In particular, they can still read only a substring of the authenticated value, but are restricted to reading specific blocks of consecutive 8 bits in their entirety. In other words, users that read 32 bits in this setting may read only one of $\binom{8}{4} = 70$ many 32-bit substrings of the out-of-band authenticated value.

Identifying the Weakness in Existing Protocols. It is quite simple to construct a contrived example of a secure protocol that is completely insecure when executed by lazy users. Thus, we chose to focus on the protocols of WhatsApp [Wha] and Naor et al. [NSS06] for the following reasons: (1) the protocol implemented by WhatsApp is among the most widely-used out-of-band authentication protocols, and (2) the protocol of Naor et al. offers the optimal tradeoff between the length of the out-of-band authenticated value and the adversary's forgery probability in the statistical setting (thus showing that both computationally-secure protocols and statistically-secure ones may become completely insecure when executed by lazy users).

Analyzing our rather simple attacks on these protocols (see Sect. 4), we identify a key property that they have in common which makes them completely insecure when executed by lazy users: Intuitively, different sections of the sender input message (i.e., the message m to be authenticated) influence different sections of the out-of-band authenticated value. Hence, if the users only consider a subset of positions of the out-of-band authenticated value that is independent in some sense from a particular part of the message to be authenticated, the adversary can replace this part of the message in an undetected manner (we refer to this property as "over locality"). In what follows, we discuss why the protocol of Vaudenay in the computational setting does not suffer from over locality; and how our general transformation in the statistical setting addresses it.

Naive Approaches that Fail. A potential approach to immunizing any comparison based out-of-band authentication protocol against lazy users, is to have the parties run the protocol and then hash the out-of-band authenticated value with a random oracle (in addition to transmitting it over the insecure channel). On the face of it, this resolves any over dependency on locality the initial protocol might have exhibited. However, this approach may generally suffer from the major shortcoming of introducing a tradeoff between the adversary's running time and its success probability (aside, of course, from relying on a random oracle which may be undesirable if the security of the underlying protocol does not require it). More concretely, an adversary that runs in time $T(\lambda)$ has forgery probability that is roughly (at least) $T(\lambda)/2^{-|\mathcal{I}|}$, where $\mathcal{I}$ is the subset of positions that the parties consider. When $\mathcal{I}$ is small (which is exactly the case with lazy users), then the asymptotics "do not kick in", and the latter forgery probability is significant. This is precisely the reason why we are interested in protocols in which for every such subset $\mathcal{I}$, the forgery probability is bounded by $\epsilon(\mathcal{I}) + \nu(\lambda)$ (where $\nu(\cdot)$ is a negligible function of the security parameter λ) *for every* polynomial-time adversary.

An additional potential approach is to have the parties apply some fixed error-correcting code to the out-of-band authenticated value. Though this may have the effect of increasing the fraction of inconsistent positions in the out-of-band authenticated value at the end of any forgery attempt, it does not provide the security guarantees we seek: If before applying the error-correcting code there was some subset of t positions for some fixed t, for which there was an attack causing the receiver to output a fraudulent message with probability ϵ, this may still be the case after applying the code. Moreover, this approach has the consequence of worsening the tradeoff between the length of the out-of-band authenticated value and the adversary's forgery probability. Similarly, adding redundancy to the input message itself (e.g., by applying an error-correcting code to it) is not necessarily helpful in immunizing protocols against lazy users.

Another possibility is to reduce the number of characters in the out-of-band authenticated value by mapping it to a larger alphabet. As discussed above, this has the effect of restricting the lazy behavior of the users; in particular, assuming that the users read at least one character of the out-of-band value, after increasing the alphabet size, this single character constitutes a larger fraction of the out-of-band value. Alas, even if the new alphabet is sufficiently large so that the out-of-band value consists just of two characters, the resulting protocol may still be insecure for lazy users who read only one of them (this is the case, for example, with the protocols of WhatsApp [Wha] and Naor et al. [NSS06]). On the other hand, our lower bounds on the bit-length of the out-of-band value (see Sect. 7) imply that in order for the out-of-band value to consists only of a single character, its alphabet size has to be at least $1/\epsilon$, where ϵ is the forgery probability. For any reasonable level of security, this means an impractical-sized alphabet has to be used.

Security for Lazy Users via "Influence Spreading". Our transformation in the statistical setting takes as input a parameter $t \in \mathbb{N}$ and any statistically-secure out-of-band authentication π with out-of-band authenticated value of length ℓ and forgery probability at most ϵ. It proceeds by having the sender S and the receiver R run t parallel executions of π with the same input message m to S. Afterwards, S parses each of the resulting t out-of-band authentication values as a single character from an alphabet of the appropriate size, concatenates them into a single string of length t (over the larger alphabet) and sends it over the out-of-band channel. When considering some subset $\mathcal{I} \subseteq [t]$ of the characters in the new out-of-band authenticated value, the receiver R accepts the message m if and only if it accepts m in each of the executions corresponding to the subset $\mathcal{I}$. We show that for every subset $\mathcal{I} \subseteq [t]$, the forgery probability in this new protocol is bounded by $\epsilon'(\mathcal{I}) \leq \epsilon^{|\mathcal{I}|}$.

In light of our observations regarding protocols that are insecure for lazy users, this transformation can be thought of in the following manner: We start with a protocol that might be insecure for lazy users and suffer from over locality, and we "spread" the influence of each bit of the input message across all characters of the new out-of-band authenticated value via the parallel invocations of the basic protocol.

When instantiated with the protocol of Naor et al. [NSS06] (while setting its security to $\epsilon = 1/2$), our transformation yields a protocol with a constant-size alphabet which is statistically-secure for lazy users: For every subset $\mathcal{I} \subseteq [t]$, the forgery probability corresponding to $\mathcal{I}$ is bounded by $2^{-|\mathcal{I}|}$. However, using the protocol of Naor et al. and their analysis "off the shelf" results in an alphabet which is, though constant-size, large and impractical (concretely, it is of size $2^{16} = 65536$). Hence, in the full version [NRS18], we show by a refined analysis of the protocol of Naor et al. that this constant can be reduced to $2^8 = 256$ (which fits nicely, for example, in the set of 333 emoji Telegram uses as the alphabet in the verification of their voice calls).

Leveraging the "Local Sensitivity" of Non-malleable Commitments. Informally speaking, the protocol of Vaudenay [Vau05] consists of the following steps: (1) On input m, S sends m to R, chooses a random r_S and commits to the message (m, r_S); (2) R sends a random r_R to S; (3) S reveals r_S; and (4) S sends $r_S \oplus r_R$ over the out-of-band authenticated channel. In the lazy user setting, where the users only read the subset $\mathcal{I}$ of positions in the out-of-band authenticated value, R accepts m if and only if the value $(r_S \oplus r_R)_\mathcal{I}$ sent over the out-of-band channel is consistent with her view of the protocol.

In Sect. 6 we prove that when the commitment scheme used in Step (1) is a non-malleable commitment scheme, then this protocol is optimal for lazy users (considering the matching lower bound from Sect. 7). Our proof goes about by considering all potential synchronizations that a man-in-the middle attacker might impose while attacking an execution of the protocol, and showing that in each of them, an attack on the protocol that succeeds with probability noticeably larger than $2^{-|\mathcal{I}|}$ can be translated into an attack on a different property of the underlying commitment scheme.

From a more conceptual point of view, our proof leverages the fact that the non-malleability of commitment schemes is a property which is "locally sensitive" in the following sense. Informally, in a non-malleable commitment scheme, it should be impossible, given a commitment c to some value v, to produce a related commitment $\widehat{c}$ for some value $\widehat{v}$ such that v and $\widehat{v}$ satisfy *any* efficiently recognizable relation. This includes, in particular, relations that are defined with respect to a subset of the positions in v and $\widehat{v}$; and namely, the relation induced by a successful forgery in Vaudenay's protocol when the users only consider the subset $\mathcal{I}$ of positions of the out-of-band authenticated value.

1.4   Paper Organization

The remainder of this paper is organized as follows. In Sect. 2 we present the notation and basic definitions that are used in this work. In Sect. 3 we introduce our framework for modeling the behavior and security of lazy users in out-of-band message authentication protocols. In Sect. 4 we show that existing out-of-band authentication protocols may become completely insecure when executed by lazy users. In Sects. 5 and 6 we present statistically-secure and computationally-secure out-of-band authentication protocols, respectively. Finally, in Sect. 7 we derive lower bounds on the tradeoff between the adversary's forgery probability and the length of the out-of-band authenticated value in out-of-band authentication protocols that are executed by lazy users.

2   Preliminaries

In this section we present the notation and basic definitions that are used in this work. For a distribution X we denote by $x \leftarrow X$ the process of sampling a value x from the distribution X. Similarly, for a set $\mathcal{X}$ we denote by $x \leftarrow \mathcal{X}$ the process of sampling a value x from the uniform distribution over $\mathcal{X}$. For an integer $n \in \mathbb{N}$ we denote by $[n]$ the set $\{1, \ldots, n\}$. For a string s and a subset $\mathcal{I} \subseteq [|s|]$ of positions, we let $s_\mathcal{I}$ (sometimes we may write $(s)_\mathcal{I}$) denote the substring of s obtained by concatenating the characters of s in the positions specified by the set $\mathcal{I}$ in increasing order. A function $\nu : \mathbb{N} \to \mathbb{R}^+$ is *negligible* if for any polynomial $p(\cdot)$ there exists an integer N such that for all $n > N$ it holds that $\nu(n) \leq 1/p(n)$.

Shannon Entropy. For a random variable X defined over a finite domain Ω, we rely the standard notion of Shannon entropy: $H(X) = - \sum_{x \in \Omega} \Pr[X = x] \cdot \log_2 \Pr[X = x]$. Note that for any such X it holds that $H(X) \leq \log_2 |\Omega|$.

Non-malleable Commitment Schemes [DDN00]. We rely on the notion of statistically-binding non-malleable commitments (for basic definitions and background on commitment schemes, we refer the reader to [Gol01]). We follow the indistinguishability-based definition of Lin and Pass [LP11], though we find it convenient to consider non-malleability with respect to content, other than with respect to identities. Intuitively speaking, a non-malleable commitment scheme has the following guarantee: Any efficient adversary cannot use a commitment to some value v in order to produce a commitment to a value $\hat{v}$ which is "non-trivially" related to v. For formal definitions regarding commitment schemes and non-malleable commitment schemes in particular, see the full version [NRS18].

Dolev et al. [DDN00] constructed non-malleable commitment schemes from any one-way function. Subsequently, Lin and Pass [LP11] and Goyal [Goy11] have shown that constant-round non-malleable commitments can be constructed from the same assumption. The round complexity was further improved by Goyal et al. [GRR+14] to 4 rounds, and by Goyal et al. [GPR16] to 3 rounds assuming the existence of an injective one-way function. Such schemes can also be constructed efficiently in a simple manner in the random-oracle model [BR93]. For further information regarding non-malleable commitment schemes in the standard model see the references above as well as, for example, [Bar02, PR08, LP09, PPV08, PW10, Wee10, GLO+12] and the references therein.

3   Modeling the Security of Lazy Users

In this section we introduce our framework for modeling the behavior and security of lazy users in out-of-band message authentication protocols. We start by reviewing the communication model and existing notions of security for out-of-band message authentication [Vau05, NSS06], and then present our notions of security for the case of lazy users.

3.1   Out-of-Band Authentication

Following the framework of Vaudenay [Vau05] and Naor et al. [NSS06], we model the interaction between the sender and the receiver as occurring over two types of channels: A bidirectional insecure channel that is completely vulnerable to man-in-the middle attacks, and an authenticated unidirectional low-bandwidth channel from the sender to the receiver. The adversary is assumed to have complete control over the insecure channel: She can read, delay and remove any messages sent by the two parties, as well as insert new messages of her choice at any point in time. In particular, this provides the adversary with considerable control over the synchronization of the protocol's execution. Nonetheless, the execution is still guaranteed to be "marginally synchronized": Each party sends her message in the ith round of the protocol only upon receiving the due message of round $i - 1$. As for the out-of-band channel, we assume that the sender is equipped with a low-bandwidth channel, through which the sender may send a short message to the receiver in an authenticated manner (but without any secrecy guarantee). The adversary may read or remove this message, and may delay it for different periods of time, but cannot modify it in an undetectable manner.

We follow the definitions of Vaudenay [Vau05] and Naor et al. [NSS06], generalizing naturally to consider out-of-band authenticated values over general alphabets and not only over the binary alphabet. As we discuss later on, this is of little importance in the standard setting (where the parties are assumed to read the entire out-of-band authenticated value), but will play a significant role when considering lazy users. Following Naor et al. we differentiate between protocols that are computationally secure and ones that are statistically secure. We formalize the notion of *statistically-secure* out-of-band authentication protocols as:

Definition 3.1. *Let $n, \ell, r \in \mathbb{N}$, let $\epsilon \in (0,1)$ and let Σ be an alphabet. A statistically-secure out-of-band (n, ℓ, r, ϵ)-authentication protocol over Σ is an r-round protocol in which the sender S is invoked on an n-bit message and sends at most ℓ characters of Σ over the out-of-band authenticated channel. The following requirements must hold:*

1. **Correctness:** *In an honest execution of the protocol, for any input message $m \in \{0,1\}^n$ on which S is invoked, R outputs m with probability 1.*

2. **Unforgeability:** *For any man-in-the-middle adversary A and for any adversarially chosen input message $m \in \{0,1\}^n$ on which S is invoked, the probability that R outputs some message $\widehat{m} \notin \{m, \bot\}$ in an execution with S that is attacked by A is at most ϵ.*

A *computationally-secure* out-of-band authentication protocol is defined similarly, except that security need only hold against efficient adversaries, and the probability of forgery is also allowed to additively grow (with respect to the statistical setting) by a negligible function of the security parameter.

Definition 3.2. *Let $n = n(\lambda), \ell = \ell(\lambda), r = r(\lambda), \epsilon = \epsilon(\lambda)$, and $\Sigma = \Sigma(\lambda)$ be functions of the security parameter $\lambda \in \mathbb{N}$. A computationally-secure out-of-band (n, ℓ, r, ϵ)-authentication protocol over alphabet Σ is an r-round protocol in which the sender S is invoked on an n-bit message and sends at most ℓ characters of Σ over the out-of-band authenticated channel. The following requirements must hold:*

1. **Correctness:** *In an honest execution of the protocol, for any input message $m \in \{0,1\}^n$ on which S is invoked, R outputs m with probability 1.*
2. **Unforgeability:** *For any probabilistic polynomial-time man-in-the-middle adversary A there exists a negligible function $\nu(\cdot)$ such that: For any input message $m \in \{0,1\}^n$ chosen by the adversary and on which S is invoked, the probability that R outputs some message $\widehat{m} \notin \{m, \bot\}$ in an execution with S that is attacked by A is at most $\epsilon + \nu(\lambda)$.*

3.2 The Security of Lazy Users

In order to formally capture the lazy-users setting, given an out-of-band authentication protocol we define a collection of "lazy protocols", one per each possible subset of positions of the out-of-band authenticated value. Informally speaking, given a protocol π in which the out-of-band authenticated value consists of ℓ characters, for a subset $\mathcal{I} \subseteq [\ell]$ of indexes, we consider the "lazy protocol" $\pi_{\mathcal{I}}$ in which the parties execute π, with the exception that S only sends over the out-of-band channel the substring of the out-of-band authenticated value that corresponds to the positions in the set $\mathcal{I}$.

Specifically, let π be a (statistically-secure or computationally-secure) out-of-band (n, ℓ, r, ϵ)-authentication protocol over an alphabet Σ (recall Definitions 3.1 and 3.2). For every subset $\mathcal{I} \subseteq [\ell]$ of the positions of its out-of-band authenticated value, the "lazy protocol" $\pi_{\mathcal{I}}$ is defined as follows:

1. On input $m \in \{0,1\}^n$ to S, the sender S and receiver R run the first $r - 1$ rounds of π. Let $v \in \Sigma^\ell$ be the out-of-band authenticated value that S is due to send in round r.
2. S receives $\mathcal{I}$ and sends only $v_{\mathcal{I}}$ over the out-of-band authenticated channel.
3. R receives $\mathcal{I}$ and $v_{\mathcal{I}}$, and decides on her output according to π.[5]

---

[5] As noted before, the protocols we consider in this paper must be defined for every substring of the out-of-band authenticated value.

Using this notion, Definitions 3.3 and 3.4 below formalize the extensions discussed above in the statistical setting and computational setting, respectively. Intuitively, we define the security of out-of-band authentication protocols for lazy users by letting the bound on the forgery probability be a function of the subset $\mathcal{I}$ considered by the users. Concretely, an out-of-band authentication protocol π is parameterized by some function ϵ, which maps each possible set of positions $\mathcal{I}$ of the out-of-band authenticated value to be read by the users to a matching upper bound on the forgery probability. That is, in case the users only read the out-of-band authentication value in positions $\mathcal{I}$, an adversary should be able to make the receiver output a fraudulent message with probability at most $\epsilon(\mathcal{I})$. This approach has the benefit of being very general on the one hand, while coinciding with the standard definitions (see Definitions 3.1 and 3.2) when $\mathcal{I} = [\ell]$. We note, however, that one may still consider a more restrictive notion where the forgery probability should only depend on the size of $\mathcal{I}$ (observe that this is a strict restriction of our notion).

Definition 3.3. *Let $n, \ell, r \in \mathbb{N}$ and let $\epsilon : 2^{[\ell]} \rightarrow [0,1]$. A protocol π is a statistically-secure out-of-band (n, ℓ, r, ϵ)-authentication protocol for lazy users over alphabet Σ if for every $\mathcal{I} \subseteq [\ell]$ the protocol $\pi_{\mathcal{I}}$ is a statistically-secure out-of-band $(n, |\mathcal{I}|, r, \epsilon(\mathcal{I}))$-authentication protocol.*

Definition 3.4. *Let $n = n(\lambda), \ell = \ell(\lambda), r = r(\lambda)$ and $\Sigma = \Sigma(\lambda)$ be functions of the security parameter $\lambda \in \mathbb{N}$, and let $\epsilon = \epsilon(\lambda, \cdot) : 2^{[\ell]} \rightarrow [0,1]$. A protocol π is a computationally-secure out-of-band (n, ℓ, r, ϵ)-authentication protocol for lazy users over alphabet Σ if for every $\mathcal{I} = \mathcal{I}(\lambda) \subseteq [\ell]$ the protocol $\pi_{\mathcal{I}}$ is a computationally-secure out-of-band $(n, |\mathcal{I}|, r, \epsilon(\cdot, \mathcal{I}))$-authentication protocol.*

4   The Insecurity of Existing Protocols

In this section we show that existing out-of-band authentication protocols may become completely insecure when executed by lazy users. We focus on the computationally-secure protocol implemented by WhatsApp [Wha] and on the statistically-secure protocol of Naor et al. [NSS06], and show that these protocols are completely vulnerable to man-in-the-middle attacks when the parties consider only a half (or less) of the out-of-band authenticated value.

Concretely, for each of these two protocols we present an efficient man-in-the-middle attacker that fools the receiver into accepting a fraudulent message with probability 1. Then, we discuss the basic underlying structure that these two protocols share, which makes them completely insecure when executed by lazy users.

WhatsApp's Protocol [Wha]. Consider any protocol where in order to authenticate a message m, the sender S partitions m into two halves $m = m_1 \| m_2$, and authenticates each half using some out-of-band authentication protocol separately and independently. The out-of-band authenticated value is then $\sigma = \sigma_1 \| \sigma_2$, where σ_1 and σ_2 are the out-of-band authenticated values of the two executions. If the underlying out-of-band authentication protocol is secure and the users read the entire string σ, then this newly-defined protocol is secure as well (though, possibly, with a sub-optimal tradeoff between the adversary's forgery probability and the length of the out-of-band authenticated value). However, consider for example the case where the parties only read σ_1 (or a substring of it). In this case, no security is guaranteed and a man-in-the-middle adversary can trivially make R output a fraudulent message of the form $\widehat{m} = m_1 \| \widehat{m_2}$ for some $\widehat{m_2} \neq m_2$. A similar problem arises when the parties read only σ_2 (or a substring of it).

The above protocol might seem like a pathological example, specifically contrived for our needs, but this is in fact exactly the approach used by WhatsApp. Concretely, a pair of WhatsApp users wishing to verify that each of them has the correct key of the other user compare a 60-digit sequence displayed on each of their screens. This sequence is derived by hashing each user's key into a 30-digit string, and concatenating the two strings.[6] It is not hard to see that if the users only compare the first half of the out-of-band authenticated value, it might very well be the case that one of them holds a fraudulent key, completely compromising the secrecy of their chat.

The Protocol of Naor et al. [NSS06]. Naor et al. [NSS06] presented a construction of a statistically-secure out-of-band authentication protocol that relies on the following idea. Loosely speaking, the two parties iteratively hash the message into shorter intermediate values until reaching a short enough value that can be transmitted out-of-band. More concretely, in each round of the protocol the parties cooperatively choose an algebraic hash function: They treat the input message and the intermediate values as polynomials over finite fields of appropriate sizes, and in each round, one party chooses a random element in the field on which the polynomial is evaluated, and the other party chooses a random shift to apply to the result. When choosing the last hash function, the sender S is the one to choose the element on which the polynomial is evaluated. The out-of-band authenticated value then consists of two parts: (1) The result of the last hash function (according to the view of S); (2) and the last element S chose.

Yet again, if the parties read and compare the entire out-of-band authenticated value, then Naor et al. proved that this protocol is secure (and provides the optimal tradeoff between the adversary's forgery probability and the length of the out-of-band authenticated value). Alas, if the users are lazy, and read only one of the two parts of the out-of-band authenticated value, then the protocol becomes completely insecure. Concretely, if the parties only read the part that corresponds to the last field element chosen by S, then a trivial attack exists:

---

[6] From WhatsApp's security white paper [Wha, p. 10]: "WhatsApp users additionally have the option to verify the keys of the other users with whom they are communicating so that they are able to confirm that an unauthorized third party (or WhatsApp) has not initiated a man-in-the-middle attack. This can be done by scanning a QR code, or by comparing a 60-digit number. [...] The 60-digit number is computed by concatenating the two 30-digit numeric fingerprints for each user's Identity Key".

The man-in-the-middle adversary simply runs two independent executions, one with the sender S and one with the receiver R, on two different input messages, with the exception of choosing the same field element as S does in the last hash function of her interaction with R.

Summary: The Underlying Weakness. The property that both of the above examples share and which makes them completely insecure in the face of rather trivial attacks can be articulated in the following manner: In both cases, different sections of the input message to be authenticated affect different sections of the out-of-band authenticated value. In the case of WhatsApp, each user's key affects only half of the out-of-band authentication value (but both keys should be verified). In the case of Naor et al. [NSS06], the input message to be authenticated goes into the computation of only half of the out-of-band authenticated value, while the other half is simply a random value generated during the execution of the protocol.

It is instructive to view our positive results also in this light, as this may provide the reader with additional intuition regarding the security of our constructions:

1. In the statistical setting, our transformation (and its resulting protocol when instantiated with that of Naor et al. [NSS06]) can be interpreted as follows. We start with an out-of-band authentication protocol that guarantees no security for lazy users to begin with (but does guarantee security for users who fully comply with the protocol), and in particular may suffer from the same problematic property described above. We transform this protocol into a protocol that provides security for lazy users by "spreading" the influence of each bit of the input message m across all characters of the out-of-band authenticated value of the resulting protocol.
2. In the computational setting we consider Vaudenay's protocol [Vau05] whose out-of-band authenticated value is simply a uniformly-distributed string that is generated during the execution of the protocol. Intuitively speaking, even though this value is determined independently of the input message, we "tie together" the message *in its entirety* and the out-of-band authenticated value using cryptographic tools (namely, a non-malleable commitment scheme).

5   Immunizing Statistically-Secure Protocols Against Lazy Users

In this section we present a generic transformation that uses any out-of-band authentication protocol that is secure under a certain form of parallel repetition for constructing an out-of-band authentication protocol for lazy users. In particular, our transformation can be applied to any statistically-secure protocol, and can thus be instantiated with the protocol of Naor et al. [NSS06]. As our transformation itself is statistically secure, this yields a statistically-secure protocol (that comes very close to matching our lower bound on the tradeoff between adversary's forgery probability and the length of the partial out-of-band authenticated value considered by the lazy users – see Corollary 7.3).

We first present and analyze our transformation for statistically-secure protocols, as well as discuss the properties of its instantiation with the protocol of Naor et al. [NSS06]. Then, we discuss the specific composability property required of computationally-secure protocols in order for them to be compatible with our transformation (this, however, is somewhat less motivated given that our computationally-secure protocol in Sect. 6 already matches our lower bound in the computational setting).

The Transformation. The building block underlying our transformation is an out-of-band authentication protocol that does not necessarily guarantee any form of security for lazy users. Loosely speaking, our transformation proceeds as follows: On input message m, the parties run ℓ parallel and independent executions of the underlying protocol with the same message m, and parse each of the resulting ℓ out-of-band authentication values as a single character from an alphabet of the appropriate size. The sender S then concatenates these ℓ characters into a single string of length ℓ (over the larger alphabet) and sends it over the out-of-band authenticated channel. In a lazy execution of the protocol, where the receiver considers only some number $t \leq \ell$ out of the ℓ out-of-band authenticated characters, the receiver accepts m if and only if it m is accepted in each of the corresponding t executions.

Intuitively, if the forgery probability of the underlying protocol is bounded by ϵ', then fooling a receiver that reads only a predetermined t-character subset of the out-of-band authenticated value requires the adversary to break the unforgeability (in the standard sense, not considering lazy users) of t copies of the underlying protocol, and hence the adversary's forgery probability is bounded by $(\epsilon')^t$ in the statistical setting.

More formally, let $n', \ell', r' \in \mathbb{N}$, let $\epsilon' \in (0,1)$, and let π' is a statistically-secure out-of-band $(n', \ell', r', \epsilon')$-authentication protocol; that is, π' is an r'-round protocol for out-of-band authentication of messages of length n', where the sender out-of-band authenticates at most ℓ' bits, and the probability of forgery is bounded by ϵ'. We use π' to construct a statistically-secure out-of-band $(n = n', \ell, r = r', \epsilon)$-authentication protocol for lazy users, denoted π_{Lazy}, for any $\ell \in \mathbb{N}$, such that $\epsilon(\mathcal{I}) = (\epsilon')^{|\mathcal{I}|}$ for every $\mathcal{I} \subseteq [\ell]$.

The protocol for lazy users, denoted π_{Lazy}, is defined as follows for every $\mathcal{I} \subseteq [\ell]$ (i.e., this is the "lazy protocol" $\pi_{\mathsf{Lazy},\mathcal{I}}$ – see Sect. 3):

1. On input message m to S, S and R run ℓ parallel executions of π' up to (and including) round $r' - 1$ with the same input message m to S in all executions. Denote the out-of-band authenticated values that S computes in these executions by $\sigma_1 \cdots \sigma_\ell \in \{0,1\}^{\ell'}$.
2. For each $i \in [\ell]$, S parses σ_i as a single character over an alphabet of size $k = 2^{\ell'}$; denote the ith character by β_i. S then receives $\mathcal{I} = \{i_1, \ldots, i_{|\mathcal{I}|}\} \subseteq [\ell]$ and sends $\sigma = \beta_{i_1} \| \ldots \| \beta_{i_{|\mathcal{I}|}}$ over the out-of-band authenticated channel.
3. R receives $\mathcal{I}$, parses $\sigma = \sigma_{i_1} \cdots \sigma_{i_{|\mathcal{I}|}}$ as $|\mathcal{I}|$ binary strings of length ℓ' each. For every $i \in \mathcal{I}$, denote by $\widehat{m}_i$ the output of R in the ith execution given

R's view of that execution (including σ_i). If for every $i, j \in \mathcal{I}$ it holds that $\widehat{m_i} = \widehat{m_j}$, then R outputs $\widehat{m_{i_1}}$. Otherwise, R outputs $\perp$.

The correctness and security of the protocol π_{Lazy} are stated in the following theorem.

Theorem 5.1. *Let* π' *be a statistically-secure out-of-band* (n, ℓ', r, ϵ') *-authentication protocol, let* $k = 2^{\ell'}$ *and let* $\ell \in \mathbb{N}$. *Then,* π_{Lazy} *is a statistically-secure out-of-band* (n, ℓ, r, ϵ)*-authentication protocol for lazy users over an alphabet of size* k, *where* $\epsilon(\mathcal{I}) = (\epsilon')^{|\mathcal{I}|}$ *for every* $\mathcal{I} \subseteq [\ell]$.

The correctness and round complexity of π_{Lazy} follow immediately from the correctness and round complexity of π', respectively. The unforgeability of π_{Lazy} for lazy users (vis-à-vis Definition 3.3) is proven in the full version [NRS18], yielding the above theorem.

A Concrete Instantiation. Naor et al. [NSS06] constructed a statistically-secure out-of-bound (n, ℓ', r, ϵ')-authentication protocol for any $n, r \in \mathbb{N}$ and any $\epsilon' \in (0, 1)$, where $\ell' \leq \log(1/\epsilon') + \log^{(r-1)} + O(1)$. Instantiating our protocol π_{Lazy} with the protocol of Naor et al. as π', while setting $r = \Omega(\log^* n)$ and $\epsilon' = 1/2$, yields a statistically-secure out-of-band authentication protocol for lazy users with the same round complexity and a constant-size alphabet. This is formalized by the following corollary.

Corollary 5.2. *For any* $n, \ell \in \mathbb{N}$, *there exists a statistically-secure out-of-band* $(n, \ell, \log^* n, \epsilon)$*-authentication protocol for lazy users over a constant size alphabet, where* $\epsilon(\mathcal{I}) = 2^{-|\mathcal{I}|}$ *for every* $\mathcal{I} \subseteq [\ell]$.

In the full version [NRS18] we also provide a refined analysis of the protocol of Naor et al. which reduces the alphabet size of the protocol from Corollary 5.2 to 2^8, and discuss how our transformation applies to computationally-secure protocols with some specific parallel-composability property.

6   Matching the Optimal Tradeoff for Computationally-Secure Protocols

In this section we show that Vaudenay's computationally-secure protocol [Vau05] can be extended to allow execution by lazy users, and that the resulting protocol matches our lower bound on the tradeoff between the adversary's forgery probability and the length of the out-of-band authenticated value for lazy users (see Theorem 7.1). That is, the protocol offers the optimal tradeoff between the adversary's forgery probability and the length of the partial out-of-band authenticated value considered by the lazy users.

The basic building block used by the protocol is any non-malleable statistically-binding commitment scheme Com. From a foundational point of view, such a scheme with a constant number of rounds can be constructed based on any one-way function in the standard model, and from a more practical point of view, such a scheme can be constructed by simply invoking a hash function modeled as a random oracle (see Sect. 2).

The protocol, which we denote by π_{Comp}, is parametrized by the security parameter $\lambda \in \mathbb{N}$, the message length $n = n(\lambda) \in \mathbb{N}$ and the length of the out-of-band authenticated value $\ell = \ell(\lambda) \in \mathbb{N}$, and is defined as follows:

1. On input the security parameter $\lambda \in \mathbb{N}$ and a message $m \in \{0,1\}^n$, the sender S chooses a random $r_S \leftarrow \{0,1\}^\ell$, sends m to the receiver R, and commits to the pair (m, r_S) to receiver R using Com. Denote the resulting commitment by c_S and its corresponding decommitment by d_S.[7] Denote the message and commitment as received by R by $\widehat{m}$ and $\widehat{c_S}$, respectively.
2. The receiver R chooses a random $r_R \leftarrow \{0,1\}^\ell$ and sends it to the sender S. Denote by $\widehat{r_R}$ the value that S receives.
3. The sender S sends the decommitment d_S to R. Denote by $\widehat{d_S}$ the decommitment R receives. If $\widehat{d_S}$ is not a valid decommitment to $\widehat{c_S}$ or if the revealed value is not of the form $(\widehat{m}, *)$, then R outputs $\perp$. Otherwise, let $(\widehat{m}, \widehat{r_S})$ be the revealed value.
4. The sender S sends $\sigma = r_S \oplus \widehat{r_R}$ over the out-of-band channel. R checks if $\widehat{r_S} \oplus r_R = \sigma$. If so, R outputs $\widehat{m}$, and otherwise R outputs $\perp$.

The following theorem captures the security of the above protocol, stating that it provides the optimal tradeoff as discussed above.

Theorem 6.1. *Let $n = n(\cdot), r = r(\cdot)$ and $\ell = \ell(\cdot)$ be functions of the security parameter $\lambda \in \mathbb{N}$ and let Com be an r-round statistically-binding non-malleable commitment scheme. Then, protocol π_{Comp} is a computationally-secure out-of-band $(n, \ell, r + 3, \epsilon)$-authentication protocol for lazy users (over the alphabet $\Sigma = \{0,1\}$), where $\epsilon(\lambda, \mathcal{I}) = 2^{-|\mathcal{I}|}$ for every $\lambda \in \mathbb{N}$ and for every $\mathcal{I} \subseteq [\ell(\lambda)]$.*

Our protocol incurs an almost minimal overhead in the number of rounds relative to the round complexity of the underlying commitment scheme: The number of rounds of insecure communication is $r + 2$ (this includes the $r + 1$ rounds necessary for commitment and decommitment), to which we add only a single message over the insecure channel, and a single message over the out-of-band authenticated channel. In the plain model, a non-malleable commitment is known to exist with $r = 3$, while in the random oracle model, there exist non-interactive non-malleable commitments (i.e., with $r = 1$).

The security proof of our protocol considers all possible synchronizations a man-in-the-middle adversary may impose on an execution of the protocol. For each such synchronization and for every possible subset $\mathcal{I} \subseteq [\ell]$ of positions of the out-of-band authenticated value, we bound the forgery probability by $2^{-|\mathcal{I}|} +$

---

[7] As a commitment scheme may be interactive, when referring to a commitment, we mean the transcript of the interaction between the committer and the receiver during an execution of the commit phase of the commitment scheme. When the scheme is non-interactive, a commitment is simply a single string sent from the committer to the receiver.

$\nu(\lambda)$, for a negligible function $\nu(\lambda)$, by converting an adversary achieving better forgery probability into an adversary that breaks a specific security property of the underlying commitment scheme (i.e., binding, hiding or non-malleability). The full proof is given in the full version [NRS18].

7 Lower Bounds on the Security of Lazy Users

Vaudenay [Vau05] and Naor et al. [NSS06] established tight bounds on the trade-off between the adversary's forgery probability and the length of the out-of-band authenticated value in out-of-band authentication. In this section we show that their lower bounds, in both the computational and statistical setting, directly translate into corresponding lower bounds for protocols that are executed by lazy users.

7.1 Computationally-Secure Protocols

In any computationally-secure out-of-band authentication protocol where the probability of forgery is bounded by $\epsilon > 0$, the sender must out-of-band authenticate at least $\log(1/\epsilon)$ bits. This can be seen, for example, by analyzing the collision probability of the random variable corresponding to the out-of-band authenticated value (see for example, [PV06]). Below, we show that this reasoning generalizes to the case of lazy users: Namely, for each number $k \in [\ell]$ of bits read from the out-of-band authenticated value, we provide a corresponding lower bound.

Theorem 7.1. *For any computationally-secure out-of-band (n, ℓ, r, ϵ) -authentication protocol for lazy users over alphabet Σ, it holds that*

$$\epsilon(\mathcal{I}) \geq 2^{-|\mathcal{I}| \cdot \log |\Sigma|} - 2^{-n}$$

for every $\mathcal{I} \subseteq [\ell]$.

Proof. Let π be any computationally-secure out-of-band (n, ℓ, r, ϵ)-authentication protocol for lazy users over alphabet Σ. Let $\lambda \in \mathbb{N}$ and $\ell = \ell(\lambda)$ and fix any $\mathcal{I} \subseteq [\ell]$. Consider the following attack:

1. Choose a random $m \leftarrow \{0,1\}^n$ and run an honest execution with S on input m (with the adversary playing the role of R). Denote by v the out-of-band authenticated value S sends at the end of the execution. Delay the relaying of v to (the real) R until the end of the attack.
2. Choose a random $\widehat{m} \leftarrow \{0,1\}^n$ and run an honest execution with R, where the adversary plays the role S on input $\widehat{m}$. Denote by $\widehat{v}$ the out-of-band authenticated value that the simulated sender sends at the end of the execution. If $\widehat{v}_{\mathcal{I}} = v_{\mathcal{I}}$, forward v to R; otherwise, terminate.

Denote by $V_\mathcal{I}$ the random variable corresponding to the substring of the out-of-band authenticated value defined by the positions in $\mathcal{I}$, where the distribution of $V_\mathcal{I}$ is induced by an honest execution of π on a randomly chosen input message to S. Then, the following holds:

$$\Pr_{(\widehat{v}_\mathcal{I}, v_\mathcal{I}) \leftarrow V_\mathcal{I} \times V_\mathcal{I}} [\widehat{v}_\mathcal{I} = v_\mathcal{I}] = \sum_{v_\mathcal{I}} (\Pr[V_\mathcal{I} = v_\mathcal{I}])^2 = 2^{\log \sum_{v_\mathcal{I}} (\Pr[V_\mathcal{I} = v_\mathcal{I}])^2}$$

$$\geq 2^{\sum_{v_\mathcal{I}} \Pr[V_\mathcal{I} = v_\mathcal{I}] \log(\Pr[V_\mathcal{I} = v_\mathcal{I}])} = 2^{-\mathrm{H}(V_\mathcal{I})}.$$

The inequality above follows from Jensen's inequality.

Let $\mathsf{Forge}_\mathcal{I}$ denote the event in which the above attack goes through; i.e., R outputs a fraudulent message. By the correctness of π, it holds that

$$\Pr[\mathsf{Forge}_\mathcal{I}] \geq \Pr[\widehat{v}_\mathcal{I} = v_\mathcal{I} \wedge \widehat{m} \neq m]$$

$$\geq \Pr[\widehat{v}_\mathcal{I} = v_\mathcal{I}] - \Pr[\widehat{m} = m]$$

$$\geq 2^{-\mathrm{H}(V_\mathcal{I})} - 2^n.$$

On the one hand, by the unforgeability of π, it must hold that $\epsilon(\mathcal{I}) \geq 2^{-\mathrm{H}(V_\mathcal{I})}$ 2^n. On the other hand, it is always the case that $\mathrm{H}(V_\mathcal{I}) \leq |\mathcal{I}| \cdot \log|\Sigma|$. Taken together, these inequalities yield the theorem. ∎

The lower bound of Theorem 7.1 should be thought of in the following terms. On the one hand, if the message to be authenticated is short (relative to the bandwidth of the out-of-band authenticated channel), then the sender can just go ahead and send it over the out-of-band channel. On the other hand, if it is long, then the term 2^{-n} is small and of little significance, and the attack from our proof succeeds with probability close to $2^{-|\mathcal{I}| \cdot \log|\Sigma|}$. Specifically, for any protocol in which the length of the out-of-band authenticated value is independent of the length of the input message to be authenticated, the success probability of our attack can be made arbitrarily close to $2^{-|\mathcal{I}| \cdot \log|\Sigma|}$ (while considering arbitrarily long input messages).

7.2   Statistically-Secure Protocols

Naor et al. [NSS06] proved a lower bound on the length of the out-of-band authenticated value in any statistically-secure out-of-band authentication protocol. More precisely, they provided a lower bound on the Shannon entropy of the random variable corresponding to the out-of-band authenticated value. If we denote this random value by V, the lower bound of Naor et al. can be articulated as follow:

Theorem 7.2 ([NSS06]). *For any statistically-secure out-of-band (n, ℓ, r, ϵ)-authentication protocol it holds that*

$$\epsilon \geq 2^{-\mathrm{H}(V)/2} - 2^{-n}$$

Theorem 7.2 implies the following, more general, lower bound for out-of-band authentication protocols for lazy users over possibly non-binary alphabets.

Corollary 7.3. *For any statistically-secure out-of-band* (n, ℓ, r, ϵ)-*authentication protocol for lazy users over alphabet* Σ*, it holds that for every* $\mathcal{I} \subseteq [\ell]$

$$\epsilon(|\mathcal{I}|) \geq 2^{-|\mathcal{I}| \cdot \log(|\Sigma|)/2} - 2^{-n}.$$

Proof. Let π be any (n, ℓ, r, ϵ)-authentication protocol for lazy users over alphabet Σ. By definition, this means that for any $\mathcal{I} \subseteq [\ell]$, the induced protocol $\pi_{\mathcal{I}}$ is an $(n, |\mathcal{I}|, r, \epsilon(\mathcal{I}))$-authentication protocol. For every $\mathcal{I} \subseteq [\ell]$, denote by $V_{\mathcal{I}}$ the random variable corresponding to the substring of the out-of-band authenticated value that is induced by the subset $\mathcal{I}$. Hence, by Theorem 7.2, for every $\mathcal{I} \subseteq [\ell]$ it holds that

$$\epsilon(|\mathcal{I}|) \geq 2^{-\mathrm{H}(V_{\mathcal{I}})/2} - 2^{-n}.$$

For every $\mathcal{I} \subseteq [\ell]$ it holds that $\mathrm{H}(V_{\mathcal{I}}) \leq |\mathcal{I}| \cdot \log |\Sigma|$, and combining this fact with the above inequality completes the proof. ∎

References

[AFJ15]   Alghamdi, D., Flechais, I., Jirotka, M.: Security practices for households bank customers in the kingdom of Saudi Arabia. In: Symposium on Usable Privacy and Security (SOUPS), pp. 297–308 (2015)

[BA04]   Besnard, D., Arief, B.: Computer security impaired by legitimate users. Comput. Secur. **23**(3), 253–264 (2004)

[Bar02]   Barak, B.: Constant-round coin-tossing with a man in the middle or realizing the shared random string model. In: Proceedings of the 43rd Annual IEEE Symposium on Foundations of Computer Science, pp. 345–355 (2002)

[BM94]   Bellovin, S.M., Merritt, M.: An attack on the interlock protocol when used for authentication. IEEE Trans. Inf. Theor. **40**(1), 273–275 (1994)

[BR93]   Bellare, M., Rogaway, P.: Random oracles are practical: a paradigm for designing efficient protocols. In: Proceedings of the 1st ACM Conference on Computer and Communications Security, pp. 62–73 (1993)

[BSJ+17]   Bellare, M., Singh, A.C., Jaeger, J., Nyayapati, M., Stepanovs, I.: Ratcheted encryption and key exchange: the security of messaging. In: Katz, J., Shacham, H. (eds.) CRYPTO 2017. LNCS, vol. 10403, pp. 619–650. Springer, Cham (2017). https://doi.org/10.1007/978-3-319-63697-9_21

[CCD+17]   Cohn-Gordon, K., Cremers, C.J.F., Dowling, B., Garratt, L., Stebila, D.: A formal security analysis of the signal messaging protocol. In: Proceedings of the 2nd IEEE European Symposium on Security and Privacy (EuroS&P), pp. 451–466 (2017)

[CGC17]   Cohn-Gordon, K., Cremers, C.: Mind the gap: where provable security and real-world messaging don't quite meet. Cryptology ePrint Archive, Report 2017/982 (2017)

[CGCG+17]   Cohn-Gordon, K., Cremers, C., Garratt, L., Millican, J., Milner, K.: On ends-to-ends encryption: asynchronous group messaging with strong security guarantees. Cryptology ePrint Archive, Report 2017/666 (2017)

[DDB+16] Dupree, J.L., Devries, R., Berry, D.M., Lank, E.: Privacy personas: clustering users via attitudes and behaviors toward security practices. In: Proceedings of the CHI Conference on Human Factors in Computing Systems, pp. 5228–5239. ACM (2016)

[DDN00] Dolev, D., Dwork, C., Naor, M.: Non-malleable cryptography. SIAM J. Comput. **30**(2), 391–437 (2000)

[Ell96] Ellison, C.M.: Establishing identity without certification authorities. In: Proceedings of the 6th USENIX Security Symposium, p. 7 (1996)

[FMB+16] Frosch, T., Mainka, C., Bader, C., Bergsma, F., Schwenk, J., Holz, T.: How secure is TextSecure? In: Proceedings of the 1st IEEE European Symposium on Security and Privacy (EuroS&P), pp. 457–472 (2016)

[GLO+12] Goyal, V., Lee, C.-K., Ostrovsky, R., Visconti, I.: Constructing non-malleable commitments: a black-box approach. In: Proceedings of the 53rd Annual IEEE Symposium on Foundations of Computer Science, pp. 51–60 (2012)

[Gol01] Goldreich, O.: Foundations of Cryptography: Basic Techniques, vol. 1. Cambridge University Press, Cambridge (2001)

[Goy11] Goyal, V.: Constant round non-malleable protocols using one way functions. In: Proceedings of the 43rd Annual ACM Symposium on Theory of Computing, pp. 695–704 (2011)

[GPR16] Goyal, V., Pandey, O., Richelson, S.: Textbook non-malleable commitments. In: Proceedings of the 48th annual ACM Symposium on Theory of Computing, pp. 1128–1141 (2016)

[Gre18a] Green, M.: Attack of the week: Group messaging in WhatsApp and Signal. A Few Thoughts on Cryptographic Engineering (2018). https://blog.cryptographyengineering.com/2018/01/10/attack-of-the-week-group-messaging

[Gre18b] Greenberg, A.: WhatsApp security flaws could allow snoops to slide into group chats. Wired Magazine (2018). https://www.wired.com/story/whatsapp-security-flaws-encryption-group-chats

[GRR+14] Goyal, V., Richelson, S., Rosen, A., Vald, M.: An algebraic approach to non-malleability. In: Proceedings of the 55th Annual IEEE Symposium on Foundations of Computer Science, pp. 41–50 (2014)

[Her09] Herley, C.: So long and no thanks for the externalities: the rational rejection of security advice by users. In: Proceedings of the Workshop on New Security Paradigms, pp. 133–144 (2009)

[HL16] Herzberg, A., Leibowitz, H.: Can Johnny finally encrypt?: evaluating E2E-encryption in popular IM applications. In: Proceedings of the 6th Workshop on Socio-Technical Aspects in Security and Trust, pp. 17–28 (2016)

[HZF+14] Harbach, M., Zezschwitz, E.V., Fichtner, A., Luca, A.D., Smith, M.: It's a hard lock life: a field study of smartphone (un)locking behavior and risk perception. In: Symposium on Usable Privacy and Security (SOUPS), pp. 213–230 (2014)

[KBB17] Kobeissi, N., Bhargavan, K., Blanchet, B.: Automated verification for secure messaging protocols and their implementations: a symbolic and computational approach. In: Proceedings of the 2nd IEEE European Symposium on Security and Privacy (EuroS&P), pp. 435–450 (2017)

[LP09] Lin, H., Pass, R.: Non-malleability amplification. In: Proceedings of the 41st Annual ACM Symposium on Theory of Computing, pp. 189–198 (2009)

[LP11] Lin, H., Pass, R.: Constant-round non-malleable commitments from any one-way function. In: Proceedings of the 43rd Annual ACM Symposium on Theory of Computing, pp. 705–714 (2011)

[LS03] Li, S., Shum, H.-Y.: Secure human-computer identification against peeping attacks (SecHCI): A survey (2003)

[Mem17] Membe, T.: A look at how private messengers handle key changes. Medium (2017). https://medium.com/@pepelephew/a-look-at-how-private-messengers-handle-key-changes-5fd4334b809a

[NRS18] Naor, M., Rotem, L., Segev, G.: The security of lazy users in out-of-band authentication. Cryptology ePrint Archive, Report 2018/823 (2018)

[NSS06] Naor, M., Segev, G., Smith, A.: Tight bounds for unconditional authentication protocols in the manual channel and shared key models. In: Dwork, C. (ed.) CRYPTO 2006. LNCS, vol. 4117, pp. 214–231. Springer, Heidelberg (2006). https://doi.org/10.1007/11818175_13

[NSS08] Naor, M., Segev, G., Smith, A.D.: Tight bounds for unconditional authentication protocols in the manual channel and shared key models. IEEE Trans. Inf. Theor. **54**(6), 2408–2425 (2008)

[PLF03] Patrick, A.S., Long, A.C., Flinn, S.: HCI and security systems. In: Proceedings of the CHI Conference on Human Factors in Computing Systems, pp. 1056–1057 (2003)

[PM16] Perrin, T., Marlinspike, M.: The double ratchet algorithm (2016). https://signal.org/docs/specifications/doubleratchet/doubleratchet.pdf. Accessed 16 May 2018

[PPV08] Pandey, O., Pass, R., Vaikuntanathan, V.: Adaptive one-way functions and applications. In: Wagner, D. (ed.) CRYPTO 2008. LNCS, vol. 5157, pp. 57–74. Springer, Heidelberg (2008). https://doi.org/10.1007/978-3-540-85174-5_4

[PR08] Pass, R., Rosen, A.: New and improved constructions of nonmalleable cryptographic protocols. SIAM J. Comput. **38**(2), 702–752 (2008)

[PV06] Pasini, S., Vaudenay, S.: An optimal non-interactive message authentication protocol. In: Pointcheval, D. (ed.) CT-RSA 2006. LNCS, vol. 3860, pp. 280–294. Springer, Heidelberg (2006). https://doi.org/10.1007/11605805_18

[PW10] Pass, R., Wee, H.: Constant-round non-malleable commitments from subexponential one-way functions. In: Gilbert, H. (ed.) EUROCRYPT 2010. LNCS, vol. 6110, pp. 638–655. Springer, Heidelberg (2010). https://doi.org/10.1007/978-3-642-13190-5_32

[RMS18] Rösler, P., Mainka, C., Schwenk, J.: More is less: on the end-to-end security of group chats in signal, WhatsApp, and Threema. In: Proceedings of the 3nd IEEE European Symposium on Security and Privacy (EuroS&P) (2018)

[RS84] Rivest, R.L., Shamir, A.: How to expose an eavesdropper. Commun. ACM **27**(4), 393–395 (1984)

[RS18] Rotem, L., Segev, G.: Out-of-band authentication in group messaging: computational, statistical, optimal. In: Shacham, H., Boldyreva, A. (eds.) CRYPTO 2018. LNCS, vol. 10991, pp. 63–89. Springer, Cham (2018). https://doi.org/10.1007/978-3-319-96884-1_3

[SKH17] Schliep, M., Kariniemi, I., Hopper, N.: Is Bob sending mixed signals? In: Proceedings of the 2017 on Workshop on Privacy in the Electronic Society, pp. 31–40 (2017)

[Tela] Telegram. End-to-end encrypted voice calls - key verification. https://core.telegram.org/api/end-to-end/voice-calls#key-verification. Accessed 16 May 2018

[Telb] Telegram. End-to-end encryption. https://core.telegram.org/api/end-to-end. Accessed 16 May 2018

[Telc] Telegram. FAQ for the technically inclined - hash collisions for Diffie-Hellman keys. https://core.telegram.org/techfaq#hash-collisions-for-diffie-hellman-keys. Accessed 16 May 2018

[Vau05] Vaudenay, S.: Secure communications over insecure channels based on short authenticated strings. In: Shoup, V. (ed.) CRYPTO 2005. LNCS, vol. 3621, pp. 309–326. Springer, Heidelberg (2005). https://doi.org/10.1007/11535218_19

[Vib] Viber encryption overview. https://www.viber.com/app/uploads/Viber-Encryption-Overview.pdf. Accessed 16 May 2018

[Wee10] Wee, H.: Black-box, round-efficient secure computation via non-malleability amplification. In: Proceedings of the 51st Annual IEEE Symposium on Foundations of Computer Science, pp. 531–540 (2010)

[Wha] WhatsApp encryption overview. https://www.whatsapp.com/security/WhatsApp-Security-Whitepaper.pdf. Accessed 16 May 2018

[Wik] Wikipedia. Instant messaging. https://en.wikipedia.org/wiki/Instant_messaging. Accessed 16 May 2018

ORAM and PRF

Is There an Oblivious RAM Lower Bound for Online Reads?

Mor Weiss$^{(\boxtimes)}$ and Daniel Wichs

Department of Computer Science, Northeastern University, Boston, MA, USA
m.weiss@northeastern.edu, wichs@ccs.neu.edu

Abstract. Oblivious RAM (ORAM), introduced by Goldreich and Ostrovsky (JACM 1996), can be used to read and write to memory in a way that hides which locations are being accessed. The best known ORAM schemes have an $O(\log n)$ overhead per access, where n is the data size. The work of Goldreich and Ostrovsky gave a lower bound showing that this is optimal for ORAM schemes that operate in a "balls and bins" model, where memory blocks can only be shuffled between different locations but not manipulated otherwise. The lower bound even extends to weaker settings such as *offline* ORAM, where all of the accesses to be performed need to be specified ahead of time, and *read-only* ORAM, which only allows reads but not writes. But can we get lower bounds for general ORAM, beyond "balls and bins"?

The work of Boyle and Naor (ITCS '16) shows that this is unlikely in the *offline* setting. In particular, they construct an offline ORAM with $o(\log n)$ overhead assuming the existence of small sorting circuits. Although we do not have instantiations of the latter, ruling them out would require proving new circuit lower bounds. On the other hand, the recent work of Larsen and Nielsen (CRYPTO '18) shows that there indeed is an $\Omega(\log n)$ lower bound for general *online* ORAM.

This still leaves the question open for online *read-only* ORAM or for *read/write* ORAM where we want very small overhead for the read operations. In this work, we show that a lower bound in these settings is also unlikely. In particular, our main result is a construction of online ORAM where *reads* (but not *writes*) have an $o(\log n)$ overhead, assuming the existence of small sorting circuits as well as very good *locally decodable codes (LDCs)*. Although we do not have instantiations of either of these with the required parameters, ruling them out is beyond current lower bounds.

1 Introduction

An *Oblivious RAM (ORAM)*, first introduced by Goldreich and Ostrovsky [Gol87, Ost90, GO96], is a scheme that allows a client to read and write to his data stored on untrusted storage, while entirely hiding the access pattern, i.e., which operations were performed and at which locations. More precisely, we think of the client's data as "logical memory" which the ORAM scheme encodes and stores in "physical memory". Whenever the client wants

© International Association for Cryptologic Research 2018
A. Beimel and S. Dziembowski (Eds.): TCC 2018, LNCS 11240, pp. 603–635, 2018.
https://doi.org/10.1007/978-3-030-03810-6_22

to read or write to logical memory, the ORAM scheme translates this operation into several accesses to the physical memory. Security ensures that for any two (equal length) sequences of access to logical memory, the resultant distributions over the physical accesses performed by the ORAM are computationally (or statistically) close. Following its introduction, there has been a large body of work on ORAM constructions and security [SCSL11, GMOT12, KLO12, WS12, SvDS+13, RFK+15, DvDF+16], as well as its uses in various application scenarios (see, e.g., [GKK+12, GGH+13, LPM+13, LO13, MLS+13, SS13, YFR+13, CKW13, WHC+14, MBC14, KS14, LHS+14, GHJR15, BCP15, HOWW18]).

One can always trivially hide the memory access pattern by performing a linear scan of the entire memory for *every* memory access. Consequently, an important measure of an ORAM scheme is its *overhead*, namely the number of memory blocks which need to be accessed to answer a *single* read or write request. Goldreich and Ostrovsky [GO96] proved a lower bound of $\Omega(\log n)$ on the ORAM overhead, where n denotes the number of memory blocks in the logical memory. There are also ORAM constructions achieving this bound [SvDS+13, WCS15], at least if the block size is set to a sufficiently large polylogarithmic term; and works [PPRY] achieving $O(\log n \log \log n)$ overhead for $\Omega(\log n)$ block size, assuming one-way functions. We note that one can circumvent the [GO96] lower bound by *relaxing* the notion of ORAM to either allow server-side computation [AKST14], or multiple non-colluding servers [LO13], and several works have obtained *sublogarithmic overhead* in these settings [AKST14, FNR+15, DvDF+16, ZMZQ16, AFN+17, WGK18, KM18]. However, in this work we focus on the standard ORAM setting with a single server and no server-side computation.

In some respects, the lower bound of [GO96] is very general. First, it applies to all block sizes. Second, it holds also in restricted settings: when the ORAM is only required to work for *offline* programs in which, roughly, all memory accesses are stated explicitly in advance; and for *read-only* programs that do not update the memory contents. However, in other respects, the bound is restricted since it only applies to ORAM schemes that operate in the *"balls and bins"* model, in which memory can only be manipulated by moving memory blocks ("balls") from one memory location ("bin") to another. Therefore, the main question left open by the work of [GO96] is: *is there an ORAM lower bound for general ORAM schemes, that are not restricted to operate in the "balls and bins" model?*

Almost 20 years after Goldreich and Ostrovsky proved their lower bound, it was revisited by Boyle and Naor [BN16], who show how to construct an ORAM scheme *in the offline setting* with $o(\log n)$ overhead, using sorting circuits of size $o(n \log n)$. Though sorting circuits of such size are not known, ruling out their existence seems currently out of our reach. This result can be interpreted in two ways. On the one hand, an optimist will view it as a possible approach towards an ORAM construction in the offline setting, which uses "small" sorting circuits as a building block. On the other hand, a pessimist may view this result as a barrier towards proving a lower bound. Indeed, the [BN16] construction shows that proving a lower bound on the overhead of offline ORAM schemes would yield lower bounds on the size of sorting circuits, and proving circuit lower bounds is notoriously difficult. We note that unlike sorting *networks*, which only contain "compare-and-swap" gates that operate on the two input words as a whole, and for which a simple $\Omega(n \log n)$ lower bound exists, sorting *circuits* can arbitrarily operate over the input bits, and no such lower bounds are known for them.

The main drawback of the Boyle and Naor result [BN16] is that it only applies to the *offline* setting, which is not very natural and is insufficient for essentially any imaginable ORAM application. More specifically, the offline setting requires that *the entire sequence of accesses* be specified in advance - including *which operation* is performed, on *which address*, and in case of a write operation, *what value* is written. However, even very simple and natural RAM programs (e.g., binary search) require dynamic memory accesses that depend on the results of previous operations. Despite this drawback, the result of Boyle and Naor is still very interesting since it shows that lower bounds which are easy to prove in the "balls and bins" model might not extend to the general model. However, it does not answer the question of whether general ORAM lower bounds exist in the *online* setting, which is the one of interest for virtually all ORAM applications.

Very recently, and concurrently with our work, Larsen and Nielsen [LN18] proved that the [GO96] lower bound *does* indeed extend to general *online* ORAM. Concretely, they show an $\Omega(\log n)$ lower bound on the *combined* overhead of read and write operations in any general online ORAM, even with computational security. Their elegant proof employs techniques from the field of data-structure lower bounds in the cell-probe model, and in particular the "information-transfer" method of Pătraşcu and Demaine [PD06].

1.1 Our Contributions

In this work, we explore the read *overhead* of general ORAM schemes *beyond the "balls and bins" model* and in the *online setting*. We first consider *read-only* ORAM schemes that only support reads – but not writes – to the logical memory. We stress that the scheme is read-only in the sense that it only supports programs that do not write to the *logical* memory. However, to emulate such programs in the ORAM, the client might write to the *physical* memory stored on the server. We note that read-only ORAM already captures many interesting applications such as private search over a database, or fundamental algorithmic tasks such as binary search. We show how to construct *online* read-only ORAM schemes with $o(\log n)$ overhead assuming "small" sorting circuits and "good" Locally Decodable Codes (LDCs). We then extend our results to a setting which also supports sub-linear writes but does not try to hide whether an operation is a read or a write and, in particular, allows different overheads for these operations. In all our constructions, the server is only used as remote storage, and does not perform any computations.

We note that, similar to [BN16], our results rely on primitives that we do not know how to instantiate with the required parameters, but also do not have any good lower bounds for. One can therefore interpret our results either positively, as a blueprint for an ORAM construction, or negatively as a barrier to proving a lower bound in these settings. For simplicity of the exposition, we choose to present our results through the "optimistic" lens.

We now describe our results in more detail.

Read-Only (RO) ORAM. We construct a read-only ORAM scheme, based on sorting circuits and smooth locally decodable codes. Roughly, a Locally Decodable Code (LDC) [KT00] has a decoder algorithm that can recover any message symbol by querying only few codeword symbols. In a smooth code, every individual decoder query is uniformly distributed. Given a logical memory of size-n, our scheme has $O(\log \log n)$ overhead, assuming the existence of linear-size sorting circuits, and smooth LDCs with constant query complexity and polynomial length codewords. Concretely, we get the following theorem.

Theorem 1 (Informal statement of Corollary 1). *Suppose there exist linear-size boolean sorting circuits, and smooth LDCs with constant query complexity and polynomial length codewords. Then there exists a statistically-secure read-only ORAM scheme for memory of size n and blocks of size* poly $\log n$, *with* $O(1)$ *client storage and* $O(\log \log n)$ *overhead.*

In Sect. 3, we also show a read-only ORAM scheme with $o(\log n)$ overhead based on milder assumptions – concretely, smooth LDCs with $O(\log \log n)$ query complexity, and the existence of sorting circuits of size $o\left(\frac{n \log n}{\log^2 \log n}\right)$; see Corollary 2. We note that under the (strong) assumption that the LDC has linear-size codewords, our constructions achieve linear-size server storage. We also note that if an a-priori polynomial bound on the number of memory accesses is known, then the constructions can be based solely on LDCs, and the assumption regarding small sorting circuits can be removed.

ORAM Schemes Supporting Writes. The read-only ORAM scheme described above still leaves the following open question: *is there a lower bound on* read *overhead for ORAM schemes supporting* write *operations?* To partially address this question, we extend our ORAM construction to a scheme that supports writes but does not hide whether an operation was a read or a write. In this setting, read and write operations may have different overheads, and we focus on minimizing the overhead of read operations while preserving efficiency of write operations as much as possible. Our construction is based on the existence of sorting circuits and smooth LDCs as in Theorem 1, as well as the existence of One-Way Functions (OWFs). (We elaborate on why OWFs are needed in Sect. 1.2.) Assuming the existence of such building blocks, our scheme has $O(\log \log n)$ read overhead and $O(n^\epsilon)$ write overhead for an arbitrarily small constant $\epsilon \in (0, 1)$, whose exact value depends on the efficiency of the LDC encoding. Concretely, we show the following:

Theorem 2 (Informal statement of Theorem 7). *Assume the existence of OWFs, as well as LDCs and sorting circuits as in Theorem 1. Then for every constant $\epsilon \in (0, 1)$, there exists a constant $\gamma \in (0, 1)$ such that if LDC encoding* *requires $n^{1+\gamma}$ operations then there is a computationally-secure ORAM scheme for memory of size n and blocks of size* poly $\log n$ *with* $O(1)$ *client storage,* $O(\log \log n)$ *read overhead, and* $O(n^\epsilon)$ *write overhead.*

Similar to the read-only setting, we also instantiate (Sect. 4, Theorem 8) the ORAM with writes scheme based on milder assumptions regarding the parameters of the underlying sorting circuits and LDCs, while only slightly increasing the read overhead. Additionally, we describe a variant of our scheme with improved write complexity, again at the cost of slightly increasing the read overhead:

Theorem 3 (Informal statement of Theorem 9). *Assume the existence of OWFs, as well as LDCs and sorting circuits as in Theorem 1, where LDC encoding requires $n^{1+o(1)}$ operations. Then there exists a computationally-secure ORAM scheme for memory of size n and blocks of size* poly $\log n$ *with* $O(1)$ *client storage, $o(\log n)$ read overhead, and $n^{o(1)}$ write overhead.*

A Note on Block vs. Word Size. In our constructions we distinguish between *words* (which are bit strings) and *blocks* (which consist of several words). More specifically, words, which are the basic unit of physical memory on the server, consist of w bits; and blocks, which are the basic unit of logical memory on the client, consist of B words. We measure the overhead as the number of words the client accesses on the server to read or write to a single logical block, divided by B. We note that it is generally easier to construct schemes with *smaller* word size. (Indeed, it allows the client more fine-grained access to the physical memory; a larger word size might cause the client to access unneeded bits on the server, simply because they are part of a word containing bits that do interest the client.) Consequently, we would generally like to support *larger* word size, ideally having words and blocks of equal size. Our constructions can handle any word size,[1] as long as blocks are poly-logarithmically larger (for a sufficiently large poylogarithmic factor). A similar differentiation between block and word size was used in some previous works as well (e.g., to get $O(\log N)$ overhead in Path ORAM [SvDS+13]).

A Note Regarding Assumptions. We instantiate our constructions in two parameter regimes: one based on the existence of "best possible" sorting circuits and smooth LDCs (as described above), and one based on milder assumptions regarding the parameters of these building blocks (as discussed in Sects. 3 and 4). We note that despite years of research in these fields, we currently seem very far from ruling out the existence of even the "best possible" sorting circuits and smooth LDCs. Concretely, to the best of our knowledge there are no specific lower bounds for sorting circuits (as opposed to sorting networks, see discussion above and in Sect. 2.2), and even for general boolean circuits only linear lower bounds of $c \cdot n$ for some constant $c > 1$ are known [Blu84,IM02,FGHK16].

---

[1] Similar to previous works (e.g., [SCSL11,SvDS+13,SS13]), we assume words are of at least logarithmic size.

Regarding LDCs, research has focused on the relation between the query complexity and codeword length in the constant query regime, but there are currently no non-trivial lower bounds for *general* codes. Even for restricted cases, such as *binary* codes, or *linear* codes over arbitrary fields, the bounds are extremely weak. Specifically, the best known lower bound shows that codewords in q-query LDCs must have length $\Omega\left(n^{(q+1)/(q-1)}\right)/\log n$ [Woo07] (which, in particular, does not rule out the existence of 4-query LDCs with codeword length $n^{5/3}$), so it is plausible that for a sufficiently large constant, constant-query LDCs with polynomial length codewords exist. We note that a recent series of breakthrough results construct *3-query* LDCs with *sub-exponential* codewords of length $\exp\left(\exp\left(O\left(\sqrt{\log n \log\log n}\right)\right)\right) = 2^{n^{o(1)}}$, as well as extensions to larger (constant) query complexity [Yek07, Rag07, Efr09, IS10, CFL+13]. Notice that lower bounds on the size of the encoding circuit of such codes will similarly yield circuit lower bounds.

A Note on the Connection to Private Information Retrieval (PIR) and Doubly-Efficient PIR (DEPIR). The notions of PIR and DEPIR, which support reads from memory stored on a remote server, are closely related to read-only ORAM, but differ from it significantly in some respects. We now discuss these primitives in more detail. In a (single-server) PIR scheme [KO97], there is no initial setup, and anybody can run a protocol with the server to retrieve an arbitrary location in the logical memory. The server is *not* used solely as remote storage, and in fact the main goal, which is to minimize the communication between the client and server, *inherently* requires the server to perform computations. One additional significant difference from ORAM is that the PIR privacy guarantee *inherently* requires the server runtime to be linear in the size of the logical memory, whereas a main ORAM goal is to have the server touch only a sublinear number of blocks (which the client reads from it to retrieve the block he is interested in). In a DEPIR scheme [BIM00, BIPW17, CHR17], there is a setup phase (as in ORAM), following which the server(s) stores an encoded version of the logical memory, and the logical memory can be accessed either with no key (in multi-server DEPIR [BIM00]), with a public key (in public-key DEPIR [BIPW17]) or with a secret key (in secret-key DEPIR [BIPW17, CHR17]). First proposed by Beimel, Ishai and Malkin [BIM00], who showed how to construct information-theoretic DEPIR schemes in the multi-server setting (i.e., with several non-colluding servers), two recent works [BIPW17, CHR17] give the first evidence that this notion may be achievable in the single-server setting. These works achieve sublinear server runtime, with a server that is only used as remote storage. Thus, these single-server DEPIR schemes satisfy all the required properties of a RO-ORAM scheme, with the added "bonus" of having a stateless server (namely, whose internal memory does not change throughout the execution of the scheme). However, these (secret-key) constructions are based on new, previously unstudied, computational hardness assumptions relating to Reed-Muller codes, and the public-key DEPIR scheme of [BIPW17] additionally requires a heuristic use of obfuscation. Unfortunately, both of the above assumptions are non-standard, poorly understood, and not commonly accepted. Additionally, these constructions do not achieve $o(\log n)$ overhead (at least not with polynomial server storage).

A Note on Statistical vs. Computational Security. Our RO-ORAM achieves *statistical* security under the assumption that the server does not see the memory *contents*, namely the server only sees which memory locations are accessed. Hiding memory contents from the server can be generically achieved by encrypting the logical memory, in which case security holds against *computationally-bounded* servers. We note that our ORAM scheme supporting writes requires encrypting the logical memory *even if the server does not see the memory contents.* Consequently, our ORAM with writes scheme achieve computational security even in the setting where the server does not see the memory contents. Alternatively, our construction can achieve statistical security if the underlying LDC has the additional property that the memory accesses during encoding are independent of the data. (This property is satisfied by, e.g., linear codes.) We elaborate on this further in Sects. 3.1 and 4.

1.2 Our Techniques

We now give a high-level overview of our ORAM constructions. We start with the read-only setting, and then discuss how to enable writes.

We note that our technique departs quite significantly from that of Boyle and Naor [BN16], whose construction seems heavily tied to the offline setting. Indeed, the high-level idea underlying their scheme is to use the sorting circuit to sort by location the list of operations that need to be performed, so that the outcomes of the read operations can then be easily determined by making one linear scan of the list. It does not appear that this strategy can naturally extend to the *online* setting in which the memory accesses are not known a-priori.

Read-Only ORAM. We first design a Read-Only (RO) ORAM scheme that is secure only for an *a-priori bounded* number of accesses, then extend it to a scheme that remains secure for *any* polynomial number of accesses.

Bounded-Access RO-ORAM Using Metadata. Our RO-ORAM scheme employs a smooth LDC, using the decoder to read from memory. Recall that a k-query LDC is an error-correcting code in which every message symbol can be recovered by querying k codeword symbols. The server in our scheme stores k copies of the codeword, each permuted using a separate, random permutation. (We note that permuted LDCs were already used – but in a very different way – in several prior works [HO08, HOSW11, CHR17, BIPW17].) To read the memory block at address j, the client runs the decoder on j, and sends the decoder queries to the server, who uses the i'th permuted codeword copy to answer the i'th decoding query. This achieves correctness, but does not yet guarantee obliviousness since the server learns, for each $1 \leq i \leq k$, which read operations induced the same i'th decoding query.

To prevent the server from obtaining this additional information, we restrict the client to use only *fresh* decoding queries in each read operation, namely a set $q_1, \ldots, q_k$ of queries such that no q_i was issued before as the i'th query. The metadata regarding which decoding queries are fresh, as well as the description of the permutations, can be stored on the server using any sufficiently efficient (specifically, polylogarithmic-overhead) ORAM scheme. Each block in the metadata ORAM will consist of a single word, so using the metadata ORAM will not influence the overall complexity of the scheme, since for sufficiently large memory blocks the metadata blocks are significantly smaller. In summary, restricting the client to make fresh queries guarantees that the server only sees uniformly random decoding queries, which reveal no information regarding the identity of the accessed memory blocks.

However, restricting the client to only make fresh decoding queries raises the question of whether the ORAM is still correct, namely whether this restriction has not harmed functionality. Specifically, *can the client always "find" fresh decoding queries?* We show this is indeed the case as long as the number of read operations is at most $M/2k$, where M denotes the codeword length. More precisely, the smoothness of the code guarantees that for security parameter λ and any index $j \in [n]$, λ independent executions of the decoder algorithm on index j will (with overwhelming probability) produce at least one set of fresh decoding queries. Thus, the construction is secure as long as the client performs at most $M/2k$ read operations.

We note that given an appropriate LDC, this construction already gives a read-only ORAM scheme which is secure for an a-priori *bounded* number of accesses, *without relying on sorting circuits*. Indeed, given a bound B on the number of accesses, all we need is a smooth LDC with length-M codewords, in which the decoder's query complexity is at most $M/2B$.

Handling an Unlimited Number of Reads. To obtain security for an *unbounded* number of read operations, we "refresh" the permuted codeword copies every $M/2k$ operations. (We call each such set of read operations an "epoch".) Specifically, to refresh the codeword copies the client picks k fresh, random permutations, and together with the server uses the sorting circuit to permute the codeword copies according to the new permutations. Since the logical memory is read-only, the refreshing operations can be spread-out across the $M/2k$ read operations of the epoch.

ORAM with Writes. We extend our RO-ORAM scheme to support write operations, while preserving $o(\log n)$ overhead for read operations. The construction is loosely based on hierarchical ORAM [Ost90, GO96]. The high-level idea is to store the logical memory on the server in a sequence of ℓ levels of increasing size, each containing an RO-ORAM.[2] We think of the levels as growing from the top down, namely level-1 (the smallest) is the top-most level, and level-ℓ (the largest) is the bottom-most. Initially, all the data is stored in the bottom level ℓ, and all the remaining levels are empty. To read the memory block at some location j, the client performs a read for location j in the RO-ORAMs of all levels, where the output is the block from the highest level that contains the j'th block. When the client writes to some location j, the server places that memory block in the top level $i = 1$. After every l_i write operations – where l_i denotes the size of level i – the i'th level becomes full. All the values in level i are then moved to level $i + 1$, a process which we call a "reshuffle" of level i into level $i + 1$. Formalizing this high-level intuition requires some care, and the final scheme is somewhat more involved. See Sect. 4 for details.

We note that our construction differs from Hierarchical ORAM in two main points. First, in Hierarchical ORAM level i is reshuffled into level $i + 1$ every l_i read *or* write *operations*, whereas in our scheme only write operations are "counted" towards reshuffle (in that respect, read operations are "free"). This is because the data is stored in each level using an RO-ORAM which already guarantees privacy for read operations. Second, Hierarchical ORAM uses $\Omega(\log n)$ levels, whereas to preserve $o(\log n)$ read overhead, we must use $o(\log n)$ levels. In particular, the ratio between consecutive levels in our scheme is no longer constant, leading to a higher reshuffle cost (which is the reason write operations have higher overhead in our scheme).

2 Preliminaries

Throughout the paper λ denotes a security parameter. For a length-n string $\mathbf{x}$ and a subset $I = \{i_1, \dots, i_l\} \subseteq [n]$, $\mathbf{x}_I$ denotes $(x_{i_1}, \dots, x_{i_l})$.

Terminology. Recall that words, the basic unit of physical memory on the server, consist of w bits; and blocks, the basic unit of logical memory on the client, consist of B words. The client may *locally* perform bit operations on the bit representation of blocks, but can only access full words on the server. We will usually measure complexity in terms of logical blocks (namely, in terms of the basic memory unit on the client). More specifically, unless explicitly stated otherwise, client and server storage are measured as the number of *blocks* they store (even though the basic storage unit on the server side is a word), and overhead measures the number of blocks one needs to read or write to implement a read or write operation on a single block. Formally:

---

[2] This is reminiscent of a construction of [OS97], which also instantiated the levels of a hierarchical ORAM with a primitive guaranteeing read privacy (specifically, they use PIR). However, our goals, and the details of our construction, differs significantly from [OS97].

Definition 1 (Overhead). *For a block size* B *and input length* n, *we say that a protocol between client* C *and server* S *has overhead* Ovh *for a function* Ovh : $\mathbb{N} \to \mathbb{N}$, *if implementing a* read *or* write *operation on a single logical memory block requires the client to access* B · Ovh (n) *words on the server.*

2.1 Locally Decodable Codes (LDCs)

Locally decodable codes were first formally introduced by [KT00]. We rely on the following definition of smooth LDCs.

Definition 2 (Smooth LDC). *A smooth* k-query *Locally Decodable Code* (LDC) *with message length* n, *and codeword length* M *over alphabet* Σ, *denoted by* $(k, n, M)_{\Sigma}$-smooth LDC, *is a triplet* (Enc, Query, Dec) *of PPT algorithms with the following properties.*

- **Syntax.** Enc *is given a message* msg $\in \Sigma^n$ *and outputs a codeword* $c \in \Sigma^M$, Query *is given an index* $\ell \in [n]$ *and outputs a vector* $\mathbf{r} = (r_1, \ldots, r_k) \in [M]^k$, *and* Dec *is given* $c_{\mathbf{r}} = (c_{r_1}, \ldots, c_{r_k}) \in \Sigma^k$ *and outputs a symbol in* Σ.
- **Local decodability.** *For every message* msg $\in \Sigma^n$, *and every index* $\ell \in [n]$,

$$\Pr[\mathbf{r} \leftarrow Query(\ell) \ : \ \mathsf{Dec}(\mathsf{Enc}(msg)_{\mathbf{r}}) = msg_\ell] = 1.$$

- **Smoothness.** *For every index* $\ell \in [n]$, *every query in the output of* Query (ℓ) *is distributed uniformly at random over* $[M]$.

To simplify notations, when $\Sigma = \{0, 1\}$ we omit it from the notation.

Remark on Smooth LDCs for Block Messages. We will use smooth LDCs for messages consisting of *blocks* $\{0, 1\}^B$ of bits (for some block size $B \in \mathbb{N}$), whose existence is implied by the existence of smooth LDCs over $\{0, 1\}$. Indeed, given a (k, n, M)-smooth LDC (Enc, Query, Dec), one can obtain a $(k, n, M)_{\{0,1\}^B}$-smooth LDC (Enc′, Query′, Dec′) by "interpreting" the message and codeword as B individual words, where the j'th word consists of the j'th bit in all blocks. Concretely, Enc′ on input a message $(msg^1, \ldots, msg^n) \in (\{0, 1\}^B)^n$, computes $y_j^1 \ldots y_j^M = \mathsf{Enc}(msg_j^1, \ldots, msg_j^n)$ for every $1 \leq j \leq B$, sets $c^i = y_1^i \ldots y_B^i$, and outputs $c = (c^1, \ldots, c^M)$. Query′ operates exactly as Query does. Dec′, on input $c^{r_1}, \ldots, c^{r_k} \in \{0, 1\}^B$, computes $z_j = \mathsf{Dec}(c_j^{r_1}, \ldots, c_j^{r_k})$ for every $1 \leq j \leq B$, and outputs $z_1 \ldots z_B$.

2.2 Oblivious-Access Sort Algorithms

Our construction employ an Oblivious-Access Sort algorithm [BN16] which is, roughly, a RAM program that sorts its input, such that the access patterns of the algorithm on any two inputs of equal size are statistically close. Thus, oblivious-access sort is the "RAM version" of boolean sorting circuits. (Informally, a boolean sorting circuit is a boolean circuit ensemble $\{C(n, B)\}_{n,B}$ such that each $C(n, B)$ takes as input n size-B tagged blocks, and outputs the blocks in sorted order according to their tags.)

Definition 3 (Oblivious-Access Sort Algorithm, [BN16]). *An Oblivious-Access Sort algorithm for input size* n *and block size* B, *with overhead* $\mathsf{Ovh}_{\mathsf{Sort}}(n, \mathsf{B})$, *is a (possibly randomized) algorithm* Sort *run by a client* C *on an input stored remotely on a server* S, *with the following properties:*

- **Operation:** *The input consists of* n *tagged blocks which are represented as length-B bit strings (the tag is a substring of the block) and stored on the server.[3] The client can perform local bit operations, but can only read and write full blocks from the server.*
- **Overhead:** *The overhead of* Sort *is* $\mathsf{Ovh}_{\mathsf{Sort}}(n, \mathsf{B})$.
- **Correctness:** *With overwhelming probability in* n, *at the end of the algorithm the server stores the blocks in sorted order according to their tags.*
- **Oblivious Access:** *For a logical memory* DB *consisting of* n *blocks of size* B, *let* $AP_{n,\mathsf{B}}(\mathsf{Sort}, DB)$ *denote the random variable consisting of the list of addresses accessed in a random execution of the algorithm* Sort *on* DB. *Then for every pair* DB, DB' *of inputs with* n *size-B blocks,* $AP_{n,\mathsf{B}}(\mathsf{Sort}, DB) \approx^s AP_{n,\mathsf{B}}(\mathsf{Sort}, DB')$, *where* $\approx^s$ *denotes* $\mathsf{negl}(n)$ *statistical distance.*

Boyle and Naor [BN16] show that the existence of sorting circuits implies the existence of oblivious-access sort algorithms with related parameters:

Theorem 4 (Oblivious-access sort from sorting circuits, [BN16]). *If there exist boolean sorting circuits* $\{C(n, \mathsf{B})\}_{n,\mathsf{B}}$ *of size* $s(n, \mathsf{B})$, *then there exists an oblivious-access sort algorithm for* n *distinct elements with* $O(1)$ *client storage,* $O\left(n \cdot \log \mathsf{B} + s\left(\frac{2n}{\mathsf{B}}, \mathsf{B}\right)\right)$ *overhead, and* $e^{-n^{\Omega(1)}}$ *probability of error.*

Remark on the Existence of Oblivious-Access Sort Algorithms with Small Overhead. We note that for blocks of poly-logarithmic size $\mathsf{B} = \mathrm{poly}\log n$, the existence of sorting circuits of size $s(n, \mathsf{B}) = O(n \cdot \mathsf{B} \cdot \log \log n)$ guarantees (through Theorem 4) the existence of oblivious-access sort algorithms with $O(n \cdot \log \log n)$ overhead.

Remark on the Relation to Sorting Networks. The related notion of a *sorting network* has been extensively used in ORAM constructions. Similar to oblivious-access sort algorithms, sorting networks sort n size-B blocks in an oblivious manner. (More specifically, a sorting network is *data oblivious*, namely its memory accesses are independent of the input.) However, unlike oblivious-access sort algorithms, and boolean sorting circuits, which can operate *locally* on the bits in the bit representation of the input blocks, a sorting network consist of a single type of *compare-exchange* gate which takes a pair of blocks as input, and outputs them in sorted order. We note that a simple information-theoretic lower bound of $\Omega(n \log n)$ on the network size is known for sorting networks (as well as matching upper bounds, e.g. [AKS83, Goo14]), whereas no such bound is known for boolean sorting circuits or oblivious-access sorting algorithms.

---

[3] In [BN16], the blocks consist solely of the tag, but the algorithm is usually run when tags are concatenated with memory blocks (which are carried as a "payload", and the overhead increases accordingly). We choose to explicitly include the data portion in the block.

2.3   Oblivious RAM (ORAM)

Oblivious RAMs were introduced by Goldreich and Ostrovskey [Gol87, Ost90, GO96]. To define oblivious RAMs, we will need the following notation of an *access pattern*.

Notation 1 (Access pattern). A length-q *access pattern* Q consists of a list $(\mathsf{op}_l, \mathsf{val}_l, \mathsf{addr}_l)_{1 \leq l \leq q}$ of instructions, where instruction $(\mathsf{op}_l, \mathsf{val}_l, \mathsf{addr}_l)$ denotes that the client performs operation $\mathsf{op}_l \in \{\mathsf{read}, \mathsf{write}\}$ at address addr_l with value val_l (which, if $\mathsf{op}_l = \mathsf{read}$, is $\perp$).

Definition 4 (Oblivious RAM (ORAM)). *An* Oblivious RAM (ORAM) *scheme with block size* B *consists of procedures* (Setup, Read, Write), *with the following syntax:*

- *Setup*$(1^\lambda, DB)$ *is a function that takes as input a security parameter* λ, *and a logical memory* $DB \in (\{0,1\}^\mathsf{B})^n$, *and outputs an initial server state* st_S *and a client key* ck. *We require that the size of the client key* $|\mathsf{ck}|$ *be bounded by some fixed polynomial in the security parameter* λ, *independent of* $|DB|$.
- *Read is a protocol between the server* S *and the client* C. *The client holds as input an address* $\mathsf{addr} \in [n]$ *and the client key* ck, *and the server holds its current state* st_S. *The output of the protocol is a value* val *to the client, and an updated server state* st'_S.
- *Write is a protocol between the server* S *and the client* C. *The client holds as input an address* $\mathsf{addr} \in [n]$, *a value* v, *and the client key* ck, *and the server holds its current state* st_S. *The output of the protocol is an updated server state* st'_S.

Throughout the execution of the Read *and* Write *protocols, the server is used only as remote storage, and does not perform any computations.*
   We require the following correctness and security properties.

- **Correctness:** *In any execution of the* Setup *algorithm followed by a sequence of* Read *and* Write *protocols between the client and the server, where the* Write *protocols were executed with a sequence* V *of values, the output of the client in every execution of the* Read *protocol is with overwhelming probability the value he would have read from the logical memory in the corresponding* read *operation, if the prefix of* V *performed before the* Read *protocol was performed directly on the logical memory.*
- **Security:** *For a logical memory* DB, *and an access pattern* Q, *let* $AP(DB, Q)$ *denote the random variable consisting of the list of addresses accessed in the ORAM when the* Setup *algorithm is executed on* DB, *followed by the execution of a sequence of* Read *and* Write *protocols according to* Q. *Then for every pair* $DB^0, DB^1 \in (\{0,1\}^\mathsf{B})^n$ *of inputs, and any pair* $Q^0 = (\mathsf{op}_l, \mathsf{val}_l^0, \mathsf{addr}_l^0)_{1 \leq l \leq q}, Q^1 = (\mathsf{op}_l, \mathsf{val}_l^1, \mathsf{addr}_l^1)_{1 \leq l \leq q}$ *of access patterns of length* $q = \mathrm{poly}(\lambda)$, $AP(DB^0, Q^0) \approx^s AP(DB^1, Q^1)$, *where* $\approx^s$ *denotes* $\mathsf{negl}(\lambda)$ *statistical distance.*
   If $AP(DB^0, Q^0), AP(DB^1, Q^1)$ *are only* computationally *indistinguishable, then we say the scheme is computationally secure.*

Definition 4 does not explicitly specify who runs the Setup procedure. It can be performed by the client, who then sends the server state st_S to the server S, or (to save on client computation) can be delegated to a trusted third party.

Remark on Hiding the Type of Operation. Notice that Definition 4 does not hide whether the performed operation is a read or a write, whereas an ORAM scheme is usually defined to hide this information. However, any such scheme can be generically made to hide the identity of operations by always performing both a read and a write. (Specifically, in a write operation, one first performs a dummy read; in a read operation, one writes back the value that was read.) Revealing the identity of operations allows us to obtain more fine-grained overheads.

Remark on Hiding Physical Memory Contents. The security property of Definition 4 implicitly assumes that the server does not see the *contents* of the physical memory: if the server is allowed to see it, he might be able to learn some nontrivial information regarding the access pattern, and thus violate the security property. As noted in Sect. 1.1, hiding the physical memory contents from the server can be achieved by encrypting the physical memory blocks, but security will then only hold against *computationally-bounded* servers, and so we choose to define security with the implicit assumption that the server does not see the memory contents (which also allows for cleaner constructions).

We will also consider the more restricted notion of a *Read-Only (RO) ORAM* scheme which, roughly, is an ORAM scheme that supports only read operations.

Definition 5 (Read-Only Oblivious RAM (RO-ORAM)). *A Read-Only Oblivious RAM (RO-ORAM) scheme consists of procedures (Setup, Read) with the same syntax as in Definition 4, in which correctness holds for any sequence of Read protocols between the client and the server, and security holds for any pair of access patterns R^0, R^1 that contain only read operations.*

3   Read-Only ORAM from Oblivious-Access Sort and Smooth LDCs

In this section we construct a Read-Only Oblivious RAM (RO-ORAM) scheme from oblivious-access sort algorithms and smooth LDCs. Concretely, we prove the following:

Theorem 5. *Suppose there exist:*

- *(k, n, M)-smooth LDCs with $M = \mathrm{poly}(n)$.*
- *An oblivious-access sort algorithm Sort with $s(n, \mathsf{B})$ overhead for input size n and block size B.*

Then there exists an RO-ORAM scheme for logical memory of size n and blocks of size $\mathsf{B} = \Omega\left(\lambda \cdot k^2 \cdot \log^3(kn) \log^7 \log(kn)\right)$ with $k + \frac{2k^2}{M} \cdot s(M, \mathsf{B}) + O(1)$ overhead, and $O(k)$ client storage.

Theorem 1 now follows from Theorem 5 (using also Theorem 4) for an appropriate instantiation of the sorting algorithm and LDC.

Corollary 1 (RO-ORAM, "dream" parameters; formal statement of Theorem 1). *Suppose there exist:*

- *(k, n, M)-smooth LDCs with $k = O(1)$ and $M = \text{poly}(n)$.*
- *Boolean sorting circuits $\{C(n, \mathsf{B})\}_{n,\mathsf{B}}$ of size $s(n, \mathsf{B}) = O(n \cdot \mathsf{B})$ for input size n and block size B.*

Then there exists an RO-ORAM scheme for logical memory of size n and blocks of size $\Omega\left(\lambda \cdot \log^4 n\right)$ with $O(\log \log n)$ overhead, and $O(1)$ client storage.

We also instantiate our construction with sorting algorithms and LDCs with more "conservative" parameters, to obtain the following corollary.

Corollary 2 (RO-ORAM, milder parameters). *Suppose there exist:*

- *(k, n, M)-smooth LDCs with $k = \text{poly} \log \log n$ and $M = \text{poly}(n)$.*
- *Boolean sorting circuits $\{C(n, \mathsf{B})\}_{n,\mathsf{B}}$ of size $s(n, \mathsf{B}) \in o\left(\frac{n \cdot \mathsf{B} \cdot \log n}{k^2}\right)$ for input size n and block size B.*

Then there exists an RO-ORAM scheme for memory of size n and blocks of size $\Omega\left(\lambda \cdot \log^4 n\right)$ with $= o(\log n)$ overhead, and $\text{poly} \log \log n$ client storage.

Construction Overview. As outlined in the introduction, our construction uses a (k, n, M)-smooth LDC. The server stores k codeword copies, each permuted using a unique uniformly random permutation. To read block j from the logical memory, the client runs the LDC decoder until the decoder generates a set of *fresh* decoding queries (i.e., a set $q_1, \ldots, q_k$ of queries such that for every $1 \leq i \leq k$, q_i was not issued before as the i'th query), and sends these queries to the server. The server uses the i'th permuted codeword copy to answer the i'th decoding query. The metadata regarding which decoding queries are fresh, as well as the description of the permutations, are stored on the server using a (polylogarithmic-overhead) ORAM scheme, which the client accesses to determine whether the decoder queries are fresh, and to permute them according to the random permutations.

The execution is divided into "epochs" consisting of $O(M/k)$ read operations. When an epoch ends, the client "refreshes" the permuted codeword copies by picking k fresh, random permutations, and running an oblivious-access sort algorithm with the server to permute the codeword copies stored on the server according to the new permutations. The description of the new permutations is stored in the metadata ORAM (the client also resets the bits indicating which decoding queries are fresh). The refreshing operations are spread-out across the $O(M/k)$ read operations of the epoch. The resultant increase in complexity depends on k (which determines the epoch length, i.e., the frequency in which refreshing is needed), and on the overhead of the oblivious-access sort algorithm.

Construction 1 (RO-ORAM from Oblivious-Access Sort and Smooth LDCs). The scheme uses the following building blocks:

- A $(k, n, M)_{\{0,1\}^B}$-smooth LDC $(\mathsf{Enc_{LDC}}, \mathsf{Query_{LDC}}, \mathsf{Dec_{LDC}})$.
- An oblivious-access sort algorithm Sort.
- An ORAM scheme $(\mathsf{Setup_{in}}, \mathsf{Read_{in}}, \mathsf{Write_{in}})$.

The scheme consists of the following procedures:

- **Setup**$(1^\lambda, \mathbf{DB})$: Recall that λ denotes the security parameter, and $\mathsf{DB} \in (\{0,1\}^B)^n$. Instantiate the LDC with message size n over alphabet $\Sigma = \{0,1\}^B$, and let k be the corresponding number of queries, and M be the corresponding codeword size. Proceed as follows.
  1. Counter initialization. Initializes a *step counter* $\mathsf{count} = 0$.
  2. Data storage generation.
     (a) Generate the codeword $\widetilde{\mathsf{DB}} = \mathsf{Enc_{LDC}}(\mathsf{DB})$ with $\widetilde{\mathsf{DB}} \in \Sigma^M$.
     (b) For every $1 \leq i \leq k$:
        - Generate a random permutation $P^i : [M] \to [M]$.
        - Let $\widetilde{\mathsf{DB}}^i \in \Sigma^M$ be a permuted version of the codeword which satisfies $\widetilde{\mathsf{DB}}^i_{P^i(j)} = \widetilde{\mathsf{DB}}_j$ for all $j \in [M]$.
  3. Metadata storage generation.
     (a) For every $1 \leq i \leq k$:
        - Initialize a length-M bit-array $\mathsf{Queried}^i$ to $\mathbf{0}$.
        - Initialize a length-M array Perm^i over $\{0,1\}^{\log M}$ such that $\mathsf{Perm}^i(j) = P^i(j)$.
     (b) Let mDB denote the logical memory obtained by concatenating $\mathsf{Queried}^1, \ldots, \mathsf{Queried}^k$ and $\mathsf{Perm}^1, \ldots, \mathsf{Perm}^k$. Run $(\mathsf{ck}_m, \mathsf{st}_m) \leftarrow \mathsf{Setup_{in}}(1^\lambda, \mathsf{mDB})$ to obtain the client key and server state for the metadata ORAM.
  4. Output. The long-term client key $\mathsf{ck} = \mathsf{ck}_m$ consists of the client key for the metadata ORAM. The server state $\mathsf{st}_S = \left(\left\{ \widetilde{\mathsf{DB}}^i : i \in [k] \right\}, \mathsf{st}_m, \mathsf{count} \right)$ contains the k permuted codewords, the server state for the metadata ORAM, and the step counter.

- **The Read protocol.** To read the logical memory block at location $\mathsf{addr} \in [n]$ from the server S, the client C with key $\mathsf{ck} = \mathsf{ck}_m$ operates as follows, where in all executions of the $\mathsf{Read_{in}}$ or $\mathsf{Write_{in}}$ protocols on mDB S plays the role of the server with state st_m and C plays the role of the client with key ck_m.
  1. Generating decoder queries. Repeat the following λ times:
     - Run $(q_1, \ldots, q_k) \leftarrow \mathsf{Query_{LDC}}(\mathsf{addr})$ to obtain decoding queries.
     - For every $1 \leq i \leq k$, run the $\mathsf{Read_{in}}$ protocol to read $\mathsf{Queried}^i[q_i]$. We say that q_i is *fresh* if $\mathsf{Queried}^i[q_i] = 0$.
     - Let $(\hat{q}_1, \ldots, \hat{q}_k)$ denote the decoding queries in the first iteration in which all queries were fresh. (If no such iteration exists, set $(\hat{q}_1, \ldots, \hat{q}_k)$ to be the decoding queries generated in the last iteration.)

2. Permuting queries. For every $1 \leq i \leq k$, run the $\mathsf{Read_{in}}$ protocol to read $\mathsf{Perm}^i[\hat{q}_i]$. Let q_i' denote the value that $\mathsf{Read_{in}}$ outputs to the client.

3. Decoding logical memory blocks. Read $\widetilde{\mathsf{DB}}^1_{q_1'}, \ldots, \widetilde{\mathsf{DB}}^k_{q_k'}$ from the server, and set the client output to $\mathsf{Dec_{LDC}}\left(\widetilde{\mathsf{DB}}^1_{q_1'}, \ldots, \widetilde{\mathsf{DB}}^k_{q_k'}\right)$.

4. Updating counter and server state. Let $\ell = \frac{M}{2k}$. Read count from the server.

   - If $\mathsf{count} < \ell - 1$, then update $\mathsf{count} := \mathsf{count} + 1$, and for every $1 \leq i \leq k$, run the $\mathsf{Write_{in}}$ protocol to write "1" to $\mathsf{Queried}^i[\hat{q}_i]$.
   - Otherwise, update $\mathsf{count} := 0$, and for every $1 \leq i \leq k$:
     - Run the $\mathsf{Write_{in}}$ protocol to write $\mathbf{0}$ to $\mathsf{Queried}^i$.
     - Replace P^i with a fresh random permutation on $[M]$ by running the Fisher-Yates shuffle algorithm (as presented by Durstenfeld [Dur64]) on Perm^i, using the $\mathsf{Read_{in}}$ and $\mathsf{Write_{in}}$ protocols.
     - Use Sort to sort $\widetilde{\mathsf{DB}}^i$ according to the new permutation P^i (each block consists of a codeword symbol, and the index in the codeword which is used as the tag of the block).

   If the complexity of these three steps is c_{epoch}, then the client performs c_{epoch}/ℓ steps of this computation in each protocol execution so that it is completed by the end of the epoch.

We prove the following claims about Construction 1.

Proposition 1 (ORAM security). *Assuming the security of all of the building blocks, Construction 1 is a secure RO-ORAM scheme.*

Proposition 2 (ORAM overhead). *Assume that:*

- *The logical memory DB has block size B, and the metadata ORAM has block size mB, satisfying $\mathsf{B} > \mathsf{mB} \geq \log M$.*
- *The metadata ORAM has overhead $\mathsf{Ovh}(N)$ for memory of size N.*
- *The oblivious-access sort algorithm has $\mathsf{Ovh_{Sort}}(n, \mathsf{B})$ overhead when operating on inputs consisting of n size-B blocks.*

Then every execution of the Read protocol in Construction 1 requires accessing

$$O\left(k\lambda + k^2\right) \cdot \mathsf{mB} \cdot \mathsf{Ovh}\left(\frac{k \cdot (M + M \log M)}{\mathsf{mB}}\right) + \left(k + \frac{2k^2}{M} \cdot \mathsf{Ovh_{Sort}}(M, \mathsf{B})\right) \cdot \mathsf{B}$$

words on the server.

Claims Imply Theorem. To prove Theorem 5, we instantiate the metadata ORAM of Construction 1 with the following variant of path ORAM [SvDS+13]:

Theorem 6 (Statistical ORAM with polylog overhead, implicit in [SvDS+13]). *Let λ be a security parameter. Then there exists a statistical*

ORAM scheme with negl (λ) *error for logical memory consisting of* N *blocks of size* mB $= \log^2 N \log \log N$ *with* $O(\log N)$ *overhead, in which the client stores* $O(\log N (\lambda + \log \log N))$ *blocks.*

Moreover, initializing the scheme requires accessing $O(N \cdot$ mB$)$ *words, and the server stores* $O(N)$ *blocks.*

Proof of Theorem 5. Security follows directly from Proposition 1 since (as noted in Sect. 2.1) the existence of a (k, n, M)-smooth LDC implies the existence of a $(k, n, M)_{\{0,1\}^B}$-smooth LDC.

As for the overhead of the construction, let $N_m = k(M + M \log M)$ denote the size (in bits) of the metadata ORAM. Substituting mB $= \log^2 N_m \log \log N_m$, and Ovh $(N) = O(\log N)$ (according to Theorem 6), Proposition 2 guarantees that every execution of the Read protocol requires accessing

$$O\left(k\lambda + k^2\right) \cdot \log^2 N_m \log \log N_m \cdot O\left(\log N_m\right) + \left(k + \frac{2k^2}{M} \cdot s\left(M, \mathsf{B}\right)\right) \cdot \mathsf{B}$$

words on the server. The first summand can be upped bounded by

$$k^2\lambda \cdot \log^2\left(kM\right) \log^3 \log\left(kM\right) \cdot O\left(\log\left(kM\right)\right) \leq k^2\lambda \cdot \log^3\left(kM\right) \log^3 \log\left(kM\right).$$

For B $= \Omega\left(\lambda \cdot k^2 \cdot \log^3\left(kn\right) \log^7 \log\left(kn\right)\right)$ (as in the theorem statement) with a sufficiently large constant in the $\Omega(\cdot)$ notation, and since $M = \text{poly}(n)$, this corresponds to accessing $O(\mathsf{B})$ words on the server, so the overhead is $k + \frac{2k^2}{M} \cdot s(M, \mathsf{B}) + O(1)$.

Finally, regarding client storage, emulating the LDC decoder requires storing k size-B blocks (i.e, the answers to the decoder queries). Operations on mDB require (by Theorem 6) storing $O(\log N_m (\lambda + \log \log N_m))$ size-mB blocks which corresponds to a constant number of size-B blocks. $\qquad\square$

Security Analysis: Proof of Proposition 1. The proof of Proposition 1 will use the next lemma, which states that with overwhelming probability, every Read protocol execution uses fresh decoding queries. This follows from the smoothness of the underlying LDC.

Lemma 1. *Let* $k, M \in \mathbb{N}$, *and let* $X = (X_1, \ldots, X_k)$ *be a random variable over* $[M]^k$ *such that for every* $1 \leq i \leq k$, X_i *is uniformly distributed over* $[M]$. *Let* $S_1, \ldots, S_k \subseteq [M]$ *be subsets of size at most* ℓ. *Then in* l *independent samples according to* X, *with probability at least* $1 - \left(k \cdot \frac{\ell}{M}\right)^l$, *there exists a sample* $(x_1, \ldots, x_k)$ *such that* $x_i \notin S_i$ *for every* $1 \leq i \leq k$.

In particular, if $\ell = \frac{M}{2k}$ *and* $l = \Omega(\lambda)$ *then except with probability* negl (λ), *there exists a sample* $(x_1, \ldots, x_k)$ *such that* $x_i \notin S_i$ *for every* $1 \leq i \leq k$.

Proof. Consider a sample $(x_1, \ldots, x_k)$ according to X. Since each X_i is uniformly distributed over $[M]$, then $\Pr[x_i \in S_i] \leq \frac{\ell}{M}$, so by the union bound, $\Pr[\exists i : x_i \in S_i] \leq k \cdot \frac{\ell}{M}$. Since the l samples are independent, the probability that no such sample exists is $(\Pr[\text{in a single sample}, \exists i : x_i \in S_i])^l \leq \left(k \cdot \frac{\ell}{M}\right)^l$. For the "in particular" part, notice that for $\ell = \frac{M}{2k}$ and $l = \Omega(\lambda)$, $1 - \left(k \cdot \frac{\ell}{M}\right)^l = 1 - 2^{-\Omega(\lambda)}$. $\qquad\square$

We are now ready to prove Proposition 1.

Proof of Proposition 1. The correctness of the scheme follows directly from the correctness of the underling LDC. We now argue security. Let DB^0, DB^1 be two logical memories consisting of n size-B blocks, and let R^0, R^1 be two sequences of read operations of length $q = \text{poly}(\lambda)$. We proceed via a sequence of hybrids. We assume that in each read operation, at least one iteration in the Read protocol succeeded in generating fresh decoder queries, and condition all hybrids on this event. This is without loss of generality since by Lemma 1, this happens with overwhelming probability.

$\mathcal{H}_0^b$: Hybrid $\mathcal{H}_0^b$ is the access pattern $\mathsf{AP}\left(\mathsf{DB}^b, R^b\right)$ in an execution of read sequence R^b on the RO-ORAM generated for logical memory DB^b.

$\mathcal{H}_1^b$: In hybrid $\mathcal{H}_1^b$, for every $1 \le i \le k$, we replace the values of $\mathsf{Queried}^i$ and Perm^i with dummy values of (e.g.,) the all-0 string. Moreover, we replace all read and write accesses to the metadata mDB with dummy operations that (e.g.,) read and write the all-0 string to the first location in the metadata. (We note that the accesses to the permuted codewords remain unchanged, where each access consists of fresh decoding queries, permuted according to $P^1, \ldots, P^k$.)

Hybrids $\mathcal{H}_0^b$ and $\mathcal{H}_1^b$ are statistically indistinguishable by the security of the metadata ORAM.

$\mathcal{H}_2^b$: In hybrid $\mathcal{H}_2^b$, for every $1 \le i \le k$, and every epoch j, we replace the permutation on which the oblivious-access sort algorithm Sort is applied, with a dummy permutation (e.g., the identity). (As in $\mathcal{H}_1^b$, the accesses to the codeword copies remain unchanged, and in particular the "right" permutations are used in all epochs.)

Hybrids $\mathcal{H}_1^b$ and $\mathcal{H}_2^b$ are statistically indistinguishable by the obliviousness property of the oblivious-access sort algorithm.

$\mathcal{H}_3^b$: In hybrid $\mathcal{H}_3^b$, for every $1 \le i \le k$, we replace the queries to the i'th permuted codeword with queries that are uniformly random subject to the constraint that they are all distinct.

Hybrids $\mathcal{H}_2^b$ and $\mathcal{H}_3^b$ are statistically indistinguishable since by our assumption all the queries sent to the codeword copies are fresh, and they are permuted using random permutations. (Notice that $\mathcal{H}_2^b, \mathcal{H}_3^b$ contain no additional information regarding these permutations.)

We conclude the proof by noting that $\mathcal{H}_3^0 \equiv \mathcal{H}_3^1$ since neither depend on $\mathsf{DB}^0, \mathsf{DB}^1, R^0$ or R^1. $\square$

Complexity Analysis: Proof of Proposition 2. We now analyze the complexity of Construction 1, proving Proposition 2. Notice that since $\mathsf{mB} \ge \log M$, an image of any random permutation $P^i : [M] \to [M]$ is contained in a single block of mDB. Notice also that the metadata mDB consists of $k \cdot (M + M \log M)$ bits, and let $N_m := \frac{k \cdot (M + M \log M)}{\mathsf{mB}}$ denote its size in size-mB blocks. Recall that a word (i.e., the basic unit of the physical memory stored on the server) consists of w bits.

Proof of Proposition 2. Every execution of the Read protocol consists of the following operations:

- Reading $k \cdot \lambda$ bits from mDB to check if the decoding queries in each of the λ iterations are fresh. Reading each bit requires reading a different block from mDB, which requires accessing $k\lambda \cdot \text{mB} \cdot \text{Ovh}(N_m)$ words on the server.
- Reading k images from $\text{Perm}^1, \ldots, \text{Perm}^k$ to permute the chosen decoding queries. This requires reading k blocks from mDB, which requires accessing $k \cdot \text{mB} \cdot \text{Ovh}(N_m)$ words on the server.
- Reading k blocks from the permuted codewords $\widetilde{\text{DB}}^1, \ldots, \widetilde{\text{DB}}^k$ to answer the decoder queries, which requires accessing $\frac{\text{B}}{w} \cdot k$ words on the server.
- Writing k bits to mDB to update the values $\text{Queried}^i [\hat{q}^i], 1 \le i \le k$, to 1, in total accessing $k \cdot \text{mB} \cdot \text{Ovh}(N_m)$ words on the server. (This operation is only performed when $\text{count} < \ell - 1$, but counting it in *every* Read execution will not increase the overall asymptotic complexity.)
- Updating the counter, which requires accessing $\frac{\lambda}{w}$ words on the server.

In total, these operations require accessing $O(k\lambda) \cdot \text{mB} \cdot \text{Ovh}(N_m) + k \cdot \frac{\text{B}}{w}$ words on the server.

In addition, every Read execution performs its "share" of the operations needed to update the server state at the end of the epoch. More specifically, it performs a $\frac{1}{\ell} = \frac{2k}{M}$-fraction of the following operations:

- Writing $k \cdot \frac{M}{\text{mB}}$ blocks to mDB to reset all entries of $\text{Queried}^i, 1 \le i \le k$, as well as reading and writing $k \cdot 2M$ blocks to mDB to update the entries of $\text{Perm}^i, 1 \le i \le k$ with the images of the new permutations, using the Fisher-Yates shuffle. In total, this requires accessing $k \cdot M \cdot \left(\frac{1}{\text{mB}} + 4\right) \cdot \text{mB} \cdot \text{Ovh}(N_m)$ words on the server.
- Running k executions of Sort on an input of M blocks of size B to re-permute the codeword copies, which requires accessing $k \cdot \text{Ovh}_{\text{Sort}}(M, \text{B})$ words on the server.

So these update operations require accessing $O(k^2) \cdot \text{mB} \cdot \text{Ovh}(N_m) + \frac{2k^2}{M} \cdot \text{B} \cdot \text{Ovh}_{\text{Sort}}(M, \text{B})$ words on the server per execution of the Read protocol.

In summary, reading a single logical block from DB requires accessing $O(k\lambda + k^2) \cdot \text{mB} \cdot \text{Ovh}\left(\frac{k \cdot (M + M \log M)}{\text{mB}}\right) + \left(\frac{k}{w} + \frac{2k^2}{M} \cdot \text{Ovh}_{\text{Sort}}(M, \text{B})\right) \cdot \text{B}$ words on the server.

3.1 Read-Only ORAM with Oblivious Setup

In this section we generalize the notion of an RO-ORAM scheme to allow the client to run the ORAM Setup algorithm, using the server as remote storage, when the logical memory is already stored at the server. We call this primitive an *RO-ORAM scheme with oblivious setup*. This primitive will be used in the next section to construct an ORAM scheme supporting writes with low read overhead.

At a high level, an RO-ORAM scheme with oblivious setup is an RO-ORAM scheme (Setup, Read) associated with an additional protocol OblSetup which allows the client to execute the Setup algorithm using the server as remote storage when the logical memory is already stored on the server, where the execution is oblivious in the sense that the scheme remains secure when the RO-ORAM is generated using OblSetup instead of Setup.

In the full version [WW18] we formalize this notion, and show that the RO-ORAM scheme of Construction 1 has oblivious setup. The oblivious setup protocol relies on the building blocks of Construction 1, and additionally uses a CPA-secure symmetric encryption scheme (whose existence follows from the existence of OWFs). The high-level idea is conceptually simple. The client first encrypts the logical memory, then generates the codeword copies by encoding the *encrypted* logical memory. This can be done by running the encoding procedure of the LDC "in the clear" (using the server as remote storage), because by the CPA-security of the encryption scheme, the access pattern of the encoding procedure reveals no information on the logical memory. (Indeed, the access pattern might depend on the *values of the ciphertexts*, but those are computationally indistinguishable from encryptions of 0.) Then, the client can use an "empty" metadata (initialized to 0) to generate his keys for the metadata ORAM, and update its contents by running the Write protocol of the metadata ORAM together with the server. Finally, the codeword copies can be obliviously permuted using the oblivious-access sort algorithm. This high-level intuition is formalized in the full version [WW18], where we prove the following:

Lemma 2 (RO-ORAM with oblivious setup). *Assuming OWFs, and assuming the security of the building blocks of Construction 1, there exists a computationally-secure RO-ORAM scheme with oblivious setup. Moreover, if:*

- *the logical memory DB has block size B, and the metadata ORAM has block size mB, satisfying $B > mB \geq \log M$,*
- *the metadata ORAM has Ovh (N) overhead for memories of size N, and its setup algorithm can be executed using the server as remote storage by accessing $T_m(N)$ words on the server, where the client (server) stores s_C (s_S) size-mB blocks,*
- *the oblivious-access sort algorithm has Ovh$_{\mathsf{Sort}}(n, B)$ overhead when operating on inputs consisting of n size-B blocks,*
- *the LDC has query complexity k, codeword length M, and on messages of length n its encoding procedure performs $T_{LDC}(n)$ operations (i.e., touches $T_{LDC}(n)$ message symbols),*

then the OblSetup protocol accesses

$$\lambda + T_m\left(\frac{k(M + M\log M)}{mB}\right) + 2n \cdot \frac{B}{w} + T_{LDC}(n) \cdot \frac{B}{w} + kM \cdot \frac{B}{w}$$

$$+ \left(\frac{kM}{mB} + kM\right) \cdot mB \cdot \mathsf{Ovh}\left(\frac{k(M + M\log M)}{mB}\right) + k \cdot B \cdot \mathsf{Ovh}_{\mathsf{Sort}}(n, B)$$

words on the server, where w denotes the word size. Moreover, the client stores $s_C \cdot \frac{mB}{B}$ size-B blocks, and the server stores $n + kM + s_S \cdot \frac{mB}{B} + \lambda$ size-B blocks.

A Note on Statistically-Secure RO-ORAM with Oblivious Setup. Our RO-ORAM with oblivious setup scheme is computationally-secure, even assuming the server does not see the memory contents. This is due to the fact that the access pattern during LDC-encoding might depend on the contents of the message being encoded, which in our case is the encrypted contents of the logical memory. Since the encryptions of two logical memories are only computationally indistinguishable, the resultant security is computational. We note that using an LDC with additional properties, we can obtain a *statistically-secure* RO-ORAM scheme with oblivious setup. Concretely, if the LDC encoding procedure is oblivious in the sense that its access pattern is independent of the contents of the message being encrypted (a property satisfied by, e.g., linear codes) then one can run the LDC encoding procedure on the logical memory itself, and encryption is not needed. Similarly, if the LDC has a sufficiently small encoding *circuit*, then encoding can be performed directly on the (un-encrypted) logical memory.

4   Oblivious RAM Supporting Writes with $o(\log n)$ Read Complexity

In this section we extend the RO-ORAM scheme of Sect. 3 to support writes, while preserving the overhead of read operations. We instantiate our construction in several parameter regimes, obtaining the following results (see the full version [WW18] for the proofs).

First, by instantiating our construction with "best possible" sorting circuits and LDCs, we prove Theorem 2:

Theorem 7 (ORAM, "dream" parameters; formal statement of Theorem 2). *Assume the existence of OWFs, as well as LDCs and sorting circuits as in Corollary 1, where the LDC has the following additional properties:*

- *$M = n^{1+\delta}$ for some $\delta \in (0, 1)$.*
- *Encoding requires $M^{1+\gamma}$ operations over size-B blocks, for some $\gamma \in (0, 1)$.*

*Then there exists an ORAM scheme for memories of size n and blocks of size $B = \Omega\left(\lambda \cdot \log^3 n \log^7 \log n\right)$ with $O(1)$ client storage, where **read** operations have $O(\log \log n)$ overhead, and **write** operations have $O(n^\epsilon)$ overhead for any constant $\epsilon \in (0, 1)$ such that $\epsilon > \delta + \gamma + \delta\gamma$.*

Using milder assumptions regarding the parameters of the underlying sorting circuit and LDC, we can prove the following:

Theorem 8 (ORAM, milder parameters). *Assume the existence of OWFs, as well as LDCs and sorting circuits as in Corollary 2, where the LDC has the additional properties specified in Theorem 7. Then there exists an ORAM scheme for memories of size n and blocks of size $B = \Omega\left(\lambda \cdot \log^3 n \log^7 \log n\right)$*

with poly log log n *client storage, where* **read** *operations have* $o(\log n)$ *overhead, and* **write** *operations have* $O(n^\epsilon)$ *overhead for any constant* $\epsilon \in (0, 1)$ *such that* $\epsilon > \delta + \gamma + \delta\gamma$.

Finally, we also obtain a scheme with improved write overhead, by somewhat strengthening the assumptions regarding the LDC.

Theorem 9 (ORAM, low write overhead; formal statement of Theorem 3). *Assume the existence of OWFs, as well as LDCs and sorting circuits as in Corollary 1, where the LDC has the following additional properties:*

- $M = n^{1+o(1)}$.
- *Encoding requires* $M^{1+o(1)}$ *operations over size-B blocks.*

Then there exists an ORAM scheme for memories of size n and blocks of size $\mathsf{B} = \Omega\left(\lambda \cdot \log^3 n \log^7 \log n\right)$ *with* $O(1)$ *client storage, where* **read** *operations have* $o(\log n)$ *overhead, and* **write** *operations have* $n^{o(1)}$ *overhead.*

Construction Overview. As outlined in Sect. 1.2, the ORAM consists of ℓ levels of increasing size (growing from top to bottom), where initially the logical memory is stored in the lowest level, and all other levels are empty. read operations look for the memory block in all levels, returning the top-most copy of the block, and write operations write the memory block to the top-most level, causing a reshuffle at predefined intervals to prevent levels from overflowing.

Transforming this high-level intuition into an actual scheme requires some adjustments. First, our RO-ORAM scheme[4] was designed for logical memories given as array data structures (namely, in which blocks can only be accessed by specifying the location of the block in the logical memory), but upper levels are too small to contain the entire logical memory, namely they require RO-ORAM schemes for *map data structure*.[5] To overcome this issue, we associate with each level i an array $\mathcal{DB}^i$ that contains the memory blocks of level i, and is stored in an RO-ORAM $\mathcal{O}^i$ (for array data structures). Additionally, we store the metadata regarding which block appears in which array location in a (standard, polylogarithmic-overhead) ORAM $\mathcal{MO}^i$ for map structures. Thus, to look for block j in level i, the client first searches for j in $\mathcal{MO}^i$. If the j'th memory block appears in level i, then $\mathcal{MO}^i$ returns the location t in which it appears in $\mathcal{DB}^i$, and so the client can read the block by performing a read for address t on the RO-ORAM $\mathcal{O}^i$ of the level.

Second, to allow for efficient "reshuffling" of level i (which, in particular, requires a traversal of both $\mathcal{DB}^i$ and $\mathcal{DB}^{i+1}$), we also store $\mathcal{DB}^i$ in every level i. Thus, every level i contains the array $\mathcal{DB}^i$, the metadata ORAM $\mathcal{MO}^i$ which

---

[4] The construction can use any RO-ORAM scheme, but the read overhead is at least the overhead of the RO-ORAM scheme. Therefore, to obtain $o(\log n)$ overhead, we need to instantiate the ORAM with our RO-ORAM scheme.

[5] We note that several ORAM schemes (such as tree-based ORAM schemes, and in particular the ORAM of Theorem 6), though described for logical memories given as arrays, can actually support logical memories given as map data structures.

maps blocks to their locations in $\mathcal{DB}^i$, and the RO-ORAM $\mathcal{O}^i$ which stores $\mathcal{DB}^i$. We note that the metadata ORAM is not needed in the lowest level, because the structure will preserve the invariant that $\mathcal{DB}^\ell$ contains all the blocks "in order" (namely, the k'th block of the logical memory is the k'th block of $\mathcal{DB}^\ell$).

Finally, every "reshuffle" of level i into level $i + 1$ requires re-generation of the RO-ORAM $\mathcal{O}^{i+1}$, since the contents of $\mathcal{DB}^{i+1}$ have changed. In general, re-generation cannot use the setup algorithm of the RO-ORAM due to two reasons. First, the setup is designed to be run by a trusted party, and so the server cannot run it, and since setup depends on the entire logical memory, it is too costly for the client to run on his own. Second, while the setup of an RO-ORAM is only required to be polynomial-time (since it is only executed once, and so its cost is amortized over sufficiently many accesses to the RO-ORAM), when executed repeatedly as part of reshuffle, a more stringent efficiency requirement is needed. The first property is captured by the ORAM with oblivious setup primitive (Sect. 3.1). For the second property we use the fact that our RO-ORAM scheme described in Sect. 3 has a highly-efficient oblivious setup protocol.

Given these building blocks, the ORAM operates as follows. To read the j'th logical memory block, the client looks for the block in every level. At the lowest level ℓ, which contains the entire logical memory, this is done by reading the block at address j from $\mathcal{O}^\ell$. For all other levels $1 \le i < \ell$, this is done by first reading j from $\mathcal{MO}^i$ to check whether the j'th memory block appears in $\mathcal{DB}^i$, and if so in which index t; and then using $\mathcal{O}^i$ to read the t'th block of $\mathcal{DB}^i$. (If the j'th block does not appear in $\mathcal{DB}^i$, a dummy read is performed on $\mathcal{O}^i$.) The output is the copy of block j from $\mathcal{DB}^{i^*}$ for the smallest level i^* such that $\mathcal{DB}^{i^*}$ contains the j'th memory block. This is the "correct" answer because the levels preserve the invariant that each level contains at most one copy of each logical memory block, and the most recent copy appears in the top-most level that contains the block.

To write value v to the block at address j, the client asks the server to write a new copy of block j with value v to the top level. As noted above, this causes a reshuffle into lower levels at predefined intervals to prevent levels from overflowing. More specifically, every l_i write operations level i will be reshuffled into level $i + 1$, where l_i denotes the size of level i. During reshuffle, all memory blocks from $\mathcal{DB}^i$ are copied into $\mathcal{DB}^{i+1}$, and multiple copies of the same memory block are consolidated by storing the level-i copy. Additionally, the ORAMs $\mathcal{MO}^{i+1}, \mathcal{O}^{i+1}$ of level $i + 1$ are updated, and level i is emptied (that is, $\mathcal{DB}^i$ is replaced with an empty array, and $\mathcal{MO}^i, \mathcal{O}^i$ are updated accordingly). See Figs. 2 and 4 for an example.

Instantiating this ORAM scheme with different values of the number of levels ℓ yields ORAM schemes with different tradeoffs between the read and write overhead. Concretely, Theorems 7 and 8 are obtained by setting ℓ to be constant, and Theorem 9 is obtained by setting $\ell = \frac{\log n}{\log^2 \log n}$.

We now formally describe the construction.

Construction 2 (ORAM with writes). The scheme uses the following building blocks:

- An RO-ORAM scheme with oblivious setup $(\mathsf{Setup}_R, \mathsf{Read}_R, \mathsf{OblSetup}_R)$.
- An ORAM scheme $(\mathsf{Setup}_m, \mathsf{Read}_m, \mathsf{Write}_m)$ for map data structures.

We define the following protocols.

- **Setup**$(1^\lambda, \mathbf{DB})$: Recall that λ denotes the security parameter, and $\mathsf{DB} \in (\{0,1\}^B)^n$. Setup does the following.
  - Initialize a writes counter. Initialize a writes counter count to 0.
  - Initialize lowest level.
    - Initialize $\mathcal{DB}^\ell = \mathsf{DB}$. We assume without loss of generality that the blocks in DB are of the form (j, b_j), namely each logical memory block contains its logical address.[6]
    - Generate an RO-ORAM scheme $\mathcal{O}^\ell$ for $\mathcal{DB}^\ell$ by running $\left(\mathsf{ck}_R^\ell, \mathsf{st}_R^\ell\right) \leftarrow$ $\mathsf{Setup}_R\left(1^\lambda, \mathcal{DB}^\ell\right)$ to obtain a client key ck_R^ℓ and a server state st_R^ℓ for $\mathcal{O}^\ell$.
  - Initialize upper levels. For every level $1 \le i < \ell$:
    - Initialize $\mathcal{DB}^i$ to consist of i dummy memory blocks.
    - Generate an RO-ORAM scheme $\mathcal{O}^i$ for $\mathcal{DB}^i$ by running $(\mathsf{ck}_R^i, \mathsf{st}_R^i) \leftarrow$ $\mathsf{Setup}_R\left(1^\lambda, \mathcal{DB}^i\right)$ to obtain a client key ck_R^i and a server state st_R^i for $\mathcal{O}^i$.
    - Generate a map data structure $\mathcal{M}^i$ mapping each block (j, b_j) in $\mathcal{DB}^i$ to its index in $\mathcal{DB}^i$. (That is, if (j, b_j) is the t'th block of $\mathcal{DB}^i$ then the entry (t, j) is added to $\mathcal{M}^i$.)
    - Generate a metadata ORAM scheme $\mathcal{MO}^i$ for $\mathcal{M}^i$, by running $(\mathsf{ck}_m^i, \mathsf{st}_m^i) \leftarrow \mathsf{Setup}_m\left(1^\lambda, \mathcal{M}^i\right)$ to obtain the client key and server state for $\mathcal{MO}^i$.
  - Output. The long-term client key $\mathsf{ck} = \left(\mathsf{ck}_R^\ell, \{\mathsf{ck}_R^i, \mathsf{ck}_m^i\}_{i \in [\ell-1]}\right)$ consists of the client keys for the RO-ORAMs $\mathcal{O}^i$ and the metadata ORAMs $\mathcal{MO}^i$ of all levels. The server state $\mathsf{st}_S = \left(\mathsf{count}, \mathsf{st}_R^\ell, \mathcal{DB}^\ell, \{\mathsf{st}_R^i, \mathsf{st}_m^i, \mathcal{DB}^i\}_{i \in [\ell-1]}\right)$ contains the counter count of the number of write operations performed, the server states in the RO-ORAMs $\mathcal{O}^i$ and the metadata ORAMs $\mathcal{MO}^i$ of all levels, as well as the memory contents $\mathcal{DB}^i$ of all levels.

---

[6] This assumption is without loss of generality since for the block sizes we consider, concatenating the address to the block would cause at most a constant multiplicative increase in the block size.

The ReShuffle$^\ell$ procedure

Inputs:

$\mathsf{ck}_R^j, j \in \{\ell - 1, \ell\}$: the client keys for the RO-ORAMs $\mathcal{O}^{\ell-1}, \mathcal{O}^\ell$ of levels $\ell - 1, \ell$.
$\mathsf{ck}_m^{\ell-1}$: the client key for the metadata ORAM $\mathcal{MO}^{\ell-1}$ of level $\ell - 1$.
$\mathsf{st}_R^j, j \in \{\ell - 1, \ell\}$: the server states for the RO-ORAMs $\mathcal{O}^{\ell-1}, \mathcal{O}^\ell$ of levels $\ell-1, \ell$.
$\mathsf{st}_m^{\ell-1}$: the server state for the metadata ORAM $\mathcal{MO}^{\ell-1}$ of level $\ell - 1$.

Operation:

- Updating contents of level ℓ. For every $1 \leq k \leq n$:
  - Read the k'th block (k, v_k) of $\mathcal{DB}^\ell$.
  - Run the Read_m protocol (with client key $\mathsf{ck}_m^{\ell-1}$ and server state $\mathsf{st}_m^{\ell-1}$) on $\mathcal{MO}^{\ell-1}$ to read the index t in which memory block k appears in $\mathcal{DB}^{\ell-1}$. (If memory block k does not appear in $\mathcal{DB}^{\ell-1}$ then Read_m returns $\bot$ to the client.)
  - Run the Read_R protocol (with client key $\mathsf{ck}_R^{\ell-1}$ and server state $\mathsf{st}_R^{\ell-1}$) on $\mathcal{O}^{\ell-1}$ to read the value v'_k of the t'th block in $\mathcal{DB}^{\ell-1}$. (If $t = \bot$, perform a dummy read of the block at index 1.)
  - If $t \neq \bot$, replace the k'th block in $\mathcal{DB}^\ell$ with (k, v'_k). Otherwise, replace the k'th block with (k, v_k) (this is a dummy write).
- Updating RO-ORAMs. Replace $\mathcal{DB}^{\ell-1}$ with an array consisting of $l_{\ell-1}$ dummy blocks. For $j = \ell - 1, \ell$, run the $\mathsf{OblSetup}_R$ protocol to generate a new RO-ORAM $\mathcal{O}^j$ for $\mathcal{DB}^j$: $\left(\widetilde{\mathsf{ck}}_R^j, \widetilde{\mathsf{st}}_R^j\right) \leftarrow \mathsf{OblSetup}_R\left(1^\lambda, \mathcal{DB}^j\right)$. Replace $\mathsf{ck}_R^j, \mathsf{st}_R^j$ with $\widetilde{\mathsf{ck}}_R^j, \widetilde{\mathsf{st}}_R^j$, respectively.
- Updating metadata ORAM. For every $1 \leq k \leq l_{\ell-1}$:
  - Read the k'th block (j, v_j) of $\mathcal{DB}^{\ell-1}$.
  - Remove the entry corresponding to k from $\mathcal{M}^{\ell-1}$ by executing the Write_m protocol on $\mathcal{MO}^{\ell-1}$ (with client key $\mathsf{ck}_m^{\ell-1}$ and server state $\mathsf{st}_m^{\ell-1}$).

Fig. 1. The ReShuffle$^\ell$ protocol used in Construction 2

The Read protocol. To read the logical memory block at location $\mathsf{addr} \in [n]$ from the server S, the client C with key $\left(\mathsf{ck}_R^\ell, \left\{\mathsf{ck}_R^i, \mathsf{ck}_m^i\right\}_{i \in [\ell-1]}\right)$ operates as follows, where in all executions of the Read_R protocol on $\mathcal{O}^i$ (respectively, all executions of the Read_m or Write_m protocols on $\mathcal{MO}^i$) S plays the role of the server with state st_R^i (respectively, st_m^i) and C plays the role of the client with key ck_R^i (respectively, ck_m^i).

- Determine block location in level i. For every level $1 \leq i \leq \ell - 1$, run the Read_m protocol on $\mathcal{MO}^i$ to read the index l in which the block appears in $\mathcal{DB}^i$. (If block addr does not appear in level i, then $l = \bot$.)
- Read block from level i. For every $1 \leq i \leq \ell - 1$, if $l = \bot$, set $l = 1$. Run the Read_R protocol on $\mathcal{O}^i$ to read the l'th block from $\mathcal{DB}^i$.
- Read block from level ℓ. Run the Read_R protocol on $\mathcal{O}^\ell$ to read the addr'th block from $\mathcal{DB}^\ell$.

– Output. Let i^* be the smallest such that block addr appears in $\mathcal{DB}^{i^*}$, and let $\overline{(\text{addr}, v)}$ denote the block returned by the execution of the Read_R protocol on $\mathcal{O}^{i^*}$. Output v to C. (All other memory blocks returned by the Read_R protocol executions are ignored.)

The Write protocol. To write value val to block addr $\in [n]$ in the logical memory, the client C with key $\left(\text{ck}_R^\ell, \{\text{ck}_R^i, \text{ck}_m^i\}_{i \in [\ell-1]}\right)$ operates as follows.

– Generate a "dummy" level 0 which contains a single memory block $(\text{addr}, \text{val})$, and send it to the server.
– Update the server state and client key as follows:
  • count := count + 1.
  • If $l_{\ell-1}$ divides count, then reshuffle level $\ell - 1$ into level ℓ using the ReShuffle$^\ell$ procedure of Fig. 1, namely execute ReShuffle$^\ell\left(\text{ck}_R^{\ell-1}, \text{ck}_R^\ell, \text{ck}_m^{\ell-1}, \text{st}_R^{\ell-1}, \text{st}_R^\ell, \text{st}_m^{\ell-1}\right)$.

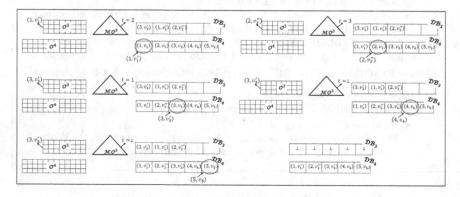

Fig. 2. ReShuffle$^\ell$ execution on a toy-example ORAM with logical memory size $n = 5$ and $\ell = 4$ levels. The red circle indicates the block which is currently updated. Arrows denote the output of the metadata and RO ORAMs, where dashes arrows denote dummy accesses. Block 1 is updated first (top left), $\mathcal{MO}^3$ is accessed and returns $t = 2$ indicating that block 1 appears as the second block of $\mathcal{DB}^3$. The block $(1, v_1')$ is then read from $\mathcal{O}^3$, and updated in $\mathcal{DB}^4$. Block 2 is updated next (top right), $\mathcal{MO}^3$ is accessed and returns $t = 3$ indicating that block 2 appears as the third block of $\mathcal{DB}^3$. The block $(2, v_2'')$ is then read from $\mathcal{O}^3$, and updated in $\mathcal{DB}^4$. Block 3 is updated next (center left), $\mathcal{MO}^3$ is accessed and returns $t = 1$ indicating that block 3 appears as the first block of $\mathcal{DB}^3$. The block $(3, v_3')$ is then read from $\mathcal{O}^3$, and updated in $\mathcal{DB}^4$. Block 4 is updated next (center right), $\mathcal{MO}^3$ is accessed and returns $t = \perp$, indicating that block 4 does not appear in $\mathcal{DB}^3$. Therefore, a dummy read is performed on $\mathcal{O}^3$, and a dummy write is performed on $\mathcal{DB}^4$. Finally, block 5 is updated (bottom left), $\mathcal{MO}^3$ is accessed and returns $t = \perp$, indicating that block 5 does not appear in $\mathcal{DB}^3$. Therefore, a dummy read is performed on $\mathcal{O}^3$, and a dummy write is performed on $\mathcal{DB}^4$. The values of $\mathcal{DB}^3, \mathcal{DB}^4$ at the end of the ReShuffle$^\ell$ execution are depicted at the bottom right (these values are used to generate new RO-ORAMs $\mathcal{O}^3, \mathcal{O}^4$, and update the metadata ORAMs $\mathcal{MO}^3, \mathcal{MO}^4$).

The ReShuffle procedure

Inputs:

i: the index of a level to reshuffle.

$\mathsf{ck}_R^j, j \in \{i, i+1\}$: the client keys for the RO-ORAMs $\mathcal{O}^i, \mathcal{O}^{i+1}$ of levels $i, i+1$.

$\mathsf{ck}_m^j, j \in \{i, i+1\}$: the client keys for the metadata ORAMs $\mathcal{MO}^i, \mathcal{MO}^{i+1}$ of levels $i, i+1$.

$\mathsf{st}_R^j, j \in \{i, i+1\}$: the server states for the RO-ORAMs $\mathcal{O}^i, \mathcal{O}^{i+1}$ of levels $i, i+1$.

$\mathsf{st}_m^j, j \in \{i, i+1\}$: the server states for the metadata ORAMs $\mathcal{MO}^i, \mathcal{MO}^{i+1}$ of levels $i, i+1$.

Operation:

- Let $m = \mathsf{count} \mod l_{i+1}$. (Notice that level $i+1$ contains at most m elements.)
- Updating level-$(i+1)$ blocks. For every $1 \le k \le m$:
  1. Read the k'th block (j, v_j) from $\mathcal{DB}^{i+1}$.
  2. Run the Read_m protocol (with client key ck_m^i and server state st_m^i) on $\mathcal{MO}^i$ to read the index t in which memory block j appears in $\mathcal{DB}^i$. (If memory block j does not appear in $\mathcal{DB}^i$ then Read_m returns $\bot$ to the client.)
  3. Run the Read_R protocol (with client key ck_R^i and server state st_R^i) on $\mathcal{O}^i$ to read the value v'_j of the t'th block in $\mathcal{DB}^i$. (If $t - \bot$, perform a dummy read to the block at index 1.)
  4. If $t \ne \bot$, replace the k'th block in $\mathcal{DB}^{i+1}$ with (j, v'_j). Otherwise, replace the k'th block with (j, v_j) (this is a dummy write).
  5. If $t \ne \bot$, remove the entry corresponding to t from $\mathcal{M}^i$ by executing the Write_m protocol on $\mathcal{MO}^i$. Otherwise, perform a dummy write to $\mathcal{MO}^i$, writing back the entry corresponding to t that was read in step 2.
- Copying level-i blocks that were not in $\mathcal{DB}^{i+1}$. Initialize a counter count' to $m+1$. For every $1 \le k \le l_i$:
  1. Read the k'th block (j, v_j) of $\mathcal{DB}^i$.
  2. Run the Read_m protocol (with client key ck_m^i and server state st_m^i) on $\mathcal{MO}^i$ to read the index t in which memory block j appears in $\mathcal{DB}^i$. (This step checks whether the k'th block has been deleted from $\mathcal{DB}^i$ in the previous step. If so, then Read_m returns $\bot$ to the client.)
  3. If $t \ne \bot$, write (j, v_j) as the count''th block of $\mathcal{DB}^{i+1}$. Otherwise, write a dummy block as the count''th block of $\mathcal{DB}^{i+1}$.
  4. If $t \ne \bot$, run the Write_m protocol (with client key ck_m^{i+1} and server state st_m^{i+1}) to write (count', j) to $\mathcal{MO}^{i+1}$. Otherwise, perform a dummy write to $\mathcal{MO}^{i+1}$.
  5. If $t \ne \bot$, remove the entry corresponding to t from $\mathcal{M}^i$ by executing the Write_m protocol on $\mathcal{MO}^i$. Otherwise, perform a dummy write to $\mathcal{MO}^i$.
  6. Update the counter: $\mathsf{count}' := \mathsf{count}' + 1$.
- Updating level ORAMs. Replace $\mathcal{DB}^i$ with an array consisting of l_i dummy blocks. For $j = i, i+1$, run the $\mathsf{OblSetup}_R$ protocol to generate a new RO-ORAM $\mathcal{O}^j$ for $\mathcal{DB}^j$: $\left(\widetilde{\mathsf{ck}}_R^j, \widetilde{\mathsf{st}}_R^j \right) \leftarrow \mathsf{OblSetup}_R \left(1^\lambda, \mathcal{DB}^j \right)$. Replace $\mathsf{ck}_R^j, \mathsf{st}_R^j$ with $\widetilde{\mathsf{ck}}_R^j, \widetilde{\mathsf{st}}_R^j$, respectively.

Fig. 3. The ReShuffle protocol used in Construction 2

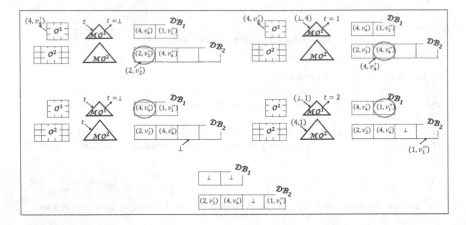

Fig. 4. ReShuffle execution for $i = 1$ on the ORAM from Fig. 2. The red circle indicates the block which is currently updated. Arrows denote the output of the metadata and RO ORAMs, where dashes arrows denote dummy accesses. The blocks of $\mathcal{DB}^2$ are updated first. The first block of $\mathcal{DB}^2$ is updated first (top left), $\mathcal{MO}^1$ is accessed and returns $t = \perp$ indicating that this block does not appear in $\mathcal{DB}^1$. Therefore, a dummy read is performed on $\mathcal{O}^1$, and dummy writes are performed on $\mathcal{MO}^1, \mathcal{DB}^2$. The second block of $\mathcal{DB}^2$ is updated next (top right), $\mathcal{MO}^1$ is accessed and returns $t = 1$ indicating that this block appears as the first block of $\mathcal{DB}^1$. The block $(4, v_4')$ is then read from $\mathcal{O}^1$, and updated in $\mathcal{DB}^2$. Then, the block is deleted from $\mathcal{DB}^1$ by updating $\mathcal{MO}^1$ (replacing the entry $(1,4)$ with $(\perp,4)$). Next, the blocks of $\mathcal{DB}^1$ are copied into $\mathcal{DB}^2$. The first block of $\mathcal{DB}^1$ is copied first. $\mathcal{MO}^1$ is accessed and returns $t = \perp$, indicating that this block was already copied into $\mathcal{DB}^2$ (and removed from $\mathcal{DB}^1$). Therefore, a dummy block is written to $\mathcal{DB}^2$, and dummy writes are performed on $\mathcal{MO}^1, \mathcal{MO}^2$. Finally, the second block of $\mathcal{DB}^1$ is copied. $\mathcal{MO}^1$ is accessed and returns $t = 2$, indicating that the block has not been removed from $\mathcal{DB}^1$. The block is then written into $\mathcal{DB}^2$, $\mathcal{MO}^2$ is updated to reflect that block 1 appears as the fourth block of $\mathcal{DB}^2$, and the block is deleted from $\mathcal{DB}^1$ by updating $\mathcal{MO}^1$ accordingly. The values of $\mathcal{DB}^1, \mathcal{DB}^2$ at the end of the ReShuffle execution are depicted at the bottom (these values are used to generate new RO-ORAMs $\mathcal{O}^1, \mathcal{O}^2$).

- For every i from $\ell - 2$ down to 0 for which l_i divides count, reshuffle level i into level $i + 1$ using the ReShuffle procedure of Fig. 3, namely execute ReShuffle $\left(i, \mathsf{ck}_R^i, \mathsf{ck}_R^{i+1}, \mathsf{ck}_m^i, \mathsf{ck}_m^{i+1}, \mathsf{st}_R^i, \mathsf{st}_R^{i+1}, \mathsf{st}_m^i, \mathsf{st}_m^{i+1}\right)$.

Remark on De-amortization. We note that using a technique of Ostrovsky and Shoup [OS97], the server complexity in Construction 2 can be de-amortized, by slightly modifying the Write protocol to allow the reshuffling process to be *spread-out* over multiple accesses to the ORAM. The reason reshuffle operations can be "spread out" is that reshuffling is performed in a "bottom-up" fashion, namely when it is time to reshuffle level i into level $i + 1$, that reshuffling is executed *before* level $i - 1$ is reshuffled into level i. Thus, the memory blocks that are involved in the reshuffle of level i into level $i + 1$ have been known for the last l_{i-1} time units, ever since level i was last updated due to a reshuffle of level $i - 1$ into it. Therefore, the operations needed to perform the reshuffle of level i into level $i + 1$ can be spread out over l_{i-1} operations.

A Note on Statistically-Secure ORAM with Writes. Our ORAM with writes constructions (Theorems 7–9) are computationally-secure due to the use of a computationally-secure RO-ORAM with oblivious setup. However, given a *statistically-secure* RO-ORAM with oblivious setup the resultant ORAM with writes would also be statistically secure. As noted in Sect. 3.1, such a scheme can be obtained assuming an LDC with a small encoding circuit, or with an oblivious encoding procedure. Thus, given an LDC with one of these additional properties we can get a statistically-secure ORAM with writes (with the parameters stated in Theorems 7–9).

Acknowledgements. Research supported by NSF grants CNS-1314722, CNS-1413964, CNS-1750795 and the Alfred P. Sloan Research Fellowship. The first author was supported in part by The Eric and Wendy Schmidt Postdoctoral Grant for Women in Mathematical and Computing Sciences.

References

[AFN+17] Abraham, I., Fletcher, C.W., Nayak, K., Pinkas, B., Ren, L.: Asymptotically tight bounds for composing ORAM with PIR. In: Fehr, S. (ed.) PKC 2017. LNCS, vol. 10174, pp. 91–120. Springer, Heidelberg (2017). https://doi.org/10.1007/978-3-662-54365-8_5

[AKS83] Ajtai, M., Komlós, J., Szemerédi, E.: An $O(n \log n)$ sorting network. In: Proceedings of the 15th Annual ACM Symposium on Theory of Computing, 25–27 April 1983, pp. 1–9 (1983)

[AKST14] Apon, D., Katz, J., Shi, E., Thiruvengadam, A.: Verifiable oblivious storage. In: Krawczyk, H. (ed.) PKC 2014. LNCS, vol. 8383, pp. 131–148. Springer, Heidelberg (2014). https://doi.org/10.1007/978-3-642-54631-0_8

[BCP15] Boyle, E., Chung, K.-M., Pass, R.: Large-scale secure computation: multiparty computation for (parallel) RAM programs. In: Gennaro, R., Robshaw, M. (eds.) CRYPTO 2015. LNCS, vol. 9216, pp. 742–762. Springer, Heidelberg (2015). https://doi.org/10.1007/978-3-662-48000-7_36

[BIM00] Beimel, A., Ishai, Y., Malkin, T.: Reducing the servers computation in private information retrieval: PIR with preprocessing. In: Bellare, M. (ed.) CRYPTO 2000. LNCS, vol. 1880, pp. 55–73. Springer, Heidelberg (2000). https://doi.org/10.1007/3-540-44598-6_4

[BIPW17] Boyle, E., Ishai, Y., Pass, R., Wootters, M.: Can we access a database both locally and privately? In: Kalai, Y., Reyzin, L. (eds.) TCC 2017. LNCS, vol. 10678, pp. 662–693. Springer, Cham (2017). https://doi.org/10.1007/978-3-319-70503-3_22

[Blu84] Blum, N.: A boolean function requiring $3n$ network size. Theor. Comput. Sci. **28**, 337–345 (1984)

[BN16] Boyle, E., Naor, M.: Is there an oblivious RAM lower bound? In: Proceedings of the 2016 ACM Conference on Innovations in Theoretical Computer Science, Cambridge, MA, USA, 14–16 January 2016, pp. 357–368 (2016)

[CFL+13]   Chee, Y.M., Feng, T., Ling, S., Wang, H., Zhang, L.F.: Query-efficient locally decodable codes of subexponential length. Comput. Complex. **22**(1), 159–189 (2013)

[CHR17]   Canetti, R., Holmgren, J., Richelson, S.: Towards doubly efficient private information retrieval. In: Kalai, Y., Reyzin, L. (eds.) TCC 2017. LNCS, vol. 10678, pp. 694–726. Springer, Cham (2017). https://doi.org/10.1007/978-3-319-70503-3_23

[CKW13]   Cash, D., Küpçü, A., Wichs, D.: Dynamic proofs of retrievability via oblivious RAM. In: Johansson, T., Nguyen, P.Q. (eds.) EUROCRYPT 2013. LNCS, vol. 7881, pp. 279–295. Springer, Heidelberg (2013). https://doi.org/10.1007/978-3-642-38348-9_17

[Dur64]   Durstenfeld, R.: Algorithm 235: random permutation. Commun. ACM **7**(7), 420 (1964)

[DvDF+16]   Devadas, S., van Dijk, M., Fletcher, C.W., Ren, L., Shi, E., Wichs, D.: Onion ORAM: a constant bandwidth blowup oblivious RAM. In: Kushilevitz, E., Malkin, T. (eds.) TCC 2016. LNCS, vol. 9563, pp. 145–174. Springer, Heidelberg (2016). https://doi.org/10.1007/978-3-662-49099-0_6

[Efr09]   Efremenko, K.: 3-query locally decodable codes of subexponential length. In: Proceedings of the 41st Annual ACM Symposium on Theory of Computing, STOC 2009, Bethesda, MD, USA, 31 May–2 June 2009, pp. 39–44 (2009)

[FGHK16]   Find, M.G., Golovnev, A., Hirsch, E.A., Kulikov, A.S.: A better-than-$3n$ lower bound for the circuit complexity of an explicit function. In: IEEE 57th Annual Symposium on Foundations of Computer Science, FOCS 2016, 9–11 October 2016, Hyatt Regency, New Brunswick, New Jersey, USA, pp. 89–98 (2016)

[FNR+15]   Fletcher, C.W., Naveed, M., Ren, L., Shi, E., Stefanov, E.: Bucket ORAM: single online roundtrip, constant bandwidth oblivious RAM. IACR Cryptology ePrint Archive 2015:1065 (2015)

[GGH+13]   Gentry, C., Goldman, K.A., Halevi, S., Julta, C., Raykova, M., Wichs, D.: Optimizing ORAM and using it efficiently for secure computation. In: De Cristofaro, E., Wright, M. (eds.) PETS 2013. LNCS, vol. 7981, pp. 1–18. Springer, Heidelberg (2013). https://doi.org/10.1007/978-3-642-39077-7_1

[GHJR15]   Gentry, C., Halevi, S., Jutla, C., Raykova, M.: Private database access with HE-over-ORAM architecture. In: Malkin, T., Kolesnikov, V., Lewko, A.B., Polychronakis, M. (eds.) ACNS 2015. LNCS, vol. 9092, pp. 172–191. Springer, Cham (2015). https://doi.org/10.1007/978-3-319-28166-7_9

[GKK+12]   Gordon, S.D., et al.: Secure two-party computation in sublinear (amortized) time. In: The ACM Conference on Computer and Communications Security, CCS 2012, Raleigh, NC, USA, 16–18 October 2012, pp. 513–524 (2012)

[GMOT12]   Goodrich, M.T., Mitzenmacher, M., Ohrimenko, O., Tamassia, R.: Privacy-preserving group data access via stateless oblivious RAM simulation. In: Proceedings of the Twenty-Third Annual ACM-SIAM Symposium on Discrete Algorithms, SODA 2012, Kyoto, Japan, 17–19 January 2012, pp. 157–167 (2012)

[GO96]   Goldreich, O., Ostrovsky, R.: Software protection and simulation on oblivious RAMs. J. ACM **43**(3), 431–473 (1996)

[Gol87] Goldreich, O.: Towards a theory of software protection and simulation by oblivious RAMs. In: Proceedings of the 19th Annual ACM Symposium on Theory of Computing, 1987, New York, NY, USA, pp. 182–194 (1987)

[Goo14] Goodrich, M.T.: Zig-zag sort: a simple deterministic data-oblivious sorting algorithm running in $O(n \log n)$ time. In: Symposium on Theory of Computing, STOC 2014, New York, NY, USA, 31 May–03 June 2014, pp. 684–693 (2014)

[HO08] Hemenway, B., Ostrovsky, R.: Public-key locally-decodable codes. In: Wagner, D. (ed.) CRYPTO 2008. LNCS, vol. 5157, pp. 126–143. Springer, Heidelberg (2008). https://doi.org/10.1007/978-3-540-85174-5_8

[HOSW11] Hemenway, B., Ostrovsky, R., Strauss, M.J., Wootters, M.: Public key locally decodable codes with short keys. In: Goldberg, L.A., Jansen, K., Ravi, R., Rolim, J.D.P. (eds.) APPROX/RANDOM - 2011. LNCS, vol. 6845, pp. 605–615. Springer, Heidelberg (2011). https://doi.org/10.1007/978-3-642-22935-0_51

[HOWW18] Hamlin, A., Ostrovsky, R., Weiss, M., Wichs, D.: Private anonymous data access. IACR Cryptology ePrint Archive 2018:363 (2018)

[IM02] Iwama, K., Morizumi, H.: An explicit lower bound of $5n - o(n)$ for boolean circuits. In: Diks, K., Rytter, W. (eds.) MFCS 2002. LNCS, vol. 2420, pp. 353–364. Springer, Heidelberg (2002). https://doi.org/10.1007/3-540-45687-2_29

[IS10] Itoh, T., Suzuki, Y.: Improved constructions for query-efficient locally decodable codes of subexponential length. IEICE Trans. 93-D(2), 263–270 (2010)

[KLO12] Kushilevitz, E., Lu, S., Ostrovsky, R.: On the (in)security of hash-based oblivious RAM and a new balancing scheme. In: Proceedings of the Twenty-Third Annual ACM-SIAM Symposium on Discrete Algorithms, SODA 2012, Kyoto, Japan, 17–19 January 2012, pp. 143–156 (2012)

[KM18] Kushilevitz, E., Mour, T.: Sub-logarithmic distributed oblivious RAM with small block size. CoRR, abs/1802.05145 (2018)

[KO97] Kushilevitz, E., Ostrovsky, R.: Replication is not needed: single database, computationally-private information retrieval. In: 38th Annual Symposium on Foundations of Computer Science, FOCS 1997, Miami Beach, Florida, USA, 19–22 October 1997, pp. 364–373 (1997)

[KS14] Keller, M., Scholl, P.: Efficient, oblivious data structures for MPC. In: Sarkar, P., Iwata, T. (eds.) ASIACRYPT 2014. LNCS, vol. 8874, pp. 506–525. Springer, Heidelberg (2014). https://doi.org/10.1007/978-3-662-45608-8_27

[KT00] Katz, J., Trevisan, L.: On the efficiency of local decoding procedures for error-correcting codes. In: Proceedings of the Thirty-Second Annual ACM Symposium on Theory of Computing, 21–23 May 2000, Portland, OR, USA, pp. 80–86 (2000)

[LHS+14] Liu, C., Huang, Y., Shi, E., Katz, J., Hicks, M.W.: Automating efficient RAM-model secure computation. In: 2014 IEEE Symposium on Security and Privacy, SP 2014, Berkeley, CA, USA, 18–21 May 2014, pp. 623–638 (2014)

[LN18] Larsen, K.G., Nielsen, J.B.: Yes, there is an oblivious RAM lower bound!. In: Shacham, H., Boldyreva, A. (eds.) CRYPTO 2018. LNCS, vol. 10992, pp. 523–542. Springer, Cham (2018). https://doi.org/10.1007/978-3-319-96881-0_18

[LO13]   Lu, S., Ostrovsky, R.: Distributed oblivious RAM for secure two-party computation. In: Sahai, A. (ed.) TCC 2013. LNCS, vol. 7785, pp. 377–396. Springer, Heidelberg (2013). https://doi.org/10.1007/978-3-642-36594-2_22

[LPM+13] Lorch, J.R., Parno, B., Mickens, J.W., Raykova, M., Schiffman, J.: Shroud: ensuring private access to large-scale data in the data center. In: Proceedings of the 11th USENIX Conference on File and Storage Technologies, FAST 2013, San Jose, CA, USA, 12–15 February 2013, pp. 199–214 (2013)

[MBC14]   Mayberry, T., Blass, E.-O., Chan, A.H.: Efficient private file retrieval by combining ORAM and PIR. In: 21st Annual Network and Distributed System Security Symposium, NDSS 2014, San Diego, California, USA, 23–26 February 2014 (2014)

[MLS+13] Maas, M., Love, E., Stefanov, E., Tiwari, M., Shi, E., Asanovic, K., Kubiatowicz, J., Song, D.: PHANTOM: practical oblivious computation in a secure processor. In: 2013 ACM SIGSAC Conference on Computer and Communications Security, CCS 2013, Berlin, Germany, 4–8 November 2013, pp. 311–324 (2013)

[OS97]   Ostrovsky, R., Shoup, V.: Private information storage (extended abstract). In: Proceedings of the Twenty-Ninth Annual ACM Symposium on the Theory of Computing, El Paso, Texas, USA, 4–6 May 1997, pp. 294–303 (1997)

[Ost90]   Ostrovsky, R.: Efficient computation on oblivious RAMs. In: Proceedings of the 22nd Annual ACM Symposium on Theory of Computing, 13–17 May 1990, Baltimore, Maryland, USA, pp. 514–523 (1990)

[PD06]   Patrascu, M., Demaine, E.D.: Logarithmic lower bounds in the cell-probe model. SIAM J. Comput. **35**(4), 932–963 (2006)

[PPRY]   Patel, S., Persiano, G., Raykova, M., Yeo, K.: Panorama: Oblivious RAM with logarithmic overhead. In: FOCS, (2018, to appear)

[Rag07]   Raghavendra, P.: A note on Yekhanin's locally decodable codes. In: Electronic Colloquium on Computational Complexity (ECCC), vol. 14, no. 16 (2007)

[RFK+15] Ren, L., et al.: Constants count: practical improvements to oblivious RAM. In: 24th USENIX Security Symposium, USENIX Security 15, Washington, D.C., USA, 12–14 August 2015, pp. 415–430 (2015)

[SCSL11] Shi, E., Chan, T.-H.H., Stefanov, E., Li, M.: Oblivious RAM with $O((\log N)^3)$ worst-case cost. In: Lee, D.H., Wang, X. (eds.) ASIACRYPT 2011. LNCS, vol. 7073, pp. 197–214. Springer, Heidelberg (2011). https://doi.org/10.1007/978-3-642-25385-0_11

[SS13]   Stefanov, E., Shi, E.: ObliviStore: high performance oblivious distributed cloud data store. In: 20th Annual Network and Distributed System Security Symposium, NDSS 2013, San Diego, California, USA, 24–27 February 2013 (2013)

[SvDS+13] Stefanov, E., et al.: Path ORAM: an extremely simple oblivious RAM protocol. In: 2013 ACM SIGSAC Conference on Computer and Communications Security, CCS 2013, Berlin, Germany, 4–8 November 2013, pp. 299–310 (2013)

[WCS15]   Wang, X., Chan, T.-H.H., Shi, E.: Circuit ORAM: on tightness of the Goldreich-Ostrovsky lower bound. In: Proceedings of the 22nd ACM SIGSAC Conference on Computer and Communications Security, Denver, CO, USA, 12–16 October 2015, pp. 850–861 (2015)

[WGK18] Wang, X., Gordon, S.D., Katz, J.: Simple and efficient two-server ORAM. IACR Cryptology ePrint Archive, 2018:5 (2018)

[WHC+14] Wang, X.S., Huang, Y., Chan, T.-H.H., Shelat, A., Shi, E.: SCORAM: oblivious RAM for secure computation. In: Proceedings of the 2014 ACM SIGSAC Conference on Computer and Communications Security, Scottsdale, AZ, USA, 3–7 November 2014, pp. 191–202 (2014)

[Woo07] Woodruff, D.P.: New lower bounds for general locally decodable codes. In: Electronic Colloquium on Computational Complexity (ECCC), vol. 14, no. 6 (2007)

[WS12] Williams, P., Sion, R.: Single round access privacy on outsourced storage. In: The ACM Conference on Computer and Communications Security, CCS 2012, Raleigh, NC, USA, 16–18 October 2012, pp. 293–304 (2012)

[WW18] Weiss, M., Wichs, D.: Is there an oblivious RAM lower bound for online reads? IACR Cryptology ePrint Archive 2018:619 (2018)

[Yek07] Yekhanin, S.: Towards 3-query locally decodable codes of subexponential length. In: Proceedings of the 39th Annual ACM Symposium on Theory of Computing, San Diego, California, USA, 11–13 June 2007, pp. 266–274 (2007)

[YFR+13] Yu, X., Fletcher, C.W., Ren, L., van Dijk, M., Devadas, S.: Generalized external interaction with tamper-resistant hardware with bounded information leakage. In: CCSW 2013, Proceedings of the 2013 ACM Cloud Computing Security Workshop, Co-located with CCS 2013, Berlin, Germany, 4 November 2013, pp. 23–34 (2013)

[ZMZQ16] Zhang, J., Ma, Q., Zhang, W., Qiao, D.: MSKT-ORAM: a constant bandwidth ORAM without homomorphic encryption. IACR Cryptology ePrint Archive 2016:882 (2016)

Perfectly Secure Oblivious Parallel RAM

T.-H. Hubert Chan[1][(✉)], Kartik Nayak[2,3], and Elaine Shi[4]

[1] The University of Hong Kong, Hong Kong, China
hubert@cs.hku.hk
[2] University of Maryland, College Park, USA
[3] VMware Research, Palo Alto, USA
nkartik@vmware.com
[4] Cornell University, Ithaca, USA
elaine@cs.cornell.edu

Abstract. We show that PRAMs can be obliviously simulated with perfect security, incurring only $O(\log N \log \log N)$ blowup in parallel runtime, $O(\log^3 N)$ blowup in total work, and $O(1)$ blowup in space relative to the original PRAM. Our results advance the theoretical understanding of Oblivious (Parallel) RAM in several respects. First, prior to our work, no perfectly secure Oblivious Parallel RAM (OPRAM) construction was known; and we are the first in this respect. Second, even for the sequential special case of our algorithm (i.e., perfectly secure ORAM), we not only achieve logarithmic improvement in terms of space consumption relative to the state-of-the-art, but also significantly simplify perfectly secure ORAM constructions. Third, our perfectly secure OPRAM scheme matches the parallel runtime of earlier statistically secure schemes with negligible failure probability. Since we remove the dependence (in performance) on the security parameter, our perfectly secure OPRAM scheme in fact asymptotically outperforms known statistically secure ones if (sub-)exponentially small failure probability is desired. Our techniques for achieving small parallel runtime are novel and we employ special expander graphs to derandomize earlier statistically secure OPRAM techniques—this is the first time such techniques are used in the constructions of ORAMs/OPRAMs.

1 Introduction

Oblivious RAM (ORAM), originally proposed in the ground-breaking work by Goldreich and Ostrovsky [21,22], is an algorithmic technique that transforms any RAM program to a secure version, such that an adversary learns nothing about the secret inputs from observing the program's access patterns to memory. The parallel extension of ORAM was first phrased by Boyle, Chung, and Pass [6]. Similar to ORAM, an Oblivious Parallel RAM (OPRAM) compiler transforms a Parallel RAM (PRAM) program into a secure form such that the resulting PRAM's access patterns leak no information about secret inputs.

An online full version of our paper [9] is available at https://eprint.iacr.org/2018/364.

© International Association for Cryptologic Research 2018
A. Beimel and S. Dziembowski (Eds.): TCC 2018, LNCS 11240, pp. 636–668, 2018.
https://doi.org/10.1007/978-3-030-03810-6_23

ORAMs and OPRAMs have been recognized as powerful building blocks in both theoretical applications such as multi-party computation [5,25,29], as well as in practical applications such as cloud outsourcing [14,37,40], and secure processor design [17,18,28,30,31,35].

Henceforth in this paper, *we consider ORAMs to be a special case of OPRAMs*, i.e., when both the original PRAM and the OPRAM have only one CPU. To characterize an OPRAM scheme's overhead, we will use the standard terminology *total work blowup* to mean the multiplicative increase in total computation comparing the OPRAM and the original PRAM; and we use the term *depth blowup* to mean the multiplicative increase in parallel runtime comparing the OPRAM and the original PRAM—assuming that *the OPRAM may employ more CPUs than the original PRAM* to help parallelize its computation [7]. Note that for the case of sequential ORAMs, total work blowup is equivalent to the standard notion of simulation overhead [21,22], i.e., the multiplicative increase in runtime comparing the ORAM and the original RAM. Finally, we use the term *space blowup* to mean the multiplicative blowup in space when comparing the OPRAM (or ORAM) and that of the original PRAM (or RAM).

The original ORAM schemes, proposed by Goldreich and Ostrovsky [21, 22], achieved poly-logarithmic overheads but required the usage of pseudo-random functions (PRFs); thus they defend only against computationally bounded adversaries. Various subsequent works [2,10,12,13,36,38,39], starting from Ajtai [2] and Damgård et al. [13] investigated information-theoretically secure ORAM/OPRAM schemes, i.e., schemes that do not rely on computational assumptions and defend against even unbounded adversaries. As earlier works point out [2,13], the existence of efficient ORAM schemes without computational assumptions is not only theoretically intriguing, but also has various applications in cryptography. For example, information-theoretically secure ORAM schemes can be applied to the construction of efficient RAM-model, information-theoretically secure multi-party computation (MPC) protocols [4]. Among known information-theoretically secure ORAM/OPRAM schemes [2,6,10–13,36,38,39], almost all of them achieve only *statistical* security [2,6,10–12,36,38,39], i.e., there is still some non-zero failure probability—either correctness or security failure—but the failure probability can be made negligibly small in N where N is the RAM/PRAM's memory size. Damgård et al. [13] came up with the first *perfectly* secure ORAM construction—they achieve zero failure probability against computationally unbounded adversaries. Although recent works have constructed statistically secure OPRAMs [6,10,11], there is no known (non-trivial) *perfectly* secure OPRAM scheme to date.

Motivation for Perfect Security. Perfectly secure ORAMs/OPRAMs are theoretically intriguing for various reasons:

1. First, to achieve $2^{-\kappa}$ failure probability (either in security or in correctness), the best known statistically secure OPRAM scheme [7,10] incurs a $O(\kappa \log N)$ total work blowup and $O(\log \kappa \log N)$ depth blowup where N is the PRAM's memory size. Although for negligibly small in N failure probability the blowups are only poly-logarithmic in N, they can be as large as

N^c for some constant $c < 1$ if one desires (sub-)exponentially small failure probability in N.

2. Second, perfectly secure ORAM schemes have been used as a building block in recent results on oblivious algorithms [3,36] and searchable encryption schemes [15]. Typically these algorithmic constructions rely on divide-and-conquer to break down a problem into smaller sizes and then apply ORAM to a small instance—since the instance size N is small (e.g., logarithmic in the security parameter), negligible in N failure probability is not sufficient and thus these works demand *perfectly secure* ORAMs/OPRAMs and existing statistically secure schemes result in asymptotically poorer performance.

3. Third, understanding the boundary of perfect and statistical security has been an important theoretical question in cryptography. For example, a long-standing open problem in cryptography is to separate the classes of languages that admit perfect ZK and statistical ZK proofs. For ORAMs/OPRAMs too, it remains open whether there are any separations between statistical and perfect security (and we believe that this is an exciting future direction). Perfect security is also useful in other contexts such as multi-party computation (MPC). For example, Ishai et al. [26] and Genkin et al. [19] show that perfectly secure MPC is required to achieve their respective goals matching the "circuit complexity" of the underlying application. Perfectly secure ORAMs/OPRAMs can enable perfectly secure RAM-model MPC, and thus we believe that they can be an important building block in other areas of theoretical cryptography.

1.1   Our Results and Contributions

In this paper, we prove the following result which significantly advances our theoretical understanding of *perfectly* secure ORAMs and OPRAMs in multiple respects. We present the informal theorem statement below and then discuss its theoretical significance.

Theorem 1 (Informal statement of main theorem). *Any PRAM that consumes N memory blocks each of which is at least $\log N$-bits long[1] can be simulated by a perfectly oblivious PRAM, incurring $O(\log^3 N)$ total work blowup, $O(\log N \log \log N)$ depth blowup, and $O(1)$ space blowup.*

The above theorem improves the theoretical state of the art on perfectly secure ORAMs/OPRAMs in multiple dimensions:

1. First, our work gives rise to the first perfectly secure (non-trivial) OPRAM construction. No such construction was known before and it is not clear how to directly parallelize the perfectly secure ORAM scheme by Damgård et al. [13].
2. Second, even for the sequential special case, we improve Damgård et al. [13] asymptotically by reducing a $\log N$ factor in the ORAM's space consumption.

---

[1] All existing ORAM and OPRAM works [21–23,27,36] make this assumption.

3. Third, our perfectly secure OPRAM's parallel runtime matches the best known statistically secure construction [7,10] for negligibly small in N failure probabilities;

4. Finally, when (sub-)exponentially small (in N) failure probabilities are required, our perfectly secure OPRAM scheme asymptotically outperforms all known statistically secure constructions both in terms of total work blowup and depth blowup. For example, suppose that we require $2^{-\kappa}$ failure probability and $N = \mathsf{poly}(\kappa)$—then all known statistically secure OPRAM constructions [6,10,11] would incur at least N^c total work blowup and $\Omega(\log^2 N)$ depth blowup and thus our new perfectly secure OPRAM construction is asymptotically better for this scenario.

Theorem 1 applies to general block sizes. We additionally show that for sufficiently large block sizes, there exists a perfectly secure OPRAM construction with $O(\log^2 N)$ total work blowup and $O(\log m + \log\log N)$ depth blowup where m denotes the number of CPUs of the original PRAM. Finally, we point out that this work focuses mostly on the theoretical understanding of perfect security in ORAMs/OPRAMs, and we leave it as a future research direction to investigate their practical performance (see also Sect. 6).

Technical Highlights. Our most novel and non-trivial technical contribution is the use of *expander graphs* techniques, allowing our OPRAM to achieve as small as $O(\log N \log\log N)$ depth blowup. To the best of our knowledge, this is the first time such techniques have been used in the construction of ORAM/OPRAM schemes. Besides this novel technique, our scheme requires carefully weaving together many algorithmic tricks that have been used in earlier works [7,10,21,22].

1.2 Related Work

Oblivious RAM (ORAM) was first proposed in a ground-breaking work by Goldreich and Ostrovsky [21,22]. Goldreich and Ostrovsky first showed a computationally secure ORAM scheme with poly-logarithmic simulation overhead. Therefore, one interesting question is whether ORAMs can be constructed without relying on computational assumptions. Ajtai [2] answered this question and showed that statistically secure ORAMs with poly-logarithmic simulation overhead exist. Although Ajtai removed computational assumptions from ORAMs, his construction has a (negligibly small) statistical failure probability, i.e., with some negligibly small probability, the ORAM construction can leak information. Subsequently, Shi et al. [36] proposed the tree-based paradigm for constructing statistically secure ORAMs. Tree-based constructions were later improved further in several works [10,12,20,38,39], and this line of works improve the practical performance of ORAM by several orders of magnitude in comparison with earlier constructions. It was also later understood that the tree-based paradigm can be used to construct computationally secure ORAMs saving yet another $\log\log$ factor in cost in comparison with statistical security [10,16].

Perfect security requires that the (oblivious) program's memory access patterns be *identically distributed* regardless of the inputs to the program; and thus with probability 1, no information can be leaked about the secret inputs to the program. Perfectly secure ORAM was first studied by Damgård et al. [13]. Their construction achieves $O(\log^3 N)$ simulation overhead and $O(\log N)$ space blowup relative to the original RAM program. Their construction is a Las Vegas algorithm and there is a negligibly small failure probability that the algorithm exceeds the stated runtime. Raskin et al. [34] and Demertzis et al. [15] achieve a *worst-case* bandwidth of $O(\sqrt{N} \frac{\log N}{\log \log N})$ and $O(N^{1/3})$, respectively. As mentioned, even for the sequential case, our paper asymptotically improves Damgård et al.'s result [13] by avoiding the $O(\log N)$ blowup in space; and moreover, our ORAM construction is conceptually simpler than that of Damgård et al.'s.

Oblivious Parallel ORAM (OPRAM) was first proposed in an elegant work by Boyle et al. [6], and subsequently improved in several followup works [7,8, 10,11,32]. All known results on OPRAM focus on the statistically secure or the computationally secure setting. To the best of our knowledge, until this paper, we know of no efficient OPRAM scheme that is perfectly secure. Chen et al. [11] introduced a generic method to transform any ORAM into an OPRAM at the cost of a $\log N$ blowup. Their techniques achieve *statistical* security since security (or correctness) is only guaranteed with high probability (specifically, when some queue does not become overloaded in their scheme).

Defining a good performance metric for OPRAMs turned out to be more interesting and non-trivial than for ORAMs. Boyle et al. [6] were the first to define a notion of simulation overhead for OPRAM: if an OPRAM's simulation overhead is X, it means that if the original PRAM consumes m CPUs and completes in parallel runtime T, then the oblivious counterpart must complete within $X \cdot T$ time also consuming m CPUs. The recent work of Chan et al. [7] observes that if the OPRAM could consume more CPUs than the original PRAM, then the oblivious simulation can benefit from the additional parallelism and be additionally sped up by asymptotic factors. Under the assumption that the OPRAM can consume more CPUs than the original PRAM, Chan et al. [7,10] show that statistically secure OPRAM schemes can be constructed with $O(\log^2 N)$ blowup in total work and only $\tilde{O}(\log N)$ blowup in depth (where depth characterizes the parallel runtime of a program assuming ample number of CPUs). Our paper is the first to construct an OPRAM scheme with perfect security, and our OPRAM's depth matches existing schemes with statistical security assuming negligible in N security failure; however, if (sub-)exponentially small failure probability is required, our new OPRAM scheme can asymptotically outperform all known statistically secure OPRAMs!

2   Technical Roadmap

In this section, we present an informal roadmap of our technical approach to aid understanding.

2.1 Simplified Perfectly Secure ORAM with Asymptotically Smaller Space

First, we propose a perfectly secure ORAM scheme that is conceptually simpler than that of Damgård et al. [13] and gains a logarithmic factor in space. Our construction is inspired by the hierarchical ORAM paradigm originally proposed by Goldreich and Ostrovsky [21,22]. However, most existing hierarchical ORAMs achieve only computational security since they rely on a pseudorandom function (PRF) for looking up hash tables in the hierarchical data structure. Thus our focus is to get rid of this PRF and achieve perfect security.

Background: Hierarchical ORAM. The recent work by Chan et al. [8] gave a clean and modular exposition of the hierarchical paradigm. A hierarchical ORAM consists of $O(\log N)$ levels that are geometrically increasing in size. Specifically, level i is capable of storing 2^i memory blocks. One could think of this hierarchical data structure as a hierarchy of stashes where smaller levels act as stashes for larger levels. In existing schemes with computational security, each level is an *oblivious hash-table* [8]. To access a block at logical address addr, the CPU sequentially looks up every level of the hierarchy (from small to large) for the logical address addr. The physical location of a logical address addr within the oblivious hash-table is determined using a PRF whose secret key is known only to the CPU but not to the adversary. Once the block has already been found in some level, for all subsequent levels the CPU would just look for a dummy element, denoted by $\perp$. When a requested block has been found, it is marked as deleted in the corresponding level where it is found. Every 2^i memory requests, we perform a rebuild operation and merge all levels smaller than i (including the block just fetched and possibly updated if this is a write request) into level i—at this moment, the oblivious hash-table in level i is rebuilt, where every block's location in the hash table is determined using a PRF.

As Chan et al. [8] point out, the hierarchical ORAM paradigm effectively reduces the problem of constructing ORAM to constructing an oblivious hash-table supporting two operations: (1) **rebuild** takes in a set of blocks each tagged with its logical address, and constructs a hash-table data structure that facilitates lookups later; and (2) **lookup** takes a request that is either a logical address addr or dummy (denoted $\perp$), and returns the corresponding block requested. Obliviousness (defined w.r.t. the joint access patterns of the rebuild and lookup phases) is guaranteed as long as during the life-time of the oblivious hash-table, the sequence of lookup requests never ask for the same real element twice—and this invariant is guaranteed by the specific way the hierarchical ORAM framework uses the oblivious hash-table as a building block (more specifically, the fact that once a block is found, it is moved to a smaller level and a dummy block is requested from all subsequent levels).

Removing the PRF. As mentioned, an oblivious hash-table relies on a PRF to determine each block's location within a hash-table instance; and both the rebuilding phase and the lookup phase use the same PRF for placing and fetching blocks respectively. Since we wish to achieve perfect security, we would like to remove the PRF. One simple idea is to randomly permute all blocks within a level— this way, each lookup of a real block would visit a random location and we could hope to retain security as long as every real block is requested *at most once* for every level (in between rebuilds)[2]. Using techniques from earlier works [7,10], it is possible to obliviously perform such a random permutation without disclosing the permutation; however, difficulty arises when one wishes to perform a look up—if blocks are randomly permuted within a level during rebuild, lookup must know where each block resides to proceed successfully. Thus if the CPU could hold a position map for free to remember where each block is in the hierarchical data structure, the problem would have been resolved: during every lookup, the CPU could first look up the physical location of the logical address requested, and then proceed accordingly.

Actually storing such a position map, however, would consume too much CPU space. To avoid storing this position map, we are inspired by the recursion technique that is commonly adopted by tree-based ORAM schemes [36]—however, as we point out soon, making the recursion idea work for the hierarchical ORAM paradigm is more sophisticated. The high-level idea is to recursively store the position map in a smaller ORAM rather than storing it on the CPU side; we could then recurse and store the position map of the position map in an even smaller ORAM, and so on—until the ORAM's size becomes $O(1)$ at which point we would have the CPU store the entire ORAM. Henceforth, we use the notation ORAM_D to denote the ORAM that stores the actual data blocks where $D = O(\log N)$; and we use ORAM_d to denote the ORAM at depth d of this recursion where $d \in [0..D-1]$. Thus, the larger d is, the larger the ORAM.

Although this recursion idea was very simple in the tree-based paradigm, it is not immediately clear how to make the same recursion idea work in the hierarchical ORAM paradigm. One trickiness arises since in a hierarchical ORAM, every 2^i requests, the ORAM would reshuffle and merge all levels smaller than i into level i — this is called a rebuild of level i. When a level-i rebuild happens, the position labels in the position-map ORAM must be updated as well to reflect the blocks' new locations. In a similar fashion, the position labels in all of $\mathsf{ORAM}_0, \mathsf{ORAM}_1, \ldots, \mathsf{ORAM}_{D-1}$ must be updated. We make the following crucial observation that will enable a *coordinated rebuild* technique which we will shortly explain:

(Invariant necessary for coordinated rebuild:) If a data block resides at level i of ORAM_D, then its position labels in all recursion depths must reside in level i or smaller[3].

This invariant enables a *coordinated rebuild* technique: when the data ORAM (i.e., ORAM_D) merges all levels smaller than i into level i, all smaller recursion depths would do the same (unless the recursion depth is too small and does

---

[2] As we point out later, randomly permuting real blocks is in fact not sufficient; we also need to allow dummy lookups by introducing an oblivious dummy linked list.

[3] A similar observation was adopted by Goodrich et al. [24] in their statistically secure ORAM construction.

not have level i, in which case the entire ORAM would be rebuilt). During this coordinated rebuild, ORAM_D would first perform its rebuild, and propagate the position labels of all blocks involved in the rebuild to recursion depth $D - 1$; then ORAM_{D-1} would perform its rebuild based on the position labels learned from ORAM_D, and propagate the new position labels involved to recursion depth $D - 2$, and so on. As we shall discuss in the technical sections, rebuilding a level (in any recursion depth) can be accomplished through the help of $O(1)$ oblivious sorts and an oblivious random permutation.

Handling Dummy Blocks with Oblivious Linked Lists. The above idea almost works, but not quite so. There is an additional technical subtlety regarding how to handle and use dummy blocks. Recall that during a memory access, if a block requested actually resides in a hierarchical level, we would read the memory location that contains the block (and this memory location could be retrieved through a special recursive position map technique). If a block does not reside in a level (or has been found in a smaller level), we still need to read a dummy location within the level to hide the fact that the block does not reside within the current level.

Recall that the i-th level must support up to 2^i lookups before the level is rebuilt. Thus, one idea is to introduce 2^i dummy blocks, and obliviously and randomly permute all blocks, real and dummy alike, during the rebuild. All dummy blocks may be indexed by a dummy counter, and every time one needs to look up a dummy block in a level, we will visit a new dummy block. In this way, we can retain obliviousness by making sure that every real block and every dummy block is visited at most once before the level is rebuilt again.

To make this idea fully work, there must be a mechanism for finding out where the next dummy block is every time a dummy lookup must be performed. One naïve idea would be to use the same recursion technique to store position maps for dummy blocks too—however, since each memory request might involve reading $O(\log N)$ dummy blocks, one per level, doing so would incur extra blowup in runtime and space. Instead, we use an *oblivious dummy linked list* to resolve this problem—this oblivious dummy linked list is inspired by technical ideas in the Damgård et al. construction [13]. In essence, each dummy block stores the pointer to the next dummy block, and the head pointer of the linked list is stored at a designated memory location and updated upon each read of the linked list. In the subsequent technical sections, we will describe how to rely on oblivious sorting to rebuild such an oblivious dummy linked list to support dummy lookups.

Putting It Altogether. Putting all the above ideas together, the formal presentation of our perfectly secure ORAM scheme adopts a modular approach[4]. First, we define and construct an abstraction called an "oblivious one-time memory". An oblivious one-time memory allows one to obliviously create a data structure

---

[4] In fact, later in our paper, we omit the sequential version and directly present the parallel version of all algorithms.

given a list of input blocks. Once created, one can look up real or dummy blocks in the data structure, and to look up a real block one must provide a correct position label indicating where the block resides (imagine for now that the position label comes from an "oracle" but in the full ORAM scheme the position label comes from the recursion). An oblivious one-time memory retains obliviousness as long as every real block is looked up *at most once* and moreover, dummy blocks are looked up at most n times where n is a predetermined parameter (that the scheme is parametrized with).

Once we have this "oblivious one-time memory" abstraction, we show how to use it to construct an intermediate abstraction referred to as a "position-based ORAM". A position-based ORAM contains a hierarchy of oblivious one-time memory instances, of geometrically growing sizes. A position-based ORAM is almost a fully functional ORAM except that we assume that upon every memory request, an "oracle" will somehow provide a correct position label indicating where the requested block resides in the hierarchy.

Finally, we go from such a "position-based ORAM" to a fully functional ORAM using the special recursive position-map technique as explained. At this point, we have constructed a perfectly secure ORAM scheme with $O(\log^3 N)$ simulation overhead. Specifically, one $\log N$ factor arises from the $\log N$ depths of recursion, the remaining $\log^2 N$ factor arises from the cost of the ORAM at each recursion depth. Intuitively, our perfectly secure ORAM is a logarithmic factor more expensive than existing computationally-secure counterparts in the hierarchical framework [8,23,27] since the computationally-secure schemes [8, 23,27] avoid the recursion by adopting a PRF to compute the pseudorandom position labels of blocks.

2.2   Making Our ORAM Scheme Parallel

Our next goal is to make our ORAM scheme parallel. Instead of compiling a sequential RAM program to a sequential ORAM, we are now interested in compiling a PRAM program to an OPRAM. In this section, we describe an informal roadmap of our technical approach to parallelism. However, due to lack of space, we defer the details to the full version of our paper [9].

When the OPRAM Consumes the Same Number of CPUs as the PRAM. Suppose that the original program is a PRAM that completes in T parallel steps consuming m CPUs. We now would like to parallelize our earlier ORAM scheme and construct an OPRAM that completes in $T \cdot O(\log^3 N)$ parallel steps consuming also exactly m CPUs. To accomplish this, first, we need to parallelize within each position-based ORAM so m CPUs can perform work concurrently. This is not too difficult to accomplish given the simplicity of our position-based ORAM construction. Next, when m CPUs have all fetched position labels at one recursion depth, they need to pass these position labels to the CPUs at the next depth. The main technique needed here is oblivious routing: when the m CPUs at recursion depth d have fetched the position labels for the next recursion depth, the m CPUs at depth d must now obliviously route the position labels to the correct fetch CPU at the next recursion depth. As shown in earlier works [6,7,10], such oblivious routing can be accomplished with m CPUs in $O(\log m)$ parallel steps.

We stress that the *simplicity of our sequential ORAM construction makes it easy to parallelize — in comparison, we are not aware how to parallelize Damgård et al. [13]'s construction*[5].

When the OPRAM May Consume Unbounded Number Of CPUs. The more interesting question is the following: *if the OPRAM is allowed to consume more CPUs than the original PRAM, can we further reduce its parallel runtime?* If so, it intuitively means that the overheads arising due to obliviousness are parallelizable in nature. This model was first considered by Chan et al. [7] and can be considered as a generalization of the case when the OPRAM must consume the same number of CPUs as the original PRAM.

So far, in our OPRAM scheme, although within each recursion depth, up to m requests can be served concurrently, the operations over all $O(\log N)$ recursion depths must be performed sequentially. There are two reasons that necessitate this sequentiality:

1. *Fetch phase:* first, to fetch from recursion depth d, one must wait for the appropriate position labels to be fetched from recursion depth $d - 1$ and routed to recursion depth d;
2. *Maintain phase:* recall that coordinated rebuilding (see Sect. 2.1) is performed across all recursion depths in the reverse direction: recursion depth d must rebuild first and then propagate the new positions labels back to recursion depth $d - 1$ before $d - 1$ can rebuild (recall that recursion depth $d - 1$ must store the position labels for blocks in depth d).

Note that for the fetch phase, oblivious routing between any two adjacent recursion depths would consume $O(\log m)$ depth; for the maintain phase, rebuilding a hierarchical level can consume up to $O(\log N)$ depth (due to oblivious sorting of up to $O(N)$ blocks). Thus, the current OPRAM algorithm incurs a depth blowup of $O(\log^2 N)$ for moderate sizes of m, e.g., when $\log m = \Theta(\log N)$. Our next goal is to reduce the depth blowup to $\widetilde{O}(\log N)$, and this turns out to be highly non-trivial.

Reducing the Depth of the Fetch Phase with Expander Graphs. Using the recursion technique, it seems inherent that one must fetch from smaller recursion

---

[5] In Damgård et al. [13], the shuffle phase incurs an $O(\log^3 N)$ depth which is the same as the overhead for accessing a block. Specifically, a $\log N$ factor arises due to oblivious sorting, a $\log N$ factor due to the existence of hierarchies, and another $\log N$ factor due to the extra $\log N$ dummies stored for every real element. Though an offline/online technique like ours may be conceivable for their scheme, the existence of the extra $\log N$ dummies makes it inherently hard to improve the depth by another $\log N$ factor.

depths before embarking on larger ones. To reduce the depth of the fetch phase, we ask whether the depth incurred by oblivious routing in between adjacent recursion depths can be reduced. In the statistically and computationally secure settings, the recent work by Chan, Chung, and Shi have tried to tackle a similar problem for tree-based OPRAMs [7]. Their idea is to construct an offline/online routing algorithm. Although the offline phase incurs $O(\log N)$ depth per recursion depth, the offline work of all recursion depths can be performed concurrently rather than sequentially. On the other hand, the online phase of their routing algorithm must be performed sequentially among the recursion depths, but happily the online routing phase incurs only $O(1)$ depth per recursion depth. Unfortunately, the offline/online routing algorithm of Chan et al. [7] is a randomized algorithm that leverages some form of statistical "load balancing", and such load balancing can fail with negligibly small probability—this makes their algorithm unsuitable for the perfect security setting.

We propose a novel offline/online routing algorithm that achieves *perfect* security using special expander graphs—our techniques can be viewed as a method for derandomizing a new variant of the offline/online routing techniques described by Chan et al. [7]. Like Chan et al. [7], our offline/online routing algorithm achieves $O(\log N)$ depth for each recursion depth in the offline stage but the work in all recursion depths can be performed in parallel in the offline stage. By contrast, the online phase must traverse the recursion depths sequentially, but the online stage of routing can be accomplished in $O(1)$ depth per recursion depth. To achieve this, we rely on a core building block called a "loose compactor". Leveraging special expander graphs, we show how to build a loose compactor with small online depth—since this part of our techniques are novel, we present a more expanded overview in Sect. 2.3 while deferring a detailed, formal description to the full version [9].

Reducing the Depth of the Maintain Phase. We also must reduce the depth of the maintain phase. Although a naïve implementation of *coordinated rebuild* is to do it sequentially from recursion depth D down to recursion depth 0, we devise a method for performing the coordinated rebuild in parallel among all recursion depths. Recall that in the naïve solution, recursion depth $d - 1$ must wait for recursion depth d to relocate its blocks and be informed of the new position labels chosen before it starts reshuffling.

In our new algorithm, we introduce the notion of a rehearsal step called "mock shuffle" which determines the new positions of each of the blocks. Note that during this step, the newly chosen block contents (position labels) at the recursion depths are not available. Now, instead of sequentially performing the shuffle, in a mock shuffle, every recursion depth performs eager reshuffling without having updated the block's contents (recall that each block in recursion depth d is supposed to store position labels for the next recusion depth $d + 1$). After this mock shuffle, all blocks' new positions are determined though their contents are not known. Each mock reshuffle incurs $O(\log N)$ depth, but they are independent and can be performed in parallel. At this moment, recursion depth d informs the newly chosen position labels to recursion depth $d - 1$—now recursion depth $d - 1$ relies on oblivious routing to deliver each block's contents to the block. Note that recursion depth $d - 1$ has already chosen each block's position at this point and thus in this content update step, each block's contents will be routed to the corresponding block and all blocks will maintain their chosen positions.

Using this idea, although each recursion depth incurs $O(\log N)$ depth for the maintain phase, all recursion depths can now perform the maintain-phase operations in parallel.

Additional Techniques. Besides the above, additional tricks are needed to achieve $\widetilde{O}(\log N)$ depth. For example, within each recursion depth, all the hierarchical levels must be read in parallel during the fetch phase rather than sequentially like in existing hierarchical ORAMs [21,22], and the result of these fetches can be aggregated using an oblivious select operation incurring $O(\log \log N)$ depth. It is possible for us to read all the hierarchical levels in parallel since each recursion depth must have received the position labels of all real blocks requested before its fetch phase starts—and thus we know for each requested block which level to look for a real element and which level to visit dummies. We defer additional algorithmic details to the full version [9].

2.3   Offline/Online Routing with Special Expander Graphs

Informal Problem Statement. Without going into excessive details, consider the following abstract problem: imagine that m CPUs at a parent depth have fetched m real or dummy blocks, and each real block contains two position labels for the next depth—thus in total up to $2m$ position labels have been fetched. Meanwhile, m CPUs at the next depth are waiting to receive m position labels before they can start their fetch. Our task is to obliviously route the (up to) $2m$ position labels at the parent depth to the m CPUs at the child depth. Using oblivious routing directly would incur $\Omega(\log m)$ depth and thus is too expensive.

A Blueprint: Using an Offline/Online Algorithm. As mentioned earlier, our high-level idea is to leverage an offline-online paradigm such that the online phase, which must be performed sequentially for all recursion depths, should have small parallel runtime for each recursion depth.

Here is another idea: suppose that we are somehow able to compress the $2m$ position labels down to m, removing the ones that are not needed by the next recursion depth—this is in fact non-trivial but for now, suppose that somehow it can be accomplished.

Our plan is then the following: in the offline phase, we obliviously and randomly permute the m position labels to be routed (without leaking the permutation), and we obliviously compute the routing permutation π preserving the following invariant: the CPU at position $\pi(i)$ (in the child depth) is waiting for the i-th position label in the permuted array. In other words, the i-th position label wants to be routed to the CPU in position $\pi(i)$; and in the offline phase, we want to route down this π.

If we can accomplish all of the above, then in the online phase we simply apply the routing permutation that has been recorded and it takes a single parallel step to complete the routing. Moreover, for the offline phase, as long as we can perform the operations in parallel across all recursion depths, we are allowed to incur $\log m$ depth.

Informally, obliviousness holds because of the following: recall that the m labels to be routed have been obliviously and randomly permuted. Now, although the routing permutation π is revealed in the online phase, the revealed permutation is uniform at random to an observer.

Technical Challenges: Compaction (and More). The above blueprint seems promising, but there are multiple technical challenges. One critical ingredient that is missing is how to perform compaction from $2m$ elements down to m, removing the labels not needed by the next recursion depth—in fact, even if we can solve this compaction problem, additional challenges remain in putting these techniques together. However, for the time being, let us focus on the compaction problem alone. The most naïve method is again to leverage oblivious sorting but unfortunately that takes $\Omega(\log m)$ depth and thus is too expensive for our purpose.

Pippenger's Factory-Facility Problem. Our approach is inspired by the techniques described by Pippenger in constructing a self-routing super-concentrator [33]. Pippenger's elegant construction can be used to solve a "factory-facility" problem described as follows. Suppose that $2m$ factories and m facilities form a special bipartite expander graph: each factory is connected to $\eth$ facilities and each facility is connected to $2\eth$ factories, where $\eth$ is a constant. Among the factories, $m/64$ of them are *productive* and actually end up manufacturing products. Each productive factory produces $\eth/2$ products; these products must be routed to a facility to be stored, and each facility has a storage capacity of $\eth/2$. Now, the question is: given the set of productive factories (and assuming that the bipartite graph is known), can we find a *satisfying assignment* for routing products to facilities, such that (1) every edge in the bipartite graph routes carries at most one unit of flow; (2) all products manufactured are routed; and (3) no facility exceeds its storage capacity.

In his ingenious work [33], Pippenger described a distributed protocol for finding such an assignment: imagine that the factories and facilities are Interactive Turing Machines. Now the factories and facilities exchange messages over edges in the bipartite graph. Pippenger's protocol completes after $O(\log m)$ rounds of interaction and a total of $O(m)$ number of messages. Pippenger proved that as long as the underlying bipartite graph satisfies certain expansion properties, his protocol is guaranteed to find a satisfying assignment.

Using Pippenger's Protocol for Oblivious Loose Compaction. Now we can reduce the problem of (loose) compaction to Pippenger's factory-facility problem. Imagine that there are twice as many factories as there are facilities. Another way to think of the factory-facility problem is the following: imagine that the factories initially store real elements (i.e., the manufactured products) as well as dummies, and in total $2m \cdot (\eth/2)$ amount of storage is consumed since each factory can produce at most $\eth/2$ products. We ensure that only $m/64$ factories are productive by appropriately adding a constant factor of dummy elements (i.e., dummy factories and facilities). Now, when routed to the facilities, the storage amount is compressed down by a factor of 2 since each facility can store up to $\eth/2$ products and the number of facilities is half that of factories. Further, for any satisfying assignment, we guarantee that no real element is lost during the routing, and that is why the compaction algorithm satisfies correctness. Note that such compaction is *loose*, i.e., we do not completely remove dummies during compaction although we do cut down total storage by a half while preserving all real elements. In our OPRAM algorithm, it turns out that such *loose* compaction is sufficient, since CPUs who have received dummy position labels can always perform dummy fetch operations.

Pippenger's protocol can be easily simulated on a PRAM incurring $O(m)$ total work and $O(\log m)$ parallel runtime—however, a straightforward PRAM simulation of their protocol is *not* oblivious. In particular, the communication patterns between the factories and facilities (which translate to memory access patterns when simulated on a PRAM) leak information about which factories are productive. Thus it remains for us to show how to *obliviously* simulate his protocol on a PRAM. We show that this can be done incurring $O(m \log m)$ total work and $O(\log m)$ parallel runtime—note that the extra $\log m$ overhead arises from the obliviousness requirement.

Finally, we apply the loose compaction algorithm in an offline/online fashion too. In the offline phase, we execute Pippenger's protocol obliviously on a PRAM to compute the satisfying assignment—the offline phase can be parallelized over all recursion depths, thus incurring $O(\log m)$ parallel runtime overall. In the online phase, we carry out the satisfying assignment that has already been recorded in the offline phase to perform the actual routing of the fetched position labels, and this can be accomplished in $O(1)$ online parallel runtime.

3   Definitions

3.1   Parallel Random-Access Machines

We review the concepts of a parallel random-access machine (PRAM) and an oblivious parallel random-access machine (OPRAM). Some of the definitions in this section are borrowed verbatim from Boyle et al. [6] or Chan and Shi [10].

Although we give definitions only for the parallel case, we point out that this is without loss of generality, since a sequential RAM can be thought of as a special case PRAM with one CPU.

Parallel Random-Access Machine (PRAM). A *parallel random-access machine* consists of a set of CPUs and a shared memory denoted by mem indexed by the address space $\{0, 1, \ldots, N-1\}$, where N is a power of 2. In this paper, we refer to each memory word also as a *block*, which is at least $\Omega(\log N)$ bits long.

In a PRAM, each step of the execution can employ multiple CPUs, and henceforth we use m_t to denote the number of CPUs involved in executing the t-th step for $t \in \mathbb{N}$. In each step, each CPU executes a next instruction circuit denoted Π, updates its CPU state; and further, CPUs interact with memory through request instructions $\boldsymbol{I}^{(t)} := (I_i^{(t)} : i \in [m_t])$. Specifically, at time step t, CPU i's instruction is of the form $I_i^{(t)} := (\mathsf{read}, \mathsf{addr})$, or $I_i^{(t)} := (\mathsf{write}, \mathsf{addr}, \mathsf{data})$ where the operation is performed on the memory block with address addr and the block content data.

If $I_i^{(t)} = (\mathsf{read}, \mathsf{addr})$ then the CPU i should receive the contents of $\mathsf{mem[addr]}$ at the beginning of time step t. Else if $I_i^{(t)} = (\mathsf{write}, \mathsf{addr}, \mathsf{data})$, CPU i should still receive the contents of $\mathsf{mem[addr]}$ at the beginning of time step t; further, at the end of step t, the contents of $\mathsf{mem[addr]}$ should be updated to data.

Write Conflict Resolution. By definition, multiple read operations can be executed concurrently with other operations even if they visit the same address. However, if multiple concurrent write operations visit the same address, a conflict resolution rule will be necessary for our PRAM to be well-defined. In this paper, we assume the following:

- The original PRAM supports concurrent reads and concurrent writes (CRCW) with an arbitrary, parametrizable rule for write conflict resolution.
- Our compiled, oblivious PRAM (defined below) is a "concurrent read, exclusive write" PRAM (CREW). In other words, our OPRAM algorithm must ensure that there are no concurrent writes at any time.

CPU-to-CPU Communication. In the remainder of the paper, we sometimes describe our algorithms using CPU-to-CPU communication. For our OPRAM algorithm to be oblivious, the inter-CPU communication pattern must be oblivious too. We stress that such inter-CPU communication can be emulated using shared memory reads and writes. Therefore, when we express our performance metrics, we assume that all inter-CPU communication is implemented with shared memory reads and writes. In this sense, our performance metrics already account for any inter-CPU communication, and there is no need to have separate metrics that characterize inter-CPU communication. In contrast, some earlier works [11] adopt separate metrics for inter-CPU communication.

Additional Assumptions and Notations. Henceforth, we assume that *each CPU can only store $O(1)$ memory blocks*. Further, we assume for simplicity that the runtime T of the PRAM is *fixed* a priori and *publicly known*. Therefore, we can consider a PRAM to be parametrized by the following tuple

$$\mathsf{PRAM} := (\Pi, N, T, m_1, m_2, \ldots, m_T),$$

where Π denotes the next instruction circuit, N denotes the total memory size (in terms of number of blocks), T denotes the PRAM's total runtime, and m_t denotes the number of CPUs in the t-th step for $t \in [T]$.

Finally, in this paper, we consider PRAMs that are *stateful* and can evaluate a sequence of inputs, carrying state in between. Without loss of generality, we assume each input can be stored in a single memory block.

3.2 Oblivious Parallel Random-Access Machines

An OPRAM is a (randomized) PRAM with certain security properties, i.e., its access patterns leak no information about the inputs to the PRAM.

Randomized PRAM. A *randomized PRAM* is a PRAM where the CPUs are allowed to generate private random numbers. For simplicity, we assume that a randomized PRAM has a priori known, deterministic runtime, and that the CPU activation pattern in each time step is also fixed a priori and publicly known.

Memory Access Patterns. Given a PRAM program denoted PRAM and a sequence inp of inputs, we define the notation Addresses[PRAM](inp) as follows:

- Let T be the total number of parallel steps that PRAM takes to evaluate inputs inp.
- Let $A_t := (\mathsf{addr}_1^t, \mathsf{addr}_2^t, \ldots, \mathsf{addr}_{m_t}^t)$ be the list of addresses such that the ith CPU accesses memory address addr_i^t in time step t.
- We define Addresses[PRAM](inp) to be the random object $[A_t]_{t \in [T]}$.

Oblivious PRAM (OPRAM). We say that a PRAM is *perfectly oblivious*, iff for any two input sequences inp_0 and inp_1 of equal length, it holds that the following distributions are identically distributed (where $\equiv$ denotes identically distributed):

$$\mathsf{Addresses}[\mathsf{PRAM}](\mathsf{inp}_0) \equiv \mathsf{Addresses}[\mathsf{PRAM}](\mathsf{inp}_1)$$

We remark that for statistical and computational security, some earlier works [8, 10] presented an adaptive, composable security notion. The perfectly oblivious counterpart of their adaptive, composable notion is equivalent to our notion defined above. In particular, our notion implies security against an adaptive adversary who might choose the input sequence inp adaptively over time after having observed partial access patterns of PRAM.

We say that OPRAM is a *perfectly oblivious simulation* of PRAM iff OPRAM is perfectly oblivious, and moreover OPRAM(inp) is identically distributed as PRAM(inp) for any input inp. In the remainder of the paper, we always assume that the original PRAM has a fixed number of CPUs (denoted m) in all steps of execution. For the compiled OPRAM, we consider two models (1) when the OPRAM always consumes exactly m CPUs in every step (i.e., the same number of CPUs as the original PRAM); and (2) when the OPRAM can consume an unbounded number of CPUs in every step; in this case, the actual number of CPUs consumed in each step may vary. We leave it as an open problem how to obliviously simulate a PRAM with a varying number of CPUs (without naïvely padding the number of CPUs to the maximum which can incur large overhead).

Oblivious Simulation Metrics. We adopt the following metrics to characterize the overhead of (parallel) oblivious simulation of a PRAM. In the following, when we say that an OPRAM scheme consumes T parallel steps (or W total work), we mean that the OPRAM scheme consumes T parallel steps (or W total work) except with negligible in N probability. In other words, the definition of our metrics allows the OPRAM to sometimes, but with negligibly small (in N) probability, exceed the desired runtime or total work bound; however, note that the security or correctness failure probability must be 0^6.

- *Simulation overhead (when the OPRAM consumes the same number of CPUs as the PRAM).* If a PRAM that consumes m CPUs and completes in T parallel steps can be obliviously simulated by an OPRAM that completes in $\gamma \cdot T$ steps also with m CPUs (i.e., the same number of CPUs as the original PRAM), then we say that the simulation overhead is γ. Note that this means that every PRAM step is simulated by *on average* γ OPRAM steps.
- *Total work blowup (when the OPRAM may consume unbounded number of CPUs).* A PRAM's total work is the number of steps necessary to simulate the PRAM under a single CPU, and is equal to the sum $\sum_{t \in [T]} m_t$. If a PRAM of total work W can be obliviously simulated by an OPRAM of total work $\gamma \cdot W$ we say that the total work blowup of the oblivious simulation is γ.
- *Depth blowup (when the OPRAM may consume unbounded number of CPUs).* A PRAM's depth is defined to be its parallel runtime when there are an unbounded number of CPUs. If a PRAM of depth D can be obliviously simulated by an OPRAM of depth $\gamma \cdot D$ we say that the depth blowup of the oblivious simulation is γ.

Note that the simulation overhead is a good standalone metric if we assume that the OPRAM must consume the same number of CPUs as the PRAM. If the OPRAM is allowed to consume more CPUs than the PRAM, we typically use the metrics total work blowup and depth blowup in conjunction with each other: total work blowup alone does not characterize how much the OPRAM preserves parallelism; and depth blowup alone does not capture the extent to which the OPRAM preserves total work.

Finally, the following simple fact is useful for understanding the complexity of (oblivious) parallel algorithms.

Fact 2. *Let $C > 1$. If an (oblivious) parallel algorithm can complete in T steps consuming m CPUs, then it can complete in CT steps consuming $\lceil \frac{m}{C} \rceil$ CPUs.*

3.3   Building Blocks

In our constructions, we use several useful building blocks such as oblivious routing, oblivious select, oblivious random permutation, etc. Due to lack of space, we describe these building blocks in detail in the full version of the paper [9].

---

[6] Similarly, the perfectly secure ORAM by Damgård et al. [13] also allowed a negligible small probability for the algorithm to exceed the desired complexity bound but the security or correctness failure probability must be 0.

4   Parallel One-Time Oblivious Memory

We define and construct an abstract datatype to process non-recurrent memory lookup requests. Although the abstraction is similar to the oblivious hashing scheme in Chan et al. [8], our one-time memory scheme needs to be perfectly secure and does not use a hashing scheme. Furthermore, we assume that every real lookup request is *tagged with a correct position label* that indicates where the requested block is—in this section, we simply assume that the correct position labels are simply provided during lookup; but later in our full OPRAM scheme, we will use a recursive ORAM/OPRAM technique reminiscent of those used in binary-tree-based ORAM/OPRAM schemes [10,12,36,38,39] such that we can obtain the position label of a block first before fetching the block.

4.1   Definition: One-Time Oblivious Memory

Intuition. We describe the intuition using the *sequential* special case but our formal presentation later will directly describe the parallel version. An oblivious one-time memory supports three operations: (1) Build, (2) Lookup, and (3) Getall. Build is called once upfront to create the data structure: it takes in a set of real blocks (each tagged with its logical address) and creates a data structure that facilitates lookup. After this data structure is created, a sequence of lookup operations can be performed: each lookup can request a real block identified by its logical address or a dummy block denoted $\perp$ — if the requested block is a real block, we assume that the correct position label is supplied to indicate where in the data structure the requested block is. Finally, when the data structure is no longer needed, one may call a Getall operation to obtain a list of blocks (tagged with their logical addresses) that have not been looked up yet—in our OPRAM scheme later, this is the set of blocks that need to be preserved during rebuilding.

We require that our oblivious one-time memory data structure retain obliviousness as long as (1) the sequence of real blocks looked up all exist in the data structure (i.e., it appeared as part of the input to Build), and moreover, each logical address is looked up at most once; and (2) at most $\tilde{n}$ number of dummy lookups may be made where $\tilde{n}$ is a predetermined parameter (that the scheme is parametrized with).

Formal Definition. Our formal presentation will directly describe the parallel case. In the parallel version, lookup requests come in batches of size $m > 1$.

A (parallel) one-time memory scheme denoted $\mathsf{OTM}^{[n,m,t]}$ is parametrized by three parameters: n denotes the upper bound on the number of real elements; m is the batch size for lookups; t is the upper bound on the number of batch lookups supported. We use three parameters because we use different versions of OTM. For the basic version in Sect. 5, we have $t = \frac{n}{m}$ number of batch lookups, whereas for the low-depth version, the number of batch lookups is larger (which means that some of the lookup addresses must be dummy).

The (parallel) one-time memory scheme $\mathsf{OTM}^{[n,m,t]}$ is comprised of the following possibly randomized, stateful algorithms to be executed on a *Concurrent-Read, Exclusive-Write* PRAM — note that since the algorithms are stateful, every invocation will update an implicit data structure in memory. Henceforth we use the terminology key and value in the formal description but in our OPRAM scheme later, a real key will be a logical memory address and its value is the block's content.

- $U \leftarrow \mathsf{Build}(\{(k_i, v_i) : i \in [n]\})$: given a set of n key-value pairs (k_i, v_i), where each pair is either real or of the form $(\bot, \bot)$, the Build algorithm creates an implicit data structure to facilitate subsequent lookup requests, and moreover outputs a list U of exactly n key-position pairs where each pair is of the form (k, pos). Further, every real key input to Build will appear exactly once in the list U; and the list U is padded with $\bot$ to a length n. Note that U does not include the values v_i's. Later in our scheme, this key-position list U will be propagated back to the parent recursion depth during a coordinated rebuild[7].
- $(v_i : i \in [m]) \leftarrow \mathsf{Lookup}(\{(k_i, \mathsf{pos}_i) : i \in [m]\})$: there are m concurrent Lookup operations in a single batch, where we allow each key k_i requested to be either real or $\bot$. Moreover, in each batch, at most n/t of the keys are real.
- $R \leftarrow \mathsf{Getall}$: the Getall algorithm returns an array R of length n where each entry is either $\bot$ or real and of the form (k, v). The array R should contain all real entries that have been inserted during Build but have not been looked up yet, padded with $\bot$ to a length of n.

Valid Request Sequence. Our oblivious one-time memory ensures obliviousness only if lookups are non-recurrent (i.e., never look for the same real key twice); and moreover the number of lookups requests must be upper bounded by a predetermined parameter. More formally, a sequence of operations is valid, iff the following holds:

- The sequence begins with a single call to Build upfront; followed by a sequence of at most t batch Lookup calls, each of which supplies a batch of m keys and the corresponding position labels; and finally the sequence ends with a single call to Getall.
- The Build call is supplied with an input array $S := \{(k_i, v_i)\}_{i \in [n]}$, such that any two real entries in S must have distinct keys.
- For every $\mathsf{Lookup}(\{(k_i, \mathsf{pos}_i) : i \in [m]\})$ query in the sequence, if each k_i is a real key, then k_i must be contained in S that was input to Build earlier. In other words, Lookup requests are not supposed to ask for real keys that do not exist in the data structure[8]; moreover, each (k_i, pos_i) pair supplied to

---

[7] Note that we do not explicitly denote the implicit data structure in the output of Build, since the implicit data structure is needed only internally by the current oblivious one-time memory instance. In comparison, U is explicitly output since U will later on be (externally) needed by the parent recursion depth in our OPRAM construction.

[8] We emphasize this is a major difference between this one-time memory scheme and the oblivious hashing abstraction of Chan et al. [8]; Chan et al.'s abstraction [8] allows lookup queries to ask for keys that do not exist in the data structure.

Lookup must exist in the U array returned by the earlier invocation of Build, i.e., pos_i must be a correct position label for k_i; and

- Finally, in all Lookup requests in the sequence, no two keys requested (either in the same or different batches) are the same.

Correctness. Correctness requires that

1. for any valid request sequence, with probability 1, for every $\mathsf{Lookup}(\{(k_i, \mathsf{pos}_i) : i \in [m]\})$ request, the i-th answer returned must be $\bot$ if $k_i = \bot$; else if $k_i \neq \bot$, Lookup must return the correct value v_i associated with k_i that was input to the earlier invocation of Build.
2. for any valid request sequence, with probability 1, Getall must return an array R containing every (k, v) pair that was supplied to Build but has not been looked up; moreover the remaining entries in R must all be $\bot$.

Perfect Obliviousness. We say that two valid request sequences are *length-equivalent*, if the input sets to Build have equal size, and the number of Lookup requests (where each request asks for a batch of m keys) in the two sequences are equal.

We say that a (parallel) one-time memory scheme is perfectly oblivious, iff for any two length-equivalent request sequences that are valid, the distribution of access patterns resulting from the algorithms are *identically distributed*.

4.2   Construction

Intuition. We first explain the intuition for the sequential case, i.e., $m = 1$. The intuition is simply to permute all elements received as input during Build. However, since subsequent lookup requests may be dummy (also denoted $\bot$), we also need to pad the array with sufficiently many dummies to support these lookup requests. The important invariant is that *each real element as well as each dummy will be accessed at most once* during lookup requests. For reals, this is guaranteed since the definition of a valid request sequence requires that each real key be requested no more than once, and that each real key requested must exist in the data structure. For dummies, every time a $\bot$-request is received, we always look for an unvisited dummy. To implement this idea, one tricky detail is that unlike real lookup requests, dummy requests do not carry the position label of the next dummy to be read—thus our data structure itself must maintain an *oblivious linked list* of dummies such that we can easily find out where the next dummy is. Since all real and dummies are randomly permuted during Build, and due to the aforementioned invariant, every lookup visits a completely random location of the data structure thus maintaining perfect obliviousness.

It is not too difficult to make the above algorithm parallel (i.e., for the case $m > 1$). To achieve this, one necessary modification is that instead of maintaining a single dummy linked list, we now must maintain m dummy linked lists. These m dummy linked lists are created during Build and consumed during Lookup.

Detailed Construction. At the end of Build, our algorithm creates an in-memory data structure consisting of the following:

1. An array A of length $n + \tilde{n}$, where $\tilde{n} := tm$ denotes the number of dummies and n denotes the number of real elements. Each entry of the array A (real or dummy alike) has four fields (key, val, next, pos) where
   - key is a key that is either real or dummy; and val is a value that is either real or dummy.
   - the field next $\in [0..n+\tilde{n})$ matters only for dummy entries, and at the end of the Build algorithm, the next field stores the position of the next entry in the dummy linked list (recall that all dummy entries form m linked lists); and
   - the field pos $\in [0..n+\tilde{n})$ denotes where in the array an entry finally wants to be—at the end of the Build algorithm it must be that $A[i].\text{pos} = i$. However, during the algorithm, entries of A will be permuted transiently; but as soon as each element i has decided where it wants to be (i.e., $A[i].\text{pos}$), it will always carry its desired position around during the remainder of the algorithm.
2. An array that stores the head pointers of all m dummy linked lists. Specifically, we denote the m head pointers as $\{\text{dpos}_i : i \in [m]\}$ where each $\text{dpos}_i \in [0..n + \tilde{n})$ is the head pointer of one dummy linked list.

These in-memory data structures, including A and the dummy pointers will then be updated during Lookup.

Build. Our oblivious Build($\{(k_i, v_i)\}_{i \in [n]}$) algorithm proceeds as follows.

1. _Initialize._ Construct an array A of length $n + \tilde{n}$ whose entries are of the form described above. Specifically, the keys and values for the first n entries of A are copied from the input. Recall that the input may contain dummies too, and we use $\perp$ to denote a dummy key from the input.
   The last $\tilde{n}$ entries of A contain _special_ dummy keys that are numbered. Specifically, for each $i \in [1..\tilde{n}]$, we denote $A_n[i] := A[n-1+i]$, and the entry stored at $A_n[i]$ has key $\perp_i$ and value $\perp$.
2. _Every element decides at random its desired final position._ Specifically, perform a perfectly oblivious random permutation on the entries of A—this random permutation decides where each element finally wants to be.
   Now, for each $i \in [0..n+\tilde{n})$, let $A[i].\text{pos} := i$. At this moment, $A[i].\text{pos}$ denotes where the element $A[i]$ finally wants to be. Henceforth in the algorithm, the entries of A will be moved around but each element always carries around its desired final position.
3. _Construct the key-position map U._ Perform oblivious sorting on A using the field key. We assume that real keys have the highest priority followed by $\perp < \perp_1 < \cdots < \perp_{\tilde{n}}$ (where smaller keys come earlier).
   At this moment, we can construct the key-position map U from the first n entries of A—recall that each entry of U is of the form (k, pos).
4. _Construct m dummy linked lists._ Observe that the last $\tilde{n}$ entries of A contain special dummy keys, on which we perform the following to build m disjoint

singly-linked lists (each of which has length t). For each $i \in [1..\tilde{n}]$, if $i \mod t \neq 0$ we update the entry $A_n[i]$.next $:= A_n[i+1]$.pos, i.e., each dummy entry (except the last entry of each linked list) records its next pointer.

We next record the positions of the heads of the m lists. For each $i \in [m]$, we set dpos$_i := A_n[t(i-1)]$.pos.

5. *Move entries to their desired positions.* Perform an oblivious sort on A, using the fourth field pos. (This restores the ordering according to the previous random permutation.)

At this moment, the data structure $(A, \{\text{dpos}_i : i \in [m]\})$ is stored in memory. The key-position map U is explicitly output and later in our OPRAM scheme it will be passed to the parent recursion depth during coordinated rebuild.

Fact 3. *Consuming $O(\tilde{n} + n)$ CPUs and setting $(\tilde{n} + n)^2 \leq \lambda \leq 2^{\tilde{n}+n}$, the Build algorithm completes in $O(\log(\tilde{n}+n))$ parallel steps, except with probability negligible in λ.*

Lookup. We implement a batch of m concurrent lookup operations $\{\text{Lookup}(\{(k_i, \text{pos}_i) : i \in [m]\})$ as follows. For each $i \in [m]$, we perform the following *in parallel*.

1. *Decide position to fetch from.* If $k_i \neq \perp$ is real, set pos $:= \text{pos}_i$, i.e., we want to use the position label supplied from the input. Else if $k_i = \perp$, set pos $:= \text{dpos}_i$, i.e., the position to fetch from is the next dummy in the i-th dummy linked lists. (To ensure obliviousness, the algorithm can always pretend to execute both branches of the if-statement.)
   At this moment, pos is the position to fetch from (for the i-th request out of m concurrent requests).
2. *Read and remove.* Read the value from $A[\text{pos}]$ and mark $A[\text{pos}] := \perp$.
3. *Update dummy head pointer if necessary.* If pos $= \text{dpos}_i$, update the dummy head pointer dpos$_i := $ next. (To ensure obliviousness, the algorithm can pretend to modify dpos$_i$ in any case.)
4. *Return.* Return the value read in the above Step 4.2.

The following fact is straightforward from the description of the algorithm.

Fact 4. *The Lookup algorithm completes in $O(1)$ parallel steps with $O(m)$ CPUs.*

Getall. Getall is implemented by the following simple procedure: obliviously sort A by the key such that all real entries are packed in front. Return the first n entries of the resulting array (and removing the metadata entries next and pos).

Fact 5. *The Getall algorithm completes in $\log(\tilde{n} + n)$ parallel steps consuming $O(\tilde{n} + n)$ CPUs.*

Lemma 1. (Perfect obliviousness of the one-time memory scheme). *The above (parallel) one-time memory scheme satisfies perfect obliviousness.*

Due to lack of space, we defer the proof to the full version of the paper [9]. Summarizing the above, we conclude with the following theorem.

Theorem 6 (One-time oblivious memory). *Let $\lambda \in \mathbb{N}$ be a parameter related to the probability that the algorithm's runtime exceeds a desired bound. Assume that each memory block can store at least $\log n + \log \lambda$ bits. There exists a perfectly oblivious one-time scheme such that* Build *takes $O(\log n)$ parallel steps (except with negligible in λ probability) consuming n CPUs,* Lookup *for a batch of m requests takes $O(1)$ parallel steps consuming m CPUs, and* Getall *takes $O(\log n)$ parallel steps consuming n CPUs.*

5   Basic OPRAM with $O(\log^3 N)$ Simulation Overhead

Recall that N denotes the number of logical memory blocks consumed by the original PRAM, and each memory block can store at least $\Omega(\log N)$ bits. In this section, we describe an OPRAM construction such that each batch of m memory requests takes $O(\log^3 N)$ parallel steps to satisfy with m CPUs. In the full version of our paper [9], we will describe how to further parallelize the OPRAM when the OPRAM can consume more CPUs than the original PRAM.

Roadmap. We briefly explain the technical roadmap of this section:

- In Sect. 5.1, we will first describe a *position-based OPRAM* that supports two operations: Lookup and Shuffle. A position-based OPRAM is *an almost fully functional OPRAM scheme except that every real lookup request must supply a correct position label.* In our OPRAM construction, these position labels will have been fetched from small recursion depths and therefore will be ready when looking up the position-based OPRAM.
  Our position-based OPRAM relies on the hierarcial structure proposed by Goldreich and Ostrovsky [21,22], as well as techniques by Chan et al. [8] that showed how to parallelize such a hierarchical framework.
- In Sect. 5.2, we explain how to leverage "coordinated rebuild" and recursion techniques to build a recursive OPRAM scheme that composes logarithmically many instances of our position-based OPRAM, of geometrically decreasing sizes.

5.1   Position-Based OPRAM

Our basic OPRAM scheme (Sect. 5.2) will consist of logarithmically many position-based OPRAMs of geometrically increasing sizes, henceforth denoted OPRAM_0, OPRAM_1, OPRAM_2, ..., OPRAM_D where $D := \log_2 N - \log_2 m$. Specifically, OPRAM_d stores $\Theta(2^d \cdot m)$ blocks where $d \in \{0, 1, \ldots, D\}$. The last one OPRAM_D stores the actual data blocks whereas every other OPRAM_d where $d < D$ recursively stores the position labels for the next depth $d + 1$.

Data Structure. As we shall see, the case OPRAM_0 is trivial and is treated specially at the end of this section (Sect. 5.1). Below we focus on describing OPRAM_d for some $1 \leq d \leq D = \log N - \log m$. For $d \neq 0$, each OPRAM_d consists of $d + 1$ *levels* geometrically growing in size, where each level is a *one-time oblivious memory scheme* as defined and described in Sect. 4. We specify this data structure more formally below.

Hierarchical Levels. The position-based OPRAM_d consists of $d+1$ levels henceforth denoted as $(\mathsf{OTM}_j : j = 0, \ldots, d)$ where level j is a one-time oblivious memory scheme,

$$\mathsf{OTM}_j := \mathsf{OTM}^{[2^j \cdot m, m, 2^j]}$$

with at most $n = 2^j \cdot m$ real blocks and m concurrent lookups in each batch (which can all be real). This means that for every OPRAM_d, the smallest level is capable of storing up to m real blocks. Every subsequent level can store twice as many real blocks as the previous level. For the largest OPRAM_D, its largest level is capable of storing N real blocks given that $D = \log N - \log m$—this means that the total space consumed is $O(N)$.

Every level j is marked as either *empty* (when the corresponding OTM_j has not been rebuilt) or *full* (when OTM_j is ready and in operation). Initially, all levels are marked as empty, i.e., the OPRAM initially is empty.

Position Label. Henceforth we assume that a position label of a block specifies (1) which level the block resides in; and (2) the position within the level the block resides at.

Additional Assumption. We assume that each block is of the form (logical address, payload), i.e., each block carries its own logical address.

Operations. Each position-based OPRAM supports two operations, Lookup and Shuffle. For every OPRAM_d consisting of $d+1$ levels, we rely on the following algorithms for Lookup and Shuffle.

Lookup. Every batch lookup operation, denoted $\mathsf{Lookup}(\{(\mathsf{addr}_i, \mathsf{pos}_i) : i \in [m]\})$ receives as input the logical addresses of m blocks as well as a correct position label for each requested block. To complete the batch lookup request, we perform the following.

1. For each level $j = 0, \ldots, d$ *in parallel*, perform the following:
   - For each $i \in [m]$ in parallel, first check the supplied position label pos_i to see if the requested block resides in the current level j: if so, let $\mathsf{addr}'_i := \mathsf{addr}_i$ and let $\mathsf{pos}'_i := \mathsf{pos}_i$ (and specifically the part of the position label denoting the offset within level j); else, set $\mathsf{addr}'_i := \bot$ and $\mathsf{pos}'_i := \bot$ to indicate that this should be a dummy request.
   - $(v_{ij} : i \in [m]) \leftarrow \mathsf{OTM}_j.\mathsf{Lookup}(\{\mathsf{addr}'_i, \mathsf{pos}'_i : i \in [m]\})$.

2. At this point, each of the m CPUs has d answers from the d levels respectively, and only one of them is the valid answer. Now each of the m CPUs chooses the correct answer as follows.
   For each $i \in [m]$ in parallel: set val_i to be the only non-dummy element in $(v_{ij} : j = 0, \ldots, d)$, if it exists; otherwise set $\mathsf{val}_i := \bot$. This step can be accomplished using an oblivious select operation in $\log d$ parallel steps consuming d CPUs.
3. Return $(\mathsf{val}_i : i \in [m])$.

We remark that in Goldreich and Ostrovsky's original hierarchical ORAM [21,22], the hierarchical levels must be visited sequentially—for obliviousness, if the block is found in some smaller level, all subsequent levels must perform a dummy lookup. Here we can visit all levels in parallel since the position label already tells us which level it is in. Now the following fact is straightforward:

Fact 7. *For* OPRAM_d, Lookup *consumes* $O(\log d)$ *parallel steps consuming* $m \cdot d$ *CPUs where* m *is the batch size.*

Shuffle. Similar to earlier hierarchical ORAMs [21,22] and OPRAMs [8], a shuffle operation merges consecutively full levels into the next empty level (or the largest level). However, in our Shuffle abstraction, there is an input U that contains some logical addresses together with new values to be updated. Moreover, the shuffle operation is associated with an update function that determines how the new values in U should be incorporated into the OTM during the rebuild.

In our full OPRAM scheme later, the update array U will be passed from the immediate next depth OPRAM_{d+1}, and contains the new position labels that OPRAM_{d+1} has chosen for recently accessed logical addresses. These position labels must then be recorded by OPRAM_d appropriately.

More formally, each position-based OPRAM_d supports a shuffle operation, denoted $\mathsf{Shuffle}(U, \ell; \mathsf{update})$, where the parameters are explained as follows:

1. An update array U in which each (non-dummy) entry contains a logical address that needs to be updated, and a new value for this block. (Strictly speaking, we allow a block to be partially updated.)
   We will define additional constraints on U subsequently.
2. The level ℓ to be rebuilt during this shuffle.
3. An update function that specifies how the information in U is used to compute the new value of a block in the OTM.
   The reason we make this rule explicit in the notation is that a block whose address that appears in U may only be partially modified; hence, we later need to specify this update function carefully. However, to avoid cumbersome notation, we may omit the parameter update, and just write $\mathsf{Shuffle}(U, \ell)$, when the context is clear.

For each OPRAM_d, when $\mathsf{Shuffle}(U, \ell; \mathsf{update})$ is called, it must be guaranteed that $\ell \leq d$; and moreover, either level ℓ must either be empty or $\ell = d$ (i.e., this is the largest level in OPRAM_d). Moreover, there is an extra OTM_0'; jumping ahead, we shall see that OTM_0' contains the blocks that are freshly fetched.

The Shuffle algorithm then combines levels $0, 1, \ldots, \ell$ (of OPRAM_d), together with the extra OTM_0', into level ℓ, updating some blocks' contents as instructed by the update array U and the update function update. At the end of the shuffle operation, all levels $0, 1, \ldots, \ell - 1$ are now marked as empty and level ℓ is now marked as full.

We now explain the assumptions we make on the update array U and how we want the update procedure to happen:

- We require that each logical address appears at most once in U.
- Let A be all logical addresses remaining in levels 0 to ℓ in OPRAM_d: it must hold that the set of logical addresses in U is a subset of those in A. In other words, a subset of the logical addresses in A will be updated before rebuilding level ℓ.
- If some logical address addr exists only in A but not in U, after rebuilding level ℓ, the block's value from the current OPRAM_d should be preserved. If some logical address addr exists in both A and in U, we use the update function to modify its value: update takes a pair of blocks (addr, data) and (addr, data') with the same address but possibly different contents (the first of which coming from the current OPRAM_d and the second coming from U), and computes the new block content data* appropriately.
  We remark that the new value data* might depend on both data and data'. Later, we will describe how the update rule is implemented.

Upon receiving Shuffle$(U, \ell; \text{update})$, proceed with the following steps:

1. Let $A := \cup_{i=0}^{\ell} \mathsf{OTM}_i.\mathsf{Getall} \cup \mathsf{OTM}_0'.\mathsf{Getall}$, where the operator $\cup$ denotes concatenation. Moreover, for an entry in A that comes from OTM_i, then it also carries a label i.
   At this moment, the old $\mathsf{OTM}_0, \ldots, \mathsf{OTM}_\ell$ instances may be destroyed.
2. We obliviously sort $A \cup U$ in increasing order of logical addresses, and moreover, placing all dummy entries at the end. If two blocks have the same logical address, place the entry coming from A in front of the one coming from U.
   At this moment, in one linear scan, we can operate on every adjacent pair of entries using the aforementioned update operation, such that if they share the same logical address, the first entry is preserved and updated to a new value, and the second entry is set to dummy.
   We now obliviously sort the resulting array moving all dummies to the end. We truncate the resulting array preserving only the first $2^\ell \cdot m$ elements and let A' denote the outcome (note that only dummies and no real blocks will truncated in the above step).
3. Next, we call $U' \leftarrow \mathsf{Build}(A')$ that builds a new OTM' and U' contains the positions of blocks in OTM'.
4. OTM' is now the new level ℓ and henceforth it will be denoted OTM_ℓ. Mark level ℓ as full and levels $0, 1, \ldots, \ell - 1$ as empty. Finally, output U' (in our full OPRAM construction, U' will be passed to the immediately smaller position-based OPRAM as the update array for performing its shuffle).

If we realize the oblivious sort with the AKS network [1] that sorts n items in $O(\log n)$ parallel steps consuming n CPUs, we easily obtain the following fact—note that there is a negligible in N probability that the algorithm runs longer than the stated asymptotic time due to the oblivious random permutation building block.

Fact 8. *Suppose that the* update *function can be evaluated by a single CPU in $O(1)$ steps. For OPRAM_d, let $\ell \leq d$, then except with negligible in N probability, $\mathsf{Shuffle}(U, \ell)$ takes $O(\log(m \cdot 2^\ell))$ parallel steps consuming $m \cdot 2^\ell$ CPUs.*

Observe that in the above fact, the randomness comes from the oblivious random permutation subroutine used in building the one-time oblivious memory data structure.

Trivial Case: OPRAM_0. In this case, OPRAM_0 simply stores its entries in an array $A[0..m)$ of size m and we assume that the entries are indexed by a $(\log_2 m)$-bit string. Moreover, each address is also a $(\log_2 m)$-bit string, whose block is stored at the corresponding entry in A.

- *Lookup.* Upon receiving a batch of m depth-m truncated addresses where all the real addresses are distinct, use oblivious routing to route $A[0..m)$ to the requested addresses. This can be accomplished in $O(m \log m)$ total work and $O(\log m)$ depth. Note that OPRAM_0's lookup does not receive any position labels.
- *Shuffle.* Since there is only one array A (at level 0), $\mathsf{Shuffle}(U, 0)$ can be implemented by oblivious sorting.

5.2 OPRAM Scheme from Position-Based OPRAM

Recursive OPRAMs. The OPRAM scheme consists of $D + 1$ position-based OPRAMs henceforth denoted as $\mathsf{OPRAM}_0, \mathsf{OPRAM}_1, \mathsf{OPRAM}_2, \ldots, \mathsf{OPRAM}_D$. OPRAM_D stores the actual data blocks, whereas every other OPRAM_d where $d \neq D$ recursively stores the position labels for the next data structure OPRAM_{d+1}. Our construction is in essence recursive although in presentation we shall spell out the recursion for clarity. Henceforth we often say that OPRAM_d is at *recursion depth d* or simply *depth d*.

Although we are inspired by the recursion technique for tree-based ORAMs [36], using this recursion technique in the context of hierarchical ORAMs/OPRAMs raises new challenges. In particular, we cannot use the recursion in a blackbox fashion like in tree-based constructions since all of our (position-based, hierarchical) OPRAMs must reshuffle in sync with each other in a non-blackbox fashion as will become clear later.

Format of Depth-d Block and Address. Suppose that a block's logical address is a $\log_2 N$-bit string denoted $\mathsf{addr}^{\langle D \rangle} := \mathsf{addr}[1..(\log_2 N)]$ (expressed in binary format), where $\mathsf{addr}[1]$ is the most significant bit. In general, at depth d, an address $\mathsf{addr}^{\langle d \rangle}$ is the length-$(\log_2 m + d)$ prefix of the full address $\mathsf{addr}^{\langle D \rangle}$. Henceforth, we refer to $\mathsf{addr}^{\langle d \rangle}$ as a depth-d address (or the depth-d truncation of addr).

When we look up a data block, we would look up the full address $\mathsf{addr}^{\langle D \rangle}$ in recursion depth D; we look up $\mathsf{addr}^{\langle D-1 \rangle}$ at depth $D - 1$, $\mathsf{addr}^{\langle D-2 \rangle}$ at depth $D - 2$, and so on. Finally at depth 0, the $\log_2 m$-bit address uniquely determines one of the m blocks stored at OPRAM_0. Since each batch consists of m concurrent lookups, one of them will be responsible for this block in OPRAM_0.

A *block with the address* $\mathsf{addr}^{\langle d \rangle}$ *in* OPRAM_d *stores the position labels for two blocks in* OPRAM_{d+1}, *at addresses* $\mathsf{addr}^{\langle d \rangle}\|0$ *and* $\mathsf{addr}^{\langle d \rangle}\|1$ *respectively*. Henceforth, we say that the two addresses $\mathsf{addr}^{\langle d \rangle}\|0$ and $\mathsf{addr}^{\langle d \rangle}\|1$ are *siblings* to each other; $\mathsf{addr}^{\langle d \rangle}\|0$ is called the left sibling and $\mathsf{addr}^{\langle d \rangle}\|1$ is called the right sibling. We say that $\mathsf{addr}^{\langle d \rangle}\|0$ is the left child of $\mathsf{addr}^{\langle d \rangle}$ and $\mathsf{addr}^{\langle d \rangle}\|1$ is the right child of $\mathsf{addr}^{\langle d \rangle}$.

Operations. Each batch contains m requests denoted as $((\mathsf{op}_i, \mathsf{addr}_i, \mathsf{data}_i) : i \in [m])$, where for $\mathsf{op}_i = \mathsf{read}$, there is no data_i. We perform the following steps.

1. **Conflict resolution.** For every depth $d \in \{0, 1, \ldots, D\}$ in parallel, perform oblivious conflict resolution on the depth-d truncation of all m addresses requested.

   For $d = D$, we suppress duplicate addresses. If multiple requests collide on addresses, we would prefer a write request over a read request (since write requests also fetch the old memory value back before overwriting it with a new value). In the case of concurrent write operations to the same address, we use the properties of the underlying PRAM to determine which write operation prevails.

   For $0 \leq d < D$, after conflict resolution, the m requests for OPRAM_d become

   $$((\mathsf{addr}_i^{\langle d \rangle}, \mathsf{flags}_i) : i \in [m]),$$

   where each non-dummy depth-d truncated address $\mathsf{addr}_i^{\langle d \rangle}$ is distinct and has a two-bit flags_i that indicates whether each of two addresses $(\mathsf{addr}_i^{\langle d \rangle}\|0)$ and $(\mathsf{addr}_i^{\langle d \rangle}\|1)$ is requested in OPRAM_{d+1}. As noted by earlier works on OPRAM [6,10,11], conflict resolution can be completed through $O(1)$ number of oblivious sorting operations. We thus defer the details of the conflict resolution procedure to the full version of the paper [9].

2. **Fetch.** For $d = 0$ to D sequentially, perform the following:
   - For each $i \in [m]$ in parallel: let $\mathsf{addr}_i^{\langle d \rangle}$ be the depth-d truncation of $\mathsf{addr}_i^{\langle D \rangle}$.
   - Call $\mathsf{OPRAM}_d.\mathsf{Lookup}$ to look up the depth-d addresses $\mathsf{addr}_i^{\langle d \rangle}$ for all $i \in [m]$; observe that position labels for the lookups of non-dummy addresses will be available from the lookup of the previous OPRAM_{d-1} for $d \geq 1$, which is described in the next step. Recall that for OPRAM_0, no position labels are needed.
   - If $d < D$, each lookup from a non-dummy $(\mathsf{addr}_i^{\langle d \rangle}, \mathsf{flags}_i)$ will return two positions for the addresses $\mathsf{addr}_i^{\langle d \rangle}\|0$ and $\mathsf{addr}_i^{\langle d \rangle}\|1$ in OPRAM_{d+1}. The

two bits in flags_i will determine whether each of these two position labels are needed in the lookup of OPRAM_{d+1}.

We can imagine that there are m CPUs at recursion depth $d+1$ waiting for the position labels corresponding to $\{\mathsf{addr}_i^{\langle d+1 \rangle} : i \in [m]\}$. Now, using oblivious routing, the position labels can be delivered to the CPUs at recursion depth $d+1$.

- If $d = D$, the outcome of Lookup will contain the data blocks fetched. Recall that conflict resolution was used to suppress duplicate addresses. Hence, oblivious routing can be used to deliver each data block to the corresponding CPUs that request it.
- In any case, the freshly fetched blocks are updated if needed in the case of $d = D$, and are placed in OTM_0' in each OPRAM_d.

3. **Maintain.** We first consider depth D. Set depth-D's update array $U^{\langle D \rangle} := \emptyset$. Suppose that $\ell^{\langle D \rangle}$ is the smallest empty level in OPRAM_D. We have the invariant that for all $0 \le d < D$, if $\ell^{\langle D \rangle} < d$, then $\ell^{\langle D \rangle}$ is also the smallest empty level in OPRAM_d.

For $d := D$ downto 0, do the following:

- If $d < \ell^{\langle D \rangle}$, set $\ell := d$; otherwise, set $\ell := \ell^{\langle D \rangle}$.
- Call $U \leftarrow \mathsf{OPRAM}_d.\mathsf{Shuffle}(U^{\langle d \rangle}, \ell; \mathsf{update})$ where update is the following natural function: recall that in $U^{\langle d \rangle}$ and OPRAM_{d-1}, each depth-$(d-1)$ logical address stores the position labels for both children addresses. For each of the child addresses, if $U^{\langle d \rangle}$ contains a new position label, choose the new one; otherwise, choose the old label previously in OPRAM_{d-1}.
- If $d \ge 1$, we need to send the updated positions involved in U to depth $d-1$.

  We use the Convert subroutine to convert U into an update array for depth-$(d-1)$ addresses, where each entry may pack the position labels for up to two sibling depth-d addresses. Convert can be realized with $O(1)$ oblivious sorting operations and we defer its detailed presentation to the full version of our paper [9].

  Now, set $U^{\langle d-1 \rangle} \leftarrow \mathsf{Convert}(U, d)$, which will be used in the next iteration for recursion depth $d-1$ to perform its shuffle.

With the above basic OPRAM construction, we can achieve the following theorem whose proof is deferred to the full version of the paper [9].

Theorem 9. *The above construction is a perfectly secure OPRAM scheme satisfying the following performance overhead:*

- *When consuming the same number of CPUs as the original PRAM, the scheme incurs $O(\log^3 N)$ simulation overhead;*
- *When the OPRAM is allowed to consume an unbounded number of CPUs, the scheme incurs $O(\log^3 N)$ total work blowup and $O((\log m + \log \log N) \log N)$ depth blowup.*

In either case, the space blowup is $O(1)$.

Proof. We defer the obliviousness proof and performance analysis to the full version of the paper [9].

Note that at this moment, even for the sequential special case, we already achieve asymptotic savings over Damgård et al. [13] in terms of space consumption. Furthermore, Damgård et al. [13]'s construction is sequential in nature and does not immediately give rise to an OPRAM scheme.

6 Conclusion and Future Work

In this paper, we constructed a perfectly secure OPRAM scheme with $O(\log^3 N)$ total work blowup, $O(\log N \log \log N)$ depth blowup, and $O(1)$ space blowup. To the best of our knowledge our scheme is the first perfectly secure (non-trivial) OPRAM scheme, and even for the sequential special case we asymptotically improve the space overhead relative to Damgård et al. [13]. Prior to our work, the only known perfectly secure ORAM scheme is that by Damgård et al. [13], where they achieve $O(\log^3 N)$ simulation overhead and $O(\log N)$ space blowup. No (non-trivial) OPRAM scheme was known prior to our work, and in particular the scheme by Damgård et al. [13] does not appear amenable to parallelization. Finally, in comparison with known statistically secure OPRAMs [10,39], our work removes the dependence (in performance) on the security parameter; thus we in fact asymptotically outperform known statistically secure ORAMs [39] and OPRAMs [10] when (sub-)exponentially small failure probabilities are required.

Exciting questions remain open for future research:

– Are there any separations between the performance of perfectly secure and statistically secure ORAMs/OPRAMs?
– Can we construct perfectly secure ORAMs/OPRAMs whose total work blowup matches the best known statistically secure ORAMs/OPRAMs assuming negligible security failures?
– Can we construct perfectly secure ORAM/OPRAM schemes whose concrete performance lends to deployment in real-world systems?

Acknowledgments. Kartik Nayak was supported by a Google Ph.D. fellowship. T.-H. Hubert Chan was supported in part by the Hong Kong RGC under grant 17200418. Elaine Shi was supported in part by NSF award CNS-1601879, a Packard Fellowship, and a DARPA Safeware grant (subcontractor under IBM).

We gratefully acknowledge Shai Halevi and Craig Gentry for helpful discussions and for suggesting the use of expander graphs to achieve low-online-depth routing of position labels. We are extremely grateful to Bruce Maggs for most patiently explaining Pippenger's result [33] to us and answering many of our technical questions. We acknowledge Kai-Min Chung for many helpful technical discussions regarding perfectly secure ORAM and OPRAM. We thank Ling Ren for many early discussions on perfectly secure ORAMs. We thank Muthuramakrishnan Venkitasubramaniam, Antigoni Polychroniadou, and Kai-Min Chung for helpful discussions on the significance of achieving perfect security in cryptographic primitives, and for helpful editorial comments. Elaine Shi is grateful to Bruce Maggs, Bobby Bhattacharjee, Kai-Min Chung, and Feng-Hao Liu for their unwavering moral support during the period this research was conducted.

References

1. Ajtai, M., Komlós, J., Szemerédi, E.: An O(N log N) sorting network. In: Proceedings of the Fifteenth Annual ACM Symposium on Theory of Computing, STOC 1983, pp. 1–9. ACM, New York (1983)
2. Ajtai, M.: Oblivious RAMs without cryptogrpahic assumptions. In: Proceedings of the Forty-Second ACM Symposium on Theory of Computing, STOC 2010, pp. 181–190. ACM, New York (2010)
3. Asharov, G., Chan, T.-H.H., Nayak, K., Pass, R., Ren, L., Shi, E.: Oblivious computation with data locality. IACR Cryptology ePrint Archive 2017:772 (2017)
4. Ben-Or, M., Goldwasser, S., Wigderson, A.: Completeness theorems for non-cryptographic fault-tolerant distributed computation. In: Proceedings of the Twentieth Annual ACM Symposium on Theory of Computing, STOC 1988, pp. 1–10 (1988)
5. Boyle, E., Chung, K.-M., Pass, R.: Large-scale secure computation: multi-party computation for (parallel) RAM programs. In: Gennaro, R., Robshaw, M. (eds.) CRYPTO 2015. LNCS, vol. 9216, pp. 742–762. Springer, Heidelberg (2015). https://doi.org/10.1007/978-3-662-48000-7_36
6. Boyle, E., Chung, K.-M., Pass, R.: Oblivious parallel RAM and applications. In: Kushilevitz, E., Malkin, T. (eds.) TCC 2016. LNCS, vol. 9563, pp. 175–204. Springer, Heidelberg (2016). https://doi.org/10.1007/978-3-662-49099-0_7
7. Chan, T.-H.H., Chung, K.-M., Shi, E.: On the depth of oblivious parallel RAM. In: Asiacrypt (2017)
8. Chan, T.-H.H., Guo, Y., Lin, W.-K., Shi, E.: Oblivious hashing revisited, and applications to asymptotically efficient ORAM and OPRAM. In: Asiacrypt (2017)
9. Chan, T.-H.H., Nayak, K., Shi, E.: Perfectly secure oblivious parallel ram. Cryptology ePrint Archive, Report 2018/364 (2018). https://eprint.iacr.org/2018/364
10. Chan, T-H.H., Shi, E.: Circuit OPRAM: a unifying framework for computationally and statistically secure ORAMs and OPRAMs. In: TCC (2017)
11. Chen, B., Lin, H., Tessaro, S.: Oblivious parallel RAM: improved efficiency and generic constructions. In: Kushilevitz, E., Malkin, T. (eds.) TCC 2016. LNCS, vol. 9563, pp. 205–234. Springer, Heidelberg (2016). https://doi.org/10.1007/978-3-662-49099-0_8
12. Chung, K.-M., Liu, Z., Pass, R.: Statistically-secure ORAM with $\tilde{O}(\log^2 n)$ overhead. In: Asiacrypt (2014)
13. Damgård, I., Meldgaard, S., Nielsen, J.B.: Perfectly secure oblivious RAM without random oracles. In: Theory of Cryptography Conference (TCC), pp. 144–163 (2011)
14. Dautrich, J., Stefanov, E., Shi, E.: Burst ORAM: minimizing ORAM response times for bursty access patterns. In: 23rd USENIX Security Symposium (USENIX Security 14), pp. 749–764, San Diego, CA, August 2014. USENIX Association
15. Demertzis, I., Papadopoulos, D., Papamanthou, C.: Searchable encryption with optimal locality: achieving sublogarithmic read efficiency. Cryptology ePrint Archive, Report 2017/749 (2017). https://eprint.iacr.org/2017/749
16. Fletcher, C.W., Ren, L., Kwon, A., van Dijk, M., Devadas, S.: Freecursive ORAM: [nearly] free recursion and integrity verification for position-based oblivious RAM. In: ASPLOS (2015)
17. Fletcher, C.W., Ren, L., Kwon, A., van Dijk, M., Stefanov, E., Devadas, S.: RAW path ORAM: a low-latency, low-area hardware ORAM controller with integrity verification. IACR Cryptol. Eprint Arch. **2014**, 431 (2014)

18. Fletcher, C.W., Ren, L., Yu, X., van Dijk, M., Khan, O., Devadas, S.: Suppressing the oblivious RAM timing channel while making information leakage and program efficiency trade-offs. In: HPCA, pp. 213–224 (2014)
19. Genkin, D., Ishai, Y., Weiss, M.: Binary AMD circuits from secure multiparty computation. In: Hirt, M., Smith, A. (eds.) TCC 2016. LNCS, vol. 9985, pp. 336–366. Springer, Heidelberg (2016). https://doi.org/10.1007/978-3-662-53641-4_14
20. Gentry, C., Goldman, K.A., Halevi, S., Jutla, C.S., Raykova, M., Wichs, D.: Optimizing ORAM and using it efficiently for secure computation. In: Privacy Enhancing Technologies Symposium (PETS) (2013)
21. Goldreich, O.: Towards a theory of software protection and simulation by oblivious RAMs. In: ACM Symposium on Theory of Computing (STOC) (1987)
22. Goldreich, O., Ostrovsky, R.: Software protection and simulation on oblivious RAMs. J ACM 43(3), 431–473 (1996)
23. Goodrich, M.T., Mitzenmacher, M.: Privacy-preserving access of outsourced data via oblivious RAM simulation. In: International Colloquium on Automata, Languages and Programming (ICALP), pp. 576–587 (2011)
24. Goodrich, M.T., Mitzenmacher, M., Ohrimenko, O., Tamassia, R.: Privacy-preserving group data access via stateless oblivious RAM simulation. In: Proceedings of the Twenty-Third Annual ACM-SIAM Symposium on Discrete Algorithms, SODA 2012, pp. 157–167, Philadelphia, PA, USA (2012). Society for Industrial and Applied Mathematics
25. Dov Gordon, S., Katz, J., Kolesnikov, V., Krell, F., Malkin, T., Raykova, M., Vahlis, Y.: Secure two-party computation in sublinear (amortized) time. In: ACM Conference on Computer and Communications Security (CCS) (2012)
26. Ishai, Y., Kushilevitz, E., Ostrovsky, R., Prabhakaran, M., Sahai, A.: Efficient non-interactive secure computation. In: Paterson, K.G. (ed.) EUROCRYPT 2011. LNCS, vol. 6632, pp. 406–425. Springer, Heidelberg (2011). https://doi.org/10.1007/978-3-642-20465-4_23
27. Kushilevitz, E., Lu, S., Ostrovsky, R.: On the (in)security of hash-based oblivious RAM and a new balancing scheme. In: ACM-SIAM Symposium on Discrete Algorithms (SODA) (2012)
28. Liu, C., Harris, A., Maas, M., Hicks, M., Tiwari, M., Shi, E.: Ghostrider: a hardware-software system for memory trace oblivious computation. SIGPLAN Not. 50(4), 87–101 (2015)
29. Liu, C., Wang, X.S., Nayak, K., Huang, Y., Shi, E.: ObliVM: a programming framework for secure computation. In: 2015 IEEE Symposium on Security and Privacy, SP 2015, San Jose, CA, USA, 17–21 May 2015, pp. 359–376 (2015
30. Maas, M., Love, E., Stefanov, E., Tiwari, M., Shi, E., Asanovic, K., Kubiatowicz, J., Song, D.: Phantom: practical oblivious computation in a secure processor. In: ACM Conference on Computer and Communications Security (CCS) (2013)
31. Nayak, K., et al.: HOP: hardware makes obfuscation practical. In: 24th Annual Network and Distributed System Security Symposium, NDSS (2017)
32. Nayak, K., Katz, J.: An oblivious parallel RAM with $o(log^2 n)$ parallel runtime blowup. IACR Cryptol. Eprint Arch. 2016, 1141 (2016)
33. Pippenger, N.: Self-routing superconcentrators. In: Proceedings of the Twenty-Fifth Annual ACM Symposium on Theory of Computing, STOC 1993, pp. 355–361. ACM, New York (1993)
34. Raskin, M., Simkin, M.: Oblivious RAM with small storage overhead. Cryptology ePrint Archive, Report 2018/268 (2018). https://eprint.iacr.org/2018/268

35. Ren, L., Yu, X., Fletcher, C.W., van Dijk, M., Devadas, S.: Design space exploration and optimization of path oblivious RAM in secure processors. In: ISCA, pp. 571–582 (2013)
36. Shi, E., Chan, T.-H.H., Stefanov, E., Li, M.: Oblivious RAM with $O(\log^3 N)$ worst-case cost. In: ASIACRYPT, pp. 197–214 (2011)
37. Stefanov, E., Shi, E.: Oblivistore: high performance oblivious cloud storage. In: IEEE Symposium on Security and Privacy (S & P) (2013)
38. Stefanov, E., van Dijk, M., Shi, E., Fletcher, C., Ren, L., Yu, X., Devadas, S.: Path ORAM - an extremely simple oblivious RAM protocol. In: ACM Conference on Computer and Communications Security (CCS) (2013)
39. Wang, X.S., Chan, T-H.H., Shi, E.: Circuit ORAM: on tightness of the Goldreich-Ostrovsky lower bound. In: ACM CCS (2015)
40. Williams, P., Sion, R., Tomescu, A.: PrivateFS: a parallel oblivious file system. In: ACM Conference on Computer and Communications Security (CCS) (2012)

Watermarking PRFs Under Standard Assumptions: Public Marking and Security with Extraction Queries

Willy Quach[(✉)], Daniel Wichs, and Giorgos Zirdelis

Northeastern University, Boston, USA
quach.w@husky.neu.edu, wichs@ccs.neu.edu, zirdelis.g@husky.neu.edu

Abstract. A software watermarking scheme can embed some information called a mark into a program while preserving its functionality. No adversary can remove the mark without damaging the functionality of the program. Cohen et al. (STOC '16) gave the first positive results for watermarking, showing how to watermark certain *pseudorandom function (PRF) families* using indistinguishability obfuscation (iO). Their scheme has a secret marking procedure to embed marks in programs and a public extraction procedure to extract the marks from programs; security holds even against an attacker that has access to a marking oracle. Kim and Wu (CRYPTO '17) later constructed a PRF watermarking scheme under only the LWE assumption. In their scheme, both the marking and extraction procedures are secret, but security only holds against an attacker with access to a marking oracle *but not* an extraction oracle. In fact, it is possible to completely break the security of the latter scheme using extraction queries, which is a significant limitation in any foreseeable application.

In this work, we construct a new PRF watermarking scheme with the following properties.

- The marking procedure is public and therefore anyone can embed marks in PRFs from the family. Previously we had no such construction even using obfuscation.
- The extraction key is secret, but marks remain unremovable even if the attacker has access to an extraction oracle. Previously we had no such construction under standard assumptions.
- Our scheme is simple, uses generic components and can be instantiated under many different assumptions such as DDH, Factoring or LWE.

The above benefits come with one caveat compared to prior work: the PRF family that we can watermark depends on the public parameters of the watermarking scheme and the watermarking authority has a secret key which can break the security of all of the PRFs in the family. Since the watermarking authority is usually assumed to be trusted, this caveat appears to be acceptable.

Supported by NSF grants CNS-1314722, CNS-1413964, CNS-1750795 and the Alfred P. Sloan Research Fellowship.

© International Association for Cryptologic Research 2018
A. Beimel and S. Dziembowski (Eds.): TCC 2018, LNCS 11240, pp. 669–698, 2018.
https://doi.org/10.1007/978-3-030-03810-6_24

1   Introduction

Watermarking allows us to embed some special information called a *mark* into digital objects such as images, movies, music files, or software. There are two basic requirements: firstly, a marked object should not be significantly different from the original object, and secondly, it should be impossible to remove an embedded mark without somehow "destroying" the object.

The works of Barak et al. [2,3] and Hopper, Molnar and Wagner [14] initiated the first theoretical study of program watermarking including rigorous definitions. However, positive results for watermarking remained elusive. A few early works [17,18,20] gave very partial results showing that certain cryptographic functions can be watermarked, but security only held against restricted adversaries with limited ability to modify the program. For example, in such schemes it is easy to remove the watermark by obfuscating the program without changing its functionality. The first positive result for watermarking against arbitrary removal strategies was given in the work of Cohen et al. [10] who showed how to watermark certain families of pseudo-random functions (PRFs). However, this result relies on the heavy hammer of *indistinguishability obfuscation (iO)* [2,3,12]. Later, the work of Kim and Wu [16] constructed a PRF watermarking scheme under only the learning-with-errors (LWE) assumption, but at the cost of weakening security. We first describe the problem of watermarking PRFs in more detail, then come back to discuss the above two works and finally present our new contributions.

Watermarking PRFs. A watermarking scheme for a PRF family $\{F_k\}$ consists of two procedures Mark and Extract. The Mark procedure takes as input a PRF F_k from the family and outputs a program P which is a marked version of the PRF. We want *approximate correctness*, meaning that $F_k(x) = P(x)$ for all but a negligible fraction of inputs x and these should be hard to find. The Extract procedure takes as input a program P' and determines whether it is marked or unmarked. The main security property that we desire is *unremovability*: if we choose F_k randomly from the family and give the marked version P to an adversary, the adversary should be unable to come up with any program P' that even ε-approximates P for some small ε (meaning that $P(x) = P'(x)$ for an ε fraction of inputs x) yet the extraction procedure fails to recognize P' as marked. Each of the procedures Mark, Extract may either be "public" meaning that it only relies on the public parameters of the watermarking scheme, or it may be "secret" meaning that it requires a secret key of the watermarking scheme. If one (or both) of the procedures is secret then the unremovability security property should hold even if the adversary gets oracle access to that procedure. We can also consider "message embedding" schemes, where the marking procedure additionally takes a message and the extraction procedure recovers the message from a marked program – the unremovability property should then ensure that the adversary cannot remove the mark or modify the embedded message.[1]

There are several reason why watermarking PRFs is interesting. Firstly, watermarking in general is a poorly understood cryptographic concept yet clearly desirable in practice – therefore any kind of positive result is fascinating since it helps us get a better understanding of this elusive notion. Secondly, software watermarking only makes sense for unlearnable functions (as formalized in [10]) so we need to focus on cryptographic programs such as PRFs rather than (e.g.,) tax preparation software. Lastly, PRFs are a basic building block for more advanced cryptosystems and therefore watermarking PRFs will also allow us to watermark more advanced primitives that rely on PRFs, such as symmetric-key encryption or authentication schemes. See [10] for further discussion and potential applications of watermarked PRFs.

Prior Work. The work of Cohen et al. [10] showed how to watermark any family of puncturable PRFs using indistinguishability obfuscation (iO). They constructed a watermarking scheme with secret marking and public extraction, where the unremovability property holds even if the adversary has access to the marking oracle. The use of obfuscation may have appeared inherent in that result. However, Kim and Wu [16] (building on [5]) surprisingly showed how to remove it and managed to construct a watermarking scheme for a specific PRF family under only the learning-with-errors (LWE) assumption. In their scheme, both the marking and the extraction procedures are secret, but the unremovability security property only holds if the adversary has access to the marking oracle *but not* the extraction oracle. In particular, an adversary that can test whether arbitrary programs are marked or unmarked can completely break the security of the watermarking scheme. Since the entire point of watermarking is to use the extraction procedure on programs that may potentially have been constructed by an adversary, it is hard to justify that the adversary does not get access to the extraction oracle. Therefore this should be considered as a significant limitation of that scheme in any foreseeable application.

Our Results. In this work, we construct a watermarking scheme for a PRF family under standard assumptions. In particular, we only rely on CCA-secure public-key encryption with pseudorandom ciphertexts, which can be instantiated under most standard public-key assumptions such as DDH, LWE or Factoring. Our watermarking scheme has public marking and secret extraction, and the

---

[1] Some previous watermarking schemes also required an *unforgeability* property, which roughly says that an adversary should not be able to produce any marked functions on his own – in fact, he should not be able to come up with a function which is marked but is far from any of the marked functions that were output by the marking oracle. This property appears to be orthogonal to the main watermarking requirement of unremovability and we do not consider it here. In particular, it crucially requires a scheme with a secret marking procedure whereas here we construct watermarking scheme with a public marking procedure.

unremovability security property holds even if the adversary has access to the extraction oracle. We emphasize that:

- This is the first watermarking scheme with a public marking procedure. Previously such schemes were not known even under iO.
- This is the first watermarking scheme under standard assumptions where unremovability holds in the presence of the extraction oracle. Previously we only had such schemes under iO, in which case it was possible to even get public extraction, but not under any standard assumptions.
- This is the first watermarking scheme altogether under assumptions other than LWE or iO.

Our basic scheme is not message embedding (whereas the constructions of [10,16] are), but we also show how to get a message embedding scheme by additionally relying on generic constraint-hiding constrained PRFs, which we currently have under LWE [4,8,9,19].

Additionally, we allow an adversary who tries to remove the mark of some program P to change a *large* fraction of its outputs, matching the security guarantee of [10] based on iO. In comparison, the work of [16] based on standard assumptions restricts an adversary to only modify a *very small* fraction of its inputs. More precisely, while [16] only allows an adversary to only change a *negligible* fraction of the outputs of P, our construction without message embedding allows him to modify *almost all* of these outputs, as long as a polynomial fraction remains the same; and our construction with message embedding allows an adversary to change almost half of the outputs which is essentially optimal (as shown in [10])

Our scheme comes with one caveat that was not present in prior works. The PRF family that we watermark depends on the public-parameters of the watermarking scheme and it is possible to break the PRF security of this family given the watermarking secret key. In particular, this means that the watermarking authority which sets up the scheme can break the PRF security of all functions in the family, even ones that were never marked. However, we ensure that PRF security continues to hold even given the public parameters of the watermarking scheme and oracle access to the extraction procedure. Therefore the PRFs remain secure for everyone else *except* the watermarking authority. Technically, this caveat makes our results incomparable with those in prior works. However, we argue that since the watermarking authority is anyway assumed to be a trusted party in order for the watermarking guarantees to be meaningful, this caveat doesn't significantly detract from the spirit of the problem and our solutions with this caveat are still very meaningful.

1.1   Our Techniques

Watermarking Unpredictable Functions. To give the intuition behind our scheme, we first describe a simplified construction which allows us to watermark an *unpredictable* (but not yet pseudorandom) function family.[2]

The public parameters of the watermarking scheme consist of a public-key pk for a CCA secure public-key encryption scheme and the watermarking secret key is the corresponding decryption key sk. Let $\{f_s\}$ be an arbitrary puncturable PRF (pPRF) family. We are able to watermark a function family $\{F_k\}$ which is defined as follows:

- The key $k = (s, z, r)$ consists of a pPRF key s, a random pPRF input z and encryption randomness r.
- The function is defined as $F_k(x) = (f_s(x), \mathsf{ct})$ where $\mathsf{ct} = \mathsf{Enc}_{\mathsf{pk}}((f_s(z), z)\,;\,r)$.

Note that this is not yet a PRF family since the ct part of the output is always the same no matter what x is. However, the first part of the output ensures that the function is unpredictable. We now describe the marking and extraction procedures.

- To mark a function F_k with $k = (s, z, r)$ we create a key $\tilde{k} = (s\{z\}, \mathsf{ct})$ where $s\{z\}$ is a PRF key which is punctured at the point z and $\mathsf{ct} = \mathsf{Enc}_{\mathsf{pk}}((f_s(z), z)\,;\,r)$. We define the marked function as $F_{\tilde{k}}(x) = (f_{s\{z\}}(x), \mathsf{ct})$. The extraction procedure gets a circuit C and let $C(x) = (C_1(x), C_2(x))$ denote the first and second part of the output respectively. The extraction procedure computes $C_2(x_i) = \mathsf{ct}_i$ for many random values x_i and attempts to decrypt $\mathsf{Dec}_{\mathsf{sk}}(\mathsf{ct}_i) = (y_i, z_i)$. If for at least one i the decryption succeeds and it holds that $C_1(z_i) \neq y_i$ then the procedure outputs marked, else it outputs unmarked.

There are several properties to check. Firstly, note that marking procedure does not require any secret keys and that the marked function satisfies $F_k(x) = F_{\tilde{k}}(x)$ for all $x \neq z$. In other words, the marking procedure only introduces only a single difference at a random point z.[3] Secondly, for any function F_k in the family which was not marked, the extraction procedure correctly outputs unmarked and for any function $F_{\tilde{k}}(x)$ that was marked it correctly outputs marked.[4]

To argue that marks are unremovable, assume that we choose a random function F_k in the family, mark it, and give the adversary the marked function

---

[2] A function family is unpredictable if, given arbitrarily many oracle calls to a random function from the family on various inputs x_i, it is hard to predict the output of the function on any fresh input x^* which was not queried.

[3] Moreover, we show the following. Given oracle access to a random unmarked function $F_k(\cdot)$ and its marked version $F_{\tilde{k}}(\cdot)$ as well as the extraction oracle, it is hard to find the point z on which they differ.

[4] Moreover, we can also ensure that any a-priori chosen circuit C is unmarked with high probability over the keys of the watermarking scheme. To achieve this we rely on an encryption scheme where legitimate ciphertexts are sparse.

$F_{\widetilde{k}}$ with $\widetilde{k} = (s\{z\}, \mathsf{ct})$. The adversary produces some circuit C which he gives to the extraction procedure and he wins if C agrees with $F_{\widetilde{k}}$ on a sufficiently large fraction of inputs but the extraction procedure deems C to be unmarked. If C agrees with $F_{\widetilde{k}}$ on a sufficiently large fraction of inputs then with very high probability for at least one x_i queried by the extraction procedure it holds that $C_2(x_i) = \mathsf{ct}$ and ct decrypts to $(f_s(z), z)$. In order for the extraction procedure to output unmarked it would have to hold that $C_1(z) = f_s(z)$ meaning that the adversary can predict $f_s(z)$. But the adversary only has a punctured pPRF key $s\{z\}$ and therefore it should be hard to predict $f_s(z)$. This argument is incomplete since the adversary also has a ciphertext ct which encrypts $f_s(z)$ and oracle access to the extraction procedure which contains a decryption key sk. To complete the argument, we rely on the CCA security of the encryption scheme to argue that extraction queries do not reveal any information about $f_s(z)$ beyond allowing the adversary to test whether $f_s(z) = y$ for various chosen values y and this is insufficient to predict $f_s(z)$.

Watermarking Pseudorandom Functions. To get a watermarking scheme for a pseudorandom function family rather than just an unpredictable one we add an additional "outer" layer of encryption. We need the outer encryption to be a "pseudorandom tagged CCA encryption" which ensures that a ciphertext encrypting some message m under a tag x looks random even given decryption queries with respect to any tags $x' \neq x$. The public parameters consist of an outer public key pk' for the "pseudorandom tagged CCA encryption" and an inner public key pk for the standard CCA encryption. The watermarking secret key consists of the decryption keys $\mathsf{sk}', \mathsf{sk}$.

We define the PRF family $\{F_k\}$ as follows:

- The key $k = (s, z, r, s')$ consists of a pPRF key s, a random pPRF input z and encryption randomness r as before. We now also include an additional PRF key s'.
- The function is defined as $F_k(x) = (f_s(x), \mathsf{ct}')$ where $\mathsf{ct}' = \mathsf{Enc}'_{\mathsf{pk}',x}(\mathsf{ct}\,;\,f_{s'}(x))$ is an encryption of ct with respect to the tag x using randomness $f_{s'}(x)$ and $\mathsf{ct} = \mathsf{Enc}_{\mathsf{pk}}(f_s(z), z\,;\,r)$ as before. Note that the inner ciphertext ct is always the same but the outer ciphertext ct' is different for each x.

The watermarking scheme is almost the same as before except that:

- To mark a function F_k with $k = (s, z, r, s')$ we create a key $\widetilde{k} = (s\{z\}, \mathsf{ct}, s')$ where $s\{z\}$ is a pPRF key which is punctured at the point z and $\mathsf{ct} = \mathsf{Enc}_{\mathsf{pk}}(f_s(z), z\,;\,r)$ as before. We define the marked function as $F_{\widetilde{k}}(x) = (f_{s\{z\}}(x), \mathsf{ct}')$ where $\mathsf{ct}' = \mathsf{Enc}'_{\mathsf{pk}',x}(\mathsf{ct}\,;\,f_{s'}(x))$.
- The extraction procedure is the same as before except that it also peels off the outer layer of encryption.

We now argue that the function family $\{F_k\}$ is pseudorandom even given the public parameter $(\mathsf{pk}, \mathsf{pk}')$ of the watermarking scheme and access to the extraction oracle. However, note that given the watermarking secret key $\mathsf{sk}, \mathsf{sk}'$, it is easy to completely break PRF security by testing if the outer ciphertexts decrypts correctly to the same value every time. To argue pseudorandomness, we rely on the security of the outer encryption. Note that the outer ciphertexts are tagged with various tags x_i corresponding to the adversary's PRF queries. However, the extraction oracle only decrypts with respect to tags x_i' corresponding to random inputs that it chooses on each extraction query. Therefore, with exponentially small probability there will be an overlap between the values x_i' and x_i, and thus we can switch all of the ciphertexts returned by the PRF queries with uniformly random values.

Watermarking with Message Embedding. Our watermarking construction that allows to embed a message $\mathsf{msg} \in \{0,1\}^\ell$ during marking is very similar to the non-message embedding one. The main difference is that we use a constraint-hiding constrained PRF (CHC-PRF) to embed a hidden pattern that allows the extraction procedure to recover the message. At a high level, to mark a key with some message msg, we consider for each message bit msg_j a sparse pseudorandom set V_j; and we constrain the key on V_j if $\mathsf{msg}_j = 1$. We use an additional set V_0 on which we always constrain when marking a key. Each set V_j is defined using a fresh PRF key t_j. The public parameters and the watermarking secret key are the same as before, but now our PRF key k grows linearly with the message length.

Let $\{f_s\}$ be an arbitrary constraint-hiding constrained PRF (CHC-PRF) family. We define the PRF family $\{F_k\}$ as follows:

- The key $k = (s, (t_0, t_1, \ldots, t_\ell), r, s')$ consists of a CHC-PRF key s, $\ell + 1$ PRF keys $\{t_i\}_{i \le \ell}$, encryption randomness r, and a PRF key s'.
- The function is defined as $F_k(x) = (f_s(x), \mathsf{ct}')$ where $\mathsf{ct}' = \mathsf{Enc}'_{\mathsf{pk}',x}(\mathsf{ct}; f_{s'}(x))$ is an encryption of ct with respect to the tag x using randomness $f_{s'}(x)$ and $\mathsf{ct} = \mathsf{Enc}_{\mathsf{pk}}(s, (t_0, t_1, \ldots, t_\ell); r)$. Again, the inner ciphertext ct is always the same but the outer ciphertext ct' is different for each x.

The marking and extraction procedures work as follows:

- To mark a function F_k with $k = (s, (t_0, t_1, \ldots, t_\ell), r, s')$ and message $\mathsf{msg} \in \{0,1\}^\ell$, we first define the following circuit C_{msg}. For each key t_j, let C_j be the circuit which on input $x = (a, b)$ accepts if $f_{t_j}(a) = b$. Here we implicitly define the set $V_j = \{(a, f_{t_j}(a))\}$, and thus the circuit C_j checks membership in V_j. We define C_{msg} as:

$$C_{\mathsf{msg}} = C_0 \vee \left(\bigvee_{\substack{j=1,\ldots,\ell \\ \mathsf{msg}_j=1}} C_j \right),$$

so that C_{msg} checks membership in the union of V_0 and the V_j's for j with $\mathsf{msg}_j = 1$.

We create a key $\widetilde{k} = (s\{C_{\mathsf{msg}}\}, \mathsf{ct}, s')$ where $s\{C_{\mathsf{msg}}\}$ is a CHC-PRF key which is constrained on the circuit C_{msg} and $\mathsf{ct} = \mathsf{Enc}_{\mathsf{pk}}(s, (t_0, t_1, \ldots, t_\ell); r)$. We define the marked function as $F_{\widetilde{k}}(x) = (f_{s\{C_{\mathsf{msg}}\}}(x), \mathsf{ct}')$ where $\mathsf{ct}' = \mathsf{Enc}'_{\mathsf{pk}', x}(\mathsf{ct}; f_{s'}(x))$.

- The extraction procedure gets a circuit C and let $C(x) = (C_1(x), C_2(x))$ denote the first and second part of the output respectively. The extraction procedure computes $C_2(x_i) = \mathsf{ct}'_i$ for many random values x_i, peels off the outer layer to obtain ct_i, and attempts to decrypt $\mathsf{Dec}_{\mathsf{sk}}(\mathsf{ct}_i) = (s, (t_0, t_1, \ldots, t_\ell))$. The extraction procedure selects the decrypted message $(s, (t_0, t_1, \ldots, t_\ell))$ which forms the majority of the decrypted messages. If such a majority doesn't exist, the extraction stops here and outputs unmarked.

  The procedure now samples many random values a_i, computes $x_i = (a_i, f_{t_0}(a_i)) \in V_0$ and tests if $C_1(x_i) \neq f_s(x_i)$. If for the majority of the values x_i it holds that $C_1(x_i) \neq f_s(x_i)$ then the procedure considers the circuit as marked and proceeds to extract a message, as described below; else it stops here and outputs unmarked.

  To extract a message $\mathsf{msg} \in \{0, 1\}^\ell$ the procedure does the following:

  It samples, for $j = 1, \ldots, \ell$, many random values $a_{j,i}$, computes the pseudorandom values $x_{j,i} = (a_{j,i}, f_{t_j}(a_{j,i})) \in V_j$, and checks if $C_1(x_{j,i}) \neq f_s(x_{j,i})$. If for the majority of the values $x_{j,i}$ it holds that $C_1(x_{j,i}) \neq f_s(x_{j,i})$ then it sets $\mathsf{msg}_j = 1$, otherwise sets $\mathsf{msg}_j = 0$. It then outputs $\mathsf{msg} = (\mathsf{msg}_1, \ldots, \mathsf{msg}_\ell)$.

To show pseudorandomness of the function family $\{F_k\}$ even given the public parameters $(\mathsf{pk}, \mathsf{pk}')$, the same argument as in the non-message embedding family goes through. Moreover, for any function F_k in the family which was not marked, the extraction procedure correctly outputs unmarked (because of the checks on V_0). Furthermore, for any message msg any function $F_{\widetilde{k}}$ where $\widetilde{k} \leftarrow \mathsf{Mark}(k, \mathsf{msg})$, $\mathsf{Extract}(\mathsf{ek}, F_{\widetilde{k}})$ correctly outputs the original message msg. This is because with overwhelming probability, a random point in V_j is constrained if and only if $\mathsf{msg}_j = 1$, by pseudorandomness and sparsity of the V_j. Then, correctness of the CHC-PRF ensures that $\mathsf{Extract}$ computes msg_j correctly when $\mathsf{msg}_j = 0$ (as the marked key is not constrained on V_j in that case), while constrained pseudorandomness ensures correctness when $\mathsf{msg}_j = 1$ (as the marked key is then constrained on V_j).

For watermarking security, we let the adversary choose a message msg. We sample a key $k = (s, (t_0, t_1, \ldots, t_\ell), r, s')$ and give him $F_{\widetilde{k}}$ where $\widetilde{k} \leftarrow \mathsf{Mark}(k, \mathsf{msg})$. However, we now only allow the adversary to modify slightly less than half of the outputs of the marked challenge circuit $F_{\widetilde{k}}$. As shown by Cohen et al. [10], this restriction is necessary when considering watermarking schemes that allow message embedding. So now, the adversary is given a marked function $F_{\widetilde{k}}$, and produces some circuit C which agrees with $F_{\widetilde{k}}$ on more than half of its input values. We use similar arguments as in the non message embedding version, but now we additionally rely on the constraint-hiding property of the CHC-PRF to argue that the sets V_j remain pseudorandom for the adversary, even given the marked circuit $F_{\widetilde{k}}$.

Now, the extraction procedure Extract(ek, C) samples sufficiently many random input values. Because C and $F_{\tilde{k}}$ agree on more than half of their input values, then with overwhelming probability the majority of the random input values will agree on their output values in both C and $F_{\tilde{k}}$ (by a standard Chernoff bound); in which case the extraction procedure recovers $(s, (t_0, \ldots, t_\ell))$. But then, by pseudorandomness of the sets V_j, we have by another Chernoff bound that with overwhelming probability, the majority of the input values sampled in V_j will agree on their output values in both C and $F_{\tilde{k}}$. By the sparsity and pseudorandomness of the sets V_j, these input values are constrained in $F_{\tilde{k}}$ if and only if $\mathsf{msg}_j = 1$; and the correctness and pseudorandomness of the CHC-PRF ensure that the extraction procedure outputs msg on input C with overwhelming probability.

2 Preliminaries

2.1 Notations

For any probablistic algorithm alg(inputs), we may explicit the randomness it uses by writing alg(inputs; coins).

For two circuits C, D, and $\varepsilon \in [0, 1]$, we write $C \cong_\varepsilon D$ if C and D agree on an ε fraction of their inputs.

We will use the notations $\overset{s}{\approx}$ and $\overset{c}{\approx}$ to denote statistical and computational indistinguishability, respectively.

We will use the following lemma:

Lemma 1 (Chernoff Bound). *Let* $X_1, \ldots X_n$ *be independent Bernoulli variables of parameter* $p \in [0, 1]$. *Then for all* $\varepsilon > 0$, *we have:*

$$\Pr\left[\sum_{i=1}^{n} X_i < n \cdot (p - \varepsilon)\right] \leq e^{-2\varepsilon^2 n}.$$

In particular for $n = \lambda / \varepsilon^2$, *this probability is exponentially small in* λ.

2.2 Constrained PRFs

We recall the definition of two variants of contrained PRFs.

Definition 1 (Puncturable PRFs *[6, 7, 13, 15]***).** *Let* $\ell_{in} = \ell_{in}(\lambda)$ *and* $\ell_{out} = \ell_{out}(\lambda)$ *for a pair of polynomial-time computable functions* $\ell_{in}(\cdot)$ *and* $\ell_{out}(\cdot)$. *A puncturable pseudo-random function (pPRF) family is defined by the following algorithms:*

- KeyGen(1^λ) *takes as input the security parameter* λ, *and outputs a PRF key* k.
- Eval(k, x) *takes as input a key* k *and an input* $x \in \{0,1\}^{\ell_{in}}$ *and deterministically outputs a value* $y \in \{0,1\}^{\ell_{out}}$.

- Puncture(k, z) *takes as input a key k and an input $z \in \{0,1\}^{\ell_{in}}$, and outputs a punctured key $k\{z\}$.*
- PunctureEval($k\{z\}, x$) *takes as input a constrained key $k\{z\}$ and an input $x \in \{0,1\}^{\ell_{in}}$, and outputs a value $y \in \{0,1\}^{\ell_{out}}$.*

We require a puncturable PRF to satisfy the following properties:

Functionality preserving under puncturing. Let $z, x \in \{0,1\}^{\ell_{in}}$ such that $x \neq z$. Then:

$$\Pr\left[\text{Eval}(k, x) = \text{PunctureEval}(k\{z\}, x) \;\middle|\; \begin{array}{l} k \leftarrow \text{KeyGen}(1^\lambda) \\ k\{z\} \leftarrow \text{Puncture}(k, z) \end{array}\right] = 1.$$

Pseudorandomness on punctured points. For all $z \in \{0,1\}^{\ell_{in}}$, we have that for all PPT adversary $\mathcal{A}$:

$$|\Pr\left[\mathcal{A}(k\{z\}, \text{Eval}(k, z)) = 1\right] - \Pr\left[\mathcal{A}(k\{z\}, \mathcal{U}_{\ell_{out}}) = 1\right]| \leq \text{negl}(\lambda),$$

where $k \leftarrow \text{KeyGen}(1^\lambda)$, $k\{z\} \leftarrow \text{Puncture}(k, z)$ and $\mathcal{U}_{\ell_{out}}$ denotes the uniform distribution over ℓ_{out} bits.

We have constructions of puncturable PRFs assuming the existence of one-way functions [6,7,13,15].

Definition 2 ((Selective) Constraint-hiding Constrained PRFs). *Let $\ell_{in} = \ell_{in}(\lambda)$ and $\ell_{out} = \ell_{out}(\lambda)$ for a pair of polynomial-time computable functions $\ell_{in}(\cdot)$ and $\ell_{out}(\cdot)$. A constraint-hiding constrained pseudo-random function (CHC-PRF) family is defined by the following algorithms:*

- KeyGen(1^λ) *takes as input the security parameter λ, and outputs a PRF key k.*
- Eval(k, x) *takes as input a key k and an input $x \in \{0,1\}^{\ell_{in}}$ and deterministically outputs a value $y \in \{0,1\}^{\ell_{out}}$.*
- Constrain(k, C) *takes as input a key k and a binary circuit $C : \{0,1\}^{\ell_{in}} \to \{0,1\}$, and outputs a constrained key k_C.*
- ConstrainEval(k_C, x) *takes as input a constrained key k_C and an input $x \in \{0,1\}^{\ell_{in}}$, and outputs a value $y \in \{0,1\}^{\ell_{out}}$.*

We require the algorithms (KeyGen, Eval, Constrain, ConstrainEval) to satisfy the following property, which captures the notions of constraint-hiding, (computational) functionality preserving and constrained pseudorandomness at the same time [9, 19]:

Selective Constraint-Hiding. Consider the following experiments between an adversary $\mathcal{A}$ and a simulator $\text{Sim} = (\text{Sim}^{\text{key}}, \text{Sim}^{\text{ch}})$:

$$\text{EXP}_{CH}^{Real}(1^\lambda): \qquad\qquad\qquad \text{EXP}_{CH}^{Ideal}(1^\lambda):$$

1. $C \leftarrow \mathcal{A}$	1. $C \leftarrow \mathcal{A}$
2. $k \leftarrow \mathsf{KeyGen}(1^\lambda)$	2.
3. $k_C \leftarrow \mathsf{Constrain}(k, C)$	3. $k_C \leftarrow \mathsf{Sim}^{\mathsf{key}}(1^{|C|})$
4. Output $b \leftarrow \mathcal{A}^{\mathsf{Eval}(\cdot)}(k_C)$	4. Output $b \leftarrow \mathcal{A}^{\mathsf{Sim}^{\mathsf{ch}}(\cdot)}(k_C)$

where $\mathsf{Sim}^{\mathsf{ch}}(\cdot)$ is defined as:

$$\mathsf{Sim}^{\mathsf{ch}}(x) = \begin{cases} R(x) & \text{if } C(x) = 1 \\ \mathsf{ConstrainEval}(k_C, x) & \text{if } C(x) = 0, \end{cases}$$

where $R : \{0,1\}^{\ell_{in}} \to \{0,1\}^{\ell_{out}}$ is a random function.
We say that $\mathcal{F}$ is a constraint-hiding contrained PRF if:

$$\left| \Pr\left[\text{EXP}_{CH}^{Real}(1^\lambda) = 1\right] - \Pr\left[\text{EXP}_{CH}^{Ideal}(1^\lambda) = 1\right] \right| \leq \mathsf{negl}(\lambda).$$

There are several constructions of constraint-hiding constrained PRFs under LWE [4,8,9,19].

2.3   Tag-CCA Encryption with Pseudorandom Ciphertexts

Definition 3 (Tag-CCA2 Encryption with Pseudorandom Ciphertexts).
Let $(\mathsf{KeyGen}, \mathsf{Enc}, \mathsf{Dec})$ *be an encryption scheme with the following syntax:*

- $\mathsf{KeyGen}(1^\lambda)$ *takes as input the security parameter* λ *and outputs keys* $(\mathsf{pk}, \mathsf{sk})$.
- $\mathsf{Enc}_{\mathsf{pk},t}(m)$ *takes as input the public key* pk, *a message* m *and a tag* t, *and outputs a ciphertext* ct.
- $\mathsf{Dec}_{\mathsf{sk},t}(\mathsf{ct})$ *takes as input the secret key* sk, *a ciphertext* ct *and a tag* t, *and outputs a message* m.

We will in the rest of the paper omit the keys as arguments to Enc *and* Dec *when they are clear from the context.*
We will consider for simplicity perfectly correct schemes, so that for all messages m *and tag* t:

$$\Pr[\mathsf{Dec}_{\mathsf{sk},t}(\mathsf{Enc}_{\mathsf{pk},t}(m)) = m] = 1.$$

over the randomness of KeyGen, Enc *and* Dec.
Denote by $\mathcal{CT} = \mathcal{CT}_{\mathsf{pk}}$ *be the ciphertext space of* $(\mathsf{KeyGen}, \mathsf{Enc}, \mathsf{Dec})$. *For security, consider for* $b \in \{0,1\}$ *the following experiments* $\mathsf{Exp}_{tag-CCA2}^b(1^\lambda)$ *between a PPT adversary* $\mathcal{A}$ *and a challenger* $\mathcal{C}$:

$$\text{EXP}_{tag-CCA2}^0(1^\lambda): \qquad\qquad\qquad \text{EXP}_{tag-CCA2}^1(1^\lambda):$$

1. $(\mathsf{pk}, \mathsf{sk}) \leftarrow \mathsf{KeyGen}(1^\lambda)$	1. $(\mathsf{pk}, \mathsf{sk}) \leftarrow \mathsf{KeyGen}(1^\lambda)$
2. $(m^*, t^*) \leftarrow \mathcal{A}^{\mathsf{Dec}_{\mathsf{sk}, \cdot}(\cdot)}$	2. $(m^*, t^*) \leftarrow \mathcal{A}^{\mathsf{Dec}_{\mathsf{sk}, \cdot}(\cdot)}$
3. $c^* \leftarrow \mathsf{Enc}_{\mathsf{pk},t^*}(m)$	3. $c^* \leftarrow \mathcal{CT}$
4. Output $b \leftarrow \mathcal{A}^{\mathsf{Dec}_{\mathsf{sk}, \cdot}(\cdot)}$	4. Output $b \leftarrow \mathcal{A}^{\mathsf{Dec}_{\mathsf{sk}, \cdot}(\cdot)}$

where $\mathsf{Dec}_{\mathsf{sk},.}(\cdot)$ *takes as input a tag* t *and a ciphertext* c, *and outputs* $\mathsf{Dec}_{\mathsf{sk},t}(c)$ *We say that* $(\mathsf{KeyGen}, \mathsf{Enc}, \mathsf{Dec})$ *is tag-CCA2 with pseudorandom ciphertexts if for all PPT* $\mathcal{A}$ *who do not make any query of the form* $(t^*, *)$ *to the decryption oracle in phases 2 and 4:*

$$\left| \Pr[\mathsf{Exp}^0(1^\lambda) = 1] - \Pr[\mathsf{Exp}^1(1^\lambda) = 1] \right| \leq \mathrm{negl}(\lambda).$$

Notice that the notion of tag-CCA2 encryption with pseudorandom ciphertexts is weaker than both CCA2 encryption with pseudorandom ciphertexts, and fully secure Identity-Based Encryption (IBE) with pseudorandom ciphertexts. To see that CCA2 schemes with pseudorandom ciphertexts imply their tag-CCA2 counterpart, notice that it suffices to encrypt the tag along with the message. Then, make the decryption output $\perp$ if the decrypted tag part does not match the decryption tag. IBEs with pseudorandom ciphertexts also directly imply a tag-CCA2 version by simply considering identities as tags.

In particular, we have construction of tag-CCA2 schemes with pseudorandom ciphertexts under various assumptions, e.g. DDH, DCR, QR [11], or LWE [1].

We will need an additional property on the encryption scheme, namely that its ciphertexts are *sparse*:

Definition 4 (Sparsity of Ciphertexts). *We say that an encryption scheme is* sparse *if for all* ct *from the ciphertext space, and all tags* t:

$$\Pr[\mathsf{Dec}_{\mathsf{sk},t}(\mathsf{ct}) \neq \perp \,|\, (\mathsf{pk}, \mathsf{sk}) \leftarrow \mathsf{KeyGen}(1^\lambda)] \leq \mathrm{negl}(\lambda).$$

Note that we can build a sparse tag-CCA2 encryption scheme with pseudorandom ciphertexts generically from any tag-CCA2 encryption scheme with pseudorandom ciphertexts. To do so, it suffices to add a random identifier $\alpha \in \{0,1\}^\lambda$ to the public key; to encrypt some message m, encrypt instead the message (m, α) using the non-sparse encryption scheme. Then, when decrypting, output $\perp$ if the identifier α does not match. For any fixed ct, the probability that it decrypts under the new encryption scheme is negligible over the randomness of α (sampled during KeyGen).

3   Watermarking PRFs

In this section, we construct a watermarking scheme and its associated watermarkable PRF family. The marking procedure is public, and security holds even when the attacker has access to an extraction oracle. We can instantiate the primitives we require under different various assumptions, e.g. DDH, LWE, or Factoring. We do not consider the case of embedding messages in the marked circuit yet though; the extraction algorithm here simply detects if the key has been marked or not. We will study the case of message embedding in Sect. 4.

3.1   Definitions

We first define the notion of watermaking. We tailor our notation and definitions to implicitly consider the setting where marking is public and extraction is secret.[5]

Definition 5 (Watermarking Scheme). *Let $\lambda \in \mathbb{N}$ be the security parameter and $\varepsilon \in [0,1]$ be a parameter. A watermarking scheme* WatMk *for a watermarkable family of pseudorandom functions* $\mathcal{F} = \{\mathcal{F}_{\mathsf{pp}} : \mathcal{X}_{\mathsf{pp}} \to \mathcal{Y}_{\mathsf{pp}}\}_{\mathsf{pp}}$ *is defined by the following polynomial-time algorithms:*

- Setup$(1^\lambda) \to (\mathsf{pp}, \mathsf{ek})$: *On input the security parameter* 1^λ, *outputs the public parameters* pp *and the extraction key* ek.
- KeyGen$(1^\lambda, \mathsf{pp}) \to k$: *On input the security parameter* 1^λ *and public parameters* pp, *outputs a PRF key* k.
- $F_k(x) \to y$: *On input a key* k *and an input* $x \in \mathcal{X}_{\mathsf{pp}}$, *outputs* $y \in \mathcal{Y}_{\mathsf{pp}}$.
- Mark$(k) \to \widetilde{k}$: *On input and a PRF key* $k \in \mathcal{F}$, *outputs a marked key* $\widetilde{k}$.
- Extract$(\mathsf{ek}, C) \to \{\mathsf{marked}, \mathsf{unmarked}\}$: *On input an extraction key* ek *and an arbitrary circuit* C, *outputs* marked *or* unmarked.

We will simply denote by F_k some circuit that computes $F_k(x)$ on input x (which is efficiently computable given k).

Definition 6 (Watermarking Properties). *A watermarking scheme* WatMk *has to satisfy the following properties:*

Non-triviality. *We require two properties of non-triviality.*

1. *We require that functions in* $\mathcal{F}$ *are unmarked:*

$$\Pr\left[\mathsf{Extract}(\mathsf{ek}, F_k) = \mathsf{unmarked} \,\middle|\, \begin{array}{l} (\mathsf{pp}, \mathsf{ek}) \leftarrow \mathsf{Setup}(1^\lambda) \\ k \leftarrow \mathsf{KeyGen}(1^\lambda, \mathsf{pp}) \end{array}\right] = 1.$$

2. *Any fixed circuit* C *(fixed independently of* pp*) should be unmarked:*

$$\Pr\left[\mathsf{Extract}(\mathsf{ek}, C) = \mathsf{unmarked} \,\middle|\, (\mathsf{pp}, \mathsf{ek}) \leftarrow \mathsf{Setup}(1^\lambda)\right] \geq 1 - \mathsf{negl}(\lambda).$$

Strong Correctness. *It should be hard to find points on which* F_k *and* $F_{\widetilde{k}}$ *output different values, given oracle access to both circuits.*
  For all PPT $\mathcal{A}$ *we require:*

$$\Pr\left[F_k(x) \neq F_{\widetilde{k}}(x) \,\middle|\, \begin{array}{l} (\mathsf{pp}, \mathsf{ek}) \leftarrow \mathsf{Setup}(1^\lambda) \\ k \leftarrow \mathsf{KeyGen}(1^\lambda, \mathsf{pp}) \\ \widetilde{k} \leftarrow \mathsf{Mark}(k) \\ x \leftarrow \mathcal{A}^{F_k(\cdot), F_{\widetilde{k}}(\cdot), \mathsf{Extract}(\mathsf{ek}, \cdot)}(\mathsf{pp}) \end{array}\right] \leq \mathsf{negl}(\lambda).$$

---

[5] We can directly extend the following definitions to the weaker setting of *secret* marking, by additionally giving the adversary oracle access to the marking algorithm in the relevant properties.

In particular, for any fixed x, the probability that $F_k(x) \neq F_{\tilde{k}}(x)$ is negligible.[6]

Extended Pseudorandomness. *We do not require PRF security to hold if the adversary is given the extraction key. We still require that the PRFs in the family remain secure even given oracle access to the extraction algorithm.*

We require that for all PPT $\mathcal{A}$:

$$\mathcal{A}^{F_k(\cdot),\, \text{Extract}(\text{ek},\cdot)}(\text{pp}) \stackrel{c}{\approx} \mathcal{A}^{R(\cdot),\, \text{Extract}(\text{ek},\cdot)}(\text{pp}),$$

where $(\text{pp}, \text{ek}) \leftarrow \text{Setup}(1^\lambda)$, $k \leftarrow \text{KeyGen}(1^\lambda, \text{pp})$, *and R is a random function.*

ε-**Unremovability.** *Define the following experiment* $\text{Exp}_{\mathcal{A}}^{\text{remov}}(1^\lambda)$ *between an adversary $\mathcal{A}$ and a challenger:*

1. *The challenger generates* $(\text{pp}, \text{ek}) \leftarrow \text{Setup}(1^\lambda)$. *It also samples a random* $k \leftarrow \text{KeyGen}(1^\lambda, \text{pp})$, *and gives the public parameters* pp *and a circuit* $\tilde{C} = F_{\tilde{k}}$ *to the adversary, where* $\tilde{k} \leftarrow \text{Mark}(k)$.
2. *The adversary* $\mathcal{A}^{\text{Extract}(\text{ek},\cdot)}(\text{pp}, \tilde{C})$ *has access to an extraction oracle, which on input a circuit C, outputs* $\text{Extract}(\text{ek}, C)$.
3. *The adversary* $\mathcal{A}^{\text{Extract}(\text{ek},\cdot)}(\text{pp}, \tilde{C})$ *outputs a circuit C^*. The output of the experiment is 1 if* $\text{Extract}(\text{ek}, C^*) = $ unmarked; *and the output of the experiment is 0 otherwise.*

We say that an adversary $\mathcal{A}$ is ε-admissible if its output C^* in phase 3. satisfies $C^* \cong_\varepsilon \tilde{C}$, *i.e. C^* and $\tilde{C}$ agree on an ε fraction of their inputs.*

We say that a watermarking scheme achieves ε-unremovability if for all ε-admissible PPT adversaries $\mathcal{A}$ we have:

$$\Pr[\text{Exp}_{\mathcal{A}}^{\text{remov}}(1^\lambda) = 1] \leq \text{negl}(\lambda).$$

Extraction Correctness. We require that:

$$\Pr\left[\text{Extract}(\text{ek}, F_{\tilde{k}}) = \text{marked} \;\middle|\; \begin{array}{l} (\text{pp}, \text{ek}) \leftarrow \text{Setup}(1^\lambda) \\ k \leftarrow \text{KeyGen}(1^\lambda, \text{pp}) \\ \tilde{k} \leftarrow \text{Mark}(k) \end{array} \right] \geq 1 - \text{negl}(\lambda),$$

but in this case this follows from ε-Unremovability, as otherwise an Adversary could just directly output the marked challenge in the ε-Unremovability game.

3.2   Construction

Let $\lambda \in \mathbb{N}$ be the security parameter and let $\varepsilon = 1/\text{poly}(\lambda)$ be a parameter. We describe our construction of a watermarkable family $\mathcal{F}_{\text{pp}}$ and its associated ε-unremovable watermarking scheme.

We will use the following primitives in our construction:

---

[6] In particular, this notion of correctness is stronger than simply requiring that the output of the original PRF and the marked version differ at most on a negligible fraction of inputs.

- $\mathcal{E}^{\text{in}} = (\mathcal{E}^{\text{in}}.\text{KeyGen}, \text{Enc}^{\text{in}}, \text{Dec}^{\text{in}})$, a CCA2 secure public-key encryption scheme
- $\mathcal{E}^{\text{out}} = (\mathcal{E}^{\text{out}}.\text{KeyGen}, \text{Enc}^{\text{out}}, \text{Dec}^{\text{out}})$, a sparse tag-CCA2 encryption scheme with pseudorandom ciphertexts
- pPRF $= (\text{pPRF.KeyGen}, \text{pPRF.Eval}, \text{Puncture}, \text{PunctureEval})$, a puncturable PRF family
- PRF $= (\text{PRF.KeyGen}, \text{PRF.Eval})$, a standard PRF family.

We will use the following notation:

- $r^{\text{in}} = r^{\text{in}}(\lambda)$ and $r^{\text{out}} = r^{\text{out}}(\lambda)$ are the number of random bits used by Enc^{in} and Enc^{out}, respectively;
- $(\mathcal{X}, \mathcal{Y}^{(1)}) = (\mathcal{X}_{\text{pp}}, \mathcal{Y}_{\text{pp}}^{(1)})$ are the input and output spaces of pPRF, where we assume that $\mathcal{X}$ and $\mathcal{Y}^{(1)}$ are of size super-polynomial in λ;
- We'll suppose that PRF has input and output spaces $(\mathcal{X}, \{0,1\}^{r^{\text{out}}}) = (\mathcal{X}_{\text{pp}}, \{0,1\}^{r^{\text{out}}})$;
- $\mathcal{CT} = \mathcal{CT}_{\text{pp}}$ is the ciphertext space of $\mathcal{E}^{\text{out}}$.
- We set the input space of our watermarkable PRF to be $\mathcal{X}$, and its output space to be $\mathcal{Y} = \mathcal{Y}^{(1)} \times \mathcal{CT}$. For $y \in \mathcal{Y}$, we will write $y = (y_1, y_2)$, where $y_1 \in \mathcal{Y}^{(1)}$ and $y_2 \in \mathcal{CT}$.

We now describe our construction of a watermarking scheme, with its associated watermarkable PRF family:

- Setup(1^λ): On input the security parameter 1^λ, sample $(\text{pk}^{\text{in}}, \text{sk}^{\text{in}}) \leftarrow \mathcal{E}^{\text{in}}.\text{KeyGen}(1^\lambda)$ and $(\text{pk}^{\text{out}}, \text{sk}^{\text{out}}) \leftarrow \mathcal{E}^{\text{out}}.\text{KeyGen}(1^\lambda)$. Output:

$$\text{pp} = (\text{pk}^{\text{in}}, \text{pk}^{\text{out}});$$

$$\text{ek} = (\text{sk}^{\text{in}}, \text{sk}^{\text{out}}).$$

- KeyGen$(1^\lambda, \text{pp})$: On input the security parameter 1^λ and the public parameters pp, sample $s \leftarrow \text{pPRF.KeyGen}(1^\lambda)$, $s' \leftarrow \text{PRF.KeyGen}(1^\lambda)$, $r \leftarrow \{0,1\}^{r^{\text{in}}}$, and $z \leftarrow \mathcal{X}$. The key of the watermarkable PRF is:

$$k = (s, z, r, s', \text{pp}).$$

For ease of notation, we will simply write $k = (s, z, r, s')$ when the public parameters pp are clear from the context.

- $F_k(x)$: On input a key k and input x, output

$$F_k(x) = \Big(f_s(x), \ \text{Enc}_x^{\text{out}}(\text{pk}_{\text{out}}, \text{Enc}^{\text{in}}(\text{pk}_{\text{in}}, (f_s(z), z); r); f'_{s'}(x)) \Big)$$

where $f_s(\cdot) = \text{pPRF.Eval}(s, \cdot)$, $f'_{s'}(\cdot) = \text{PRF.Eval}(s', \cdot)$, and Enc^{out} encrypts $\text{Enc}^{\text{in}}(\text{pk}_{\text{in}}, (f_s(z), z); r)$ using tag x and randomness $f'_{s'}(x)$.
- Mark(k): On input a key $k = (s, z, r, s')$, do the following:
  - Puncture the key s at point z: $s\{z\} \leftarrow \text{pPRF.Puncture}(s, z)$.
  - Compute $c^{\text{in}} = \text{Enc}^{\text{in}}(\text{pk}_{\text{in}}, (f_s(z), z); r)$.

- Output the marked key

$$\widetilde{k} = (s\{z\}, c^{\text{in}}, s'),$$

where the associated evaluation circuit computes:

$$F_{\widetilde{k}}(x) = \big(\ \mathsf{PunctureEval}(s\{z\}, x)\,,\ \mathsf{Enc}_x^{\text{out}}(\mathsf{pk}_{\text{out}}, c^{\text{in}}\,;\, f_{s'}'(x))\ \big).$$

- Extract(ek, C): Let $w = \lambda/\varepsilon = \text{poly}(\lambda)$. On input the extraction key ek and a circuit C do the following:
  - If the input or output length of C do not match $\mathcal{X}$ and $\mathcal{Y}^{(1)} \times \mathcal{CT}$ respectively, output unmarked.
  - For all $i \in [w]$ sample uniformly at random $x_i \leftarrow \mathcal{X}$, and do the following:
    * Parse $C(x_i) = (C_1(x_i), C_2(x_i))$ where $C_1(x_i) \in \mathcal{Y}^{(1)}$ and $C_2(x_i) \in \mathcal{CT}$.
    * Compute $c_i^{\text{in}} = \mathsf{Dec}_{\mathsf{sk}^{\text{out}}, x_i}^{\text{out}}(C_2(x_i))$ (using secret key sk^{out} and tag x_i);
    * If $c_i^{\text{in}} \neq \perp$, compute $(y_i, z_i) = \mathsf{Dec}_{\mathsf{sk}^{\text{in}}}^{\text{in}}(c_i^{\text{in}})$. If $C_1(z_i) \neq y_i$, output marked.
  - If the procedure does not output marked after executing the loop above, output unmarked.

Note that when it is clear from the context, we will omit writing $\mathsf{pk}_{\text{out}}, \mathsf{pk}_{\text{in}}$.

3.3   Correctness Properties of the Watermarking Scheme

We first show that our watermarking scheme satisfies the non-triviality properties.

Claim (Non-triviality). Assume $\mathcal{E}^{\text{in}}$ and $\mathcal{E}^{\text{out}}$ are perfectly correct, and that $\mathcal{E}^{\text{out}}$ is sparse. Then our watermarking scheme satisfies the non-triviality properties.

Proof. 1. Let $(\mathsf{pp}, \mathsf{ek}) \leftarrow \mathsf{Setup}(1^\lambda)$ and $k = (s, z, r, s') \leftarrow \mathsf{KeyGen}(1^\lambda, \mathsf{pp})$; then Extract(ek, F_k) always outputs unmarked. This is because by perfect correctness of $\mathcal{E}^{\text{in}}$ and $\mathcal{E}^{\text{out}}$, we have that $(y_i, z_i) = (f_s(z), z)$ for all $i \in [w]$, and therefore $C_1(z_i) = y_i = f_s(z)$.
2. Fix a circuit $C = (C_1, C_2)$, and sample $(\mathsf{pp}, \mathsf{ek}) \leftarrow \mathsf{Setup}(1^\lambda)$. By sparsity of $\mathcal{E}^{\text{out}}$, we have that for all $x_i \in \mathcal{X}$, the probability that $c_i^{\text{in}} := \mathsf{Dec}_{\mathsf{sk}^{\text{out}}, x_i}^{\text{out}}(C_2(x_i)) \neq \perp$ is negligible (over the randomness of $\mathsf{Setup}(1^\lambda)$ alone). In particular, taking a union bound over the $w = \text{poly}(\lambda)$ points $\{x_i\}_{i \in [w]}$ sampled by Extract, we have that $c_i^{\text{in}} = \perp$ with overwhelming probability, and therefore

$$\Pr\big[\mathsf{Extract}(\mathsf{ek}, C) = \mathsf{unmarked} \,|\, (\mathsf{pp}, \mathsf{ek}) \leftarrow \mathsf{Setup}(1^\lambda)\big] \geq 1 - \mathsf{negl}(\lambda).$$

Claim (Strong Correctness). Suppose pPRF is a punctured PRF, PRF is secure and $\mathcal{E}^{\text{out}}$ is tag-CCA2 with pseudorandom ciphertexts. Then the watermarking scheme satisfies strong correctness.

Proof. We show that the view of the adversary is essentially independent of z.

First, notice that it suffices to argue strong correctness when the adversary $\mathcal{A}$ only has oracle access to $F_k(\cdot)$ but not the marked version $F_{\widetilde{k}}(\cdot)$. This is because if we have the seemingly weaker version of correctness where the adversary doesn't have oracle access to $F_{\widetilde{k}}(\cdot)$, we can simulate oracle access to $F_{\widetilde{k}}(\cdot)$ by simply forwarding the output of $F_k(\cdot)$ on the same input. Now, an adversary can only tell the difference if he makes a query on z, which breaks the weaker notion of correctness (with a polynomial loss equal to his number of PRF queries).

Therefore, we focus on proving

$$\Pr\left[F_k(x) \neq F_{\widetilde{k}}(x) \;\middle|\; \begin{array}{l} (\mathsf{pp}, \mathsf{ek}) \leftarrow \mathsf{Setup}(1^\lambda) \\ k \leftarrow \mathsf{KeyGen}(1^\lambda, \mathsf{pp}) \\ \widetilde{k} \leftarrow \mathsf{Mark}(k) \\ x \leftarrow \mathcal{A}^{F_k(\cdot), \mathsf{Extract}(\mathsf{ek}, \cdot)}(\mathsf{pp}) \end{array}\right] \leq \mathrm{negl}(\lambda).$$

We prove the claim by a sequence of hybrids.

Hybrid 0. In this hybrid, the adversary $\mathcal{A}$ has oracle access to $F_k(\cdot)$ and $\mathsf{Extract}(\mathsf{ek}, \cdot)$ where $(\mathsf{pp}, \mathsf{ek}) \leftarrow \mathsf{Setup}(1^\lambda)$ and $k = (s, z, r, s') \leftarrow \mathsf{KeyGen}(1^\lambda, \mathsf{pp})$.

Hybrid 1. We modify how PRF queries are answered. Now, instead of using $f'_{s'}(x)$ as randomness to encrypt $c^{\mathsf{in}} = \mathsf{Enc}^{\mathsf{in}}(f_s(z), z; r)$ using $\mathsf{Enc}^{\mathsf{out}}$ with tag x, we pick a random function $R^{(1)} : \mathcal{X} \to \{0,1\}^{r^{\mathsf{out}}}$ and use $R^{(1)}(x)$ as the encryption randomness to output:

$$(f_s(x), \mathsf{Enc}^{\mathsf{out}}_x(c^{\mathsf{in}}; R^{(1)}(x))),$$

where the function $R^{(1)}$ is common across all the PRF queries.

Hybrid 2. Now we keep track of the PRF queries x from the adversary, as well as all the x_i's that are sampled during the calls to the extraction oracle. We abort the experiment if at any point there is some x that has been both queried by the adversary and sampled during an extraction call.

Hybrid 3. We now pick a random function $R^{(3)} : \mathcal{X} \to \mathcal{CT}$ and answer to PRF oracle queries x from the adversary with:

$$(f_s(x), R^{(3)}(x)).$$

Now, by functionality preserving under puncturing of pPRF, z is the only point such that $F_k(z) \neq F_{\widetilde{k}}(z)$. However the view of the adversary is independent of z, and therefore the probability that he outputs z is negligible, over the random choice of z (sampled during $\mathsf{KeyGen}(1^\lambda, \mathsf{pp})$).

We prove the indistinguishability of the hybrids in the next section, as our proof of extended pseudorandomness uses the same hybrids.

3.4   Security Properties of the Watermarking Scheme

Unremovability. We first prove that our construction is ε-unremovable (where $\varepsilon = 1/\mathrm{poly}(\lambda)$ is a parameter of our scheme).

Claim (ε-unremovability). Suppose $\mathcal{E}^{in}$ is CCA2-secure, and f is a puncturable PRF. Then the watermarking scheme is ε-unremovable.

Proof. We prove the claim by a sequence of hybrids.

Hybrid 0. This is the ε-Unremovability game $\mathsf{Exp}_{\mathcal{A}}^{\mathsf{remov}}(1^\lambda)$.

Hybrid 1. We now change how extraction oracle queries are answered (including the call used to determine the output of the experiment). Let $k = (s, z, r, s') \leftarrow \mathsf{PRF}_{\mathsf{pp}}.\mathsf{KeyGen}(1^\lambda, \mathsf{pp})$ be the (unmarked) PRF key sampled to produce the challenge marked circuit, and $c^{in} = \mathsf{Enc}^{in}(s, z\,;\, r)$ be the associated ciphertext (which is used to produce the challenge marked circuit $\widetilde{C}$). On extraction query C from the adversary, the extraction procedure samples x_i's for $i \in [w]$ as before. Denote by E the event that $\mathsf{Dec}^{out}_{\mathsf{sk}^{out}, x_i}(C_2(x_i)) = c^{in}$, i.e. the second part $C_2(x_i)$ decrypts to c^{in} when decrypting using tag x_i. If E occurs, then instead of decrypting this inner ciphertext c^{in} in the extraction procedure, we directly check $C_1(z) \neq f_s(z)$; in particular c^{in}, z and $f_s(z)$ are now hard-coded in the modified extraction procedure.

Hybrid 2. We change how extraction calls are answered and how the challenge marked circuit is generated. Let $0_{\mathcal{X}}$ and $0_{\mathcal{CT}}$ be arbitrary fixed values in $\mathcal{X}$ and $\mathcal{CT}$ respectively. We now set

$$c^{in} = \mathsf{Enc}^{in}(0_{\mathcal{X}}, 0_{\mathcal{CT}}),$$

which is used as the ciphertext hard-coded in the extraction oracle (used to handle event E), and used to produce challenge marked circuit $\widetilde{C}$.

Hybrid 3. We change how we answer extraction queries (including the one determining the output of the experiment). Now pick a uniformly random $R \in \mathcal{Y}^{(1)}$. Whenever E occurs during an extraction oracle call, we check $C_1(z) \neq R$ instead. In particular, the modified extraction oracle now has $c^{in} = \mathsf{Enc}^{in}(0_{\mathcal{X}}, 0_{\mathcal{CT}})$, z, and R hard-coded.

Hybrid 4. Now if there is any extraction oracle call such that E occurs and $C_1(z) = R$, we abort the experiment.

Now, all the outputs of the extraction oracle queries are independent of R, as R only affects the output of extraction queries only when E occurs, and the extraction oracle queries now outputs marked whenever there exists some index i such that E occurs, independently of R. Recall that the adversary wins the game if he outputs a circuit C^* such that $C^* \cong_\varepsilon \widetilde{C}$ and $\mathsf{Extract}(\mathsf{ek}, C^*) = $ unmarked. By construction, we have that during the execution of $\mathsf{Extract}(\mathsf{ek}, C^*)$ that defines the output of the experiment, $\mathsf{Extract}$ samples at least one x_i such that $C^*(x_i) = \widetilde{C}(x_i)$ with overwhelming probability. This is because C^* and $\widetilde{C}$ agree on a fraction $\varepsilon = 1/\mathrm{poly}(\lambda)$ of inputs, so that the probability that none of the $w = \lambda/\varepsilon$ samples x_i's satisfies $C^*(x_i) = \widetilde{C}(x_i)$ is at most $(1 - \varepsilon)^{\lambda/\varepsilon} \leq e^{-\lambda} = \mathsf{negl}(\lambda)$. Now by correctness of the outer encryption scheme $\mathcal{E}^{out}$, we have $\mathsf{Dec}^{out}_{\mathsf{sk}^{out}, x_i}(C^*(x_i)) = c^{in}$, so that event E occurs, and $\mathsf{Extract}$ outputs unmarked only if $C_1^*(z) = R$. As the view of the adversary in the experiment is now independent of R, the experiment outputs marked with overwhelming probability (over the randomness of R alone).

Indistinguishability of the Hybrids. We now show that the hybrids above are indistinguishable.

Lemma 2. *Assuming $\mathcal{E}^{in}$ is perfectly correct, we have* **Hybrid 0** $\equiv$ **Hybrid 1**.

The view of the adversary is identical in Hybrid 0 and Hybrid 1 by perfect correctness of the inner encryption $\mathcal{E}^{in}$: in the latter we simply hardcode the result of the decryption whenever we have to decrypt c^{in} during an extraction oracle call.

Lemma 3. *Assuming $\mathcal{E}^{in}$ is CCA2-secure, we have* **Hybrid 1** $\overset{c}{\approx}$ **Hybrid 2**.

We build a reduction that turns any distinguisher between Hybrid 1 and Hybrid 2 to a CCA2 adversary for $\mathcal{E}^{in}$. The reduction essentially does not pick any secret key for Enc^{in} but can still answer extraction oracle queries by interacting with the CCA2 challenger. More precisely, the reduction does not sample the secret key sk^{in} associated to the CCA2 scheme $\mathcal{E}^{in}$, but samples the other parts of $(\mathsf{pp}, \mathsf{ek})$ as in Hybrid 1. It then sends CCA2 challenge messages $(f_s(z), z)$, and $(0_\mathcal{X}, 0_{\mathcal{CT}})$, and gets back a challenge ciphertext c^{in}, and sets the challenge circuit as $F_{\tilde{k}}$ where $\tilde{k} = (s\{z\}, c^{in}, s')$. To answer extraction oracle queries for the distinguisher, it uses the CCA2 challenger to get the decryption of any $c \neq c^{in}$ (which correspond to sampling x_i and event E does not occur); and whenever E occurs (which correspond to having $c_i^{in} = c^{in}$), it uses the hard-coded values $(f_s(z), z)$ to produce the output of the extraction oracle, by checking if $C_1(z) \neq f_s(z)$ directly without decrypting c^{in}. Now if c^{in} is an encryption of $(f_s(z), z)$, the view of the distinguisher is as in Hybrid 1; and if c^{in} is an encryption of $(0_\mathcal{X}, 0_{\mathcal{CT}})$ then its view is as in Hybrid 2.

Lemma 4. *Assuming* pPRF *satisfies constrained pseudorandomness, we have* **Hybrid 2** $\overset{c}{\approx}$ **Hybrid 3**.

This is done by a simple reduction to the constrained pseudorandomness property of pPRF: the reduction samples some random z and gets a constrained key $s\{z\}$ from the constrained pseudorandomness game. Then, it gets a value y^*, which is used whenever event E occurs, to check $C_1(z) \neq y^*$. If $y^* = f_s(z)$, the view of the adversary is as in Hybrid 2; if y^* is random, then his view is as in Hybrid 3.

Lemma 5. *We have* **Hybrid 3** $\overset{s}{\approx}$ **Hybrid 4**.

For any C queried by the adversary as an extraction oracle query, the probability that E occurs and $C_1(z) = R$ is negligible over the randomness of R alone (where we use that $\mathcal{Y}^{(1)}$ has super-polynomial size). Therefore, with overwhelming probability, all extraction oracle queries where E occurs output marked, independently of R. In particular, an union bound over the polynomial number of extraction queries made by the adversary gives that the probability that the experiment aborts is negligible.

Extended Pseudorandomness. Next, we show that our construction satisfies the extended pseudorandomness property.

Claim (Extended Pseudorandomness). Suppose pPRF and PRF are secure and $\mathcal{E}^{out}$ is tag-CCA2 with pseudorandom ciphertexts. Then the watermarking scheme satisfies extended pseudorandomness.

Proof. We prove the claim by a sequence of hybrids.

Hybrid 0. In this hybrid, the adversary $\mathcal{A}$ has oracle access to $F_k(\cdot)$ and Extract(ek, $\cdot$) where (pp, ek) $\leftarrow$ Setup(1^λ) and $k = (s, z, r, s') \leftarrow$ KeyGen(1^λ, pp).

Hybrid 1. We modify how PRF queries are answered. Now, instead of using $f'_{s'}(x)$ as randomness to encrypt $c^{in} = \text{Enc}^{in}(f_s(z), z; r)$ with tag x, we pick a random function $R^{(1)} : \mathcal{X} \to \{0, 1\}^{r^{out}}$ and use $R^{(1)}(x)$ as randomness, and output:

$$(f_s(x), \text{Enc}_x^{out}(c^{in}; R^{(1)}(x))),$$

where the function $R^{(1)}$ is common throughout the experiment.

Hybrid 2. Now we keep track of the PRF queries x from the adversary, as well as all the x_i's that are sampled during the calls to the extraction oracle. We abort the experiment if at any point there is some x that has been both queried by the adversary and sampled during an extraction call.

Hybrid 3. We now pick a random function $R^{(3)} : \mathcal{X} \to \mathcal{CT}$ and answer to PRF oracle queries x from the adversary with:

$$(f_s(x), R^{(3)}(x)).$$

Hybrid 4. We now additionally pick a random function $R^{(4)} : \mathcal{X} \to \mathcal{Y}^{(1)}$, and answer to PRF oracle queries x from the adversary with:

$$(R^{(4)}(x), R^{(3)}(x)).$$

Hybrid 5. Now we do not abort the experiment even if some x is both queried by the adversary and sampled during an extraction call.

Now the adversary has oracle access to $R(\cdot) = (R^{(4)}(\cdot), R^{(3)}(\cdot))$ and Extract(ek, $\cdot$).

Indistinguishability of the Hybrids. We now show that the hybrids above are indistinguishable.

Lemma 6. *Assuming the security of* PRF, *we have* **Hybrid 0** $\overset{c}{\approx}$ **Hybrid 1**.

We build a reduction from any distinguisher to an attacker for the PRF security game for PRF. On PRF query x from the distinguisher, the reduction queries x in the PRF game, and uses the answer as encryption randomness for the outer scheme $\mathcal{E}^{out}$. If the value is $f'_{s'}(x)$, the view of the distinguisher is as in Hybrid 0; if it is random $R^{(1)}(x)$ then its view is as in Hybrid 1.

Lemma 7. *We have* **Hybrid 1** $\overset{s}{\approx}$ **Hybrid 2**.

We argue that the probability that the experiment aborts is negligible.

Suppose that some x has been both queried by the adversary as a PRF query, and sampled during an extraction oracle call.

If it has been sampled by the extraction procedure after the adversary queried it, this means that the extraction procedure sampled an x_i that the adversary queried previously, which happens with probability at most $Q^{PRF}/|\mathcal{X}|$, where Q^{PRF} is the number of PRF queries the adversary makes. An union bound on the polynomial number of samples used in every extraction call and the polynomial number of extraction calls imply that the probability that this event happens is negligible (where we use that $\mathcal{X}$ has super-polynomial size).

Otherwise, it means that the adversary queries an x_i that has previously been sampled by the extraction procedure. However, each output of the extraction oracle leaks at most 1 bit of entropy on the fresh x_i's it sampled during its execution. Therefore the adversary can only succeed in outputting such an x_i with negligible probability.

Lemma 8. *Assuming* $\mathcal{E}^{\mathrm{out}}$ *is a tag-CCA2 encryption scheme with pseudorandom ciphertexts, then* **Hybrid 2** $\overset{c}{\approx}$ **Hybrid 3**.

We replace the right part $\mathsf{Enc}_x^{\mathrm{out}}(c^{\mathrm{in}}; R^{(1)}(x))$ of the outputs to every PRF queries with $R^{(3)}(x)$ for some random $R^{(3)}$, one by one, using a hybrid argument.

To change the output to some query x^*, we reduce any distinguisher using our assumption on $\mathcal{E}^{\mathrm{out}}$. The reduction answers extraction queries using the decryption oracle provided by the tag-CCA2 game, and sends as a challenge message $c^{\mathrm{in}} = \mathsf{Enc}^{\mathrm{in}}(f_s(z), z; r)$ and challenge tag x^*, and uses the challenge ciphertext from the tag-CCA2 game as a right part of the output to the PRF query on x^*. As we make our experiment abort if an extraction call uses some tag that is queried at any point by the distinguisher, we never have to decrypt any ciphertext with tag x^*, so that we can faithfully answer all the extraction queries by using the decryption oracle from the tag-CCA2 game. Note that we have to change the output of all the PRF queries on x^* in this hybrid.

If the challenge ciphertext from the tag-CCA2 game is a proper encryption of c^{in} under tag x^*, then the view of the distinguisher is as in Hybrid 2; and if it is random, then its view is as in Hybrid 3.

Lemma 9. *Assuming the security of* pPRF, *we have* **Hybrid 3** $\overset{c}{\approx}$ **Hybrid 4**.

We reduce any distinguisher to an attacker for the PRF security game. Our reduction, on PRF query x from the distinguisher, forwards it as a query in the PRF game. If it receives PRF values $f_s(x)$, the view of the distinguisher is as in Hybrid 3; if it receives a random $R^{(4)}(x)$, the view of the distinguisher is as in Hybrid 4.

Lemma 10. *We have* **Hybrid 4** $\overset{s}{\approx}$ **Hybrid 5**.

The same argument as to prove Hybrid 1 $\overset{s}{\approx}$ Hybrid 2 applies here.

4   Watermarking PRFs with Message-Embedding

In this section we describe our construction of a watermaking scheme that supports message embedding. Our construction is very similar to the non message embedding version: the main difference is that we now use a constraint-hiding constrained PRF as a base PRF.

4.1   Definitions

Let $\lambda \in \mathbb{N}$ be the security parameter, $\varepsilon \in [0, 1]$ and $\ell = \ell(\lambda)$ be parameters. We make a few syntactical changes to the notions introduced in Sect. 3.1 when considering message-embedding watermarking schemes:

- Mark$(k, \mathsf{msg}) \to \widetilde{k}$: On input a key k and a message $\mathsf{msg} \in \{0, 1\}^\ell$, outputs a marked $\widetilde{k}$;
- Extract$(\mathsf{ek}, C) \to \mathsf{msg}$: On input an extraction key ek and an arbitrary circuit C, outputs a message $\mathsf{msg} \in \{0, 1\}^\ell \cup \{\mathsf{unmarked}\}$.
- Strong correctness: The adversary can now adaptively choose which message to mark.

  For all PPT $\mathcal{A}$ we require:

$$\Pr\left[F_k(x) \neq F_{\widetilde{k}}(x) \;\middle|\; \begin{array}{l} (\mathsf{pp}, \mathsf{ek}) \leftarrow \mathsf{Setup}(1^\lambda) \\ k \leftarrow \mathsf{KeyGen}(1^\lambda, \mathsf{pp}) \\ \mathsf{msg}^* \leftarrow \mathcal{A}^{F_k(\cdot), \mathsf{Extract}(\mathsf{ek}, \cdot)}(\mathsf{pp}) \\ \widetilde{k} \leftarrow \mathsf{Mark}(k, \mathsf{msg}^*) \\ x \leftarrow \mathcal{A}^{F_k(\cdot), F_{\widetilde{k}}(\cdot), \mathsf{Extract}(\mathsf{ek}, \cdot)}(\mathsf{pp}) \end{array} \right] \leq \mathsf{negl}(\lambda).$$

- ε-unremovability: the adversary now additionally chooses some message msg^* given oracle access to the extraction procedure, and wins if he produces a circuit C^* that is ε-close to the marked challenge circuit such that Extract$(\mathsf{ek}, C^*) \neq \mathsf{msg}^*$, as described by the following experiment $\mathsf{Exp}^{\mathsf{remov-msg}}(1^\lambda)$:

  1. The challenger generates $(\mathsf{pp}, \mathsf{ek}) \leftarrow \mathsf{Setup}(1^\lambda)$. It also samples a random $k \leftarrow \mathsf{KeyGen}(1^\lambda, \mathsf{pp})$, and gives the public parameters pp to the adversary.
  2. The adversary computes a challenge message $\mathsf{msg}^* \in \{0, 1\}^\ell \leftarrow \mathcal{A}^{\mathsf{Extract}(\mathsf{ek}, \cdot)}(\mathsf{pp})$, given access to an extraction oracle, which on input a circuit C, outputs Extract(ek, C).
  3. The challenger computes $\widetilde{C} \leftarrow \mathsf{Mark}(k, \mathsf{msg}^*)$ and sends it to the adversary.
  4. The adversary $\mathcal{A}^{\mathsf{Extract}(\mathsf{ek}, \cdot)}(\mathsf{pp}, \widetilde{C})$ can make further extraction oracle queries.
  5. The adversary $\mathcal{A}^{\mathsf{Extract}(\mathsf{ek}, \cdot)}(\mathsf{pp}, \widetilde{C})$ outputs a circuit C^*. The output of the experiment is 1 if Extract$(\mathsf{ek}, C^*) \neq \mathsf{msg}^*$; and the output of the experiment is 0 otherwise.

We now say that an adversary $\mathcal{A}$ is ε-*admissible* if its output C^* in phase 5. satisfies $C^* \cong_\varepsilon \widetilde{C}$.

We say that a watermarking scheme achieves ε-unremovability if for all ε-admissible PPT adversaries $\mathcal{A}$ we have:

$$\Pr[\mathsf{Exp}_{\mathcal{A}}^{\mathsf{remov-msg}}(1^\lambda) = 1] \leq \mathsf{negl}(\lambda).$$

- Extraction correctness: we could now require that for all message $\mathsf{msg} \in \{0,1\}^\ell$:

$$\Pr\left[\mathsf{Extract}(\mathsf{ek}, \mathsf{Mark}(k, \mathsf{msg})) = \mathsf{msg} \;\middle|\; \begin{matrix} (\mathsf{pp}, \mathsf{ek}) \leftarrow \mathsf{Setup}(1^\lambda) \\ k \leftarrow \mathsf{KeyGen}(1^\lambda, \mathsf{pp}) \end{matrix}\right] \geq 1 - \mathsf{negl}(\lambda),$$

but again, this property follows from ε-Unremovability.

4.2 Construction

Let $\lambda \in \mathbb{N}$ be the security parameter, let $\rho = 1/\mathsf{poly}(\lambda)$, and $\ell = \mathsf{poly}(\lambda)$ be parameters. Let $\varepsilon = 1/2 + \rho$. We describe our construction of a watermarkable family $\mathcal{F}_{\mathsf{pp}}$ and its associated ε-unremovable watermarking scheme supporting the embedding of messages of length ℓ.

We'll use the following primitives in our construction:

- $\mathcal{E}^{\mathsf{in}} = (\mathcal{E}^{\mathsf{in}}.\mathsf{KeyGen}, \mathsf{Enc}^{\mathsf{in}}, \mathsf{Dec}^{\mathsf{in}})$, a CCA2 secure public-key encryption scheme
- $\mathcal{E}^{\mathsf{out}} = (\mathcal{E}^{\mathsf{out}}.\mathsf{KeyGen}, \mathsf{Enc}^{\mathsf{out}}, \mathsf{Dec}^{\mathsf{out}})$, a sparse tag-CCA2 encryption scheme with pseudorandom ciphertexts
- $\mathsf{chcPRF} = (\mathsf{chcPRF}.\mathsf{KeyGen}, \mathsf{chcPRF}.\mathsf{Eval}, \mathsf{Constrain}, \mathsf{ConstrainEval})$, a constraint-hiding constrained PRF
- $\mathsf{PRF} = (\mathsf{PRF}.\mathsf{KeyGen}, \mathsf{PRF}.\mathsf{Eval})$, a PRF family
- $\mathsf{PRF}' = (\mathsf{PRF}'.\mathsf{KeyGen}, \mathsf{PRF}'.\mathsf{Eval})$, another PRF family.

We will use the following notations:

- $r^{\mathsf{in}} = r^{\mathsf{in}}(\lambda)$ and $r^{\mathsf{out}} = r^{\mathsf{out}}(\lambda)$ are the number of random bits used by $\mathsf{Enc}^{\mathsf{in}}$ and $\mathsf{Enc}^{\mathsf{out}}$, respectively;
- $(\mathcal{X}, \mathcal{Y}^{(1)}) = (\mathcal{X}_{\mathsf{pp}}, \mathcal{Y}_{\mathsf{pp}}^{(1)})$ are the input and output spaces of chcPRF; where we assume that $\mathcal{X}$ and $\mathcal{Y}^{(1)}$ are of size super-polynomial in λ;
- We'll suppose that PRF has input and output spaces $(\mathcal{X}, \{0,1\}^{r^{\mathsf{out}}}) = (\mathcal{X}_{\mathsf{pp}}, \{0,1\}^{r^{\mathsf{out}}})$;
- $\mathcal{CT} = \mathcal{CT}_{\mathsf{pp}}$ is the ciphertext space of $\mathcal{E}^{\mathsf{out}}$.
- We set the input space of our watermarkable PRF to be $\mathcal{X}$, and its output space to be $\mathcal{Y} = \mathcal{Y}^{(1)} \times \mathcal{CT}$. For $y \in \mathcal{Y}$, we will write $y = (y_1, y_2)$, where $y_1 \in \mathcal{Y}^{(1)}$ and $y_2 \in \mathcal{CT}$.
- We'll suppose that PRF' as input space $\mathcal{X}^{(1)}$ and output space $\mathcal{X}^{(2)}$ such that $\mathcal{X} = \mathcal{X}^{(1)} \times \mathcal{X}^{(2)}$, where we will suppose that both $\mathcal{X}^{(1)}$ and $\mathcal{X}^{(2)}$ have super-polynomial size. In particular, for $x \in \mathcal{X}^{(1)}$, and $t \leftarrow \mathsf{PRF}'.\mathsf{KeyGen}$, we have $(x, \mathsf{PRF}'.\mathsf{Eval}(t, x)) \in \mathcal{X}$.

- For t a key for PRF′, define $V_t := \{(x, \mathsf{PRF'.Eval}(t, x)) \mid x \in \mathcal{X}^{(1)}\}$. Let C_t the circuit, which, on input $x \in \mathcal{X}$, parses x as $(x_1, x_2) \in \mathcal{X}^{(1)} \times \mathcal{X}^{(2)}$, and outputs 1 if $x_2 = \mathsf{PRF'.Eval}(x_1)$, and outputs 0 otherwise; in other words, C_j tests membership in V_j. If the key t_j is indexed by some j, we will write V_j and C_j instead of the more cumbersome V_{t_j} and C_{t_j}.

We now describe our construction of a watermarking scheme, with its associated watermarkable PRF family:

- Setup(1^λ): On input the security parameter 1^λ, sample $(\mathsf{pk^{in}}, \mathsf{sk^{in}}) \leftarrow \mathcal{E}^{in}.\mathsf{KeyGen}(1^\lambda)$ and $(\mathsf{pk^{out}}, \mathsf{sk^{out}}) \leftarrow \mathcal{E}^{out}.\mathsf{KeyGen}(1^\lambda)$. Output:

$$\mathsf{pp} = (\mathsf{pk^{in}}, \mathsf{pk^{out}});$$

$$\mathsf{ek} = (\mathsf{sk^{in}}, \mathsf{sk^{out}}).$$

- KeyGen($1^\lambda, \mathsf{pp}$): On input the security parameter 1^λ, and the public parameters pp, sample $s \leftarrow \mathsf{chcPRF.KeyGen}(1^\lambda)$, $s' \leftarrow \mathsf{PRF.KeyGen}(1^\lambda)$ and $r \leftarrow \{0,1\}^{r^{in}}$. Sample for $j \in \{0, \ldots, \ell\}$: $t_j \leftarrow \mathsf{PRF'.KeyGen}(1^\lambda)$. The key of the watermarkable PRF is:

$$k = (s, (t_0, t_1 \ldots, t_\ell), r, s', \mathsf{pp}).$$

For ease of notation, we will simply write $k = (s, (t_0, t_1 \ldots, t_\ell), r, s')$ when the public parameters pp are clear from the context.

- $F_k(x)$: On input a key k and input x, output

$$F_k(x) = \left(f_s(x), \; \mathsf{Enc}_x^{out}(\mathsf{pk_{out}}, \mathsf{Enc}^{in}(\mathsf{pk_{in}}, (s, t_0, \ldots, t_\ell); r); f_{s'}'(x)) \right)$$

where $f_s(\cdot) = \mathsf{pPRF.Eval}(s, \cdot)$, $f_{s'}'(\cdot) = \mathsf{PRF.Eval}(s', \cdot)$ and Enc^{out} encrypts $\mathsf{Enc}^{in}(\mathsf{pk_{in}}, (s, t_1, \ldots, t_\ell); r)$ using tag x and randomness $f_{s'}'(x)$.

- Mark(k, msg): On input a key $k = (s, (t_0, t_1 \ldots, t_\ell), r, s')$, and a message $\mathsf{msg} \in \{0,1\}^\ell$, do the following:
  - Compute the circuit

  $$C_{\mathsf{msg}} = C_0 \vee \bigvee_{\substack{j=1 \\ \mathsf{msg}_j = 1}}^{\ell} C_j,$$

  which on input $x \in \mathcal{X}$ outputs 1 if and only if $x \in V_0$ or if there exists some $j \in [\ell]$ such that $\mathsf{msg}_j = 1$ and $x \in V_j$, and 0 otherwise, where $V_j = \{(x_1, \mathsf{PRF'.Eval}(t_j, x_1))\}_{x_1 \in \mathcal{X}^{(1)}}$.
  - Constrain the key s with respect to C_{msg}: $s_{\mathsf{msg}} \leftarrow \mathsf{chcPRF.Constrain}(s, C_{\mathsf{msg}})$.
  - Compute $c^{in} = \mathsf{Enc}^{in}(\mathsf{pk_{in}}, (s, t_0, \ldots, t_\ell); r)$.
  - Output the marked key:

  $$\widetilde{k} = (s_{\mathsf{msg}}, c^{in}, s'),$$

  where the associated circuit computes:

  $$F_{\widetilde{k}}(x) = \left(\mathsf{ConstrainEval}(s_{\mathsf{msg}}, x), \; \mathsf{Enc}_x^{out}(\mathsf{pk_{out}}, c^{in}; f_{s'}'(x)) \right).$$

- Extract(ek, C): Let $w = \lambda/\rho^2 = \text{poly}(\lambda)$. On input the extraction key ek and a circuit C do the following:
  - If the input or output length of C do not match $\mathcal{X}$ and $\mathcal{Y}^{(1)} \times \mathcal{CT}$ respectively, output unmarked.
  - For all $i \in [w]$ sample uniformly at random $x_i \leftarrow \mathcal{X}$, and do the following:
    * Parse $C(x_i) = (C_1(x_i), C_2(x_i))$ where $C_1(x_i) \in \mathcal{Y}^{(1)}$ and $C_2(x_i) \in \mathcal{CT}$.
    * Compute $c_i^{\text{in}} = \text{Dec}^{\text{out}}_{\text{sk}^{\text{out}}, x_i}(C_2(x_i))$ (using secret key sk^{out} and tag x_i);
    * If $c_i^{\text{in}} \neq \bot$, compute $(s_i, t_{0,i}, \ldots, t_{\ell,i}) = \text{Dec}^{\text{in}}_{\text{sk}^{\text{in}}}(c_i^{\text{in}})$.
  - Let $(s, t_0, \ldots, t_\ell)$ the majority of the w values $(s_i, t_{0,i}, \ldots, t_{\ell,i})$, where $i \in [w]$ (that is if $\text{Dec}^{\text{in}}_{\text{sk}_{\text{in}}}$ outputs some $(s, t_0, \ldots, t_\ell)$ more than $w/2$ times in the loop above). If such a majority does not exist, stop here and output unmarked.
  - For $i \in [w]$, do the following:
    * Sample $z_{0,i} \leftarrow V_0$ where $V_0 = \{(x, \text{PRF}'.\text{Eval}(t_0, x)) \mid x \in \mathcal{X}^{(1)}\}$. This is done by picking a random $z_1 \leftarrow \mathcal{X}^{(1)}$ and setting $z = (z_1, \text{PRF}'.\text{Eval}(t_0, z_1))$.
    * Test $C_1(z_{0,i}) \neq f_s(z_{0,i})$.
    * If a majority are equal, stop here and output unmarked.
  - For $j \in [\ell]$, do the following:
    * For $i \in [w]$ sample $z_{j,i} \leftarrow V_j$ where $V_j = \{(x, \text{PRF}'.\text{Eval}(t_j, x)) \mid x \in \mathcal{X}^{(1)}\}$.
    * Test for $i \in [w]$: $C_1(z_{j,i}) \neq f_s(z_{j,i})$.
    * If a majority are different (for $i \in [w]$), set $\text{msg}_j = 1$, otherwise set $\text{msg}_j = 0$.
  - Output $\text{msg} = (\text{msg}_1, \ldots, \text{msg}_\ell)$.

Note that when it is clear from the context, we will omit writing $\text{pk}_{\text{out}}, \text{pk}_{\text{in}}$.

4.3 Correctness Properties of the Watermarking Scheme

Claim. Assuming $\mathcal{E}^{\text{in}}$ and $\mathcal{E}^{\text{out}}$ are perfectly correct and $\mathcal{E}^{\text{in}}$ is sparse, the scheme above satisfies the non-triviality properties.

Proof. 1. For $(\text{pp}, \text{ek}) \leftarrow \text{Setup}(1^\lambda)$ and $k = (s, (t_0, t_1 \ldots, t_\ell), r, s') \leftarrow \text{KeyGen}(1^\lambda, \text{pp})$, we have that Extract, on input F_k, gets $(s, t_0, \ldots, t_\ell)$ as the majority, by perfect correctness of $\mathcal{E}^{\text{in}}$ and $\mathcal{E}^{\text{out}}$. Therefore, the first check (corresponding to $j = 0$) makes $\text{Extract}(\text{ek}, F_k)$ output unmarked (as $(F_k)_1(z) = f_s(z)$ for all $z \in \mathcal{X}$).

2. Let C be a fixed circuit, and let $(\text{pp}, \text{ek}) \leftarrow \text{Setup}(1^\lambda)$. By sparsity of $\mathcal{E}^{\text{out}}$, the probability that any of the w values $C_1(x_i)$ decrypts, for $i \in [w]$, is negligible. Therefore, $\text{Extract}(\text{ek}, C)$ outputs unmarked.

Claim. Assuming PRF and PRF' are secure, chcPRF preserves functionality on unconstrained inputs, and $\mathcal{E}^{\text{out}}$ is tag-CCA2 with pseudorandom ciphertexts, then the scheme above satisfies strong correctness.

Proof. We use the exact same hybrids as in the non-message embedding case, after which the view of the adversary is independent of $(t_0, \ldots, t_\ell)$. We then conclude in two steps. First, the probability that the adversary outputs a constrained point is negligible. This is by PRF security of PRF'. Actually, the adversary cannot even find a point in any V_j, $j \in \{0, \ldots, \ell\}$ (where the set of constrained points the union of a subset of the V_j's defined by msg*), as it would be indistinguishable from predicting one of $\ell + 1$ random values (in $\mathcal{X}^{(2)}$, the output space of PRF').

Second, the probability that the adversary finds an unconstrained point on which F_k and $F_{\tilde{k}}$ differ is also negligible; this is by functionality preserving of chcPRF on unconstrained inputs (which is implied by our definition of constraint-hiding).

4.4   Security Properties of the Watermarking Scheme

Extended Pseudorandomness. We show here that our scheme satisfies Extended Pseudorandomness.

Claim (Extended Pseudorandomness). Suppose chcPRF and PRF are secure, and that $\mathcal{E}^{\mathsf{out}}$ is tag-CCA2 with pseudorandom ciphertexts. Then the watermarking scheme satisfies extended pseudorandomness.

Proof. The proof is similar to the one for Claim 3.4. The only difference is that we now also keep track of the points $z_{j,i}$ sampled from the sets V_j during the calls to the extraction oracle, and we abort in Hybrids 2 to 4 if any of the points $z_{j,i}$ is queried to the PRF oracle. This event only occurs with negligible probability as the sets V_j are of super-polynomial size.

Unremovability. We prove that our construction is ε-unremovable (where $\varepsilon = 1/2 + \rho$ where $\rho = 1/\mathrm{poly}(\lambda)$ is a parameter of our scheme).

Claim. Suppose that $\mathcal{E}^{\mathsf{in}}$ is CCA2-secure, chcPRF is a constraint-hiding constrained PRF, and PRF' is a PRF. Then the watermarking scheme is ε-unremovable.

Proof. We prove the claim via a sequence of hybrids.

Hybrid 0. This is the ε-Unremovability game $\mathsf{Exp}_{\mathcal{A}}^{\mathsf{remov-msg}}(1^\lambda)$.

Hybrid 1. We now change how extraction calls are answered (including the one used to determine the output of the experiment). Let $k = (s, (t_0, \ldots, t_\ell), r, s') \leftarrow \mathsf{PRF}_{\mathsf{pp}}.\mathsf{KeyGen}(1^\lambda, \mathsf{pp})$ be the (unmarked) PRF key sampled to produce the challenge marked circuit, and $c^{\mathsf{in}} = \mathsf{Enc}^{\mathsf{in}}(s, t_0, \ldots, t_\ell; r)$ be the associated ciphertext (which is used to produce the challenge marked circuit $\widetilde{C}$). On extraction query C from the adversary, the extraction procedure samples x_i's for $i \in [w]$ as before. Let denote by E the event that $\mathsf{Dec}^{\mathsf{out}}_{\mathsf{sk}^{\mathsf{out}}, x_i}(C_2(x_i)) = c^{\mathsf{in}}$, i.e. the second part $C_2(x_i)$ decrypts to c^{in} when decrypting using tag x_i. If E occurs, then instead of decrypting this inner ciphertext c^{in} in the extraction procedure, we directly consider it as outputting $(s, t_0, \ldots, t_\ell)$ (used to pick the majority of decryption outputs); in particular c^{in}, s and $(t_0, \ldots, t_\ell)$ are now hard-coded in the modified extraction procedure.

Hybrid 2. We change how extraction calls are answered and how the challenge marked circuit is generated. Let $0_\mathcal{K}$ and $0_{\mathcal{K}'}$ be arbitrary fixed keys for chcPRF and PRF' respectively. We now use:

$$c^{in} = \mathsf{Enc}^{in}(0_\mathcal{K}, 0_{\mathcal{K}'}^{\ell+1}),$$

which is used as the ciphertext hard-coded in the extraction oracle (used to handle event E), and used to produce the challenge marked circuit $\widetilde{C}$. Furthermore, we abort the experiment if the adversary makes any extraction query before submitting his challenge message such that $C_2(x_i)$ gets decrypted to c^{in} for any $i \in [w]$ (where c^{in} is defined before giving the adversary oracle access to the extraction oracle).

Hybrid 3. We change how we produce the challenge marked circuit $\widetilde{C}$ and how we answer extraction queries (including the one determining the output of the experiment). First, to generate the challenge marked circuit, we use the simulator from the constraint-hiding experiment to generate a simulated key $\widehat{s}_{\mathsf{msg}^*} \leftarrow \mathsf{Sim}^{\mathsf{key}}(1^{|C_{\mathsf{msg}^*}|})$.

On extraction query C, we now abort if it considers any $c_i^{in} \neq c^{in}$ such that $\mathsf{Dec}_{sk^{in}}^{in}(c_i^{in}) = (s, *, \ldots, *)$. Furthermore, if we have $\mathsf{Dec}_{sk^{out}, x_i}^{out}(C_2(x_i)) = c^{in}$ for more than $w/2$ samples $i \in [w]$ in the same execution of the extraction procedure, we use the constraint-hiding simulator and check $C_1(z_{j,i}) \neq \mathsf{Sim}^{\mathsf{ch}}(z_{j,i}, C_{\mathsf{msg}^*}(z_{j,i}))$ where $z_{j,i} \leftarrow V_j$ for $i \in [w]$ and $j \in \{0, \ldots, \ell\}$ (instead of checking $C_1(z_{j,i}) \neq f_s(z_{j,i})$).

If c^{in} appears in less than $w/2$ samples, we ignore it in the majority election.

Hybrid 4. We modify how we answer extraction queries (including the one determining the output of the experiment). We now pick $\ell + 1$ random functions $R_j : \mathcal{X}^{(1)} \rightarrow \mathcal{X}^{(2)}$ for $j \in \{0, \ldots, \ell\}$. Define $W_j := \{(x, R_j(x)) \mid x \in \mathcal{X}^{(1)}\}$. If c^{in} appears in more than $w/2$ samples $i \in [w]$, we now sample $z_{j,i} \leftarrow W_j$, and check $C_1(z_{j,i}) \neq \mathsf{Sim}^{\mathsf{ch}}(z_{j,i}, d_{\mathsf{msg}^*}(z_{j,i}))$ instead, where $d_{\mathsf{msg}^*}(z) = 1$ if $z_2 = R_0(z_1)$ or if there exists some j such that $\mathsf{msg}_j^* = 1$ and $z_2 = R_j(z_1)$, where $z = (z_1, z_2)$.

Hybrid 5. Now if c^{in} appears in more than $w/2$ indices $i \in [w]$, for $j \in \{0, \ldots, \ell\}$ we sample $z_{j,i} \leftarrow W_j$, and check:

- $C_1(z_{0,i}) \neq \mathsf{Sim}^{\mathsf{ch}}(z_{0,i}, 1)$ for $j = 0$;
- $C_1(z_{j,i}) \neq \mathsf{Sim}^{\mathsf{ch}}(z_{j,i}, \mathsf{msg}_j^*)$ for $j \in [\ell]$.

We now argue that in Hybrid 5, the experiment outputs 0 with overwhelming probability.

Consider the execution of the extraction algorithm that determines the output of the experiment. We have $C^* \cong_{(1/2 + \rho)} \widetilde{C}$ by admissibility of the adversary.

Hence, a Chernoff bound on the $w = \lambda/\rho^2$ random samples x_i picked by the extraction call gives that with probability at least $(1 - e^{-2\lambda})$, the majority of the x_i satisfy $C^*(x_i) = \widetilde{C}(x_i)$. In particular, by perfect correctness of $\mathcal{E}^{\mathrm{out}}$, we have $c_i^{\mathrm{in}} = c^{\mathrm{in}}$ for a majority of indices $i \in [w]$.

Therefore, for all $j \in \{0, \ldots, \ell\}$, the extraction algorithm now samples $z_{j,i} \leftarrow W_j$ for $i \in [w]$, and tests $C_1(z_{0,i}) \neq \mathsf{Sim}^{\mathrm{ch}}(z_{0,i}, 1)$ for $j = 0$, and $C_1(z_{j,i}) \neq \mathsf{Sim}^{\mathrm{ch}}(z_{j,i}, \mathsf{msg}_j^*)$ for $j \in [\ell]$. But then, by randomness of R_j, the probability that a random $z_{j,i} \leftarrow W_j$ satisfies $C^*(z_{j,i}) = \widetilde{C}(z_{j,i})$ is at least $1/2 + \rho$ (up to some negligible statistical loss upper bounded by $wQ/|X^{(1)}|$ due to the previous $Q = \mathrm{poly}(\lambda)$ extraction queries). Therefore, another Chernoff bound states that with overwhelming probability, the majority of those $z_{j,i}$'s (over $i \in [w]$) satisfy $C^*(z_{j,i}) = \widetilde{C}(z_{j,i})$.

Now, if $\mathsf{msg}_j^* = 0$, we have $\widetilde{C}_1(z_{j,i}) = \mathsf{Sim}^{\mathrm{ch}}(z_{j,i}, \mathsf{msg}_j^*)$ with overwhelming probability by (computational) correctness of chcPRF.

If $\mathsf{msg}_j^* = 1$ we have $\mathsf{Sim}^{\mathrm{ch}}(z_{j,i}, \mathsf{msg}_j^*) = R(z_{j,i})$ for a random function $R : \mathcal{X} \to \mathcal{Y}^{(1)}$ (picked independently of $\widetilde{C}$), so the probability that some index i satisfies $\widetilde{C}(z_{j,i}) = R(z_{j,i})$ is negligible over the randomness of R (again, even conditioned on the polynomial number $(\ell+1)wQ$ of evaluations to R during the extraction queries, as $\mathcal{Y}^{(1)}$ has super-polynomial size). Overall, an union bound gives that the extraction procedure, on input C^*, does not output unmarked with overwhelming probability (corresponding to $j = 0$), and then outputs msg^* with overwhelming probability.

Indistinguishability of the Hybrids. We now show that the hybrids above are indistinguishable.

Lemma 11. *Assuming $\mathcal{E}^{\mathrm{in}}$ is perfectly correct, we have* **Hybrid 0** $\equiv$ **Hybrid 1**.

The view of the adversary is identical in Hybrid 0 and Hybrid 1 by perfect correctness of the inner encryption $\mathcal{E}^{\mathrm{in}}$: in the latter we simply hardcode the result of the decryption whenever we have to decrypt c^{in} during an extraction oracle call.

Lemma 12. *Assuming $\mathcal{E}^{\mathrm{in}}$ is CCA2-secure, we have* **Hybrid 1** $\overset{c}{\approx}$ **Hybrid 2**.

The same argument as for Lemma 3 holds, by additionally noting that any adversary who queries, before receiving the marked circuit, some C such that the extraction call on C gets c^{in} with substantial probability can be directly used to break CCA securiy of $\mathcal{E}^{\mathrm{in}}$.

Lemma 13. *Assuming chcPRF is a constraint-hiding constrained PRF, we have* **Hybrid 2** $\overset{c}{\approx}$ **Hybrid 3**.

First, any adversary who queries some C such that the extraction call on C gets some c_i^{in} such that $\mathsf{Dec}_{\mathsf{sk}^{\mathrm{in}}}^{\mathrm{in}}(c_i^{\mathrm{in}}) = (s, *, \ldots, *)$ can be directly used to break constraint-hiding (as the challenger has $\mathsf{sk}^{\mathrm{in}}$, he can extract the PRF key s using such an adversary). Then, the reduction is very similar to the proof of Lemma 4, by receiving both the constrained key $\tilde{k}$ and values y_i^* from the constraint-hiding experiment to answer the extraction queries where c^{in} form the majority. This is because c^{in} is now the only possible ciphertext that makes the extraction procedure use evaluations to the constrained PRF $f_s(\cdot)$.

Lemma 14. *Assuming the security of* PRF$'$, *we have* **Hybrid 3** $\overset{c}{\approx}$ **Hybrid 4**.

As the challenge marked circuit does not depend on $(t_0, \ldots, t_\ell)$ anymore, all the steps involving PRF$'$ in Hybrid 3 can be simulated given only oracle access to PRF$'$.Eval (on different keys $t_0, \ldots, t_\ell$). More precisely, we have to sample random points in V_j and compute $C_{msg^*}(z_{j,i})$ (given as input to Sim^{ch} if c^{in} form the majority). This gives a simple reduction to the PRF security of PRF$'$, using a standard hybrid argument over the $\ell + 1$ PRF keys $t_0, \ldots, t_1$.

Lemma 15. *We have* **Hybrid 4** $\overset{s}{\approx}$ **Hybrid 5**.

Hybrids 4 and 5 differ exactly when there is some point $z_{j,i} \leftarrow W_j$ such that $d_{msg^*}(z_{j,i}) \neq msg_j^*$, which happens exactly when $msg_j^* = 0$ but $d_{msg^*}(z_{j,i}) = 1$, that is, when $msg_j^* = 0$ but $z_{j,i} \in W_{j'}$ for some $j' \neq j$ such that $msg_{j'}^* = 1$. By definition, this implies having $R_j(z_1) = R_{j'}(z_1)$ for some $j' \neq j$ for some independently chosen random functions R_j and $R_{j'}$; and the probability that this happens, even conditioned on the $\ell = \text{poly}(\lambda)$ functions R_j' and the $Q \cdot w = \text{poly}(\lambda)$ samples $z_{j,i}$ picked accross all the extraction queries made by the adversary (where Q denotes the number of extraction queries he makes), is negligible, as $\mathcal{X}^{(2)}$ has super-polynomial size.

References

1. Agrawal, S., Boneh, D., Boyen, X.: Efficient lattice (H)IBE in the standard model. In: Gilbert, H. (ed.) EUROCRYPT 2010. LNCS, vol. 6110, pp. 553–572. Springer, Heidelberg (2010). https://doi.org/10.1007/978-3-642-13190-5_28

2. Barak, B., et al.: On the (im)possibility of obfuscating programs. In: Kilian, J. (ed.) CRYPTO 2001. LNCS, vol. 2139, pp. 1–18. Springer, Heidelberg (2001). https://doi.org/10.1007/3-540-44647-8_1

3. Barak, B., et al.: On the (im)possibility of obfuscating programs. J. ACM **59**(2), 6 (2012). http://dblp.uni-trier.de/db/journals/jacm/jacm59.html#Barak GIRSVY12

4. Boneh, D., Kim, S., Montgomery, H.: Private puncturable PRFs from standard lattice assumptions. In: Coron, J.-S., Nielsen, J.B. (eds.) EUROCRYPT 2017. LNCS, vol. 10210, pp. 415–445. Springer, Cham (2017). https://doi.org/10.1007/978-3-319-56620-7_15

5. Boneh, D., Lewi, K., Wu, D.J.: Constraining pseudorandom functions privately. In: Fehr, S. (ed.) PKC 2017. LNCS, vol. 10175, pp. 494–524. Springer, Heidelberg (2017). https://doi.org/10.1007/978-3-662-54388-7_17

6. Boneh, D., Waters, B.: Constrained pseudorandom functions and their applications. In: Sako, K., Sarkar, P. (eds.) ASIACRYPT 2013. LNCS, vol. 8270, pp. 280–300. Springer, Heidelberg (2013). https://doi.org/10.1007/978-3-642-42045-0_15

7. Boyle, E., Goldwasser, S., Ivan, I.: Functional signatures and pseudorandom functions. In: Krawczyk, H. (ed.) PKC 2014. LNCS, vol. 8383, pp. 501–519. Springer, Heidelberg (2014). https://doi.org/10.1007/978-3-642-54631-0_29

8. Brakerski, Z., Tsabary, R., Vaikuntanathan, V., Wee, H.: Private constrained PRFs (and more) from LWE. In: Kalai, Y., Reyzin, L. (eds.) TCC 2017. LNCS, vol. 10677, pp. 264–302. Springer, Cham (2017). https://doi.org/10.1007/978-3-319-70500-2_10

9. Canetti, R., Chen, Y.: Constraint-hiding constrained PRFs for NC^1 from LWE. In: Coron, J.-S., Nielsen, J.B. (eds.) EUROCRYPT 2017. LNCS, vol. 10210, pp. 446–476. Springer, Cham (2017). https://doi.org/10.1007/978-3-319-56620-7_16

10. Cohen, A., Holmgren, J., Nishimaki, R., Vaikuntanathan, V., Wichs, D.: Watermarking cryptographic capabilities. In: Wichs, D., Mansour, Y. (eds.) 48th ACM STOC, pp. 1115–1127. ACM Press, June 2016

11. Cramer, R., Shoup, V.: Universal hash proofs and a paradigm for adaptive chosen ciphertext secure public-key encryption. In: Knudsen, L.R. (ed.) EUROCRYPT 2002. LNCS, vol. 2332, pp. 45–64. Springer, Heidelberg (2002). https://doi.org/10.1007/3-540-46035-7_4

12. Garg, S., Gentry, C., Halevi, S., Raykova, M., Sahai, A., Waters, B.: Candidate indistinguishability obfuscation and functional encryption for all circuits. In: 54th FOCS, pp. 40–49. IEEE Computer Society Press, October 2013

13. Goldreich, O., Goldwasser, S., Micali, S.: How to construct random functions. J. ACM **33**(4), 792–807 (1986)

14. Hopper, N., Molnar, D., Wagner, D.: From weak to strong watermarking. In: Vadhan, S.P. (ed.) TCC 2007. LNCS, vol. 4392, pp. 362–382. Springer, Heidelberg (2007). https://doi.org/10.1007/978-3-540-70936-7_20

15. Kiayias, A., Papadopoulos, S., Triandopoulos, N., Zacharias, T.: Delegatable pseudorandom functions and applications. In: Sadeghi, A.R., Gligor, V.D., Yung, M. (eds.) ACM CCS 13, pp. 669–684. ACM Press, November 2013

16. Kim, S., Wu, D.J.: Watermarking cryptographic functionalities from standard lattice assumptions. In: Katz, J., Shacham, H. (eds.) CRYPTO 2017. LNCS, vol. 10401, pp. 503–536. Springer, Cham (2017). https://doi.org/10.1007/978-3-319-63688-7_17

17. Naccache, D., Shamir, A., Stern, J.P.: How to copyright a function? In: Imai, H., Zheng, Y. (eds.) PKC 1999. LNCS, vol. 1560, pp. 188–196. Springer, Heidelberg (1999). https://doi.org/10.1007/3-540-49162-7_14

18. Nishimaki, R.: How to watermark cryptographic functions. In: Johansson, T., Nguyen, P.Q. (eds.) EUROCRYPT 2013. LNCS, vol. 7881, pp. 111–125. Springer, Heidelberg (2013). https://doi.org/10.1007/978-3-642-38348-9_7

19. Peikert, C., Shiehian, S.: Privately constraining and programming PRFs, the LWE Way. In: Abdalla, M., Dahab, R. (eds.) PKC 2018. LNCS, vol. 10770, pp. 675–701. Springer, Cham (2018). https://doi.org/10.1007/978-3-319-76581-5_23

20. Yoshida, M., Fujiwara, T.: Toward digital watermarking for cryptographic data. IEICE Trans. **94–A**(1), 270–272 (2011). http://dblp.uni-trier.de/db/journals/ieicet/ieicet94a.html#YoshidaF11

Exploring Crypto Dark Matter:
New Simple PRF Candidates and Their Applications

Dan Boneh[1(✉)], Yuval Ishai[2], Alain Passelègue[3], Amit Sahai[3],
and David J. Wu[1]

[1] Stanford University, Stanford, USA
{dabo,dwu4}@cs.stanford.edu
[2] Technion, Haifa, Israel
yuvali@cs.technion.ac.il
[3] UCLA, Los Angeles, USA
alapasse@gmail.com,sahai@cs.ucla.edu

Abstract. Pseudorandom functions (PRFs) are one of the fundamental building blocks in cryptography. Traditionally, there have been two main approaches for PRF design: the "practitioner's approach" of building concretely-efficient constructions based on known heuristics and prior experience, and the "theoretician's approach" of proposing constructions and reducing their security to a previously-studied hardness assumption. While both approaches have their merits, the resulting PRF candidates vary greatly in terms of concrete efficiency and design complexity.

In this work, we depart from these traditional approaches by exploring a new space of plausible PRF candidates. Our guiding principle is to maximize *simplicity* while optimizing complexity measures that are relevant to cryptographic applications. Our primary focus is on *weak* PRFs computable by very simple circuits—specifically, *depth-2* ACC⁰ circuits. Concretely, our main weak PRF candidate is a "piecewise-linear" function that first applies a secret mod-2 linear mapping to the input, and then a public mod-3 linear mapping to the result. We also put forward a similar depth-3 *strong* PRF candidate.

The advantage of our approach is twofold. On the theoretical side, the simplicity of our candidates enables us to draw many natural connections between their hardness and questions in complexity theory or learning theory (e.g., learnability of ACC⁰ and width-3 branching programs, interpolation and property testing for sparse polynomials, and new natural proof barriers for showing super-linear circuit lower bounds). On the applied side, the piecewise-linear structure of our candidates lends itself nicely to applications in secure multiparty computation (MPC). Using our PRF candidates, we construct protocols for distributed PRF evaluation that achieve better round complexity and/or communication complexity (often both) compared to protocols obtained by combining standard MPC protocols with PRFs like AES, LowMC, or Rasta (the latter two are specialized MPC-friendly PRFs).

Y. Ishai—Work done in part at UCLA.

Finally, we introduce a new primitive we call an *encoded-input PRF*, which can be viewed as an interpolation between weak PRFs and standard (strong) PRFs. As we demonstrate, an encoded-input PRF can often be used as a drop-in replacement for a strong PRF, combining the efficiency benefits of weak PRFs and the security benefits of strong PRFs. We conclude by showing that our main weak PRF candidate can plausibly be boosted to an encoded-input PRF by leveraging standard error-correcting codes.

1   Introduction

Today, there are two primary paradigms for designing cryptographic primitives. The "theory-oriented" or "provable security" approach is to develop constructions whose security can be *provably* reduced to the hardness of well-studied computational problems (e.g., factoring, discrete log, or learning with errors). The second and "practice-oriented" approach aims at obtaining efficient constructions for specific functionalities (e.g., block ciphers or hash functions). Here, designers typically try to maximize concrete efficiency at the expense of relying on heuristic arguments and prior experience to argue security. But ultimately, confidence in the underlying security assumptions or cryptographic designs only grows if they withstand the test of time.

There are several limitations to these approaches. On the one hand, both the efficiency and the structure of provably-secure constructions are inherently limited by the underlying computational problems. This leads to constructions that are far less efficient than those obtained from the practice-oriented approach. On the other hand, despite the efficiency of practical constructions, their designs are often complex, thereby complicating their analysis. Consequently, it is difficult to argue whether the lack of cryptanalysis against practical constructions is due to their actual security or due to the complexity of their design. The structure of both types of constructions often makes them poorly suited as building blocks for cryptographic applications that are different from the ones envisioned by their designers (e.g., secure multiparty computation).

In this work, we depart from these traditional approaches and consider a surprisingly unexplored space of cryptographic constructions. Our approach is driven by *simplicity*, and aims at circumventing some of the limitations of the existing approaches. Our hope is to obtain constructions that are (1) relatively easy to describe and analyze, (2) concretely efficient, and (3) well-suited for different applications. In particular, we aim at relying on assumptions that are *simple* to state, and yet at the same time, breaking them would likely require new techniques that may themselves have other applications. In a sense, the assumptions we introduce have a win-win flavor and can be of independent interest beyond the cryptographic community (e.g., to complexity theorists, learning theorists, or mathematicians). A notable example for prior work in this direction is Goldreich's proposal of a simple one-way function candidate [29], which had an unexpected impact in different areas of cryptography and beyond (see [4] for a survey).

What Do We Mean by Simplicity? The concrete direction we take is exploring whether the simple operation of *changing moduli* can be a source of hardness in the context of secret-key cryptographic primitives. Our starting observation is that computing the sum of m binary-valued variables modulo 3 is actually a *high-degree* polynomial over $\mathbb{Z}_2$. More precisely, the mapping function map: $\{0,1\}^n \to \mathbb{Z}_3$ where $\mathsf{map}(x) := \sum_{i \in [m]} x_i$ (mod 3) is a polynomial of high-degree over the *binary* field $\mathbb{Z}_2$ (but a simple linear function over $\mathbb{Z}_3$). Surprisingly, this simple idea of mixing different moduli enables new constructions of "piecewise-linear" symmetric primitives that are conceptually simple to describe, can plausibly achieve strong security guarantees, and are well-suited for many cryptographic applications.

Our Focus: Pseudorandom Functions. In this work, we focus specifically on pseudorandom functions (PRFs) [31]—one of the most fundamental building blocks of modern cryptography. Our primary focus is on *weak* pseudorandom functions, namely, functions whose behavior looks indistinguishable from that of a random function to any adversary who only observes the input-output behavior of the function on *random* domain elements. Since weak PRFs cannot replace standard (or strong) PRFs in all cryptographic applications, we then show how our construction can be adapted to yield a new primitive we call an *encoded-input* PRF. An encoded-input PRF is defined similarly to a standard (strong) PRF, except that its input domain is restricted to an efficiently recognizable set. Encoded-input PRFs can be viewed as an intermediate primitive between strong PRFs and weak PRFs that combines the security advantages of the former and efficiency advantages of the latter. Indeed, we show that in many cases they can be used as a replacement for a strong PRF. At the same time, we exhibit simple candidates of encoded-input PRFs in complexity classes where strong PRFs are not known to exist. Finally, a unique feature of our new PRF candidates is that they are very "MPC-friendly." As we show in Sect. 5, our PRFs can be computed more efficiently in a distributed fashion compared to standard block ciphers like AES and even custom-built MPC-friendly block ciphers like LowMC [2] or Rasta [23].

Previous Work on Simple PRFs. Before describing our contributions, it is useful to survey some closely relevant previous works on low-depth PRFs (see Sects. 1.2 and 3.2 for a broader survey). We denote by AC^0 the class of polynomial-size, constant-depth circuits with unbounded fan-in AND, OR, and NOT gates and by $\mathsf{ACC}^0[m]$ the class of such circuits that can additionally have unbounded fan-in MOD_m gates, which return 0 or 1 depending on whether the sum of their inputs is divisible by m. We denote by ACC^0 the union over all m of $\mathsf{ACC}^0[m]$.

With the goal of minimizing the depth complexity of weak PRFs, Akavia et al. proposed in [1] the first candidate that can be computed by $\mathsf{ACC}^0[2]$ circuits. More precisely, their candidate construction can be computed by depth-3 circuits where the first layer consists of MOD_2 gates computing a matrix-vector product $\mathbf{A}x$, where $\mathbf{A} \in \mathbb{Z}_2^{n \times n}$ is the secret key and $x \in \mathbb{Z}_2^n$ is the input. The second and third layer define a public DNF formula. While the Akavia et al. candidate could plausibly provide exponential security,[1] Bogdanov and Rosen [17] recently showed that this candidate (on n-bit inputs) can be approximated by a rational function of degree $O(\log n)$, which in turn gives rise to a quasi-polynomial-time attack. Applebaum and Raykov [6] show that low-complexity PRFs can be based on one-wayness assumptions. In particular, under a variant of Goldreich's one-wayness assumption [29], they present a weak PRF with quasi-polynomial security that can be implemented (on any fixed key) by depth-3 AC^0 circuits.

These recent results leave several open questions regarding the complexity of low-depth (weak) PRFs. First, even if one settles for quasi-polynomial time security, there is no proposed PRF candidate of any kind that can be realized by *depth-2* circuits over any standard basis. When restricting attention to (weak) PRFs that offer a better level of security, the situation is even worse. While it is known that weak PRFs with better than quasi-polynomial security do not exist in AC^0,[2] and that strong PRFs with similar security do not exist in $\mathsf{ACC}^0[p]$ for any prime p,[3] it is plausible that weak PRFs with *exponential* security could still exist in $\mathsf{ACC}^0[2]$. But to the best of our knowledge, there are currently no weak PRF candidates in ACC^0 with exponential (or even sub-exponential) security. Note that if we settle for *quasi-polynomial* security, then the result of Kharitonov [36, Theorem 9] (resp., Viola [51, Theorem 11]) gives a weak PRF in AC^0 (resp., strong PRF in $\mathsf{ACC}^0[p]$ for any p) based on the hardness of factoring. This raises the question of whether it is possible to construct (weak or strong) PRFs with exponential (or even sub-exponential) security in ACC^0. In this work, we propose a new candidate weak PRF that can be computed by depth-2 ACC^0 circuits. Our candidate is conceptually simple and can plausibly satisfy exponential security, thus addressing both of the above challenges simultaneously. We also propose other variants of this candidate, including a candidate for an exponentially secure strong PRF that can be computed by depth-3 ACC^0 circuits.

1.1   Our Contributions

In this section, we give a more detailed overview of the main results of this paper.

New Weak PRF Candidates. We put forward several new (weak) PRF candidates that mix linear functions over different moduli. We start by describing our most useful candidate, and will discuss other variants later. Our primary weak PRF candidate follows a very similar design philosophy as that taken by Akavia et al. [1]. Recall first that in the Akavia et al. construction, the secret key

---

[1] Roughly speaking, we say that a weak PRF is *exponentially* secure if the distinguishing advantage of any adversary (modeled as a Boolean circuit) of size 2^λ is bounded by $2^{-\Omega(\lambda)}$.

[2] Specifically, the classic learning result of Linial et al. [38] showed that AC^0 circuits can be learned from *random* examples in quasi-polynomial time.

[3] The recent learning result by Carmosino et al. [19] showed that for any prime p, $\mathsf{ACC}^0[p]$ circuits can be learned using membership queries in quasi-polynomial time. Extending this result to the setting of learning from uniformly random examples (without membership queries) or to composite moduli seems challenging.

is a matrix $\mathbf{A} \in \mathbb{Z}_2^{m \times n}$ and the input is a vector $x \in \mathbb{Z}_2^n$. The output of the PRF is defined as $\mathsf{F_A}(x) := g(\mathbf{A}x)$, where the function g is a non-linear mapping (in the case of the Akavia et al. construction, the function g is a "tribes" function and can be expressed as a DNF formula). In our setting, we adopt the same high-level structure, but substitute a different and conceptually simpler non-linear function g. In our candidate, we define the non-linear function to be the function that interprets the binary outputs of $\mathbf{A}x$ as $0/1$ values over $\mathbb{Z}_3$, and the output of the function is simply the sum of the input values over $\mathbb{Z}_3$. Specifically, we define the mapping function $\mathsf{map}: \{0,1\}^m \to \mathbb{Z}_3$ that maps $y \in \{0,1\}^m \mapsto \sum_{i \in [m]} y_i$ (mod 3). Our weak PRF candidate (with key $\mathbf{A}$) is then defined as

$$\mathsf{F_A}(x) := \mathsf{map}(\mathbf{A}x) \text{ where } \mathsf{map}(y) = \sum_{i \in [m]} y_i \pmod{3}. \tag{1}$$

We formally introduce our candidate (and discuss several generalizations[4]) in Sect. 3. We state our formal conjectures regarding the hardness of our candidate in Sect. 3.1. There are several properties of our weak PRF candidate that we want to highlight:

- **Conceptual simplicity.** Our candidate is conceptually very simple to describe. It reduces to computing a matrix-vector product over $\mathbb{Z}_2$, reinterpreting the output vector as a $0/1$ vector mod-3 and then computing their sum. The simplicity of our construction is fairly apparent compared to block cipher candidates likes AES or number-theoretic constructions of PRFs. In spite of its simplicity, to the best of our knowledge, such a candidate has not previously been proposed, let alone studied.
- **Low complexity.** Our candidate can be computed by *depth-2* $\mathsf{ACC}^0[2, 3]$ circuits. More precisely, the first layer consists entirely of MOD_2 gates to compute the matrix-vector product $\mathbf{A}x$, and the second layer consists of two MOD_3 gates that computes the binary representation of the output. We refer to Remark 3.9 for a more precise definition.
- **MPC friendliness.** The simplicity of our candidate also lends itself nicely for use in MPC protocols. In Sect. 5, we give an efficient protocol that enables *distributed* evaluation of our PRF in a setting where both the key and the input are secret-shared. We discuss this further in the sequel. As we show in Table 1, the round complexity and communication complexity of our distributed evaluation protocol outperform existing MPC protocols for distributed evaluation of not only AES, but even those for MPC-friendly block ciphers like LowMC [2] and Rasta [23].

Cryptanalysis. In Sect. 4, we consider several classic cryptanalytic techniques on our weak PRF candidate. While our analysis is by no means exhaustive, we

---

[4] An immediate generalization is replacing 2 and 3 by different numbers. However, the particular choice of 2 and 3 turns out to be the most useful for our purposes. A more useful generalization replaces the above choice of map by a suitable compressive mod-3 linear mapping, which yields a weak PRF with a longer output.

are able to rule out several classes of attacks, thereby providing some confidence into the security of our new candidate. Following the work of Akavia et al. [1], we focus on two primary classes of attacks:

- **Lack of correlation with fixed function families.** First, we rule out the learning-type attacks of Linial et al. [38] by showing that there are no *fixed* function families of *exponential* size that are noticeably correlated with our PRF candidate. (Previously, Linial et al. showed that for all AC^0 functions, there exists a quasi-polynomial-size function family such that any AC^0 function is noticeably correlated with a function in that class; this implies a quasi-polynomial time learning algorithm for AC^0.)

- **Inapproximability by low-degree polynomials.** Next, we show that there does not exist a low-degree polynomial approximation to our PRF candidate. Our argument here follows from the well known Razborov-Smolensky lower bounds [46,48] for ACC^0 circuits, which say that for distinct primes p, q, the MOD_p function is not computable by a polynomial-size circuit in $ACC^0[q]$. We conjecture that the Razborov-Smolensky lower bounds also generalize to rule out low-degree *rational* approximations: namely, for distinct primes p, q, there does not exist a low-degree rational function that approximates MOD_p gates over $GF(q^\ell)$ for any ℓ (Conjecture 4.3). We believe that this question is of independent interest from a complexity-theoretic perspective, and leave it as an interesting challenge.

Given the above, we conjecture that our main weak PRF candidate is exponentially secure. We hope that our exploratory analysis will encourage further study and refinement of our conjectures.

Theoretical Implications. We next turn to studying the implications and applications of our new PRF candidates. We first describe several theoretical implications related to complexity theory and learning theory that are implied by our conjectures:

- **Hardness of learning for depth-2 ACC^0 and width-3 branching programs.** As mentioned earlier, one of the key structural properties of our weak PRF candidate is that it can be computed by a depth-2 ACC^0 circuit. Another low-complexity feature, which crucially depends on the choice of the moduli 2 and 3, is that it can be computed by (polynomial-length) *width-3 permutation branching programs* [11]. The existence of a weak PRF in any complexity class rules out learning algorithms for that class even with uniformly random examples. This means that, assuming the exponential security of our weak PRF candidate in Eq. (1), the classes of depth-2 ACC^0 circuits and width-3 permutation branching programs are not learnable (in the standard sense of PAC-learnability [49] *without* membership queries), even under the uniform distribution and even when allowing sub-exponential time learning algorithms. We explore these connections in greater detail in the full version. We note that efficient learning algorithms for the above classes would imply an efficient learning algorithm for DNF formulas [25]. While there are quasi-polynomial time learning algorithms for DNF formulas (in fact, even for AC^0

circuits) under the uniform distribution [38,50], no such learning algorithm (even a sub-exponential one) is known for depth-2 ACC^0 or width-3 branching programs.

- **Hardness of interpolating and property-testing sparse polynomials.** In the full version, we give an alternative characterization of Eq. (1) as essentially implementing a *sparse* multilinear polynomial over $\mathbb{Z}_3$, where the monomials are determined by the key $\mathbf{A}$. We then show that the conjectured hardness of our weak PRF candidate implies that sparse polynomials over $\mathbb{Z}_3$ (with sufficient degree and sparsity) are hard to interpolate given *random* evaluations drawn from a subset of the domain, namely from $\{1, 2\}^n$. Similar to the previous connections to hardness of learning, if it is easy to interpolate the polynomial corresponding to the operation of the PRF (on random inputs), then the interpolation algorithm gives a trivial distinguisher for the scheme. While the problem of sparse polynomial interpolation has been the subject of extensive study [8,13,27,35,52,56,57], much less is known when the interpolation algorithm only sees random evaluations from a subset of the domain. Our conjectures imply hardness results for this variant of the sparse interpolation problem. In fact, as we show in the full version, our conjectures even rule out property-testing algorithms [3,22,34,44] for sparse polynomials.

- **Natural proofs barrier for super-linear circuit lower bounds.** Our work also has relevance to minimizing the *sequential time complexity* or *circuit size* of *strong* PRFs. We consider the problem of constructing "asymptotically optimal" strong PRFs, namely ones that have exponential security in the input length and can be computed by linear-size circuits. This problem is motivated by the goal of ruling out *natural proofs* of super-linear circuit lower bounds, in the sense of Razborov and Rudich [47]. While previous works constructed PRFs that can be evaluated by linear-size circuits [33] or in linear time on a RAM machine [6], these PRFs fail to achieve full exponential security. The work of Miles and Viola [39] presented a simplified abstraction of existing block cipher designs and proved their security under a class of natural attacks. One of their constructions can be implemented by *quasi-linear* size circuits and is shown to have *exponential security* against a wide class of attacks, thus falling a bit short of the asymptotic optimality goal. In Sect. 6.3, we present a depth-3 variant of our main weak PRF candidate that can plausibly meet this goal (Remark 6.7). Thus, we give the first candidate construction for an asymptotically optimal strong PRF, which in turn rules out natural proofs of super-linear circuit lower bounds.

Applications to MPC and Distributed PRF Evaluation. A particularly appealing property of our weak PRF candidate is that it is very MPC-friendly. Protocols for PRF evaluation in a distributed setting (where the secret key and input are distributed or secret-shared between two or more parties) have received a significant amount of attention recently, and new block ciphers have been proposed specifically to be MPC-friendly [2,23]. The structure of our weak PRF lends itself nicely to an efficient MPC protocol (with semi-honest security) for evaluating the PRF with a secret-shared key and a secret-shared input. Consider a scenario where the PRF key and input are secret-shared across multiple servers. Our protocol proceeds roughly as follows:

- If we use a *linear* secret-sharing scheme to share the keys and the inputs over $\mathbb{Z}_2$ (alternatively, a field or characteristic 2), then the matrix-vector product $\mathbf{A}x$ can be computed *non-interactively*: each party simply operates locally on their shares (of the key and input).[5]
- Next, the servers engage in a simple interactive protocol to convert their secret-shared values (over $\mathbb{Z}_2$) to a linear secret-sharing of the same value over $\mathbb{Z}_3$ (effectively implementing the non-linear step in our PRF). Working in the 3-server setting (in a semi-honest model tolerating at most one corruption), we can implement this protocol very efficiently using the protocol of Araki et al. [7]. Here, the "share conversion" procedure essentially requires 13 bits of communication for each bit of $\mathbf{A}x$.
- Once the parties have a linear secret-sharing of $\mathbf{A}x$ over $\mathbb{Z}_3$, computing the output can again be done non-interactively. Note that to extend our weak PRF candidate to output multiple bits, we replace the summation over $\mathbb{Z}_3$ with a matrix-vector product. Namely if $y \leftarrow \mathbf{A}x \in \{0,1\}^m$, then we define the PRF output to be $\mathbf{G}y$ (mod 3), where $\mathbf{G}$ here is a fixed *public* matrix in $\mathbb{Z}_3^{t \times m}$ (Remark 3.3). Even with this extension, computing the output (given a $\mathbb{Z}_3$ secret-sharing of the values $\mathbf{A}x$) still corresponds to computing a *linear* function over $\mathbb{Z}_3$. Again, this is possible non-interactively.

The takeaway is that even though our weak PRF candidate is *highly nonlinear* (due to the mixing of mod-2 and mod-3 operations), the piecewise-linear structure means that it can be securely computed by a constant-round *information-theoretic* MPC protocol with $O(|x|)$ bits of communication. In Table 1, we provide some *concrete* comparisons of our protocol for distributed evaluation of our PRF candidate to some of the existing candidates. As the baseline for our comparisons, we use the protocol of Araki et al. [7] as the representative for 3-party secret-sharing-based MPC protocols, and optimized garbled circuit constructions [37,55] for 2-party protocols. We compare against both the AES block cipher as well as several settings of LowMC [2] and Rasta [23], two custom-designed block ciphers tailored for MPC applications. We describe our precise methodology for deriving these estimates in Sect. 5.2.

From Table 1, we see that using an optimistic setting of parameters for our candidate, the communication and round complexity of our 3-server protocol for distributed (weak) PRF evaluation is better than the generic MPC protocols applied to existing (strong) PRF candidates in terms of both round complexity and communication complexity in almost all cases. The only case where another protocol has smaller communication complexity is the case of evaluating the AND-gate-optimized variant of LowMC (using the Araki et al. protocol);

---

[5] More precisely, one needs here a linear secret-sharing scheme that supports multiplication. In our 3-server implementation we use replicated additive shares (also known as "CNF secret-sharing") to achieve this. We refer to Sect. 5.1 for the full details.

Table 1. Comparison of semi-honest oblivious PRF evaluation protocols. In all cases, we assume that the keys and inputs have been secret-shared between the (2 or 3) servers. We estimate the round complexity and the *total* communication complexity (in bits) needed to evaluate the PRF on the shared key and input. All of our comparisons assume semi-honest servers with up to one corruption and assuming a concrete security parameter of $\lambda = 128$. When comparing to the LowMC block cipher [2] and the Rasta block cipher [23], we compare against two variants: a depth-optimized variant (min-depth) that minimizes the multiplicative depth of the circuit implementing the block cipher, and a gates-optimized variant (min-gates) that minimizes the number of AND gates. We refer to Sect. 5.2 for the parameter settings we use for our estimates. For our protocol, we set the dimensions m, n according to our concrete parameter estimates from Table 2 (in particular we let $m = n$), and set the output dimension to be $t = 128$ (for output space $\mathbb{Z}_3^{128}$).

Construction	Number of servers	Round complexity	Communication complexity
Araki et al. (AES)	3	40	$\approx 1.6 \cdot 10^4$
Araki et al. (LowMC, min-depth)	3	14	$\approx 7.9 \cdot 10^3$
Araki et al. (LowMC, min-gates)	3	252	$\approx 2.3 \cdot 10^3$
Araki et al. (Rasta, min-depth)	3	2	$\approx 2.6 \cdot 10^{10}$
Araki et al. (Rasta, min-gates)	3	6	$\approx 6.3 \cdot 10^3$
Garbled Circuit (AES)	2	2	$\approx 1.4 \cdot 10^6$
Garbled Circuit (LowMC, min-gates)	2	2	$\approx 1.9 \cdot 10^5$
Garbled Circuit (Rasta, min-gates)	2	2	$\approx 5.4 \cdot 10^5$
Our Protocol (Optimistic)	3	2	$\approx 3.8 \cdot 10^3$
Our Protocol (Conservative)	3	2	$\approx 5.5 \cdot 10^3$
Our Protocol (General)	3	2	$13n + 4t$

however, evaluating this variant of LowMC requires over 250 rounds of communication compared to the 2 rounds needed for our protocol.

Compared to the communication-intensive protocols based on garbled circuits, the communication complexity of our protocol is roughly two orders of magnitude smaller than garbled circuit evaluation of LowMC and Rasta, and three orders of magnitude smaller than garbled circuit evaluation of AES. The secret-sharing-based protocols are much more competitive in terms of communication, but these protocols generally have much larger round complexities, which can be problematic in high-latency networks. To summarize, our new PRFs have the advantage that they are very friendly to compute in a distributed MPC setting when both the key and the input are secret-shared. We note that even *weak* PRFs are still useful in a variety of application scenarios. In the full version we describe a concrete application of MPC-friendly weak PRFs for implementing distributed flavors of secure keyword search and searchable symmetric encryption. Moreover, for applications that require strong PRFs, one can apply the *encoded-input* variant of our weak PRF with a modest loss of efficiency.

Alternative Weak PRF Candidate with Better Garbling Efficiency. The structure of our main weak PRF candidate makes it well-suited for three-party distributed evaluation. In a two-party setting, it is natural to rely on a "garbling scheme" such as that of Yao [53] or its optimized variants. However, the cost of this approach will be high because of the super-linear number of multiplications needed for computing the matrix-vector product. In Sect. 5.3, we introduce a variant of our weak PRF candidate (Construction 5.3) that is more suitable for two-party distributed evaluation. The core ingredient in our two-party evaluation protocol is a lightweight *information-theoretic* garbling scheme using arithmetic randomized encoding techniques (cf. [5]). The full two-party distributed evaluation protocol additionally relies on a single (parallel) invocation of a 1-out-of-6 oblivious transfer (OT) protocol; the overall two-party distributed evaluation protocol for this alternative candidate is thus 4 rounds (rather than the usual 2 rounds with Yao's protocol). The output size of this garbling scheme (as well as the total communication complexity of the distributed evaluation protocol) is linear in the input size *times* the output size of the PRF. Thus, this candidate is particularly attractive when the PRF output is short. As we show in the full version, the garbling size of our alternative candidate (which constitutes the bulk of the protocol's communication complexity) with 40 bits of output is smaller than that of an optimized Yao-style garbling applied to LowMC, Rasta, and AES. Thus, for applications that only require such a short PRF output (e.g., using a PRF to compute tags for a set of keywords), the better garbling complexity of our alternative candidate implies a secure two-party protocol for PRF evaluation that is better than that of protocols for evaluating AES, LowMC, or Rasta.[6] While this alternative candidate seems better suited for distributed *two-party* evaluation than our main weak PRF candidate given in Eq. (1), it also has several limitations; most notably, it can at best provide (slightly) *sub-exponential* security. In contrast, our main candidate can plausibly provide exponential security. We give a more thorough discussion of the alternative candidate and its security in Sect. 5.3.

Towards Strong Pseudorandomness. Turning now to strong pseudorandomness, we show in the full version that our candidate is not a strong PRF, and in fact, can be learned in polynomial time given *adaptive* queries. Specifically, we can recast our PRF as an automaton with multiplicity, and then apply known learning results for these function families [14]. However, this attack is unlikely to extend to the setting of weak pseudorandomness. Here, we show that if the learning attack in [14] can be generalized to the weak pseudorandomness setting (where the learning algorithm is only provided function evaluations on a random subset of the domain), then the same algorithm implies a polynomial-time attack on the learning with rounding (LWR) [10] assumption with any polynomial moduli p and q.

Encoded-Input PRFs and Strong PRFs. Motivated by the fact that many applications of PRFs (e.g., message authentication codes (MACs)) do not naturally follow from weak pseudorandomness, we introduce an intermediate notion

---

[6] It is not clear whether LowMC or Rasta can be further optimized in settings where few output bits are needed, or when only weak PRF security is required. If longer outputs are needed for the particular application, then the garbling complexities of LowMC and Rasta will be better than that of our construction.

between weak PRFs and strong PRFs we refer to as *encoded-input PRFs*. Our new notion suffices for instantiating most applications of strong PRFs, and at the same time, still admits simple constructions (and circumvents known lower bounds on the existence of strong PRFs in various complexity classes). At a high-level, an encoded-input PRF is a function that behaves like a PRF on some (possibly sparse) subset of its domain. Moreover, this subset is specific to the PRF family, and in particular, *independent* of the key. For instance, a suitable subset might be the set of valid codewords in a linear error-correcting code. In Sect. 6, we formally define this notion, and then show that many standard applications of PRFs (e.g., MACs, CCA-secure encryption) can be instantiated from encoded-input PRFs by incorporating an additional validity check for the encoded input. The validity check can be made more efficient by using an additional proof provided by the evaluator. We then propose an efficient candidate construction of encoded-input PRFs by combining our weak PRFs with error-correcting codes. The resulting construction resists the adaptive attacks we describe in the full version and can remain MPC-friendly. Using our candidate encoded-input PRFs, we are able to construct MACs with low-complexity verification and CCA-secure encryption with low-complexity decryption (that is, both operations can be computed by a depth-3 ACC^0 circuit). In fact, for a suitable instantiation of our encoding function (e.g., using a *linear* error-correcting code), we obtain a candidate *strong PRF* that can be computed by a *depth-3* ACC^0 circuit (Remark 6.6). Concretely, our depth-3 strong PRF candidate is obtained from our main weak PRF candidate by first applying a mod-3 linear encoding to the input. We also propose a variant of this candidate that can be implemented by linear-size circuits. This variant is used for the new natural proofs barrier discussed above.

1.2 Related Work

There is a large body of work on minimizing different complexity measures of (weak or strong) PRFs. Most relevant to the present work are works proposing PRF constructions that can be evaluated by different classes of low-depth circuits such as AC^0, ACC^0, TC^0 [1,6,9,10,15,18,41–43,51,54]. Of these candidates, those in AC^0 [6] and in ACC^0 [1,51] are either vulnerable to quasi-polynomial time attacks [1,6] or can only be shown to have quasi-polynomial time security [51]. In more detail, the result of Viola [51, Theorem 11] says that assuming hardness of factoring against 2^{n^ε}-time adversaries (for some constant ε), there is a strong PRF in ACC^0 with security against quasi-polynomial time adversaries. We discuss these candidates and their cryptanalysis in greater detail in Sect. 3.2.

2 Preliminaries

We begin by defining some basic notation that we will use throughout this work. For a positive integer n, we write $[n]$ to denote the set of integers $\{1, \ldots, n\}$. We use bold uppercase letters (e.g., $\mathbf{A}$, $\mathbf{B}$) to denote matrices.

For a finite set S, we write $x \xleftarrow{R} S$ to denote that x is drawn uniformly at random from S. For a distribution $\mathcal{D}$, we write $x \leftarrow \mathcal{D}$ to denote a draw from a distribution $\mathcal{D}$. Unless otherwise noted, we write λ to denote the security parameter. We say that a function $f(\lambda)$ is negligible in λ if $f(\lambda) = o(1/\lambda^c)$ for all $c \in \mathbb{N}$. We write $f(\lambda) = \mathrm{poly}(\lambda)$ to denote that f is bounded by some (fixed) polynomial in λ. We say that an algorithm is efficient if it runs in probabilistic polynomial time in the length of its input.

For two sets $\mathcal{X}$ and $\mathcal{Y}$, we write $\mathsf{Funs}[\mathcal{X}, \mathcal{Y}]$ to denote the set of all functions from $\mathcal{X}$ to $\mathcal{Y}$. For two functions f and g on a common domain $\mathcal{X}$, we say that f is ε-close to g if $\Pr_x[f(x) \neq g(x)] \leq \varepsilon$ and that it is ε-far from g if $\Pr_x[f(x) \neq g(x)] > \varepsilon$. Next, we review the definition of a pseudorandom function (PRF) [30].

Definition 2.1 (Pseudorandom Function). *Denote by $\mathcal{K} = \{\mathcal{K}_\lambda\}_{\lambda \in \mathbb{N}}$, $\mathcal{X} = \{\mathcal{X}_\lambda\}_{\lambda \in \mathbb{N}}$, and $\mathcal{Y} = \{\mathcal{Y}_\lambda\}_{\lambda \in \mathbb{N}}$ three ensembles of finite sets indexed by a security parameter λ. Let $\{\mathsf{F}_\lambda\}_{\lambda \in \mathbb{N}}$ be an efficiently-computable collection of functions $\mathsf{F}_\lambda \colon \mathcal{K}_\lambda \times \mathcal{X}_\lambda \to \mathcal{Y}_\lambda$. Then, we say that the function family $\{\mathsf{F}_\lambda\}_{\lambda \in \mathbb{N}}$ is a (t, ε)-strong pseudorandom function if for all adversaries $\mathcal{A}$ running in time $t(\lambda)$, and taking $k \xleftarrow{R} \mathcal{K}_\lambda$ and $f_\lambda \xleftarrow{R} \mathsf{Funs}[\mathcal{X}_\lambda, \mathcal{Y}_\lambda]$, we have that*

$$\left| \Pr[\mathcal{A}^{\mathsf{F}_\lambda(k, \cdot)}(1^\lambda) = 1] - \Pr[\mathcal{A}^{f_\lambda(\cdot)}(1^\lambda) = 1] \right| \leq \varepsilon(\lambda).$$

We say that the function family $\{\mathsf{F}_\lambda\}_{\lambda \in \mathbb{N}}$ is an (ℓ, t, ε)-weak pseudorandom function if for all adversaries $\mathcal{A}$ running in time $t(\lambda)$ and taking $k \xleftarrow{R} \mathcal{K}_\lambda$, $f_\lambda \xleftarrow{R} \mathsf{Funs}[\mathcal{X}_\lambda, \mathcal{Y}_\lambda]$, $x_1, \ldots, x_\ell \xleftarrow{R} \mathcal{X}_\lambda$, we have that

$$\left| \Pr\left[\mathcal{A}\left(1^\lambda, \{(x_i, \mathsf{F}_\lambda(k, x_i))\}_{i \in [\ell]}\right) \right] - \Pr\left[\mathcal{A}\left(1^\lambda, \{(x_i, f_\lambda(x_i))\}_{i \in [\ell]}\right) \right] \right| \leq \varepsilon(\lambda).$$

To simplify the notation, we will often drop the index λ on F. We will also write F_k to denote $\mathsf{F}(k, \cdot)$.

Domains and Their Representations. The key-space, domain, and range of all of the PRF candidates we consider in this work consist of vector spaces over finite fields (i.e., $\mathbb{Z}_p^k$ for some p and k). For notational convenience, we write everything using vector space notation. However, when measuring the complexity of evaluating the PRF, we measure everything in terms of Boolean operations (as opposed to arithmetic or finite field operations). Specifically, we view the keys, inputs, and outputs of our PRF candidates as vectors of bit-strings, where each bit-string encodes the binary representation of its respective field element. For example, a vector $v \in \mathbb{Z}_p^k$ would be represented by a binary string of length $k \cdot \lceil \log p \rceil$, where each block of $\lceil \log p \rceil$ bits represents a single component of v. This way, we can discuss the *Boolean* circuit complexity of evaluating a PRF over a key-space $\mathbb{Z}_p^{m \times n}$, domain $\mathbb{Z}_p^n$, and range $\mathbb{Z}_q^t$.

Circuit Classes. We also recall the definition of several basic complexity classes. First, the circuit class AC^0 consists of all circuits with constant depth, polynomial size, and unbounded fan-in (containing only $\mathsf{AND}, \mathsf{OR}$, and NOT gates).

The circuit class TC^0 (resp., TC^1) consists of all circuits with constant (resp., logarithmic) depth, polynomial size, unbounded fan-in and threshold gates.

Definition 2.2 (Modular Gates). *For any integer m, the MOD_m gate outputs 1 if m divides the sum of its inputs, and 0 otherwise.*

Definition 2.3 (Circuit Class ACC^0). *For integers $m_1, \ldots, m_k > 1$, we say that a language $\mathcal{L}$ is in $\mathsf{ACC}^0[m_1, \ldots, m_k]$ if there exists a circuit family $\{C_n\}_{n \in \mathbb{N}}$ with constant depth, polynomial size, and consisting of unbounded fan-in AND, OR, NOT, and $\mathsf{MOD}_{m_1}, \ldots, \mathsf{MOD}_{m_k}$ gates that decides $\mathcal{L}$. We write ACC^0 to denote the class of all languages that is in $\mathsf{ACC}^0[m_1, \ldots, m_k]$ for some $k \geq 0$ and integers $m_1, \ldots, m_k > 0$.*

3   Candidate Weak Pseudorandom Functions

In this section, we introduce our candidate weak pseudorandom function families. We begin with a basic candidate below (Construction 3.1), and then describe several generalizations and extensions. When describing our applications in the subsequent sections, we will focus primarily on our basic construction.

Construction 3.1 (Mod-2/Mod-3 Weak PRF Candidate). Let λ be a security parameter, and define parameters $m = m(\lambda)$ and $n = n(\lambda)$. The weak PRF candidate is a function $\mathsf{F}_\lambda : \mathbb{Z}_2^{m \times n} \times \mathbb{Z}_2^n \to \mathbb{Z}_3$ with key-space $\mathcal{K}_\lambda = \mathbb{Z}_2^{m \times n}$, domain $\mathcal{X}_\lambda = \mathbb{Z}_2^n$ and output space $\mathcal{Y}_\lambda = \mathbb{Z}_3$. For a key $\mathbf{A} \in \mathbb{Z}_2^{m \times n}$, we write $\mathsf{F}_\mathbf{A}(x)$ to denote the function $\mathsf{F}_\lambda(\mathbf{A}, x)$. We define $\mathsf{F}_\mathbf{A}$ as follows:

- On input $x \in \mathbb{Z}_2^n$, compute $y' = \mathbf{A}x \in \mathbb{Z}_2^m$.
- The output is defined by applying a non-linear mapping to y'. In this case, we take our non-linear mapping to be the function $\mathsf{map} : \{0, 1\}^m \to \mathbb{Z}_3$ that outputs the sum of the inputs values modulo 3. Specifically, for $y' \in \{0, 1\}^m$, we write $\mathsf{map}(y') := \sum_{i \in [m]} y_i' \pmod 3$.

We define $\mathsf{F}_\mathbf{A}(x) := \mathsf{map}(\mathbf{A}x)$. Note that we compute the matrix-vector product $\mathbf{A}x$ over $\mathbb{Z}_2$, and then re-interpret the values as their integer values 0 and 1.

Remark 3.2 (Weak PRF Candidate for Arbitrary p and q). The weak PRF candidate in Construction 3.1 can be generalized to work over two arbitrary fields $\mathbb{Z}_p$ and $\mathbb{Z}_q$ where $p \neq q$. In particular, we define the key-space to be $\mathcal{K}_\lambda = \mathbb{Z}_p^{m \times n}$, the domain to be $\mathcal{X}_\lambda = \mathbb{Z}_p^n$, and the range to be $\mathcal{Y}_\lambda = \mathbb{Z}_q$. We define the non-linear mapping $\mathsf{map}_{p,q} : \{0, 1, \ldots, p-1\}^m \to \mathbb{Z}_q$ that computes the sum of input values modulo q:

$$\mathsf{map}_{p,q}(y') := \sum_{i \in [m]} y_i' \pmod q.$$

Putting all the pieces together, the PRF is defined to be $\mathsf{F}_\mathbf{A}(x) := \mathsf{map}_{p,q}(\mathbf{A}x)$. In this case, Construction 3.1 corresponds to the special case where $p = 2$ and $q = 3$. Note that for certain choices of p, q, the output of this mapping might not be balanced (this is not the case for $p = 2$ and $q = 3$), and pseudorandomness is then defined with respect to the corresponding distribution. We now describe several variations on our general candidate:

- We can consider a binary input space $\mathcal{X}_\lambda = \mathbb{Z}_2^{n'}$ rather than a mod-p input. In this case, we require that the key $\mathbf{A}$ to be compressing so that the product $\mathbf{A}x$ for a random $x \in \mathbb{Z}_2^{n'}$ is statistically close to the uniform distribution over $\mathbb{Z}_p^m$. For instance, this holds by the leftover hash lemma [32] if we take $n'(\lambda) = \Omega(m \log p)$.

- We can consider more complex input spaces and non-linear mappings. As a concrete example, we can define a PRF where the input domain is an elliptic curve group $E(\mathbb{Z}_q)$ of prime order p. That is, we take the domain to be $\mathcal{X}_\lambda = E(\mathbb{Z}_q)^n$; the key-space and range are unchanged: $\mathcal{K}_\lambda = \mathbb{Z}_p^{m \times n}$ and $\mathcal{Y}_\lambda = \mathbb{Z}_q$. In this case, the linear mapping $\mathbf{A}x$ corresponds to computing a linear combination of elliptic curve points. We can define the non-linear mapping $\mathsf{map}_{p,q}$ from $E(\mathbb{Z}_q)$ into $\mathbb{Z}_q$ to be the mapping that returns the x-coordinate of the curve point (recall that each element in $E(\mathbb{Z}_q)$ can be represented by a pair of (x, y)-coordinates in $\mathbb{Z}_q$).

Remark 3.3 (Multiple Output Bits). The output of our weak PRF candidate from Construction 3.1 consists of a single element in $\mathbb{Z}_3$. In many scenarios (such as the ones we describe in Sect. 5), we require a PRF with longer output. One way to extend Construction 3.1 to provide longer outputs is to take the vector $\mathbf{A}x \in \mathbb{Z}_2^m$, reinterpret it as a 0/1 vector $y' \in \mathbb{Z}_3^m$, and output $\mathbf{G}y' \in \mathbb{Z}_3^t$, where $\mathbf{G} \in \mathbb{Z}_3^{t \times m}$ is a *fixed* public matrix. Formally, we define the mapping $\mathsf{map}_\mathbf{G} \colon \{0,1\}^m \to \mathbb{Z}_3^t$ that maps $y' \mapsto \mathbf{G}y'$, and define the PRF candidate $\mathsf{F} \colon \mathbb{Z}_2^{m \times n} \times \mathbb{Z}_2^n \to \mathbb{Z}_3^t$ to be $\mathsf{F}_\mathbf{A}(x) := \mathsf{map}_\mathbf{G}(\mathbf{A}x)$. Construction 3.1 then corresponds to the special case where $\mathbf{G} = \mathbf{1}^{1 \times m}$, where $\mathbf{1}^{1 \times m}$ denotes the all-ones matrix of dimension 1-by-m. In our constructions, we propose taking $\mathbf{G}$ to be the generator matrix of a linear error-correcting code over $\mathbb{Z}_3$. This choice is motivated by the fact that the generator matrix of a linear code with sufficient distance implements a good extractor for a bit-fixing source [20]. As a concrete candidate for our constructions, we propose taking $\mathbf{G}$ to be the generator matrix of a BCH code over $\mathbb{Z}_3$. Note that we require $t < m$. Otherwise, if $t \geq m$, then we can use linear algebra (over $\mathbb{Z}_3$) to recover $y' = \mathbf{A}x$ from the output $\mathbf{G}y'$ (since $\mathbf{G}$ is public). Given multiple pairs (x, y'), we can recover the secret key $\mathbf{A}$ (over $\mathbb{Z}_2$). In particular, in our concrete parameter settings, we require $m - t \geq \lambda$.

Remark 3.4 (Using Structured Matrices as the PRF Key). We can improve the asymptotic (and concrete) efficiency of our weak PRF candidate (Construction 3.1) by taking the key to be a *structured* matrix rather than a random matrix. For example, we can take $\mathbf{A}$ to be a uniformly random *Toeplitz* matrix rather than a uniformly random matrix. In particular, if $\mathbf{A} \in \mathbb{Z}_2^{m \times n}$ is Toeplitz, then computing the matrix-vector product $\mathbf{A}x$ can be done in time that is *quasi-linear* rather than quadratic in the input dimension. A similar optimization of using a random Toeplitz matrix in place of a random matrix was previously proposed to improve the concrete efficiency of authentication schemes based on the learning parity with noise (LPN) problem [28,45].

3.1   Conjectures on the Security of Weak PRF Candidates

We now state three conjectures on our new family of weak PRF candidates, sorted in order from the weakest to the strongest:

Conjecture 3.5 (General Mod-p/Mod-q Weak PRF Candidate). Let λ be a security parameter. Then, there exist fixed primes p and q and $m, n = \text{poly}(\lambda)$ such that for all $\ell, t = \text{poly}(\lambda)$, there exists a function $\varepsilon = \text{negl}(\lambda)$ such that the family $\{F_\lambda\}_{\lambda \in \mathbb{N}}$ from Remark 3.2 is an (ℓ, t, ε)-weak PRF.

Conjecture 3.6 (Mod-2/Mod-3 Weak PRF Candidate). Let λ be a security parameter. Then, there exist $m, n = \text{poly}(\lambda)$ such that for all $\ell, t = \text{poly}(\lambda)$, there exists $\varepsilon = \text{negl}(\lambda)$ such that the function family $\{F_\lambda\}_{\lambda \in \mathbb{N}}$ from Construction 3.1 is an (ℓ, t, ε)-weak PRF.

Conjecture 3.7 (Exponential Hardness of Mod-2/Mod-3 Weak PRF Candidate). Let λ be a security parameter. Then, there exist $m, n = O(\lambda)$ such that for all $\ell = \text{poly}(\lambda)$ and $t = 2^\lambda$, there exists $\varepsilon = 2^{-\Omega(\lambda)}$ such that the function family $\{F_\lambda\}_{\lambda \in \mathbb{N}}$ from Construction 3.1 is an (ℓ, t, ε)-weak PRF.

Remark 3.8 (Further Generalizations). As stated, Conjectures 3.6 and 3.7 are specific to the security of our mod-2/mod-3 weak PRF candidate from Construction 3.1. But more generally, we can consider an analogous pair of conjectures for any fixed mod-p/mod-q candidate (where p and q are distinct primes). Going further, we can even conjecture that the analogous claims hold for *all* choices of p and q. In this work however, we focus on the security of the mod-2/mod-3 candidate, since that candidate is most well-suited for our MPC applications.

Remark 3.9 (Weak PRF in ACC^0). An appealing property of the mod-2/mod-3 PRF candidate from Construction 3.1 is that the PRF can be computed by a depth-2 ACC^0 circuit (in fact, a depth-2 $\text{ACC}^0[2, 3]$ circuit suffices). Specifically, if $\mathbf{A} \in \mathbb{Z}_2^{m \times n}$ is the secret key to the PRF, then the function $F_\mathbf{A}$ can be computed by a depth-2 circuit where the first layer consists of m MOD_2 gates, one associated with each row of $\mathbf{A}$ (concretely, each MOD_2 gate takes as input the subset of input bits on which the corresponding row of $\mathbf{A}$ depends). All of the MOD_2 gates feed into two MOD_3 gates, each computing one bit of the binary encoding of the output value (more precisely, the MOD_3 gate computing the most significant bit of the output outputs 1 if the sum of the inputs is 2 mod 3 and the MOD_3 gate computing the least significant bit of the outputs outputs 1 if the sum of its input bits is 1 mod 3). Note that we can also implement the PRF in depth-2 $\text{ACC}^0[6]$, that is, ACC^0 with MOD_6 gates only (using essentially the same construction). In either case, we conclude that under Conjecture 3.6, there exists a weak-PRF candidate in depth-2 ACC^0. Intuitively, this means that under Conjecture 3.6, the complexity class ACC^0 should be hard to learn. We formalize this intuition in the full version.

3.2 Comparison with Other Weak PRF Candidates

In the full version, we compare our weak PRF candidate (Construction 3.1) to previous candidate low-complexity PRFs, and in particular to the Akavia et al. construction [1], candidates based on hard learning problems or on expander graphs by Blum et al. [15] and by Applebaum and Raykov [6], and to number-theoretic [41–43,51] and lattice-based candidates [9,10,18]. Here, we also discuss several advantages of our construction.

Advantages of Our Construction. We now describe two appealing properties of our new weak PRF candidate compared to the existing ones:

- **Low complexity:** Our weak PRF candidate is the first that can be computed by an ACC^0 circuit and plausibly satisfy exponential security (Conjecture 3.7). Previous PRF candidates in ACC^0 (or AC^0) only provided quasi-polynomial [1,6] or sub-exponential security [51]. In fact, our candidates are computable by a *depth-2* ACC^0 circuit, which is the *minimal* depth possible for any PRF candidate. To our knowledge, there are no other candidates that can be computed by a depth-2 AC^0 or ACC^0 circuit (even if we just require polynomial hardness).
- **MPC-friendliness:** Another advantage of our construction is that our PRF is very MPC-friendly. Specifically, we consider scenarios where multiple parties hold shares of the PRF key as well as the PRF input, and the goal is for the parties to compute the PRF output on their joint inputs. The structure of our PRF is very amenable for use in MPC protocols. Notably, much of the computation is *linear* (over $\mathbb{Z}_2$ and $\mathbb{Z}_3$). Using (standard) MPC protocols based on linear secret-sharing, computing linear functions on secret-shared values can be done *non-interactively*. Communication is only needed to handle the non-linear transformation from values over $\mathbb{Z}_2$ to values over $\mathbb{Z}_3$. In Sect. 5, we show that this step can be done very efficiently using the recent protocol of Araki et al. [7]. In contrast, evaluating the tribes function (in the case of Akavia et al. [1]) or the majority function (in the case of Blum et al. [15]) over secret-shared values will either incur additional overhead in either round complexity or communication complexity (or both).

4 Rationales for Security

In this section, we provide a brief overview of several rationales to support the conjectured security of our candidate. The detailed analysis (including proofs and further discussions) is available in the full version. First, we follow the security analysis of the weak-PRF candidate proposed by Akavia et al. [1] and show that (1) standard learning algorithms cannot break the security of our construction, and (2) our candidate cannot be approximated by low-degree polynomials over finite fields. In addition, we conjecture that it is difficult to approximate our construction with low-degree rational functions. Finally, we suggest concrete parameters for our candidate weak PRF.

4.1 Lack of Correlation with Fixed Function Families

The most natural way to rule out the existence of pseudorandom functions in a complexity class is to provide a learning algorithm for the class. In the the full version, we show that a randomly chosen function in our PRF family does not have a noticeable correlation with any sufficiently small (but still exponential-size) collection of functions $\mathcal{H} = \{h \colon \{0,1\}^n \to \{0, \pm 1\}\}$. Our analysis relies on techniques similar to those used by Akavia et al. [1, Proposition 16]. This rules out distinguishers based on learning algorithms of the form of the one by Linial et al. [38]. Specifically, in the the full version, we show the following lemma.

Lemma 4.1 (No Correlation with Fixed Function Families). *Let $\mathcal{H} = \{h \colon \{0,1\}^n \to \{0, \pm 1\}\}$ be a collection of functions of size s. Then,*

$$\Pr_{\mathbf{A}} \left[\exists h \in \mathcal{H} \mid \Pr_x \left[\mathsf{map}(\mathbf{A}x) = h(x) \right] > \frac{1}{3} + \frac{1}{2^{n-1}} + \varepsilon \right] \leq \frac{5s}{2^n \cdot \varepsilon^2},$$

where $\mathbf{A} \xleftarrow{\text{R}} \{0,1\}^{n \times n}$.

4.2 Inapproximability by Low-Degree Polynomials and Rational Functions

Another necessary condition for a PRF family is that the family should be hard to approximate by low-degree polynomials (resp. rational functions). Specifically, assume there exists a degree-d multivariate polynomial f (resp. f, g) over GF(2) such that $\mathsf{F}_k(x) = f(x)$ (resp. $\mathsf{F}_k(x) \cdot g(x) = f(x)$) for all $x \in \{0,1\}^n$. Then, given (sufficiently many) PRF evaluations $(x_i, \mathsf{F}_k(x_i))$ on uniformly random values x_i, an adversary can set up a linear system where the unknowns corresponds to the coefficients of f (resp. f, g). Since f (resp. f, g) has degree d, the resulting system has $N = \sum_{k=0}^{d} \binom{n}{k}$ (resp. $2N$) variables. Thus, given $O(2^d \cdot N)$ random samples, the adversary can solve the linear system and recover the coefficients of f (resp. f, g) (and therefore, a complete description of F_k). We note that this attack still applies even if F_k is $1/O(2^d \cdot N)$-close to a degree-d polynomial (resp. rational function). In this case, the solution to the system will be $1/O(2^d \cdot N)$-close to F_k with constant probability (which still suffices to break pseudorandomness). Thus, for a candidate PRF family to be secure, the family should not admit a low-degree polynomial (resp. rational function) approximation.

In our setting, we are able to rule out low-degree polynomial approximations by appealing to the classic lower bounds for ACC^0 by Razborov and Smolensky [46,48], which essentially says that for distinct primes p and q, MOD_p gates cannot be computed in $\mathsf{ACC}^0[q^\ell]$ for any $\ell > 1$. We show the following lemma in the full version.

Lemma 4.2 (Inapproximability by Low-Degree Polynomials). *For $n > 0$ and $d < n/2$, let $B(n, d) = \frac{1}{2^n} \cdot \sum_{i=0}^{n/2-d-1} \binom{n}{i}$. Then, for all primes $p \neq q$, the function $\mathsf{map}_p \colon \{0,1\}^n \to \mathbb{Z}_q$ on n-bit inputs that maps $x \mapsto \sum_{i \in [n]} x_i \pmod{p}$ is $B(n, d)$-far from all degree-d polynomials over GF(q^ℓ) for all $\ell \geq 1$.*

The low-degree polynomial approximation attack described above directly generalizes to the setting where the PRF F_k can be approximated by a low-degree *rational* function. For instance, suppose there exist multivariate polynomials f, g over GF(2) of degree at most d such that $f(x) = F_k(x) \cdot g(x)$ for all $x \in \{0,1\}^n$. Then, a similar attack can be mounted, as any random input-output pair corresponds to an equation in the $2N$ variables (with $N = \sum_{k=0}^{d} \binom{n}{k}$) defining polynomials f and g. Thus, if our PRF candidate is $1/O(2^d \cdot N)$-close to a degree-d rational function, then there is an $O(2^d \cdot N)$-time attack given $O(2^d \cdot N)$ evaluations of the PRF.

While the Akavia et al. weak PRF candidate [1] cannot be approximated by a low-degree polynomial, Bogdanov and Rosen [17] showed that the function can be approximated by a degree $O(\log(n))$ rational function, where n is the length of the key. This gives a quasi-polynomial distinguisher against the Akavia et al. candidate.

In our case, we conjecture that the map_p function (respectively, the $\mathsf{map}_{p,q}$ function for our more general candidates from Remark 3.2) cannot by approximated by a low-degree rational function over $GF(q^\ell)$, for any $q \neq p$ and $\ell \geq 1$. While the Razborov-Smolensky argument used to argue hardness of approximation of map_p by low-degree polynomials over $GF(q^\ell)$ does not generalize to rational functions, we still believe that this is a very plausible conjecture.

Conjecture 4.3 (Inapproximability by Rational Functions). For any primes $p \neq q$, any integer $\ell \geq 1$, and any $d = o(n)$, there exists a constant $\alpha < 1$ such that the function $\mathsf{map}_p \colon \{0,1\}^n \to \mathbb{Z}_p$ that maps $x \mapsto \sum_{i \in [n]} x_i \pmod{p}$ is $1/(2^d \cdot N)^\alpha$-far from all degree-d rational functions over $GF(q^\ell)$.

We believe that studying this conjecture is a natural and well-motivated complexity problem. Proving or disproving this conjecture would lead to a better understanding of ACC^0.

4.3   Resilience to Standard Cryptanalysis Techniques

In this section, we survey several other relevant cryptanalytic techniques and their impact on the conjectured security of our weak PRF candidate.

Pairwise Independence. First, we note that our candidate is pairwise independent. This is immediate as for any pair of distinct inputs, the value of $\mathbf{A}x$ will be uniformly random and independent over $\mathbb{Z}_2^m$. Pairwise-independence is sufficient to argue that basic versions of differential and linear cryptanalysis (in the sense of the definitions proposed in [39]) do not apply to our candidate. We note that these linear and differential cryptanalysis are particularly relevant when evaluating the security of our encoded-input PRF (Sect. 6.3), since there, the adversary can make adaptive queries (over a restricted subset of the domain).

Blum-Kalai-Wasserman Attacks. Due to the structural similarities between our candidate and the learning parity with noise (LPN) assumption, the Blum-Kalai-Wasserman (BKW) attack [16] seems particularly relevant.

We do not see a way to adapt such attacks to our candidate as it does not seem possible to create "fresh" samples given a collection of samples. In particular, the mixing of the mod-2 and the mod-3 operations in our basic candidate destroys the linear structure exploited by BKW.

Other Classical Techniques. Several other classical techniques used in cryptanalysis, such as algebraic or correlation attacks, are closely related to the degree of approximation by polynomials or by rational functions. Thus, we can appeal to our previous analysis and conjectures (Sects. 4.1 to 4.2) to argue that our weak PRF candidate plausibly resists those attacks.

Further Cryptanalysis. To conclude, we emphasize that the analysis we have done is not intended to be exhaustive, and we invite the community to further evaluate the security of our candidate. We believe though that the initial exploratory study we have conducted provides evidence to support the security of our candidate.

4.4 Concrete Parameters

We now propose some concrete parameters for our candidate. Our proposals (summarized in Table 2) are based on our exploration of possible attacks as well as concrete parameters for LPN with constant noise rate. Specifically, we use the parameters suggested by [26, Table 4] based on the estimated runtime on a machine with 2^{60} bits of memory and assuming a constant noise rate $\tau = 1/4$.[7] We propose optimistic and conservative parameters. Our optimistic choice of parameters ($n = m = 2\lambda$, where λ is the security parameter) suggests better parameters than those for LPN, which is in part justified by the fact that the most efficient attacks against LPN (e.g., BKW) do not seem to apply to our candidate. Our conservative parameters are the same as those suggested for LPN. We further conjecture that choosing a structured key (e.g., a Toeplitz matrix) does not significantly affect the parameters. Based on our exploratory analysis, we see no need to use larger parameters to instantiate our candidate. We encourage further cryptanalysis to support or disprove the validity of our proposals.

5   Applications to Multiparty Computation

An attractive feature of our candidate is that it supports efficient evaluation in a fully distributed setting, where both the PRF key and the PRF input are secret-shared between multiple parties. We highlight one such application of this primitive to distributed searchable symmetric encryption (SSE) in the full version.

---

[7] Better algorithms for LPN are possible if we allow for machines with even larger memory, but as noted in [26], a machine with 2^{60} bits of memory is already significantly larger than the largest existing supercomputers today.

Table 2. Proposed parameters (for Construction 3.1, we set $m = n$) and comparison with parameters for LPN.

Assumption	$\lambda = 80$	$\lambda = 128$
LPN	300	384
Construction 3.1 (Optimistic)	160	256
Construction 3.1 (Conservative)	300	384

5.1 Fully-Distributed Weak PRF Evaluation

In this section, we describe a 3-party protocol with security against one passive corruption for secure evaluation of our weak PRF candidate (Construction 3.1).[8] At the beginning of the protocol, we assume that the servers hold a secret-sharing of both the input x and the PRF key k. At the end of the protocol execution, each server should hold a fresh secret-sharing of the output.

We assume the parties use an additive secret sharing scheme (over a ring), so additions on secret-shared values are free. For multiplications, we use the multiplication protocol from [7] that allows 3 servers to take shares of ring elements a and b and compute a share of the product ab where each server only needs to broadcast a single ring element. In particular, if we work over the binary field $\mathbb{Z}_2$, computing XOR is free while computing an AND requires 1-bit of communication. The protocol relies on pseudorandom secret sharing (PRSS) [21] and requires a one-time setup of replicated PRF keys. We note that we can achieve information-theoretic security without the need for the (trusted) setup at twice the cost of the basic protocol.

We now describe our protocol π_{fde} for distributed evaluation of our mod-2/mod-3 candidate (Construction 3.1). We assume a structured key (e.g., a Toeplitz matrix), so the key can be compactly represented by a single vector $k \in \mathbb{Z}_2^n$. This assumption is only needed to simplify the protocol description. Our protocol naturally generalizes to the setting with an unstructured (i.e., fully random) key with no overhead (in either communication or round complexity). To recall, to evaluate our PRF, we first evaluate the matrix-vector product between the key and the input: $k, x \mapsto h \in \mathbb{Z}_2^m$. We then reinterpret h as an m-dimensional vector over $\mathbb{Z}_3$. The output $\mathsf{map}_{\mathbf{G}}(h) \in \mathbb{Z}_3^t$ can then be computed as a linear function $\mathsf{map}_{\mathbf{G}}$ on h. We begin by defining the fully-distribution evaluation functionality that we seek to instantiate.

Definition 5.1 (Fully-Distributed Evaluation Functionality). *The ideal fully-distributed PRF evaluation functionality is defined as follows:*

- *Inputs: The servers hold replicated additive shares of the input and the key over $\mathbb{Z}_2$. Concretely, let k_1, k_2, k_3 be vectors in $\mathbb{Z}_2^n$ such that $k_1 \oplus k_2 \oplus k_3 = k$ and similarly x_1, x_2, x_3 vectors in $\mathbb{Z}_2^n$ such that $x_1 \oplus x_2 \oplus x_3 = x$. Server i holds k_j, x_j with $j \neq i$.*

---

[8] The protocol uses two rounds of interaction between the servers.

- **Outputs:** The first two servers hold random $y_1, y_2 \in \mathbb{Z}_3^t$ such that $y_1 + y_2 = F_k(x)$.

We write $[h]_p$ to denote an additive sharing of h over $\mathbb{Z}_p$—that is, a tuple of values whose sum is $h \bmod p$. Depending on the context, this will sometimes be a triple of shares held by the 3 servers and sometimes a pair of shares held by the first 2 servers. Our protocol uses a sub-protocol $\pi_{2,3}$ that transforms an additive sharing $[h]_2$ (i.e., a mod-2 secret-sharing of h) held by the 3 servers into an additive sharing $[h]_3$ (i.e., a mod-3 secret-sharing of h) held by the first two servers. We define this functionality f_{23} below.

Definition 5.2 (Share Conversion Functionality). *The share-conversion functionality f_{23} converts a 3-party mod-2 secret sharing of a value $h \in \{0,1\}$ into a 2-party mod-3 secret sharing of the same value h. Specifically, the functionality's input/output behavior is as follows:*

- **Inputs:** *Every server $i \in [3]$ has an input $b_i \in \{0,1\}$. Server 1 has an additional input $c \in \mathbb{Z}_3$.*
- **Outputs:** *Servers 1 and 3 receive no output. Server 2 receives an output $d \in \mathbb{Z}_3$ such that $c + d = b_1 \oplus b_2 \oplus b_3 \pmod 3$.*

It is straightforward to design a Boolean circuit that implements the ideal share-conversion functionality from Definition 5.2. We give the circuit in Fig. 1 below. The circuit consists of 3 AND gates and 10 XOR gates. To obtain our final share-conversion protocol, we use the PRSS-based protocol by Araki et al. [7] to evaluate the circuit in Fig. 1.

Simple Circuit that Implements f_{23}

- **Input:** $((c_0 c_1, b_1), b_2, b_3) \in \{0,1\}^5$, where $c_0 c_1$ is the 2-bit representation of $c \in \mathbb{Z}_3$.
- **Output:** $d_0 d_1 \in \{0,1\}^2$, representing $d \in \mathbb{Z}_3$.
- **Computation:**
  $d_0 = c_1 \cdot (1 \oplus b_1 \oplus b_2 \oplus b_3) \oplus c_0 \cdot (b_1 \oplus b_2 \oplus b_3)$
  $d_1 = c_0 \oplus (1 \oplus c_1) \cdot (b_1 \oplus b_2 \oplus b_3)$.

Fig. 1. A simple circuit that implements the share-conversion functionality f_{23} (Definition 5.2).

The Protocol π_{fde}. We now describe our protocol π_{fde} for fully-distributed evaluation of our mod-2/mod-3 weak PRF candidate. Recall that at the beginning of the protocol, we assume that the three servers have a replicated additive secret-sharing of the input and the key. The protocol π_{fde} then consists of three phases:

- During the first phase, each server S_i computes an additive share $h_i \in \mathbb{Z}_2^m$ of the linear mapping $(k, x) \mapsto h$ defined by the key. This can be done *locally*

using the replicated additive shares of the input and the key. This follows
from the fact that for any two secret-shared values a, b split into 3 shares
(i.e., $a = a_1 + a_2 + a_3$ and $b = b_1 + b_2 + b_3$), we have that $ab = (a_1 + a_2 + a_3)(b_1 + b_2 + b_3) = \sum_{1 \leq i,j \leq 3} a_i b_j$. In a replicated secret-sharing scheme, server
S_i knows a_j, b_j for $j \neq i$. This means that every term $a_i b_j$ in the sum can be
computed by at least 1 of the servers.

- In the second step of the protocol, the three servers evaluate the share-
conversion protocol $\pi_{2,3}$ to their secret-shared values. For each component
of their additive share, the servers runs the interactive protocol $\pi_{2,3}$ to transform additive shares (held by the 3 servers) modulo 2 into additive shares
(held by the first 2 servers) modulo 3. At the end of this phase, servers S_1
and S_2 hold a share $[h]_3$ of the linear mapping.
- In the final step of the protocol, the two parties evaluate $\mathsf{map}_{\mathbf{G}}$ on their
share. Since the matrix $\mathbf{G}$ is public, this is a linear operation, and can be
done non-interactively. The output is the output of the protocol.

Observe that by construction, only the second step of the protocol is interactive.
Moreover, the protocol requires just two rounds of interaction. We give the full
protocol in the full version.

5.2   Concrete Efficiency of Distributed PRF Evaluation

In this section, we compare the *concrete* efficiency of secure evaluation of our
PRF to alternative constructions. Here, we assume that both the input x and
the key k to the PRF are secret-shared across multiple servers. We measure the
concrete cost in terms of the round complexity and the communication complexity needed for joint evaluation of the PRF. For all of our estimates, we use a
concrete security parameter of $\lambda = 128$.

In Table 1, we provide a concrete comparison of the communication complexity and round complexity for oblivious evaluation of our PRF candidate.
We compare them to the corresponding costs of using the Araki et al. protocol
or an optimized garbled-circuit protocol to evaluate standard block ciphers like
AES and MPC-optimized block ciphers like LowMC and Rasta. We describe the
methodology we used to derive these estimates in the full version.

5.3   An Alternative Candidate with Better Garbling Complexity

While our weak PRF candidate in Construction 3.1 can be computed efficiently
when the input and key are secret shared across 3 servers, the large number
of multiplications makes it less amenable for garbled circuit evaluation. In this
section, we introduce a variant of our weak PRF candidate that is well-suited
for garbling (even compared to MPC-friendly block ciphers like LowMC and
Rasta), and yet, is still plausibly secure. We give the candidate below, but defer
the description of the efficient information-theoretic garbling of the candidate
(based on [5]) to the full version.

Construction 5.3 (Alternative Mod-2/Mod-3 Weak PRF Candidate).
Let λ be a security parameter, and let $n = n(\lambda)$ be the key length (and input length). The weak PRF candidate is a function $F_\lambda : \{0,1\}^n \times \{0,1\}^n \to \mathbb{Z}_3$ with key-space $\mathcal{K}_\lambda = \{0,1\}^n$, domain $\mathcal{X}_\lambda = \{0,1\}^n$ and output space $\mathcal{Y}_\lambda = \mathbb{Z}_3$. For a key $\mathbf{k} \in \mathbb{Z}_2^n$, we write $F_\mathbf{k}(x)$ to denote the function $F_\lambda(\mathbf{k}, x)$. We define $F_\mathbf{k}$ as follows:

– On input $x \in \{0,1\}^n$,

$$F_\mathbf{k}(x) = \sum_{i \in [n]} \mathbf{k}_i x_i \bmod 2 + \sum_{i \in [n]} \mathbf{k}_i x_i \bmod 3 \pmod 2.$$

– In other words, the PRF evaluation consists of computing the inner product between the key $\mathbf{k}$ and the input x modulo 2 and modulo 3, and then combining the results modulo 2, Alternatively, it can be viewed as a variant of LPN with noise rate $1/3$ where the noise is derived deterministically from the input and key (with the noise being 1 if and only if $\langle \mathbf{k}, x \rangle = 1 \pmod 3$).

Security of Construction 5.3. In the full version, we provide additional discussion on the security of our construction. In particular, while many of the rationales we discussed in Sect. 4 for security of our main candidate (e.g., lack of correlation with fixed function families and inapproximability by low-degree rational functions) also apply to the alternative candidate, there are two key limitations of this new candidate compared to Construction 3.1: (1) the BKW attack now applies to this candidate due to its structural similarity with the LWE or LPN problems, and (2) there exist non-adaptive attacks on this candidate.

6   Encoded-Input Pseudorandom Functions

In this section, we examine the security of our weak PRF candidate against *adaptive* attacks. In fact, we show in the full version that strong PRFs do not exist in a large class of depth-2 circuits (including our weak PRF candidate (Construction 3.1), thus ruling out adaptive security of our candidate). Our lower bound relies on a learning algorithm for automata with multiplicity by Bergadano and Varricchio [14].

There are many scenarios where a weak PRF does not suffice for security. For instance, if we consider the distributed SSE application described in the full version and impose the additional requirements of security against *malicious* clients, then a weak PRF no longer suffices. To address this limitation, we introduce a new notion we call an *encoded-input pseudorandom function* that can often be used as a drop-in replacement for strong PRFs. At a high-level, an encoded-input PRF is a function that behaves like a PRF on some (possibly sparse) subset of the domain. As a concrete example, a suitable subset might be the set of codewords under a linear error-correcting code.

In this section, we describe several natural applications of encoded-input PRFs, and then describe a candidate encoded-input PRF whose efficiency is comparable to that of our weak PRF candidate. This candidate remains MPC-friendly, and can thus be useful for MPC applications that require a strong PRF.

6.1   Definitions of (P)EI-PRFs

We define two versions of our notion: *encoded-input pseudorandom function* (EI-PRF) and *protected encoded-input pseudorandom function* (PEI-PRF).

Definition 6.1 (Encoded-Input PRF). *Let* $\mathcal{K} = \{\mathcal{K}_\lambda\}_{\lambda \in \mathbb{N}}$, $\mathcal{X} = \{\mathcal{X}_\lambda\}_{\lambda \in \mathbb{N}}$, $\mathcal{X}' = \{\mathcal{X}'_\lambda\}_{\lambda \in \mathbb{N}}$, *and* $\mathcal{Y} = \{\mathcal{Y}_\lambda\}_{\lambda \in \mathbb{N}}$ *be ensembles of finite sets indexed by a security parameter* λ. *Let* $\{\mathsf{F}'_\lambda\}_{\lambda \in \mathbb{N}} = \{(\mathsf{E}_\lambda, \mathsf{F}_\lambda)\}_{\lambda \in \mathbb{N}}$ *be an efficiently-computable collection of functions where* $\mathsf{E}_\lambda \colon \mathcal{X}'_\lambda \to \mathcal{X}_\lambda$ *is an encoding function and* $\mathsf{F}_\lambda \colon \mathcal{K}_\lambda \times \mathcal{X}_\lambda \to \mathcal{Y}_\lambda$ *is a keyed evaluation function. Then, we say that* $\{\mathsf{F}'_\lambda\}_{\lambda \in \mathbb{N}}$ *is a* (t, ε)-*encoded-input PRF (EI-PRF) if the function* $\mathcal{K}_\lambda \times \mathcal{X}'_\lambda \to \mathcal{Y}_\lambda$ *defined via* $(k, x') \mapsto \mathsf{F}_\lambda(k, \mathsf{E}_\lambda(x'))$ *is a* (t, ε)-*strong pseudorandom function. Moreover, we say that* F'_λ *is computable in* $\mathcal{C}$ *if* F_λ *is computable in* $\mathcal{C}$.

While the definition of an encoded-input PRF may seem equivalent to that of a standard PRF, the important point is that the encoding function is a *keyless* procedure. This means that an honest user can evaluate for itself the encoding algorithm on an input to obtain a valid *encoded input*, and then ask for the PRF value on the encoded input. The holder of the PRF secret key only needs to evaluate F. This is the reason we define the complexity of an EI-PRF to be the complexity of its evaluation function (rather than the composition of its evaluation and encoding functions). Furthermore, we note that even though the overall function $\mathsf{F}(\cdot, \mathsf{E}(\cdot))$ is a strong PRF, the function F itself may live in a complexity class where strong PRFs do not exist.

One of the main reasons we are interested in EI-PRFs is that we can potentially use them as a drop-in replacement for strong PRFs in concrete applications. In many of these scenarios, however, it does not make sense to assume that the evaluator behaves honestly and will only evaluate the F on properly-encoded inputs. This motivates our stronger notion of a *protected encoded-input PRF* (PEI-PRF), which augments an EI-PRF with an additional verification algorithm. The inputs to a PEI-PRF consists of a point x as well as a proof w that x is a proper encoding (with respect to the encoding function of the underlying EI-PRF). The guarantee is that the output of the PEI-PRF are pseudorandom on all properly-encoded inputs, and $\perp$ on improperly-encoded inputs.

Definition 6.2 (Protected EI-PRF). *Let* $\{\mathsf{F}'_\lambda\}_{\lambda \in \mathbb{N}} = \{(\mathsf{E}_\lambda, \mathsf{V}_\lambda, \mathsf{F}_\lambda)\}_{\lambda \in \mathbb{N}}$ *be an efficiently-computable collection of functions where* $\mathsf{E}_\lambda \colon \mathcal{X}'_\lambda \to \mathcal{X}_\lambda \times \mathcal{W}_\lambda$ *is a protected encoding function whose range is polynomial-time checkable by* $\mathsf{V}_\lambda \colon \mathcal{X}_\lambda \times \mathcal{W}_\lambda \to \{0, 1\}$. *That is,* $\mathsf{V}_\lambda(x, w) = 1$ *if and only if* (x, w) *is a valid encoding. Finally,* $\mathsf{F}_\lambda \colon \mathcal{K}_\lambda \times \mathcal{X}_\lambda \times \mathcal{W}_\lambda \to \mathcal{Y}_\lambda$ *is a keyed evaluation function. Denote by* $\perp$ *a special element of* $\mathcal{Y}_\lambda$. *For a function* $f \in \mathsf{Funs}[\mathcal{X}_\lambda, \mathcal{Y}_\lambda]$, *define* $\mathsf{Eval}^f_\lambda \colon \mathcal{X}_\lambda \times \mathcal{W}_\lambda \to \mathcal{Y}_\lambda$ *as:*

$$\mathsf{Eval}^f_\lambda(x, w) = \begin{cases} f(x) & \text{if } \mathsf{V}_\lambda(x, w) = 1 \\ \perp & \text{otherwise.} \end{cases}$$

Then, we say that $\{F'_\lambda\}_{\lambda \in \mathbb{N}}$ *is a* (t, ε)*-PEI-PRF if for all adversaries* $\mathcal{A}$ *running in time* $t(\lambda)$, *and taking* $k \xleftarrow{\text{R}} \mathcal{K}_\lambda$ *and* $f \xleftarrow{\text{R}} \mathsf{Funs}[\mathcal{X}_\lambda, \mathcal{Y}_\lambda]$, *we have that*

$$\left| \Pr[\mathcal{A}^{F_\lambda(k, \cdot, \cdot)}(1^\lambda) = 1] - \Pr[\mathcal{A}^{\mathsf{Eval}^f_\lambda(\cdot, \cdot)}(1^\lambda) = 1] \right| \leq \varepsilon(\lambda).$$

We say that F'_λ *is* computable in a circuit class $\mathcal{C}$ *if the mapping* $(k, x, w) \mapsto F_\lambda(k, x, w)$ *is computable in* $\mathcal{C}$. *Finally, we say that a PEI-PRF is* systematic *if the witness* w *has the form* $x' \| w'$ *such that* $V_\lambda(x, (x' \| w')) = 1$ *if and only if* $(x, w) = E_\lambda(x')$.

Remark 6.3 (Relation between EI-PRFs and PEI-PRFs). PEI-PRFs are more powerful objects than EI-PRFs: If $(\mathsf{E}, \mathsf{V}, \mathsf{F})$ is a PEI-PRF, then (E, F) is an EI-PRF.

We first show that that PEI-PRFs can be generically constructed from EI-PRFs.

Lemma 6.4 (PEI-PRFs from EI-PRFs). *Let* $\{(\mathsf{E}^*_\lambda, \mathsf{F}^*_\lambda)\}_\lambda$ *be an EI-PRF. Then, assuming* F_λ *and CNF formulas can be computed by depth-d circuits in a class* $\mathcal{C}$, *there exists a systematic PEI-PRF* $\{(\mathsf{E}_\lambda, \mathsf{V}_\lambda, \mathsf{F}_\lambda)\}_\lambda$ *computable by a depth-$(d+1)$ circuit.*

Proof. The lemma follows from the fact that we can check the correctness of any Boolean circuit computation using a CNF formula. In particular, we define a variable associated with each wire in the circuit, and construct a constant-size CNF associated with each gate in the circuit (checking that the gate is implemented correctly). The conjunction of all of these gate-by-gate CNFs gives a CNF for the overall circuit. For notational convenience, we drop the λ subscripts in the description below. We now define a systematic PEI-PRF $(\mathsf{E}_\lambda, \mathsf{V}_\lambda, \mathsf{F}_\lambda)$ as follows:

- $\mathsf{E}(x') \to (x, w)$: On input a point $x' \in \mathcal{X}'$, output $(\mathsf{E}^*(x'), w)$, where w is the set of all of the wire values for the Boolean circuit computing $\mathsf{E}^*(x')$. Specifically, we can write $w = x' \| w'$, where x' is the input to E^* and w' contain the internal (and output) wire values of $\mathsf{E}^*(x')$.
- $\mathsf{V}(x, w) \to \{0, 1\}$: On input an encoded input $x \in \mathcal{X}$ and a witness $w \in \mathcal{W}$, the verification algorithm interprets $w = x' \| w'$. Then, it invokes the CNF verification procedure (for checking correct computation of E^*) to check that $\mathsf{E}^*(x') = (x, w)$.
- $\mathsf{F}(k, x, w) \to y$: On input the key $k \in \mathcal{K}$, an encoded input $x \in \mathcal{X}$, and a witness $w \in \mathcal{W}$, the evaluation algorithm outputs $y \leftarrow \mathsf{F}^*(k, x)$ if $V(x, w) = 1$, and $\perp$ otherwise. This can be implemented by computing an AND between the output of $\mathsf{V}(x, w)$ and $\mathsf{F}^*(k, x)$.

Since the verification algorithm V can be expressed as a CNF formula, and moreover, both F^* and CNFs can be computed by a circuit of depth $d > 2$, the evaluation algorithm F can be implemented by a circuit of depth $d + 1$.

6.2   Applications of (P)EI-PRFs

Certainly, we can instantiate any application of strong PRFs using an EI-PRF, since EI-PRFs are PRFs if we consider the combination of the encoding and the evaluation functions. However, we note here that our notions of EI-PRFs and PEI-PRFs allow us to obtain interesting alternative instantiations of many of the classic applications of PRFs. We provide details on the constructions and proofs in the full version.

Theorem 6.5 (Symmetric Low-Depth Primitives). *Let C be a class of circuits. Then, if there exists an EI-PRF computable in C, there exists a symmetric encryption scheme with decryption in C (assuming C is closed under composition with 2-bit* XOR*). Similarly, if there exists a systematic PEI-PRF computable in C, there exists a MAC with verification in C (assuming C is closed under composition with equality testing). Together, this yields a CCA-secure symmetric encryption scheme (in fact, an authenticated encryption scheme [12]) with decryption in C.*

6.3   Candidate Constructions of (P)EI-PRFs

In the full version, we give a heuristic construction of PEI-PRFs from weak-PRFs in the random oracle model. This construction is primarily of conceptual interest and follows from some basic observations on the connection between weak PRFs and strong PRFs [40]. We also propose a candidate PEI-PRF based on our mod-2/mod-3 weak PRF candidate (Construction 3.1) that remains MPC-friendly. We briefly describe our candidate below.

(P)EI-PRF from our candidate. At a high level, the adaptive attack on our weak PRF candidate (based on [14], see the full version) relies on querying inputs that are close (in terms of Hamming distance) and on the fact that each component of the input of the second mapping (i.e. the components of $\mathbf{A}x$) can be computed by a read-once computation (by some automaton to be precise). This suggests that using a code with large minimal distance to encode the input x should prevent this attack. For MPC-friendliness, we would like to use a linear code, as verifying that an input is a valid codeword can be done efficiently (by multiplying by the parity-check matrix for the code).

A natural candidate is to use a linear code $(\mathbf{G}, \mathbf{H})$ over $\mathbb{Z}_2$: the encoding of an input x' is the codeword $\mathbf{G} \cdot x'$. Unfortunately, the same attack still applies since we can always view the PRF evaluation as $\mathbf{A} \cdot (\mathbf{G} \cdot x') = (\mathbf{A} \cdot \mathbf{G}) \cdot x'$ and interpret $(\mathbf{A} \cdot \mathbf{G})$ as the key. To defend against this, we instead use a linear code over $\mathbb{Z}_3$ and define the encoded bitstring x to be the binary representation of the codeword obtained by applying the code to x' (where we interpret $x' \in \{0,1\}^{n'}$ as a vector over $\mathbb{Z}_3$). By mixing mod-2 and mod-3 operations, the encoding procedure becomes non-linear, but verification can still be expressed as a linear function. At the same time, the use of the linear code ensures that (1) encoded inputs are far from each other, (2) verification is MPC-friendly as the code is linear, and (3) the input of the second mapping *cannot* be expressed as a read-once computation. We give the full description in the the full version.

Remark 6.6 (Candidate Strong PRF in Depth-3 $\mathsf{ACC}^0[2,3]$). Our candidate EI-PRF gives a strong PRF candidate if we consider the composition of the encoding function E with the evaluation function F. In fact, since the encoding function E computes a *linear* function over $\mathbb{Z}_3$, it can be computed by a depth-1 $\mathsf{ACC}^0[3]$ circuit. As noted in Remark 3.9, the PRF evaluation function F can be computed by a depth-2 $\mathsf{ACC}^0[2,3]$ circuit. Thus, the composition of E and F can be computed by a *depth-3* ACC^0 circuit (note that the binary decomposition in the encoding function is easily handled via fan-in and does not increase the depth of the circuit). Thus, our construction gives a candidate *strong PRF* in depth-3 $\mathsf{ACC}^0[2,3]$.

Remark 6.7 (Asymptotically-Optimal PRFs and Natural Proof Barriers). As we note in Remark 6.6, our candidate EI-PRF gives a strong PRF candidate if we consider the composition of the encoding function E with the evaluation function F. If both E and F can be computed by a circuit of linear size (in the length of the key and input), then we obtain a candidate strong PRF with exponential security that can be computed by linear-size circuits. This gives an "asymptotically optimal" PRF that rules out natural proofs of super-linear circuit lower bounds in the sense of Razborov and Rudich [47]. We now describe a variant of our EI-PRF that gives the first candidate instantiation of an asymptotically-optimal PRF, and correspondingly, the first natural proof barrier for proving super-linear circuit lower bounds.

Evaluating our EI-PRF candidate consists of three main steps: encoding the input over $\mathbb{Z}_3$, computing the binary decomposition of the encoded vector, and then multiplying the encoded input with the secret key $\mathbf{A}$ over $\mathbb{Z}_2$. If we instantiate the $\mathbb{Z}_3$-encoding with a linear-time encodable code over $\mathbb{Z}_3$ and then replace the key $\mathbf{A}$ with the generator matrix of a linear-time encodable code over $\mathbb{Z}_2$, then the resulting construction can be computed by a linear-size circuit. For instance, we can instantiate the code with the linear-time encodable code family proposed by Druk and Ishai [24] (building on the hash function from [33]). This family gives a randomized construction of a linear-time encodable code that has many of the combinatorial properties of a *random* linear code. Thus, we conjecture that sampling the key to be the generator matrix of a Druk-Ishai code does not compromise the security of our candidate. Putting these pieces together, we obtain a plausible candidate of a strong PRF with exponential security and which can be computed by a linear-size circuit. As far as we know, this is the first candidate instantiation of such an asymptotically-optimal strong PRF. Assuming it is indeed exponentially secure, natural proof techniques cannot prove super-linear circuit lower bounds.

Conclusions. We believe that *the conjectures we have made in this section are strong and a healthy dose of skepticism is warranted.* We hope that the applications and implications we point out will motivate further study and constructions of (P)EI-PRFs, as well as additional cryptanalysis of our concrete candidates. We also leave open the question of setting concrete parameters for our new PEI-PRF and strong PRF candidates (Remark 6.6).

Acknowledgments. We thank Benny Applebaum, Andrej Bogdanov, Arkadev Chattopadhyay, Itai Dinur, Neeraj Kayal, Sam Kim, Hart Montgomery, Alexander Sherstov, Emanuele Viola, and the anonymous TCC reviewers for helpful discussions and pointers. D. Boneh and D. J. Wu are supported by NSF, DARPA, a grant from ONR, and the Simons Foundation. Y. Ishai, A. Passelègue, and A. Sahai are supported in part from a DARPA/ARL SAFEWARE award, NSF Frontier Award 1413955, NSF grants 1619348, 1228984, 1136174, and 1065276, BSF grant 2012378, NSF-BSF grant 2015782, a Xerox Faculty Research Award, a Google Faculty Research Award, an equipment grant from Intel, and an Okawa Foundation Research Grant. Y. Ishai is additionally supported by ERC grant 742754, ISF grant 1709/14, and a grant from the Ministry of Science and Technology, Israel and Department of Science and Technology, Government of India. This material is based upon work supported by the Defense Advanced Research Projects Agency through the ARL under Contract W911NF-15-C-0205. The views expressed are those of the authors and do not reflect the official policy or position of the Department of Defense, the National Science Foundation, or the U.S. Government.

References

1. Akavia, A., Bogdanov, A., Guo, S., Kamath, A., Rosen, A.: Candidate weak pseudorandom functions in AC^0 o MOD_2. ITCS **2014**, 251–260 (2014)
2. Albrecht, M.R., Rechberger, C., Schneider, T., Tiessen, T., Zohner, M.: Ciphers for MPC and FHE. In: Oswald, E., Fischlin, M. (eds.) EUROCRYPT 2015. LNCS, vol. 9056, pp. 430–454. Springer, Heidelberg (2015). https://doi.org/10.1007/978-3-662-46800-5_17
3. Alon, N., Kaufman, T., Krivelevich, M., Litsyn, S., Ron, D.: Testing low-degree polynomials over $GF(2)$. In: Arora, S., Jansen, K., Rolim, J.D.P., Sahai, A. (eds.) APPROX/RANDOM -2003. LNCS, vol. 2764, pp. 188–199. Springer, Heidelberg (2003). https://doi.org/10.1007/978-3-540-45198-3_17
4. Applebaum, B.: Cryptographic hardness of random local functions-survey. In: TCC, p. 599 (2013)
5. Applebaum, B., Ishai, Y., Kushilevitz, E.: How to garble arithmetic circuits. In: FOCS, pp. 120–129 (2011)
6. Applebaum, B., Raykov, P.: Fast pseudorandom functions based on expander graphs. In: Hirt, M., Smith, A. (eds.) TCC 2016. LNCS, vol. 9985, pp. 27–56. Springer, Heidelberg (2016). https://doi.org/10.1007/978-3-662-53641-4_2
7. Araki, T., Furukawa, J., Lindell, Y., Nof, A., Ohara, K.: High-throughput semi-honest secure three-party computation with an honest majority. In: ACM CCS, pp. 805–817 (2016)
8. Arnold, A., Giesbrecht, M., Roche, D.S.: Sparse interpolation over finite fields via low-order roots of unity. In: Proceedings of the 39th International Symposium on Symbolic and Algebraic Computation, pp. 27–34. ACM (2014)
9. Banerjee, A., Peikert, C.: New and improved key-homomorphic pseudorandom functions. In: Garay, J.A., Gennaro, R. (eds.) CRYPTO 2014. LNCS, vol. 8616, pp. 353–370. Springer, Heidelberg (2014). https://doi.org/10.1007/978-3-662-44371-2_20
10. Banerjee, A., Peikert, C., Rosen, A.: Pseudorandom functions and lattices. In: Pointcheval, D., Johansson, T. (eds.) EUROCRYPT 2012. LNCS, vol. 7237, pp. 719–737. Springer, Heidelberg (2012). https://doi.org/10.1007/978-3-642-29011-4_42

11. Barrington, D.A.: Width-3 permutation branching programs. Technical Memorandum TM-293 (1985)
12. Bellare, M., Namprempre, C.: Authenticated encryption: relations among notions and analysis of the generic composition paradigm. In: Okamoto, T. (ed.) ASIACRYPT 2000. LNCS, vol. 1976, pp. 531–545. Springer, Heidelberg (2000). https://doi.org/10.1007/3-540-44448-3_41
13. Ben-Or, M., Tiwari, P.: A deterministic algorithm for sparse multivariate polynominal interpolation (extended abstract). In: ACM STOC, pp. 301–309 (1988)
14. Bergadano, F., Varricchio, S.: Learning behaviors of automata from multiplicity and equivalence queries. SIAM J. Comput. **25**(6), 1268–1280 (1996)
15. Blum, A., Furst, M., Kearns, M., Lipton, R.J.: Cryptographic primitives based on hard learning problems. In: Stinson, D.R. (ed.) CRYPTO 1993. LNCS, vol. 773, pp. 278–291. Springer, Heidelberg (1994). https://doi.org/10.1007/3-540-48329-2_24
16. Blum, A., Kalai, A., Wasserman, H.: Noise-tolerant learning, the parity problem, and the statistical query model. In: ACM STOC, pp. 435–440 (2000)
17. Bogdanov, A., Rosen, A.: Pseudorandom functions: three decades later. Tutorials on the Foundations of Cryptography. ISC, pp. 79–158. Springer, Cham (2017). https://doi.org/10.1007/978-3-319-57048-8_3
18. Boneh, D., Lewi, K., Montgomery, H., Raghunathan, A.: Key homomorphic PRFs and their applications. In: Canetti, R., Garay, J.A. (eds.) CRYPTO 2013. LNCS, vol. 8042, pp. 410–428. Springer, Heidelberg (2013). https://doi.org/10.1007/978-3-642-40041-4_23
19. Carmosino, M.L., Impagliazzo, R., Kabanets, V., Kolokolova, A.: Learning algorithms from natural proofs. In: CCC, pp. 10:1–10:24 (2016)
20. Chor, B., Goldreich, O., Håstad, J., Friedman, J., Rudich, S, Smolensky, R.: The bit extraction problem of t-resilient functions (preliminary version). In: FOCS, pp. 396–407 (1985)
21. Cramer, R., Damgård, I., Ishai, Y.: Share conversion, pseudorandom secret-sharing and applications to secure computation. In: Kilian, J. (ed.) TCC 2005. LNCS, vol. 3378, pp. 342–362. Springer, Heidelberg (2005). https://doi.org/10.1007/978-3-540-30576-7_19
22. Diakonikolas, I., et al.: Testing for concise representations. In: FOCS, pp. 549–558 (2007)
23. Dobraunig, C., et al.: Rasta: a cipher with low ANDdepth and Few ANDs per bit. In: Shacham, H., Boldyreva, A. (eds.) CRYPTO 2018. LNCS, vol. 10991, pp. 662–692. Springer, Cham (2018). https://doi.org/10.1007/978-3-319-96884-1_22
24. Druk, E., Ishai, Y.: Linear-time encodable codes meeting the gilbert-varshamov bound and their cryptographic applications. In: ITCS 2014, pp. 169–182 (2014)
25. Ergün, F., Kumar, R., Rubinfeld, R.: On learning bounded-width branching programs. In: COLT, pp. 361–368 (1995)
26. Esser, A., Kübler, R., May, A.: LPN decoded. In: Katz, J., Shacham, H. (eds.) CRYPTO 2017. LNCS, vol. 10402, pp. 486–514. Springer, Cham (2017). https://doi.org/10.1007/978-3-319-63715-0_17
27. Garg, S., Schost, É.: Interpolation of polynomials given by straight-line programs. Theor. Comput. Sci. **410**(27–29), 2659–2662 (2009)
28. Gilbert, H., Robshaw, M.J.B., Seurin, Y.: HB$^\sharp$: increasing the security and efficiency of HB$^+$. In: Smart, N. (ed.) EUROCRYPT 2008. LNCS, vol. 4965, pp. 361–378. Springer, Heidelberg (2008). https://doi.org/10.1007/978-3-540-78967-3_21
29. Goldreich, O.: Candidate one-way functions based on expander graphs. Cryptology ePrint Archive, Report 2000/063 (2000). http://eprint.iacr.org/2000/063

30. Goldreich, O., Goldwasser, S., Micali, S.: On the cryptographic applications of random functions (extended abstract). In: Blakley, G.R., Chaum, D. (eds.) CRYPTO 1984. LNCS, vol. 196, pp. 276–288. Springer, Heidelberg (1985). https://doi.org/10.1007/3-540-39568-7_22

31. Goldreich, O., Goldwasser, S., Micali, S.: How to construct random functions. J. ACM **33**(4), 792–807 (1986)

32. Håstad, J., Impagliazzo, R., Levin, L.A., Luby, M.: A pseudorandom generator from any one-way function. SIAM J. Comput. **28**(4), 1364–1396 (1999)

33. Ishai, Y., Kushilevitz, E., Ostrovsky, R., Sahai, A.: Cryptography with constant computational overhead. In: ACM STOC, pp. 433–442 (2008)

34. Jutla, C.S., Patthak, A.C., Rudra, A., Zuckerman, D.: Testing low-degree polynomials over prime fields. In: FOCS, pp. 423–432 (2004)

35. Kaltofen, E., Yagati, L.: Improved sparse multivariate polynomial interpolation algorithms. In: Gianni, P. (ed.) ISSAC 1988. LNCS, vol. 358, pp. 467–474. Springer, Heidelberg (1989). https://doi.org/10.1007/3-540-51084-2_44

36. Kharitonov, M.: Cryptographic hardness of distribution-specific learning. In: ACM STOC, pp. 372–381 (1993)

37. Kolesnikov, V., Schneider, T.: Improved garbled circuit: free XOR gates and applications. In: Aceto, L., Damgård, I., Goldberg, L.A., Halldórsson, M.M., Ingólfsdóttir, A., Walukiewicz, I. (eds.) ICALP 2008. LNCS, vol. 5126, pp. 486–498. Springer, Heidelberg (2008). https://doi.org/10.1007/978-3-540-70583-3_40

38. Linial, N., Mansour, Y., Nisan, N.: Constant depth circuits, fourier transform, and learnability. In: FOCS, pp. 574–579 (1989)

39. Miles, E., Viola, E.: Substitution-permutation networks, pseudorandom functions, and natural proofs. In: Safavi-Naini, R., Canetti, R. (eds.) CRYPTO 2012. LNCS, vol. 7417, pp. 68–85. Springer, Heidelberg (2012). https://doi.org/10.1007/978-3-642-32009-5_5

40. Naor, M., Reingold, O.: Synthesizers and their application to the parallel construction of pseudo-random functions. In: FOCS, pp. 170–181 (1995)

41. Naor, M., Reingold, O.: Synthesizers and their application to the parallel construction of pseudo-random functions. J. Comput. Syst. Sci. **58**(2), 336–375 (1999)

42. Naor, M., Reingold, O.: Number-theoretic constructions of efficient pseudo-random functions. J. ACM **51**(2), 231–262 (2004)

43. Naor, M., Reingold, O., Rosen, A.: Pseudo-random functions and factoring (extended abstract). In: ACM STOC, pp. 11–20 (2000)

44. Parnas, M., Ron, D., Samorodnitsky, A.: Testing basic Boolean formulae. SIAM J. Discret. Math. **16**(1), 20–46 (2002)

45. Pietrzak, K.: Cryptography from learning parity with noise. In: Bieliková, M., Friedrich, G., Gottlob, G., Katzenbeisser, S., Turán, G. (eds.) SOFSEM 2012. LNCS, vol. 7147, pp. 99–114. Springer, Heidelberg (2012). https://doi.org/10.1007/978-3-642-27660-6_9

46. Razborov, A.A.: Lower bounds on the size of bounded-depth networks over a complete basis with logical addition (russian). Matematicheskie Zametki **41**(4), 598–607 (1987). english translation in Mathematical Notes of the Academy of Sci. of the USSR, 41(4):333–338, 1987

47. Razborov, A.A., Rudich, S.: Natural proofs. In: ACM STOC, pp. 204–213 (1994)

48. Smolensky, R.: Algebraic methods in the theory of lower bounds for Boolean circuit complexity. In: ACM STOC, pp. 77–82 (1987)

49. Valiant, L.G.: A theory of the learnable. In: ACM STOC, pp. 436–445 (1984)

50. Verbeurgt, K.A.: Learning DNF under the uniform distribution in quasi-polynomial time. In: COLT, pp. 314–326 (1990)

51. Viola, E.: The communication complexity of addition. In: SODA, pp. 632–651 (2013)
52. Werther, K.: The complexity of sparse polynomial interpolation over finite fields. Appl. Algebr. Eng. Commun. Comput. **5**(2), 91–103 (1994)
53. Yao, A.C.C.: How to generate and exchange secrets (extended abstract). In: FOCS, pp. 162–167 (1986)
54. Yu, Y., Steinberger, J.: Pseudorandom functions in almost constant depth from low-noise LPN. In: Fischlin, M., Coron, J.-S. (eds.) EUROCRYPT 2016. LNCS, vol. 9666, pp. 154–183. Springer, Heidelberg (2016). https://doi.org/10.1007/978-3-662-49896-5_6
55. Zahur, S., Rosulek, M., Evans, D.: Two halves make a whole. In: Oswald, E., Fischlin, M. (eds.) EUROCRYPT 2015. LNCS, vol. 9057, pp. 220–250. Springer, Heidelberg (2015). https://doi.org/10.1007/978-3-662-46803-6_8
56. Zippel, R.: Probabilistic algorithms for sparse polynomials. In: Ng, E.W. (ed.) Symbolic and Algebraic Computation. LNCS, vol. 72, pp. 216–226. Springer, Heidelberg (1979). https://doi.org/10.1007/3-540-09519-5_73
57. Zippel, R.: Interpolating polynomials from their values. J. Symb. Comput. **9**(3), 375–403 (1990)

Author Index

Agrawal, Shashank I-659
Agrawal, Shweta II-473
Ananth, Prabhanjan II-455
Applebaum, Benny I-152, I-317
Arkis, Barak I-317

Badrinarayanan, Saikrishna I-629
Bartusek, James II-544
Benhamouda, Fabrice I-175
Bitansky, Nir I-209
Block, Alexander R. II-36
Boneh, Dan II-699
Brakerski, Zvika I-152, II-370

Campanelli, Matteo II-66
Canetti, Ran I-476
Cash, David II-159
Chan, T.-H. Hubert II-636
Chen, Yilei II-341
Chongchitmate, Wutichai I-370
Chung, Kai-Min I-563

Damgård, Ivan II-225
Döttling, Nico II-370
Dryja, Thaddeus I-33
Dupuis, Frédéric II-282

Fehr, Serge II-282, II-315

Garg, Sanjam I-123, I-689, II-425
Gennaro, Rosario II-66
Guan, Jiaxin II-544
Guo, Yue I-563
Gupta, Divya II-36

Haitner, Iftach I-539
Hajiabadi, Mohammad I-448, I-689
Halevi, Shai II-255
Hazay, Carmit I-263

Ishai, Yuval I-123, II-255, II-699

Jost, Daniel I-345
Jutla, Charanjit S. I-235

Kazana, Tomasz II-225
Khurana, Dakshita I-286, I-629
Kiyoshima, Susumu I-67
Koppula, Venkata I-659
Kushilevitz, Eyal II-255

Lamontagne, Philippe II-282
LaVigne, Rio II-3
Libert, Benoît II-391
Lichtenberg, Amit I-476
Lin, Huijia I-175, I-209
Lin, Wei-Kai I-563
Liu, Quanquan C. I-33
Liu, Tianren I-98
Liu-Zhang, Chen-Da II-3
Lombardi, Alex II-455

Ma, Fermi II-513, II-544
Mahmoody, Mohammad I-689
Maitra, Monosij II-473
Maji, Hemanta K. II-36
Makriyannis, Nikolaos I-539
Maurer, Ueli I-345, II-3
Mennink, Bart II-192
Moran, Tal II-3
Morgan, Andrew I-507, I-597
Mularczyk, Marta II-3

Naor, Moni II-575
Narayanan, Varun I-389
Nayak, Kartik II-636
Nguyen, Hai H. II-36

Obremski, Maciej II-225
Omri, Eran I-539
Ostrovsky, Rafail I-286, I-370

Park, Sunoo I-33
Pass, Rafael I-507, I-563, I-597
Passelègue, Alain II-699
Polychroniadou, Antigoni I-175
Prabahakaran, Vinod M. I-389

Quach, Willy II-669

Rabin, Tal   II-255
Rahimi, Ahmadreza   I-689
Raj, Varun   II-225
Ribeiro, João L.   I-345
Rosulek, Mike   II-98
Rotem, Lior   I-421, II-575
Roy, Arnab   I-235

Sahai, Amit   I-629, II-699
Salvail, Louis   II-282
Segev, Gil   I-421, II-177, II-575
Shahaf, Ido   II-177
Shi, Elaine   I-563, II-636
Shirley, Morgan   II-98
Siniscalchi, Luisa   II-225
Srinivasan, Akshayaram   I-123, I-286, II-425
Stehlé, Damien   II-391

Tessaro, Stefano   I-3
Thiruvengadam, Aishwarya   I-3
Titiu, Radu   II-391
Tsabary, Rotem   I-152
Tschudi, Daniel   II-3

Vaikuntanathan, Vinod   II-341
Venkitasubramaniam, Muthuramakrishnan
        I-175, I-263

Waters, Brent   I-629, I-659, II-341
Wee, Hoeteck   II-341
Weiss, Mor   II-603
Wichs, Daniel   II-341, II-603, II-669
Wu, David J.   II-699

Zhandry, Mark   II-129, II-513, II-544
Zhang, Cong   II-129, II-159
Zirdelis, Giorgos   II-669

Printed in the United States
By Bookmasters